Sevilla

0 200 meters
0 200 yards

TO SAN LORENZO Y JESÚS DEL GRAN PODER (100m)
TO ALAMEDA DE HÉRCULES (150m)
TO SAN BERNARDO (250m)
TO PARQUE DE MARÍA LUISA (300m) & MUSEO ARQUEOLÓGICO (800m)

EL CENTRO
SANTA CRUZ
EL ARENAL
TRIANA
LOS REMEDIOS

Museo Provincial de Bellas Artes
El Corte Inglés
Casa de las Dueñas
Convento de Sta. Inés
La Anunciación
Iglesia de la Magdalena
El Salvador
San José
Ayuntamiento
Casa de Pilatos
Monolitos Romanos
Palacio Arzobispal
Catedral
Encarnación
Santa María la Blanca
Casa de Murillo
Convento de San José
Hospital de los Venerables
Plaza de Toros de la Real Maestranza
Hospital de la Caridad
Teatro de la Maestranza
Casa Lonja
Alcázar
Jardines del Alcázar
Puerta de Jerez
Torre del Oro
Universidad
Palacio de San Telmo
Estación Prado San Sebastián
Prado de San Sebastián
Jardines de Murillo
Río Guadalquivir
U.K.
Canada
United States

PL. GAVIDIA
PL. DUQUE DE LA VICTORIA
PL. DE LA ENCARNACIÓN
PL. PONCE DE LEÓN
PL. SAN PEDRO
PL. CRISTO DE BURGOS
PL. DEL CARMEN
PL. GODINAS
PL. ALFALFA
PL. DEL SALVADOR
PL. PESCADERÍA
PL. PILATOS
PL. NUEVA
PL. DE SAN FRANCISCO
PL. DE LAS MERCENARIAS
PL. V. REYES
PL. DEL CABILDO
PL. DE TRIUNFO
PL. STA. CRUZ
PL. DOÑA ELVIRA
PL. CONTRATACIÓN
PL. DE SAN SEBASTIÁN
PL. DON JUAN DE AUSTRIA
PL. CUBA
PL. GLORIETA S. DIEGO
PL. DE ESPAÑA

C. Baños
C. San Vicente
C. Miguel Cid
C. A. Gordillo
C. Jesús de la Veracruz
C. San Juan de Ávila
C. Jesús del Gran Poder
C. Trajano
C. Amor de Dios
C. D. Pedro Niño
C. Atienza
C. Amparo
C. Jerónimo Hernández
C. Sor Ángela de la Cruz
C. Dueñas
C. Peñuelas
C. Bustos Tavera
C. del Sol
C. Dña. María Coronel
C. Gerona
C. Vega
C. Gestoso
C. Alfonso XII
C. la Campaña
C. Moscardo
C. Martín Villa
C. Laraña
C. Imagen
C. Alhóndiga
C. S. Felipe
C. Azafrán
C. Monsalves
C. Ferrán
C. San Eloy
C. O'Donnell
C. Velázquez
C. Goyeneta
C. Galdós
C. Santillana
C. Escarpín
C. Golfo
C. O. Zuñiga
C. Cañón
C. Santiago
C. San Roque
C. de Ballén
C. Rivero
C. Acetres
C. Don Sabio
C. P. Galdós
C. Canalejas
C. Murillo
C. Morati
C. Rioja
C. Cerrajería
C. Imperial
C. Boteros
C. Cabeza del Rey
C. Caballerizas
C. Méndez Núñez
C. Tetuán
C. Sierpes
C. Cuna
C. Herbolarios
C. Huelva
C. Alfalfa
C. Rosario
C. Sagasta
C. Villegas
C. Almirante Hoyos
C. Águilas
C. San Pablo
C. Moratín
C. Jovellanos
Fabiola
C. Lirio
C. S. Isidoro
C. Luchana
C. Virgenes
C. Bilbao
C. Granada
C. Carlos Cañal
C. Conde de Ibarra
C. Madrid
C. Pajaritos
Corral del Rey
C. Muñoz y Pavón
C. Santas Patronas
C. Zaragoza
C. Francos
C. Álvarez Quintero
C. Galera
C. Padre Marchena
C. Guichot
C. Argote de Molina
C. F. Rubio
C. San José
C. Levíes
C. Aire
Av. de la Constitución
C. Castelar
C. Gamazo
C. Harinas
C. Jimios
C. Placentines
C. Remondo
C. Famesio
C. Céspedes
C. Dos Hermanos
C. Pastor y Leandro
C. Adriano
C. Alemanes
C. Abades
C. Mateos Gago
C. Fabiola
C. Sta. María la Blanca
C. Archeros
C. G. de Vinuesa
C. M. del Moro
Ximénez de Enciso
C. Cruces
C. Mariscal
C. Doncella
C. Antonio Díaz
C. Varflora
C. R. Caro
Paseo de Cristóbal Colón
P. Alcalde Marqués de Contadero
C. Castaño
C. Dos de Mayo
C. Temprado
Gloria
C. de Cifuentes
Av. de Menéndez Pelayo
C. Santander
Av. Málaga
C. Almirante Lobo
C. San Fernando
Av. Sanjurjo
C. del Betis
C. Fortaleza
Av. de Roma
Rosario Vega
Pte. San Telmo
Av. Carlos V
C. Inf. Orleáns
C. de Rivera
C. Inf. Carlos
Paseo de las Delicias
Palos de la Frontera
C. Cruz Conde
Av. de la República Argentina
C. Juan Sebastián Elcano
C. Virgen de la Consolación
C. Asunción
C. de la Rábida
Av. María Luisa
Av. de Isabel la Católica
Av. de Portugal
Av. Bécquer

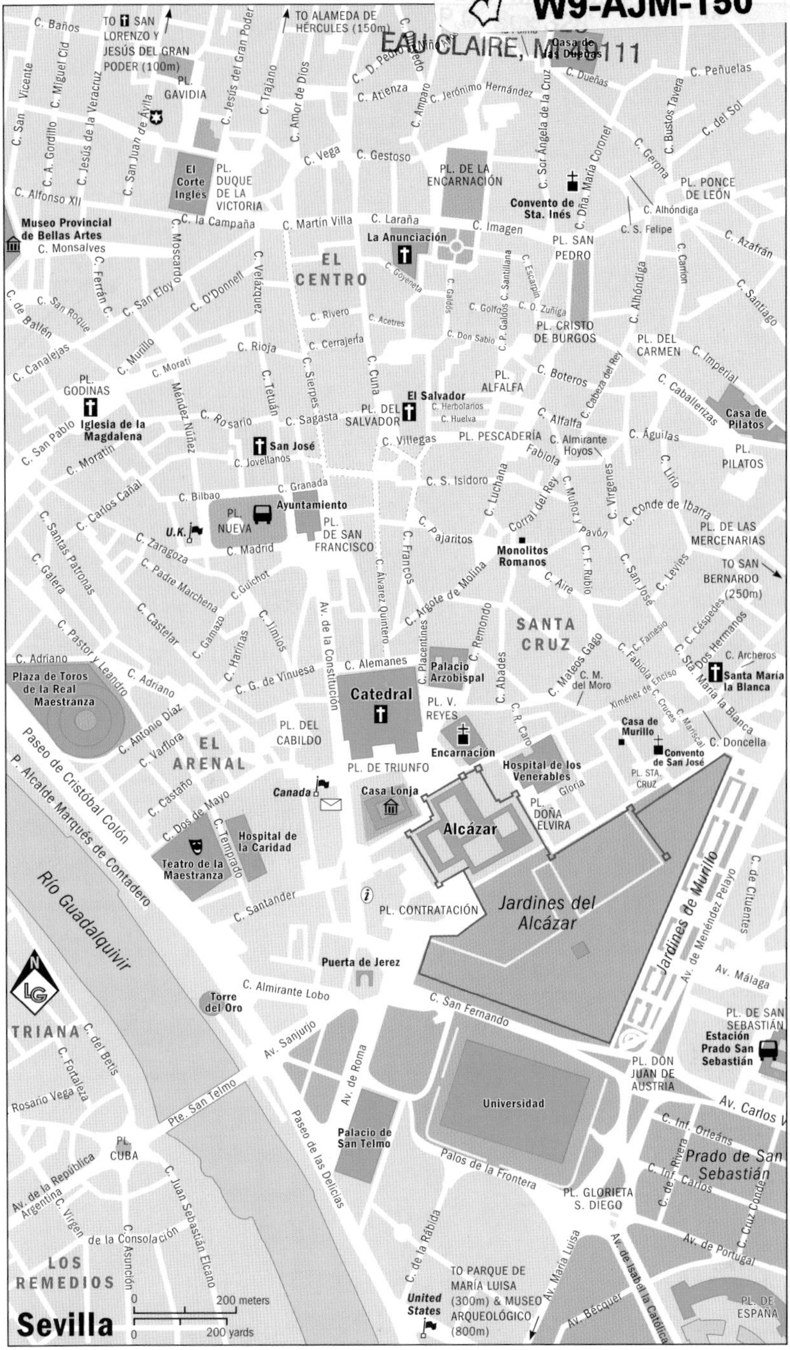

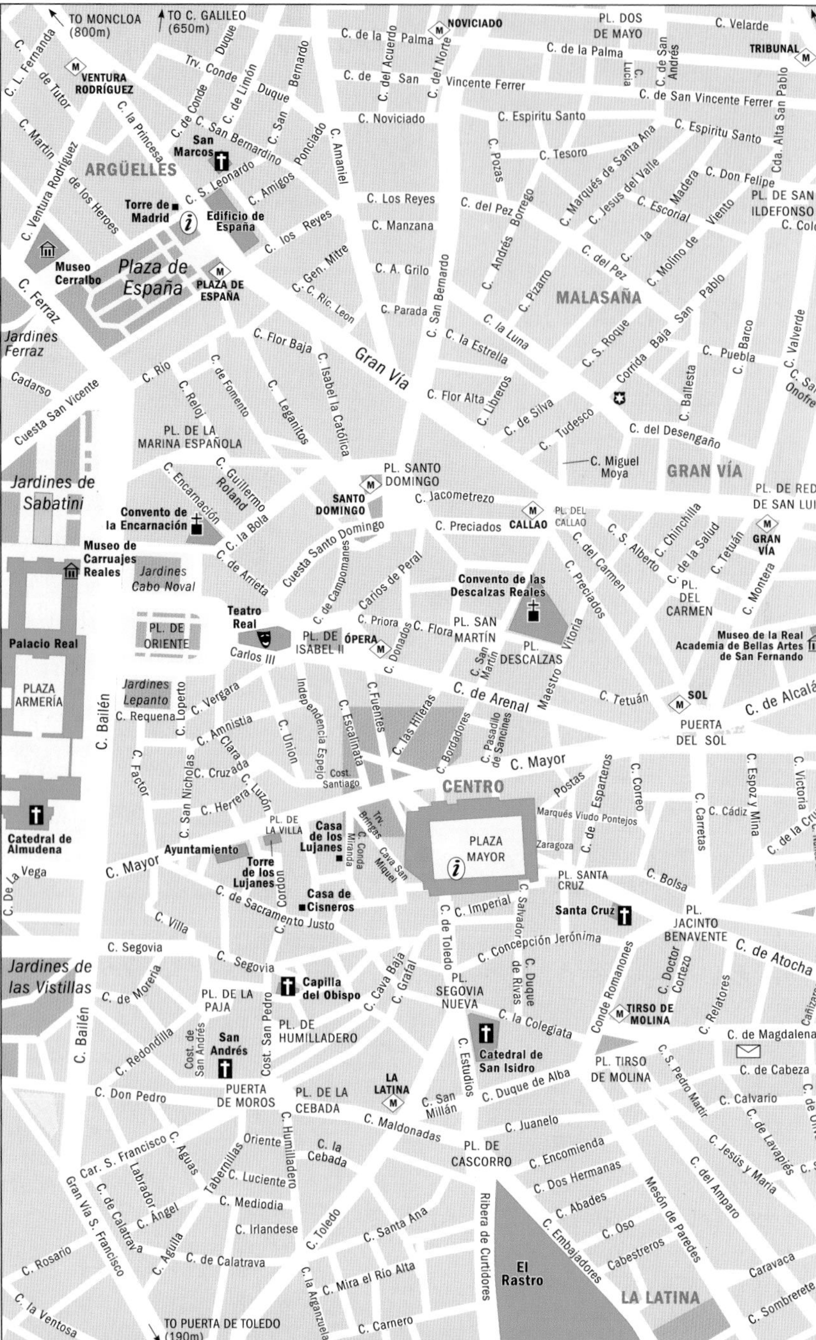
TO MONCLOA (800m)
TO C. GALILEO (650m)
NOVICIADO
PL. DOS DE MAYO
C. Velarde
TRIBUNAL
VENTURA RODRÍGUEZ
ARGÜELLES
San Marcos
Torre de Madrid
Edificio de España
Museo Cerralbo
Plaza de España
PLAZA DE ESPAÑA
Jardines Ferraz
MALASAÑA
PL. DE SAN ILDEFONSO
Gran Vía
PL. DE LA MARINA ESPAÑOLA
PL. SANTO DOMINGO
SANTO DOMINGO
GRAN VÍA
PL. DE RED. DE SAN LUIS
Jardines de Sabatini
Convento de la Encarnación
Museo de Carruajes Reales
Jardines Cabo Noval
CALLAO
PL. DEL CALLAO
Convento de las Descalzas Reales
PL. DEL CARMEN
Teatro Real
PL. DE ORIENTE
Palacio Real
PLAZA ARMERÍA
PL. DE ISABEL II
ÓPERA
PL. SAN MARTÍN
PL. DESCALZAS
Museo de la Real Academia de Bellas Artes de San Fernando
SOL
PUERTA DEL SOL
Jardines Lepanto
CENTRO
Catedral de Almudena
Ayuntamiento
PL. DE LA VILLA
Torre de los Lujanes
Casa de los Lujanes
Casa de Cisneros
PLAZA MAYOR
PL. SANTA CRUZ
Santa Cruz
PL. JACINTO BENAVENTE
Jardines de las Vistillas
Capilla del Obispo
PL. DE LA PAJA
PL. SEGOVIA NUEVA
San Andrés
PL. DE HUMILLADERO
Catedral de San Isidro
TIRSO DE MOLINA
PL. TIRSO DE MOLINA
PUERTA DE MOROS
PL. DE LA CEBADA
LA LATINA
PL. DE CASCORRO
El Rastro
LA LATINA
TO PUERTA DE TOLEDO (190m)
C. de la Palma
C. de San Vincente Ferrer
C. Noviciado
C. Espiritu Santo
C. Tesoro
C. Los Reyes
C. del Pez
C. Manzana
C. A. Grilo
C. Parada
C. San Bernardo
C. Flor Baja
C. Isabel la Católica
C. Flor Alta
C. de Silva
C. Tudesco
C. del Desengaño
C. Miguel Moya
C. Jacometrezo
C. Preciados
C. del Carmen
C. Montera
C. de Arenal
C. Tetuán
C. de Alcalá
C. Mayor
C. Bailén
C. Segovia
C. de Toledo
C. Imperial
C. Concepción Jerónima
C. de Atocha
C. la Colegiata
C. Duque de Alba
C. de Magdalena
C. de Cabeza
C. Calvario
C. Maldonadas
C. Juanelo
C. Encomienda
C. Dos Hermanas
C. Abades
C. Oso
C. Embajadores
Cabestreros
Mesón de Paredes
Ribera de Curtidores
C. Santa Ana
C. Mira el Río Alta
C. Carnero
C. de Calatrava
Gran Vía S. Francisco
C. la Ventosa
C. Rosario
C. Don Pedro
C. Redondilla
C. de Morería
Cuesta San Vicente
Cadarso
C. Ferraz
C. Ventura Rodríguez
C. la Princesa
Carlos III
C. Requena
C. de Sacramento
C. Cava Baja
C. Estudios
C. Toledo

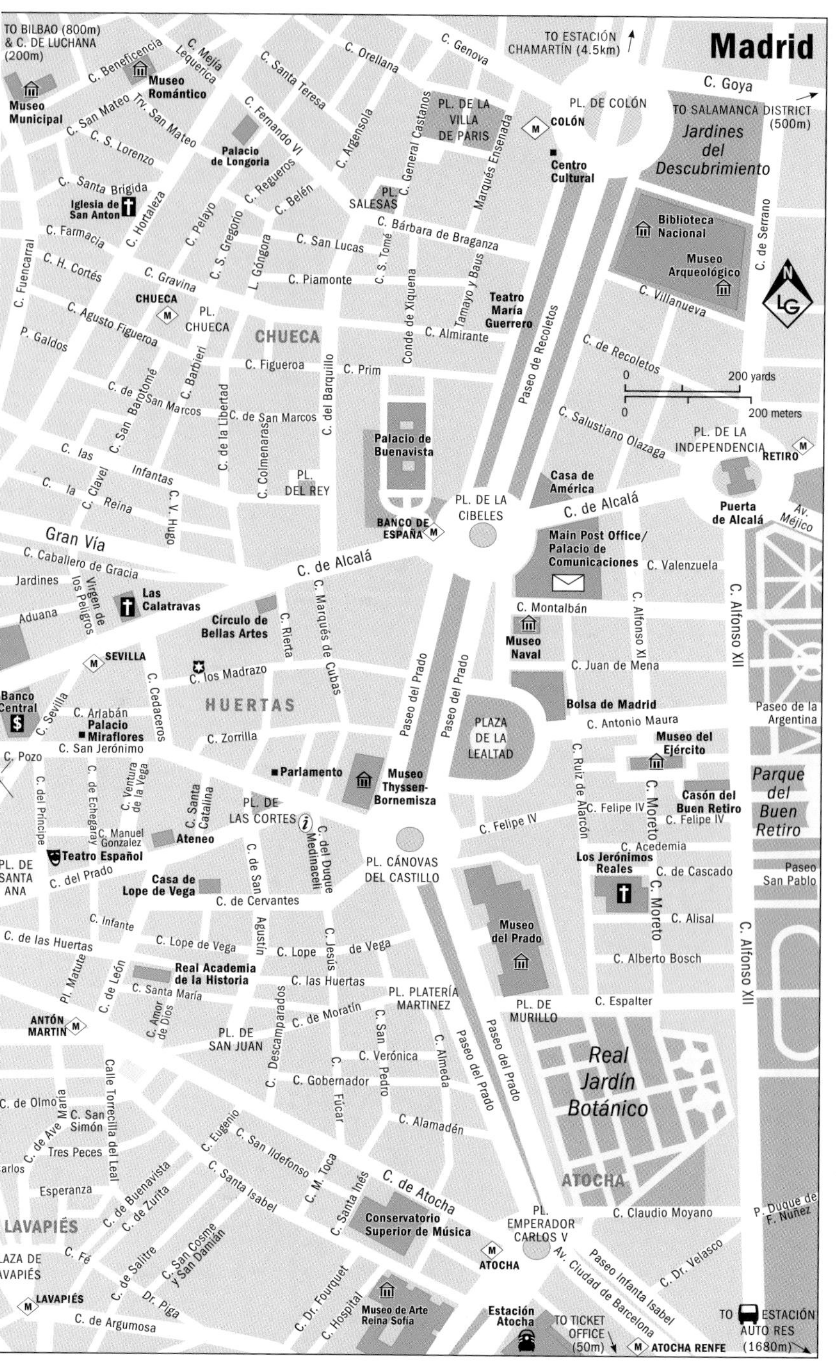
Madrid
TO BILBAO (800m) & C. DE LUCHANA (200m)
TO ESTACIÓN CHAMARTÍN (4.5km)
TO SALAMANCA DISTRICT (500m)
Museo Municipal
Museo Romántico
Palacio de Longoria
Iglesia de San Anton
PL. DE LA VILLA DE PARIS
PL. SALESAS
PL. DE COLÓN
COLÓN
Centro Cultural
Jardines del Descubrimiento
Biblioteca Nacional
Museo Arqueológico
Teatro María Guerrero
CHUECA
PL. CHUECA
Palacio de Buenavista
PL. DEL REY
PL. DE LA CIBELES
BANCO DE ESPAÑA
Casa de América
PL. DE LA INDEPENDENCIA
RETIRO
Puerta de Alcalá
Main Post Office/ Palacio de Comunicaciones
Museo Naval
Las Calatravas
Círculo de Bellas Artes
SEVILLA
Banco Central
Palacio Miraflores
HUERTAS
PLAZA DE LA LEALTAD
Bolsa de Madrid
Museo del Ejército
Casón del Buen Retiro
Parque del Buen Retiro
Parlamento
Museo Thyssen-Bornemisza
PL. DE LAS CORTES
Ateneo
Teatro Español
PL. DE SANTA ANA
Casa de Lope de Vega
PL. CÁNOVAS DEL CASTILLO
Los Jerónimos Reales
Museo del Prado
Real Academia de la Historia
PL. PLATERÍA MARTINEZ
PL. DE MURILLO
ANTÓN MARTIN
PL. DE SAN JUAN
Real Jardín Botánico
ATOCHA
LAVAPIÉS
PLAZA DE LAVAPIÉS
Conservatorio Superior de Música
PL. EMPERADOR CARLOS V
Museo de Arte Reina Sofia
Estación Atocha
TO TICKET OFFICE (50m)
ATOCHA RENFE
TO ESTACIÓN AUTO RES (1680m)
0 200 yards
0 200 meters
C. Genova
C. Goya
C. Orellana
C. Santa Teresa
C. Mejía Lequerica
C. Beneficencia
C. San Mateo
Trv. San Mateo
C. S. Lorenzo
C. Fernando VI
C. Argensola
C. General Castanos
Marqués Ensenada
C. Santa Brigida
C. Hortaleza
C. Pelayo
C. S. Gregorio
C. Regueros
C. Belén
C. Bárbara de Braganza
C. San Lucas
C. S. Tomé
C. de Serrano
C. Farmacia
C. H. Cortés
C. Fuencarral
C. Gravina
L. Góngora
C. Piamonte
Conde de Xiquena
Tamayo y Baus
Paseo de Recoletos
C. Villanueva
C. Agusto Figueroa
P. Galdos
C. Almirante
C. de Recoletos
C. Barbieri
C. Figueroa
C. Prim
C. del Barquillo
C. de San Barotomé
C. de San Marcos
C. de la Libertad
C. Colmenares
C. Salustiano Olazaga
C. San Marcos
C. las Infantas
C. la Reina
C. Clavel
C. V. Hugo
C. de Alcalá
Av. Méjico
Gran Vía
C. Caballero de Gracia
Jardines
Virgen de los Peligros
Aduana
C. Marqués de Cubas
C. Rierta
C. Valenzuela
C. Montalbán
C. Alfonso XI
C. Alfonso XII
C. los Madrazo
Paseo del Prado
C. Juan de Mena
Paseo de la Argentina
C. Sevilla
C. Arlabán
C. Cedaceros
C. Antonio Maura
C. Zorrilla
C. San Jerónimo
C. Pozo
C. del Principe
C. de Echegaray
C. Ventura de la Vega
C. Santa Catalina
C. Ruiz de Alarcón
C. Moreto
C. Felipe IV
C. Manuel Gonzalez
C. de San Agustín
C. del Duque Medinaceli
C. Acedemia
C. del Prado
C. de Cascado
Paseo San Pablo
C. de Cervantes
C. Infante
C. Alisal
C. de las Huertas
C. Lope de Vega
C. Jesús
C. Alberto Bosch
Pl. Matute
C. de León
C. Santa María
C. las Huertas
C. Amor de Dios
C. Descamparados
C. de Moratín
C. San Pedro
C. Almeda
C. Espalter
C. Verónica
C. Gobernador
C. Fúcar
Calle Torrecilla del Leal
C. de Olmo
C. San Simón
C. de Ave María
C. Alamadén
Tres Peces
Carlos
C. Eugenio
C. San Ildefonso
C. M. Toca
C. de Atocha
C. Santa Isabel
C. Santa Inés
Esperanza
C. de Buenavista
C. de Zurita
C. Claudio Moyano
P. Duque de F. Nuñez
C. Fé
C. de Salitre
C. San Cosme y San Damián
C. Dr. Fourquet
C. Hospital
Av. Ciudad de Barcelona
Paseo Infanta Isabel
C. Dr. Velasco
Dr. Piga
C. de Argumosa

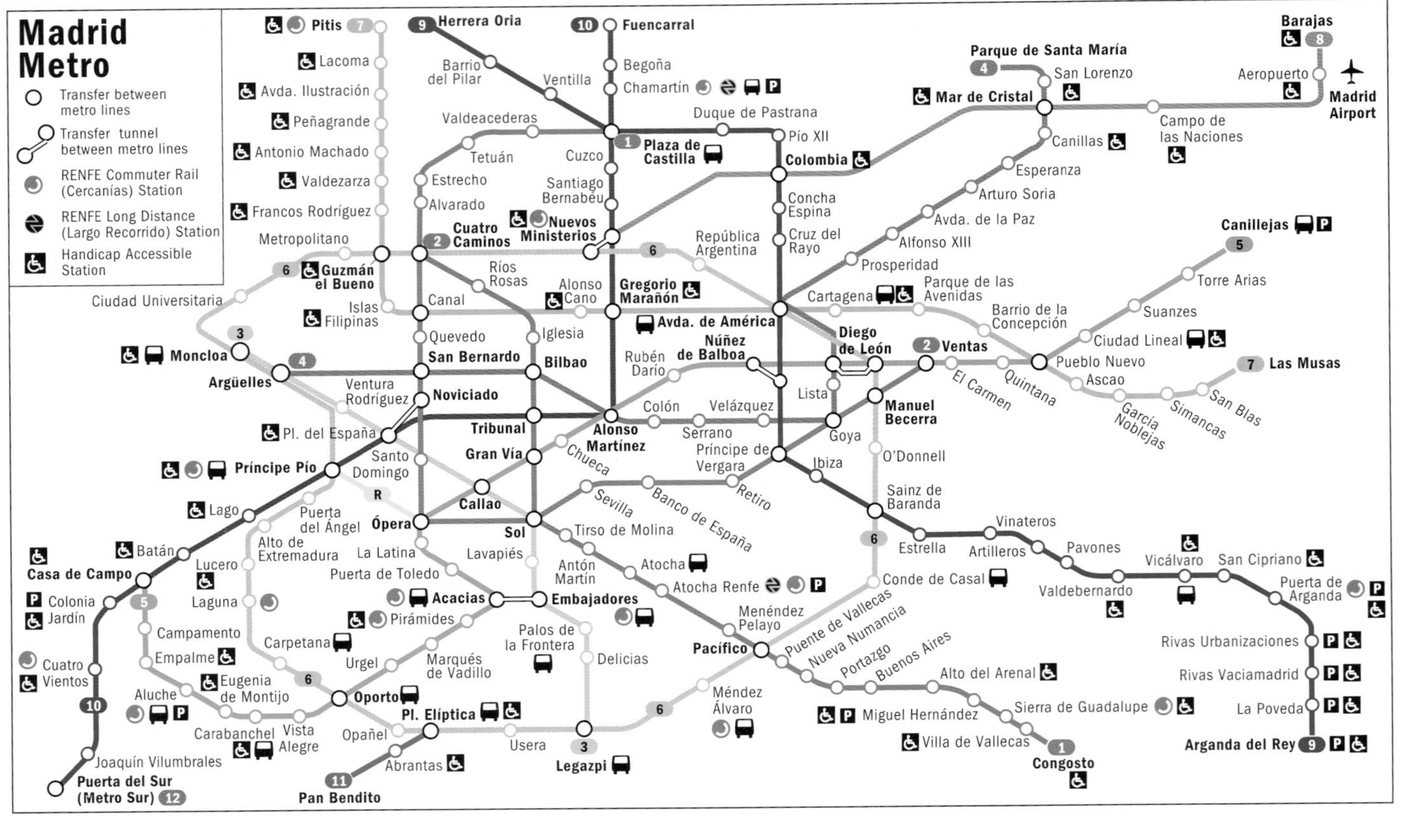
Madrid Metro
Transfer between metro lines
Transfer tunnel between metro lines
RENFE Commuter Rail (Cercanías) Station
RENFE Long Distance (Largo Recorrido) Station
Handicap Accessible Station
Pitis
Lacoma
Avda. Ilustración
Peñagrande
Antonio Machado
Valdezarza
Francos Rodríguez
Metropolitano
Guzmán el Bueno
Ciudad Universitaria
Islas Filipinas
Moncloa
Argüelles
Herrera Oria
Barrio del Pilar
Ventilla
Valdeacederas
Tetuán
Estrecho
Alvarado
Cuatro Caminos
Ríos Rosas
Canal
Quevedo
San Bernardo
Iglesia
Bilbao
Ventura Rodríguez
Noviciado
Pl. del España
Santo Domingo
Príncipe Pío
Tribunal
Gran Vía
Callao
Ópera
Sol
R
Lago
Batán
Casa de Campo
Colonia Jardín
Cuatro Vientos
Joaquín Vilumbrales
Puerta del Sur (Metro Sur)
Lucero
Laguna
Campamento
Empalme
Aluche
Eugenia de Montijo
Carabanchel
Vista Alegre
Puerta del Ángel
Alto de Extremadura
Carpetana
Urgel
Oporto
Opañel
Abrantas
Pan Bendito
Pl. Elíptica
Usera
Legazpi
La Latina
Puerta de Toledo
Acacias
Pirámides
Marqués de Vadillo
Lavapiés
Embajadores
Palos de la Frontera
Delicias
Fuencarral
Begoña
Chamartín
Duque de Pastrana
Plaza de Castilla
Cuzco
Santiago Bernabéu
Nuevos Ministerios
Pío XII
Colombia
Concha Espina
Cruz del Rayo
República Argentina
Alonso Cano
Gregorio Marañón
Avda. de América
Rubén Darío
Núñez de Balboa
Alonso Martínez
Chueca
Colón
Serrano
Velázquez
Lista
Diego de León
Goya
Manuel Becerra
Príncipe de Vergara
Retiro
Banco de España
Sevilla
Tirso de Molina
Antón Martín
Atocha
Atocha Renfe
Menéndez Pelayo
Pacífico
Méndez Álvaro
Cartagena
Parque de las Avenidas
Barrio de la Concepción
Prosperidad
Alfonso XIII
Avda. de la Paz
Arturo Soria
Esperanza
Canillas
Mar de Cristal
Parque de Santa María
San Lorenzo
Campo de las Naciones
Aeropuerto
Barajas
Madrid Airport
Canillejas
Torre Arias
Suanzes
Ciudad Lineal
Pueblo Nuevo
Ventas
El Carmen
Quintana
Ascao
García Noblejas
Simancas
San Blas
Las Musas
O'Donnell
Ibiza
Sainz de Baranda
Conde de Casal
Estrella
Vinateros
Artilleros
Pavones
Valdebernardo
Vicálvaro
San Cipriano
Puerta de Arganda
Rivas Urbanizaciones
Rivas Vaciamadrid
La Poveda
Arganda del Rey
Puente de Vallecas
Nueva Numancia
Portazgo
Buenos Aires
Alto del Arenal
Miguel Hernández
Sierra de Guadalupe
Villa de Vallecas
Congosto

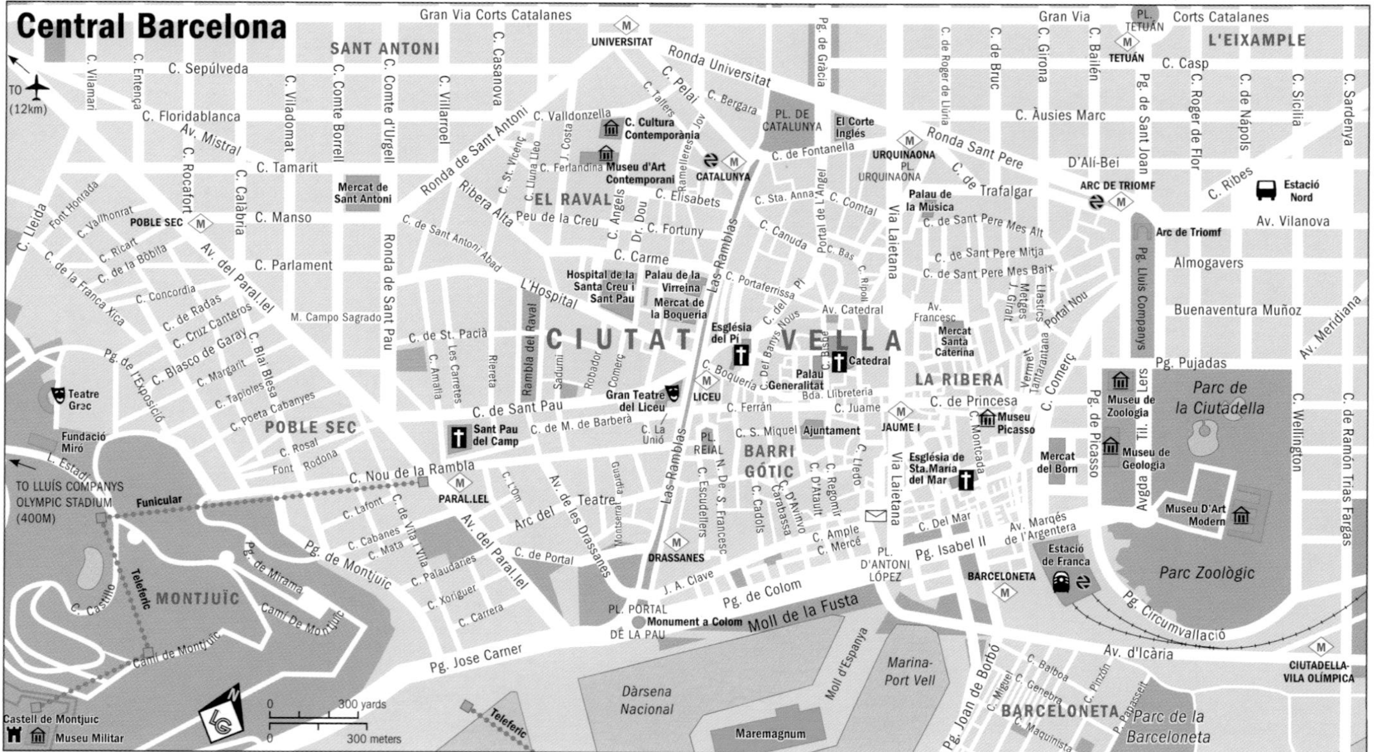

Central Barcelona
TO (12km)
TO LLUÍS COMPANYS OLYMPIC STADIUM (400M)
SANT ANTONI
L'EIXAMPLE
EL RAVAL
CIUTAT VELLA
LA RIBERA
BARRI GÒTIC
POBLE SEC
MONTJUÏC
BARCELONETA
Gran Via Corts Catalanes
C. Sepúlveda
C. Floridablanca
Av. Mistral
C. Tamarit
C. Manso
C. Parlament
C. Vilamari
C. Entença
C. Rocafort
C. Calàbria
C. Viladomat
C. Comte Borrell
C. Comte d'Urgell
C. Villarroel
C. Casanova
Ronda de Sant Pau
Ronda de Sant Antoni
Ronda Universitat
Ronda Sant Pere
C. de Fontanella
C. de Trafalgar
Pg. de Gràcia
C. de Roger de Llúria
C. de Bruc
C. Girona
C. Bailén
Pg. de Sant Joan
C. Roger de Flor
C. de Nápols
C. Sicília
C. Sardenya
C. Casp
C. Àusies Marc
D'Alí-Bei
C. Ribes
Av. Vilanova
Almogavers
Buenaventura Muñoz
Av. Meridiana
Pg. Lluis Companys
Pg. Pujadas
C. Wellington
C. de Ramón Trias Fargas
Parc de la Ciutadella
Parc Zoològic
Pg. Circumvallació
Av. d'Icària
Pg. de Picasso
Avgda Til. Lers
Museu de Zoologia
Museu de Geologia
Museu D'Art Modern
Mercat del Born
Estació de Franca
Museu Picasso
C. de Princesa
C. Comerç
C. Montcada
Església de Sta.Maria del Mar
Pg. Isabel II
Av. Marqués de l'Argentera
C. Del Mar
Via Laietana
Palau de la Música
Mercat Santa Caterina
Av. Francesc
C. de Sant Pere Mes Alt
C. de Sant Pere Mitja
C. de Sant Pere Mes Baix
Portal Nou
C. Sta. Anna
C. Comtal
Portal de L'Angel
C. Canuda
C. Bas
C. Ripoll
Av. Catedral
Catedral
Palau Generalitat
Bda. Llibreteria
C. Jaume
Ajuntament
C. Lledo
C. Regomir
C. D'Atault
C. Ample
C. Mercé
C. D'Avinyo
Carabassa
C. Cadols
N. De. S. Francesc
C. Escudellers
C. S. Miquel
C. Ferrán
PL. REIAL
Las Ramblas
Església del Pi
C. Boqueria
C. Portaferrissa
Gran Teatre del Liceu
C. La Unió
C. de M. de Barberà
C. de Sant Pau
Sant Pau del Camp
Hospital de la Santa Creu i Sant Pau
Palau de la Virreina
Mercat de la Boqueria
C. Carme
C. Fortuny
C. Elisabets
C. Angels
Dr. Dou
Peu de la Creu
Ribera Alta
L'Hospital
Rambla del Raval
C. de Sant Antoni Abad
C. de St. Pacià
Les Carretes
C. Amalia
Riereta
Sadurni
Robador
Comerç
C. Cultura Contemporània
Museu d'Art Contemporani
C. Valldonzella
C. Ferlandina
C. Lluna Lleo
C. St. Vicenç
J. Costa
C. Tallers
C. Pelai
C. Bergara
PL. DE CATALUNYA
El Corte Inglés
Mercat de Sant Antoni
M. Campo Sagrado
Av. del Paral.lel
C. Nou de la Rambla
Av. de les Drassanes
C. de Portal
Arc del Teatre
C. Blai Blesa
C. Poeta Cabanyes
C. Rosal
Font Rodona
C. Lleida
Font Honrada
C. Vallhonrat
C. Ricart
C. de la Bòbila
C. de la Franca Xica
C. Concordia
C. de Radas
C. Cruz Canteros
C. Blasco de Garay
C. Margarit
C. Tapioles
Pg. de l'Exposició
Teatre Grec
Fundació Miró
L. Estadi
Funicular
Teleferic
Pg. de Miramar
Camí De Montjuïc
C. Castillo
Castell de Montjuïc
Museu Militar
Pg. de Montjuïc
Pg. Jose Carner
Pg. de Colom
Moll de la Fusta
PL. PORTAL DE LA PAU
Monument a Colom
J. A. Clave
PL. D'ANTONI LÓPEZ
Dàrsena Nacional
Maremagnum
Moll d'Espanya
Marina-Port Vell
Pg. Joan de Borbó
C. Balboa
C. Genebra
C. Miguel
C. Pinzón
C. Maquinista
Parc de la Barceloneta
UNIVERSITAT
CATALUNYA
URQUINAONA
PL. URQUINAONA
ARC DE TRIOMF
Arc de Triomf
Estació Nord
TETUÁN
PL. TETUÁN
LICEU
JAUME I
DRASSANES
PARAL.LEL
POBLE SEC
BARCELONETA
CIUTADELLA-VILA OLÍMPICA
0 300 yards
0 300 meters

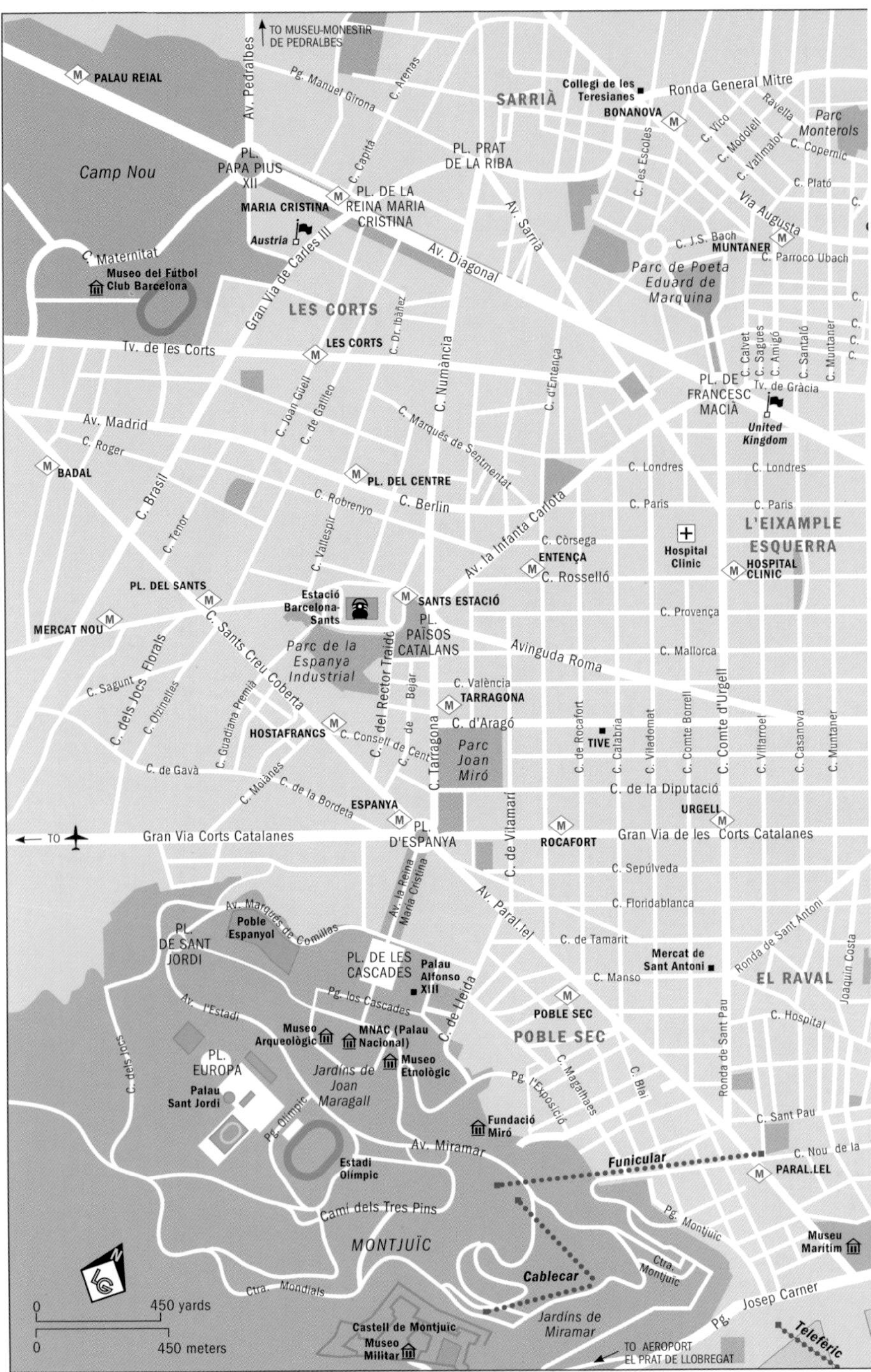

TO MUSEU-MONESTIR DE PEDRALBES
PALAU REIAL
Av. Pedralbes
Pg. Manuel Girona
C. Arenas
SARRIÀ
Collegi de les Teresianes
Ronda General Mitre
BONANOVA
Ravella
Parc Monterols
C. Vico
C. Modolell
C. Vallmalor
C. Copernic
C. les Escoles
C. Plató
Camp Nou
PL. PAPA PIUS XII
C. Capità
PL. PRAT DE LA RIBA
PL. DE LA REINA MARIA CRISTINA
MARIA CRISTINA
Av. Sarrià
Via Augusta
Austria
C. Maternitat
Gran Via de Carles III
Av. Diagonal
C. J.S. Bach
MUNTANER
C. Parroco Ubach
Museo del Fútbol Club Barcelona
Parc de Poeta Eduard de Marquina
LES CORTS
C. Dr. Ibáñez
C. Numància
C. Calvet
C. Sagues
C. Amigó
C. Santaló
C. Muntaner
Tv. de les Corts
LES CORTS
C. d'Entença
PL. DE FRANCESC MACIÀ
Tv. de Gràcia
United Kingdom
Av. Madrid
C. Joan Güell
C. de Galileo
C. Marquès de Sentmenat
C. Roger
BADAL
PL. DEL CENTRE
C. Londres
C. Londres
C. Robrenyo
C. Berlin
C. Paris
C. Paris
C. Brasil
C. Tenor
C. Vallespir
Av. la Infanta Carlota
L'EIXAMPLE ESQUERRA
C. Còrsega
Hospital Clinic
ENTENÇA
C. Rosselló
HOSPITAL CLINIC
PL. DEL SANTS
Estació Barcelona-Sants
SANTS ESTACIÓ
MERCAT NOU
PL. PAÏSOS CATALANS
C. Provença
C. Sants Creu Coberta
Parc de la Espanya Industrial
Avinguda Roma
C. Mallorca
C. dels Jocs Florals
C. Sagunt
C. Olzinelles
C. Guadiana Premià
C. del Rector Triadó
Bejar
C. València
TARRAGONA
C. d'Aragó
HOSTAFRANCS
C. Consell de Cent
C. de Rocafort
C. Calabria
C. Viladomat
C. Comte Borrell
C. Comte d'Urgell
C. Villarroel
C. Casanova
C. Muntaner
TIVE
C. Tarragona
Parc Joan Miró
C. de Gavà
C. Moianes
C. de la Bordeta
C. de la Diputació
ESPANYA
URGELL
TO
Gran Via Corts Catalanes
PL. D'ESPANYA
C. de Vilamarí
ROCAFORT
Gran Via de les Corts Catalanes
Av. la Reina Maria Cristina
C. Sepúlveda
Av. Marquès de Comillas
Poble Espanyol
C. Floridablanca
Av. Paral.lel
Ronda de Sant Antoni
PL. DE SANT JORDI
C. de Tamarit
Joaquín Costa
PL. DE LES CASCADES
Palau Alfonso XIII
Mercat de Sant Antoni
EL RAVAL
C. Manso
Pg. los Cascades
Av. l'Estadi
C. de Lleida
POBLE SEC
C. Hospital
Museo Arqueològic
MNAC (Palau Nacional)
POBLE SEC
Ronda de Sant Pau
C. dels Jocs
PL. EUROPA
Museo Etnològic
Jardins de Joan Maragall
C. Magalhaes
C. Blai
Pg. l'Exposició
Palau Sant Jordi
Pg. Olímpic
Fundació Miró
C. Sant Pau
Av. Miramar
C. Nou de la
Funicular
Estadi Olímpic
PARAL.LEL
Camí dels Tres Pins
Pg. Montjuïc
MONTJUÏC
Museu Marítim
Ctra. Montjuïc
Cablecar
Ctra. Mondials
Pg. Josep Carner
0
450 yards
0
450 meters
Jardins de Miramar
Castell de Montjuïc
Museo Militar
TO AEROPORT EL PRAT DE LLOBREGAT
Telefèric

Barcelona
PARK GÜELL
Parc Carmel
C. Balmes
C. Pàdua
PÀDUA
C. Zaragoza
C. Vallirana
Av. La República Argentina
C. Verdi
C. Muntanya
C. de Marianao
C. de Molist
C. de Castillejos
PL. DE LESSEPS
LESSEPS
Travessera de Dalt
SAN GERVASI
C. Sanjoanistes
C. Guillem Tell
Canada
PL. MOLINA
C. Lincoln
C. Alfons XII
Madrazo
Laforja
de Marià Cubí
de l'Avenir
Casa Vicens
C. Gran de Gràcia
FONTANA
C. Sant Salvador
C. de Martí
C. Providència
C. Robí
C. d'Astúries
C. de l'Or
C. Sant Lluís
C. Torrent de l'Olla
C. Torrent de les Flors
C. Sors
C. l'Escorial
C. Alegre de Dalt
C. Coloma
C. Camèlies
Av. de Montserrat
PL. ALFONS EL SAVI
ALFONS X
Tenerife
Parc de les Aïgües
Ronda Guinardó
C. de Cartagena
Hospital de la Santa Creu i Sant Pau
C. Sant Marc
C. Montseny
GRÀCIA
C. Ros de Olano
C. Terol Bruniguer
C. Ramón y Cajal
JOANIC
C. Pi. i Margall
Tv. de Gràcia
C. Siracusa
Tusset
Via Agusta
C. Sant Antoni Maria Claret
HOSPITAL DE SANT PAU
C. Indústria
Av. Diagonal
C. Martínez
C. Bonavista
PL. JOAN CARLES I
C. Còrsega
DIAGONAL
C. de Ballen
Pg. de Sant Joan
C. Roger de Flor
C. Nàpols
C. Sicilia
C. Sardenya
C. Marina
L'EIXAMPLE DRETA
Av. de Gaudí
C. Còrsega
C. Rosselló
C. Aribau
C. Granados
PROVENÇA
La Pedrera
LA SAGRADA FAMILIA
ENCANTS
C. Provença
VERDAGUER
La Sagrada Familia
C. Mallorca
C. de Balmes
Rambla de Catalunya
Pg. de Gràcia
C. Pau Claris
C. Roger Llúria
C. València
PL. JACINT VERDAGUER
Fundació Tàpies
PG. DE GRÀCIA
PL. DEL DOCTOR LETAMENDI
Manzana de la Discòrdia
C. d'Aragó
PL. PABLO NERUDA
C. Consell de Cent
GIRONA
C. Bruc
C. de la Diputació
(Pg. Carles I)
PL. DE LES GLÒRIES CATALANES
PL. UNIVERSITAT
UNIVERSITAT
PG. DE GRÀCIA
TETUÁN
PL. TETUÁN
Plaza de Toros Monumentales
Gran Via de les Corts Catalanes
Teatre Nacional de Catalunya
MONUMENTAL
GLÒRIES
Auditori Municipal
C. Pelai
Ronda Universitat
C. Casp
C. Girona
C. Ballen
CATALUNYA
PL. DE CATALUNYA
Museu d'Art Contemporani
Aero-bus
URQUINAONA
C. d'Ausiàs Marc
C. de Marina
Ronda de Sant Pere
Fontanella
ARC DE TRIOMF
Estació Nord
C. Tànger
CIUTAT VELLA
Portal de l'Àngel
Palau de la Música Catalana
S. Pere Més Alt
Av. Meridiana
MARINA
C. Carme
Las Ramblas
S. Pere Més Baix
C. dels Almogàvers
Mercat Boqueria
PL. DE PÍ
Sta. Maria del Pi
Palau de la Generalitat
LA RIBERA
United States
C. Comerç
C. Pamplona
C. d'Alaba
C. d'Àvila
Gran Teatre de Liceu
LICEU
PL. DE ST. JAUME
Pg. Pujades
BOGATELL
C. Princesa
C. Llull
Ajuntament
Museu Picasso
POBLE NOU
Rambla
Palau Güell
PL. REIAL
JAUME I
C. Ciutat
Via Laietana
Pg. Born
Pg. Picasso
Museu d'Art Modern
C. Wellington
C. Ramón Turró
Santa Maria del Mar
Parlament de Catalunya
C. del Doctor Trueta
BARRI GÒTIC
Av. Marques de l'Argentera
DRASSANES
Estació França
PARC DE LA CIUTADELLA
Parc Zoologic
Av. Bogatell
PL. PORTAL DE LA PAU
Pg. Colom
Monument a Colom
Av. d'Icària
Pg. Circumvallació
Av. d'Icària
Vila Olímpica
Moll de la Fusta
CIUTADELLA-VILA OLÍMPICA
Moll d'Espanya
The Towers
PORT OLÍMPIC
BARCELONETA

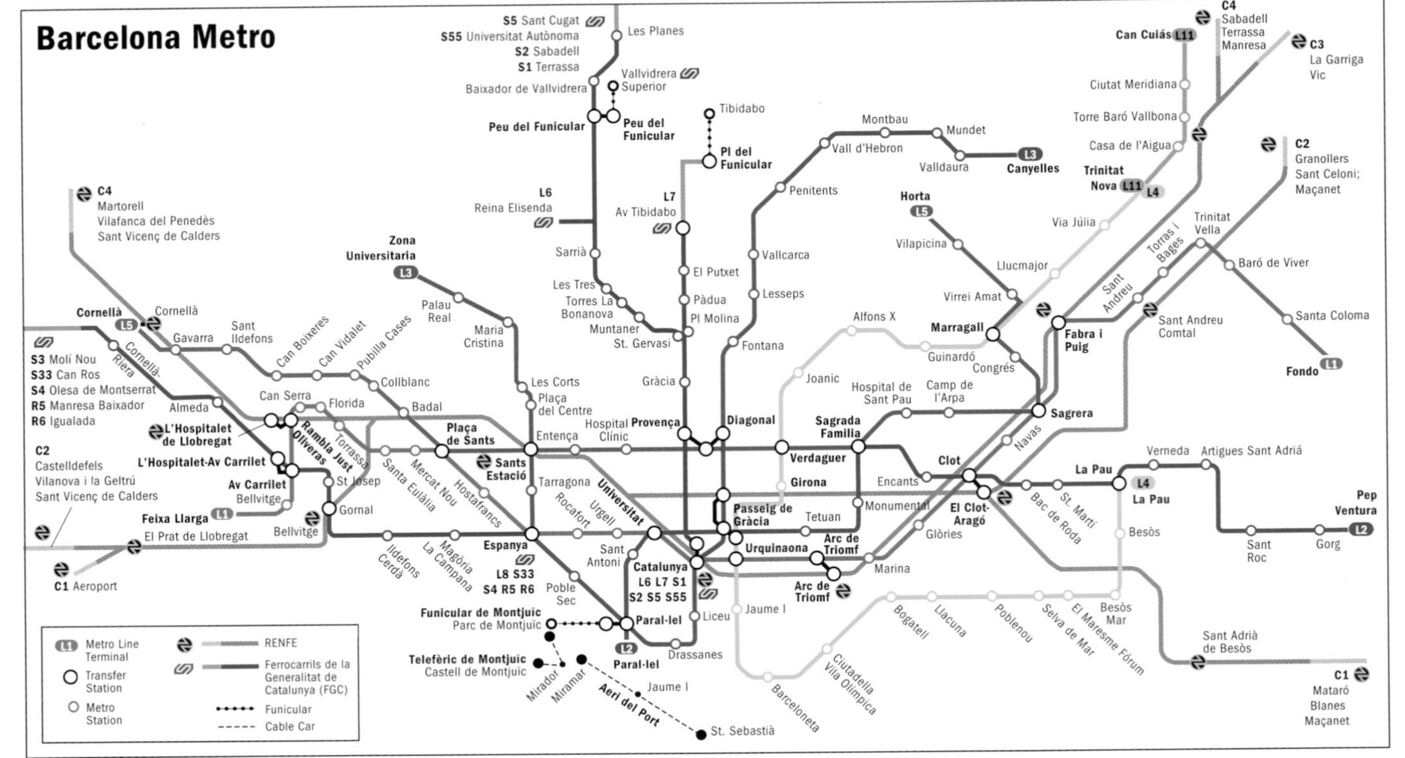

Barcelona Metro
S5 Sant Cugat
S55 Universitat Autònoma
S2 Sabadell
S1 Terrassa
Les Planes
Baixador de Vallvidrera
Vallvidrera Superior
Peu del Funicular
Peu del Funicular
Tibidabo
Pl del Funicular
L6 Reina Elisenda
L7 Av Tibidabo
Sarrià
Les Tres Torres
La Bonanova
Muntaner
St. Gervasi
El Putxet
Pàdua
Pl Molina
Gràcia
Montbau
Mundet
Vall d'Hebron
Valldaura
Canyelles
Penitents
Vallcarca
Lesseps
Fontana
Horta
Vilapicina
Llucmajor
Virrei Amat
Can Cuiás
Ciutat Meridiana
Torre Baró Vallbona
Casa de l'Aigua
Trinitat Nova
Via Júlia
C4 Sabadell Terrassa Manresa
C3 La Garriga Vic
C2 Granollers Sant Celoni; Maçanet
Trinitat Vella
Torras i Bages
Baró de Viver
Sant Andreu
Sant Andreu Comtal
Santa Coloma
Fondo
Fabra i Puig
Marragall
Alfons X
Guinardó
Congrés
Joanic
Hospital de Sant Pau
Camp de l'Arpa
Sagrera
Navas
C4 Martorell Vilafanca del Penedès Sant Vicenç de Calders
Zona Universitaria
Palau Real
Maria Cristina
Les Corts
Plaça del Centre
Entença
Hospital Clínic
Provença
Diagonal
Sagrada Familia
Verdaguer
Girona
Encants
Clot
El Clot-Aragó
Verneda
Artigues Sant Adrià
La Pau
La Pau
Pep Ventura
Sant Roc
Gorg
Bac de Roda
St. Martí
Besòs
Cornellà
Cornellà
Cornellà-Riera
Gavarra
Sant Ildefons
Can Boixeres
Can Vidalet
Pubilla Cases
Collblanc
Badal
Plaça de Sants
Sants Estació
Can Serra
Florida
Torrassa
Rambla Just Oliveras
Santa Eulàlia
Mercat Nou
Hostafrancs
S3 Molí Nou
S33 Can Ros
S4 Olesa de Montserrat
R5 Manresa Baixador
R6 Igualada
Almeda
L'Hospitalet de Llobregat
L'Hospitalet-Av Carrilet
Av Carrilet
St Josep
Tarragona
Rocafort
Urgell
Universitat
Passeig de Gràcia
Tetuan
Monumental
Glòries
C2 Castelldefels Vilanova i la Geltrú Sant Vicenç de Calders
Bellvitge
Feixa Llarga
Bellvitge
Gornal
El Prat de Llobregat
C1 Aeroport
Ildefons Cerdà
Magòria La Campana
Espanya
L8 S33 S4 R5 R6
Sant Antoni
Catalunya L6 L7 S1 S2 S5 S55
Urquinaona
Arc de Triomf
Arc de Triomf
Marina
Poble Sec
Funicular de Montjuïc Parc de Montjuïc
Paral·lel
Paral·lel
Liceu
Jaume I
Drassanes
Telefèric de Montjuïc Castell de Montjuïc
Mirador
Miramar
Aeri del Port
Jaume I
St. Sebastià
Barceloneta
Ciutadella Vila Olímpica
Bogatell
Llacuna
Poblenou
Selva de Mar
El Maresme Fórum
Besòs Mar
Sant Adrià de Besòs
C1 Mataró Blanes Maçanet
Metro Line Terminal
Transfer Station
Metro Station
RENFE
Ferrocarrils de la Generalitat de Catalunya (FGC)
Funicular
Cable Car

LET'S GO

PAGES PACKED WITH ESSENTIAL INFORMATION

"Value-packed, unbeatable, accurate, and comprehensive."

—*The Los Angeles Times*

"The guides are aimed not only at young budget travelers but at the independent traveler; a sort of streetwise cookbook for traveling alone."

—*The New York Times*

"Unbeatable; good sight-seeing advice; up-to-date info on restaurants, hotels, and inns; a commitment to money-saving travel; and a wry style that brightens nearly every page."

—*The Washington Post*

THE BEST TRAVEL BARGAINS IN YOUR BUDGET

"All the dirt, dirt cheap."

—*People*

"Let's Go follows the creed that you don't have to toss your life's savings to the wind to travel—unless you want to."

—*The Salt Lake Tribune*

REAL ADVICE FOR REAL EXPERIENCES

"The writers seem to have experienced every rooster-packed bus and lunar-surfaced mattress about which they write."

—*The New York Times*

"[Let's Go's] devoted updaters really walk the walk (and thumb the ride, and trek the trail). Learn how to fish, haggle, find work—anywhere."

—*Food & Wine*

"A world-wise traveling companion—always ready with friendly advice and helpful hints, all sprinkled with a bit of wit."

—*The Philadelphia Inquirer*

A GUIDE WITH A SPIRIT AND A SOCIAL CONSCIENCE

"Lighthearted and sophisticated, informative and fun to read. [Let's Go] helps the novice traveler navigate like a knowledgeable old hand."

—*Atlanta Journal-Constitution*

"The serious mission at the book's core reveals itself in exhortations to respect the culture and the environment—and, if possible, to visit as a volunteer, a student, or a teacher rather than a tourist."

—*San Francisco Chronicle*

LET'S GO PUBLICATIONS

TRAVEL GUIDES

Australia
Austria & Switzerland
Brazil
Britain
California
Central America
Chile
China
Costa Rica
Eastern Europe
Ecuador
Egypt
Europe
France
Germany
Greece
Hawaii
India & Nepal
Ireland
Israel
Italy
Japan
Mexico
New Zealand
Peru
Puerto Rico
Southeast Asia
Spain & Portugal with Morocco
Thailand
USA
Vietnam
Western Europe

ROADTRIP GUIDE

Roadtripping USA

ADVENTURE GUIDES

Alaska
Pacific Northwest
Southwest USA

CITY GUIDES

Amsterdam
Barcelona
Boston
Buenos Aires
London
New York City
Paris
Rome
San Francisco
Washington, DC

POCKET CITY GUIDES

Amsterdam
Berlin
Boston
Chicago
London
New York City
Paris
San Francisco
Venice
Washington, DC

LET'S GO

SPAIN & PORTUGAL WITH MOROCCO 2009

ANNA KATHRYN KENDRICK EDITOR
MEAGAN MICHELSON ASSOCIATE EDITOR
DANIEL BARBERO ASSOCIATE EDITOR

RESEARCHER-WRITERS

JORGE ALVAREZ
GABRIELA BORTOLOMEDI
CHIMDIMNMA ESIMAI
JEFFREY PHANEUF
RUSSELL RENNIE
JESSICA RIGHTHAND
MOLLY STRAUSS
CHARLES FISHER-POST

ILLIANA QUIMBAYA MAP EDITOR
DWIGHT LIVINGSTONE CURTIS MANAGING EDITOR

ST. MARTIN'S PRESS NEW YORK

HELPING LET'S GO. If you want to share your discoveries, suggestions, or corrections, please drop us a line. We appreciate every piece of correspondence, whether a postcard, a 10-page email, or a coconut. Visit Let's Go at **http://www.letsgo.com,** or send email to:

feedback@letsgo.com
Subject: "Let's Go: Spain & Portugal"

Address mail to:

Let's Go: Spain & Portugal
67 Mount Auburn St.
Cambridge, MA 02138
USA

In addition to the invaluable travel advice our readers share with us, many are kind enough to offer their services as researchers or editors. Unfortunately, our charter enables us to employ only currently enrolled Harvard students.

Distributed outside the USA and Canada by Macmillan.

ISBN-13: 978-0-312-38573-6
ISBN-10: 0-312-38573-0
First edition
10 9 8 7 6 5 4 3 2 1

Let's Go: Spain & Portugal with Morocco is written by Let's Go Publications, 67 Mount Auburn St., Cambridge, MA 02138, USA.

HOW TO USE THIS BOOK

COVERAGE LAYOUT. *Let's Go: Spain & Portugal with Morocco* launches out of Madrid. Coverage spirals out counter-clockwise, ending in Galicia. Your travels begin anew in Portugal, starting in Lisboa and then sweeping from the south to the north. Morocco coverage is based around the travel hubs of Tangier, Casablanca, and Marrakesh, proceeding from north to south.

TRANSPORTATION INFO. For making connections between destinations, information is generally listed under both the arrival and departure cities. Parentheticals usually provide the trip duration followed by its frequency and price. To plan a rail jouney, check out the **Spain and Portugal Transportation** map (p. XVII). For more general information on travel, consult **Essentials** (p. 10).

COVERING THE BASICS. The first chapter, **Discover Spain, Portugal, and Morocco** (p. 1), contains highlights of the Iberian Peninsula and Morocco, complete with **Suggested Itineraries.** The **Essentials** (p. 10) chapter contains useful travel tips and practical information. The **Life and Times** chapters introduce each separate country (Spain p. 60; Portugal p. 566; Morocco p. 701) and briefly sum up the history, culture, and customs of each destination. The **Appendix** (p. 759) has climate information, a list of bank holidays, measurement conversions, and a glossary. For study abroad, volunteer, and work options in Spain and Portugal, **Beyond Tourism** (p. 49) is all you need.

LANGUAGE. Translations of words and phrases in Spanish, Portuguese, and regional languages appear in parentheses directly folloing them. City and provincial names in this guide are listed in Castilian first, followed by the regional language in parentheses where appropriate. For details on Spanish, Portuguese, Arabic, French, and regional languages like català, euskera, and gallego, see the Language sections for each country (Spain p. 60; Portugal p. 566; Morocco p. 706), or the Appendix (p. 760).

PRICE DIVERSITY. Our researchers list establishments in order of value from best to worst, with absolute favorites denoted by the Let's Go thumbs-up (☒). Since the cheapest price does not always mean the best value, we have incorporated a system of price ranges for food and accommodations; see p. XII.

PHONE CODES AND TELEPHONE NUMBERS. Area codes for each region appear opposite the name of the region and are denoted by the ☎ icon. Phone numbers in text are also preceded by the ☎ icon.

A NOTE TO OUR READERS. The information for this book was gathered by Let's Go researchers from May through August of 2008. Each listing is based on one researcher's opinion, formed during his or her visit at a particular time. Those traveling at other times may have different experiences since prices, dates, hours, and conditions are always subject to change. You are urged to check the facts presented in this book beforehand to avoid inconvenience and surprises.

ih
totally loved my time studing at
Kristin, Iceland
The teachers make learning Spanish fun. They really love it and it shows.
Micki, Germany
DONALD, CANADA X
After studying at IH I now have
of friends from all over the world
Nasim, Sweden
Selina USA
Todos, desde las secretarias hasta las profesores, todos nos hicieron sentir como en nuestra casa.
Carl, Group Leader – USA
yo ♥ ihSpain
Love to learn Spanish whilst travelling in Spain
Come and study with International House Spain. We offer a wide range of quality Spanish language courses and accommodation options, wonderful social and cultural activities and an experience you will never forget.
Combine your travels with a Spanish course at one or more schools.
IH Barcelona . IH Cordoba . IH Madrid . IH Palma de Mallorca
IH San Sebastian . IH Seville . IH Valencia . IH Vejer (Cadiz)
www.iloveihspain.com

CONTENTS

DISCOVER SPAIN, PORTUGAL AND MOROCCO 1
ESSENTIALS 10
BEYOND TOURISM 49
A Philosophy for Travelers 49
Volunteering 49
Studying 53
Working 56
SPAIN (ESPAÑA) **60**
History 60
Current Events 66
People and Culture 67
MADRID 78
San Lorenzo de El Escorial 123
Comunidad de Madrid 125
Sierra De Guadarrama 129
Cercedilla 129
CASTILLA Y LEÓN 131
Segovia 131
Ávila 137
Salamanca 141
Zamora 149
León 151
Astorga 155
Valladolid 157
Burgos 161
Palencia 166
Soria 168
CASTILLA LA MANCHA AND EXTREMADURA 172
Toledo 172
Cuenca 179
Extremadura 184
Cáceres 184
Trujillo 189
Mérida 192
Badajoz 196
SEVILLA 200
ANDALUCÍA 220
Córdoba 220
Costa de la Luz 229
Jerez de la Frontera 230
Sanlúcar de Barrameda 234
Arcos de la Frontera 236
Cádiz 238
Vejer de la Frontera 243
Tarifa 244
Gibraltar 247
Costa del Sol 250
Málaga 250
Marbella 255
Almería 259
Mojácar 263
Ronda 266
Antequera 270
Granada 273
Guadix 284
Las Alpujarras 285
VALENCIA AND MURCIA 289
Valencia 289
Castellón 301
Morella 303
Costa Blanca 304
Alicante (Alacant) 306
Benidorm 312
Denia 314
Murcia 316
LAS ISLAS BALEARES 322
Mallorca (Majorca) 324
Palma 324
Western Mallorca 330
Northern Mallorca 332
Southeastern Mallorca 334
Menorca 334
Mahón (Maó) 334
Ciutadella (Ciudadela) 339
Beaches 341
Ibiza (Eivissa) 343
San Antonio de Portmany (Sant Antoni) 350
Formentera 351
BARCELONA 353
Montserrat 391
CATALUÑA (CATALUNYA) **394**
Costa Dorada 394
Sitges 394
Tarragona 399
Reus 403
Costa Brava 406
Tossa de Mar 406
Calella de Palafrugell 409
Girona (Gerona) 410
Figueras (Figueres) 415
Cadaqués and Port Lligat 418
Inland Catalunya 421
Lérida (Lleida) 421
THE PYRENEES 424
Catalan Pyrenees 424
Ripoll 424
Puigcerdà 429
Parc Nacional d'aigüestortes I Estany de Sant Maurici 432
Espot 434
Boí 435

Val d'Aran 436
Vielha 436
La Seu d'Urgell 439
Andorra 441
Aragonese Pyrenees 444
Jaca 444
Parque Nacional de Ordesa 447
Valle de Benasque 450
Navarran Pyrenees 452
Valle de Roncal 454
ARAGÓN, LA RIOJA, AND NAVARRA (NAVARRE) 456
Aragón 456
Zaragoza 456
Teruel 465
La Rioja 467
Logroño 468
Navarra (Navarre) 473
Pamplona (Iruña) 473
PAÍS VASCO (EUSKADI) **484**
San Sebastián (Donostia) 484
Bilbao (Bilbo) 492
Guernica (Gernika) 498
Vitoria-Gasteiz 500
ASTURIAS AND CANTABRIA..... 506
Asturias 506
Oviedo 507
Gijón 512
Cangas de Onís 515
Parque Nacional Picos de Europa 517
Cantabria 527
Santander 527
GALICIA (GALIZA) **536**
Santiago De Compostela 536
Rías Bajas (Rías Baixas) 545
Vigo 545
Pontevedra 553
Rías Altas 557
La Coruña (A Coruña) 557
Lugo 562
The Northern Coast 564
PORTUGAL 566
History 566
Current Events 571
People and Culture 571
LISBOA 579
Belém 604
Cascais 607
Ericeira 608
Sintra 609
Setúbal 613
ALGARVE AND ALENTEJO 616
Algarve 616
Lagos 616
Sagres 622
Albufeira 624
Faro 626
Olhão 628
Alentejo 630
Évora 631
Beja 636
Sines 638
RIBATEJO AND ESTREMADURA .. 641
Santarém 641
Peniche 645
Nazaré 649
Leiria 653
Fátima 656
Tomar 659
Castelo Branco 662
THE NORTH 664
Douro and Minho 664
Porto (Oporto) 664
Braga 671
Parque Nacional da Peneda-Gerês 678
Viana do Castelo 680
The Three Beiras 684
Coimbra 684
Buçaco Forest and Luso 689
Aveiro 690
Trás-Os-Montes 696
Bragança 696
MOROCCO 701
Life and Times 701
People and Culture 706
Essentials 710
EXPLORING MOROCCO 715
Tangier 715
Chefchaouen (Chaouen) 722
The Middle Atlas 725
Meknes 725
Fez 731
The Atlantic Coast 741
Asilah 741
Casablanca 743
Essaouira 748
The High Atlas 751
Marrakesh 753
APPENDIX 760
Climate 760
Measurements 760
Glossary 768
INDEX 774
MAP INDEX 782

RESEARCHER-WRITERS

Jorge Alvarez *Lisboa, Alentejo, Ribatejo, Estremadura, Northern Portugal*

Jorge got to the core of Portugal and rose above all challenges, from overzealous train authorities to the Portuguese wilderness. From encounters with Metallica to journeys through castles and cathedrals, Jorge's adventures, whether in fast-paced Lisboa or quiet Monsanto, never failed to liven up his editors' summers.

Gabriela Bortolomedi *Galicia, Asturias, Castilla y León*

Hailing from the warm shores of Puerto Rico, Gabi arrived in chilly Salamanca in June and promptly sought out a winter jacket and lots of *café con leche.* But when she hit the Atlantic coast, Gabi truly came alive. Whether writing about the islands of Vigo or the sunny streets of Santiago, her words brimmed with good humor, artistic joy, and a genuine love of the road. From shells to sardines, Gabi gave herself fully to the spirit of the Northwest.

Chimdimnma Esimai *Andalucía, Extremadura, the Algarve*

Chi-Chi's passion for all things Spanish led her to strap on a backpack for one blazing hot summer. Endlessly fascinated by cities like Córdoba and Cáceres, Chi-Chi took the time to talk to everyone from immigration workers to bartenders, sending back dispatches full of personal spark. We wish her all the best in graduate school, and eagerly await stories of her next jaunt through *al-Andalus*.

Charles Fisher-Post *Granada*

After a semester studying in the beautiful city of Granada, Charles was eager to bring his insider knowledge to *Let's Go* readers everywhere. And he did, with spirit and a smile. A two-time vet, Charles previously brought his professionalism to *Let's Go: Greece 2008* and *Australia 2009.* We are the luckier for having had him join our team.

Jeffrey Phaneuf *Asturias and Cantabria, País Vasco, the Pyrenees*

Jeff's route was "hahd"—there's no denying it—but he took it by the horns with unbelievable determination. For Jeff, unforeseen snowstorms in the Pyrenees made Massachusetts winters seem like paradise. Buses failed to show up, and Phaneuf prevailed. Elderly female hostel owners got a little too friendly, and still Phaneuf prevailed. On top of it all, he stared down the bulls of Pamplona. Jeff Phaneuf was truly a champ of an RW—and that's no bull.

RESEARCHER-WRITERS

Russell Rennie *Madrid and Morocco*

Part-time *aficionado* and full-time cultural voyeur, Russell hit the ground running in Madrid. Once in Morocco, he infiltrated markets and tanneries and kept his editors laughing, awestruck, all summer long. Expats, hippies, hustlers: no one was safe when Russell came to town. Whether scaling hostel roofs or Rif peaks, Russell was a tirelessly intrepid researcher. Yes, we are so glad he said yes.

Jessica Righthand *Valencia, Murcia, and Las Islas Baleares*

Jess island-hopped like a rockstar. Always on the lookout for artsy, hip coverage, Jess found her way into film festivals, hot nightclubs, and nudist colonies. She sunned on the white sands of Valencia and Murcia, jammed with the jazzy locals in an Ibizan nightclub, and met some unforgettable people along the way. Her most impressive feat? She managed to bring her guitar home in one piece.

Molly Strauss *Barcelona, Catalunya, Aragón, La Rioja, and Navarra*

Molly's enthusiasm was infectious. This easy-going Santa Monica girl brought her sunny ways to Spain, and despite a twisted ankle and a stolen pack, she powered through her research with unwavering commitment. From Gaudí's lizards to mooing dogs, her time in Barcelona was an adventure. She often told her editors that she fell in love with the city, and frankly, her editors fell in love with her.

CONTRIBUTING WRITERS

Antonio Córdoba was born in Sevilla, where he earned his B.A. in English Literature. He got his Ph.D. in Latin American literature from Harvard University in June of 2008, and is currently a lecturer in History and Literature at Harvard. Córdoba is completing a book on a 17th-century Andalucian poet.

Silvia Killingsworth was Editor-in-Chief of the 2008 *Let's Go* series. She graduated from Harvard in 2007 and now lives in New York City.

Victoria Norelid graduated from Harvard in 2007 with a degree in History. She has edited for *Let's Go: Italy 2007*, *Let's Go: Mexico 2008*, and *Let's Go: London 2008*, and most recently was a Researcher-Writer for *Let's Go: Australia 2009*. She is currently getting a Masters degree at Oxford University.

PRICE RANGES
SPAIN & PORTUGAL

Our researchers list establishments in order of value from best to worst, honoring our favorites with the Let's Go thumbs-up (☒). Because the best *value* is not always the cheapest *price*, we have incorporated a system of price ranges based on a rough expectation of what you will spend. For **accommodations,** we base our range on the cheapest price for which a single traveler can stay for one night. For **restaurants** and other dining establishments, we estimate the average amount a traveler will spend in one sitting. The table below tells you what you'll typically find in Spain and Portugal at each price range, but keep in mind that no system can allow for the quirks of individual establishments.

ACCOMMODATIONS	RANGE	WHAT YOU'RE *LIKELY* TO FIND
❶	under €20	Campgrounds, HI hostels, basic dorm rooms, *albergues* or *refugios.* Expect bunk beds and a communal bath; you may have to provide or rent towels and sheets.
❷	€20-29	Upper-end hostels or lower-end *pensiones.* You may have a private bathroom, or there may be a sink in your room and a communal shower in the hall. Breakfast is often included, or meals may be available cheaply to hostel guests.
❸	€30-37	A small room with a private bath, probably in a budget hotel, *hostal,* or *pensión.* Should have decent amenities, like a phone and TV. Breakfast may be included.
❹	€38-50	Similar to ❸, but should have more amenities or be in a more highly-touristed or conveniently-located area. Breakfast is often included in the price of your room.
❺	above €50	Large hotels, upscale chains, or government-run luxury *paradores.* If it's a ❺ and it doesn't have the perks or service you're looking for, you've probably paid too much.

FOOD	RANGE	WHAT YOU'RE *LIKELY* TO FIND
❶	under €6	Probably a *kebap* or fast-food stand, *cafetería,* bar, or bakery. Rarely a sit-down meal, unless you're sitting at the bar feasting on free tapas with your drinks.
❷	€6-12	*Bocadillos* (sandwiches), salads, tapas, and some entrees and set *menús.* May be sit-down or take-out, but expect to be served by a waiter or bartender.
❸	€13-17	Typically a sit-down meal. Many set menús include a 3-course meal that includes wine and dessert.
❹	€18-25	Entrees are more expensive than ❸, but you're paying for quality service, ambience, and decor. Few restaurants in this range have a dress code, but you'll want to clean yourself up after a day of travel.
❺	over €25	Your meal might cost more than your hostel, but here's hoping it's something fabulous or famous. Just don't plan on wearing flip-flops.

ACKNOWLEDGMENTS

TEAM SP&M THANKS: Our fabulous **RWs.** Dwight, for bustin' our chops. Nathaniel, for managing our tickets all summer long. Illiana, for seeing the world as it is. Ronan, for bringing S&P to the masses. Sam, Inés, and the Prod team, for making this book a reality.

ANNA THANKS: SPadThai. Meg for being shooptastic. Sr. Barbero for caravels and alfajores. Ashley for calming grace. Dwight for guiding brilliance. Nathaniel for outbursts and laughs. ROAD for Monday nights and the Garden of Life. Here's to RW love, sunlight, foreign muses, RadCrew, *Let's Go*, and my family.

MEAGAN THANKS: Our fantabulous RWs. Anna for her smiles and love of Lorca. DBarbs, a.k.a. "bro," for being silent but deadly. Dwight for being an honorary shoop, and shaking it like one. Ash for being a real person—and an amazing one. Nathaniel for his format prowess and coupons. Dube for Dunkin. Mapland for their dance parties. Mrs. O'Brien. Nicole. Hemingway. HRST 2009. *Let's Go*. Mom for being there through it all.

DANIEL THANKS: Anna, *para todo*, and for being the perfect foil to her crazy AEs; Meg, for singing to us (and more); Nathaniel and Ashley for completing wondrous SpadThai; my comrades at LG for making this a superb summer; as always, my family, for their support, understanding, and *pastafrola*.

ILLIANA THANKS: Anna for her constant smiles and hard work. Meg for her shoop-shoop dance moves. Dan for tolerating his split AE status with cheer. Mapland for all the laughs (most notably, Derek's Prince moments). All the SPaM RWs for bringing down the house. And Nemo for keeping me sane during the entire summer.

Editor
Anna Kathryn Kendrick
Associate Editors
Meagan Michelson, Daniel Barbero
Managing Editor
Dwight Livingstone Curtis
Map Editor
Illiana Quimbaya
Typesetter
C. Alexander Tremblay

LET'S GO

Publishing Director
Inés C. Pacheco
Editor-in-Chief
Samantha Gelfand
Production Manager
Jansen A. S. Thurmer
Cartography Manager
R. Derek Wetzel
Editorial Managers
Dwight Livingstone Curtis,
Vanessa J. Dube, Nathaniel Rakich
Financial Manager
Lauren Caruso
Publicity and Marketing Manager
Patrick McKiernan
Personnel Manager
Laura M. Gordon
Production Associate
C. Alexander Tremblay
Director of IT & E-Commerce
Lukáš Tóth
Website Manager
Ian Malott
Office Coordinators
Vinnie Chiappini, Jenny Wong
Director of Advertising Sales
Eric Alberto Claros
Business Manager of Advertising
Nicole J. Bass
Senior Advertising Associates
Kipyegon Kitur, Jeremy Siegfried,
John B. Ulrich
Junior Advertising Associate
Edward C. Robinson Jr.

President
Timothy J. J. Creamer
General Manager
Jim McKellar

CANTABRIAN SEA
Gijón
At Coruña
Asturias and Cantabria
p. 506
ASTURIAS
Oviedo
Cangas de Onís
Santander
Bilbao
CANTABRIA
Santiago de
Compostela
Galicia
p. 536
León
Burgos
Castilla y León
p. 131
Viana do
Castelo
Bragança
Valladolid
DOURO AND
MINHO
TRÁS-OS-MONTES
The North
p. 624
Porto
Salamanca
THE THREE BEIRAS
Aveiro
Guarda
Segovia
Madrid
p. 78
Coimbra
PORTUGAL
Madrid
Toledo
Ribatejo and
Estremadura
p. XXX
Cáceres
Castilla la Mancha
and Extremadura
p. 172
CASTILLA
Lisboa
p. 579
EXTREMADURA
Lisboa
Mérida
Setúbal
Badajoz
Ciudad Real
ALENTEJO
Évora
Beja
Córdoba
Algarve and Alentejo
p. 616
Sevilla
p. 200
Andalucía
p. 220
ALGARVE
Lagos
Faro
Granada
Málaga
ATLANTIC
OCEAN
Gibraltar
Algeciras
ALBORAN
SEA
Morocco
p. 701
MOROCCO

Spain and Portugal Chapters
País Vasco
p. 484
FRANCE
Vitoria-Gasteiz
Pamplona
NAVARRA
ANDORRA
The Pyrenees
p. 424
Logroño
LA RIOJA
Girona
Zaragoza
Cataluña
p. 394
Aragón, La Rioja, and Navarra
p. 456
Barcelona
p. 353
Tarragona
Sigüenza
SPAIN
ARAGÓN
Teruel
Castellón
Cuenca
Mallorca
Palma
Valencia
LA MANCHA
VALENCIA
Las Islas Baleares
p. 322
Ibiza
Eivissa/Ibiza City
Formentera
TO MENORCA
Menorca
Ciudadela
Mahón
Alicante
Murcia
Valencia and Murcia
p. 289
MURCIA
MEDITERRANEAN SEA
Almería
ALGERIA
0
75 miles
0
75 kilometers

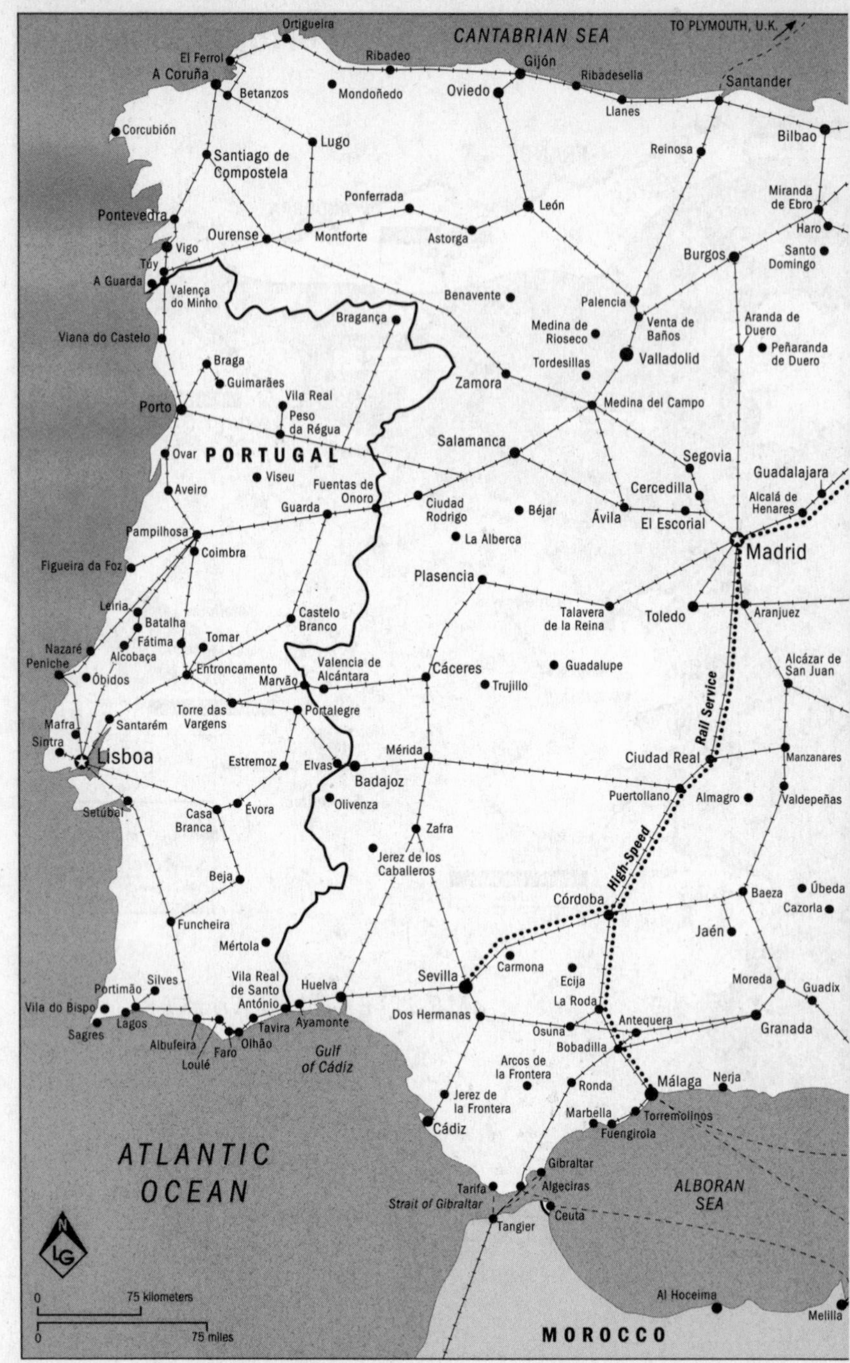
CANTABRIAN SEA
TO PLYMOUTH, U.K.
Ortigueira
El Ferrol
A Coruña
Betanzos
Ribadeo
Mondoñedo
Gijón
Oviedo
Ribadesella
Llanes
Santander
Bilbao
Corcubión
Lugo
Santiago de Compostela
Reinosa
Miranda de Ebro
Haro
Santo Domingo
Pontevedra
Ponferrada
León
Ourense
Montforte
Astorga
Vigo
Tuy
A Guarda
Valença do Minho
Burgos
Benavente
Palencia
Venta de Baños
Bragança
Medina de Rioseco
Aranda de Duero
Peñaranda de Duero
Viana do Castelo
Valladolid
Tordesillas
Braga
Guimarães
Zamora
Vila Real
Peso da Régua
Medina del Campo
Porto
Salamanca
Ovar
PORTUGAL
Segovia
Guadalajara
Viseu
Fuentas de Onoro
Cercedilla
Aveiro
Ciudad Rodrigo
Béjar
Ávila
El Escorial
Alcalá de Henares
Guarda
Pampilhosa
La Alberca
Madrid
Coimbra
Figueira da Foz
Plasencia
Leiria
Castelo Branco
Talavera de la Reina
Toledo
Aranjuez
Batalha
Fátima
Nazaré
Tomar
Alcobaça
Peniche
Valencia de Alcántara
Alcázar de San Juan
Guadalupe
Óbidos
Entroncamento
Cáceres
Marvão
Trujillo
Torre das Vargens
Portalegre
Mafra
Santarém
Rail Service
Sintra
Lisboa
Estremoz
Elvas
Mérida
Ciudad Real
Manzanares
Badajoz
Puertollano
Almagro
Valdepeñas
Setúbal
Évora
Olivenza
Casa Branca
Zafra
High-Speed
Jerez de los Caballeros
Beja
Úbeda
Córdoba
Baeza
Cazorla
Funcheira
Jaén
Mértola
Carmona
Sevilla
Ecija
Moreda
Guadix
Silves
Portimão
Vila Real de Santo António
Huelva
La Roda
Vila do Bispo
Lagos
Dos Hermanas
Sagres
Tavira
Ayamonte
Antequera
Granada
Albufeira
Faro
Olhão
Osuna
Loulé
Bobadilla
Gulf of Cádiz
Arcos de la Frontera
Ronda
Málaga
Nerja
Jerez de la Frontera
Marbella
Torremolinos
Cádiz
Fuengirola
ATLANTIC OCEAN
Gibraltar
Tarifa
Algeciras
ALBORAN SEA
Strait of Gibraltar
Tangier
Ceuta
N
LG
0
75 kilometers
0
75 miles
Al Hoceima
Melilla
MOROCCO

Spain and Portugal Transportation

DISCOVER SPAIN, PORTUGAL, AND MOROCCO

The Iberian Peninsula is a land apart. Cordoned from Europe and Africa by mountain and sea, Spain and Portugal are themselves cultural mosaics. Despite being fiercely proud of their individuality, Spain's regions share a common rhythm. Late-night parties segue into afternoon siestas, fast-paced cities shut down as citizens linger over lunch, and everything happens *mañana*. The dizzying Pyrenees and Picos de Europa exhilarate adventurers, while Spain's sands entice sun-lovers young and old. Pilgrims tread the path across northern Spain to the soaring cathedral of Santiago de Compostela, while other visitors make their pilgrimage to Madrid's famed art museums. Northeastern and central Spain are aesthetic wonders. Trendy, quirky Barcelona hugs a rugged coastline characterized by famed architecture like Antoni Gaudí's fantastical conjurings and Bilbao's shining Guggenheim Museum. The south, meanwhile, is the passionate Spain of popular imagination, home to bullfights, flamenco, tapas, and Moorish intricacies. The nocturnal energy of Madrid, Barcelona, and Ibiza could exhaust the most hardcore clubbers, but the Spanish tradition of *churros con chocolate* at dawn goes a long way to starting the next day off right. Spain is a paradise for partiers, a mecca for art lovers, a kick-start for thrill-seekers, and a rest stop for the restless.

Today, travelers will discover one of Europe's fastest-growing hotspots in Portugal. Lisboa, the capital and largest city, has the country's most impressive imperial monuments, while the southern Algarve, boasting spectacular beaches and wild nightlife, draws backpackers in droves. Northern Coimbra crackles with the energy of a university town, and Porto surpasses even Lisboa in elegance. Portugal's inland towns have a timeless feel, with medieval castles overlooking rushing rivers and peaceful town squares. The wild northern region, including the land in Trás-Os-Montes, is among the most pristine in all of Europe—some villages have remained unchanged for nearly a millennium.

While Morocco lies only 13 km from the southern tip of Spain, visitors will feel like they've stumbled into another world. Whether fascinated by the roots of Iberia's Muslim past, eager to experience the sounds and scents of bustling markets, or just longing to sit in a cafe with a steaming glass of mint tea, travelers consistently find that the bursting color and cultural hybridity of modern Morocco make a visit south from Iberia an unforgettable experience.

FACTS AND FIGURES

OFFICIAL NAMES: Kingdom of Spain, Portuguese Republic, Kingdom of Morocco

SPAIN POPULATION: 40.5 million

PORTUGAL POPULATION: 10.7 million

NUMBER OF PILGRIMS TO SANTIAGO DE COMPOSTELA IN 2007: 114,026

NUMBER OF CASTLES IN THE PORTUGUESE REPUBLIC: 101

NUMBER OF SPANISH SPEAKERS IN THE WORLD: 332 million

PORTUGAL'S MOST FAMOUS INVENTION: The hot air balloon, flown in Lisboa on August 8, 1709

HIGHEST PEAK IN IBERIA: 3478.6m (Mulhacén in Granada's Sierra Nevadas)

KILOMETERS SEPARATING SPAIN AND MOROCCO: 13

WHEN TO GO

Summer is **high season** *(temporada alta)* for coastal and interior regions in Spain and Portugal; winter is high season for ski resorts. In many areas, high season begins during **Semana Santa** (Holy Week; March 14-23 in 2008) and includes festival days. July and August see some of the hottest weather, especially in the central plains, where the mercury can creep up to 36°C (97°F). Tourism on the Iberian Peninsula peaks in August, when the coast overflows as inland cities empty out, leaving closed offices, restaurants, and lodgings. As a general rule, make **reservations** if you plan to travel in June, July, or August.

Traveling in the **low season** *(temporada baja)* has many advantages, most noticeably lighter crowds and lower prices. Many hostels cut their prices by at least 30%, and reservations are seldom necessary. While major cities and university towns may exude energy during these months, many smaller seaside spots are ghost towns, and tourist offices and sights cut their hours nearly everywhere. The weather is also ideal in spring and early summer, when temperatures are around 20-25°C (68-77°F). For a table of temperatures and rainfall, see **Climate,** p. 760. For a chart of **National Holidays** and **Festivals** in Spain, see p. 77; in Portugal, p. 578; and in Morocco, p. 709.

WHAT TO DO

Two millennia of invaders have swept over these countries, resulting in an edgy and eclectic culture ripe with custom, religion, history, and an irrepressible energy. You can see it in **Madrid's** famous nightlife (p. 119), in the sidewalk cafes of **Lisboa** (p. 579), and in extravagant festivals from small towns to big cities. There are countless ways to see Spain and Portugal: some choose to search out every Baroque chapel, while others spend weeks trekking on some of Europe's best trails. For those with time to spare, a trip down to Morocco adds more than a dash of spice to the Iberian experience.

IMAGES OF IBERIA

The insatiable frenzy of the **Queima das Fitas** in Coimbra (p. 688), **Las Fallas** in Valencia (p. 300), the **Feria de Abril** in Sevilla (p. 217), and the infamous **San Fermín** in Pamplona (p. 478) make it difficult to deny the overwhelming exuberance of the Iberian peninsula. But underneath Iberian fervor is a rich sonority of feeling—the poignant expressions of heartbreak are often as gripping and adrenaline-charged as the celebrations. The ritually tragic emotions of Portuguese **fado** would bring tears to the eyes of even the most macho bullfighters, who in turn create their own tragedies on Spanish sands. Meanwhile, art and architecture like Picasso's powerfully symbolic **Guernica** (p. 109) and the propagandistic **Valle de los Caídos** (p. 125) immortalize the real tragedies that scarred Spain during the last century. But ample opportunity exists for peace and quiet in the thin-aired reverence of **Montserrat** (p. 391), the serenity of a rowboat in **El Retiro** (p. 107), or the surreal calm of **Parc Güell** (p. 380).

CASAS TO CASTLES

From traditionally conservative to unconventionally decadent, the buildings and monuments of Iberia form a collage of architectural styles. The remains of ancient civilizations are everywhere—from the Celtiberian tower of **O Castro de**

Baroña (p. 544) and the Punic walls of **Cartagena** (p. 320) to Roman ruins like the aqueduct in **Segovia** (p. 131) and the amphitheater in **Mérida** (p. 192). Hundreds of years of Moorish rule left breathtaking monuments, including Granada's spectacular **Alhambra** (p. 278), Córdoba's **Mezquita** (p. 226), and Sintra's **Castelo dos Mouros** (p. 612). The Catholic church has spent immense sums of money to build some of the world's most ornate religious complexes, ranging from the pastiche of the **Convento de Cristo** (p. 661) to the imposing **El Escorial** (p. 123). Spain's magnificent cathedrals are Gothic, Plateresque, or just plain bizarre, like Gaudí's unfinished *Modernista* **Sagrada Família** in Barcelona (p. 380). Recent additions to the architectural landscape include Lisboa's expansive **Parque das Nações** (p. 604), Bilbao's gleaming **Guggenheim Museum** (p. 497), and Valencia's huge **Ciudad de las Artes y las Ciencias** (p. 296). The Roman ruins of **Volubulis** (p. 730) and Casablanca's **Hassan II Mosque** (p. 747) provide two very different glimpses of the societies that have shaped these lands.

AU NATUREL

Iberia's best-kept secrets are its sprawling national parks and soaring, snow-covered mountain ranges. **Andorra** (p. 441), in the heart of the Pyrenees, has easily accessible glacial valleys, rolling forests, and wild meadows. In northern Spain, the **Parque Nacional de Ordesa** (p. 447) features well-kept trails, rushing rivers, and thundering waterfalls, while the **Parc Nacional d'Aigüestortes** (p. 432) hides 50 ice-cold mountain lakes in its 24,700 acres of rugged peaks and valleys. The **Picos de Europa** (p. 517) offer some of Europe's best mountaineering. Northern Portugal's **Parque Natural de Montesinho** (p. 698) is probably the most isolated, untouched land in all of Europe. Farther south, greenery-starved *madrileños* hike the **Sierra de Guadarrama** (p. 129), and nature-lovers are drawn to Andalucía's huge **Parque Nacional Coto de Doñana** (p. 217), which protects nearly 60,000 acres of land for threatened wildlife. In the south, **Las Alpujarras** (p. 285) are perfect for hiking among Spain's famous *pueblos blancos* (white towns). Morocco's fertile, green **Rif Mountains** (p. 724) contrast with the deep oranges of the dramatic **High Atlas** (p. 751), both popular with trekkers.

SUN AND SAND

Iberia's stunning shores deserve their reputation as Europe's playground. **San Sebastián's**) calm,

WAYS TO SAVE IN SPAIN AND PORTUGA

Exchange rate pinching you pocket? Travel in style while stick ing to a budget with these tips fo cheap eats, low-cost lodgings, and free entertainment.

1. Buy food in **open-air mar kets** and **grocery stores** instead of restaurants. If you do go out, try sharing a selection of tapas.

2. Stay in **alternative lodgings** such as monasteries, university dorms, or *refugios.*

3. Be on the lookout for days when you can get into sights and museums for **free.**

4. Clubbing is pricey enough without depending on overpriced sangria; start the night off with **market-purchased booze.**

5. Keep an eye out for flyers and coupons (in weekly papers o from promoters) that offer heav discounts at **clubs.**

6. Take **public transportation** or **walk** as much as possible.

7. Relax on one of the Iberian peninsula's many **beaches** o **parks,** where the scenery is worth while and your tan is free!

8. **Bargain** where appropriate like in Madrid's El Rastro.

9. Get cheap tickets for fla menco and bullfighting show by attending semi-professiona events. They're less touristy, too.

10. Enjoy the **great outdoors** hike in the Pyrenees, or enjoy the view of the Alhambra from the hills rising above Granada.

voluptuous Playa de la Concha attracts young travelers from around the world, while **Santander** (p. 527) caters to an elite, refined crowd. The beaches of **Galicia** (p. 536) curve around crystal-green, misty inlets. On the **Islas Baleares** (p. 322), glistening bodies crowd the chic beaches, and southern Spain's infamous **Costa del Sol** (p. 250) draws tourists to its scorched Mediterranean bays by the plane-load. The eastern **Costa Blanca** (p. 304) mixes small-town charm with ocean expanses, while the looming cliffs and turquoise waters of Portugal's southern **Algarve** (p. 616) make for a relaxed vacation. Thrill-seekers will not be disappointed by the endless watersports opportunities—surfing, sailing, kiteboarding, scuba diving, and windsurfing are all popular. Morocco's **Essaouira** has a past of pirates and hippies, but today it's better known for music festivals and laid-back vibes.

ALL NIGHT LONG

Nightlife in Spain and Portugal ranges from laid back to debaucherous. With countless bars and clubs and intoxicating energy, **Madrid** (p. 78) has earned international renown as one of the greatest party cities in the world. **Barcelona's** (p. 353) wild, edgy nightlife reflects the city's outrageous sense of style. Residents of **Sevilla** (p. 200) pack discotecas floating on the Río Guadalquivir, and on **Ibiza** (p. 343) you will find the world's largest club, filled with 10,000 decadent partiers. Student-packed **Salamanca** (p. 141) is a crazed, international frat party, and **Lagos,** in Portugal (p. 566), has more bars and backpackers per square meter than any town in the world. In **Morocco,** visitors channel expats of old by drinking espresso at outdoor cafes and lounging on open rooftops under the night sky.

LET'S GO PICKS

BEST PLACE TO STUPIDLY ENDANGER YOUR LIFE: Pamplona, during the infamous Running of the Bulls (p. 478).

BEST PLACE TO SPOON A STRANGER: A *refugio* in Picos de Europa, where close quarters make for fast friends (p. 517).

BEST PLACE TO CRY LIKE A BABY: A fado house in Lisboa's Bairro Alto district, where melancholy music brings audiences to tears (p. 579).

BEST PLACE TO BUMP INTO MIRA SORVINO: Ibiza International Film Festival on the Islas Baleares (p. 343).

BEST PLACE TO HAVE A SURREALIST HALLUCINATION: Figueres at the Teatre-Museu Dalí (p. 417).

BEST MEDIEVAL RECYCLING PROJECT: The macabre Capela dos Ossos, in Évora, made from 5000 unwitting skeletons (p. 631).

BEST PLACE TO ATTACK UNSUSPECTING TOURISTS: Porto's Festa de São João, where for one evening in June townspeople beat each other over the head with plastic hammers (p. 671).

BEST PLACE TO BE LOUD AND PROUD: Madrid, during Orgullo Gay, one of the biggest gay festivals in the world, with parades and free concerts (p. 117).

BEST PLACE TO SIT ON THE THRONE: Sintra's Palácio da Pena, home of the Queen's golden toilet (p. 612).

BEST GNARLY WAVE: Peniche, at the Praia do Molho, site of "supertubos," also known as the "Portuguese pipeline," comparable to Hawaii's biggest surf (p. 647).

BEST PLACE TO CHARM A SNAKE: Djemaa el-Fna, Marrakesh's bizarre bazaar. And when that's done, enjoy storytellers and magicians (p. 756).

OFF THE BEATEN CAMINO

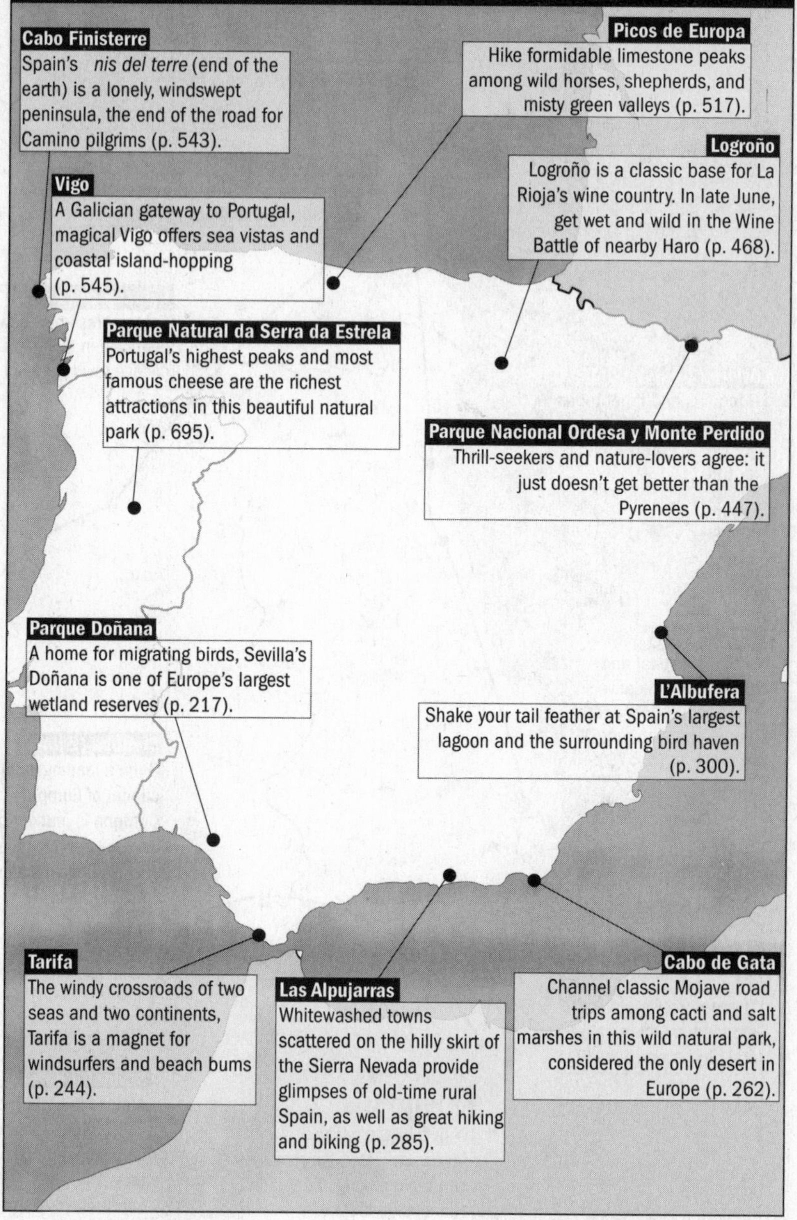

Cabo Finisterre
Spain's *nis del terre* (end of the earth) is a lonely, windswept peninsula, the end of the road for Camino pilgrims (p. 543).

Picos de Europa
Hike formidable limestone peaks among wild horses, shepherds, and misty green valleys (p. 517).

Logroño
Logroño is a classic base for La Rioja's wine country. In late June, get wet and wild in the Wine Battle of nearby Haro (p. 468).

Vigo
A Galician gateway to Portugal, magical Vigo offers sea vistas and coastal island-hopping (p. 545).

Parque Natural da Serra da Estrela
Portugal's highest peaks and most famous cheese are the richest attractions in this beautiful natural park (p. 695).

Parque Nacional Ordesa y Monte Perdido
Thrill-seekers and nature-lovers agree: it just doesn't get better than the Pyrenees (p. 447).

Parque Doñana
A home for migrating birds, Sevilla's Doñana is one of Europe's largest wetland reserves (p. 217).

L'Albufera
Shake your tail feather at Spain's largest lagoon and the surrounding bird haven (p. 300).

Tarifa
The windy crossroads of two seas and two continents, Tarifa is a magnet for windsurfers and beach bums (p. 244).

Las Alpujarras
Whitewashed towns scattered on the hilly skirt of the Sierra Nevada provide glimpses of old-time rural Spain, as well as great hiking and biking (p. 285).

Cabo de Gata
Channel classic Mojave road trips among cacti and salt marshes in this wild natural park, considered the only desert in Europe (p. 262).

BEST OF SPAIN AND PORTUGAL (6 WEEKS)

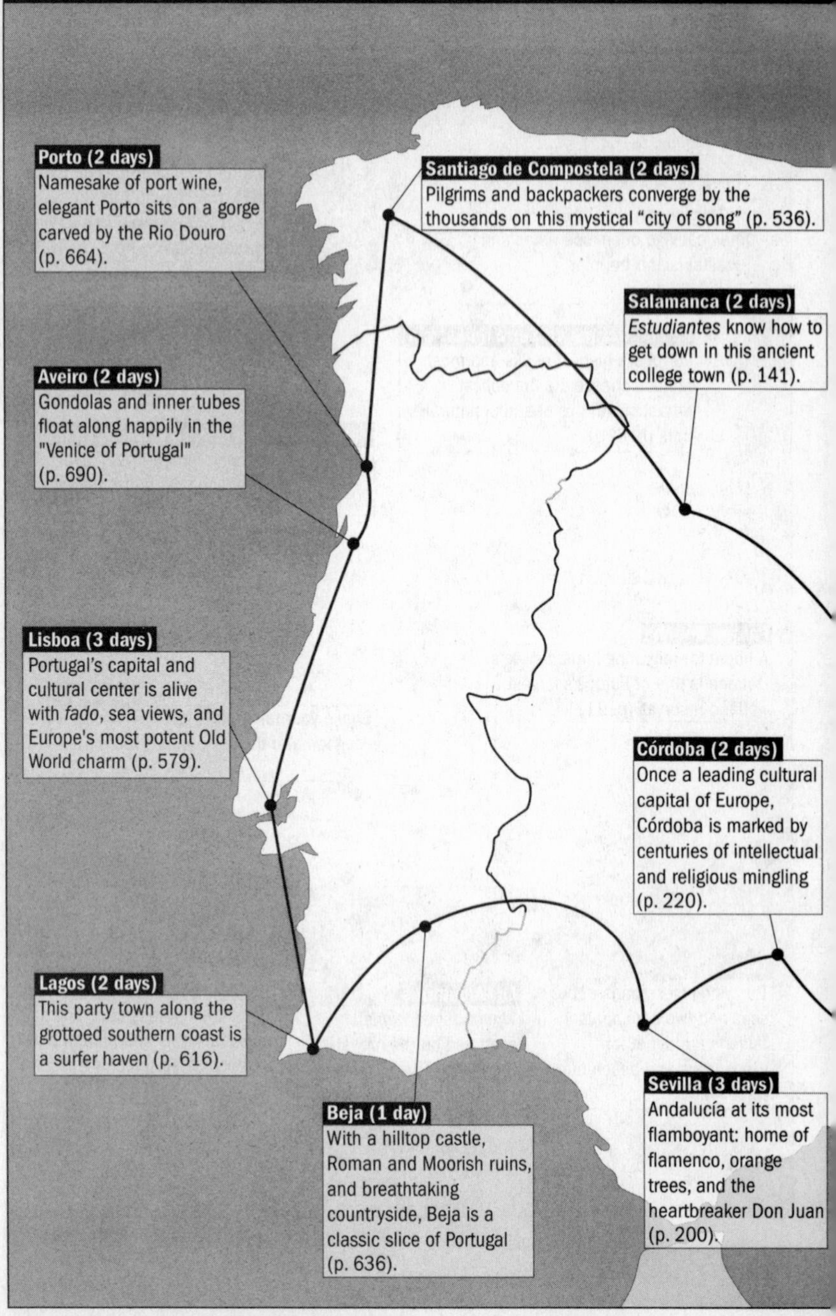

Porto (2 days)
Namesake of port wine, elegant Porto sits on a gorge carved by the Rio Douro (p. 664).

Santiago de Compostela (2 days)
Pilgrims and backpackers converge by the thousands on this mystical "city of song" (p. 536).

Salamanca (2 days)
Estudiantes know how to get down in this ancient college town (p. 141).

Aveiro (2 days)
Gondolas and inner tubes float along happily in the "Venice of Portugal" (p. 690).

Lisboa (3 days)
Portugal's capital and cultural center is alive with *fado*, sea views, and Europe's most potent Old World charm (p. 579).

Córdoba (2 days)
Once a leading cultural capital of Europe, Córdoba is marked by centuries of intellectual and religious mingling (p. 220).

Lagos (2 days)
This party town along the grottoed southern coast is a surfer haven (p. 616).

Beja (1 day)
With a hilltop castle, Roman and Moorish ruins, and breathtaking countryside, Beja is a classic slice of Portugal (p. 636).

Sevilla (3 days)
Andalucía at its most flamboyant: home of flamenco, orange trees, and the heartbreaker Don Juan (p. 200).

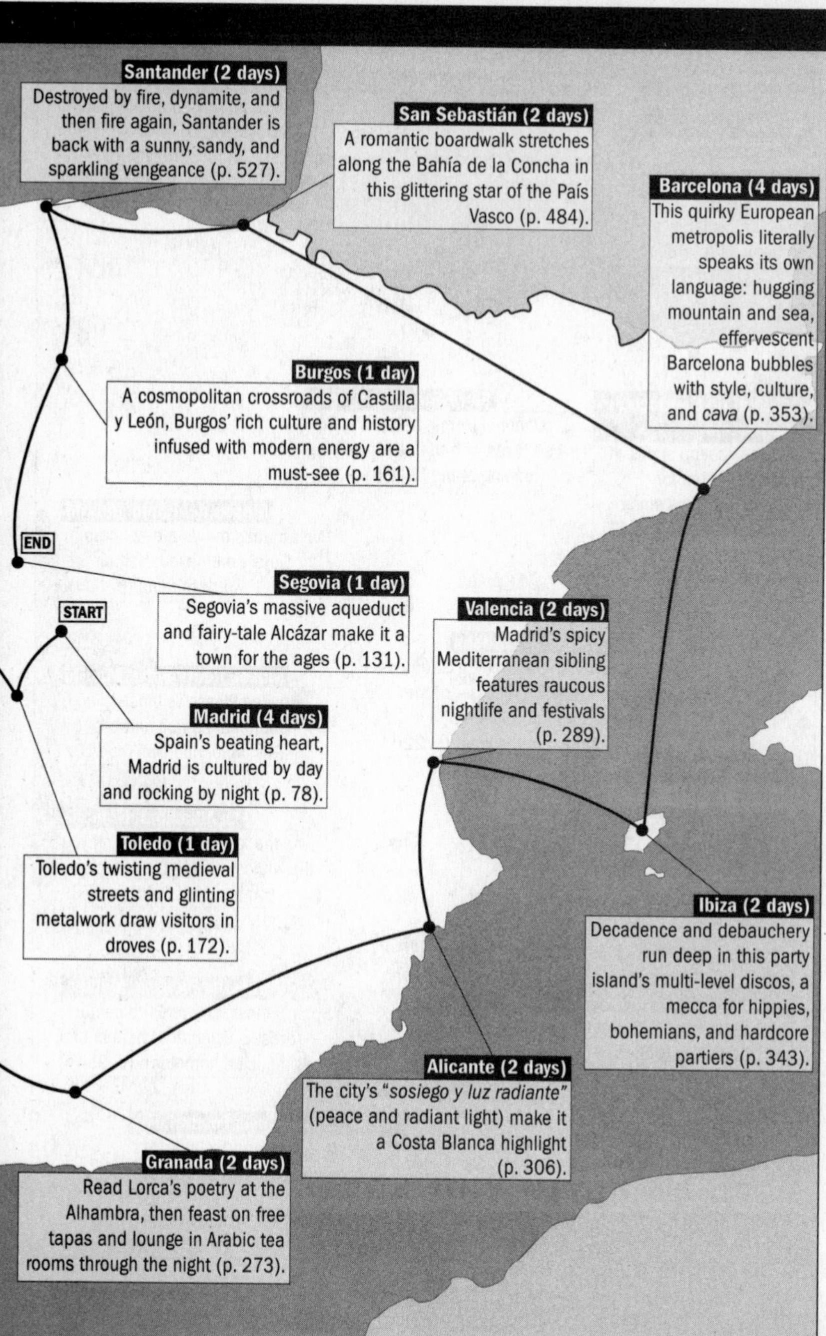
Santander (2 days)
Destroyed by fire, dynamite, and then fire again, Santander is back with a sunny, sandy, and sparkling vengeance (p. 527).
San Sebastián (2 days)
A romantic boardwalk stretches along the Bahía de la Concha in this glittering star of the País Vasco (p. 484).
Barcelona (4 days)
This quirky European metropolis literally speaks its own language: hugging mountain and sea, effervescent Barcelona bubbles with style, culture, and *cava* (p. 353).
Burgos (1 day)
A cosmopolitan crossroads of Castilla y León, Burgos' rich culture and history infused with modern energy are a must-see (p. 161).
END
Segovia (1 day)
Segovia's massive aqueduct and fairy-tale Alcázar make it a town for the ages (p. 131).
START
Valencia (2 days)
Madrid's spicy Mediterranean sibling features raucous nightlife and festivals (p. 289).
Madrid (4 days)
Spain's beating heart, Madrid is cultured by day and rocking by night (p. 78).
Toledo (1 day)
Toledo's twisting medieval streets and glinting metalwork draw visitors in droves (p. 172).
Ibiza (2 days)
Decadence and debauchery run deep in this party island's multi-level discos, a mecca for hippies, bohemians, and hardcore partiers (p. 343).
Alicante (2 days)
The city's "*sosiego y luz radiante*" (peace and radiant light) make it a Costa Blanca highlight (p. 306).
Granada (2 days)
Read Lorca's poetry at the Alhambra, then feast on free tapas and lounge in Arabic tea rooms through the night (p. 273).

THE CULTURED LIFE

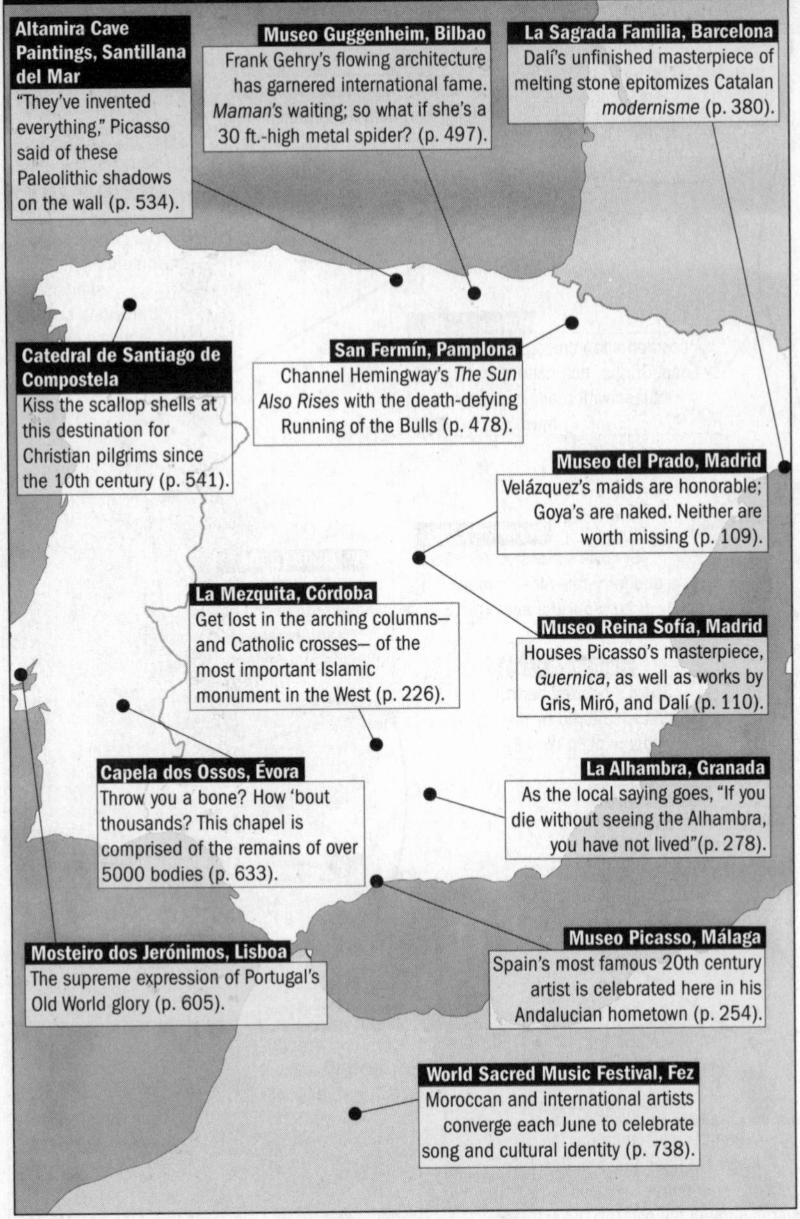

Altamira Cave Paintings, Santillana del Mar
"They've invented everything," Picasso said of these Paleolithic shadows on the wall (p. 534).

Museo Guggenheim, Bilbao
Frank Gehry's flowing architecture has garnered international fame. *Maman's* waiting; so what if she's a 30 ft.-high metal spider? (p. 497).

La Sagrada Familia, Barcelona
Dalí's unfinished masterpiece of melting stone epitomizes Catalan *modernisme* (p. 380).

Catedral de Santiago de Compostela
Kiss the scallop shells at this destination for Christian pilgrims since the 10th century (p. 541).

San Fermín, Pamplona
Channel Hemingway's *The Sun Also Rises* with the death-defying Running of the Bulls (p. 478).

Museo del Prado, Madrid
Velázquez's maids are honorable; Goya's are naked. Neither are worth missing (p. 109).

La Mezquita, Córdoba
Get lost in the arching columns– and Catholic crosses– of the most important Islamic monument in the West (p. 226).

Museo Reina Sofía, Madrid
Houses Picasso's masterpiece, *Guernica*, as well as works by Gris, Miró, and Dalí (p. 110).

Capela dos Ossos, Évora
Throw you a bone? How 'bout thousands? This chapel is comprised of the remains of over 5000 bodies (p. 633).

La Alhambra, Granada
As the local saying goes, "If you die without seeing the Alhambra, you have not lived"(p. 278).

Mosteiro dos Jerónimos, Lisboa
The supreme expression of Portugal's Old World glory (p. 605).

Museo Picasso, Málaga
Spain's most famous 20th century artist is celebrated here in his Andalucian hometown (p. 254).

World Sacred Music Festival, Fez
Moroccan and international artists converge each June to celebrate song and cultural identity (p. 738).

AL-LOVIN' AL-ANDALUS (4 WEEKS)

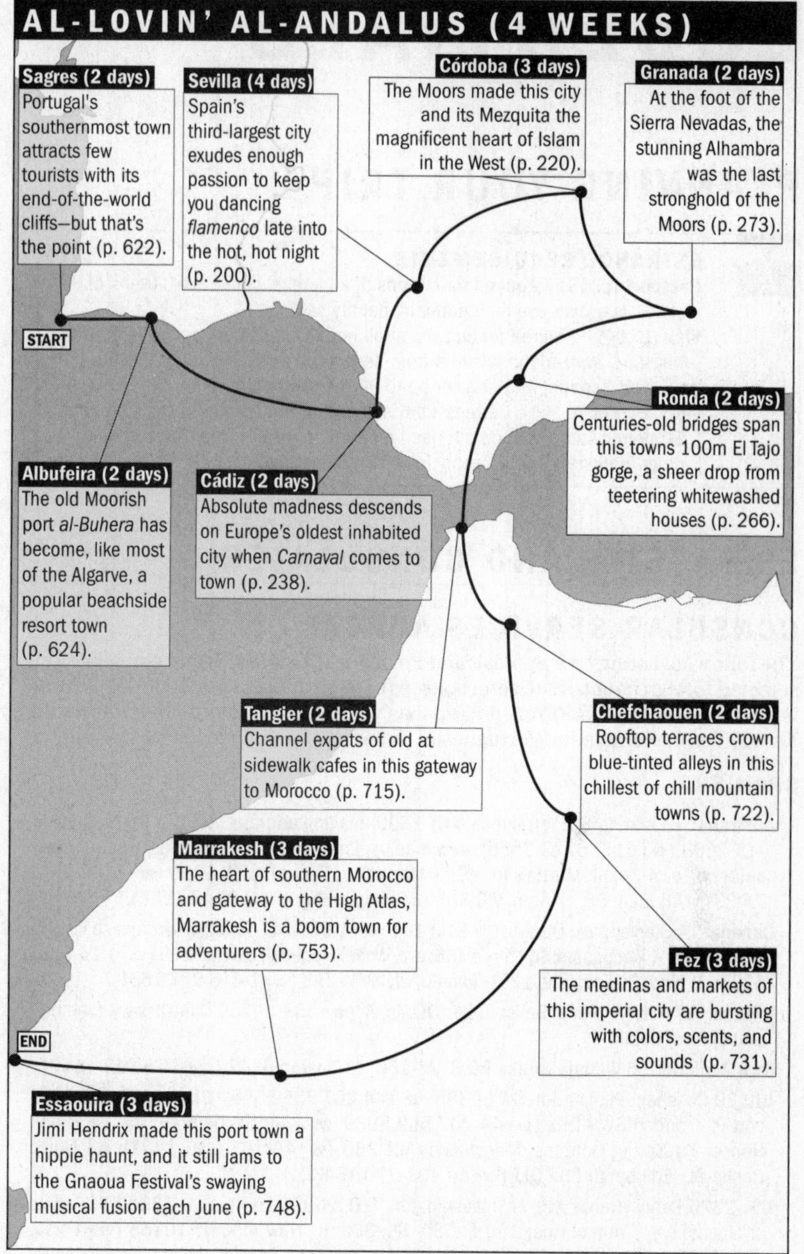

Sagres (2 days)
Portugal's southernmost town attracts few tourists with its end-of-the-world cliffs—but that's the point (p. 622).
Sevilla (4 days)
Spain's third-largest city exudes enough passion to keep you dancing *flamenco* late into the hot, hot night (p. 200).
Córdoba (3 days)
The Moors made this city and its Mezquita the magnificent heart of Islam in the West (p. 220).
Granada (2 days)
At the foot of the Sierra Nevadas, the stunning Alhambra was the last stronghold of the Moors (p. 273).
START
Ronda (2 days)
Centuries-old bridges span this towns 100m El Tajo gorge, a sheer drop from teetering whitewashed houses (p. 266).
Albufeira (2 days)
The old Moorish port *al-Buhera* has become, like most of the Algarve, a popular beachside resort town (p. 624).
Cádiz (2 days)
Absolute madness descends on Europe's oldest inhabited city when *Carnaval* comes to town (p. 238).
Tangier (2 days)
Channel expats of old at sidewalk cafes in this gateway to Morocco (p. 715).
Chefchaouen (2 days)
Rooftop terraces crown blue-tinted alleys in this chillest of chill mountain towns (p. 722).
Marrakesh (3 days)
The heart of southern Morocco and gateway to the High Atlas, Marrakesh is a boom town for adventurers (p. 753).
Fez (3 days)
The medinas and markets of this imperial city are bursting with colors, scents, and sounds (p. 731).
END
Essaouira (3 days)
Jimi Hendrix made this port town a hippie haunt, and it still jams to the Gnaoua Festival's swaying musical fusion each June (p. 748).

ESSENTIALS

PLANNING YOUR TRIP

ENTRANCE REQUIREMENTS

Passport (p. 13). Required for citizens of all foreign countries. Citizens of EU states may also use their national identity card.

Visa (p. 14). Required for citizens of all non-EU states, except Iceland, Norway, and Switzerland. Visitors from select countries, including the US, the UK, and Canada, may stay for up to 90 days without a visa.

Work Permit (p. 14). Citizens from states that participate in the European Economic Area (EEA) do not need a permit to work in Spain or Portugal. All other foreigners should apply for work visas at their nearest embassy.

EMBASSIES AND CONSULATES

CONSULAR SERVICES ABROAD

The following listings are Spanish and Portuguese embassies and consulates in selected foreign countries. Useful sources of such information include the Ministerio de Asuntos Exteriores de España (www.mae.es) and the Secretaria de Estado das Comunidades Portuguesas (www.secomunidades.pt/postos.php).

SPANISH

Australia: 15 Arkana St., Yarralumla, ACT 2600; mailing address: P.O. Box 9076, Deakin ACT 2600 (☎+61 2 6273 3555; www.mae.es/Embajadas/Canberra/es/Home). **Consulates:** Level 24, St. Martin's Tower, 31 Market St., Sydney, NSW 2000 (☎+61 2 9261 24 33); 146 Elgin St., Carlton, VIC 3053 Melbourne (☎+61 3 9347 1966).

Canada: 74 Stanley Ave., Ottawa, ON K1M 1P4 (☎+1-613-747-2252; www.embaspain.ca). **Consulates:** 1 Westmount Sq., Ste. 1456, Ave. Wood, Montreal, QC H3Z 2P9 (☎+1 14-935-5235); 2 Bloor St. East. Ste. 1201, Toronto, ON M4W 1A8 (☎+1-416-977 1661).

Ireland: 17 Merlyn Park, Ballsbridge, Dublin 4 (☎+353 1 269 1640; www.mae.es/embajadas/dublin).

New Zealand: 56 Victoria Street, P.O.B. 24-150, Wellington 6142 (☎+64 4 913 1167).

UK: 39 Chesham Pl., London SW1X 8SB (☎ +44 207 235 5555). **Consulates:** 20 Draycott Pl., London SW3 2RZ (☎+44 207 589 8989; www.conspalon.org); Ste. 1A, Brook House, 70 Spring Gardens, Manchester M2 2BQ (☎+44 161 236 1262); 63 North Castle St., Edinburgh EH2 3LJ (☎+44 131 220 1843.)

US: 2375 Pennsylvania Ave. NW, Washington, D.C. 20037 (☎+1-202-728-2330; www.spainemb.org). **Consulates:** 150 E. 58th St., 30th fl., New York, NY 10155 (☎+1-212 355-4080s); branches in Boston, Chicago, Houston, Los Angeles, Miami, New Orleans, San Francisco, and San Juan (PR).

PORTUGUESE

Australia: 23 Culgoa Circuit, O'Malley, Canberra, ACT 2606; P.O. Box 92, Deakin, ACT 2600 (☎+61 2 6290 1733). **Consulate:** Level 9, 30 Clarence St., Sydney, NSW 2000; P.O. Box 3309, Sydney, NSW 2001 (☎+61 2 9262 2199; www.consulportugalsydney.org.au).

Canada: 645 Island Park Dr., Ottawa, ON K1Y 0B8 (☎+1-613-729-2270; www.embportugal-ottawa.org). **Consulates** in Toronto, Edmonton, Halifax, Kingston, Montreal, Quebec, Vancouver, and Winnipeg.

Ireland: Knocksinna House, Knocksinna, Foxrock, Dublin 18 (☎+353 1 289 4416).

New Zealand: See Australian embassy in Canberra. **Consulates:** 16 Fisher Crescent, Mt Wellington; PO Box 305, Auckland (☎+64 9 259 4014), Suite 1, 1st Fr, 21 Marion St., PO Box 1024 Wellington ☎+64 4 382 7655).

UK: 3 Portland Pl., London W1B-1HR (☎+44 20 7291 3770).

US: 2012 Massachusetts Ave. NW, Washington, D.C. 20036 (☎+1-202-350-5400). **Consulates:** 590 5th Ave., 3rd fl., New York, NY 10036 (☎+1-212-221-3165); branches in Boston, New Bedford, New Orleans, Newark, Providence, San Francisco.

CONSULAR SERVICES IN SPAIN

Embassies and consulates are usually open Monday through Friday mornings and late afternoons, with siestas in between. Many consulates are only open mornings. Call ahead for exact hours.

Australia: Pl. del Descubridor Diego de Ordás, 3, Madrid 28003 (☎913 53 66 00; www.spain.embassy.gov.au). **Consulates:** Pl. Gala Placidia, 1-3, 1st fl., Barcelona 08006 (☎934 90 90 13); Federico Rubio, 14, Sevilla 41004 (☎954 22 09 71).

Canada: C. Núñez de Balboa, 35, Madrid 28001 (☎914 23 32 50; www.canada-es.org). **Consulates:** Elisenda de Pinós, 10 Barcelona 08034 (☎932 04 27 00); Pl. de la Malagueta, 2, 1st fl., Málaga 29016 (☎952 22 33 46).

Ireland: Po. de la Castellana, 46, 4th fl., Madrid, 28046 (☎914 36 40 93; www.dfa.ie). **Consulate:** Gran Vía de Carlos III, 94, 10th fl., Barcelona 08028 (☎934 91 50 21).

New Zealand: Pinar 7, 3rd fl., Madrid 28006 (☎915 23 02 26; www.nzembassy.com). **Consulate:** Tr. de Gràcia, 64, 4th fl., Barcelona 08006 (☎932 09 03 99).

UK: Po. de Recoletos, 7-9, 4th fl., Madrid 28004 (☎915 24 97 00; www.ukinspain.com). **Consulate-General:** Av. Diagonal, 477, 13th fl., Barcelona 08036 (☎933 66 62 00). **Consulates** in Alicante, Bilbao, Ibiza, Las Palmas, Málaga, Santa Cruz de Tenerife, and Palma de Mallorca.

US: C. de Serrano, 75, Madrid 28006 (☎915 87 22 40; www.embusa.es). **Consulate General:** Po. Reina Elisenda de Montcada, 23, Barcelona 08034 (☎932 80 22 27). **Consulates** in A Coruña, Las Palmas, Málaga, Palma de Mallorca, Sevilla, Valencia.

CONSULAR SERVICES IN PORTUGAL

Australia: Embassy: Av. da Liberdade, 200, 2nd fl., 1250-147 Lisboa (☎213 10 15 00; www.portugal.embassy.gov.au).

Canada: Av. da Liberdade, 198-200, 3rd fl., 1269-121 Lisboa (☎213 16 46 00; www.portugal.gc.ca. **Consulate:** R. Frei Lourenço de Santa Maria, 1, 1st fl., Apdo. 79, 8001 Faro (☎289 80 37 57).

Ireland: R. da Imprensa à Estrela, 1-4, 4th fl., 1200-684 Lisboa (☎213 92 94 40).

New Zealand: Contact New Zealand embassy in Rome: Via Zara 28, Rome 00198, Italy (☎396 441 7171; www.nzembassy.com). **Consulate:** Rua do Periquito, Lote A-13, Quinta da Bicuda, Cascais 2750-712 (☎213 705 779).

UK: R. de São Bernardo, 33, 1249-082 Lisboa (☎213 92 41 59; www.britishembassy.gov.uk). **Consulates** in Portimao (☎282 49 07 50) and Oporto (☎226 18 47 89).

United States: Av. das Forças Armadas, 1600-081 Lisboa (☎217 27 33 00; http://portugal.usembassy.gov).

TOURIST OFFICES

IN SPAIN

Spain's official tourist board provides information at www.tourspain.es.

Canada: Tourist Office of Spain, 2 Bloor St. West, 34th fl., Toronto, ON M4W 3E2 (☎+1 416 961 3131; www.tourspain.toronto.on.ca).

UK: Spanish National Tourist Office, 22-23 Manchester Sq., London W1M 5AP (☎+44 207 486 8077; http://www.spain.info/uk/TourSpain).

US: Tourist Office of Spain, 666 5th Ave., 35th fl., New York, NY 10103 (☎+1 212 265 8822; www.okspain.org). Additional offices in Beverly Hills, CA (☎+1-323-658-7188), Miami, FL (☎+1-305-358-1992), and Chicago, IL (☎+1-312-642-1992).

IN PORTUGAL

The official Portuguese tourism website is located at www.visitportugal.com.

Canada: Portuguese Trade and Tourism Commission, 60 Bloor St. West, Ste. 1005, Toronto, ON M4W 3B8 (☎+1-416-921-7376).

UK: Portuguese Trade and Tourism Office (ICEP), 11 Belgrave Sq., London SWIX 8PP (☎+44 207 201 6666; www.visitportugal.com).

US: Portuguese National Tourist Office, 590 5th Ave., 4th fl., New York, NY 10036 (☎+1-212-354-4403; www.portugal.com).

DOCUMENTS AND FORMALITIES

PASSPORTS

REQUIREMENTS

Citizens of Australia, Canada, Ireland, New Zealand, the UK, and the US need valid passports to enter **Spain** and to re-enter their home countries. To enter **Portugal,** citizens from EU states need only a national identity card and are not required to present a passport. Neither Spain nor Portugal allow entrance if the holder's passport expires in under 6 months; returning home with an expired passport is illegal and may result in a fine.

NEW PASSPORTS

Citizens of Australia, Canada, Ireland, New Zealand, the UK, and the US can apply at any passport office or at selected post offices and courts of law. Citizens of these countries may also download passport applications from the official website of their country's government or passport office. Any new passport or renewal applications must be filed well in advance of the departure date, though most passport offices offer rush services for a very steep fee. "Rushed" passports still take up to two weeks to arrive.

ONE EUROPE. European unity has come a long way since 1958, when the European Economic Community (EEC) was created to promote European solidarity and cooperation. Since then, the EEC has become the European Union (EU), a mighty political, legal, and economic institution. What does this have to do with the average non-EU tourist? The EU's policy of **freedom of movement** means that most border controls have been abolished and visa policies harmonized. Under this treaty, formally known as the **Schengen Agreement,** you're still required to carry a passport (or government-issued ID card for EU citizens) when crossing an internal border, but, once you've been admitted into one country, you're free to travel to other participating states. Britain and Ireland have also formed a **common travel area,** abolishing passport controls between the UK and the Republic of Ireland.

PASSPORT MAINTENANCE

Photocopy the page of your passport with your photo, as well as your visas, traveler's check serial numbers, and any other important documents. Carry one set of copies in a safe place and leave another set at home. Consulates also recommend that you carry an expired passport or an official copy of your birth certificate in a part of your baggage separate from other documents.

If you lose your passport, immediately notify the local police and nearest embassy or consulate of your home government. To expedite its replacement, you must show ID and proof of citizenship. Have a record of all information recorded in the passport. In some cases, a replacement may take weeks to process, and it may be valid only for a limited time. Any visas stamped in your old passport will be lost. In an emergency, ask for immediate temporary traveling papers that will permit you to re-enter your home country.

VISAS AND WORK PERMITS

VISAS

As of August 2008, EU citizens do not need a visa to enter Spain or Portugal. Citizens of Australia, Canada, New Zealand, and the US do not need a visa for stays of up to 90 days, though this three-month period begins upon entry into any of the countries that belong to the EU's freedom of movement zone. For more information, see **One Europe** (p. 13). Those staying longer than 90 days must apply for a visa in person at their local embassy or consulate. Double-check entrance requirements at the nearest embassy or consulate of Spain or Portugal (see **Embassies and Consulates, p. 10**) for up-to-date info before departure. US citizens can also consult http://travel.state.gov. Entering Spain or Portugal to study requires a visa (see **Beyond Tourism,** p. 49).

WORK PERMITS

Admission as a visitor does not include the right to work, which is authorized only by a work permit (see **Beyond Tourism,** p. 56).

IDENTIFICATION

When you travel, always carry at least two forms of identification on your person, including a photo ID. A passport and a driver's license or birth certificate should suffice. Never carry all of your IDs together; instead, split them up in case of theft or loss and keep photocopies in your luggage and at home.

STUDENT, TEACHER, AND YOUTH IDENTIFICATION

The **International Student Identity Card (ISIC),** the most widely accepted form of student ID, provides discounts on some sights, accommodations, food, and transportation, access to a 24hr. emergency help line, and insurance benefits for US cardholders. In Spain, the ISIC can provide discounts like 20% off Alsa bus tickets. Applicants must be full-time secondary or post-secondary school students at least 12 years old. Because of the proliferation of fake ISICs, some services (particularly airlines) require additional proof of student identity.

The **International Teacher Identity Card (ITIC)** offers teachers the same insurance coverage as the ISIC and similar but limited discounts. To qualify for the card, teachers must be currently employed and have worked a minimum of 18hr. per week for at least one school year. For travelers who are under 26 years old but who are not students, the **International Youth Travel Card (IYTC)** also offers many of the same benefits as the ISIC does.

Each of these identity cards costs US$22. ISICs, ITICs, and IYTCs are valid for one year from the date of issue. To learn more about ISICs, ITICs, and IYTCs, visit www.myisic.com. Many student travel agencies (p. 26) issue the cards; for a list of issuing agencies or more information, see the **International Student Travel Confederation (ISTC)** website (www.istc.org).

The **International Student Exchange Card (ISE Card)** is a similar identification card available to students, faculty, and ages 12 to 26. The card provides discounts, medical benefits, access to a 24hr. emergency help line, and the ability to purchase student airfares. An ISE Card costs US$25. Call ☎+1-800-255-8000 in North America or ☎+1-480-951-1177 from all other continents for more info, or visit www.isecard.com.

CUSTOMS

CUSTOMS IN THE EU. As well as freedom of movement of people (p. 13), travelers in the European Union can also take advantage of the freedom of movement of goods. This means that there are no customs controls at internal EU borders (i.e., you can take the blue customs channel at the airport), and travelers are free to transport whatever legal substances they like as long as it is for their own personal (non-commercial) use—up to 800 cigarettes, 10L of spirits, 90L of wine (including up to 60L of sparkling wine), and 110L of beer. Duty-free allowances were abolished on June 30, 1999, for travel between the original 15 EU member states; this now also applies to Cyprus and Malta. However, travelers between the EU and the rest of the world still get a duty-free allowance when passing through customs.

Upon entering Spain or Portugal, you must declare certain items from abroad and pay a duty on the value of those articles if they exceed the allowance established by the Spanish or Portuguese customs service. Goods and gifts purchased at duty-free shops abroad are not exempt from duty or sales tax; "duty-free" only means that you won't pay tax in the country of purchase. Duty-free allowances were abolished for travel between EU member states on June 30, 1999, but still exist for those arriving from outside the EU. Upon returning home, you must likewise declare all articles acquired abroad and pay a duty on the value of articles in excess of your home country's allowance. In order to expedite your return, make a list of any valuables brought from home and register them with customs before traveling abroad. It's a good idea to keep receipts for all goods acquired abroad.

MONEY

CURRENCY AND EXCHANGE

CURRENCY

AUS$1 = EUR €0.59	EUR €1 = AUS$1.70
CDN$1 = EUR €0.62	EUR €1 = CDN$1.62
NZ€1 = EUR €0.47	EUR €1 = NZ$2.15
UK£1 = EUR €1.26	EUR €1 = UK£0.79
US$1 = EUR €0.65	EUR €1 = US$1.54

The currency chart above is based on August 2008 exchange rates between local currency and Australian dollars (AUS$), Canadian dollars (CDN$), European Union euro (EUR€), New Zealand dollars (NZ$), British pounds (UK£), and US dollars (US$). Check the currency converter on websites like www.xe.com or www.bloomberg.com for the latest exchange rates. As a general rule, it is cheaper to convert money in Spain or Portugal than at home. While currency exchange will probably be available in your arrival airport, it is wise to bring enough foreign currency to last for at least a few days.

When changing money abroad, try to go only to banks or *casas de cambio* that have at most a 5% margin between their buy and sell prices. Since you lose money with every transaction, it makes sense to convert large sums at one time (unless the currency is depreciating rapidly).

If you use traveler's checks or bills, carry some in small denominations (the equivalent of US$50 or fewer) for times when you are forced to exchange money at poor rates, but bring a range of denominations since charges may be applied per check cashed. Store your money in a variety of forms; ideally, at any given time you will be carrying some cash, some traveler's checks, and an ATM or credit card. All travelers should also consider carrying some US dollars (about US$50 worth), which are often preferred by local tellers.

TRAVELER'S CHECKS

Traveler's checks are one of the safest and most convenient means of carrying funds. American Express and Visa are the most recognized brands. Many banks and agencies sell them for a small commission. Check issuers provide refunds if the checks are lost or stolen, and many provide additional services, such as toll-free refund hotlines abroad, emergency message services and assistance with lost and stolen credit cards or passports. Traveler's checks are readily accepted in most parts of Spain and Portugal, though less convenient than ATMs or credit cards. Ask about toll-free refund hotlines and the location of refund centers when purchasing checks, and always carry emergency cash.

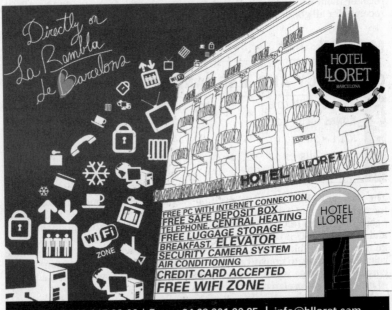

American Express: Checks available with commission at select banks, at all AmEx offices, and online (www.americanexpress.com; US residents only). AmEx cardholders can also purchase checks by phone (☎+1-800-528-4800). AmEx also offers the Travelers Cheque Card, a prepaid, reloadable card. Cheques for Two can be signed by either of 2 people traveling together. For purchase locations or more information, contact AmEx's service centers: in Australia ☎+61 2 9271 8666, in New Zealand +64 9 367 4567, in the UK +44 1273 696 933, in the US and Canada +1-800-221-7282; elsewhere, call the US collect at +1-336-393-1111. For emergency services in Spain, call ☎917 43 70 00, or in Portugal, ☎214 27 04 00/04 02.

Travelex: Visa TravelMoney prepaid cash card and Visa traveler's checks available. For information about Thomas Cook MasterCard in Canada and the US, call ☎+1-800-223-7373, in the UK +44 0800 622 101; from elsewhere, call the UK collect at +44 1733 318 950. For information about Interpayment Visa in the US and Canada, call ☎+1-800-732-1322, in the UK +44 0800 515 884; from elsewhere, call the UK collect at +44 1733 318 949. For more information, visit www.travelex.com.

Visa: Checks available (generally with commission) at banks worldwide. For the location of the nearest office, call the Visa Travelers Cheque Global Refund and Assistance Center: in the UK ☎+44 0800 895 078, in the US +1-800-227-6811; from elsewhere, call the UK collect at +44 2079 378 091. Checks available in British, Canadian, European, Japanese, and US currencies, among others. Visa also offers TravelMoney, a prepaid debit card that can be reloaded online or by phone. For more information on Visa travel services, see http://usa.visa.com/personal/using_visa/travel_with_visa.html.

ESSENTIALS

CREDIT, DEBIT, AND ATM CARDS

PINS AND ATMS. To use a cash or credit card to withdraw money from a cash machine (ATM) in Europe, you must have a four-digit Personal Identification Number (PIN). If your PIN is longer than four digits, ask your bank whether you can use just the first four or whether you'll need a new one. Credit cards don't usually come with PINs, so, if you intend to hit up ATMs in Europe with a credit card to get cash advances, call your credit card company before leaving to request one.

Travelers with alphabetic rather than numerical PINs may also be thrown off by the lack of letters on European cash machines. The following are the corresponding numbers to use: 1 = QZ; 2 = ABC; 3 = DEF; 4 = GHI; 5 = JKL; 6 = MNO; 7 = PRS; 8 = TUV; 9 = WXY. If you mistakenly punch the wrong code into the machine three times, it will swallow your card for good.

Where they are accepted, credit cards often offer superior exchange rates—up to 5% better than the retail rate used by banks and other currency exchange establishments. Credit cards may also offer services like insurance or emergency help and are sometimes required to reserve hotel rooms or rental cars. **MasterCard** and **Visa** (a.k.a. Carte Bleue) are the most frequently accepted; **American Express** cards work at some ATMs and at AmEx offices and major airports.

ATM cards are widespread in Spain and Portugal. Depending on the system that your home bank uses, you can most likely access your personal bank account from abroad. ATMs get the same wholesale exchange rate as credit cards, but there is often a limit on the amount of money you can withdraw per day, usually around US$500. There is also typically a surcharge of US$1-5 per withdrawal. Debit cards are as convenient as credit cards but withdraw money directly from the holder's checking account. A debit card can be used wherever its associated credit card company (usually MasterCard or Visa) is accepted. Debit cards often also function as ATM cards and can be used to withdraw cash from associated banks and ATMs throughout Spain and Portugal.

The two major international money networks are **MasterCard/Maestro/Cirrus** (for ATM locations ☎+1-800-424-7787 or www.mastercard.com) and Visa/PLUS (for ATM locations ☎+1-800-847-2911 or www.visa.com). Most ATMs charge a transaction fee that is paid to the bank that owns the ATM.

GETTING MONEY FROM HOME

If you run out of money while traveling, the easiest and cheapest solution is to have someone back home make a deposit to your bank account. Otherwise, consider one of the following options.

WIRING MONEY

It is possible to arrange a **bank money transfer,** which means asking a bank back home to wire money to a bank in Spain or Portugal. This is the cheapest way to transfer cash, but it's also the slowest, often taking several days. Some banks may only release your funds in local currency, potentially sticking you with a poor exchange rate; inquire about this in advance. Money transfer services like **Western Union** are faster and more convenient than bank transfers—but also much pricier. Western Union has many locations worldwide. To find a local agent in Spain or Portugal, visit www.westernunion.com.

US STATE DEPARTMENT (US CITIZENS ONLY)

In serious emergencies only, the US State Department will forward money within hours to the nearest consular office, which will then disburse it according to instructions for a US$30 fee. If you wish to use this service, you must contact the Overseas Citizens Services division of the US State Department (☎+1-202-501-4444, from US 888-407-4747).

COSTS

The cost of your trip will vary considerably, depending on where you go, how you travel, and where you stay. The most significant expenses will probably be your round-trip (return) airfare (see **Getting to Spain and Portugal: By Plane,** p. 25) and your internal transport and accommodation costs. Before you go, spend some time calculating a reasonable daily budget.

STAYING ON A BUDGET

To give you a general idea, a bare-bones day in Spain or Portugal (camping or sleeping in hostels/guesthouses, buying food at supermarkets) would cost about €40 (US$62); a slightly more comfortable day (sleeping in hostels/guesthouses and the occasional budget hotel, eating one meal per day at a restaurant, going out at night) would cost closer to €60 (US$93); and, for a luxurious day, the sky's the limit. Don't forget to factor in emergency reserve funds (at least US$200) when planning how much money you'll need.

TIPS FOR SAVING MONEY

Some simpler ways include searching out opportunities for free entertainment, splitting accommodation and food costs with trustworthy fellow travelers, and buying food in supermarkets rather than eating out. Bring a sleepsack (p. 19) to save on sheet charges in hostels and do your laundry in the sink (unless you're explicitly prohibited from doing so). Museums often have certain days once a month or once a week when admission is free, so plan accordingly. If you are eligible, consider getting an ISIC or an IYTC card (p. 14) to reap the benefits of reduced admission at museums and sights. Bikes are a great way to get around, and renting a bike is cheaper than renting a moped or scooter. Don't forget about walking, though; you can learn a lot about a city by seeing it on foot. Drinking at bars and clubs quickly becomes expensive, so many Spanish youths continue the tradition of *botellón* (buying alcohol in the supermarket and partying in the street), though authorities tend to frown on public drunkenness.

TIPPING AND BARGAINING

IN SPAIN

Tipping is not widespread in Spain or Portugal. In restaurants, all prices include a service charge. Satisfied customers occasionally toss in some spare change and while it is purely optional, tipping is becoming customary in restaurants and other places that cater to tourists. Many people give train, airport, and hotel porters €1 per bag while taxi drivers sometimes get 5-10%. Bargaining is common at flea markets and with street vendors.

IN PORTUGAL

Tips are customary in fancy restaurants and hotels. Cheaper restaurants include a 10% service charge; if they don't and you'd like to leave a tip, round up and leave the change. Taxi drivers do not expect a tip unless the trip was especially long. Bargaining is not customary in shops, but give it a shot at the local *mercado* (market) or when looking for a private room.

TAXES

Both Spain and Portugal have a 7-8% **value added tax,** known as **IVA,** on all meals and accommodations. The prices listed in *Let's Go* include IVA unless otherwise mentioned. Retail goods bear a much higher 16% IVA, although listed prices are usually inclusive. Non-EU citizens who have stayed in the EU fewer than 180 days can claim back the tax paid on purchases at the airport. Ask the shop where you have made the purchase to supply you with a tax return form, though stores will often provide them only for purchases of more than €50-100. **Taxes,** presently 21%, are included in all prices in Portugal. Request a refund form, *Isenção de IVA,* which is presented to customs upon departure.

PACKING

Pack lightly: lay out only what you absolutely need, then take half the clothes and twice the money. The **Travelite FAQ** (www.travelite.org) is a good resource for tips on traveling light. The online **Universal Packing List** (http://upl.codeq.info) will generate a customized list of suggested items based on your trip length, the expected climate, your planned activities, and other factors. If you plan on doing a lot of hiking, also consult **The Great Outdoors,** p. 42.

Luggage: If you plan to cover most of your itinerary by foot, a sturdy internal-frame backpack is unbeatable. In addition, a smaller pack is useful for daily use.

Clothing: Depending on destination and season, pack rain gear and breathable, cotton or linen clothing, a warm jacket or wool sweater, sturdy shoes or hiking boots, and thick socks. Pack modest and respectful dress for visting religious sites. Flip-flops or waterproof sandals are useful for grubby hostel showers.

Sleepsack: Some hostels require that you either provide your own linen or rent sheets. Save cash by making your own sleepsack: fold a full-size sheet in half the long way, then sew it closed along the long side and one of the short sides.

Converters and Adapters: In Spain and Portugal, electricity is 230 volts AC, enough to fry any 120V North American appliance. 220/240V electrical appliances won't work with a 120V current, either. Americans and Canadians should buy an adapter and a converter.

Don't make the mistake of using only an adapter (unless appliance instructions explicitly state otherwise). Australians and New Zealanders (who use 230V at home) won't need a converter, but will need a set of adapters.

Toiletries: Condoms, deodorant, tampons, and toothbrushes are readily available.

First-Aid Kit: Pack bandages, a pain reliever, antibiotic cream, a thermometer, a multi-function pocketknife, tweezers, moleskin, decongestant, motion-sickness remedy, diarrhea or upset-stomach medication (Pepto Bismol® or Imodium®), an antihistamine, sunscreen, insect repellent, and burn ointment.

Other Useful Items: Bring a money belt and a small padlock. Basic outdoors equipment (water bottle, compass, matches, pocketknife, sunglasses, sunscreen, hat) may also prove useful. Quick clothing repairs of torn garments can be done with a needle and thread or electrical tape. For laundry by hand, bring detergent and string for a makeshift clothes line. Consider packing an umbrella, alarm clock, flashlight, and earplugs. A cell phone can be a lifesaver on the road, and don't forget your camera.

Important Documents: Your passport, traveler's checks, ATM and/or credit cards, adequate ID, and photocopies of your documents are essential (p. 13). Other useful documents include a hosteling membership card (p. 14); driver's license (p. 34); travel insurance forms (p. 23); ISIC (p. 14), and/or rail or bus pass (p. 30).

SAFETY AND HEALTH

GENERAL ADVICE

In any type of crisis situation, the most important thing to do is stay calm. Your country's embassy abroad (p. 10) is usually your best resource when things go wrong. Register with that embassy upon arrival in the country. The government offices listed in the Travel Advisories box (p. 21) can provide a number of services to their citizens in the case of an emergency abroad.

LOCAL LAWS AND POLICE

Travelers are not likely to break major laws unintentionally while visiting Spain or Portugal. You can contact your embassy if arrested, although they often cannot do much to assist you beyond finding you legal counsel. You should feel comfortable approaching the police, although few officers speak English. There are three types of police in Spain. The **Policía Nacional** wear blue or black uniforms and white shirts; they deal with crime investigation (including theft), guard government buildings, and protect dignitaries. The **Policía Local** wear blue uniforms, deal with more local issues, and report to the mayor or town hall in each municipality. The **Guardia Civil** wear olive green uniforms and are responsible for issues more relevant to travelers: customs, crowd control, and national security. In Portugal, the **Polícia de Segurança Pública** is the police force in all major cities and towns. The **Guarda Nacional Republicana** polices more rural areas, while the **Brigada de Trânsito** is the traffic police, with red armbands. All three branches wear light blue uniforms.

DRUGS AND ALCOHOL

Recreational drugs are illegal in Spain and Portugal, and police take these laws seriously. The legal minimum drinking age in Spain and Portugal is 16. Spain and Portugal have the highest road mortality rates in Europe. Do not drive while intoxicated, and be cautious on the road.

SPECIFIC CONCERNS

TERRORISM

Basque terrorism concerns all travelers in Spain, with the active presence of a militant wing of Basque separatists called the Euskadi Ta Askatasuna (**ETA;** Basque Homeland and Freedom). March 2006, ETA declared a permanent cease-fire that officially ended in June 2007. ETA's attacks are typically targeted and are not considered random terrorist acts. The March 11, 2004 train bombings in Madrid were linked to **al-Qaeda,** and in June 2008, Spanish police arrested eight men in Barcelona, Pamplona, and Castellón under suspicion of involvement with an Algerian terrorist group linked to al-Qaeda. (See **Current Events,** p. 66, for more information.) While terrorism is rarely an issue in Portugal, Spain has experienced more than its fair share of troubles in recent years.

TRAVEL ADVISORIES. The following government offices provide travel information and advisories by telephone, by fax, or via the web:

Australian Department of Foreign Affairs and Trade: www.dfat.gov.au.

Canadian Department of Foreign Affairs and International Trade (DFAIT): www.dfait-maeci.gc.ca.

New Zealand Ministry of Foreign Affairs: www.mfat.govt.nz.

United Kingdom Foreign and Commonwealth Office: www.fco.gov.uk.

US Department of State: http://travel.state.gov.

ESSENTIALS

PERSONAL SAFETY

EXPLORING AND TRAVELING

To avoid unwanted attention, try to blend in as much as possible. Respecting local customs (in many cases, dressing more conservatively than you would at home) may ward off would-be hecklers. Familiarize yourself with your surroundings before setting out and carry yourself with confidence. Check maps in shops and restaurants rather than on the street. If you are traveling alone, be sure someone at home knows your itinerary and never tell anyone you meet that you're by yourself. When walking at night, stick to busy, well-lit streets and if you ever feel uncomfortable, leave the area as quickly as you can. A good **self-defense course** will give you concrete ways to react to unwanted advances.

If you are using a **car,** learn local driving signals and wear a seatbelt. Study route maps before you hit the road and, if you plan on spending a lot of time driving, consider bringing spare parts. For long drives in desolate areas, invest in a cellular phone and a roadside assistance program, and do not sleep in your car. For info on the perils of **hitchhiking,** see p. 37.

POSSESSIONS AND VALUABLES

There are a few steps you can take to minimize the financial risk associated with traveling. First, bring as few valuables as possible. Second, buy a few padlocks to secure your belongings either in your pack or in a locker. Third, carry as little cash as possible. Keep your traveler's checks and ATM/credit cards in a money belt—not a "fanny pack"—along with your passport and ID cards. Fourth, keep a small cash reserve separate from your primary stash. This should be about US$50 (US dollars or euros are best) sewn into or stored in the depths of your pack, along with your traveler's check numbers, photocopies of your passport, your birth certificate, and other important documents.

Never let your passport or bags out of your sight. Hostel workers will sometimes stand at bus and train-station arrival points to recruit tired and disoriented travelers to their hostel; never believe strangers who tell you that theirs is the only hostel open. Beware of **pickpockets** in city crowds, especially on public transportation. Also, be alert in public telephone booths: if you must say your calling card number, do so very quietly; if you punch it in, make sure no one can look over your shoulder. If you will be traveling with electronic devices, such as a laptop computer or a PDA, check whether your homeowner's insurance covers loss, theft, or damage when you travel. If not, you might consider purchasing a low-cost separate insurance policy. **Safeware** (☎+1-800-800-1492; www.safeware.com) specializes in covering computers and charges $90 for 90-day comprehensive international travel coverage up to $4000.

IN SPAIN

Spain has a low crime rate, but visitors can always fall victim to tourist-related crimes. Tourists should take particular care in Madrid, especially in El Centro, and in Barcelona around Las Ramblas. If you happen to experience car problems, be careful about accepting help from anyone other than a uniformed Spanish police officer or Guardia Civil (Civil Guard). Travelers who accept unofficial assistance should keep their valuables secure. For those travelers using public transportation, be aware of your belongings and surroundings.

IN PORTUGAL

In Portugal, the highest rates of crime have been in the Lisboa area, especially on buses, in train stations, and in airports. Exercise the most caution in the Alfama district, the Santa Apolonia and Rossio train stations, Castelo de São Jorge, and in Belém. The towns around Lisboa with the most reported crimes in recent years are Cascais, Fátima, and Sintra. Thieves often try to distract people by staging loud arguments, passing a soccer ball back and forth on a crowded street, asking for directions, pretending to dance with their victim, or spilling something on their victim's clothing.

PRE-DEPARTURE HEALTH

In your passport, write the names of any people you wish to be contacted in case of a **medical emergency** and list any allergies or medical conditions. Matching a prescription to a foreign equivalent is not always easy, safe, or possible, so if you take **prescription drugs,** carry up-to-date prescriptions or a statement from your doctor. While traveling, keep all medication with you in your carry-on luggage. Spanish and Portuguese names for common drugs are quite similar to their English names (aspirina, ibuprofen, acetaminofén), and brand names are generally recognizable in both countries.

IMMUNIZATIONS AND PRECAUTIONS

Travelers over two years old should make sure that the following vaccines are up to date: MMR (for measles, mumps, and rubella), DTaP or Td (for diphtheria, tetanus, and pertussis), IPV (for polio), Hib (for *haemophilus influenzae* B), and HepB (for Hepatitis B).

USEFUL ORGANIZATIONS AND PUBLICATIONS

The American **Centers for Disease Control and Prevention** (**CDC;** ☎+1-877-FYI-TRIP; www.cdc.gov/travel) maintains an international travelers' hotline and an informative website. Consult the appropriate government agency of your home country for consular information sheets on health, entry requirements, and other issues for various countries (see the listings in the box on **Travel Advisories,** p. 21). For quick information on health and travel warnings, call the **Overseas Citizens Services** (From overseas +1-202-501-4444, from US 888-407-4747; line open M-F 8am-8pm EST). For information on medical evacuation services and travel insurance firms, see the US government's website at http://travel.state.gov/travel/abroad_health.html or the **British Foreign and Commonwealth Office** (www.fco.gov.uk). For general health information, contact the **American Red Cross** (☎+1-202-303-4498; www.redcross.org).

ONCE IN SPAIN OR PORTUGAL

ENVIRONMENTAL HAZARDS

Common sense is the simplest prescription for good health while you travel. Drink lots of fluids to prevent dehydration and constipation and wear sturdy, broken-in shoes and clean socks.

Heat exhaustion and dehydration: Summer temperatures in southern and central Spain can reach a scorching 36˚C/97˚F. Heat exhaustion leads to nausea, excessive thirst, headaches, and dizziness. Avoid it by drinking plenty of fluids, eating salty foods (e.g., crackers), avoiding excessive caffeine and alcohol, and wearing sunscreen.

Sunburn: Always wear sunscreen when spending excessive amounts of time outdoors. If you get sunburned, drink more fluids than usual and apply an aloe-based lotion.

Hypothermia and frostbite: A rapid drop in body temperature is the clearest sign of overexposure to cold. Victims may shiver, feel exhausted, have poor coordination or slurred speech, hallucinate, or suffer amnesia. To avoid hypothermia, keep dry, wear layers, and stay out of the wind. When the temperature is below freezing, watch out for frostbite. Drink warm beverages, stay dry, and slowly warm the area with dry fabric or steady body contact until a doctor can be found.

High altitude: Allow your body a couple of days to adjust to lower levels of oxygen before exerting yourself. Alcohol is more potent and UV rays are stronger at high elevations. You'll want to be careful in parts of the Pyrenees, the Picos de Europa, the Sierra Nevada, or in Spain and Portugal's other high-altitude areas.

INSECT-BORNE DISEASES

Many diseases are transmitted by insects—mainly mosquitoes, fleas, ticks, and lice. Be careful of insects in wet or forested areas, especially while hiking and camping. Wear long pants and long sleeves, tuck your pants into your socks, and use a mosquito net. Use insect repellents with DEET and soak or spray your gear with permethrin (licensed in the US only for use on clothing). **Ticks**—which can carry Lyme and other diseases—can be particularly dangerous in rural and forested regions of Spain and Portugal.

Lyme disease: A bacterial infection carried by ticks and marked by a circular bull's-eye rash. Advanced symptoms include fever, headache, fatigue, and aches and pains. Antibiotics are effective if administered early. Left untreated, Lyme can cause problems in joints, the heart, and the nervous system. If you find a tick attached to your skin, grasp the head with tweezers as close to your skin as possible and apply slow, steady traction. Do not try to remove ticks with petroleum jelly, nail polish remover, or a hot match.

FOOD- AND WATER-BORNE DISEASES

Prevention is the best cure: be sure that your food is properly cooked and the water you drink is clean. Watch out for food from markets or street vendors that may have been cooked in unhygienic conditions. Other culprits are raw shellfish, unpasteurized milk, and sauces containing raw eggs. Salmonella bacteria, transmitted by raw eggs and egg shells, has been a prevalent problem in Spain in the past decade.

Traveler's diarrhea: Results from drinking fecally contaminated water or eating contaminated foods. Symptoms include nausea, bloating, and urgency. Try quick-energy, non-sugary foods with protein and carbohydrates to keep your strength up. Over-the-counter anti-diarrheals (e.g., Imodium®) may counteract the problem. The most dangerous side effect is dehydration; drink 8 oz. of water with tsp. of sugar or honey and a pinch of salt, try uncaffeinated soft drinks, or eat salted crackers. If you develop a fever or your symptoms don't go away after 4-5 days, consult a doctor.

Giardiasis: Transmitted through parasites and acquired by drinking untreated water from streams or lakes. Symptoms include diarrhea, cramps, bloating, fatigue, weight loss, and nausea. If untreated, it can lead to severe dehydration.

OTHER INFECTIOUS DISEASES

The following diseases exist all over the world. Travelers should know how to recognize them and what to do if they suspect they have been infected.

Hepatitis B: A viral infection of the liver transmitted via blood or other bodily fluids transmitted through unprotected sex and unclean needles. Symptoms may not surface until years after infection, but include jaundice, appetite loss, fever, and joint pain. A 3-shot vaccination sequence is recommended for sexually active travelers and anyone planning to seek medical treatment abroad; it must begin 6 months before traveling.

Hepatitis C: IV drug users, those exposured to blood, hemodialysis patients, and recipients of blood transfusions are at the highest risk, but the disease can also be spread through sexual contact or sharing items like razors and toothbrushes with traces of blood. No symptoms are usually exhibited. Hepatitis C can lead to liver failure.

AIDS and HIV: For detailed information on Acquired Immune Deficiency Syndrome (AIDS) in Spain or Portugal, call the 24hr. AIDS Hotline at ☎+1-800-342-2437 (USA).

Sexually transmitted infections (STIs): Gonorrhea, chlamydia, genital warts, syphilis, herpes, HPV, and other STIs are easier to catch than HIV and can be just as serious. Though condoms may protect you from some STIs, oral or even tactile contact can lead to transmission. If you think you may have contracted an STI, see a doctor immediately.

OTHER HEALTH CONCERNS

MEDICAL CARE ON THE ROAD

The public health-care system in Spain is very reliable; in case of emergency, seek out the *urgencias* (emergency) section of the nearest hospital. For smaller concerns, private clinics let you avoid long waits. Expect to pay cash up front (though most travel insurance will pick up the tab later, so request a receipt) and bring your passport and other forms of identification. *Farmacias* in Spain are also very helpful. A duty system has been set up so that at least one *farmacia* is open at all times in each town. Look for a flashing green cross. Spanish pharmacies are not the place to find your cheap summer flip-flops or greeting cards, but they sell contraceptives, common drugs, and many prescription drugs, answer simple medical questions, and can help you find a doctor. **Portugal's** public health system is equally good. A private clinic may be worth the money for quick, covenient service, and most travel insurance providers will cover the tab. Portuguese *farmacias* offer basic drugs and advice.

If you are concerned about obtaining medical assistance while traveling, you may wish to employ special support services. The **MedPass** from **GlobalCare, Inc.** (☎+1-800-860-1111; www.globalcare.net), provides 24hr. international medical assistance, support, and medical evacuation resources. The **International Association for Medical Assistance to Travelers** (**IAMAT;** US ☎+1-716-754-4883, Canada +1-519-836-0102; www.iamat.org) has free membership, lists English-speaking doctors worldwide, and offers information on immunization and sanitation.

Those with diabetes, allergies to antibiotics, epilepsy, heart conditions, or other health problems may want to obtain a **MedicAlert** membership (US$40 per year), which includes among other things a 24hr. collect-call number and ID tag. Contact the MedicAlert Foundation International (☎888-633-4298, outside US +1-209-668-3333; www.medicalert.org). If your regular insurance policy does not cover travel abroad, you may wish to purchase additional coverage.

WOMEN'S HEALTH

Vaginal yeast infections may flare up in hot and humid climates, but wearing loosely fitting trousers or a skirt and cotton underwear can help. Bring supplies from home if you are prone to infection, as they may be difficult to find on the road. Tampons, pads, and contraceptive devices are widely available, though your favorite brand may not be stocked. Abortion is illegal in Spain and Portugal, except in the first trimester for health reasons or in the case of rape. For sexual health information in Spain, contact the **Federación de Planificación Familiar de España (FPFE),** C. Ponce de Leon 8, 28010 Madrid (www.fpfe.org). In Portugal, contact the **Associação Para o Planeamento da Família (APF),** 38 Rua da Artilharia, 1250-040 Lisboa (www.apf.pt).

GETTING TO SPAIN OR PORTUGAL

BY PLANE

When it comes to airfare, a little research can save you a bundle. Courier fares are cheapest for those whose plans are flexible enough to deal with the restrictions. Tickets sold by consolidators and standby seating are also good deals, but last-minute specials, airfare wars, and charter flights often beat these fares. The key is to hunt around, be flexible, and ask about discounts. Students, seniors, and those under 26 should never have to pay full price for a ticket.

AIRFARES

Airfares to Spain and Portugal peak between the end of May and early September, and holiday periods are also expensive. The cheapest times to travel to the Iberian Peninsula are typically between December and February. Midweek (M-Th morning) round-trip flights run US$40-50 cheaper than weekend flights, but they are generally more crowded and less likely to permit frequent-flier upgrades. Not fixing a return date ("open return") or arriving in and departing from different cities ("open-jaw") can be pricier than round-trip flights. Patching one-way flights together is the most expensive way to travel. Flights between Spain and Portugal's capitals or regional hubs—Madrid, Barcelona, Lisboa—will tend to be cheaper.

If Spain or Portugal is only one stop on a more extensive globe-hop, consider a round-the-world (RTW) ticket. Tickets usually include at least five stops and are valid for about a year, and prices range US$1200-5000. Try **Northwest Airlines/KLM** (☎+1-800-225-2525; www.nwa.com) or **Star Alliance,** a consortium of 16 airlines including United Airlines (www.staralliance.com).

FLIGHT PLANNING ON THE INTERNET. The internet may be the budget traveler's dream when it comes to finding and booking bargain fares, but the array of options can be overwhelming. Many airline sites offer special last-minute deals on the web. Iberia Airlines (www.iberia.com) serves the entire peninsula, as well as other international destinations.

STA (www.statravel.com) and **StudentUniverse** (www.studentuniverse.com) provide quotes on student tickets, while **Orbitz** (www.orbitz.com), **Expedia** (www.expedia.com), and **Travelocity** (www.travelocity.com) offer full travel services. **Priceline** (www.priceline.com) lets you specify a price and obligates you to buy any ticket that meets or beats it. **Hotwire** (www.hotwire.com) offers bargain fares but won't reveal the airline or flight times until you buy. Other sites include www.bestfares.com, www.flights.com, www.lowestfare.com, www.onetravel.com, and www.travelzoo.com.

SideStep (www.sidestep.com) and **Booking Buddy** (www.bookingbuddy.com), and **Kayak** (www.kayak.com) help you sift through multiple offers; these let you enter your trip information once and search multiple sites.

BUDGET AND STUDENT TRAVEL AGENCIES

While knowledgeable agents specializing in flights to Spain and Portugal can make your life easy, they may not spend the time to find you the lowest possible fare—they get paid on commission. Travelers holding ISICs and IYTCs (p. 14) qualify for big discounts from student travel agencies. Most flights from budget agencies are on major airlines, but in peak season some may sell seats on less reliable chartered aircraft.

STA Travel, 5900 Wilshire Blvd., Ste. 900, Los Angeles, CA 90036, USA (24hr. reservations and info ☎+1-800-781-4040; www.statravel.com). A student and youth travel organization with over 150 offices worldwide.

Travel CUTS (Canadian Universities Travel Services Limited), 187 College St., Toronto, ON M5T 1P7, Canada (Toronto Toll Free ☎+1-888-359-2887, Toronto Office ☎+1-416-979-2406; www.travelcuts.com). Offices across Canada and the US including Los Angeles, New York, Seattle, and San Francisco.

USIT, 19-21 Aston Quay, Dublin 2, Ireland (☎+353 1 602 1906; www.usit.ie). Ireland's leading student/budget travel agency has 20 offices throughout Northern Ireland and the Republic of Ireland. Offers programs to work, study, and volunteer worldwide.

COMMERCIAL AIRLINES

The commercial airlines' lowest regular offer is the **APEX (Advance Purchase Excursion)** fare, which provides confirmed reservations and allows "open-jaw" tickets. Generally, reservations must be made seven to 21 days ahead of departure, with seven- to 14-day minimum-stay and up to 90-day maximum-stay restrictions. These fares carry hefty cancellation and change penalties. Book peak-season

APEX fares early. Use **Expedia** (www.expedia.com) or **Travelocity** (www.travelocity.com) to get an idea of the lowest published fares, then use the resources outlined here to try to beat those fares. Low-season fares should be appreciably cheaper than the high-season (mid-June to August) ones listed here.

TRAVELING FROM NORTH AMERICA

Basic round-trip fares to Spain and Portugal range from roughly US$200-750: to Barcelona, $450-1200; to Lisboa, $550-1200; to Madrid, $400-900; to Málaga, $400-800. Standard commercial carriers like American and United will probably offer the most convenient flights, but they may not be the cheapest, unless you snag a special promotion or airfare-war ticket. You will probably find flying one of the following "discount" airlines a better deal, if any of their limited departure points is convenient for you.

Iberia, USA (☎+1-800-772-4642; www.iberia.com). Extensive service from North America to major Spanish cities, as well as within Europe.

Spanair, (☎+1-888-545-5757; www.spanair.com). Flies out of New York, Boston, Houston, Los Angeles, Philadelphia, and other North American gateways to various cities in Spain and Portugal.

TRAVELING FROM IRELAND AND THE UK

Because of the many carriers flying from the British Isles to the continent, we only include discount airlines or those with cheap specials here. **ABTA, The Travel Association** in London (☎+44 020 7637 2444; www.abta.com) provides information on several participating travel agencies and tour operators in Spain and Portugal. **Cheapflights** (www.cheapflights.co.uk) publishes airfare bargains.

Aer Lingus, Ireland (☎+353 818 365 000; www.aerlingus.ie). Return tickets from Dublin, Cork, and Shannon to Madrid, Barcelona, and Málaga (EUR€16-280).

easyJet, UK (www.easyjet.com). London to Barcelona, Madrid, Majorca, Lisboa, and other Iberian destinations.

KLM Royal Dutch Airlines (☎+44 871 222 7474; www.klmuk.com). Cheap return tickets from London and elsewhere to many destinations in Spain and Portugal, including Madrid, Barcelona, and Lisboa.

Ryanair, Ireland (☎+353 818 303 030, UK +44 8712 460 000; www.ryanair.com). Many flights from Ireland and the UK to Spain and Portugal. From Dublin, Liverpool, and London to Madrid, Barcelona, and Porto, to name a few.

TRAVELING FROM AUSTRALIA AND NEW ZEALAND

Singapore Air, Australia (☎+61 13 10 11), New Zealand (+64 800 808 909; www.singaporeair.com). Auckland, Christchurch, Melbourne, Perth, and Sydney to Barcelona.

Thai Airways, Australia (☎+61 1300 651 960), New Zealand (☎+64 9 377 3886; www.thaiair.com). Auckland, Melbourne, Perth, and Sydney to Madrid.

AIR COURIER FLIGHTS

Those who travel light should consider courier flights. Couriers help transport cargo on international flights by using their checked luggage space for freight. Generally, couriers are limited to carry-ons and must deal with complex flight restrictions. Most flights are round-trip only, with short fixed-length stays (usually one week) and a limit of one ticket per issue. Most of these flights also operate only out of major gateway cities, mostly in North America. Generally, you must be over 18, in some cases 21. In summer, the most popular destinations usually require an advance reservation of about two weeks (you can usually book up to two months ahead). Super-discounted fares are common for "last-minute" flights (three to 14 days ahead).

Air Courier Association/CheapTrips, 1767 Denver West Blvd., Golden, CO 80401 (☎800-211-5119; www.aircourier.org). Several departure cities throughout US and Canada to Madrid and throughout Western Europe. One-year membership US$49.

International Association of Air Travel Couriers (**IAATC;** www.courier.org). Flights to Western Europe from Chicago, Los Angeles, Miami, Newark, San Francisco, and Washington, DC. One-year membership US$45.

Courier Travel (www.couriertravel.org). Searchable online database. Multiple departure points in the US to various European destinations.

STANDBY FLIGHTS

Traveling standby requires considerable flexibility in arrival and departure dates. Companies dealing in standby flights sell vouchers rather than tickets, along with the promise to get you to your destination (or nearby) within a certain window of time (typically 1-5 days). You call in before your specific window of time to hear your flight options and the probability that you will be able to board each flight. You can then decide which flights you want to try to catch, show up at the appropriate airport at the appropriate time, present your voucher, and board if space is available. Vouchers can usually be bought for both one-way and round-trip travel. You may receive a monetary refund only if every available flight within your date range is full; if you opt not to take an available (but perhaps less convenient) flight, you can only get credit toward future travel. To check on a company's service record in the US, contact the **Better Business Bureau** (☎+1-703-276-0100; www.bbb.org). It is difficult to receive refunds, and clients' vouchers will not be honored when an airline fails to receive payment in time.

TICKET CONSOLIDATORS

Ticket consolidators, or **"bucket shops,"** buy unsold tickets in bulk from commercial airlines and sell them at discounted rates. The best place to look is in the Sunday travel section of any major newspaper (try *The New York Times*), where many bucket shops place tiny ads. Call quickly, as availability is extremely limited. Not all bucket shops are reliable, so insist on a receipt that gives full details of restrictions, refunds, and tickets, and pay by credit card (in spite of the 2-5% fee) so you can stop payment if you never receive your tickets. For more info, see www.travel-library.com/air-travel/consolidators.html.

BY TRAIN

You can either buy a **railpass,** which allows you unlimited travel within a particular region for a given period of time, or rely on buying individual **point-to-point** tickets as you go. Almost all countries give students or youths (usually defined as anyone under 26) direct discounts on regular domestic rail tickets, and many also sell a student or youth card that provides 20-50% off of fares.

SHOULD YOU BUY A RAILPASS? Railpasses were conceived to allow you to jump on any train in Europe, go wherever you want whenever you want, and change your plans at will. In practice, it's not so simple. You still must stand in line to validate your pass, pay for supplements, and fork over cash for seat and couchette reservations. More importantly, railpasses don't always pay off. If you plan to spend extensive time on trains hopping between big cities, a railpass will probably be worth it. But in many cases, especially if you are under 26, point-to-point tickets may prove a cheaper option. It may be tough to make your railpass pay for itself in Spain and Portugal, where train fares are reasonable, distances short, and buses often preferable.

MULTINATIONAL RAILPASSES

EURAIL PASSES. Eurail is valid in much of Europe: Austria, Belgium, Bulgaria, Croatia, Czech Republic, Denmark, Finland, France, Germany, Greece, Hungary, Italy, Luxembourg, Montenegro, the Netherlands, Norway, Poland, Portugal, The Republic of Ireland, Romania, Serbia, Slovenia, Spain, Sweden, and Switzerland. It is not valid in the UK. **Eurail Global Passes,** valid for a given number of consecutive days, are best for those planning on spending extensive time on trains every few days. Global passes valid for any 10 or 15 (not necessarily consecutive) days within a two-month period are more cost-effective for those traveling longer distances less frequently. **Eurail Pass Saver** provides first-class travel for travelers in groups of two to five (prices are per person). **Eurail Pass Youth** provides parallel second-class perks for those under 26. Passholders receive a timetable for major routes and a map with details on possible bike rental, car rental, hotel, and museum discounts. Passholders often also receive reduced fares or free passage on many boat, bus, and private railroad lines. The **Eurail Select Pass** is a slimmed-down version of the Eurail Pass: it allows five, six, eight, 10, or 15 days of unlimited travel in any two-month period within three, four, or five bordering countries of 23 European nations.

SHOPPING AROUND FOR A EURAIL. Eurail Passes are designed by the EU itself and can be bought only by non-Europeans almost exclusively from non-European distributors. These passes must be sold at uniform prices determined by the EU. However, some travel agents tack on a handling fee, and others offer certain bonuses with purchase, so shop around. Also, keep in mind that pass prices usually go up each year, so save cash by purchasing before January 1 (you have 6 months from the purchase date to validate your pass in Europe). Because only a few places in major European cities sell them, and at a marked-up price, it is best to buy your pass before leaving. You can get a replacement for a lost pass only if you have purchased insurance under the Pass Security Plan (€10). Eurail Passes are available through travel agents, student travel agencies like **STA** (p. 26), as well as **Rail Europe** (www.raileurope.com) or directly from Eurail's website, www.eurail.com.

OTHER MULTINATIONAL PASSES. If your travels will be limited to one area, regional passes are often the best value. Visit www.raileurope.com and www.eurail.com for Portugal-Spain Pass options. If you have lived for at least six months in one of the European countries where **InterRail Passes** are valid, they prove an economical option. The InterRail Pass allows travel within 30 European countries excluding the passholder's country of residence. The **Global Pass** is valid for a given number of days (not necessarily consecutive) within a 10-day to one-month period. The **One Country Pass** limits travel to one European country. Passholders receive free admission to many museums as well as discounts on accommodations, food, and ferries. Passes are available at www.interrailnet.com as well as from travel agents, at major train stations throughout Europe, and through online vendors (like www.railpassdirect.co.uk).

GETTING AROUND SPAIN AND PORTUGAL

BY PLANE

Many national airlines offer multi-stop tickets for travel within Spain and Portugal. These tickets are particularly useful for travel between the Spanish mainland and the Islas Baleares and Islas Canarias. Outside of the peninsula, the recent emergence of no-frills airlines has made hopscotching around Europe by air increasingly affordable and convenient. Though these flights often feature inconvenient hours or serve less-popular regional airports, it's never been faster or easier to jetset across the Continent.

easyJet, UK (☎+44 871 244 2366; www.easyjet.com). Serves 78 destinations across Europe and northern Africa.

Ryanair, Ireland (☎+353 1 249 7791, UK 0871 246 0000; www.ryanair.com). Serves over 100 airports across Europe and northern Africa.

Vueling, Spain (☎902 33 39 33; www.vueling.com). Based in Barcelona, Vueling serves major cities in Spain and the rest of western Europe.

The Star Alliance European Airpass offers economy class fares for travel within Europe to more than 200 destinations in 44 countries. The pass is available to non-European passengers on Star Alliance carriers, including ANA, Austrian Airlines, BMI, LOT Polish Airlines, Lufthansa, Scandinavian Airlines, SWISS, TAP Portugal, Turkish Airlines, and US Airways. See www.staralliance.com for more information. In addition, a number of European airlines offer discount coupon packets. Most are only available as tack-ons for transatlantic passengers, but some are stand-alone offers. Most must be purchased before departure, so research in advance.

Europe by Air (☎+1-888-321-4737; www.europebyair.com). FlightPass allows you to country-hop to over 150 European cities. US$99 per flight.

Iberia (☎+1-800-772-4642; www.iberia.com). Offers discount airfare to and within Spain and Europe.

IN SPAIN

All major international airlines offer service to Madrid and Barcelona, most serve Las Islas Baleares and Canarias, and many serve Spain's smaller cities. **AirEuropa** (☎902 401 501; www.aireuropa.com) flies between major European cities. **Iberia** (Canada and US ☎+1-800-772-4642, Spain 902 40 05 00, UK +44 870 609 0500; www.iberia.com) serves all domestic locations and all major international cities. **SpanAir** (Spain ☎902 13 14 15 or 971 74 50 20, US +1-888-545-5757; www.spanair.com/en) offers international and domestic flights.

IN PORTUGAL

Most major international airlines serve Lisboa; some serve Faro, the Madeiras, and Porto. **TAP Air Portugal** (US and Canada ☎+1-800-221-7370, UK +44 845 601 0932, Lisboa 707 20 57 00; www.tap.pt) is Portugal's national airline, serving all domestic locations and many major international cities.

BY BUS

Though European trains and rail passes are popular, in some cases buses prove a better option. In Spain, the bus and train systems are on par; in Portugal, bus networks are more extensive, efficient, and often more comfortable. In the rest of Europe, bus travel is more of a gamble, and scattered offerings from private companies are often cheap but unreliable. Generally cheaper than rail passes, international bus passes allow unlimited travel on a hop-on, hop-off basis between major European cities. Prices below reflect high-season travel.

Eurolines, Estación Sur de Autobuses, Local 10, C. Méndez Álvaro 83, Madrid, Spain (☎+34 915 063 360; www.eurolines.com). The largest operator of Europe-wide coach services. Unlimited 15-day pass high season €329, under 26 €279, low season €199/169; 30-day pass high season €439/359, low season €299/229. Passes offer unlimited transit between hundreds of European cities and Morocco.

Busabout, 258 Vauxhall Bridge Rd., London SW1V 1BS, UK (☎+44 020 7950 1661; www.busabout.com). Offers 3 interconnecting bus circuits covering 60 cities and towns in Europe. Purchase a pass for the Western, Northern, or Southern loop starting at US$639, or for all of Europe starting at $549 (6 stops, additional stops $59). Also offers adventure tours throughout Europe, including Spain, Portugal, and Morocco.

IN SPAIN

Bus routes, far more comprehensive than the rail network, provide the only public transportation to many isolated areas, and almost always cost less than trains. They are generally quite comfortable, though leg room may be limited. For those traveling primarily within one region, buses are the best method of transport. We list below the major national companies, along with the phone number of their Madrid office; you will likely use many other companies. For more information, see the section for your transportation destination.

ALSA (☎913 27 05 40; www.alsa.es). Serves Madrid, Galicia, Asturias, and Castilla y León. Runs to many surrounding countries, including France, Germany, Italy, Morocco, the Netherlands, and Portugal.

Alosa (☎902 21 07 00; www.alosa.es). Operates primarily in northeastern Spain. Alosa serves a number of cities, including Barcelona, Huesca, Jaca, Pamplona, and Zaragoza.

Auto-Res (☎902 02 00 52; www.auto-res.net). Runs buses across much of central and western Spain.

Samar (☎917 23 05 06; www.samar.es). Serves Madrid, Zaragoza, and Sevilla, as well as international routes to Andorra, France, Italy, Morocco, Portugal, and Moscow.

IN PORTUGAL

Buses are cheap and frequent. They connect just about every town in Portugal. **Rodoviária** (☎212 94 71 00; www.rodotejo.pt), the national bus company, was recently privatized. Private regional companies also operate. Be wary of non-express buses in small regions like Estremadura and Alentejo, which stop every few minutes. Express coach service *(expressos)* between major cities is especially good; inexpensive city buses often run to nearby villages. Schedules *(horarios)* are usually printed and posted, but double-check with the ticket vendor to make sure they are accurate. Portugal's main Euroline affiliates are Intercentro, Internorte, and Intersul.

BY TRAIN

Trains in Spain and Portugal are generally comfortable, convenient, and reasonably swift. Almost all countries give students or youths (usually defined as anyone under 26) direct discounts on regular domestic rail tickets, and many also sell a student or youth card that provides 20-50% off for up to a year.

RESERVATIONS. While seat reservations are required only for selected trains (usually on major lines), you are not guaranteed a seat without one (usually US$5-30). You should strongly consider reserving in advance during peak holiday and tourist seasons (at the very latest, a few hours ahead). You will also have to purchase a supplement (US$10-50) or special fare for high-speed or high quality or trains such as Spain's AVE. Supplements are often unnecessary for Eurail pass and Europass holders.

OVERNIGHT TRAINS. Overnight trains can be one of the most time-efficient ways to travel, saving you valuable daylight hours and possibly even hotel fare. That efficiency, however, comes at the cost of comfort, scenery, and safety. Sleeping arrangements differ, but you can typically either sleep upright or in *couchettes* (berths), which typically have four to six seats per compartment (supplement about US$10-50 per person). Sleepers (beds) in private sleeping cars offer more privacy and comfort, but are considerably more expensive (supplement US$40-150). If you are using a railpass valid only for a restricted number of days, inspect train schedules to maximize the use of your pass: an overnight train or boat journey often uses up only one of your travel days if it departs after 7pm.

EURAIL PASSES

There is no reason to buy a Eurail Pass if you plan to travel only within Spain and Portugal. Trains are cheap, so a pass saves little money. Visit www.raileurope.com for more specific information on the passes below.

Spain Pass: Offers 3 days of unlimited travel over a 2-month period. 1st-class US$296, 2nd-class $231. Each additional rail-day (up to 10 days total) $40-50 for 1st-class, $30-40 for 2nd-class.

Portugal-Spain Pass: Good for 3 days of unlimited 1st-class travel in Spain and Portugal within a 2-month period. Travel may be on consecutive or non-consecutive days. US$341. Each additional rail-day (up to 10 days total) $40-50.

Spain Rail 'n Drive Pass: Good for 3 days of unlimited 1st-class train travel and 2 days of unlimited mileage in a Hertz rental car within a 2-month period in Spain. Prices US$316 and up, depending on number of travelers, type of car, and type of train ticket. Up to 7 additional rail-days and 7 additional car days available.

IN SPAIN

Spanish trains are clean, punctual, and reasonably priced, but tend to bypass many small towns. Spain's national railway is **RENFE** (☎902 24 02 02; www.renfe.es). Avoid *transvía*, *semidirecto*, or *correo* trains—they tend to be slow. **Alta Velocidad Española (AVE)** high-speed trains connect several major Spanish hubs, soaring above trains in comfort, price, and speed. Student discounts are available. Consult the RENFE website for complete listings and schedules of all train destinations, but for the most part, buses are an easier and more efficient means of traveling around Spain.

IN PORTUGAL

Caminhos de Ferro Portugueses (☎213 18 59 90; www.cp.pt) is Portugal's national railway, but for long-distance travel outside of the Braga-Porto-Coimbra-Lisboa line, the bus is better. The exception is around Lisboa, where local trains are fast and efficient. Most trains have first- and second-class cabins, except for local and suburban routes. Check the station ticket booth for the departure schedule; trains often run at irregular hours, and posted schedules *(horarios)* aren't always accurate. You can save 10% by buying a return ticket, but unless you own a Eurail pass the return on round-trip tickets must be used before 3am the following day. Keep your ticket with you; if you're caught without one, you'll be fined. Though there is a Portugal Flexipass, it is not worth buying.

BY CAR

Cars offer speed, freedom, access to the countryside, and an escape from the town-to-town mentality of trains. Although a solo traveler won't save by renting a car, four usually will. For a primer on European road signs and conventions, check out www.travlang.com/signs. The **Association for Safe International Road Travel** (**ASIRT**; www.asirt.org) can provide information on road conditions.

RENTING

You can rent a car from a US-based firm (Alamo, Avis, Budget, or Hertz) with European offices, from a European-based company with local representatives (Europcar), or from a tour operator (Auto Europe, Europe By Car, and Kemwel Holiday Autos) that will arrange a rental for you from a European company. Multinationals offer greater flexibility, but tour operators often strike better deals. Ask airlines about special fly-and-drive packages; you may get up to a week of free or discounted rental. Expect to pay US$80-400 per week, plus tax (5-25%), for a tiny car. Always check if prices quoted include tax and collision insurance. At most agencies, all that's needed to rent a car is a license from home and proof that you've had it for a year.

RENTAL AGENCIES

You can generally make reservations before you leave by calling major international offices in your home country. However, sometimes the price and availability information they give doesn't jive with what the local offices in Spain or Portugal will tell you, so try calling both numbers to make sure you get the best price. Local desk numbers are included in town listings; for home-country numbers, call your toll-free directory.

To rent a car from most establishments in Spain and Portugal, you need to be at least 21 years old. Some agencies require renters to be 25, and most charge those aged 21-24 an additional insurance fee. Policies and prices vary from agency to agency. Small local operations occasionally rent to people under 21, but be sure to ask about the insurance coverage and deductible, and always check the fine print. Rental agencies in Spain and Portugal include:

Auto Europe (US and Canada ☎+1-888-223-5555; www.autoeurope.com).

Avis (US ☎+1-800-331-1212, Spain 93 344 3700; www.avis.com).

Budget (US ☎+1-800-527-0700, international +1-800-472-3325; www.budget.com).

Europe by Car (US ☎+1-800-223-1516 or 212-581-3040; www.ebctravel.com).

Europcar (US ☎+1-877-940-6900, Spain 913 43 45 12; www.europcar.com).

Hertz (☎+1-800-654-3001; www.hertz.com).

Kemwel (US ☎+1-877-820-0668; www.kemwel.com).

COSTS AND INSURANCE

Renting a car in Spain is cheaper than in many other European countries. Prices start at around €50 per day from national companies, €25 from local agencies. In Portugal, prices start at around €50 per day from national companies, or €35 per day from local agencies. Expect to pay more for larger cars and for 4WD. Cars with automatic transmission can cost up to €30 per day more than standard manuals (stick shift), and in some places, automatic transmission is hard to find. It is virtually impossible, no matter where you are, to find an automatic with 4WD. Rental agencies are listed in the Practical Information at the start of each city.

Many rental packages offer unlimited kilometers, while others offer a limited number of kilometers per day with a surcharge per kilometer after that. Return the car with a full tank of gasoline (petrol) to avoid high fuel charges at the end. Insurance plans from rental companies almost always come with an excess charge for younger drivers and for 4WD. This means that the insurance bought from the rental company only applies to damages over the excess; damages up to that amount must be covered by your existing insurance plan. Many rental companies in Spain and Portugal encourage you to buy a Collision Damage Waiver (CDW), which will waive the excess in the case of a collision. Loss Damage Waivers (LDWs) do the same in the case of theft or vandalism.

National chains often allow one-way rentals (picking up in one city and dropping off in another). There is usually a minimum hire period and sometimes an extra drop-off charge of several hundred dollars.

DRIVING PERMITS AND CAR INSURANCE

INTERNATIONAL DRIVING PERMIT (IDP)

If you plan to drive a car while in Spain or Portugal, you must be over 18 and have an **International Driving Permit (IDP).** However, in Spain, a US licence is valid for six months in a calendar year, after which a driving school can help you apply for a Spanish license. A driver's license from any EU state is valid in Spain. In Portugal, only a valid license from one's home country is required.

It may be a good idea to get an IDP, in case you're in a situation (e.g., an accident or stranded in a small town) where the police do not know English; information on the IDP is printed in 11 languages, including Spanish and Portuguese. The **Jefatura Provincial de Tráfico** (www.dgt.es/portal) in Madrid is a source for help with such matters.

Your IDP, valid for one year, must be issued in your own country before you depart. An application for an IDP usually requires one or two photos, a current local license, an additional form of identification, and a fee. To apply, contact your home country's automobile association. Be vigilant when purchasing an IDP online or anywhere other than your home automobile association. Many vendors sell permits of questionable legitimacy for higher prices.

CAR INSURANCE

Most credit cards cover standard insurance. If you rent, lease, or borrow a car, you will need a **green card,** or **International Insurance Certificate,** to certify that you have liability insurance and that it applies abroad. Green cards can be obtained at car rental agencies, car dealers (for those leasing cars), some travel agents, and some border crossings. Rental agencies may require you to purchase theft insurance in countries that they consider to have a high risk of auto theft.

ON THE ROAD

Spain's highway system connects major cities by four-lane *autopistas* (highways) with plenty of service stations. Traffic moves quickly and drivers can get annoyed if you don't; study your map before you leave. The speed limit in Spain is 31mph/50kph in cities, 55mph/90kph on open roads, and 74mph/120kph on highways. Speeders beware: police can "photograph" the speed and license plate of your car and issue a ticket without pulling you over. Purchase gas in both Spain and Portugal in super (97-octane), normal (92-octane), diesel, and unleaded. The average price for unleaded gas in Spain is approximately double the US price, and slightly higher in Portugal.Seatbelts are required in Spain, and drunk driving incurs hefty fines; be aware that allowed blood levels of alcohol are lower than in other countries in Europe.Portugal has the highest rate of car accidents per capita in Western Europe. The narrow, twisting roads are difficult to negotiate. Speed limits are ignored, recklessness is common, and lighting and road surfaces are often inadequate.

DRIVING PRECAUTIONS. When traveling in the summer or in the desert, bring substantial amounts of water (a suggested 5L of water per person per day) for drinking and for the radiator. You should always carry a spare tire and jack, jumper cables, extra oil, flares, a flashlight, and heavy blankets (in case your car breaks down at night or in the winter). If you don't know how to change a tire, learn before heading out, especially if you are planning on traveling in deserted areas. If your car breaks down, stay in your vehicle.

CAR ASSISTANCE

The Spanish automobile association is **Real Automóvil Club de España** (RACE, ☎902 40 45 45; www.race.es). It functions much like AAA, offering roadside assistance and general advice on driving in Spain. Portugal's automobile association, the **Automóvel Clube de Portugal,** or ACP (☎213 71 47 20; www.acp.pt) provides breakdown, towing, and first-aid services.

BY BICYCLE

With a mountain bike, you can also do some serious sightseeing. Some airlines will count your bike as your second piece of luggage, but others charge extra. The additional fee runs about US$50-150 each way. Airlines sell bike boxes at the airport, although it is easier and cheaper to get one from a local bike store. Most ferries let you take your bike for free or for a nominal fee. You can almost always ship your bike on trains, though the cost varies. Renting a bike beats bringing your own if your touring will be confined to one or two regions. *Let's Go* lists bike rental shops for larger cities and towns, when they exist. Some youth hostels rent bicycles for low prices. Some train stations rent bikes and often allow you to drop them off elsewhere.

BY MOPED AND MOTORCYCLE

In both Spain and Portugal, motorized bikes are a popular method of transportation for locals, and they can be a fun alternative for tourist daytrips. However, they're uncomfortable for long distances, dangerous in the rain, and unpredictable on rough roads and gravel. Always wear a helmet, and never ride with a backpack. If you've never been on a moped, the windy roads of the Pyrenees and the congested streets of Madrid are not the place to start. Before renting, ask if the quoted price includes tax and insurance, or you may be hit with an unexpected additional fee. Pay ahead of time instead—do not hand over your passport.

BY THUMB

LET'S NOT GO. *Let's Go* never recommends hitchhiking as a safe means of transportation, and none of the information here is intended to do so.

Let's Go strongly urges you to consider the risks before you choose to hitchhike. Hitching means entrusting your life to a stranger and risking assault, sexual harassment, theft, and unsafe driving. For women traveling alone (or even in pairs), hitching is a risky proposal. A man and a woman are a less dangerous combination; two men will have a harder time getting a lift. In Spain, hitchers report that Castilla and Andalucía are long, hot waits, and hitchhiking out of Madrid is virtually impossible. The Mediterranean Coast and the islands are more promising, and remote areas in Cataluña, Galicia, or the Pyrenees may be most accessible by hitching (if renting a car is not an option). In Portugal, hitchhikers are rare. Beach-bound locals occasionally hitch in summer, but otherwise stick to the inexpensive bus system.

KEEPING IN TOUCH

BY EMAIL AND INTERNET

Email is easy to access in Spain and Portugal. Internet costs only about €1-3 per hour in most cafes. Many hostels, libraries, and schools also provide free access. In small towns, if internet acess is not listed, check the library or the tourist office, where travelers occasionally get access for a small fee. These establishments are listed in the **Practical Information** sections of each city. Lucky travelers with wireless-enabled laptops may be able to take advantage of an increasing number of internet "hot spots," where they can get online for free or for a small fee, or at internet cafes with Wi-Fi. Newer computers can detect these hot spots automatically; otherwise, websites like www.jiwire.com, www.wififreespot.com, and www.wi-fihotspotlist.com can help you find them. For information on insuring your laptop while traveling, see p. 21.

WARY WI-FI. Wireless hot spots make internet access possible in public and remote places. Unfortunately, they also pose **security risks.** Hot spots are public, open networks that use unencrypted, unsecured connections. They are susceptible to hacks and "packet sniffing"—ways of stealing passwords and other private information. To prevent problems, disable "ad hoc" mode, turn off file sharing and network discovery, encrypt your email, turn on your firewall, beware of phony networks, and watch for over-the-shoulder creeps.

BY TELEPHONE

CALLING HOME FROM SPAIN AND PORTUGAL

Prepaid phone cards are a common and relatively inexpensive means of calling abroad. Each one comes with a Personal Identification Number (PIN) and a toll-free access number. You call the access number and then follow the directions for dialing your PIN. To purchase prepaid phone cards, check online for the best rates; www.callingcards.com is a good place to start. Online providers generally send your access number and PIN via email, with no actual "card" involved. Another option is to purchase a **calling card,** linked to a major national telecommunications service in your home country. Calls are billed collect or to your account. Placing a collect call through an international operator can be expensive, but may be necessary in case of an emergency. You can frequently call collect without a company's calling card just by calling its access number and following the instructions.

PLACING INTERNATIONAL CALLS. Dial:

1. Your **International dialing prefix.** From Australia, dial 0011; Canada or the US, 011; Ireland, New Zealand, Portugal, Spain, or the UK, 00.
2. The **country code** of the country you want to call. To call Australia, dial 61; Canada or the US, 1; Ireland, 353; New Zealand, 64; the UK, 44; Spain, 34; Portugal, 351; Morocco, 212.
3. The **city/area code.** *Let's Go* lists the city/area codes for cities and towns in opposite the city or town name, next to a ☎, as well as in every phone number. If the first digit is a zero (e.g., 020 for London), omit the zero when calling from abroad (e.g., dial 20 from Canada to reach London).
4. The **local number.**

CALLING WITHIN SPAIN AND PORTUGAL

The simplest way to call within the country is to use a coin-operated phone. **Prepaid phone cards** (available at newspaper kiosks and tobacco stores), which carry a certain amount of phone time depending on the card's denomination, may be more convenient, and usually save time and money in the long run. Phone rates typically tend to be highest in the morning, lower in the evening, and lowest on Sunday and late at night.

CELLULAR PHONES

GSM PHONES. Having a GSM phone doesn't necessarily mean you're good to go when you travel abroad. The majority of GSM phones sold in the United States operate on a different frequency (1900) than international phones (900/1800) and will not work abroad. Tri-band phones work on all three frequencies (900/1800/1900) and will operate through out most of the world. Additionally, some GSM phones are SIM-locked and will only accept SIM cards from a single carrier. You'll need a SIM-unlocked phone to use a SIM card from a local carrier when you travel.

Some tourists find that the availability and usefulness of cell phones in Spain and Portugal make them worth their moderate cost. **Telefónica Movistar** (www.movistar.com) and **Vodafone** (www.vodafone.com) sell relatively inexpensive cell phones to travelers. The international standard for cell phones is **Global System for Mobile Communication (GSM).** You will need a GSM-compatible phone and a **SIM (Subscriber Identity Module) card,** a country-specific, thumbnail-sized chip that gives you a local phone number and plugs you into the local network. Many SIM cards are prepaid, and incoming calls are frequently free. You can buy additional cards or vouchers (usually available at convenience stores) to "top up" your phone. For more information on GSM phones, check out www.telestial.com, www.orange.co.uk, www.roadpost.com, or www.planetomni.com. Companies like **Cellular Abroad** (www.cellularabroad.com) rent cell phones that work in a variety of destinations around the world.

TIME DIFFERENCES

Spain is one hour ahead of Greenwich Mean Time (GMT), while Portugal operates at GMT. Both countries observe Daylight Saving Time. The following table realtes Spain and Portugal's capitals to other localities at noon GMT.

BY MAIL

SENDING MAIL HOME FROM SPAIN AND PORTUGAL

Airmail is the best way to send mail home from Spain and Portugal. **Aerogrammes,** printed sheets that fold into envelopes and travel via airmail, are available at post offices. Write "airmail," "*par avion,*" "*por avión,*" "*por avião,*" or "*via aerea*" on the front. In Spain, airmail usually takes from five to 10 business days to reach the US or Canada. **Express mail** may be the most reliable way to send a letter or parcel, and takes four to seven business days. Be aware that Spain's **overnight mail** may not exactly be "overnight." For faster service, try companies like DHL, UPS, or SEUR, under *mensajerías* in the yellow pages. Stamps are sold at post offices and tobacconists (*estancos* or *tabacos*). Mail letters and postcards from the yellow mailboxes scattered throughout cities, or from the post office in small towns. Mail in Portugal can be inefficient—airmail can take from one to two weeks longer to reach the US. Again, stamps are available at post offices (which can have automatic stamp machines) and at central locations around cities. Fax machines are often available at post offices. **Surface mail** is by far the cheapest and slowest way to send mail. It takes one to two months to cross the Atlantic and one to three to cross the Pacific—good for heavy items you won't need for a while, such as souvenirs that you've acquired along the way.

SENDING MAIL TO SPAIN AND PORTUGAL

In addition to the standard postage system whose rates are listed below, **Federal Express** (www.fedex.com) handles express mail services from most countries to Spain and Portugal. Service tends to be best between major cities like Barcelona, Lisboa, and Madrid. Rural areas often have slower service. There are several ways to arrange the pick up of letters sent to you while you are abroad. Mail can be sent via **Poste Restante** (General Delivery; **Lista de Correos (S); Lista de Correiros (P)**) to almost any city or town in Spain or Portugal with a post office, but it is not very reliable. Address **Poste Restante** letters like so:

Miguel de CERVANTES
Lista de Correos
Salamanca, España

The mail will go to a special desk in the central post office, unless you specify a post office by street address or postal code. Itiss best to use the largest post office, since mail may be sent there regardless. It is usually safer and quicker, though more expensive, to send mail express or registered. Bring your passport (or other photo ID) for pickup; there may be a small fee. If the clerks insist that there is nothing for you, ask them to check under your first name as well. *Let's Go* lists post offices in the **Practical Information** section for each city and most towns. **American Express's** travel offices throughout the world offer a free **Client Letter Service** (mail held up to 30 days and forwarded upon request) for cardholders who contact them in advance. Some offices provide these services to non-cardholders (especially AmEx Travelers Cheque holders), but call ahead to make sure. *Let's Go* lists AmEx locations for most large cities in **Practical Information** sections; for a complete list, call ☎+1-800-528-4800 or visit www.americanexpress.com/travel.

ACCOMMODATIONS

HOSTELS

Many hostels are laid out dorm-style, often with large single-sex rooms and bunk beds, with some private rooms that sleep two to four. They often have kitchens and utensils for your use, bike or moped rentals, storage areas, transportation to airports, breakfast and other meals, laundry facilities, and internet. There can, however, be drawbacks: some hostels close during certain daytime "lockout" hours, have a curfew, don't accept reservations, impose a maximum stay, or, less frequently, require that you do chores.

A HOSTELER'S BILL OF RIGHTS. There are certain standard features that we do not include in our hostel listings. Unless we state otherwise, you can expect that every hostel has no lockout, no curfew, free hot showers, some system of secure luggage storage, and no key deposit.

HOSTELLING INTERNATIONAL

Joining the youth hostel association in your own country (listed below) automatically grants you membership privileges in **Hostelling International (HI)**, a federation of national hosteling associations. Non-HI members may be allowed to stay in some HI hostels, but will have to pay extra to do so. HI hostels are scattered throughout Spain and Portugal, and can be less expensive than private hostels. HI's umbrella website (www.hihostels.com), which lists the websites and phone numbers of all national associations, can be a great place to begin researching hosteling in a specific region. Other comprehensive hosteling websites include www.hostels.com and www.hostelplanet.com.

Most HI hostels also honor **guest memberships**—you'll get a blank card with space for six validation stamp, each night you'll pay a nonmember supplement (one-sixth the membership fee) and earn one guest stamp, and six stamps make you a member. Most student travel agencies (p. 26) sell HI cards, as do all of the national hosteling organizations listed below. All prices listed below are for one-year memberships unless otherwise noted.

Australian Youth Hostels Association (AYHA), 422 Kent St., Sydney, NSW 2000 (www.yha.com.au). AUS$52, under 18 $19.

Hostelling International-Canada (HI-C), 205 Catherine St., Ste. 400, Ottawa, ON K2P 1C3 (www.hihostels.ca). CDN$35, under 18 free.

Hostelling International Northern Ireland (HINI), 22-32 Donegall Rd., Belfast BT12 5JN (www.hini.org.uk). UK£15, under 25 UK£10.

Youth Hostels Association of New Zealand Inc. (YHANZ), Level 1, 166 Moorhouse Ave., P.O. Box 436, Christchurch (www.yha.org.nz). NZ$40, under 18 free.

Youth Hostels Association (England and Wales), Trevelyan House, Dimple Rd., Matlock, Derbyshire DE4 3YH (www.yha.org.uk). UK£16, under 26 UK£10.

Hostelling International (USA), 8401 Colesville Rd., Ste. 600, Silver Spring, MD 20910 (www.hiayh.org). US$28, under 18 free.

OTHER TYPES OF ACCOMMODATIONS

HOTELS, GUESTHOUSES, AND PENSIONS

Spanish accommodations have many aliases distinguished by the different grades of rooms. The cheapest and barest options are **casas de huéspedes** and **hospedajes.** While **pensiones** and **fondas** (like a B&B) tend to be a bit nicer, all are essentially just boarding houses; these establishments provide basic and well-used rooms with a shared bath, possibly a sink, but no A/C. Another relatively comfortable option is the **hostal,** which provides sheets and lockers. The government rates *hostales* on a two-star system, and even one-star establishments can be quite comfortable. *Hostal* owners tend to dip below official rates in the off season (Sept.-May), so bargain away.

The highest-priced accommodations are **hoteles,** which have a bathroom in each room but are usually on the pricey side, and rated with one to five stars. The top-notch hotels are the government **Paradores Nacionales**—castles, palaces, convents, and historic buildings that have been converted into luxurious hotels. They often are interesting sights in their own right.

In Portugal, **pensões,** also called **residencias,** are a budget traveler's mainstay. They are cheaper than hotels and only slightly more expensive than youth hostels. **Hotels** in Portugal tend to be pricey. Room prices typically include breakfast and showers, and most rooms that lack a bath or shower have a sink. When business is weak, try bargaining in advance. **Pousadas,** like Spanish *paradores*, outperform standard hotels, but are more expensive. Most are castles, palaces, or monasteries converted into luxurious, government-run hotels.

HOME EXCHANGES AND HOSPITALITY CLUBS

Home exchange offers travelers various types of homes (houses, apartments, condominiums, villas, even castles in some cases). For more information, contact **HomeExchange.com Inc.,** P.O. Box 787, Hermosa Beach, CA 90254, USA (☎+1-310-798-3864 or toll-free +1-800-877-8723; www.homeexchange.com) or **Intervac International Home Exchange** (☎934 53 31 71; www.intervac.com).

Hospitality clubs link their members with individuals or families abroad who are willing to host travelers for free or for a small fee to promote cultural exchange. In exchange, members must be willing to host travelers in their own homes, and a small fee may also be required. **The Hospitality Club** (www.hospitalityclub.org) is a good place to start. **Servas** (www.servas.org) requires a fee and an interview to join. An internet search will yield many similar organizations, some of which cater to special interests. Be sure to use common sense when planning to stay with or host someone you do not know.

LONG-TERM ACCOMMODATIONS

Travelers planning to stay in Spain or Portugal for extended periods of time may find it most cost-effective to rent an **apartment.** Many students spend time living in sublets, and there are plenty of places to be found. A basic one-bedroom (or studio) apartment in Madrid, Barcelona, or Lisboa will range €400-800 and beyond per month. In addition to the rent itself, prospective tenants usually are also required to front a security deposit (often one month's rent) and the last month's rent. Expatriates.com (www.expatriates.com) lists apartments for rent, with extensive entries for Spain and Portugal.

CAMPING

Campgrounds exist throughout Spain and Portugal, and their popularity varies by region. They are frequently located on the outskirts of cities and towns, making for inconvenient or extensive commutes. Campers heading to Europe should consider buying an **International Camping Carnet.** Similar to a hostel membership card, it is required at a few campgrounds and sometimes provides discounts. The card is available in North America from the **Family Campers and RVers Association** and in the UK from the **Caravan Club** (see below).

Most **campgrounds** charge separate fees per person, per tent, and per car; others charge for a *parcela*—a small plot of land—plus per-person fees. Be aware that although camping may seem like a budget option, prices can get high for lone travelers and even for pairs. Most tourist offices provide info on official areas, including the hefty *Guía de campings.* In Portugal, you will find many official campgrounds *(parques de campismo)* with amenities. Most have a supermarket or cafe, and many are even beach-accessible. Some may require reservations. Do not take the risk of illegal camping. A useful resource is *Portugal: Camping and Caravan Sites*, a free guide to official campgrounds. Otherwise, contact the **Federação de Campismo e Montanhismo de Portugal** (☎218 12 68 90/1; fcmportugal.com). For more information on outdoor activities in Spain and Portugal, see **The Great Outdoors,** below.

THE GREAT OUTDOORS

LEAVE NO TRACE. *Let's Go* encourages travelers to embrace the "Leave No Trace" ethic, minimizing their impact on natural environments and protecting them for future generations. Trekkers and wilderness enthusiasts should set up camp on durable surfaces, use cookstoves instead of campfires, bury human waste away from water supplies, bag trash and carry it out with them, and respect wildlife and natural objects. For more detailed information, contact the **Leave No Trace Center for Outdoor Ethics,** P.O. Box 997, Boulder, CO 80306 USA (☎+1-800-332-4100 or 303-442-8222; www.lnt.org).

USEFUL RESOURCES

A variety of publishing companies offer guidebooks to meet the educational needs of novicesor expert hikers. For information about camping, hiking, and biking, write or call the publishers listed below to receive a free catalog.

The **Great Outdoor Recreation Page** (www.gorp.com) provides excellent general information for travelers planning on camping or enjoying the outdoors.

Automobile Association, Contact Centre, Lambert House, Stockport Rd., Cheadle SK8 2DY, UK (www.theAA.com). Publishes *Caravan and Camping Europe* and *Britain & Ireland* (UK£10) as well as road atlases for Europe, Britain, France, Germany, Ireland, Italy, Spain, and the US.

Sierra Club Books, 85 2nd St., 2nd fl., San Francisco, CA 94105, USA (☎+1-415-977-5500; www.sierraclub.org). Publishes general resources on hiking and camping.

The Mountaineers Books, 1001 SW Klickitat Way, Ste. 201, Seattle, WA 98134, USA (☎+1-206-223-6303; www.mountaineersbooks.org). Over 600 titles on hiking, biking, mountaineering, natural history, and conservation.

Vayacamping, (☎935 94 61; www.vayacamping.net). Publishes guides, maintains a website with resources for camping across Spain and Portugal. Also offers card-holding membership that gives discounts at participating establishments on the peninsula.

The Caravan Club, East Grinstead House, East Grinstead, West Sussex, RH19 1UA, UK (www.caravanclub.co.uk). For UK£34, members receive access to sites, insurance services, equipment discounts, maps, and a monthly magazine. Provides some European information covering Spain and Portugal.

NATIONAL PARKS

Spain and Portugal have extensive national park systems with opportunities for hiking, mountaineering, and other outdoor adventures. Camping within national park boundaries is usually illegal, but campgrounds can be found in most nearby towns. The general procedure is to stock up on equipment and supplies, stop by the visitor information center to pick up free maps, and head into the park. More detailed maps, with specific hiking or adventure information, can be purchased both at the visitors centers and in nearby towns.

The Spanish **Ministry of Natural Environment** operates a website (reddeparquesnacionales.mma.es/parques/index.htm) that provides information, mostly in Spanish but with some English, about the national park system, including trip-planning tools. The Spanish government's tourism portal also provides information, contact information, and listings for national parks at www.spain.info/TourSpain/Naturaleza. **Turismo de Portugal** (www.visitportugal.com), the official Portuguese tourist office website, offers some information in English and links to details about the parks, mostly in Portuguese.

WILDERNESS SAFETY

Staying warm, dry, and well hydrated is key to a happy wilderness experience. For any hike, prepare yourself for an emergency by packing a first-aid kit, a reflector, a whistle, high-energy food, extra water, rain gear, a hat, mittens, and extra socks. For warmth, wear wool or insulating synthetic materials designed for the outdoors. Check weather forecasts often and pay attention to the skies when hiking, as weather patterns can change suddenly. Always let someone—a friend, your hostel, or a park ranger—know when and where you are going. See **Safety and Health,** p. 20, for information on outdoor medical concerns.

ORGANIZED ADVENTURE TRIPS

Organized adventure tours offer another way of exploring the wild. Activities include hiking, biking, skiing, canoeing, kayaking, rafting, climbing, photo safaris, and archaeological digs. Tourism bureaus often can suggest parks, trails, and outfitters. Organizations that specialize in camping and outdoor equipment like REI and EMS are good sources for info, or contact the **Specialty Travel Index,** P.O. Box 458, San Anselmo, CA 94979, USA (www.specialtytravel.com).

SPECIFIC CONCERNS

SUSTAINABLE TRAVEL

As the number of travelers on the road rises, their detrimental effect on natural environments is an increasing concern. *Let's Go* promotes the philosophy of sustainable travel with this in mind. Through a sensitivity to issues of ecology and sustainability, today's travelers can be a powerful force in preserving and restoring the places they visit.

Ecotourism, a rising trend in sustainable travel, focuses on the conservation of natural habitats—mainly, on how to use them to build up the economy without exploitation or overdevelopment. Travelers can make a difference by doing advance research, by supporting organizations and establishments that pay attention to their carbon "footprint," and by patronizing establishments that strive to be environmentally friendly.

Staying at organic farms, campgrounds, or long-established monasteries and convents is one way to minimize your mark in fragile areas. Supporting local markets and shops instead of tourist restaurants and chains also helps. You can take part in more specialized conservation efforts, like preventing desertification in Spain (See **Beyond Tourism**, p. 49).

ECOTOURISM RESOURCES. For more information on environmentally responsible tourism, contact one of the organizations below:

Conservation International, 2011 Crystal Dr., Ste. 500, Arlington, VA 22202, USA (☎+1-800-406-2306 or 703 341 2400; www.conservation.org).

Green Globe 21, Green Globe vof, Verbenalaan 1, 2111 ZL Aerdenhout, the Netherlands (☎+31 23 544 0306; www.greenglobe.com).

International Ecotourism Society, 1333 H St. NW, Ste. 300E, Washington, DC 20005, USA (☎+1-202-347-9203; www.ecotourism.org).

United Nations Environment Program (UNEP), 39-43 Quai André Citroën, 75739 Paris Cedex 15, France (www.uneptie.org/pc/tourism).

RESPONSIBLE TRAVEL

Your tourist dollars can make a big impact on the destinations you visit. Travelers who care about the destinations and environments they explore should make themselves aware of the social and cultural implications of their choices. Simple decisions such as buying local products, paying fair prices for products or services, and attempting to speak the local language can have a strong, positive effect on the community.

Community-based tourism aims to channel tourist dollars into the local economy by emphasizing tours and cultural programs run by members of the host community. This type of tourism also benefits the tourists themselves, as it often takes them beyond traditional sightseeing in the region. *The Ethical Travel Guide* (UK£13), a project of Tourism Concern (☎+44 20 7133 3330; www.tourismconcern.org.uk), is an excellent resource for information on community-based travel, with a directory of 300 establishments in 60 countries.

TRAVELING ALONE

Traveling alone can provide a sense of independence and a greater opportunity to connect with locals. On the other hand, solo travelers are more vulnerable to harassment and street theft. If you are traveling alone, look confident, try not to stand out as a tourist, and be especially careful in deserted or very crowded areas. Stay away from areas that are not well lit. If questioned, never admit that you are traveling alone. Maintain regular contact with someone at home who knows your itinerary, and always research your destination before traveling. For more tips, pick up *Traveling Solo* by Eleanor Berman (Globe Pequot Press; US$18), visit www.travelaloneandloveit.com, or subscribe to **Connecting: Solo Travel Network,** 689 Park Rd., Unit 6, Gibsons, BC V0N 1V7, Canada (☎+1-604-886-9099; www.cstn.org; membership US$30-48).

WOMEN TRAVELERS

Women exploring on their own inevitably face some additional safety concerns. Single women can consider staying in hostels that offer single rooms that lock from the inside or in religious institutions with single-sex rooms. It's a good idea to stick to centrally located accommodations and to avoid solitary late-night treks or metro rides. Always carry extra cash for a phone call, bus, or taxi. Hitchhiking is never safe for lone women, or even for two women traveling together. Look as if you know where you're going and approach older women or couples for directions if you're lost or feeling uncomfortable. Dress conservatively, especially in rural areas. Wearing a conspicuous wedding band sometimes helps to prevent unwanted advances.

Your best answer to verbal harassment is no answer at all. Feigning deafness, sitting motionless, and staring straight ahead at nothing in particular will usually do the trick. Persistent aggressors sometimes be dissuaded by a firm, loud, and very public "go away!" in the appropriate language. Don't hesitate to seek out a police officer or a passerby if you are being harassed. Memorize the emergency numbers in places you visit, and consider carrying a whistle on your keychain. A self-defense course will both prepare you for a potential attack and raise your level of awareness of your surroundings (see **Personal Safety,** p. 21). Consider talking with your doctor about the health concerns that women face when traveling (See **Women's Heath,** p. 25).

GLBT TRAVELERS

Attitudes toward gay, lesbian, bisexual, and transgendered (GLBT) people in Spain and Portugal vary by region. GLBT travelers may feel out of place in the more traditional, rural areas of Spain and Portugal, given the countries' strong Catholic heritage, but overt homophobia is rare. In Spain, Sitges (p. 394), Benidorm (p. 312), and Ibiza (p. 343) are internationally renowned as gay party destinations, and Madrid (see Chueca, p. 94) hosts the famous party *Orgullo*

Gay (Gay Pride) party in June. The website www.guiagay.com has info about gay Spain, and www.portugalgay.pt offers listings in Portuguese and English.

Listed below are contact organizations, mail-order catalogs, and publishers that offer materials addressing some specific concerns. **Out and About** (www.planetout.com) offers a weekly newsletter addressing travel concerns and a comprehensive site addressing gay travel concerns. The online newspaper **365gay.com** has a travel section (www.365gay.com/travel/travelchannel.htm).

ADDITIONAL RESOURCES: GLBT

International Lesbian and Gay Association (ILGA), www.ilga.org.

Spartacus International Gay Guide 2008 (US$22).

Damron Travel Guides (US$18-24). www.damron.com.

The Gay Vacation Guide: The Best Trips and How to Plan Them, by Mark Chesnut. Kensington Books (US$15).

Gayellow Pages, by Frances Green. (US$20), http://gayellowpages.com.

TRAVELERS WITH DISABILITIES

Wheelchair accessibility varies widely in Iberia but is generally inferior to that in the US. Handicapped access is common in modern and big city museums. Some Spanish tourist offices abroad can provide useful listings of accessible (but often expensive) accommodations and sights.

Barcelona is particularly accessible to travelers with disabilities, having revamped much of its infrastructure in preparation for the 1992 Olympics. Other large cities may be amenable as well, but rural and small-town Iberia will be difficult to manage for the budget traveler with disabilities. Those with disabilities should inform airlines and hotels of their disabilities when making reservations, as some time may be needed to prepare special accommodations. Call ahead to restaurants, museums, and other facilities to find out if they are wheelchair-accessible. Guide-dog owners should inquire as to the quarantine policies of each destination country.

Trains are probably the easiest form of travel for disabled travelers in Europe: many stations have ramps, and some trains have wheelchair lifts, special seating areas, and specially equipped toilets. All Eurostar, some InterCity (IC), and some EuroCity (EC) trains are wheelchair-accessible, and CityNightLine trains and Conrail trains feature special compartments. Some car rental agencies (e.g., Hertz) offer hand-controlled vehicles.

USEFUL ORGANIZATIONS

Accessible Journeys, 35 W. Sellers Ave., Ridley Park, PA 19078, USA (☎+1-800-846-4537; www.disabilitytravel.com). Designs tours for wheelchair users and slow walkers. The site has tips and forums for all travelers.

Flying Wheels Travel, 143 W. Bridge St., Owatonna, MN 55060, USA (☎+1-507-451-5005; www.flyingwheelstravel.com). Specializes in escorted trips to Europe for people with physical disabilities; plans custom trips worldwide.

The Guided Tour, Inc., 7900 Old York Rd., Ste. 114B, Elkins Park, PA 19027, USA (☎+1-800-783-5841; www.guidedtour.com). Organizes travel programs for persons with developmental and physical challenges in Canada, Hawaii, Ireland, Italy, Mexico, Spain, the UK, and the US.

Mobility International USA (MIUSA), P.O. Box 10767, Eugene, OR 97440, USA (☎+1-541-343-1284; www.miusa.org). Provides a variety of books and other publications containing information for travelers with disabilities.

Society for Accessible Travel and Hospitality (SATH), 347 5th Ave., Ste. 610, New York, NY 10016, USA (☎+1-212-447-7284; www.sath.org). Advocacy group that publishes free online travel info. Annual membership US$49, students and seniors US$29.

MINORITY TRAVELERS

The cities of Spain are increasingly cosmopolitan due to immigration and tourism. The infrequent incidents of racism reported are rarely violent or threatening. However, after the arrest of Moroccans for the terrorist attack of 11-M (p. 66), travelers who appear Middle Eastern may face some harassment. Portugal, with its increasingly diverse ethnic composition and long history with Africa, Asia, and South America, is actively anti-racist, but travelers should always be aware of and sensitive to their surroundings.

DIETARY CONCERNS

The travel section of **The Vegetarian Resource Group's** website, at www.vrg.org/travel, has a comprehensive list of organizations and websites geared toward helping vegetarians and vegans traveling abroad. Vegetarians will also find numerous resources on the web; try www.vegdining.com, www.happycow.net, and www.vegetariansabroad.com, for starters.

Travelers who keep **kosher** should contact synagogues in larger cities for information. Your own synagogue or college Hillel should have access to lists of Jewish institutions across the nation. If you are strict in your observance, you may have to prepare your own food on the road. A good resource is the *Jewish Travel Guide* edited by Michael Zaidner (Vallentine Mitchell; US$18). Travelers looking for **halal** restaurants may find www.zabihah.com a useful resource. The database at http://shamash.org/kosher provides listings of Jewish centers and restaurants providing kosher food, mostly in Spain and Morocco.

OTHER RESOURCES

Let's Go tries to cover all aspects of budget travel, but we can't put everything in our guides. Listed below are books and websites that will help you conduct your own research.

WORLD WIDE WEB

Almost every aspect of budget travel is accessible via the web. In 10min. at the keyboard, you can make a hostel reservation, get advice on travel hot spots from other travelers, or find out how much a train from Lleida to Lisboa costs. Listed here are some regional and travel-related sites to start off your surfing; other relevant websites are listed throughout the book. Because website turnover is high, use search engines (like Google) to strike out on your own.

LET'S GO ONLINE. Plan your next trip on our newly redesigned website, **www.letsgo.com.** It features the latest travel info on your favorite destinations as well as tons of interactive features: make your own itinerary, read blogs from our trusty researcher-writers, browse our photo library, watch exclusive videos, check out our newsletter, find travel deals, and buy new guides. We're always updating and adding new features, so check back often!

THE ART OF TRAVEL

Backpacker's Ultimate Guide: www.bugeurope.com. Tips on packing, transportation, and where to go. Also tons of country-specific travel information.

BootsnAll.com: www.bootsnall.com. Numerous resources for independent travelers, from planning your trip to reporting on it when you get back.

How to See the World: www.artoftravel.com. A compendium of great travel tips, from cheap flights to self defense to interacting with local culture.

Travel Intelligence: www.travelintelligence.net. A large collection of works by distinguished travel writers.

INFORMATION ON SPAIN, PORTUGAL, AND MOROCCO

CIA World Factbook: www.odci.gov/cia/publications/factbook/index.html. Tons of vital statistics on geography, government, economy, and people.

Geographia: www.geographia.com. Highlights the culture and peoples of Spain, Portugal, and Morocco.

TravelPage: www.travelpage.com. Links to official tourist office sites.

PlanetRider: www.planetrider.com. A list of links to the "best" websites covering the culture and tourist attractions of Spain, Portugal, and Morocco.

World Travel Guide: www.travel-guides.com. Helpful practical info.

BEYOND TOURISM

A PHILOSOPHY FOR TRAVELERS

HIGHLIGHTS OF SPAIN, PORTUGAL, AND MOROCCO

SIMMER and slice with Basque chefs in San Sebastián (p. 484).

SPEAK Portuguese (almost) like the Portuguese in Lisboa (p. 579).

SWEAT as you plant cherry trees in the mountains of Morocco's High Atlas (p. 751).

FLIP to our "Giving Back" sidebar feature for more on Beyond Tourism (p. 49).

There comes a point when tourism and traveling diverge. Whether exploring Spain, Portugal, or Morocco, you will be surrounded by chances to immerse yourself in your environment. And as you do, certain realities around you become more obvious: environmental destruction, poverty, and discrimination, to name a few. Even as tourism plays a heavy role in the development of local economies, it contributes to some of the worst environmental and cultural erosion. Responsible and socially-conscious tourism, therefore, is not only essential but also one of the most rewarding ways to travel.

As a **volunteer** in Spain, Portugal, or Morocco, you can unleash that inner superhero with projects from fighting racism in Barcelona to painting murals in Marrakesh. This chapter is full of ideas to help get your search for NGOs and other relevent organizations started, whether you're hoping to pitch in for a few days or run away to a whole new life of Iberian activism.

The power of **studying** abroad is beyond comprehension. Thousands of students descend on Spain every year to take advantage of a broad array of language programs, and Portugal and Morocco offer equally incredible learning experiences. If you want to brush up your Arabic, birdwatch in the Pyrenees, or conquer the Spanish lisp, there is probably a course out there for you.

Working abroad can bring some of the most meaningful relationships and experiences of your life. (And it doesn't hurt that a job helps pay for more globetrotting.) High rates of unemployment in Spain, Portugal, and Morocco can make it difficult to find a job or obtain a work visa, and travelers should also realize that they could be taking away jobs from locals. That said, English speakers are always in high demand as teachers, au pairs, or workers in seasonal resort towns. In order to work abroad, you must meet the legal requirements for either short-term or long-term work (see **Working,** p. 56).

SHARE YOUR EXPERIENCE. Have you had a particularly enjoyable volunteer, study, or work experience that you'd like to share with other travelers? Post it to our website, www.letsgo.com.

VOLUNTEERING

Feel like saving the world this week? Volunteering can be a powerful and fulfilling experience, especially when combined with the thrill of traveling. While Spain, Portugal, and Morocco face very different realities, key problems unite them. Pressing issues like immigration, the environment, poverty, and women's rights make volunteering in these countries a compelling option.

Most people who volunteer do so on a short-term basis at organizations that make use of drop-in or once-a-week volunteers. The best way to find opportunities that match your interests and schedule may be to check with local or national volunteer centers. In Spain, contact the **Plataforma del Voluntariado de España,** C. Fuentes, 10, Madrid (☎902 12 05 12) in order to best match your interests to local needs. In Portugal, the **Plataforma Portuguesa das ONGD,** Rua da Madalena, 91, Lisboa (☎218 87 22 39) is a central coordinator of NGOs and volunteer opportunities. As always, read up before heading out.

Those looking for longer, more intensive volunteer opportunities usually choose to go through a parent organization that takes care of logistical details and often provides a group environment and support system—for a fee. There are two main types of organizations—religious and secular—although there are rarely restrictions on participation in either. Websites like **www.volunteerabroad.com, www.servenet.org,** and **www.idealist.org** allow you to search for volunteer openings both in your country and abroad. The following listings are just a starting point; local opportunities are endless.

I HAVE TO PAY TO VOLUNTEER? Many volunteers are surprised to learn that some organizations require large fees or "donations," but don't go calling them scams just yet. While such fees may seem ridiculous at first, they often keep the organization afloat, covering airfare, room, board, and administrative expenses for the volunteers. (Other organizations must rely on private donations and government subsidies.) If you're concerned about how a program spends its fees, request an annual report or finance account. A reputable organization won't refuse to inform you of how volunteer money is spent. Pay-to-volunteer programs might be a good idea for young travelers who are looking for more support and structure (such as pre-arranged transportation and housing) or anyone who would rather not deal with the uncertainty of creating a volunteer experience from scratch.

SOCIAL ACTIVISM

Here's your chance to work toward goals of justice and equity, whether in Spain, Portugal, or Morocco. A diverse network of social organizations addresses all manner of problems, from homelessness to domestic abuse to human rights. Such volunteering can help you better understand the global scope of these issues and immerse you in a foreign environment with a community of like-minded individuals. The following is a brief selection of organizations to help you begin your search.

Abraço, Larco José Luis Champalimaud, 4a, 1600-110 Lisboa, Portugal (☎217 99 75 00; www.abraco.org.pt). With multiple offices in Portugal, this non-profit offers support services and fights HIV/AIDS discrimination.

Asociacion del Sur del Trabajo Voluntario y Social (ASTVS), N°480 Lot, Boutalamine 52000 Errachidia, Morocco (☎212 67 41 76 30; www.astvs.org). Works to further educational, cultural, and social goals in Morocco's southern region, organizing work camps with foreign and Moroccan volunteers. 2- to 4-week project €160.

Banco Alimentar, Av. de Ceuta, Estação C.P. Alcântara-Terra, Armazém 1, 1300-125 Lisboa, Portugal (☎213 64 96 55; www.bancoalimentar.pt). This federation of food banks operates branches throughout Portugal, providing much-needed food for the hungry.

Equanimal, Apdo. 14454, 28080 Madrid, spain (☎902 10 29 45; www.equanimal.org). Works for animal rights, including the abolition of bullfighting, through education. Volunteers can participate in demonstrations, distribute pamphlets, and organize events.

Fundación Triángulo, C. Eloy Gonzalo, 25, 28010 Madrid, Spain (☎915 93 05 40; www.fundaciontrangulo.es). Combats discrimination and promotes equality for gay, lesbian, bisexual, and transgendered people in Spain and around the world.

Stop SIDA, C. Muntaner, 121, Entresuelo 1, Barcelona, Spain (☎902 10 69 27; www.stopsida.org). A member of the federation Coordinadora GaiLesbiana, Stop SIDA helps combat the spread of AIDS by providing prevention information and support services.

IMMIGRATION

Today, Spain absorbs more immigrants than any other country in the European Union. Over the past decade, the number of immigrants has risen from 2 percent of the Spanish population to more than 10 percent, changing the face of Spanish cities and making booming economic growth possible. Though popular images suggest a flood of immigrants crossing the Strait of Gibraltar from Morocco, in reality only about 20 percent of Spain's immigrants come from Africa. The vast majority, in fact, emigrate from Europe and Latin America. Portuguese society has become just as multicultural and is now home to a huge number of immigrants, largely from former African colonies and Brazil.

Unlike both Spain and Portugal, Morocco's migration flows outward; thousands of workers attempt to reach Spanish shores each year. But with rising unemployment on the peninsula, attitudes toward foreign workers seem to be shifting as immigration policy becomes controversial for the first time. Below is a partial list of organizations that attempt to level social inequalities while alleviating the burdens placed on immigrants.

ARSIS, C General Weyler, 257, 08912 Barcelona, Spain (☎902 88 86 07; www.arsis.org). Opportunities to tutor underprivileged children, work in a women's center, or run food and clothing drives for recent immigrants.

Comisión Española de Ayuda al Refugiado (CEAR), Avda. General Perón 32, 2° 28020 Madrid, Spain (☎915 98 05 35; www.cear.es) Aims to protect the right to asylum with branches in Madrid, Barcelona, Bilbao, Sevilla, Gran Canarias, Mérida, and Valencia. Work in outreach, legal assistance, translation, and human rights.

Ecos do Sur, C. Ángel Senra, 25, 15007 La Coruña, Spain (☎981 15 01 18; www.ecosdosur.org). Works to ease recent immigrants' transitions into Galician society with English, Spanish, and Gallego classes and support services. Teach, assist with HIV/AIDS prevention programs, conduct tuberculosis tests, or do other community outreach.

Federació Catalana de Voluntariat Social, C. Grassot, 2, 3er, 08025 Barcelona, Spain (☎933 14 19 00; www.federacio.net). Umbrella organization of Catalan social service organizations. Volunteers can assist with projects to achieve better standards of living and equality for immigrants in the region.

SOS Racisme, C. Hospital, 49, 08001 Barcelona, Spain (☎934 12 00 34; www.sosracisme.org) and Quinta da Torrinha, Lote 11A, 1750 Ameixoeira, Lisboa, Portugal (☎217 55 27 00; www.sosracismo.pt). Volunteers strive to combat racism and achieve equal rights for non-citizens and migrant workers in Spain and Portugal.

ENVIRONMENTAL WORK

Development, abuse of natural resources, and rampant tourism all threaten the land and water of Spain, Portugal, and Morocco. Many tourists already make an effort to choose the most environmentally friendly travel possible, whether by using public transit or reducing their local consumption, but some go even further. Working with environmental conservation organizations can reduce the impact of your tourism, and working in the beauty of the landscapes you are helping to protect is its own reward.

Ecoforest, Apdo. 29, Coin 29100, Málaga, Spain (☎661 07 99 50; www.ecoforest.org). Fruit farm and vegan community in southern Spain that uses environmental education to develop a sustainable lifestyle for residents. Visitors are welcome to stay, contributing €5-15 per day toward operating costs.

High Atlas Foundation, Park West Station, P.O. Box 21081, New York, NY 10025, USA (☎+1-646-688-2946; http://highatlasfoundation.org). Formed by former Peace Corps volunteers in Morocco, this foundation works with community-based projects in rural areas of Morocco to plant fruit trees, ensure potable water, improve irrigation, and work for the rights of women and children. Contact the foundation for ways to contribute.

Sunseed Desert Technology, Apdo. 9, 04270, Sorbas, Almería, Spain (☎950 52 57 70; www.sunseed.org.uk). Researches methods of preventing desertification in the driest regions of Spain. Volunteers come for a mimimum of 2 weeks for a part-time position, or stay on with a full time residency. Costs range from €91-165 per week, room and board included. Student discounts available.

World Wide Opportunites on Organic Farms (WWOOF), Yainz 33, Casa 14, Cereceda, Cantabria, Spain (☎902 01 08 14; www.wwoof.es). Connects members with organic farms in Spain and Portugal, which offer work in exchange for food and board. Membership to the Spanish national organization costs €20 per year.

FOR THE UNDECIDED ALTRUIST

The possibilities for meaningful volunteer work in Spain, Portugal, or Morocco are endless. These volunteer agencies are great resources; explore their options and find an opportunity that excites you and speaks to your talents.

Service Civil International, 5505 Walnut Level Road, Crozet, VA 22932, USA (☎+1-206-350-6585; www.sci-ivs.org). Organizes a huge variety of short- and long-term work camps in Spain, Portugal, and Morocco. All overseas camps cost $235, which includes simple shared housing and communal meals.

Volunteers for International Partnership, 70 Landmark Hill, Suite 204, Brattleboro, VT 05301 (☎802 246 1154; www.partnershipvolunteers.org) Coordinates 2- or 3-month volunteer programs in Morocco focusing on social welfare, the environment, teaching, and cultural tourism. Includes language courses and homestay. Must be 21 or older; 3-month program $2635 plus airfare.

Volunteers for Peace, 1034 Tiffany Road, Belmont, VT 05730, USA (☎+1-801-259-2759; www.vfp.org). Organizes 2-3 week group projects in Spain, Portugal, and Morocco on a wide range of social and environmental issues. Average project cost $300.

STUDYING

Study-abroad programs range from basic language and culture courses to university-level classes, often for college credit. In order to choose a program that best fits your needs, research as much as you can before making your decision—determine costs and duration, as well as what kind of students participate in the program and what sorts of accommodations are provided. Many American universities, as well as student travel organizations, provide international programs for undergraduates.

VISA INFORMATION. Most foreigners planning to study in Spain or Portugal must obtain a student visa, but those studying for fewer than three months in Spain need only a passport. Visa applications for study in Spain and Portugal can be completed in your home country, at your destination country's consulate (listed under **Consular Services Abroad,** p. 10). Obtaining a visa can be an arduous process; the consulate will often require you to apply in person and demands loads of paperwork (letter verifying enrollment, medical certificate, proof of health insurance, etc.) before they process your application. They are also likely to charge a processing fee of around $100. To study more than 90 days, you must obtain a student residency card (student visa) once in Spain for as long as you are enrolled in the university. For residents of most countries, a stay in Portugal or Morocco of less than three months requires a passport; beyond three months, a visa is necessary.

UNIVERSITIES

Most university-level study-abroad programs are conducted in the country's native language, although many programs offer classes in English as well as courses geared toward non-fluent speakers. Savvy linguists may find it cheaper to enroll directly in a university abroad, although getting college credit may be more difficult. You can search **www.studyabroad.com** for various semester- or summer-abroad programs that meet your criteria, including your desired location and focus of study. If you're a college student, your local study-abroad office is often the best place to start.

AMERICAN PROGRAMS

American Institute for Foreign Study (AIFS), College Division, River Plaza, 9 W. Broad St., Stamford, CT 06902, USA (☎+1-800-727-2437; www.aifsabroad.com). Organizes programs for high school and college study in universities in Spain. Offers study-abroad opportunities in Barcelona in the summer, and Granada and Salamanca in the summer and academic year.

Council on International Educational Exchange (CIEE), 300 Fore St., Portland, ME 04101, USA (☎+1-207-553-4000 or 800-40-STUDY/407-8839; www.ciee.org). One of the most comprehensive resources for work, academic, and internship programs around the world, including in Portugal. Students of all levels of Portuguese can study in Lisboa, where the curriculum focuses largely on the humanities and social sciences.

International Association for the Exchange of Students for Technical Experience (IAESTE; www.iaeste.org). IAESTE runs several branches across Spain and Portugal. Chances are that your home country has a local office, too: contact it to apply for hands-on technical internships abroad. You must be a college student studying science, technology, or engineering. Cost-of-living allowance is provided.

School for International Training (SIT) Study Abroad, 1 Kipling Rd., P.O. Box 676, Brattleboro, VT 05302, USA (☎+1-888-272-7881 or 802-258-3212; www.sit.edu/studyabroad). Semester-long programs in Spain run approximately US$23,000-24,000. In Morocco they run approximately US$18,300-19,300. Summer intensive language program in Morocco runs US$10,190. SIT also runs **The Experiment in International Living** (☎+1-800-345-2929; www.usexperiment.org), with its 3- to 5-week summer programs that offer high-school students cross-cultural homestays, community service, ecological adventure, and language training in Spain and Morocco (US$5300-6800).

SPANISH AND PORTUGUESE PROGRAMS

The European Union sponsors programs encouraging study abroad opportunities within Europe, and Spain and Portugal have not missed the train. From Valencia to Lisboa, Madrid to Coimbra, these countries are studded with dynamic university communities, and in less than a decade the number of foreign students in Barcelona alone has doubled. Information on Spanish study programs is provided by the **Organismo Autónomo de Programas Educativos Europeos** (www.oapee.es). For Portuguese programs, check out the **Programa de Aprendizagem ao Longo da Vida** (www.proalv.pt).

Agencia Nacional Erasmus, Vicesecretaría General del Consejo de Universidades, Juan del Rosal, 14, Ciudad Universitaria, 28040 Madrid, Spain (☎914 53 98 42; http://ec.europa.eu/education/index_en.html). Spanish branch of the European Union's study abroad program, which offers EU members the opportunity to study within Europe.

Agência Nacional para os Programas Comunitários Sócrates e Leonardo da Vinci, Av. Infate Santo, 2, Piso 1, 1350-178 Lisboa, Portugal (☎213 94 47 00; www.socleo.pt). Portuguese division of the European Union's study abroad program.

Universidad Complutense de Madrid, Vicerectorado de Relaciones Internacionales, C. Isaac Peral, 28040 Madrid, Spain (☎913 94 69 22/23; www.ucm.es/info/ucmp/index.php). The largest and one of the oldest universities in Spain. Hosts hundreds of foreign students annually. Opportunities for study in a variety of fields.

Universidade de Lisboa, Rectorate Al. da Universidade, Cidade Universitária, Campo Grande, 1649-004 Lisboa, Portugal (☎217 96 76 24; www.ul.pt). Allows foreign students to enroll directly.

MOROCCAN PROGRAMS

Morocco can be a great option for speakers of French or Arabic, or those with particular interests in subjects like development, religion, and contemporary politics in Africa and the Middle East.

Amideast, 35, Zanqat Oukaimeden, Agdal, Rabat Morocco (☎+212 2 225 9393; www.amideast.org). In partnership with Mohammed V University-Agdal in Rabat, offers a four-month-long program with classes in Arabic, French, humanities, and social sciences.

International Studies Abroad, 35, 1640-B E. 2nd St., Suite 200, Austin, TX 78702, USA (☎+1-800-580-8826; www.studiesabroad.com). Offers fall, winter, and summer programs in Meknès.

LANGUAGE SCHOOLS

Enrolling at a language school has two big perks: a slightly less rigorous course load and the promise that you'll learn exactly what those kids in Cadaqués are calling you under their breath. There is a great variety of language schools—independent, affiliated with a larger university, local, international—but one thing is constant: they rarely offer college credit. Their programs are best for younger high-school students who might not feel comfortable with older students in a university program. Some worthwhile organizations include:

Eurocentres, 56 Eccleston Sq., London SW1V 1PH, UK (☎+44 20 7963 8450; www.eurocentres.com). Language programs for beginning to advanced students with homestays in Barcelona and Valencia.

Language Immersion Institute, State University of New York at New Paltz, 1 Hawk Dr., New Paltz, NY 12561, USA (☎+1-845-257-3500; www.newpaltz.edu/lii). Short, intensive summer language courses and some overseas courses in Spanish, Portuguese, Arabic, and French. Program fees are around US$1000 for a 2-week course, not including accommodations.

Enforex, Alberto Aguilera, 26, 28015 Madrid, Spain (☎915 943 776; www.enforex.com). Offers 20 Spanish programs in Spain, ranging from 1 week to a year in duration. Opportunities in 12 Spanish cities, including Granada, Sevilla, Barcelona, and Madrid.

Amerispan Study Abroad, 1334 Walnut St, 6th Floor, Philadelphia, PA 19107, USA (☎+1-215-751-1100; www.amerispan.com). Offers language courses around the world, many including homestays. Arabic language programs in Fez, Rabat, and Tetouan. Also offers several programs in Spain and Portugal.

OTHER PROGRAMS

Associació per a Defensa i L'Estudì de la Natura (ADENC), Ca l'Estruch, C. Sant Isidre, 08208 Sabadell, Spain (☎937 17 18 87; www.adenc.org). Catalan conservation group offering short courses on bird-watching, landscape photography, and other ecotourism-related fields.

Escuela de Cocina Luis Irizar, C. Mari, 5, 20003 San Sebastián, Guipuzcoa, Spain (☎943 43 15 40; www.escuelairizar.com). Learn how to cook Basque cuisine at this culinary institute. Offers a 2-year diploma course. Professionals and amateurs alike can enroll in 1-week summer programs.

Taller Flamenco School, C. Peral, 49, E-41002 Sevilla, Spain (☎954 56 42 34; www.tallerflamenco.com). Offers courses in flamenco dance (€180-240 per week) and guitar (€225 per week) at varying levels of difficulty.

WORKING

As with volunteering, work opportunities tend to fall into two categories. Some travelers want long-term jobs that allow them to integrate into a community, while others seek out short-term jobs to finance the next leg of their travels. The most common form of long-term work in Spain and Portugal is teaching English, while short-term employment is centered on the tourist industry, whether it's bartending or giving tours of sherry bodegas. *Let's Go* discourages working in developing countries such as Morocco, as employment is scarce enough for locals; however, those with specialized skills may be able to make a positive contribution. **Transitions Abroad** (www.transitionsabroad.com) also offers updated online listings for work over any time span.

For Spain, begin your search at the **INEM (Instituto de Empleo).** The address and telephone number of regional employment offices *(Oficinas de Empleo)* can be found in any telephone guide or at www.inem.es. Many seasoned travelers, however, go straight to a particular town's Yellow Pages *(Páginas Amarillas)* or even go door-to-door. In Portugal, the English-language weekly **The News** (www.the-news.net) carries job listings. Note that working abroad often requires a special work visa.

MORE VISA INFORMATION. Travelers from within the European Union can work without a permit in Spain and Portugal, but those from outside the EU need a work permit. Obtaining a work permit requires extensive documentation, often including a passport, police background check, and medical records, and the cost varies. Contact your nearest consulate (p. 10) for a complete list of requirements. Any foreigner wishing to work in Morocco must obtain a residency permit, which requires a contract, passport, application forms, an AIDS test, and a fee. Again, contact your consulate for details.

LONG-TERM WORK

If you're planning on spending a substantial amount of time (more than three months) working in Spain, Portugal or Morocco, search for a job well in advance. International placement agencies are often the easiest way to find employment abroad, especially for those interested in teaching. Although they are often only available to college students, **internships** are a good way to ease into working abroad. Many say the interning experience is well worth it, despite low pay (if you're lucky enough to be paid at all). Be wary of advertisements for companies claiming to be able get you a job abroad for a fee—often the same listings are available online or in newspapers. Some reputable organizations include:

Council on International Educational Exchange (CIEE), 300 Fore St., Portland, ME 04101, USA (☎+1-207-553-4000 or 800-40-STUDY/407-8839; www.ciee.org). They assist with both studying and teaching abroad. Tucked among their study-abroad listings is a resource for international internships.

Career Journal (www.careerjournaleurope.com). The Wall Street Journal publishes this online journal listing thousands of jobs throughout Europe. There are both short- and long-term as well as part- and full-time jobs.

Escape Artist (www.escapeartist.com/jobs/overseas1). Offers information on living abroad, including job listings for Spain and Portugal.

Expat Exchange (www.expatexchange.com). Provides message boards where individuals seeking employment in Spain and Portugal can advertise.

Trabajos (www.trabajos.com). Contains job listings for all regions of Spain.

EURES (www.europa.eu.int/eures). EU agency providing job listings and opportunities across Europe, including Spain and Portugal.

TEACHING ENGLISH

As an English speaker, you have the chance to contribute your skills while forming lasting relationships with students and a community. In almost all cases, you must have at least a bachelor's degree to be a full-fledged teacher, although college undergraduates can often get summer positions teaching or tutoring. Many schools require teachers to have a **Teaching English as a Foreign Language (TEFL)** certificate. You may still be able to find a teaching job without one, but certified teachers often find higher-paying jobs. Teachers in public schools will likely work in both English and the local language, but private schools usually hire native English speakers for English-immersion classrooms where no Spanish, Portuguese, or Arabic is spoken. Placement agencies or university fellowship programs are the best resources for finding teaching jobs. The alternative is to contact schools directly or to try your luck once you arrive in the country. In the latter case, the best time to look is several weeks before the start of the school year. The following organizations are extremely helpful in placing teachers in Spain, Portugal, and Morocco.

International Schools Services (ISS), 15 Roszel Rd., P.O. Box 5910, Princeton, NJ 08543, USA (☎+1-609-452-0990; www.iss.edu). Hires teachers for more than 200 overseas schools. Candidates should have teaching experience and a bachelor's degree. 2-year commitment is the norm.

Teach Abroad (www.teach.studyabroad.com). Brings you to listings around the world for paid positions teaching English, including some in Spain and Portugal.

TESOL-Spain (www.tesol-spain.org). Non-profit association of English teachers in Spain. Site features a jobs board among its many resources.

TEFL Job Placement (www.tefljobplacement.com). Places teachers in countries across the world, including Morocco. Requirements and durations vary.

AU PAIR WORK

Au pairs are typically women aged 18-27 who work as live-in nannies, caring for children and doing light housework in foreign countries in exchange for room, board, and a small spending allowance or stipend. One perk of the job is that it allows you to get to know Spain or Portugal without the costs of traveling. An au pair can expect to make €50 and up per week. Drawbacks, however, can include mediocre pay and long hours. Much of the au pair experience depends on your relationship with the family with which you are placed. The agencies below are a good starting point for looking for employment.

InterExchange, 161 6th Ave., New York City, NY 10013, USA (☎+1-212-924-0446 or 800-AU-PAIRS/287-2477; www.interexchange.org). Families post messages seeking help. Organized by country for both Spain and Portugal.

Childcare International, Trafalgar House, Grenville Pl., London NW7 3SA, UK (☎+44 20 8906 3116; www.childint.co.uk). Offers opportunities in Spain.

International Au Pair Association (IAPA), Store Kongensgade 40 H, DK-1264 Copenhagen K, Denmark (☎+453 317 0066; www.iapa.org). Non-profit organization that connects to smaller au pair agencies in many nations, including Spain.

SHORT-TERM WORK

Many travelers try their hand at odd jobs to help pay for another few months of travel. However, obtaining a work permit is a long, complicated, and bureaucratic process, and requires a prior job contract, which can be difficult for short-term workers. It is illegal for non-EU citizens to work in Spain or Portugal without this work permit. However, many establishments hire travelers under-the-table for jobs like bartending, waiting tables, or promoting bars and clubs. Another popular option is to work several hours a day at a hostel in exchange for free or discounted room and/or board. Most often, these short-term jobs are found by word of mouth or by expressing interest to the owner of a hostel or restaurant. *Let's Go* lists temporary jobs of this nature whenever possible; look in a city's **Practical Information** listings or see below. *Let's Go* does not recommend working illegally.

EcoForest, Apdo. Correos, 29, 29100 Coin, Málaga, Spain (☎661 07 99 50; www.ecoforest.org). Exchanges free camping space for 3hr. of work per day. €20 initial fee.

Bodega Tour Guide, Jerez de la Frontera, Spain (p. 230).

Intern Jobs (www.internjobs.com). Lists not only internships, but also many ideal short-term jobs like camp counseling and bartending. Applies to Spain, not Portugal.

Transitions Abroad (www.transitionsabroad.com). Lists organizations in Spain and Portugal that hire short-term workers and provides links to articles about working abroad.

FURTHER READING ON BEYOND TOURISM

Alternatives to the Peace Corps: A Guide of Global Volunteer Opportunities, edited by Paul Backhurst. Food First, 2005 (US$12).

The Back Door Guide to Short-Term Job Adventures: Internships, Summer Jobs, Seasonal Work, Volunteer Vacations, and Transitions Abroad, by Michael Landes. Ten Speed Press, 2005 (US$22).

Green Volunteers: The World Guide to Voluntary Work in Nature Conservation, by Fabio Ausenda. Universe, 2007 (US$15).

How to Get a Job in Europe, by Cheryl Matherly and Robert Sanborn. Planning Communications, 2003 (US$23).

Live and Work Abroad: A Guide for Modern Nomads, by Huw Francis and Michelyne Callan. Vacation Work Publications, 2001 (US$20).

Work Abroad: The Complete Guide to Finding a Job Overseas, edited by Clayton A. Hubbs. Transitions Abroad, 2002 (US$16).

Work Your Way Around the World, by Susan Griffith. Vacation Work Publications, 2007 (US$22).

walking the walk

A Pilgrims' Path on the Camino de Santiago

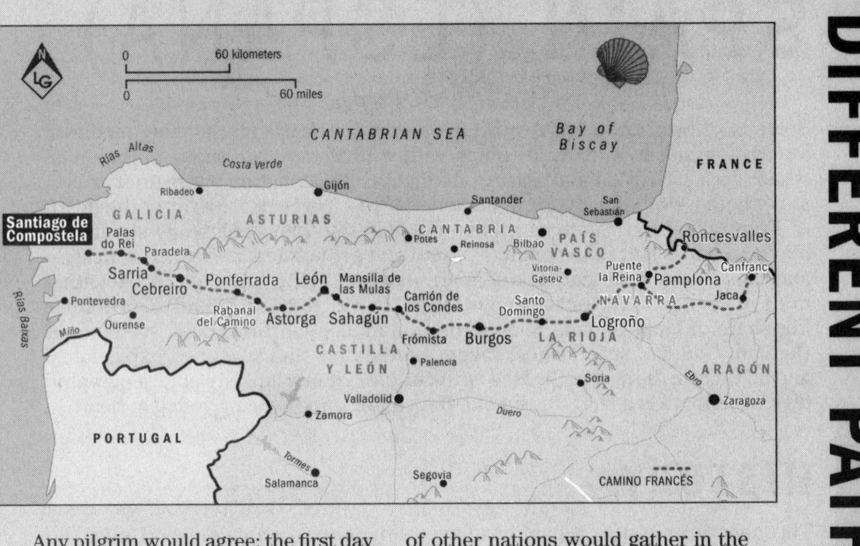

Any pilgrim would agree: the first day of the Camino de Santiago is the hardest. From St-Jean-Pied-de-Port, we hiked 23km uphill into the Pyrenees and then 4km downhill to the *albergue* (pilgrim hostel) in Roncesvalles. We faced drenching rain and impenetrable fog, blisters and scrapes, but we kept walking. And each day, we woke up a little less tired and sore than the day before. As the miles wore on and paths stretched to the horizon, we began to see the rolling wheat fields and *terra rossa* vineyards as calming. We appreciated the silence when our company was limited to grazing cows and the occasional roaming chicken. We encountered locals who offered us cake and cookies with our tea, apples for the road, and homemade *albóndigas* (meatballs). And we looked forward to each evening, when pilgrims from Australia, Italy, Japan, Germany, Venezuela, France, Spain, and a host of other nations would gather in the kitchen to cook and regale each other with stories of the road.

Thirty-four days after that painful first day, we found ourselves sitting in the pews at the Cathedral of St. James in Santiago, awaiting the pilgrims' daily mass. We completed all the traditional rituals, including hugging the golden statue of St. James in an awkward but oddly comforting metallic embrace. We were fumigated by the incense from the *botafumeiro*, a massive swinging contraption rigged to overpower the stench of sweaty pilgrims. Sitting there, we couldn't help but contemplate how many others had gone through the same motions days, months, and even centuries ago. And as we thought back to the first days of our journey, we took solace in the fact that that either we hadn't made a mistake after all, or we had done so in very good company.

"We began to see the rolling wheat fields and *terra rossa* vineyards as calming."

Silvia Killingsworth was the Editor-in-Chief of the 2008 Let's Go series. She graduated from Harvard in 2007 and now lives in New York City. Victoria Norelid, a fellow Let's Go vet, graduated from Harvard with a degree in History. She is currently getting a Masters degree at Oxford University.

SPAIN (ESPAÑA)

Spain is colorful and playful, austere and refined. It is a place where medieval Moorish arches in Andalucía collide with wild *Modernista* spires in Cataluña, where classical royal paintings inspire flights of imagination by abstract artists, and where Celtic rock overlays flamenco beats. Three decades after the death of Franco and the country's rebirth as a liberated and politically significant player, Spain is still riding out its cultural and economic renaissance with style and flair. Today, whether travelers are making their pilgrimage to the cathedrals of León or to the pulsing nightlife of Madrid, they are bound to meet their fair share of hippies, nuns, shepherds, and mullet-sporting youth; speakers of Catalan, Gallego, and Basque; recent immigrants and seasoned expatriates; and all those in between. Blessed with cultural vitality and enviable geographic diversity, Spain is a land for the old, the young, and the truly young at heart.

HISTORY

Throughout its history, Spain has been both colony and colonizer. Under the rule of the Iberians, Celts, Romans, Visigoths, Arabs, and French, the country inherited an exotic mélange of influences. In the 16th century, it became a world superpower, ruling from Argentina to Austria. After the 1588 defeat of the Armada, Spain began a long and arduous descent from international empire to Pyrenean pauper, though artistic and literary achievements offset constant military defeats. In 1936, democracy disintegrated into civil war, bringing Generalissimo Francisco Franco to power. Now a thriving democracy with the ninth largest economy in the world, Spain surges into the 21st century with a glorious past and a promising future.

RULE HISPANIA (PREHISTORY-AD 711). Spain played host to a succession of civilizations—**Basque, Celtiberian,** and **Greek**—before the Romans came for an extended visit in the 3rd century BC. Over the next seven centuries, the Romans infused Spanish culture with their langauge, architecture, roads, and food (particularly grapes, olives, and wheat). Following the Romans, a slew of Germanic tribes swept through Iberia, and the **Visigoths**--newly converted Christians--emerged victorious. In AD 419 they established their court at Barcelona and ruled Spain for the next 300 years.

PLEASE, SIR, MAY I HAVE SOME MOORS? (711-1492). A small force of Arabs, Berbers, and Syrians invaded Spain in AD 711 following Muslim unification. The **Moors** encountered little resistance from the divided Visigoths, and the peninsula fell to the caliph of Damascus, the spiritual leader of Islam. The Moors established their Iberian capital at Córdoba (p. 220), which by the 10th century was the largest city in Western Europe with over 500,000 inhabitants. During Abderramán III's rule (929-961), many considered Spain the wealthiest and most cultivated country in the world. Abderramán III's successor, Al-Mansur, snuffed out opposition in his court and undertook a series of military campaigns that culminated with the destruction of Santiago de Compostela (p. 536) in AD 997 and the kidnapping of its bells. It took the Christians 240 years to get them back, and centuries more to retake Spain.

LOS REYES CATÓLICOS (1469-1516). The marriage of **Fernando de Aragón** and **Isabel de Castilla** in 1469 joined Iberia's two mightiest Christian kingdoms. During their half-century rule, these Catholic monarchs established Spain as the prime European exponent of Catholicism, and as an international power. They introduced the brutal **Inquisition** in 1478, which mandated execution or burning of heretics, principally Jews. The policy prompted a mass exodus, as Jews and Muslims who stayed faced conversion to Christianity or imprisonment and death. In 1492, the royal couple captured Granada from the Moors, victoriously ending the centuries-long *Reconquista* and uniting Spain under Catholic rule. This dominance continued to flourish with lucrative conquests in the Americas, beginning in 1492 when they agreed to finance **Christopher Columbus's** first adventure.

HABSBURGS TAKE THE STAGE (1516-1713). The daughter of Fernando and Isabel, **Juana la Loca** (the Mad) married **Felipe el Hermoso** (the Fair) of the powerful Habsburg family. When the young king died, La Loca, a possible schizophrenic, walked his coffin to Granada, opening it occasionally to kiss his corpse. Juana and Felipe secured their genetic legacy with the birth of **Carlos I,** better known as Holy Roman Emperor Charles V (1516-1556).

Under Carlos, the Spanish empire grew exponentially. Royal marriages placed the country in control of European territories in Sicily and Naples, while in the New World conquistadors plundered Mexico, Peru, and Chile, destroying the vast empires of the Aztec and Inca civilizations. They brought their booty back to Spain by the galleon, providing Carlos with funds for his battles and conquests. Gold and silver were complemented by the potatoes, corn, and exotic fruits that were introduced as new crops in Europe.

When Carlos retired to a monastery, **Felipe II** (1556-1598) inherited simmering rebellion in the Protestant Netherlands. His marriage to Mary Tudor, Queen of England, in 1554 created an international Catholic alliance, and Felipe made it his life's mission to create a true Catholic empire. In 1581, a year after Felipe II annexed Portugal, the Dutch declared their independence from Spain, starting a war and becoming embroiled with England's Elizabeth I. The conflict ground to a halt when Sir Francis Drake defeated Spain's "invincible" **Armada** in 1588. With much of his European empire lost and his wealth from the Americas sapped, Felipe retreated to **El Escorial** (p. 123) and sulked in its monastery until his death.

In 1609, **Felipe III** (1598-1621) expelled nearly 300,000 of Spain's remaining Moors. **Felipe IV** (1621-1665) painstakingly held the country together through his long, tumultuous reign while patronizing the arts (painter Diego Velázquez and playwright Lope de Vega both graced his court) and architecture (he commissioned the Parque del Buen Retiro in Madrid; p. 107). Defending Catholicism began to drain Spain's resources after the outbreak of the **Thirty Years' War** (1618-1648), which ended with the marriage of Felipe IV's

1100 BC
Phoenicians found the ports of Cádiz and Málaga.

500 BC
Celts cross the Pyrenees.

200 BC
The Roman Empire sets up camp.

409-711
Visigoths arrive in Iberia after sacking Rome, but fall to the Moors 300 years later.

900-1000
Córdoba claims the title of largest city in Western Europe.

1478
The Inquisition begins.

1492
Fernando and Isabel conquer Granada, the last Moorish holdout; Columbus sets sail with royal funding.

1519
Hernán Cortéz lands in Mexico in search of gold, silver, and chocolate.

1559
St. Teresa of Ávila has a vision of Christ that lasts for almost two years.

1588
Britain's Elizabeth I defeats Spain's "invincible" armada.

1605
Cervantes publishes *Don Quixote* in Madrid.

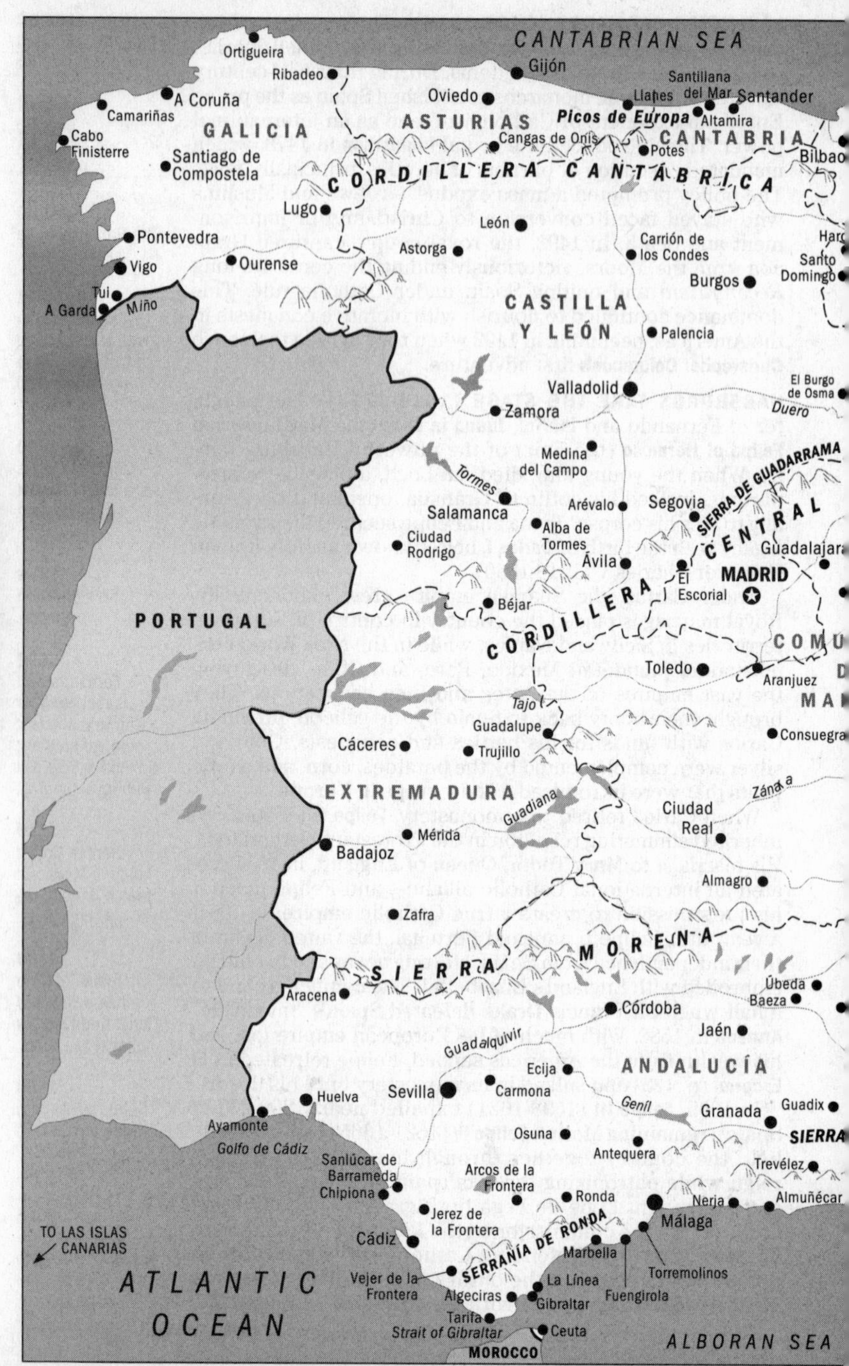
CANTABRIAN SEA
Ortigueira
Ribadeo
Gijón
Santillana del Mar
Santander
A Coruña
Oviedo
Llanes
Camariñas
GALICIA
ASTURIAS
Picos de Europa
Altamira
Cabo Finisterre
Cangas de Onís
Potes
CANTABRIA
Bilbao
Santiago de Compostela
CORDILLERA CANTÁBRICA
Lugo
León
Pontevedra
Carrión de los Condes
Astorga
Vigo
Ourense
Santo Domingo
Burgos
Tui
A Garda
Miño
CASTILLA Y LEÓN
Palencia
Valladolid
El Burgo de Osma
Zamora
Duero
Medina del Campo
SIERRA DE GUADARRAMA
Tormes
Arévalo
Segovia
Salamanca
CENTRAL
Alba de Tormes
Ciudad Rodrigo
Guadalajara
Ávila
El Escorial
MADRID
PORTUGAL
Béjar
CORDILLERA
Toledo
Aranjuez
Tajo
Guadalupe
Consuegra
Cáceres
Trujillo
EXTREMADURA
Záncara
Guadiana
Ciudad Real
Mérida
Badajoz
Almagro
Zafra
MORENA
SIERRA
Úbeda
Aracena
Baeza
Córdoba
Jaén
Guadalquivir
ANDALUCÍA
Ecija
Sevilla
Carmona
Huelva
Genil
Granada
Guadix
Ayamonte
Osuna
Golfo de Cádiz
Antequera
Sanlúcar de Barrameda
Arcos de la Frontera
Trevélez
Chipiona
Ronda
Nerja
Almuñécar
Jerez de la Frontera
Málaga
TO LAS ISLAS CANARIAS
Cádiz
SERRANÍA DE RONDA
Marbella
Torremolinos
ATLANTIC OCEAN
Vejer de la Frontera
La Línea
Algeciras
Gibraltar
Fuengirola
Tarifa
Strait of Gibraltar
Ceuta
ALBORAN SEA
MOROCCO

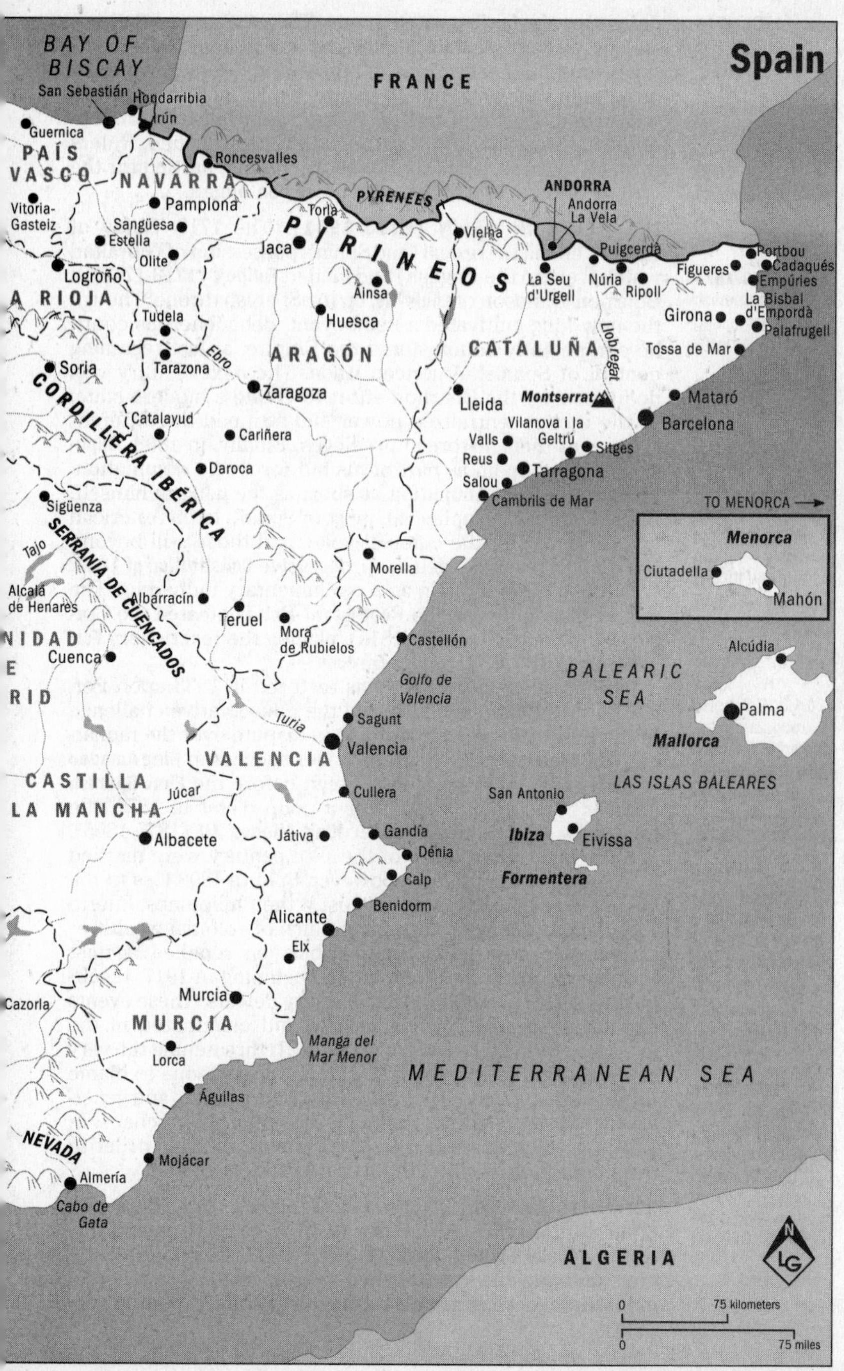
Spain
BAY OF BISCAY
FRANCE
San Sebastián
Hondarribia
Irún
Guernica
PAÍS VASCO
NAVARRA
Roncesvalles
Vitoria-Gasteiz
Pamplona
Sangüesa
Estella
Olite
Logroño
LA RIOJA
PYRENEES
Torla
Jaca
PIRINEOS
Aínsa
Huesca
Vielha
ANDORRA
Andorra La Vela
La Seu d'Urgell
Puigcerdà
Núria
Ripoll
Figueres
Portbou
Cadaqués
Empúries
La Bisbal d'Empordà
Girona
Palafrugell
Tossa de Mar
Tudela
Tarazona
Ebro
ARAGÓN
CATALUÑA
Llobregat
Soria
Zaragoza
Lleida
Montserrat
Mataró
Barcelona
CORDILLERA IBÉRICA
Catalayud
Cariñera
Daroca
Vilanova i la Geltrú
Valls
Reus
Salou
Sitges
Tarragona
Cambrils de Mar
TO MENORCA
Menorca
Ciutadella
Mahón
Sigüenza
Tajo
SERRANÍA DE CUENCADOS
Alcalá de Henares
Albarracín
Teruel
Morella
Mora de Rubielos
Castellón
NIDAD
E
RID
Cuenca
Golfo de Valencia
BALEARIC SEA
Alcúdia
Palma
Mallorca
Turia
Sagunt
Valencia
VALENCIA
CASTILLA LA MANCHA
Júcar
Cullera
San Antonio
LAS ISLAS BALEARES
Albacete
Játiva
Gandía
Dénia
Ibiza
Eivissa
Calp
Formentera
Benidorm
Alicante
Elx
Murcia
Cazorla
MURCIA
Manga del Mar Menor
Lorca
MEDITERRANEAN SEA
Águilas
NEVADA
Mojácar
Almería
Cabo de Gata
ALGERIA
0
75 kilometers
0
75 miles
SPAIN

1701-1714
Europe jockeys for control of the Spanish monarchy in the War of Spanish Succession.

1808
Napoleon occupies Spain and rules for a short six years.

1873-1874
The first Spanish Republic forms and quickly dissolves.

1893
Anarchists bomb Barcelona's Liceu, killing 20 opera-goers.

1898
Spain loses the Spanish-American War and its last three colonies.

1921
14,000 Spanish troops are massacred in Morocco after their attempt to consolidate Spain's hold on its new protectorate.

1923
Spain's first dictator, General Primo de Rivera, rises to power in a coup.

1933-1936
The country is polarized by radical governments, the increased presence of the military, and the Fascist Falange.

daughter María Teresa to Louis XIV of France. Felipe's successor **Carlos II el Hechizado** (the bewitched; 1665-1700), the product of generations of inbreeding, was known to fly into fits of rage and epileptic seizures. From then on, little went right: Carlos II left no heirs, Spain fell into an economic depression, and cultural bankruptcy ensued. Rulers from all over, particularly Habsburg Vienna, battled for the crown, and the **War of Spanish Succession** began.

THE REIGN IN SPAIN (1713-1931). The 1713 Treaty of Utrecht ended the ordeal (and Spain's possession of Gibraltar, which went to the English) and landed **Felipe V** (1713-1746), a Bourbon grandson of **Louis XIV**, on the Spanish throne. Though the new king cultivated a flamboyant, debaucherous court, he competently administered the Empire, at last regaining control of Spanish-American trade. The next century was dominated by the Bourbon effort to create a modern state, as the crown centralized power and stripped the different regions of their historical privileges. Finally, in 1808, **Napoleon** invaded Spain as part of his bid for world domination, inaugurating an occupation as short as the general himself. In the midst of the upheaval, most of Spain's Latin American empire threw off the colonial yoke, and those still beyond Napoleon's reach penned the progressive **Constitution of 1812**, which established Spain as a parliamentary monarchy. The violence ended when the Protestant Brits defeated the Corsican troops at Waterloo (1815), placing the reactionary **Fernando VII** (1814-1833) on the throne.

Parliamentary liberalism was restored in 1833 upon Fernando VII's death, and survived the conservative challenge of the first **Carlist War** (1833-1839), a dispute over the monarchy of **Queen Isabel II** (1843-1868). Her successor, **King Amadeo I** (1870-1873), enjoyed a short reign before the **First Spanish Republic** was proclaimed. After a coup d'etat in 1875, the monarchy was restored under **King Alfonso XII** (1875-1885), and the last two decades of the 19th century were marked by rapid industrialization. However, Spain's 1898 loss to the US in the **Spanish-American War** cost it the Philippines, Puerto Rico, Cuba, and any remaining dreams of colonial wealth.

Closer to home, Moroccan tribesmen rebelled against Spanish troops in northern Africa beginning in 1917, resulting in a series of embarrassing military defeats. These events further weakened Spanish morale and culminated in the massacre of 14,000 royal troops in 1921, threatening the very survival of the monarchy. The search for someone to blame for the disaster occupied aristocrats, bureaucrats, and generals for the next decade, throwing the country into chaos. In 1923, **General Miguel Primo de Rivera** sought to bring order to the situation in the form of Spain's first dictatorship.

REPUBLIC AND REBELLION (1931-1939). King Alfonso XIII (1902-1931) abdicated the throne in April 1931, giving rise to the **Second Spanish Republic** (1931-1939). Republican Liberals and Socialists established safeguards for farmers and industrial workers, granted women's suffrage, assured religious tolerance, and chipped away at traditional military dominance. National euphoria, however, faded fast. The 1933 elections split the Republican-Socialist coalition, increasing the power of right-wing and Catholic parties in parliament. Military dissatisfaction led to a heightened profile of the **Fascist Falange** (founded by Primo de Rivera's son José Antonio), which further polarized national politics. By 1936, radicals, anarchists, Socialists, and Republicans had formed a **Popular Front** coalition to win the February elections. Their victory, however, was short lived. After increasing polarization, **Generalísimo Francisco Franco** led a militarist uprising and the nation plunged into war, as the infectious ideology of **La Guerra Civil** (**The Spanish Civil War;** 1936-1939) diffused across the globe. Germany and Italy readily supplied Franco with troops and munitions, while the US and liberal European states instituted the Non-Intervention Treaty. The Soviet Union organized the **International Brigades,** an amalgamation of Communists and other leftist volunteers from all over Europe and the US, to battle Franco's fascism. Foreign aid waned as Stalin began to see the benefits of an alliance with Hitler. Bombings, executions, combat, starvation, and disease took nearly 600,000 lives and forced almost one million Spaniards to emigrate. In April 1939, Franco bid a "farewell to arms," marching into Madrid and ending the War.

1936-1939
Civil War engulfs Spain. Europe joins the fray.

1937
Nazi planes bomb the Basque town of Guernica; in response, Picasso paints *Guernica*.

1939
Franco begins his reign and the country enters a period later known as the "national tragedy."

FRANCO AND THE NATIONAL TRAGEDY (1939-1975). Franco's dictatorship was largely centered around the church, the army, and the Falange. Thousands of scientists, artists, intellectuals, and sympathizers were exiled, imprisoned, or executed in the name of order and purity. Franco initially pursued an isolationist economic policy, but stagnant conditions eventually forced him to adopt a more open policy. With prosperity came unrest. Dissatisfied workers and students engaged in protests, hoping to draw attention to the dark underside of Franco's reign. Groups like the Basque **ETA** also provided resistance throughout the dictatorship, often via terrorist acts, producing turmoil that undermined the legitimacy of the regime. In his old age, the general tried to smooth international relations by joining NATO, courting the Pope, and encouraging tourism. However, the **"national tragedy,"** as the tense period under Franco was later called, did not officially end until Franco's death in 1975. **King Juan Carlos I** (1975-), grandson of Alfonso XIII and nominally a Franco protégé, carefully set out to undo Franco's damage.

1959
Twenty years into Franco's rule, the Euskadi Ta Askatasuna (ETA) forms.

1975
Franco dies, and "La Movida" begins: the nation explodes in a burst of creative expression.

DEMOCRACY RISES (1975-2005). In 1978, under centrist Prime Minister **Adolfo Suárez,** Spain adopted a new constitution and restored parliamentary government and regional autonomy. The post-Franco years have been marked by progressive social change in the economic and political arenas. The period was also characterized by a movement known in Madrid as "La Movida," which saw an unprecedented outburst of artistic, cultural, and social expression after decades of censorship and inhibition. Suárez's resignation in early 1981 left the country ripe for an attempted coup on February

1982
Felipe González is elected prime minister and works over the course of the next decade to expand the economy.

1986
Spain joins the European Economic

23rd of that year, when a group of rebels took over parliament in an effort to impose a military-backed government. King Juan Carlos I used his personal influence to convince the rebels to stand down, paving the way for the charismatic **Felipe González** to lead the PSOE (Spanish Socialist Worker's Party) to victory in the 1982 elections. González opened the Spanish economy and championed consensus policies, overseeing Spain's integration into the European Community (now the EU) four years later. Despite unpopular economic policies, González was reelected in 1986 and continued a program of massive public investment to rejuvenate the nation's economy. By the end of 1993, however, recession and revelations of large-scale corruption led to a resounding Socialist defeat at the hands of the Popular Party (PP) in the 1994 European parliamentary elections. The leader of the PP, **José María Aznar,** managed to maintain a fragile coalition with the support of the Catalan and Islas Canarias regional parties. He won an absolute majority in 2000. Since then Spain has moved in a more liberal direction. On July 1, 2005 it legalized gay marriage, eliminating all legal distinctions between same sex and heterosexual couples

Community, later to become the European Union (EU).

1995
The Barcelona Process begins an EU effort to strengthen European ties with the Middle East and Maghreb.

1996-2004
Popular Party leader José Maria Aznar is elected prime minister and works to quell terrorism.

2004
Bombings linked to Al-Qaeda rock Madrid and kill 192 people. Days later, the Spanish elect José Luis Rodriquez Zapatero as prime minister.

2005
The Spanish parliament legalizes same-sex marriage.

2006
ETA announces the end of its terrorist attacks.

2007
ETA revokes the cease-fire, dashing hopes of peace.

2008
Francisco Javier Lopez, the suspected leader of ETA, is arrested in France.

SPAIN

GLOBAL TERRORISM. Under the conservative Aznar, Spain became one of the US's most prominent allies in the war on terror, but the relationship has since been strained. On **March 11, 2004,** days before the national elections, the country suffered its own grievous attack, often referred to as **11-M** *(el once eme).* In an attack linked to Al-Qaeda, 10 bombs exploded on four trains heading to Madrid from the suburbs, killing 191 passengers and injuring more than 1800. Immediately thereafter, the conservatives lost the election to **José Luis Rodríguez Zapatero** of the PSOE. Many attributed the loss to the popular reaction against Aznar's attempt to shirk responsibility for the attacks. Under the new government, Spain withdrew its troops from Iraq in 2004.

CURRENT EVENTS

ETA TERRORISM. Spain has a long history of domestic terrorism, due to separatist movements, particularly in the Basque region in northwestern Spain. Since 1968, over 800 people have been killed in bombings planned by the movement's militant wing, the Euskadi Ta Askatasuna (**ETA;** Basque Homeland and Freedom). Violence continued into 2005 with a series of car bombings in Madrid. In March 2006, ETA declared a permanent cease-fire, promising to promote Basque separation through democratic means, but in December 2006 two bombs exploded in the Madrid airport. In June 2007, the cease-fire officially came to an end. In May 2008, Francisco Javier Lopez, the suspected leader of ETA, was arrested in France. While there may be some danger to travelers, the ETA's attacks are typically targeted and are not considered random acts of terrorism. In more recent years, the organization has tended to provide advance warning.

WE WILL ROCK YOU. For the past 300 years, Spain has fought an uphill battle to regain control of **Gibraltar** (p. 247), a strategic 6km territory in the south currently under British rule. Britain's desire to improve relations with Spain paved the way for a 2002 proposal to share sovereignty of the rock between the two nations, but Gibraltar residents, who remain overwhelmingly loyal to the UK and enjoy salaries almost a third higher than the Spanish average, rejected the measure.

STRAITENED RELATIONS. In July 2002, a handful of Moroccan soldiers occupied **Perejil,** an island in Spanish territorial water known for its abundance of goats. The occurence sparked a minor international event. Amid much fanfare and grandstanding, the soldiers and their Moroccan flag were promptly removed. Its sovereignty and military prowess secured, Spain could once again direct its attention to pressing internal affairs, including increased **immigration** from northern Africa. The Canary Islands and Spain's outposts in Morocco, Ceuta, and Melilla are typical places of entry. In 2005, Spain granted amnesty to 700,000 of the illegal immigrants within its borders, and has continued to experiment with temporary worker programs.

FURTHER READING. These texts provide additional background on the history and culture of Spain.

Homage to Catalonia, by George Orwell (1938). A personal account of Orwell's time in uniform during the Spanish Civil War.

South from Granada, by Gerald Brenan (1957). A British writer's classic account of uprooting himself to a rural village life in Granada's Alpujarras.

Iberia, by James Michener (1968). A bestselling travelogue that captures Spain's past and present as they appeared in the 1960s.

The New Spaniards, by John Hooper (1995). An excellent introduction to contemporary, post-Francoist Spanish society.

The Ornament of the World, by María Rosa Menocal (2003). An insightful account of medieval Moorish, Christian, and Jewish coexistence in Toledo.

PEOPLE AND CULTURE

LANGUAGE

Castellano (Castilian) Spanish, spoken almost everywhere, is Spain's official language; other languages are official regionally. **Català** (Catalan) is spoken throughout Cataluña in the northeast and is the official language of Andorra. Permutations of català gave rise to the dialects **valencià** (Valencian), the regional tongue of Valencia, and **mallorquí,** the principal dialect of the Islas Baleares. Even tiny Asturias has its own dialect, **bable,** spoken mostly among older generations. The once-Celtic northwest corner of Iberia gabs in **gallego** (Galician), which is closely related to Portuguese and most prevalent in the countryside. **Euskera** (Basque), spoken in País Vasco and northern Navarra, is one of the oldest languages in Europe and known by only about 2% of the nation's population.

City and provincial names in this guide are listed in *castellano* first, followed by the regional language in parentheses where appropriate. Information within cities (e.g. street and plaza names) is listed in the regional language. For a **phrasebook, glossary,** and **pronunciation guide,** see p. 760.

RELIGION

The **Roman Catholic Church** has prevailed in Spain since 1492. In 2005 the Center for Sociological Investigation determined that almost 80 percent of the population still identified as Catholic. As a testament to the increasing secularism of the country, however, only 20% claimed to attend church regularly. Moreover, one need only look at Spanish art and architecture to see the influence of other religions, like **Islam** and **Judaism,** that once thrived in Spain. Before Fernando and Isabel's completion of the *Reconquista* in 1492, the Moors controlled the Iberian Peninsula for seven centuries, leaving buildings such as the 10th-century *mezquita* (mosque) in Córdoba to attest to their once dominant presence. The *Reyes Católicos* (Catholic kings) began the Spanish Inquisition in 1478, even before they had completely reclaimed the Iberian Peninsula from the Moors. Anyone who was suspected of practicing Judaism was tried, usually found guilty, and punished, often with death. The ultimate goal of the *Reyes Católicos* was the expulsion of all Jews and Moors from the peninsula. Many Jews converted to Catholicism or emigrated to North Africa to avoid persecution. In 1834 the Inquisition finally came to an end, after nearly 45,000 heresy trials and thousands of executions.

FOOD AND DRINK

Sometimes Spain's best cuisine is served not in expensive restaurants, but in private homes or steet-side bars. Many locals opt for tapas barhopping in lieu of a formal meal. Fresh, local ingredients play an integral part of every menu, varying according to each region's climate, geography, and history. Spanish fare is becomingly increasingly innovative, as the avant-guarde cuisine movement continues to gain prominence.

LOCAL FARE

ANDALUCÍA. Flavorful Andalucian cuisine boasts a rich past, as it maintains the cooking methods introduced by Islamic tribes in the first millennium AD. Centuries later, it was through **Sevilla** (p. 200) that New World products like corn, peppers, tomatoes, and potatoes first entered Europe. Andalucians have since mastered the art of *gazpacho*, a cold tomato-based soup perfectly suited to the hot southern climate. Andalucía is famous for its olive oil, which is found in a vast number of the region's dishes. The area is also known for its *pescadito frito* (fried fish), *rabo de toro* (bull's tail), egg yolk desserts, sherry wines, and tasty tapas. Spain's best cured ham, *jamón ibérico*, comes from the town of Jabugo, where black-footed pigs are pampered with daily oak acorn feasts.

THE CASTILLAS. Sheep share space with more of the prized black-footed pigs in nearby **Extremadura** (p. 184), where the pastoral life has inspired *cocidos* (hearty stews), cheeses, and unique meals based on *migas* (bread crumbs). This type of dry-land "shepherd's cuisine" dominates central Spain. **Castilla La Mancha** (p. 172) is famous for its sheep's milk *queso manchego*, the most widely eaten cheese in Spain, and the deliciously vegetarian *pisto manchego*, a mix of zucchini, tomatoes, and eggplant. Spain's most prized spice, *azafrán* (saffron), is also grown in La Mancha. Lamb and roasted game are essential menu items both here and in **Castilla y Léon** (p. 131). *Escabeche*, an Arab tradition of sautéing with vinegar, has become a specialty, as has *tortilla española* (potato omelette) and *menestra de verduras*, a succulent vegetable mix. **Madrid** (p. 78) rivals Andalucía with its tapas and renowned *cocido*, a heavy stew of meat, cabbage, carrots, and potatoes.

CANTABRIAN COAST. Farther north, the 800 miles of coastline in **Galicia** (p. 536) provide fresh ingredients for local shellfish dishes. Octopus, spider crab, and mussels are popular here, as is *empanada gallega*, a Galician pastry filled with anything from pork to chicken to fish. In **Asturias** (p. 506), dried beans rule the kitchen and *fabada asturiana*, a hearty bean and sausage stew, is the best way to refuel after a long day of work. Apples, *sidra* (cider), and cow's milk are also especially good here. **Cantabrian** (p. 527) sardines and tuna are among the best in Spain and are often included in a seafood stew. Food in the **País Vasco** (p. 484) rivals that of Cataluña in national prominence. The combination of coastal and mountain cultures has created a unique style of food in the Basque Country. Popular dishes include *bacalao* (salt cod), *angulas* (baby eels), *calamar en su tinta* (squid in its own ink), and suckling lamb.

THE PYRENEES. **Navarra** (p. 473) boasts the best red peppers in Spain, as well as the famous Roncal cheese. Game meats, sausages, and cauldron stews are popular here. Neighboring **La Rioja** (p. 467) is known for its pork, vegetables, and above all its *vino* (wine). The region, which boasts seven grape varieties, has been host to wineries and vineyards since before the arrival of the Moors. **Aragón's** (p. 456) hearty cuisine reflects the region's varied character. *Migas de pastor* (bread crumbs fried with ham) and lamb are ubiquitous, while a sweeter option is *melocotones al vino* (native peaches steeped in wine).

MEDITERRANEAN COAST. In **Cataluña** (p. 394), the Roman triumvirate of olives, grapes, and wheat prevails, and seafood, grilling, and even pasta play key roles in many meals. Cataluña is at the forefront of the avant-garde movement in cooking, led by innovative chef Ferran Adrià of El Bulli. On the Mediterranean coast, **Valencia** (p. 289) is renowned for its oranges and its *paella*—which has evolved profoundly since Arabic short-grained rice was first introduced to the area in the 8th century AD. It had matured from a simple dish into an increasingly elaborate mix of rice, vegetables, seafood, and meat. The island of **Menorca** is known for its *mahón* cheese, often grated over meat or vegetables.

BEERS, BEERS, BEERS

Ordering in Spanish bars can be intimidating for an outsider. If you wish to partake of the fermented nectar, Spanish *cerveza*, it helps to talk like a local:

Quinto: This miniature bottle of beer, though non-existent in the States, maintains a distinct popularity in Spain. Normally taken straight from the bottle.

Caña (Can-ya): If you seek an inexpensive draft beer, ask for this cup-full of the house beer, usually marked with its logo on the tap at the bar.

Mediana (in Madrid and central Spain, *Tercio*): This is your standard bottled beer, often served with a glass, sometimes frosted. If you simply ask for a cerveza, this is what you will most likely receive.

Jarra: This large mug of beer is ordered more often by tourists than locals; it is your best bet for uninterrupted imbibing.

Lata: If you want cans of beer, ask for *latas*. These are normally sold in stores, but not in bars.

Para Llevar: Many Spanish bar owners will gladly pour your beer into a plastic cup to-go. Just ask for your drink *para llevar* (to carry out).

Litro: Those who really mean business stop by the supermarket and pick up a *litro* (liter) of *cerveza* and party in the streets with their *amigos*.

DRINKS

VINO. When in doubt, the *vino de la casa* (house wine) is an economical and often delectable choice. Castilla y León's **Ribera del Dueros** are smooth and full-bodied reds, and Biezo has recently been unearthed as a red wine haven. Cataluña's whites and *cavas* (champagnes) and **Galicia's** *albariños* pack a refreshing punch, while the reds and whites of **La Rioja** are famous—and rightfully so. As the saying goes: *"El vino, para que sepa a vino, bébelo con un amigo"* (For wine to taste of wine, you must drink it with a friend). *Sidra* (cider) from Asturias and *sangria* (red-wine punch with fruit, seltzer, and sugar) are other delicious alcoholic options. *Jerez* (sherry), Spain's most famous libation, hails from **Jerez de la Frontera** (p. 230) in Andalucía. Try the dry *fino* and *amontillado* as aperitifs, or finish off a rich supper with the sweet *dulce*.

CERVEZAS. A normal-sized draft beer is a *caña de cerveza*, while a *tubo* is a little bigger. Small beers go by different names—*corto* in Castilian and *zurito* in Basque. Pros refer to mixed drinks as *copas:* beer and soda water make a *clara*, *calimocho* is a mix of Coca-Cola and red wine; another famous drink is *tinto de verano*, a mix of red wine and lemon soda. Spain whips up non-alcoholic quenchers as well, notably *horchata de chufa* (made by blending almonds and ice) and flavored crushed-ice *granizados*. *Café solo* means black coffee; add a touch of milk for a *nube;* a little more and it's a *café cortado;* half milk and half coffee makes a *café con leche*.

MEALS AND DINING HOURS

TYPICAL SPANISH MEALS. In Spain, mealtime is a social event. Spaniards start their day with *el desayuno*, a continental breakfast of coffee or thick, liquid chocolate accompanied by *bollos* (rolls), *churros*, or *porros* (dough fritters). Mid-morning they often have another coffee with a tapa to tide them over to the main meal of the day, *la comida*, which is eaten around 2 or 3pm. *La comida* consists of several courses: soup or salad, meat, fish, or, on special occasions, *paella*, and a dessert of fruit, cheese, or sweets. Supper at home, *la cena*, tends to be lighter—usually a sandwich or *tortilla española* anywhere from 8pm to midnight. Eating out starts anywhere between 9pm and midnight. Going out for tapas is part of the Spanish lifestyle; groups of friends will often spend several hours bar-hopping.

RESTAURANT DINING. While some restaurants are open from 8am to 1 or 2am, most serve meals from 1 or 2 to 4pm only and in the evening from 8pm until midnight. Some hints: eating at the bar is cheaper than at tables or on a terrace, and the check won't be brought to a table unless it is requested. Also, even though a server may bring bread to the table, it is often not free and the unwitting tourist falls prey to the "you touched it, you bought it" policy of most Spanish restaurants. Service is notoriously slow. Spaniards commonly choose the **menú del día**—two or three dishes, bread, a drink, and dessert—a good deal at roughly €7-12. *Raciones* are large tapas, comparable in size to entrees.

CUSTOMS AND ETIQUETTE

Spaniards are generally polite and courteous to foreigners and attempts to be culturally correct will not go unnoticed.

TABOOS. Spaniards are very proud and take offense to criticism about their country or customs. Foreigners should be careful when approaching Spanish women; fathers, husbands, or boyfriends can be aggressive. Be aware that shorts and short skirts are not common in most parts of Spain, save the coasts. Wearing these and other especially revealing clothing away from the beaches may garner unwanted attention, or at the very least, scream "I am a foreigner!" Women with bare shoulders should carry a shawl to tour churches and monasteries, and it is considered disrespectful to wear shorts in these places.

PUBLIC BEHAVIOR. The people of Spain are very polite in mannerisms and social behavior, so it's a good idea to be as formal as possible in first encounters. Be sure to address Spaniards as *Señor* (Mr.), *Señora* (Mrs.), or *Señorita* (Ms.), and don't be surprised if you get kissed on both cheeks, in place of a handshake. Machismo is very apparent, especially in Andalucía, and women may be the object of whistling and catcalling when walking alone or in groups without any men. The best response to this type of display is to ignore it.

TIPPING. Though a service charge is generally included in the check at bars and restaurants, an additional tip is common for good service: 5-10% will generally do the trick. Taxi drivers, theater ushers, and hotel porters will also expect small tips for their services.

THE ARTS

ARCHITECTURE

ANCIENT AND EARLY MODERN. A testament to six centuries of occupation, **Roman ruins** are scattered throughout the country, seen in the magnificent **aqueduct** in Segovia (p. 135), the **amphitheater** in Mérida (p. 195), and the town of Tarragona (p. 399). Other vestiges of Spain's Roman past lie in the ruined town of Itálica (near Sevilla; p. 217). Moorish rule began in 711 and left intricately-decorated mosques and palaces throughout the country's southern regions, rich in geometric designs, red-and-white horseshoe arches, and ornate tiles. The spectacular 14th-century **Alhambra** in Granada (p. 278) and the **Mezquita** in Córdoba (p. 226) epitomize the Moorish style. Periods of peaceful coexistence between Muslims and Christians inspired the synthetic **mudéjar** architectural movement, created by Moors living under Christian rule in the years between the Christian resurgence (11th century) and the *Reconquista* (1492). Sevilla's **Alcázar** (p. 209) is an exquisite example of this tradition.

The **Spanish Gothic** style (13th-16th centuries) fused *mudéjar* influences with European innovations of the Renaissance, including pointed arches, flying buttresses, airy spaces, and stained-glass windows. Along with those in Toledo (p. 172) and León (p. 151), the cathedral of Burgos is one of the finest examples of the Spanish Gothic style. Sevilla boasts the largest Gothic cathedral (p. 209) in the world. Spain also contains important **Romanesque** sculpture: Maestro Mateo's **Pórtico de la Gloria,** completed in 1188 in Santiago de Compostela (p. 536), is considered one of the finest examples.

RENAISSANCE AND BAROQUE. New World riches inspired the **Plateresque** ("silversmith") style, which brought ornamentation to shining new levels with the extravagant use of silver and gold. Intricate stonework and gleaming metals grace the facades of 15th- and 16th-century buildings like those of **La Universidad de Salamanca** (p. 145). In the late 16th century, Italian innovations in perspective and symmetry arrived in Spain and sobered the Plateresque style. These innovations influenced **Juan Bautista de Toledo** in his design for the austere **El Escorial** (p. 123), Felipe II's immense palace-cum-monastery. Opulence took center stage in 17th- and 18th-century **Baroque** Spain. The Churriguera family of Salamanca pioneered the new, aptly-named **Churrigueresque** style, whose elaborate ornamentation fused sculpture and architecture, giving buildings of this period a rich exuberance. Churrigueresque is perhaps most resonant in Salamanca's **Plaza Mayor** (p. 136).

MODERN AND POSTMODERN. In the late 19th and early 20th centuries, Cataluña's **Modernistas** burst on the scene in Barcelona, led by the eccentric geniuses **Antoni Gaudí, Lluís Domènech i Montaner,** and **Josep Puig i Cadafalch.** *Modernista* structures defied all precedents with their voluptuous curves, vibrant colors and striking textures. Unbridled imagination and organic forms inspired Gaudí's **La Sagrada Família** (p. 380) and the **Casa Milà** (p. 381), which stand as some of the most famous examples of Catalan *Modernisme.*

Spain's outstanding architectural tradition has continued through the 20th century. In the midst of Civil War, Catalan architect **Josep Lluís Sert** designed the Spanish Pavilion at the 1937 International Exposition in Paris. The pavilion played host to artistic protests against war and fascism, including Pablo Picasso's *Guernica* (p. 111) and works by **Joan Miró.** Today Spain boasts stars like **Rafael Moneo,** who designed the 2007 enlargement of the **Prado** in Madrid (p. 109), and **Santiago Calatrava,** who built elegant steel-and-crystal buildings in Valencia (p. 289) and unmistakable bridges in Sevilla, Mérida, and Bilbao. Spain has also acquired several new landmarks from foreign architects, most notably Frank Gehry's stunning **Guggenheim Museum** in Bilbao (p. 492).

SPAIN

PAINTING AND SCULPTURE

MEDIEVAL AND RENAISSANCE. The earliest art in Spain can be found at the caves at **Altamira** (p. 534), near Santander in Cantabria, which are home to some of the oldest Paleolithic cave paintings in the world. Frescoes and illuminated manuscripts from the 11th and 12th centuries adorn churches along the Camino de Santiago and in many Spanish cities.

During Spain's imperial ascent in the 16th century, Spanish painting reached its **Siglo de Oro** (Golden Age; roughly 1492-1650). Felipe II, one of the era's presiding monarchs, imported foreign art and artists to jump-start native production and embellish his palace, El Escorial. One hopeful artist, Crete-born Doménikos Theotokópoulos, a.k.a. **El Greco** (1541-1614), failed to earn the patronage of Felipe II, supposedly because of his daring use of bright, saturated colors and radical notions of form and space. El Greco's haunting, elongated figures and dramatic use of light have since garnered widespread appreciation. One of his most famous canvases, *El entierro del Conde de Orgaz* (*The Burial of Count Orgaz,* 1586) graces the Iglesia de Santo Tomé in Toledo (p. 177), the city whose landscape he painted so vividly.

Felipe IV's foremost court painter, **Diego Velázquez** (1599-1660), is considered one of the world's greatest artists. Whether depicting the family of Felipe IV or commoners buying water, Velázquez painted scenes with naturalistic precision and a virtually photographic quality. Nearly half of this Sevilla-born artist's works reside in the Prado, perhaps most notably his famous *Las Meninas* (1656; p. 109). Other distinguished Golden Age painters include **Francisco de Zurbarán** (1598-1664) and **Bartolomé Murillo** (1617-1682).

FROM MODERN TO AVANT-GARDE. While Spain's political power declined, its cultural capital flourished. **Francisco de Goya** (1746-1828) ushered European painting into the modern age. Hailing from provincial Aragón, Goya rose to the position of official court painter under Carlos IV. Goya cast flattery aside: his depictions of the royal family come close to caricature, as Queen María Luisa's haughty jaw line in Goya's famous *The Family of Carlos IV* (1800) can attest. His series of etchings, *The Disasters of War* (1810-1814), records the horrific Napoleonic invasion of 1808. Deaf and alone in his later years, Goya painted nightmarishly fantastic visions, inspiring expressionist and surrealist artists of the next century with his free and loose brushstrokes and dramatic presentation. His chilling **Black Paintings** (1820-1823) fill a room in the Prado.

Few artists influenced 20th-century painting as deeply as Málaga-born **Pablo Picasso** (1881-1973). During his Blue Period, characterized by somber depictions of society's outcasts, Picasso alternated between Barcelona and Paris. His permanent move to Paris in 1904 caused a shift in his artistic trajectory, and the Rose Period ushered in a new fascination with harlequins, clowns, and acrobats. With his French colleague Georges Braque, he founded **Cubism,** a method of abstraction in painting achieved by the geometric fragmentation of form. His 1937 mural *Guernica* portrays the bombing of the Basque city (p. 111) by Nazi planes during the Spanish Civil War. *Guernica* now resides in the Museo Nacional Centro de Arte Reina Sofía in Madrid (p. 110).

The chaotic, abstract lines and vivid colors of Catalan painter and sculptor **Joan Miró** (1893-1983) rebelled against the authoritarian society of post-Civil War years. **Salvador Dalí** (1904-1989), in contrast, scandalized society and leftist intellectuals in France and Spain by claiming to support the Fascists. His name has become synonymous with **Surrealism,** the artistic expression of the liberated, subconscious imagination. A self-congratulatory fellow, Dalí founded the Teatro-Museu Dalí in Figueres (p. 417), Spain's second-most visited museum after the Prado. A new generation of painters and sculptors has flourished with new museums as active platforms for their work. Today, **Antoni Tàpies** (1923-) constructs unorthodox collages and is a founding member of the self-proclaimed "Abstract Generation," while **Antonio López García** (1936-) paints hyperrealist works.

LITERATURE

A GOLDEN AGE. Spain's literary tradition first blossomed in the late Middle Ages (1000-1500). The 13th-century *El Cantar del Mío Cid* (Song of My Cid) is Spain's most important epic poem. It chronicles the life and military triumphs of national hero Rodrigo Díaz de Vivar, from his exile to his eventual return to grace in the king's court. At the end of the 15th century, **Fernando de Rojas** wrote the famous novel *La Celestina* (1499), a tragicomedy beloved for its witch-like matchmaker and star-crossed lovers Calixto and Melibea. The anonymous work *Lazarillo de Tormes* (1554) established the genre of the picaresque: a tale following the adventures of a roguish young rascal, in this case, an orphaned servant boy in Salamanca. Literature bloomed during Spain's literary **Siglo de Oro** (Golden Age; 16th and 17th centuries); some consider the sonnets of Garcilaso de la Vega (1503-1536) the most perfect ever written in *castellano*. The dense, difficult verse of **Luis de Góngora** (1561-1627) found a new following in the poets of the famed *Generación de 1927* years later. The Golden Age also produced outstanding dramatists, including **Pedro Calderón de la Barca** (1600-1681) and **Lope de Vega** (1562-1635), who collectively wrote over 2,300 plays. **Tirso de Molina's** (1584-1648) famed *El Burlador de Sevilla* (1630) introduced the character of Don Juan into the national psyche. **Miguel de Cervantes's** *Don Quixote* (1605-1615) is without a doubt the most famous work of Spanish literature. This humorous and satirical novel follows a hapless knight and his servant, Sancho Panza, as they undertake a chivalric quest to save the world.

ROMANTICS AND INNOVATORS. The 18th century brought a belated Enlightenment, while the 19th century inspired new heights of romanticism and realism. The lyrical verse of **Rosalía del Castro** (1837-1885) made her the most distinguished modern writer in Galician, while the naturalistic novels and bold critiques of **Leopoldo Alas** ("Clarín") made him one of Spain's most powerful voices. Essayist and philosopher **Miguel de Unamuno** and critic **José Ortega y Gasset** led the **Generación de 1898,** along with novelist **Pío Baroja,** playwright **Ramón del Valle Inclán,** and poets **Antonio Machado** and **Juan Ramón Jiménez.** Reacting to Spain's defeat in the Spanish-American War (1898), they contributed to reawakening Spain's culture of literary innovation and helped form a new national consciousness. This group, though not organized or unified, was a critical influence on the **Generación de 1927,** a group of experimental lyric poets including **Federico García Lorca** and **Rafael Alberti** that experimented with Surrealist and avant-garde poetry. This vibrant and cohesive group scattered at the onset of Civil War, with several of its artists persecuted for Republican or communist leanings. Lorca was executed by the Nationalists in 1936, while **Miguel Hernández** was condemned to life imprisonment. Others such as **Jorge Guillén, Pedro Salinas,** and **Luis Cernuda** joined Spain's long history of intellectual and ideological exiles, writing and teaching in the United States, Mexico, and Europe.

SPAIN

MODERN MARVELS. Spanish Nobel Prize recipients include playwright and essayist **Jacinto Benavente y Martínez** (1922), poet **Vicente Aleixandre** (1977), and novelist **Camilo José Cela** (1989). Female writers, like **Mercè Rodoreda, Carmen Martín Gaite,** and **Almudena Grandes,** have likewise earned critical international acclaim. After the death of Franco, Spanish artists flocked to Madrid as they once did earlier in the century, and an avant-garde, liberated spirit—known as *La Movida*—was reborn. Writers like **Ana Rossetti** led a new generation of erotic poets into the 80s, placing women at the forefront of Spanish literature for the first time. Today, **Arturo Pérez-Reverte** is one of Spain's most translated and bestselling contemporary writers.

FICTION AND NONFICTION

The Sun Also Rises, by Ernest Hemingway (1926). Immortalizes bullfighting, machismo, and expatriates of the so-called Lost Generation.

San Manuel Bueno, Mártir, by Miguel de Unamuno (1933). Acclaimed novella of a saintly priest who has lost his faith.

The House of Bernarda Alba, by Federico García Lorca (1936). A drama about a family of repressed women stifled by Andalucían society.

Driving Over Lemons: An Optimist in Spain, by Chris Stewart (1999). A sunny read for those who dream of living amongst olive groves and oranges.

MUSIC

FLAMENCO. Spain's most famous art form combines *cante* (song), *baile* (dance), and *guitarra* (guitar). True flamenco artists are said to perform with *duende*, the soul or spirit behind any passionate performance. The music originated among Andalucian gypsies in the late 18th century and remains an extremely popular tradition that continues to engage audiences around the world. While it is possible to buy flamenco recordings, nothing compares to seeing a live performance. Flamenco heroes include **Andrés Segovia** (1893-1987), who was instrumental in giving the flamenco guitar the same renown as the violin and the cello, and singer **Antonio Mairena** (1909-1983). Today, bands like the **Gipsy Kings** mix flamenco with dance rhythms like salsa and rumba for a pop-oriented sound that has caught on across the globe.

CLASSICAL. Spain bred two of the world's greatest Renaissance composers in **Francisco Guerrero** and **Tomás Luis de Victoria,** who composed both sacred and secular masterpieces. Spain's classical tradition continued centuries later when **Pau (Pablo) Casals** (1876-1973), cellist, conductor, composer, pianist, and humanitarian, became one of the most influential classical musicians of the 20th century. Arguably the greatest Spanish composer of the last two centuries, Cádiz native **Manuel de Falla** (1876-1946) wrote the popular opera *El sombrero de tres picos (The Three-Cornered Hat)*, which premiered in London in 1919 with stage design by Picasso. Spain also claims two of the world-famous "Three Tenors," Barcelona-born **José Carreras** and **Plácido Domingo,** who hails from Madrid.

FOLK MUSIC. While flamenco has come to epitomize Spanish music, every region adds its own rhythm. Accordion-based **trikitrixa** music defines Basque folk, while the **zambomba** drum, played by pulling on a rope inside the drum, is a staple of Extremadura. Valencia takes pride in its **brass bands,** and Cataluña celebrates with a hearty **sardana,** or circle dance.

CONTEMPORARY MUSIC. *Cantautores* (singer-songwriters) **Luis Eduardo Aute, Joaquin Sabina,** and **Joan Manuel Serrat** have been forces on the Spanish music scene since the 60s and 70s. Since Franco's demise, Spanish music has exploded. While the popular music scene is heavily influenced by American and Latin American artists, singers like **Julio** and **Enrique Iglesias,** as well as **Alejandro Sanz,** have gained international acclaim. Successful Spanish bands in recent years include the rock and pop groups **Mecano, Heroes del Silencio, Jarabe de Palo, La Oreja de Van Gogh,** the Celtic-infused **El Sueño de Morfeo,** and **Ojos de Brujo,** whose music is a socially conscious fusion of hip-hop and flamenco.

FILM

FILM UNDER FRANCO. Spain's first film, *Riña en un café* (directed by Fructuoso Gelabert), dates back to 1897, and technically-innovative director **Segundo de Chomón** is recognized worldwide as a pioneer of early cinema. **Luis Buñuel** produced several early classics, most notably his collaboration with **Salvador Dalí,** *Un Chien Andalou* (1929), a surrealist montage of startling and disturbing images. Buñuel followed up this controversial offering with the acclaimed *L'Âge d'or* (1930), banned for nearly 50 years for its perceived attack on Catholicism. Meanwhile, Franco's censors stifled most creativity, leaving the public with cheap westerns and innocuous spy flicks. As censorship waned in the early 1970s, Spanish cinema showed signs of life, led by **Carlos Saura's** dark, subversive hits such as *El jardín de las delicias* (1970) and *Cría cuervos* (1976).

CONTEMPORARY CINEMA. Domestic censorship laws were revoked in 1977. The move brought artistic freedom and financial hardship for Spanish filmmakers, who found their films shunned domestically in favor of newly permitted foreign films. Depictions of the exuberant fervor of a super-liberated Spain found increased attention and international respect. Basque director **Eloy de la Iglesia** portrays this radical shift in *El diputado* (1978). One of Spain's most highly acclaimed directors today, **Pedro Almodóvar**, is the creative force behind *Todo sobre mi madre* (1999) and *Hable con ella* (2002), and his *Volver* (2006) won Best Screenplay at the Cannes Film Festival. Chilean-born Spanish director **Alejandro Amenábar** received critical acclaim as well as the Best Foreign Language Film award at the 2004 Oscars for his poignant *Mar adentro (The Sea Inside)*. Most recently, Mexican writer/director Guillermo del Toro's *El laberinto del fauno (Pan's Labyrinth;* 2006) reached international audiences with its disturbing fantasy of post-Civil War Spain.

SPORTS

FÚTBOL

Soccer is a nationally unifying and locally divisive passion for Spaniards. Historically, Spanish national teams have underperformed at international tournaments, and for forty years their failure to punch their weight was both debated and lamented. Happily, Spanish fans' misery was ended in 2008, when **Fernando Torres** *et al* brought home the Euro 2008 trophy. Spanish club teams constantly bring back honors from European leagues, led by international icons like Brazilian **Ronaldinho,** Argentine **Lionel Messi,** and Cameroonian **Samuel Eto'o.** Squads in the Spanish "La Liga" Premier League, like Real Madrid, FC Barcelona, and Valencia, bring Spaniards to their feet and into the street on game days. La Liga competition starts up every September.

BULLFIGHTING

The national spectacle of *la corrida* (bullfighting) derives from earlier Roman and Moorish practices, but its modern form dates to around 1726. A bullfight has three stages: first, *picadores* (lancers on horseback) pierce the bull's neck muscles to lower his head for the kill. Next, assistants on foot thrust *banderillas* (decorated darts) into the bull's back to provoke the tiring animal. Finally, the *matador* (bullfighter) has ten minutes to kill his opponent with a sword between the shoulder blades, executing artful passes with confidence and grace while daring the bull closer with agility and nerve. If the matador shows special skill and daring, the audience waves white *pañuelos* (handkerchiefs), imploring the bullfight's president to award the *matador* the coveted ears. The techniques of the modern *matador* were refined around 1914 by **Juan Belmonte,** considered one of the greatest *matadores* of all time (others include **Joselito, Manolete,** and **Cristina,** the first female *matadora*). Bullfighting has always had its critics: in the 17th century, it was the Church; more recently, the challenge comes from animal rights activists. Cataluña banned bullfighting in 2006, owing perhaps as much to Catalan nationalism as to cross-species sympathy.

JAI ALAI

Known as *pelota vasca* in Spanish, the Basque government promotes jai alai (meaning "Merry Game" in Basque) as the "fastest game on earth." Jai alai is a game played with a wicker *cesta* basket, used to hurl a ball against a *fronton* (open-walled arena). Points are awarded when the other team drops, misses, or sends the ball out of bounds. These deadly projectiles have been clocked in at incredible speeds of up to 188 mph.

OTHER SPORTS

Fans fondly remember five-time consecutive Tour de France champion **Miguel Indurain,** a Navarran hero and Spain's most decorated athlete. The Vuelta de España is a crucial piece of the European **cycling** circuit, along with the Tour de France and the Giro d'Italia. Spain is a contender on the international **rowing** circuit, with the 1992 Olympic course in Banyoles remaining a popular foreign training site. Old **tennis** favorites like **Arantxa Sánchez-Vicario** and **Carlos Moya** and up-and-comers like **Rafael Nadal,** one of the sport's top-ranked players, have all made names on the court.

NATIONAL HOLIDAYS

The following table lists the national holidays for 2009.

DATE	HOLIDAYS
January 1	Año Nuevo (New Year's Day)
January 6	Epifanía (Epiphany)
April 3-12	Semana Santa (Holy Week)
April 9	Jueves Santo (Maundy Thursday)
April 10	Viernes Santo (Good Friday)
April 12	Pascua (Easter)
May 1	Día del Trabajador (Labor Day)
August 15	La Asunción (Feast of the Assumption)
October 12	Día de la Hispanidad (National Day)
November 1	Día de Todos Santos (All Saints' Day)
December 6	Día de la Constitución (Constitution Day)
December 8	La Inmaculada Concepción (Feast of the Immaculate Conception)
December 25	Navidad (Christmas)
December 31	Noche Vieja (New Year's Eve)

SPANISH FESTIVALS IN 2009

The following table lists selected Spanish festivals for 2009.

DATE	HOLIDAYS
Mid-January to early February	Carnaval (Cadiz, Islas Canarias, Barcelona, and Sitges). Hedonism and frivolity at its best.
Late February to early March	Jerez Flamenco Festival (Jerez de la Frontera). A celebration with the nation's best singers and dancers.
March 12-19	Fallas de San José (Valencia). A pyromaniac's dream—fireworks and burning effigies.
April 3-12	Semana Santa (Sevilla). The city's Easter processions are justifiably famous. Join the crowd.
April 23	La Diada de Sant Jordi (Barcelona). Las Ramblas fills up with roses and booksellers for Cataluña's patron saint: a day for romantics and readers.
May 15	San Isidro (Madrid). Spain's biggest and most prestigious bullfighting exhibition.
June 20-29	Hogueras de San Juan (Alicante). Celebrate the summer solstice with fires and feasts.
June 22	Paso do Fuego (Soria). Fire walking: only the strong (and some say, only the locals) survive.
June 29	Wine Battle (Haro, La Rioja). Just what it sounds like: wet and wild.
Last week of June	Orgullo Gay (Madrid). One of Europe's biggest gay pride festivals.
July 6-14	San Fermín (Pamplona). Featuring the famous "running of the bulls," this festival was immortalized in Hemingway's *The Sun Also Rises*.
August 26	La Tomatina (Buñol). An organized food fight for those who really like tomatoes.
September 24	Festes de la Merce (Barcelona). Wood giants, human towers, and cava—all for a patron saint.
October 12	Día de la Hispanidad (nationwide). A celebration of the arrival of Christopher Columbus in the Americas.

MADRID

Welcome to Spain's political, intellectual, and cultural center—the country's wild, pulsing heart. While theoretically subject to the earth's rotations, Madrid seems to transcend traditional hours. In this city, morning commuters collide with stragglers leaving after-hour clubs at dawn. Tourists spend their days absorbed in its monuments, world-renowned museums, and raging nightlife, mingling with the 5.5 million *madrileños* sprawled in the city's plazas, tapas bars, and parks. Businessmen scoot along on mopeds, old women compare vegetables at the markets, and teens text furiously in search of the next hot club. Stock up on energy with a late afternoon siesta in the Parque del Buen Retiro or in your hostel; the city only truly comes awake after the sun has set.

Though Madrid witnessed the coronation of Fernando and Isabel, it did not achieve prominence until Habsburg monarch Felipe II moved his court here in 1561. It served as Spain's artistic hub during the *Siglo de Oro* (Golden Age), becoming a seat of wealth, culture, and imperial glory, despite its considerable distance from vital ports and rivers. In the 18th century, Madrid experienced a Neoclassical rebirth when Carlos III embellished the city with wide, tree-lined boulevards and scores of imposing buildings, but things took a turn for the worse during the Peninsular wars against Napoleon (1808-1814), the bloody inspiration of some of Francisco de Goya's most famous canvases. Madrid was the base of the 20th-century Republican government and resisted Franco's troops until the spring of 1939, when the Civil War had already washed most of the peninsula in blood. It was the second-to-last city in Spain to fall; immediately after, the Nationalists took Valencia and brought the four-year conflict to a close. For the next four decades, Madrid served as the seat of Franco's government. When the dictator died in 1975, Madrid, and the rest of Spain, came out in what is known today as *la movida* ("shift" or "movement") or *el destapeo* ("uncovering"). A 200,000-strong student population took to the streets and stayed there—and it hasn't stopped moving yet.

HIGHLIGHTS OF MADRID

MUSE over world-famous museums along the **Avenida del Arte** (p. 109).

RELIVE royal dreams at the luxurious 18th-century **Palacio Real** (p. 103).

RETREAT in kingly fashion to the **Parque del Buen Retiro** (p. 107).

TRIP along the cobblestones in quirky **Malasaña** and **Chueca** (p. 86).

INTERCITY TRANSPORTATION

BY PLANE

All flights land at **Aeropuerto Internacional de Barajas** (☎902 40 47 04, flight information 35 35 70; www.aena.es.), 16km and 20min. northeast of Madrid. The regional **tourist office** in the international terminal has maps and info. (☎913 05 86 56. Open M-Sa 8am-8pm, Su 9am-1pm.) **Luggage storage** *(consigna)* is sometimes available. (☎913 93 68 05. 1 day €3.70, 2-15 days €4.78 per day. Max. storage 15 days. Open 24hr.)

The **Barajas metro stop** connects the airport to all of Madrid (€1 for metro ride plus €1 extra from the airport). From the airport arrivals area, follow signs to the metro, located in Terminals 2 and 4. Take Line 8 (pink) to Nuevos Ministerios and switch to Line 10 (dark blue, dir.: Puerta del Sur). At Tribunal, change to Line 1 (light blue, dir.: Valdecarros), and two stops later you'll find yourself at Sol, smack in the middle of Madrid's best accommodations and sights. The **Bus-Aeropuerto #200** leaves from the national terminal **T2** and runs to the city center. (☎902 50 78 50. Look for "EMT" signs just outside the airport doors. Daily every 10-15min. 6am-11pm, last bus 11:30pm, €1.) The bus stops in the metro station **Avenida de América.** Line 101 leaves from T1, 2, and 3 and goes to Canillejas, and Line 204 leaves from T4 and goes to Avenida de América as well. Fleets of **taxis** swarm the airport. Taxi fare to central Madrid should cost €35-40, including the €5.25 airport surcharge, depending on traffic and time of day.

BY TRAIN

Two largo *recorrido* (long-distance) **RENFE** stations, **Atocha** and **Chamartín**, connect Madrid to surrounding areas and the rest of Europe. Both stations are easily accessible by metro. Call RENFE (☎902 24 02 02; www.renfe.es) for reservations and info. Buy tickets at the station or online.

Estación Atocha, Av. Ciudad de Barcelona (☎915 06 61 37). M: Atocha Renfe. The cast-iron atrium of the original station has been turned into an urban rainforest, with lush plants, a small marsh with a colony of turtles, and the occasional bird. Galleries, boutiques, and restaurants provide more commercial diversions. There is a **tourist office** in the station. (☎913 15 99 76; open M-Sa 8am-8pm, Su 9am-2pm.) **RENFE information office** located in the main terminal (☎902 24 02 02). Open daily 6:30am-10:30pm. **Luggage storage** (*consignas automáticas;* €2.40-4.50), at the back right corner of the atrium. Open daily 6:30am-11:45pm. Ticket windows open 6:30am-10:30pm, advance purchases 7am-9:30pm. No international service. **AVE** (☎91 506 63 29) offers high-speed service to southern Spain, including **Sevilla** (2hr., 22 per day 6:30am-11:30pm, €67-74) via **Córdoba** (1hr., €55-61), **Valladolid** (1hr., 6 per day 7:30am-9:45pm, €32), and **Barcelona** (3hr., 20 per day 6am-9pm, €105-124).

Estación Chamartín, C. Agustín de Foxa (☎913 00 69 69). M: Chamartín. Bus #5 runs to and from **Puerta del Sol** (45min.); the stop is just beyond the lockers. Alternatively, get off at M: Atocha Renfe and take a red Cercanías train (15min., every 5-10min., €1.05) to Chamartín. Be sure to keep your ticket, or you won't be able to exit the turnstiles. Chamartín is a mini-mall of useful services, including a **tourist office** (*Vestíbulo,* Puerta 14; ☎913 15 99 76; open M-Sa 8am-8pm, Su 8am-2pm), **currency exchange, accommodations service, post office, car rental, police,** and **luggage storage** (*consignas;* €2.40-4.50; open daily 7am-11pm). Call RENFE at ☎902 24 34 02 for international destinations, and ☎902 24 02 02 (Spanish only) for domestic. Ticket windows open 5:30am-midnight, advance sales 8am-9pm. Chamartín serves both international and domestic destinations to the northeast and south. Most Cercanías (local) trains stop at both Chamartín and Atocha. Major destinations include: **Barcelona** (9hr., 10pm on intermittent days, call ahead, €40-53); **Bilbao** (4hr., 8am, €45-70; or 6hr., 3:50pm, €40-53); **Lisboa** (9 hr., 10:45pm, €56); **Paris** (13hr., 7pm, €115-130).

BY BUS

Numerous private companies serve Madrid, each with its own station and set of destinations. Most buses pass through **Estación Sur de Autobuses** or **Estación de Moncloa,** both easily accessible by metro. The Pl. Mayor tourist office and any other branch in the city has information on the most relevant intercity buses.

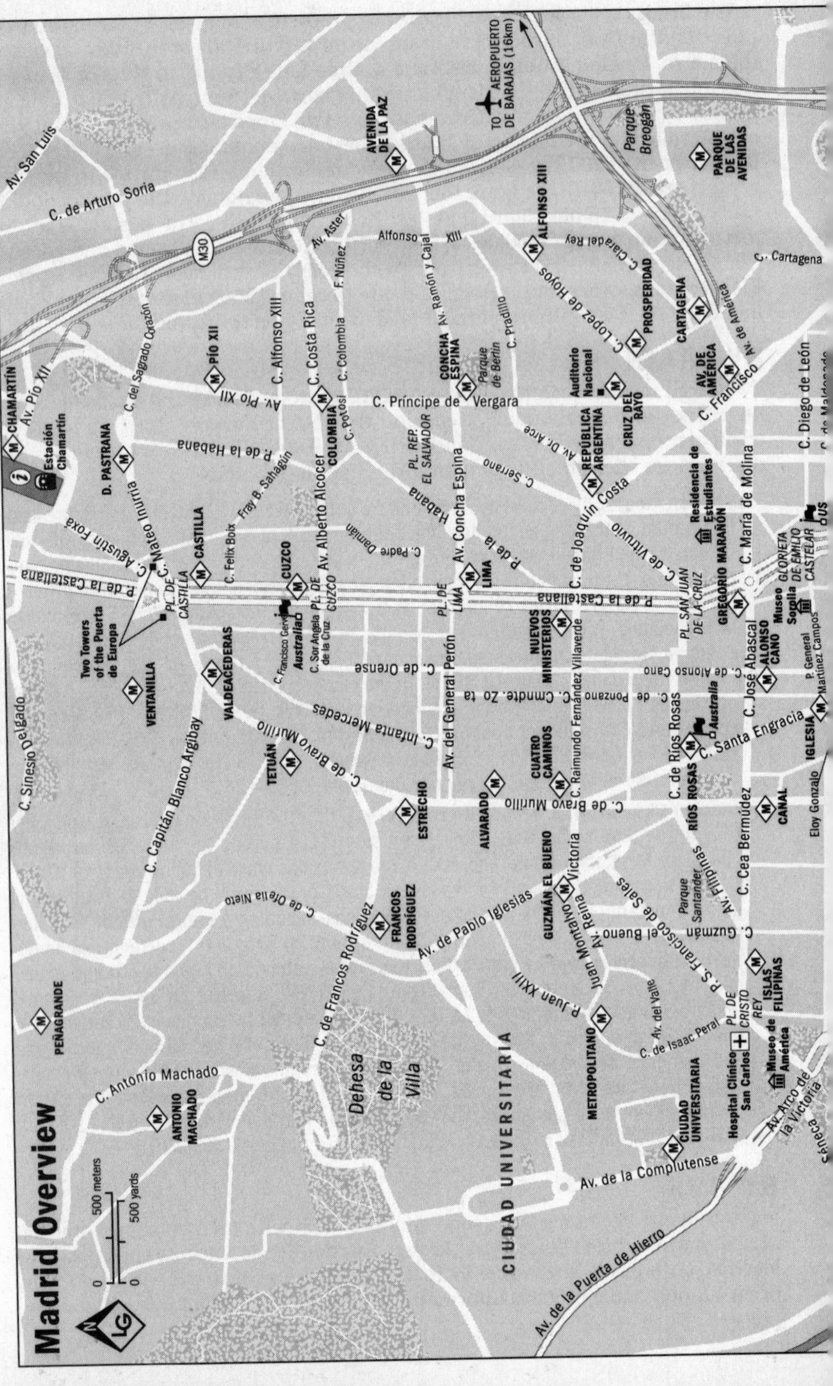

Madrid Overview

0 — 500 meters
0 — 500 yards

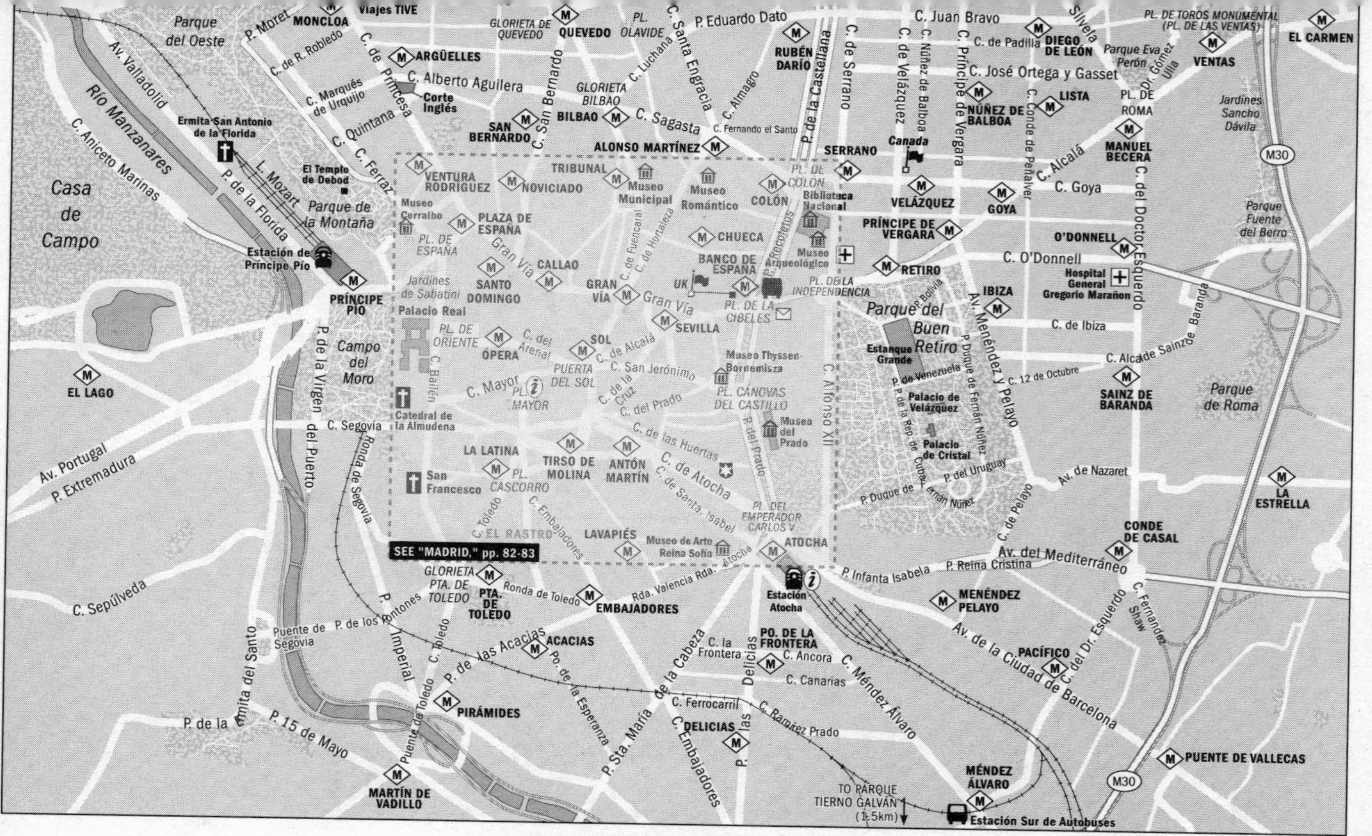
SEE "MADRID," pp. 82-83
Parque del Buen Retiro
Estanque Grande
Palacio de Velázquez
Palacio de Cristal
Casa de Campo
Río Manzanares
Parque del Oeste
Parque de la Montaña
Campo del Moro
Parque de Roma
Parque Fuente del Berro
Jardines Sancho Dávila
Jardines de Sabatini
Palacio Real
Catedral de la Almudena
San Francesco
Ermita San Antonio de la Florida
El Templo de Debod
Estación de Príncipe Pío
Estación Atocha
Estación Sur de Autobuses
Hospital General Gregorio Marañon
Museo Arqueológico
Biblioteca Nacional
Museo del Prado
Museo Thyssen-Bornemisza
Museo de Arte Reina Sofía
Museo Romántico
Museo Municipal
Museo Cerralbo
Corte Inglés
Viajes TIVE
Canada
UK
TO PARQUE TIERNO GALVÁN (1.5km)
MONCLOA
ARGÜELLES
VENTURA RODRÍGUEZ
PLAZA DE ESPAÑA
SANTO DOMINGO
ÓPERA
LA LATINA
SAN BERNARDO
NOVICIADO
CALLAO
TRIBUNAL
GRAN VÍA
SOL
TIRSO DE MOLINA
LAVAPIÉS
EMBAJADORES
ACACIAS
PIRÁMIDES
MARTÍN DE VADILLO
PTA. DE TOLEDO
QUEVEDO
BILBAO
ALONSO MARTÍNEZ
CHUECA
BANCO DE ESPAÑA
SEVILLA
ANTÓN MARTÍN
ATOCHA
DELICIAS
PO. DE LA FRONTERA
MÉNDEZ ÁLVARO
MENÉNDEZ PELAYO
PACÍFICO
CONDE DE CASAL
SAINZ DE BARANDA
IBIZA
RETIRO
PRÍNCIPE DE VERGARA
GOYA
O'DONNELL
MANUEL BECERA
LISTA
NÚÑEZ DE BALBOA
VELÁZQUEZ
SERRANO
COLÓN
RUBÉN DARÍO
DIEGO DE LEÓN
VENTAS
EL CARMEN
LA ESTRELLA
PUENTE DE VALLECAS
EL LAGO
PRÍNCIPE PÍO
PL. DE TOROS MONUMENTAL (PL. DE LAS VENTAS)
M30
C. Juan Bravo
C. Príncipe de Vergara
C. Núñez de Balboa
C. de Velázquez
C. de Serrano
P. de la Castellana
P. Eduardo Dato
C. Santa Engracia
C. Sagasta
C. San Bernardo
C. Alberto Aguilera
C. de Princesa
C. Ferraz
Gran Vía
C. de Alcalá
C. Mayor
C. Bailén
C. de Atocha
C. Segovia
Ronda de Segovia
Ronda de Toledo
C. Embajadores
P. de la Virgen del Puerto
P. de la Florida
Av. Valladolid
C. Aniceto Marinas
Av. Portugal
P. Extremadura
C. Sepúlveda
P. de la Ermita del Santo
P. 15 de Mayo
Puente de Segovia
Puente de Toledo
P. Imperial
P. de las Acacias
Po. de la Esperanza
P. Sta. María de la Cabeza
Delicias
C. Méndez Álvaro
Av. de la Ciudad de Barcelona
Av. del Mediterráneo
P. Reina Cristina
P. Infanta Isabela
C. Alfonso XII
P. del Prado
Recoletos
Av. Menéndez y Pelayo
C. O'Donnell
C. Goya
C. del Doctor Esquerdo
C. Conde de Peñalver
C. José Ortega y Gasset
C. de Ibiza
C. Alcalde Sainz de Baranda
C. Fernandez Shaw
Av. de Nazaret
PL. DE LA INDEPENDENCIA
PL. DE LA CIBELES
PL. CÁNOVAS DEL CASTILLO
PL. DEL EMPERADOR CARLOS V
PUERTA DEL SOL
PL. MAYOR
PL. DE ORIENTE
PL. DE ESPAÑA
PL. DE COLÓN
GLORIETA BILBAO
GLORIETA DE QUEVEDO
GLORIETA PTA. DE TOLEDO
C. EL RASTRO
PL. CASCORRO

MADRID

A
B
C
Centro Cultural Conde Duque
TO MONCLOA, MUSEO DE AMÉRICA (1.4km), AND EL PARDO
TO C. GALILEO (650m)
TO (500m)
TO HOSPITAL DE MADRID (600m) AND
PL. DEL DOS DE MAYO (325m)
C. Velarde
TRIBUNAL
VENTURA RODRÍGUEZ
Motocicletas Antonio Castro
Iglesia de San Marcos
Princesa
ARGÜELLES
Torre de Madrid
Edificio de España
Museo Cerralbo
NOVICIADO
TO TEMPLO DE DEBOD (225m)
PL. DE ESPAÑA
PLAZA DE ESPAÑA
Atesa Car Rental
Jardines Ferraz
MALASAÑA
C. de la Palma
C. de San Vincente Ferrer
C. del Espíritu Santo
PL. DE JUAN PUJOL
C. Tesoro
C. del Pez
PL. DE SAN ILDEFONSO
C. de la Luna
C. Puebla
COGAM
SATE
Gran Vía
C. Flor Alta
C. de Ferraz
C. Cadarso
Cuesta de San Vicente
TO CAMPO DEL MORO (400m)
PL. DE LA MARINA ESPAÑOLA
Jardines de Sabatini
C. de Encarnación
Convento de la Encarnación
C. de la Bola
SANTO DOMINGO
PL. DE SANTO DOMINGO
C. de Jacometrezo
CALLAO
PL. DEL CALLAO
C. de Preciados
GRAN VÍA
C. Miguel Moya
Casa del Libro
PL. VÁSQUEZ DE MELLA
Cuesta Santo Domingo
Jardines Cabo Noval
C. de Arrieta
Convento de las Descalzas Reales
C. del Carmen
PL. DEL CARMEN
C. de la Montera
Palacio Real
PL. DEL ORIENTE
Teatro Real
PL. DE ISABEL II
ÓPERA
PL. SAN MARTÍN
PL. DE LAS DESCALZAS
El Corte Inglés
C. de Arenal
PL. SAN GINES
C. de Tetuán
SOL
PUERTA DEL SOL
C. de Alcalá
Jardines Lepanto
C. Requena
C. de Bailén
C. Mayor
CENTRO
C. Carretas
C. Cádiz
Catedral de Ntra. Sra. de la Almudena
Torre de los Lujanes
PL. DE SAN MIGUEL
PL. MAYOR
Ayuntamiento
PL. DE LA VILLA
Casa de los Lujanes
Casa de Cisneros
PL. DE SANTA CRUZ
C. de la Bolsa
PL. JACINTO BENAVENTE
Santa Cruz
C. Imperial
C. de Toledo
C. de Concepción Jerónima
C. Segovia
C. de Segovia
Parque de las Vistillas
PL. DE LA PAJA
Iglesia de San Pedro
PL. SEGOVIA NUEVA
Dia%
C. de la Colegiata
TIRSO DE MOLINA
PL. TIRSO DE MOLINA
Filmoteca Española
San Andrés
Museo de San Isidro
Catedral de San Isidro
LA LATINA
PL. DE HUMILLADERO
PL. DE LA CEBADA
C. del Duque de Alba
C. de Don Pedro
C. Maldonadas
C. de Juanelo
PL. DE CASCORRO
C. de la Ruda
LA LATINA
C. de Toledo
PL. DEL GENERAL VARA DEL REY
El Rastro
C. de la Ribera de Curtidores
C. Embajadores
C. de Calatrava
TO GLORIETA PUERTA DE TOLEDO (190m), ESTADIO VICENTE CALDERON (1.6km)
Gran Vía de San Francisco
C. de la Ventosa
C. del Carnero
C. de Lavapiés
C. del Amparo
Champ Supermar

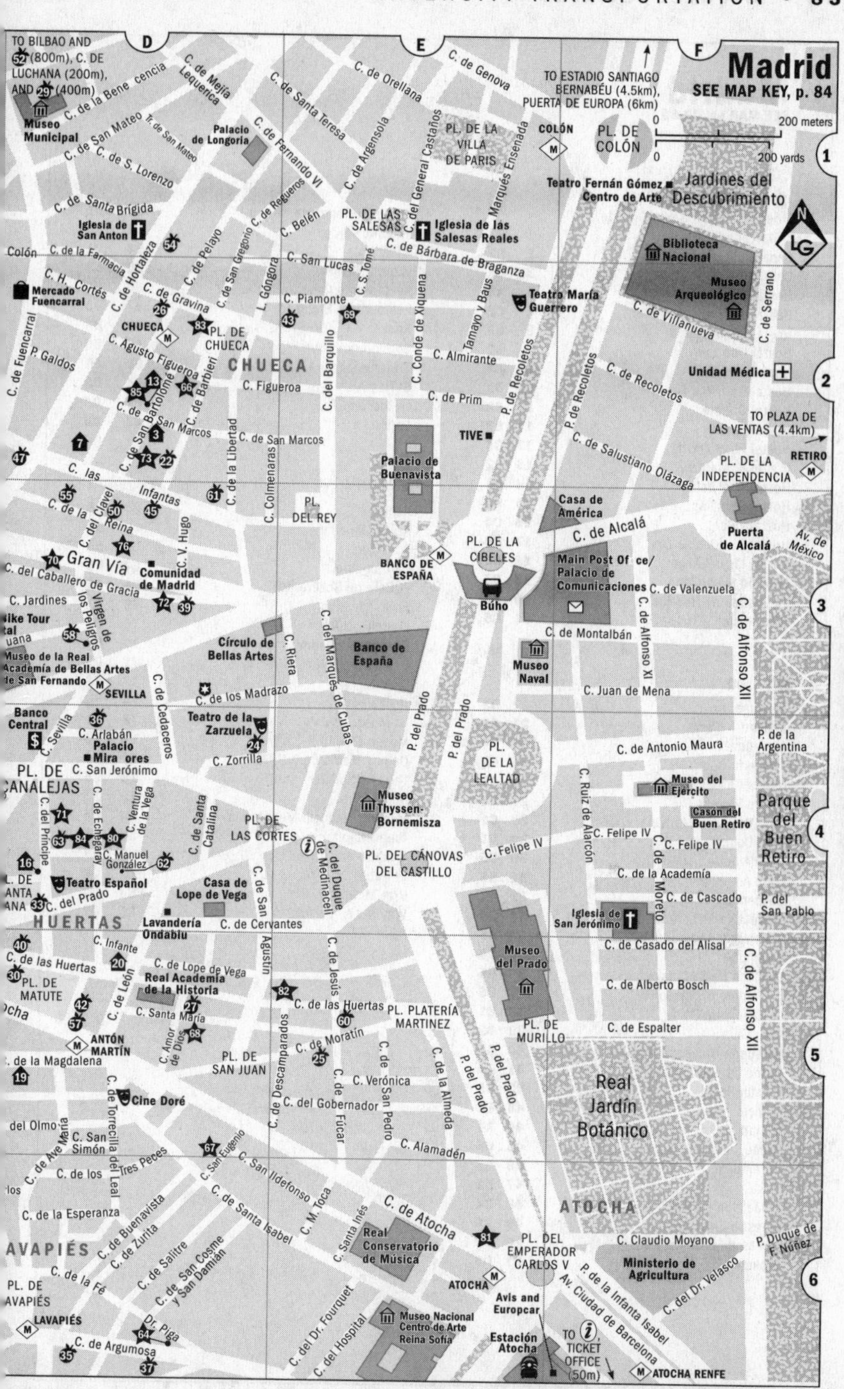
Madrid
SEE MAP KEY, p. 84
TO BILBAO AND (800m), C. DE LUCHANA (200m), AND (400m)
TO ESTADIO SANTIAGO BERNABÉU (4.5km), PUERTA DE EUROPA (6km)
TO PLAZA DE LAS VENTAS (4.4km)
Museo Municipal
Palacio de Longoria
PL. DE LA VILLA DE PARIS
COLÓN
PL. DE COLÓN
Teatro Fernán Gómez Centro de Arte
Jardines del Descubrimiento
Iglesia de San Anton
PL. DE LAS SALESAS
Iglesia de las Salesas Reales
Biblioteca Nacional
Museo Arqueológico
Mercado Fuencarral
Teatro María Guerrero
CHUECA
PL. DE CHUECA
Unidad Médica
TIVE
Palacio de Buenavista
PL. DEL REY
PL. DE LA INDEPENDENCIA
RETIRO
Casa de América
Puerta de Alcalá
PL. DE LA CIBELES
BANCO DE ESPAÑA
Main Post Office/Palacio de Comunicaciones
Búho
Gran Vía
Comunidad de Madrid
Círculo de Bellas Artes
Banco de España
Museo Naval
Museo de la Real Academía de Bellas Artes de San Fernando
SEVILLA
Banco Central
Teatro de la Zarzuela
Palacio Miraflores
PL. DE CANALEJAS
PL. DE LA LEALTAD
Museo del Ejército
Casón del Buen Retiro
Museo Thyssen-Bornemisza
Parque del Buen Retiro
PL. DE LAS CORTES
PL. DEL CÁNOVAS DEL CASTILLO
Teatro Español
Casa de Lope de Vega
Lavandería Ondabiu
HUERTAS
Iglesia de San Jerónimo
Museo del Prado
Real Academia de la Historia
PL. DE MATUTE
PL. PLATERÍA MARTINEZ
PL. DE MURILLO
ANTÓN MARTÍN
PL. DE SAN JUAN
Real Jardín Botánico
Cine Doré
ATOCHA
AVAPIÉS
PL. DE AVAPIÉS
LAVAPIÉS
Real Conservatorio de Música
PL. DEL EMPERADOR CARLOS V
Ministerio de Agricultura
Museo Nacional Centro de Arte Reina Sofía
Avis and Europcar
Estación Atocha
TO TICKET OFFICE (50m)
ATOCHA RENFE
C. de Genova
C. de Orellana
C. de Santa Teresa
C. de Fernando VI
C. de Argensola
C. del General Castaños
Marqués Ensenada
C. de Mejía Lequerica
C. de la Beneficencia
C. de San Mateo
C. de S. Lorenzo
C. de Santa Brígida
C. de Hortaleza
C. de Pelayo
C. de Barbara de Braganza
C. San Lucas
C. Piamonte
C. Almirante
C. de Prim
P. de Recoletos
C. de Recoletos
C. de Villanueva
C. de Serrano
C. de Salustiano Olázaga
C. de Alcalá
C. de Alfonso XII
C. de Montalbán
C. Juan de Mena
C. de Antonio Maura
C. Felipe IV
C. de la Academía
C. de Cascado
C. de Casado del Alisal
C. de Alberto Bosch
C. de Espalter
P. del Prado
C. de Atocha
C. Claudio Moyano
Av. Ciudad de Barcelona
P. de la Infanta Isabel
C. de Argumosa
C. de Fuencarral
C. de la Libertad
C. de San Marcos
C. Figueroa
C. de Cedaceros
C. de Cervantes
C. de las Huertas
C. de Lope de Vega
C. de Moratín
C. Infante
C. de León
C. San Ilfonso
C. de Santa Isabel
C. de la Esperanza
Av. de México
P. de la Argentina
P. del San Pablo
P. Duque de F. Núñez
200 meters
200 yards

MADRID

Madrid

SEE MAP, pp. 82-83

ACCOMMODATIONS

Albergue Juvenil Santa Cruz de Marcenado (HI),	1	B1
Casa Chueca,	2	D2
Cat's Hostel,	3	C5
Hostal A. Nebrija,	4	A2
Hostal Concepción Arenal,	5	C2
Hostal Condestable,	6	C2
Hostal Don Juan,	7	D2
Hostal Esparteros,	8	C4
Hostal Gran Via 44,	9	C3
Hostal Oriente,	10	B3
Hostal Paz,	11	B3
Hostal Plaza D'Ort,	12	C5
Hostal R. Arantza,	13	D2
Hostal Real Valencia,	14	A3
Hostal Santillan,	15	B2
Hostal Villar,	16	D4
Hostal-Residencia Luz,	17	B4
Hostel Miguel Ángel,	18	B3
Pensión Magdalena,	19	D5
La Posada de Huertas,	20	D5
Mad Hostel,	21	C5

FOOD

Al-Jaima,	22	D2
Almendro 13,	23	B5
Al Natural,	24	D4
Arrocería Gala,	25	E5
BAires Café,	26	D2
La Bio Tika,	27	D5
Café-Botillería Manuela,	28	C1
Cafe Comercial,	29	D1
Casa Alberto,	30	D5
Casa Amadeo,	31	B6
Cáscaras,	32	A1
Cervecería Alemana,	33	D4
El Estragón Vegetariano,	34	A5
Eucalipto,	35	D6
La Finca de Susana,	36	D4
El Granero de Lavapies,	37	D6
La Granja de Said,	38	C1
Gula Gula,	39	D3
Heladería Giuseppe Ricci,	40	D5
Horno La Santigüesa,	41	A4
El Imperfecto,	42	D5
El Inca,	43	E2
Inshala,	44	A4
Isolée,	45	D3
El Jamonal,	46	C3
Maoz,	47	D2
El Mejillón de Madrid	48	C4
Maestro Churrero,	49	C5
The Modern Dining Room,	50	D3
Olokun,	51	C3
Osteria Il Regno de Napoli,	52	D1
Pimento Verde,	53	A1
Il Pizzaiolo,	54	D1
Pizzeria Vesuvio,	55	D3
Restaurante Casa Granada,	56	C5
Restaurante El Basha,	57	D5
Root,	58	D3
Sobrino del Botín,	59	B5
Taberna Maceira,	60	E5
El Tigre,	61	D3
La Toscana,	62	D4
La Trucha,	63	D4

NIGHTLIFE

Achuri,	64	D6
Azúcar Palador,	65	B1
Bar Nike,	66	D2
Cardamomo,	67	D5
El Cafe de Schérezad,	68	D5
El Clandestino	69	E2
Costello Club,	70	D3
Cuevas de Sésamo,	71	D4
De Las Letras Restaurante,	72	D3
l'levn	73	D2
Joy Eslava,	74	B4
La Musa,	75	B1
Museo Chicote,	76	D3
Ocho y Medio Club,	77	C3
The Penthouse,	78	C4
Reinabruja,	79	B3
Taberna Vinoçola Mentridana,	80	D4
Teatro Kapital,	81	E6
Trocha,	82	E5
El Truco,	83	D2
Viva Madrid,	84	D4
Why Not?,	85	D2

MADRID

Estación Sur de Autobuses: C. Méndez Álvaro (☎914 68 42 00; www.estacionautobusesmadrid.com). M: Méndez Álvaro; metro stop inside station. Info booth open daily 6:30am-1am. **ATMs, food,** and **luggage storage** (€1.30 per bag per day, open 6:30am-10:30pm). Serves 40+ private bus companies. National destinations include: **Algeciras, Alicante, Aranjuez, Benidorm, Cartagena, Gijón, A Coruña, Lugo, Murcia, Oviedo, Santiago de Compostela,** and **Toledo.** Check at the station or call for specific info on routes and schedules. Among others, it serves:

AISA-Empresa Semar (☎915 27 12 94). Buses to **Aranjuez** (45min.; M-F every 30min. 6:30am-11:45pm, Sa-Su every 30min., 7am-11:30pm; €3.50).

ALSA (☎915 06 33 60; www.alsa.es). International destinations include: **Czech Republic, France, Germany, Holland, Italy, Poland, Portugal, Romania,** and **Switzerland,** but flying can actually be cheaper. Contact **Eurolines** for more information (reservations ☎902 40 50 40, www.eurolines.es). Open daily 7am-11pm.

Auto-Res (auto-res.net). Offers service to many domestic destinations. Prices and times are given with regular service first, then express service. Goes to **Badajoz** (5½hr., 4 per day 1am-4:30pm, €26; or 4½hr., 5 per day 10am-9pm, €32), **Cáceres** (5hr., 5 per day 8am-6:30pm, €19; or 3½hr., 2 per day 3:30 and 8pm, €23; 3:30pm express bus only on weekends), **Cuenca** (2½hr., 7 per day 6:45am-10pm, €11; or 2hr., 2 per day 10am and 6:30pm, €14; 10am express only on weekends), **Mérida** (4½hr., 4 per day 1am-4:30pm, €22; or 4hr., 5 per day 10am-9pm, €28), **Salamanca** (3hr., 7 per day 8:30am-10:30pm, €12, or 2½hr., 16 per day 7am-10pm, €17.50), **Trujillo** (4hr., 10 per day 1am-6:30pm, €16; or 2½hr., 7 per day 10am-9pm, €22.50), and **Valencia** (4hr., 16 per day 1am-11pm, €23-29).

Empresa Larrea (☎913 98 38 05). Goes to **Ávila** (1hr.; M-F 8 per day 7am-8:30pm, Sa 6 per day 9:30am-10pm, Su 4 per day 10am-8:30pm; €7.30).

Empresa La Sepulvedana. Buses to: **Segovia** (1hr.; every 30min. 6:30am-10:30pm; €6.50, round-trip €10).

Estación Autocares Herranz: Headquarters located on C. Juan de Toledo, 5 (☎918 96 90 28), in the Intercambio de Moncloa. M: Moncloa. To **Valle de los Caídos** (20min.; Tu-Su departs **El Escorial** 3:15pm, returns 5:30pm; round-trip plus admission €8).

Estación Empresa Alacuber: Pl. del Caudillo, 2 (☎913 76 01 04). M: Moncloa. To **El Pardo** (20min.; every 15min. M-F 6:25am-1am, Sa 6:25am-2am, Su 7:15am; €1.25).

Estación Empresa Continental Auto: Av. de América, 9 (☎902 42 22 42). M: Av. de América. To **Alcalá de Henares** (40min.; M-Sa every 15min. 6:15am-11pm, Su every 20min. 7-11pm; €2.20).

ORIENTATION

THE NEIGHBORHOODS OF MADRID

EL CENTRO: SOL, ÓPERA, AND PLAZA MAYOR

Puerta del Sol is the center of the city in the center of the country. The "Kilómetro 0" sign in front of the police station marks the intersection of eight of Madrid's most celebrated streets and the starting point of the country's major highways. Tourist shops and fast-food restaurants mingle with ancient churches, gardens, and plazas. The heart of 16th- and 17th-century **Habsburg Madrid** *(Madrid de los Austrias)* is vibrant **Plaza Mayor,** out of which radiate small, maze-like streets. Farther west of Sol by way of C. del Arenal lies the chief monument of Bourbon Madrid, the **Palacio Real,** its gray facade rising above sprawling gardens.

LA LATINA AND LAVAPIÉS

South of Sol and west of Huertas is the neighborhood around the metro stops **La Latina** and **Lavapiés**, multicultural hot spots whose immigrant roots are starting to attract bohemian gentrification. Trendy *madrileños* socialize in the small markets that line the area's winding streets, perfect for an evening of gourmet treats. Just a 10min.walk down the hill from Huertas, the area is easily accessible and well worth the climb back up. **El Rastro,** an ancient, gargantuan flea market, is held here every Sunday morning.

HUERTAS

Huertas is the wedge carved out by C. de San Jerónimo and C. de Atocha, with C. de las Huertas running through the southern portion of the district. A seedy area in the not-too-distant past, Huertas has grown into a clean, popular cluster of theaters, restaurants, and bars. **Plaza Santa Ana, C. del Príncipe,** and **C. de Echegaray** contain some of the best bars in Madrid, but every hidden side street is worth investigating. Once the cradle of Spanish literary giants,the area is now home to the city's three great museums along the **Avenida del Arte** (p. 109), not to mention the lush **Parque del Buen Retiro** (p. 107).

STAYING SAFE IN MADRID. Madrid is just as safe as most major European cities, but Pta. del Sol, Pl. de España, Pl. Chueca, C. Gran Vía, and Malasaña's Pl. 2 de Mayo can be intimidating late at night. As a general rule, avoid parks and quiet residential streets after dark, and always watch out for thieves and pickpockets in crowds.

GRAN VÍA

North of Sol, busy **Gran Vía** is the commercial center of Madrid, called *"el broadway madrileño"* after its model in New York. Once an impressive feat of architectural ingenuity and determination, it has slowly given itself over to American fast food, crumbling theaters, sirens fighting their way through traffic, and designer apparel outlets. The parade of flashing cars, swishing skirts, and high-heeled shoes makes Gran Vía worth a quick look, but not much more.

MALASAÑA AND CHUECA

Across the Gran Vía to the north, and split down the middle by C. de Fuencarral, **Malasaña** and **Chueca** are Madrid's hub for all things alternative or funky. Small boutiques and delicious restaurants provide ample daytime activities; by night, the GLBT scene blooms into an outrageous, colorful bar and club atmosphere. Despite the alternative vibe, these two neighborhoods are diverse enough to offer something for everyone. Traditional tapas bars and raging discos, old fruit markets, and sex shops sit in peaceful accord. Beyond Gran Vía and east of Malasaña and Chueca lies modern Madrid.

ARGÜELLES AND MONCLOA

Just outside the core of the city, north and northwest of the Palacio Real, the neighborhood of **Argüelles** and the zone around **C. San Bernardo,** together with **Moncloa,** form a cluttered mixture of middle-class homes, student apartments, tranquil parks, and bohemian hangouts. Located near the **Ciudad Universitaria,** the area is full of teenagers and university students.

BILBAO

Located slightly north of the city's cultural nexus, **Bilbao** is the area north of Glorieta de Bilbao (M: Bilbao), in the "V" formed by C. Fuencarral and C. Luchana including Pl. de Olavide. Like its neighbors, Argüelles and Moncloa, Bilbao is a student district filled with cheap eateries and neon nightclubs.

MAPS

The free *Plano de Madrid* (street map) and *Plano de Transportes* (public transport map) are fantastic. Pick them up at any tourist office. Public transport info is also available by phone (☎012) or on the web (www.ctm-madrid.es). **El Corte Inglés** (p. 118) offers a free one-page map of Madrid. For a comprehensive map with street index, pick up the *Almax* map (€7) at any newsstand.

LOCAL TRANSPORTATION

METRO

Safe, speedy, spotless, and almost always under *obras* (improvements), Madrid's metro puts most major subway systems to shame. Trains run frequently; green timers above most platforms show increments of five minutes or less between trains. The free *Plano del Metro* (available at any ticket booth) and the wall maps of surrounding neighborhoods are clear and helpful. Fare and schedule info is posted in every station; trains run daily 6am-2am.

Twelve lines, totaling 284km, connect Madrid's 282 stations, making the city's metro the third most extensive in the world, after London and New York. Line 12 now extends coverage from Casa de Campo to the Puerta del Sur, Móstoles, and Getafe regions south of the city. An individual metro ticket costs €1, or €1.90 if you leave the city limits, but frequent riders opt for the **Metrobus** (ticket of 10 rides valid for both the metro and bus system; €6.70). Children under the age of four travel free. Buy them at machines in metro stops, *estancos* (tobacco shops), or newsstands. Remember to keep your ticket until you leave the metro—riding without one can subject you to outrageous fines. There is also the **abonos turísticos** (tourist ticket of unlimited rides for a period of 1, 2, 3, 5, or 7 days; €4-42). These are available at all metro stations or online. For information, call **Metro Info** (☎902 44 44 03) or visit www.metromadrid.es.

Violent crime in metro stations is almost unheard of, and women usually feel safe traveling alone. Be advised, however, that crowded subway cars are a pickpocket's land of milk and honey. Metro stations such as Tirso de Molina, La Latina, Lavapiés, Gran Vía, Pl. de España, Chueca, and Sol can be intimidating after midnight if alone. These areas are usually busy all through the night, but many crimes are reported in the area; use caution and common sense.

BUS

While the metro makes the most sense for trips across Madrid, buses cover areas inaccessible by metro and are a great way to see the city. Most stops are clearly marked, but if you want extra guidance in finding routes and stops, try the handy *Plano de Transportes* or the English-language *Visiting the Downtown on Public Transport*, free at the tourist office.

Bus fares are the same as the metro, and tickets are interchangeable. Buses run 6am-11pm, generally at intervals of 10-15min. From midnight-6am, the **Búho** (owl), or night bus, travels from Pl. de Cibeles and other marked routes to the outskirts of the city (every 30min. midnight-3am, hourly 3-6am; F-Sa every 20min.) These buses, marked on the essential *Red de autobuses nocturnos*, available at any tourist office, run along 26 lines covering regular daytime routes. For info, call **Empresa Municipal de Transportes.** (☎902 50 78 50 or 914 06 88 10; www.emtmadrid.es. Open M-F 8am-2pm.)

TRAIN

The Cercanías trains run through the city and into the suburbs of the city, reaching areas inaccessible or impractical by metro and bus. There are 33 stations, 13 of which connect directly to metro stations, among them Atocha Renfe (line 1) and Nuevos Ministerios (lines 7 and 10). The timetables

MADRID

FROM THE ROAD

THE TOUR SANS PANTS

Civil liberties have come a long way in Spain since Franco died. While this fact almost goes without saying, it was borne out vividly for me as I walked through the Plaza de Oriente the other day.

Traffic stopped and a din arose from down C. Bailén, which runs in front of the Palacio Real. Then hundreds—perhaps thousands—of naked protesters came riding by on bicycles. Some chanted *"Gasolina es asesina"* ("gas is an assassin"), others merely *"Coches = mierda"* (cars are shit). Whatever it was, they were out in force with children, wives, and co-workers, drinking beer and taking photos as they rode slowly by.

I stopped and talked to a few of the unclad riders. "We're protesting for urban transport," one said, patting his bicycle. Riding your bicycle in Madrid, he told me, is often dangerous, because drivers don't care about cyclists. They rode on, followed by a police escort, ostensibly protecting the group from traffic.

Enjoying the irony, I paused and saw the mass of naked riders being escorted past one of the most beautiful royal palaces in the world, an image that won't leave me soon. Riding naked in my puritanical country, much less past the Capitol or the home of the president, would not be tolerated. *Madrileños* cherish their rights, and that is the naked truth.

—Russell Rennie

are regular and are available at the train stations. Fares are the same as those for the bus and metro, and are interchangeable. Trains run from 5:30am until 11:30am every day.

TAXI

Taxis stream through Madrid around the clock. Call **Radio Taxi Madrid** (☎915 47 82 00), **Radio-Taxi Independiente** (☎914 05 55 00 or 91 405 12 13), or **Teletaxi** (☎913 71 21 31; www.tele-taxi.es). A *"libre"* sign or a green light indicates availability. Base fare is €1.85 (or €2.90 after 10pm), plus €0.87-1.00 per km from 6am-10pm and €1-1.10 from 10pm-6am. **Teletaxi** charges a flat rate of €1 per km. Fare supplements include airport (€5.25) and bus and train stations (€2.75). Official taxis are white with a red stripe on the door; avoid impostors.

Check that the driver starts the meter. If you have a complaint or think you've been overcharged, demand a *recibo oficial* (official receipt) and an *hoja de reclamaciones* (complaint form), which the driver is required to supply. Take down the license number, route taken, and fare charged. Take the forms and information to the **Oficina Municipal del Taxi,** C. Albarracín, 31 (☎914 80 46 23; M: García Noblejas). Open M-F July-Sept. 9am-1pm; Oct.-June 9am-2pm) or the *Ayuntamiento* (City Hall), Pl. de la Villa, 4 (info ☎010 or 915 88 10 00; M: Ópera) to request a refund. To request taxi service for the handicapped, call ☎915 47 85 00 or 47 86 00. Rates are the same as other taxis. If you leave belongings in a taxi, visit or call the **Negociado de Objetos Perdidos,** Paseo del Molino, 7 (☎915 27 95 90. M: Legazpi. Open M-F 9am-2pm.)

CAR RENTAL

There is no reason to rent a car in Madrid. If congested traffic and nightmarish parking don't drive you into hysterics, aggressive drivers, annoying mopeds, and sky-high gasoline prices will. If you do choose to drive, parking permits are available on the street from column-like machines with "P" signs. If you plan to drive to places outside of Madrid, a larger car rental chain is your best bet. See **By Car,** p. 33, for listings of multinational chains with offices in Spain.

MOPED AND BIKE RENTAL

Fortunately for pedestrians, Madrid is not scarred by the moped mayhem that has taken over most of Europe. Though mopeds are swift, Madrid's stellar public transport system is more than sufficient for getting around. If you choose to ride, you'll need a lock and helmet. **Motocicletas Antonio Castro,** C.

Conde Duque, 13, rents mopeds from €26-85 per day or €120-340 per week, including unlimited mileage and insurance. (☎915 42 06 57. M: San Bernardo. 21+ with **International Driver's Permit** only (see **Driving Permits,** p. 34). €300 deposit required for 1-day rentals, €650 for 1-week rentals. Open M-F 8am-1:30pm and 5-8pm.) For bike rental, try **Madrid Bike Rental and Tours,** C. Jardines, 12 (☎915 23 15 47; www.trixi.com. M: Gran Vía. Rental €8 for 4 hrs., €12 for 8hrs., €15 for 24hrs., and €50 for the week. Open Mar.-Oct. M-F 10am-2pm and 4-8pm, Sa-Su 10am-8pm; Nov.-Feb. 10am-3pm. Tours daily 11am; €22 for 3hr. tour with English-speaking guide, drink included. No reservations needed.)

PRACTICAL INFORMATION

TOURIST AND FINANCIAL SERVICES

Tourist Offices: English and French are spoken at most tourist offices. Those planning trips outside the Comunidad de Madrid can visit region-specific offices within Madrid; ask at any tourist office for their addresses.

Regional Office of the Comunidad de Madrid, C. del Duque de Medinaceli, 2 (☎914 29 49 51, info 902 10 00 07; www.madrid.org). M: Banco de España. Brochures, transportation info, and maps for the Comunidad. Extremely helpful; if you are planning to travel beyond Madrid, make this your first stop. Open M-Sa 8am-8pm, Su 9am-2pm.

Madrid Tourism Centre, Pl. Mayor, 27 (☎915 88 16 36; www.esmadrid.com). M: Sol. Hands out indispensable city and transportation maps and a complete guide to accommodations, as well as *In Madrid,* a monthly activity and information guide in English and interactive information available in 7 others. Branches at Estación Chamartín (p. 79), Estación Puerta de Atocha (p. 79), and the airport (p. 78), also at Plaza de Cibeles, Plaza de Callao, and Plaza de Felipe II. All open daily 9:30am-8pm.

General Info Line: Turespaña (☎901 30 06 00 or 010). Info on anything about Madrid, from police stations to zoo hours. Ask for *inglés* for an English-speaking operator.

Tours: Tours can be informative but pricey, so read the fine print before signing on. The *Ayuntamiento* offers walking tours in English and Spanish called **Descubre Madrid** (☎915 88 29 06. Open M-F 9:30am-8:30pm. €3.10; students, children, and seniors €2.50) or pick up more info at the municipal tourist office. **Madrid Vision** (☎917 79 18 88; www.madridvision.es) operates double-decker bus tours. There are 2 routes (Madrid Histórico and Moderno) each of which makes 15-20 stops around the city, featuring monuments and museums. Get on and off the bus as you please. €16, ages 7-16 and seniors €8.50; 2-day ticket €20.

Budget Travel: TIVE, C. Fernando el Católico, 88 (☎915 43 74 12). M: Moncloa. Walk straight down C. Arcipreste de Hita (one street over, parallel to C. Princesa) and turn left on C. Fernando el Católico. A great resource for long-term visitors. Lodging, tourism, and student residence info. Organizes group excursions and language classes and cheap trips to other European cities. Some English spoken. Some services only for Spanish nationals. Sells cheap **ISIC** cards (€6) and **Hostelling International (HI)** memberships (€5), along with discount memberships for teachers and people above 26. Open M-F 9am-2pm. Arrive early to avoid lines. Another smaller branch is located at Paseo de Recoletos, 7 (☎917 20 13 24). M: Banco de España. Open M-F 9am-2pm.

Consulates: see **Embassies and Consulates,** p. 10.

Currency Exchange: The airport is the best place to change your cash, but if you need to change more in the city later, head to **Banco Santander Central Hispano,** which does not charge commission on American Express Travelers Cheques, but will charge around €12-15 commission on all others. Max. exchange €300. Main branch, Po. Castellana, 7 (☎915 58 11 11). M: Sol. Follow C. San Jerónimo 100m to Pl. Canalejas. Open Apr.-Sept. M-F 8:30am-2pm; Oct.-Mar. M-F 8:30am-2pm, Sa 8:30am-1pm. Banks usually charge 1-2% commission (min. charge €3). Booths in Sol and Gran Vía, though open as late as midnight and on weekends, have poor rates and are not a good deal. **ServiRed, ServiCaixa,** and **Telebanco** machines accept bank cards with Cirrus, PLUS, EuroCard, or NYCE logos. Withdrawal fees approx. $5 per withdrawal and $3 per balance check.

American Express: Currency exchange only at the airport. Open M-F 9am-7:30pm, Sa 9am-2pm. Airport Branch (☎91 393 82 16 or 93 82 16). To report lost Travelers Cheques, call toll free ☎90 099 44 26.

LOCAL SERVICES

Luggage Storage: At the airport (€3.70 for the first day, €4.78 per day for the next two weeks) and bus and train stations (€2.75 per bag per day).

English-language Periodicals: International editions available at kiosks everywhere, especially on Gran Vía, Paseos del Prado, Recoletos, Castellana, and around Pta. del Sol. *In Madrid* is an English-language guide to what's going on in the city, available at tourist offices. For English-language books, try **Book Sellers,** C. José Abascal, 48 (☎914 42 81 04). M: Gregorio Marañon. Open M-Sa 10am-1pm and 5-9pm.

Language Service: A "Language Exchanges Meeting Night" happens every Th at 9:30pm at **Café Madrid,** C. Escalinata s/n. M: Ópera. Locals and travelers come to sip coffee, practice Spanish, or try to pick up a little of another language. (Info ☎647 01 00 67).

Libraries: The municipal tourist office has a comprehensive list of libraries around the city. These include **Bibliotecas Municipales Especializadas,** numerous branches of the **Bibliotecas Públicas Municipales por Distritos** (23 locations), and **Bibliotecas Públicas de la Comunidad de Madrid** (18 locations). Large branch **Biblioteca Centro-Pedro Salinas** (☎913 66 54 07) at M: Pta. de Toledo, has English-language periodicals. Open M-F 8:30am-8:45pm, Sa 9am-1:45pm.

Women's Resources: For general information on women's services in Spain or to report an incident, call **Instituto de la Mujer,** C. Genova, 11 (☎900 13 10 10; www.mtas.es/mujer). M: Colón or Alonso Martinez. Open M-F 9am-2pm.

GLBT Resources: Most establishments in Chueca carry *Shangay* and *Shanguide,* free guides to gay nightlife in Spain. The guide also offers detailed listings and maps of the many gay establishments in and around Madrid. Alternatively, you can purchase **Zero** magazine (€5) at any kiosk, with a guide to nightlife and gay activities.

Colectivo de Gais y Lesbianas de Madrid (COGAM), C. Puebla, 9 (☎915 22 45 17; www.cogam.org). M: Callao. Provides a wide range of services and organizes activities. Reception open M-Th 10am-2pm and 5-8pm, F 10am-2pm.

GAY-INFORM/Línea Lesbos, a gay info line and hotline (☎915 23 00 70), provides counseling from 5-9pm every night. Th 7-9pm in English. F staffed by and for lesbians, but takes all calls. Also provides information in Spanish and English (Th 7-9pm) about gay associations, activities, health issues, sports, and dinners. Open M-F 10am-2pm, 5-8pm. The city of Madrid has its own GLBT info line (☎900 72 05 69) open M-F 10am-2pm and 5-9pm.

Laundromat: Lavandería Ondablu, C. León, 3 (☎913 69 50 71). M: Antón Martín, Sol, or Sevilla. Wash €3.50, dry €1. Open M-F 9:30am-10pm, Sa 10:30am-7pm. Also at C. Hortaleza, 84 (☎915 31 28 73). M: Chueca. €4.50 each for wash and dry. Open daily 9:30am-10:30pm. Laundry also available in most hostels for €5 wash and dry.

EMERGENCY AND COMMUNICATIONS

Emergency: ☎112 for all emergencies, medical or otherwise.

Police: C. de los Madrazo, 9 (☎ 913 22 11 60 or 900 15 00 00). M: Sevilla. Largely administrative. English forms available. Open daily 9am-2pm. **Policía Municipal,** C. Montera 18, has staff 24hr. **Servicio de Atención al Turista Extranjero (SATE)** are police who deal exclusively with tourists; they help with administrative formalities, reporting crimes, canceling credit cards, contacting embassies and family members, finding lost objects, and finding counseling. (C. Leganitos, 19. ☎915 48 85 37 for the office or ☎902 102 112 to report a crime. M: Plaza de España. Open daily 9am-10pm.)

Hotlines: Poison Control (24hr. ☎915 62 04 20). **Rape Hotline** (☎915 74 01 10). Open M-F 10am-2pm and 4-8pm.

Late-Night Pharmacy: Dial ☎098 for locations. One at C. Mayor, 13 (☎913 66 46 16), off Pta. del Sol; **Antigua Farmacia de la Reina Madre** at C. Mayor, 59 (☎915 48 00 14), closer to M: Ópera. Open 8am-midnight.

Hospitals: Emergency rooms are the best option for immediate attention. US insurance is not accepted, but if you get a receipt your insurance may pay. For non-emergency concerns, **Unidad Médica Angloamericana,** C. del Conde de Aranda, 1, 1st fl. (☎914 35 18 23; www.unidadmedica.com). M: Serrano or Retiro. Regular English-speaking personnel on duty M-F 9am-8pm, Sa 10am-1pm. English-speaking specialists in every branch of medicine do non-urgent consultations. Initial visit €125; appointment needed. AmEx/MC/V. Embassies and consulates keep lists of English-speaking doctors.

Emergency Clinics: In a medical emergency, dial ☎061 or 112. **Hospital de Madrid,** Pl. del Conde del Valle Suchil, 16 (☎914 47 66 00; www.hospitaldemadrid.com). M: Bilbao. **Hospital Ramón y Cajal,** Ctra. Colmenar Viejo, km 9100 (☎91 336 80 00). Bus #135 from Pl. de Castilla. **Red Cross** (☎915 22 22 22, info 902 22 22 92). **Centro de Salud Sandoval,** C. Sandoval, 7 (☎914 45 23 28). M: Bilbao. Free, confidential government clinic specializing in HIV/AIDS and other STDs. Open M-F 9am-2pm.

Telephones: Directory services ☎1003. (See **Keeping in Touch,** p. 37.)

Internet Access: Hundreds of internet cafes are spread across the city, and most hostels provide free internet access as well. Rates are generally consistent (roughly €1-1.50 per 30min. and €2 per hour). **Kioscocity,** C. Montera 47, above the Argentine bar/convenience store. €1 for 15min., €1.50 for 30min., €2 per hour. Offers domestic and international fax services. Open daily 9am-2am.

Post Office: Palacio de Comunicaciones, C. Alcalá, 51, on Pl. de Cibeles (☎902 19 71 97). M: Banco de España. Enormous palace on the far side of the plaza from the metro. Info (main vestibule) open M-Sa 8:30am-9:30pm. Windows open M-Sa 8:30am-9:30pm, Su 8:30am-2pm for stamp purchases. To find a more convenient location near you, check the website at www.correos.es. **Postal Code:** 28080.

ACCOMMODATIONS

The demand for rooms in Madrid is always high, and rises dramatically in summer. Though the city is filled with hostels, good quality at good prices can be hard to find. Most listings below include breakfast and internet, and offer laundry services. Prices range from €15 to €50 per person, depending on location, amenities, and season. Don't be deceived; higher prices don't necessarily indicate nicer accommodations. Try negotiating the price if you plan on staying for over a week. Those staying in Madrid for long periods may want to check out **The Broadsheet** (€2.50), an English periodical with classifieds and events.

In Madrid, the difference between a one-star *hostal* and a *pensión* is often minimal. In winter, heating is standard; in summer, air-conditioning is not. Unless otherwise noted, communal bathrooms (toilet and shower) are the norm, although it is not unusual to get a shower and sink in your room, with just a communal toilet. Reservations are recommended in summer and on weekends, especially in the Puerta del Sol area and at the first few places *Let's Go* lists in each neighborhood; on summer weekends reservations are essential. A "*completo*" sign indicates that there are no vacancies. Owners are accustomed to opening doors, albeit groggily, at all hours, or providing keys for guests, but check before returning at 3am to a locked door. *Pensiones* are inexpensive, sometimes have curfews, and often host guests staying for longer periods of time. The tourist office in the airport has a full list of lodgings; also check out www.hosteleriademadrid.com.

CAMPING

Tourist offices have the *Guía Oficial de Campings*, which provides info on the 22 campsites surrounding Madrid, as well as in the Comunidad de Madrid. For further camping info, contact the Consejería de Educación (☎901 51 06 10).

Camping Alpha (☎916 95 80 69; www.campingalpha.com). Site 12.4km down Ctra. de Andalucía in Getafe. M: Legazpi. From the metro, walk down Vado Santa Catalina, cross the bridge, and bear right. Take the green bus #447, which stops across from the Museo de Jamón (10min., every 20-30min. 6am-10pm, €1.25). Ask for the Camp Alpha stop. Cross the footbridge and walk 1.5km back toward Madrid along the busy highway; follow the signs. Welcoming reception, paved roads, pool, tennis courts, showers, and laundry. Oct-June €5.44 per person; June-Sept. €6.80 per person. €7 per tent and per car. Bungalows for 1-2 €52/63; for 3-4 €79/94; for 5 €85-100. IVA not included. ❶

EL CENTRO: SOL, ÓPERA, AND PLAZA MAYOR

The following listings lie between the Sol and Ópera metro stops. For better deals in quieter spots, stray several blocks from Sol. Price and location in El Centro are ideal, especially if you are planning to brave its legendary nightlife. Buses #3, 25, 39, and 500 serve Ópera; buses #3, 5, 15, 20, 50, 51, 52, 53, and 150 serve Sol. Hotels here are largely indistinguishable, with the same pieces of furniture and pretty much the same rates, which are not the cheapest you'll find in Madrid, but the uniformity guarantees a good standard of cleanliness.

Hostel Miguel Ángel, Pl. Celenque, 1, 4th fl. (☎915 22 23 55; www.hostelmiguelangel.com), one block up off C. Arenal. M: Sol or Callao. The cleanest "backpacker hostel" around and the best deal in the *centro*. Immaculate rooms have clean, toy-like blue and yellow beds with bright curtains and comforters. Communal bathrooms are big and very clean. Sheets, safe, and breakfast included. Wi-Fi available. English spoken. Make reservations. Dorms €18-21; triple €70. ❶

Hostal Oriente, C. de Arenal, 23, 1st fl. (☎915 48 03 14). M: Ópera. Rooms have magnificently clean white tile, creamy peach walls and bedspreads. Glass enclosed balconies at this elegant *hostal* add breeze but unexciting view. 17 rooms have TV, phone, A/C, and bath. Reserve ahead. Singles €43; doubles €60; triples €82. MC/V. ❹

Hostal Paz, C. Flora, 4, 1st and 4th fl. (☎915 47 30 47). M: Ópera. Simple but well-lit rooms, and a wonderful couple who make you feel at home. Spotless rooms have satellite TV and A/C. Laundry €10. Singles €30; doubles €38, with shower €43; triples €60. Monthly rentals available, but reserve far in advance. MC/V. ❸

Hostal-Residencia Luz, C. de las Fuentes, 10, 3rd fl. (☎915 42 07 59; www.hostalluz.com). M: Ópera. Bathrooms are luxurious and modern, and rooms are decorated in an attractive white scheme. Faux-*azulejo* tiling in the hallways is a nice touch. Satellite TV, free Wi-Fi, and A/C. Laundry €5. Singles €38, with bath €45; doubles with bath €60. Discount for longer stays. MC/V. ❸

Hostal Real Valencia, Pl. del Oriente, 2, 3rd fl. (☎915 59 84 50; www.hostalvalencia.tk). M: Ópera. Narrow glass elevator lifts you to 7 elegant rooms with the splendor of deep carpets and upholstered satin. Huge bathrooms. Ask for a view over the Pl. del Oriente. Rooms have TV and fan. Reserve ahead—the one single is booked weeks in advance. Singles €42; doubles €75-95, with extra bed €100; master suite €115. MC/V. ❺

Hostal Esparteros, C. de Esparteros, 12, 4th fl. (☎915 21 09 03). M: Sol. Unbeatable location. Sparkling rooms with balconies or large windows are worth the 4-flight hike, as are the peace and quiet. Some rooms have private bath, TV, and fans. Laundry €9-10. Singles €25; doubles €35; triples €45. Discount for longer stays. Cash only. ❷

HUERTAS

Smaller and quieter than El Centro nearby, Huertas has top-notch hostels and budget accommodations within walking distance of all of the city's sights, live music and hundreds of bars, and some of the world's finest art. Sol-bound buses stop on C. del Príncipe, C. Núñez de Arce, and C. San Jerónimo; buses #10, 14, 27, 34, 37, and 45 run along Po. del Prado. Buses #6, 26, and 32 run up C. Atocha; get off at C. San Sebastián for Pl. Santa Ana. The closest metro stops are Sol, Sevilla, Antón Martín, and Tirso de Molina.

Cat's Hostel, C. Cañizares, 6 (☎913 69 28 07; www.catshostel.com). M: Antón Martín. This renovated 18th-century palace features clean dorms (2-16 beds), small doubles with private baths, a patio area with a fountain and cushions to lie back and stare up at the stained-glass skylight, bar, and cafe. Warm community, and cave-like bar in the basement. Breakfast, luggage storage, and internet access. Laundry €5 wash and dry. Reserve ahead, as it fills up quickly. Dorms €20; doubles with bath €44. MC/V. ❷

La Posada de Huertas, C. Huertas, 21 (☎914 29 55 26; www.posadadehuertas.com). M: Antón Martín or Sol. Rooms of 4 or 8 are well-kept, with comfortable beds. Spotless bathrooms. Kitchen, Wi-Fi, and breakfast. €5 wash and dry. Check out 10:30am, luggage storage available. Beds from €18; singles €50; doubles €70. MC/V. ❶

Pension Magdalena, C. Magdalena, 26 (☎ 913 69 36 38). M: Antón Martín. The ordered clutter of the central room gives a homey feel to the small, warmly colored rooms. Shared baths are well-maintained. Some doubles have huge beds and balconies. Ask about discounts for longer stays. Singles €25; doubles €35. Cash only. ❷

Mad Hostel, C. Cabeza, 24 (☎915 06 48 40; www.madhostel.com) M: Tirso de Molina. The owners of Cat's Hostel bring the same high-tech flair and relaxed atmosphere to this brand-new hostel, which features sparkling dorms (2-6 beds), a bar area with pool table, free Wi-Fi, gym, kitchen, and a sweet rooftop terrace. Breakfast, sheets, and safe included. Laundry €5 wash and dry. Reserve ahead. Dorms €20-22. MC/V. ❷

Hostal Villar, C. del Príncipe, 18 (☎915 31 66 00; www.villar.es). M: Sol or Sevilla. Winding staircases and long corridors lead to quiet rooms with full baths. Beds are comfortable, even with thin sheets. Small, bright common rooms with couches dot the floors. Singles €28, with bath €36; doubles €36/50; triples €50/66. MC/V. ❷

Hostal Plaza D'Ort, Pl. del Angel, 13 (☎914 29 90 41; www.plazadort.com). M: Antón Martín. Friendly staff and immaculate rooms with bright blankets, TV, A/C, phone, and safe. Conveniently located outside the Pl. Santa Ana, so it fills up quickly. Internet access and in-room movies €11. The quality is well worth the price. Singles €42-45, depending on bathroom; doubles €52-59; triples €75-85; suite €110. MC/V. ❹

GRAN VÍA

Hostal Santillan, Gran Vía, 64, 8th fl. (☎915 48 23 28; www.hostalsantillan.com). M: Pl. de España. Take the glass elevator to the top of this gorgeous building. Leaf-patterned curtains and wooden furniture give rooms a homey feel. All have shower, sink, TV, and fan. A little more can you get you a bath and much bigger room (by half); explore the options. Singles €30-35; doubles €55; triples €72. MC/V. ❸

Hostal Gran Vía 44, Gran Vía, 44, 8th fl. (☎915 21 00 51; www.hostalgranvia44.com). M: Callao. Cheerful rooms with high ceilings and bright, colorful bedspreads. Southward views over the city's red roofs. Private bath, TV, fan, and balcony. Lounge area and free Wi-Fi. Breakfast included. Singles €40; doubles €50; triples from €60. MC/V. ❹

Hostal Concepción Arenal, C. Concepción Arenal, 6, 3rd fl. (☎915 22 68 83). M: Callao. Breezy and just far enough from Gran Vía to be tranquil, with brown decor. Quiet rooms have short but soft beds and well-scrubbed showers. Rooms come with shower and TV. Singles €25-28, with toilet €33; doubles €35/45; triples €55. Cash only. ❷

Hostal A. Nebrija, Gran Vía, 67, 8th fl., elevator A (☎915 47 73 19). M: Pl. de España. Knick-knacks and religious paintings in the lobby lead to spacious, unadorned rooms with spectacular views of the Palacio Real, cathedral, and gardens west. Rooms come with TV, fan, and shared bath. No smoking. Singles €36, with bath €40; doubles €42/46; triples €60/64. AmEx/MC/V. ❸

MALASAÑA AND CHUECA

Hostales and *pensiones* in Malasaña and Chueca are usually located on the upper floors of older buildings, so be prepared to climb. Accommodations can be a bit pricier here than other areas, but they are usually well-equipped and well-maintained. Buses #3, 40, and 149 run along C. de Fuencarral and C. Hortaleza. Metro stops Chueca, Gran Vía, and Tribunal serve the neighborhoods.

Hostal Don Juan, Pl. Vasquez de Mella, 1, 2nd fl. (☎915 22 31 01). M: Chueca. Luxury fit for the romancing namesake himself. Chinese vases, wall tapestries, and old wooden chests fill the lobby, adjacent to an Art Deco common room with sofas and chandeliers. Rooms come with beautiful wooden flooring and hand-carved furniture, A/C, TV, and gleaming bath. Singles €38; doubles €53; triples €70. MC/V. ❹

Hostal R. Arantza, C. San Bartolomé, 7. 1st floor. M: Chueca. Dark wooden doors and dark brown leather everywhere give the feeling of a classy old professor's study. Airy rooms with pink sheets and newly-tiled balconies with plants. Communal and private showers all very clean. Singles €35, with shower €40; doubles €40/45. Cash only. ❸

Casa Chueca, C. de San Bartolomé 4, 2nd fl. (☎915 23 81 27; www.casachueca.com). M: Chueca. Marine blue walls with polka dots impart a cool vibe. Bathrooms are small, but clean and modern. Rooms have A/C, free internet, and satellite TV. "Mini-breakfast" included. Reservations required. Singles €40; doubles €55; triples €70. MC/V. ❹

Hostal Condestable, C. Puebla, 15, 2nd fl. (☎915 31 62 02; www.hostalcondestable.com). M: Callao. Rich, fully-carpeted lobby fronts rooms with tall ceilings, comfy beds, and nifty wardrobes built into the walls. Very tranquil. Communal baths are clean and bright. Rooms with TV and A/C. Singles €30; doubles €40; triples €50. ❸

ARGÜELLES AND MONCLOA

Accommodations are few here, and quite a hike from the sights in the *centro*. These neighborhoods are excellent for those looking for a little peace, but anyone who wants noise and nightlife will feel left out of the action.

Albergue Juvenil Santa Cruz de Marcenado (HI), C. de Santa Cruz de Marcenado, 28 (☎915 47 45 32; fax 48 11 96). M: Argüelles. From the metro, walk 1 block down C. de Alberto Aguilera away from C. de la Princesa, turn right onto C. de Serrano Jóver, then left onto C. de Santa Cruz de Marcenado. The 72 beds fill quickly, even in winter. Single-sex floor. Breakfast and sheets included. Laundry €2. Max. 6-day. stay. Quiet hours after midnight. Reception daily 9am-10pm. 1:30am curfew. Reserve in advance. Closed Christmas and New Year's Eve. For Spaniards, dorms €8.50, 26 and over €12.84. Flat rate for foreigners €21. €3.50 extra per night without HI card. Cash only. ❶

FOOD

Madrid prides itself on simple fare: bread, cheese, and every fathomable part of pig and cow—from tail to brains—that can be had on a plate. But even the most devoted meat eater will need a break, and the city provides plenty of seafood and vegetarian restaurants. Trawling from bar to bar savoring tapas is an alternative to a full sit-down meal and a fun way to sample local food. Most tapas bars (*tascas* or *tabernas*) are open noon-4pm and 8pm-midnight or later. Some double as restaurants, and many are clustered around **Plaza Santa Ana** and **Plaza Mayor.** Madrid's cafes offer ambience as well as caffeine, giving contemplative coffee drinkers a shot of historical ambience with their *café con leche.* For those on a shoestring budget, the absolute cheapest choices are *bocadillos de jamón* (ham sandwiches) or *kebaps* from Turkish or Middle Eastern joints. Wherever you eat, you won't be bothered with the check until you ask.

FOOD BY TYPE

A Argüelles and Moncloa **B** Bilbao **C** El Centro: Ópera, Sol, and Plaza Mayor **GV** Gran Vía **H** Huertas **L** Lavapiés and La Latina **M** Malasaña and Chueca

CAFES

BAires Café (p. 100)	M	❷
Café Comercial (p. 101)	B	❶
Café-Botillería Manuela (p. 100)	M	❶
El Imperfecto (p. 98)	H	❶
Eucalipto (p. 97)	L	❶

ITALIAN

Osteria Il Regno de Napoli (p. 101)	B	❸
Il Pizzaiolo (p. 99)	M	❷
Pizzeria Vesuvio (p. 100)	M	❷

LATIN AMERICAN

El Inca (p. 99)	M	❹

NORTH AFRICAN/MIDDLE EASTERN

Al-Jaima, Cocina del Desierto (p. 99)	M	❸
Olokun (p. 101)	B	❷
Inshala (p. 96)	C	❸
La Granja de Said (p. 99)	M	❷
Restaurante El Basha (p. 98)	H	❷

SPANISH

Arrocería Gala (p. 97)	H	❸
Cervecería Alemana (p. 98)	C	❷
El Jamonal (p. 99)	GV	❷
El Mejillón de Madrid (p. 96)	C	❷
Gula Gula (p. 99)	GV	❹
La Finca de Susana (p. 97)	H	❷
Maoz (p. 100)	M	❶
Pimiento Verde (p. 100)	A	❷
Sobrino del Botín (p. 96)	C	❹
Taberna Maceira (p. 98)	H	❸

SWEETS

Heladería Giuseppe Ricci (p. 98)	H	❶
Horno La Santiagüesa (p. 96)	C	❶
La Mallorquina (p. 96)	C	❶
Maestro Churrero (p. 122)	C	❶

TAPAS

Almendro 13 (p. 97)	L	❷
Casa Alberto (p. 98)	H	❷
Casa Amadeo (p. 97)	L	❷
El Tigre (p. 100)	M	❶
La Toscana (p. 98)	H	❷
Restaurante Casa Granada (p. 98)	H	❷
La Trucha (p. 98)	H	❸

VEGETARIAN

Al Natural (p. 97)	H	❷
Cáscaras (p. 100)	A	❷
El Estragón Vegetariano (p. 97)	L	❸
El Granero de Lavapiés (p. 97)	L	❷
La Bio Tika (p. 98)	H	❷

OTHER

Isolée (p. 100)	M	❷
The Modern Dining Room (p. 99)	GV	❸
Root (p. 99)	GV	❷

FOOD SHOPPING

In general, the bigger the market and the farther from the city center, the cheaper the groceries. Specialty items may require a visit to a pricey store, but *supermercados* are generally the best bet. Also look for shops labeled *"alimentaciones"* or *"frutos secos,"* small convenience stores that generally have low prices.

Groceries: Champion and **Día%** are the cheapest city-wide supermarket chains, though they are mostly far from the city center. There is, however, a **Día%,** C. Toledo, 32 (☎914

65 55 22), in La Latina at the corner of C. Toledo and C. de la Colegiata. M: La Latina. Open M-Sa 9:30am-9:30pm, Su 10am-6pm. MC/V.

Markets: Mercado de San Miguel, a covered market on Pl. de San Miguel, off the northwest corner of Pl. Mayor, sells the finest seafood and produce in the city, albeit at high prices. Open M-F 9am-2pm and 4:30-8pm, Sa 9am-2pm.

Pastry Shops: These are everywhere. **La Mallorquina,** C. Mayor, 2 (☎915 21 12 01) is the most famous in all Madrid, and their desserts live up to their reputation (€.90-1.90 each, or €14-22 per kg). Open daily Sept.-July 9am-9:15pm. The sublime **Horno La Santiagüesa,** C. Mayor, 73 (☎915 59 62 14) sells everything from *roscones de reyes* (sweet bread for the Feast of the Epiphany) to *empanadas* (€18-23 per kg) and pastries doused in chocolate. Try the *tarta de Santiago* (almond bread). Open daily 8am-9pm.

Red-Eye Establishments: *Guía del Ocio* lists late-night eateries under *"La última hora"*. Street vendors, some disguised as normal citizens, may catch you unawares offering beer and sandwiches at ungodly hours. You may see these sandwich-sellers fleeing into the darkness at the first hint of police presence. *Cervecerías* and *kebap* restaurants that stay open until 2am aren't hard to find, but nothing's open much past 3.

EL CENTRO: SOL ÓPERA, AND PLAZA MAYOR

Tourists flood the *centro*, fostering a neighborhood packed with overpriced places serving mediocre fare. Wandering into the streets just south of Sol and the *centro*, though, leads to some cheap food with character.

RESTAURANTS

MADRID

El Mejillón de Madrid, Pasaje de Matheu, 4, just off Espoz y Mina. No-frills seafood under umbrellas right on Madrid's shellfish row. Try the heaping plate of mussels (€8), the restaurant's namesake, or the plate of *paella* (€25) for two or more. Four orders of *raciones* (€4-8) bring a free jug of sangria for up to 4 people—a sweet deal. Open M-Th, Su 11:30am-12:30am, F-Sa 11:30am-1:30am. Cash only. ❷

Sobrino del Botín, C. Cuchilleros, 17 (☎913 66 42 17; www.botin.es), off Pl. Mayor. Advertising itself as the oldest restaurant in the world, Sobrino del Botín has seen its share of the famous since it opened in 1725. Goya washed dishes here when he was 19, and Hemingway ate here when he was in town. Ancient wooden doors and patterned red walls with gold filigree lend the class only age can. Dishes €8-20. Suckling pig €38.10. Open daily 1-4pm and 8pm-midnight. AmEx/MC/V. ❹

Inshala, C. de la Amnistía, 10 (☎915 48 26 32). M: Ópera. Perfect for a fancy date, but cheap enough for a backpacker's meal. Moroccan decor, but decidedly eclectic international fare, ranging from Japanese to Argentine. Weekday lunch *menú* €9. Dinner €12-20. Reservations strongly recommended. Open in summer M-Th noon-5pm and 8pm-1am, F-Sa noon-5pm and 8pm-2am; in winter M-Sa noon-2am. MC/V. ❸

TAPAS BARS AND CAFES

Maestro Churrero, Pl. de Jacinto Benavente, 3 (☎913 69 24 06; www.maestrochurrero.com). M: Sol. This cafe has been serving pastries since 1902, and it's a must-stop for churros and chocolate (€2.20 at the bar, €3.60 sitting down)—definitely tastier than your hostel's toast. Breakfast rolls €1.50-2. Open daily 7:30am-11:30pm. MC/V. ❶

LA LATINA AND LAVAPIÉS

From the *centro*, a few narrow, mazy streets, chief among them **Calle Almendro** and **La Cava Baja,** wind down toward Lavapiés and La Latina, which are quieter, more local, and brimming with exciting new restaurants, tapas bars, and terraces. It's easy to wander from *taberna* to *bodega* and back for hours on end and then down into Lavapiés, which has cheap Chinese and Indian food. Not the place to come for a sit-down meal, but tapas and wine aplenty.

RESTAURANTS

El Estragón Vegetariano, Pl. de la Paja, 10 (☎913 65 89 82; www.guiadelocio.com/estragonvegetariano). M: La Latina. This unobtrusive restaurant, with its quiet decor and patio feel, would blush at any superlatives we might give it, but its vegetarian delights could convince even the most die-hard carnivores to switch teams. *Menús* M-F €10, Sa-Su and evenings €25. Open daily 1:30-4pm and 8pm-midnight. AmEx/MC/V. ❸

El Granero de Lavapiés, C. Argumosa, 10 (☎914 67 76 11). M: Lavapiés. For 18 years, rotating art exhibits and inventive specials have kept this hideaway packed with locals. Free-trade, organic food at low, low prices. F night is the *tiramisu* special (€4). *Menú* €10. Dinner €5.80-6.90. Open daily 1-4pm and 8:30-11pm. MC/V. ❷

TAPAS BARS AND CAFES

Almendro 13, C. Almendro, 13 (☎913 65 42 52). M: La Latina. Locals dive into plates of *huevos rotos* (eggs and ham over fried potatoes; €8.40) and the tomato salad (€5) on top of barrels crammed in tightly—add your voice to the orderly clamor for a cheap *caña* (€1.40). Open M-F 1-4pm and 7:30pm-12:30am, Sa-Su 1-5pm and 8pm-1am. ❷

Eucalipto, C. Argumosa, 4 (☎629 33 49 98), south of Huertas. M: Lavapiés. Take a break from normal coffee fare for refreshing *zumos tropicales* (fresh juice; €2.60-3.50). The *batidos* (€3-3.50) are delicious. Spike up the night with a daiquiri (€6), or enjoy a huge fruit salad (€7). Lively sidewalk seating. Open daily 5pm-2am. ❶

Casa Amadeo, Pl. de Cascorro, 18 (☎913 65 94 39). M: La Latina. The owner of 68 years supervises the preparation of specialty *caracoles* (snails; €4.50). Good stop after a day at El Rastro. *Raciones* €4-11. Open M-Th 11am-4pm, F-Su 10:30am-8pm. ❷

HUERTAS

Huertas is, without a doubt, the best place to eat in the center of the city. The area is chock-full of seafood, salad, and vegetarian spots, a much-needed break from the heavy tapas fare that Madrid cherishes. Popular with locals, **Plaza de Santa Ana** is perfect for passing time with a drink and some good food. Quality is generally high, and if you head into the less-crowded streets, prices are low. As the evening grows and the wine flows, the streets and squares of Huertas become the first stop for a night out in Madrid.

RESTAURANTS

Arrocería Gala, C. de Moratín, 22 (☎914 29 25 62; www.paellas-gala.com). M: Antón Martín. Pastoral Spanish scenes of bulls on hillsides are gracefully overlaid in vine and shadows from the gorgeous chandeliers. The specialty *paellas* (€10 per person) are second to none. Quality sangria €10 per pitcher. Reserve ahead on weekends. Open Tu-Su 1-5pm and 9pm-1:30am. Cash only. ❸

La Finca de Susana, C. Arlaban, 4 (☎913 69 35 57, www.lafinca-restaurant.com). M: Sevilla. Simple, elegant dining at shockingly low prices. The beef and arugula sushi (€7.80) is one of countless top-notch plates. Arrive early to avoid the ever-present line down the street. Open daily 1-3:45pm and 8:30-11:45pm. AmEx/MC/V. ❸

Al Natural, C. de Zorrilla, 11 (☎913 69 47 09; www.alnatural.biz). M: Sevilla. Dark ochre walls set a tranquil mood here, where fresh salads (€8) and light Mediterranean dishes (€9-12) rule the menu. An ideal break from crowded salty ham stand-up joints. Open M-Sa 1-4pm and 9pm-midnight, Su 1-4pm. AmEx/MC/V. ❷

Restaurante El Basha, Plaza Matute, 7 (☎914 29 96 10). M: Antón Martín. A fountain centering the upstairs dining is one of many exotic touches to this youthful Middle Eastern joint. The *baba ghanoush* (€5) perfectly complements their flavored teas (€2.50). Top it off in the basement with hookah (€8) on camel-hide stools along with the rest of Madrid's young bohemians. Open daily 1:30pm-1:30am. ❶

Taberna Maceira, C. de Jesús, 7 (☎914 29 15 84), also C. Huertas, 66 (☎914 29 58 18). M: Antón Martín. Yellow-green walls and grog barrels make this funky seafood place feel like a psychedelic pirate ship. Try the *mejillones Maceira* (mussels in cream sauce; €5) or the towering plate of baked clams (€12). Open M 8pm-12:45am, Tu-F 1-4:15pm and 8:30pm-12:45am, Sa-Su 1-4:45pm and 8:30pm-1:30am. Cash only. ❸

Heladeria Giuseppe Ricci (Gelato & Cafe), C. de las Huertas, 9 (☎914 29 33 45; www.heladeriaricci.com). M: Antón Martín. Forget tapas and *jamón;* this gelato is the best relief from a hot Madrid summer's day. Most patrons request 2 flavors, which still counts as 1 scoop. Small cones €2, large €3. Rich *batidos* (milkshakes) €3. Open M-Th and Su 10am-10pm, F-Sa 10am-10:30pm. ❶

La Bio Tika, C. Amor de Dios, 3 (☎914 29 07 80). M: Antón Martín. An unobtrusive vegetarian/macrobiotic restaurant serving up a *menú* of wholesome food (healthy dessert included) in a simple setting, with a shop for all your macrobiotic grocery needs. *Menú* €9.50 for lunch, €11.50 for dinner. Open daily 1-4:30pm and 8-11:30pm. MC/V. ❷

TAPAS BARS AND CAFES

Casa Alberto, C. de las Huertas, 18 (☎914 29 93 56; www.casaalberto.es). M: Antón Martín. The manual-wash bar and shanks hanging from the walls are throwbacks to the early days of this bar, founded in 1827. It's the place to be, so getting a table during bustling meal hours can be difficult. Sweet vermouth (€1.45) is served with original house tapas. Try the delicious *gambas al ajillo* (shrimp with garlic) or the *patatas ali-oli* (garlic potatoes; €4.50). Open Tu-Sa noon-5:30pm and 8pm-1:30am. MC/V. ❷

Restaurante Casa Granada, C. Doctor Cortezo, 17, 6th fl. (☎914 20 08 25). The unmarked door on the left side of C. Doctor Cortezo as you head downhill is easy to miss, but the experience of the rooftop tapas terrace at the top is hard to forget. Come around 8pm and stay for the sunset, but don't forget to put your name on the outdoor seating list when you arrive. *Cañas* of beer (€2.20) come with tapas. *Raciones* €6.50-8. Open M-Sa noon-midnight, Su noon-9pm. MC/V. ❷

Cervecería Alemana, Pl. de Santa Ana, 6 (☎914 29 70 33). M: Antón Martín. Food orders come out of the kitchen as fast as they go in, but the locals here linger over drinks from the massive bar selection for a lot longer. Spanish cider (€2.25) goes well with the exquisite *chorizo* (sausage; €9). *Bocadillos* €4-7. Open M, W-Th, Su 11am-12:30am, F-Sa 11am-2am. MC/V. ❷

El Imperfecto, Plaza Matute, 2 (☎913 66 72 11). M: Antón Martín. The potpourri of sombreros, birdcages, suspended globes, and sequined shawls work together in a surprisingly hip way in this diminutive bar, which offers up alcoholic coffees (€4) and flavored tea infusions (€2.50). Open M-Th and Su 3pm-2am, F-Sa 3pm-2:30am. Cash only. ❶

La Trucha, C. Manuel Fernández González, 3 (☎914 29 58 33). M: Sol. Also at C. Núñez de Arce, 6 (☎915 32 08 90), without terrace. Local seasonal fruits (€5) like summer strawberries are a good bet. Grab the *rabo de toro* (bull's tail with potatoes; €11.80). Entrees €12-15. Open daily 12:30-4pm and 7:30pm-midnight. AmEx/MC/V. ❸

La Toscana, C. Manuel Fernández González, 10-12 (☎914 29 60 31). M: Sol or Sevilla. A local crowd hangs out over tapas of *morcillo asado* (€11.50). The more intrepid should try the *sezos rebozados* (fried brains; €5.50). Antique lettering and wrought-iron decor lend a medieval feel. Open M-Sa 1-4pm and 8pm-midnight. ❷

GRAN VÍA

Good food is hard to find when American burger joints, overpriced tourist diners, and cumbling cinemas occupy every foot of real estate. Fear not—there are still some culinary diamonds in the rough, especially in the side streets just off of the colossus itself. Small markets with fresh fruit and cheap food can be found in Chueca, a couple streets north of Gran Vía.

Root, C. Virgen de los Peligros, 1 (☎912 75 81 18). M: Gran Vía. Mellow environment, sophisticated white leather mixes with soft light diffused through lots of glass walls. A professional crowd comes in for the lunch *menú* (M-F 1-3pm, €12.50) and the desserts. "Death by Chocolate" €4.50. Open M-Th and Su 1:30-4:30pm and 8:30-11:30pm, F-Sa 1:30-4:30pm and 8:30pm-1am. MC/V. ❸

El Jamonal, Mesonero Romanos, 7 (☎915 31 51 04). M: Gran Vía or Callao. Skip the metal bar that runs the perimeter of the cramped, littered interior and sit in the peaceful, tree-shaded area outside, miles away from the grime of Gran Vía. *Menú* €9.60 in the terrace, €8.60 inside. Open M-Th and Su 7am-1am, F-Sa 7am-1:30am. Cash only. ❷

The Modern Dining Room, C. Clavel, 6 (☎915 23 92 75). M: Gran Vía. The dark ceiling and floral prints give a touch of secluded romance to the small, candlelit tables. *Menú* contains small but fancy dishes like *brochette* meats (€9). Open M-Th and Sun 1-5pm and 9pm-midnight, Fr-Sa 1-5pm, 9pm-12:30am. MC/V. ❸

Gula Gula, Gran Vía, 1 (☎915 22 87 64; www.gulagula.net). M: Gran Vía. Nondescript buffet restaurant by day, outrageous drag show by night. Good variety of salad and vegetable dishes. Cold lunch buffet €6, hot €9. Dinner €23. Performances M-Th and Su 10pm, F-Sa 10:30pm and midnight. Reserve 1 week ahead for weekend dinner. Open daily 1-5pm and 9pm-last customer. AmEx/MC/V. ❷

MALASAÑA AND CHUECA

Exceptional vegetarian, Middle Eastern, Italian, and fusion cuisine dominate the scene in Chueca and Malasaña. Both neighborhoods offer high quality and low prices and a glorious reprieve from the salty tapas that rule the rest of the city. Don't worry about choice; you'll find something funky and worthwhile down any street. For seriously fresh fruit, try **Frutas Eloy,** C. Barbieri, 26. Right off the metro in Plaza de Chueca, this fruit stand makes you feel healthier just by walking in. (☎917 01 01 91. Open M-F 9am-9pm, Sa-Su 9am-3pm. Cash.)

RESTAURANTS

La Granja de Said, C. de San Andrés, 11 (☎915 32 87 93). M: Tribunal or Bilbao. Moorish designs in the doorways, beautiful tiling, and the dim glow of light through lamps and tapestries brings the Middle East to Chueca. Dine well, then puff peacefully on hookah (€8). *Tabouleh* salad €6. Falafel plate €7. Open daily 1pm-2am. MC/V. ❷

Il Pizzaiolo, C. de Hortaleza, 84 (☎913 19 29 64). M: Chueca. Authentic thin-crust Italian pizzas made with fresh ingredients. Friendly staff and bright, casual atmosphere. Pizzas €7.50-10. Tiramisu €4.50. Open daily noon-4pm and 8:30pm-12:30am. MC/V. ❷

Al-Jaima, Cocina del Desierto, C. de Barbieri, 3 (☎915 23 11 42). M: Gran Vía or Chueca. Ambience is a serious business here—waiters in Moroccan *djellabas* scurry through the heavily incensed air, bringing tea and Maghrebi dishes to patrons on the floormats. Try the *pollo con higos y miel* (chicken with figs and honey, €6.90). Most dishes €12-18. Open daily 1:30-4pm and 9pm-midnight. Reserve ahead. MC/V. ❸

El Inca, C. Gravina, 21 (☎915 32 77 45). M: Chueca. Colonial paintings, small tables, and soft music greet guests into this intimate Peruvian restaurant, which serves up massive seafood dishes aloing with other far-off favorites. Try the *solterito arequipeño* (vegetable and cheese dish; €10) or the *yucas fritas* (fried potatoes; €6.50). Open daily 1:30-4pm and 8:30pm-midnight. MC/V. ❹

Maoz, C. Hortaleza, 5. M: Gran Vía. One of several locations in the city, another at C. Mayor, 4. Minimalist decor matches the stripped-down menu, which offers falafel sandwiches (€3.90) and salad (also €3.90). Huge portions are a good break from salty ham, and service is quick. Open daily noon-2am. Cash only. ❶

Pizzeria Vesuvio, C. de Infantas, 32 (☎915 21 65 06). M: Gran Vía. Fresh pizza in 27 varieties. Artfully exposed brick around the kitchen gives it the good ol' brick-oven feel. At lunch, counters are packed with a rowdy crowd. Pizzas €5-8. Extra ingredients €0.90 each. Open M-Th 1-3pm and 8pm-midnight, F-Sa 1-4pm and 8pm-1am. Cash only. ❷

Isolée, C. de las Infantas, 19 (☎915 22 81 38; www.isolee.com). White leather sets the hipster mood at this restaurant with 25+ varieties of bottled water. Don't miss the black and gold Moët and Chandon champagne lounge, or the store selling handbags, space helmets, and pretentious home decor for all of one's lifestyle needs. *Menú* €9.50. Free Wi-Fi. Takeout available. Open M-Sa 10:30am-11pm, Su 3:30-10:30pm. MC/V. ❷

TAPAS BARS AND CAFES

Café-Botillería Manuela, C. de San Vicente Ferrer, 29 (☎915 31 70 37; www.manuelacafe.com). M: Tribunal. Old World Parisian café with a golden touch—a player piano stacked high with everyone's favorite board games. Enjoy conversation over a *caña* (€2.50). Tapas €3-8. Mixed drinks €6. Live music last Sa of every month, 9:30pm. Open June-Aug. M-Th 6pm-2am, F-Su 4pm-3am; Sept.-May daily 4pm-2am. ❶

BAires Café, C. Gravina, 4 (☎915 32 98 79), corner of Pelayo. M: Chueca. Lurid paintings of glamorous women smoking cover the walls. Laid-back joint with soft music piping in; sit down and take a load off with your *caña* (€2) or wine (€2-2.50). Red Bull *"bebida energética"* €3. Open M-W and Su 3pm-1am, Th-Sa 3pm-2:30am. ❶

El Tigre, C. Infantas, 30 (☎915 32 00 72), is Chueca's most happening *cañas* spot. The marvelous, salty tapas—included with your drink—get tastier with each sip. Beer €1.80. *Raciones* €4-7. Open M-F 12:30pm-1:30am and Sa-Su 1pm-2am. Cash only. ❶

ARGÜELLES AND MONCLOA

Argüelles and Moncloa, in the heart of a modest Madrid residential area outside of the touristy center, brim with inexpensive markets and picnicking spots. If you're still in need of crowds and coffee, hit up the chic terrazas on Po. del Pintor Rosales overlooking the park.

Cáscaras, C. Ventura Rodríguez, 7 (☎915 42 83 36; www.restaurantescascaras.com). M: Ventura Rodríguez. A sprawling restaurant with panoramic city shots and shelves crammed with all manner of books to match the intellectual table talk. Well-dressed 30-somethings fill up on *pinchos* and specialty vegetarian dishes (€8-9). Open M-F 6am-1am, Sa-Su 10am-2pm. AmEx/MC/V. ❷

Pimiento Verde, C. Quintana, 1 (☎915 41 21 40), on the corner of Princesita just north of Ventura Rodríguez. The tall ceiling and wooden tables hold a little Basque soul and a lot of Basque cooking. The flowers and farm implements on the wall give a rustic feeling, but the prices are urban enough. For starters, try the green Guernika peppers (€8.20). Cider €7.80. Seafood plates €20. Open daily 1:30-5pm and 9pm-midnight. MC/V. ❹

BILBAO

Although discotecas and cheap drinks are easy to find, the student-filled streets and plazas usually empty out after a few cocktails, when the crowd heads to nearby Malasaña or Chueca. C. Hartzenbusch, C. Cisneros, C. de Fuencarral, and C. de Luchana all offer cheap tapas and beers.

RESTAURANTS

Olokun, C. Fuencarral, 5 (☎914 45 69 16). From Gl. de Bilbao, walk south on Fuencarral. Beach scenes, tropical cocktails, and delicacies like *tostones* (fried plantains; €6) served on wooden barrels bring Cuba to Malasaña. The wall is covered with the names of patrons, phone numbers, and indelicate suggestions—add some of your own. Mixed drinks €5-7. *Menú* €9. Salsa Th 5:30pm. Open M-Th and Su noon-4pm and 8:30pm-midnight, Fri-Sa noon-4pm and 8pm-2am. MC/V. ❷

Osteria Il Regno de Napoli, C. San Andrés, 21 (☎914 45 63 00). From Gl. de Bilbao, head 1 block down C. Carranza; turn left onto C. San Andrés. Exquisite Neapolitan food arrives quickly. A quiet place to eat a calm lunch. The bruschetta (€4) is unbeatable. Lunch *menú* €10. Dinner entrees €9-15. Reservations advisable on weekends. Open M-F 2-4pm and 9pm-midnight, Sa 9pm-midnight, Su 2-4pm. AmEx/MC/V. ❸

TAPAS BARS AND CAFES

Café Comercial, Glorieta de Bilbao, 7 (☎915 21 56 55). M: Bilbao. The marble and high mirrors of Madrid's oldest cafe have reflected the city's artists, politicians, journalists, and bullfighters since 1887, but they don't discriminate. Huge, well-lit, and open late. Coffee at the bar €1.20, at a table €1.90. Internet access 50min. for €1. Open M-Th 7:30am-1am, F 7:30am-2am, Sa 8:30am-2am, Su 10am-1am. ❶

SIGHTS

While Madrid is small enough to walk in a day, its sights are enough to keep you for weeks. Two dynasties, a dictatorship, and a cultural rebirth have bequeathed the city a wealth of parks, palaces, plazas, cathedrals, and art museums. Soak it all in, strolling from Sol to Cibeles and Pl. Mayor to the Palacio Real.

For hard-core visitors with a checklist of destinations, the municipal tourist office's **Plano de Transportes,** also called *Visiting the Downtown on Public Transport*, is indispensable for mapping monuments and public transport. In this chapter, sights are arranged by neighborhood. If you are trying to design a walking tour of the entire city, it is best to begin in El Centro, the nucleus of Madrid. A good few days of sightseeing might move from historic Madrid, to the cafes of Huertas, to the celebrated *paseos*, to a stroll through El Retiro (see **The Paseos: A Walking Tour,** p. 104). El Pardo is best visited as a daytrip.

EL CENTRO

The sunlit buildings in El Centro radiate from the **Puerta del Sol** (Gate of the Sun), ultimately dividing into two sections named after the families that financed their famous monuments: **Habsburg Madrid** *(Madrid de los Austrias)*, full of old plazas, convents, and churches, and **Bourbon Madrid** *(Madrid de los Borbones)*, with its immense palace and sculpted gardens. The directions for most of the sights in Habsburg Madrid are given from Puerta del Sol, and directions for sights in Bourbon Madrid originate in Ópera.

PUERTA DEL SOL

Named for the Puerta del Sol (Gate of the Sun) that stood here in the 1500s, Puerta del Sol bustles day and night with taxis, performers, hawkers selling "designer" watches and sunglasses, and countless locals-in-transit trying to evade the luggage-laden tourists. A web of pedestrian-only streets originating at **Gran Vía** funnels a rush of consumers into Sol, where today the sun shines over department stores, restaurants, a throng of pedestrians, and the ever-present crowd snapping photos with **El oso y el madroño,** a bronze statue of the

MADRID

bear and strawberry tree from the city's heraldic coat of arms. The *"kilométro cero"* (kilometer 0) sign on the pavement is the beginning of the national road system and marks the symbolic center of Spain. On New Year's Eve, citizens meet here to gobble one grape per clock chime at midnight, ensuring good luck in each month of the coming year.

HABSBURG MADRID

El Centro, the city's central neighborhood, is most densely packed with monuments and tourists. In the 16th century, the Austrian dynasty of the Habsburgs funded the construction of **Plaza Mayor** and the **Catedral de San Isidro.** After moving the seat of Castilla from Toledo to Madrid (then only a town of 20,000) in 1561, Felipe II and his descendants commissioned the court architects (including Juan de Herrera, the master behind El Escorial) to update many of Madrid's buildings, creating a distinctive set of churches and palaces with wide central patios and scrawny black towers—the "Madrid style." Another Juan, Juan de Villanueva, added his architectural mark to the mix under Carlos III, designing the palace which houses the permanent collection of the Prado.

PLAZA MAYOR. In 1620, the Pl. Mayor was completed for Felipe III; his statue, installed in 1847, graces the plaza's center. He commissioned Juan de Herrera, the same architect who built the stolid El Escorial, to redesign the cluttered, dirty area around the old Plaza del Arrabal. Its elegant arcades, spindly towers, and pleasant verandas are defining elements of the aforementioned "Madrid style." In the 17th century, nobles on horseback spent Sunday afternoons chasing bulls in the plaza; citizens joined the fun on foot. The tradition came to be known as a *corrida*, from the verb *correr* (to run). As the site of Inquisition's grand *auto-da-fé* (trials, or "acts of faith") and public executions, Pl. Mayor saw bloodbaths of a different kind. In the evening, Pl. Mayor awakens as *madrileños* resurface, tourists multiply, and cafe tables fill with lively patrons. Live performances of flamenco and music are a common treat. During the annual **Fiesta de San Isidro** (p. 117), held the Friday before May 15 through the following Sunday, the plaza explodes with celebration and dancing in traditional dress. *(From Pta. del Sol, walk down C. Mayor 5-10 min. M: Sol.)*

CATEDRAL DE SAN ISIDRO. Though Isidro, patron saint of crops, farmers, and Madrid, was humble, his final resting place is anything but. The church was designed in the Jesuit Baroque style in the 17th century, before San Isidro's remains were disinterred and brought here in 1769 at Carlos II's command. The cathedral, restored after workers razed it to the ground during the Civil War, reigned as Madrid's cathedral from the late 19th century until the **Catedral de la Almudena** (p. 106) was consecrated in 1993. The church's nine gilded chapels are the main draw—the chapel dedicated to San Isidro, third on the right, is made of marble with gold leaf inlay, and has a cupola dwarfed by the grand one in the center. *(From Pta. del Sol, take C. Mayor to Pl. Mayor, cross the plaza, and exit onto C. de Toledo. Cathedral is at the intersection of C. Toledo and C. de la Colegiata. M: Latina. Open daily in summer 7:30am-1:30pm and 5:30-9pm; in winter 7:30am-1pm and 5:30-8:30pm. Free.)*

CONVENTO DE LAS DESCALZAS REALES. In 1559 Juana of Austria, Felipe II's sister, converted the former royal palace into a convent; today it is home to Franciscan nuns who watch over Juana's tomb. Claudio Coello's magnificent 17th-century frescoes line the staircase. The **Salón de Tapices** contains 11 renowned tapestries along with Santa Úrsula's jewel-encrusted bones. The highlights of the tour are in the final rooms, which include a portrait of Carlos II (the final, most terribly inbred Habsburg monarch), an allegorical Flemish painting of demons assaulting society, a dark portrait of San Francisco by Zurbarán, and Titian's *Tributo de la Moneda al César.* Lines are long in the summer; arrive early to buy tickets, and enjoy the mandatory 1hr. tour in Spanish. *(Pl. de las Descalzas, between Pl. de Callao and Pta. del Sol. ☎914 54 88 00; www.patrimonionacional.es; M: Callao, Ópera, or Sol. Open Tu-Th and Sa 10:30am-12:30pm and 4-5:30pm, F 10:30am-12:30pm, Su 11am-1:30pm. €5, students €2.50.*

CONVENTO DE LA ENCARNACIÓN. Spain's finest reliquary is housed in this monastery, designed by Juan Gómez de Mora. It holds more than 1500 saintly relics, including a vial of San Pantaleón's blood believed to liquefy every year on July 27, his feast day. According to legend, disaster will strike Madrid if it fails to do so. Rumor has it that the blood stayed liquid just before the outbreak of the Civil War, but the Church insists that the transformation has been an annual event. The ceiling in the reliquary, flaunting intricately patterned tesselating figures separated by gold veins, was done by Vicente Carducho, as was the ominous painting of the Last Supper. *(Pl. de la Encarnación. ☎915 47 53 50; www.patrimonionacional.es. M: Ópera. From the metro stop, facing the Ópera building, bear diagonally right up C. Arrieta. Mandatory 1hr. tour in Spanish. Open Tu-Th and Sa 10:30am-12:45pm and 4-5:45pm, F 10:30am-12:45pm, Su 11am-1:45pm. €3.60; students, under 18, and over 65 €2.90. Visita de conjunto with the Convento de las Descalzas Reales €6/4.60. EU citizens free W.)*

ALONG THE RÍO MANZANARES. Madrid's notoriously puny "river" snakes its way around the city past the **Puerta de Toledo.** The triumphal arch was commissioned by Joseph Bonaparte to celebrate his brother Napoleon, but was completed in honor of Fernando VII, the "exterminator of the French usurpers." The Baroque **Puente de Toledo** makes up for the river's inadequacies. Sandstone carvings by Juan Ron on both sides of the bridge depict the martyrdom of San Isidro and his family. The **Puente de Segovia,** which spans the river along C. Segovia, was conceived by Juan de Herrera and constructed in the late 16th century, making it the oldest bridge in Madrid. *(To reach Puente de Toledo from Pta. del Sol, take C. Mayor through the Pl. Mayor and onto C. Toledo; follow C. Toledo to the bridge; approx. 15min. M: Puerta de Toledo or Ópera.)*

BOURBON MADRID

Weakened by plagues and political losses, the Habsburg era in Spain ended with the death of Carlos II in 1700. Felipe V, the first of Spain's Bourbon monarchs, ascended to the throne in 1714 after the 12-year War of the Spanish Succession. Bankruptcy, economic stagnation, and disillusionment compelled Felipe V to embark on a crusade of urban renewal, and his successors pursued the same ends with astounding results. Today, their lavish palaces, churches, and parks are the most spectacular (and touristed) in Madrid.

PALACIO REAL. The Palacio Real overlooks the Río Manzanares at the western tip of central Madrid. Felipe V commissioned Giovanni Sachetti to replace the Alcázar, which burned down in 1734, with a palace that would dwarf all others—and the architect succeeded. When Sachetti died, Filippo Juvara took over, basing his new facade on rejected designs for the Louvre. Decorating its 2000 rooms with a vast collection of porcelain, tapestries, furniture, and art lasted over a century. Today the palace is used by the royal couple only on official occasions, but it continues to stand as one of Europe's most grandiose residences and a testament to the cultural wealth of Spain.

The palace's most impressive rooms are decorated in the Rococo style. The **Salón del Trono** (Throne Room) contains the two magnificent Spanish thrones, supported by two golden lions. The **Salón de Columnas** (Column Room) is decked out in tapestries and an enormous royal carpet. This room was the scene of the official integration of Spain into the E.U. in 1985. The **Salón de Gasparini,** site of the king's ceremonial dressing before the court, houses one of Goya's many portraits of Carlos IV. The stunning **Porcelain Room** is composed

START: M: Estación Atocha

FINISH: M: Lima

DISTANCE: 7km

DURATION: From 3-6hr.

Madrid's *paseos* are a great starting point for walking tours, since most major sights are located on these main avenues. Trees in the the grassy medians offer shade and provide a nice buffer from the zooming traffic. You may be tempted to head to El Retiro after the Museo del Prado, or venture to Puerta del Sol once you have reached Pl. de Cibeles. Regardless of the path chosen, the paseos are a simple way to acquaint yourself with the city and organize a daily itinerary.

1. REINA SOFÍA. Directly across from Estación Atocha, the **Museo Nacional Centro de Arte Reina Sofía,** home to Picasso's *Guernica,* presides over Pl. del Emperador Carlos V. Its glass elevators hint at the impressive collection of modern art within.

2. MUSEO DEL PRADO. Walking up Po. del Prado, you'll pass the **Real Jardín Botánico** on the right. Next to the botanical garden is the world-renowned art museum, the **Museo del Prado.** Behind the Prado, on C. Ruíz de Alarcón, stands the **Iglesia de San Jerónimo,** Madrid's royal church. Built by Hieronymite monks, the church has witnessed the coronation of Fernando and Isabel and the marriage of King Alfonso XIII. These days, the church hosts the weddings of Madrid's modern-day elites. *(Open daily 10am-1pm and 5-8:30pm.).*

3. PLAZA DE LA LEALTAD. Back on Po. del Prado, to the north in Pl. de la Lealtad, stands the Obelisco a los Mártires del 2 de Mayo, filled with the ashes of those who died in the 1808 uprising against Napoleon. Its four statues represent constancy, virtue, valor, and patriotism. Behind the memorial sits the colonnaded, classical Bolsa de Comerico (Madrid's Stock Exchange). Ventura Rodríguez's Fuente de Neptuno, in Pl. Cánovas de Castillo, is one of three aquatic masterpieces along the avenue, famous enough to have earned him a Metro stop. Crossing the plaza brings you to another great museum, the **Museo Thyssen-Bornemisza.** One block up San Jerónimo on the right towards Sol is El Congreso de los Diputados, which houses the chambers of the Spanish Parliament.

4. PLAZA DE CIBELES. The arts of the Po. del Prado transition into the Po. de Recoletos at the overwhelming **Plaza de Cibeles.** From the plaza, the small **Museo Naval** is to the right. *(Entrance on C. Juan de Mena, 1. ☎913 79 52 99; www.museonavalmadrid.com. Open Sept.-July Tu-Su 10am-2pm. Free.)* In the southeast corner of the plaza sits the spectacular **Palacio de Comunicaciones,** designed by Antonio Palacios and Julián Otamendi of Otto Wagner's Vienna School in 1920, which functions as Madrid's central post office. On the corner opposite the Palacio lies the equally impressive **Banco de España.**

5. PALACIO DE BUENAVISTA. Across C. Alcalá from Banco de España is the **Palacio de Buenavista,** occupying the heart of an entire city block. The stately palace was built in 1777 by Juan Arnal and passed through succeeding generations of noble families. The entrance facing Cibeles is fronted by a gorgeous rose garden. Sadly, both the palace and garden must be observed from behind the gate, as they are now home to **Cuartel General de Ejército** (Army Headquarters).

6. BARRIO DE SALAMANCA. Continuing north toward the brown **Torres de Colón** (Towers of Columbus), you'll pass the **Biblioteca Nacional** (National Library), which often hosts temporary exhibitions and celebrations in the summer. *(Entrance at P. de Recoletos, 20-22. ☎915 80 78 23; www.bne.es. Open Tu-Sa 10am-9pm, Su 10am-2pm. Free.)* Behind the library is the massive **Museo Arqueológico Nacional.** Madrid's display of the history of the Western world, including a 4th-century urn, Felipe II's astrolabe, and a 16th-century porcelain clock, settled in this huge museum in 1895 after countless moves. *(C. Serrano, 13. M: Serrano. ☎915 77 79 12; www.man.mcu.es. Open in summer Tu-Sa 9:30am-8:00pm, Su 9:30am-3pm. €3, Sa after 2:30pm and Su free.)* The museum entrance is on C. Serrano, an avenue lined with pricey boutiques in the posh Barrio de Salamanca. Across Recoletos from the museums, down C. Braganza, is **Iglesia de las Salesas Reales,** whose gorgeous neoclassical façade complements the ornate interior. The church houses the tomb of Rey Fernando VI, who commissioned its construction.

7. PLAZA DE COLÓN. The museum and library are just before the modern **Plaza de Colón** (M: Colón) and the **Jardines del Descubrimiento** (Gardens of Discovery). On one side loom huge clay boulders, inscribed with trivia about the New World, including Seneca's prediction of its discovery, the names of the mariners onboard the caravels, and passages from Columbus's diary. A neo-Gothic spire honoring Columbus rises opposite a thundering fountain in the center of the plaza. An inlaid map detailing Columbus's journey covers the wall behind the waterfall. Concerts, lectures, ballets, and plays are held here in the **Teatro Fernán Gómez Centro de Arte,** a municipal art center. *(☎914 80 03 00; www.esmadrid.com/ccvilla/jsp/index.jsp. Box office open Tu-Su 11am-1:30pm and 5-7pm, or check on www.telentrada.com.)*

8. MUSEOS. The next stretch takes you past's Madrid's financial district and embassies and to a few good smaller museums. Just south of the **American Embassy,** between Pl. de Colón and Glorieta de Emilio Castelar, is a very small **open-air sculpture garden** with works by Joan Miró and Eduardo Chillida. Smaller museums, including the **Museo Sorolla,** are just off the Paseo. Further up on the right is the **Museo de Ciencias Naturales,** which houses an impressive collection of displays on geology and paleontology, including the full skeleton of a *Diplodocus.* *(☎914 11 13 28. Open Tu-Sa 10am-6pm, Su 10am-2:30pm. €5, students €3.)*

9. PLAZA DE LIMA. At **Plaza de Lima** is the 110,000-seat **Estadio Santiago Bernabéu** (M: Lima), home to the beloved **Reall Madrid** soccer club, which won its 9th European Championship in 2002 and its 31st Spanish La Liga Championship in 2008. Diametrically opposed to it are the **Torre de Europa** and the impassive but impressive **Torre de Picasso.**

of a wooden frame entirely covered in porcelain designs of fat cherubim; the edges are executed to perfection, with no roughess or inconsistency. The **Real Oficina de Farmacia** (Royal Pharmacy) has crystal and china receptacles used to hold royal medicine. Also open to the public is the **Real Armería** (Armory), which has an entire floor devoted to an impressive collection of knights' armor sitting atop their fully decorated horses. Behind closed doors is the only complete Stradivarius quintet in the world, a collection of the finest stringed instruments ever made. *(From Pl. de Isabel II, head toward the Teatro Real. M: Ópera. ☎914 54 87 88. Open Apr.-Sept. M-Sa 9am-6pm, Su 9am-3pm; Oct.-Mar. M-Sa 9:30am-5pm, Su 9am-2pm. Arrive early to avoid lines. Changing of the guard Sept.-May 1st W of every month at noon. €8, with tour €10; students €3.50/6. Under 5 free. EU citizens free W.)*

PLAZA DEL ORIENTE. The statues progress through old kings and princes, from old Ataulfo (died 415 AD) into the beginnings of the second millennium. The centerpiece is the imposing Felipe IV on horseback, a tribute to the monarch who oversaw so much of the decline of the Habsburg monarchy. *(From Pl. Isabel II, walk past Teatro Real. Across from the Palacio Real. M: Ópera.)*

CATEDRAL DE NUESTRA SEÑORA DE LA ALMUDENA. Take a break from the cherub-filled frescoes of most Spanish cathedrals for refreshingly modern decor. Begun in 1879 and finished a century later, this cathedral is a stark contrast to the gilded Palacio Real. After a 30-year hibernation, the building, dedicated to Madrid's other patron saint, received a controversial face-lift. The reasons for the controversy are apparent, as the cathedral's frescoes and stained glass windows sport a discordant mix of traditional and abstract styles: gray stone walls clash with the ceiling panels of brilliant colors and sharp geometric shapes that verge on Art Deco or graphic art. The fragmented figures in the stained glass show more than a little influence of modernist multiple perspective. *(C. Bailén, 10. ☎91 542 22 00. Left of the Palacio Real on C. Bailén. M: Ópera. Closed during mass. Open daily 9am-9pm. Confession 11am-12:45pm and 5-8:30pm. Free. Call 80 722 00 22 for a telephonic guided tour of the church. Various parts of church €1.50-4.50.)* The blindingly white chapel below (C. Mayor, 92) is worth a visit, but make sure you aren't interrupting any nuptials—it is a popular place for weddings. There is a museum that details the construction of the church and also leads tours up into the cupola, which affords spectacular views of the Campo del Moro, the Palace, and the city below. *(Behind the church, on the side facing the Palacio. ☎91 559 28 94; www.archimadrid.es. Open M-Sa 10am-2:30pm. €4.)*

MUSEO DE LA REAL ACADEMÍA DE BELLAS ARTES DE SAN FERNANDO. In 1752, Fernando VI established a royal academy to train the country's most talented artists. Goya, who was an early member of the *Academía*, is well-represented with two of his self-portraits and his *Niños (Children)* series. From time to time the Prado will loan some of his notable works to the collection. Other artists on display include Luca Giordano, Rubens, Ribera, and Archimboldo, whose delightful *La Primavera*, a portrait of Maximilian II made entirely of flowers, is on the first floor. The top floor holds Picasso sketches. The **Calcografía Real** (Royal Print and Drawing Collection) holds Goya's studio and organizes exhibitions, along with an extensive collection of his engravings, many of them disturbing wartime scenes of hunger and execution.. *(C. Alcalá, 13. ☎915 24 08 64; http://rabasf.insde.org. M: Sol or Sevilla. Open Tu-Fr 9am-7pm, Sa 9am-2:30pm and 4-7pm, Su 9am-2:30pm.. €3, students €1.50. W free. Top 2 fl. often closed; call ahead.)*

OTHER SIGHTS. The **Campo del Moro,** visible from the west side of the Palacio, is worthy of the King, better than the Retiro, and worth the hike to the entrance. Well-groomed trails lead through lush deciduous groves with the odd palm tree thrown in. The central lawn offers an unbroken view up to the Palacio. The secluded gardens are full of rosebushes and benches, and hide a small lake. Don't be afraid to stray from the path to check out the statues overgrown with vine, or to get a better glimpse of the rare and ostentatious **peacocks** haughtily preening themselves in the shade. *(From the palace, turn left onto C. Bailén, left again down Cuesta de San Vicente, and at the bottom of the hill turn left onto C. Puerto. From M: Príncipe Pío, cross the plaza to the entrance on C. del Puerto. Open in winters M-Sa 10am-6pm, Su 9am-6pm; in summer M-Sa 10am-8pm, Su 9am-8pm; last entrance 30min. before closing.)* The **Jardines de Sabatini,** to the right when facing the palace, is the everyman's park. Lovers canoodling, poets dreaming, and the homeless sleeping all share the park's manicured hedges, dipping their feet in the wading pool. Be sure to catch the sunset from the garden walls. *(Open daily 9am-9pm.)*

HUERTAS

Huertas is bordered by C. de Alcalá to the north, C. de Atocha to the south, and Po. del Prado to the east. Off C. San Jerónimo, streets slope downward, outward, and eastward toward various points along Po. del Prado and Pl. Cánovas de Castillo. Plaza de Santa Ana and its *terrazas* are the center of this old literary neighborhood, once home to Cervantes, Lope de Vega, and Quevedo during its heyday in the Siglo de Oro (see **Literature,** p. 73). Huertas's sights, from authors' houses to famous cafes, reflect its artistic past. A stroll down the neighborhood's namesake street, impressed in bronze with quotations and trivia related to its authors, gives a taste of their writing and time in Huertas.

PARQUE DEL BUEN RETIRO

With the construction of the 300-acre Parque del Buen Retiro in the 1630's, Felipe IV intended to transform the former hunting grounds into a personal retreat, *un buen retiro.* Today, "the lungs of Madrid" are a menagerie of art exhibits and magicians doing tricks, students reading, families strolling, and tourists and locals alike milling around the lake and breathing deeply away from the sweat and dirt of the city. The northeast corner of the park enchants with medieval monastic ruins and waterfalls. The park houses the spectacular **Palacio de Cristal** and **Estanque Grande,** along with a running track, a sports complex with tennis courts and soccer pitches, a rose garden featuring the famous **Fuente del Ángel Caído,** inspired by Milton, and smaller gardens and plazas.

On weekends, the promenades fill with musicians, families, and young lovers; on summer nights (when only the north gate remains open), the lively bars and cafes scattered around the park come alive with conversation and clinking glasses. Try to avoid the park after dark if you're alone—a slew of shady characters retires here by night, and the Retiro isn't signposted, making navigation difficult even during daylight. The park is accessible from the Retiro **metro** stop. There are four entrances: C. Alfonso XII, C. Alcalá, Pl. de la Independencia, and Av. Menéndez y Pelayo. *(Park open Oct.-May 6am-10pm., Apr.-Sept. 6am-midnight Guided tours every Saturday, check in the info. kiosk near the Estanque or in the Jardín del Recuerdo.)*

ESTANQUE GRANDE. Amateur rowers young and old haphazardly manuever their boats around this artificial lake, replacing the gondolas that used to glide across it. The colonnaded mausoleum of Alfonso XII, featuring a marble statue of a horsebacked *"El Pacificador"* (the Peacemaker), is a gathering place for friends and a great spot for relaxation and people-watching. While away lazy afternoons in a **rowboat** on the lake, or take in puppet shows and street perfomers on shore. Sundays from 5pm to midnight, over 100 percussionists gather for an immense drum circle by the monument on the Estanque; synchronistic rhythms and hash smoke fill the air. *(Boats €4.40 per 45min. for 4 people. The Pl. de la Independencia entrance leads to Av. de Méjico, the path to the lake.)*

PALACIO DE VELÁZQUEZ. Built in 1883, this Ricardo Velázquez creation has billowing ceilings, marble floors, and tiles by Daniel Zuloaga. The palace exhibits frequently changing contemporary and experimental works in conjunction with the **Reina Sofía** (p. 110). *(From the Estanque, walk straight to Pl. de Honduras and turn left onto Po. Venezuela. The palace will be on your right. ☎915 73 62 45. Open Apr.-Sept. M and W-Sa 11am-8pm, Su 11am-6pm; Oct.-Mar. M-Sa 10am-6pm, Su 10am-4pm. Free.)*

PALACIO DE CRISTAL. Built by Ricardo Velázquez to exhibit flowers from the Philippines in 1887, this exquisite steel-and-glass structure hosts a variety of art shows and exhibits, with subjects ranging from Bugs Bunny to Spanish portraiture to vocal recognition of bird calls. The little pond out front, with its rowdy family of ducks, has a beautiful reflection of the dome. *(From Palacio de Velázquez, head out the main door until you reach the lake and the palace. ☎915 74 66 14. Open Apr.-Sept. M-Sa 11am-8pm, Su 11am-6pm; Oct.-Mar. M-Sa 10am-6pm, Su 10am-4pm. Free.)*

PUERTA DE ALCALÁ AND CASÓN DEL BUEN RETIRO. Bullets from the 1921 assassination of Prime Minister Eduardo Dato permanently scarred the eastern face of the **Puerta de Alcalá** (1778), outside El Retiro's Puerta de la Independencia. To the south, the **Casón del Buen Retiro** faces the park; behind it sits the **Museo del Ejército.** *(☎902 10 70 77. Casón open W-Su 10am-8pm. The permanent collection, 19th- and 20th-century works from the Prado, is closed, but it hosts temporary exhibits.)* In this stately edifice is a vast collection of over 27,000 artifacts tracing the history of the Spanish military, including the Tizona sword of El Cid Campeador and a fragment of the cross Columbus wore when he arrived in the New World. The two buildings are remnants of Felipe IV's palace, which burned in the Napoleonic Wars. *(C. Mendez Nunez, 1. ☎915 22 89 77. M: Retiro or Banco de España. The Museo is being relocated to the Alcázar in Toledo, but had not completed the move as of August 2008.)*

MADRID

OTHER SIGHTS

REAL JARDÍN BOTÁNICO. Opened during reign of Carlos III in 1781, the garden showcases over 30,000 species of plants, ranging from traditional roses to medicinal herbs from the furthest reaches of Asia and the Americas to familiar Spanish plants. The tall European cypresses and secluded rose gardens are an even better getaway than **El Retiro.** Botanical courses on plants and flowers are periodically offered; call for details. Perfect escape for both those with horticultural interests and those who just like gorgeous gardens. *(Pl. de Murillo, 2, next to the Prado. ☎914 20 30 17; www.rjb.csic.es. Open daily in summer 10am-9pm; in winter 10am-6pm. €2, students €1, under 10 and over 65 free.)*

CASA DE LOPE DE VEGA. A prolific playwright and poet of Spain's Golden Age, Lope de Vega spent the last 25 years of his life writing plays in this house. None of the objects here belonged to him, but they are all period pieces collected using a catalog he left behind. Though Lope de Vega and Miguel de Cervantes were bitter rivals, Lope de Vega's 17th-century home is ironically now located on C. Cervantes. *(C. Cervantes, 11. With your back to Pl. de Santa Ana, turn left onto C. del Prado, right onto C. León, and left onto C. de Cervantes. ☎91 429 92 16. Open Tu-F 9:30am-2pm, Sa 10am-2pm. Free.)*

CÍRCULO DE BELLAS ARTES. The Círculo is the hub of Madrid's performing arts scene, organizing performances and shows around the city. Their quarterly magazine, *Minerva*, is available at the entrance (€15). Many facilities are for *socios* (members) only, but the galleries are open to the public. Exhibitions range from photography to video art to abstract sculpture, and it sponsors **Radio Círculo,** 100.4 FM. They also hold concerts, festivals, films, and theater events. Attached cinema shows student and art film (€3-4). Pick up a free program at the front desk. *(C. Alcalá, 42. From Pl. de Santa Ana, go up C. del Príncipe, cross C. San Jerónimo to C. Sevilla, and turn right onto C. Alcalá. ☎913 60 54 00; www.circulobellasartes.com. Open Tu-F 5-9pm, Sa 11am-2pm and 5-9pm, Su 11am-2pm. €1. Cafe open daily 10am-1am.)*

AVENIDA DEL ARTE

If Madrid were reduced to a moonscape with nothing left but its art, it would still be worth a visit. Considered to be among the world's best art galleries individually, the Museo del Prado, Museo de Thyssen-Bornemisza, and the Museo Nacional Centro de Arte Reina Sofía together form the impressive "Avenida del Arte." While the Prado overshadows its smaller sisters, their collections of modern and avant-garde art pick up where it leaves off. From Goya in the Prado and Rothko in the Thyssen-Bornemisza to Picasso in the Reina Sofía, Madrid's museums form one of the most comprehensive collections in the world.

MUSEO DEL PRADO

Po. del Prado at Pl. Cánovas del Castillo. M: Banco de España or Atocha. ☎902 10 70 77; www.museodelprado.es. Open Tu-Su 9am-8pm. €6, students €3, under 18, over 65 free. free Tu-Sa 6-8pm, Su 5-8pm.

One of Europe's finest centers for 12th- to 17th-century art, the Prado is Spain's most prestigious museum and home to the world's greatest collection of Spanish paintings. Following Carlos III's order for a museum of natural history and sciences, architect **Juan de Villanueva** began construction of the Neoclassical building in 1785. In 1819, Fernando VII transformed it into the royal painting archive; the museum's 7000 pieces are the result of hundreds of years of collecting by the houses of Habsburg and Bourbon. The walls are filled with Spanish and foreign masterpieces, including a comprehensive selection from the Flemish and Venetian schools. The museum is well-organized: the ground floor houses Spanish painting from the 12th through 16th centuries and 15th- to 16th-century Flemish, German, and Italian works. The first floor contains Spanish art from the 17th to the 19th centuries, with all the *"Siglo de Oro"* painters here, along with French and Italian art from the Neoclassical and Baroque eras. The sheer quantity of paintings means you'll have to be selective. The museum provides a free and indispensable guide upon entry which describes each numbered room, and a guide to where the most famous paintings are by room. **Audio guides** in English are available for the best €3 you've spent in this city, and the museum's **guidebooks** (€10-25) offer extensive art history and criticism.

MADRID

DIEGO VELÁZQUEZ. The first floor houses Spanish, French, Dutch, and Italian works. The most notable is its collection of works by Diego Velázquez (1599-1660). Known for his unforgiving realism and use of light, Velázquez was the court painter and majordomo to Felipe IV (there are 6 portraits of the foppish monarch, on horseback, hunting, etc). Several of his most famous paintings are here, including *Las hilanderas* (The Spinners), *El Dios Marte* (Mars), and *Portait of the Count-Duke of Olivares on Horseback*. The painter's *magnum opus* and perhaps the museum's most famous work is **Las Meninas** (The Maids of Honor), a scene of the artist painting the young maids with the king and the queen in the background. The painting's novel use of perspective and complex ambient lighting are Velázquez hallmarks. In the painting, Velázquez sports the cross of the order of Santiago, first created in 1658. Since the work was completed two years earlier, in 1656, art historians suggest that either Felipe the IV or Velázquez added it later to ennoble the painter. Regardless, the snapshot quality of Velázquez's figures transformed painting in the 17th century.

FRANCISCO DE GOYA. In 1785, Francisco de Goya y Lucientes (1746-1828) became the court portraitist. Despite his controversial depictions of the royal family (some argued that Goya manipulated light and shadow to focus the viewer's gaze on the figure of the queen—rather than the king—in *La familia de Carlos IV,* discreetly pointing to the true power behind the monarchy), Goya was never expelled from court. (He didn't escape punishment completely, however, and was hauled before the Inquisition in 1815.) His painting evolved as profound political changes—the French Revolution, the Napoleonic wars, and the Spanish defeat—shook Spain and Europe. Goya consciously imitated the techniques of his national predecessors, including himself in the shadows of a royal portrait, in a nod to Velázquez's *Las Meninas*. The stark *2 de Mayo* and *Fusilamientos de 3 de Mayo* depict the terrors of the 1808 Napoleonic invasion, and may be Goya's most recognized works, along with the expressionless woman in *La maja vestida* and *La maja desnuda*, thought to be Goya's mistress, the Duchess of Alba. The *Pinturas Negras (Black Paintings)* are the most evocative, featuring grotesques and dark subject matter on even darker, obscure canvases. Goya painted them at the end of his life, when he was deaf and alone. *Saturno devorando a su hijo (Saturn Devouring His Son)* stands out; Goya captures the crazed eyes of Saturn as he bites off the head of his son after a prophecy that one of his children would overthrow him. The blurry *Perro semihundido (Half-Sunken Dog)* is unsettling in its obscurity.

ITALIAN, FLEMISH, AND OTHER SPANISH ARTISTS. The ground floor of the Prado displays many of **El Greco's** (Doménikos Theotokópoulos, 1541-1614) religious paintings. *La Trinidad (The Holy Trinity)* and *San Andrés y San Francisco (St. Andrew and St. Francis)* are characterized by El Greco's luminous colors, elongated figures, and mystical subjects. On the first floor are works by Spanish artists like **Bartolomé Murillo, José de Ribera, and Francisco Zurbarán.**

The collection of Italian works is formidable, with massive collections by **Tintoretto,** including the wonderfully detailed *El lavatorio (Christ Washing the Disciples' Feet)*, **Veronese,** and **Titian,** whose *Danäe and the Shower of Gold* is emblematic of mythologically-inspired Renaissance themes. Several enormous canvases by **Raphael,** like *The Transfiguration of the Lord*, are on the ground floor. Some minor **Botticellis** and a slew of imitations are on display. Among the works by **Rubens,** *The Adoration of the Magi* and *The Three Graces* best show his grand style. *The Annunciation*, **Fra Angelico's** symbolic work with gilt halos and sunbeams and mesmerizing blues, is equally striking.

As a result of the Spanish Habsburgs' control of the Netherlands, the Flemish holdings are also top-notch. Works like **Albrecht Dürer's** Adam and Eve diptych, **Peter Brueghel the Elder's** terrifying *The Triumph of Death*, and **Hieronymus Bosch's** moralistic triptych **The Garden of Earthly Delights** are equally striking.

LA AMPLIACIÓN. The Prado's newest expansion—the biggest in the museums's 200-year history—opened at the end of 2007. Designed by Rafael Moneo, the new building houses the cloisters of the former monastery of Los Jerónimos and a 440-seat auditorium, in addition to space for temporary exhibitions, restorations and painting storage.

MUSEO NACIONAL CENTRO DE ARTE REINA SOFÍA

Pl. Santa Isabel, 52. ☎917 74 10 00; www.museoreinasofia.es. M: Atocha. Open M and W-Sa 10am-9pm, Su 10am-2:30pm. €3; students €1.50; Sa after 2:30pm, Su, holidays, under 18, over 65 free.

Since Juan Carlos I declared this renovated hospital a national museum in 1988 and named it after his wife, this collection of 20th-century art has burgeoned. The building is a work of art in itself, with two futuristic-looking glass elevators ferrying visitors up and down the museum as they look north over the skyline. With over 10,000 pieces, the museum has an amazing collection of paintings,

MADRID

sculptures, experimental space, and film. The second and fourth floors are mazes of permanent exhibits charting the Spanish avant-garde and contemporary movements. If that's not for you, head straight to the rooms dedicated to **Juan Gris, Joan Miró,** and **Salvador Dalí,** which display Spain's vital contributions to the Surrealist movement. Miró's works show spare, colorful abstraction, visible in the *Mujer y pájaro* (Woman and Bird) series, highlighting his love of both. Meanwhile, Dalí's paintings, like *El gran masturbador (The Great Masturbator)*, portray the artist's Freudian nightmares and sexual fantasies. Another must-see is the film room dedicated to **Luis Buñuel,** the surrealist Spanish director famous for *Le chien andalou (The Andalucian Dog)*, a project undertaken with Dalí, infamous for its unsettling images.

Pablo Picasso's masterpiece, **Guernica,** is the highlight of the Reina Sofía's permanent collection. Now freed from its restrictive glass cover and long exile in New York, it depicts the Basque town bombed by the German and Nationalist air forces during the Spanish Civil War (p. 498). Commissioned to produce a piece large enough for the main wall in the Spanish Pavilion at the Paris World's Fair in August 1937, Picasso began work on the painting on May 1st and completed the mammoth work just over a month later. In a huge, colorless work of contorted, agonized figures, Picasso denounced the violence unconditionally. When one German minister asked him, "You did this?" Picasso replied, "No, you did." While many have attempted to explain the allegories at work, Picasso himself refused to acknowledge its symbolism; still, most critics insist that the screaming horse represents war and the twisted bull represents Spain. The contortions of the figures and the painful sharp points, like tongues and nipples, are offset by more optimistic symbols: the dove, for peace; the horseshoe, for luck; and the flower, for rebirth. Picasso stipulated that the painting was not to return to Spain as long as a Fascist government was in place, and loaned the canvas to the Museum of Modern Art in New York on the condition that it be repatriated when democracy was restored. In 1981, six years after Franco's death, Guernica was delivered to the Prado and housed in El Casón del Buen Retiro (p. 107). The subsequent move to the Reina Sofía sparked an international controversy—Picasso's other request was that the painting hang only in the Prado, among the works of masters like El Greco, Goya, and Velázquez.

MUSEO THYSSEN-BORNEMISZA

Paseo del Prado, 8, on the corner of Po. del Prado and C. Manuel González. M: Banco de España or Atocha. Buses #1, 2, 5, 9, 10, 14, 15, 20, 27, 34, 37, 45, 51, 52, 53, 74, 146, and 150. ☎91 369 01 51; www.museothyssen.org. Open Tu-Su 10am-7pm. Last entrance 6:30pm. €6, students with ISIC and seniors €4, under 12 free. Audio guides €4.

Unlike the Prado and the Reina Sofía, the Thyssen-Bornemisza covers many periods and diverse media; exhibits range from 14th-century canvases to 20th-century sculptures, and its collection encompasses periods of art overlooked by the other two. The museum is housed in the 18th-century **Palacio de Villahermosa** and contains the former collection of the late Baron Heinrich Thyssen-Bornemisza. The baron donated his collection in 1993, and today the museum is the world's most extensive private showcase. In June 2004, a new wing was opened to house the collection of his wife, Baroness Carmen, whose taste, if not her collection, rivals her husband's. More manageable than the Prado or Reina Sofía, the pieces are hung chronologically from the second floor down.

The top floor of the baron's collection is dedicated to the **Old Masters,** with stars like Hans Holbein's austere *Portrait of Henry VIII* and El Greco's *Anunciación.* You can chart the changing attitudes and representations of the body, from Lucas Cranach's *The Nymph of the Spring* to Titian's *Saint Jerome in the Desert* to Anthony van Dyck's *Portrait of Jacques Le Roy.* The Thyssen-

MADRID

Bornemisza's **Baroque** collection, with pieces by Caravaggio, Ribera, and Claude Lorraine, rivals the Prado's. The baroness' collection on the 2nd floor is eclectic, featuring both the old Italian masters and 5 Rodin sculptures and moving toward early Impressionism, with work by Winslow Homer and John Constable. The museum's finest collection is down a floor, encompassing renowned works of **Impressionism, Fauvism,** and early **avant-garde** that paved the way to modern art. The Impressionist and **Post-Impressionist** works in the Baroness' collections explode with texture and color—look for works by Sisley, Renoir, Manet, Degas, Monet, Cézanne, and Matisse. Van Gogh's brushstrokes make their mark here, as do the island scenes of Gauguin. Edvard Munch's strange work and pre-Cubist Picasso are also featured on this floor.

The conclusion of the tour is the museum's 20th-century collection, which reflects a diversity of styles and philosophies. You can trace the deconstruction of figurative painting, starting with Picasso, Georges Braque, and Juan Gris, moving toward the sterility of Piet Mondrian and the **Constructivists.** A cluster of pieces by Magritte, Chagall, and Kandinsky follows, and American **Abstract Expressionism** (Pollock, Mark Rothko, Morris Louis, and Willem de Kooning) has its place here too. Look for Georgia O'Keefe's desert flowers and Rothko's enigmatic *Green on Maroon.* **German Expressionist** artists are also well-represented. The second-to-last room holds Lucien Freud's disturbing work and some early **pop art,** but doubling back to the exit brings perhaps some more optimistic work amid modernist abstraction: Maxim Gorky's *Hugging* and Dalí's *Dream Caused by the Flight of a Bumblebee around a Pomegranate.*

MALASAÑA AND CHUECA

Devoid of the numerous historic monuments and palaces that characterize most of Madrid, the labyrinthine streets of Malasaña and Chueca house countless undocumented "sights," from street performers and sex shops to some of Madrid's best fashion. These streets are a funky, colorful, and relaxing break for travelers weary of crucifixes and brushstrokes. Chueca in particular is great for people-watching and boutique shopping. By night, both districts bustle with Madrid's alternative and gay scene. Although the area between **Calle de Fuencarral** and **Calle de San Bernardo** plays host to Madrid's avant-garde—architecture and art galleries included—the streets and the people are the real draw.

IGLESIA DE LAS SALESAS REALES. Bourbon King Fernando VI commissioned this church in 1758 at the request of his wife. The Baroque/Neoclassical church, with a facade of angels made of Carrera marble, towers over a lush rose garden and tall European cypresses. Inside is the massive sepulcher of the king, who died before the church's completion. The soaring dome is frescoed with various biblical scenes, among them the image of the dove returning to Noah after the Flood. Untouristed and uncrowded, the church offers a quiet retreat in which to contemplate its treasures. *(C. Bárbara de Braganza, 1. M: Colón. From Pl. Colón, go down Po. de Recoletos and take a right onto C. de Bárbara de Braganza. ☎913 19 48 11. Open M-F 8:30am-1pm and 5:30-9pm. Not open to tourists during mass.)*

MUSEO DE HISTORIA (ANTIGUO MUNICIPAL). An intricate facade welcomes visitors to explore Madrid's history through its art. Exhibits feature paintings, prints, and photographs, all of which document the changes and consistencies of this dynamic city over the past four centuries. Though the museum undergoes relatively frequent renovation projects, small, well-curated exhibits are open to the public. Highlights include lithographs of the 1837 revolution and paintings of chivalric festivities in the Pl. Mayor. The 3D model of the city is a lifesaver for the disoriented tourist. *(C. de Fuencarral, 78, right outside M: Tribunal. ☎917 01 18 63. Open Tu-F 9:30am-8pm, Sa-Su 10am-2pm. Free.)*

GRAN VÍA

Urban planners paved Gran Vía in 1910 to link C. Princesa with Pl. de Cibeles, creating a cosmopolitan center of life in the city. The controversial project required the demolition of more than 300 buildings, several churches included, and the diversion or destruction of some 50 streets. After Madrid gained wealth as a neutral supplier during WWI, the city funneled much of its earnings into making Gran Vía one of the world's great thoroughfares. In its heyday, Hemingway described it as a cross between Broadway and Fifth Avenue. Today the lights, traffic, and tourist excess are much closer to New York's Times Square than anything else, and while it lacks much of historical note, is worth a look.

Sol's shopping streets converge at Gran Vía's highest elevation in **Plaza del Callao** (M: Callao). C. Postigo San Martín splits off southward, where you'll find the famed **Convento de las Descalzas Reales** (p. 102). Westward from Pl. de Callao, Gran Vía heads up toward **Plaza de España** (M: Pl. de España). Locals relax on the shady grass, but you're better off going to the bottom of the park and turning left toward the **Jardines de Sabatini,** or right to **El Templo de Debod** (p. 113). Next to Pl. de España are two of Madrid's tallest skyscrapers, the **Telefónica building** (1929) and the **Edificio de España** (1953). Lewis S. Weeks of the Chicago School designed the Telefónica building, the tallest concrete building at the time (81m), which supposedly was used as a lookout by Republican forces during the Civil War. The best perspective of Gran Vía is from its eastern end, where it intersects with C. Alcalá. Walking a little bit from Pl. de Cibeles toward Gran Vía affords a long view up the thoroughfare past the dome of the Metropolis building and the state of Victory on top of it. This distance hides the noise and commercialism and lends a little of the grandeur that must have been the vision of its architects.

ARGÜELLES AND MONCLOA

TEMPLO DE DEBOD. Built by King Adijalamani of Meröe, the Templo de Debod is the only Egyptian temple in Spain. In 1968. The Egyptian government shipped the temple stone by stone to Spain in appreciation of Spanish archaeologists who helped to rescue the Abu Simbel temples from the floods of the Aswan Dam. The 2200-year-old temple was originally built to honor Isis and Ammon; the structure was elaborated by Egyptian monarchs and later, Roman emperors Augustus and Tiberius, reliefs of whom accompany Egyptian gods performing offerings. Walk through the original archways outside to see the temple juxtaposed with urban Madrid. Left, behind the temple, which is nested in Parque de la Montaña, is a *mirador* (lookout point) with commanding views of the city and the Catedral de la Almudena. *(M: Pl. de España or Ventura Rodríguez. Buses #1 and 74. From the metro, walk down C. Ventura Rodríguez to Parque de la Montaña; the temple is on the right. ☎913 66 74 15; www.munimadrid.es/templodebod. Guided tours available. Open Apr.-Sept. Tu-F 10am-2pm and 6-8pm, Sa-Su 10am-2pm; Oct.-Mar. Tu-F 9:45am-1:45pm and 4:15-6:15pm, Sa-Su 10am-2pm. Closed M. Free. Park open daily. Free.)*

EL PARDO. Built as a hunting lodge for Carlos I in 1547, El Pardo was enlarged by generations of Habsburgs and Bourbons. Though Spain's growing capital eventually extended into the old hunting grounds and enveloped the country palace, the Pardo remains one of the nation's most compelling constructions. In 1940, centuries after its heyday as a hunting lodge, El Pardo opened its doors to its most trigger-happy resident when Franco, who fancied himself Felipe II reincarnate, decided to move in, remaining there until his death in 1975. Though the house's master has changed, the palace is still the official reception site for foreign dignitaries. Renowned for its collection of vivid pastoral tapestries—several of which were designed by Goya—the palace also holds a Velázquez painting and Ribera's *Techo de los Hombres Ilustres (Ceiling of the Illustrious Men)*. You can also see Franco's bathroom, and the bedroom cabinet in which he kept Santa Teresa's silver-encrusted arm. Entrance to the palace's *capilla* and the nearby **Casita del Príncipe,** created by Juan de Villanueva of Museo del Prado fame, is free. *(Take bus #601 from the stop in front of the Ejército del Aire building above M: Moncloa; every 15min., €1. ☎913 76 15 00. Palace open Apr.-Sept. M-Sa 10:30am-5:45pm, Su 9:30am-1:30pm; Oct.-Mar. M-Sa 10:30am-4:45pm, Su 10am-1:30pm. Mandatory 45min. guided tour in Spanish. €4, over 65 and students with ID €2.70. EU citizens free W. The Casita del Príncipe may be undergoing restorations; call ahead.)*

MUSEO DE AMÉRICA. The museum houses an impressive collection of artifacts from Native American cultures, extending from Alaska to the tip of South America. Most comprehensive are the treasures from pre-Columbian cultures the Spanish conquered, including plumed Amazon headdresses, Mayan funerary urns and sculptures, and a massive Aztec calendar stone, with a reconstructed Sioux teepee upstairs. Colonial accounts and artwork provide a glimpse into the conquistadors' perspectives on the peoples they encountered. Especially compelling are paintings depicting interracial families and the various ethnic identities assigned to their offspring, which help form a picture of the colonial mindset. *(Av. de los Reyes Católicos, 6, next to the Faro de Moncloa. ☎915 49 26 41; www.museodeamerica.mcu.es. M: Moncloa. Open Tu-Sa 9:30am-3pm, Su 10am-3pm. €3.01, students and EU citizens €1.50, under 18 and over 65 free. Sa after 2:30pm, Su free.)*

ERMITA DE SAN ANTONIO DE LA FLORIDA. Slightly off the beaten path, the Ermita (hermitage) is Goya's final resting place, and over his tomb is an elaborate fresco painted by Goya himself. On June 13th, single *madrileñas* offer their faith (and blood) to San Antonio in exchange for his help in the husband-hunt. The women line the baptismal fount with thirty pins and then press their hands into them. The number of resulting pin-pricks represents how many *novios* (boyfriends) they'll have in the next year. *(M: Príncipe Pío. From the metro, go right onto Po. de la Florida and walk to the first traffic circle. The Ermita is on the right. ☎915 42 07 22. Open Tu-F 9:30am-8pm, Sa-Su 10am-2pm. Free.)*

CASA DEL CAMPO. Take the Teleférico *(☎915 41 11 18; open M-F noon-2pm and 3-9:30pm, Sa-Su noon-9:30pm; one-way €3.25, round-trip €4.65)* from Po. del Pintor Rosales into Madrid's largest park. Or head down from M: Príncipe Pío, left of the traffic circle and over the Río Manzanares. Practically a town in itself, the park offers shaded areas, running and biking trails, and long walks around the lake, where you can rent a kayak or rowboat (€4.40 for 45min.) and row past the massive fountain in the middle. *(Much of it is unattended and prostitutes have been occasionally seen along the main road, so be careful and stick to daytime visits.)* Inside the amusement park, **Parque de Atracciones,** relive your childhood on the roller coaster. One of Madrid's largest pools is in the corner of the park, next to M: Lago. *(Take bus #33 or 65 or M: Batán. Turn right out of the metro and walk up the main street away from the lake. ☎914 63 29 00; www.parquedeatracciones.es. €9.30 to enter, €27.50 to ride. Schedule changes daily, see website for hours.)* The **Zoo/Aquarium,** 5min. away, is a more exciting prospect, featuring a panda, the extremely rare Barbary lion, gorillas, and a dolphin show. *(☎915 12 37 70; www.zoomadrid.com. Open in summer M-W 10:30am-9pm, Th-Sa 10:30am-midnight, in winter M-F 10:30-8pm, Sa-Su 10:30am-9:30pm. Schedule changes daily; check website for details. €16.90, under 7 €12.20, guided tour €4.70.)*

MUSEO CERRALBO. This museum displays the collections of the Marqués de Cerralbo in all their ornate, eclectic, 19th-century *fin-de-siècle* glory. Highlights include El Greco's *Ecstasy of St. Francis* in the chapel, collections of battle-scarred European and Japanese arms, a quaint green garden, and a golden ballroom capped by a ceiling fresco of tumbling revelers. *(C. Ventura Rodríguez, 17.*

☎915 47 36 46. M: Ventura Rodríguez or Pl. de España. Open Tu-Sa 9:30am-3pm, Su 10am-3pm. €2.40, students €1.20, under 18 and over 65 free. W and Su free. As of Aug. 2008, it was closed for renovations, so call ahead.)

OTHER SIGHTS. The **Parque del Oeste** is a large, sloping park known for the **Rosaleda** (rose garden) at its bottom and the statues of prominent *madrileños* that stand in every grove. A yearly competition determines which rosebush will be added to the permanent collection. *(M: Moncloa. From the metro, take C. Princesa. Garden open daily 10am-8pm.)* A prime example of Fascist Neoclassicism, the arcaded **Cuartel General del Aire** *(Ejército del Aire;* Air Force Headquarters) commands the view on the other side of the Arco de la Victoria (by the Moncloa metro station). One of Madrid's finest cultural centers, the **Centro Cultural Conde Duque,** hosts traveling exhibitions and is home to the **Museo Municipal de Arte Contemporáneo.** *(C. Conde Duque, 9. Museo ☎915 88 59 28; www.munimadrid.es/museoartecontemporaneo. M: San Bernardo. Open Tu-Sa 10am-2pm and 6pm-9pm, Su 10:30am-2:30pm. Free.)*

BILBAO

MUSEO SOROLLA. The former residence of the Valencian painter Joaquín Sorolla Bastida (1863-1923) displays the work of late 19th-century painters. The collection also includes centuries of colorful Spanish ceramics. Sorolla's vibrant works, known for their complex depiction of light, include *Mis Hijos* and *La Siesta.* His three-part garden, with fountains and myrtle taken from the Alhambra, is as fantastic as his art. *(Po. General Martínez Campos, 37. M: Iglesia or Rubén Darío. ☎913 10 15 84; www.museosorolla.mcu.es. Open in summer Tu-Su 9am-11:30pm; in winter Tu-Su 9:30am-3pm, Su 10am-3pm. Check dates online. €2.40, students €1.20. Su free.)*

MUSEO LÁZARO GALDIANO. This small palace displays a private collection of Italian Renaissance bronzes and Celtic and Visigoth brasses. Paintings include *Young Christ,* a painting unofficially attributed to Leonardo da Vinci, and Hieronymus Bosch's *Ecce Homo,* along with the classic Spanish trifecta: El Greco, Velázquez, and Goya. *(C. Serrano, 122. M: Gregorio Marañón. Turn right off Po. de la Castellana onto C. María de Molina. ☎915 61 60 84; www.flg.es. Open M and W-Su 10am-4:30pm. €4, students €3. EU citizens free W.)*

ENTERTAINMENT

Anyone interested in live entertainment—from music to dance to theater—should stop by the **Círculo de Bellas Artes,** C. Alcalá, 42 (☎913 60 54 00) at M: Sevilla or Banco de España. The six-floor building houses performance venues and art exhibits, and is also an organizing center for events throughout Madrid. It has current information on virtually all performances. The *Guía del Ocio* (€1, comes out every F) is an indispensable guide to all entertainment in the city.

MUSIC

In summer, Madrid sponsors free concerts, ranging from classical and jazz to bolero and salsa, at **Pl. Mayor, Lavapiés, Oriente,** and **Villa de París;** check the *Guía del Ocio* for the current schedule. The city is undergoing a live music explosion in all genres, with a relatively cheap *consumición* (cover) giving you access to the music in an intimate venue. Flamenco *tablaos* have music every week; call ahead to see who's playing. Most theaters close in July and August, but many participate in **Veranos en la Villa,** hosting summer events or productions.

Huertas is a quiet capital of jazz and swing, with Europe's best acts in every week. In the darkened streets south of Gran Vía, a small rock enclave has sprouted up. **Costello,** Caballero de Gracia, 10, has 3-5 rock concerts a week in the long, fairly soundproof basement concealed under its bar. (☎915 23 01 74; www.costelloclub.com. Cover €7-20, depending on the band. Call for showtimes.) **El Sol,** Jardines, 3, showcases rock, salsa, ska—whatever's on the marquee—about 4 times per week. Cover free-€6. (☎915 32 64 90; www.elsolmad.com. Open daily 6pm-end of show.) Madrid's major performance venues are listed below.

Auditorio Nacional, C. Príncipe de Vergara, 146 (☎913 37 01 40; www.auditorionacional.mcu.es). M: Cruz del Rayo. Home to the National Orchestra, and features Madrid's best classical music performances. Tickets €6-100. Box office open M 4-6pm, Tu-F 10am-5pm, Sa 11am-1pm.

Fundación Joan March, C. Castelló, 77 (☎914 34 42 40; www.march.es). M: Núñez de Balboa. Hosts summer activities like lectures (usually Tu and Th 7:30pm; free), poetry readings, and concerts. Concerts M, W, Sa; no events June-Oct. Call ahead for details.

Teatro Monumental, C. Atocha, 65 (☎915 81 72 11, tickets 91 581 72 08). M: Antón Martín. Home to Madrid's Symphonic Orchestra. Reinforced concrete–a Spanish invention–was first used in its construction in the 1920s, so be prepared for unusual acoustics. Tickets €6.50-18. Box office open M-F 9:30am-2pm and Th 5-7pm; July open mornings only. closed. No regular concerts from mid-Apr. to mid-Oct.)

Teatro de la Zarzuela, C. Jovellanos, 4 (☎915 24 54 10; www.teatrodelazarzuela.mcu.es.) M: Sevilla or Banco de España. The city's base for opera and *zarzuela* (light opera native to Madrid). Built in 1856, it was modeled on Milan's La Scala. No performances from late July to Aug. Box office open noon-8pm on days with shows, noon-6pm on days without; closed Su with no shows.

Teatro Real, Pl. de Oriente (☎915 16 06 60.) M: Ópera. Madrid's principal performance venue, featuring the city's best ballet and opera. Tickets sold M-Sa 10am-8pm, Su with shows 2 hours before curtain, closed Su with no shows.

MADRID

FLAMENCO

Flamenco in Madrid is tourist-oriented and expensive, but a few nightlife spots are authentic (see **Cardamomo,** p. 121). **Las Tablas,** Pl. de España, 9 on the corner of C. Bailén and Cuesta San Vicente, has lower prices than most other clubs (€24). Shows start every night at 10:30pm. Funk and jazz shows on occasion after the flamenco's over (☎915 42 05 20; www.lastablasmadrid.com. M: Pl. de España.) **Casa Patas,** C. Cañizares, 10, offers excellent quality (*espectáculo* M-Th €25, F-Sa €30), and teaches weekly lessons starting in the fall, 1-2hrs. per week for €51-68 (☎914 29 84 71; www.casapatas.com. M: Antón Martín. Call for reservations. Shows M-Th at 10:30pm, F-Sa at 9pm and midnight.) **Teatro Albéniz,** C. la Paz, 11, hosts the *Certamen de Coreografía de Danza Española* (Choreography Competition; 3-4 days in June) with original music and extraordinary flamenco. (☎915 47 69 79; www.certamenflamenco.com. M: Sol.)

THEATER

Theaters are scattered throughout the city, with older ones in Huertas and newer venues for musicals around Callao. In July and August, Pl. Mayor, Lavapiés, and Villa de París frequently host outdoor performances. Tickets range from €3-30; student and senior discounts are often available. Theatergoers should consult magazines published by state-sponsored theaters, like **TeatroMADRID,** available outside most theaters. Some principal theaters are **Teatro Español,** C. del Príncipe, 25, in Pl. de Santa Ana (☎913 60 14 80; M: Sol or Sevilla), **Teatro Infanta Isabel,** C. Barquillo, 24 (☎915 19 47 69 or 915 21 02 12; M: Banco de España), **Teatro Fernán Gómez,** Pl. de Colón, 4 (☎914 80 03 00; M: Serrano or Colón), and the superb **Teatro María Guerrero,** C. Tamayo y Baus, 4 (☎913

10 15 00; M: Colón or Banco de España). Tickets can be purchased at theater box offices or at ticket agencies. (**El Corte Inglés** ☎902 40 02 22; **FNAC** 91 595 62 00; **Crisol** 902 11 83 12; **TelEntrada** 902 10 12 12; **Entradas.com** 902 48 84 88.)

FÚTBOL

Fútbol (soccer) festivities start hours before matches begin as fans with headphones congregate in the streets, listening to pre-game commentary and discussing it with other die-hard fans. If either **Real Madrid** (in all white) or **Atlético de Madrid** (in red and white stripes) wins a match, count on streets clogged with honking cars. Real, named the greatest club of the 20th century by FIFA, captured the **La Liga** title again last year, while Atlético finished a very solid 4th. Suburban **Getafe** doesn't quite have the same support, but only a few years ago won promotion to La Primera Liga, joining the other two. Every Sunday and some Saturdays between September and June, one of these three teams plays at home. Real Madrid plays at **Estadio Santiago Bernabéu,** Av. Cochina Espina, 1. (☎914 57 11 12. M: Santiago Bernabéu.) In the summer, the club offers tours of the stadium. (☎902 29 17 09; www.realmadrid.com. Tours daily 10:30am-6:30pm. €7-9.) Atlético de Madrid plays at **Estadio Vicente Calderón,** Po. de la Virgen del Puerto, 67. (☎913 64 22 34; www.clubatleticodemadrid.com. M: Pirámides or Marqués de Vadillos.) Getafe plays at **Coliseum Alfonso Pérez,** Avenida Teresa de Calcuta s/n. (☎916 95 97 71. M: Los Espartales.) Tickets for Real games sell out well in advance and will probably run €50-100; tickets for Atlético are a little cheaper, and lower still for Getafe.

BULLFIGHTS

Some call it animal torture, others tradition; either way, the Plaza de Ventas remains the most important bullfighting arena in the world since its opening in 1931. The ring plays host to the real professionals; you can also catch a summer *Novillada* (beginner), when a younger and less experienced bullfighter takes on smaller bulls. The cheap seats are in the sun, where it can get hot, but still afford an exceptional view of the action and are the best value. Wherever you sit, bring a cushion—the concrete is not comfortable.

From early May to early June, the **Fiestas de San Isidro** stage a daily *corrida* (bullfight) with top *matadores* and the fiercest bulls in the largest ring in Spain, **Plaza de las Ventas,** C. Alcalá, 237. (☎913 56 22 00; www.las-ventas.com or www.taquillatoros.com. M: Ventas.) A seat costs €2-115, depending on its location in the *sol* (sun) or *sombra* (shade). Tickets are available, in person only, the Friday and Saturday before and Sunday of a bullfight. There are bullfights every Sunday from March to October and less frequently the rest of the year. Look for posters in bars and cafes for upcoming *corridas* (especially on C. Victoria, off C. San Jerónimo). **Plaza de Toros Palacio de Vistalegre** also hosts bullfights and cultural events. (☎914 22 07 80. M: Vista Alegre. Call for schedule and prices.) To watch amateurs, head to the **Escuela de Tauromaquia,** a training school with its own *corridas* on Saturdays at 7:30pm. At the Casa de Campo, Avda. de Portugal Lago. Open M-F 10am-2pm. €7, children €3.50.)

FESTIVALS

The city bursts with dancing and processions during **Carnaval** in February, culminating on Ash Wednesday with the beginning of Lent and the *Entierro de la Sardina* (Burial of the Sardine), which commemorates the arrival of a shipload of rotting sardines to Madrid during the reign of Carlos III, who ordered them promptly buried. Goya's painting of these popular feasts and festivals hangs in the Real Academia de Bellas Artes. In March, the city gets dramatic for the renowned **International Theater Festival.** The Comunidad de Madrid celebrates its struggle against the French invasion of 1808 during the **Fiestas del 2 de Mayo** with bullfights and concerts. Starting May 15, the week-long **Fiestas de San Isidro** honor Madrid's patron saint with concerts, parades, and Spain's best bullfights. In the last week of May is the small but wonderful **Fería de la Tapa,** where restaurants and chefs put out their best for Madrid with fantastically cheap, exquisite tapas and beer. In the last week of June or the first week of July, Madrid goes mad with **Orgullo Gay** (Gay Pride). Outrageous floats filled with drag queens, muscle boys, and rambunctious lesbians shut down traffic between El Retiro and Puerta del Sol on the festival's first Saturday. Free concerts in Pl. Chueca and bar crawls among the congested streets of Chueca are popular weekend activities. Last year over 3 million people poured through Chueca during the course of the week. Throughout the summer, the city sponsors the **Veranos de la Villa.** Movies play nightly at 10:30pm in Parque de la Bombilla, Av. de Valladolid. (M: Príncipe Pío; June 29-Sept. 3. Ticket office opens 9:30pm. €5, students €4.50; schedule at tourist office.) The **Festivales de Otoño** (Autumn Festivals), from September to November, offer more refined music, theater, and film events. In November, an **International Jazz Festival** entices great musicians to Madrid. On New Year's Eve, **El Fin del Año,** crowds gather at Puerta del Sol to count down to the new year. The brochure *Madrid en Fiestas*, available at tourist offices, contains comprehensive details on Spain's festivals. The *Guía de Fiestas* details all the festivals for the year around the Comunidad de Madrid.

SHOPPING

For upscale shopping, throw on your oversized Gucci sunglasses and sashay down the swanky Calle Serrano and Calle Velázquez in the famous Salamanca district (near Pl. de Colón), where fine boutiques and specialty stores like Pedro del Hierro line the streets next to stores like Mango, Zara, and Armani. Most major department stores can be found between Puerta del Sol and Callao, with smaller clothing stores scattered along Gran Vía. **El Corte Inglés,** Spain's unavoidable all-in-one store, sports over 10 locations throughout the city. (www.corteingles.es. Some convenient locations include: C. Preciados, 3. ☎913 79 80 00. M: Sol. C. Goya, 76. ☎914 32 93 00. M: Goya. C. Princesa, 56 ☎ 914 54 60 00. M: Argüelles. Open daily 10am-10pm. AmEx/MC/V.)

Countless funky boutiques in Chueca display hot clubwear, tight jeans, and sexy street clothes. **Mercado Fuencarral,** C. Fuencarral, 45, specializes in funky attire and is home to many tattoo and piercing parlors. (☎915 21 41 52; www.mdf.es. Open M-Sa 11am-9pm.) By law, *grandes almacenes* (department stores) may open only the first Sunday of every month to allow smaller businesses to compete. Many boutiques close in August, when almost everyone flees to the coast. Non-EU residents can shop tax-free at major stores, as long as they remember to ask for their VAT return form and spend more than €100. (☎900 43 54 82 for more info. Don't forget to bring your passport.) The municipal tourist office has the *Rutas de Compras en Areas y Centros Comerciales de la Comunidad de Madrid*, a map with shopping routes.

EL RASTRO (FLEA MARKET)

For hundreds of years, **El Rastro** has been a Sunday-morning tradition in Madrid. The market begins in La Latina at Pl. Cascorro off C. Toledo and ends at the bottom of C. Ribera de Cortidores. El Rastro sells everything from zebra hides to jeans to antique tools to pet birds. As crazy as the market seems, it is actually thematically organized, and for many, a weekly ritual. The main street is a labyrinth of clothing, cheap jewelry, leather goods, incense, and sunglasses, branching out into side streets, each with its own repertoire of vendors and wares. As you descend further into the market, the typical shoestands disappear and more eclectic stalls appear, selling all manner of goods: back-issues of pornographic comic books, tarnished old silver tea services, and animal hides. Fantastic collections of old books and LPs are sold in Pl. del Campillo del Mundo at the bottom of C. Carlos Arnides. Whatever price you're thinking (or being offered), it can probably be bargained in half. The flea market is a pickpocket's paradise, so ditch your camera, bust out the money belt, and turn that backpack into a frontpack. Take a hint from the locals and always keep your hand on your bag while walking. (Open Sundays and holidays 9am-3pm.)

BOOKS

Books in English tend to be outrageously expensive in Spain. If you read Spanish, however, it's worthwhile to buy books here and ship or carry them home. **The Rastro,** Paseo del Duque Fernán Nuñez, at the bottom of El Retiro and just across the Paseo del Prado from the Reina Sofia Museum, and the many little shops in Huertas, are great places to find antique and more recent books on the cheap. **Casa del Libro,** Gran Vía, 29, is a chain of Spanish bookstores with a wide offering of books in every genre. (☎902 02 64 02. Open daily 9:30am-9:30 pm. Also at C. Fuencarral, 119, and C. Alcalá, 96.) **Altair,** C. Gaztambide, 31, is a comprehensive travel bookstore, with some excellent travel guides and knowledgeable staff. (M: Moncloa or Argüelles. ☎915 43 53 00. Open M-F 10am-2pm and 4:30-8:30pm, Sa 10:30am-2:30pm and 4:30-8pm. AmEx/MC/V.) The **Berkana Librería Gay y Lesbiana,** C. Hortaleza, 64, is a gay and lesbian bookstore with loads of contacts and a free map of gay Madrid. (M: Chueca. ☎915 22 55 99.)

NIGHTLIFE

We might as well title this section "Life." Nightlife, especially in the summer months, is not optional. The city does nightlife bigger and better, later and harder, with more bars, clubs, and discos—gay and straight—than perhaps anywhere else on earth. People hit the streets around 10 or 11 when music and liquor begin pouring out of bars and *cervecerías*, and the crowds and traffic are just as heavy at 2am on a Saturday night as at any point of the week. Proud of their nocturnal offerings, *madrileños* will tell you with a straight face that they were bored in Paris or New York—they insist that no one goes to bed until they've "killed the night" and, usually, a good part of the following morning.

A successful night involves several neighborhoods and countless venues. An evening might start in the tapas bars of Huertas, move to a bar in Malasaña, and then continue on to a wild disco in El Centro or Chueca. While bars open their doors around dinner, most clubs and discotecas don't start raging until 1 or 2am; *"los afters"*, semi-mythical clubs that continue partying past the legal hour of 6am, constantly change and require an ear to the ground. The only (relatively) quiet nights of the week are Monday and Tuesday. For clubs and discotecas, *entrada* (cover) often includes a drink and can be as high as €18; men may be charged up to €3 more than women, who may not be charged at all. Venues often change prices depending on the night; Saturdays are the most expensive. Keep an eye out for *invitaciones* and *oferta* cards—in stores, restaurants, tourist publications, and on the street—that offer a free *chupito* (shot) to lure you in the door. Walking home alone is obviously not as safe as walking with company, but if you must walk solo, avoid unlit areas like El Retiro, Salamanca, and some of the seedier metro stops around Sol, La Latina, and Lavapiés. Check a bus map for the best **Búho** (p. 87) home from Pl. de Cibeles. Alternatively, taxis are a safe ride home.

NIGHT READING. For info on the latest hotspots, scan Madrid's entertainment guides. The *Guía del Ocio,* available behind the counter of any news kiosk, should be your first purchase in Madrid (€1). Although it's in Spanish, alphabetical listings of clubs and restaurants are invaluable even to non-speakers. The *Guía* comes out on Fridays; buy the latest issue. For an English magazine with articles on new finds in and around the city, pick up *In Madrid*, free at tourist offices and many restaurants. For articles as well as listings, do what the cool *madrileños* do and check out *Salir Salir Madrid* (€2) at any kiosk. Gay travelers can pick up the free magazine *Shanguide,* which lists activities and nightspots, or buy *Zero* magazine at any kiosk (€5).

EL CENTRO

In the middle of Madrid and at the heart of the action are the spectacular clubs of El Centro. With multiple floors, swinging lights, cages, and disco balls, they meet even the wildest clubber's expectations. Some of the most happening tapas bars in town huddle southwest of Pl. Mayor, closer to M: Latina.

Joy Eslava, C. Arenal, 11 (☎913 66 54 39; www.joy-madrid.com). M: Sol. Madrid's sexy, rich, and famous come here to dance to R&B and club hits under artsy projections and frenetic strobing. This is the place to be—dress well and come early so you don't stand outside while Madrid's young and gorgeous are streaming through the VIP entrance. Drinks €15. Cover M-Th and Su €12-15, Fr-Sa €18, includes one drink; look for drink coupons to ease the pain in the pocket. Open daily midnight-6am.

Reinabruja, C. Jacometrezo, 6 (☎915 42 81 93). M: Callao. A sinuous, subterranean jungle of neon. Stenciled pillars and curving honeycombed walls constantly change color around the bumping central dance floor. Come ready and raring to dance—there's practically nowhere to sit down. Beer €6, mixed drinks €10-12. Cover €10 includes one drink. Open W-Sa 11pm-6am.

De Las Letras Restaurante, C. Gran Vía, 11 (☎915 23 79 80; www.hoteldelasletras.com). Situated right on the border between El Centro, Chueca, and Gran Vía, this beautiful terrace atop the hotel fills with an urbane, champagne-sipping crowd. The view from the top is good enough to offset the drink prices. Wine €3.15, mixed drinks €12. Open M-Th and Su 7:30pm-midnight, Fri-Sa 7:30pm-12:30am. MC/V.

MADRID

LA LATINA AND LAVAPIÉS

Away from the clubs of the centro are the bars of La Latina and Lavapiés, which cater to all groups, old, hip, and alternative, but all offer the same trusty old bar favorites—beer and tapas.

La Cabra en el Tejado, C. Santa Ana, 31, a right just off C. Toledo. A funky place, packed as local acts stand on tables and sing Spanish favorites. Sing or mumble along, enjoying the art exhibit along the walls while enjoying the Mediterranean tapas (hummus and *tzatziki* €3.50). Beer €2.50. Cheap glass of Rioja €1.30. No cover. Check the posters outside for concerts. Open M-W and Su 5:30pm-midnight, Th-Sa 5:30pm-2am.

Taberna Vinoçola Mentridana, C. San Eugenio, 9 (☎915 27 87 60) M: Antón Martín. A block off C. Atocha as you head towards Atocha. A popular local tapas bar during the day, at night this place revs up with locals thirsty for a glass of wine (€1.50-5). Countless varieties of red, white, and rosé line the walls. The wooden tables and the students sipping lend the place an earthy feel, so go with the red *(tinto).* Beer €1.20. MC/V.

Achuri, C. Argumosa, 21 (☎914 68 78 56). M: Lavapiés. An alternative crowd—mohawks and Marxists—pile in and spill out onto the sidewalk for the alcohol and huge sandwiches at proletarian prices. *Caña* of beer €1.10, liter €4.70. Wine €1-2 per glass. *Bocadillos* €4. Open M-Th and Su 1:30pm-2am, F-Sa 1:30pm-2:30am. Cash only.

HUERTAS

Plaza de Santa Ana and the long **C. Huertas** brim with *terrazas*, bars, and jazz cafes. Many discobars convert to clubs as the night unfolds, spinning house and techno on intimate dance floors. Its variety makes Huertas is one of the best places to party. **C. del Príncipe** is lined with smaller spots, in contrast to the pricey, thumping discotecas of **C. de Atocha.** Most locals begin their nights in Huertas and end them in El Centro or Chueca. If you do, skip the bars offering the same five mixed drinks in favor of more original choices elsewhere.

Trocha, C. Huertas, 55 (☎91 429 78 61; www.trochabar.com). M: Antón Martín. Watch the barman squeeze the lemons and limes into your *caipirinha* (€6-7), the house specialty, as you sit back and take in the smooth jazz and and art prints on the walls. The ultimate place to relax. Other drinks €4-7. Open daily 4:30pm-2:30am.

Teatro Kapital, C. de Atocha, 125 (☎91 420 29 06). M: Atocha. 7 fl. of justly famed discoteca insanity. From hip-hop to house, open *terrazas* to cinemas and karaoke, it is easy to lose yourself, your dignity, and all your money in the madness. Drinks €9-12. Cover €12-18 includes 1 drink, but look for people handing out cards that will get you 2 drinks included if you head in before 1:30am. Open Th-Su midnight-6am.

El Café de Schérezad, C. Santa Maria, 18 (☎ 91 369 24 74). M: Antón Martín. Young *madrileños* lie on plush cushions and carpets and savor the hookah smoke and Moroccan music. Delicious herbal teas come with fresh fruit and small pastries. Tea €3.50 and hookah €7-10. Open Th and Sun 6pm-2am, M-W and F-Sa 6pm-3am.

Cuevas de Sésamo, C. del Príncipe, 7 (☎914 29 65 24). M: Antón Martín. "Descend into these caves like Dante!" (Antonio Machado) is one of the many colorful literary tidbits that welcome you to this smoky, underground gem. Charmingly worn plush seats and live jazz from an unassuming upright piano (Tu-Su) bring in Madrid's bohemian youth. Beer €2.50, bottles of red wine €9. Open daily 7pm-2am.

Cardamomo, C. de Echegaray, 15 (☎913 69 07 57; www.cardamomo.net). M: Sevilla. Flamenco and Latin music spin all night. Those who prefer to relax retreat to the lounge area. Live music at midnight on W nights brings out a dancing crowd, while mobs cram in to see professional dancing on Tu and Th at midnight. Come early for a good spot. Admission to shows €10-15. Beer €5, mixed drinks €7-10. Open Tu-Sa 9pm-3:30am.

Viva Madrid, C. Manuel Fernández González, 7 (☎914 29 36 40), off C. Echegaray. M: Sol or Sevilla. This is the country for old men and the young in one another's arms, who have been shouting down the bar and carousing here since 1870. It is worth the little extra for the breeze and ambience of the outdoor seating, but there's plenty of room in the elegantly-tiled area upstairs. Beer €3-4, mixed drinks €8. Open daily 1pm-2am.

The Penthouse, Pl. Santa Ana, 16 (☎917 01 60 20). M: Antón Martín or Sol. Directly across the lively Plaza Santa Ana from the Teatro Español, the Penthouse is a swanky hangout for the elite. Atop a fancy hotel, the bar overlooks the Plaza for an expansive view of the city and its insomniac nightlife. The line can be long, and the seating is limited, so arrive early. Drinks €10-14. Sushi €21. Open daily from 9pm-3am. MC/V.

GRAN VÍA

Drum and bass beats pound well into the early morning in the boisterous landmark clubs on the neon-lit side streets of Gran Vía. Subtlety has never been a strong suit of this area, nor is it known for its safety; a mix of seedy tourists and locals makes Gran Vía less than ideal for late-night wandering.

Museo Chicote, C. Gran Vía, 12 (☎915 32 67 37). M: Gran Vía. Recline in green leather chairs amid glamorous black-and-white pictures of silver screen celebrities. Share mixed drinks with Madrid's chic socialites after 11pm. Beer €4-5. Famous mixed drinks €9. Open daily 4pm-4am. AmEx/MC/V.

Costello Club, C. Caballero de Gracia, 10 (☎915 23 01 74). M: Gran Vía. Packed spot with alternative rock for Madrid's scenesters. 3-4 concerts per week (free to €6). Beer €4. Mixed drinks €8-10. Happy hr. M-Tu 6-8pm. Open daily 6pm-last out. MC/V.

Ocho y Medio Club, C. Mesonero Romanos, 13 (☎91 541 35 00; www.tripfamily.com). Where the cool kids go for their late-night discoteca fix; the line will probably be long, so come early. Local hipsters dance to electronica remixes of their favorite tunes. Each F offers a new DJ or live performance. Sa is Dark Hole, a goth extravaganza. Check the website for schedule. Drinks €7-10. Cover €10-12 includes 1 drink. Open F-Sa 1-6am.

MALASAÑA AND CHUECA

Plaza Chueca and Plaza Dos de Mayo are social hubs. For those cutting costs, handing a bottle around in the the plaza is just about the norm. Outside the plazas are traditional and more modern bars and shifty clubs with dark fronts and ominously closed doors. As you branch out along the smaller radiating streets, bars become less frequent. Many partygoers migrate to other areas, but the area vibrates deep into *la madrugada* (dawn). Chueca also has a good number of gay establishments. The area is ideal for bar-hopping until 2 or 3am, when people hit the clubs near Sol, El Centro, and Gran Vía.

Bar Nike, C. Augusto Figueroa, 22 (☎915 21 07 51). M: Chueca. A colorless *cafetería* where half of Chueca comes to drink before clubbing. Absolutely packed from wall to wall. Fight your way to the bar for an enormous, sticky *calimocho* (red wine and cola; €4.20). Beer €4.50. Sangria €5. Open daily noon-3am.

El Clandestino, C. del Barquillo, 34 (☎915 21 55 63). M: Chueca. Chill crowd nurses drinks under diffuse red light, then heads down into the caves and dark corners downstairs to nod and dance to the DJ's acid jazz, fusion, and funk selections. Beer €3. Mixed drinks €6. Live music most Th-Sa at 11:30pm. Open M-Sa 6:30pm-3am.

El Truco, C. de Gravina, 10 (☎915 32 89 21). M: Chueca. It's a miracle that dancers find room to move their bodies in this packed, gay- and lesbian-friendly disco-bar. Marvel at the feat or jockey for your own hip space. The line is long, but outdoor seating helps avoid the €4 cover on weekends. Beer €3.50. Same owners also run the popular Escape, also on the plaza. Open Th 10pm-late, F-Sa midnight-late.

Why Not?, C. de San Bartolomé, 7. M: Chueca. A super-hip underground bunker playing Europop and salsa. Well-dressed patrons sip drinks under the domed ceiling and gazes of black-and-white Hollywood stars of olden days. Beer €6. Mixed drinks €8-10. Cover €8 when crowded, includes 1 drink. Open daily 11:30pm-6am.

l'Ievn, Pl. Vasquez de Mella, 11 (☎918 24 13 10). M: Chueca. A bar designed by dictionary aesthetes. Blue neon scattered through wire mesh and piled rocks suspended behind metal grating vie with artsy definitions of food, music, and sound on the front window. Jazz piano lends old-world class; shows at noon on Su. Beer €3, mixed drinks €9-12. Veuve Cliquot €55. Open M-Th and Su noon-1:30am, Fr-Sa noon-2:30am. MC/V.

ARGÜELLES AND MONCLOA

The only reason to leave Madrid's better nighttime areas for Moncloa is **Los Bajos,** a concrete megaplex of diminutive bars serving incredibly cheap *chupitos*. As student population comes out looking for cheap drinks, decor is secondary here. Bars are usually only open Fridays and Saturdays and close around 2-3am. From M: Moncloa, align yourself with the center of the imposing

Ejército del Aire building on C. de la Princesa and cross the street under the double archway. Walk one block up C. de Hilarion Eslava and turn left onto C. de Fernando el Católico. Los Bajos is a few blocks down on the left.

BILBAO

Azúcar Paladar, C. Manuela Malasaña, 20 (☎91 447 77 99), two blocks off Gl. de Bilbao. Salsa and faded prints of Havana set the island mood in this small but happening bar. Comes replete with all manner of tropical mixed drinks (€6), so don't order the beer (€3). Open M-W and Su 5pm-midnight, Th-Sa 5pm-2am.

La Musa, C. Manuela Malasaña, 18 (☎914 48 75 78; www.lamusa.com.es). Hip, chain resto-bar made hipper by a funky collection of shadowbox artwork. At night fills with couples sipping on the vast selection of reds and rosés. Wine €2.50 per glass. Vermouth €1.80. Open daily 1:30-5pm and 9pm-midnight.

DAYTRIPS FROM MADRID

SAN LORENZO DE EL ESCORIAL ☎918

El Escorial—half monastery and half mausoleum—is the most popular daytrip from Madrid. Although Felipe II constructed El Escorial for himself and God, the complex, with its magnificent library, palaces, and works of art, seems made for tourists. Visits are popular during August's Fiestas de San Lorenzo, when parades line the streets and fireworks fill the sky, and on Romería a la Ermita de la Virgen de Gracia, the second Sunday in September, when folk dancing contests fill the forests. The whole town shuts down on Mondays.

TRANSPORTATION AND PRACTICAL INFORMATION

El Escorial's train station (☎918 90 00 15), on Ctra. Estación, is 2km outside of town. **Trains** run to Atocha and Chamartín stations in Madrid (1hr.; 30 per day M-F and Su 5:47am-10:15pm, Sa 19 per day 5:47am-10:15pm; €2.90). Autocares Herranz **buses** (☎918 96 90 28) run from Madrid's Moncloa metro station (bus #661, in the bus interchange just above the metro platform; 50min.; every 10-30min. M-F 6:15am-10pm, Sa 8am-8pm, Su 8am-10pm; €3.20) and back (every 15min. M-F 7:15am-10pm, Sa 9am-9:30pm, Su 9am-11pm; €3.20). **Shuttles** go between the bus and train stations (M-F every 20min. 7:23am-10:38pm, Sa-Su every 20min.-1hr. 9:44am-10:38pm; €1.15).

The **tourist office** is located at C. Grimaldi, 4. (☎918 90 53 13; www.sanlorenzoturismo.org. Open Tu-F 11am-6pm, Sa-Su 10am-3pm.) With your back to the bus station, turn right down C. Juan de Toledo, then make a right onto C. Floridablanca. Follow C. Floridablanca until the first archway on the left. From the train station, take the shuttle to the bus station or exit the train station, walk straight ahead, and follow the signs uphill (25min.). For a more peaceful walk, exit the train station and enter the Casita del Príncipe entrance directly in front of you. Start walking uphill and take the C. de los Tilos path, which leads to the monastery (25min.). The **police** are at Pl. de la Constitución, 3 (☎918 90 52 23). Many 24hr. **ATMs** can also be found along this street.

SIGHTS

EL ESCORIAL

☎918 90 59 03. Complex open Tu-Su Apr.-Sept. 10am-7pm; Oct.-Mar. 10am-6pm. Last entry to palaces, pantheons, and museums 30min. before closing. Complete visit 2hr.

Guided tour €10. Spanish tours every 15min.; English times vary. Monastery €8, students and seniors €4. Admission to tombs and library €8/4. EU citizens free W.

MONASTERIO. "*El escoria*" translates roughly to "scum." Indeed, the regal Escorial sits atop a mound that was once a refuse heap of bones and dung. Ironically, the pile of leftovers includes royal bones dating back to Charles V. Felipe II built the Monasterio de San Lorenzo de el Escorial as a gift to God and his people, and perhaps to alleviate his conscience for sacking a French church at the battle of San Quintín in 1557. In 1563, he commissioned Juan Bautista de Toledo to design the monastery-mausoleum complex on the side of Mt. Abantos, but Toledo died just four years into the project and the job fell to his pupil Juan de Herrera. With the exception of the Panteón Real and minor additions, the monastery was completed in just 21 years. Felipe oversaw the work from a chair-shaped rock, the Silla de Felipe II, 7km away.

What distinguishes El Escorial from other huge royal palaces is its utter simplicity. Four towers surround the central basilica in a perfect rectangle. Its "*herreriano*" style focuses on straight lines in preference to decorative pattern, which the architect thought distracted from the unity of the whole. Felipe himself described it as "majesty without ostentation." Majesty indeed, the complex has 16 patios, 88 fountains, 1200 doors, and some 2700 windows, an incredible number for a building used only during religious festivals.

GALLERIES AND LIVING QUARTERS. To avoid the worst of the crowds, enter El Escorial through the gateway on C. Floridablanca, where you'll find a collection of Flemish art. Though much of the work is standard religious fare, keep an eye out for some exceptions. Bosch's famous "Garden of Earthly Delights" hangs in replica on a tapestry in the first room. In the next room is El Greco's "El Martirio de San Mauricio,", which was apparently hidden away on a wall in the sacristy because it failed to please his majesty. Other works by Dürer, Zurbarán, Tintoretto, and Ribera also grace the walls of the galleries. The newly opened **Museum of Architecture,** after the art galleries, has plaster models of El Escorial, early building plans, and enormous 16th-century construction machinery that shows how the huge blocks of stone were lifted.

Azulejo tiles from Toledo line the Palacio Real, which includes the **Salón del Trono** (Throne Room) and two dwellings: Felipe II's spartan 16th-century apartments and the more luxurious 18th-century rooms of Carlos III and Carlos IV. As the retreat was only used during religious holidays, Felipe II's rooms were designed so he could listen to and see masses from his own bed. The **Puertas de Marguetería,** crafted by German artist Jacob Weisshaupt, are doors inlaid with 18 kinds of wood in masterfully intricate patterns. The **Sala de Batallas** (Battle Room) links the two parts of the palace with frescoes by Italian artists Grabelo and Castello. The walls and ceiling trumpet first Castilla's and then united Spain's greatest victories—including Juan II's 1431 triumph over the Muslims at Higueruela, Felipe II's successful expeditions in the Azores, and the Battle of San Quintín. Look closer for comic details of the everyday; bowmen share a laugh during battle as two peasants look on, passing a wineskin.

LIBRARY. The *biblioteca* on the second floor holds over 40,000 priceless folios and manuscripts. Though several fires have reduced the collection, the extant volumes—some bound as early as 1500—are in remarkably good condition; the bindings, made of scraped hide, can last for hundreds of years. St. Agustin's *De Baptismo*, placed between the 5th and 6th centuries, Alfonso X's *Cantigas de Santa María*, Santa Teresa's manuscripts and diary, the gold-scrolled *Aureus Codex* of 1039 by German Emperor Conrad III, and an 11th-century *Commentary on the Apocalypse* by Beato de Liébana provide just a sampling.

BASÍLICA. Under the gigantic central dome is the basilica, which for years was seen as a direct link between the kings and God. Up the stairs are gilded statues of the entire royal family, genuflecting before Jesus and the more earthly retinue of Popes, saints, and clergymen. Felipe II's room overlooks Titian's ceiling fresco of the martyrdom of San Lorenzo.

PANTHEONS. The impressive—and creepy—**Panteón Real** contains the remains of Spanish kings since Charles V (and a lone queen, Isabel II); their stacked green marble tombs lie in a circular room. The nearby **Panteón de los Infantes** was built to house the remains of royal children.

VALLE DE LOS CAÍDOS

The Valle de los Caídos is accessible only via El Escorial. Autocares Herranz runs Bus #660 to the monument from the Pl. de la Virgen de Gracia (☎918 90 41 25 or 96 90 28. 20min.; Tu-Su 3:15pm, returns 5:30pm; round-trip plus admission €8.30.) Abadía Benedictina de Santa Cruz del Valle de los Caídos (☎ 918 90 56 11 or 918 90 13 98; patrimonionacional.es) holds mass M-Sa 11am; Su 11am, 12:30, 1, and 5:30pm. Entrance gate open Tu-Su 10am-6pm. €5.30. EU citizens free W.

In a valley 8km north of **El Escorial,** General Franco forced Republican prisoners to build the overpowering monument of **Santa Cruz del Valle de los Caídos** (Holy Cross of the Valley of the Fallen) as a memorial to those who gave their lives in the Spanish Civil War. As a historical wonder, this site should not be missed—but it also should not be misunderstood. Although ostensibly a monument to both sides, the inscription over the door to the crypt that reads "Caídos por Díos y España" (Fallen for God and Spain) suggests it is more a Nationalist memorial than anything else. Construction of the massive granite cross claimed the lives of at least 14 forced laborers. To climb to the base of the cross, follow the paved road up to the trailhead just past the monastery on the right (30min.), or take the **funicular.** Apocalyptic tapestries line the vast, austere, cave-like **basilica,** where the ghost of Fascist architecture rests. Muscular warrior monks watch the pews, while gigantic death-angels guard the crucified Jesus. Forty thousand dead Nationalists and many unidentified other soldiers are buried behind the chapel walls; **José Antonio Primo de Rivera** (godfather of Spanish fascism and the **Falange** party) and General Franco himself rest beside the high altar, underneath the imposing cross with its giant statues. While the monument could be seen as a testament to the glory of Franco's dictatorship, for most Spaniards it persists as a stain on the central Spanish landscape.

COMUNIDAD DE MADRID

The Comunidad de Madrid is an autonomous administrative region smack in the middle of Spain, bordered by Castilla y León to the north and west and Castilla La Mancha to the south and east. Beyond Madrid proper, the Comunidad offers travelers a variety of daytrips to exquisite cultural landscapes and small-town serenity; these are just a start to possible explorations.

ALCALÁ DE HENARES ☎918

The one-time home of Golden Age authors Miguel de Cervantes, Francisco de Quevedo, and Lope de Vega, and site of a university dating to 1498, the Renaissance city of Alcalá de Henares (pop. 191,000) is packed with old stone churches and equally ancient literary history but doesn't get much press. Packed with students, families, and stores with the name "Cervantes" on them, the town is worth a quick train ride from Madrid.

TRANSPORTATION. The train station is on Po. de la Estación (☎902 24 02 02). Cercanías trains run to Estación Atocha in Madrid (40min., every 10min. 5:54am-11:26pm, €2.45). To get to the center from the train station, turn right on to Paseo de la Estación, then left on to Libreros. Continental Auto, Av. Guadalajara, 5 (☎918 88 16 22), runs buses between Alcalá and Madrid (45min.; M-Sa every 15min. 5:10am-11pm, Su every 30min. 7-9am and every 20min. 9am-11pm; €2.13). To reach the city center from the bus station, turn right onto Av. De Guadalajara and walk 5 blocks. Taxis can be summoned at ☎918 82 21 88.

ORIENTATION AND PRACTICAL INFORMATION. The **tourist office,** Pl. de Cervantes, 1, offers a list of local cultural events and has maps and suggestions for accommodations and restaurants. To get there, walk the length of Pl. Cervantes toward the bell tower and turn left down the small street. There is also an office in the Pl. de los Santos Niños. (☎918 89 26 94; www.alcalaturismo.com. Open daily in summer 10am-2pm and 5-7:30pm. July-Aug closed Monday.) On weekends the tourist office leads tours in Spanish to major sites in the city. (☎918 82 13 54. Leaves at noon and 5:30pm).

FOOD. Alcalá's famed *almendras garrapiñadas* (honey- and sugar-coated almonds) beg to be sampled. At night, it seems that the whole town comes out to eat on the terrazas on **C. Mayor** and **Pl. de Cervantes.** Dinner *menús* can be pricey (€18-25), so the tapas that come with your drink at **Rocio Chico ❶**, C. Ramón y Cajal, 3, are a good alternative. You can feed two with the fantastically huge *tortilla patata bocadillo* (*tortilla* sandwich) for €3.50. *Menú* €21. (☎918 83 10 75. Drinks €2-3. Open daily 8pm-2am. Cash only.)

SIGHTS. The **Capilla del Oidor,** where Cervantes was christened, survives. Nowadays it displays the baptismal font and shows a video on the history of the church and the Cervantes' life in Alcalá. (☎918 79 73 80. Open June-Sept. Tu-Su noon-2pm and 6-9pm; Oct.-May Tu-Su noon-2pm and 5-8pm. Free.) Just before Pl. de Cervantes in Pl. de San Diego, take a left off C. de Libreros onto C. Bedel to see the **Colegio Mayor de San Ildefonso** (☎918 85 64 87). In the main hall, where doctorates were once awarded, the king now presents the Premio Cervantes, Spain's most prestigious literary award, during the week-long **Festival de Cervantes.** The hall and Capilla de San Ildefonso both have spectacular *mudéjar* ceilings. (Mandatory tours in summer M-F 6 per day 11am-2pm and 5-7pm, Sa-Su every 30min. 11am-2pm and 5-7:30pm. €3.) Down C. Mayor from Pl. de Cervantes is the **Casa Natal de Cervantes,** the reconstructed house where the author was born in 1547, replete with editions of Don Quixote in languages Cervantes never knew existed. Bronze statues of the delusional knight and his long-suffering squire sit on a bench outside. (☎918 89 96 54; www.museo-casa-natal-cervantes.org. Open Tu-Su 10am-6pm. Free.)

On the way back to the bus station, stop at the **Palacio de Laredo,** a strange neo-*mudéjar* mansion on Po. de la Estación tucked between tall, boxy apartments. Built by an eccentric 19th-century writer and painter, it is a composite of styles ranging from Gothic to Renaissance to *mudéjar.* Unable to afford tile and marble, Laredo cleverly painted imitation versions on tile throughout the house. From the Alhambra he brought the idea of the *Sala de los Secretos,* with its acoustic tricks, and built a secret door to his Persian minaret, where he'd hide from unwelcome visitors. Today it holds several old Bibles, one of which was used to produce the first English Bible. (☎918 85 64 87. Mandatory 30min. tours leave every 30min. M-F 4:40-7pm and Sa-Su 11am-7pm. €2.50).

ARANJUEZ ☎918

Once a getaway for Habsburg and Bourbon royalty and now named a World Heritage Cultural Landscape by UNESCO, Aranjuez remains a worthwhile retreat for its dazzling gardens and palaces, as well as famous asparagus and strawberries.

TRANSPORTATION. RENFE trains, C. de la Estación (☎902 24 00 42), go to **Cuenca** (2hr.; M-F 4-5 per day 6:10am-8:14pm, Sa-Su 9:23am-8:14pm; €7.70), and **Madrid** (45min.; to Estación Atocha M-F every 15-30min.; 5:30am-11:30pm, Sa-Su 6am-11:30pm; to Estación Chamartín M-F 8-10 per day 6:57am-9:27pm, Sa-Su 8:57am-9:27pm; €2.90). AISA, C. de las Infantas, 16 (☎902 198 788; www.aisa-grupo.com) also runs buses to **Toledo** (30min., 8am and 4:15pm, €2.60.) and **Madrid** (45min, every 15min. 5am-midnight, €3.20).

ORIENTATION AND PRACTICAL INFORMATION. To reach the city, exit left from the train station parking lot and follow signs to the Palacio Real. With your back to the bus station, head left onto C. de las Infantas toward the main fountain. Alternatively, climb aboard the **Chiquitren de Aranjuez,** a sightseeing train, to catch all the major sights. (☎918 08 80 89. €4, under 13 €2, not including admission to museums and sights.) The helpful **tourist office** in Pl. San

Antonio, 9, stores luggage and distributes maps with a complete list of sights, restaurants, and accomodations. (☎918 91 04 27; www.aranjuez.net. Open daily Apr.-Sept. 10am-6pm; Oct.-Mar. 9am-5:30pm.) Services include: **police,** C. Príncipe, 42, on the corner of Montesinos. (☎091 or 918 09 09 80); **pharmacy,** C. Real, 25, on the corner of C. del Capitán Angosto Gómez Castrillón and C. Real (☎918 91 08 62. Open M-F 9:30am-1:45pm and 5:30-8:30pm, Sa 10am-1:45pm. MC/V). **Internet** access at **Locutorio Casablanca,** on C. Florida at the corner of C. de la Rosa, 5 blocks south of the Palacio Real. Internet €0.70 for 30min., €1.20 for an hour. Open daily noon-4pm and 7-10pm. The **post office** is on C. de Peñarredonda, 3, off C. del Capitán Angosto Gómez Castrillón. (☎918 91 11 32. Open M-F 8:30am-8:30pm, Sa 9:30am-1pm.) **Postal Code:** 28300.

ACCOMMODATIONS AND FOOD. Aranjuez smiles on tourists with money, as do most of its hotels, which charge a lot for a night's rest. The only real budget option in town is **Hostal Rusiñol ❷,** C. de San Antonio, 76. Rooms are small and square but have windows overlooking a sunny central courtyard. Rooms with TV and sink. Communal baths are big and clean. Some doubles have A/C. (☎918 91 01 55; www.hostalesaranjuez.com. Singles €24, with bath €40; doubles €44/52. MC/V.) Most dining options around the Palace and gardens cater to tourists and are quite pricey. For cheaper eats, try the indoor **Mercado de Abastos** on Ctra. de Andalucía. With your back to the tourist office, go left through the arch; the market is on the left. It sells fish, meat, and fruits for reasonable prices, if you're inclined to cook. Massive baskets of strawberries €5. (Open M-F 9am-2pm and 6-9pm, Sa 9am-3pm.) Be sure to grab some delicious **fresones con nata** (strawberries and cream), the local delicacy, from the vendors just over the small bridge near the main fountain in front of the palace gardens. **El Rana Verde** 3, C. de la Reina, 1, by the water, has been serving up *ancasa de rana* (€11.50) and tasty asparagus (€10.70) in a lime-green waterfront setting since 1903. (☎918 01 15 71; www.aranjuez.com/ranaverde. Dinner €15-20. Open daily 9am-midnight. AmEx/D/MC/V.)

SIGHTS. The chief architect of El Escorial, Juan de Herrera, designed the resplendent white **Palacio Real** under the direction of Felipe II. Later monarchs Felipe V, Fernando VI, and Carlos III enlarged and embellished the palace, but it was Isabel II who left her mark in the mid-19th century with over-the-top draperies and decor. The work of Luca Giordano and Sabatini, whose gardens flank the Palacio Real in Madrid, decorate the walls and drawing rooms of the palace, along with Flemish tapestries. Among the best items are Isabel's strangely proportioned royal bed, and the Arabian study, a smoking room covered in Arabesque traceries, which was designed by Rafael Contreras, restorer of the Alhambra. On your way out, the **Museo de la Vida en Palacio** contains a collection of toys of the royal children, a large collection of ornate fans, and the wedding dresses of the current Queen Sofia and her daughters. *(☎918 91 07 40; www.patrimonionacional.es. Open Apr.-Sept. Tu-Su 10am-6:15pm; Oct.-Mar. Tu-Su 10am-5:15pm. 1hr. tours in English or Spanish approx. every 15min. The 1hr. tour gives access to 12 extra rooms. €4.50, students €2.50; with guided tour €5/€3. Museo de la Vida free.)*

Just outside the palace is a labyrinth of river walkways, freshly trimmed hedges, and mythological statues, all part of the **Jardín del Parterre** and the adjacent **Jardín de la Isla,** surrounded by rivers on both sides. The largest garden in Aranjuez is Jardín del Príncipe, a short walk from the palace on C. de la Reina. *(Open daily Apr.-Sept. 8am-8:30pm; Oct.-Mar. 8am-6:30pm. Free.)* At the very top of the garden is the **Falúas Museum,** once home to the Tajo's sailing squad. Nowadays it stores royal gondolas. *(☎918 91 03 05. Open Tu-Su Oct.-Mar. 10am-5:15pm; Apr.-Sept. 10am-6:15pm. €2, for students and under 16 €1. €8 combined ticket for Palacio Real. W EU* *citizens free.)* The last weekend in May, when the **strawberry harvest** reaches its pinnacle, Aranjuez holds parades, concerts, and bullfights in the Plaza de Toros, Av. Pl. de Toros, 1, at the very southern end of C. Capitán. The bullring is open for visitors and has a small museum. *(Open M-Sa 10:30am-1:30pm and 4:30-7:30pm, Su 10:30am-1:30pm. Free.)*

SIERRA DE GUADARRAMA

The Sierra de Guadarrama is a cold, clear, and dry retreat from Madrid's noise and pollution. If Madrid's urbane sophistication has got you down, consider spending an afternoon (or a few days) in the Sierra, a pine-covered mountain range halfway between Madrid and Segovia. With *La Mujer Muerta* (The Dead Woman) to the west, the *Sierra de la Maliciosa* (Mountains of the Evil Woman) to the east, and the less imaginatively named *Siete Picos* (Seven Peaks) along its northern perimeter, the Sierra draws visitors in all seasons to hike and ski.

CERCEDILLA ☎918

A picturesque chalet town graced with mild summer heat and ample winter snow, Cercedilla (pop. 6,000) is the ideal base for venturing into the Sierra. Summertime sees an invasion of city-dwellers escaping the smog and dirt and enjoying the mountain scenery.

TRANSPORTATION. The **train station** (☎918 52 00 57), at the base of the hill on C. Emilio Serrano, goes to: **Los Cotos** (45min.; M-F and Su 8 per day 9:35am-6:35pm, Sa hourly 9:35am-7:35pm except 2:35pm; €3.80, round-trip €6.55) via **Puerto de Navacerrada** (€3.70); **Madrid's Atocha** and **Chamartín** stations (1hr.; over 20 per day M-F and Su 6:07am-10:35pm, Sa 6:37am-9:35pm; €3.80) via **Villalba** (30min., €1.30); and **Segovia** (45min., 8-9 per day 7:27am-9:23pm, €2.70). **Larrea** (☎918 52 02 39) sends **buses** from the stop across from the *Ayuntamiento* in Plaza Mayor, with a stop by the train station, to **Madrid** (1hr.; M-F every 20-30min. 5:30am-10:20pm, Sa-Su every 20-30min. 6:20am-10:20pm; €3.65).

PRACTICAL INFORMATION. Upon arrival in Cercedilla, proceed a few kilometers up the hill along Carretera las Dehesas to the **Valle de la Fuentría: Centro de Educación Ambiental,** which has tourist info and great hiking maps (some in English) and is the starting point for several hikes (**Hiking,** p. 130). To get there from either station, you may want to call a **taxi** (Manolo ☎619 80 64 52; Francisco 650 26 30 43; and Juan 619 226 272; each about €7) or wait for one, though they do not come often. **Larrea** buses run from the train station to the centro intermittently (every 50min. daily 8am-7:40pm, €1). The *centro* is roughly 3km from the train station on Carretera de las Dehesas. By foot (40min.), go straight uphill and bear right on C. Mayor with all the signs, then walk for 20 minutes. Local services include the **police** (☎918 52 15 53) and the **health center,** the **Centro de Salud** (☎918 52 30 31, emergency 52 04 97).

ACCOMMODATIONS AND FOOD. Cercedilla makes an easy daytrip from Madrid. Most albergues and hostels are booked in summer, so reservations should be made at least 15 days in advance. Conveniently located near the trails, **Albergue Juvenil "Las Dehesas" (HI) ❶,** Ctra. de las Dehesas km. 2.5h, is a beautiful government-subsidized hostel at the foot of the mountains. Rooms (for 2-6 people) are bright and clean with shared bath. Guests mingle in the large common spaces and basketball court. (☎918 52 01 35; www.madrid.org/

inforjoven. Blankets provided, but not sheets or towels. Open Jan. 2-Aug. 15 and Sept. 21-Dec. 30. HI card required and available for purchase. With breakfast €8.50, with 2 meals €11.50, with 3 meals €14; over 26 €12/15.50/18.50.Cash only.) **Villa Castora (HI)** ❶ is about 1km up Ctra. de las Dehesas from the fork that leads to the Centro on the left, and has rooms with two to four beds and private bath. (☎918 52 03 34; fax 52 24 11. Reception 8am-10pm. Reservations strongly recommended. With breakfast €8.50, with 2 meals €11.50, with 3 meals €14; over 26 €12/15.50/18.50.) **Camping** is strictly controlled throughout the Sierra de Guadarrama and is prohibited in the area surrounding Cercedilla. Since you'll be staying in town, ask the Centro de Educación Ambiental for a list of Cercedilla's restaurants. For groceries, find **Supermarket Gigante,** C. Doctor Cañados, 2, in the town center off Av. del Generalísimo. (☎918 52 23 19. Open M-Sa 9:30am-2pm and 5-9pm, Su 10am-2:30pm.)

HIKING. The **Valle de la Fuentría: Centro de Educación Ambiental** offers hiking information for visitors. (☎918 52 22 13. Open daily 10am-6pm. Some English spoken.) The Centro provides detailed maps of six trails and day hikes ranging from the challenging (14.3km, 5-6hr.) **El GR-10** to the more relaxed **Camino Puricelli** (4km, 1hr.), which conveniently leads from the trailhead to the train station. Set aside an afternoon for the orange trail, **Los Miradores** (9.3km, 3hr.), a hike with fantastic views of the valley. Most of the hiking around Cercedilla begins up **Carretera las Dehesas,** near the Centro de Educación Ambiental. At the top of the Carretera, the **Calzada Romana** (about 1.5km from the Centro) follows a Roman road between Madrid and Segovia (1hr.). Springs marked with a blue dot on the trail map should have potable water, but double check at the Centro. Weather is unpredictable, so bring a rain jacket and sweater. Those who prefer wheels over heels should check out the bike trails.

CASTILLA Y LEÓN

Culture and grandeur pervade the province of Castilla y León. Spanish icons like the fairy-tale Alcázar and Roman aqueduct of Segovia, the Gothic cathedrals of Burgos and León, the Romanesque belfries along the Camino de Santiago, the sandstone of Salamanca, and the city walls of Ávila all belong to this ancient region. Well before Fernando of Aragón and Isabel of Castilla were joined in a world-shaking matrimony, Castilla was the political and military powerhouse of Spain. During the High Middle Ages, it emerged from obscurity to lead the Christian charge against Islam. Its nobles, enriched by the spoils of combat, made their success official: *castellano* became the dominant language of the nation. Castilla's comrade in arms, León, though chagrined to be lumped with Castilla in a 1970s reorganization, shares many cultural similarities with its neighbor while bringing its own wealth of historical and natural beauty.

HIGHLIGHTS OF CASTILLA Y LEÓN

GUSH over the Roman aqueduct in **Segovia** (p. 135).

LOSE yourself in the medieval library of the **Universidad de Salamanca** (p. 145).

SMILE with the saints on the facade of **León's** stunning cathedral (p. 154).

WIN a golden ticket to the Museo de Chocolate in medieval **Astorga** (p. 156).

SEGOVIA ☎921

Segovia's famous aqueduct and imposing castle, set high above lush green hills, make it feel like something out of a picture-book. Its beauty hasn't gone unnoticed, with tourists streaming in every day, cameras out, to try and capture a little of the magic. It was here, too, that Columbus charmed the crown into financing his journey to the New World. Though Segovia is a city of 60,000, you'd hardly notice—stay for a few days and you're sure to recognize a few faces by the end. If you do make it to this "stone ship" (so called because the stone aqueduct resembles a ship's helm), expect to shell out a little more cash; but trust us, Segovia should not be missed.

TRANSPORTATION

Trains: Po. Obispo Quesada (☎902 24 02 02). To **Madrid** (2hr.; 7-9 per day M-F 5:55am-8:55pm, Sa-Su 8:55am-8:55pm; €5.90) and **Villalba** (1hr., 7-9 per day M-F 5:55am-8:55pm, €3.90). Transfers to **Ávila, El Escorial, León,** and **Salamanca.**

Buses: Estación Municipal de Autobuses, Po. Ezequiel González, 12 (☎921 42 77 07). **Linecar** (☎921 42 77 06) to **Valladolid** (2hr.; M-F 12 per day, Sa 8 per day 6:45am-9pm, Su 6 per day 9am-9pm; €6.85). **La Sepulvedana** (☎921 42 77 07) to **Ávila** (1hr.; M-Sa 7:45am, 6pm; €4.25); **La Granja** (20min.; 9-15 per day M-Sa 7:40am-9:30pm, Su 10:30am-10:30pm; €1.05); **Madrid** (1hr.; 2 per hr. M-F 6:30am-10:30pm, Sa 8am-10:30pm, Su hourly 8am-10:30pm; €6.43).

Public Transportation: Transportes Urbanos de Segovia, C. Juan Bravo, in the Centro Comercial Almuzara (☎921 46 27 27). €0.80; discounted electronic passes available.

Taxis: Radio Taxi (24hr. ☎921 44 50 00). Taxis pull up by the train and bus stations. Stands in the Pl. Mayor and just beyond the Pl. Azoguejo.

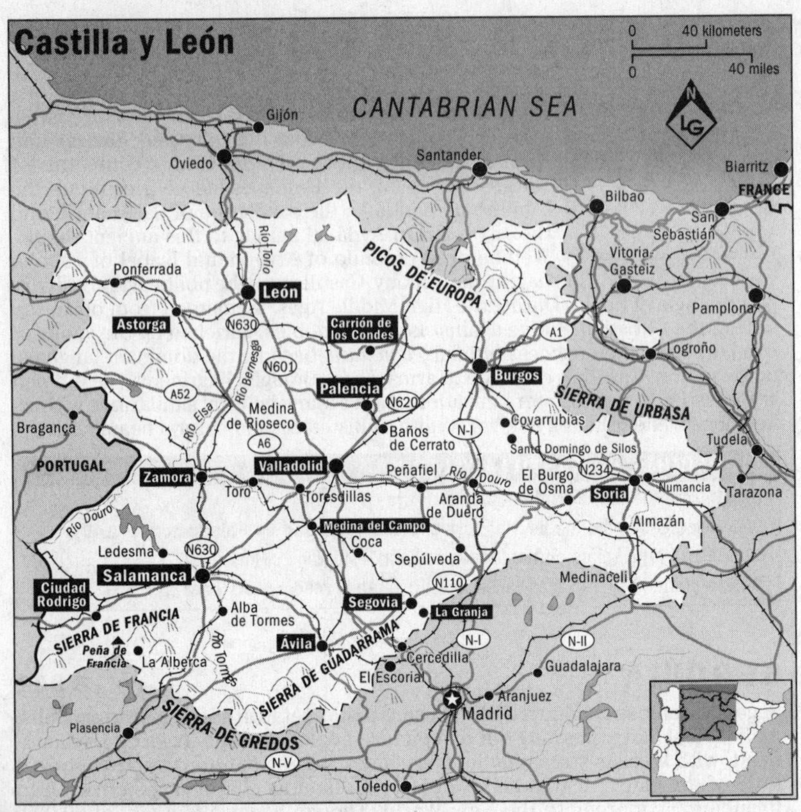

ORIENTATION AND PRACTICAL INFORMATION

Take bus #8 from the train station to **Acueducto,** which drops off near **Plaza del Azoguejo** and the municipal **tourist office.** (M-F every 15-30min. 7:25am-10:03pm, Sa every 30-45min. 8:18am-10pm, Su 2 per hr. 8:50am-10pm). The office is just downhill in the plaza, at the foot of the aqueduct, along **Calle Real** (the main route from the Aqueduct to the Pl. Mayor, the city's historic center, composed of C. Cervantes, C. Juan Bravo, and C. Isabel la Católica). On foot from the train station (30min.), turn right, cross the street, and walk toward town along Po. Obispo Quesada, which becomes Av. Conde de Sepúlveda and then Po. Ezequiel González, before coming to the bus station. From there, (15min.) cross Po. Ezequiel González and follow Av. de Fernández Ladreda to Pl. del Azoguejo, or take bus #4 to the aqueduct. A taxi to the aqueduct is €3-4.

Tourist Office: Regional office, Pl. Mayor, 10 (☎921 46 03 34). Open July-Sept. 15 M-Th and Su 9am-8pm, F-Sa 9am-9pm; Sept. 16-June 9am-2pm and 5-8pm.

Municipal office (Centro de Recepción de Visitantes), Pl. del Azoguejo, 1 (☎921 46 67 20). Open M-F and Su 10am-7pm, Sa 10am-8pm.

Currency Exchange: Banco Santander Central Hispano, Av. de Fernández Ladreda, 12. Open Apr.-Sept. M-F 8:30am-2pm; Oct.-Mar. M-F 8:30am-2pm, Sa 8:30am-1pm. ATMs and other banks, which also change cash, line Av. de Fernández Ladreda.

CASTILLA Y LEÓN

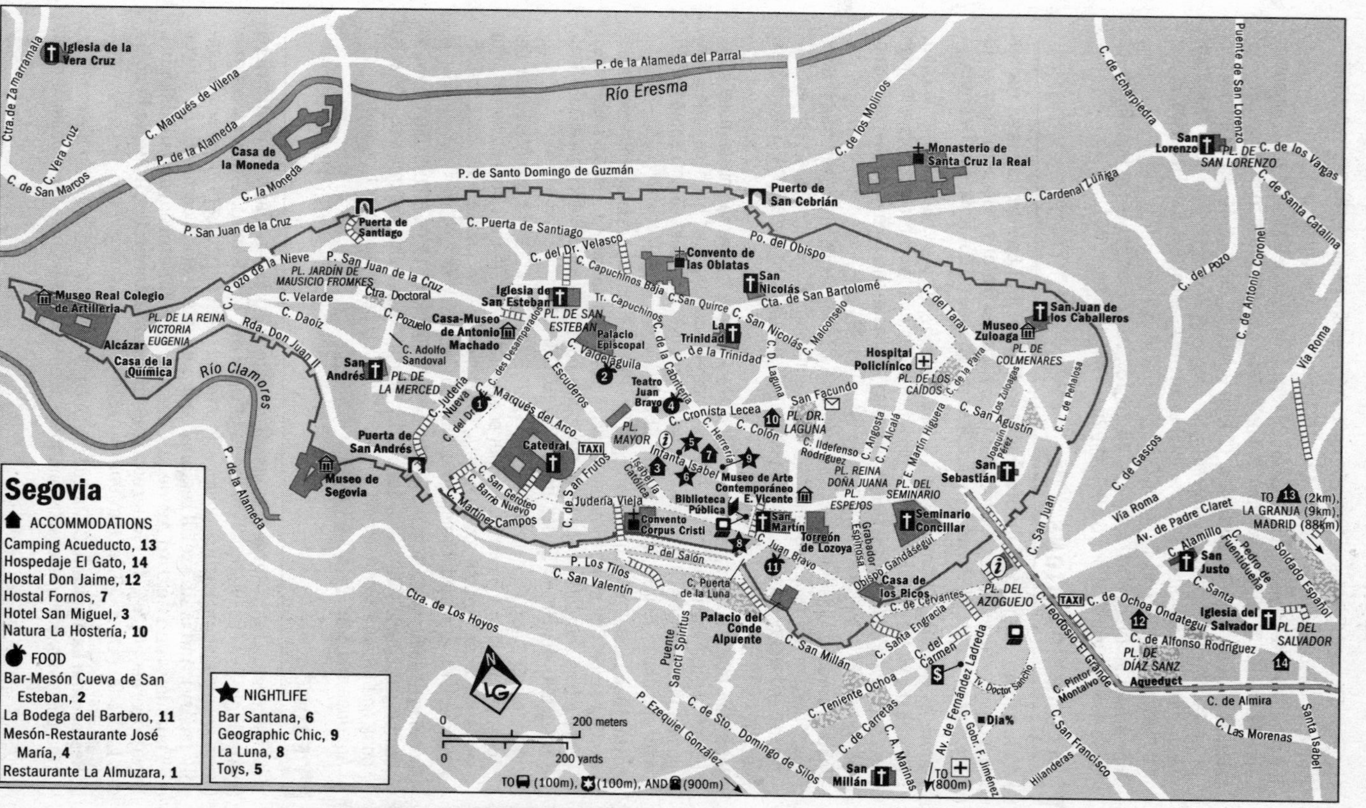

CASTILLA Y LEÓN

Luggage Storage: Lockers at the train station (€3 per day). Open daily 6am-10:30pm.

Police: C. Guadarrama, 24 (☎921 43 12 12 or ☎091 for emergencies).

Hospital: Hospital General de Segovia, Crta. de Ávila s/n, (☎921 41 91 01, emergencies 41 91 00). A 10min. walk from the police station on the road to Ávila, on left.

Internet Access: Biblioteca Pública, C. Juan Bravo, 11 (☎ 921 46 35 33). Free and fast. Max. 30min. Passport required. Open July-Aug. M-F 9am-3pm, Sa 9am-2pm; Sept.-June M-F 9am-9pm, Sa 9am-2pm. **Locutorio Aceducto,** C. San Francisco, 6, just off Plaza de Azoguejo. €1 per hour. Open noon-11pm daily.

Post Office: Pl. Dr. Laguna, 5 (☎921 46 16 16), up C. Cronista Lecea from Pl. Mayor. Open M-F 8:30am-8:30pm, Sa 9:30am-2pm. **Postal Code:** 40001.

ACCOMMODATIONS

Segovia's many sights and its proximity to Madrid and La Granja make rooms scarce during the summer. Reservations are a must for any hotels in or around major plazas. *Pensiones* can be significantly cheaper than hotels in Segovia.

Natura La Hostería, C. Colón, 5 and 7 (☎921 46 67 10; www.naturadesegovia.com), outside the Pl. Mayor. Every room is decorated in beautiful, bright solid colors, with huge soft beds. Free Wi-Fi. Prices change according to season and time of week—call ahead. Singles €35-40; doubles as low as €50-80. MC/V. ❸

Hostal Fornos, C. Infanta Isabel, 13 (☎921 46 01 98). Beige and green pastel walls and flowers make for a soothing feel. Well-maintained rooms with glass-enclosed balconies and pretty curtains. Rooms comes with TV, A/C, and large bath. Singles €41; doubles €55; triples €67. MC/V. ❹

Hotel San Miguel, C. Infanta Isabel, 6 (☎921 46 36 57; www.sanmiguel-hotel.com). Full of bright, modern amenities. Huge full bath is sparkling, and big beds have downy patchwork comforters. Balconies have good views over the street. Rooms come with TV, A/C, and phone. Singles €35; doubles €60. MC/V. ❸

Hostal "Don Jaime", C. Ochoa Ondátegui, 8 (☎921 44 47 87; hostaldonjaime@hotmail.com). A stone's throw from the aqueduct, visible from some of the room's balconies. Bright rooms with lots of space. Some rooms have bath for a higher price. July-Sept. singles €30, doubles €45; Oct.-June, €35/50. MC/V. ❸

Hospedaje El Gato, Pl. del Salvador, 10 (☎921 42 32 44; fax 43 80 47). Follow the aqueduct uphill to modern rooms with comfortable beds. The bar downstairs fills with locals day and night. All rooms have A/C, satellite TV, and private bath. Singles €25; doubles €40; extra bed for single/double €15/24. MC/V. ❷

Camping Acueducto, C. Borbón, 49/Highway CN-601, km 112 (☎921 42 50 00; www.campingacueducto.com), 2km toward La Granja. Restaurant, supermarket, showers, pool, and laundry. July-Aug. and *Semana Santa* €5 per person, per tent, and per car; Apr.-June and Sept. €4.50. MC/V. ❶

CASTILLA Y LEÓN

FOOD

The restaurants in the larger plazas all cater to tourists, and jack up their prices accordingly—steer clear of any menu printed on "parchment." *Sopa castellana* (soup with eggs and garlic), *cochinillo asado* (roast suckling pig), *ponche* (egg-yolk pastry), and lamb are all regional specialties. A market comes to Pl. Mayor on Thursdays and next to Av. de la Constitución on Saturdays (9am-2:30pm). Buy groceries at **Día%,** C. Gobernador Fernández Jiménez, 3, off Av. de Fernández Ladreda. (Open M-Sa 9am-9pm.)

Restaurante La Almuzara, C. Marqués del Arco, 3 (☎921 46 06 22), past the cathedral. The pastel flowers on the walls and the real ones in vases make for a pastoral meal.

Massive salads €9-12. Creative vegetarian plates €9.50. Open Tu 8-11:30pm, W-Su 12:45-4pm and 8-11:30pm. MC/V. ❷

Bar-Mesón Cueva de San Esteban, C. Valdeláguila, 15 (☎921 46 09 82). The owner knows his wines (he's still celebrating his 2002 victory in the national "nose of gold" competition), and with a prize-winning pork carver on his staff, food is excellent as well. *Menú* M-F €9, Sa-Su €10. Meat dishes €12-20. Open daily 11am-midnight. MC/V. ❸

Restaurante-Mesón José María, C. Cronista Lecea, 11 (☎921 46 11 11; www.rtejose-maria.com). With somber wood, yellow walls, and iron chandeliers, this restaurant is an ultra-typical Spanish *mesón,* but it distinguishes itself with succulent, if pricey, *cochinillo asado* (roast suckling pig; €21.35). Open M-W and Su 1-4pm and 8:30-11pm, Th-Sa 1-4pm and 8:30pm-12:30am. MC/V. ❹

La Bodega del Barbero, C. Alhóndiga, 2. (☎921 46 27 70), just off C. Juan Bravo. An easy-to-miss terrace that makes a perfect mid-day break. Technically a *"vinoteca"* (winery) with tastings and exhibitions, the bodega also keeps an inventive kitchen year-round. Glasses of wine €1.50-2.50. Mouth-watering salads €5.80-8.80 and lunch *menú* €10. Open Tu 11am-3:30pm, W-Su 11am-3:30pm and 7:30-11:30pm. MC/V. ❷

SIGHTS

Though dominated by its aqueduct and the romantic Alcázar, Segovia is packed with churches, convents, and palaces dating from medieval and Renaissance times, all worth exploring. When you tire of the cobblestones, head south out of the city into the massive hills and copses of the Pinarillo or explore one of the villages you can see from the city.

AQUEDUCT. The Romans built Segovia's aqueduct around 50 BC with 20,000 blocks of granite and not a drop of mortar. The two tiers of 166 arches supported by 128 pillars span 813m, reaching a height of 29m near Pl. del Azoguejo. This spectacular feat of engineering piped in water from the Río Fuenfría, 14km away, and was capable of transporting 30 liters of water per second to the Alcázar. It was in use until 60 years ago, but today the aqueduct primarily pipes in tourists from Madrid.

ALCÁZAR. Walt Disney reportedly modeled the Disney castle off the Alcázar's spiral towers and pointed turrets, and it does give a magical sense of *déjà vu.* Fortifications have commanded the site since Celtic occupation. Alfonso X beautified the original 11th-century fortress in the 13th century. Successive monarchs increased the grandeur; final touches were added for the coronation of Isabel I in 1474. In the Throne Room, the inscription above the throne reads *"Tanto Monta,"* a phrase meant to suggest that Fernando and Isabel had equal authority to rule. Process through various luxe royal bedrooms and halls. The **Tower of Juan II,** 152 steps up, offers incredible views of Segovia and the surrouding hills. *(Pl. de la Reina Victoria Eugenia. ☎921 46 07 59. Open daily Apr.-Sept. 10am-7pm; Oct.-Mar. 10am-6pm. Tower closed Tu. Buy tickets in the Real Laboratorio de Chimia, to the left of the Alcázar. Palace €4, seniors and students €2.50. Tower €2. Audio tours in English €3.)*

CASA-MUSEO DE ANTONIO MACHADO. Antonio Machado (1875-1939), literature professor, playwright, and, above all, poet, never made much money. The poet rented this small *pensión* from 1919 to 1932 for three *pesetas* per day while he taught French in the nearby university. A short, informative tour details major influences on Machado's poetry, including the 1909 death of his teenage wife and his affair with a married woman. The poet's room, filled with manuscripts and portraits (including a Picasso), has been left untouched. His last letter, written weeks before he died in France, is a poignant account of the hardships he would endure because of his flight from Spain in 1939. *(C. des*

Desamparados, 5. ☎921 46 03 77. Open M-Tu 4:30-7:30pm, W-Su 11am-2pm and 4:30-7:30pm. Mandatory guided tour in Spanish every 30min. €1.50, W free.)

CATHEDRAL. In 1525, Carlos V commissioned a cathedral in Pl. Mayor to replace the 12th-century edifice destroyed in the *Revuelta de las Comunidades*, a political uprising against the crown that lasted from 1520-1521. When the cathedral was finished 200 years later with an impressive 23 chapels topped with stained glass, it earned the nickname "The Lady of All Cathedrals." The altar was designed by Sabatini, creator of the gardens in Madrid, and features the four saints of Segovia. The **Sala Capitular,** hung with 17th-century tapestries, displays an ornate silver-and-gold chariot. Off the cloister (moved from the Alcázar) is the **Capilla de Santa Catalina,** filled with crosses, chalices, and candelabra. A framed coin collection on the cloister wall has currency from the royal mint going back 5 centuries. *(☎921 46 22 05. Open daily Apr.-Oct. 9am-6:30pm; Nov.-Mar. 9:30am-5:30pm; last entry 30min. before closing. Mass M-Sa 10am, Su 11am and 12:30pm. €3, under 14 free. Guided tours leave from the entrance at 11am, 4:30, 5:30pm.)*

NIGHTLIFE AND FESTIVALS

Plaza Mayor is the heart of Segovia's after-hours scene. Crowded **Calle Infanta Isabel,** toward the aqueduct, definitely earns its local nickname, *"calle de los barres,"* where locals fill the street sipping beers. The bars filling **Plaza del Azoguejo, Calle Fernandez de Ladreda,** and **Calle Carmen,** near the aqueduct, are frequented by a younger set, and club central is **C. Ruiz de Alda,** off **Pl. del Azoguejo.**

June 23rd-29th, Segovia holds a fiesta in honor of San Juan and San Pedro, with free open-air concerts on Pl. del Azoguejo, a pilgrimage to the hermitage of Juarrillos, 5km distant, and dances and fireworks on June 29. Zamarramala, 3km northwest of Segovia, hosts the **Fiestas de Santa Águeda** (the closest Su to Feb. 5). Women take over the town for a day and dress in period costumes to commemorate a **sneak attack** on the Alcázar in which women distracted the castle guards with wine and song. The all-female local council takes advantage of its authority to ridicule men and, at the festival's end, burns a male effigy.

Toys, C. Infanta Isabel, 13. *Copas* and childhood knick-knacks mix in the eclectic atmosphere of Toys. Techno music plays on a small dance floor as the crowd sips cocktails under red lights upstairs. Beer €1. Mixed drinks €4.50-5.50. Open daily 10pm-4am.

Geographic Chic, C. Infanta Isabel, 13 (☎921 46 30 38). Carries on Toys' doll fetish with mannequins lining the windows and cherubs smiling on the bar. A mixed crowd sips and dances as lights sweep the bar. Mixed drinks €5. Open W-Sa 10:30pm-4am.

Bar Santana, C. Infanta Isabel, 18 (☎921 46 35 64). Tasty tapas and rock music draw a casual older crowd, which loiters outside with drinks along the exterior bar. Photo and poetry exhibits line the back wall, but few are looking. Beer €1.10. Mixed drinks €4.50. Open Th-Sa 10:30pm-3:30am.

La Luna, C. Pta. de la Luna, 8 (☎921 46 26 51). From Pl. Mayor, head down C. Isabel la Católica onto C. Juan Bravo and take the first right. If you're looking for a club, this is the place. You can also count on a raucous American crowd and a lot of testosterone. Beer €1.50. *Chupitos* (shots) €3. Open daily 5pm-4am.

DAYTRIP FROM SEGOVIA

LA GRANJA DE SAN ILDEFONSO

La Sepulvedana buses (☎921 42 77 07) run from Segovia (20min.; 12-14 per day M-Sa 7:40am-9:30pm, Su 10:30am-10:30pm; return M-Sa 7:20am-9pm, Su 11am-10pm; €1.05). From the bus stop in La Granja, walk uphill through the gates and follow signs to the Palacio de La Granja. ☎921 47 00 19. Open Apr.-Sept. Tu-Su 10am-6pm; Oct.-Mar.

Tu-Sa 10am-1:30pm and 3-5pm, Su 10am-2pm. Tours, in Spanish, depart every 15min. €4.50, with guide €5; students and under 16 €3.

La Granja, a must-see located 11 km southeast of the city, is the most extravagant of Spain's royal summer retreats (the others being El Pardo, El Escorial, and Aranjuez). Felipe V, the first Bourbon King of Spain and grandson of Louis XIV, detested the Habsburgs' austere El Escorial. Nostalgic for Versailles, he commissioned La Granja in the early 18th century, choosing the site for its hunting and gardening potential. A fire destroyed the living quarters in 1918, but the structure was rebuilt in 1932. Today it houses the **Museo de Tapices,** one of the world's best collections of Flemish tapestries, which were popular in Spanish royal palaces. The usual marble clocks, oriental porcelain, and paintings by Luca Giordano round out the palace's decoration. French architect René Carlier designed the immense French **gardens** around the palace. Hedges surround impressive flowerbeds and lead to endless waterworks, including the decadent **Cascadas Nuevas,** an ensemble of illuminated fountains and pools representing the continents and seasons.The **Baños de Diana** is a massive pool with a bronze statue of the goddess, backed by a wall meticulously inlaid with hundreds of seashells. (Gardens open daily 10am-9pm. *Baños de Diana* July 22-Sept. 2 Sa from 10:30am-11:30pm. Other fountains suspended due to lack of water. Palace open June 17-Aug. 10am-9pm; May-June 16 and Sept. 10am-8pm; Apr. 10am-7pm; Mar. and Oct. 10am-6:30pm; Nov.-Feb. 10am-6pm.)

ÁVILA ☎920

Ávila (pop. 50,000) is a popular retreat from Madrid summer heat and winter bustle. The city makes its name with its incredible 12th-century stone walls and as the birthplace of the mystical Santa Teresa de Jesús (1515-1582). The old city, though, is full of beautiful buildings from Spain's glory days, and half the fun is stumbling upon half-hidden churches and palaces in a city almost totally untouched by urban grime and traffic.

TRANSPORTATION

Trains: Po. de la Estación (☎902 24 02 02). Info office open daily 7:30am-1:30pm and 3:30-9:30pm. To **El Escorial** (1hr.; 6-9 per day M-F 5:30am-8:15pm, Sa-Su 9:15am-10:15pm; €4.50); **Madrid** (1-2hr.; 15-23 per day M-F 5:30am-8:15pm, Sa-Su 7am-10:15pm; €7.55) via **Villalba** (1hr., €6.40); **Salamanca** (1½hr., 7-9 per day 7:10am-10:50pm, €8.35); **Valladolid** (1hr.; 5 per day 7:30am-9:30pm, €7.55).

Buses: Av. de Madrid, 2 (☎920 22 01 54).To **Madrid** (1hr.; 10-13 per day 6am-10:30pm, Su 6 per day 10am-10:15pm; €7.27) and **Segovia** (1hr.; M-F 5 per day 6:30am-7pm, Sa-Su 10:15am and 7:15pm; €4.25).

Taxis: Radio Taxis (☎920 35 35 45), in Pl. Sta. Teresa and the bus and train stations.

ORIENTATION AND PRACTICAL INFORMATION

The winding old city streets meet in the Plaza del Mercado Chico inside the walls and the recently revamped Plaza de Santa Teresa just outside. Bus #1 (€0.65) departs a block from the train station towards Pl. del Mercado Chico. To get from the bus station to Pl. Sta. Teresa, cross the intersection in front, follow the park, and turn left onto C. Duque de Alba.

Tourist Office: Pl. Pedro Dávila, 4 (☎920 21 13 87). English spoken. Open July-Aug. M-Th 9am-8pm, F-Sa 9am-9pm; Sept.-June M-Sa 9am-2pm and 5-8pm.

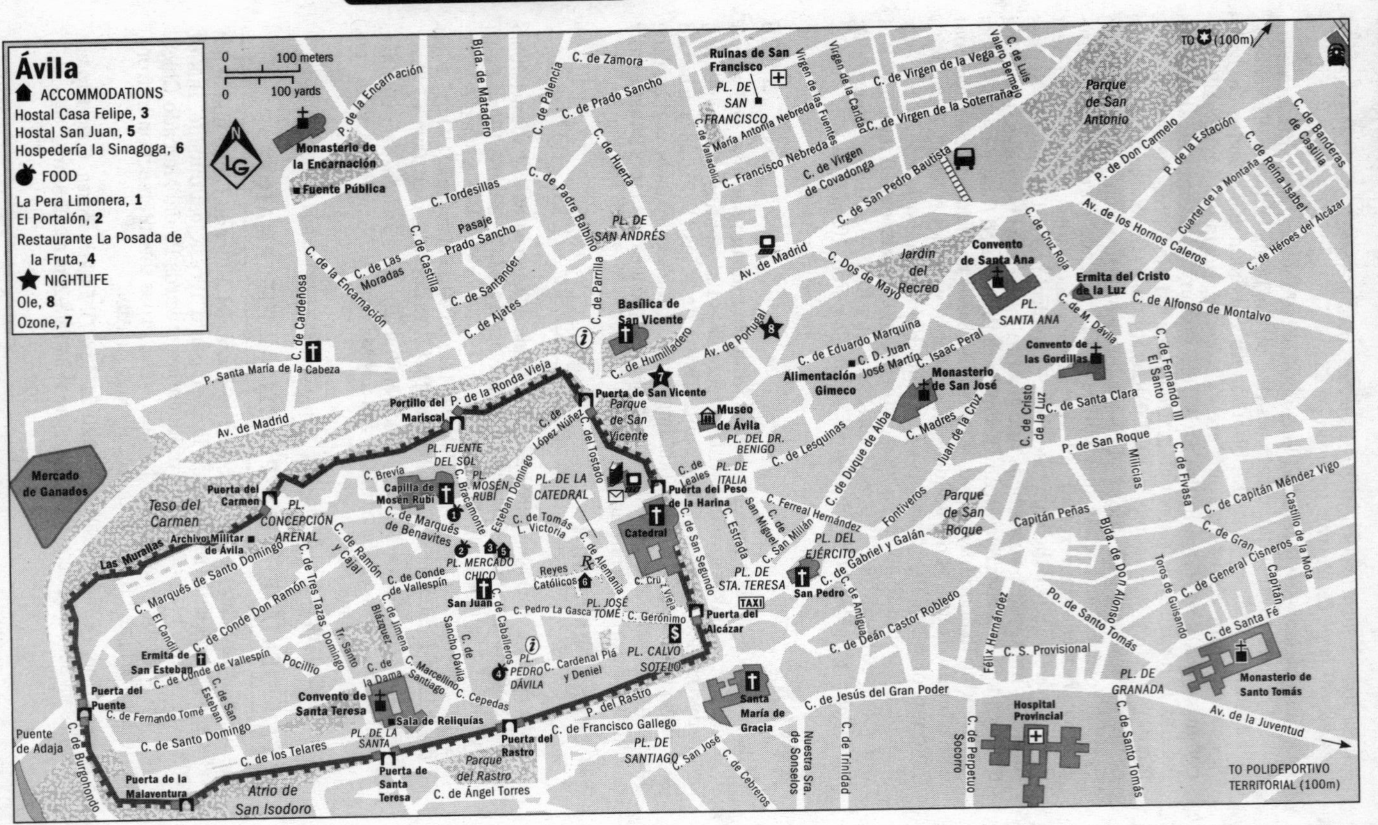
Ávila
ACCOMMODATIONS
Hostal Casa Felipe, 3
Hostal San Juan, 5
Hospedería la Sinagoga, 6
FOOD
La Pera Limonera, 1
El Portalón, 2
Restaurante La Posada de la Fruta, 4
NIGHTLIFE
Ole, 8
Ozone, 7
0 100 meters
0 100 yards
TO (100m)
TO POLIDEPORTIVO TERRITORIAL (100m)
Monasterio de la Encarnación
Fuente Pública
Ruinas de San Francisco
PL. DE SAN FRANCISCO
Parque de San Antonio
PL. DE SAN ANDRÉS
Basílica de San Vicente
Jardín del Recreo
Convento de Santa Ana
PL. SANTA ANA
Ermita del Cristo de la Luz
Convento de las Gordillas
Monasterio de San José
Alimentación Gimeco
Museo de Ávila
PL. DEL DR. BENIGO
PL. DE ITALIA
Puerta de San Vicente
Parque de San Vicente
Portillo del Mariscal
PL. FUENTE DEL SOL
Capilla de Mosén Rubí
PL. MOSÉN RUBÍ
PL. DE LA CATEDRAL
Puerta del Peso de la Harina
Catedral
PL. MERCADO CHICO
San Juan
PL. JOSÉ TOMÉ
PL. CALVO SOTELO
PL. PEDRO DÁVILA
Puerta del Alcázar
PL. DE STA. TERESA
TAXI
San Pedro
PL. DEL EJÉRCITO
Parque de San Roque
PL. DE GRANADA
Monasterio de Santo Tomás
Hospital Provincial
Santa María de Gracia
PL. DE SANTIAGO
Mercado de Ganados
Puerta del Carmen
Teso del Carmen
PL. CONCEPCIÓN ARENAL
Archivo Militar de Ávila
Las Murallas
Ermita de San Esteban
Puerta del Puente
Puente de Adaja
Convento de Santa Teresa
Sala de Reliquías
PL. DE LA SANTA
Puerta del Rastro
Parque del Rastro
Puerta de Santa Teresa
Puerta de la Malaventura
Atrio de San Isodoro
C. de Zamora
Bjda. de Matadero
C. de Palencia
C. de Prado Sancho
P. de la Encarnación
C. de Huerta
C. de Padre Balbino
C. Tordesillas
Pasaje Prado Sancho
C. de Las Moradas
C. de Castilla
C. de Santander
C. de Ajates
C. de la Encarnación
C. de Cardeñosa
C. de Parrilla
P. Santa María de la Cabeza
C. de Valladolid
C. María Antonia Nebreda
C. Francisco Nebreda
Virgen de las Fuentes
Virgen de la Caridad
C. de Virgen de Covadonga
C. de Virgen de la Vega
C. de Luis Valero Bermejo
C. de Virgen de la Soterraña
C. de San Pedro Bautista
P. de Don Carmelo
P. de la Estación
Cuartel de la Montaña
C. de Reina Isabel
C. de Banderas de Castilla
C. de Héroes del Alcázar
Av. de los Hornos Caleros
C. de Cruz Roja
Av. de Madrid
C. Dos de Mayo
C. de Alfonso de Montalvo
C. de M. Dávila
Av. de Portugal
C. de Humilladero
C. de Eduardo Marquina
C. D. Juan José Martín
C. Isaac Peral
C. de Fernando III El Santo
C. de Santa Clara
C. de Cristo de la Luz
C. Madres
Juan de la Cruz
C. de Duque de Alba
C. de Lesquinas
P. de San Roque
Milicias
C. de Fivasa
C. de Capitán Méndez Vigo
Castillo de la Mota
C. de Gran Capitán
C. de General Cisneros
P. de la Ronda Vieja
Av. de Madrid
C. de López Núñez
C. del Tostado
C. Brevía
C. Bracamonte
Esteban Domingo
C. de Tomás L. Victoria
C. de Marqués de Benavites
C. de Alemania
C. de Leales
C. de San Segundo
C. Estrada
San Miguel
C. de San Millán
C. Ferreal Hernández
Fontiveros
Capitán Peñas
Bjda. de Don Alonso
Toros de Guisando
C. de Gabriel y Galán
C. de Antigua
Po. de Santo Tomás
C. de Santa Fé
C. de Deán Castor Robledo
Félix Hernández
C. S. Provisional
C. de Jesús del Gran Poder
Av. de la Juventud
C. de Santo Tomás
C. de Perpetuo Socorro
C. de Trinidad
Nuestra Sra. de Sonselos
C. de Cebreros
C. San José
C. de Francisco Gallego
P. del Rastro
C. de Ángel Torres
C. de los Telares
C. de Santo Domingo
C. de Burgohondo
C. de Fernando Tomé
C. de San Esteban
C. de Conde de Vallespín
El Candil
Pocillo
C. de Conde Don Ramón
C. Marqués de Santo Domingo
C. de Tres Tazas
Tr. Santo Domingo
C. de Ramón y Cajal
C. de Conde de Vallespín
Reyes Católicos
C. Cruz Vieja
C. Gerónimo
C. Pedro La Gasca
C. de Caballeros
C. Cardenal Plá y Deniel
C. de Sancho Dávila
C. Cepedas
C. Marcellino Santiago
C. de la Dama
C. de Jimena Blázquez

Centro de Recepción de Visitantes, Av. de Madrid, 39 (☎920 10 21 21), across the street from the northwest tower of the wall. Open summer 9am-8pm; winter 9am-6pm.

Currency Exchange: Banco Santander Central Hispano, C. Don Gerónimo, 8 (☎920 21 11 39). Open Apr.-Sept. M-F 8:30am-2pm; Oct.-May also Sa 8:30am-1pm.

Luggage Storage: At the train station (€3). Open daily 6am-11pm.

Police: Policía Municipal, C. Molino del Carril, 1 (☎920 35 24 24).

Pharmacy: Farmacia Vinuesa, C. Reyes Católicos, 31 (☎920 21 13 35). Open M-F 9:30am-2pm and 4:30-8pm, Sa 10am-2pm.

Hospital: Hospital Provincial, C. de Jesús del Gran Poder, 42 (☎920 35 72 00). Ambulance: ☎920 22 22 22. Open daily 9am-9pm.

Internet Access: Cybernet Locutorio DG, Av. de Madrid, 25 (☎920 253 800). €2 per hr., but you don't have to use all your time at once. Open daily 10am-3pm and 4-10:30pm. Also available at the **Biblioteca Municipal,** Pl. de la Catedral, 3 (☎920 25 46 38). max. 30 min., with passport. Open July-Aug. M-F 8:30am-2:45pm, Sa 9am-2pm, Sept.-June M-F 9am-9pm, Sa 9am-2pm.

Post Office: Pl. de la Catedral, 2 (☎920 35 31 06). Fax service available. Open M-F 8:30am-8:30pm, Sa 9:30am-2pm. **Postal Code:** 05001.

ACCOMMODATIONS

Comfortable, affordable accommodations can be found within the city walls. True budget options are a long march down the Av. de la Juventud, about 25min. outside of the old city. Those near the cathedral and Pl. de Sta. Teresa fill fast in summer, so call early. Many hotels double as restaurants, and breakfast can be had on the cheap with the price of a room; ask the receptionist or barman.

Hostal San Juan, C. Comuneros de Castilla, 3 (☎920 25 14 75). Excellent bargain hidden off the plaza. Huge full bath is sparkling. Bright green beds and yellow walls. Rooms with phone and TV. Oct.-May singles €24, doubles €38; June-Sept. €30/48. MC/V. ❷

Hostal Casa Felipe, Pl. Mercado Chico, 12 (☎920 21 39 24). Rooms with windows overlooking the plaza offer fresh air and light. All rooms have TV, phone, and sink. Singles €25; doubles €38, with bath €44. MC/V. ❷

Hospedería la Sinagoga, C. Reyes Católicos, 22 (☎920 35 23 21; www.lasinagoga.net). This former synagogue—now sharing space with a convent—offers tranquility and rooms with enormous full baths and balconies overlooking the quiet street. Beautiful central patio with couches and plants, brass-framed mirrors and old wooden beams. Great deal for groups and doubles. Singles €50; doubles €60. MC/V. ❺

FOOD

Ávila is filled with sober *mesones*, where vested waiters serve pricey meat dishes; variety is not Ávila's strong suit. Fridays, the **market** in Pl. Mercado Chico sells produce 10am-2pm. The supermarket, **Alimentación Gimeco,** C. Juan José Martín, 6, stocks basics. (Open in summer M 10:30am-2pm and 5:30-8:30pm, Tu-Su 9:45am-2pm and 5:30-8:30pm; winter M-Sa 9:45am-2pm and 5-8pm.)

El Portalón, Pl. del Mercado Chico, 4 (☎920 21 43 29). Nothing fancy, but big plates and a lively atmosphere right on the plaza. Cheapest terrace dining you'll find in town. The *platos combinados* (€9-11), combinations of meat, eggs, and fries, are a good bet. Hamburgers €5. *Menús* €12-18. Open daily noon-4pm and 8:30pm-1am. MC/V. ❷

Restaurante La Posada de la Fruta, Pl. Pedro Dávila, 8 (☎920 25 47 02; www.posadadelafruta.com). Four seating locations at different prices—the shaded *terraza* is the most pleasant and cheapest. *Platos combinados* €6-8. *Menú* €9-11. Restaurant open daily 1-4:30pm and 8:30-11:30pm. Bar open 9am-midnight. MC/V. ❷

CASTILLA Y LEÓN

La Pera Limonera, Pl. Mosén Rubí, 5 (☎920 25 04 72) Cool lime-green walls and napkins, orchids, and black leather are a welcome break from endless "medieval-themed" fare. Style comes at a price, though: seafood and meat dishes €18-20. Smaller appetizers €13. Open Tu-Sa 1:30-4pm and 9pm-midnight, Su 1:30-4pm. MC/V. ❹

SIGHTS

LAS MURALLAS. These gigantic city walls were originally built to keep foreigners out. They now let thousands of them in each year for rampart-scaling and city views. Research dates the 2500 battlements, 88 towers, and 9 gates to the 12th century, though legend maintains that they are the oldest in Spain, dating back to 1090. **Cimorro,** the most imposing tower, doubles as the cathedral's apse. The walls can be reached from both **Puerta del Peso de la Harina** and **Puerta del Alcázar,** on either side of the cathedral. There are three walks along the ramparts, all included in the price of admission, but once you've done one, you've probably seen it all. **Tramo de la Carnicería** commands the best views of the city and its environs. *(☎920 25 50 88. Open Apr.-Oct. 15 M-W and Su 10am-8pm and 10pm-12:30am; Oct. 16-Mar. daily 11am-6pm. Theatrical tour June 16-Sept. 17 Th-Sa 10-11:30pm, last entry 45min. before closing. €4; students, groups, over 65, and under 8 €2.50; at night €6/4. 3-person theatrical tour €4.50.)* The best view of the walls and of Ávila is from the Cuatro Postes, past the Río Adaja, 1.5km along the highway to Salamanca. *(From Pl. de Sta. Teresa, walk out the Puerta del Puente. Cross the bridge and follow the road to the right for about 1km. The walk to Cuatro Postes takes approx. 25min.)*

CATEDRAL. Begun in the late 12th century, Ávila's is the oldest Spanish cathedral in the transitional style between Romanesque and Gothic. Look for the **Altar de La Virgen de la Caridad,** where 12-year-old Santa Teresa prostrated herself after the death of her mother. Behind the main altar is the alabaster tomb of Cardinal Alonso de Madrigal, a bishop of Ávila and prolific writer whose dark complexion won him the title "El Tostado" (The Swarthy, literally "Toasted"). The museum displays an El Greco portrait, enormous *libros de canti* (hymnals), and Juan de Arfe's silver, six-story Custodia de Asiento, complete with swiveling bells. *(Pl. de la Catedral. ☎920 21 16 41. Open July-Sept. M-F 10am-7:30pm, Sa 10am-8pm, Su noon-6pm; Nov.-Mar. M-F 10am-5pm, Sa 10am-6pm, Su noon-5pm; Apr.-June and Oct. M-F 10am-6pm, Sa 10am-7pm, Su noon-6pm. Last entry 45min. before closing. Front entrance only free; full cathedral and museum €4.)*

MONASTERIO DE LA ENCARNACIÓN. The monastery's museum holds items from Teresa's childhood in the lap of luxury, which she renounced for a life of asceticism. The mandatory tour visits Santa Teresa's tiny cell and the main staircase where she had a mystical encounter with the child Jesus; a mannequin on the stairs recreates the experience. Upstairs are personal effects given to the convent by wealthier nuns as bribes to procure entrance. *(Po. de la Encarnación. ☎920 21 12 12. Museum open in summer M-F 9:30am-1pm and 4-7pm, Sa-Su 10am-1pm and 4-7pm; in winter M-F 9:30am-1:30pm and 3:30-6pm, Sa-Su 10am-1:30pm and 3:30-6pm. Admission and tour €1.70.)*

EL MONASTERIO DE SANTO TOMÁS. One of the most strange and wonderful sights in the city is this untouristed Dominican monastery, built at the behest of Fernando and Isabel. Three cloisters hold various rooms and a church with the tomb of Prince Juan, a son of the monarchs, who died at 19. The Dominicans traveled widely as missionaries, and their souvenirs are on display in the **Museo de Arte Oriental,** off the third cloister, featuring kimonos, buddha statues, Chinese screens and paintings, and gorgeous calligraphy. Even stranger is the **Museo de Ciencias Naturales** (2nd cloister), which has all manner of exotic preserved animals, from birds to cattle to sharks and crocodiles; the **full-sized African lion** is the best. Take a break from Teresa and enjoy—it's the only church in Spain where you'll find an entombed prince and a snarling, mutant lamb. *(Pl. Granada, down Paseo de Santo Tomás. ☎920 35 22 37. Open daily 10am-1pm and 4-7pm. €3.*

OTHER SIGHTS. Santa Teresa's admirers built the 17th-century **Convento de Santa Teresa** at the site of her birth. *(Inside the city walls, near Puerta de Sta. Teresa. ☎920 21 10 30. Open daily 9:30am-1:30pm and 3:30-7:30pm. Free.)* If you see only one site related to Santa Teresa, visit **Sala de Reliquías,** near the convent, where you will find a small scrapbook of Santa Teresa relics, including her preserved ring finger, the sole of her sandal, and the cord she used to flagellate herself. Two bones of St. John of the Cross complete the collection. *(Open daily Apr.-Oct. 9:30am-1:30pm and 3:30-7:30pm; Nov.-Mar. Tu-Su 10am-1:30pm and 3:30-7pm. Free.)* For a larger display of items that Santa Teresa may have touched, looked at, or lived among, as well as artifacts of lesser-known Teresas, visit the **Museo de Santa Teresa,** built into a crypt. *(☎920 22 07 08. Open Apr.-Oct. daily 10am-2pm and 4-7pm; Nov.-Mar. Tu-Su 10am-1:30pm and 3:30-5:30pm. Last entry 30min. before closing. €2.)*

NIGHTLIFE

After nightfall, the Ávila's *centro* empties of its youth, as if St. Teresa's asceticism is still too strong within the city walls for late-night revelry. The **Parque San Vicente,** just to the left out of the Puerto del Peso de la Harina, is the gathering place of Ávila's teenagers, passing around 40s in paper bags, fighting, and flirting, occasionally relieving themselves on the city's sacrosanct 800-year-old walls. Across the street are the *terrazas* on **San Segundo,** where a more sedate crowd eats tapas and nurses drinks well into the night. The clubs and bars are just up the road and to the right on Av. de Portugal. Many only open on weekends. **Ozone,** Av. de Portugal, 4, is a lively place with a disco ball, Spanish alt-rock, and intense darts competitions in the corner. (Beer €2. Mixed drinks €5-6. Open F-Sa 11:30pm-5:30am.) Further down is **Ole,** Av. de Portugal, 18, a lively hive of conversation and European flags. (☎920 226 475. Beer €2-3. Mixed drinks €5-6. Open W-Sa 10pm-4am.)

SALAMANCA ☎923

Salamanca (pop. at term-time 363,000) is Spain's golden city. Once a battleground of Arabs and Christians, Salamanca has since become the home of the prestigious Universidad de Salamanca, in medieval times considered one of the four leading lights of the world. The city seems to radiate its own light, with massive buildings built of yellow Villamayor stone flaunting ornate facades that exemplify Spanish Plateresque architecture. Salamanca's location is also golden. While accessible from Spain's major transportation hubs, the city's mild summers make it a welcome retreat from the heat that the rest of Spain's interior can suffer. Salamanca remains steadfastly a university town; even in summer, thousands of students flood the streets, giving rise to a student scene that rivals those of major cities like Barcelona and Madrid.

TRANSPORTATION

Flights: Aeropuerto de Salamanca, Ctra. Madrid, km 14 (☎923 32 96 00).

Trains: Vialia Estación de Salamanca, Po.de la Estación (☎902 24 02 02). To: **Ávila** (65min., 7-8 per day 6am-7:53pm, €8.05); **Lisboa** (6hr., 4:51am, €47); **Madrid** (2hr., 6-7 per day 6am-7:53pm, €15); **Palencia** (2hr., 1:50pm, €9-21); **Valladolid** (2hr., 4-6 per day 7:35am-8:35pm, €6.05-13.40). The station offers **luggage storage,** a Carrefour supermarket, restaurants, and a movie theater.

Buses: Av. Filiberto Villalobos, 71-85 (☎923 23 67 17). Take C. Ramón y Cajal to Po. de San Vicente. Cross Po. de San Vicente, and C. Ramón y Cajal becomes Av. Filiberto Villalobos. Open M-F 8am-8:30pm, Sa 9am-2:30pm and 4:30-6:30pm, Su 10am-2pm and 4-7:30pm. **Avanza Grupo** (☎902 02 09 99) sends buses to: **Ávila** (1hr.; M-Th 4 per day 6:30am-8:30pm, F 6 per day 6:30am-8:30pm, Sa-Su 4 per day 8:30am-8:30pm; €5); **Alsa** (☎902 42 22 42, www.alsa.es) sends buses to **Barcelona** (11hr; M-Th and Sa 10am and 8pm, F 10am, 4:30, 8pm, Su 10am, 2:30, 8pm; €47, round-trip €73); **Linea Zamora** (☎923 223 587, www.zamorasalamanca.com) sends buses to **León** (2hr.; M-F 7 per day 7am-7:30pm, Sa 4 per day 10:15am-5pm, Su 4 per day 10:15-11pm, €12.80. **Avanza Grupo** to **Madrid** (2hr.; M-Sa 16 per day 6am-9:30pm, Su 16 per day 8am-11pm; €11.40-17); **Segovia** (2hr.; M-F 6:30am, 1:15pm, Sa-Su 8:30am, 5:30pm; €9.42, round-trip €17.29); **Valladolid** (1hr.; M-Sa 7-9 per day 7am-8pm, Su 6 per day 9am-10pm; €7, round-trip €13.20); **Linea Zamora** to **Zamora** (1hr.; M-F 21 per day 6:30am-9:40pm, Sa 10 per day 7:45am-8:30pm, Su 10 per day 8:45am-10:15pm; €4.25). **El Pilar** (☎923 22 26 08; www.elpilar-arribesbus.com) to **Ciudad Rodrigo** (1hr.; M-F 13 per day 7am-9:30pm, Sa 7 per day 8:30am-8pm, Su 4 per day 11am-9:30pm; €6).

Taxis: Radio Taxi (☎923 25 00 00). 24 hr.

Car Rental: Avis, Po. de Canalejas, 49 (☎923 26 97 53). Open M-F 9:30am-1:30pm and 4-7pm, Sa 9am-1:30pm. **Europcar,** C. Calzada de Medina 7-9 (☎923 25 02 70). Open M-F 9am-1:30pm and 4:30-8pm, Sa 9am-1:30pm.

ORIENTATION AND PRACTICAL INFORMATION

The majestic **Plaza Mayor** is the social and geographical center of Salamanca. Most hostels are to the south on **Rúa Mayor** and **Plaza de Anaya,** as are the **University** and most sights. From the train station, catch bus #1 (€0.80) to Gran Vía and get off at the Pl. Mayor (20min. from train station, 15min. from bus station).

Tourist Office: Municipal office, Pl. Mayor, 32 (☎923 21 83 42 or 923 27 24 08). Open June-Sept. M-F 9am-2pm and 4:30-8pm, Sa 10am-8pm, Su 10am-2pm; Oct.-May M-F 9am-2pm and 4-6:30pm, Sa 10am-6:30pm, Su 10am-2pm. **Regional office,** R. Mayor (☎923 26 85 71), in the Casa de las Conchas. Open July-Sept. M-Th and Su 9am-8pm, F-Sa 9am-9pm; Oct.-June daily 9am-2pm and 5-8pm. Look out for **DGratis,** a free listing of goings-on distributed every Friday available at tourist offices and distributors in Pl. Mayor. See www.salamanca.es for details.

Currency Exchange: EuroDivisas, R. Mayor, 2 (☎923 21 21 80). Open M-F 8:30am-10pm, Sa-Su 10am-7pm. ATMs can be found on every major street.

Luggage Storage: At the **train station** (24hr.; €3-4.50) and **bus station** (open daily 7am-7:45pm; €2).

Women's Resources: Office for the Assistance of Victims of Sexual Assault and Harassment, Gran Vía, 39-31, 4th fl. (☎923 12 68 75). **Association for the Assistance of Victims of Sexual Assault and Domestic Abuse,** Pl. Nueva de San Vincente, 5 (☎923 26 15 99).

Laundromat: Pasaje Azafranal, 18 (☎923 36 02 16), off C. Azafranal. Wash and dry €4. Open M-F 9:30am-2pm and 4-8pm, Sa 9:30am-2pm.

Police: In the Ayuntamiento, Pl. Mayor, 2 (☎923 19 44 40 or locally 923 27 91 00).

Red Cross: C. Cruz Roja, 1 (☎923 22 22 22).

Pharmacy: Amador Felipe, C. Toro, 25 (☎923 21 41 24). Open daily 9:30am-10pm.

Hospital: Hospital Clínico Universitario, Po. de San Vicente, 108 (☎923 29 11 00).

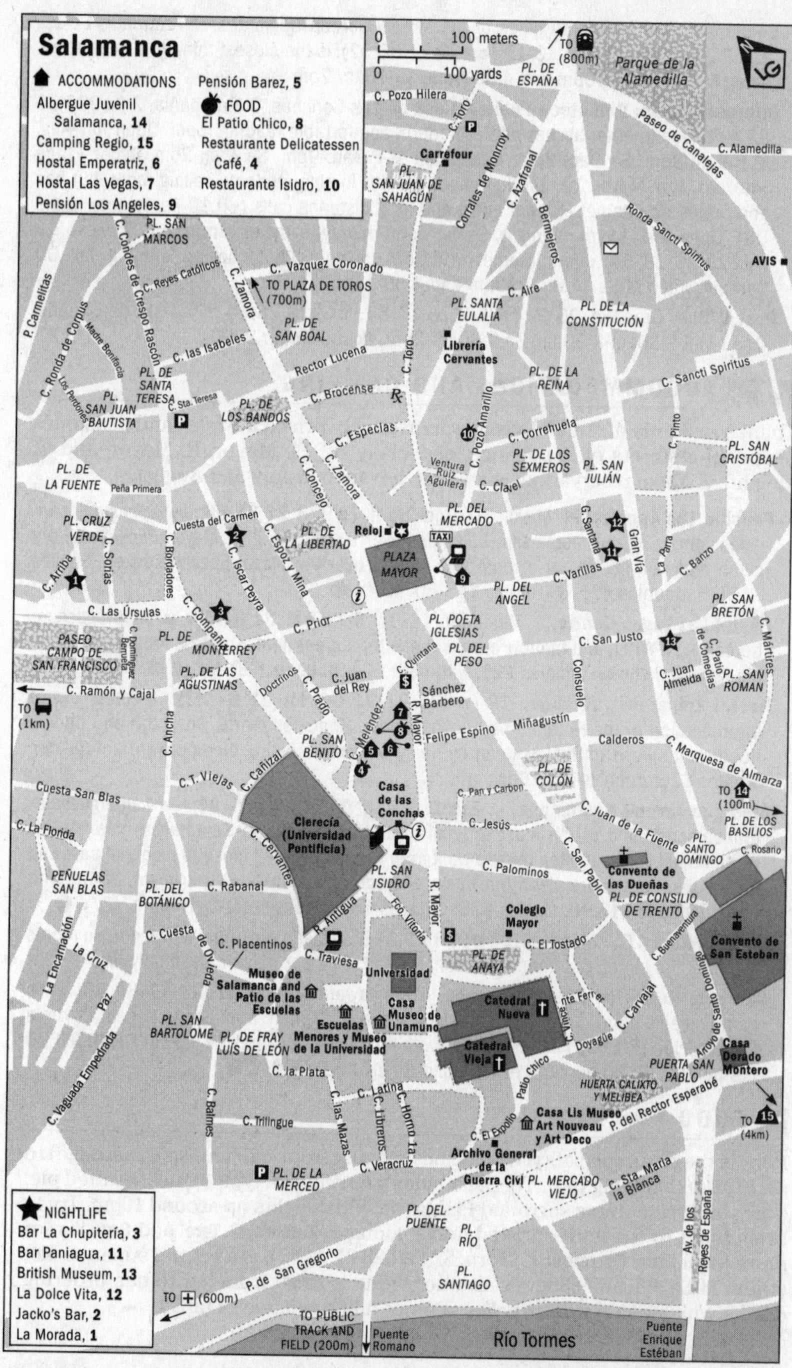
Salamanca
ACCOMMODATIONS
Albergue Juvenil Salamanca, 14
Camping Regio, 15
Hostal Emperatriz, 6
Hostal Las Vegas, 7
Pensión Los Angeles, 9
Pensión Barez, 5
FOOD
El Patio Chico, 8
Restaurante Delicatessen Café, 4
Restaurante Isidro, 10
NIGHTLIFE
Bar La Chupitería, 3
Bar Paniagua, 11
British Museum, 13
La Dolce Vita, 12
Jacko's Bar, 2
La Morada, 1
0 100 meters
0 100 yards
TO (800m)
PL. DE ESPAÑA
Parque de la Alamedilla
Paseo de Canalejas
C. Alamedilla
C. Pozo Hilera
C. Toro
Carrefour
PL. SAN JUAN DE SAHAGÚN
Corrales de Monrroy
C. Azafranal
C. Bermejeros
Ronda Sancti Spiritus
AVIS
PL. SAN MARCOS
C. Condes de Crespo Rascón
C. Reyes Católicos
C. Zamora
C. Vazquez Coronado
TO PLAZA DE TOROS (700m)
P. Carmelitas
C. Ronda de Corpus
Madre Bonifacia
C. las Isabeles
PL. DE SAN BOAL
Rector Lucena
C. Aire
PL. SANTA EULALIA
Librería Cervantes
PL. DE LA CONSTITUCIÓN
PL. DE SANTA TERESA
C. Sta. Teresa
Los Perdones
PL. SAN JUAN BAUTISTA
PL. DE LOS BANDOS
C. Brocense
C. Especias
PL. DE LA REINA
C. Sancti Spiritus
C. Pozo Amarillo
C. Correhuela
PL. DE LOS SEXMEROS
PL. SAN JULIÁN
C. Pinto
PL. SAN CRISTÓBAL
PL. DE LA FUENTE
Peña Primera
C. Concejo
Ventura Ruiz Aguilera
C. Clavel
PL. CRUZ VERDE
C. Sorias
Cuesta del Carmen
C. Iscar Peyra
C. Espoz y Mina
PL. DE LA LIBERTAD
Reloj
PL. DEL MERCADO
TAXI
G. Santana
Gran Vía
La Parra
C. Banzo
C. Arriba
C. Bordadores
PLAZA MAYOR
C. Varillas
PL. DEL ANGEL
C. Las Úrsulas
C. Compañía
C. Prior
PL. POETA IGLESIAS
PL. SAN BRETÓN
PASEO CAMPO DE SAN FRANCISCO
C. Dominguez Berrueta
PL. DE MONTERREY
PL. DEL PESO
C. San Justo
C. Patio de Comedias
C. Mártires
PL. DE LAS AGUSTINAS
Doctrinos
C. Juan del Rey
C. Quintana
Sánchez Barbero
Consuelo
C. Juan Almeida
PL. SAN ROMAN
C. Ramón y Cajal
TO (1km)
C. Prado
R. Mayor
C. Meléndez
Felipe Espino
Miñagustín
Calderos
C. Marquesa de Almarza
C. Ancha
PL. SAN BENITO
C. T. Viejas
C. Cañizal
PL. DE COLÓN
C. Pan y Carbon
TO (100m)
Cuesta San Blas
Casa de las Conchas
C. Jesús
C. Juan de la Fuente
PL. DE LOS BASILIOS
C. La Florida
C. Cervantes
Clerecía (Universidad Pontificia)
PL. SANTO DOMINGO
C. Rosario
C. San Pablo
Convento de las Dueñas
PEÑUELAS SAN BLAS
PL. DEL BOTÁNICO
C. Rabanal
PL. SAN ISIDRO
C. Palominos
PL. DE CONSILIO DE TRENTO
Colegio Mayor
Fco. Vitoria
R. Antigua
C. La Encarnación
C. Cuesta
de Oviedo
C. Placentinos
C. Traviesa
C. El Tostado
C. Buenaventura
Convento de San Esteban
La Cruz
PL. DE ANAYA
Museo de Salamanca and Patio de las Escuelas
Universidad
Catedral Nueva
Paz
Casa Museo de Unamuno
C. Vince nte Ferrer
C. Carvajal
PL. SAN BARTOLOME
PL. DE FRAY LUÍS DE LEÓN
Escuelas Menores y Museo de la Universidad
Catedral Vieja
Doyagüe
Arroyo de Santo Domingo
C. Vaguada Empedrada
C. la Plata
Patio Chico
PUERTA SAN PABLO
Casa Dorado Montero
HUERTA CALIXTO Y MELIBEA
C. Latina
C. Balmes
C. las Mazas
C. Libreros
C. Horno 1a
C. Trilingue
C. El Expolio
Casa Lis Museo Art Nouveau y Art Deco
P. del Rector Esperabé
TO (4km)
PL. DE LA MERCED
C. Veracruz
Archivo General de la Guerra Civil
PL. MERCADO VIEJO
C. Sta. María la Blanca
PL. DEL PUENTE
PL. RÍO
Av. de los Reyes de España
P. de San Gregorio
PL. SANTIAGO
TO (600m)
TO PUBLIC TRACK AND FIELD (200m)
Puente Romano
Río Tormes
Puente Enrique Estéban

Bookstore: Spanning both sides of the street, Librería Cervantes, C. Azafranal, 11-13, and Pl. de Santa Eulalia, 13-19 (☎923 21 86 02), is the closest thing to a superstore. Open M-F 10am-1:30pm and 4:30-8pm, Sa 10am-2pm.

Internet Access: Biblioteca Pública, Casa de Las Conchas, C. Compañía, 2 (☎923 26 93 17). Free internet access and a modern, comfortable reading room. Open July-Aug. M-F 9am-3pm, Sa 9am-2pm; Sept.-June M-F 9am-9pm, Sa 9am-2pm. **Cyber Place Internet,** Pza. Mayor, 10, 1st fl., is flooded with foreign students calling mom, but has good rates on internet (€1 per hour) and long distance calls (€0.10 per minute to the US). Open M-F 11am-midnight, Sa-Su noon-midnight. **Cyber Anuario,** C. Traviesa 16 (☎923 26 13 54) offers internet at €1.50 per hour. Photocopying, printing, fax, CD burning. Open M-Sa 11am-2:30pm and 4:30-11pm.

Post Office: Gran Vía, 25-29 (☎923 28 14 57, fax 923 28 14 57). Lista de Correos. Open M-F 8:30am-8:30pm, Sa 9:30am-2pm. **Postal Code:** 37001.

ACCOMMODATIONS AND CAMPING

Thanks to floods of student visitors, reasonably priced *hostales* and pensiones pepper the streets of Salamanca, especially off Pl. Mayor, R. Mayor, and C. Meléndez. Make reservations a week in advance in July and August.

Pensión Los Ángeles, Pl. Mayor, 10, 2nd-3rd fl. (☎923 21 81 66; www.pensionlosangeles.com). Colorful rooms with balconies over the stunning Pl. Mayor. *Pensión* is very clean and well lit. Ask for a room with a view over the plaza. English spoken. Singles €15-25; doubles €25-60; triples €45-80. MC/V. ❷

Hostal Las Vegas Centro, C. Meléndez, 13, 1st fl. (☎923 21 87 49; www.lasvegascentro.com). TV, Wi-Fi, and friendly owners make for a great deal. Spotless rooms with white tile floor and shower. Singles €20, with bath €24; doubles €30. MC/V. ❷

Hostal Emperatriz, R. Mayor, 18 (☎923 21 91 56; fax 21 87 83). Operates out of the reception of the Hotel Emperatriz next door. Spacious rooms with bath and phone. Rooms with views of R. Mayor can be noisy, but rooms facing the courtyard are quieter. Singles €26; doubles €35. Cash only.

Albergue Juvenil Salamanca, C. Escoto 13-15 (☎923 26 91 41; www.alberguesalamanca.com). One of the least expensive student options in Salamanca, this friendly youth hostel is about a ten minute walk from Plaza Mayor but close to plenty of bars and nightclubs. Rooms are clean but basic. Storage of valuables €1 per night. Dorms with up to 20 beds €12.90; singles €25; doubles €36. Deposit for reservation. MC/V. ❶

Pensión Barez, C. Meléndez, 19 (☎923 21 74 95). Clean pink-and-yellow double rooms overlook the street. Common room with terrace. €14 per person. Cash only. ❶

Camping Regio, on Ctra. Salamanca, 4 km toward Madrid (☎923 13 88 88; www.campingregio.com). **Salmantino** buses leave every 30min. from Gran Vía near Pl. de la Constitución (€0.80). First-class sites with hot showers. Laundry €3. Pool €1.30. €3.20 per person; €2.80 per tent, per car, and for electricity. MC/V. ❶

FOOD

Pork is the city's speciality, with dishes ranging from *chorizo* (spicy sausage) to *cochinillo* (suckling pig). Try Salamanca's *hornazo*, a type of meat-stuffed pie. Cafes and restaurants surround Pl. Mayor, which lights up around 10pm. Try to branch out to the less-touristed north, along **C. Zamora, C. Toro,** and **Gran Vía** for more local fare. **Carrefour,** C. Toro, 82 (☎923 21 22 08), is a central supermarket (Open M-Sa 9:30am-9:30pm). Another tactic is to go from bar to bar, ordering drinks which come with *pinchos*, a more filling relative of tapas.

Restaurante Delicatessen Café, C. Meléndez, 25 (☎ 923 28 03 09). A dramatic departure from the traditional taverns that dominate the restaurant scene, this trendy locale serves up a wide variety of *platos combinados* (€11) and a lunch *menú* (€11) in a colorful solarium. Enjoy breakfast (€2.50) under the glass cupula, or enjoy the fresh air with the chatty, hip crowd sitting outside. Open daily 10am-midnight. MC/V. ❷

El Patio Chico, C. Meléndez, 13 (☎923 26 51 03). *Salmantinos* crowd this rustic joint, but the hefty portions of dishes like the *Farinato* are worth the wait. Try the *morcilla picante* (spicy blood sausage) and expect *pinchos* with your drink at the bar. Entrees €6-17. *Menú* €14. Open daily 1-4pm and 8pm-midnight. MC/V. ❷

Restaurante Isidro, C. Pozo Amarillo, 19 (☎923 26 28 48), a block from Pl. Mayor. Prompt and friendly service, big crowds, and generous portions. Numerous vegetable, seafood, and meat entrees (€4-15.50). You can't go wrong with the great *tortilla de chorizo*. *Menú* €10. Open M-Sa 1-3:30pm and 8-11:30pm. MC/V. ❷

SIGHTS

LA UNIVERSIDAD DE SALAMANCA. Salamanca's highlight is its renowned university, established in 1218. The entrance is one of the country's best examples of Spanish Plateresque, a 15th and 16th century architectural style named after the work of *plateros* (silversmiths) and characterized by the ornate motifs that cover the sandstone walls of Salamanca. Sculpted into the facade is a tiny frog atop a skull, now a mascot for Salamanca. Legend has it that if you find the croaker without assistance, good luck or marriage follow—but it's likely your chances will be spoiled by everyone else already pointing at it.

The old lecture halls inside the university are open to the public. The 15th-century classroom **Aula Fray Luis de León** has been left in more or less its original state; medieval students considered the hard benches luxurious, as most students then sat on the floor. Look for carved graffiti on the benches, an inheritance of 500 years of gossip and unrequited loves. The **Biblioteca Antigua,** one of Europe's oldest libraries, is the most spectacular room of all. The magnificent Plateresque staircase that ascends toward the library is said to represent the perilous path to true knowledge through youth, love, and adventure.

The University would administer its rigorous oral tests in front of the **chapel,** *La Capilla del Estudiante*, 800 years ago. That evening, the town would host a bullfight in honor of those who passed; the fresh blood of the bull was mixed with flour and used to paint the names of the new doctors on the university and cathedral walls. Look closely and you'll see faded red stamps and text on the sandstone. Across the street from the university and through the hall on the left corner of the patio is the **University Museum.** The reconstructed **Cielo de Salamanca,** Fernando Gallego's famous 15th-century fresco of the zodiac which used to crown the ceiling of the Capilla, is preserved here. *(From Pl. Mayor follow R. Mayor, veer right onto R. Antigua, then left onto C. Libreros; the University is on the left. University ☎923 29 45 00, ext. 1225, museum ext. 1150. Museum open M-Sa 10am-2pm and 4-8pm, Su 10am-2pm. University open M-F 9:30am-1:30pm and 4-7:30pm, Sa 9:30am-1:30pm and 4-7pm, Su 10am-1:30pm. €4, students and seniors €2.)*

CATEDRAL NUEVA. It took 220 years (1513-1733) to build this spectacular Gothic structure. Successive architects decided to retain the original late Gothic style but couldn't resist adding touches from later periods, particularly apparent in the Baroque tower. Modern renovators have left their marks too: look for an astronaut and a dragon eating ice cream on the left side of the main door. The church is best viewed first from the ground, but be sure to visit the **Ieronimus** exhibition in the heart of the tower, which offers a spectacular artifactual and architectural exhibition and an even more stunning **view** of the city and the New Cathedral. *(Pl. de Anaya. Cathedral open daily Apr.-Sept. 9am-8pm; Oct.-Mar. 9am-1pm and 4-6pm. Free. Ieronimus open daily 10am-8pm, last entry 7:15pm. €3.)*

CATEDRAL VIEJA. Constructed in 1140, the Romanesque **Catedral Vieja** has one of the most detailed cupolas in Spain, assembled from intricately carved pieces. The oldest part of the cathedral is the **Capilla de San Martín,** with frescoes dating from 1242. Look for the golden-hued statue of the Virgen de la Vega, Salamanca's patron saint. The **museum** features works by Renaissance artists Fernando Gallego and Pedro Bello. Visit the **Patio Chico** behind the cathedral, where students congregate and tourists head for a view of both cathedrals. *(Enter through the Catedral Nueva. Museum ☎923 21 74 76. Cathedral open daily Oct.-Mar. 10am-12:30pm and 4-5:30pm; Apr.-Sept. 10am-7:30pm. €4.25, students €3.50, children €2.75.)*

PLAZA MAYOR. Built on the orders of Bourbon King Philip V, the renowned Plaza Mayor owes its beauty to French architecture. Designed by Alberto Churriguera (see **Architecture**, p. 71) between 1729 and 1755, the plaza contains 88 towering arches, the **Ayuntamiento,** and three pavilions. The **Pabellón Real,** to the right of the *Ayuntamiento*, honors the Spanish monarchy (and, quite controversially, the 20th-century dictator Francisco Franco, behind the blue tarpaulin); the **Pabellón del Sur,** in front of the *Ayuntamiento*, is dedicated to famous Spanish conquistadors; and the **Pabellón del Oeste,** to the left of the *Ayuntamiento*, pays homage to important *salmantinos* like San Juan de Sahagún and Miguel de Unamuno. Additional spaces of honor were left intentionally blank for future generations. Plaza Mayor is a common meeting place for the young and old alike, right under the *reloj* (clock).

MUSEO DE SALAMANCA. Across from the university in the Patio de las Escuelas, the Museo de Salamanca occupies an astounding building that was once home to Álvarez Albarca, physician to Fernando and Isabel. Along with the Casa de las Conchas, this structure is among Spain's most important examples of 15th-century architecture. The museum has an intriguing collection of sculptures and paintings including *Mesa Alegre (Happy Table)* by Vincenzo Camp and *Viejo Bebedor (Old Drunk)* by Esteban March, Juan de Flandes's portrait of San Andrés, and Luis de Morales's *Llanto por Cristo muerto (Cry for the Dead Christ)*. *(Patio de las Escuelas, 2. ☎923 21 22 35. Open June-Sept. Tu-Sa 10am-2pm and 5-8pm, Su 10am-2pm; Oct.-May Tu-Sa 10am-2pm and 4-7pm, Su 10am-2pm. €1.20; students, children, and over 65 €0.60. Free Sa and Su.)*

CASA LIS MUSEO ART NOUVEAU Y ART DECO. This early 20th-century stained-glass palace houses an extensive collection of 19th- and 20th- century glassware, statues of **flappers** in various states of undress, and a set of bottles depicting curmudgeonly old Dickens characters. Walking through the *museo* feels like entering an F. Scott Fitzgerald parlor or Edith Wharton's most animated boudoir. *(C. El Explolio, 14. ☎923 27 10 89; www.museocasalis.org. Open Apr.-Oct. 15 Tu-F 11am-2pm and 5-9pm, Sa-Su 11am-9pm; Oct. 16-Mar 31 Tu-F 11am-2pm and 4-7pm, Sa-Su 11am-8pm. €3, students €2, under 14 free. Free Th 11am-2pm.)*

CASA MUSEO DE UNAMUNO. Miguel de Unamuno, a founding figure of the prolific Spanish literary movement known as the *Generación de 1898*, lived here as rector of the university in the early 20th century. His stand against General Miguel Primo de Rivera's 1923 coup led to his dismissal and exile, though he was triumphantly reinstated some years later. It is said that he began his first lecture back with the line, "As we were saying yesterday..." Poet, author, and intellectual badass, Unamuno's extensive library testifies to his fascination with religious philosophy and his ability to read in 14 different languages. *(C. Libreros, 25. To the right of the university's main entrance. Ring bell if house appears closed. ☎923*

29 44 00, ext. 1196. Open July-Sept. Tu-F 9:30am-1:30pm, Sa-Su 10am-1:30pm; Oct.-June Tu-F 9:30am-1pm and 4-6pm, Sa-Su 10am-1:30pm. Research room open M-F 9am-2pm. Mandatory tour in Spanish every 30min. €3, students €1.50.)

EL ARCHIVO GENERAL DE LA GUERRA CIVIL ESPAÑOLA. Once a vital organ in Franco's anti-Communist repression, this early 18th-century hospital now houses Spain's most extensive collection of Republican documents and rotating exhbitions. During the Spanish Civil War (1936-1939), Franco converted the building into a storage and work facility for the Office of Anti-Communist Investigation and Propaganda, which accumulated information on Republican forces. In 1938, the office was christened the State Delegation for the Recuperation of Documents. After Franco's death in 1975 and the end of his dictatorship, the collection of documents became a general archive, part of Spain's system of study and documentation centers. *(C. El Expolio, 2. ☎923 21 28 45; www.mcu.es/archivos/MC/AGC/index.html. Archive open M-Th 8am-8:30pm, F 8am-7:45pm. Museum on ground floor open Tu-Su 11am-2pm and 5-9pm. To consult documents, bring a passport and acquire a pass from the guards at the front door. Free.)*

CASA DE LAS CONCHAS. Follow R. Mayor from the Plaza Mayor until you reach a plaza with an organ-pipe fountain. On the right, you'll find the 15th-century Casa de las Conchas (House of Shells), with over 300 scallop halves on the facade, one of Salamanca's most famous landmarks. Pilgrims who journeyed to Santiago de Compostela (p. 536) traditionally wore shells to commemorate their visit to the tomb of Santiago. Legend has it that the Jesuits bought and leveled every house in the area to build their college—except the Casa de las Conchas, though they offered to pay one gold coin for every shell. Inquire about periodic *tertulias* (cultural or artistic social gatherings). *(C. Compañía, 2. Library ☎923 26 93 17. Open M-F 9am-9pm, Sa 9am-2pm. Casa open M-F 9am-9pm, Sa-Su 9am-2pm and 4-7pm, Su 10am-2pm and 4-7 pm. Free.)* Directly across from the Casa de las Conchas is **La Clerecía** (Royal College of the Holy Spirit), the main building of La Universidad Pontificia de Salamanca. *(☎923 27 71 00. Open Tu-F 10:30am-12:50pm and 5-7:30pm, Sa 10am-1:20pm and 5-8pm, Su 10am-1:20pm. €2.)*

PUENTE ROMANO. A 2000-year-old Roman bridge spans the scenic Río Tormes at the southern edge of the city. It was once part of the *Camino de la Plata* (Silver Way), a Roman trade route running from Mérida in Extremadura to Astorga. In medieval times, that was the route most Andalucian and Castilian Christians took to complete their pilgrimage to Santiago de Compostela. A headless granite bull called the **Toro Ibérico** guards one end of the bridge. Though it dates to pre-Roman times, the bull gained fame in the 16th century when it appeared in *Lazarillo de Tormes*, the prototype of the picaresque novel and a predecessor of *Don Quixote*. In one karmic episode, Lazarillo gets his head slammed into the bull's ear after cheating his blind employer. *(To reach the bridge, walk downhill toward the river.)*

NIGHTLIFE

Salmantinos claim Salamanca is the best place in Spain **para ir de marcha** (to go out on the town). With some 5,000 bars, Salamanca is not lacking in supplies. *Chupiterías* (bars selling mostly shots), *barres*, and discotecas line nearly every street, and the party doesn't wind down until it's time for *churros con chocolate* at dawn. For out-of-towners, the *marcha* starts in Pl. Mayor, where members of local *tunas* (medieval-style student troubadour groups) strut around the plaza dressed in traditional black capes, serenading women with mandolins and tambourines in hand. Student nightlife spreads out to **Gran Vía, Calle Bordadores,** and side streets, full of disco-bars. **Calle Prior** and **Rúa Mayor** are good bar spots; **Plaza de San Juan Bautista** fills with students kicking off their evening, date in one hand, infamous *litro* of beer in the other. On **C. Prior** and **C. Compañía,** tipsy young Americans and clubby *salmantinos* mix at **Niebla,** C. Bordadores, 14 (☎923 21 45 30) and **Gatsby,** C. Bordadores, 16 (☎923 21 73 62). Both host the same tight pants and free-flowing alcohol. Dress to impress; though none of the clubs have cover charges, bouncers can be picky. Club promoters are often in the streets handing out cards for free drinks.

Bar La Chupitería, Pl. de Monterrey. Make your way through the crowds and psychedelic Beatles posters to order from Los Exóticos, their extensive menu of specialty shots. Absinthe, anyone? *Chupitos* (shots) €1. Beer €2.50. Open daily 10pm-very late.

La Dolce Vita, Gran Vía, 48. Groove to salsa and pop in a Hollywood-themed disco. Unbeatable weeknight promotions on unlimited beer and sangria. Shots €1. Beer €3. Mixed drinks from €5. Open M-Th 10:30pm-3:30am, F-Sa 11pm-4:30am.

Jacko's Bar, C. Iscar Peyra, 22. Cheap shots and *litros* keep students—mostly American—coming to this Michael Jackson-inspired bar. *Litro* of beer, sangria, or *tinto de verano* €2. Specialty *litros* €3.90-7. *Chupitos* €1-1.50. Open daily 9:30pm-3am.

Bar Paniagua, C. Varillas, 1. Smartly dressed student crowd. Rumor has it that Paniagua is the place for foreigners to meet their *salmantino* mate. *Litro* of beer or *calimocho* (wine and Coke) €3.50. Open M-Th and Su 8pm-3am, F-Sa 8pm-5am.

British Museum, C. San Justo, 36. Despite the nerdy name, this bar attracts a laid-back, local student crowd who dig the Beatles, R.E.M., and American blues. Beer €1.50. Open M-Th 7pm-3am, F-Sa 7pm-4:30am.

ENTERTAINMENT AND FESTIVALS

Guia del Ocio, a free pamphlet distributed at the tourist office and at some bars, lists movies, special events, and bus schedules. Posters at the **Colegio Mayor,** Pl. de Anaya, advertise university events, free films, and student theater. On June 12, in honor of San Juan de Sahagún, the **Plaza de Toros** hosts a bullfight for charity. Take **C. Zamora** to **Po. Dr. Torres Villarroel;** the bullring is just beyond Pl. de la Glorieta. (Seats in the sun from €35.) A **Renaissance fair** runs until June 15. Between the end of July and September, Salamanca puts on **Verano en La Cueva,** a weekend music and theater festival in a cave in the Villena Antigua Muralla, across from the Convento de San Esteban. (Shows start at 9:15pm. For more info, visit www.salamanca.es.) Salamanca celebrates the week-long **Fiestas de Salamanca** in honor of their patroness the Virgen de la Vega; exhibitions abound, most honoring the bullfighting that has made the region's *ganaderías* (bull farms) the best in all of Spain. Salamanca goes all out during **Semana Santa,** with local traditions like *Lunes de Aguas*. In the 16th century, King Felipe II ordered all prostitutes to leave the city from Ash Wednesday until the end of Holy Week. A priest known as *El Padre Putas* would escort them across the Tormes and supervise their week of exile while the city put on its pious face. Then, on the Monday after Easter, jubilant students would ferry their Magdalene ladies back triumphantly as *salmantinos* drank and feasted on shore.

DAYTRIP FROM SALAMANCA

CIUDAD RODRIGO

Buses arrive from Salamanca (1hr.; M-F 12-13 per day 7am-9:30pm, Sa 6 per day 8:30am-6pm, Su 4 per day 11am-9:30pm; last return to Salamanca M-F 7:30pm, Sa 5:45pm, Su 8pm; €5.50). Buy tickets from El Pilar, windows 23 and 24. Save about 25min. walking from the Plaza Mayor to the bus station, or take the #4 bus (€0.80).

The hushed, labyrinthine streets and 18th-century ramparts of Ciudad Rodrigo (pop. 16,000), a sleepy town just 27km from Portugal, harbor sandstone churches, Roman ruins, and medieval masonry. The town was a Roman outpost, but its namesake is Conde Rodrigo González Girón, the count who brought the site back to life in 1100 after Moorish invasions. Fortified during border wars between Spain and Portugal, Ciudad Rodrigo soon grew into an outpost for the Spanish military. The **cathedral** is the town's main attraction. Originally a Romanesque church, it was later modified to conform to 16th-century Gothic tastes. The cathedral's **claustro** (cloister) is the highlight of any trip to Ciudad Rodrigo. The capitals of the ruined columns are covered with figures doing everything from making love to playing peek-a-boo to flirting with cannibalism. (Cathedral open July-Sept. Tu-Sa noon-2pm and 4-7pm, Su 1-2pm and 4-6pm; Oct.-June daily 10am-1pm and 4-7pm. €2.50, students €2, groups €1.50. Cloister and museum open Tu-Su 10am-2pm and 4-8pm, Sa-Su 10am-8pm. Free; includes tour in Spanish. Tower open Tu-Su at 12:30, 1:30, 5:30pm). Aside from its cathedral, Ciudad Rodrigo makes a worthwhile stop for its daytime tranquility and rollicking festivals. The **bus station** (☎923 46 10 09) is on Campo de Toledo, 3-25. From the entrance, walk uphill on Av. Yurramendi and through the stone arch; the cathedral is ahead. Stop by **Supermercado El Arbol,** Av. Yurramendi, s/n. (☎923 48 00 56. Open M-Sa 9:15am-9:15pm. MC/V.) The **tourist office,** Pl. de Amayuelas, 5, is to the left through the arch. (☎923 46 05 61; turismociudadrodrigo@jcyl.es. English spoken. Open M-F 9am-2pm and 5-7pm, Sa-Su 11:30am-2pm and 4:30-8:30pm.) There is also a **visitor's center** just before the arch, on Avda. de Sefarad. (☎923 16 33 73). To get to Pl. Mayor from the tourist office, go straight on Pl. de Amayuelas into town, turn left onto C. del Cardenal Pacheco before Pl. de San Salvador, and take a right onto C. Julián Sánchez; Pl. Mayor is at the end of this street.

ZAMORA ☎980

Perched atop a cliff over the Río Duero, Zamora (pop. 70,000) blends medieval and modern: 11th-century churches rub shoulders with stylish Mango and Zara, while the 12th-century cathedral overlooks modern subdivisions and steel bridges. With more than 20 churches, the city overflows with monuments of religious fervor. But it also has an earthly past, as Zamora was historically one of the most powerful cities in medieval Castilla. *Zamoranos* have, without a doubt, stayed true to their roots: nearly every plaza venerates Zamora's infamous historical figures, including the fierce Roman warrior Viriato, who was born here; El Cid, who fled here; and Sancho II, who died here during an attempt to overthrow his sister and claim the crown of Castilla as his own. The nearby town of Sanabria was also the inspiration for Miguel de Unamuno's famous novella, *San Manuel Bueno, Mártir.*

TRANSPORTATION

The bus station on Av. Alfonso Peña (☎980 52 12 82; 24hr.; lockers €0.85 per bag per day) sends **buses** to **Madrid** (2-3hr.; M-F 6 per day 7am-7:30pm, Sa 3 per day 10:30am-5:30pm, Su 6 per day 10:30am-9pm; €13-20), **Salamanca** (1hr.; M-F 15 per day 6:30am-9:35pm, Sa 10 per day 7:45am-8:30pm, Su 7 per day 8:45am-10:15pm; €4), and **Valladolid** (1hr.; M-F hourly 7am-8:30pm, Sa 6 per day 8:00am-6:30pm, Su 4 per day 10:30am-8pm; €6). **Trains** leave C. de la Estación (☎980 52 11 10; 24hr.) at the end of Av. Alfonso Peña to **Madrid** (3hr.; M-F and Su 4am, 6:47pm; Sa 4am, 2:30pm; €26) and **Valladolid** (1hr., 8:32am, €7.15). Both stations are a 20min. walk from Pl. Mayor.

PRACTICAL INFORMATION

To reach the **tourist office** at Av. Príncipe de Asturias, 1, exit the bus station through the arrival platform and turn left onto Av. Alfonso Peña, which becomes Av. de Tres Cruces. Take a left at Pl. Alemania onto C. Alfonso IX, and then a left onto Av. Príncipe de Asturias. (☎980 53 18 45. Open July to mid-Sept. M-Th and Su 9am-8pm, F-Sa 9am-9pm; mid-Sept. to June daily 9am-2pm and 5-8pm.) There is a second office closer to the monuments at Pl. Arias Gonzalo, 6. (☎987 53 36 94; www.ayto-zamora.org. Open daily Oct.-Mar. 10am-2pm and 4-7pm; Apr.-Sept. 10am-2pm and 5-8pm.) **Banco Santander** is at Ave. de las Tres Cruces, 31. (Open M-F 8:30am-2pm, Sa 8:30am-1pm.) **Municipal police** are in the Plaza Mayor in the *Ayuntamiento Viejo* (☎930 52 50 92). There is a **pharmacy** in Pl. Mayor on C. Ramos Carrión, 2. (☎980 53 01 62. English spoken. Open M-F 9:45am-2pm and 5-8pm, Sa 10am-1:45pm.) In a medical emergency, head to **Hospital Virgen de la Concha,** Av. Requejo, s/n (☎980 54 82 00, emergencies 54 82 12). The **Biblioteca Pública,** Pl. Moyano, has free **internet.** (☎980 53 15 51. Max. 1hr. Passport required. Open M-F 9am-9pm, Sa 9am-2pm.)

ACCOMMODATIONS AND FOOD

Zamora has a number of options in the old part of the city. **Hostal Siglo XX ❷**, Pl. del Seminario, 3, a few blocks off the Pl. Mayor, has beautiful, antique rooms and a serene location across from a historic seminary. (☎980 53 29 08 Singles €20; doubles €35. Cash only.) **Hostal La Reina ❷,** C. Reina, 1, conveniently located right off Pl. Mayor, is also a safe bet, with some rooms featuring TVs and private baths. (☎980 53 39 39. Singles €19-26; doubles €28-35. Cash only.) The Pl. Mayor also houses a number of inviting restaurants. **Casa Bernardo ❶,** Plazuela de San Miguel, 2, has a terrace right on the Pl. Mayor next to the picturesque Iglesia de San Juan. The entrees (€5-9), tapas (€3-7) and sandwiches (€3-4.50) are fit for any traveler's budget. (☎980 53 27 41. Open M and W-Su 1-4pm and 9-11:30pm.) Alternatively, **El Arbol** supermarket, Ave. de las Tres Cruces, 26-28, stocks all the basics. (Open M-Sa 9:30am-9:30pm.)

SIGHTS

Zamora's foremost monument is its Romanesque cathedral, built in the 12th-15th centuries. In the cloister, the **Museo de la Catedral** features the 15th-century Black Tapestries, illustrating the story of the Trojan War. From the tourist office, go one block up C. del Obispo. (☎980 53 06 44. Cathedral and museum open Tu-Su 10am-2pm and 5-8pm; mass daily 10am, also Sa 6pm and Su 1pm. €3, students €1.50.) Beyond its medieval heritage, Zamora also hosts the contemporary **Museo Etnográfico,** C. Sacramento, a seven-story glass building just off the Pl. Mayor. The museum has a collection of over 1000 eclectic works that explore life in Castilla y León over the last few centuries. (☎980 53 17 08. Open Mar.-Sept. Tu-Sa 10am-2pm and 5-8pm, Su 10am-2pm; Oct.-Dec. Tu-Sa 10am-2pm and 4:30-6:30pm, Su 10am-2pm. €3, students €1.) The **Museo de Semana Santa,** Pl. Santa María la Nueva, shows just how significant Holy Week, *Semana Santa*, is to the city of Zamora. Hooded mannequins guard sculpted floats, used during the *romería* processions depicting the stations of the cross. The crypt-like setting and collected pieces dating back to the 16th century make this museum one of the eeriest stops in town. (☎980 53 22 95. Open Tu-Sa 10am-2pm and 5-8pm, Su 10am-2pm. €3, under 12 €1.50.)

Twelve striking, recently restored Romanesque churches reside within the walls of the old city. Almost all date from the 11th and 12th centuries, but their ornate altars were added in the 15th and 16th centuries. In Pl. Mayor, the

Iglesia San Juan is notable for its marble-veined windows. **Iglesia Santa María la Nueva** was the site of *El Motín de la Trucha;* in 1158 villagers set the church on fire (with the nobles inside) to protest a law giving the nobility priority over the commoners in buying trout. From the Pl. Mayor, walk up C. Sacramento and turn right onto C. Barandales; the church is in Pl. Santa María la Nueva. (All open Tu-Sa Feb.-Sept. 10am-1pm and 5-8pm; Oct.-Jan. 6 10am-2pm and 4:30-6:30pm. Free.) Located directly behind the cathedral is another venerable building of Zamora: **El Castillo.** Built in the Middle Ages on pre-Roman foundations, the castle of Zamora stands formidably on the cliff overlooking the countryside surrounding Zamora. Although it is not open to the public, the park and area around the castle offer great views of Zamora and the surrounding land.

HIKING

The tourist office has info on hikes about 25km west of the city. Two popular routes start from **Muelas del Pan** and **Ricobayo de Alba,** both of which feature great views and undisturbed countryside. **Vivas** runs buses from the Zamora station (M-Th 1:30, 5:45, 6pm; F 1:30, 6pm; Sa 1:30pm; return M-Sa 8:30am; €1.10). Trails are well marked, and the hikes are 8-9km each. Going to either town requires an overnight stay, since buses only return in the morning. **Pensión Tomasita ❹,** Ctra. Alcañices, has rooms along Muelas del Pan (☎980 55 30 07. Breakfast included. Doubles €40.) Those traveling to Ricobayo can stay at **Hostal del Rio ❶,** Ctra. Alcañices, 90. (☎980 55 32 45. Singles €18; doubles €36.)

LEÓN ☎987

León (pop. 165,000) is the last big city along the Camino de Santiago where pilgrims have a chance to rest, enjoy delicious tapas, and visit a gorgeous cathedral. It's easy to feel at home in León; though big, its streets are easy to navigate and its natives are friendly and welcome. They are also fiercely proud of León's distinct identity, apart from the enveloping province of Castilla y León. The Roman Legion named the town *Legio* in AD 68, but derivations over the years have led the name to *León,* or lion. The city was also a stronghold against the Moors during the *Reconquista.* The spectacular blue stained-glass windows of its famous cathedral have earned León the nickname *La Ciudad Azul.* This Gothic masterpiece is only a starting point for exploration of León's parks, bustling cafes, and raucous nightlife.

TRANSPORTATION

Flights: Aeropuerto de León (☎987 87 77 00). **Air Nostrum** (☎902 40 05 00) flies to **Barcelona** and **Madrid. Lagun Air** (☎902 34 03 00) services **Alicante, Ibiza, Málaga, Menorca, Palma, Sevilla,** and **Valencia.**

Trains: RENFE, Av. de Astorga, 2 (☎902 24 02 02). Open 24hr. To: **Barcelona** (9hr.; 2-3 per day M-F and Su 12:25am-9:28pm, Sa 12:25am-1:21pm; €45-52); **Bilbao** (5hr., 2:54pm, €27); **Burgos** (2-3hr.; 3-4per day 12:25am-9:28pm, Sa until 2:54pm; €19-22); **La Coruña** (7hr., express 4hr. W-F; 2-3 per day 5:40am-2:07pm; M, Th, Sa-Su 5:40am-4:40pm; €29-34); **Gijón** (3hr.; 5-7 per day M-F 9:07am-9:10pm, Sa until 5:39pm, Su 1:15pm-9:10pm; €10-20) via **Oviedo** (2hr., €7-18); **Madrid** (4hr.; 6-8 per day M-Sa 3:34am-8:35pm, Su 7:10am-8:35pm; €23-40); **Valladolid** (2hr.; 10-11 per day M-Sa 3:34am-8:50pm, Su 7:10am-8:50pm; €10-23). Updated train schedules are printed daily in *Diario de León* (€0.65).

Buses: Estación de Autobuses, Po. del Ingeniero Sáenz de Miera (☎987 21 00 00). Station open M-Sa 5:15am-2:30am, Su 6am-2:30am. Information open M-F

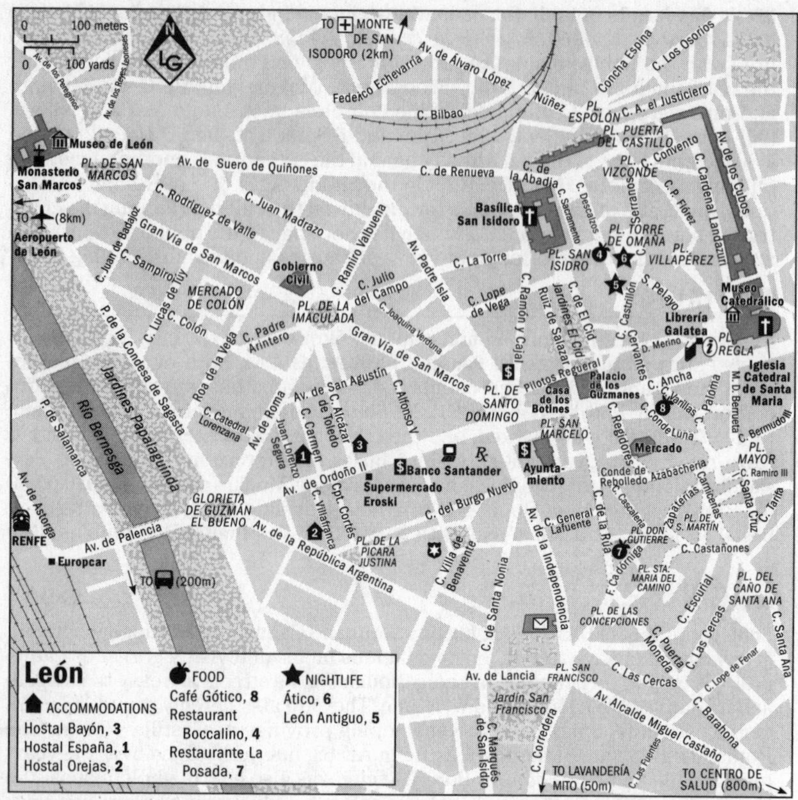

7:30am-9pm, Sa 8am-1pm, Su 3:30-8:30pm. To: **Madrid** (4hr.; 9-13 per day M-F and Su 2:30am-10:30pm, Sa 2:30am-8:30pm; €20-30); **Salamanca** (2hr.) via **Zamora** (1 hr.; M-F 6 per day 8am-6:30pm, Sa 4 per day 8am-5pm, Su 4 per day 10:15am-7pm); **Santander** (5hr.; M-Th 9-10 per day 3:40am-10pm, F 14 per day 3:40am-10pm, Sa 6 per day 3:40am-3:30pm, Su 12 per day 3:40am-12pm; €11-28); **Valladolid** (2hr., 19-21 per day 12:30am-11:59pm, €8).

Taxis: Radio Taxi (☎987 26 14 15). 24hr.

Car Rental: Europcar, Av. de Astorga, next to the train station (☎987 23 02 51). 21+, must have had license for 1 year. From €80 per day with 350km limit. Open M-F 9am-1:30pm and 4-7:30pm, Sa 9am-1pm.

ORIENTATION AND PRACTICAL INFORMATION

Most of León, including the old city *(León Gótico)* and the modern commercial district, lies on the east side of the Río Bernesga. The **bus** and **train** stations are across the river on the west side. **Av. de Palencia** leads across the river to **Glorieta de Guzmán el Bueno,** and after the rotary becomes **Av. de Ordoño II,** which bisects the new city. At Pl. de Santo Domingo, Av. de Ordoño II becomes **C. Ancha,** a pedestrian street that splits the old town in two and leads to the cathedral.

Tourist Office: Pl. Regla, 3 (☎987 23 70 82; www.turismocastillayleon.com). Free city maps, regional brochures, and accommodations guide. Look out for the monthly city guide *Guía del Ocio.* Sept 16-June M-F 9am-2pm and 5-8pm, Sa-Su 10am-2pm and 5-8pm; July-Sept. 15 M-F 9am-8pm, Sa-Su 10am-8pm.

Currency Exchange: ATMs and **banks** line Pl. de Santo Domingo. **Banco Santander Central Hispano,** Pl. de Santo Domingo (☎987 29 23 00). Open Apr.-Sept. M-F 8:30am-2pm; Oct.-Mar. M-F 8:30am-2pm, Sa 8:30am-1pm. **Citibank,** on Av. de la Independencia at C. Legión VII. Open M-F 8:30am-2pm.

Luggage Storage: At the train station (€3). Open 24hr. At the bus station (€2). Buy tokens M-F 7:30am-9pm, Sa 8am-1pm, Su 3:30-8:30pm.

English-Language Bookstore: Librería Galatea, C. Sierra Pambley, 1 (☎987 27 26 52). Open M-F 10am-2pm and 4:30-8:30pm.

Police: National C. Villa de Benavente, 6 (☎987 21 89 00). Municipal Paseo del Parque (☎987 25 55 00).

Medical Services: Emergency service (☎987 22 22 22). **Hospital Monte de San Isidro,** Ctra. Asturias (☎987 22 72 50).

Late-Night Pharmacy: Farmacia Mata Espeso, Av. de Ordoño II, 3 (☎987 20 73 15). Open M-F 9:30am-2pm and 4:30-10pm, Sa 9:30am-2pm; every night 10pm-9:30am.

Internet Access: Cafetería Santo Domingo, Av. de Ordoño II, 3 (☎987 26 13 84). €1.80 per hr., min. 30min. (€1). Free Wi-Fi with meal or drink. Open M-F Su 8am-noon. **Locutorio La Rua,** C. Varillas, 3 (987 21 99 94). €1 per hr., €0.20 per min. for calls to the U.S. Open M-F 9:30am-9:30pm, Sa 10:30am-2:30pm and 5:30-9pm.

Laundromat: Lavandería Mito, C. Arcipreste de Hita. (☎987 20 08 77). From the Pl. Santo Domingo walk down Av. de la Independencia. When you reach Pl. San Francisco, continue straight onto C. Corredera. After about 5 blocks turn right onto C. Arcipresta de Hita. Open M-F 9am-1:30pm and 4-8pm, Sa 9am-1pm.

Post Office: Jardín de San Francisco (☎987 87 60 81). **Lista de Correos** (windows #12-13) and fax. Open M-F 8:30am-8:30pm, Sa 9:30am-2pm. **Postal Code:** 24070.

ACCOMMODATIONS

Moderately priced hostels are fairly easy to find, thanks to the yearly influx of pilgrims on their way to Santiago, but they tend to fill up during the June fiestas. If you plan to visit León on a weekend, book rooms at least a week in advance. Find rooms on **Avenida de Roma, Avenida de Ordoño II,** and **Avenida de la República Argentina,** which lead into the old town from **Glorieta de Guzmán el Bueno.**

Hostal Bayón, C. Alcázar de Toledo, 6, 2nd fl. (☎987 23 14 46). Wicker chairs, old photos of León, sun-drenched rooms, and bright colors make this hostel a good retreat from the hustle and bustle of the city. Hall baths and a dining room with TV. Breakfast €1.50. Singles €18, with shower €25; doubles €28/35. Cash only. ❶

Hostal España, C. Carmen, 3, 1st floor (☎987 23 60 14). This hostel features antique-looking rooms with beautiful white fixtures and a friendly staff. Daily meals served in large dining room €7. Call in advance because this place fills quickly. Singles €17; doubles with shower €35. Cash only. ❶

Hostal Orejas, C. Villafranca, 8, 2nd fl. (☎987 25 29 09; www.hostal_orejas.com,). Sunny, white rooms complete with modern fixtures, big, comfy beds, showers, and cable TV. Cozy dining hall has free Wi-Fi access. Daily breakfast served 7:30-11am €2.50. Singles €25, with bath €35-45; doubles €50; triples €62. MC/V. ❷

FOOD

Inexpensive eateries fill the area near the cathedral and the small streets off **Calle Ancha;** also check **Plaza de San Martín** near Pl. Mayor. Pork-lovers will rejoice, as local menus are heavily porcine. The **Eroski Center Supermercado** is on Av. de Ordoño II, 16 (☎987 25 60 53. Open daily 9:30am-9:30pm. AmEx/MC/V.)

Café Gótico, C. Varillas, 5 (☎987 08 49 56). Conveniently located, with a loungy, romantic ambience and pleasant outdoor patio. Delicious fresh food fills the daily *menú* (€11.40), which includes a vegetarian option. Offers wide variety of salads, *platos combinados, raciones,* and tempting desserts like coffee flan. Excellent service. Entrees €4-11. Open daily 1-4:30pm and 8:30-11:30pm. AmEx/MC/V. ❷

Restaurante La Posada, C. La Rúa, 33 (☎987 25 82 66). Laid-back family restaurant off the beaten path. Savory *raciones* (€3-6) in a relaxed, rustic atmosphere. Saturday's *menú del día* features a traditional meal from Castilla y León. *Menú* €9. Open M-Th and Su 1-3:45pm and 7-11:45pm, F-Sa 1-3:45pm and 8:30-11:45pm. MC/V. ❷

Restaurante Boccalino, Pl. de San Isodoro, 9 (☎987 22 30 60). Set right next to the picturesque Basílica San Isidoro, Boccalino features an incredibly wide selection of Italian and Spanish dishes: moderately priced salads, pasta, fish, meat, and pizza. Terrace overlooks the church. *Menú* €10.30 Kitchen open noon-4pm and 8pm-1am. MC/V. ❷

SIGHTS

León has several significant historical and religious sights, crowned by its magnificent cathedral. The city still retains a provincial feel, and is filled with attractive parks where weary travelers can sit and laze away the day.

IGLESIA CATEDRAL DE SANTA MARÍA. A breathtakingly beautiful 13th-century Gothic cathedral, *La Pulchra Leonina* exhibits the country's best Gothic architecture. Silhouetted against a clear sky, the cathedral is best seen in the early morning or evening, when the stained-glass windows dazzle in phenomenal color and detail. The grand facade depicts serene saints floating among monsters munching on the damned. Tours allow you to visit the cathedral's museum, which houses an impressive collection of seventh-16th century religious artwork. *(On Pl. Regla. ☎987 87 57 70; www.catedraldeleon.org. Open Oct. 1-June 30 M-Sa 8:30am-1:30pm and 4-7pm, Su 8:30am-2:30pm and 5-7pm; July 1-Sept. 30 8:30am-1:30pm and 4-8pm, Su 8:30am-2:30pm and 5-8pm. Free. Museum tour in Spanish. Museum open Oct 1-June 30 M-F 9:30am-1:30pm and 4-7pm, Sa 9:30am-1:30pm; July 1-Sept 30 M-F 9:30am-1:30pm, and 4-7:30pm, Sa 9:30am-1:30pm and 4-7pm. €4, cloisters €1.)*

BASÍLICA SAN ISIDORO. The Romanesque Basílica San Isidoro was dedicated in the 11th century to San Isidoro of Sevilla, a Visigoth bishop whose philosophical treatises were influential throughout the Middle Ages and Renaissance. After his death, his remains were brought from Muslim-controlled Andalucía to the Christian stronghold of León. Countless royals rest in the **Panteón Real,** covered in vibrant 12th-century frescoes with themes of infancy, passion, and apocalypse. *(On Pl. San Isidoro. Open July-Aug. M-Sa 9am-8pm, Su 9am-2pm; Sept.-June M-Sa 10am-1:30pm and 4-6:30pm, Su 10am-1:30pm. Museum €4, Th afternoons free.)*

MUSEO DE ARTE CONTEMPORANEO DE CASTILLA Y LEON (MUSAC). This museum was inaugurated in 1998 as part of Castilla y Leon's efforts to provide a space of expression for contemporary artists. The museum has a repertoire of rotating, interactive exhibitions and activities, and the colorful, funky restaurant and cafe/bar serves up salads and meals 10am-4pm and 8:30pm-midnight. Free Wi-Fi and internet access in the library. *(Ave. de los Reyes Leoneses, 24. www.musac.es. Open Tu-Su 10am-3pm and 4-9pm. Free.)*

OTHER SIGHTS. Casa de los Botines, on C. Ancha just off of Pl. Santo Domingo, is one of the few buildings outside Cataluña designed by architect **Antoni Gaudí** in 1891, the most famous member of the *Modernista* movement. The building now contains private bank offices, but the first floor hosts public exhibitions.

NIGHTLIFE AND FESTIVALS

For bars, discos, and techno, head to the *barrio húmedo* ("wet neighborhood," for its free-flowing alcohol) around **Pl. de San Martín** and **Pl. Mayor.** Walk up C. Ancha toward the cathedral and turn right onto C. Varillas (which becomes C. Cardiles Platerías). Walk to the intersection with C. Carnicerías. To reach Pl. de San Martín, go right; to reach Pl. Mayor, go left onto C. Plegaría. If you're looking for a slightly older crowd, head to the **Pl. Torres de Omaña** and C. Astrilión and C. Cervantes. To reach either area, turn up C. Cervantes from the main pedestrian street C. Ancha, close to the cathedral. For a relaxed drink, head to **León Antiguo,** Pl. del Cid, 16. (Drinks €2-5. Open M-W 7pm-midnight, Th-Sa 7pm-4am.) For a bigger party later in the evening, head down the street to **Ático,** which features funky dance music and strong drinks. (☎987 24 86 53. Beer €3, mixed drinks €6. Open M-Sa.) In the first week of June, León's 3500km of streams host the **International Trout Festival.** Festivals commemorating **San Juan** and **San Pedro** occur June 21-30. Highlights include a *corrida de toros* (bullfight), a massive chess tournament, clowns, artisans, and dance lessons on Pl. Regla. The high point is the feast day of San Juan (June 24).

ASTORGA ☎987

In the 15th century, Astorga was a vital stop on both the Roman silver route and the Camino de Santiago. It became one of the world's main chocolate-making centers in the 17th century, and until the turn of the 20th century, there were 49 chocolate factories in Astorga alone. Today, *confiterías* still infuse the streets with their sweet aromas. One of the oldest towns in Castilla y León, Astorga still houses the vestiges of centuries of history, which seem to whisper from the walls that protect it. Modern sights include the fantastically odd Palacio Episcopal, a Gaudí masterpiece sitting atop this hillside city.

TRANSPORTATION. The **train station** (☎987 61 64 44) is located on Pl. de la Estació and runs to: **Barcelona** (11hr.; 12:38, 11:48pm, via **Lugo** and **Burgos;** €45-56); **Burgos** (2hr.; 12:38, 2:20, 11:48pm; €21-25); **Gijón** (2hr.; 12:24pm, M-F Su 6:23pm; €12); **León** (40min., 8 per day 3:02am-11:48pm, €3.15-14); **Madrid** (3-5hr.; 3:02am, 6:23pm; €30-41); **Vigo** (6hr.; 6:09am, 2:44, 5:10pm; €26-35). **Buses** (☎987 61 91 00) run from the station at Av. las Murallas, 54, to **Ponferrada** (M-F 14 per day 6:40am-10:10pm, Sa-Su 6 per day 8:20am-9:15pm; €4.60), **Vitoria/Bilbao** (F and Su 3am, 1:30pm; €26), and **Oviedo** (5 per day 9:50am-8pm, €10.28).

PRACTICAL INFORMATION AND ORIENTATION. There is a **tourist office** at Glorieta Eduardo de Castro, 5. (☎987 60 30 65; www.ayuntamientodeastorga.com. Open Oct.-June daily 10am-1:30pm and 4-6:30pm; July-Sept. 10am-2pm and 4-7pm.) From the **train station,** head straight uphill onto Av. Estación. Continue uphill until the Pl. de Ponfidio Lopez, and head straight onto C. de las Enfermeras, diagonally across the street. At the Pl. de Obispo Alcolea, turn right onto C. Los Sitios. The tourist office is on your left in the Pl. I. Eduardo de Castro. To get there from the **bus station,** cross the street into the park with the cathedral in front of you. Walk up the stairs, then turn left on the street in front of cathedral. The tourist office will be on your right in the following plaza. A **bank, Santander Central Hispano,** is on Pl. Obispo Alcolea. From the tourist office, go down Los Sitios, which becomes Pl. Obispo Alcolea. (Open M-F 8:30am-2pm; Oct.-Mar. 8:30am-1pm.) Local services include **police** (☎987 61 60 80) and **ambulance** (☎987 61 85 62). **Internet** access is at **Ciber@stoR,** C. Manuel Gullón, 2. (☎987 61 80 17. €2 per hr. 15min., min. €0.50. Open daily 10am-2pm and 4pm-midnight, Su noon-2pm and 4pm-midnight.) **Postal Code:** 24700.

ACCOMMODATIONS AND FOOD. Cheap accommodations are scarce in Astorga; some may prefer to stay in León and visit Astorga as a daytrip. **Pensión García ❷,** Bajada del Postigo, 3, situated on a sloping, cozy little street overlooking a small park, has moderately priced rooms with worn pine floors, clean hall bathrooms, and a bright common room. (☎987 61 60 46. Singles €20; doubles €30.) Another option is **Hostal San Narciso ❷,** Ctra. Madrid-Coruña, km 325. Although a bit out of the way and located above an all-night bar, this *hostal* offers spacious, standard rooms for decent prices. To get there, take the C. Leon from the plaza right behind the cathedral out to the highway. (☎987 615 370. Singles €20, with bathroom €25; doubles €30/36.)

Astorga is one place where no one could blame you for eating dessert first: the streets are lined with beckoning *chocolaterías* and pastry shops. For a full meal, the area around **Plaza Mayor** has plenty to offer the hungry traveler. The restaurant **Ruta Romana ❷** and the more informal **Cafeteria/Cervecería Imperial ❷,** under the same ownership, are located at Pl. Santocildes, 9. Cafeteria has standard tapas fare: ham croquettes (€3) and a variety of salads (€5-7) fill out the menu. For a more formal meal, visit the restaurant downstairs. (☎987 60 30 20. *Menú* €11. Tapas and *raciones* €3-9. Desserts €2-4. Open daily 8am-midnight. Restaurant open 1-4pm and 9pm-midnight. MC/V.) **Taberna los Hornos ❷,** Pl. de España, 3, serves good traditional food in a relaxed, tavern-like atmosphere, or on its outdoor terrace. (☎987 61 89 00. Entrees €8-11, tapas €3-4. Open daily 8am-1am, kitchen open 9am-1pm.) For the basics, try **Gadis Supermercado,** Pl. Santocildes, 6. (Open daily 9am-2:30pm and 5-9pm. MC/V.)

SIGHTS. Created by Antoni Gaudí, the **Palacio Episcopal** (Bishop's Palace) is Astorga's main attraction. The palace is set upon a section of the ancient Roman wall, and the turrets, main entryway, and beveled stone exterior, as well as the funky, colorful interior, are pure Gaudí. The palace houses the **Museo de los Caminos,** which exhibits historic and contemporary interpretations of the Santiago de Compostela pilgrimage, as well as a permanent exposition of contemporary work from Leonese artists. (☎987 61 68 82. Open July-Sept. Tu-Sa 10am-2pm and 4-8pm, Su 10am-2pm; Oct.-June Tu-Sa 11am-2pm and 4-6pm, Su 11am-2pm. €2.50, over 65 or under 18 €1.50.) Sugar fiends must stop by the **Museo de Chocolate,** C. José María Goy, 5. This museum chronicles the history of chocolate that is so dear to Astorgans, given the city's past as chocolate pioneer and factory-central since the 17th century. With cocoa beans, chocolate molds, cocoa grinders, vintage ads, and samples of local chocolate, this little museum is a sweet find. From the Palacio Episcopal, walk up C. los Sitios to Pl. Obispo Alcolea; veer to the right onto C. Lorenzo Segura and C. José María Goy is on the right. (Open May-Sept. Tu-Sa 10:30am-2pm and 4:30-7pm, Su 11am-2pm; Oct.-Apr. 10:30am-2pm and 4-6pm, Su 11am-2pm. €2.) The **Museo Romano,** Pl. San Bartolomé, offers a joint ticket (€3), and features artifacts and relics from Astorga's Roman and pre-Roman past. (Open July-Sept. 10am-1:30pm and 4:30-7pm, Su 10am-1:30pm; Oct.-June Tu-Sa 10am-1:30pm and 4-6pm, Su 10am-1:30pm. €2.) If you have an hour to spare, walk the Roman walls encircling the city for magnificent views of Astorga and the far-off mountains.

VALLADOLID ☎983

When Fernando and Isabel married in Valladolid in 1469, the city stood at the helm of Spanish politics, finance, and culture. Explorers such as Fernão Magelhães (Ferdinand Magellan) came here to discuss navigation plans; Miguel de Cervantes, the mind behind *Don Quixote*, lived here; and in 1506, Christopher Columbus died here. Today, the administrative capital of Castilla y León has a reputation of class, sophistication, and architectural diversity. Wandering through cobblestone streets past outdoor cafes, fountains, statues, and plazas, visitors to Spain's original capital find that the heart of Spain's majesty is just as evident in its current incarnation as a lively but laid-back town.

TRANSPORTATION

Flights: Villanubla Airport, CN-601, km 13 (☎983 41 55 00). Taxi to airport €17-20. Daily flights to **Barcelona, Islas Baleares, Vigo, Brussels, Lisboa, London,** and **Paris.** Info open daily 8am-8pm. **Iberia** (☎983 56 01 62). Open daily 8am-8pm.

Trains: Estación del Norte, C. Recondo (☎902 24 02 02; www.renfe.es), south of Parque del Campo Grande. Info. office open daily 7am-8:30pm. Trains to: **Barcelona** (9-11hr.; daily 9:15am, Sa-Su also 9:40pm; €42); **Bilbao** (4hr.; Tu-Sa 9:20-11:45am, M 8-11:45am; €23); **Burgos** (1-2hr., M-Su 9-13 per day, €7-17); **León** (2-3hr.; M-Sa 10-11 per day 12:37am-9:08pm, Su 7 per day 12:30pm-9:08pm; €9.20-23); **Madrid** (3-3hr.; 17-22 per day M-Sa 5am-12:40am, Su 8:30am-12:40am; €14-24); **Oviedo** (4-5hr., 2-3 per day 8:00am-7:40pm, €27); **Paris** (11hr., 9:20pm, €127); **Salamanca** (1-2hr., 6-9 per day 3:20am-10:17pm, €7.20-18); **Santander** (3-6hr.; 5-7 per day M-Th and Sa 1:42am-6:54pm, F 1:42am-7:18pm, Su 7:15am-6:54pm; €14-27).

Buses: C. de Puente Colgante, 2 (☎983 23 63 08). Info open daily 8am-10pm. **ALSA** (☎902 42 22 42; www.alsa.es) to: **Barcelona** (10hr., 11am and 9pm, €40); **Bilbao** (4-6hr.; M-Sa 4-5 per day 5:45am-4:15pm, Su 3 per day 5:45am-5pm; €16; Eurobus service 3hr., 11am, €18); **Burgos** (2-3hr., 4-8 per day 5:15am-9pm, €8, Eurobus service, 1½hr., 11am, €11); **León** (2hr.; M-Sa 11-13 per day 12:15am-8pm, Su 10 per day 2:45am-8pm; €8.50); **Madrid** (2hr.; 19-22 per day M-Sa 12:30am-9:30pm, Su 4:50am-10pm; €12-16); **Oviedo** (3-4hr., 5 per day 2am-8pm, €16); **Santander** (4hr., 4-5 per day 7:30am-6pm, €11. **La Regional** (☎983 27 15 87; www.laregionalvsa.com) to **Palencia** (45min.; M-F hourly 7am-9pm, Sa 6 per day 8am-8:15pm, Su 3 per day 10am-8pm, €3) and **Zamora** (1hr.; M-F hourly 7am-8:30pm, Sa 6 per day 8:30am-8:30pm, Su 4 per day 8:30am-8:30pm; €6).

Taxis: Radio Taxi (☎983 29 14 11). 24hr. Train and bus stations to Pl. Mayor €4-5.

Bike Rental: Monta y Pedalea (☎626 70 90 45), Playa de las Morenas. €2.50 for 1hr., €10 per day, €50 per week. Open Tu 5-9pm, W-Su 11:30am-2pm and 5-9pm.

ORIENTATION AND PRACTICAL INFORMATION

The bus and train stations are on the southern edge of town, near the Parque del Campo Grande. To get from the **bus station** to the **tourist office** (15min.), leave the bus station through the left exit as you get off the bus. Turn right onto C. San José and take the first left on Po. del Arco de Ladrillo. Keep right onto C. Ladrillo at the rotary and follow it until Po. de Los Filipinos. Turn right and walk along the park until Pl. de Colón. Turn left onto Av. Acera de Recoletos, with the park on your left, and continue to the tourist office. From the front entrance of the **train station** (10min.), walk up the street perpendicular to the station, C. Estación del Norte, and follow it to Pl. de Colón. Follow the rotary to the right; Av. Acera de Recoletos will be the third street on the right. The tourist office is at the top of Av. Acera de Recoletos on your left. From the tourist office, continue up Av. Acera de Recoletos until you reach Pl. de Zorilla. **C. Santiago,** the main pedestrian street, is the second to the right. **Pl. Mayor** is straight up C. Santiago from the tourist office.

Tourist Office: Av. Acera de Recoletos (☎983 34 40 13; www.ava.es). Helpful staff. English spoken. Open daily 9am-2pm and 5-8pm.

Currency Exchange: Citibank, C. Miguel Iscar, 7, off Pl. de Zorrilla. Open M-F 8:30am-2pm. **BBVA,** Av. Acera de Recoletos, 1, on the corner with C. Miguel Iscar. (☎902 22 44 66; www.bbva.es). Open M-F 8:30am-2:15pm, Sa 8:30am-1pm. Banks line **Av. Acera de Recoletos;** most exchange cash and travelers checks.

Luggage Storage: At the train station at the end of Platform 1. Lockers €3-4.50 per hr. At the bus station (€0.70 per bag 1 day; extra days €1). Open M-Sa 8am-10pm.

Police: In the *Ayuntamiento* (municipal police) (☎983 42 61 07 or 091).

Late-Night Pharmacy: Da. Esther Vicente Reguero Po. de Zorilla, 85 at C. Luna. (☎983 23 15 44). Open M-F 10pm-2pm and 5pm-8pm; Sa 10pm-2pm; Su 24hr.

Medical: Hospital Pío del Río Hortega, Rnda. de Sta. Teresa (☎983 42 04 00).

Internet Access: Ciberc@fé Segafredo Zanetti, Po. de Zorrilla, 46 (☎983 33 80 63). From Pl. de Zorrilla, walk down Po. de Zorrilla alongside the park; the cafe is on right before Av. García Morato. €0.50 per 15 min. Open daily 8am-11pm.

Post Office: Pl. Rinconada (☎983 36 22 70; www.correos.es). 2 blocks from Pl. Mayor, up C. Jesús on the right. *Lista de correos*, photocopying, fax, and phone cards available. Open M-F 8:30am-8:30pm, Sa 8:30am-2pm. **Postal Code:** 47001.

ACCOMMODATIONS

Cheap lodgings and *pensiones* pack the streets off Av de Recoletos near the train station, the area by the cathedral, and behind Pl. Mayor at Pl. del Val.

Hostal los Arces, C. San Antonio de Padua, 2, 1st fl. (☎983 35 38 53). 3 blocks from Pl. Mayor, just off Pl. de los Arces. Under the same ownership as Hostal del Val. Features cozy rooms with old European charm, complete with wooden floors, elegant rugs, windows overlooking the plaza, and comfortable sofas and chandeliers. Lounge with TV. Singles €18, with shower €33; doubles €30/42. MC/V. ❷

Pension Zamora, C. Arribas 14, 2nd fl. (983 30 30 52). Right across from the Catedral Metropolitana, this hostel offers a quiet spot to rest after a long day of travel. Rooms are very white, fresh, and clean. Try to get hold of one of the sunny rooms with large windows. Wi-Fi €4. Singles €18, with shower €30; doubles €30/€38. MC/V.

Hostal Del Val, Pl. del Val, 6 (☎983 37 57 52). Centrally located in a historic building with views of the plaza. Rooms with private bathrooms have TVs. Book in advance. Singles €18, with bath €33; doubles €30/42. MC/V.

FOOD

Terraced restaurants and cafes lie between Pl. Mayor and Pl. del Val and near the cathedral. The *castellano* restaurants around Pl. Martí y Monsó, off Pl. Mayor, boast local specialties like *lechazo* (roast lamb) and roast quail. Mercado del Val, in Pl. del Val, has fresh fruit and vegetables and lots of fish and meat. (Open M-Sa 9am-3:30pm.) For a supermarket, head to **Carrefour** on C. Santiago, 13. (☎983 35 92 11. Open M-Sa 9:30am-9:30pm.)

Restaurante Covadonga, C. Zapico, 1 (☎983 33 07 98). This lively establishment with a tastefully decorated interior and reasonable prices will leave you satisfied. Three *menús* offer an appetizer, main course, and dessert (€9.20-22.80, wine included). Open M-Sa

1-4pm and 9-11:30pm; Sundays open mornings. Variety of salads, meat and fish dishes; try the *lomillo de cerdo con patatas*. MC/V. ❷

La Toscana, P. de Zorilla, 30 (☎983 35 22 27). This bright, casual cafe opened originally in Cuba over 100 years ago, before bringing its all-natural ice cream (€1-3) back to Spain. A good choice for coffee (€1.10), pastries (€2-5), and frozen drinks (€1-3). Open daily summer 9:30am-11:30pm. Cash only. ❶

El Rincón del Val, Pl. del Val (☎983 33 18 88), a few blocks off the Pl. Mayor. This small, bustling spot boasts specialties from the sea (entrees €9-18), vegetarian options (salads €7-12), beer (€2.60), and sangria (€7 per liter). Ask for a table on the romantic terrace. Opens M-F 11am, Sa 12:30pm, Su 12:45pm. Closing time varies. MC/V. ❷

SIGHTS

Valladolid is surrounded by churches, bridges, and pastures. Although the city's main sights revolve around the art, religion, and culture of centuries past, these attractions make a graceful counterpoint of medieval and modern.

CASA DE CERVANTES. The windmill-chasing, barmaid-wooing idealist Don Quixote may have been a fictional character, but his presence is almost tangible in the Valladolid house where Cervantes penned his groundbreaking *Don Quixote* from 1603 to 1606. Home to the author's vast library, the home offers tours of the writer's living and working spaces, embellished with beautiful woodwork on the low ceilings. *(C. Rastro. From Pl. de Zorrilla, walk up C. Miguel Iscar; C. Rastro is 2 blocks up on the right. ☎983 30 88 10. Open Tu-Sa 9:30am-3pm, Su 10am-3pm. €2.40, students with ID €1.20, under 18 and over 65 free. Su free.)*

MUSEO NACIONAL DE ESCULTURA. This vast museum boasts a fascinating chronological collection of Spanish sculpture, from a Gothic *pietà* of the 16th century to more recent Baroque works. It features the works of Renaissance and Baroque masters Alonso Berruguente, Juan de Juni, and Gregorio Fernández. Due to construction on the original museum building, the Colegio de San Gregorio, the museum is currently located in the Palacio de Villena. *(Palacio de Villena, C. Cadenas de San Gregorio, 1-3. ☎983 25 03 75; www.mne.es. Open Tu-S Mar 20-Sept 30 10am-2pm and 4-9pm; Oct 1-Mar 19 10am-2pm and 4-6pm; Su throughout the year 10am-2pm. €2.40, students €1.20, under 18 and over 65 free. Sa afternoon and Su free.)*

MUSEO PATIO HERRERIANO. Housed in a former convent, the stone arches and prim gardens of Valladolid's contemporary art museum give no hint of the riotous art that rules inside. The museum is home to works by renowned Spanish artists like Salvador Dalí, Antoni Tàpies, Joan Miró, and Eduardo Chillida in its permanent collection, and hosts rotating exhibitions of contemporary work. *(C. Jorge Guillén, 6. ☎983 36 27 71; www.museopatioherreriano.org. Open Tu-F 11am-8pm, Sa 10am-8pm, Su 10am-3pm. €3, students €2, €1 on Wednesdays.)*

CATEDRAL METROPOLITANA. Designed by Juan de Herrera, creator of El Escorial (p. 123), this grand cathedral is an excellent example of Herrera's *desornamentado* style of plain masonry. The extensive **Museo Diocesano,** in the Gothic addition, houses the remains of the original 11th- to 13th-century structure as well as Herrera's model of the basilica. *(C. Arribas, 1. From Pl. Mayor, walk up C. Ferrari. After 2 blocks, veer left onto Bajada de la Libertad. At Pl. de la Libertad, turn right. ☎983 30 43 62. Open Tu-F 10am-1:30pm and 4:30-7pm, Sa-Su 10am-2pm. Mass Su and festivals 10:45am, noon, 1:30, 6pm. Museum €2.50. Cathedral free.)*

NIGHTLIFE AND ENTERTAINMENT

Lively cafes and bars are spread throughout the city. Students fill the countless bars on **C. Paraíso,** near the cathedral. From Pl. de la Universidad at the cathedral, turn left onto C. Duque de Lerma, then right onto C. Marqués del Duero; C. Paraíso will be on the right. To reach **Pl. San Miguel** from Pl. Mayor, walk up Pl. Corrillo, turn left onto C. Val; after the plaza, continue onto C. Zapico, and at Pl. los Arces, turn left onto C. San Antonio de Padua, which brings you to Pl. San Miguel. The area around **Pl. Martí y Monsó,** just off Pl. Mayor, hosts the most central nightlife.

Vino Tinto Jóven, C. Campanas, 12. Tiny, chic wine bar fills up with 20- and 30-somethings gathering for *copas de vino* (wine €1.50-2.50) and refreshingly unusual tapas choices, like savory grilled vegetables. Open M-Sa 9am-4pm, 8pm-midnight.

Salobanco, C. Doctor Cazalla, 4, on Pl. San Miguel. A lively pub with modern Spanish music and an equally lively bartending team. Particularly popular among university students and a young backpacking crowd. Beer €2.60. Open M-Tu 10:30pm-2:30am, W-Th 11pm-3:30am, F-Sa 10pm-4:30am.

Baqur, C. Pasión, 13. Baqur lasts club music and Spanish pop on two floors for a student crowd. Spaces for electronica and chill-out music open after 1am. Open 8:30pm-6am.

Café España, Pl. Fuente Dorada, 8 (☎983 37 17 64). Hosts regular concerts; call for details. Open M-Th 8:30am-12:30am, F-Sa 8:30pm-3am, Su 9pm-1am. Cash only.

DAYTRIPS FROM VALLADOLID

MEDINA DEL CAMPO

La Regional V.S.A. runs buses to Medina del Campo from Valladolid (45min.-1hr., M-F 4 per day 9:15am-8:15pm, €3). Buses back to Valladolid leave from the bus stop at the Pl. de San Agustín (M-F 8 per day 7am-7pm, Sa 4 per day 8am-7:30pm; €3.30, round-trip €5.50). Tickets and information are available at the neighboring Bar Punto Rojo (☎983 80 12 98). Open daily 6am-midnight.

Medina del Campo's greatest claim to fame is its association with the illustrious Queen Isabel; the town houses her majesty's summer getaway, and Isabel signed her will and died in Medina del Campo. At its peak, the town was famous for banking and the sheep industry, drawing tens of thousands of visitors every year and serving as the country's gateway for art imports. The **Palacio Real Testamentario,** on the corner of the Pl. Mayor, has exhibits on the queen's childhood, reign, and final days, along with copies of her signed will. (☎983 81 00 63; www.palaciorealtestamentario.com. Open M-Sa May-Sept. 10am-1:30pm and 5-8pm; Oct.-Feb. 10am-1:30pm and 4-7pm. €2, seniors and under 26 €1.80. English audio tours €1.80.) Medina del Campo's most impressive sight is the 15th-century brick **Castillo de la Mota** on a hilltop overlooking the town. To get there, exit Pl. Mayor from the corner opposite the tourist office on C. Maldonado. Turn left at the intersection, cross the bridge over the dry riverbed, walk beneath the highway (access on C. Claudio Moyano), exit on the second stairwell to your right before the tunnel ends, and go uphill onto Av. del Castillo. Queen Isabel and her daughter, Juana la Loca, once lived in the castle; it has also served as an arsenal and prison. Today, tourists come to see the **chapel** of Santa María del Castillo and a mural-sized world map from 1500. Only the ground floor is open to visitors, but the Castillo is worth the hike. (☎983 80 10 24. Open M-Sa 11am-2pm and 4-7pm, Su 11am-2pm. Free.) To get to **Pl. Mayor** from the bus stop, walk past the bar El Punto Rojo on your right and continue up the street. At the intersection, turn left onto C. de Gamaza and continue straight until you reach the Plaza; the **tourist office,** Pl. Mayor 48, is to your right. (☎983 81 13 57; www.ayto-medinadelcampo.es. Open M 8am-3pm, Tu-F 8am-3pm and 4-7pm, Sa 10am-2pm and 4-7pm, Su 10am-2pm.)

BURGOS ☎947

By day, Burgos (pop. 346,000) is a city celebrated for its rich history, breathtaking art, and unique cuisine. By night, it is infused with a different kind of energy; behind the magnificently lit cathedral and luminous plazas, narrow streets glow with the neon signs from local bars and clubs. Unlike many other cities of Castilla y Leon, Burgos is cosmopolitan in every sense of the word—as you walk through its cafe and restaurant-filled winding streets, you'll smell cuisines from every corner of the world and hear chatter in foreign languages. Still, Burgos holds fast to its traditions and history. The region's hero, El Cid Campeador, a crusader of medieval lore, was born and eventually buried here. Today you can trace the Route of El Cid that begins at his birthplace in Vivar and enters Burgos through the Portal de San Martín south of the city.

TRANSPORTATION

Trains: Pl. de la Estación (☎947 20 35 60). 10min. walk or €3 taxi ride to the city center. Info open 24hr. (☎902 24 02 02). To: **Barcelona** (9-14hr.; M-F and Su 4 per day 2:17am-11:24pm, Sa 3 per day 2:17am-3:07pm; €39-47); **Bilbao** (2-4hr., 4-5 per day 9:20am-7:13pm, €16-22); **La Coruña** (6-9hr., 3 per day 3:43am-2:42pm, €37-43); **León** (2-3hr., 3-4 per day 3:43am-2:42pm, €19-21); **Lisboa** (8-10hr., 2am, €60); **Madrid** (3-5hr., 6-7 per day 8:44am-7:31pm, €23-37); **Palencia** (45min.; M-F and Su 7-9 per day 3:43am-8:35pm, Sa until 7:18pm; €3.90-13.60); **Valladolid** (1-2hr.; M-Th and Sa-Su 10-11 per day 1:59am-9:06pm, F 11 per day 1:49am-11:53pm; €8.20-19.50).

Buses: C. Miranda, 4 (☎947 28 88 55). Information open 24hr.; if there isn't someone in the booth, look around the station for help. **ALSA** (www.alsa.es; ☎902 422 242) runs to: **Bilbao** (2-3hr., M-Th and Sa 4 per day 8:30am-7pm, F 5 per day 8:30am-9pm, Su 5 per day 10:30am-10:30pm; €11); **Gijón** (4hr.; daily 6:45am, 5:45pm and Sa 2:20am; €17.09) via **Oviedo** (4hr.; 6:46am, 5:40pm, Sa 2:20am; €15.69); **León** (3hr.; M-F 4 per day 6:45am-6:15pm, Sa 4 per day 2:20am-4:30pm, Su 3 per day 6:45am-6:15pm; €13); **Salamanca** (3-4hr.; M-Sa 11:30am, 5:45, 9pm; Su 12:45, 6:15, 7:45, and 9pm; €14-18); **Valladolid** (2-3hr.; M-Th, Sa-Su 5-6 per day 6:30am-9pm, F 6 per day 6:30am-9:45pm; €8). **Continental-Auto** runs to: **Madrid** (2hr.; M-Sa 11-13 per day 3:15am-10:30pm, Su 17 per day midnight-10:30pm; €15); **San Sebastián** (4-5hr.; M-Th and Sa 7 per day 3:15am-10pm, F 9 per day 3:15am-11:59pm, Su 7 per day 3:15am-11:59pm; €14.50); **Santander** (3hr., 5-7 per day 3:15am-10pm, €10.50); **Vitoria-Gasteiz** (2hr.; M-Th and Sa 8 per day 3:45am-11:59pm, F and Su 8-11 per day 3:15am-11:59pm; €7).

Taxis: Abutaxi (☎947 27 77 77) or **Radio Taxi** (☎947 48 10 10). 24hr.

ORIENTATION AND PRACTICAL INFORMATION

The Río Arlanzón splits Burgos into north and south. While the **train** and **bus** stations are to the south, the **Catedral Santa Iglesia** and most other sights of interest are in the north. To get to the main part of the city from the **train station,** exit out the front of the station and walk straight up C. de la Estación, crossing the small bridge. At the end of the bridge, you will come to a small rotary. Take the second right, Calle de Aparicio y Ruiz. Follow it until you come to an intersection with C. de Eduardo Martinez del Campo (right in front of the University building). Turn right onto C. de Eduardo Martinez del Campo, and in about 50m, turn left onto C. Asunción de Ntra. Señora. This street will bring you right into the center of the city, in plain view of the cathedral. **From the bus station,** exit left out of the front entrance onto C. de Miranda. Walk down the street until the intersection then turn right onto C. de Madrid—you will see the

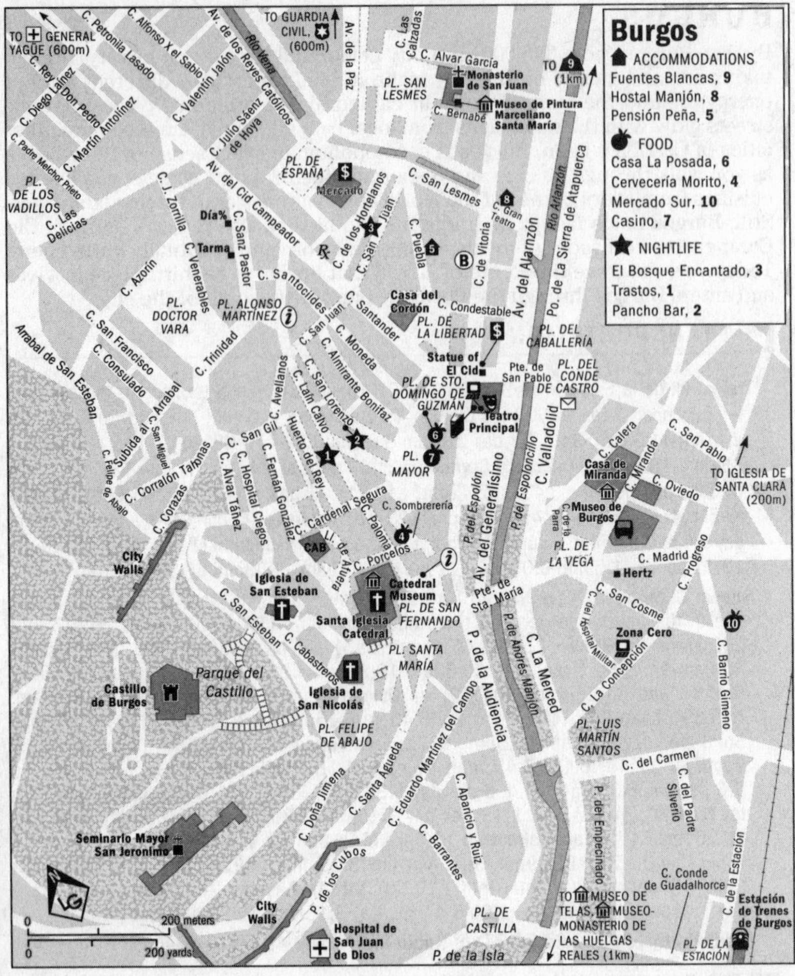

spires of the cathedral ahead. Continue up the street, staying to the left at the rotary and then crossing over a small bridge. Then, go through the arch in front of you into the Pl. del Rey San Fernando.

Tourist Office: Regional Office, Pl. Alonso Martínez, 7 (☎947 20 31 25). Open July-Sept. M-Th and Su 9am-8pm, F-Sa 9am-9pm; Oct.-June daily 9am-2pm and 5-8pm. The **Municipal Office** is next to the Catedral, Pl. de San Fernando, 2 (☎947 28 88 74). Open July-Sept. daily 10am-8pm; Oct.-June M-F 10am-2pm and 4:30-7:30pm, Sa-Su and holidays 10am-1:30pm and 4-7:30pm.

Currency Exchange: Banco Santander Central Hispano, Pl. del Mío Cid, 6 (☎902 24 24 24). Open Apr.-Sept. M-F 8:30am-2pm; Oct.-Mar. also Sa 8:30am-1pm. There are 24hr. **ATMs** on C. San Juan near C. Santander and along C. del Cid.

Luggage Storage: 24hr. lockers at train station €3 per day; bus station €2 per day. Tickets available for purchase at information desk.

Police: Av. Cantabria, 54 (☎947 28 88 39).

Medical Services: Ambulance SACYL 9 (☎947 23 75 76). **Hospital General Yagüe,** Av. del Cid Campeador, 96 (☎947 28 18 00).

Internet Access: Zonacero, C. la Concepción, 18 (947 208 649). €1.80 per hr. Open daily 10:30am-2:30pm and 4-10pm. **Biblioteca del Teatro Principal,** Po. del Espolón (☎947 28 88 73). Free 30min. slots. Wi-Fi. ID required. Open July M-F 8:30am-2:30pm; Aug. M-F 8:30am-9pm; Sept.-June M-F 9am-9pm, Sa 9:30am-2pm.

Post Office: Pl. del Conde de Castro (☎/fax 947 25 66 11). Lista de Correos and fax. Open M-F 8:30am-8:30pm, Sa 9:30am-4pm. **Postal Code:** 09002.

ACCOMMODATIONS

Cheap and desirable accommodations are hard to find in Burgos, but some reasonably priced *hostales* and *pensiones* lie along or near **Calle San Juan** and **Calle Puebla,** leading from the **Plaza de la Libertad.** Otherwise try hostels on **Calle Vitoria,** at the eastern end of the city, and along Ctr. N-1 toward Irún. Reservations are crucial on summer weekends, given all the festivals from June-August.

Hostal Manjón, C. Gran Teatro, 1, 7th fl. (☎947 20 86 89). A short walk from the city center, this hostel has palatial, well-lit rooms with TV and sink, and an elevator—no luggage lugging here. Single €27, with bathroom €33; doubles €33/42. MC/V. ❷

Pensión Peña, C. Puebla, 18 (☎947 20 63 23). Newly renovated rooms, relatively close to all-night bars and across from an internet cafe, **Cabaret.** Walls are thin, but the pensión offers good value. Shared bath. Singles €17; doubles €26. Cash only. ❶

Fuentes Blancas, Parque de Fuentes Blancas. (☎947 48 60 16). Catch the #26 bus ("Fuentes Blancas") from Pl. de España June-Aug. (M-F every 30min. 7:45am-10:45pm, €0.70). Sept.-May ride the #7 from the same plaza (4 per day, 9:30am-7:15pm). Common shower pavilion and restaurant. Open Apr.-Sept. Camping is €4.30 per person, €3 per child, €3.50-7 per tent, €4 per car. About 24 dorm beds in *albergue*, €7; or bungalows, €20 per person. MC/V. ❶

FOOD

Burgaleses take pride in their *morcilla* sausage and their *queso de Burgos*, a soft cheese usually served with honey or in a *tarta* as dessert. Look near the cathedral for these staples. **Calle San Lorenzo** is tapas heaven. **Mercado Sur,** on **Calle Barrio Gimeno,** has fresh meat and bread (Open M-Th 8am-3pm, F-Sa 7:30am-3:15pm). For groceries, try **Dia%,** Sanz Pastor, 16 (Open M-Sa 9:30am-2:15pm and 5-8:15pm). Or if you just need a midday sugar infusion, duck into **Chocolates Valor,** a Spanish chain, for rich *churros con chocolate*, right next to the cathedral on C. Nuño Rasura.

Casa La Posada, Pl. Santo Domingo de Guzmán, 18 (☎947 20 85 13). Although a bit pricey, this warm, cozy restaurant features a daily vegetable specialty, an ever-changing *menú* (€15), and an excellent *natilla* custard for dessert. Fish and meat entrees €7-18. Friendly, attentive service. Open daily 1-4pm and 8pm-midnight. AmEx/MC/V. ❸

Cervecería Morito, C. Sombrerería, 27 (☎947 26 75 55). The line for the Cervecería's good, cheap food often snakes out the door. *Raciones* €1-5.30, sandwiches €2.50-4.50, *revueltos* €3.60-4.50. Sangria €1.50. Open daily noon-3:30pm, 7pm-midnight, kitchen opens at 1pm. Cash only. ❶

Casino, Pl. Mayor (☎947 27 81 56). Located in the heart of the Plaza Mayor, this cafeteria-restaurant features a variety of *paella* dishes (€8-9). If you're hankering for classic Spanish cuisine, head here to find it on the cheap. Open daily 9am-midnight. ❷

SIGHTS

CATEDRAL DE BURGOS. The Catedral de Burgos, designated an UNESCO Word Heritage site in 1984, is one of the most stunning in Spain. Its majestic spires, which find their way into every view of the city, are matched only by its Gothic interior. Originally a Romanesque church built by 13th-century *Reconquista* hero Fernando III (El Santo), the cathedral was transformed over three centuries into a Gothic marvel. The cathedral is the product of hundreds of years of work, and its 29 magnificent chambers reflect different time periods, artistic styles, and religious events. Visitors can enter the **Chapel of Christ** to see the cathedral's holiest and most infamous arch: a crucified Jesus constructed of buffalo skin with human hair and nails. The cathedral has other wonders for those not attending services: the 16th-century stained-glass dome of the **Capilla Mayor,** the eerily life-like *papamoscas* (flycatcher), and, under the transept, marked by a small brick beneath a star-shaped lantern, the remains of **El Cid** himself. The cathedral's **museum** displays a Visigoth Bible and El Cid's nuptial documents, as well as chalices, paintings, and tapestries. *(☎947 20 47 12; www.catedraldeburgos.es. Open Nov. 1-Mar. 18 10am-7pm; Mar, 19-Oct. 31 9:30am-7:30pm. Chapel of Christ free, entered by the left side door of the cathedral. Cathedral and museum €4, students €2.50, pilgrims €12.50. Audio tour in English €3.50.)*

CENTRO DE ARTE CAJA BURGOS (CAB). Housed in a striking hilltop space next to the Iglesia Gótica de San Esteban and the Castillo de Burgos, this contemporary art center stands out in radical contrast to its historic neighbors. The Center is home to a permanent collection of more than 300 works by renowned contemporary artists and hosts rotating exhibitions of international work. Offering a constant cultural dialogue, this is a great place to provoke the mind and senses. The climb uphill is well worth it for the museum's breathtaking city vistas. Visit the website for ongoing exhibitions. *(C. Saldaña s/n. ☎947 25 65 60; www.cabdeburgos.com. Open Tu-F 11:30am-2pm and 5:30-8:30pm, Sa 11am-2:30pm and 5-9pm, Su 11am-2:30pm and 5-8:00pm. Free.)*

MUSEO-MONASTERIO DE LAS HUELGAS REALES. Built by King Alfonso VIII in 1187, the Museo-Monasterio de las Huelgas Reales was once a summer palace for Castilian kings and later an elite convent for Cistercian nuns. Today's monastery-cum-museum allows visitors a glimpse of the glory of medieval Castilian royalty. *(Take the "Barrio del Pilar" bus from Pl. de España to the Museo stop; €0.70. ☎947 20 16 30. Open Tu-Sa 10am-1pm and 3:45-5:30pm, Su 10:30am-2pm. Mandatory tours in Spanish every 30min. €5, students and under 14 €2.50, under 5 free. EU citizens free W.)*

MUSEO DE BURGOS. This sprawling 16th-century mansion has four floors of provincial Burgalese art and archaeology, with everything from paleolithic skulls to Roman relics from the nearby town of Clunia. The adjacent Casa de Inigo Angulo also features four floors of art. Included in the exhibits are a piece of the Santo Domingo de Silos monastery's facade, the sepulchre of Don Juan de Padilla, and paintings from the 14th to 20th centuries. *(C. Miranda, 13. ☎947 26 58 75. Open Oct.-May Tu-Sa 10am-2pm and 4-7pm, Su 10am-2pm; June-Sept. M-Sa 10am-2pm and 5-8pm, Su 10am-2pm. €1.20; under 18, seniors, and students with ID free. Sa and Su free.)*

NIGHTLIFE AND FESTIVALS

Burgaleses start the night out by sampling *pinchos* and sipping glasses of wine in tapas bars throughout the city; **Calle San Lorenzo** and **Calle la Puebla** are popular locations. By midnight, **Calle Avellanos** (across from Pl. Alonso Martínez) fills with night owls migrating onto nearby **Calle Huerto del Rey.** Behind the church, **Llanes de Afuera** is lined with hip bars and dance clubs. On Sunday mornings, the crowds will still be dancing at discotecas along **Calle San Juan** and **Calle la Puebla** and in the complex on **Plaza San Lesmes.** During the last week of June, Burgos honors its patron saints with parades, fireworks, and bullfights.

Pancho Bar, C. San Lorenzo, 15. This cosmopolitan, modern bar just off Plaza Mayor is always packed, but the bartenders are relaxed and attentive. Adjacent restaurant serves meals; order the *Postre del Abuelo,* (creamy Burgos cheese smothered in honey and walnuts). Sangria €1.90, wine €1.30, tapas €1.25-3. Open M-Sa 10am-midnight, Su 11am-midnight. AmEx/MC/V.

El Bosque Encantado, C. San Juan, 31 (☎658 64 19 06). This funky bar owes its name to the apple-laden tree rooted front and center. Eden-esque revelry meets the house of the Seven Dwarves, where teacups and dollhouses perch next to bottles of rum and vodka. Beer €2. Teas €1.50-3. Open M-Th 5pm-midnight, F-Sa 5pm-4am.

Trastos, C. Huerto del Rey, 7. The DJ at this discoteca keeps a young European crowd bouncing to Europop and trance well into morning. Drinks €2-5. Open W-Su 8pm-4am.

DAYTRIP FROM BURGOS

CARRIÓN DE LOS CONDES

Buses run to Carrión de los Condes from Burgos (1hr.; M-F 11:45am, 6:15pm, Sa 11:45am, Su 6:15pm; return M-F 11:15am, 4:50pm, Sa 11:15am, Su 5:30pm; €6). Buses also run from Palencia (45min.; M-Sa 7:45am, 1:30, 6:00pm; Su 1:30, 7:15pm; return M-Sa 9am, 2:10, 5:10pm; Su 5 and 6:10pm; €2.30).

It is easy to bypass this sleepy riverside town, but many pilgrims consider Carrión de los Condes (pop. 2500) one of the most important stops on the Camino de Santiago. The **Iglesia de Santiago,** the town's most famous church, was built in the 12th century. It was rebuilt after Spanish troops burned it down to prevent the French army from using it as a stronghold in the 1811 War of Independence. The adjacent *museo* has a small but impressive collection of embroidered frocks and paintings from the 16th century. (Church and museum open daily 11am-2pm and 4:30-8pm. €1.) On the way to this church from the bus stop, you'll pass the **Iglesia Santa María del Camino,** the oldest church in Carrión, built in 1130. (Open in summer daily 9am-2pm and 4:30-6pm; in winter M-Sa 11am-1:30am and 6-9pm, Su noon-1:30pm and 6-9pm. Free.) Across the river is the 11th-century **Real Monasterio de San Zollo,** which houses one of the most beautiful cloisters of the Spanish Renaissance. (☎979 88 09 02. Open from Apr. to mid-Oct. daily 10:30am-2pm and 4:30-8pm; from mid-Oct. to Mar. M-F 10:30am-2pm, Sa-Su 4-6:30pm. €1.50, pilgrims €1.) If you need to spend the night, **Camping El Eden** is in a shaded area on the riverbank, in the Parque Municipal. (☎979 88 01 95. €4 per person; €3.50-3.90 per tent; €4 per car. Electricity €3.50.) Many restaurants along C. Santa María offer a three-course *menú del peregrino* (pilgrim menu) for €7-8. **Cervecería "J. M."**, Pl. Marques de Santillana, 10, has all a pilgrim could want for dinner—sandwiches, eggs, salads, meat, and fish. (Open daily noon-4pm and 6-10pm. Cash only.) The tourist office is across the street from the bus stop in front of Bar España and offers internet access for €2 per hour. (☎979 88 09 32. Open July-Aug. 10am-2pm, 4:30pm-7pm.) There is also another tourist office located in the Monasterio de San Zoilo open year-round. (☎979 880 902. Open Tu-Su 10am-2pm and 5-8pm.)

PALENCIA ☎979

Palencia's lack of notoriety only adds to its ambience; like its beautiful and haunting Gothic cathedral, it is often called *La Bella Desconocida* (The Unknown Beauty). Palencia (pop. 80,000) has been the home of Romans, Visigoths, Arabs, and even El Cid Campeador, and its historic center is studded with 14th- to 16th-century churches. Laid-back and unassuming, Palencia is a quiet city well worth a short visit for its museums, churches, and graceful squares.

TRANSPORTATION

Trains: Jardinillos de la Estación (☎902 24 02 02). **Renfe** runs to: **Barcelona** (8-9hr.; daily 1:30 and 2:23pm, M-Su excluding Sa 10:40pm; €41-49); **Bilbao and San Sebastián** (4hr., 3:57pm, €20); **Burgos** (1hr.; M-F and Su 8-9 per day 1:30am-10:40pm, Sa 7 per day 1:30am-7:35pm; €4-14); **La Coruña** (8hr.; daily 4:30am and 1pm; M, Th, Sa-Su also 3:31pm; €33-43); **León** (1hr.; M-Sa 14-15 per day 1:04am-9:42pm, Su 10 per day 4:30am-9:42pm; €7-18); **Madrid** (3-5hr.; M-Sa 12-14 per day 4:30am-10pm, Su 11 per day 8:15am-10pm; €18-34); **Salamanca** (2hr.; daily 1:20 pm, M, Th, Sa 8:07am; €11-22); **Santander** (3-4hr.; 5-6 per day M-Sa 9:26am-10:20pm, Su 10:20am-10:20pm; €12-23); and **Valladolid** (45min.; 24-28 per day M-F 4:34am-10pm, Sa 4:34am-10pm, Su 8:15am-10:08pm; €4-14).

Buses: Depart from the same station (☎979 74 32 22, info open M-F 9:30am-7pm, Sa 9:30am-2pm) to **Burgos** (1hr.; M-Th 8:45am and 3pm, F 8:45am, 3, 6:45pm, Su 8:45am; €6) and **Valladolid** (45min.; M-F hourly 7am-9pm, Sa 6 per day 8am-7:30pm, Su 3 per day 11am-9pm; €3).

ORIENTATION AND PRACTICAL INFORMATION

Palencian life is centered along C. Mayor. From the bus or train station, head past the Jardinillos de la Estación to Pl. León; from there you can see C. Mayor, the fourth street on the right from the rotary.

Tourist office: C. Mayor, 105 (☎979 74 00 68). A 15min. walk down C. Mayor from Pl. León. Open July to mid-Sept. M-Th and Su 9am-8pm, F-Sa until 9pm; mid-Sept. to June daily 9am-2pm and 5-8pm. There is a smaller office located closer to the train and bus stations off Pl. León in the Pl. de San Pablo. Open daily 10:30am-2pm and 5-8:30pm.

Currency Exchange: Banco Santander Central Hispano, on the corner of C. Mayor and C. Martínez de Azcotita. Open Apr.-Sept. M-F 8:30am-2pm; Oct.-Mar. Sa 8:30am-1pm.

Municipal Police, C. Ortega y Gasset (☎979 71 82 00)

Taxis: Radiotaxi stops at Estación Renfe and C. Mayor (☎979 72 00 16).

Hospital: Hospital Río Carrión, Av. Donanter de Sangre (☎979 16 70 00).

Internet Access: Biblioteca Pública, C. Eduardo Dato (☎979 75 11 00). Open M-F 8am-9:30pm, Sa 9am-2pm; time limit 30min.; free.

Post Office, Pl. León, 8 (☎979 70 68 09), by the train station. Open M-F 8:30am-8:30pm, Sa 9:30am-2pm). **Postal Code:** 34001.

ACCOMMODATIONS

Palencia has fewer tourists than many of its neighbors, so accommodations are less abundant and more expensive. Hostels can be found off C. Mayor. Reserve ahead, as hostels tend to fill up quickly in the summer.

Pensión El Salón, Av. República Argentina, 10. (☎979 72 64 42). From the tourist office on C. Mayor continue down C. Mayor and cross the street onto Av. República Argentina; the pensión is on your right after C. Los Tintes. Brings a touch of home with friendly staff, lace curtains, flowers and comfortable TV lounge. Rooms are basic, but some have sinks. Singles €15; doubles €25. No private bathrooms. Cash only. ❷

Hostal Ávila, C. Conde de Vallellano, 5. (☎979 71 19 10; www.hostalavila.com). From C. Mayor, turn left onto C. San Bernardo, which becomes C. Empedrada. The hostel features spacious rooms, private bathrooms, telephones, TVs, a common room, parking, and a cafeteria. Singles €33; doubles €41-49. MC/V. ❸

FOOD

Cafeterias and restaurants fill the *zona vieja* and the streets off C. Mayor, and there is an **El Árbol** supermarket at C. Mayor, 99. (Open M-Sa 9:30am-9pm.)

Cervecería Gambrinus, C. Patio Castaño, 1. (☎979 75 08 28). Off C. Mayor from Pl. León. Serves good *raciones* and house-specialty homemade beer at reasonable prices on its outdoor terrace. *Raciones* €2.50-11. Open daily 7:30am-1am. MC/V. ❶

La Trebede, Pl. Mayor, 14 (☎979 74 12 12). Shaded by white umbrellas and the trees lining Pl. Mayor, La Trebede offers a pleasant view and delicious food; the *sopa de pescado* (fish soup) is especially good. Salads €6-8. Entrees €4-14. Menú €9. MC/V. ❷

Rincón de Istanbul, C. San Bernardo, 4. (☎979 74 75 33). This has earned a name for itself among locals with delicious Turkish fare (€3-8). The restaurant's specialty, a vegetarian dish aptly called the Rincón de Istanbul (€5), is particularly good, as are the *döner kebap* and *kofte*. Open daily noon-2am. Cash only. ❶

SIGHTS

CATEDRAL DE PALENCIA. Palencia's greatest sight is its gargoyle-laden Gothic **cathedral,** known as *La Bella Desconocida.* The elegant old beauty has an air of mystery about her, with medieval memories of times like the marriage of 14-year-old Catherine of Lancaster to 10-year-old Enrique III in 1388. Visitors can descend to the **Cripta de San Antolín,** a 7th-century sepulcher containing the remains of the Roman/Visigoth structure upon which the cathedral was built. The cathedral's **museum** contains El Greco's *San Sebastián,* some 16th-century Flemish tapestries, and a tiny caricature of Carlos V. *(From Pl. León, walk down C. Eduardo Dato and turn left at Pl. Carmelitas onto C. Santa Teresa de Jesús; the cathedral is at the end in Pl. de la Inmaculada Concepción. ☎979 70 13 47. Cathedral is open M-Sa 9am-1:30pm and 4:30-7:30pm, Su 9am-1:30pm. Tours of the museum, crypt and cathedral in Spanish M-Sa hourly 10:30am-12:30pm and 4:30-6:30pm, Su 11:15am. Cathedral free. Museum €3.)*

CRISTO DEL OTERO. Located on top of a hill on the outskirts of the city, Palencia's statue *Cristo del Otero,* built in 1931, is the second tallest statue of Jesus Christ in the world—only Rio de Janiero's *Corcovado* is taller. The statue can be reached by a path that winds to the top of the hill. The short walk (approx. 15min.) to the top also offers fantastic views of Palencia and the surrounding countryside of Castilla y León. *(To reach the statue, take the B-line bus from Pl. de Leon to Camino La Miranda. Get off at the third stop, Po. de Otero. From the bus stop, continue walking up the street; the enormous statue rises ahead. Follow the street until you reach the park on your right, and take one of the numerous paths to the top.)*

NIGHTLIFE AND FESTIVALS

Midweek nightlife is tame, but on weekends, plenty of *palentinos* roam the streets of the *zona vieja,* off **C. Mayor,** into the wee hours of the morning. **Merlin,**

C. Conde de Vallellano, 4, packs in a young crowd for drinks, dancing and revelry in what looks like a medieval castle. (Beer €2. Mixed drinks €4. Open Th-Sa 7pm-4:30am, Su 7pm-2:30am.) **Disco-Bar Cendal,** across from Merlin on C. Conde de Vallellano, is a tapas bar by day, then transforms into a dark, pop music-infused favorite at night. (Beer €1.50. Mixed drinks €4.50. Open M-Th and Su 7:30pm-2:30am, F-Sa until 4:30am.) If you happen to drop by Palencia on September 2, join in the **Fiesta de San Antolín.** Feasts commemorate the city's patron saint, while some brave locals head to the cathedral's crypt for a supposedly auspicious sip of holy water.

SORIA ☎975

Known for its raucous Fiesta de San Juan, the poet Antonio Machado, and surrounding architectural sites, Soria (pop. 38,000) is a vibrant small city. Though things really heat up around the fiesta, there is plenty to do in the low season. In the center of city lies the lush Parque Alameda de Cervantes. The Monasterio de San Jaun de Duero and Ermita de San Saturio rest at the outskirts of Soria. Though it was initially built as a fortress to protect against invasions from neighboring Aragón, today the small city is anything but bellicose. Bars with outdoor seating fill Soria's plazas, and the banks of the Río Ebro are a serene setting for sunbathing, relaxing, or swimming.

TRANSPORTATION

Trains: Estación El Cañuelo (☎975 23 02 02), Ctra. de Madrid. Buses (€0.45) run from Pl. Mariano Granados to the station 20-25min. before trains depart, returning immediately after new arrivals. Trains to: **Madrid** (3hr.; M-F 7:40am, 5:40pm, Sa 8:45am, 5:40pm, Su 8:45am, 5:40, 6:25pm; €13.85) via **Alcalá de Henares** (2hr., €11).

Buses: Av. de Valladolid, 40 (☎975 22 51 60). Desk open daily 9am-7pm and 8-10pm. **Continental Auto** (☎975 22 44 01; www.continental-auto.es) sends buses to **Logroño** (1hr.; M-Th and Sa 6 per day 11am-10:15pm, F and Su 9 per day 11am-12:15am; €6.19), **Madrid** (2hr.; M-Th and Sa 10 per day 9:25am-3:30am, F and Su 17 per day 8:15am-11:50pm; €14.08-22), and **Pamplona** (2hr.; M-Th and Sa per day 10:45am-10:45pm, F and Su 10 per day 10:45am-1:45am; €12). **La Serrana** (☎975 22 20 60) to **Burgos** (2hr.; M-Sa 1-3 per day 7am-6:30pm, Su 4, 6pm; €10). **Therpasa** (☎975 22 20 60) goes to **Zaragoza** (2hr.; 6 per day M-Sa 7:30am-8pm, Su 3 per day noon-9pm; €9.40) via **Tarazona** (1hr., €4.50). **Linecar** (☎975 22 15 55) runs to **Valladolid** (3hr.; M-Sa 3 per day 9:45am-6:45pm, Su 4 per day 11:15am-9:30pm; €12.45).

Car Rental: AVIS, Av. de Mariano Vicén, 1/3 (☎975 21 10 19). 23+. Open M-F 9am-1pm and 4-7pm, Sa 10am-1pm. AmEx/MC/V. **Europcar,** C. Ángel Terrel, 3-5 (☎975 22 05 05). 21+. Open M-F 9:30am-1:30pm and 4-7pm, Sa 10:30am-1pm. AmEx/MC/V.

Taxis: At Pl. Ramón y Cajal (☎975 21 30 34) and bus station (☎975 23 13 13).

ORIENTATION AND PRACTICAL INFORMATION

The city center is a 10min. walk from the bus station and a brisk 15min. walk from the train station. There's a map just to the left of the traffic circle in front of the bus station; you should head out from the traffic circle in the direction you're facing while reading the map. Walk along **Avenida de Valladolid** downhill towards the *centro ciudad* for five blocks and bear right at the fork onto Po. del Espolón, which borders the **Parque Alameda de Cervantes.** At the end of the park, the main intersection, **Plaza Mariano Granados**, will be directly in front of you. To reach the center from the **train station,** take the shuttle, or turn left onto Calle Madrid and follow the signs to *centro ciudad.* Continue on C. Almazán as it becomes Av. de Mariano Vicén, follow the road for six blocks, and keep left at the fork onto **Avenida Alfonso VIII** until you reach Pl. Mariano Granados. **Carrer Marqués de Vadillo** is the main pedestrian street extending from the city center. It becomes C. El Collado, cutting through the old quarter to **Plaza Mayor.**

Tourist Office: C. Medinaceli, 2 (☎975 21 20 52; www.turismocastillayleon.com). From the bottom of Pl. Mariano Granados, walk 1 block toward the train station on Av. Alfonso VIII. It's on the corner to your left, but not well marked upon approach. English, French, and German spoken. Open July-Sept. 15 M-Th and Su 9am-8pm, F-Sa 9am-9pm; Sept 16.-June daily 9am-2pm and 5-8pm; holidays 9am-9pm.

Currency Exchange: Banco Santander Central Hispano, C. El Collado, 56 (☎975 22 02 25), 1 block from the plaza. Open Apr.-Sept. M-F 8:30am-2pm; Oct.-May M-F 8:30am-2pm, Sa 8:30am-1pm. **Branch** at Av. Navarra, 6-8. Several other banks cluster around Pl. Mariano Granados.

Luggage Storage: At the **bus station.** 1st day €0.60, €0.30 each additional day. Open daily 9am-7pm and 8-10pm.

Police: Guardia Civil, C. Eduardo Saavedra, 6 (☎975 22 03 50). **Municipal:** C. Obispo Agustín, 1 (☎975 21 18 62). **National:** C. Nicolás Rabal, 9 (☎975 23 93 23).

Hospital: Hospital General Santa Bárbara, Po. de Santa Bárbara (☎975 23 43 00).

Pharmacy: Many around Pl. Mariano Granados. Pharmacies post lists of which locations will be open that evening (*"en guardia"*).

Internet Access: Cyber Centro, Pje. Tejera, 16 (☎975 23 90 85), up the stairs and on the left in the small tunnel between C. las Casas and C. Caro on Po. Tejera. €2.50 per 30min., €3.75 per hr., €8.20 per 3hr. Open M-F 10am-2:30pm and 5:30-9:30pm. **Locutorio Nuevo Mundo,** C. Campo, 18 (☎975 23 92 34). Open 11am-2pm and 5pm-midnight. **Locutorio Alô Brasil,** Po. Florida, 4. Open daily 11am-3pm and 5-10:30pm.

Post Office: Po. del Espolón, 6 (☎975 23 35 70). Open M-F 8:30am-8:30pm, Sa 9:30am-2pm. **Postal Code:** 42001.

ACCOMMODATIONS

Reservations are always a good idea during fiesta week (June 27-July 2).

Hostal Residencia Alvi, C. Alberca, 2 (☎975 22 81 12). 24 large rooms with simple decor, TV, phone, free Wi-Fi, full baths, and big beds. Hotel quality for half the price. Large sitting room with homey furnishings. Reserve ahead. Breakfast €2.41. Singles €31; doubles €49. MC/V. ❸

Residencia Juvenil Juan Antonio Gaya Nuño (HI), Po. San Francisco (☎975 22 14 66). With your back to Pl. Mariano Granados, take C. Nicolás Rabal left along the park. Take the 2nd left onto C. Santa Luisa de Marillac; look for yellow dorms. Turn right at Po. San Francisco to enter. TV room. Laundry €1. Reception 24hr. Open July-Sept. 15. Wheelchair-accessible. HI card required. Reserve in advance. €7.65-11.60 person. Breakfast included. Cash only. ❶

Camping Fuente la Teja (☎975 22 29 67; www.fuentedelateja.com), 2km from town on Ctra. de Madrid. Only accessible by car or long walk on the highway (N-111 km 233). Restaurant, huge bar-cafeteria, laundry, and playground. Dogs allowed. Pool open July-Aug. Wheelchair-accessible. Open *Semana Santa*-Sept. €3.60 per person, €3.30 per car, €4.20 per tent, €2.50 per child. IVA not included. AmEx/MC/V. ❶

FOOD

Countless bars and inexpensive restaurants along C. El Collado and Pl. Mayor offer local specialties like roast lamb and *migas* (bread crumbs fried with garlic and paprika). Buy Soria's famed butter at *mantequerías* in the town center, or opt for fruits and vegetables at the thriving **market** in Pl. Bernardo Robles on C. los Estudios, off C. El Collado. (Open M-Sa 8:30am-2pm.) A **SPAR** supermarket is at Av. de Mariano Vicén, 10, four blocks from Pl. Mariano Granados toward the train station. (Open M-Sa 9am-2pm and 5:30-8:30pm. MC/V.)

Collado 58, C. El Collado, 58 (☎975 24 00 53). Huge sandwiches and burgers at this popular, laid-back bar/restaurant. Limited seating. Ice cream concoctions (€4.25-6.10), shakes (€3.65-4.40), and banana splits (€4.60-5.50). Combo plates €9.35-14.10. M-Sa daily 8am-midnight. Cash only. ❷

Nuevo Siglo, C. Almazán, 9 (☎975 22 13 32), quite a trek, two-thirds of the way down Av. Mariano Vicén toward the train station. Chinese food served under chandeliers. Entrees €3-9.15, 4-course lunch weekday *menú* €5.85. Open daily 11:30am-4:30pm and 7:30pm-midnight. MC/V. ❶

SIGHTS

ERMITA DE SAN SATURIO. Soria's most popular sight is definitely worth the 1.5km trek downstream, and is a refreshing departure from the more traditional cathedrals found nearby. From ground-level caves with stained-glass windows to passageways carved out of stone, the 17th-century *ermita* is a fitting tribute to San Saturio, Soria's patron saint. On foot, take the scenic route through the lush island of **Soto Playa.** Turn right just before the main bridge on C. San Augustín and cross the first green footbridge, then take the small wooden bridge at the end. Keeping the river to your left, walk off the small island, following small footpaths and boardwalks (you'll be on the same side of the river you started on). After the footpath ends, continue on the black and yellow brick roadsidewalk above and to your right, next to the pavement road. The *ermita* is on your left, accessed across the bridge and up the stairs.*(Open July-Aug. 10:30am-2pm and 4:30-8:30pm; Apr.-June and Sept.-Oct. 10:30am-2pm and 4:30-7:30pm; Nov-Mar 10:30am-2pm and 4:30-6:30pm. Free.)*

MONASTERIO DE SAN JUAN DE DUERO. The Monasterio San Juan de Duero sits quietly by the river amid fields of cottonwoods. The church, dating from the 12th century, is one of the most visited in Castilla y León. The graceful arches of its cloister blend romanesque and Islamic styles. Inside, a few cases display medieval artifacts. *(Turn left after crossing the main bridge. Paseo de las Ánimas s/n ☎975 23 02 18. Open Tu-Sa July-Sept. 10am-2pm and 5-8pm, Oct.-June 10am-2pm and 4-7pm; Su year-round 10am-2pm. €0.60; groups of 15 or more with appointment €0.30 per person; under 18, over 65, and students free. Sa-Su free.)*

MUSEO NUMANTINO. Across from the *alameda* park, the *museo* exhibits a collection of Celtiberian and Roman artifacts excavated from nearby Numancia. *(Po. del Espolón, 8. ☎975 22 14 28. Same hours as Monasterio. €1.20; groups of 15 or more €0.60 per person with prior arrangement; under 18, over 65, and students free. Sa-Su free.)*

NIGHTLIFE AND FESTIVALS

For a town of its size, Soria has a vibrant nightlife, especially during fiesta month (almost all of June). As the moon rises, revelers of all ages flood the outdoor seating at bars in **Plaza Ramón Benito Aceña,** a stone's throw from Pl. Mariano Granados and the adjacent **Plaza San Clemente,** off C. El Collado. Late-night discotecas center on the intersection of Rota de Calatañazor and Calle Cardenal Frías, near **Pl. de Toros. Greens,** near the Plaza de Toros, has outdoor seating, and is a good place to have a *calimocho* (wine and coke; €1.50) and people-watch. Nearby, **Mitos** has loud music and a dance floor, as do many of its neighbors. A few small clubs and a number of bars with a more relaxed atmosphere lie near **Calle Zapatería.** Spend a night surrounded by quirky Irish decor while hanging out with hip *sorianos* at the intimate tables of **Bar Ogham,** C. Nicolás Rabal, 3, on the side of the park opposite Po. del Espolón. (☎975 22 57 71. Open daily noon-3am. Cash only.)

In summer, Soria hosts concerts and street theater. Pick up the free *Actividades Culturales* at the tourist office for specific dates. Late June brings Soria's biggest celebration, the **Fiestas de San Juan,** which floods the city with celebrants from all over the country, and three weeks of smaller (but equally fun) preceding "*prefiestas.*" Beginning at midnight the Thursday after Día de San Juan (June 24th) and lasting until Monday, the entire city hits the streets to dance, play music at all hours, drink wine from *botas* (leather wineskins), watch processions, and, of course, go to bullfights. Patron **San Saturio** is celebrated on October 2 with a more low-key, day-long festival.

CASTILLA LA MANCHA AND EXTREMADURA

Castilla La Mancha and Extremadura are the Spanish Outback. Stark and barren compared to the rest of the country, these arid lands hardened New World conquistadors like Hernán Cortés and Francisco Pizarro and inspired some of Spain's greatest fictional characters, including the Man of La Mancha himself, Cervantes's Don Quixote. While much of Castilla La Mancha remains unexplored by tourists, Extremadura is undiscovered even by most Spaniards, despite the radiant beauty of its Roman ruins and traditional towns.

HIGHLIGHTS OF CASTILLA LA MANCHA AND EXTREMADURA

REMINISCE in **Toledo** about the days when everyone got along (see below).

EXPLORE the "Cradle of the Conquistadors" in hilltop **Trujillo** (p. 189).

LIVE on the edge in one of the hanging houses of **Cuenca** (p. 179).

ROAM around the astoundingly well-preserved Roman ruins of **Mérida** (p. 192).

CASTILLA LA MANCHA

Filled with sleepy medieval towns, cliffs, and—of course—windmills, Castilla La Mancha provokes the imagination with its solitary beauty. Drawing its name from the Arabic word *manza* (parched earth) and the Spanish *mancha* (stain), the province remains one of Spain's least-developed regions. Long ago, it was the epicenter of conflict between Christians and Muslims, and so became the domain of military orders modeled after crusading institutions like the Knights Templar, a society of powerful warrior-monks. In the 14th and 15th centuries, the region saw struggles between Castilla and Aragón before they were united in 1492 by the Reyes Católicos, Fernando and Isabel. Castilla La Mancha is Spain's largest wine-producing region, if not its best (Valdepeñas is a popular table wine), and the abundant olive groves and wild game influence local recipes, including Toledo's famed partridge dish. Stews, roast meats, and game are all *manchego* staples, as is *queso manchego*, Spain's beloved national cheese.

TOLEDO ☎925

Toledo (pop. 75,500), the pride of Castilla La Mancha, is, like any good medieval city, fraught with myth and legend. Cervantes called the hilltop town the "glory of Spain and light of her cities"; it is commonly called the "Ciudad de las Tres Culturas" (City of Three Cultures), at one time or another a flourishing capital of Muslims, Jews, and Christians. Locals will tell you the history has been a bit romanticized; still, with more monuments per cobblestone than almost any other city in the world, the hometown of El Greco holds a special mystique. With the Reconquista and the expulsion of the Jews and Muslims from Spain, the Christians reconsecrated the mosques and synagogues, creating the fusion of styles and faiths that makes Toledo so remarkable. On every twisting corner

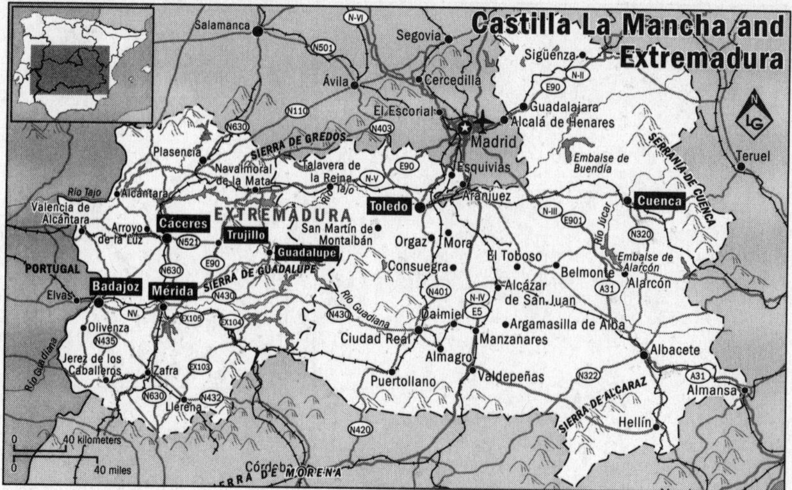

is a store selling Damascene swords (used on the set of *The Lord of the Rings)* or Toledo's famous marzipan, and you'll be lucky to get out of the city without having bought one or the other. In June, Toledo's movie-set-like facades come alive with costumed processions during the Corpus Cristi celebration.

TRANSPORTATION

Trains: Po. de la Rosa, 2 (**RENFE** info ☎902 24 02 02), in an exquisite *neo-mudéjar* station just over Puente de Azarquiel. High speed AVE train to Atocha station in **Madrid.** (30min.; M-F 11 per day 6:55am-9:25pm, Sa-Su 9 per day 9:25am-9:25pm; €9)

Buses: Av. Castilla La Mancha (☎925 21 58 50), 10min. from Puerta de Bisagra. Open daily 7am-11pm. **Alsina Graells** (in Toledo ☎925 21 58 50, in Valencia 963 49 72 30) goes to **Valencia** (5hr., M-F 3pm, €25.05; buy ticket on board). **Continental Auto** (in Toledo ☎925 22 36 41, in Madrid 915 27 29 61) runs to Estación Sur in **Madrid** (1hr.; every 30min. M-F 6am-10:30pm, Sa 6:30am-10:30pm, Su 8am-11:30pm; €4.53).

Public Transportation: Buses 8.1 and 8.2 head from the bus station into the center of town. Buses 1-7 leave from Pl. de Zocodóver on various circular routes through town. Ask for routes at the tourist office. (€0.95, at night €1.25).

Taxis: Radio Taxi (☎925 22 70 70) and **Gruas de Toledo** (☎925 25 50 50).

Car Rental: Avis, in the train station (☎925 21 45 35). From €80 per day. 23+. Open M-F 9:30am-1:30pm and 4:30-7:30pm, Sa 9:30am-1pm.

ORIENTATION AND PRACTICAL INFORMATION

Consider yourself warned: the way in Toledo is uphill. To walk from the train station to the Plaza de Zocodóver (derived from the Arabic name for the market once held there, "Souk al Dawar") in the center, turn right and follow the left fork uphill to an incredible and ornate stone bridge, the Puente de Alcántara. Cross the bridge to the stone staircase; after climbing it, turn left and go up, veering right at C. Cervantes, which leads to Pl. de Zocodóver. The bus avoids the sidewalk-less uphill hike. To get to the Plaza from the bus station, exit via the cafeteria, head toward the traffic circle, and continue on the highway until

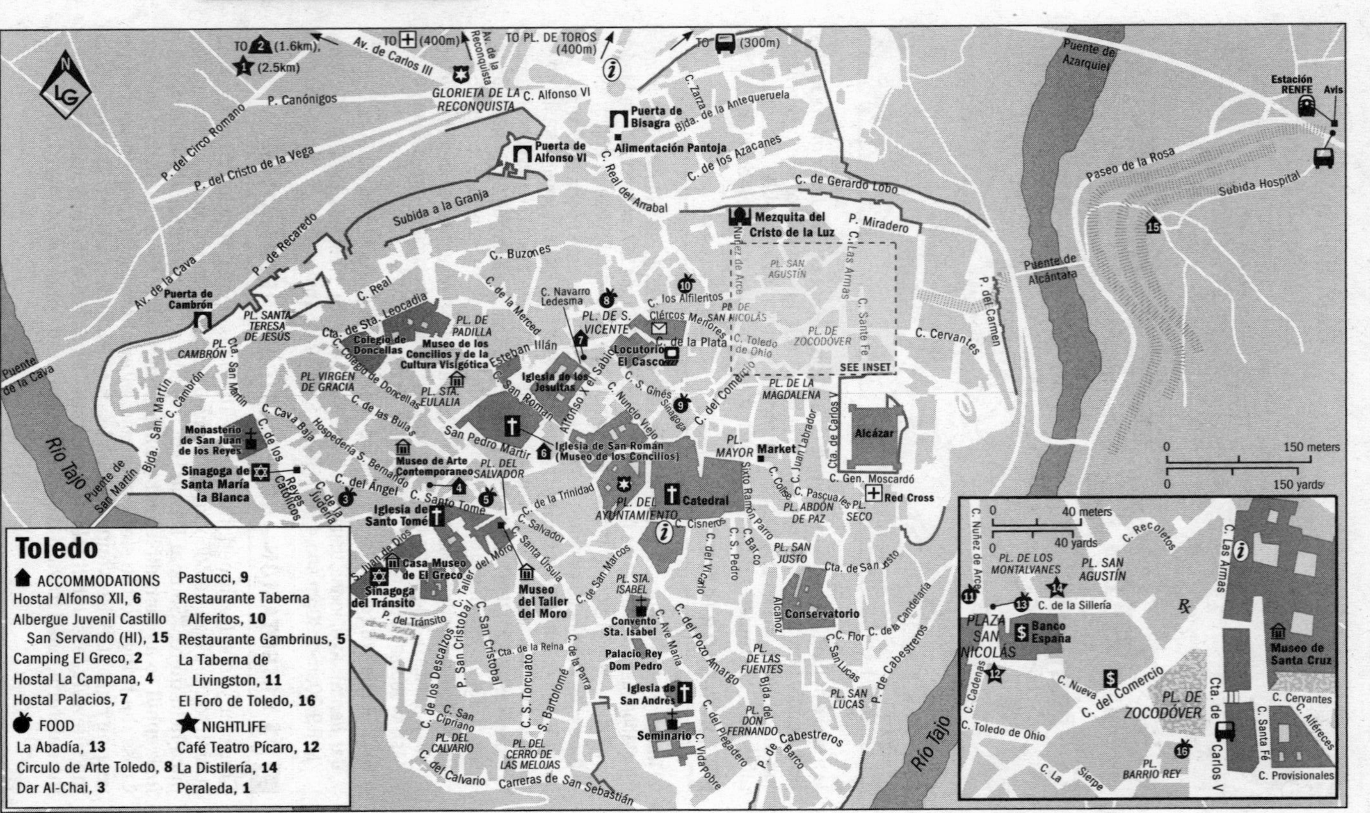
Toledo
ACCOMMODATIONS
Hostal Alfonso XII, 6
Albergue Juvenil Castillo San Servando (HI), 15
Camping El Greco, 2
Hostal La Campana, 4
Hostal Palacios, 7
FOOD
La Abadía, 13
Circulo de Arte Toledo, 8
Dar Al-Chai, 3
Pastucci, 9
Restaurante Taberna Alferitos, 10
Restaurante Gambrinus, 5
La Taberna de Livingston, 11
El Foro de Toledo, 16
NIGHTLIFE
Café Teatro Pícaro, 12
La Distilería, 14
Peraleda, 1
Río Tajo
Estación RENFE
Avis
Puente de Azarquiel
Puente de Alcántara
Paseo de la Rosa
Subida Hospital
150 meters
150 yards
SEE INSET
Alcázar
Red Cross
Catedral
Mezquita del Cristo de la Luz
Puerta de Bisagra
Alimentación Pantoja
Puerta de Alfonso VI
Puerta de Cambrón
TO PL. DE TOROS (400m)
GLORIETA DE LA RECONQUISTA
Museo de Santa Cruz
Banco España
PL. DE ZOCODOVER
PL. SAN AGUSTÍN
PLAZA SAN NICOLÁS
Conservatorio
Iglesia de San Andrés
Seminario
Palacio Rey Dom Pedro
Convento Sta. Isabel
Museo del Taller del Moro
Iglesia de Santo Tomé
Casa Museo de El Greco
Sinagoga del Tránsito
Sinagoga de Santa María la Blanca
Monasterio de San Juan de los Reyes
Museo de Arte Contemporaneo
Iglesia de San Román (Museo de los Concilios)
Iglesia de los Jesuitas
Museo de los Concilios y de la Cultura Visigótica
Colegio de Doncellas
Locutorio El Casco
Puente de San Martín
Puente de la Cava

you reach the bridge on your left. Then, turn right up the stone steps and continue up toward the city. A map is essential; the streets in Toledo fork deviously at every opportunity, and a wrong turn is just about inevitable.

Tourist Office: The **municipal** office, Pl. del Ayuntamiento (☎925 25 40 30) hands out indispensable maps and information about accommodations and eating. Some English spoken. Open M 10:30am-2:30pm, Tu-Su 10:30am-2:30pm and 4:30-7pm. Another branch is located at the Casa del Mapa under the arches in Pl. de Zocodóver. Maps and similar information. Open daily 11am-7pm. **Regional** office, Puerta de Bisagra (☎925 22 08 43). From the train station, turn right and take the right-hand fork across the bridge (Puente de Azarquiel), following the walls until you reach the 2nd traffic circle; the office is across the road, outside the walls. Staff offers handy maps. Open July-Sept. M-F 9am-7pm, Sa 10am-6pm, Su 10am-2pm; Oct.-June M-F 9am-6pm, Sa 10am-6pm, Su 10am-2pm.

Currency Exchange: Banco Santander Central Hispano, C. del Comercio, 47 (☎925 22 98 00). No commission and 24hr. **ATM.** Open Apr.-Sept. M-F 8:30am-2pm; Oct.-Mar. M-F 8:30am-2pm, Sa 8:30am-1pm.

Luggage Storage: At the bus station (€1.80/3 per day for small/large bags). Open daily 7am-11pm.

Police: (☎925 25 04 12). At the corner of Av. de la Reconquista and Av. de Carlos III.

Pharmacy: Pl. de Zocodóver (☎925 22 17 68). Some English spoken Open daily 9:30am-2pm and 5-8pm. MC/V.

Hospital: Hospital Virgen de la Salud, Av. de Barber (☎925 26 92 00), outside the city walls. With your back to Puerta de Bisagra, go left until Glorieta de la Reconquista (300m). Take Av. de la Reconquista to Pl. de Colón; Av. de Barber is to the left. It's a 10min walk up the road. No English spoken.

Internet Access: Options are limited, but access is available at Locutorio El Casco, C. La Plata, 2, (☎925 22 61 65), across from the post office. €1.50 per hr. Open daily 11am-11pm.

Post Office: C. de la Plata, 1 (☎925 22 36 11; fax 21 57 64). Lista de Correos. Open M-F 8:30am-8:30pm, Sa 9:30am-2pm. **Postal Code:** 45070.

ACCOMMODATIONS AND CAMPING

Toledo has plenty of accommodations in the old city, but finding a bed in summer can be a hassle, especially on weekends. Reservations are strongly recommended; try the tourist office if you run into trouble. There are also several campgrounds around Toledo.

Albergue Juvenil Castillo de San Servando (HI), C. de San Servando (☎925 22 45 54; alberguesclm@jccm.es). Cross the street from the train station, then turn right up Subida del Hospital. Continue up the windy, uphill street past Hospital Provincial to the *hostal,* housed in a 14th-century castle. From the bus station, go toward the traffic circle and continue uphill; cross the footbridge to the left and head up to the castle. Incredible stone fortress that once gave refuge to El Cid Campeador, Spain's medieval hero. 38 spacious rooms, each with 2-4 bunks, bath, and wooden floors. Pool in the summer, TV room, and internet access €1/hr. Reservations recommended at least 15 days in advance in summer. Lockout from 11am-2pm. Dorms €9.50, with breakfast €11.50; over 30 €12.50/15. MC/V. ❶

Hostal Alfonso XII, C. Alfonso XII, 18 (☎925 25 25 09; www.hostal-alfonso12.com). Turn off C. Santo Tomé up Campana and follow it to C. Alfonso XII. Scented herbs and flowers fill the halls and rooms with nice aromas. Wooden beams traverse the ceilings and add the finishing note to an elegant, deceptively rustic place with modern amenities. Rooms with TV, A/C, WiFi. Singles €40; doubles €55; triples €70. MC/V. ❹

Hostal Palacios, C. Navarro Ledesma, 4 (☎925 28 00 83; www.hostalpalacios.net), straight up C. Nuncio Viejo from the cathedral. This hotel has big beds and long, glass-enclosed balconies that fill the rooms with light. Rooms come with TV, A/C, phone, and WiFi. Singles €30, with breakfast/lunch/dinner at adjoining restaurant €32/40/45; doubles €50/54/65/80. AmEx/MC/V. ❸

Hostal La Campana, C. de la Campana, 10-12 (☎925 22 16 59 or 925 22 16 62; www.hostalcampana.com). The small, soft beds and wooden furniture feel like a country cottage, but for the balcony overlooking the narrow street. Great location—monuments at the doorstep. Rooms have bath, TV, phone, A/C, and Wi-Fi. Breakfast included. Reserve well in advance.Singles €36; doubles €60. MC/V. ❹

Camping El Greco, Ctra. CM-4000 km 0.7 (☎925 22 00 90; www.campingelgreco.es.vg), 1.5km from town. Take bus #7 from Pl. de Zocodóver. Clean, shady site between the Río Tajo and an olive grove. Restaurant, bar, supermarket, and pool. €5.94 per person, per tent, and per car. Pool €3.50. IVA not included. MC/V. ❶

FOOD

Many restaurants are a bit steep, but if you know where to look, reasonable eats are available. For those in a crunch, cheap *cafeterías* and the occasional kebab joint can be found in the streets snaking off Pl. de Zocodóver. Pastelería windows on every corner in Toledo beckon with *mazapán* (marzipan) of every shape and size, from colorful nuggets to half-moon cookies. For a wide array, stop by the market in Pl. Mayor, behind the cathedral. (Open M-Sa 9am-8pm.)

La Abadía, Pl. de San Nicolás, 3 (☎925 25 11 40; www.abadiatoledo.com). From Pl. de Zocodóver, bear left when C. de la Sillería splits; Pl. de San Nicolás is to the right. Dine on tapas (€3.25) or the delicious lunch *menú* (€11) in a maze of cave-like underground rooms. Excellent selection of German and American beers on tap (€2-2.50). Combo tapas plates €5-10. Open daily 8am-midnight. AmEx/MC/V. ❷

Restaurante Gambrinus, C. Santo Tomé, 10 (☎925 21 44 40). The shadiest outdoor seating in the old city is perfect for people-watching as you slowly conquer a hearty traditional Spanish plate. Has big soups (€6) as well as the whole partridge (€19.80) for the hungry. Meat dishes €10-11. Open daily 11am-4pm and 8pm-midnight. MC/V. ❸

Pastucci, C. Sinagoga, 10 (☎925 25 77 42; www.aplinet.com/pastucci). From Pl. de Zocodóver take C. del Comercio; turn right below the underpass just past the Rodier store. Pizza joint produces stunning array of gourmet hand-made pizzas. Pastas €5.60-7.50. Small pizzas €6.50-9.50. Open Tu-Su noon-4pm and 8pm-midnight. MC/V. ❷

Restaurante Taberna Alferitos, 24. C. Alferitos, 24 (☎902 10 65 77; www.alferitos24.com). Modern white decor meets old Toledo stone. Ground floor is a popular tapas stop (€5-8), while the levels above seat a dining crowd. Glass-roofed top floor. Woks €10-11. Entrees €12-15. Taberna *menú* €10.Open daily 8pm-midnight. AmEx/MC/V. ❸

El Foro de Toledo, Pl. de Zocodóver, 8 (☎925 28 95 55). Right in the middle of the action. Pay the extra €1 per plate to eat on red plush chairs outside, among tourists and guitar-strummers. Sells marzipan (bulk 250g pieces €7.80) for a sweet dessert. *Platos combinados* €4-7. *Bocadillos* €4-6. Open daily noon-midnight. AmEx/MC/V. ❶

La Taberna de Livingston, C. Alferitos, 4. Take C. Sillería from Pl. de Zocodóver and keep walking straight. Colonialism gone way overboard. Zebra-print stools and walls crammed with black and white pictures of big game and various native peoples set the mood, along with posters from British boys' schools. Look for the fake skull in the floor. Despite the aggressive decor, serves up regular *raciones* (€9-12) like meat *croquetas* (€9)—no rhino meat here. Mixed drinks €5. Open M-Th and Su 10am-2pm and 8-11pm, F-Sa 10am-2pm and 8pm-1:30am. Cash only. ❷

CAFES

Dar Al-Chal, Pl. de Barrio Nuevo, 6 (☎925 22 56 25; www.daralchai.com). Moorish arches straight from Alhambra and hilarious, squat little stools crowd this hip, busy tea joint, a favorite with local students. The crepes (€2.80-3.40) are sweet, fruity, and gigantic. Tea €2.30 per person or €10 for 6 people. Open M-Th and Su 9:30am-10pm, F-Sa 4pm-1am. MC/V. ❷

Circulo de Arte Toledo, Pl. de San Vicente, 2 (☎925 21 43 29; www.circuloartetoledo.org). A local university and hipster cafe that hosts regular concerts, exhibits, dance recitals, and theater. Gorgeously set in a 12th century *mudéjar* temple, the stage sits under a massive Moorish arch. Full bar. Tapas €5 and breakfast €1.90-2.30. Open daily,; hours and food availability change according to performance schedule. ❷

SIGHTS

Toledo is bursting with old churches, mosques, museums, and synagogues, all of which demand a visit and adequate time. Toledo's attractions wrap around its middle within the fortified 7th-century walls. An east-west tour beginning in Pl. de Zocodóver is largely downhill. Many sights are closed on Mondays.

CATEDRAL. Built between 1226 and 1498, Toledo's cathedral flaunts its architectural and artistic riches, coming from multiple periods and styles, with Gothic, Renassiance, and Baroque ornament all vying for attention. The cathedral consists of 5 naves, built around a central altarpiece and an adjacent courtyard, with chapels clustering around the sides. The **Capilla de San Ildefonso,** dedicated to Toledo's patron saint, portrays a scene replicated in various media all over town, of the Virgin descending to impose on Ildefonso a chasuble, the garment of a Catholic priest. Behind it is **Capilla de la Descensión,** which has a small red jasper box containing the stone the Virgin is rumored to have tread on when she descended. The newly restored **Capilla de San Blas,** beyond the courtyard, boasts bright, intricate designs. The treasury flaunts a 400 lb. 16th-century gold monstrosity that gets lugged through the streets during the annual Corpus Cristi procession on June 10th. The priestly vestments are hardly the main attraction in la Sacristía, which is practically a small art museum in itself. 18 of El Greco's portraits of the saints, along with works by Rafael, Titian, Caravaggio, Rubens, Goya, and Velásquez (to name a few) adorn the walls. *(☎925 22 22 41. Entrance down C. Chapinería. Open M-Sa 10am-6:30pm, Su 2-6:30pm. Audio tour in English, French, and Italian; €7, students €6. Tickets sold at the store opposite the entrance. Modest dress required.)*

EL GRECO SIGHTS. Greek painter Doménikos Theotokópoulos, better known as El Greco, spent most of his life in Toledo. Many works are displayed throughout town, but the majority of his masterpieces have been carted off to the Prado and other big-name museums. The best place to start is the **Casa Museo de El Greco,** the master's former home, which contains 19 of his paintings, among them glowing portraits of a sad-eyed Christ and a San Bartolomé who is poised to kill a *diablito* with a large knife. *(C. Samuel Leví, 2. ☎925 22 44 05. Open in summer Tu-Sa 10am-2pm and 4-9pm, Su 10am-2pm; in winter Tu-Sa 10am-2pm and 4-6pm, Su 10am-2pm. €2.40; students, under 18, and over 65 free. Sa-Su afternoons free. Closed due to renovation; call ahead to see if open.)* Up the hill and to the right is the **Iglesia de Santo Tomé,** which still houses one of his most famous and recognized works, *El Entierro del Conde de Orgaz (The Burial of Count Orgaz)*. The stark figure staring out from the back is El Greco himself, and the boy is his son, Jorge Manuel, architect of Toledo's city hall. Arrive early to beat out the tour groups. *(Pl. del Conde, 4. ☎925 25 60 98; www.santotome.org. Open daily Mar.-Oct. 15 10am-7pm; Oct.16-Feb.*

10am-6pm. €2.30, students and over 65 €1.80.) The **Hospital de Talavera,** built in 1541, also holds some of his paintings (C. Cardenal Tavera, 2, north of the city walls; ☎925 22 04 51; open daily 10am-1:30pm and 3-5:30pm; €4.50), as does the convent of **Santo Domingo el Antiguo,** along with his sepulcher. *(Pl. Santo Domingo el Antiguo. ☎925 22 29 30. Open daily 11am-1:30pm and 4-7pm. €2.30.)*

SYNAGOGUES. Only two of the many synagogues once in Toledo's *judería* (Jewish quarter) have been preserved. Samuel Ha Leví, diplomat and treasurer to Pedro el Cruel, built the Sinagoga del Tránsito in 1366, which now houses the **Museo Sefardí.** Stare up at the Hebrew letters carved into the *mudéjar* plasterwork and a stunning *artesonado* (coffered) wood ceiling. The museum documents the history of the Jews in Spain and Morocco and their diaspora abroad, with old relics and Hebrew bibles on display. *(Paseo del Tránsito, C. Samuel Leví. ☎925 22 36 65; www.museosefardi.net. Open Mar.-Nov. Tu-Sa 10am-2pm and 4-9pm, Su 10am-2pm; Dec.-Feb. Tu-Sa 10am-2pm and 4-6pm, Su 10am-2pm. €2.40; students, over 65, and under 18 free. Sa after 4pm and Su free.)* **Sinagoga de Santa María la Blanca,** built by Rabbi Joseph, one of Alfonso VIII's ministers, served as the principal synagogue in Toledo until 1405, when it was consecrated as a Christian temple, leaving the city's Jews to pray elsewhere until they were expelled entirely in 1492. The white Moorish arches and tracery along the ceiling betray its Islamic influences, harking back to the city's more multicultural days and the intolerant ones to follow. Now secular, its arches and tranquil garden are pleasant for any denomination.*(C. de los Reyes Católicos, 4. ☎925 22 72 57. Open daily June-Aug. 10am-7pm; Sept.-May 10am-6pm. €2.30.)*

IGLESIA DE LOS JESUITAS. This Jesuit church, former home of Juan de Mendoza, Count of Orgaz, and the birthplace of San Ildefonso, has **amazing views** of Toledo from its top towers. Completed in 1765, two years before the Jesuits were expelled from Spain, the interior is gleaming white and filled with art dating from the Counter-Reformation. Located at one of the highest points in the city, the roof offers a panorama of all the tower and tiled roofs in the old city and the hills for miles around. *(Pl. Padre Juan de Mariana, 1, up C. Nuncio Viejo from the Cathedral, and then a left on Alfonso X El Sabio. ☎925 25 15 07. Open daily Apr.-Sept. 10am-6:45pm, Oct.-March 10am-5:45pm. €2.30.)*

MONASTERIO DE SAN JUAN DE LOS REYES. At the far western edge of the city stands this Franciscan monastery, commissioned by Fernando and Isabel to commemorate their victory over the Portuguese in the Battle of Toro (1476). Over the church's entrance, a grinning skeleton awaits resurrection. The church is elegant but simple, with a single nave, and free of the gilded chapels that overwhelm other cathedrals. Better, though, is the cloister, with blossoming flowers and orange trees you can look down on from the upper level, largely by yourself; the monastery is relatively untouristed and the birdsong is the noisiest thing here. *(☎925 22 38 02. Ticket sales stop 20min. before closing. Open daily Apr.-Sept. 10am-7pm; Oct.-Mar. 10am-6pm. €2.30.)*

MEZQUITA DEL CRISTO DE LA LUZ. The only wholly preserved mosque remaining the city, La Mezquita has strangely syncretic name—meaning literally "Mosque of Christ of the Light"—of unknown origin. Legend has it that the monarch Alfonso VI's horse stumbled and would go no further as they approached the mosque, in those days called Bab al-Mardum. A strange light was observed, and hidden behind the wall was a cross illuminated continuously by a lamp for four centuries. The spot is marked on the paving in front of the mosque. The Arabic script on the facade is striking, as is the *qibla*, the wide arch that points toward Mecca. *(Cuesta de Carmelitas Descalzos, 10, just south of the Puerta de Sol. ☎925 25 41 91. Open daily May-Sept. 10am-7pm, Oct.-April 10am-6pm. €2.30.)*

MUSEUMS. Toledo was the seat of Visigoth rule and culture for three centuries prior to the Muslim invasion in 711. The exhibits at the **Museo de los Concilios y de la Cultura Visigótica** pale in comparison to their beautiful setting, the **Iglesia de San Román.** The temple is an awesome fusion of Muslim and Christian elements, with painted images of saints fringed by inscriptions in Arabic and Christian martyrs decorating the underside of striped Moorish arches. The vivid artwork on the walls depicts heaven and hell, church elders, and saints battling dragons. *(C. San Román. ☎925 22 78 72. Open Tu-Sa 10am-2pm and 4-6:30pm, Su 10am-2pm. Free.)* The impressive and under-touristed **Museo de Santa Cruz** (1504) is an impressive example of ornate renaissance architectural embellishment. Inside, explore a handful of El Grecos, attributed El Grecos, and copies of El Grecos, along with temporary art exhibits. The basement is open intermittently but holds remains from local archaeological digs; check out the mastodon skull with tusks intact. Around the courtyard is a hodgepodge of marble slates from the Renaissance and older stone ones with Arabic inscriptions. *(C. Miguel de Cervantes, 3. ☎925 22 10 36; www.jccm.es. Open Tu-Sa 10am-6pm, Su 10am-2pm. Free.)*

NIGHTLIFE

Toledo's thick stone does a good job of concealing the nightlife, but if you keep an ear to the ground you'll find they can party, too. That said, the city doesn't really pull out the stops except on the weekends. Head downstairs into the dark at **La Destilería,** C. Sillería, 3, where local youth line the bar and cram into corners to listen to the mix and sip their cocktails (€6), getting up to dance when the salsa comes on. (☎925 25 47 74; www.casontoledo.com. Beer €2. Open Tu-Sa 10pm-3am.) Calle de la Sillería and Calle de los Alfileritos host a few upscale bars and clubs, including a bar at **La Abadía,** packed with locals, old, and young, with beers and *bocadillos* until late. (☎925 25 11 40. Open daily 1:30-4pm and 8pm-1am. For directions, see Food, p. 176.) To escape the raucous noise, check out the chill **Café Teatro Pícaro,** C. Cadenas, 6, where lights play on abstract art, and it's just as cool to be sipping on a *batido* (milkshake, €3, with Bailey's, €4) as a mixed drink. (☎925 22 13 01; www.picarocafeteatro.com. Mixed drinks €5. Beer €1.50-2.50. Open M-F 4pm-3am, Sa-Su 4pm-5am.) For die-hard partygoers, head past the hospital to the summer discos in **Peraleda** (Open Th-Sa, 11pm-4am). Inquire at the tourist office for more info.

CUENCA

☎969

Cuenca (pop. 50,000) is a quiet hill-top retreat, which owes its fame to the marvelous geological foundations on which it stands. The city spills over a hill and is flanked by two rivers and the stunning rock formations they have carved. The cobblestone streets, meandering up and down and around corners, alternatively lead to frustrating dead ends and stunning, abrupt vistas of the gorges and the buildings that cascade down the hillside, in particular the **casas colgadas** (hanging houses), which jut out over the Río Huécar hundreds of feet below. The rest of the *casco antiguo* (old city), declared a World Heritage site in 1996, is densely packed with ancient buildings and churches that aren't to be missed. Since the 19th century, the city has strained against its natural boundaries, depositing modern and uninspired commercial life downhill in New Cuenca with graffiti and highrise apartments. It's definitely worth a night's stay to get lost in the old city's streets and see the *casas* lit up at sunrise from the footbridge across the gorge.

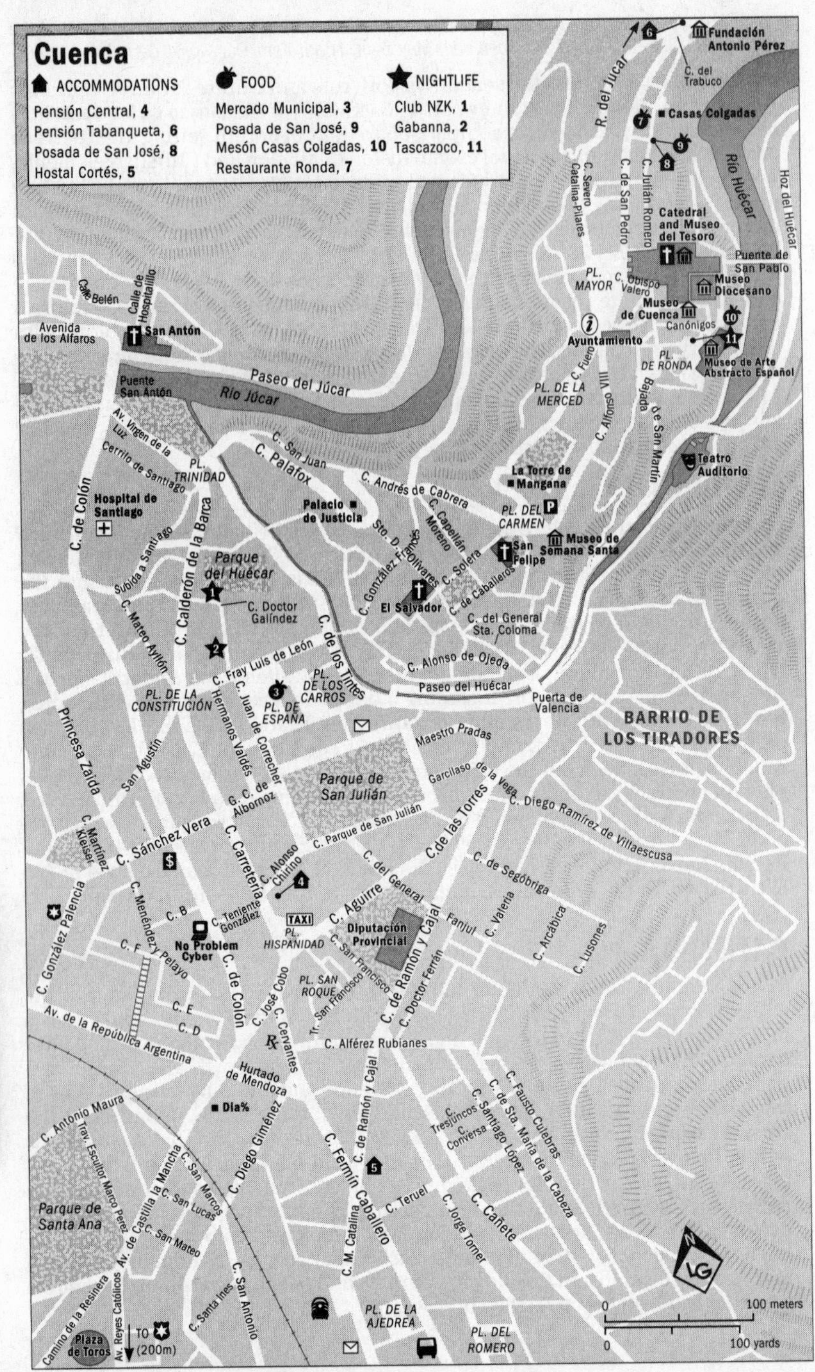

CASTILLA LA MANCHA AND EXTREMADURA

TRANSPORTATION

Trains: C. Mariano Catalina, 10 (☎902 24 02 02). To Aranjuez (2hr., 5-6 per day 7:05am-6:55pm, €7.70), Madrid (2-3hr., 5-6 per day 7:05am-6:55pm, €10.65), and Valencia (3-4hr., 3-4 per day 7:35am-6:50pm, €10.75).

Buses: C. Fermín Caballero, 20 (☎969 22 70 87). Info open M-F 6am-9pm, Sa-Su 7am-2:30pm and 4-9pm. AutoRes (☎969 22 70 87) to Madrid (2hr.; 8-9 per day M-F 6:45am-10pm, Sa 6:45am-9pm, Su 6:45am-12:30am; €10.75-14). AISA to Toledo via Ciudad Directo (2hr.; M-F 6:30am and 4pm, Sa 8am and 4pm,Su 5pm; €12-14). Samar buses go to Barcelona (9hr., M-Sa 9am, Su 2pm, €34.41).

Taxis: Radio Taxi (☎969 23 33 43). From the train station to Pl. Mayor €6.

ORIENTATION AND PRACTICAL INFORMATION

Upon exiting the train station, the back of the bus station (a large brick building) will be on the street in front of you; head up the steps to C. Fermín Caballero and turn right to enter the bus station. To reach the Plaza Mayor in the old city from either station, take a left onto C. Fermín Caballero, following it as it becomes C. Cervantes, C. José Cobo, and, bearing left through Pl. de la Hispanidad, Calle Carretería. Street signs point the way. From C. Carretería, head toward the river. The winding route up is more scenic; for a busier but much quicker route, turn right onto C. Fray Luis de León; it's a long hike uphill to Pl. Mayor and the old city (20-25min.) until you get the hang of it. Alternatively, take bus #1 or 2 (every 30min.; €0.70, Su €0.85) to Pl. Mayor from the bus stop right outside the bus station or from the one off Pl. de la Constitución, at the intersection of C. Carretería and C. Frey Luis de León.

Tourist Office: Pl. Mayor, 1 or C. Alfonso VII, 2 (☎969 24 10 51; www.cuenca.org). Distributes comprehensive maps with all of Cuenca's sights and accommodations. Open July-Sept. daily 9am-9pm; Oct.-June M-Sa 9am-2pm and 4-6:30pm, Su 9am-2pm. Another branch in Plaza de Hispanidad, bearing right on José Cobo as it becomes Carretería. Open M-Th 10am-2pm and 5-8pm, F-Sa 10am-8pm, and Su 10am-2pm.

Currency Exchange: Banco Santander Central Hispano, C. Sánchez Vera, 5 (☎969 22 36 51). Open Apr.-Sept. M-F 8:30am-2pm; Oct.-Mar. also Sa 8:30am-2pm.

Luggage Storage: At the bus station (☎969 22 70 87. €1.50-3 per day; open daily 7am-2pm and 4-9pm.

Police: (☎091 or 969 22 48 59). At the intersection of C. González Palencia and C. Duque de Alhumada.

Pharmacy: Farmacia Castellanos, C. Cervantes, 20 (☎969 21 23 37), at the corner of C. Alférez Rubianes. Open Apr.-Oct. M-F 9:30am-2pm and 5-8pm, Sa 10am-2pm; Nov.-Mar. M-F 9:30am-2pm and 4:30-7:30pm, Sa 10am-2pm.

Internet: No Problem Cyber, C. Colón, 36 (www.noproblem.es), left off Carretería down Teniente González and then right across the street. Internet €1.60/hr. Open daily noon-10pm.

Post Office: Parque de San Julián, 16 (☎969 22 10 42). Open M-F 8:30am-8:30pm, Sa 9:30am-2pm. A smaller branch with fewer services is right next to the train station. Open M-F 8:30am-2:30pm, Sa 8am-2pm. **Postal Code:** 16001/16002.

ACCOMMODATIONS

Lodging in the old city makes nightlife a bit of an excursion—but the views and clean breezes are definitely worth it. Reserve ahead, as these places are generally very small. Cheap rooms are abundant in the newer part of town, but not always in the prettiest places.

Posada de San José, C. Julián Romero, 4 (☎969 21 13 00; www.posadadesanjose.com). Housed in a 17th-century choir school, it has gorgeous, simply decorated rooms with elegant tiled baths. All are airy, some with balconies overlooking the gorge and garden. Restaurant attached (see below). Reserve ahead. Breakfast €8. Singles €25, with bath €50; doubles €38/75; triples with bath €83; quads with bath €128. *Semana Santa* higher prices; weeknights and Oct.-Apr €3-5 discount. AmEx/MC/V. ❷

Hostal Cortés, C. Ramón y Cajal, 45 (☎969 22 04 00; www.hostalcortes.com), just off Fermín Caballero. Bright red bedspreads with matching curtains liven up sober wood in these spacious, modern rooms. Rooms come with huge full bath, soft beds, phone, and A/C. Singles Oct.-June €33, July-Sept. €38; doubles €44/53. MC/V. ❸

Pensión Tabanqueta, C. del Trabuco, 13 (☎969 21 12 90), up C. San Pedro from the cathedral past Pl. del Trabuco. Quite a hike from New Cuenca, but the view over the Río Júcar and the breeze are worth it. Small rooms fill up quickly, so reserve ahead. Don't miss the terrace bar. Singles €15; doubles €30. Cash only. ❷

Pensión Central, C. de Alonso Chirino, 7, 2nd fl. (☎969 21 15 11). Long corridors lead the way to clean, high-ceilinged rooms with big beds and balconies at the cheapest price you will find anywhere in Cuenca. Rooms with TV. Communal baths are large and clean. Singles €14 Oct.-June, €16 July-Sept. and *Semana Santa;* doubles €24/26; triples €32/35. Cash only. ❶

FOOD

The area around Pl. Mayor is filled with mid- to high-priced restaurants and only mediocre eats, but side streets near the plaza yield cheaper alternatives. Budget spots line **Calle Cervantes** and **Avenida de la República Argentina** in New Cuenca; the cafes off **Calle Fray Luis de León** are even cheaper. Area specialties include *resoli* (a liqueur of coffee, sugar, orange peel, and *aguardiente*) and glorious *alajú* (a nougat of honey, almonds, and figs). The **mercado municipal** is on C. Fray Luis de León (open M-Sa 8:30am-2pm), and groceries are at **Dia%,** Av. Castilla La Mancha, 5. (Open M-Th 9:30am-2pm and 5:30-8:30pm, F-Sa 9am-2:30pm and 5:30-9pm.)

Restaurante Ronda, C. San Pedro, 20 (☎969 23 29 42). Dark, formal tables inside, and a pleasant stone terrace by the Mirador Florencio Cañas, fringed by trees with songbirds. From here, the surrounding hills and their statues are all visible. Big meat dishes €8-10. *Menú del día* €14. Open daily 1-3:30pm and 8:30-11pm. Cash only. ❷

Posada de San José, C. Julián Romero, 4 (☎969 21 13 00). Arrive early to grab a terrace seat, with a breeze and climbing rose bushes. Fried eggs are a staple (€6), and come with ham, *pisto* (thick tomato stew), or potatoes. To top it off, the *alajú* (€2.25) is unbeatable here. Open Tu-Su 8-11am and 6-10:30pm. AmEx/MC/V. ❶

Mesón Casas Colgadas, C. Canónigos, s/n (☎969 22 35 09; www.mesoncasascolgadas.com). Gourmet cooking inside a hanging house comes at a hefty price, but the food and the view of the gorge over the overhanging porch are stunning. *Menú* €28. Small meat dishes €15-20. Open M and W-Su. 1:30-4pm and 9-11pm. AmEx/MC/V. ❹

SIGHTS

CASAS COLGADAS. Cuenca derives its fame from the 14th-century *casas colgadas* that dangle over its riverbanks. These "hanging houses," built precariously on the edges of Cuenca's cliffs, are believed to have been the summer homes of 14th-century monarchs. Restored in the 1920s, the houses are best seen from the other side of the Río Huécar, across the iron Puente de San Pablo. The Paseo del Huécar continues up, affording a broader view of the town, especially spectacular at night, when the *casas* are illuminated.

CATEDRAL DE CUENCA. Constructed under Alfonso VIII in the 12th century, the cathedral is a fantastic centerpiece of the Pl. Mayor. Renovated throughout the centuries, the cathedral is a strange but unified composite of styles, with a Romanesque layout, Gothic arches, Renaissance statues, neoclassical chapels and a neo-Gothic façade. The 20 chapels are decked out in gold, marble, and fantastic artwork, with 571 statues in all. Among them is the Virgin of the Shrine, a figure that Alfonso VIII carried into battle against the Moors. The sheer amount of wealth, artistic and historical, makes the cathedral a must-see. *(Pl. Mayor. Cathedral open July-Sept. M-F 10am-2pm and 4-7pm, Sa 10am-7pm, Su 10am-6:30pm; Oct.-Apr. open daily 10:30am-1:30pm and 4-6pm; May-June Sa 10:30am-2pm and 4-6pm, Su 10:30am-2pm and 4-6:30pm. Cathedral, museum, and audio tour €2.80.)*

MUSEO DE ARTE ABSTRACTO ESPAÑOL. Inside the only *casa colgada* open to the public, the award-winning Museo de Arte Abstracto Español exhibits works by the odd yet renowned Abstract Generation of Spanish painters. The museum, designed by Zóbel and the painter Gustavo Torner, flows smoothly along grouped stylistic and thematic lines. All pieces, most by Canogar, Tàpies, Chillida, and Fernando Zóbel, were chosen by Zóbel himself. La Sala Blanca (the White Room) and striking views of the gorge are not to miss. *(Pl. de Ronda; follow signs from Pl. Mayor. ☎969 21 29 83. Open July-Sept. Tu-F 11am-2pm and 5-7pm, Sa 11am-2pm and 4-9pm, Su 11am-2:30pm; Oct.-June Tu-F 11am-2pm and 4-6pm, Sa 11am-2pm and 4-8pm, Su 11am-2:30pm. €3, students and seniors €1.50.)*

OTHER SIGHTS. The **Fundación Antonio Pérez,** C. Julian Romero, 20, is near the top of the street. Antonio Pérez, a contemporary writer and critic, has opened his impressively eclectic collection of 20th-century art to the public. Highlights include surrealist collages, Pérez's *objetos encontrados* (found objects), a couple of Warhols, and, notably, Ximo Amigó's "Michelin Man" works, which haunt various nooks and corners of the regal casa. The downstairs gallery hosts exhibits. *(☎969 23 06 19. Open daily 10am-9pm. Free.)* Around the cathedral, down C. Obispo Valero, is the **Museo Diocesano,** whose exhibits include Juan de Borgoña's altarpiece from the local Convento de San Pablo, some colossal Flemish tapestries, splendid rugs, and an old *mudéjar* door. The stars of the collection are two El Grecos—*Oración del huerto* and the well-known *Cristo con la cruz*. *(☎969 22 42 10. Open in summer Tu-Sa 11am-2pm and 4-6pm, Su 11am-2pm; in winter Tu-Sa 11am-2pm. €2.)* Down Calle Alfonso VIII is the **Torre de Mangana,** an old clocktower assembled in the 15th century. It occupies one of the highest points in the *casco antiguo*, and its *mirador* offers some of the best views of the Río Júcar. Further down the street is the **Museo de la Semana Santa,** showcasing the town's devotion to the festival, which it celebrates with solemn, silent parades. *(Open W-Sa 11am-2pm and 4:30-7pm, Su 11am-4pm. €3, students €1.50.)*

NIGHTLIFE

Cuenca's nightlife scene extends into the wee hours of the morning from Thursday to Saturday, and bars tend to only open on the weekend. The older, and early-to-bed crowd stays near **Pl. Mayor,** while teens and twenty-somethings flock to the new city. Numerous bars with young, well-dressed partiers line **C. Doctor Galíndez,** off C. Fray Luis de León. It's a hot spot in the new city, but a long, dark walk down the hill from Old Cuenca; a taxi costs about €5.50, but the Buho (night bus) #1 runs from nearby Pl. de la Constitución to Pl. Mayor until 3am (€1.15). *Botellón*, the Spanish institution of communal drinking in public, is an integral part of the nightlife in Cuenca, and people begin setting up in **Pl. de España** at 10 or 11pm. Black and white **Gabbana,** C. Dr. Galíndez, 5, draws both young people breaking it down and older people out for a drink. The DJ spins a strange mix of American pop and rock favorites—not always danceable, but no one's self-conscious here. (Open Th-Sa 11pm-4am.) At the end of the street is **Club NZK,** C. Dr. Galíndez, 28, which plays remixed dance music for a dance floor owned by the girls. Sip an astrological cocktail (potent mixes, one for each sign, €6) in the darkness. (Open Th-Sa 11pm-4am.) If you stay around the Pl. Mayor, head to the Pl. de Ronda, facing the Cathedral. Hug the right side and head downhill to **Tascazoco,** Pl. de Ronda, with an airy terrace and impressive wine cellar (☎969 23 78 87; open W-Sa 10:30am-4pm and 8-close, Su 11am-4:30pm.)

EXTREMADURA

At first glance, Extremadura seems in no hurry to step into the 21st century. With an endless landscape of thirsty soil, scattered lakes, occasional sunflower fields, and gorgeous stone towns, the region seems stilled by time. Even Extremaduran cuisine reflects a pastoral age; local specialties include rabbit, partridge, lizard with green sauce, wild pigeon with herbs, and *migas extremeñas* (fried bread crumbs). Fittingly, Mérida's ancient Roman ruins and the hushed beauty of Trujillo and Cáceres are now beginning to draw flocks of admirers looking for the "classic" Spanish countryside.

CÁCERES ☎927

Cáceres's *barrio antiguo* (old city) is like a sudden time warp. The bustle of the modern city is silenced by an overwhelming wave of medieval antiquity. Built between the 14th and 16th centuries by rival noble families in a sort of architectural war for prestige and socio-political control, the *barrio antiguo* is comprised of miniature palaces once used to show off each family's power and wealth. Wander through this magnificent maze of tiny streets with palaces on almost every corner, and don't forget to pay your respects to the city's modern sentinels: innumerable storks keep watch from their posts on the roofs and towers. The cheerful nightlife and intriguing old city provide more than enough amusement for a one- or two-night stay.

TRANSPORTATION

Trains: RENFE (☎927 23 37 61), on Av. de Alemania, 3km from the old city. Across the highway from the bus station. Open daily 9am-9pm. To: **Badajoz** (2hr., 4 per day 6:40am-10pm, €15); **Madrid** (4hr., 6 per day 4:10am-6:51pm, €16-35); **Sevilla** (4hr., 8:33am, €15) via **Mérida** (1hr., €5.25).

Buses: (☎927 23 25 50), on Av. de la Hispanidad. Info open daily 8:30am-7:30pm; closed Su 2-3pm. Fewer buses available in July and August. Buses to: **Badajoz** (1hr.; 2-6 per day M-F 7:30am-7:30pm, Sa 8:30am and 2:30pm, Su 2:30pm-9pm; €6.48); **Madrid** (4-5hr., 7-9 per day 1:45am-6pm, €18.35); **Mérida** (1hr.; 2-6 per day M-Th 6:30am-7:30pm, F 6:30am-8:30pm, Sa 1 and 5pm, Su 10am-9:30pm; €4.33); **Salamanca** (4hr.; 7-28 per day M-F 7:15am-9:25pm, Sa 7:15am-10:15pm, Su 9:30am-12:45am; €12.83-13); **Sevilla** (4hr., 8-14 per day 4:10am-1:45am, €16.09); **Trujillo** (45min.; M-F 4 per day 11am-5:30pm, Sa 1pm, Su 7:30pm; €3); **Valladolid** (5hr.; noon, 6:15pm; €18.50).

Taxis: Phono Taxi (☎927 21 21 21) or **Radio Taxi** (☎927 23 23 23). Stands at Pl. Mayor, Pl. de San Juan, and bus and train stations.

Car Rental: Avis (☎927 23 57 21), in the bus station. 23+. 1-day rental from €80. Open summer M-F 9:30am-1pm and 5-8pm, Sa 9:30am-1pm; winter M-F 5-8pm.

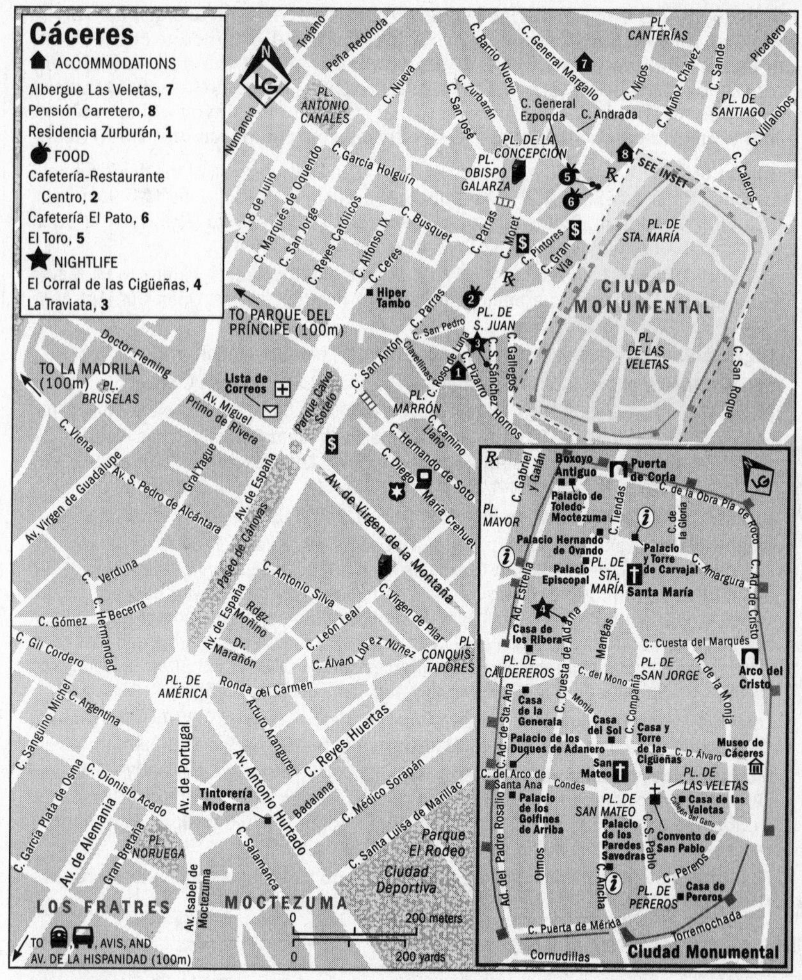

ORIENTATION AND PRACTICAL INFORMATION

The *ciudad monumental* (also called the *barrio antiguo*) and the commercial **Avenida de España** flank the **Plaza Mayor.** The plaza is 3km from the bus and train stations, which face each other across the rotary intersection of Av. de la Hispanidad and Av. de Alemania. From the bus or train station, the best way to get to the center of town is via **Bus #1** (€0.75 per ride, 10 rides for €5.50); from the station, walk out the exit opposite the buses, and turn left uphill. Turn right at the intersection, and the bus stop is past the gas station on the same side of the street. Hop off at **Plaza Obispo Galarza.** Facing the bus stop, walk right and take the first left down the steps across from the "Pl. Mayor 80m" sign. At the first intersection, turn right, then left to continue downhill and past the next street, following the "Centro Historico" signs. When you reach the arches, Pl. Mayor will be on the left. **Bus #2** stops on Av. de la Hispanidad, around the corner from the bus station, and runs to Pl. de América, the hub of the new downtown. From there, signs point up tree-lined Av. de España (Paseo de Cánovas) toward the Pl. Mayor. Walking from the bus or train station to Pl. Mayor will take about a half hour and can be trying in the sweltering Extremaduran afternoon heat.

Tourist Office: Pl. Mayor, 9-10 (☎927 01 08 34), in the outer wall of the *ciudad monumental.* Open July-Sept. M-F 8am-3pm, Sa-Su 10am-2pm; Oct.-June M-F 9am-2pm, Sa-Su 9:45am-2pm. Branch office at C. Ancha, 7 (☎927 24 71 72). Open Tu-Su in summer 10am-2pm and 5:30-8:30pm; in winter 4:30-7:30pm.

Currency Exchange: Banks line the Av. de España and the streets leading to Pl. Mayor. Caja de Extremadura has a branch on Pl. Mayor near C. Pintores. Open Oct.-Apr. M-W and F 9am-2pm, Th 5-6:45pm.

Luggage Storage: Train station (€3 per bag per day) and bus station (€2).

Police: Municipal (☎092/091, 112 emergency), on C. Diego María Crehuet.

Pharmacies: Farmacia Castel, Pl. Mayor, 28A (☎927 24 50 87). Open M-F 9:30am-2pm and 5:30-8:30pm, Sa-Su 9:30am-2pm. **Farmacia Jiménez Robledo,** C. los Pintores, 27 (☎927 24 55 28). Posts a list of 24hr. pharmacies. **24hr. pharmacy:** D. Matilde Torres Muñoz, Av. Virgen de la Montaña, 6. (☎927 62 66 60).

Hospital: Hospital Virgen de la Montaña (☎927 25 68 00), on Av. de España, 2.

Libraries: Biblioteca Municipal, Pl. de la Concepción, 2 (☎927 26 00 15). Located inside the Palacio de la Isla, 1st fl. exhibits local art. Building open for tourist visits M-F 9am-9pm, Sa 9am-2pm. Library on the 2nd fl. has 4 computers with internet access. Open M-F 10am-9pm, Sa 10am-2pm. **Biblioteca Pública,** on the corner of Av. Virgen de la Montaña and C. León Leal (☎927 00 68 60). Renovated in marble and glass, the library has computers on the 2nd fl. for internet access. Open M-F 9:30am-1:30pm and 5-8pm, Sa-Su 9am-2pm and 5-9pm. July-Aug. daily 8:15am-2:45pm.

Laundry: Tintorería Moderna, Av. de Antonio Hurtado, 16 (☎927 22 00 66; www.tintoreriamoderna.com). Open M-F 9:30am-2pm and 5-8pm, Sa 9:30am-2pm.

Internet Access: Ciberjust, C. Diego María Crehuet, 7 (☎927 21 46 77). €1 per 25min. Free coffee 10am-noon and 4:30-6pm. Open M-F 10:30am-2:30pm and 4:30pm-midnight, Sa noon-2:30pm and 5-11:30pm, Su 5-11:30pm. Free internet access available at the public and municipal libraries.

Post Office: Av. Miguel Primo de Rivera (☎927 62 66 81). Stamps and Lista de Correos. Open M-F 8:30am-8:30pm, Sa 9:30am-2pm. **Postal Code:** 10071.

ACCOMMODATIONS

Hostels are scattered throughout the new city and line Pl. Mayor in the old town. Prices rise during festivals, and advance reservations are recommended on summer weekends, especially for *pensiones* near Pl. Mayor.

Pensión Carretero, Pl. Mayor, 22 (☎927 24 74 82; pens_carretero@yahoo.es). Spacious rooms with painted tile floors and some with balcony views of the plaza. Hospitable, informative staff. Prime location; the balconies allow you to take in the sounds, not just the views, of the main square. Communal bath. Curfew 1am. Singles €20; doubles €30; triples €40. Sept.-May €15/20/35. AmEx/MC/V. ❷

Albergue Turistico "Las Veletas," C. Margallo, 36 (☎927 21 12 10). Located on a side street off the Pl. Mayor, this tranquil haven has a garden, a spectacular view of Caceres from its south facade, and free Wi-Fi access if you ask the wonderful owner, Juani. Rooms come in 3 packages: *peregrino* (up to 6 beds in a room) €18.50, *turistas* (singles) €20, or *turistas* with breakfast included, €21, with two large single-sex communal baths on each of its floors. Ask for other meal options (up to €8 for dinner) or laundry service on W (up to €5 for a big load). Curfew 1am. MC/V. ❷

Residencia Zurbarán, C. Roso de Luna, 11 (☎927 21 04 52). Popular with study-abroad students who live here all semester or summer. Clean rooms are basic; all have desks and some have TVs. Two hall baths. Singles €20; doubles €35. Cash only. ❷

FOOD

Pl. Mayor overflows with restaurants and cafes serving up *bocadillos*, *raciones*, and *extremeño* specialties. Side streets and newer parts of the city offer less-touristy bars and pastry shops. **Hiper Tambo,** C. Alfonso IX, 25, has wine and groceries and boasts an impressive deli and counters with ready-to-eat meals. (☎927 21 17 71. Open M-Sa 9:30am-9pm. AmEx/MC/V.)

El Toro, C. General Ezponda, 2 (☎927 21 15 48). Spanish cuisine in an upscale setting glorifying the bullfight—costumes, brands, and autographed pictures. Animal rights activists may want to ask for a table facing away from the stuffed bull's head. Entrees €8-14. Open Sa-Su 11am-afternoon. MC/V. ❸

Cafetería El Pato, (☎927 24 67 36) in the Pl. Mayor, 14. Co-owned with El Toro. Take in the stork-scattered walls of the old city while the friendly staff dishes out everything from ham and eggs to ewe's milk cheese sandwiches. Entrees €6.60-15. *Menú* €10-13. Open Tu-Sa noon-4pm and 8pm-midnight. V. ❷

Cafetería-Restaurante Centro, C. Pintores, 34 (☎927 26 00 09). This convenient *extremeño* restaurant has outdoor seating right in the middle of the square (Pl. San Juan). Social atmosphere and a local crowd. Ask for the menu in English to help navigate through the local specialties. Entrees €4-12. Combination plates €7-9. *Menú* €8.50-9.50. Open daily 11am-11pm. AmEx/MC/V. ❷

SIGHTS

The golden *ciudad monumental* is a melting pot of styles: wealthy Spanish families incorporated Roman, Arabic, Gothic, Renaissance, and even Incan influences (brought back by the *conquistadores*) into their palaces. The main attraction is the neighborhood itself, since most buildings don't let tourists in beyond a peek into the patio from an open door. From Pl. Mayor, take the stairs from the left of the tourist office to the Arco de la Estrella.

MUSEO DE CÁCERES. The **Casa de las Veletas** (House of the Weathervanes) displays ethnographic and archeological pieces about Cáceres's early history, Celtiberian stone animals, Visigothic tombstones, and an astonishing **Almohade aljibe** (cistern). Through a garden adjoinng the main building, morning visitors can access the must-see **Casa de los Caballos,** the museum's Fine Arts Collection, which houses a tiny but brilliant "Who's Who" of Spanish art. It features originals by El Greco, Picasso, Miró, and recent abstractionist stars, along with rotating exhibits. *(Pl. de las Veletas, 1. ☎927 01 08 77. Open Apr.-Sept. Tu-Sa 9am-2:30pm and 5-8:15pm, Su 10:15am-2:30pm; Oct.-Apr. Tu-Sa 9am-2:30pm and 4-7:15pm, Su 10:15am-2:30pm. €1.20; students, seniors, and EU citizens free. Free on Su.)*

IGLESIA CONCATEDRAL DE SANTA MARÍA. A statue of San Pedro de Alcántara, one of Extremadura's two patron saints, eyes Pl. de Sta. María from a corner pedestal outside the cathedral—his shiny toes are the result of many years of good-luck foot rubs. The Gothic cathedral, built between the 15th and 16th centuries, with uncharacteristically visible outlines of its stone composition, looks almost as if it were built inside-out. The red sun painted on the ceiling overlooks the intricate, 16th-century wooden altar and the eroded tombstones on the cathedral's floor. Climb up the bell tower for a panoramic view of Cáceres.

(Pl. de Sta. María. ☎927 21 53 13. Open M-Sa 10am-2pm and 5-8pm, Su 9:30am-2pm and 5-7:30pm. €1. Audio tour near right sub-altar €1. Entrance to the bell tower €1.)

CONVENTO DE SAN PABLO. This late-Gothic convent is eye candy for architecture addicts. Cloistered nuns sell delicious **homemade pastries** through a peculiar rotating window called a *torno*, which protects the sisters from the unholy gaze of customers. Locals highly recommend the *bocaditos de almendra* (almond-paste cupcakes). Make sure you bring an appetite—these babies come by the kilo (€19). Have your pastry selection ready from the list on the wall, ring the bell by the window, even if the door seems closed, and ask politely. *(Pl. de San Pablo. To the left of Casa y Torre de las Cigüeñas. Open M-Sa 9am-1pm and 5-8pm. Pastries €2.50-12 per dozen, up to €24 per kilo.)*

CASA Y TORRE DE LAS CIGÜEÑAS. Cáceres's aristocracy was a warring lot, so in the 15th century, the monarchy removed all battlements and spires from local lords' houses as punishment. Due to Don Golfin's loyalty to the ruling family, however, his Casa y Torre de las Cigüeñas (House and Tower of the Storks) was the lone estate allowed to keep its battlements. The storks are still grateful. Only the ground floor is accessible to the public, but its imposing collection of medieval arms and fully armored knight in the stairwell are certainly worth a peek. *(From Arco de la Estrella, take a right up the hill, a left onto Adarve de Sta. Ana, then a right and a quick left onto C. de los Condes. Cross Pl. de San Mateo to Pl. de San Pablo; the house and the tower are on the left. Free.)*

PALACIO Y TORRE DE CARVAJAL. This mansion's roof houses a tourist office, museum, and art exhibit, but its real selling point is that it's one of the few *palacios* in the city open to the public. The museum has three rooms of colorful models, stuffed wildlife, photos, and video clips of *extremeño* villages and artisans. The tourist office hands out large maps of the *ciudad monumental* and information about upcoming festivals and events. Outside, the 500-year-old garden is still lovingly maintained, backed by a wall of roses and centered with a beautiful fig tree. *(From C. Arco de la Estrella, walk up to Pl. Santa Maria la Mayor; it is to the left of the cathedral, on the corner of C. Amargura. Open M-F 8am-8pm, Sa-Su 10am-2pm. Free.)*

OTHER SIGHTS. Most *palacios* and *casas* in the *ciudad monumental* are still inhabited and closed to visitors. The 16th-century **Casa del Sol** is the most famous of Cáceres's numerous mansions; its crest is the city's emblem. The **Casa de Toledo-Moctezuma** was built by the grandson of the Aztec princess Isabel Moctezuma to represent the union of two worlds, and holds spectacular friezes with Roman and Aztec personages. *(On Pl. del Conde de Canilleros, to the left as you enter Arco de la Estrella.)* On October 26, 1936, in the **Palacio de los Golfines de Arriba,** Franco was proclaimed head of the Spanish state and general of its armies. *(Between C. de Olmos and C. Adarve del Padre Rosalío, just before the Restaurante Los Golfines.)* For enthusiasts of the old city's Arabic past, the **Casa Museo Árabe de Cáceres** holds its own against its neighbors. The small museum, flanking a beautiful patio, is filled with weaponry and curiosities. *(On C. Cuesta de Marques, 4. Facing la Iglesia de Sta. Maria, walk forward to the right onto C. Cuesta de Marques.*

CASTILLA LA MANCHA AND EXTREMADURA

NIGHTLIFE

Just follow the noise for a tipsy evening in Cáceres—old nobles never had it this good. Local revelry begins in Pl. Mayor and along C. Pizarro, lined with bars showcasing live music. **La Traviata,** C. Sergio Sánchez, 8, is a colorful, artsy, and hip musical cafe that blasts a mix of lounge, techno, and pop, and hosts one-man shows on Thursdays at 10:30pm. (☎927 21 13 74. Giant espresso €1. Beer €2.50. Mixed drinks €4.50. Open M-Th and Su 4pm-3am, F-Sa 4pm-3:30am. Cash only.) For live jazz, poetry festivals, and free tarot card readings in a backyard setting, head to **El Corral de las Cigüeñas,** Cuesta de Aldana, 6, in the old city. Enclosed by vine-covered walls but open to a star- and sparrow-filled sky in the *ciudad monumental*, El Corral offers mellow music and occasional Friday night concerts for €3-8. (Beer €1.80-2.20. Mixed drinks from €5. Breakfast 8am-1pm. Open daily 7pm-last customer. AmEx/MC/V.) Later, the party migrates to **La Madrila,** an area near Pl. del Albatros in the new city, where clubs pound through the night. From Pl. Mayor, head to main strip Av. de España, take a right onto Av. Miguel Primo de Rivera, and cross the intersection onto C. Dr. Fleming. You'll hear the party.

DAYTRIP FROM CÁCERES

GUADALUPE

Transportation to and from Guadalupe can be somewhat tricky; most visitors arrive via tour bus or in their own cars. Empresa Mirat (☎927 23 48 63) sends buses from Cáceres to Guadalupe (2hr.; M-Sa 1pm, 5:30pm; €7.70) and back (M-Sa 6:45 and 7:30am).

Guadalupe rests on a mountainside in the Sierra de Guadalupe, 2hr. east of Trujillo and 4hr. southwest of Madrid. Considered the religious center of Extremadura, the eclectic **Real Monasterio de Santa María de Guadalupe** is worth a daytrip, particularly for pilgrims and those with an interest in history, art, and architecture. A World Heritage Site, the fairy-tale monastery has been compared to a Spanish Sistine Chapel. Its 25,000 square meters host an incredible collection of artwork, including works by Zurbarán and El Greco, and a *mudéjar*-style central courtyard. At the Battle of Salado in 1340, Alfonso XI, believed to have been aided by the Virgin Mary, defeated the superior Muslim army. As a token of his gratitude, he commissioned the lavish Real Monasterio. Years later, it became customary to grant licenses for foreign expeditions on the premises; in fact, Columbus finalized his contract with Fernando and Isabel here. In homage to the city, he named one of the islands he discovered Guadalupe. The most prominent object in the basilica is the **Icon of the Virgin,** carved out of wood, blackened with age, and cloaked in robes of silver and gold. Look for a score of illuminated manuscripts and marvel at the embroidered robes and gowns, sculptures, and paintings. (☎927 36 70 00; www.monasterioguadalupe.com. Monastery open daily 9:30am-1pm and 3:30-6:30pm. €4, discounts for seniors, groups and those younger than 14.) The **tourist office** in Pl. Mayor posts information on the door; follow signs from the bus station. (☎927 15 41 28. Open June-Aug. Tu-F 10am-2pm and 5-7pm, Sa-Su 10am-2pm; Sept.-May Tu-F 10am-2pm and 4-6pm, Sa-Su 10am-2pm.) Travelers looking for *bocadillos* or beds (singles generally €20) should head to Pl. Mayor.

TRUJILLO ☎927

An enchanting Old World town, hilltop Trujillo is the gem of Extremadura. Often called the "Cradle of Conquistadors," Trujillo furnished history with over 600 explorers of the New World, including Peru's conqueror, Francisco Pizarro, and the Amazon's first European explorer, Francisco de Orellana. Scattered with medieval palaces, Roman ruins, an Arabic fortress, and churches from every era, Trujillo, a perfect get-away from the big city, bears the imprint of the various cultures here throughout history. A past haven for kings and queens, Trujillo's friendly locals continue to extend a warm welcome.

TRANSPORTATION

The bus station (☎927 32 12 02), Av. de Miajadas, s/n, is at the bottom of town. Look for the AutoRes sign. Since most buses stop only en route to larger destinations, reserve a seat in advance. Buses run to **Badajoz** (2hr., 10 per day 4:15am-11:55pm, €9.65-14.30, **Cáceres** (45min., 9per day 7:05am-10:30pm, €3.07), and **Madrid** (2hr., 5-8 per day 10am-6:40pm, €16.18). Bus station open M-Sa 6:15am-10:30pm; Su 8:15am-10:30pm.

PRACTICAL INFORMATION

An English-speaking staff sells *bono* tickets (multi-day tourist passes) at the **tourist office** in Pl. Mayor, on the left when facing Pizarro's statue. Info is posted on the windows when it is closed. Guided tours (€6.75) leave from in front of the tourist office at 11am and 5pm. (☎927 32 26 77; www.trujillo.es. Open daily June-Sept. 10am-2pm and 4:30-7:30pm; Oct.-May 9:30am-2pm and 4-7pm.) Local services include: **currency exchange** and **ATM** at **Banco Santander Central Hispano,** Pl. Mayor, 25 (☎927 24 24 24; open Apr.-Sept. M-F 8:30am-2:30pm; Oct.-Mar. M-F 8:30am-2:30pm, Sa 8:30am-1pm); **police,** C. Carnicería, 2, just off Pl. Mayor (☎927 32 01 08); **Centro de Salud,** Av. Ramón y Cajal, s/n, (☎927 32 20 16) for **medical emergencies; internet access** at Ciberalia, C. Tiendas, 18, off Pl. Mayor (☎927 65 90 89; €2 for 1hr.; open daily noon-midnight); and the **post office,** Po. Ruiz de Mendoza, 28, on the way from the bus station to Pl. Mayor (☎927 32 05 33; open M-F 8:30am-2:30pm, Sa 9:30am-1pm). **Postal Code:** 10200.

ACCOMMODATIONS

Alojamientos "Plaza Mayor," Pl. Mayor, 6 (☎927 32 23 13). One of the best deals in town. Complete bathrooms, TV, and A/C. If no one responds to the bell, it's because the owner mans an *artesanía* shop next to the public bathrooms in the Pl. Mayor. Singles €20; doubles €36; rooms overlooking the plaza €5 more. MC/V. ❷

Pensión Boni, C. Mingos Ramos, 11 (☎927 32 16 04). Off Pl. Mayor, and run by a friendly German/Spanish couple. Rooms have large windows and small balconies over a winding street. Hostel is steps away from major sights. Singles €15; doubles €20; triples €40, with bath €30-35. Extra bed €10. Cash only. ❶

Hostal Trujillo, C. Francisco Pizarro, 4-6 (☎927 32 22 74; www.hostaltrujillo.com). From the bus station, turn left onto C. de las Cruces, right onto C. de la Encarnación, then right again onto C. Francisco Pizarro. Get medieval with armor, lance, and shield-bedecked halls in this renovated 15th-century hospital. Rooms have cushy beds, bath, A/C, and satellite TV. Reception 9am-11pm. Singles €40; doubles €50; triples €70; quads €90. Parking €7. AmEx/MC/V. ❹

FOOD

Meals in Trujillo's historic center are overpriced, but cheaper deals hide on the side streets and at the bottom of the hill leading to Pl. Mayor. For groceries, head to **Eroski**, Av. Monfragüe (open M-Sa 9:30am-10pm; AmEx/MC/V).

Churrería El Paseo, Po. Ruiz de Mendoza (☎927 32 21 67). Made fresh all morning, these *churros* (€0.25 each) are best dipped in *café con leche* or hot chocolate (both €1.10). Open daily 8am-noon. Cash only. ❶

Restaurante El Paseo, Po. Ruiz de Mendoza (☎609 30 75 33). With eclectic world music, a friendly staff, and a great lunch atmosphere, this welcoming restaurant up the steps from the *churrería* offers *bocadillos* (€3-5), *raciones* (€8-12), and a 4-course *menú* for only €14. Try the mixed salads. Open daily 9am-3pm and 7pm-midnight. ❷

La Tahona, C. Afueras, 2 (☎927 32 18 49). Serves affordable homemade pizzas (€3.50-9), pastas (€4-5.20), and sandwiches (€2.10-3). Exit Pl. Mayor by the church and walk 3 blocks. Open M 7:30pm-midnight, Tu-Su 1-4pm. Cash only. ❶

SIGHTS

Though much of Trujillo is walkable within an hour, its over 30 sites of interest offer diversions worthy of a much larger city. A **bono ticket** (€4.70), available at the tourist office, allows entrance to the Casa-Museo de Pizarro, the Castillo Árabe, the Museo del Queso y del Vino, and Iglesia de Santiago, and includes a guidebook. The tourist office runs tours of the old city (€6.75), including the Museo del Traje and the Aljibe Palacio Altamirano, twice daily. Crowning the hill are the ruins and cistern of the 10th-century Castillo Árabe. Enjoy a view of unspoiled landscape, with Trujillo on one side and fields scattered with ancient battlements on the other.

IGLESIA DE SANTA MARÍA LA MAYOR. Take a left from the 13th-century Puerta de Santiago onto C. de las Cambroneras and turn right on C. Santa María. Visit the church's breathtaking 25-panel Gothic altarpiece, painted by master Fernando Gallego in 1480, and the church tower. The 100 steps leading to the top of the Romanesque church tower are a workout, but you'll feel Extremaduran winds before a **panoramic view** of brick rooftops, castle ruins, church towers, distant mountains, and lakes. *(Open daily May-Oct. 10am-2pm and 4:30-8:30pm; Nov.-Apr. 10am-2pm and 4-6:30pm. Mass Su 11am. €1.25.)*

MUSEO DEL TRAJE. To the left of the Iglesia de Santa María and up the steps is this restored convent. Step inside for a spectacular exhibition of evening gowns worn by royalty, songstresses, and actresses from the 17-20th centuries. *(C. Ballesteros, 8. Open daily 10:30am-2pm and 4:30-7:30pm. €1.50.)*

CASA-MUSEO DE PIZARRO. To reach the Casa-Museo, take a right from the Museo del Traje and walk up the street about 2min. The ground floor reproduces a 15th-century nobleman's living quarters, while the top floor is dedicated to the life and times of Francisco Pizarro, with a focus on his time in Peru. The beautiful museum courtyard features Latin American plants introduced to Europe. *(Open daily 10am-2pm and 5-8pm. €1.40. English or Spanish guides €0.50.)*

MUSEO DEL QUESO Y DEL VINO. This *museo* is far from the other sights, at the bottom of the hill. To get there, turn left on Ruiz de Mendoza at the post office, and look for the sign at the corner of Ruiz de Mendoza and C. Francisco Pizarro. Exhibits tell the centuries-old story of wine production and shares tips on how to enjoy artisanal wine and cheese. Locals recommend also visiting a local cheese shop for further tastings. *(☎927 32 30 31. Open daily May-Sept. 11am-3pm and 6-8pm; Oct.-Apr. 11am-3pm and 5:30-7:30pm. Tickets €1.30, with tasting €2.40.)*

PLAZA MAYOR. Trujillo's Plaza Mayor was the inspiration for the Plaza de Armas in Cuzco, Peru, constructed after Francisco Pizarro defeated the Incas. Festooned with stork nests, **Iglesia de San Martín** dominates the plaza's northeastern corner and offers a nice respite from the heat. *(Open M-Sa 10am-2pm and 5-7:45pm, Su 10am-2pm and 4:30-7pm. €1.40. Mass in summer M-Sa 8:30pm, Su 1 and 8:30pm; in winter M-Sa 7:30pm, Su 1 and 7:30pm. Free.)* Across the street, visit the **Palacio de los Duques de San Carlos,** built in the 16th century to celebrate the powerful family alliance of Vargas and Carvajal. The palace now houses a cloistered convent for the females of the St. Jerónimo order and has a sanctuary dedicated to la Virgen de Guadalupe. They, too, sell sweets by the dozen for up to €10. *(Open M-Sa 9:30am-1pm and 4:30-6:30pm, Su 10am-12:30pm. €1.40.)*

NIGHTLIFE

Don't be surprised if you find yourself pre-gaming under the statue of Hernán Cortes. Although relatively quiet during the day, the city fills with crowds at the three local spots until the wee hours of the morning. "¡*Sólo uno más!* (Just one more!)" seems to be the rallying cry of Trujillanos.

Vilu, C. Sillerías, 1 (☎659 20 06 43). This small bar is a popular student hangout frequented by locals of all ages. If you happen to lose in one of the common drinking games, beware of the *chupitos* that come from the barrel in the center of the bar—these kicks are a lot to handle. Beers €2. Mixed drinks €4. Open daily 3pm-late.

Vendetta, C. de las Palmas. From Pl. Mayor, walk to the right of the statue past the Iglesia de San Martín on C. Afuera. Follow the noise on the 2nd street on the right. A central spot for partiers of all ages, where an unapologetic "We Own the Night!" emblazoned on the wall, next to shaded gangsters, encourages unabashed partying and dancing—no wonder the place is always full. Beers €2.50. Mixed drinks €4. Open Th-Sa 11pm-late.

MÉRIDA ☎924

For Roman ruins per square foot, Mérida can't be beat. In 26 BC, as a reward for services rendered to the Roman Empire, Augustus Caesar granted a group of veteran legionnaires a new city in Lusitania, a province comprising Portugal and part of Spain. The veterans chose a lovely spot surrounded by hills on the banks of the Río Guadiana to found their new home, which they named Emerita Augusta. Itching to gossip with fellow patricians in Sevilla and Salamanca, the soldiers built the largest bridge in Lusitania, the Puente Romano. The nostalgic crew adorned their "little Rome" with baths, aqueducts, a hippodrome, an arena, and a famous amphitheater. Modern Mérida complements the Roman buildings with walkways, small plazas, and the world-class Museo Nacional de Arte Romano. In July and August, the spectacular Festival de Teatro Clásico offers some of Europe's best classical and modern theater and dance.

TRANSPORTATION

Trains: C. Carderos (☎902 24 02 02). Info open daily 7am-10pm. Tickets sold 9am-9pm. To: **Badajoz** (1hr.; M-Sa 8 per day 7:44am-9:25pm, Su 6 per day 9:48am-10:25pm; €2.80-11.50); **Barcelona** (11hr.; 7:17, 8:20am; €30.60-76.80); **Cáceres** (1hr., 3-6 per day 5:30am-8:45pm, €3.40-12.50); **Madrid** (4-6hr., 4-5 per day 5:30am-3:27pm, €15.30-40); **Sevilla** (4hr., 9:45am, €11.30).

Buses: Av. de la Libertad (☎924 37 14 04). Info open M-F 7am-11pm, Sa-Su 7am-1pm. **ALSA** (☎902 42 22 42) to **Sevilla** (3hr., 6-7 per day 2:35am-10:45pm, €11). **AutoRes** (☎924 37 19 55) to **Madrid** (5hr.; 7-9 per day M-Sa 1:15am-4:45pm, F also at 7:15pm, Su 9:55am-7:15pm; €19-24). **LEDA** (☎924 37 14 03) to **Badajoz** (1hr.; 4-11 per day M-F 6:45am-12:50am, Sa 8:45am-10:50pm, Su noon-10:50pm; €4.28); **Cáceres** (1hr.; 1-4 per day M-F 9:20am-9:15pm, Sa 9:55am and 3:50pm, Su 7:10pm; €4.76); and **Sevilla** (3hr.; 7-9 per day M-F 5:45am-8:30pm, Sa 7am-9:50pm, Su 9am-11:05pm; €12.25).

Taxis: Teletaxi (☎924 31 57 56) or **Radio Taxi** (☎924 37 11 11). Both 24hr.

Car Rental: Avis (☎924 37 33 11), at the bus station. 23+. From €94.23 per day plus taxes. Insurance included. Open M-F 9am-1pm and 4:30-7:30pm, Sa 9:30am-1pm.

ORIENTATION AND PRACTICAL INFORMATION

Everything in Mérida is relatively close together and easily accessible by foot, but you'll be hard-pressed to pack it all into one day. **Plaza de España,** the town center, is two blocks up from the **Puente Romano** and easily accessible from the Teatro Romano. Walking outward from the center, cafes and shops around the plaza quickly transform into quiet residential neighborhoods, and streets often lose their signs. To reach Pl. de España from the bus station, cross the suspension bridge and turn right onto Av. de Roma. Better yet, catch the **#4 bus** at the stop across the street from the bus station (€1). Continue along the river until you reach the Puente Romano, then turn left onto C. del Puente. From the train station, take C. Carderos and its continuation, C. Camilo José Cela; bear right onto C. Félix Valverde Lillo and follow it to Pl. de España. Banks and currency exchange line C. Santa Eulalia leading to Pl. de España.

Tourist Office: Municipal Office, C. Santa Eulalia, 64 (☎924 33 07 22). Maps and information on monuments and municipal events. English spoken. Open daily in summer 10am-2pm and 5-8pm; in winter 10am-2pm and 4-7pm.

Centro Cultural Alcazaba, C. John Lennon, 5 (☎924 33 06 02). Walk up the winding ramp or take the glass elevator to the 4th fl., to an extensive DVD collection and free internet access at the city library. (☎92433 06 02. Open in summer M-F 8:30am-2:30pm; in winter M-F 9am-2:30pm and 5-8pm, Sa 10:30am-1pm.) While you're there, peruse the geology museum, municipal historical records, regional collection of prehistory, or examine the Roman ruins found during the center's construction. Ask for a schedule of cultural events and shows. Open until 5pm in summer; in winter 9pm.

Banks: Caixa Galicia, Av. Almendralejo, 12. Open M-F 8:30am-2pm. Banks also line C. Santa Eulalia.

Laundry: Tintoreria Guerrero Lavanderia, Pl. del Rastro, 10, near C. Romero Leal Político (☎ 924 31 42 57). Open M-F 10am-2pm and 5-8pm, Sa 10am-2pm.

Police: Av. Almendralejo (☎092 or 924 38 01 38).

Pharmacy: Juan Vacas Angulo, corner of S. San Salvador and C. Holguín (☎924 31 34 08). Open daily 9:30am-10pm. Several pharmacies also on the corner of C. Los Maestros and C. Cuarez Somonte.

Hospital: Residencia Sanitaria de la Seguridad Social Centralita (☎924 38 10 00). **Red Cross,** Ctra. de Caceres (☎924 33 03 53). Emergencies (☎112).

Internet Access: Friends Online Ciber, C. Romero Leal, 7. €1 per 30min. (☎924 30 41 54. Open M-Sa 11am-2pm and 5pm-10pm. **Centro Cultural Alcazaba** (see above).

Post Office: Pl. de la Constitución (☎924 31 24 58; fax 30 24 56). Open July 15-Sept. 15 M-F 8:30am-2:30pm, Sa 9:30am-1pm; Sept. 16-July 14 M-F 8:30am-8:30pm, Sa 9:30am-1pm. **Postal Code:** 06800.

ACCOMMODATIONS

Despite the flocks of tourists, finding a reasonably priced room in Mérida won't leave you in ruins. Check the tourist office for complete listings.

Hostal El Alferero, C. Sagasta, 40 (☎924 30 31 83; www.hostalelalfarero.com). Colorful luxury in gorgeously decorated rooms, all with bath (with hydromassage shower), TV, and A/C, and some with balconies. Ceramics and pottery cover every available surface. Check in before 10pm. Apr.-Oct. and Dec. 22-31 doubles €50; triples €65; quads €80. Nov.-Dec. 21 and Jan.-Mar. €40/55. MC/V. ❷

Hostal Senero, C. Holguín, 12 (☎924 31 72 07; www.hostalsenero.com). A beautifully tiled staircase leads to large, white-walled rooms, all with TV and A/C, some with balconies over the quiet street. English spoken. Reception open 8am-midnight. Mar. 14-Oct. 15 and Dec. 1-31, singles €25, with bath €28; doubles €34/40. Jan. 1-Mar. 13 and Oct. 16- Nov. 30, singles €22/24; doubles €30/34. AmEx/MC/V. ❷

Hostal Nueva España, Av. de Extremadura, 6 (☎924 31 33 56). This well-located *hostal,* steps away from the Basílica, offers spacious rooms with private bath. Singles with A/C €25; doubles €35/38; triples €50. MC/V. ❷

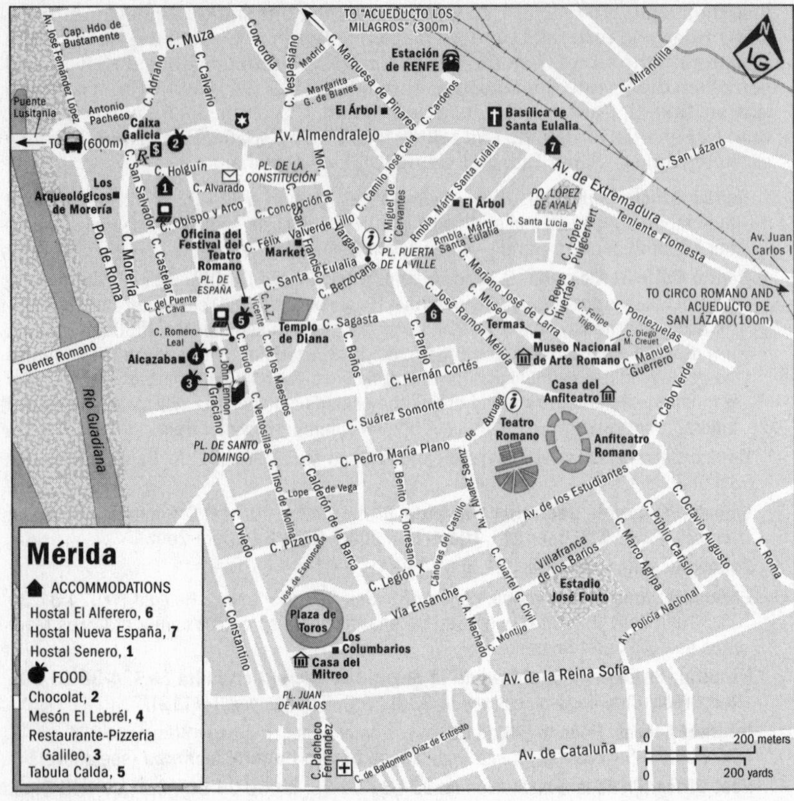

FOOD

Pl. de España is filled with cafes, but none is a steal. Look for cheaper options on nearby C. John Lennon or in cafes near the train station, or buy fresh food at the **Mercado Municipal de Calatrava** on the corner of C. Félix Valverde Lillo and C. Camilo José Cela. (Open M-Sa 8am-2pm.) There are several branches of the supermarket **El Árbol** including one at C. Félix Valverde Lillo, 8 (☎924 30 13 56; open M-F 9:30am-2pm and 6-9pm, Sa 9:30am-2:30pm; MC/V) with others closer to the train station on C. Marquesa de Pinares or on Rambla Sta. Eulalia.

Restaurante-Pizzeria Galileo, C. John Lennon, 28 (☎924 31 55 05). A partially glass-floored dining room reveals Roman ruins below. 34 creative varieties of pizza are popular with local families. Desserts are imported from Italy weekly or made fresh in the restaurant. Entrees €3.50-11. Open Tu-Su 1:30-4pm and 8:30pm-12:30am. MC/V. ❶

Chocolat, C. Almendralejo, 8 (☎924 31 29 96). Start your day in true Spanish fashion, with a *café con leche* and the buzz of morning conversation in this old-world cafe. Filling breakfast for around €2, especially if you opt for the nearly solid hot chocolate and *churros* (both €1.20); *bocadillos* €1.50-3. Open M-F 8:30am-2pm and 6-10pm, Sa 9:30am-1:30pm and 6-10pm. Cash only. ❶

Mesón El Lebrel, C. John Lennon, 4 (☎924 31 57 57). Take the hallway to the right of the bar to treat yourself to the shade of cypresses and the stately Alcázar wall, if you don't mind the traffic nearby. A full range of rustic *extremeño* flavors, from just-right gazpacho to rare rabbit *pâté*. Entrees €5-10. *Bocadillos* €2-5. Open M and W-Su noon-4:30pm and 6:30pm-12:30am. MC/V. ❷

Tabula Calda, C. Romero Leal, 11 (☎924 30 49 50; www.tabulacalda.com). The delicious house special, a Sephardic Jewish salad with orange, sugar, and olive oil, comes free with every meal. Eclectic art surrounds tables in an intimate interior garden. Entrees €12. 3-course *menú* €14. Open daily June-Sept. 1-5:30pm and 8pm-12:30am; Oct.-May 1-4:30pm and 7:30pm-midnight. AmEx/MC/V. ❷

SIGHTS

From the **Puente Romano** to aqueducts to astrological mosaics, Mérida offers Spain's best glimpse at the Romans in Iberia. A **combined ticket,** valid for all the listings below except the Museo Nacional de Arte Romano, can be purchased at any of the sights. (Ticket is valid for several days; includes a guidebook to the ruins. €10, EU students €6, seniors and children 9-16 €7. €4 for each individual sight. Ruins open daily June-Sept. 9:30am-1:45pm and 5-7:15pm; Oct.-May 9:30am-1:45pm and 4-6:15pm.)

TEATRO ROMANO AND ANFITEATRO ROMANO. The spectacular *teatro* was a gift from Agrippa, a Roman administrator, in 16 BC. Its 6000 seats face a *scaenae frons*, an incredible marble colonnade. Today, the stage features performances of Spanish classical theater during the popular **Festival de Teatro Clásico** every July and August. *(Performances on alternate days July-Aug. 10:45pm. Info at the Oficina del Festival, C. Santa Eulalia, 4. ☎924 00 49 30; www.festivaldemerida.com. Tickets €10-40. Combined ticket for all performances €100-250. Consult tourist office Sept.-June for more info.)* Inaugurated in 8 BC, the *anfiteatro* was used for contests between all possible combinations of animals and men. The seats in some sections have succumbed to the elements, but the caves where the combatants were kept, now re-enforced with brick, are safe for an adventurous crawl. *(In the park across from the Museo Nacional; also accessible by tunnel from the crypt.)*

MUSEO NACIONAL DE ARTE ROMANO. The monumentality of this site, with more than three floors of columns, statues, coins, housewares, and other relics, testifies to the grandeur of the city's Roman heritage. The museum's giant mosaics are almost completely intact and cover the multi-story expanse between statues and ceiling. Downstairs, the crypt gives a glimpse into parts of an ancient street found during the museum's construction. A marked tunnel leads to theater/amphitheater areas. Budget at least a solid hour for the museum *(C. José Ramón Mélida, 2. ☎924 31 16 90. Open Mar.-Nov. Tu-Sa 10am-2pm and 4-9pm, Su and holidays 10am-2pm; Dec.-Feb. Tu-Sa 10am-2pm and 4-6pm, Su and holidays 10am-2pm. €2.40, students €1.20. Free for EU citizens, those under 18, and seniors 65 or older.)*

CASA DEL MITREO AND LOS COLUMBARIOS. Although the **Casa del Mitreo** is a bit of a hike from downtown, you'll thank your lucky stars when you see its Mosaico Cosmológico. Attributed as a probable shrine of the Mithraic cult, which gained popularity in the Roman empire near the end of the 1st century, the work is renowned among historians for its depiction of the Romans' conception of the world and the forces of nature. Sadly, only a third of the mosaic remains. It is worth the walk if you have a combination ticket. Adjoining the Casa del Mitreo are the **Columbarios,** communal Roman burial spaces.

CASA DEL ANFITEATRO. Do not be deterred by the **Casa del Anfiteatro's** unimpressive entrance; venture a few steps farther downhill, and you will find yourself walking on expanses of beautifully preserved mosaic floors. The site also features foundations, a Roman graveyard, and arrangements of residential quarters. *(Casa del Anfiteatro is between the Anfiteatro Romano and the Museo de Arte Romano.)*

OTHER SIGHTS AND RUINS. Two blocks directly behind the Museo de Arte Romano on C. Reyes Huertas are the ruins of **Las Termas** (the Baths). Apart from their obvious function, these baths were used to store ice year-round before their restocking at wintertime. Slightly farther down is the **Circo Romano,** also called the hippodrome or circus. The arena (capacity 30,000) is closed to the public, though the view from outside is still worth the trip. Next to the Circo are the remains of the Acueducto de San Lázaro. *(From C. Cabo Verde, take the pedestrian walkway under the train tracks.)* Don't miss the impressive **Acueducto Los Milagros** (Aqueduct of Miracles), complete with a row of ever-present storks. *(From Sta. Eulalia, turn right onto Av. de Extremadura, which becomes C. Marquesa de Pinares. The aqueducts are next to the train track.)* The last two stops on the combined ticket are the **Arqueológicos de Morería** and the **Alcazaba Árabe,** both of which are on Av. de Roma. Built from materials discarded by the Visigoths, the Alcazaba was designed by the Moors to guard the Roman bridge. Take a stroll around the **Templo de Diana** and the **Portico del Foro,** the best surprises on the mostly residential C. Sagasta; it is the only surviving Roman temple of worship and displays an impressive colonnaded facade. *(Pl. del Rastro near the Puente Romano.)*

BADAJOZ ☎924

Badajoz (pop. 120,000) is generally regarded as a transportation hub on the way into Portugal, but the city has recently refreshed its ruins, cleared up much of its industrial pollution, and added a tourist office, making forced layovers significantly more pleasant. Free sights and a contemporary art museum provide for an afternoon's distraction, while lively *zonas de pubs* and nightlife entice even Portuguese neighbors to cross the border and join the fun. If you find yourself in Badajoz during the Feria de San Juan (June 23-July 1), a one-week festival on the Spanish/Portuguese border with nightly bullfights, you will surely remember it—unless the partying leaves your memory a bit spotty.

TRANSPORTATION

From Badajoz, buses to Portugal are faster and more convenient than trains.

Trains: Av. Carolina Coronado (☎924 27 11 70). Open daily 9am-10pm. From the train station to Pl. de la Libertad, take bus #1. To: **Cáceres** (2hr.; M-F and Su 7:35am, 2:40pm, Sa 7:35am; €13.75-15); **Madrid** (5hr.; M-F and Su 3 per day 8:15am-2:30pm, Sa 8:15am, 12:30pm; €28-32); and **Mérida** (1hr., 4-7 per day 6:40am-7:45pm, €3-11).

Buses: Central Station, C. José Rebollo López, 2 (☎924 25 86 61). Info booth open daily 7:45am-12:30am. Buses #3, 6a, 6b, and 9 run between the station and Pl. de la Libertad (€0.70). Schedules are flexible; call ahead or ask the tourist office for a schedule. Intercity buses run more frequently Oct.-June.

ALSA to **Cáceres** (1hr.; M 3 per day 8am-4:30pm, Tu-Sa 9:30am, 4:30pm, Su 4:30pm; €7) via **Salamanca** (5hr., €15.30) and **Lisboa** (3hr.; 4am, 2:45pm; €17).

AutoRes (☎924 23 85 15) to **Cáceres** (1hr.; M-F 6per day 7:30am-7:30pm, Sa 8:30am and 2:30pm, Su 4 per day 2:30-9pm, €6.66); **Lisboa** (2hr., 4:15am and 7:15pm, €39); **Madrid** (4hr., 5:15am and 8pm, €25.83-32.25); **Trujillo** (2hr., 3:15pm and 12:15am; €10-14.30.

V. Caballero (☎924 25 57 56) to **Cáceres** (1hr.; M-F 3 per day 8:30am-7:30pm, Sa 8:30am and 2:30pm, Su 8pm; €6).

Damas to **Sevilla** (4hr.; M-F 6 per day 6:45am-8pm, Sa-Su 3-4 per day 9am-8pm; €12.20).

LEDA (☎924 23 34 78) to **Mérida** (1hr.; M-F 9 per day 6:45am-9:30pm, Sa 4 per day 9:30am-9:30pm, Su 3 per day 3-9:30pm; €4.28).

Taxis: At bus and train stations and Pl. de España. **Radio Taxi** (☎924 24 31 01). 24hr.

Car Rental: Hertz, Av. Adolfo Diaz Ambrona, 13 (☎924 27 35 10). From the train station, turn right just before the Puente de las Palmas onto Av. Adolfo Diaz Ambrona. Averages €70 per day.

ORIENTATION AND PRACTICAL INFORMATION

Across the Río Guadiana from the train station, **Plaza de España** is the heart of Badajoz. From the plaza, C. Juan de Ribera and C. Pedro de Valdivia lead to **Pl. Dragones Hernán Cortés;** one block to the right is **Plaza de la Libertad** and the regional tourist office. Bus #1 from the train station stops across from the regional tourist office. Otherwise, follow Av. Carolina Coronado straight to **Puente de las Palmas,** cross the bridge, then continue on C. de Prim. Turn left onto C. Juan de Ribera at Pl. Minayo to get to **Pl. de España,** or right to get to Pl. de la Libertad (35min.). To get from the bus station to the center of town, walk through the parking lot until you reach C. Damián Téllez la Fuente. Take a left onto this street and go straight through Pl. de la Constitución and Pl. Dragones Hernán Cortés to Pl. de España (20min.).

Tourist Office: Municipal Office, Po. de San Juan (☎924 22 49 81; www.turismobadajoz.es). English, French, and Portuguese spoken. Open May-Sept. M-F 10am-2pm and 5-7pm, Sa-Su 10am-2pm; Oct.-Apr. M-F 10am-2pm and 4-6pm, Sa 10am-2pm. **Regional Office,** Pl. de la Libertad, 3 (☎924 01 36 58/59; www.turismoextremadura.com). Open M-F 9am-2pm and 5-7pm, Sa 10am-2pm.

Banks: Banks line Av. de Europa, Pl. de España, and every major road in Badajoz.

Luggage Storage: In the bus station (€0.60) and train station (€3).

Police: Pl. de San José, Siglo 1, near Pl. Alta (☎092 or 924 21 00 72).

Pharmacy: Doctor Camacho, Pl. de España, 10, on the corner of C. Muñoz Torrero and Pl. de España. Open M-F 9:30am-1:45pm and 5:30-8:30pm, Sa 10am-1:45pm (☎924 22 27 50).

Hospital: Hospital Infanta Cristina, Av. de Elvas, off Ctra. de Elvas (☎924 21 81 00).

Biblioteca Bartolomé Gallardo, Av. de Europa, 2 (☎901 60 16 01). Free internet access. Open M-F 9:30am-1:30pm and 5-8pm, Sa-Su 9am-2pm and 5-9pm. During the Feria de San Juan, open M-F 9am-2pm, Sa-Su 8:30am-2:30pm.

Internet access: Cyberia, C. de Rafael Lucenqui, 22 (☎924 22 93 20), near the bus station. €1.70 per hr. until 2:45pm, €2.10 per hr. after. Open M-F 11am-2:45pm and 5pm-midnight, Sa noon-2:45pm and 5pm-midnight, Su noon-2:45pm.

Post Office: Po. de San Francisco, 4 (☎924 22 25 48). Lista de Correos. Open M-F 8:30am-8:30pm, Sa 9:30am-2pm. **Postal Code:** 06001.

ACCOMMODATIONS

Most *hostales* are found on streets adjacent to the Plaza de España, but weary backpackers can still find cheaper options close to the heart of town.

Pensión Pintor, C. Arco Agüero, 26 (☎924 22 42 28). From Pl. de España, take C. San Blas downhill, then the 1st right onto C. Arco Agüero. You may need to ring at #33. Rooms are simple but have huge windows and come with TV, baths, free internet access, and A/C. Singles €27; doubles €42; triples €55. AmEx/MC/V. ❷

Hostal Niza I and II, C. Arco Agüero, 34-35 (☎924 22 31 73; www.hostal-niza.com) has 2 locations. Reception is in I. Both I and II (across the street) offer spacious rooms with TV, private bath, free internet access, and A/C. Steps away from Pl. de España.

SÍ, SOMOS IGUALES

At the crossroads of Spain and Portugal, the province of Badajoz has recently become home to a large number of immigrants. But increasing unemployment, coupled with the challenges of social integration, have made the lives of immigrants increasingly difficult. With little independent political or social agency, many find themselves in straits more dire than those of the countries they left.

Several organizations, however, are working to meet the needs of families struggling for political and financial autonomy. Asociación "Todos Iguales, Todos Legales," C. de Cristobál Oudrid, 22, is a haven to the Moroccan, Romanian, Colombian, Brazilian, Senegalese, and other immigrants that need a helping hand. Run by the fiercely protective Maria Gemio, whom many call "Mother," the association aims to provide legal and practical assistance to any and all who need it.

Among other things, the staff at "Todos Iguales" provides courses in cooking, music, language, computers, and elderly assistance, free of charge to the mostly female immigrant population. Those seeking to make their own contribution to the effort can offer to help in whatever capacity they are most comfortable, whether by giving classes or volunteering at the Association.

For more information, please contact Maria Gemio at ☎924 22 20 36/ 49 10/ 21 25, or at mariagemio@yahoo.es.

Ask for a room with a terrace. Apartments with shared bathrooms are available. Singles €27; doubles €43; triples €54. Cash only. ❷

Hostal de las Heras, C. Pedro de Valdivia, 6 (☎924 22 40 14). From Pl. de España, take C. Obispo San Juan de Ribera, which turns into C. Pedro de Valdivia after the Pl. de Minayo. Rooms are simple, neat, and quaint, with desk, TV, and large closet. Singles €19, with bath €25; doubles €27/36; triples €38/44. AmEx/MC/V. ❶

FOOD

Cafes and eateries crowd Po. de San Francisco and Pl. de España. **Eroski,** next to the post office on Po. de San Francisco, s/n (☎924 24 18 66) sells groceries. (Open M-Sa 9:30am-9:30pm. MC/V.)

La Casona, Pl. Alta (☎924 23 26 94; www.tabernalacasona.com). From the Alcazaba Árabe entrance, make a left onto Pl. Alta. Friendly, laidback La Casona is popular with a local Spanish clientele, serving upscale tapas (€0.80-2.50) and entrees (€6-14) all day. Open M-Sa 11:30am-midnight. ❷

Bar-Restaurante La Ría, Pl. de España, 7 (☎924 22 20 05). Behind the glitzy bar and fast-food decor lie large portions of traditional Spanish and *extremeño* foods, including fresh fish and meat. Lunch menú €7. Open daily 10am-midnight. MC/V. ❷

SIGHTS

The greatest part about Badajoz is that almost every sight in the city is free. The municipal tourist office has a complete listing of sights as well as recommendations for an afternoon's tour.

MUSEO EXTREMEÑO E IBEROAMERICANO DE ARTE CONTEMPORÁNEO (MEIAC). Recent works from Spain, Portugal, and Latin America are exhibited in what was, until the mid-1980s, the site of the city's high-security prison. *(C. del Museo, 2. ☎924 01 30 60. Open Tu-Sa 10am-1:30pm and 5-8pm, Su 10am-1:30pm. Free.)*

CATEDRAL DE BADAJOZ. In the heart of the old quarter sits the city's 13th-century cathedral. A converted mosque, the cathedral is a veritable artistic timeline with one Renaissance, one Gothic, and one Plateresque window. *(☎924 23 90 27. Open Tu-Sa 11am-1pm and 6-8pm. €3, groups €2.)*

ALCAZABA. Badajoz's 9th-century foundation is still evident in the ruins of the Alcazaba, the Moorish citadel atop of the hill on Pl. Alta. From the Pl. de España, take a left on C. Virgen de la Soledad. Walk right on C. S. Pedro Alcantara until you Pl. de San Jose. Pl. Alta is on your right. Climb the ancient walls to see rural Extremadura beyond the city limits. Enclosed within the Alcazaba's walls, the **Palacio de los Duques de la Roca** holds an archaeological museum with an impressive collection of Visigothic, Roman, and other pieces showcasing the history of the Lower Extremadura region. *(☎924 00 19 08. Open Tu-Su 10am-3pm, during the Feria de San Juan 10am-2pm. Free.)*

NIGHTLIFE

Locals rave about Badajoz's weekend nightlife and pub culture. City maps proudly display three **zonas de pubs.** The largest and best one is in the old quarter, where every street off Pl. de España has at least three bars.

Mercantil, C. Zurbarán, 10 (☎924 22 06 91; www.salamercantil.com). A mainstay of Badajoz's nightlife, Mercantil covers the music scene with live bands every Thursday and Friday starting at 11pm and a DJ spinning a mix of Spanish hip-hop, jazz, soul, and pop on non-concert days. Beer €2.50. Mixed drinks from €5. Open June-Aug. daily 4pm-2am; Sept.-May M-Th 8pm-2am, F-Sa 8pm-5am. MC/V.

Café Samarkanda, C. Virgen de la Soledad, 9 (☎924 22 53 68; www.cafesamarkanda.com). One of the hottest spots in Badajoz, Samarkanda offers intimate alcoves and throw pillows to lounge until late. An attentive staff, full bar, and eclectic music entices locals of all ages here after 11pm. Beers €2.50. Mixed drinks from €5.50. Open daily 4:30pm-2:30am. Stays open 1hr. later during the *feria*.

SEVILLA

Sevilla (pop. 700,000) is the most famously romantic of Spain's great cities. Narrow, tangled streets unfold from the center, leading to an awe-inspiring cathedral, the third largest in the world, and the city's tremendous Alcázar, a Moorish and Catholic palace and the official residence of the king and queen of Spain. Once the site of a Roman acropolis founded by Julius Caesar, Sevilla later became the capital of the Moorish empire and a focal point of the Spanish Renaissance. The city is now the guardian of traditional Andalucian culture and embodies the Spain of popular imagination: flamenco, tapas, and bullfighting. Tourists, locals, and students infuse Sevilla with an energy that is hard to match. The budget traveler's experience here can be one of the best in Spain—with so many students packed in during the academic year, the opportunities for things to do and see on a tight budget are almost overwhelming. For a taste of Sevilla fully unhinged, visit during its most prominent festivals—*Semana Santa* and the *Feria de Abril* are among the most lavish celebrations in Europe.

HIGHLIGHTS OF SEVILLA

FEEL the **duende** and see what the **flamenco** fuss is all about (p. 215).

SHOUT ¡OLÉ! and cover your eyes at a bullfight in the **Plaza de Toros** (p. 212).

SCREAM with a stadium full of crazed fans at a Betis-Sevilla **fútbol game** (p. 216).

WANDER the tangled, winding streets of Sevilla's bustling **Judería** (p. 204).

INTERCITY TRANSPORTATION

BY PLANE

All flights arrive at **Aeropuerto San Pablo,** Ctra. de Madrid (☎954 44 90 00), 12km outside town. A taxi from the center costs about €25. **Los Amarillos** (☎954 98 91 84) runs a bus from outside the Prado de San Sebastián bus stop across from the university (M-F every 30-45min., Sa-Su every hr. 6:15am-11pm; €2.10. Also stops at the train station). **Iberia,** C. Guadaira, 8 (☎954 22 89 01, nationwide 902 40 05 00; open M-F 9am-1:30pm) books six flights daily to Barcelona (55min.) and Madrid (45min.). For student fares, head to **Barceló Viajes** (p. 205).

BY TRAIN

Estación Santa Justa, Av. de Kansas City. (☎902 24 02 02. Info and reservations open daily 4:30am-12:30am.) Services include **luggage storage, car rental,** and **ATM.** In town, the RENFE office, C. Zaragoza, 29, posts prices and schedules on the windows and also handles bookings. (☎954 54 02 02. Open in summer 9:30am-2pm and 5:30-8pm; in winter M-F 9am-1:15pm and 4-7pm.)

Altaria and **Talgo** trains run to: **Barcelona** (9-13hr., 3 per day 8:20am-10:22pm, €57.10-94.10); **Córdoba** (1hr., 6 per day 6:45am-8:30pm, €14.40); **Valencia** (9hr., 8:20am, €48.50); **Zaragoza** (5hr, 4:15pm, €99.50).

AVE trains run to **Córdoba** (45min., 15-20 per day 6:30am-10pm, €25.30-28.10) and **Madrid** (2hr., 15-21 per day 6:30am-10pm, €67.10-74.60).

Regionales trains run to: **Almería** (5hr., 4 per day 7am-5:40pm, €34.60); **Antequera** (2hr., 3 per day 7am-5:40pm, €13); **Cádiz** (2hr., 15 per day 6:35am-9:35pm, €9.80); **Córdoba** (1hr., 6 per day 7:50am-7:55pm, €8.20); **Granada** (3hr., 4 per day 7am-5:40pm, €21.65); **Huelva** (1hr., 2-3 per day 9:10am-8:30pm, €7.50); **Jaén** (2-3hr., 6:46pm, €17.10); **Málaga** (2hr., 5-6 per day 7:35am-8:10pm, €17.30).

BY BUS

Estación Prado de San Sebastián, C. Manuel Vázquez Sagastizábal (☎954 41 71 11), serves most of Andalucía. (Open daily 5:30am-1am.) **Estación Plaza de Armas,** Av. Cristo de la Expiración (☎954 90 80 40), goes outside of Andalucía, including to many international destinations. (Open daily 5am-1:30am.)

ESTACIÓN PRADO DE SAN SEBASTIÁN

Alsina Graells (☎954 41 88 11). Open daily 6:30am-11pm. To: **Almería** (7hr., 3 per day 7am-midnight, €30.53); **Córdoba** (2hr., 7-9 per day 7:45am-9:45pm, €9.96); **Granada** (3hr., 10 per day 8am-11pm, €18.57); **Jaén** (4hr.; M-F 4 per day 9am-6pm, Sa-Su 2-3 per day 1:30-6pm; €17.93); **Málaga** (2hr., 10-12 per day 7am-midnight, €15.16); **Murcia** (8hr., 3 per day 8am-11pm, €36.36).

Los Amarillos (☎954 98 91 84 or 902 21 03 17). Open M-F 7:30am-2pm and 2:30-9pm, Sa-Su 7:30am-2pm and 2:30-8:30pm. To: **Arcos de la Frontera** (2hr., 2 per day 9:30am-5pm, €7.39); **Marbella** (3hr., 2-3 per day 8am-4pm, €15.70); **Ronda** (2hr., 3-5 per day 7am-5pm, €10.80); **Sanlúcar de Barrameda** (2hr.; M-F 12 per day 8am-9pm, Sa-Su 9-10 per day 8am-8pm; €7.25).

Transportes Comes (☎902 19 92 08). Open M-Su 6:30am-10pm. To: **Algeciras** (3hr., 4 per day 9am-8pm, €17.40); **Cádiz** (1hr., 10-12 per day 7am-10pm, €10.95); **Jerez de la Frontera** (1hr., 6-9 per day 9am-10:30pm, €6.50); **Tarifa** (3hr., 4 per day 9am-8pm, €14.80).

ESTACIÓN PLAZA DE ARMAS

ALSA (☎954 90 78 00 or 902 42 22 42). Open M-F 5:45am-10:45pm, Sa-Su 7:30am-10:45pm. To: **Cáceres** (4hr., 9 per day 6am-9pm, €16.54); **León** (11hr., 3 per day 6-9pm, €41.55); **Lisboa** (6hr., 4 per day 3-11:59pm, €45); **Salamanca** (8hr., 5 per day 6am-9pm, €29.53); **Valencia** (9-11hr., 4 per day 10am-10:30pm, €48.28-55.27).

Damas (☎954 90 77 37; www.damas-sa.es). Open daily 6am-10pm. To: **Badajoz** (3hr., 3-5 per day 6:45am-8pm, €13.25); **Faro** (4hr., 4 per day 6:30am-4:15pm, €16); **Lisboa** (6hr., 3 per day 6:30am-4:15pm, €29.50); **Lagos, Portugal** (7hr., 4 per day 6:30am-4:15pm, €18.90); **Huelva** (1hr., 25-28 per day 6am-10pm, €7.05).

Socibus (☎902 22 92 92; www.socibus.es). Open daily 7:30-10:30am and 11am-12:45am. To Madrid (6hr., 14 per day 8am-midnight, €19.25).

ORIENTATION

The **Río Guadalquivir** flows north to south through the city, bordered by Po. de Cristóbal, which becomes Po. de las Delicias by the municipal tourist office. Most of Sevilla's touristed areas, including **Santa Cruz** and **El Arenal,** are on the east bank. The historic *barrios* (neighborhoods) of **Triana, Santa Cecilia,** and **Los Remedios** lie on the western bank. **Avenida de la Constitución,** home of the *Andaluz* tourist office, runs along the cathedral. **El Centro,** a busy commercial pedestrian zone, starts at the intersection of Av. de la Constitución, **Plaza Nueva,** and **Plaza de San Francisco,** site of the *Ayuntamiento*. **Calle Tetuán** and **Calle Sierpes,** both popular shopping areas, run off from Pl. Nueva and through El Centro.

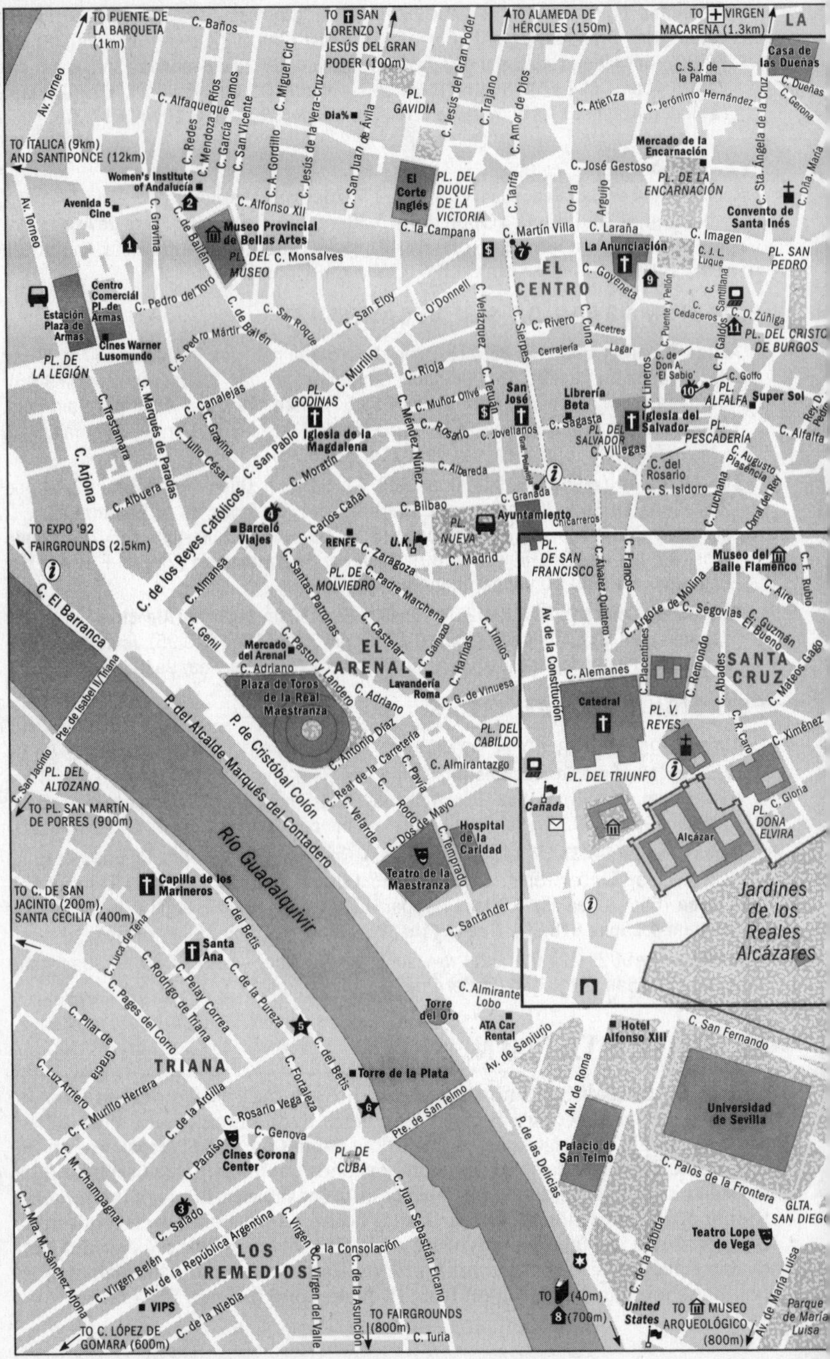

TO PUENTE DE LA BARQUETA (1km)
C. Baños
TO SAN LORENZO Y JESÚS DEL GRAN PODER (100m)
TO ALAMEDA DE HÉRCULES (150m)
TO VIRGEN MACARENA (1.3km)
LA
Casa de las Dueñas
C. S. J. de la Palma
C. Dueñas
C. Gerona
C. Jerónimo Hernández
C. Atienza
C. Sta. Ángela de la Cruz
C. Dña. María
Av. Torneo
C. Alfaqueque
C. Redes
C. Mendoza Ríos
C. García Ramos
C. San Vicente
C. Miguel Cid
C. A. Gordillo
C. Jesús de la Vera-Cruz
Dia%
C. San Juan de Ávila
PL. GAVIDIA
C. Jesús del Gran Poder
C. Trajano
C. Amor de Dios
TO ÍTALICA (9km) AND SANTIPONCE (12km)
Women's Institute of Andalucía
Avenida 5 Cine
C. Gravina
C. de Bailén
C. Alfonso XII
El Corte Inglés
PL. DEL DUQUE DE LA VICTORIA
C. Tarifa
Or la
Arguijo
Mercado de la Encarnación
C. José Gestoso
PL. DE LA ENCARNACIÓN
Convento de Santa Inés
Museo Provincial de Bellas Artes
PL. DEL MUSEO
C. Monsalves
C. la Campana
C. Martín Villa
C. Laraña
C. Imagen
La Anunciación
C. J. L. Luque
PL. SAN PEDRO
EL CENTRO
C. Goyeneta
C. Puente y Pellón
C. Santillana
Centro Comercial Pl. de Armas
Estación Plaza de Armas
C. Pedro del Toro
C. San Roque
C. San Eloy
C. O'Donnell
C. Velázquez
C. Sierpes
C. Rivero
C. Cuna
Acetres
C. Cedaceros
C. O. Zúñiga
PL. DEL CRISTO DE BURGOS
Cines Warner Lusomundo
C. S. Pedro Mártir
PL. DE LA LEGIÓN
C. Murillo
C. Rioja
Cerrajería
Lagar
C. Lineros
C. de Don A. 'El Sabio'
C. P. Galdós
C. Golfo
PL. ALFALFA
Super Sol
Rey D. Pedro
C. Trastamara
C. Marqués de Paradas
C. Canalejas
PL. GODINAS
C. Méndez Núñez
C. Muñoz Olivé
C. Tetuán
San José
Librería Beta
C. Sagasta
Iglesia del Salvador
PL. DEL SALVADOR
C. Villegas
PL. PESCADERÍA
C. Alfalfa
C. Gravina
C. Julio César
C. San Pablo
Iglesia de la Magdalena
C. Rosario
C. Jovellanos
Gral. Polavieja
C. del Rosario
C. S. Isidoro
C. Augusto Plasencia
C. Arjona
C. Albuera
C. de los Reyes Católicos
C. Moratín
C. Albareda
C. Granada
C. Luchana
Corral del Rey
C. Bilbao
PL. NUEVA
Ayuntamiento
Chicarreros
TO EXPO '92 FAIRGROUNDS (2.5km)
Barceló Viajes
C. Carlos Cañal
RENFE
U.K.
C. Zaragoza
C. Madrid
PL. DE SAN FRANCISCO
C. Álvarez Quintero
C. Francos
Museo del Baile Flamenco
C. F. Rubio
C. El Barranca
C. Almansa
C. Santas Patronas
PL. DE MOLVIEDRO
C. Padre Marchena
Av. de la Constitución
C. Argote de Molina
C. Segovias
C. Aire
C. Guzmán El Bueno
C. Genil
Mercado del Arenal
C. Pastor y Landero
C. Castelar
EL ARENAL
C. Gamazo
C. Harinas
C. Jimios
C. Placentines
C. Remondo
SANTA CRUZ
C. Mateos Gago
C. Adriano
Plaza de Toros de la Real Maestranza
Lavandería Roma
C. G. de Vinuesa
C. Alemanes
Catedral
C. Abades
Pte. de Isabel II/Triana
P. del Alcalde Marqués del Contadero
P. de Cristóbal Colón
C. Antonio Díaz
C. Real de la Carretería
PL. DEL CABILDO
PL. V. REYES
C. R. Caro
C. Ximénez
C. San Jacinto
PL. DEL ALTOZANO
C. Pavía
C. Almirantazgo
PL. DEL TRIUNFO
TO PL. SAN MARTÍN DE PORRES (900m)
C. Velarde
C. Rodo
C. Dos de Mayo
Hospital de la Caridad
Cañada
PL. DOÑA ELVIRA
C. Gloria
Alcázar
Río Guadalquivir
Teatro de la Maestranza
C. Temprado
Capilla de los Marineros
TO C. DE SAN JACINTO (200m), SANTA CECILIA (400m)
C. del Betis
Jardines de los Reales Alcázares
C. Santander
C. Luca de Tena
Santa Ana
C. Rodrigo de Triana
C. Pelay Correa
C. de la Pureza
C. Pages del Corro
C. Almirante Lobo
Torre del Oro
C. Pilar de Gracia
ATA Car Rental
Hotel Alfonso XIII
C. San Fernando
Av. de Sanjurjo
C. Luz Arriero
TRIANA
C. del Betis
C. Fortaleza
Torre de la Plata
Av. de Roma
Universidad de Sevilla
C. F. Murillo Herrera
C. de la Ardilla
C. Rosario Vega
Pte. de San Telmo
C. Genova
P. de las Delicias
Palacio de San Telmo
C. M. Champagnat
C. Paraíso
Cines Corona Center
PL. DE CUBA
C. Juan Sebastián Elcano
C. Palos de la Frontera
C. Salado
GLTA. SAN DIEGO
C. J. Mra. M. Sánchez Arjona
C. Virgen Belén
Av. de la República Argentina
C. Virgen de la Consolación
C. Virgen del Valle
C. de la Asunción
C. de la Rábida
Teatro Lope de Vega
LOS REMEDIOS
TO (40m), (700m)
VIPS
C. de la Niebla
TO FAIRGROUNDS (800m)
C. Turia
United States
TO MUSEO ARQUEOLÓGICO (800m)
Av. de María Luisa
Parque de María Luisa
TO C. LÓPEZ DE GOMARA (600m)

SEVILLA

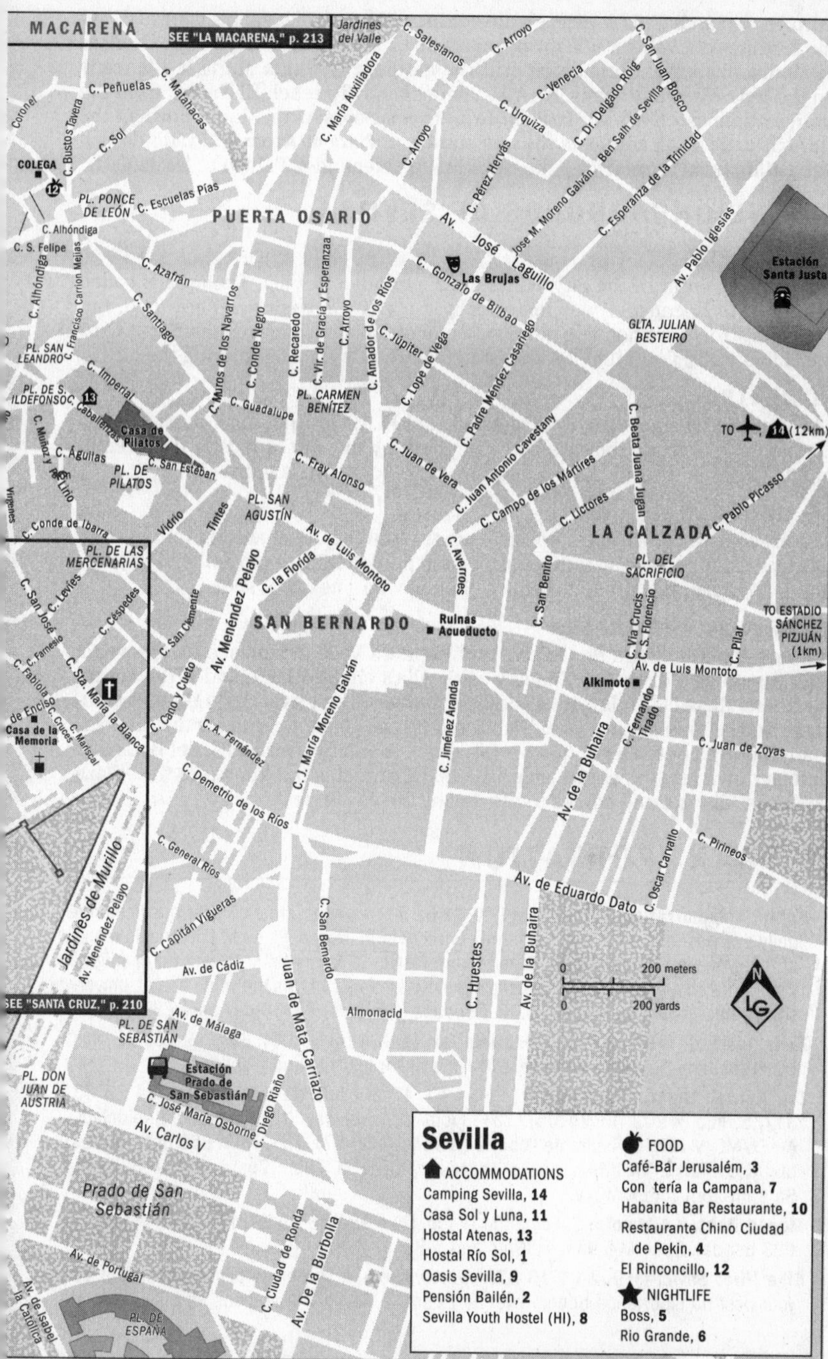
MACARENA
SEE "LA MACARENA," p. 213
Jardines del Valle
C. Salesianos
C. Arroyo
C. San Juan Bosco
C. Peñuelas
C. Matahacas
C. María Auxiliadora
C. Venecia
C. Urquiza
C. Dr. Delgado Roig
Ben Salh de Sevilla
Coronel
C. Bustos Tavera
C. Sol
C. Arroyo
C. Pérez Hervás
C. Esperanza de la Trinidad
COLEGA
12
PL. PONCE DE LEÓN
C. Escuelas Pías
PUERTA OSARIO
Av. José Laguillo
Jose M. Moreno Galván
C. Alhóndiga
C. S. Felipe
C. Alhóndiga
C. Francisco Carrion Mejias
C. Azafrán
C. Santiago
C. Muros de los Navarros
C. Conde Negro
C. Recaredo
C. Vir. de Gracia y Esperanzaa
C. Arroyo
C. Amador de los Ríos
C. Gonzalo de Bilbao
Las Brujas
Av. Pablo Iglesias
Estación Santa Justa
PL. SAN LEANDRO
C. Imperial
C. Júpiter
C. Lope de Vega
C. Padre Méndez Casariego
GLTA. JULIAN BESTEIRO
PL. DE S. ILDEFONSO
13
C. Caballerizas
Casa de Pilatos
C. Guadalupe
PL. CARMEN BENÍTEZ
C. Beata Juana Jugan
TO 14 (12km)
C. Muñoz y Pavón
C. Águilas
PL. DE PILATOS
C. San Esteban
C. Lirio
C. Fray Alonso
C. Juan de Vera
C. Juan Antonio Cavestany
C. Campo de los Mártires
Vírgenes
C. Conde de Ibarra
Vidrio
Tintes
PL. SAN AGUSTÍN
C. Lictores
LA CALZADA
C. Pablo Picasso
PL. DE LAS MERCENARIAS
C. San José
C. Levíes
C. Céspedes
Av. Menéndez Pelayo
C. la Florida
Av. de Luis Montoto
C. Averroes
C. San Benito
PL. DEL SACRIFICIO
C. San Clemente
SAN BERNARDO
Ruinas Acueducto
C. Via Crucis
C. S. Florencio
TO ESTADIO SÁNCHEZ PIZJUÁN (1km)
C. Pilar
C. Farnesio
C. Fabiola
C. Sta. María la Blanca
C. Cano y Cueto
C. J. María Moreno Galván
Av. de Luis Montoto
Alkimoto
de Enciso
Casa de la Memoria
C. Cruces
C. Mariscal
C. A. Fernández
C. Jiménez Aranda
C. Fernando Tirado
Av. de la Buhaira
C. Juan de Zoyas
C. Demetrio de los Ríos
C. General Ríos
C. Pirineos
C. Oscar Carvallo
Av. de Eduardo Dato
Jardines de Murillo
Av. Menéndez Pelayo
C. Capitán Vigueras
C. San Bernardo
Juan de Mata Carriazo
C. Huestes
Av. de la Buhaira
0 200 meters
0 200 yards
LG
Av. de Cádiz
SEE "SANTA CRUZ," p. 210
Av. de Málaga
Almonacid
PL. DE SAN SEBASTIÁN
Estación Prado de San Sebastián
PL. DON JUAN DE AUSTRIA
C. José María Osborne
C. Diego Riaño
Av. Carlos V
Prado de San Sebastián
C. Ciudad de Ronda
Av. De la Burbolla
Av. de Portugal
Av. de Isabel la Católica
PL. DE ESPAÑA
Sevilla
ACCOMMODATIONS
Camping Sevilla, 14
Casa Sol y Luna, 11
Hostal Atenas, 13
Hostal Río Sol, 1
Oasis Sevilla, 9
Pensión Bailén, 2
Sevilla Youth Hostel (HI), 8
FOOD
Café-Bar Jerusalém, 3
Con tería la Campana, 7
Habanita Bar Restaurante, 10
Restaurante Chino Ciudad de Pekin, 4
El Rinconcillo, 12
NIGHTLIFE
Boss, 5
Rio Grande, 6

To get to Santa Cruz from the train station, take bus C-2 and transfer to C-3 at the Jardines del Valle; it will drop you off on C. Menéndez Pelayo at the **Jardines de Murillo.** Walk right one block past the gardens; C. Santa María la Blanca is on the left. Without the bus, it's a 15-20min. walk. To reach El Centro from the train station, catch bus #32 to **Plaza de la Encarnación,** several blocks north of the cathedral. Bus C-4 connects the bus station at **Plaza de Armas** to Prado de San Sebastián; from there it's a 5min. walk up Av. Menéndez Pelayo to Santa Cruz.

THE NEIGHBORHOODS OF SEVILLA

SANTA CRUZ

In the very center of the city, Santa Cruz embodies Sevilla. The area is called the *Judería* because it was historically the city's Jewish neighborhood, but today its streets are home to more souvenir shops than synagogues. Santa Cruz has a lively and youthful vibe and is a great place to start exploring the city.

EL CENTRO

El Centro, a mess of narrow streets around Pl. de la Encarnación and Pl. del Duque de la Victoria, bustles with shoppers by day but is mostly deserted at night. The area near Pl. Alfalfa, a prime tapas location, is more lively.

LA MACARENA

The area north of El Centro doesn't cater to tourists. Its character ranges from quirky to familiar—from tattoo parlors and punk boutiques to authentic bars—and many residents predict that it will be Sevilla's next hot spot.

EL ARENAL AND TRIANA

Immortalized by Siglo de Oro writers Lope de Vega, Francisco de Quevedo, and Miguel de Cervantes, Triana was Sevilla's chaotic 16th- and 17th-century mariners' district. Today, it is home to many of the city's best ethnic restaurants and retains a gritty feel, contrasted by the elegant ceramics that are still manufactured in the local *talleres* (studios). Avoid overpriced C. del Betis and plunge down less expensive side streets. El Arenal is the known as the "Plaza de Toros" district and comes to life during the *Feria de Abril.*

TRANSPORTATION

Public Transportation: TUSSAM (☎900 71 01 71; www.tussam.es). Most bus lines run daily every 10min. 6am-11:15pm and converge in Pl. Nueva, Pl. de la Encarnación, and at the cathedral. Night service departs from Pl. Nueva (every hr. M-Th and Su midnight-2am; F-Sa all night). C-3 and C-4 circle the center and #34 hits the youth hostel, university, cathedral, and Pl. Nueva. €1.10. *Bonobús* (10 rides) €5, 30-day pass €30.

Taxis: TeleTaxi (☎954 62 22 22). **Radio Taxi** (☎954 58 00 00). Base rate €1.25 plus €0.40 per km, Su 25% surcharge. Extra charge for luggage and night taxis.

Car Rental: Hertz, at the airport (☎954 51 47 20) and train station (☎954 25 83 31/35, info ☎902 40 24 05). 25+. From €94 per day. Open daily 7am-midnight. AmEx/MC/V. **ATA,** C. Almirante Lobo, 2 (☎954 22 09 57). 25+. From €60 per day plus tax. Also offers 24hr. driver service; prices vary. Open M-F 9am-2pm and 4:30-8:30pm, Sa 9am-2pm. AmEx/MC/V.

Moped Rental: Alkimoto, C. Fernando Tirado, 5 (☎954 58 49 27; www.alkimoto.com). €23 per day. Open M-F 9am-1:30pm and 5-8pm.

Bike Hire: Sevici (☎902 01 10 32; www.sevici.es). If you enjoy biking, this might be your best transportation option. With an extensive network of stations for bike hire and returns, Sevici offers 1hr. (€0.50-1), 2hr. (€1-2), one week (€5), or one year (€10) rentals. Credit card required to activate the kiosk machines and retrieve PIN.

PRACTICAL INFORMATION

TOURIST AND FINANCIAL SERVICES

Tourist Offices: There are 4 tourist offices in town: municipal, provincial, and regional.

Centro de Información de Sevilla Laredo, Pl. de San Francisco, 19 (☎954 59 01 88; www.turismo.sevilla.org). English spoken. Internet access M-F 8am-2pm and 5-7:30pm; 1st hour free. Sign up at the desk near the computers. Open M-F 8am-3pm.

Naves del Barranco, C. Aronja, 28, near the bridge to Triana (☎954 22 17 14; barranco@sevilla.org). Takes over when the Centro office is closed. Open M-F 1-8pm, Sa-Su 8am-3pm.

Turismo de la Provincia, Pl. del Triunfo, 3 (☎954 21 00 05; info@dipusevilla.es). Info on daytrips and specific themed itineraries. Open M-F 10am-2:30pm and 3:30-7:30pm, Sa 10am-2pm.

Turismo Andaluz, Av. de la Constitución, 21B (☎954 22 14 04; fax 22 97 53). English spoken. Info on all of Andalucía. Free maps of the region. Open M-F 9am-7pm, Sa 10am-2pm and 3-7pm (until 7:30pm in winter), Su 10am-2pm.

Budget Travel Agency: Barceló Viajes, C. de los Reyes Católicos, 11 (☎954 22 61 31; www.barceloviajes.com). Open June-Sept. M-F 9:30am-1:30pm and 5-8:30pm, Sa 10am-1pm; Oct.-May M-F 9:30am-1:30pm and 4:30-7:30pm, Sa 10am-1pm.

Currency Exchange: Banco Santander Central Hispano, C. Tetuán, 10, and C. Martín Villa, 4 (☎902 24 24 24). Open M-F 8:30am-2pm, Sa 8:30am-1pm. Apr.-Sept. closed Sa. Banks and *casas de cambio* (currency exchange) crowd Av. de la Constitución, El Centro, and the sights in Santa Cruz.

LOCAL SERVICES

Luggage Storage: Estación Prado de San Sebastián (€0.90 per bag per day; open 6:30am-10pm); **Estación Plaza de Armas** (€3 per day); **train station** (€3 per day).

English-Language Bookstore: Vertice International Bookstore, C. San Fernando, in front of the university. Best selection of English-language books in Sevilla. Open July-Aug. M-W 10am-2pm and 5-8:30pm, Th-F 9am-3pm; Sept.-June M-F 9:30am-2pm and 5-8:30pm, Sa 11am-2pm. **Trueque,** C. Pasaje de Vila, 2 (☎954 56 32 66). Used books in English and a smattering of other languages. Open M-F 10:30am-1:30pm and 5-8pm, Sa 10:30am-1:30pm. MC/V.

Women's Resources: Women's Institute of Andalucía, C. Alfonso XII, 56 (24hr. toll-free hotline ☎900 20 09 99 or 955 03 59 50, office 954 03 49 53; www.juntadeandalucia.es/institutodelamujer). Info on feminist and lesbian organizations, plus legal and psychological counseling for rape victims. Office open to the public M-F 10am-1pm.

Laundromats: Lavandería y Tintorería Roma, C. Castelar, 2C (☎954 21 05 35). Wash, dry, and fold €6 per load. Open M-F 9:30am-2pm and 5:30-8:30pm, Sa 9am-2pm.

EMERGENCY AND COMMUNICATIONS

Police: Av. Paseo de las Delicias (☎091).

Medical Services: Red Cross (☎913 35 45 45). **Ambulatorio Esperanza Macarena** (☎954 42 01 05). **Hospital Virgen Macarena,** Av. Dr. Fedriani, 56 (☎955 00 80 00).

Library: Paseo de las Delicias, close to Puente de los Remedios. Modern space with free internet access. Open M-F 9am-8:30pm.

Internet Access: It is substantially cheaper to use pre-paid minutes; most places offer internet *bonos,* which amount to wholesale bulk minutes (most come with a min. of 2hr.

or more). Ask about *bonos* at the counter before using the computers. **Distelco,** C. Ortiz de Zuñiga, 3 (☎954 22 99 66; www.distelco.com). €2 per hr. minimum, or 20min. for €0.70 with no minimum; pre-paid cards start at €1.10 per hr. Int'l fax €2.40 for first page, €1.50 per additional page. Open M-F 10:30am-11pm, Sa-Su 6-11pm. MC/V.

Post Office: Av. de la Constitución, 32 (☎954 21 64 76). **Lista de Correos** and fax. Have your mail addressed to the *Lista de Correos de la Constitución* (otherwise mail may end up in any of the Sevilla post offices). Open M-F 8:30am-8:30pm, Sa 9:30am-2pm. **Postal Code:** 41080.

ACCOMMODATIONS

During *Semana Santa* and the *Feria de Abril*, vacant rooms vanish and prices at least double; reserve several months in advance. The tourist office has lists of *casas particulares* (private residences) that open for visitors on special occasions. Outside of these weeks, you should reserve a few days in advance and about a week ahead if you're staying for the weekend.

SANTA CRUZ

The narrow streets east of the cathedral around C. Santa María la Blanca are full of cheap, nearly identical hostels. The neighborhood is highly touristed; it's best to reserve early, but last-minute rooms are not impossible to come by. Santa Cruz's location is excellent, but many so-called *"hostales"* have the prices of hotels, and cheap lodging rarely shares the neighborhood's charm.

Pensión Vergara, C. Ximénez de Enciso, 11, 2nd fl. (☎954 21 56 68; www.pension-vergara.com). Above a souvenir shop at C. Mesón del Moro. Quirky, antique decor and perfect location. Rooms come with A/C. Singles, doubles, triples, and quads, all with common bath; €20 per person. Cash only. ❷

Pensión Bienvenido, C. Archeros, 14 (☎ 954 41 36 55; www.pensionbienvenido.com). Five comfortable, rooftop rooms surround a social patio; downstairs rooms overlook inner atrium. All have A/C. Ask for room #101, the largest and classiest in the *pensión.* Singles €20; doubles €38, with bath €50; triples and quads €60-64. MC/V. ❷

EL CENTRO

Hostal Atenas, C. Caballerizas 1 (☎954 21 80 47; www.hostal-atenas.com), off Pl. de Pilatos. Everything about this hostel is appealing, from the *mudéjar*-style arches and traditional patio to the cheery rooms. All have A/C and bath. Internet access €1 per hr. Singles €35; doubles €54; triples €75. MC/V. ❸

Oasis Sevilla, reception at Pl. Encarnación, 29 1/2, rooms above reception and at C. Alonso el Sabio, 1A (☎954 29 37 77; www.hostelsoasis.com). Young, international crowd. Co-ed dorms are centrally located above the client-only **Hiro** lounge. On C. Alonso doubles and 4-person dorms share bathrooms and fridges and are roomier and quieter. Free Wi-Fi and internet, terrace pool, weekly tapas tours, and free breakfast in the 3rd-floor kitchen (8-11am). Reserve early. Dorms €20; doubles €46. MC/V. ❷

Casa Sol y Luna, C. Pérez Galdós, 1A (☎954 21 06 82 or 626 55 96 10; www.casasoly-luna1.com). Magnificent arched doorway and marble staircase are a prelude to antique mirrors, plush living room, and bright and spacious themed rooms. Friendly staff and quiet atmosphere make this a gem of a hostel. Laundry €10. Singles €22; doubles €38, with bath €45; triples €60; quads €80. Min. stay 2-nights. Cash only. ❷

LA MACARENA

Hostal Macarena, C. San Luis, 91 (☎954 37 01 41; www.hostalmacarena.es). Large yellow and green rooms have matching rainbow-colored bedspreads and curtains. Each comes with A/C and TV. If you're looking for a quiet place to crash, this is it. Singles €22; doubles €33, with bath €45; triples €48/54. MC/V. ❷

Hostal Alameda, Alameda de Hércules, 31 (☎954 90 01 91; www.hostalalameda.es). Immaculate rooms with Wi-Fi, A/C, TV, and small roof top balcony. Singles €27; doubles with bath €48; triples €65. MC/V. ❷

NEAR ESTACIÓN PLAZA DE ARMAS

Several hostels line **C. Gravina,** parallel to C. Marqués de las Paradas two blocks from the station. Hostels here tend to be cheaper than those in other neighborhoods and are convenient for exploring **El Centro** (5min.) and **C. del Betis** and **Triana** on the west bank of the river (10-15min.).

Hostal Rio Sol, C. Marqués de Paradas, 25 (☎954 22 90 38; www.hostalriosol.com). Convenient location across from the bus station. Tiled walls, colorful bed covers, and private baths. Singles €25; doubles €45; triples €60; quads €70-75. AmEx/MC/V. ❷

Pensión Bailén, C. Bailén, 75 (☎ 954 22 16 35; www.pensionbailen.com). Rooms are clean, colorful and airy. Can't beat the location and prices. Singles €20; doubles €30, wth bathroom €40; triples €40/50; quads €65; quints €75. MC/V. ❷

Sevilla Youth Hostel (HI), C. Isaac Peral, 2 (☎955 05 65 00; inturjoven.com). Take bus #34 across from the tourist office on Av. de la Constitución; the 5th stop is the hostel. Doubles, triples, and quads, many with private bath and all with big windows. A/C and breakfast included. Other meals €7. Dorms Mar.-Oct. €16, over 26 €20; Nov.-Feb. €14/18. HI card necessary, but can be purchased here. ❶

Camping Sevilla, Ctra. Madrid-Cádiz, km 534 (☎954 51 43 79), near the airport. Take bus #70 (stops 800m away at Parque Alcosa) from Prado de San Sebastián. Showers, market, and pool. €3.75 per 1-person tent, €3.25 per car. IVA not included. MC/V. ❶

FOOD

Sevilla loves its tapas. Locals spend their evenings relaxing and socializing over plates of *caracoles* (snails) and fresh seafood, while sipping glasses of sangria and *tinto de verano* (red wine and lemon soda). For those on a tight budget, markets such as **Mercado de la Encarnación,** Pl. de la Encarnación (open M-Sa 8am-2pm), and the more modern **Mercado del Arenal,** on C. Pastor y Landero (open M-Sa 9am-3pm), have fresh meat and produce. For a supermarket, try the mammoth basement of **El Corte Inglés** in Pl. del Duque de la Victoria (☎954 27 93 97), the **Mercadona** in the Centro Commercial Plaza de Armas next to the bus station, or any of the smaller ones like **%Día, Mas,** and **Super Sol.**

SANTA CRUZ

Restaurants near the cathedral cater almost exclusively to tourists. Food quality and prices improve in the backstreet establishments between the cathedral and the river in El Arenal and on side streets in Santa Cruz. Despite the droves of tourists, locals can always be spotted sharing mixed drinks at the bars.

San Marco, C. Mesón del Moro, 6 (☎954 56 43 90). Serves great dishes and Italian desserts in an 18th-century house with old Arab baths. A full menu of creative salads (€4.30-9.25) and pizza (€7.50-8.90). Open daily 1:15-4:30pm and 8:15pm-12:30am. Branches in equally impressive settings at C. del Betis, 68 (☎954 28 03 10) and C. Santo Domingo de la Calzada, 5 (☎954 58 33 43). MC/V. ❷

Bar Entrecalles, C. Ximenez de Enciso, 14 (☎617 86 77 52). Situated at the center of the tourist buzz, but the reggae music and relaxed Cuban theme help maintain a local following. Tapas (only available inside, €2) and delicious *gazpacho* are unusually generous. Open daily 1pm-2am. Kitchen open starting at 1:30 and 8pm. Cash only. ❶

Histórico Horno San Buenaventura, SA, Av. de la Constitución, 16 (☎954 22 18 19). A restaurant/bar/deli/pastry shop, Histórico Horno hosts a delightfully indulgent selection of everything from ice cream and pastries to stews and gourmet *jamón*. Takeout available. Many locations. Open M-Sa 8am-11pm, Su 9am-11pm. AmEx/D/MC/V. ❷

Levíes Café-Bar, C. San José, 15 (☎954 21 53 08). The bar at this tapas restaurant predominates, pouring out deliciously liberal and refreshing glasses of sangria (€2.20). Tapas €2.60-3.10, entrees €6-12. Open 8am-2am. ❶

EL CENTRO

Pl. Alfalfa, Pl. de la Encarnación, and Pl. San Pedro frame a maze of tiny streets full of unassuming tapas bars and affordable international restaurants.

Habanita Bar Restaurante, C. Golfo, 3 (☎606 71 64 56), off C. Pérez Galdós. Popular vegetarian/vegan-oriented cafe-restaurant serving Cuban fare, pastas, and salads. Tapas €2.15-4.35. Entrees €6.50-16. Open M-Sa 12:30-4:30pm and 8pm-12:30am, Su 12:30-4:30pm. Reserve ahead. MC/V. ❷

Confitería La Campana, C. Sierpes 1 and 3 (☎954 22 35 70). Founded in 1885, Sevilla's most famous cafe has twice made an appearance in Spanish short stories, and it continues to serve up *granizadas de limón* (lemon-flavored crushed ice), ice cream (€2-2.50), and homemade pastries (€1.50-3.40). Open daily 8am-11pm. AmEx/MC/V. ❶

El Rinconcillo, C. Gerona, 40 (☎954 22 31 83). Founded in 1670, in an abandoned convent, this bodega is the epitome of a local hangout, teeming with grey-haired men deep in conversation and locals stopping in for a quick glass of wine. The bartender tallies up your tab in chalk on the wooden counter. Tapas €1.80-3.20. *Raciones* €6-14.50. Open daily 1:30pm-1:30am. AmEx/MC/V. ❷

Ancha de la Feria, C. Feria, 61 (☎954 90 97 45). Serves tapas (€2; *raciones* from €5) in a breezier version of the traditional *taberna*. The place feels like one big family reunion. Open Tu-Su noon-5pm and 8:30pm-12:30am. Cash only. ❶

La Plazoleta Bodega, C. San Juan de la Palma (☎954 38 27 91), just past the church on the same side of the street. Serves up generous portions of traditional Spanish fare, including sacred bull's tail (€2.40). Open M-Sa 12:30pm-12:30am, Su 4:30-8pm. ❶

EL ARENAL AND TRIANA

Café-Bar Jerusalém, C. Salado, 6. Neighborhood kebab bar with falafel (€3.50) and chicken, lamb, pork, and cheese shawarma (€3.10-4.90). A popular pit stop for a quick bite. Open M, W-Th, and Su 8pm-2am, F-Sa 8pm-3am. AmEx/MC/V. ❶

Restaurante Chino Ciudad de Pekin, C. Zaragoza, 6, enter on C. Santas Patrona (☎954 21 84 78). Granted, you didn't come to Spain to eat Chinese food, but such is life. Steaming bowls of soup (€2.50-4.50), rice (€3-5), and lightly sauced meat (€5-8) fill you up fast. Open daily noon-4:30pm and 8pm-midnight. ❶

SIGHTS

While most visits center around the Catedral and Alcázar, there is much more to Sevilla. Around these central icons are winding streets full of tapas joints, *artesanía*, and quirky finds. The **Plaza de Toros** is nestled along the riverbank and serves as an ideal place to begin a scenic tour along the Guadalquivir. Heading south toward the **Torre del Oro,** garden oases offer respite from the city.

The gardens behind the **Alcázar** are flanked by the **Jardines de Murillo,** and from there it's a short jaunt to the **Plaza de España** and nearby **Parque de María Luisa.**

SANTA CRUZ

CATEDRAL

Entrance by Pl. de la Virgen de los Reyes. ☎954 21 49 71; www.catedralsevilla.com. Open M-Sa 9:30am-4pm, Su 2:30-6pm. Last entrance 1hr. before closing. €7.50, seniors and students under 26 €2, under 16 free. Audio tour €3. Mass held in the Capilla Real M-Sa 8:30, 10:30am, noon; Su 8:30, 10:30, 11am, noon, and 1pm. Free.

Legend has it that the *reconquistadores* wanted to demonstrate their religious fervor by constructing a church so great that "those who come after us will take us for madmen." Sevilla's immense cathedral does appear to be the work of an extravagant madman—with 44 individual chapels, it is the third largest in the world, after St. Peter's Basilica in Rome and St. Paul's Cathedral in London, and it is the biggest Gothic edifice ever constructed.

In 1402, a 12th-century Almohad mosque was destroyed to clear space for the cathedral. All that remains is the **Patio de Los Naranjos,** where the faithful washed before prayer, the **Puerta del Perdón** entryway from C. Alemanes, and **La Giralda** minaret, built in 1198. The tower and its twins in Marrakesh and Rabat are the oldest and longest-surviving Almohad minarets in the world. The 35 ramps leading to the tower's top were installed to replace the stairs that once stood there, allowing a disabled *muezzín* to ride his horse up to issue the call to prayer. Climbing the ramps will leave you breathless, as will the views from the top—the entire city of Sevilla lies just on the other side of the bells. Be warned that the very loud, gong-like iron bells sound every fifteen minutes.

The 42m tall central **nave,** decorated with 3 tons of gold leaf, is considered one of the greatest in the Christian world—take a good look at its four tiers via a well-placed mirror on the nave's floor. In the center of the cathedral, the Renaissance-style **Capilla Real** stands opposite choir stalls made of mahogany recycled from a 19th-century Austrian railway. The **retablo mayor,** one of the largest in the world, is an intricately wrought portrayal of saints and disciples. Nearby, the bronze **Sepulcro de Cristóbal Colón** (Columbus's tomb) is supported by four heralds representing the ancient kingdoms of Spain united by Fernando and Isabel. The coffin holds Columbus' remains, brought back to Sevilla from Cuba in 1898. Farther on stands the **Sacristía Mayor,** which holds works by Ribera, Zurbarán, Goya, and Murillo, and a glittering Corpus Cristi icon.

ALCÁZAR

Pl. del Triunfo, 7. ☎954 50 23 23. Open Tu-Sa 9:30am-7pm, Su 9:30am-5pm. €7, students, handicapped, over 65, and under 16 free. Tours of private residence every 30min. Aug.-May 10am-1:30pm and 3:30-5:30pm; June-July 10am-1:30pm. Max. 15 people per tour, so buy tickets ahead. €4. English audio tours (€3) offer anecdotes and a route through the complex.

The oldest European palace still used as a private residence for royals, Sevilla's Alcázar exudes extravagance. The palace, built by the Moors in the seventh century and embellished in the 1600s, displays Moorish, Gothic, Renaissance, and Baroque architecture, but its intricacies are most prominently displayed in the *mudéjar* style of many of the arches, tiles, and ceilings. Fernando and Isabel are the palace's best known former residents; Carlos V also lived here after marrying his cousin Isabel of Portugal in the **Salón Techo Carlos V.**

The Alcázar is a network of splendid patios and courtyards, around which court life revolved. From the moment you step through the **Patio de la Montería,** the melange of cultures is apparent; an Arabic inscription praising Allah is carved in Gothic script. Through the archway is the **Patio del Yeso,** an exquisite

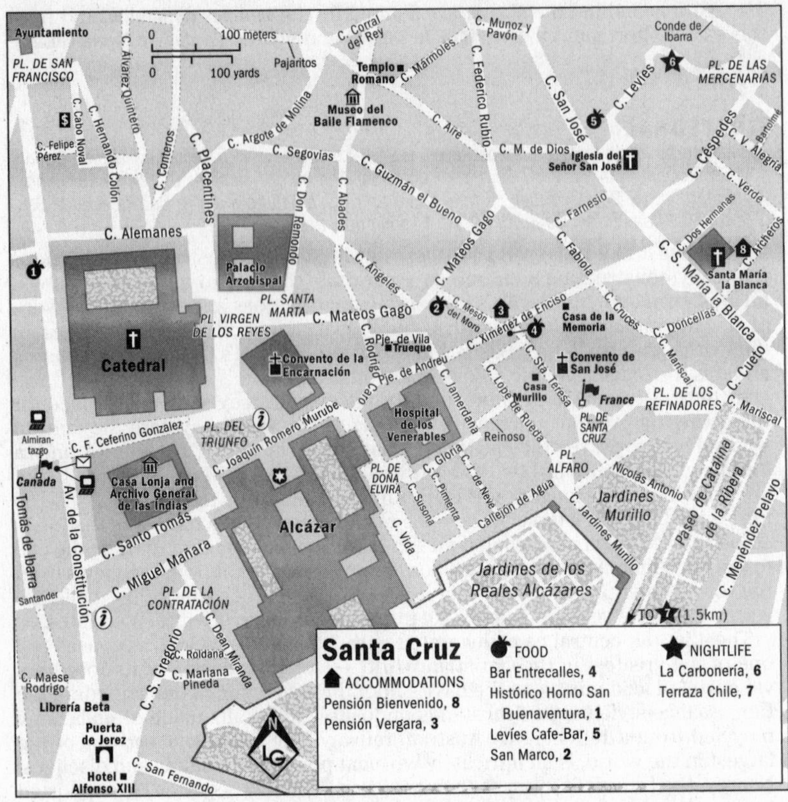

geometric space first used by Moorish governors. The center of public life at the Alcázar, however, was the **Patio de las Doncellas** (Patio of the Maids), a colonnaded quadrangle encircled by tiled archways. The **Patio de las Muñecas** (Patio of the Dolls), served as a private area for Moorish kings; the room had an escape path so that the king would not have to cross a wide-open space in an attack. The columns are thought to have come from the devastated **Madinat Al-Zahra** (p. 229), built at the height of the caliph period. Look for the little faces at the bottom of one column for a hint at how the patio got its name.

The interior is a sumptuous labyrinth where even the walls are works of art. In the **Sala de los Azulejos del Alcázar,** history's stain is literally visible—the room was the stage of a bloody duel between Pedro I and his half brother, and even today the traces of Fadrique's blood can be seen on the floor. On a more peaceful note, the golden-domed **Salón de los Embajadores** (Ambassadors' Room) is rumored to be the site where Fernando and Isabel welcomed Columbus back from the New World. Their son, Juan, was born in the red-and-blue tiled **Cuarto del Príncipe.** The private residences upstairs, the official home of the King and Queen on their visits to Sevilla, have been renovated and redecorated throughout the years, and most of the furniture today dates from the 18th and 19th centuries. These rooms are accessible only by 25min. guided tours.

AROUND SANTA CRUZ

CASA LONJA. Between the cathedral and the Alcázar stands the 16th-century Casa Lonja, built as a commercial center for trade with the Americas. Today, it contains a collection of over 44,000 documents relating to the conquest of the New World. Highlights include Juan de la Costa's wildly inaccurate **Mapa Mundi** (world map) and letters from Columbus. Swing by for the building's magnificent artistry. *(Av. de la Constitución, 3, across from the post office. ☎954 50 05 28. Open M-Sa 10am-4pm, Su 10am-2pm. Free. Access to documents is limited to scholars.)*

TEMPLO ROMANO. Rising on C. Mármoles are the ruins of the Templo Romano. Its two columns ascend 15m from below street level and offer a glimpse of the depth of Sevilla's history; river sediment, accumulated after the construction of the temple, caused the ground level to rise.

OTHER SIGHTS. After Fernando III forced Jews who had been exiled from Toledo during the Inquisition to live in Santa Cruz, the area thrived as a lively **Jewish quarter.** C. Gloria leads to the **Hospital de los Venerables,** a hospital-church adorned with art from the Sevillana School. The small garden and courtyard are calming respites from the city. *(☎954 56 26 96. Open daily for guided visits 10am-1:30pm and 4-7:30pm. €4.75, students €2.40. Children under 12 and Su Free.)* **Calle Lope de Rueda,** off C. Ximénez de Enciso, is graced with two noble mansions, beyond which lies the fragrant **Plaza de Santa Cruz,** built on the former site of the neighborhood's main synagogue. South of the plaza are the **Jardines de Murillo,** a shady expanse of shrubbery, benches, and hidden waterworks of art.

EL CENTRO

MUSEO PROVINCIAL DE BELLAS ARTES. This museum contains Spain's finest collection of works by painters of the Sevillana School, most notably Murillo, Valdés Leal, and Zurbarán, as well as El Greco and Dutch master Peter Brueghel. Much of the art was cobbled together from convents in the mid-1800s, finding a stately home amid the traditional tiles and courtyards of this impressive building. *(Pl. del Museo, 9. ☎954 78 64 82; www.museosdeandalucia.es. Open Tu 2:30-8:30pm, W-Sa 9am-8:30pm, Su 9am-2:30pm. €1.50, students and EU citizens free.)*

MUSEO DEL BAILE FLAMENCO. See flamenco as you've never seen it before. Let life-size virtual dancers whisk you away to the heart of a gypsy camp, where screen after screen lights up with color and song to convey the history, music, and technique of this Spanish art. The visual art and photo-heavy exhibitions put corner-store postcards to shame. *(C. Manuel Rojas Marcos, 3. ☎954 34 03 11; www.museoflamenco.com. Open daily 9am-7pm. €10, students and groups €8, children €6. MC/V.)*

CASA DE PILATOS. This palatial residence has been inhabited continuously by Spanish aristocrats since the 15th century, and it effortlessly merges Andalucian architecture and art. On the ground floor, Roman artifacts coexist with tropical gardens in *mudéjar* patios. The second floor features rooms decorated over the centuries with oil portraits, sculptures, painted ceilings, and tapestries. *(Pl. de Pilatos, 1. ☎954 22 52 98. Open daily 9am-6pm. Guided tours every 30min. 10am-6pm. Ground level only €5, with upper chambers €8; EU citizens free Tu 1-5pm.)*

OTHER SIGHTS. Calle Sierpes, which starts in Pl. San Francisco, cuts through the Aristocratic Quarter. At the beginning of this street, a plaque marks the spot where the royal prison once loomed. Some scholars believe that Cervantes began writing Don Quixote here. Taste a sweet Spanish tradition at the **Convento de Santa Inés:** the nuns sell pastries and cakes through the courtyard's *torno* (revolving window). *(C. María Coronel. Sweets €2.50-7, sold by the kg. and dozen. Mixed box of pastries €10-12. Open*

M-Sa 9am-1pm and 5-6:45pm.) The **Ayuntamiento,** Sevilla's city hall, has 16th-century Gothic and Renaissance interior halls, a domed ceiling, and a Plateresque facade. Art exhibitions take place here, framed by the building's beautiful stone work. *(Pl. de San Francisco, enter from Pl. Nueva. ☎954 59 01 01. Open Sept.-July Tu-Th 5:30-6pm, call in advance. Closed Aug. and holidays. Passport or other official documentation required. Free.)*

LA MACARENA

CONVENTO DE SANTA PAULA. The Convento de Santa Paula includes a church with Gothic, *mudéjar*, and Renaissance elements, as well as Montañés sculptures and Ribera's **San Jerónimo.** Nuns peddle **homemade marmalade** (300g, €2.70) and angel hair pastries. Knock if the door is closed. *(Pl. Santa Paula, 11. ☎954 53 63 30. Museum open Tu-Su 10am-6:30pm. Church officially open for visits Tu-Su 10am-1pm and 4:30-6:30pm, though often randomly closed during these hours. €2.)*

CHURCHES. A stretch of *murallas* (walls) built in the 12th century runs between Pta. de and Pta. de Córdoba on Ronda de Capuchinos. Flanking the west end of the walls, the **Basílica de la Macarena** houses the venerated *Nuestra Señora de la Esperanza*, borne through the streets at the climax of the Semana Santa processions. *(C. Bécquer, 1. ☎954 90 18 00. Basílica open daily 9:30am-2pm and 5-9pm. Basilica free. Museum €3.50, students €1.50. Mass M-F 9, 11:30am, 8, and 8:30pm; Sa 9am and 8pm; Su 10:30am, 12:30, and 8pm.)* Nearby, the Baroque **Iglesia de San Luis** has an unparalleled stained glass altar flanked by relics, including two skulls. *(C. San Luis. ☎954 55 02 07. Open Tu-Th 9am-2pm, F-Sa 9am-2pm and 6-8pm. Free.)* Toward the river is **Iglesia de San Lorenzo y Jesús del Gran Poder,** with Montañés's lifelike sculpture, *El Cristo del gran poder*; worshippers come to kiss Jesus's ankle. *(Pl. San Lorenzo. ☎954 91 56 72. Open M-Th 8am-1:30pm and 6-9pm, F 7am-2pm and 5-10pm, Sa-Su 8am-1:30pm and 6-9pm. Free.)*

OTHER SIGHTS. A large garden beyond the *murallas* and the Basílica leads to the **Hospital de las Cinco Llagas,** a spectacular Renaissance building recently renovated to host the Andalucian parliament. Thursday mornings from 9am to 2pm, a large flea market is held along **C. Feria.** The **Alameda de Hércules** is filled with outdoor cafes, and its side streets burgeon with funky restaurants.

EL ARENAL AND TRIANA

A riverside esplanade stretches along the banks of the Guadalquivir from the base of the Torre del Oro. Somewhat kitschy boat tours of Sevilla leave from in front of the tower (1hr., €15). To head out solo, look for **Lipasam Piragüismo** or head to **Pedalquivir Kayaking** (☎679 19 40 46. Open daily noon-9:30pm.)

PLAZA DE TOROS DE LA REAL MAESTRANZA. Bullfighting has been a staple of *sevillano* culture for centuries, as evidenced by the city's beautiful and world-renowned Plaza de Toros. Home to one of the two great bullfighting schools (the other is in Ronda, p. 266), the plaza fills to capacity (13,800) for the 13 *corridas* of the **Feria de Abril.** Multilingual tours take visitors through a small museum, the chapel where *matadores* pray before fights, and the emergency room used when their prayers go unanswered—though only three matadors have died in the history of bullfighting in Sevilla. *(☎954 22 45 77; www.realmaestranza.com. Open May-Oct. 9:30am-8pm; Nov.-Apr. 9:30am-7pm. Mandatory tours every 20min. in English and Spanish. €5; seniors 20% discount. See Bullfighting, p. 238, for ticket info.)*

TORRE DEL ORO Y MUSEO NAVAL. The 12-sided **Torre del Oro** (Tower of Gold), built by the Almohads in the early 13th century, overlooks the river from Po. de Cristóbal Colón. Today, a tiny yellow dome is the only remnant of the golden tiles that once covered the tower. Inside is the small **Museo Naval,** a storehouse

of maritime antiquities. Museum officers enthusiastically tend to visitors. *(☎954 22 24 19. Open Sept.-July Tu-F 10am-2pm, Sa-Su 11am-2pm. €2, students €1. Tu free.)*

OTHER SIGHTS. The **Torre de la Plata** (Tower of Silver) was once connected to the Torre del Oro by underwater chains designed to protect the city from river-borne trespassers. With old-fashioned piracy no longer a concern, the Torre is now a bank. One block farther inland, between Pte. de Isabel II and Pte. de San Telmo, is the **Iglesia de Santa Ana,** Sevilla's oldest church and the focal point of the fiestas that take over in July. *(C. Pelay Correa. Open M and W 7:30-8:30pm.)*

OUTER NEIGHBORHOODS

PLAZA DE ESPAÑA. The twin spires of **Plaza de España** gracefully mark the ends of this 200m-long wonder of a building. Designed by Aníbal González, one of Sevilla's most prominent 20th-century architects, the aristocratic-looking structure hugs a sweeping plaza, featuring mosaic floors and a large marble fountain within the semicircle. Mosaics depicting every Spanish province line the colonnade, and balconies offer a view of the surrounding gardens. The popular, nearby **Parque de María Luisa** is a grand reminder of Sevilla's 1929 plans for an Ibero-American World's Fair. *(Adjacent to Pl. de España. Open daily 8am-10pm.)*

NEAR ESTACIÓN PLAZA DE ARMAS

CENTRO ANDALUZ DE ARTE CONTEMPORÁNEO. If you're interested in Spain's vibrant art scene, the trek here is worth it. The interior of this restored monastery is a labyrinth of clean spaces exhibiting everything from optical illusions to a skull made of Christmas lights. Frequently hosts special exhibitions and film series. *(Av. Américo Vespucio, 2, on Isla de la Cartuja. ☎955 03 70 70. Open Tu-F 10am-9pm, Sa 11am-9pm, Su 10am-3pm. Complete visit €3, monastery only €1.80. Tu free.)*

NIGHTLIFE

Sevilla's nightlife is as hot as its scorching summer afternoons. A typical night out on the town begins with tapas and drinks, continues with dancing at discotecas, and ends with an early morning breakfast of *churros con chocolate.* Popular bars can be found around **Calle Mateos Gago** near the cathedral, **Calle Adriano** by the bullring, and **Calle del Betis** across the river in Triana; several popular summertime clubs lie along the river near **Puente de la Barqueta.** Many gay clubs cluster around the Pl. de Armas, and some can be found around the **Alameda de Hercules** in the Macarena neighborhood. Sevilla recently cracked down on the Spanish institution of *botellón,* a (mostly student) tradition of starting the night by drinking among massive crowds in city plazas, but nightlife is still just as raucous. In summer, crowds head to the river in hopes of a breeze, and most *terrazas* stay open until 4am. During the school year, bars and clubs are packed regardless of the night.

SANTA CRUZ

La Carbonería, C. Levies, 18 (☎954 22 99 45). A gigantic bar frequented by students and young summer travelers. Free live flamenco shows nightly at 11pm. Agua de Sevilla pitchers €21, M-W, €16. Sangria pitchers €8.50. Open daily 8pm-3 or 4am. Cash only.

Terraza Chile, Po. de las Delicias. A packed dance club and bar. Loud salsa and pop bring together young *sevillanos,* foreign students, and tourists. Beer €2.50. Mixed drinks €5. Open June-Sept. daily 8pm-5am; Oct.-May Th-Sa 8pm-5am. MC/V.

LA MACARENA

The area near Puente de la Barqueta is the place to go dancing during summer. The near side of the river features several outdoor discotecas, while the far side hosts a more rowdy clubbing scene. From , follow C. Resolana to C. Nueva Torneo, by Pte. de la Barqueta. (The A2 night bus runs at midnight, 1, and 2am from Pl. Nueva; ask to be let off near Pte. de la Barqueta. Taxi from Pl. Nueva €5-8.)

Palenque, Av. Blas Pascal (☎954 46 74 08). Gigantic dance club, complete with 2 dance floors—one of which is inexplicably called "Alabama"—2 musical choices, and a small ice skating rink (€3, including skate rental; closes at 4am). Beer €3.50. Mixed drinks €5-6. F-Sa cover €7, Th free. Open June-Sept. Th-Sa midnight-7am. MC/V.

Tribal, Av. de los Descubrimientos, next to Pte. de la Barqueta. Hip, tropical, tent-like discoteca playing American hip-hop, Latin favorites, and lots of reggaeton. W hip-hop is popular with the international crowd. Drinks served in pitchers €5-10 per person depending on group size. Open W-Sa midnight-6am. MC/V.

EL ARENAL AND TRIANA

Boss, C. Fortaleza, 13, off C del Betis (☎954 00 01 01). In Sevilla, the night is always young, and Boss is...boss. Irresistible beats, a packed dance floor, and hazy blue lights make this a top nocturnal destination. Beer €3.50. Mixed drinks €6. Open daily 9pm-5am. Closed in summer. MC/V.

Rio Grande, C. del Betis, (☎954 27 39 56; www.riogrande-sevilla.com), on the right as you cross into Triana on the San Telmo bridge. Right on the bank of the river, it's hard to believe this palmy oasis has no cover charge. Recline in a wicker couch or curl up in a pillow-strewn beached dingy. Dressy casual will get you past the bouncers and to the bar (drinks €6 and up). Open only in summer daily 11pm-4:30 or 5am.

ENTERTAINMENT

The tourist office distributes *El Giraldillo.* and its English counterpart, *The Tourist*, free monthly magazines with listings on music, art exhibits, theater, dance, fairs, and film. It can also be found online at www.elgiraldillo.es.

THEATERS

Sevilla is a haven for the performing arts. The venerable **Teatro Lope de Vega** (☎954 59 08 67; www.teatrolopedevega.org), near Parque de María Luisa, has long been the city's leading stage. Ask about scheduled events at the tourist office or check the bulletin board in the university lobby on C. San Fernando. **Sala la Herrería** and **Sala la Imperdible** put on avant-garde productions in Pl. San Antonio de Padua. (Both ☎954 38 82 19; www.imperdible.org.) **Teatro de la Maestranza,** on the river between the Torre del Oro and the bullring, is a splendid concert hall accommodating orchestral performances, opera, and dance. (☎954 22 65 73; www.teatromaestranza.com. Box office open M-F 10am-2pm and 6-9pm.) On spring and summer evenings, neighborhood fairs are often accompanied by **free open-air concerts** in Santa Cruz and Triana. **Avenida 5 Cines,** C. Marqués de las Paradas, 15 (☎954 29 30 25), and **Corona Center,** in the mall between C. Salado and C. Paraíso in Triana (☎954 27 80 64), screen films from various countries subtitled in Spanish. For more theaters, look under "Cinema" in *El Giraldillo* or any local newspaper.

FLAMENCO

Sevilla would not be Sevilla without flamenco. Born of a *gitano* (gypsy) musical tradition, flamenco consists of dance, guitar, and songs characterized by spontaneity and passion. Rhythmic clapping, intricate fretwork on the guitar, throaty wailing, and rapid foot-tapping accompany the swirling dancers. Flamenco can be seen either in the highly-touristed *tablaos*, where skilled professional dancers perform, or in *tabernas*, bars where locals dance *sevillanas.* Both are good, but the *tabernas* tend to be free. The tourist office provides a complete list of both *tablaos* and *tabernas;* ask about student discounts.

TABLAOS

Signs advertising *tablao* shows are everywhere, from souvenir shops to internet cafes, and the majority of flamenco *tablaos* in Sevilla cater to the tourist crowd rather than to true flamenco aficionados. Many *tablaos* are *tablao*-restaurantes, so you can eat while watching the show, but dinner tends to be very expensive. Less expensive alternatives are the impressive 1hr. shows at the cultural center **Casa de la Memoria Al-Andalus,** C. Ximénez de Enciso, 28, in the middle of Santa Cruz. Ask at the tourist office or swing by their ticket

SEVILLA

office for a schedule of different themed performances, including traditional Sephardic Jewish concerts. (☎954 56 06 70; www.casadelamemoria.es. Shows nightly 9pm, in summer also 10:30pm; seating is very limited, so reserve your tickets a day or two ahead, and up to four days in advance for weekend shows. €14, students €12, under 10 €8.) **Los Gallos,** Pl. de Santa Cruz, 11, is arguably the best tourist show in Sevilla. Buy tickets in advance and arrive early. (☎954 21 69 81; www.tablaolosgallos.com. 2hr. shows nightly 8 and 10:30pm. Cover €29, includes 1 drink.) **Casa Carmen Arte Flamenco,** C. Marqués de Paradas, 30, draws a student crowd. (☎954 21 28 89; www.casacarmenarteflamenco.com. Shows nightly 9:30pm and 11pm. Reserve in advance. Cover €16, students €12.) Consult the tourist office or entertainment listings for more venues.

TABERNAS

La Carbonería, C. Levies, 18, fills with students and backpackers. **El Tamboril,** Pl. de Santa Cruz, hosts a primarily middle-aged tourist crowd for midnight singing and dancing. (☎954 56 15 90. Open daily June-Sept. 5pm-3am; Oct.-May noon-3am.) Bar-filled Calle del Betis, across the river, houses several other *tabernas:* **Lo Nuestro, El Rejoneo,** and **Taberna Flamenca Triana.**

FÚTBOL

Sevilla has two professional teams, and soccer fever engulfs the city, especially when the cross-town rivals play each other. **Real Betis** wears green and white, **Sevilla FC** white and red. Sevilla FC plays at **Estadio Sánchez Pizjuán** (☎954 53 53 53) on Av. de Eduardo Dato, and Real Betis plays at **Estadio Manuel Ruiz de Lopera** (☎954 61 03 40) on Av. de la Palmera. Buy tickets at the stadium; price and availability depend on the quality of the match-up. Both teams struggle against the competitive **Barcelona** and **Real Madrid** clubs.

BULLFIGHTING

Sevilla's bullring hosts bullfights from *Semana Santa* through October. The cheapest place to buy tickets is at the ring on Po. Alcalde Marqués de Contadero. When there's a good *cartel* (line-up), buy tickets at booths on **C. Sierpes, C. Velázquez,** and **Pl. de Toros**. Prices can run from €20 for a *grada de sol* (nosebleed seat in the sun) to €75+ for a *barrera de sombra* (front-row seat in the shade). *Corridas de toros* (bullfights) or *novillada* (fight with apprentice bullfighters and younger bulls). During July and August, *corridas* occasionally occur on Thursday at 9pm; check posters around town. (For tickets, call the Plaza de Toros ticket office at ☎954 50 13 82. For more on bullfighting, see p. 76.)

SHOPPING

Sevilla is a great place to find Andalucian crafts, such as hand-embroidered silk, lace shawls, and traditional flamenco wear, albeit often at inflated tourist prices. **El Centro,** the area including C. las Sierpes, C. San Eloy, C. Velázquez, and C. Francos, offers a wide array of crafts, including ceramic shops, the most popular Spanish clothing chains, and hundreds of tiny shoe boutiques and jewelry stores. In **Santa Cruz,** the streets are packed with identical souvenir shops selling bullfighting and flamenco-themed clothing, trinkets, and postcards. A large, eclectic **flea market** is held Thursday 9am-2pm, extending along C. Feria in . In February, July, and August, all of the stores hold huge **rebajas** (sales), where everything is marked down 30-70%.

SEVILLA

FESTIVALS

Sevilla swells with tourists during its fiestas, and with good reason: the parties are world-class. If you're in Spain during any major festivals, head straight to Sevilla—you won't regret it. Reserve a room a few months in advance, and expect to pay at least twice what you would normally.

SEMANA SANTA. Sevilla's world-famous *Semana Santa* lasts from Palm Sunday to Easter Sunday. In each neighborhood, thousands of penitents in hooded cassocks guide *pasos* (huge, extravagantly-decorated floats) through the streets, illuminated by hundreds of candles; the climax is Good Friday, when the entire city turns out for a procession along the bridges and through the oldest neighborhoods. Americans should be prepared for costumes eerily like those of the Ku Klux Klan. Book rooms well in advance. The tourist office has a helpful booklet on accommodations and food during the festivities.

FERIA DE ABRIL. From April 28 to May 3, the city rewards itself for its Lenten piety with the *Feria de Abril*, held in the southern end of Los Remedios. Begun as part of a 19th-century revolt against foreign influence, the Feria has grown into a massive celebration of all things Andalucian, with circuses, bullfights, and flamenco. A spectacular array of flowers and lanterns decorates over 1000 kiosks, tents, and pavilions, known as *casetas*, which each have a small kitchen, bar, and dance floor. Though there are a few large public ones, most are private, and the only way to get invited is by making friends with locals. The city holds bullfights daily during the festival; buy tickets in advance.

DAYTRIPS FROM SEVILLA

PARQUE DOÑANA

Doñana is accessible from almost any city in Andalucía. Bus schedules vary, but both Empresa Damas (☎954 90 77 37) and Los Amarillos (☎954 98 91 84) run to towns in the park's boundaries. Buses leave Sevilla's Pl. de Armas station 6 times per day. The easiest way to see Doñana is by car. Take A-483 off of A-92; 45min.

One of Europe's largest national parks, with everything from cork trees to wild buzzards, the immense and diverse Doñana park is both daunting and inspiring. The southern zone is the Parque Nacional, while the northern area is called the Parque Natural, a distinction that often proves confusing for visitors. The Parque Natural is more popular with long-term visitors and nature enthusiasts; there are ample opportunities for horseback-riding and hiking. Like the Marismas del Odiel, Doñana has its fair share of flamingos. The provincial tourist offices in Sevilla provide information on the park, including detailed driving directions, hiking suggestions, campsites, restaurants, and lodging in nearby towns. See www.donana.es for more details. To visit the Parque Nacional, it's necessary to make a reservation for a 4hr., 80km tour that includes a boat ride across the Río Guadalquivir and a trip in an all-terrain vehicle through the three ecosystems of the park—dunes, wetlands, and pinar, arid coniferous forrest. (Call ahead to reserve ☎959 43 04 32; www.infodonana.com/donanavisitas. Open daily 9am-7pm. Trips leave Tu-Su May-Sept. 14 8:30am and 8pm; Sept. 15-Apr. 8:30am and 3pm. €23.)

ITÁLICA

Take the Empresa Casal (Área de Sevilla) bus (☎954 41 06 58) toward Santiponce from the Pl. de Armas bus station, platform 34, off to the left of the rest of the platforms. Get off at the last stop (30min.; M-Sa every 10-30min. 6:35am-2:30am, Su hourly 7:35am-midnight;

€1.15, pay onboard). The entrance to the ruins is to the left of the gas station, across the street from the bus stop. When returning to Sevilla, wait by the faded bus sign in front of the top of the driveway marking the entrance to Itálica (☎955 99 65 83; italica.ccul@juntadeandalucia.es). Ruins open Apr.-Sept. Tu-Sa 8:30am-8:30pm, Su 9am-3pm; Oct.-Mar. Tu-Sa 9am-5:30pm, Su 10am-4pm. €1.50; free for EU citizens.

Just 9 km northwest of Sevilla and right outside the village of Santiponce (pop. 7000) lie the excavated ruins of Itálica, the first permanent Roman settlement in southern Iberia. Founded by general Publius Cornelius Scipio in 206 BC as a kind of "wellness camp" for soldiers injured in the Battle of Ilipa, Itálica was used as a strategic military outpost. The ruins you can visit today are a testament to the cosmopolitan trading center started by emperor Trajan (AD 53) and his son Hadrian (AD 76), a center gradually abandoned and forgotten as Sevilla took over as the regional seat of power. Archaeological excavations continue today, although the oldest neighborhoods in Itálica and its mysterious forum are still buried under downtown Santiponce, and may never be recovered.

The most interesting ruin is the mighty **Amphitheatre,** one of the empire's largest with a seating capacity of nearly 25,000. Follow the fighters' path from the holding room, where the rules of the games, carved in metal, still hang on the wall. You can also walk through the musty tunnels under the stands until they spit you into the shadeless ring at the mercy of the unforgiving crowd and Andalucian sun. Treading the grid of ancient streets, you'll find fragments of columns and porticos leading into the intricately patterned floors of dignitaries' homes. There is also a **House of Birds,** with 30 bird species depicted in lightly-restored mosaic, and a **House of the Planetarium,** with seven planetary divinities representing the days of the week.

Sevilla's Holy Week

Unbridled Exuberance and Popular Religiosity

For hundreds of years, Sevilla's Holy Week *(Semana Santa)* has demonstrated how tradition, religion, and tourism can create a unique phenomenon. The processions featuring hooded penitents and floats depicting images of the Passion often strike outsiders as conventional manifestations of Catholicism, but things are more complicated (and interesting) than that.

"Processions were tapping into spiritual energies that went beyond dry precepts."

Although some religious brotherhoods were founded around 1400, the Holy Week festival was born around 1550. It was then that dozens of brotherhoods began their activities. The militant Catholicism of the Counter-Reformation welcomed this movement, which sought to take the symbols of the Church to the streets. The brotherhoods also offered Sevillians ways to create affiliated networks to the city and to their peers, as brotherhoods were usually support groups defined by social class, profession, or ethnic background. The result was a complex patchwork of communities that provided Sevilla with some needed social cement. Furthermore, the exuberance toward the cult of the Virgin Mary revealed that the processions were tapping into spiritual energies that went beyond dry precepts to attain salvation. Social and anthropological forces were colliding to create spectacular religious rituals, which gained international recognition by the 16th century.

Declining in importance for two centuries, the festival was revived with a different character in the late 19th century. By then Andalucía had become a frequent destination for European travelers who created an exotic image of a region outside modernity. Andalucians looked at themselves through the lens of these writings and fashioned themselves according to what they saw. Also of great significance to the changing of the festival was the economic force of tourism, already operating by the turn of the 20th century. Local businessmen and the municipal government in Sevilla decided to actively promote tourism: a revival of the Holy Week festival was part of this effort. Splendor and spectacle were institutionalized for the sake of visitors and natives, and brotherhoods were subjected to more rational arrangements. "Eternal Sevilla" was in the making, and a crucial element was a popular religiosity that manifested itself not in the temple, but on the streets, opening the door for alternative ways to be religious. At the same time, modern ways of thought had taken many individuals away from a strict adherence to organized religion.

"Spectacle...was institutionalized... 'Eternal Sevilla' was in the making."

Nevertheless, the festival's traditional image of the drama of the Passion, with its two protagonists, Christ and his suffering mother, still deeply affected many Sevillians who did not necessarily follow the teachings of the Church.

Today, participation in the brotherhoods still thrives, and individuals who have never set foot in church weep at the passing of the processions. And of course, Semana Santa still attracts thousands and thousands of baffled and enraptured tourists.

Antonio Córdoba *was born in Sevilla, where he earned his B.A. in English Literature. He got his Ph.D. in Latin American literature from Harvard University in June of 2008, and is currently a lecturer in History and Literature at Harvard. Córdoba is completing a book on a 17th-century Andalucian poet.*

ANDALUCÍA

Situated at the crossroads between Western Europe and Africa, Andalucía is steeped in thousands of years of cultural heritage. Its intoxicating mix of Roman, Moorish, and *gitano* cultures can be found anywhere from the cities of Sevilla and Granada to the tiniest mountain villages of the Alpujarras. Andalucía has no single image: Roman ruins, monumental churches, medieval castles, sun-drenched beaches, snowy peaks, orange trees, and shimmering silver olive groves all have their place. But while Andalucía is far more than a stereotype, it is also home to Spain's most notorious icons. Bullfighting, sherry, and flamenco are all *andaluz*, and the region celebrates holidays and festivals like *Semana Santa* (Holy Week) and Carnaval with famously wild abandon.

The ancient kingdom of Tartessus grew wealthy off the Sierra Nevada's rich ore deposits, and the Greeks and Phoenicians established colonies and traded up and down the coast. The Romans cultivated wheat, olive oil, and wine from the fertile soil watered by the Guadalquivir, and in the AD 5th century, the Vandals passed through on their way to North Africa, leaving little more than a name—Vandalusia (House of the Vandals). The Moors, in control under various dynasties from 711 until 1492, had the most enduring influence, forming lasting ties to Africa and the Islamic world. They preserved and perfected Roman architecture (creating the distinctive Andalucian patio), furthered industry and technology, and developed the region's greatest cities. Sevilla and Granada reached the pinnacle of Islamic art and scholarship in these centuries, while Córdoba matured into the most culturally influential medieval Muslim city.

Through the turbulent 20th century, Andalucía retained its strength and solidarity—the region was one of the last strongholds against Franco during the Civil War. Many residents still describe themselves as Andalucian before Spanish and proudly draw from the melange of cultures that first made the region famous. As for visitors, whether they come to wander the medieval streets of the *juderías* (Jewish quarters) or clap along with a *sevillana*, Andalucía will leave its golden light and vibrant colors warmly imprinted on the mind.

HIGHLIGHTS OF ANDALUCÍA

SCRUB like a sultan in the Arab baths of **Córdoba** (p. 220).

SAMPLE enough sherry to get sufficiently silly in **Jerez de la Frontera** (p. 230).

SIGH like the last of the royal Moors when you too must leave **Granada** (p. 273).

SKI until sundown amidst ocean views of Africa in the **Sierra Nevada** (p. 285).

CÓRDOBA ☎957

Abundant courtyards, flowers dangling from balconies, and narrow, winding streets make Córdoba (pop. 323,600) a captivating and unhurried city. Perched on the southern bank of the Río Guadalquivir, it was once the largest city in Western Europe. For three centuries, Córdoba was the hub of the Moorish Empire and capital of the mighty Umayyad Caliphate, rivaled only by Baghdad and Cairo. Today's city preserves its past glory with monuments of Roman, Jewish, Islamic, and Christian origin. The *Judería* is one of Spain's oldest

Andalucía
TO CÁCERES (130km)
TO MADRID (150km)
TO MURCIA (60km) AND ALICANTE (120km)
TO VALENCIA (245km)
TO LAGOS (125km)
PORTUGAL
CORDILLERA CANTÁBRICA
Río Guadiana
Río Guadiana Menor
Río Guadalquivir
Tharsis
Alosnol
Ayamonte
Vila Real de Santo António
Punta Umbría
Huelva
Valverde del Camino
Aracena
Zufre
Cazalla de la Sierra
El Pedroso
Constantina
Monasterio de la Rábida
Matalascañas
Almonte
Parque Nacional de Doñana
Itálica
Sevilla
Carmona
Utrera
Écija
Osuna
Estepa
Madinat Al-Zahra
Almodóvar del Río
Córdoba
Montoro
Montilla
Linares
Úbeda
Baeza
Jaén
Cazorla
Quesada
Parque Natural de Cazorla, Segura y Las Villas
Orcera
Segura de la Sierra
Baza
Vélez Rubio
Lorca
Huércal-Overa
Águilas
Mojácar
Carboneras
San José
Cabo de Gata
Níjar
Almería
Golfo de Almería
Costa de Almería
Roquetas de Mar
Laroles
Guadix
Granada
Pico Veleta
Mulhacén
SIERRA NEVADA
Trevélez
Bubión
Pampaneira
Capileira
Lanjarón
LAS ALPUJARRAS
Motril
Salobreña
Almuñécar
Nerja
Cuevas de Nerja
Málaga
Antequera
Villanueva de la Concepción
El Torcal
Garganta del Chorro
Álora
Torremolinos
Benalmádena
Mijas
Marbella
Puerto Banús
San Pedro de Alcántara
Costa del Sol
MEDITERRANEAN SEA
Ronda
SERRANÍA DE RONDA
Olvera
Setenil
Benaoján
Cueva de la Pileta
Algatocín
Gaucín
Estepona
Bornos
Arcos de la Frontera
Jerez de la Frontera
Sanlúcar de Barrameda
Chipiona
Rota
El Puerto de Santa María
Cádiz
San Fernando
Chiclana de la Frontera
Conil de la Frontera
Vejer de la Frontera
Costa de la Luz
Golfo de Cádiz
ATLANTIC OCEAN
Algeciras
Tarifa
La Línea de la Concepción
Gibraltar
Strait of Gibraltar
Ceuta
Tangier
MOROCCO
N630
E803
N435
N433
A49
N502
N432
NIV
A4
A92
A382
N340
E15
N331
N420
E5
A91
A7
0
40 kilometers
40 miles

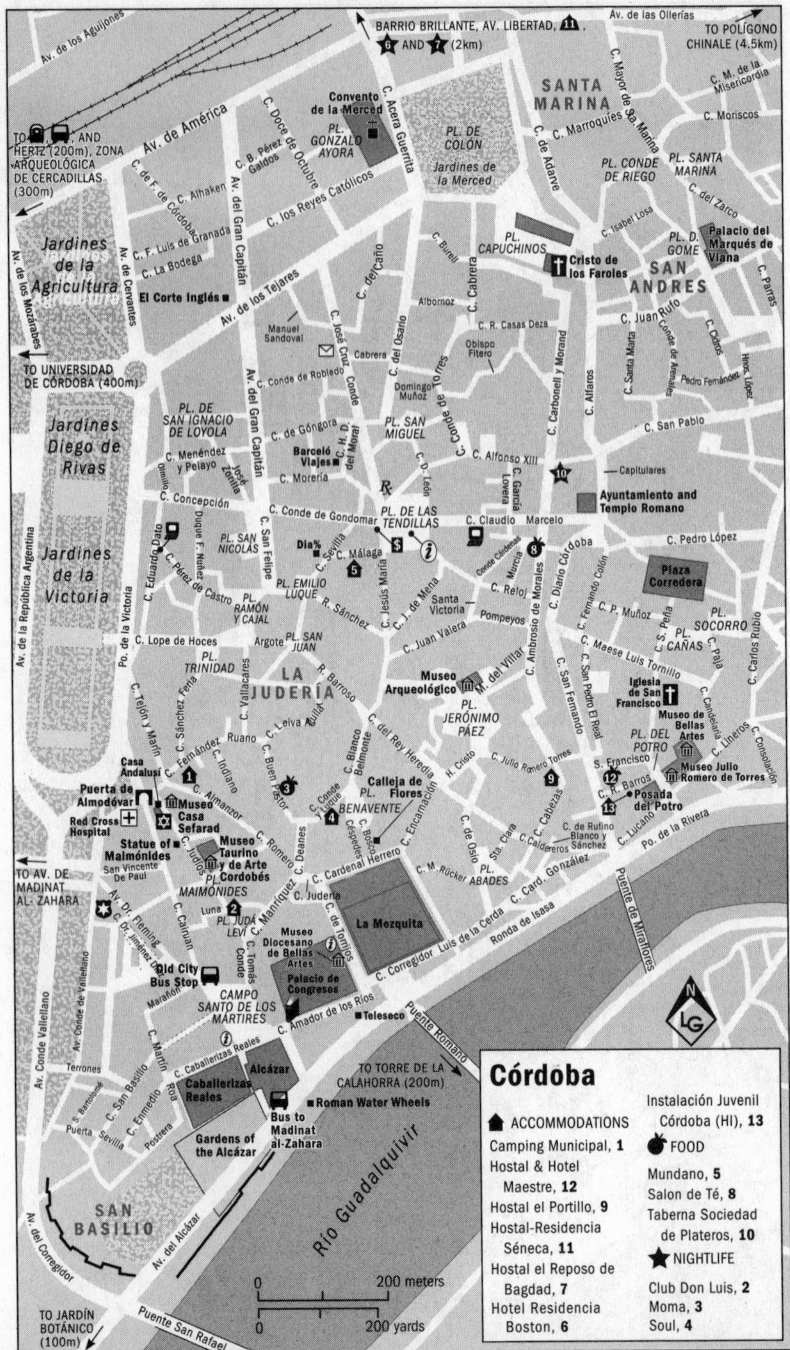
Córdoba
ACCOMMODATIONS
Camping Municipal, 1
Hostal & Hotel Maestre, 12
Hostal el Portillo, 9
Hostal-Residencia Séneca, 11
Hostal el Reposo de Bagdad, 7
Hotel Residencia Boston, 6
Instalación Juvenil Córdoba (HI), 13
FOOD
Mundano, 5
Salon de Té, 8
Taberna Sociedad de Plateros, 10
NIGHTLIFE
Club Don Luis, 2
Moma, 3
Soul, 4
BARRIO BRILLANTE, AV. LIBERTAD, 11, 6 AND 7 (2km)
TO POLÍGONO CHINALE (4.5km)
AND HERTZ (200m), ZONA ARQUEOLÓGICA DE CERCADILLAS (300m)
TO UNIVERSIDAD DE CÓRDOBA (400m)
TO AV. DE MADINAT AL- ZAHARA
TO TORRE DE LA CALAHORRA (200m)
TO JARDÍN BOTÁNICO (100m)
SANTA MARINA
SAN ANDRES
LA JUDERÍA
SAN BASILIO
Convento de la Merced
Jardines de la Merced
Jardines de la Agricultura
Jardines Diego de Rivas
Jardines de la Victoria
El Corte Inglés
Cristo de los Faroles
Palacio del Marqués de Viana
Ayuntamiento and Templo Romano
Plaza Corredera
Barceló Viajes
Dia%
Museo Arqueológico
Iglesia de San Francisco
Museo de Bellas Artes
Museo Julio Romero de Torres
Posada del Potro
Calleja de Flores
Casa Andalusí
Puerta de Almodóvar
Museo Casa Sefarad
Red Cross Hospital
Statue of Maimónides
Museo Taurino y de Arte Cordobés
La Mezquita
Museo Diocesano de Bellas Artes
Palacio de Congresos
Old City Bus Stop
Teleseco
Alcázar
Caballerizas Reales
Roman Water Wheels
Bus to Madinat al-Zahara
Gardens of the Alcázar
Río Guadalquivir
Puente Romano
Puente San Rafael
Puente de Miraflores
Av. de América
Av. de los Tejares
Av. del Gran Capitán
Av. de la República Argentina
Po. de la Victoria
Av. Conde Vallellano
Av. del Corregidor
Av. del Alcázar
Ronda de Isasa
Po. de la Rivera
PL. DE COLÓN
PL. DE LAS TENDILLAS
PL. SAN MIGUEL
PL. DE CAPUCHINOS
PL. DEL POTRO
PL. MAIMÓNIDES
PL. JERÓNIMO PÁEZ
CAMPO SANTO DE LOS MÁRTIRES
0 200 meters
0 200 yards

Jewish quarters, containing one of the three remaining synagogues on the Iberian peninsula, and the decadent, visionary 14th-century Palacio del Marqués de Viana. A lively city today, Córdoba welcomes visitors with the same peaceful hospitality that gave the city its fame.

TRANSPORTATION

Trains: Pl. de las Tres Culturas (☎957 40 02 02, 902 24 02 02), off Av. de América. To: **Algeciras** via **Bobadilla** (2 per day 10:43am and 5:06pm, €35-54); **Barcelona** (10-11hr., 3 per day 10am-10:52pm, €55-91); **Cádiz** (2hr., 5 per day 7:20am-8:13pm, €18-55); **Madrid** (2-4hr., 21-33 per day 7:29am-10:28pm, €48-61); **Málaga** (2-3hr., 5 per day 7:12am-11:27pm, €19.05-40.70); **Sevilla** (45min., 4-8 per day 6:50am-9:30pm, €8-15). For tickets, visit the **RENFE** office, Av. Ronda de los Tejares, 10.

Buses: Estación de Autobuses (☎957 40 40 40), on Glorieta de las Tres Culturas across from the train station.

Alsina Graells Sur (☎957 27 81 00) to: **Algeciras** (5hr.; 8am, 3:15pm; €24); **Almería** (5hr., 8am, €23); **Antequera** (2hr.; 9am, 4pm; €9); **Cádiz** (4-5hr.; M-F 10am, 6pm; Sa-Su 10am; €21); **Granada** (3-4hr.; M-Sa 9-10 per day 8am-7pm, Su 11 per day 8am-8:30pm; €12); **Málaga** (3hr.; 5 per day 8am-7pm, more frequent June-Aug; €12).

Bacoma (☎902 42 22 42) to **Baeza** (3hr.; 12:20, 5:15pm; €9); **Barcelona** (10hr., 3 per day 5:15pm-12:35am, €64); and **Valencia** (4 per day 12:20pm-12:35am, €39-44).

Secorbus (☎902 22 92 92) runs cheap buses to **Madrid** (5hr., 6 per day 1am-6pm, €14.40).

Transportes Ureña (☎957 40 45 58) runs to **Jaén** (2hr.; M-Sa 7-8 per day 7:30am-8pm, Su 6 per day 7:30am-8pm; €8).

Autocares Priego (☎957 40 44 79), **Empresa Carrera** (☎957 40 44 14), and **Empresa Rafael Ramírez** (☎957 42 21 77) run buses to surrounding towns and campsites.

Local Transportation: 17 bus lines (☎957 25 57 00) cover the city, running from the wee hours until 11pm. **Bus #3** makes a loop from the bus and train stations through Pl. de las Tendillas, up to the Santuario, and back along the river and up C. Dr. Fleming. **Bus #10** runs from the train station to Barrio Brillante. €1.

Taxis: Radio Taxi (☎957 76 44 44). From bus and train stations to the *Judería* €4-5.

Car Rental: Hertz (☎957 40 20 61; www.hertz.com), in the bus station. 25+. Compact car €70 per day. Open M-F 8:30am-2pm and 5-9pm, Sa 9am-2pm.

ORIENTATION

Córdoba is divided into the new city and the old. The modern, commercial northern half extends from the train station on Av. de América down to **Plaza de las Tendillas,** the center of the city. The section in the south is a medieval maze known as the **Judería** (Jewish quarter). This tangle of disorienting streets extends from Pl. de las Tendillas to the banks of the Río Guadalquivir, winding past the **Mezquita** and **Alcázar.** The easiest way to reach the old city from the train or bus station is either the **#3** or **#4 bus** (€1) to the Pl. de Tendillas. Otherwise, it is a 20min. walk. From the train station, with your back to the platforms, exit through the left doors, then turn right and cross the parking lot. Continue right onto Av. de los Mozárabes. It is best to walk through the gardens, **Jardines de la Victoria,** in the middle of the boulevard. When the gardens end, the **Puerta Almodóvar,** one of the entrances into the *Judería,* will be on the left.

PRACTICAL INFORMATION

Tourist Offices: Andalucía Regional Office, C. Torrijos, 10 (☎957 35 51 79). From the train station, take bus #3 along the river until the Puente Romano. Walk under the stone arch and the office will be on your left. Open July-Aug. M-F 9:30am-7:30pm,

Sa 10am-7:30pm, Su 10am-2pm; Sept.-June M-Sa 9am-7:30pm, Su 10am-2pm. **Turismo de Córdoba** (☎902 20 17 74; www.turismodecordoba.org) has booths in the train station (open daily 9:30am-2pm and 5-8pm), on C. Caballerizas Reales (open daily 9:30am-2:30pm and 5-8pm), and in Pl. de Tendillas (open daily 10am-1:30pm and 6-9:30pm). Offers walking tours of the city at night (€15), a patio guide and an audioguide (€15).

Currency Exchange: Banco Santander Central Hispano, Pl. de las Tendillas, 1 (☎902 24 24 24). Open M-F 8:30am-2pm, Sa 8:30am-1pm.

Luggage Storage: At the bus station. €2 per day. Open 24hr. Library (see below) offers free locks for temporarily guarding purses and valuables while you sightsee.

Laundry: Teleseco, Ronda de Isasa, 10 (☎957 48 33 56), 1 block from La Mezquita, near the river. Coin service and dry cleaning. Washers €5, dryers €3. Full service with wash, dry, and fold €11.

Budget Travel Agency: Barceló Viajes, C. Historiador Díaz del Moral, 1 (☎957 48 55 55; www.barceloviajes.com), on the corner on C. Morería. Open M-F 9:30am-1:30pm and 5-8:30pm, Sa 10am-1:30pm.

Police: Av. Doctor Fleming, 2 (☎092 or 957 23 87 00).

Medical Services: Red Cross Hospital, Po. de la Victoria, near Puerta de Almodóvar (☎957 42 06 66, emergencies 22 22 22). English spoken.

Library: C. Amador de los Rios, a block from the Mezquita (☎957 35 54 92). Free internet access on 1st and 2nd floors. Open M-F 9am-9pm, Sa 9am-2pm.

Internet Access: Tele-Click, C. Eduardo Dato, 9 (☎957 94 06 15). New machines, A/C, and assorted refreshments. €1.80 per hr., €0.50 per 15min. Open M-F 10am-3pm and 5:30-10:30pm, Sa-Su noon-11pm. **Ch@t-is,** C. Claudio Marcelo, 15 (☎957 47 45 00). €1.80 per hr.; *bonos* from €9 per 10hr. Fax and copies available (€0.06-0.40, discount for students). Open M-F 10am-2pm and 5:30-9pm.

Post Office: C. José Cruz Conde, 15 (☎957 47 97 96). **Lista de Correos.** Open M-F 8:30am-8:30pm, Sa-Su 9:30am-2pm. **Postal Code:** 14070.

ACCOMMODATIONS

Hostels abound in the *Judería* and between La Mezquita and C. de San Fernando. Córdoba is especially crowded during *Semana Santa,* May, and June, and then dies down during the months of July and August. Still, it is generally a good idea to call in advance for reservations. Prices are higher in summer.

IN AND AROUND THE JUDERÍA

The *Judería*'s whitewashed walls and proximity to sights make it a great place to stay. During the day, souvenir booths and cafes keep the streets lively, but the area feels more deserted at night. Take bus #5 from the train station to the "Hotel Melia" stop across the street from the Puerta de Almodóvar. Go under the archway to reach the neighborhood.

Instalación Juvenil Córdoba (HI), Pl. Judá Levi, down C. Judios from Puerta Almodóvar (☎957 29 01 66). A mental asylum converted into a backpacker's paradise. Most rooms have bath and A/C. Courtyards surrounded by orange trees and graffiti art. Breakfast included. Lockers €1.80-2 per day. Towels €1.20. Laundry €2.50, dry €1.50. March-Oct. €19.50-€20.50; Nov.-Feb. €2.10 less. HI discount €3.50. MC/V. ❶

Hostal-Residencia Séneca, C. Conde y Luque, 7 (☎957 47 32 34). A beautiful Córdoba courtyard greets you at the entrance. Fans or A/C. Room size differs greatly, so ask to see one first. Breakfast included; special breakfast on Su. Singles €26, with bath €38; doubles €45/51; triples and 1 huge quad €89. MC/V. ❷

BETWEEN LA MEZQUITA AND CALLE DE SAN FERNANDO

Hostal El Reposo de Bagdad, Fernández Ruano, 11 (☎957 20 28 54). A beautiful Islamic-inspired hostel with large sunlit rooms with bathroom and fan. Pillow-strewn corner where you can eat breakfast in the morning (€3.50) and smoke hookah after dark. Singles €25; doubles €38. ❷

Hostal el Portillo, C. Cabezas, 2 (☎957 47 20 91; www.hostalelportillo.com). A traditional Andalucian house decorated with quirky flair in a quieter part of the neighborhood. Spacious rooms with wrought-iron beds, bath, Wi-Fi (ask for the code), and A/C; some have balconies. Singles €18-20; doubles €30-35. MC/V. ❶

Hostal and Hotel Maestre, C. Romero Barros, 6 (☎957 47 24 10; www.hotelmaestre.com), off C. de San Fernando. Both the hotel and *hostal* have similar royal-hued decor, but the *hostal's* corridors, a maze of Spanish trinkets, are more unique. All rooms with private bath and A/C, most with TV. Breakfast buffet €5. *Hostal* singles €23-28; doubles €30-40. Hotel singles €30-38; doubles €42-50. MC/V. ❷

ELSEWHERE

Hotel Residencia Boston, C. Málaga, 2 (☎957 47 41 76; www.hostel-boston.com), a 10min. walk from the *Judería.* Plain rooms equipped with A/C, TV, phone, safe, and bath. Breakfast in large dining room and lounge area €4. Internet €1 per 30min. Singles €32-35; doubles €50-57. AmEx/MC/V. ❸

Camping Municipal, Av. del Brillante, 50 (☎957 40 38 36). From the train station, turn left on Av. de América, left on Av. del Brillante, and walk uphill (20min.). Buses #10 and 11 from Av. Cervantes stop across the street. Supermarket, restaurant, hot showers. Laundry €3. 1-2 people and tent €18; 2 people, car, and tent €19.05; 2 people and camper €19. IVA not included. Cash only. ❷

FOOD

Touristy restaurants have taken over the Mezquita area, but a 5min. walk in any direction reveals good local spots. In the evenings, locals converge at the outdoor *terrazas* between **Calle Severo Ochoa** and **Calle Dr. Jiménez Díaz** for drinks and tapas. Cheap eateries are farther from the *Judería* in **Barrio Cruz Conde** and around **Avenida Menéndez Pidal** and **Plaza de las Tendillas.** Regional specialties include *salmorejo* (a gazpacho-like cream soup topped with hard-boiled egg and pieces of ham) and *rabo de toro* (bull's tail simmered in tomato sauce). For groceries, try **%Dia,** on C. Sevilla, 4, near Pl. de las Tendillas. (Open M-Sa 9am-3pm and 5:30-9pm.) **El Corte Inglés,** Av. Ronda de los Tejares, 30, has a supermarket on the bottom floor. (Open M-Sa 10am-10pm. AmEx/MC/V.)

Taberna Sociedad de Plateros, C. San Francisco, 6 (☎957 47 00 42). A mainstay since 1872, this place has the biggest *raciones* for the best prices (€4.80-14.80); a half-*ración* of salad can serve as a filling lunch. Open M-F 8am-3:45pm and 8-11:45pm, Sa 8am-3:45pm and 7:30-1:45pm. AmEx/MC/V. ❷

Mundano, C. Conde de Cárdenas, 3 (☎957 47 37 85). Back-alley locale combines homemade fare with funky style and art shows. Breakfast (€1.50-1.80), tapas (gazpacho €1.10), teas, and entrees (€3-5). Vegetarian options. Live music some weekends. Open M-F 10am-5pm and 10pm-2am, Sa noon-6pm and 10pm-2am. Cash only. ❶

Salon de Té, C. Buen Pastor (☎957 48 79 84). Lie back on satin pillows in this recreated 12th-century teahouse while savoring a huge selection of teas, juices, and Arab pastries. Try the mint lemonade for a refreshing variation on a summer favorite (€2.50). Open daily 11am-10:30pm. Cash only. ❶

SIGHTS

LA MEZQUITA

C. Cardenal Herrero, 1. ☎957 47 05 12. Open Mar.-Oct. M-Sa 8:30am-7pm, Su 8:30-10:30am and 2-7pm. €8, 10-14 €4, under 10 free. Wheelchair-accessible. Last ticket sold 30min. before closing. Mass M-Sa 8:30-10am, Su 11am and 1pm. Take advantage of the free admission M-Sa 8:30-10am (during mass). Silence is enforced; no groups.

Built in AD 785 on the site of a Visigoth basilica, this masterpiece is considered the most important Islamic monument in the Western world. Over the course of two centuries, La Mezquita was enlarged to cover an area the size of several city blocks. With more than 850 columns, it was the third-largest mosque in the Islamic world at the time, after only those of Mecca and Medina.

Visitors enter through the **Patio de los Naranjos,** an arcaded courtyard featuring carefully spaced orange trees, palms, and fountains, where the dutiful performed their ablutions before prayer. The **Torre del Alminar** encloses remains of the minaret from which the *muezzin* called the faithful to prayer. The grand entrances to the mosque were closed during its conversion to a Gothic cathedral, and today you must enter through the right corner of the facade.

Beginning in the oldest part of the mosque, built under Abd Al-Rahman I, the multiple pillars carved from granite and marble are capped by striped arches. Look for the rails that guard the remaining mosaic of the Visigothic basilica near the entrance. La Mezquita's most elaborate additions—the dazzling *mihrab* (prayer niche) and the triple *maksourah* (caliph's niche)—were created in the 10th century. Holy Roman Emperor Constantine VII gave the nearly 35 tons of intricate gold, pink, and blue marble Byzantine mosaics that shimmer across the arches of the *mihrab* to the caliphs. The *mihrab* formerly housed a gilt copy of the Qur'an and remains covered in Kufic inscriptions of the 99 names of Allah. To this day, historians remain stumped as to why the *mihrab* does not face Mecca, as Muslim architects had highly precise methods of calculation and would be unlikely to make such a mistake.

At the far end of the Mezquita lies the **Capilla Villaviciosa,** which in 1371 was the first Christian chapel to be built in the mosque, thus beginning the transition into a place of Christian worship. In 1523, Bishop Alonso Manriquez, an ally of Carlos V, proposed the construction of a cathedral in the center of the mosque. The town rallied violently against the idea, promising painful death to any worker who helped tear down La Mezquita. The bishop nevertheless erected a towering *crucero* (transept) and *coro* (choir stall), incongruously planting a richly adorned Baroque cathedral amid far more austere environs.

The cathedral's most noteworthy part is the **choir,** which depicts the entire Bible in mahogany panels. On one side of the transept, atop the church tower, the angel Raphael (the protector of Córdoba), watches over the faithful, proud that his is the most popular male name in the city.

IN AND AROUND THE JUDERÍA

ALCÁZAR DE LOS REYES CRISTIANOS. Along the river, to the left of La Mezquita, lies the Alcázar, built in 1328 during the *Reconquista* on the site of a strategic Roman trade and transport holding. Fernando and Isabel bade farewell to Columbus here (as seen by the towering statue in the gardens), and from 1490 to 1821, it served as a headquarters for the Inquisition. The reception hall directly above the hot rooms of the royal baths displays first-century Roman mosaics and a marble sarcophagus. Don't leave without visiting the endless gardens with hedges, flowers, dancing fountains, and fish pools. *Cor-*

dobeses come to cool down in this tranquil setting, which also serves as a stage for concerts. *(☎957 42 01 51. Open Tu-Sa 8:30am-2:30pm, Su and holidays 9:30am-2:30pm. €4, students €2; F free. Gardens open June 21-Sept. 8pm-midnight. €2, F Free.)*

SINAGOGA. Built in 1315, the synagogue, where famed philosopher Maimonides (1135-1204) once prayed, evokes the memory of Córdoba's once-vibrant Jewish community. Adorned with carved Mozárabe patterns and Hebrew inscriptions, the walls of the small temple have been restored to much of their original intricacy. The first floor is open to the public, but the upper hall, where women once prayed, is closed. *(C. Judíos, 20, just past the statue of Maimonides. ☎957 20 29 28. Open Tu-Sa 9:30am-2pm and 3:30-5:30pm, Su 9:30-1:30pm. €0.30, EU citizens free.)*

CASA DE SEFARAD. Located between the synagogue and Casa Andalusí, the permanent exhibition of the Casa de Sefarad, "Memories of Sefarad," explores the legacy of the Jewish presence in Spain and in Córdoba. It also highlights the men and women who were historic pillars of the Jewish community in Córdoba and throughout al-Andalus. *(From the synagogue, turn left on C. Judíos and make the first right at C. Averroes. ☎957 42 14 04; www.casadesefarad.com. Open M-Sa 10am-6pm, Su 11am-2pm. Free guided tours M-Sa noon and 5pm, Su noon. €4, students €3.*

CASA ANDALUSÍ. A restored 12th-century house, this private museum boasts a Visigothic basement with mosaic floors, a gorgeous flower-filled fountain, old Arabic texts and coins, and an interesting display on Córdoba's role in the rise of paper-making, complete with replicas of the old tools used in the process. Calligraphic posters (€2.50-7) and gorgeous paper samples are also on sale. *(C. Judíos, 12, next to the the synagogue. ☎957 29 06 42; www.lacasaandalusi.com. Open daily 10:30am-8pm. €2.50, students €2.)*

MUSEO TAURINO Y DE ARTE CORDOBÉS. Get ready for a lot of bull. Dedicated to the history and lore of the bullfight, rooms contain uniforms, posters, and artifacts from decades of bullfighting in Spain. The main exhibit includes a replica of the tomb of Spain's most famous matador, the dashing Manolete (1917-1947), and the hide of the bull that killed him. *(Pl. Maimónides. ☎957 20 10 56. The museum is currently undergoing renovations; call to confirm hours and prices).*

OTHER SIGHTS. **El Jardín Botánico** (Botanic Garden) is one of the Córdoba's best-kept secrets. Complete with an arboretum, glass houses, ethnobotanical museum, rose gardens, and a water wheel, the gardens offer a peaceful and educational retreat from the city. The gardens host many of the city's cultural and musical events at night. *(☎957 20 00 18; www.jardinbotanicodecordoba.com. Open Tu-Sa 10am-9pm, Su 10am-3pm. Museums open Tu-Sa 10am-2:30pm and 5-8pm, Su 10am-2:30pm. €2, students €1.30, groups of 20+ €1).* Townspeople take great pride in their traditional **patios.** Among the most beautiful streets are **Calleja del Indiano,** off C. Fernández Ruano at Pl. Ángel Torres, and the **Calleja de Flores,** off C. Blanco Belmonte, where geraniums cluster along the walls of the alley.

OUTSIDE THE JUDERÍA

MUSEO JULIO ROMERO DE TORRES. Romero (1874-1930) mastered the subtleties of mixing a dark palette and applied this talent to renditions of sensual *cordobesa* women. Exhibited here in the artist's former home is the lauded *Naranjas y limones* (Oranges and Lemons) and *La Chiquita Piconera* (The Little Coal Girl), along with dozens of other works. (*Pl. Potro, 5-10min. from La Mezquita. ☎957 49 19 09. Open Tu-Sa 8:30am-2:30pm, Su and holidays 9:30am-2:30pm. Last entry 30min. before closing. €4, students €2. F free.)*

MUSEO DE BELLAS ARTES. Across the courtyard from Museo Julio Romero de Torres, this art museum's building was a hospital during the reign of Fernando and Isabel. It hosts a vast collection of Renaissance religious art, works by the de Torres family, as well as works by more modern *cordobés* artists. *(Pl. del Potro. From la Mezquita, pass the Puento Romano, the Puente de Miraflores (the next bridge), and walk 5-10min to C. Torres. Pl. del Potro is next to the fountain. Alternately, Bus #3, 7, and 16 also pass by. ☎957 35 55 50; www.museosdeandalucia.es. Open Tu 2:30-8:30pm, W-Sa 9am-8:30pm, Su and holidays 9am-2:30pm. Last entry 30min. before closing. €1.50, EU citizens free.)*

PALACIO DEL MARQUÉS DE VIANA. An elegant 14th-century mansion, the palace displays 12 traditional patios complete with sprawling gardens, majestic fountains, tapestries, furniture, and porcelain. *(Pl. Don Gome, 2, a 20min. walk from La Mezquita. ☎957 49 67 41. Open July-Sept. M-Sa 9am-2pm; Oct.-June M-F 10am-1pm and 4-6pm, Sa 10am-1pm. Closed June 1-16. Complete tour €6, garden and courtyards only €3.)*

OTHER SIGHTS. Across the river on the Puente Romano is the Puerta del Puente, which houses the **Museo Torre de la Calahorra,** a lively and beautiful testament to the coexistence of the Muslim, Christian, and Jewish communities in Córdoba. *(☎ 957 29 39 29. Open daily 10am-2pm, 4:30-8:30pm. €4.50, groups and children €3. Price includes an 1½hr. audio guide and guidebook.)* Near the Palacio del Marqués de Viana in Pl. Capuchinos (also known as Pl. de los Dolores) and next to a monastery is the **Cristo de los Faroles** (Christ of the Lanterns), one of the most famous religious icons in Spain and the site of many all-night vigils. The eight lanterns symbolize the eight provinces of Andalucía. Remnants of second-century **Roman water wheels** line the sides of the Río Guadalquivir. Believed to have been used by Romans as mills, they were later used to bring water to the caliph's palace and the gardens around the city. The mills continued to function until Isabel la Católica demanded they be shut down—they disturbed her sleep.

NIGHTLIFE

Nightlife is tame in the old city, and hip bars and clubs tend to cluster together. Nearest to the old city, **Calle Alfonso XIII** and the adjacent **Calle Alfaros** host limited options. Farther away, the **Barrio Brillante** is a true nightlife hot spot, though its bars and clubs tend to open only on weekends. Bus #10 goes to Brillante from the train station until about 11pm, but the bars are empty until 1am and stay open until 4am. A taxi costs about €3-6, or it's a 45min. uphill hike. **Avenida Libertad,** close to the Brillante, offers a more chic (and costly) ambience with diverse and consistently gorgeous pubs.

In the winter, nightlife centers around the neighborhood where the Universidad de Córdoba used to be, especially in pubs on **Calle Los Alderetes** and **Calle Julio Pellicer,** and near the **Plaza de la Corredera.** An alternative to partying is a cool stroll along the **walk-through fountains** and falling sheets of water that line Av. de América between Pl. de Colón and the train station.

Soul, C. Alfonso XIII, 3 (☎957 49 15 80). Spontaneous dancing and a crazy young crowd. Bring earplugs or a fever for bass. Free Wi-Fi. Beer €2.10. Mixed drinks €4.50 and up. Open daily 9am-2pm and 4pm-3am, later on weekends. Cash only.

Moma, Av. Libertad, 4 (☎957 27 19 12). This ethnic-chic bar has African-styled stools and fake mosaic lamp shades. Beer €2-2.50. Mixed drinks from €5. Open M-Th and Su 9am-3am, F-Sa 10am-4am. AmEx/MC/V.

Club Don Luis, Av. del Brillante, 18. Trendy club draws local university students who dance to Spanish pop. Though there's a large outdoor terrace, most people pack inside. Beer €2.50. Mixed drinks €5. Open Th-Sa midnight-4:30am. Cash only.

ENTERTAINMENT

For the latest cultural events, pick up a free copy of the *Guía del Ocio* at the tourist office. Though *flamenco* is not cheap in Córdoba, the shows are high-quality and worth a visit for those not heading to Sevilla. Prize-winning dancers perform at **Tablao Cardenal**, C. Torrijos, 10, facing La Mezquita. Reserve seats there or at your hostel. (☎957 48 31 12; www.tablaocardenal.com. Shows M-Sa 10:30pm. Cover €18, includes one drink.) A cheaper but equally entertaining option is **La Bulería,** C. Pedro López, 3, with nightly shows also at 10:30pm. (☎957 48 38 39. €11, includes one drink.) Every July, Córdoba hosts a **guitar festival,** bringing talent from all over the world.

DAYTRIP FROM CÓRDOBA

MADINAT AL-ZAHRA

Bravo buses leave from Po. de la Victoria or in front of the Alcázar on Av. del Alcázar. A video with English subtitles plays on the ride. (30min.; Tu-Sa 11am and 6pm, Sa also 10am, Su 10, 11am; €6, reserve tickets at a Turismo de Córdoba office or at most accommodations.) Buses return to Córdoba 1hr. after arriving in al-Zahra. Visión Córdoba offers transportation and 1hr. tour in both Spanish and English (☎957 76 02 41, Tu-Su at 10:30am, €28). Alternatively, Bus #1 leaves from Po. de la Victoria; get off at Cruz de Madinat al-Zahra for a 3km walk to the ruins. (☎957 35 55 06/07; www.juntadeandalucia.es/cultura/madinatalzahra. Open May-Sept. 15 Tu-Sa 10am-8:30pm, Su 10am-2pm; Sept. 16-Apr. Tu-Sa 10am-6:30pm, Su 10am-2pm. €1.50, EU citizens free.)

In 940, the self-appointed caliph Abd al-Rahman III decided to move the region's seat of power 7km to the northwest of Córdoba. There, with the muscle of an estimated 10,000 workers and 3000 pack animals, the ruler constructed an indulgent 277-acre wonderland of courtyards, gardens, porticos, and salons in a symbolic effort to strengthen and reunify the steadily diminishing Moorish empire. Legend, on the other hand, attributes the grand palace-town to the caliph's desire to impress his favorite concubine, al-Zahra. Weakened by an internal power stuggle, the medina was soon ransacked by civilian mobs and foreign Berber armies; its precious colored marble, swirling columns, and jasper were looted. In less than 80 years, al-Zahra's glory faded completely, and looting continued into the 14th century.

The ruins are worth a visit for the historically inclined, but don't expect its dazzling former grandeur. The restoration process is ongoing; almost 90% of al-Zahra is still hidden underground. Once you enter through the gate, you'll be standing atop the town's third and highest terrace, offering a bird's-eye view of the medina and minuscule Córdoba below. Follow the city wall, reconstructed in 1920s, into the old town, keeping left until you reach the site where the mosque once stood. Although you can't reach the lower terrace, you can admire the excavated earthen foundation paved with flagstones in the caliph's prayer nave. A minaret once stood high above the sloping landscape, calling those in al-Zahra and Córdoba's Alcázar to prayer. The most striking part of the ruins is the caliph's royal reception hall. The High Garden, one terrace above the Lower Gardens, is a structural part of the hall and is a kind of organic red carpet for any worthy enough to be greeted by the ruler. Palm trees, hedges, and flowers were replanted in the 1920s to emphasize the geometrical mazes that once held murmuring fountains and an aviary. Inaccessible to the general public, the gardens are best viewed from the top terrace.

COSTA DE LA LUZ

While most of Andalucía is the domain of foreign tourists seeking wild nightlife and miles of beaches, the Costa de la Luz remains a destination populated primarily by Spanish vacationers looking for some fun in the sun. Beyond the *bodegas* of Jerez de la Frontera, the region offers picture-perfect *pueblos blancos* (white towns), opportunities to catch some wind or waves, and the golden light that is its namesake. Backed by dry pines and golden-hued dunes of fine sand, the expansive beaches of Costa de la Luz are home to strong winds and waves that make it a paradise for windsurfers and surfboarders. Less developed than other vacation destinations, this region is also known for its wealth of protected natural reserves.

JEREZ DE LA FRONTERA ☎956

Jerez de la Frontera (pop. 203,000) is the cradle of three staples of Andalucian culture: flamenco, Carthusian horses, and, of course, *jerez* (sherry). The sheer quantity and quality of the third staple draws hordes of tourists, most of whom are older Europeans. On the other end of the spectrum, the newest generations of flamenco performers take the stage throughout the city and give live rhythmic form to *el duende* (soul, emotion) itself. Jerez also makes a good departure point for the *ruta de los pueblos blancos* (white village route). Those not interested in *bodegas* or horses will still find flavor in Jerez: the local zest for flamenco, as well as a veritable list of historical sites, is worth a day or two.

TRANSPORTATION

Flights: Jerez Airport, Ctra. Jerez-Sevilla (☎956 15 00 00; www.aena.es), 7km from town. Taxi to the airport about €15. Airport shuttle (☎956 01 21 00; www.cmtbc.com). **Iberia** (☎956 18 43 94) has an office at the terminal. Most international flights connect to Jerez through Sevilla or Madrid.

Trains: Pl. de la Estación (☎956 34 23 19). **RENFE,** C. Larga, 34 (☎902 24 02 02). To: **Barcelona** (12hr.; 8:22am and 8:10pm; €95.80); **Cádiz** (45min.; M-F 18 per day 6:30am-10:25pm, Sa 4 per day 8:31am-5:29pm, Su 5 per day 8:31am-5:29pm; €3.65); **Madrid** (4hr.; 8:22am and 5:02pm; €62.30); **Sevilla** (1hr.; M-F 12 per day 7:39am-10:08pm, Sa 4 per day 7:39am-3:46pm, Su 5 per day 7:39am-3:46pm; €6.70).

Buses: Pl. de la Estación, next to the train station (☎956 33 96 66).

Linesur (☎956 34 10 63; www.linesur.com) to **Algeciras** (1hr.; M-F 9 per day 7:15am-9:45pm, Sa-Su 7 per day 8:30am-9:45pm; €10), **Sanlúcar** (45min.; M-F hourly 7am-9pm, Sa-Su every 2hr. 9am-9pm; €1.30), and **Sevilla** (1hr., 7-10 per day 6:30am-10:30pm, €7.

Secorbus (☎956 34 59 71; www.socibus.es) to **Madrid** (5hr., 6 per day 8:50am-11:50pm, €21.90).

Transportes Generales Comes (☎956 32 14 64 or 902 19 92 08; www.tgcomes.es) service to: **Cádiz** (50min.; M-F 22 per day 7am-11:15pm, Sa-Su 11 per day 7am-11:15pm; €2.90); **Granada** (4hr., 1pm, €25.77); **Ronda** (2hr., 3-6 per day 9:45am-7pm, €10.34); **Sevilla** (1hr.; M-Sa 5 per day 9am-11:30pm, Su 4 per day 10:30am-11:30pm; €7.20).

Transportes Los Amarillos (☎956 32 93 47 or 902 21 03 17; www.losamarillos.es) to **Arcos de la Frontera** (30min.; M-F 19 per day 7am-9pm, Sa 9 per day 7:45am-8:15pm, Su 11 per day 9am-9pm; €2.40).

Public Transportation: Most of the 17 bus lines run every 15-20min. (though less frequently at night). Most pass through Pl. del Arenal or next to Pl. Romero Martínez. Fare €1.10. Info office (☎956 34 34 46; www.cojetusa.com) in Pl. del Arenal. A *Jerez en tu bolsillo* guide, free from the tourist office, lists all the lines and schedules.

Car Rental: Niza, Ctra. N. IV Madrid-Cádiz, Km. 634 (☎956 30 28 60 or 956 18 15 75; www.nizacars.es). Take Av. Alcalde Álvaro Domecq to Hwy. N-IV toward Sevilla (next to El Corte Inglés). 21+ and must have had license for at least 1 yr. From €75 per day. Open daily 8:30am-8pm. AmEx/MC/V. **Bahía Rent A Car,** in the train station in Pl. de la Estación (☎956 32 25 92 or 669 86 17 89; www.bahiarentacar.com). Open M-F

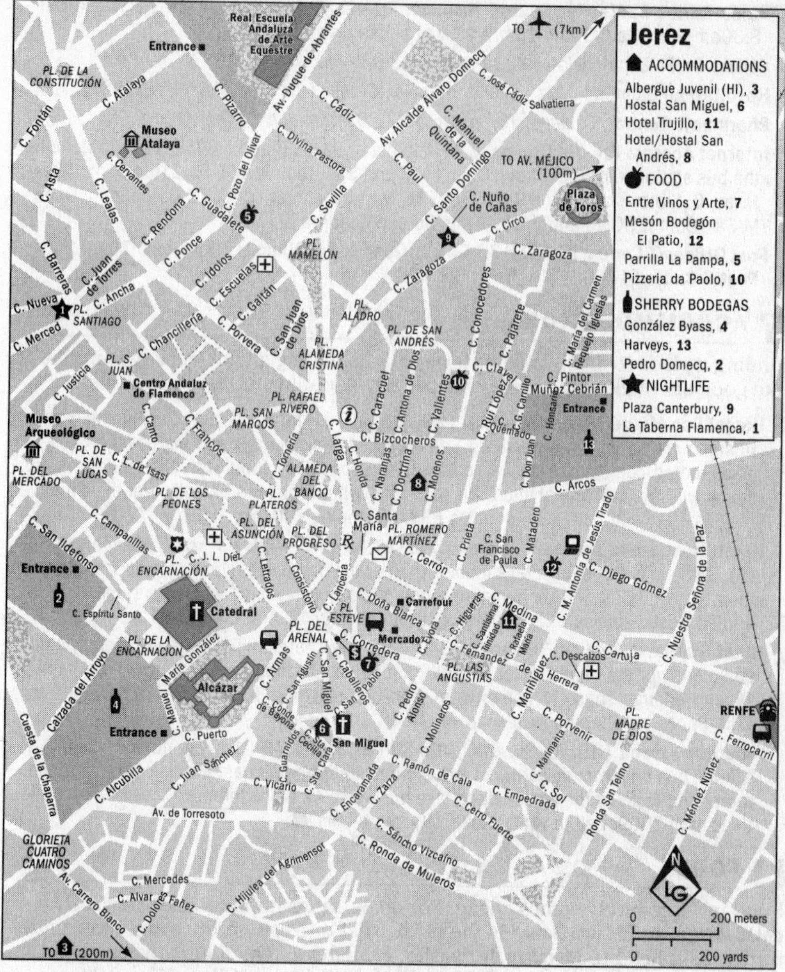

9:30am-1:30pm and 5-8pm, Sa 9:30am-1:30pm. AmEx/MC/V. There are 7 car rental agencies at the airport.

Taxis: Teletaxi (☎956 34 48 60).

ORIENTATION AND PRACTICAL INFORMATION

The streets of Jerez are difficult to navigate without a map. Get a free one from the tourist office or at any of the major sights or *bodegas*. **Plaza Romero Martínez** is the city's center. **Calle Lancería/Calle Larga** is the main pedestrian road in the center, and *bodegas* are scattered along the outskirts of the old city.

Tourist Office: Pl. Alameda Cristina (☎956 34 17 11). Open M-F 10am-3pm and 5-7pm, Sa-Su 10am-2:30pm.

Bank: Banco Santander Central Hispano, Pl. Arenal, 5 (☎902 24 24 24). Open M-F 8:30am-2pm, Sa 8:30am-1pm. A slew of banks also lines C. Larga.

Police: On Pl. Encarnación (☎092 or 956 33 03 46).

Hospital: Ambulatorio de la Seguridad Social, C. José Luis Díaz (☎956 32 32 02).

Pharmacy: Central, C. Larga, 28 (☎956 34 28 93). Open daily 9am-10pm.

Internet Access: The Big Orange, C. M. Antonía de Jesús Tirado (☎956 35 01 01), near the bus station. €1.80 per hour. Open M-Th and Su 11am-1am, F-Sa 11am-3am. **Ciber Jerez,** C. Santa Maria, 3 (☎956 33 40 16; www.ciberjerez.com). €0.03 per min. Open M-Sa 10am-2:30pm and 5:30-11pm, Su and holidays 5-11pm.

Post Office: C. Cerrón, 2 (☎956 32 67 33). Open M-F 8:30am-8:30pm, Sa 9:30am-2pm. **Postal Code:** 11480.

ACCOMMODATIONS

Finding a place to crash in Jerez is as easy as finding a wine cork to sniff, but, like good sherry, it won't come cheap. Prices double during fall festivals.

Hostal San Miguel, Pl. San Miguel, 4 (☎956 34 85 62; http://galeon.com/hsanmiguel/Hostal.htm), behind the Iglesia de San Miguel. Marble details and statues surround a glass-roofed courtyard. Pleasant, colorful, and spacious rooms with A/C and TV, mere steps away from Pl. Arenal and C. Larga, in the center. Ask for a balcony over the church. Singles €22, with bath €33; doubles €37/43; triples €60/65. AmEx/MC/V. ❷

Hotel/Hostal San Andrés, C. Morenos, 12-14 (☎956 34 09 83; www.hotelsanandres.es). Some of the cheapest digs in the center of the city. Large rooms provide the basics; the adjacent hotel, with TV common room, offers pricier rooms with private baths, A/C, and TV. Hostal singles €22; doubles €30. Hotel €26/40. AmEx/MC/V. ❷

Hotel Trujillo, C. Medina, 36 (☎ 956 34 24 38; www.hoteltrujillo.com). The friendly staff complements the hotel's quiet locale. Rooms have wooden bed frames, private baths, TV, and enough space to flamenco in. Apr.-Oct. singles €30; doubles €42.80; triples €60. Prices cheaper in low season. MC/V. ❸

Albergue Juvenil (HI), Av. Blase Infante, 30 (☎856 81 40 01; www.inturjoven.com), a 15min. bus ride from downtown. From the bus station, walk past the train station to the rotary and cross at the crosswalk to take bus #9 to Av. Blase Infante. Closed for renovations until 2009. Call to verify availability and prices. ❶

FOOD

Food in Jerez rarely comes cheap. For deals, tapas-hoppers take on **Pl. del Arenal, C. Larga,** and **Pl. del Banco** in the old town. For fresh produce and the aroma of raw fish, head to **Mercado de Abastos,** Pl. Esteve. (Open M-Sa 8:30am-3pm.) For groceries, **Carrefour** is on C. Doña Blanca 13 (Open M-Sa 9:15am-9:30pm.)

Entre Vinos y Arte, C. Corredera, 30-32 (☎956 33 38 65), 3 blocks from Pl. del Arenal. Low on tourists, high on hospitality. Don't leave without sampling the bull's tail; a half-*ración* of this delicacy is enough to keep your stomach full. Vegetarian and meat tapas €1.50-2.50. *Raciones* €6. Open daily 8:30am-4pm and 7pm-midnight. MC/V. ❶

Parrilla La Pampa, C. Guadalete, 24 (☎956 34 17 49), near Pl. Mamelón. The hides dotting the walls hint at this spot's specialty—authentic, imported Argentine beef (€8.75-19.70). Pork, chicken, veal, and ostrich (€16.20-17.70) round out the menu menagerie. Open M-Sa 12:30-4:30pm and 8:30pm-12:30am. AmEx/MC/V. ❸

Mesón Bodegón El Patio, C. San Francisco de Paula, 7 (☎956 34 07 36). Sumptuous traditional fare made with local produce in a refurbished sherry warehouse. Old portraits, antiques, and game heads fill the dining room. Tapas €1.50-4.25. *Raciones* €5-19. *Menú* €18. Open M-Sa 11:30am-4:30pm and 8pm-12:30am. MC/V. ❷

Pizzeria da Paolo, at the corner of C. Clavel and C. Valientes. Like a fancy Italian restaurant, but affordable. Tasty pizzas (€5-9) and pastas (€4.50-7.50). Plenty of vegetarian options. Open Tu-Su 1:15-4pm and 9pm-midnight. MC/V. ❷

SHERRY BODEGAS

People come to Jerez for the *bodegas* (wineries), and while many smaller *bodegas* offer tours, it's worth indulging your inner tourist and checking out the more famous ones. Tour guides explain the city's trademark *solera* (sherry-making process), leading visitors through heavenly-smelling barrel storage rooms and under grape-covered trellises before topping off the tour with free samples. The best time to visit is early September during the harvest; the worst is August, when many *bodegas* close down and wait for the grapes to ripen. Group reservations for tours must be made at least one week in advance. Looking for a job? Many *bodegas* hire English-speaking tour guides for two or three months, depending on need. *Bodegas* accept solicitations by mail, and if selected, workers undergo an intense training program before starting.

Pedro Domecq, C. San Ildefonso, 3 (☎956 15 15 00; www.bodegasfundadorpedrodomecq.com). Founded in 1730, Domecq is Jerez's oldest, most prestigious *bodega.* 1hr. tours include 20min. video. Unlimited sampling. Hourly tours in English and Spanish M-F 10am-1pm, Sa noon. Tour with tapas Tu, Th, Sa 2pm. Tour with tapas and flamenco May-Sept. Th 2pm. Regular tour €6, 2pm tour with tapas €11. AmEx/MC/V.

González Byass, C. Manuel María González, 12 (☎956 35 70 16 or 902 44 00 77; www.gonzalezbyass.es; www.bodegastiopepe.com). The makers of the popular Tío Pepe brand. The Disney World of *bodegas:* a bit commercial, but worth visiting and very kid-friendly. Trolleys whisk visitors past the world's largest weathervane and a storage room designed by Gustave Eiffel. June-Sept. tours in English M-Sa every hr. 11:30am-2pm and 4:30-6:30pm. Oct.-May tours in English M-Sa hourly 11:30am-5:30pm, Su 11:30am-1:30pm. €10, 2pm tour with tapas €15. AmEx/D/MC/V.

Harveys, C. Pintor Muñoz Cebrián (☎956 15 15 00 or 956 15 15 51; www.bodegasharveys.com). Makers of Harveys Bristol Cream, the best-selling sherry in the world. Reservations required; call in advance. 1hr. tours M-F 10am and noon. Tour and tasting Th 10am includes video and entrance to the Harveys museum. €8. MC/V.

SIGHTS

ALCÁZAR AND LA CÁMERA OSCURA. Along the southeastern axis of the city, the 12th century **Alcázar** of Jerez is one of the best preserved in the Iberian Peninsula. Visitors can also explore vestiges of the castle's renovations in the 15th and 18th centuries, including a Baroque palace and olive oil mill. The palace's tower houses the **Cámera Oscura,** the highest spot in Jerez, from which visitors can see live images of the city below. The Octagonal Tower, Torre del Homenaje, and Palacio de Doña Blanca are undergoing renovations until 2009. *(☎956 32 69 23. Open May-Sept. 15 M-Sa 10am-7:30pm, Su 10am-2:30pm; Sept. 16-Apr. daily 10am-7:30pm. Alcázar €3, students €1.80; Alcázar and Cámera Oscura €5.40/€4.20. Reservations for the guided tour are welcomed. €3. Visits to the Camera Oscura occur every 30min. with approx. 15 people per group.)*

REAL ESCUELA ANDALUZA DE ARTE EQUESTRE. Jerez's love for wine is almost matched by its passion for horses. During May, the Royal Andalucian School of Equestrian Art sponsors the **Feria del Caballo**—a horse fair with carriage competitions and races of Jerez-bred Carthusian horses. During the rest of the year, weekly shows feature a troupe of horses dancing in choreographed sequences. *(Av. Duque de Abrantes. ☎956 31 80 08; www.realescuela.org. Training sessions M* *and W 11am-2pm, July-Sept. also F. €6. Shows Tu and Th noon; Aug. also F noon. €13-21, depending on seat; children and seniors 40% off. Museum and training session €7, museum only €3. MC/V.)*

YEGUADA LA CARTUJA HIERRO DEL BOCADO. Every Saturday at 11am, the horses from the largest Carthusian thoroughbred stud farm in Spain strut their stuff for an appreciative audience. *(Ctra. Medina–El Portal, km 6.5. ☎956 16 28 09; www.yeguadacartuja.com. Sa 11am.)*

ENTERTAINMENT AND NIGHTLIFE

Rare footage of Spain's most talented flamenco singers, dancers, and guitarists is available for viewing at the **Centro Andaluz de Flamenco,** in Palacio Pemartín, on Pl. de San Juan. (☎956 34 92 65; www.centroandaluzdeflamenco.es. Open M-F 9am-2pm. Videos every hr. 10am-2pm. Free.) Most *peñas* and *tablaos* (clubs and bars that host flamenco) are in the old town and hold special performances in July and August. Occasionally there are free performances in some plazas, especially Pl. de Toros. For more frequent shows, walk over to Pl. Santiago to **La Taberna Flamenca,** Angostillo de Santiago, 3, which hosts some of Jerez's youngest flamenco dancers in an intimate setting reminiscent of the days of the gypsy camps. (☎956 32 36 93; www.latarbernaflamenca.com. Mid-May to Oct. shows daily 10:30pm, Tu-Th and Sa also 2:30pm. Nov. to mid-May shows Tu-Sa 10:30pm. Reservations recommended for dinner M-Sa noon-4pm and 8pm-midnight. Cover €15, includes 2 drinks; with dinner €30 min. AmEx/MC/V.)

Visitors to Jerez tend to be on the older side, and nightlife in the city center caters directly to them; to find a younger scene, head to the city outskirts. The Irish-themed bar and disco **Plaza Canterbury,** C. Nuño, is a hot spot for tourists and students alike, with two bars (O'Donoghue's and Gambrinus, the latter serving tapas), an outdoor patio, and a popular club. (Beer at bars €1.50-2, mixed drinks €4.50-5; at club €2.50/5. Club cover €8. **Gambrinus Bar** open M-Sa 9am-1:30pm, Su 4pm-1:30am. **O'Donoghue's** open daily 6pm-6am. Club open F-Sa 1:30-7am.) A slew of bars and clubs lines the well-lit **Avenida Méjico** between C. Santo Domingo and C. Salvatierra (a 25min. walk from Pl. del Arenal). Bars and pubs also cluster on the lively **Avenida Lola Flores** near the *fútbol* stadium.

Autumn, in addition to being grape harvest season, is festival season, when Jerez showcases its best equine and flamenco traditions. These festivals are collectively known as the **Fiestas de Otoño,** held from early September until the end of October. In September, the **Fiesta de la Bulería** and the **Festival de Teatro, Música y Baile** celebrate flamenco. The largest horse parade in the world, with races in Pl. del Arenal, is the highlight of the final week. Check at the tourist office for details; schedules are available in September for the upcoming year. And, for those with endless amounts of energy, the world-famous **Festival Internacional de Flamenco de Jerez** electrifies the city during February and March.

SANLÚCAR DE BARRAMEDA ☎956

Sanlúcar de Barrameda (pop. 63,000), at the mouth of the Río Guadalquivir, borders the Parque Nacional Coto de Doñana. Christopher Columbus sailed from here on his third voyage, while Magellan too took off from its ports. This seaside corner of the illustrious "sherry triangle" (along with Jerez and El Puerto de Santa María) specializes in *manzanilla*, the saltiest member of the sherry family. Visitors come to quiet Sanlúcar for sherry *bodegas*, sands, and sun without all the tourists of nearby Jerez and Cádiz.

TRANSPORTATION. The bus station is on Av. de la Estación, one block from the main Calzada del Ejército. Transportes Los Amarillos (☎956 38 50 60; office open M-F 7:30am-12:15pm, 1:15-2pm, and 6-10pm; Sa-Su 10am-2:15pm, 4-10pm) runs **buses** to **Cádiz** (1hr., 5-9 per day 6:15am-6:20pm, €3.08); **Sevilla** (2hr., 6-12 per day 6:45am-9pm, €7). Linesur (☎956 34 10 63) goes to **Jerez** (45min.; M-F every hr. 8:10am-9:10pm, Sa-Su every 2hr.; €2). If ticket booths are closed, you can buy tickets on the bus. For **taxis,** call ☎956 36 00 04.

ORIENTATION AND PRACTICAL INFORMATION. The tourist office is on **Calzada del Ejército,** which runs perpendicular to the beach. Staff has info on the **Parque Nacional Coto de Doñana.** (☎956 36 61 10. Open daily July-Aug. M-F 10am-2pm and 6-8pm, Sa-Su 10am-1:30pm; Sept.-Feb. M-F 10am-2pm and 4-6pm, Sa-Su 10am-2pm; Mar.-Jun. M-F 10am-2pm and 5-7pm, Sa-Su 10am-2pm.) To hit the beach from the bus station, exit from the stairs facing the supermarket (**Super Sol,** open M-Sa 10am-10pm) and turn left; turn left again at the intersection. Local services include: medical at **Ambulatorio de la S.S.** on Calzada del Ejército (☎956 04 72 00 or 04); **police,** Av. de la Constitución, 1 (☎956 38 80 11); **internet** access at **Cyber Guadalquivir,** C. Infanta Beatriz, 11, off Calzada del Ejército (☎956 36 74 03; €1.80 per hr.; open M-Sa 10am-1am, Su 11am-1am); and **post office,** C. Correos and Av. Cerro Falcón (☎956 36 09 37; open M-F 8:30am-2:30pm, Sa 9am-1pm). **Postal Code:** 11540.

ACCOMMODATIONS AND FOOD. Few bargains exist in Sanlúcar; it may be worthwhile to inquire at doorway signs reading *"se alquilan habitaciones"* (rooms for rent). **Hostal La Blanca Paloma ❶,** Pl. San Roque, 9, keeps clean rooms, some of which have balconies. Its central location makes it a good option. (☎956 36 36 44. Singles €18; doubles €30; triples €45; prices vary with season. Cash only.) For a sit-down meal, head for the side streets off **C. San Juan** or to the *casco antiguo* up the hill. *Terrazas* fill **Pl. San Roque** and **Pl. del Cabildo.** Food prices are low across town, and you can find a decent meal for under €8 at any of the cafe-bars off of the two main plazas. Women in pink get-ups scoop the most popular ice cream in town at **Helados Artesanos Toni ❶,** Pl. del Cabildo, 2. (☎956 36 22 13. Small cone €1.60, large €2.30. Banana split €4.20. Shakes €2-4.10. Open daily 11am-2am.)

SIGHTS AND ENTERTAINMENT. The enormous 14th-century **Iglesia de Nuestra Señora de la O,** Pl. de la Paz, competes with two impressive palaces for the attention of sun-worshipping tourists. The church, with a Rococo-style altar, along with nine adjoining chapels of Gothic and Baroque, is the focal point of the religious community in Sanlúcar. (☎956 36 05 55. Open Tu-Sa 10am-1pm, Su 10am-noon. Mass M and F 8pm, Su 9am, noon, 8pm. Free.) The **Palacio Medina Sidonia,** Pl. Condes de Niebla, is the home of the Duque de Medina Sidonia. Built in 1524, this home has quartered French troops during Spain's War of Independence and soldiers during the Civil War. (☎956 36 01 61; www.fcmedinasidonia.com. Guided tours Su 11am and noon. Open M-F 8am-9pm, Sa 9am-2pm, Su 9am-9pm. Free.) Sanlúcar's sandy **beaches** stretch from the mouth of the Río Guadalquivir toward the open Atlantic, and several **bodegas** dot Sanlúcar. (Tours M-Sa, more info at tourist office. €1.80-3.) In August, the **Carreras de Caballos** (horse races) thunder along the beach, and the **Festival de la Exaltación del Río Guadalquivir** brings poetry readings, flamenco, and bullfights.

DAYTRIP FROM SANLÚCAR: THE MARISMAS DEL ODIEL. The **Marismas del Odiel,** a protected wetland near the Parque Nacional de Doñana, certainly merits a daytrip. An obligatory stop for thousands of migratory birds, including the grey and purple heron, black stork, and 30% of Europe's spoonbill population, the UNESCO reserve is 7185 hectares of marshy estuary at the mouth of the Odiel river. The Marismas are a favored breeding and nesting ground for **African flamingos** in winter. Keep an eye out for **chameleons** and **lynxes,** the park's terrestrial residents. To protect the habitat, only guided visits are permitted, and **Erebea** offers tours by Jeep, boat, mini-train, or foot. Even if bird-watching isn't your passion, the opportunity to see over a thousand flamingos take flight at once doesn't come along every day. *(☎660 41 49 20 to reserve a tour. Open W-Su 10am-2pm and 6-8pm. €20. The marshes are difficult to reach by public transportation, and are usually accessed from nearby Punta Umbria. Though this small town is best reached by car—a short drive from Huelva down H414—Empresa Damas (☎959 25 69 00) also runs buses (15min.) from Huelva's bus station several times a day. The tourist office at Marismas can also give you info and make reservations. ☎959 50 90 11. Open M-F 10am-2pm and 3-6pm, Sa 10am-2pm.)*

ARCOS DE LA FRONTERA ☎956

Arcos de la Frontera (pop. 33,000) has inspired many a poet, including Cristóbal Romero, who described it as a "Town extended in the sun/Winged, raised up in flight..." With whitewashed houses wrapped around a narrow ridge, Arcos is considered one of the most perfect *pueblos blancos* in Spain. Its plazas and churches, huddled in convoluted medieval streets flush with geraniums, make it a historical and romantic gem. The city comes alive in the evening after the heat dies down and locals congregate in the plazas and bars of the old city.

TRANSPORTATION

Buses: Station on C. Corregidores. Los Amarillos (☎956 32 93 47) runs buses to **Jerez** (30min.; M-F 19 per day 7am-8pm, Sa 9 per day 8am-8pm, Su 11 per day 8am-9pm; €2) and **Sevilla** (2hr.; 7am, 3pm; €7). Transportes Generales (☎ 956 70 49 77) to: **Cádiz** (1hr., 6 per day 7:20am-7:15pm, €4), **Costa del Sol** (3-4hr., 4pm, €10-13), and **Ronda** (1hr., 4 per day 8:15am-4pm, €6). Confirm times and prices at the tourist office, and buy tickets on the bus.

Taxis: C. Debajo del Corral. **Radio/Tele Taxi** (☎956 70 13 55/00 66). 24hr.

ORIENTATION AND PRACTICAL INFORMATION

To reach the town center from the bus station, exit left, follow the road, and turn left again. Continue uphill for two blocks on C. Josefa Moreno Seguro, taking a right onto C. Muñoz Vázquez. From there it's a 20min. walk uphill. Continue until reaching **Pl. de España,** then veer left onto C. Debajo del Coral, which quickly changes into C. Corredera; the old quarter is 500m ahead. **Manolo Blanco** minibuses run every 30min. from the bus station to C. Corredera (€0.80). A taxi costs around €4. If the tourist office is closed when you arrive, make your way to **Bar Hostal Zindicato,** a short climb uphill from the bus stop, where you'll find an invaluable tile map of the city complete with street key.

Tourist Office: Pl. del Cabildo (☎956 70 22 64). Runs **tours** of the old city, monuments, and patios M-F 11am, noon, and 6pm. €7, children under 12 free. Call ahead to reserve for Sa and 6pm tours. Open mid-Mar. to mid-Oct. M-Sa 10am-2pm and 4-8pm, Su 10am-2pm; mid-Oct. to mid-Mar. M-Sa 10am-2pm and 3:30-7:30pm, Su 10am-2pm. One computer with **internet** access (€1 per 15min., €2.50 per hr.) and **printing** (€0.50 per page). An information kiosk with a more detailed street map is located on the island between C. Maldonado and C. Boticas near Pl. Boticas.

Bank and Currency Exchange: Banco Santander Central Hispano, C. Corredera, 63 (☎902 24 24 24). Open Oct.-Mar. M-F 8:30am-2pm, Sa 8:30am-1pm; Apr.-Sept. M-F 8:30am-2pm.

Laundry: Pressto, C. Debajo del Corral (☎914 48 58 61; www.pressto.com). Open M-F 9:30am-1:30pm and 5-8pm, Sa 9:30am-1:30pm.

Internet: Ciber-Locutorio "El Barrio," Pl. de las Aguas, 5 (☎956 70 45 69). €0.50 per 30min., €0.90 per hr. International phone service and phone credit recharging available. Snacks for sale. Open M-Sa 9:30am-2pm and 5:30-10pm, Su 10am-2pm.

Police: Av. Miguel Mancheño (☎092 or 956 70 16 52).

Medical Emergency: (☎061 or 956 51 15 53).

Hospital: Centro de Salud, C. Rafael Benot Rubio (☎956 70 07 87), in Barrio Bajo.

Pharmacy: Ldo. Ildefonso Guerrero Seijo, C. Corredera, 34 (☎956 70 02 13). Open M-F 9am-9pm. A list of doctors on call and available after hours is posted in the window.

Post Office: C. Murete, 24 (☎956 70 15 60). Open M-F 8:30am-2:30pm, Sa 9:30am-1pm. **Postal Code:** 11630.

ACCOMMODATIONS AND CAMPING

Arcos has a few budget hostels, but they are only slightly less expensive than classier hotels in town. Many restaurants on C. Corredera and in the old town have inexpensive rooms. Call ahead during Semana Santa and in the summer.

Hotel La Fonda, C. Corredera, 83 (☎956 70 00 57; www.hotelafonda.com), at the bottom of the hill leading to the old city. Originally a 19th-century inn, La Fonda retains a refined, old-fashioned feel. Plushly carpeted hallways lead to high-ceilinged rooms with A/C, full bath, TV, telephone, and balconies, some with terraces. Breakfast €1.70. Ask staff to use the computer downstairs for quick internet access. Singles €30; doubles €50; triples €65. Prices lower in winter. AmEx/MC/V. ❸

Pensión Callejon de las Monjas, C. Deán Espinosa, 4 (☎956 70 23 02). Rooms with incredible views, some with TV, bath, and A/C. Ask for the top floor, which has the best views, as well as a terrace. Singles €22, with bath €25; doubles €35, with terrace €40; triple €52; 4-person suite €66. MC/V, but cash preferred. ❷

Camping Lago de Arcos, Urbanización El Santiscal (☎956 70 83 33), at the foot of the hill by the lake. Has showers, pool, and electricity (€3). €3.95 per person, €3.30 per child, €4.70-4.95 per tent, €3.60 per car. ❶

FOOD

Cheap cafes and restaurants huddle at the bottom end of **C. Corredera,** while you can ascend to tapas nirvana in the old quarter uphill. Stock up on fresh fruit and produce at the small **market** on Pl. Boticas. (Open M-Sa 9am-3pm.)

Mabrouka, C. Debajo del Corral, 8 (☎956 70 06 12), downhill from C. Corredera. Enjoy authentic and filling Spanish fare in a Middle Eastern setting, complete with colorful cushions, soft music, and incense. Tapas €1.50-3.50, *montaditos* €2.50. Infusions and coffee €1-3. Extensive vegetarian *menú* €11; normal *menú* €9. Open Tu-Su 9am-5:30pm and 8pm-midnight. Cash only. ❷

Mesón "El Patio," C. Callejón de las Monjas, 4 (☎956 70 23 02; www.mesonelpatio.com). Located right next to the *pensíon,* this small establishment was originally a convent—it now specializes in *comida familiar* (local food) of all varieties. Salads €4.50-6. Tapas €2-3. *Raciones* €5-7.50. *Platos combinados* €8-10. Open daily noon-5pm and 7pm-midnight. AmEx/MC/V. ❷

SIGHTS AND FESTIVALS

The most beautiful sights in Arcos are the winding alleys, hanging flowers of the old quarter, and the stunning view from the **Plaza del Cabildo.** Festivals are spirited; on Easter Sunday is the **Toro de Aleluya,** in which two bulls run through the streets amid flamenco and general merriment. **Velada de San Pedro** is a celebration of the town's patron saint. Following a marching band processional and elaborate mass, 16 men provide the horsepower to move a larger-than-life icon of San Pedro out of the Iglesia de San Pedro and into the streets.

BASÍLICA DE SANTA MARÍA DE LA ASUNCIÓN. Built over an Arab mosque, the Basilica Baroque, Renaissance, and Gothic Plateresque styles. A symbol of the Inquisition—a circular design where exorcisms were once performed—is still etched into the ground outside on the church's left side. *(In the Plaza del Cabildo. Closed for repairs until 2009.)*

IGLESIA DE SAN PEDRO. This late-Gothic affair stands on the former site of an Arab fortress. Its gold altar is bookended by life-size icons, below which lie two saints removed from the Roman catacombs of St. Calixto. *(From Pl. Cabildo, follow C. Marqués Torresoto until Pl. Boticas. Follow C. Boticas, right on C. Núñez del Prado, which turns into C. San Pedro.Open daily 10am-2pm, 5-7pm. €1. Mass in winter 11:30am. Free.)*

EL SANTISCA. An artificial lake laps at Arcos' feet, and while it's not open to swimmers, the beach is a popular spot for a stroll. Ask about boat tours and rentals at the tourist office. *(Buses run from the bus station M-Sa 5 per day 9:15am-8:15pm, Su 2-4 per day 12:15-8:15pm; €0.90).*

CÁDIZ ☎956

If every city told its story, Cádiz would be spinning yarns well into the night. Founded by the Phoenicians in 1100 BC, Cádiz (pop. 155,000) is thought to be the oldest inhabited city in Europe. Located on a peninsula, the city has a powerful ocean on one side and a placid bay on the other. In the late 16th century, this unique geography triggered the first step in the eventual defeat of the Spanish Armada: Queen Elizabeth's fleet of small, quick ships surprised King Philip II's mighty battalion in Cádiz's harbor, causing significant damage in an event referred to as the "singeing of the King of Spain's beard." Despite Spain's eventual defeat, the Spanish colonial shipping industry transformed Cádiz into one of the wealthiest ports in Europe. Today, the narrow pedestrian streets and soaring churches of the old town, popular beaches in the new city, and thriving cafe culture give Cádiz a dynamic yet easy-going atmosphere.

TRANSPORTATION

Trains: RENFE, Pl. de Sevilla (☎956 25 43 01 or 902 24 02 02. Open 7:35am-11:35pm). To: **Barcelona** (12hr., 7:40am and 7:30pm, €96); **Córdoba** (3hr., 7:40am and 7:30pm, €18); **Jerez** (40min., 16-22 per day 6:15am-10:10pm, €4); **Madrid** (5hr., 8am, €65-100); **Sevilla** (2hr., 7-12 per day 5:45am-8:10pm, €10-32).

Buses: Several private companies operate out of small stations in Cádiz.

Transportes Generales Comes, Pl. de la Hispanidad, 1 (☎956 80 70 59 or 902 19 92 08; open M-Sa 9am-9pm; Su 10am-9pm). To: **Algeciras** (3hr., 10 per day 6:45am-8pm, €10); **Córdoba** (5hr., 7am and 3:45pm, €21); **Granada** (5hr., 4 per day 9am-9pm, €30); **Jerez de la Frontera** (45min., 11-29 per day 5:15am-9pm, €3); **La Línea** (3hr., 3 per day 11:30am-5pm, €12); **Málaga** (4hr., 6 per day 6:45am-8pm, €21); **Ronda** (3hr.; M-F 3 per day 9am-6pm, Sa 3 per day 9am-1:45pm, Su 9am and 1:45pm; €13); **Sevilla** (2hr.; M-Sa 10-11 per day 7am-9pm, Su 12 per day 7am-10pm; €11); **Vejer de la Frontera** (1hr., 6-8 per day 9am-9:15pm, €5).

Transportes Los Amarillos (☎956 29 08 00). Departs from beside the port in front of Po. de Canalejas. Purchase tickets on buses or at the **Viajes Socialtur** office on Av. Ramón de Carranza,

31 (open M-F 9:30am-1:30pm and 5-8:30pm). To **Arcos de la Frontera** (1hr., 2-4 per day 8:30am-8:15pm, €5.42).

Municipal Buses: (☎956 26 28 06). Pick up a **Bonobus** (discount packet of 10 tickets for €6.20, seniors €2.75) in the cafe at the **Transportes Generales Comes** bus station. Most lines run through Pl. de España. **Bus #1** (Cortadura), a favorite with beach bums, runs along the shore to new Cádiz (every 10min. 6:40am-1:30am, last bus from new Cádiz to Pl. de España 1:10am €0.93). **Bus #2** or **#7** runs the same route, leaving from Playa de la Caleta.

Ferry: El Vaporcito (☎902 45 05 50. www.cmtbc.es) departs from the dock behind the Estación Marítima near the Transportes Generales Comes station and runs to **Puerto de Santa María** (30-45min.; M-F 18 per day 7:40am-10pm, return 7:10am-9:15pm, Sa 6 per day 11:45am-9pm, return 10am-6pm, Su 5 per day 11:45am-8pm, return 10am-6pm; €3, round-trip €4).

Car Rental: Booth located inside the train station. **Bahía Rent A Car** (☎956 27 18 95 or 609 54 29 33; www.bahiarentacar.com. Open M-F 9:30am-1:30pm and 5-8pm, Sa 9:30am-1:30pm). Starting at €52 per day, €190 per week. AmEx/MC/V. **Europcar** (☎956 28 05 07. Open M-F 9am-3pm and 5-8pm, Sa 9-3pm). Starting at €54 per day, €172 per week. Personal insurance (PAI) and extras not included.

Taxis: Radio Taxi (☎956 21 21 21). Across from the library on Av. Ramón de Carranza.

ORIENTATION AND PRACTICAL INFORMATION

Cádiz's **old town** was built on the end of the peninsula. The **new town** formed behind it, farther inland. The old town hosts most of the cheap hostels, historic sights, and the bus and train stations, while the new town is home to high-rise hotels, bars and restaurants, and kilometers of hot sand. Old Cádiz is quite pedestrian friendly—most of the main streets do not allow cars. From the bus station, walk straight and pass through Pl. de la Hispanidad to **Plaza de España.** From Pl. de España, walk along Av. Ramón de Carranza until the tourist office kiosk. Turn left at the first street behind the kiosk (C. Nuevo), which turns into **Plaza de San Juan de Díos,** the town center. From the train station, walk out of the parking lot to **Plaza Sevilla** on Av. del Puerto; follow it past the port on your right. Pass Ción. de los Negros on your left and turn left onto the next street, which leads into Pl. San Juan de Dios. When you take the bus into new Cádiz (down the main avenue), hop off at **Glorieta Ingeniero La Cierva** (before the corner with McDonald's); the beach is directly behind it.

Tourist Office: Municipal, in Paseo de Canalejas (☎956 24 10 01). Has useful maps that include four suggested walking tours. English spoken. Open M-F in summer 9am-2pm and 5-8pm; in winter 9:30am-2pm and 4-7pm. Kiosk in front of the main office open June-Sept. M-F 9am-7pm, Sa-Su 9am-5pm; Oct.-May M-F 8:30am-6pm, Sa-Su 9am-5pm. **Regional (Junta de Andalucía),** Av. Ramón de Carranza (☎956 20 31 91). Open M-F 9am-7:30pm, Sa-Su 9:30am-3pm.

Currency Exchange: Banco Santander Central Hispano, C. Columela 13 (☎902 24 24 24). Open M-F 8:30am-2pm, Sa 8:30am-1pm.

Banks: Banks and **ATMs** line Av. Ramón de Carranza and C. San Francisco.

Pharmacy: Farmacia Central, Pl. del Palillero, right across the Banco Santander (☎956 22 48 01). Open 9am-10pm.

Laundromat: Pressto, on the corner of C. San José and C. Benjumeda (☎914 48 58 61; www.pressto.com). Open M-F 9:30am-1:30pm and 5-8pm, Sa 9:30am-1:30pm.

Police: Municipal, C. Campo del Sur, in the new city (☎092). **National,** Av. de Andalucía, 28, in the new city (☎091).

Medical Services: Ambulatorio Vargas Ponce (☎956 28 38 55). **Centro de Salud,** Pl. Iglesia de la Merced (☎956 28 64 11).

Internet Access: Free internet (30min. limit) is available at the public library, **Biblioteca Pública Provincial de Cádiz,** Av. Ramón de Carranza, 16 (☎956 20 33 24; www.juntadeandalucia.es/cultura/bibliotecas/bibcadiz/). Open in summer M-F 9am-9pm, in winter M-F 9am-9pm, Sa 9am-2pm. **Lu@r,** Plaza de Mina, 4, near the art museum (☎956 21 42 05). €0.80 per 30min., €1.50 per hr. Open daily 10:30am-1am. Free Wi-Fi can also be found in some of the city's plazas, including Pl. Palillero, Pl. de Mina, Pl. de de San Antonio, and Pl. de la Catedral.

Post Office: Pl. Topete (☎956 21 05 11). Open M-F 8:30am-8:30pm, Sa 9:30am-2pm. **Postal Code:** 11001.

ACCOMMODATIONS

Most hostels huddle around the harbor, in and around Pl. de San Juan de Dios. In the summer, they fill with young beachgoers, so singles and private baths will be scarce. Call months in advance for February's *Carnaval.*

Casa Caracol, C. Suárez de Salazar, 4, (☎956 26 11 66; www.caracolcasa.com) is where a young beach-loving crowd comes to rest tired surfer bods. Hammocks on the rooftop terrace offer a breezy *siesta* (and the cheapest bed in Cádiz), music plays all day, and the staff whips up tasty dinners (€5). Free Wi-Fi throughout. Kitchen access and breakfast included. Dorms €16; doubles €34; hammocks €10. Cash only. ❶

Pensión España, C. Marqués de Cádiz, 9 (☎956 28 55 00; www.pensionespana.com). Modern, red leather couches contrast with a traditional Spanish interior. Colorful rooms, close to the main Pl. de San Juan de Díos, overlook a quiet street. High-season singles €30; doubles €45, with bath €55. Low season €27/40/42. Cash only. ❸

Pensión Marqués, C. Marqués de Cádiz, 1 (☎956 28 58 54). Pleasant rooms with clean common baths and wrought-iron terraces. High season singles €30, with bath €35; doubles €45/55, triples with bath €60. Low season €20/35/45. Reception hours 9:30am-6:30pm daily. Cash only. ❸

FOOD

It is easy to find cafes in Cádiz's plazas, but the streets off **C. San Francisco** have cheaper tapas bars. To stock up for beach trips, head to **Carrefour,** off Pl. Topete (open M-Sa 9:15am-9:15pm), or try the **market** in the same plaza (open Tu-Sa 9am-2pm). Unless you're a minotaur, you'll want to use the entrance across from Carrefour, where you'll find a detailed layout of the labyrinthine market.

La Gorda Te Da de Comer, C. General Luque, 1 with another branch on C. Rosario, 4 (☎956 28 94 937). "The Fat Woman Gives You Food" is a trendy, New Age tapas bar that puts a 21st-century spin on age-old cuisine. Tapas €1.80-6. Open M 9-11:30pm, Tu-Th 1:30-4pm and 9-11:30pm, F-Sa 1:30-4pm and 9pm-midnight. MC/V. ❶

Cantina Cantinflas, C. Javier de Burgos, 19 (☎856 17 17 37). A Mexican-themed restaurant that celebrates authentic Mexican food in a festive space. Nacho plates (€5.40-7), house specialties, salads (€6-8.80), burritos (€5-7) and vegetarian options. Don't leave without a margarita (€2.50-5.30). Entrees up to €13.60. Delivery available. Open in summer daily 8pm-midnight; in winter open M and W-Su 8pm-midnight. ❷

Taberna El Garbanzo Negro, C. Sacramento, 18 (☎956 22 23 17). Bold blue walls, a laid-back atmosphere, and an extensive menu featuring variations on traditional Spanish staples. Tapas €1.50-2.50. *Raciones* €4-7. *Menú* €9. Open M-Sa 1:30-4pm and 8:30-11:30pm. AmEx/MC/V. ❶

Bar Rosario, Beato Diego de Cádiz, 3 (☎956 22 51 73). Rise and dine. The welcoming diner-like atmosphere of this tiny resto-bar tends to draw tourists with its €6.50 *menú* (€9 after 7:30pm and on Su and holidays), but the real reason to come here are the *churros* and coffee offered until 10am (€1.60). *Bocadillos* €2.20. Beer €1.20. Open daily 8am-3pm and 7:30-10pm. Cash only. ❶

SIGHTS

CATEDRAL. This gold-domed 18th-century masterpiece was financed by colonial riches, and took 116 years to be built, picking up Baroque, Rococo, and Neoclassical influences along the way. The treasury is bursting with valuables—the **Custodia del Millón** is said to be set with a million precious stones. The chapel holds a gazebo-like main altar encircled by sixteen side chapels, one of which is the **Capilla de las Reliquia,** full of cases of relics barely visible through the bars that guard the entrance. Visit the nearby museum for old treasures and art. *(Pl. de la Catedral. ☎956 25 98 12. Mass Su noon. Open Tu-F 10am-6pm, Sa 10am-2pm. Last entrance 30min. before close. Admission to cathedral and museum €5, students €3, children €2.50. Admission to museum, Torre de Poniente, Sanctuario Romano, Templos de Apolo, Esculapio, and Hygia €6. Free entrance to cathedral Tu-F 7-8pm and Su 11am-1pm.)*

MUSEO DE CÁDIZ. Cádiz's **Fine Arts** and **Provincial Archaeological** museums merged in 1975, and today Murillo, Rubens, and Zurbarán works reside here alongside Phoenician sarcophagi, ancient jewelry, and blown glass. *(Pl. de Mina. ☎956 20 33 68; www.juntadeandalucia.es/cultura/museocadiz. Open Tu 2:30-8:30pm, W-Sa 9am-8:30pm, Su 9am-2pm. Guided tours by appointment only Tu 9am-2:30pm. Wheelchair-accessible. €1.50, EU citizens and students free.)*

PASEO. Since Cádiz's seaside *paseo* runs around the old town and along the Atlantic, walking the path is a good way to get a feel for the city's layout. Fantastic views of ships leaving the harbor recall Spain's golden age. Exotic trees and fanciful hedges enliven the adjacent **Parque Genovés.** *(Paseo accessible via Pl. Argüelles or C. Fermín Salvochea, off Pl. de España.)*

BEACHES

Fortunately for beach-lovers, the exhaust-spewing ships on one coast of Cádiz don't pollute the pristine beaches on the other. **Playa de la Caleta** is the most convenient beach from the old town, at the peninsula's far tip. Better sand and more space can be found in the new town, serviced by bus #1 from Pl. de España (€0.93), or along the paseo by the water (20-30min. walk from the cathedral). The first beach beyond the rocks is the unremarkable **Playa de Santa María del Mar,** which is located at the bus stop near the police station. Next to it is the clean, endless **Playa de la Victoria,** recognized by the EU for its excellence and transformed into a sea of bodies on land and water in the summer. Get off bus #1 at **Glorieta Ingeniero La Cierva** in front of the McDonald's. A more unspoiled landscape can be found at **Playa de Cortadura.** Take bus #1 until its last stop. The beach is 200m away to the right.

NIGHTLIFE

In winter Cádiz's nightlife centers in the old town, while summer takes the party closer to the beach. In the old town, look for bars on the side streets off **C. Columela** and **C. San Francisco.** In the new town, **C. General Muñoz Arenillas,** off Glorieta Ingeniero La Cierva, and **Paseo Marítimo,** the main drag along Playa Victoria, have some of Cádiz's best bars. Hard-core clubbers will prefer **Punto de San Felipe,** a strip of bars and clubs north along the sea from Pl. de España (take a right before the tunnel); these spots don't get going until 4 or 5am.

La Nahu, C. Beato Diego de Cádiz (☎856 07 09 22). An African-themed hookah bar and pub. Beer €2. Mixed drinks €3-5. W hip hop night; €1 beer. See club roster (posted on door) for DJ listings, music nights, and drink specials. Open daily 8pm-3am, F and Sa until 4am. MC/V.

Medussa, C. Beato Diego, 10, on the corner of C. Manuel Ronces (www.lamedussa.com). A younger bohemian crowd congregates here for *la música,* as DJs spin dance, funk, garage, rock, and retro tunes. Beer €2.50. Mixed drinks €4-5. W International Night with €1 beers. Open Tu-Sa 10pm-4am.

Deep Ocean, Po. Maritimo 28 (☎956 07 80 32), is one among a string of bars and discotecas in Nuevo Cádiz. The 2 dance floors move to Tu ballroom lessons, Th salsa, F themed parties, and Sa erotic shows. Su, tapas come free with drinks. Beer €2. *Copas* €4. Open daily 4:30pm-dawn.

FESTIVALS

Carnaval insanity is legendary. The gray of winter gives way to dazzling color as the city hosts one of the most raucous *carnavales* in the world in late February and early March. Costumed dancers, street singers, ebullient residents, and spectators from around the world take to the streets in a week-long frenzy that makes New Orleans's Mardi Gras look like Thursday night bingo at the old folks' home (www.carnavaldecadiz.com).

VEJER DE LA FRONTERA ☎956

Arguably the most charming of the *pueblos blancos*, Vejer (pop. 20,000) is a true village: its pace is steady, its nights are black, its cobblestone alleys are narrow, and its houses are a collection of cozily clustered white buildings. From its perch atop a little mountain, Vejer offers breathtaking views of the unspoiled landscape, as well as a workout for the calves. The village is a good base for exploring the region's many pristine natural reserves and beaches. If simply basking in its quiet grace sounds appealing, plan to spend the night; if you crave a quicker pace, take a relaxing walk, then go on your merry way.

TRANSPORTATION

Vejer's buses are run by **Transportes Generales Comes** on C. La Plazuela, 2b. (☎956 45 16 80. Open M-F 9:30am-2:30pm and 6-9pm, Sa-Su 10:30am-2:30pm and 6-9pm.) When the office is closed, buy tickets on the bus. The office has snacks, public telephones, and internet access for €2 per hr. From the stop on Av. de Los Remedios next to the tourist office, buses leave for **Cádiz** (1hr., M-F 6 per day 8am-9:30pm, €5). For other destinations, take a taxi (€7-8) to **Restaurante Venta Pinco Meson Rústico** (the stop name is La Barca de Vejer. Buses depart from the parking lot next to the restaurant; make yourself visible when you see the bus coming or it will pass by). Buses go to: **Algeciras** (2hr., 10 per day 7:50am-10:25pm, €6); **Málaga** (4hr., 7:50am and 5:05pm, €18); **Sevilla** (3hr.; M-Sa 4 per day 7:15am-5:45pm, Su 4 per day 8:30am-5:45pm; €13); **Tarifa** (1hr., 10 per day 7:50am-10:25pm, €4). For a **taxi,** call ☎956 45 17 44 (Av. Los Remedios) or ☎956 45 01 85 (La Barca de Vejer).

ORIENTATION AND PRACTICAL INFORMATION

Some buses stop at the end of **Avenida de Los Remedios** (which leads uphill into **La Plazuela**), but many leave passengers by the highway at Restaurante Venta Pinco Meson Rustico at the base of the hill. Taxis to the top cost €7-8, or it is a steep 20min. walk. The staff at the **tourist office,** Av. de Los Remedios, 2, have information on nearby towns. (☎956 45 17 36; www.turismovejer.com. Open M-F 10am-2:30pm and 6-8pm, Sa 11am-2pm and 6-8pm, Su 11am-2pm. Hours change frequently, but are posted in the front window. Get there at least half an hour before closing). **Local services** include: **Banco Santander Central Hispano,** C. Divino Salvador, 5 (☎902 24 24 24. Open M-F 8:30am-2pm, Sa 8:30am-1pm); **Centro de Salud,** Av. de Andalucía (☎956 44 76 25); and **police,** Av. de Andalucía, 9 (☎956 45 04 00). **Internet access** is free at the public **library,** C. Marques de Tamarón, 10 (inside La Casa de la Cultura) or at the **Casa de la Juventud** on La Plazuela—use the entrance on C. Juan Relinque, and ask for access at the desk (☎956 44 72 24. Open M-Sa 10am-2pm). The **post office** is in Pl. Juan Carlos I (☎956 45 02 38. Open M-F 8:30am-2:30pm, Sa 9:30am-1pm). **Postal Code:** 11150.

ACCOMMODATIONS

The most affordable places in Vejer are *casas particulares* (private houses), and the tourist office has an extensive list of *hostales* and *casas*. Several options line C. San Filmo; to get there, follow C. Juan Relinque from La Plazuela, go right through the Pl. del Mercado, and head left uphill. From the tourist office, turn left, head around the curve to the left still on Av. Los Remedios, and take the first stairs you see to the right. C. San Filmo is to the right at the top. **Casa Los Cántaros ❷,** C. San Filmo, 14, is a restored Andalucian home with a grape-vined patio. Affordable rooms with private bath are small but comfortable, and the terrace is a perfect for cooking a meal or watching the sunrise. (☎956 44 75 92. June-Sept. singles €20; doubles €30; Oct.-May €20/25. Cash only.)

FOOD

The cheapest eats are tapas or *raciones* at the bars around **La Plazuela,** as full-service restaurants are more expensive. Relax under a grape trellis and laze away in the heat at **La Bodeguita ❶** tapas bar, C. Marqués de Tamarón, 9. (☎956 45 15 82. Tapas €1.50. Beer €1. Mixed drinks €4. Open daily in winter noon-3:30pm and 7pm-late, closed M in summer. Cash only.) Renowned for its *jamón ibérico* (Iberian ham), family-run **Mesón Pepe Julián ❷,** C. Juan Relinque, 7, serves reasonably priced entrees (€4.20-10) and tapas (€1.50) to a largely local crowd; plan to eat at the bar. (☎956 45 10 98. Open daily July-Aug. 11:30am-4pm and 7:30pm-midnight; Sept.-June closed Su. MC/V.) Locals swear by **Bar Navarro ❷,** C. Juan Bueno, 8, a popular restaurant-bar just off La Plazuela that offers cheap tapas and beer (both €1), mixed drinks (€3.50), and an affordable menu. (☎956 45 02 74. Entrees €5-14. Open daily 6:30pm-midnight. MC/V.)

SIGHTS AND FESTIVALS

The best way to enjoy Vejer is to wander along its streets and cliffside *paseos*. Ten kilometers down the road to Los Caños is **El Palmar,** 7km of fine sand and clear waters accessible by car or bus (June-Aug. 4 per day 11:45am-8:45pm, €1.10). To reach the beach, catch the Cádiz-bound bus to **Conil de la Frontera** and walk along the shore for 3-4km. For info on outdoor activities, consult **Discover Andalucía,** Av. de los Remedios, 45b, across from the bus stop. (☎956 44 75 75; www.discoverandalucia.com. Bikes €12-15 per day. Surfboards from €6 per day. Open M-F 10am-2pm and 6-9pm. AmEx/MC/V.)

Vejer throws brilliant fiestas. After the Corpus Cristi revelry in June comes the **Candelas de San Juan** on June 23rd, culminating in the midnight release of the **toro de fuego** (bull of fire). A local with a death wish dresses in an iron bull costume and charges the crowd as firecrackers attached to his body fly off in all directions. During the delirious *Semana Santa* celebrations, a *toro embolao* (sheathed bull) with wooden balls affixed to the tips of his horns is set loose through the narrow streets of Vejer on Easter Sunday.

TARIFA ☎956

Prepare for wind-blown hair—when the breezes pick up in the southernmost city of continental Europe, it becomes clear why Tarifa (pop. 20,000) is known as the Hawaii of Spain. World-renowned winds combined with kilometers of empty, white beaches bring some of the best kite and windsurfers from around the world, while the tropical, relaxed environment beckons divers and beach bums. Directly across the Strait of Gibraltar from Tangier, Morocco, Tarifa boasts incomparable views of Morocco to the south, the Atlantic to the east, and the Mediterranean to the west. From few other places in the world can you see two continents and two wide open seas at once.

TRANSPORTATION

Buses: Transportes Generales Comes buses go to the bus station, a trailer-like building on C. Batalla del Salado, 19. (☎956 68 40 38. Open M-F 7:30-9:30am, 10-11am, and 2:30-6:30pm, Sa-Su 3-7:45pm. Bus schedule posted on the window; if office is closed, buy tickets from driver.) Buses run to: **Algeciras** (30min., 7-11 per day 6:30am-8:15pm, €2); **Cádiz** (2hr., 7 per day 7:25am-8:55pm, €8); **La Línea** (1hr., 6 per day 12:05pm-11:15pm, €4); **Sevilla** (3hr., 4 per day 8am-5:15pm, €16).

Ferries: FRS boats (☎956 68 18 30; www.frs.es) leave from the port at the end of Po. de la Alameda for **Tangier** (35min.; daily every 2hr. 9am-11pm, F and Su last ferry at 9pm; return 9:30am-11:15pm, F and Su last return at 9:15pm Morocco time; €39, ages 3-12 €21. Small car €99).

Taxis: Parada Taxi can be reached at ☎956 68 42 41.

ORIENTATION

The **bus station** is on C. Batalla del Salado. Turn right toward the Repsol gas station and walk 10min. to the intersection with **Av. de Andalucía.** To reach the center of the old town, cross Av. de Andalucía and pass under the arch. To the left is C. Nuestra Señora de la Luz, which becomes **C. Sancho IV el Bravo,** home to many cafes and restaurants. To reach the tourist office, turn right on Av. de Andalucía before passing the arch. Take the first left onto Av. de la Constitución, then the first left into **Parque de la Alameda.**

PRACTICAL INFORMATION

Tourist Office: ☎956 68 09 93; www.tarifaweb.com. Located in Parque de la Alameda. Has detailed maps and information on adventure sports, including kite-surfing. (Open in summer M-F 10:30am-2pm and 6-8pm, Sa-Su 9am-2pm; in winter M-F 10am-2pm and 4-6pm, Sa-Su 9:30am-3pm.)

Currency Exchange: Banco Santander Central Hispano, C. Batalla del Salado, 17 and C. Sancho IV El Bravo in the walled town. (☎902 24 24 24. Open M-F 8:30am-2pm, Sa 8:30am-1pm.)

Police: Pl. Santa María, 3 (☎092 or 956 68 21 74).

Medical Services: Centro Salud, C. Amador de los Ríos, on the left after Punta de Europa when walking from the town center (☎956 02 77 00 or 956 02 77 01). **Pharmacy** on C. Batalla des Salado, 22, is nameless but conspicuous. (☎956 68 05 61. Open M-F 9:30am-10pm, Sa 9:30am-12:30pm.)

Laundry: Tarifa Top Clean, Av. Andalucía, 24 (☎956 68 03 03). A combination internet cafe, coffee bar, and laundry service. €11 for a large wash, dry, and fold. Internet €1.50 per 30min., €2.50 per hr. Open M-F 10am-2pm and 6pm-10pm.

Internet Access: Tarifa Top Clean (see Laundry, above). Cafes line Av. de Andalucía, but they aren't cheap; 1hr. of online access can cost you anywhere from €2-3. If you have a laptop, look for bars and cafes like **Bamboo** (see Food, below) which offer free Wi-Fi.

Post office: C. Coronel Moscardó, 9, is near Pl. San Mateo. (☎956 68 42 37. Open M-F 8:30am-2:30pm, Sa 9:30am-1pm.) **Postal Code:** 11380.

ACCOMMODATIONS

The cheapest rooms line C. Batalla del Salado and its side streets. Prices rise significantly in summer; those visiting in August and on weekends from June to September should call ahead and arrive early. Hard-core windsurfers often stay at one of the six campgrounds along the beach several kilometers from town; all have full bath and shower facilities, bars, and mini-supermarkets (see www.campingsdetarifa.com). Guests must bring their own tents. Cádiz-bound buses will drop you off if you ask, but flagging one down to get back is next to impossible; some surfers call for taxis or befriend fellow surfers with cars.

Hostal Facundo, C. Batalla del Salado, 47 (☎956 68 42 98; www.hostalfacundo.com). Draws the budget crowd with its "Welcome backpackers" sign. Common kitchen (8am-10pm), small TV room, and internet room provide a place to chat with your fellow travelers. Dorms €18-22; singles €25; doubles €38-45, with bath €42-50. Cash only. ❶

Hostal Villanueva, Av. de Andalucía, 11 (☎956 68 41 49). Villanueva has a restaurant and rooftop terrace with an ocean view. Spotless rooms all have bath and TV. Singles €25; doubles €45; triples €60. MC/V. ❶

Camping Río Jara, 4km from town on hightway CN-340 (☎956 68 05 70). A summer camp feel. €6.20 per person, €10 per site including tent, car, and electricity. ❶

FOOD

For cheap sandwiches (€1.50-3), try any one of the many *bagueterías* around C. Sancho IV el Bravo, or look for affordable options on C. San Francisco. To stock up for your beach trip, go to **Eroski Center** on C. San Jose, parallel to C. Batalla del Salado. (☎956 68 14 14. Open M-Sa 9:30am-9:30pm.)

Bamboo 1, Po. de la Alameda, 2 (☎956 62 73 04). A sensory wave of color, music, and both familiar and exotic tastes. Take off your shoes and lounge on eclectic, pillow-covered couches in the open-air seating area or log on for free Wi-Fi. The lounge becomes a bar at night. Teas €1.60-2. Fresh juices €3.50. Panini €2.80-4. Full breakfast €4. F-Sa Live DJ. Open M-Th 10am-2pm, F-Sa to 3am, Su to 2pm. AmEx/MC/V. ❶

Pizzería Horno de Leña, C. San Sebastián, 6, inside the Tarifa EcoCenter (☎956 62 72 20). Uses only organic local ingredients in its pizzas, staying true to its "Don't panic, it's organic" mantra. Free Wi-Fi, an organic and fair-trade shop, yoga and therapy room, bookstore, and local crafts make the EcoCenter a one-stop shop for healthy living. Live music Friday and Saturday. Pizzas €4.50-9. Tapas €2.50. Organic pastas €8-12. Open Su and M 9am-1:30pm, Tu-Sa 9am-2am. Cash only. ❷

Café Zumo, C. Sancho IV el Bravo, 26b (☎956 62 72 51). A small, lively nook that dishes out plates of vegetarian delights. Sip fresh-squeezed juice and read a book from the shelf or make an exchange. Meals from €3-9. Books €2 with an exchange, €6 without. Open M-F 10:30am-2pm and 6-8pm, Sa-Su 10am-2pm. Cash only. ❷

Vaca Loca 3, C. Cervantes, 6, is a rare steakhouse in the midst of Iberian ham country. Check the board for daily offerings (€11-23) and have your mind made up by the time you're seated. Open daily 11am-3am; food served until 1am. MC/V. ❷

SIGHTS AND OUTDOOR ACTIVITIES

Next to the port and just outside the old town are the facade and ruins of the **Castillo de Guzmán el Bueno,** built in AD 960. In the 13th century, the Moors kidnapped Guzmán's son and threatened his life if Guzmán didn't relinquish the castle. The father didn't surrender, even after his son's throat was slashed before his very eyes. (Open Apr.-Oct. Tu-Su 11am-2pm and 6-8pm; Nov.-May Tu-Su 11am-2pm and 4-6pm. €1.80.) Those with something less historical (or less gruesome) in mind can head 200m south to **Playa de los Lances** for 5km of the finest white sand on the Atlantic coast. Bathers should be aware of the occasional high winds and strong undertow. Adjacent to Playa de los Lances is **Playa Chica,** which is tiny but sheltered from the winds. **Tarifa Spin Out Surfbase,**

9km up the road toward Cádiz (ask the bus driver on the Cádiz route to stop, or take a taxi for €6), rents windsurfing and kitesurfing boards and instructs all levels. (☎956 23 63 52; www.tarifaspinout.com. Book ahead. Windsurf rental €26 per hr., €60 per day; 90min. lesson including all equipment €50. Kite and board rental €28 per hr., €58 per day; 2hr. lesson with all equipment €120.) Many campgrounds along CN-340 between km 70 and km 80 provide instruction and gear for outdoor sports. Ask at the tourist office for their list of kite- and windsurfing schools and rental shops.

NIGHTLIFE

At night, sunburned travelers mellow out in the old town's many bars, which range from jazz to psychedelic to Irish. People migrate to the clubs around 1 or 2am. The *terrazas* on C. Sancho IV el Bravo fill with locals and surfers chatting over beer or coffee. Almost every bar and club on **C. San Francisco** is a hot spot for backpackers and locals to meet, drink, and move to the music.

Moskito, C. San Francisco, 11, is a combination bar-club with a Caribbean motif, dance music, and tropical cocktails. Free salsa lessons W night 10:30pm. Beer €2.50. Mixed drinks €5-6. Open in summer daily 11pm-3am; in winter Th-Sa 11pm-later.

La Tribu, C. Nuestra Señora de la Luz, 7, a favorite among kite surfers, makes some of the most creative cocktails in town. Trance and techno pump energy into this otherwise mellow nightspot. Beer €2-3. Mixed drinks €6. Shots €1.50.

La Ruina, corner of C. San Francisco and C. Santísima Trinidad. This renovated hot spot is appropriately located in the ruins of a long-deserted Roman stronghold. Blasting house music amidst a funky surfboard-themed interior, La Ruina serves it up all night long. Beers €2-4. Mixed drinks €5-6. Open M-F 12am-3pm, Sa-Su 12am-4am. Cash only.

GIBRALTAR ☎350 OR 9567

Emerging from the morning mist, the Rock of Gibraltar's craggy face menaces those who pass by its shores. Ancient seafarers referred to the rock as one of the Pillars of Hercules, believing that it marked the end of the world. Today, it is known affectionately to locals as "Gib" and is home to more fish 'n' chips and pints of bitter per capita than anywhere in the Mediterranean. Though Gibraltar is a self-governing British colony, Spain continues to campaign for sovereignty. When a 1969 vote showed that Gibraltar's populace favored its colonial ties to Britain—at 12,138 to 44—Franco sealed the border. After 16 years of isolation and a decade of negotiations, the border re-opened on February 4, 1985. Tourists and residents cross with ease, but Gibraltar has a culture all its own, one that remains detached from Spain. While the mix of wild primates and Union Jacks makes Gibraltar worthwhile, it is also a tourist trap full of duty-free shops and pocket-burning prices. Cross the border and explore the Rock, then scurry back to España before nightfall.

TRANSPORTATION

Flights: Airport (☎730 26). **British Airways** (☎793 00) flies to London (2½hr., 2 per day, £168/€212) and Madrid (1hr., 2 per day, £142.60/€180).

Buses: From **La Línea,** on the Spanish border, to: **Algeciras** (40min.; M-F every 30min. 7:45am-11:15pm, Sa, Su, and holidays every 45min. 8:45am-11:15pm; €2); **Cádiz** (3hr., 4 per day 6:30am-8pm, €13); **Granada** (5hr., 7:15am and 2:15pm, €20); **Jerez de la Frontera** (4hr., 9:30am, €13); **Madrid** (7hr., 1:10 and 10:15pm, €26); **Málaga** (3hr.; 4 per day 7:15am-5:30pm, Su also 8:45pm; €11); **Marbella** (1hr.,

4 per day 7:15am-5:30pm, €5); **Sevilla** (6hr., 4 per day 7am-4:15pm, €21); **Tarifa** (1hr., 7 per day 6:30am-8pm, €4).

Ferries: Turner & Co., 65/67 Irish Town St. (☎783 05; fax 720 06). Open M-F 8am-3pm. To **Tangier,** Morocco (1hr.; F 6pm, return Sa 5:30pm Moroccan time; £18/€32, under 12 £9/€16.20).

Public Transport: Most bus lines run from one end of the Rock base to the other. Buses #9 and #10 go between the border and the Rock for £0.60/€1. Round-trip £0.90/€1.50. Unlimited day pass £1.50/€2.50.

Taxis: Gibraltar Taxi Association (☎956 77 00 27).

EURO OR POUNDS? Although euro are accepted almost everywhere (except at pay phones and post offices), the pound sterling (£) is the preferred method of payment in Gibraltar. ATMs dispense money in pounds. Merchants and sights sometimes charge a higher price in euros than in pounds. Unless stated otherwise, however, assume that establishments accept euros; change is often given in British currency. The exchange rate fluctuates around £1 to €1.50. As of July 2008, £1 = €1.26.

ORIENTATION AND PRACTICAL INFORMATION

Make sure you have a valid passport before heading to Gibraltar, or you'll be turned away at the border. If you need a visa, the UK embassy in Madrid takes roughly a day to process them. Buses from Spain terminate in the nearby town of La Línea. From the bus station, walk directly toward the Rock (it's impossible to miss; the border is 5min. away). Once through customs and passport control, catch bus #9 or #10 or carefully walk across the airport tarmac into town (20min.); stay left on Winston Churchill Ave. when the road forks with Corral Ln. Cars take longer to enter and exit Gibraltar—often an hour or more.

Tourist Office: Duke of Kent House, Cathedral Sq. (☎450 00). Open M-F 9am-5:30pm, Sa 10am-3pm, Su 10am-1pm. Info booth at Spanish border in the immigration building. Open M-F 9am-4:30pm, Sa 10am-1pm.

Luggage Storage: Bus station in **La Línea.** €3 per day. Buy token for locker at a bus ticket booth. Open daily 7am-10pm.

Bookstore: Gibraltar Bookshop, 300 Main St. (☎718 94).

Emergency: ☎199.

Police: 120 Irish Town St. (☎725 00).

Pharmacy: Calpe Centre, Casemates Sq. (☎779 77). Open M-F 9am-7pm, Sa 10:30am-1:30pm.

Hospital: St. Bernard's Hospital, on Hospital Hill (☎797 00).

Internet Access: Call Shop, Main St., 293A (☎496 45). £2.50/€4 per hr. Accepts pounds, euros, and dollars; all change given in pounds. Open daily 9am-9pm.

Post Office: 104 Main St. (☎756 62). Open June to mid-Sept. M-F 9am-2:15pm, Sa 10am-1pm; mid-Sept. to May M-F 9am-4:30pm, Sa 10am-1pm. Pounds (£) only.

ACCOMMODATIONS AND FOOD

Gibraltar is best visited as a daytrip. The few accommodations in the area are pricey and often full, especially in the summer, and camping is illegal. At worst, you can crash across the border in La Línea. Back on the Rock, **Emile Youth Hostel Gibraltar ❷,** in Montague Bastian on Linewall Road, has bunk beds and clean communal baths. (☎511 06; www.emilehostel.com. Breakfast included.

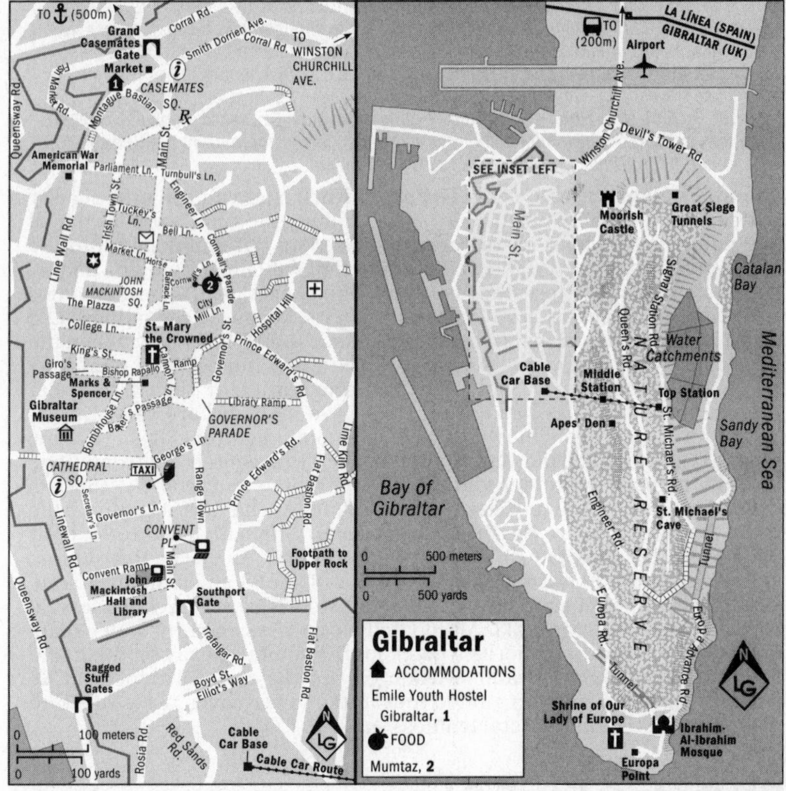

Lockout 10:30am-4:30pm. £1 for luggage storage or towels. Dorms £15/€20; doubles £34/€51. Cash only.) International restaurants are easy to find—try sampling the spices of Gibraltar's thriving Hindu community at **Mumtaz ❶**, 20 Cornwalls Ln., where authentic tastes and true *dhaba* style come at the lowest of prices. (☎442 57. Entrees £2.50-7, with ample vegetarian selection. Takeout available. Open daily 11am-3pm and 6pm-12:30am. Cash only.) **Marks & Spencer** on Main St. has a small grocery/bakery. (Open M-F 9am-7pm, Sa 9:30am-5pm. AmEx/MC/V.) The cheapest and freshest food can be found at the local **market,** behind Casemates Square. (Open M-Sa 8am-2:30pm.)

SIGHTS

THE ROCK OF GIBRALTAR

The top of the Rock Nature Reserve is accessible by car or cable car, or for the truly adventurous, by foot. Cable cars (☎778 26) depart daily every 10min. 9:30am-5:15pm; last return 5:45pm. Tickets sold until 5:15pm. It's possible to buy a ticket for only the cable car (round-trip £8/€13.50), but if you plan on visiting any of the sights, it's better to buy a combined admission ticket (£16/€26.50). At the top, don't forget to ask for the interactive guided tour, an audio tour that comes in eight languages, including Hebrew and Swedish. Included with the cable car ticket. The walk down takes 2-3hr., including stops at the sights. Tour operators offer van or taxi tours that take visitors to all attractions in about 1hr. The official Taxi Tour booth is in the immigrations building across from the tourist booth; make sure you take the official tour sponsored by the Taxi Association. Prices for the Taxi Tour include all sights so it may be slightly cheaper than the cable car. For those traveling by car, there is a £8/€13.50 entrance fee per person, plus £1.50/€3 per car. On foot, take Library St. to Library Ramp from Main St., follow it uphill to the end, and turn right. At the next intersection there is a sign for the footpath to the Rock. Follow the footpath for 20min. until you hit a road, and turn left.

Gibraltar's claim to fame is the legendary Rock, and you can't do the city justice without seeing this titanic crag. Climbing the giant white rock will give you many a photo op to capture the severe cliffs plunging into the ocean. About halfway up the Rock (at the first cable car stop, or a 25min. walk down from the top stop) is the infamous **Apes' Den,** where colonies of **Barbary apes** cavort atop taxis and tourists' heads. These tail-less Old World monkeys have inhabited Gibraltar since the 18th century. When the ape population nearly went extinct in 1944, Churchill ordered reinforcements from North Africa; now they are procreating at such a rate that population control has become an issue. The monkeys are very tourist-friendly, but have been known to steal food and other items from visitors; keep all food hidden and bags closed to avoid unwanted confrontations with the animals. Although the monkeys are cute and friendly, tourists are advised not to touch them or their young. At the northern tip of the Rock, facing Spain, are the **Great Siege Tunnels.** Originally used to fend off a combined Franco-Spanish siege at the end of the American Revolution, the tunnels were expanded during WWII to span 33 miles underground. Nearby, on the way back to town, is the old Moorish castle, rebuilt several times, most recently in 1333. Although the castle is currently under renovation, the exterior still merits a quick look if you're already on the Rock. Thousands of years of water erosion carved the eerie chambers of **St. Michael's Cave.** Ask about a guided tour to the lower caves, which feature an underground lake and stalagmites.

COSTA DEL SOL

Artifice has replaced the once-natural charms of the Costa del Sol, as chic promenades, swanky hotels, and apartment buildings spring up between the small towns and the shoreline. The Costa del Sol extends from Tarifa in the southwest to Cabo de Gata, east of Almería; post-industrial Málaga lies directly between the two. To the northeast, hills dip straight into the ocean, and rocky beaches enhance the shore's natural beauty. To the southwest, however, waves seem to wash up onto more concrete than sand. Still, nothing detracts from the coast's major attraction: eight months of spring and four months of summer. News of the fantastic weather has spread, and July and August bring swarms of pale northern Europeans. Reservations are recommended in the summer anywhere on the coast, especially at hostels.

MÁLAGA ☎952

Málaga (pop. 561,250) is the busiest city on the coast, and while its beaches are better known for their bars than their natural beauty, the city has much to offer. The Alcazaba commands a hill to the west of the city, offering magnificent—and telling—views of Málaga: cranes and industrial ports in the distance contrast with the charming *casco antiguo* and verdant gardens. One of Málaga's most famous exports is the painter Pablo Picasso, whose hometown museum opened in 2003. As a critical transportation hub, Málaga is often seen as a stopover en route to other coastal cities, but the thriving city's bustle, beaches, palm trees, and dove-filled plazas are a worthy destination in their own right.

TRANSPORTATION

Flights: (☎952 04 88 04 or 902 40 47 04). From the airport, Bus #19 (2 per hr. 6:35am-11:35pm, €1) runs from the "City Bus" sign, stopping at the bus station and at the corner of C. Molina Lario and Postigo de los Abades. RENFE trains connect the city and the airport (12min., €1). **Iberia,** C. Molina Lario, 13 (☎952 13 61 66, 24hr. reservations 902 40 05 00), has daily international flights, mostly to England.

Trains: Estación de Málaga, Explanada de la Estación (☎952 12 80 79; www.renfe.es). Take bus #3 at Po. del Parque or #4 at Pl. de la Marina to the station. **RENFE** office, C. Strachan, 4 (☎902 24 02 02). To: **Barcelona** (13hr.; 7:20am, 8:35pm; €58); **Córdoba** (2hr., 9 per day 6:45am-8:20pm, €19); **Fuengirola** (30min., every 30min. 8am-10:30pm, €1); **Madrid** (5hr., 7 per day 6:35am-9pm, €71-79); **Sevilla** (3hr., 5-6 per day 7:40am-8:10pm, €17-33); **Torremolinos** (20min., every 30min. 5:45am-10:10pm, €2). Reservations for long-distance trains highly recommended.

Buses: Po. de los Tilos (☎952 35 00 61; **ALSA** 902 42 22 42; **Alsina Graells Sur** 952 31 82 95; **Casado** 952 31 59 08; **Daibus** 952 31 52 47; **Portillo** 902 14 31 44; www.ctsa-portillo.com), 1 block from the RENFE station along C. Roger de Flor, buses #3, 4, C1 and 19 stop at the station. To: **Algeciras** (3hr., 9-10 per day 5am-7:15pm, €10.82-11.39); **Almería** (6-9 per day 3:15am-7pm, €15.37); **Antequera** (1hr.; M-F 13 per day 7am-8:45pm, Sa 8 per day 9:30am-10pm, Su 9 per day 9:30am-11pm; €4.85); **Barcelona** (3.5hr., 6 per day 8:30am-12:31am, €75.17); **Cádiz** (4hr., 6 per day 6:45am-8pm, €21.59); **Córdoba** (3hr., 7 per day 9am-8pm, €12.21); **Granada** (2hr., 22 per day 7am-10pm, €9.38); **La Línea** (3hr., 5 per day 7am-7:15pm, €10.61); **Madrid** (7hr., 8-12 per day 8:30am-1am, €20.14 or 17.80 for youth); **Marbella** (1½hr.; M-F 25 per day 6:45am-9:45pm, Sa 22 per day 8:30am-9:45pm, Su 21 per day 9am-9:45pm; €4.64-4.97); **Murcia** (6hr., 5 per day 8:30am-9:45pm, €26); **Ronda** (3hr., 4-12 per day 8am-8:30pm, €9.57-9.90); **Salamanca** (9hr; daily 6pm, €42.41); **Sevilla** (3hr., 11-13 per day 7am-3:15am, €15.16).

Taxis: Radio Taxi (☎952 32 00 00). Town center to waterfront €6; to the airport €18-23; from the train and bus station to town center €5; from **Málaga** to **Balmádena** €20.

ORIENTATION AND PRACTICAL INFORMATION

The bus and train stations lie a block away from each other along C. Roger de Flor, on the other side of the **Río Guadalmedina** from the historical center and the majority of sights. To get to the town center from the **bus station,** exit right onto Callejones del Perchel, walk straight through the big intersection with Av. de la Aurora, take a right onto Av. de Andalucía, and cross Puente de Tetuán. From here, **Alameda Principal** leads into **Plaza de la Marina** (20min.). Alternatively, take bus #3, 4 or 21 along the same route (€1). From Pl. de la Marina, C. Molina Lario leads to the **cathedral** and the old town. C. Marqués de Larios, the main shopping and pedestrian street, connects Pl. de la Marina to **Plaza de la Constitución.** Behind the latter plaza, C. Granada leads to many good tapas bars and **Plaza de la Merced,** renowned for its *botellón.* Av. Cánovas del Castillo leads to **Playa de la Malagueta** (20min. walk), the closest beach worth visiting. After dark, be wary of the **Cruz del Molinillo** area (near the market) and desolate beaches.

Tourist Offices: Municipal, Av. de Cervantes, 1, Pl. de la Aduana (☎952 12 20 20; www.malagaturismo.com). Open daily 9am-7pm. **Branch:** Pl. de la Marina (☎952 12 20 20).

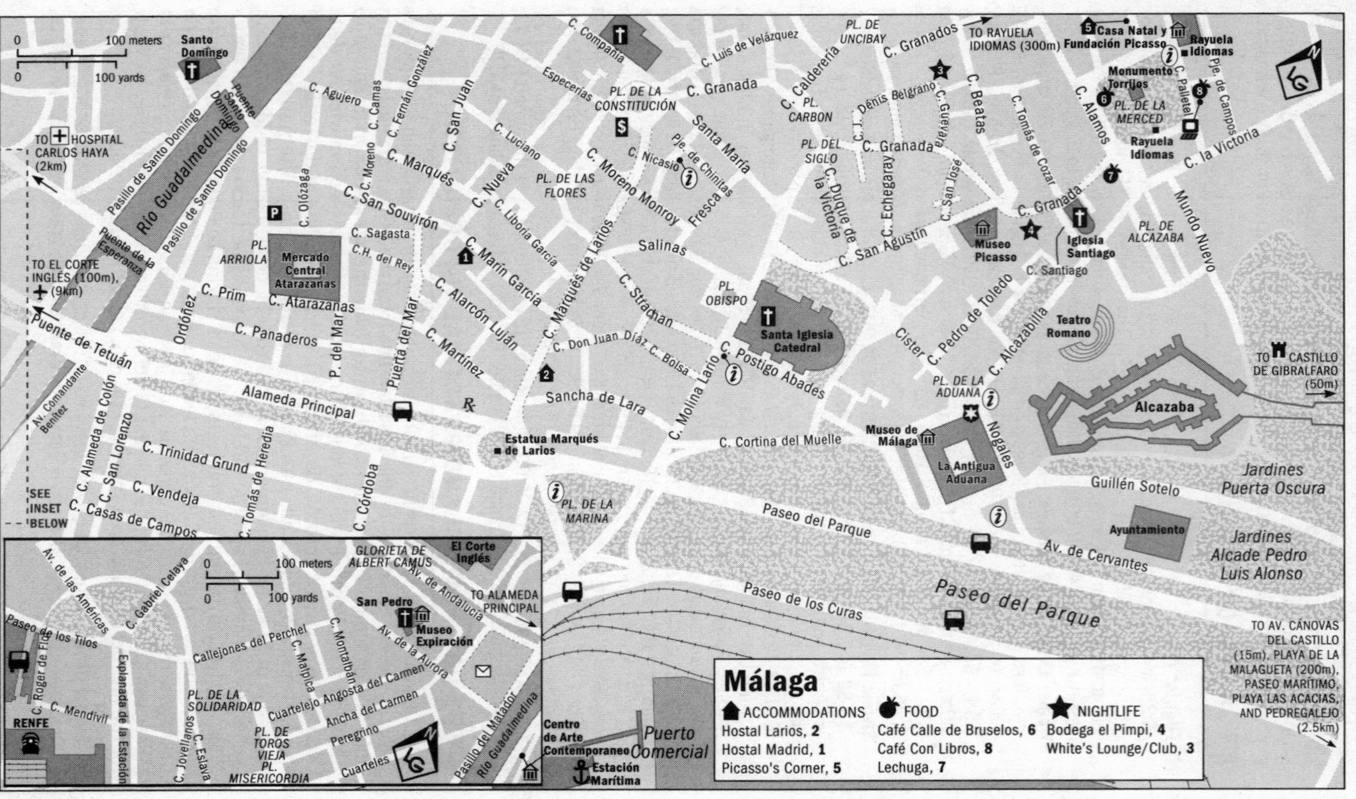
Málaga
ACCOMMODATIONS
Hostal Larios, 2
Hostal Madrid, 1
Picasso's Corner, 5
FOOD
Café Calle de Bruselos, 6
Café Con Libros, 8
Lechuga, 7
NIGHTLIFE
Bodega el Pimpi, 4
White's Lounge/Club, 3
TO RAYUELA IDIOMAS (300m)
Casa Natal y Fundación Picasso
Rayuela Idiomas
Monumento Torrijos
PL. DE LA MERCED
Museo Picasso
Iglesia Santiago
Teatro Romano
Alcazaba
TO CASTILLO DE GIBRALFARO (50m)
Santa Iglesia Catedral
Museo de Málaga
La Antigua Aduana
Ayuntamiento
Jardines Puerta Oscura
Jardines Alcade Pedro Luis Alonso
Paseo del Parque
Paseo de los Curas
Alameda Principal
Estatua Marqués de Larios
Mercado Central Atarazanas
Río Guadalmedina
TO HOSPITAL CARLOS HAYA (2km)
TO EL CORTE INGLÉS (100m), (9km)
SEE INSET BELOW
TO AV. CÁNOVAS DEL CASTILLO (15m), PLAYA DE LA MALAGUETA (200m), PASEO MARÍTIMO, PLAYA LAS ACACIAS, AND PEDREGALEJO (2.5km)
Puerto Comercial
Centro de Arte Contemporaneo
Estación Marítima
El Corte Inglés
San Pedro
Museo Expiración
TO ALAMEDA PRINCIPAL
RENFE

Open M-F 9am-7pm. **Branch:** Pl. de la Aduana. Open M-F 9am-7pm, Sa 10am-7pm, Su 10am-2pm. **Junta de Andalucía,** Pje. de Chinitas, 4 (☎952 21 34 45). Open M-F 9am-8pm, Sa 10am-7pm, Su 10am-2pm. In winter offices may close earlier.

Currency Exchange: Banks (and **ATMs**) line most major roads and cluster around the intersection of Alameda Principal and C. Marqués de Larios.

Luggage Storage: Lockers at the train station (open daily 7am-10:45pm) and bus station (open daily 6:30am-11pm). Both €2.40-4.50 per day.

English-Language Bookstore: Rayuela Idiomas, Pl. de la Merced, 17 and C. Carcer, 1. (☎952 22 48 10). Open M-F 9:45am-1:30pm and 5-8:30pm, Sa 10am-2pm. MC/V.

Women's Center: Área de Igualdad de Opportunidades de la Mujer, C. Merced, 1 (☎952 13 47 56). Open M-F 9am-2pm.

Police: Policía Nacional, Plaza de la Aduana, 1 (☎952 04 62 00). **Policía Municipal,** Av. de la Rodaleda, 19 (☎952 12 65 00).

Pharmacy: Farmacia Caffarena, Alameda Principal, 2 (☎952 21 28 58), at the intersection with C. Marqués de Larios. Open 24hr.

Medical Services: ☎952 39 04 00, emergency ☎952 30 30 34. **Hospital Carlos Haya,** Av. Carlos Haya (☎951 29 00 00).

Internet Access: Across from the Picasso Foundation, **Telsat,** C. Gomez Pallete, 7 (☎952 21 28 22), offers access for €1 per hr., minimum €0.50. Open daily 9am-1am.

Post Office: Av. de Andalucía, 1 (☎902 19 71 97). **Lista de Correos.** Open M-F 8:30am-8:30pm, Sa 9:30am-2pm. **Postal Code:** 29080.

ACCOMMODATIONS

Budget accommodations in Málaga are just a little pricier than the Andalucian average—expect to pay about €18-30 for a single or dorm bed. Most *hostales* are in the old town between Pl. de la Marina and Pl. de la Constitución.

Picasso's Corner, C. San Juan de Letrán, 9, off of Pl. de la Merced (☎952 21 22 87; www.picassoscorner.com). This king of the hostels boasts a large DVD selection, free internet, large kitchen, and an elegant bathroom with massaging shower. Dorms are social, but staff enforces quiet hours for weary travelers looking to catch some winks. Breakfast and 24hr. coffee and tea included. Laundry €3 per wash/dry cycle. Roof-top hammocks €10. 4- to 6-bed dorms €18-19; doubles €22.50 per person. MC/V. ❶

Hostal Larios, C. Marqués de Larios, 9, 3rd fl. (☎952 22 54 90). Don't pay for a room with a private bath; the common ones are clean and new. TV and A/C. Singles €32-37, with bath €35-42; doubles €42-49/53-60; triples with bath €75-89. MC/V. ❸

Hostal Madrid, C. Marín García, 4, 2nd fl. (☎646 15 86 99). Some of the cheapest digs in Málaga. Rooms have showers and balconies, some with views of a peaceful street. Singles €30-40; doubles €30-60. During Aug. and *ferias* €40/60. Cash only. ❷

FOOD

Beachfront restaurants specialize in fresh seafood; *malagueños* love *pescaíto frito* (fried fish) and sardines roasted over open flames. Restaurants in the streets around C. Granada, Pl. de la Constitución, and Pl. de la Merced display a combination of classic and inventive salad menus. Try your hand at your own salad creation with fresh produce from the **market** on C. Ataranzas (open daily 8am-2pm). There is also a supermarket in **El Corte Inglés,** Av. de Andalucía, 4-6. (☎952 07 65 00. Open M-Sa 10am-10pm. AmEx/MC/V.)

Café Con Libros, Pl. de la Merced, 19 (☎952 21 51 89). Sit amid stacks of books and magazines as you sip on milkshakes, smoothies, tea, infusions, and coffee (€1.20-4), breakfast *menús* (€2.30-3.20), crepes and pastries (€2-3.40), tapas (€1.30-1.80), and salads (€6-7.50). The plush chairs, rotating paintings by local artists, and friendly English-speaking staff will tempt you to stay. Open daily 11am-2am. Cash only. ❶

Café Calle de Bruselas, Pl. de Merced, 16 (☎952 60 39 48; www.calledebruselas.com). Located right across from the information kiosk in the plaza, this Art Deco-influenced restaurant and bar offers a welcoming atmosphere, good fare, and free Wi-Fi. Thriving nightlife with live music and jazz, and a lively community feel. Breakfast €2.80. Lunch €5.50-7.50. Beer €2-3. Mixed drinks €5. Open daily 9am-3am. MC/V. ❶

Lechuga, Pl. de la Merced, 1(☎610 39 14 94). Despite its unassuming name, "Lettuce" offers a variety of creative concoctions of vegetarian delight, while the combination of airy interior and eclectic funky pop offers the perfect escape from the noisy Pl. de la Merced. Ten large salads (€8-9), starters (€4-8), and 3-course daily menu (€8) are tasty and quick. Wine €2.90-4. Open daily 1:30pm-12:30am. MC/V. ❷

SIGHTS

ALCAZABA. Towering high above the city, the Alcazaba is Málaga's most imposing sight. The fortress offers great views of the harbor from its medieval brick and stone walls. Guarding the east end of Po. del Parque, the 11th-century structure was originally used as both a military fortress and a royal palace by Moorish kings. *(Open June-Aug. Tu-Su 9:30am-8pm; Sept.-May Tu-Sa 8:30am-7pm. €2, students and seniors €0.60, under 7 free. Su free after 2pm.)*

SANTA IGLESIA CATEDRAL DE MÁLAGA. Málaga's commanding cathedral mixes a Renaissance aesthetic with a touch of Baroque. The intricate structure, complete with detailed columns, stained glass windows, and more than 15 side chapels, was built on the site of a former mosque. On the outside, the cathedral looks a bit off balance—it should have two towers, but one of them is only half-built—hence the cathedral's nickname *La Manquita* ("One-Armed Lady"). The small museum upstairs displays religious art. *(C. Molina Lario, 4. ☎952 22 03 45. Open M-F 10am-6pm, Sa 10am-5pm. Mass daily 9am. €3.50, includes audio tour.)*

CASTILLO DE GIBRALFARO. A Moorish lighthouse was built in this Phoenician castle, which offers sweeping vistas of Málaga and the Mediterranean. After admiring the cityscape, stop by the **Centro de Interpretación,** which has artifacts from the city's seafaring past. *(Bus #35 leaves every 20min. from the Alameda Principal; otherwise it's a shadeless 30min. uphill hike. Open daily Apr.-Oct. 9am-8pm; Nov.-March 9am-6pm. €1.95, students and seniors €0.60, combined with Alcazaba €3.20. Su free after 2pm.)*

CASA NATAL Y FUNDACIÓN PICASSO. Picasso left Málaga at a young age, but according to local officials, he always "felt himself to be a true *malagueño.*" The artist's birthplace now houses the **Picasso Foundation,** which organizes a series of exhibitions and lectures. The first floor is a seasonal gallery; upstairs is a permanent collection of photographs, drawings, and pottery by the artist. The Foundation also houses a Picasso Library on the 3rd floor. *(Pl. de la Merced, 15. ☎952 06 02 15; www.fundacionpicasso.es. Museum open daily 9:30am-8pm. Library open daily 9:30-2:30pm. €1, seniors, under 17, and students under 26 free.)*

MUSEO PICASSO. Though the collection isn't as impressive as those in Spain's larger museums, this relatively new exhibition dedicated to Málaga's most famous son traces his transition from child prodigy to renowned master. Visit the projection room, with its multilingual look at Picasso's methods, and the archaeological site in the basement, which explores Málaga's Phoenician, Roman, and Moorish roots through stone and ceramic arts. *(C. San Agustín, 8. ☎902 44 33 77; www.museopicassomalaga.org. Open Tu-Th, Su, and holidays 10am-8pm; F-Sa*

10am-9pm. €6 permanent collection, €4.50 temporary, €8 combined; students, ages 11-16, and large groups €3; under 10 free. Free entrance last Su of each month 3-8pm. Free guided tours in Spanish Tu and Sa 6pm and 7pm, Th 6pm. Limit 20.)

CENTRO DE ARTE CONTEMPORÁNEO. Some of today's foremost artists, such as Gerhard Richter and the controversial Chapman brothers, have exhibited in this renovated marketplace by the river. In addition to a hefty 400-piece permanent collection, which boasts a noteworthy selection of post-1950s American art, the museum's temporary exhibits uphold a fresh, avant-garde vibe. *(C. Alemania. ☎952 12 00 55; www.cacmalaga.org. Open Tu-Su 10am-2pm and 5-9pm. Free.)*

NIGHTLIFE

Many nightlife spots are only open Thursday through Saturday. **Bodega El Pimpi** is an ultra-popular traditional *bodega* with lots of little nooks and tiny rooms. The bar fills up early in the evening and stays crowded until about 1am. (Beer €1.70-3.40. Mixed drinks €4.30-6.50. Open Tu-Su 12pm-3am.) For a change in scenery, head to **Playa de la Malagueta,** a beach where young locals party by night at beachfront bars called *chiringuitos*. (30min. walk, but a quick and affordable taxi ride; buses don't run during late party hours.) When the city's bar scene is winding down, its clubs are just getting started. Head to **White's Lounge/Club,** C. José Denis Belgrano, 19, where small wall mirrors, bright fluorescent lights, and two semi-divided dance spaces serve as a backdrop to pulsing hip-hop and Spanish pop beats. (Beer €4. Mixed drinks €6. Open daily noon-6am.)

MARBELLA ☎952

While much of Spain draws visitors looking to engage with the country's history and culture, people come to Marbella (pop. 125,000) looking for something quite different: a tan. The city has a long history as a key merchant town occupied by the Phoenicians, Greeks, Romans, and Arabs. The influence of these groups is evident in the structure and architecture of the *casco antiguo*, though old buildings now frequently house upscale restaurants and designer boutiques. Once a sleepy fishing village, the town's fortunes changed in 1947 when Prince Alfonso de Hohenlohe's Rolls-Royce broke down in Marbella. Captivated by the sunny countryside and friendly locals, Alfonso seized the opportunity to develop Marbella's white sands into an endless strip of umbrellas and seaside cafes. While today Marbella serves primarily as a Mediterranean playground, the attractive old city provides life beyond yachts and watersports.

TRANSPORTATION

Buses: Marbella, 56km south of Málaga, is best reached by bus, from **Ctra. del Trapiche** station (☎952 76 44 00). To: **Cádiz** (2hr., 6 per day 7:30am-8:45pm, €16.71); **Fuengirola** (1hr.; approx. every 20min. 6:50am-10:50pm, Su 10:40pm; €2.65); **Granada** (3hr., 7 per day 8:25am-8:15pm, €14.02); **Málaga** (1hr., 22-27 per day 7am-8pm, €4.64); **Ronda** (1hr., 7-8 per day 9am-9pm, €5.25); **Sevilla** (4hr.; M-Th and Sa 9am, 4pm, F and Su 9am, 4, 8:30pm; €15.60).

Ferries: To **Puerto Banús** from the port (30min.; every hr.; €7, round-trip €10).

Taxis: Taxi Sol (☎952 77 44 88) serves Marbella **center** (€5) and **Puerto Banús** (€10). Taxi stands on the corner of Av. Ramón y Cajal and C. Huerta Chica.

Car Rental: Hertz, Av. Arias Maldonado, 4 (☎952 77 31 91). Compact car €75 per day. Open M-F 9am-1:30pm and 4:30-7:30pm, Sa 9am-2pm.

ORIENTATION AND PRACTICAL INFORMATION

The bus station is at the top of Ctra. del Trapiche. To reach the city center, exit the station, walk left, make the first right onto Ctra. del Trapiche, and turn right at the end of the road onto C. Salvador Rueda. Continue downhill on Av. del Mercado and turn left onto C. Castillejos, which leads to the perpendicular **Avenida Ramón y Cajal,** the main street in the new town; this becomes Av. Ricardo Soriano on the way to the harbor of **Puerto Banús** (7km away). C. Peral curves up from C. Huerta Chica off of Av. Ramón y Cajal around the *casco antiguo.* The old town's center, **Plaza de los Naranjos,** leads to a jumble of pedestrian streets. From C. Peral, the most direct route to the plaza is down C. Cabelleros.

Tourist Office: Pl. de los Naranjos (☎952 82 35 50; www.marbella.es). Sells detailed maps of the city and nearby San Pedro de Alcantara (€1); small ones are free. Open M-F 9am-9pm, Sa 10am-2pm. **Municipal Office,** Glorieta de la Fontanilla (☎952 77 14 42), across from and several blocks to the right of the main beach when facing the water. English spoken. Open M-F 9:30am-9pm, Sa 10am-2pm.

Currency Exchange: Banco Santander Central Hispano, Av. Ramón y Cajal, 9 (☎902 24 24 24). Open M-F 8:30am-2pm, Sa 8:30am-1pm; Apr.-Sept. closed Sa. **ATMs** abound, especially near the *casco antiguo* and along Av. Ramón y Cajal.

English-Language Bookstore: Arthúrica Libros, C. Puerta del Mar, 11 (☎952 86 28 24; www.arthuricalibros.com. Open M-F 10am-2pm and 5-9pm) and **Libreria Mata,** C. Castillo, 3 (☎952 77 01 44. Open M-F 9:30am-1 and 5-9pm, Sa 5-9pm).

Luggage Storage: At the bus station (€3). Open daily 6:30am-11:30pm.

Laundry: Lavomatic, on the corner of Av. Cánovas del Castillo, 70 (☎952 24 59 02). Wash and dry €13. Open daily 7am-11pm.

Police: Av. Juan de la Cierva (☎952 89 99 00 or 092).

Pharmacy: Farmacia Espejo, Pl. de los Naranjos, 4 (☎952 77 12 91). Open daily 9:30am-midnight. 24hr. pharmacies **Mingorance,** Av. Ricardo Soriano, 44 (☎952 77 57 73), and **Jacinto Berdaguer,** Av. Ricardo Soriano, 4 (☎952 77 31 87).

Hospital: Comarcal, CN-340, km 187 (☎952 86 27 48).

Internet Access: Neotel Locutorios, Pl. Puente de Ronda, 6 (☎952 82 85 24). €2 per hr. Try the €5 *bono* pass, good for 5hr. Open M-F 9am-1am, Sa-Su 10am-1am. MC/V. **Telekom Locutorio,** Av. Puerta del Mar, 1 (☎952 82 44 27). €1.50 per hr. Open daily 10am-midnight. Cash only.

Post Office: C. Jacinto Benavente, 14 (☎952 77 28 98), uphill from C. Ricardo Soriano. Open M-F 8:30am-8:30pm, Sa 9:30am-1pm. **Postal Code:** 29600.

ACCOMMODATIONS

Marbella has a wealth of accommodations catering to the foreign, high-flying crowds that fill its glitzy shores, but budget options are also available.

Hostal del Pilar, C. Mesoncillo, 4 (☎952 82 99 36; www.hostel-marbella.com). Backpackers enjoy the pool table, bar, and fireplace. Friendly, English-speaking staff. Roof mattresses available when rooms are full (€15). Maximum of 6 people in the dorms (typically same-sex). Wi-Fi. July-Aug. dorms €25, doubles €35, triples €50; Sept.-June €15/25/36. Weekly and monthly rates available in winter. Cash only. ❷

Hostal Paco, C. Isaac Peral, 16 (☎952 77 12 00; www.hostalpacomarbella.com). Near many nightclubs on one of the *casco antiguo's* main arteries. Reasonably sized, airy rooms have bath and TV; some have A/C. Singles €33-40; doubles €40-65; triples €60-80; quads €75-95. Highest prices in Aug. and *Semana Santa.* AmEx/MC/V. ❸

Hostal Enriqueta, C. de los Caballeros, 18 (☎952 82 75 52; www.hostalenriqueta.com). Located just steps away from Pl. de los Naranjos, the airy, personal touch of this hostel offers a quiet refuge from the bustle of nearby beaches. Rooms have bath, A/C, and TV. Singles €30-40; doubles €40-60; triples €60-80. Prices highest in Aug. and *Semana Santa.* AmEx/MC/V. ❸

FOOD

Terrazas on Pl. de los Naranjos are not particularly budget-friendly—the multilingual menus spell tourist trap. Restaurants farther uphill or hidden in alleys are easier on the wallet and offer more authentic cuisine. The waterfront has similar eateries, but a livelier and younger atmosphere. Locals retreat to Av. Nabeul for cheap eats. The **municipal market,** on Av. del Mercado, uphill from C. Huerta Chica, sells affordable produce and meat. (Open M-Sa 8am-2pm.)

El Gallo, C. Lobatas, 44 (☎952 82 79 98). A truly local restaurant and a perennial favorite with backpackers. Reasonable meals in a family-friendly atmosphere. Tapas from €1. The €8 *menú* is the best bargain, but the rabbit in garlic sauce (€6) steals the show. Open M-W and F-Su 11am-4pm and 7-11pm. MC/V. ❷

La Casa del Té, C. Ancha, 7 (☎639 16 79 18). Loud music and incense make this place feel like a nightclub crossed with a teahouse. The crepes (€2.30-2.60) and great selection of teas and juices (€1.20-3) are sure to please. Breakfast €2-3.20. Open May-Sept. 10am-1:30pm and 5-11:30pm; Oct.-Apr. 4-10:30pm. Cash only. ❶

Cantero, C. Castillejo, 7 (☎952 82 21 12). If you're going to do Spanish pastry, you've got to do it right. Cantero does, with enormous cookies and slices of cake for only €1-1.50. Juices and smoothies €2.25-2.75. Sit inside or take your whopping dessert to a nearby park bench. Open M-F 8:15am-2:15pm and 5-9:15pm, Sa 5-9:15pm. ❶

SIGHTS

Don't leave Marbella without taking a stroll through its narrow cobbled streets and whitewashed facades trimmed with wild roses. Or for a break from the beach, head over to the dazzling **Museo del Grabado Español Contemporáneo,** C. Hospital Bazán, in a restored hospital for the poor. It contains a captivating collection of modern artistic pieces with works by greats like Miró, Picasso, and Dalí, as well as rotating exhibits. *(☎952 76 57 41. Open M and Sa 9am-2pm, Tu-F 9am-2pm and 6-9pm. €3, students €1.50.)* To the northeast is the **Museo del Bonsai,** Av. del Dr. Maiz Viñals, a Zen experience brought to you by a large and varied collection of centuries-old miniature trees maintained by Rodrigo García, son of bonsai artist and museum founder Michael Angel García. *(☎952 86 29 26; www.fkbbonsai.com. Open daily 10:30am-1:30pm and 4-7pm. €4, under 12 €2.*

NIGHTLIFE

Except for the busiest weeks of the summer, bars in the *casco antiguo* and along the waterfront only get packed on weekend nights. Typical nightlife in Marbella means hitting up bars in the *casco antiguo* at midnight or 1am then proceeding to clubbing capital Puerto Banús in the early morning, around 3am. **Plaza de los Olivos** has a handful of bars and clubs, the best of which is **O'Brian's Irish Bar**—popular for its fusion of traditional Celtic music with funky new-age beats. The bar often hosts theme nights on quieter evenings; check the window for upcoming events. (☎952 76 46 95. Beer €2.50. Mixed drinks €5. Open M-Th 6pm-3am, F-Sa 6pm-4am, Su 3pm-3am. Cash only.) After-hours clubbing happens at **Puerto Banús,** a short drive by taxi (€10) from Marbella's old city. Though open relatively early, the clubs don't fill up until around 4am. Budget travelers beware—drink prices are exorbitant and many places charge huge covers, even when the bars are mostly empty. One option is **Comedia,** C. Ribera, which attracts a dancing crowd with an artistic ambience and high-energy music. (☎952 81 40 04. Beer €8. Mixed drinks €10. Open daily 11pm-5am. MC/V.)

BEACHES

The 7km stroll from Marbella center to Puerto Banús, almost entirely along a boardwalk, is one of the most beautiful ways to spend an hour and a half. If you prefer to sit back and enjoy the ride, city buses along Av. Ricardo Soriano, heading for San Pedro or Hipercor (#6, 7, 25, and 26; €1), bring you to the chic port dominated by imposing white yachts and row upon row of boutiques and restaurants. On clear days, the Moroccan coast is just faintly visible. Throngs of well-dressed Europeans mill about the marina—the port has been frequented by the likes of Sean Connery, King Fahd of Saudi Arabia, Antonio Banderas, and the late Princess Diana. With 22km of beach, Marbella offers a choice of seaside ambience. Shores to the east of the port are popular with British backpackers; those to the west attract a more posh crowd. **Funny Beach,** popular with families, is a 10min. bus ride (take the bus to Fuengirola and ask the driver to stop, €1), or a 2km walk east along the beach. Waterskiing and jet-skiing are focused along the strip between Marbella and Puerto

Banús, although companies offer an array of watersports. Try calling **Álvaro** (☎686 48 80 68) for lessons. For sailing try **Club Marítimo** (☎952 77 25 04) or **Club de Mar Puerto Banús** (☎952 81 77 50).

ALMERÍA ☎950

A small city on the coast, Almería is known as the sunniest place in Europe. It has recently become an incredibly popular spot for wealthy weekend travelers and beach-hungry backpackers. Densely packed and bustling, Almería shows its age with unabashed grace; old stone facades melt into the hillside, streets crack, and colors fade, all beneath a unique hue of sunlight. Busy promenades lined with fountains, sculptures, and palm trees stretch between the shoreline and *casco antiguo*. A Moorish fortress, the Alcazaba, presides over the city and stands as testament to Almería's historical prowess. The city's rocking nightlife and kilometers of sand are not too shabby either; as the region's capital, Almería has a little bit of everything.

TRANSPORTATION

The **airport** (☎950 21 37 00), 9km outside town, has daily flights to **Barcelona** (1hr.; M-Sa 3 per day, Su 1 per day) and **Madrid** (1hr.; M-F 6 per day, Sa 5 per day, Su 3 per day). The combined **bus/train station,** is located in Pl. de la Estación. **RENFE** (☎902 24 02 02) sends trains to: **Barcelona** (14hr., W, F, Su 7:40am, €53.10); **Granada** (2hr., 4 per day 6am-6:25pm, €13.40); **Madrid** (7hr., 7:15am, 4:15pm, €33.90-38); **Sevilla** (5-5hr., 4 per day 6am-6:25pm, €32.50); and **Valencia** (9hr.; W, F, Su 7:40am; €43). **Buses** (☎950 26 20 98) are fairly frequent and the schedules are reliable. **ALSA/Enatcar** runs to **Barcelona** (14hr., 5 per day 9:30am-9:30pm, €56.32; express daily 10am, €68.38); **Murcia** (3hr., 8-9 per day 5:30am-9:30pm, €16.59-19.50); **Valencia** (6-7hr., 6 per day 8:45am-9:30pm, €34.25-41.47; 6hr. express daily 9:15am, €41.47). **Alsina Graells** sends buses to: **Córdoba** (5hr., 4:30pm, €23.54); **Granada** (2hr., 15 per day 7am-8pm, €11.50-12.93); **Málaga** (3-5hr.; M-F 9 per day 6:30am-11pm, Sa-Su 8-9 per day 8am-11pm; €15.37); **Sevilla** (6-9hr.; 7:30, 9:30am, 1, 11pm; €30.07-30.53). **Almeraya** goes to **Madrid** (7hr., 5 per day 9:30am-midnight, €23.81).

ORIENTATION

The city revolves around the fountain-laden **Puerta de Purchena,** a six-way intersection ten blocks from the port. The bus and train stations are closer to the port but in a less desirable area of town; the walk to Puerta de Purchena is 15-20 min. To get there, walk straight from either station to the second roundabout (Pl. Barcelona) and take the second left onto Av. de la Estacíon. From there, walk to **Av. Federico García Lorca,** an enormous traffic thoroughfare leading straight to the port. Take a right, and then take a left onto Rambla Obispo Orberá. Pta. de Purchena is at the end of the street. **Paseo de Almería,** a landscaped avenue that leads to the port, is lined with 19th-century monuments, chic shops, cafes, banks, and pharmacies. This street borders the *casco antiguo* and intersects with Av. Federico García Lorca near the port. The beaches are on the opposite side of the port along the marble-lined **Paseo Maritimo.**

PRACTICAL INFORMATION

The portside is traversed by the **Parque de Nicolás Salmerón,** site of the **municipal tourist office,** two blocks from where Av. Federico García Lorca meets the port. (☎950 27 43 60; www.almeria-turismo.org. Open M-F 9am-7:30pm, Sa, Su and holidays 9:30am-3pm.) The heart of the *casco antiguo* is just above, bordered by Calle Real and Calle de la Reina. Other services include: **police,** on C. Santos

Zarate, 13 (☎950 62 12 05); **Hospital Torre-Cárdenas,** on Paraje Torre-Cárdenas (☎950 21 21 00 or 01 68 15); **internet** access at **Locutorio PCO,** C. Tiendas 20, near Puerta de Purchena (☎600 82 04 76; €1 per hr.; open daily 10:30am-2:30pm and 5:30pm-midnight); and the **post office,** Pl. Juan Cassinello, 1, on Po. de Almería (☎950 28 15 12; open M-F 8:30am-8:30pm, Sa 9:30am-2pm). **Postal Code:** 04080.

ACCOMMODATIONS

Almería hosts an impressive range of hotels, from rooms in skyscrapers to luxurious suites beside 16th-century monuments. Bargain accommodations are more difficult to come by, though reserving a room is typically easy.

Hostal Delfin Verde, C. García Cañas, 2, (☎950 26 79 27). A merry stucco establishment offering the best budget rooms along the Po. Marítimo, about a 15min walk from the intersection of La Rambla and Po. de Almería. Ocean views, new furnishings, TV, A/C, and a private bath make for a relaxing stay. July-Aug. singles €33; doubles €60; triples €70; Sept.-June €29/45/50. AmEx/MC/V. ❸

Hostal Residencia Nixar, C. Antonio Vico, 24, (☎950 23 72 55) Ideally located near the *casco antiguo,* a few blocks along Pl. de Carmen off the Pta. de Puchena. Lobby is a haven of wicker chairs and potted palms. Rooms have A/C, TV, and bathroom. Reservations only held until 8pm, so arrive early. Breakfast €2.50. July-Aug. singles €31, doubles €44, triples €57; Sept.-June €27/44/55. MC/V. ❸

FOOD

While the beaches and Po. de Almería are littered with wallet-denting cafes and *gelaterías*, the *casco antiguo* is the zenith of cheap tapas restaurants, most in aging taverns overflowing with locals. Most restaurants are located between Po. de Almería and C. Real in the seven blocks below Pta. de Purchena, especially on C. Jovellanos, C. Trajanos, and C. Egea. **Arbol** supermarkets are located throughout town in Pl. S. Sebastian, Av. Federico García Lorca (by the port), and Po. Marítimo (open daily 9am-2pm and 5-9pm). The central **market,** on C. Aguilar de Campo, is in an ornate 19th-century edifice between Po. de Almería and Rambla del Obispo Obrera. (☎950 25 72 95; open daily 9am-3pm.)

Bodega La Aldea, C. Mendez Nunez 6 (☎950 253 597). Off Po. de Almeria away from the *casco antiguo.* A tiny tavern with a ribbed ceiling and roughly hewn rock walls. Stop by for selections from the enormous tapas menu, posted on the wall, or for the night's first glass of wine. Tapas €2-5. Open M-Sa 1-4pm and 8:30pm-midnight. MC/V. ❶

Casa Puga, C. Jovellanos, 7, (☎950 23 15 30; www.barcasapuga.es). Just off C. Real. Locals of all ages congregate here. Faded pictures, walls of liquor, and open doors surround a standing bar, which remains loud and packed until late. Try their sinfully delicious fried popcorn shrimp. Tapas €1-6. *Raciones* €6-9 (half), €11-18 (whole). Open M-Sa noon-4pm and 8:30pm-midnight. MC/V. ❷

Taberna El Postigo, C. Guzmán, (☎950 24 56 52). A sizzling tapas bar with tons of outdoor seating, nestled in a dead end. Packed with a garrulous crowd downing beer as fast as the tapas (€3-7) are prepared. Open M-Sa 8pm-midnight. Cash only. ❶

SIGHTS

ALCAZABA. A magnificent 14-acre adobe Moorish fortress built in 995 by Abderramán III of Córdoba, this is the second largest Muslim edifice in Spain. In the 15th century, the fortress was found partially destroyed by an earthquake. Christian reconstruction left it divided into three definitive parts: the first two Muslim and the second Christian. The first, now a lush garden, was a residential area during the city's 11th-century peak. The second, still undergoing renovations, was a small palatial city and a governmental hub with public baths and the Caliph wells. The third showcases gunpowder towers. The view at sunset is spectacular, when Almería's famed evening lighting bathes the mosaic of rooftops in a golden glow. *(☎950 17 55 00. Open Tu-Su 9am-8:30pm. Closes at 6:30pm Oct.-Mar. Free. Guided tours Su.)*

CATHEDRAL. The city's vast cathedral was built after a 1522 earthquake. Don't be fooled by its harsh appearance; the cathedral was built to resemble a fortress as a deterrent against raids by Berber, Turkish, and Moorish pirates. To reach the cathedral, follow the signs leading off C. Real. *(☎690 02 49 57. Open M-F 10am-2pm and 4-5:30pm, Sa 10am-2pm, and during mass. €2.)*

PASEO DE ALMERÍA. The walk up Po. de Almería from the port reveals an architectural transition from the medieval to the contemporary. Notable spots are the **Teatro Cervantes,** a neo-Baroque edifice that still shows movies daily, the open courtyard of the **Escuela de Artes,** which occasionally showcases Andalucian photography in its open courtyard, and the **Casino Cultural,** once an aristocratic mansion. At the cusp of the Pr. de Purchena sit the **Aljibes de Jayran,** Arabic water tanks used in the 11th century to store 630,000L of water channeled from 6.5km away. *(☎950 27 30 39. Open M-F 10am-2pm. Free.)* Around the Puerta, three **16th-century churches** fan out amidst Moorish bazaars. A 10min. walk from the Puerta leads up a set of stairs to the **Cerro San Cristobal,** where an exalted white statue of Jesus Christ stands over the town.

NIGHTLIFE

Nightlife in Almería centers on the raucous tapas bars in the upper part of town; relaxed barhopping begins early and ends late. Until recently, the city of Almería was one of the only cities in Spain where *botellón* (literally meaning large bottle), defined plainly as alcohol-fueled public merriment, was legal. Though the city officially banned *botellones* in the fall of 2007, the raucous spirit of the city still lingers. The bar scene is a gradual movement toward the port from the restaurant-heavy areas. Popular spots are never far from the Po. de Almería, clustered around four winding streets behind the post office in the *casco antiguo*, appropriately called Cuatro Calles.

Chambao, C. San Pedro, 13, a trendy spot in town that has two sleek bars for mingling, a flat-screen TV for soccer-watching, and a small dance floor for, well, you know. Beer €2.50. Mixed drinks €6. Shots €2. Open M-W 3:30pm-2am, Th-Su 3:30pm-4am.

Mae West, Parque Nicolás Salmerón, 9, (☎950 25 35 20). Where students have the first drink of the night before dinner. A funky red building with vintage, vampy ambience and seats beneath dark stone archways. Late-night dancing brings crowds back in droves during the wee hours of the night. Beer €3. Mixed drinks €6. Sa cover €10, includes drink. Open daily 10pm-6am. MC/V.

Teatro Dolce Vita, C. Marqués de Comillas, 18, (☎950 25 33 10). A discoteca designed to look like an old-fashioned theater. Another entrance on Po. Almería. Beer €3. Mixed drinks €5-7. M-F no cover, Sa €5; includes 1 drink. Open daily 3pm-7am.

BEACHES

Tourists swarm Almería's beaches, taking refuge from the city's stifling mid-day heat. The shores may be crowded, but the seaside atmosphere is peaceful—Po. de Marítimo is pedestrian-only, and the town is little more than a swathe of seafood cafes and apartment complexes. Po. de Almería and Av. de Federico García Lorca are only a few blocks left from the shore. The first couple of bays are rocky and churned up by yacht traffic—keep left until the start of Po. de Marítimo, which marks the calm-watered stretch of **Playa Ciudad Luminosa** and **Playa del Zapillo.** If it's seclusion you seek, you're more likely to find it in the *casco antiguo*, or on the vacant shores of Cabo de Gata.

CABO DE GATA ☎950

Alsina Graells (☎950 23 81 97) sends buses to San Miguel de Cabo de Gata (1hr.; 6 per day 8am-9:15pm, return 7 per day 7am-10:15pm; €2.26). Autocares Bernardo (☎950 25 04 22) runs to San José (45min.; M-F 10am, 1:15, 6:30pm, Sa 10am, 2:14, 6:30pm; Su 10am, 6:30pm; €3). Buses leave Cabo de Gata from the Estación de Autobuses en route to Salinas. Buses leave from Almería (6 per day 8, 11am, 1, 3, 7, 9:15pm), and Salinas (45-60min.; M-F 7 per day, 7, 9am, noon, 2, 4, 8, 10:15pm; €2.26.)

TRANSPORTATION TROUBLES? Though it's entirely possible to reach the Cabo de Gata region by bus via San José or San Miguel, both towns present difficulties for exploring the park. San José is closer, but bus service there is infrequent and often unreliable. San Miguel has reliable bus service from Almería, but is farther from the reserve. The easiest, most reliable, and most efficient way to explore Cabo de Gata is by car. Be sure to ask about return times at the bus station in Almería, as they change frequently.

Long stretches of quiet beaches await in the fishing town of **San Miguel de Cabo de Gata** (simply known as Cabo de Gata), which lies at the head of the **Parque Natural de Cabo de Gata-Níjar,** a 60km stretch of protected coast and inland environs 30km east of urban Almería. The near-desolate peninsula features salt marshes, sand dunes, and phenomenal geographical contrasts. Flamingos flock to the tropical salt marshes, while desert and mountains lie farther inland. Bird tracks often collect more thickly along the sand than human footprints. As towns along Cabo de Gata are typically small fishing hubs rather than tourist destinations, come prepared with food, cash, and anything else you might need for a day of beach-trekking. The quiet resort town of **San José** boasts an unspoiled beach and serves as a base for visiting the park. Contact the **tourist office** in San José for information on water sports, bike and car rentals, and maps for visiting the secluded *calas* (coves) along the coast. (☎950 38 02 99. Some English spoken. Open in summer daily 10am-2pm and 5-8pm; in winter M-Sa 10am-2pm and 5-8pm, Su 10am-2pm.)

The best beaches begin at **San Miguel de Cabo de Gata.** The area begins beside a hazy stretch of mountains and peters off into vacant beaches and deep-green marshes. The town itself is comprised of stilled streets and utilitarian stucco buildings—the only standout feature is an old watchtower by the fishing boats. Savvy beachgoers dive at **Mermaid's Reef** or windsurf off **Playa de San Miguel. Grupo J. 126** (☎950 38 02 99) provides information and tours in English, Spanish, French, and German; contact them a day or two in advance for tours and equipment. Three kilometers from San Miguel is **Las Salinas,** a natural salt marsh reserve home to the Laguna de Rosa and miles of sand dunes, where 169 species of birds, including flamingos, storks, and herons, roost in the summertime. **Playa Miramar** is the town's main beach. Farther up the coast, past the fishing boats, is a secluded and sparsely populated beach, bordered by a small grassy ridge with mountain views.

Hostal Las Dunas ❹, C. Barrionuevo, 5, the only budget option in town, is easy to find—simply follow the weather-worn signs from the bus-stop roundabout. A small marble staircase leads up to clean rooms with A/C, TV, and bath. (☎950 37 00 72; www.lasdunas.net. Breakfast €2. Singles €40; doubles €55. Cash only.)

Camping Cabo de Gata ❶ is 6km from the town and has a pool and restaurant. (☎950 16 04 43. €5.90 per person, €5.35 per child. Electricity €4.50.) The beachfront area offers a string of seafood cafes that quickly gives way to empty kilometers of beach. **Chiribus** ❷, tucked between the watch tower and fishing boats, offers wide ocean vistas underneath craggy mountain shadows. (☎679 18 36 69. Open daily 11am until close.)

The **tourist office** for the park and Las Salinas is a tiny wooden cabin, toward the entrance to the town, next to the large hotel. (Open M-F 9am-10:30pm, Sa-Su 10am-2pm.) A 24hr. **ATM** is in the same plaza as the **supermarket.** Phone and **internet** access are available at a small corner store, located at the intersection of C. Emilio Pérez and C. La Morena. Watch for the yellow sign on the beach, as streets tend not to be clearly marked. (€2.50 per hr.; open M-Sa 8am-2pm and 4-10pm, Su 8am-2pm.)

MOJÁCAR ☎950

Mojácar's postcard-perfect whitewashed buildings spread peacefully over the jagged crest of a green hillside. The town's steep knot of rocky, unmarked streets are accented by thick wooden doors and flowered balconies, all decorated with the region's ancient symbol of protection from evil, the *Indalo*. During the day, the village clears out as tourists escape down to the turquoise Mediterranean. Later, residents and small crowds of tourists take to rooftop terraces to enjoy the sunset, while others fill the boardwalk. Beachfront resorts fill up quickly in July and August, when hordes of international visitors join the large contingent of German, British, and American expats who have made Mojácar their home—don't be surprised to hear as much English as Spanish.

TRANSPORTATION

Getting to and from Mojácar is difficult, though it is well worth the effort.The main bus stop (there is no station) on Po. del Mediterraneo connects the many kilometers of Mojácar's coastline (the auxiliary tourist office is just across the street and to the left). The stop is on the beach, around the corner from the stop that takes passengers to the hilltop part of town every half hour (€1). Although there are long-distance buses that run from Mojacar, the small neighboring city of Vera has more extensive schedules and destinations. Blue "BARAZA" Buses (☎950 39 03 11 or 950 39 00 53) run to Vera every hour from Mojácar's beach stops. **ALSA/Enatcar** buses (☎902 42 22 42) leave from the central bus stop on Po. del Mediterráneo, across from the taxi stand, for **Almería** (1hr.; M-F 5 per day 8:05am-9:10pm, Sa 3 per day 7:56am, 1:15, 9:10pm, Su3 per day 1:15, 5:55, and 9:10pm; €6.41); **Madrid** (9hr.; 3 per day, 6:55am, 1:10, 8:55pm; €34.13); **Murcia** (1-2hr., 5-6 per day 6:55am-8:55pm, €10.17). From **Vera,** buses also run to **Barcelona** (reserve ahead of time; 12hr., 3 per day; 9:45am, 7:35pm and 10:30pm; €53.78); and **Alicante** (4hr.; 4 per day, 9:45am-10:30pm; €14.51). Be aware that bus schedules may not be strictly observed. For a **taxi** call ☎950 22 61 61, or wait at the Pl. Nueva stop in town. The tourist office has a list of nearly a dozen **car rental** agencies, or try **Mo-Car** (☎950 47 83 07). For **bikes** and **scooters,** visit **Susana's,** Po. del Mediterraneo, Pl. del Cantal (☎649 51 03 660).

STUCK IN PARADISE. Once you are in Mojácar, the city will do its best to keep you from leaving—return buses and their schedules are difficult to come by anywhere but the tourist office. Planning your route in advance is imperative.

ORIENTATION

Mojácar is split by the rocky green hills between the town and its 17km stretch of beaches. The town centers around Pl. Nueva; the steep, tangled surrounding streets here offer panoramic ocean vistas framed by rooftop terraces. Below, **Paseo Mediterráneo** links the city's 11 beaches. The beach area is decidedly more urban (you will find more banks and supermarkets here). Transportation within Mojácar is a breeze; the yellow **Transportes Urbanos** buses stop at each of the 11 beaches and travels to town mid-loop, beginning at Hotel Indalo at the far right beach, facing the water. (In summer daily 2 per hr. 8:10am-11:25pm; F-Sa service until 12:25am. In winter daily 2 per hr. 8:55am-8:55pm. €1.) The stop leading to town is in front of the central **Playa de las Ventanicas** on **Av. de Andalucía,** which diverges from Po. del Mediterraneo at an enormous roundabout. The second stop, in **Pl. Ray Alabez,** is preferable and closest to the town's main square. From the plaza, take a left on **Av. Paris** and head up the steep, slightly-hidden stairs to your immediate right; these lead to **C. Aire,** a rockside street that funnels into Pl. Nueva, the only place in town that caters to tourist needs.

PRACTICAL INFORMATION

Below the plaza, a small complex houses the **tourist office,** C. Glorieta, 1 (☎950 61 50 25; www.mojacar.es. Open M-F 10am-2pm and 5:30-8pm, Sa 10:30am-1:30pm. Services include: **Unicaja Bank,** Pl. Nueva; laundry service at **Bish's Lavandería,** Po. del Mediterráneo, by Playa del Cantal (☎950 47 80 11. €2.75 per kg. Self-serve washers €5-9.50; dryers €1.50 per 15min. Open M-F 9am-5pm, Sa 9am-2pm. Last wash 4pm.); **internet** access at Ciber Koko (€2 per hr.; open daily 11:30am;-1am); **police** (☎950 47 20 00); **auxiliary post office** (open M-F 12:30-2:30pm, Sa-Su 10:30-11:30am), and **central post office** on Po. Mediterráneo. (☎950 47 87 03. Open M-Sa 9am-2pm.) by the main bus stop. **Postal Code:** 04638.

ACCOMMODATIONS

Mojácar is not as heavily touristed as the rest of the Costa del Sol, but that means that lodging options are more limited. Reserve well in advance if you plan to visit in late summer or during the summer solstice (end of June) or the festival of the Moors and Christians (beginning of June). Hostels in town often provide affordable, luxurious rooms with stunning views of the hazy sea horizon. For beachfront accommodations, the stretch from Playa del Cantal to Playa de las Ventanicas offers the best shores, boardwalks, and restaurants.

Hostal Arco Plaza, Pl. Nueva, (☎950 47 27 77). Ideally located, this *hostal* offers elegant, blue-walled rooms and fantastic views. All rooms have huge beds, private bathrooms, TV, and A/C, making Arco well worth the price. June-July singles €33, doubles €43, triples €53; *Semana Santa,* Aug., and Christmas €36/53/65. Jan-Mar. and Oct.-Nov. €28/35/40. MC/V. ❸

Pensión Torreón, C. Jazmín, 4-6, (☎950 47 52 59). A toll-house-turned-hostel with rooms surrounding a foyer with stained glass doors. The vine-covered terrace has sea views worth writing home about. From Pl. Nueva, follow signs to the hostel. Reserve ahead. Breakfast €5. Doubles with shared bath €55. Cash only. ❺

Camping El Cantel Playa de Mojácar, (☎950 47 82 04). An enclosed, wooded campground across the highway from Playa del Cantal. €4 per person, €3 per child, €4.50 per car, €6.50 per camper. Electricity €2.75. Discounts Oct.-Mar. ❶

FOOD

As with accommodations, you're better off eating in town, where you'll find more variety and better *bocadillos* for your buck. If you are looking for a meal close to the water, look no further than the *chirringuitos*, open-air beach bars. Most restaurants, including many with rooftop terraces, are found in town around Pl. Nueva, Pl. del Sol, and Pl. Fronton.

Gelateria Italiana Alberto, Po. del Mediterraneo, 35, (☎950 47 86 64). World-class gelato with flavors that range from local cactus to chili-chocolate. €3-7. Open daily March-Oct. 10am-1am, July-Sept 2pm-2am. MC/V. ❶

Sinaloa Fanny's, (☎950 47 22 73). Loud colors, a sunset terrace, and a pool table help Sinaloa Fanny's, just above Pl. Nueva, attract a young crowd hungry for hearty Mexican cuisine and thirsty for the first mojitos of the night. Open daily from 11am-late. ❷

El Antler, C. Enmedio, (☎600 54 06 61), just down from the plaza at the top of town. Serves meats, *pâté*, and chicken, and has a warmly lit dining room and upscale ambience. Entrees from €10. Open M-Sa 8pm-11pm. MC/V. ❷

La Cantina, Playa de Ventanicas, (☎950 47 88 41; www.lacantinamojacar.com). Has a raucous ambience, sheltered beach view, and authentic Mexican tacos and quesadillas (€7-12) on a wooden deck overlooking the sea. Reserve ahead on weekends. Open daily 7:30pm-midnight. ❷

SIGHTS AND BEACHES

Mojácar was the heart of a 1488 pact of free association between Christians, Jews, and Moors. Vestiges of this convivial history are present in several standout sites concentrated around Pl. Nueva. At the lower border of town, along Cuesta de la Fuente, is the **Fuente Mora,** a Moorish fountain from which residents still bottle water. Part of the city's rocky old facade rises from the Jewish quarter by Pl. Flores to C. Enmedio, leading to the arching Puerta de la Ciudad. Along C. Enmedio, the modest *Ayuntamiento* stands in the shadows of the 16th-century **Iglesia de Santa Maria,** surrounded by flower groves and quiet streets. This bucolic architectural charm is accented by views from the terraces on **Pl. Nueva** and the **Mirador del Castillo,** the highest point in town. **C. Aire** is a quiet stretch leading away from Pl. Nueva that curves beneath the rocky hillside and old facades. Below, Mojácar's string of 11 beaches is the undisputed main attraction: stretches of sands interspersed with small, rocky promontories afford plenty of personal space for the discerning sunbather. Buses run every 30min. between the town and the beaches.

The choice stretch is between **Playa del Cantal** and **Playa de las Ventanicas,** where traffic is quieter and sands are softer. For the most part, this is also the hub of beachside nightlife. If you're walking from town, take a right from Av. de Andalucia along Po. del Mediterráneo; beaches and bars improve in this direction. **Playa de las Ventanicas** marks the start of a palm-lined street that stretches several kilometers to the south (right at the bottom of the hill from town). If you're craving total seclusion, take a taxi beyond the **Macenas Castle** (an 18th-century watchtower visible from Pl. de las Ventanicas), where a dirt track leads to **Bordenares** and **Sombrerico.** Parts of these beaches are now subject to construction, due to finish in 2011. You can also follow the dirt road at the end of **Playa de las Ventanicas,** which quickly disintegrates into a thin trail and leads up the cliff along the water, eventually spitting you out a short walk from the castle. If you opt for this **incredible hike,** be sure to bring your boots for the steep, shale path. For watersports, head to **Samoa Surf/Club** on the Playa del Cantal by Pueblo Indalo. (☎950 47 84 90t. Banana boats €10 per 15min. Sea kayaks for 1 person €6 per 30min., €9 per hr.; for 2 people €7/10. Windsurfing €15 per hr., €50 for 5hr. Wakeboarding and waterskiing €35 per 20min.)

NIGHTLIFE AND ENTERTAINMENT

Nightlife in Mojácar is surprisingly energetic and diverse. The town is dotted with hole-in-the-wall taverns and funky dives filled with loud, mixed crowds. Dozens of tented beach bars *(chirringuitos)* invite a vigorous nightlife crowd to the breezy shore—the "in" place changes constantly, but tourist offices offer helpful lists of popular spots. *Chirringuitos*, offering seaside lounging and mixed drinks, are concentrated at Playa del Cantal and become steadily more upscale and spread out toward Playa de las Ventanicas. Buses stop running at midnight on weekdays and at 1am on weekends, and taxis disappear at sundown—you can call one, but it will set you back at least €8 and up to an hour in waiting time after about 2 am. Walking the poorly lit road, however, is a dangerous and exhausting alternative. The **BúhoBus** runs from Hotel Indalo (Playa de las Ventanicas) to the neighboring towns of Garrucha and Vera every two hours (June 14-Sept. 15; every 2hr. midnight-4am; €1). Though they're a bit out of the way, **Tito's Beach Bar,** at the end of Playa de las Ventanicas, **Budu Pub,** C. Estacion 9, 23, and **Café Calima,** Pl. Arbollón, 1, are all worth the trek. (**Tito's Beach Bar** ☎950 61 50 30; open daily 10am-8pm. Bar open 7pm-2:30am. **Budu Pub** ☎630 23 11 43; open daily 8pm-5am. **Café Calima** ☎950 47 87 65; open daily 9am-1pm and 7pm-2:30am.)

Lua, Playa de las Ventanicas. Almost entirely engulfed in lush landscaping, Lua is accented with an arching mahogany bar, bamboo, and Buddha statues. Beer €2.50. Mixed drinks €5.50. Open daily noon-4am.

El Patio 2000, Playa del Cantal, (☎629 28 72 65). Offers a laid-back atmosphere amid tropical trees and tiki torches. Local rock and salsa bands play in the afternoons and nights on weekends. Beer €2. Mixed drinks €3-5. Open daily 10am-2am.

BBme, right next to El Patio 2000. A peeling wooden shack with cool lounges, a crammed dance floor, and delicious Argentine food. Open daily 10am-4am.

Mandala, Po. de Mediterráneo. One of the newest additions to the Mojácar disco circuit. The club has ornately carved wooden walls and elegant chandeliers, which are periodically obscured by the fog machines and enormous crowds dancing to house and techno. Open daily midnight-6am. Mixed drinks €7. Cover €10, includes drink before 2am.

RONDA ☎952

When you first see Ronda (pop. 370,000), you'll think you've stumbled onto the pages of a fairy-tale. Centuries-old arches span the 100m El Tajo gorge, connecting the *casco antiguo* to the newer part of town, which is less romantic but full of life. The old city dates from Roman times, and the city earned fleeting political prominence under Moorish rule. The birthplace of modern bullfighting, Ronda has attracted such literary luminaries as Rainer Maria Rilke, who wrote his *Spanish Elegies* here, Ernest Hemingway, who based *For Whom the Bell Tolls* on the city, and Orson Welles, whose ashes are buried on a bull farm outside of town. While Ronda may hold you entranced for days, the city also makes an excellent base for exploring Andalucía's best *pueblos blancos* and the nearby Cuevas de la Pileta.

TRANSPORTATION

Train and bus stations are 3 blocks apart in the new city on Av. de Andalucía.

Trains: Av. Alférez Provisional (☎952 87 16 73 or 902 24 02 02). Ticket booth at C. Infantes, 20 (☎952 87 16 62). Open M-F 7am-10pm. To: **Algeciras** (2hr., 4 per day 7:10am-7:35pm, €6.70); **Granada** (3hr., 3 per day 8:57am-5:35pm, €12.25); **Madrid** (4hr., 10am and 4:46pm, €59.90); **Málaga** (2hr., M-Sa 7:12am, €8.85); or take the train to **Bobadilla** (1hr., 4 per day 7:52am-5:19pm, €4.40), which has more frequent trains to **Málaga** (1hr., 6 per day 8am-9:49pm, €4.40-13.70).

Buses: Pl. Concepción García Redondo, 2 (☎952 18 70 61). To: **Cádiz** (4hr.; 2-3 per day 9:30am-4:30pm, Sa-Su last bus 6pm; €12.61); **Málaga** (2hr., 8-11 per day 7am-7:45pm, €9.63); **Marbella** (1hr., 5-6 per day 6:30am-8:15pm, €5.02); **Sevilla** (3hr., 3-5 per day 7am-7pm, €10.17).

Taxis: (☎952 87 23 16 or 670 20 74 38). From the train station to Pl. de España €4.

ORIENTATION AND PRACTICAL INFORMATION

The 18th-century **Puente Nuevo** connects Ronda's old and new cities. On the new side, **Carrera Espinel** (the main street, which includes the pedestrian walkway known as La Bola) runs perpendicular to C. Virgen de la Paz, intersecting it between the bullring and **Plaza de España.** To reach the tourist office and town center, leave the train station and go straight on Av. Martínez Astein. Turn right when the road ends onto the pedestrian C. Espinel. From the bus station, turn left onto C. Naranja, walk four blocks, and then turn right onto pedestrian Carrera Espinel, which leads to the Pl. de España.

Tourist Office: Municipal, Po. Blas Infante (☎952 18 71 19), near the bullring. English spoken. Open June-Aug. M-F 10am-7:15pm, Sa-Su 10am-2pm and 3:30-6:30pm; Sept.-May M-F 9:30am-6:30pm, Sa-Su 10am-2pm and 3:30-6:30pm. **Regional** office, Pl. de España, 1 (☎952 87 12 72). English spoken. Open June-Aug. M-F 9am-8pm, Sa-Su 10am-2pm; Sept.-May M-F 9am-7pm, Sa-Su 10am-2pm. The tourist office also sells *bono* tickets for discounted entrance to Ronda's major sights.

Currency Exchange: Banco Santander Central Hispano, Carrera Espinel, 17 (☎902 24 24 24), near C. Virgen de los Remedios. Open M-F 8:30am-2pm; Oct.-May also Sa 8:30am-1pm. If banks are closed, try **Ronda Change,** C. Virgen de la Paz, 2 (☎952 87 96 04). Open M-F 10am-2pm and 4-8pm, Sa 10am-3pm.

Luggage Storage: At the bus station (€3 per day). Open daily 9am-8pm.

Police: Pl. Duquesa de Parcent (☎092), 3, near the town hall

Medical Emergency: ☎952 06 52 18 or 50 50 61. **Hospital de la Serranía** (☎951 06 50 01), en route to El Burgo.

Pharmacy: Farmacia Santos, Pl. de España, 5 (☎952 87 15 80). Open in summer M-F 9:30am-2pm and 5-8:30pm; winter M-F 9:30am-2pm and 5-8pm, Sa 9:30am-2pm.

Internet Access: Ciber Locutorio Rondatelecom, C. Jerez, 4-Bajo (☎952 87 25 57). Internet €1.40 per hr. Copies €0.20 per page. Public telephones available. Open M-Sa 11am-2pm and 5-10pm.

Laundry: Pressto, C. Mariano Soubirón, 17 (☎952 87 91 77; www.pressto.com). Open M-F 9:30am-2pm and 5-8:30pm, Sa 9:30am-2pm.

Post Office: C. Virgen de la Paz, 20 (☎952 87 25 57), across from Pl. de Toros. **Lista de Correos.** Open M-F 8:30am-8:30pm, Sa 9:30am-1pm. **Postal Code:** 29400.

ACCOMMODATIONS

Hotels in the old city are expensive, so you'll be better off staying in the new city. Most *pensiones* are concentrated around the bus station on side streets off Carrera Espinel—try C. Naranja, C. Lorenzo Borrego, or C. Sevilla. Expect room shortages in August and during the *Feria de Ronda* in September.

Hotel Arunda I, C. Espinel, 120 (☎952 19 01 02; www.hotelesarunda.com). Carved-wood-furnished rooms have bath, A/C, TV, and sunny windows. A little classier than its sister hotel. Internet access €2 per hr. **Arunda II,** C. José M.C. Madrid, 10-12 (☎952 87 25 19) has the same white-walled, dark-fixtured decor and internet prices but offers breakfast. Singles €27, with breakfast €29; doubles €44/47. AmEx/MC/V. ❸

Pensión La Purísima, C. Sevilla, 10 (☎952 87 10 50). Plant-filled hallways lead to bright rooms decorated with tasteful religious art. Some have private bath. Singles €17; doubles €30, with bath €35; triples with bath €50. Cash only. ❷

Hotel Morales, C. Sevilla, 51 (☎952 87 15 38; www.hotelmorales.es). A nature theme carries from the corridor into each room by way of wildlife posters and earth tone bedspreads; singles are small but cozy. All have private bath, A/C, and TV. Singles €23-25; doubles €39-42. MC/V. ❷

FOOD

Restaurants and cafes abound in Ronda, although many are geared to tourists and tend to be overpriced, especially those near Pl. de España. Rabbit and stewed bull's tail *(rabo de toro)* are local specialties.

El Pataton, C. San José, 8 (☎678 87 06 26), tucked between C. Molino and C. Sevilla. A popular takeout spot with locals. For only €3.50, the friendly chefs prepare a delicious variation on Spanish cuisine: tapas ingredients stuffed into potatoes. Choose from one of 11 options or try the €4.50 "El Pataton" for a giant potato with a filling of your choice. Open Tu-Su 8pm-midnight. Closed 1 month per year, usually July-early Aug. ❶

Casi Ke No, C. Molino, 6B. If choosing a sandwich is an existential struggle for you, beware of Casi Ke No. Serves 50 types of *montaditos* (€1.20), small but substantial sandwiches, as well as innovative tapas such as goat cheese topped with raspberry (€3). Open Tu-Su noon-4pm and 7pm-midnight. Cash only. ❶

Los Cántaros, C. Sevilla, 66 (☎952 87 63 23). A small local bar with big food. The bull's tail (€9) is heaping and melts off the bone. Soups (€2-6), fish (€6-11), and meat dishes (€6-15). Open Tu-Sa 9am-5pm and 8-11pm, Su and M 9am-5pm. ❷

Panadería Rondeña, C. Sevilla, 53 (☎952 87 52 82). Lines of sizable fresh pastries (€1-1.40). Pop in for a lemon *granizado* (small €0.70, large €1.40), a perfect refreshment after a day of sightseeing. Open Su and M 8am-8pm, Tu-Sa 7am-8:30pm. ❶

Chocolat, C. Sevilla, 16 (☎952 87 69 84) offers a gourmet chocolate experience in an airy, light cafe. Coffees (€2.25-2.50). Over forty varieties of green, black, white, and red teas (€1-3). Pastries and chocolate (€1-3.50). Open 8:30am-2pm and 4-8:30pm. ❶

SIGHTS

CASA DEL REY MORO. The name, "House of the Moorish King," is rather misleading. Despite its Moorish facade, the house dates from the 18th century and is not the main attraction; you enter it only to pay your admission. Descend the seemingly endless stairways—60m into the depths of a 14th-century mine, which has housed more than its share of prisoners and slaves over the centuries. A strategic defense point, the mine also has a room used to hold cauldrons of boiling oil and a "Room of Secrets," where whispers travel from one corner of the room to the other but are inaudible in the middle. The other main attractions are Forestier's serene gardens, high atop the cliffs and house, designed and constructed in the 1920s by the famous French landscape architect. *(Cuesta de Santo Domingo, 17. Take the first left after crossing the Puente Nuevo. ☎952 18 72 00. Open daily in summer 10am-7pm; in winter 10am-7pm. €4, children €2.)*

PLAZA DE TOROS AND MUSEO TAURINO. Bullfighting lies at the heart of Ronda's livelihood, as evidenced by the careful construction of this stunning bullring, the oldest in Spain (est. 1785). The attached museum traces the history of the sport, focusing largely on Ronda's native matadors. Ronda has had its share of famous bullfighters, including the Romero dynasty—three generations of fighters from the same family. Pedro, the most famous, killed his first bull at age 17 in 1771; over the course of his career, it is said he fought more than 5600 bulls without a single injury. The museum's hallways are filled with Goya prints of bullfights, authentic costumes, weapons, and the heads of the bravest bulls. Perhaps of greater interest are the actual bullring and stables. In early September, the Plaza de Toros hosts *corridas goyescas* (bullfights in traditional costumes) as part of the **Feria de Ronda.** *(☎952 87 41 32; www.rmcr.org. Open daily Apr. 16-Oct. 10am-8pm; Nov.-Feb. 10am-6pm; Mar.-Apr. 15 10am-7pm. €6, students €4. Museum audio tour €3. Wheelchair-accessible.)*

MUSEO DE LARA. The private collection of Juan Antonio Lara Jurado—who still lives above the museum—is a collection of, well, collections. He covers traditional Spanish culture with fans, bullfighting costumes, and a *bodega* room, and delves into the more bizarre with a guillotine and roomful of witchcraft and Inquisition torture devices. In the summer, the museum hosts weekend flamenco shows. *(C. Armiñán, 29. ☎952 87 12 63; www.museolara.org. Open daily 11am-8pm. €4, students and seniors €2, children free. Flamenco €23 at 10pm, includes museum admission. First floor wheelchair-accessible.)*

OTHER SIGHTS. Carved by the Río Guadalquivir, Ronda's **gorge** extends 100m below the Puente Nuevo, across from Pl. de España. Arrested highwaymen were once held in a prison cell beneath the bridge's center, and during the Civil War, political prisoners were thrown from the top. Supposedly, even as they faced certain death, they were told that if they were to survive the fall they would be free. Take a stroll through **Alameda del Tajo** for a cliffside walk. The **view** from the center is unparalleled. The innovative **Puente Viejo** was rebuilt in 1616 over an Arab bridge with the Arco de Felipe V, built in 1742, presiding over one end. Farther down, the **Puente San Miguel** (or Puente Árabe) is an Andalucian hybrid of a Roman base and Arabic arches. To reach them, walk on C. Santo Domingo past the Casa del Rey Moro. The tiny but informative **Museo del Bandolero,** C. Armiñán, 65, is dedicated to presenting "pillage, theft, and rebellion in Spain since Roman time," recounting the stories of bandits and the men who tracked them. *(☎952 87 77 85; www.museobandolero.com. Open daily in summer 10:30am-8pm; in winter 10am-6pm. €3, students and children €2.50, groups over 10 €2.)*

NIGHTLIFE

Locals congregate in the pubs and discotecas along C. Jerez and the streets behind Pl. del Socorro, and both local families and young people can be found in *heladerías* (ice cream parlors) along Carrera Espinel. With cheap drinks and hearty tapas, it's no surprise that **Bar Antonio,** C. San José, 1, is popular. (Beer €1. Mixed drinks €3.50. Tapas €1-2. Giant *bocadillos* €2-2.50. Open M-Sa 7:30am-2am.) A 20-something crowd heads to **Huskies Sport Bar-Café,** C. Molino, 1, for beer and sports. Taking its name from the UConn mascot, the bar is lined with posters of American sports teams—very popular with foreigners. (www.huskiesbar.com. Beer €2. Mixed drinks €3.50. Open Tu-Su 4:30pm-3am, M 8:30pm-3am.) For a boisterous and ageless local scene, try **Bodeja-Bar 7,** C. Blas Infante, 7. Enjoy the moonlight at one of the outdoor tables on the patio. (☎952 87 60 97. Glass of sangria €1.70. Open noon-4pm and 8pm-late.)

DAYTRIP FROM RONDA

CUEVA DE LA PILETA

By car, take highway C-339 North (Ctra. Sevilla from the new city). The turnoff to Benaoján and the caves is about 22km out, in front of an abandoned restaurant. Taxis will go round-trip from Ronda for €50. A cheaper alternative is the train to Benaoján (20min.; 3 per day 7am-4:33pm, return 3 per day 1:39-8pm; round-trip €3.50). From the train station, it's a tough 1-2hr. climb to the caves, through the town of Benaoján, then along the highway. Ask locals for the way from Benaoján to the road, and don't stray off the highway or you might find yourself on an obscure mountainside path. ☎952 16 73 43. Caves open daily 10am-1pm and 4-6pm. Mandatory 1hr. tours begin on the hr., but call beforehand to hold your place. €8, groups of 10 or more €7 per person, student groups and under 12 €5.

The Cueva de la Pileta, 22km west of Ronda, is one of the few remaining privately owned caves in Spain, and as a national monument, one of the best preserved. The cave, which stretches over 2km underground, was discovered in 1905 by a local farmer looking for guano to use as fertilizer. Gas-lantern tours of this otherworldly expanse lead visitors along the 500m-long main gallery of the cave, past underground lakes, majestic mineral formations, and cathedral-like chambers. Inside, you'll find remarkably preserved Paleolithic and Neolithic paintings that represent a uniquely wide time frame, with some over 30,000 years old. Ceramics, animal bones, and human skeletons have also been discovered deep in the cave. The lamina formation nicknamed "the organ" is fascinating: years of falling water droplets carved its columns out of one giant sheet of rock, and each plays a different tone when struck. Visits are limited to 25 people, and reservations are accepted only in winter, so come early. Bring sturdy shoes and a sweatshirt—the caves are cool and slippery.

ANTEQUERA ☎952

The Romans bequeathed Antequera (pop. 42,000) its name (Antikaria), but other civilizations gave the city historical fame. On the outskirts of town, ancient *dólmenes* (stone tombs) showcase primitive art, and the abundance of beautiful churches in Antequera testify to its religious heritage. With no water in sight, the city has avoided the throngs of beachgoers who flock to nearby towns, making Antequera a relaxing detour from the bustling coast.

TRANSPORTATION

Trains: Av. de la Estación (☎952 84 32 26 or 902 24 02 02). To: **Algeciras** (3hr., 3 per day 8:41-9:14pm, €12.25); **Almería** (4hr., 4 per day 8:42am-7:43pm, €21.65); **Granada** (1hr., 7 per day 8:42am-10:16pm, €6.70-8); **Ronda** (1hr., 3 per day 8:39am-7:15pm, €5.80); **Sevilla** (1hr., 4 per day 9:43am-11:20pm, €13).

Buses: Po. García Olmo (☎952 84 19 57 or 84 13 65). To: **Córdoba** (1-1hr.; 4 per day 9:45am-6:15pm, less frequent in Aug.; €8.30); **Granada** (1-1hr., 9 per day 7:15am-1am, €6.85); **Málaga** (1hr., 9-12 per day 7am-10pm, €4.67); **Murcia** (5hr., 3 per day 9:45am-1am, €25.30); **Sevilla** (1-1½hr., 9 per day 4am-1am, €12.21).

Taxis: Taxi Radio Antequera (☎952 84 55 30) services Antequera and will go to **Sierra de Torcal.** Fare to town center approx. €4, but the walk is manageable.

ORIENTATION AND PRACTICAL INFORMATION

From the train station, it is a 10min. hike up Av. de la Estación to reach **Plaza de San Sebastián,** the town center. At the top, continue straight past the market, turn right onto C. de la Encarnación, and pass the Museo Municipal to reach the plaza. Alternatively, from the bus station it's a 10min. walk downhill. Exit the station at the top, cross the intersection, and turn right on Ctra. del Albergue; when you reach Pl. de la Constitución, cross the street at the gas station and walk left along **Alameda de Andalucía,** which becomes C. Infante Don Fernando and leads to the tourist office and Pl. de San Sebastián.

Tourist Office: Pl. de San Sebastián, 7 (☎952 70 25 05; www.turismoantequera.com). English spoken. Open mid-June to mid-Sept. M-Sa 11am-2pm and 5-8pm, Su 11am-2pm; mid-Sept. to mid-June M-Sa 10:30am-1:30pm and 4-7pm, Su 11am-2pm.

Bank: Banco Santander Central Hispano, C. Infante Don Fernando, 51 (☎952 24 24 24). Open M-F 8:30am-2pm, Sa 8:30am-1pm; Apr.-Sept. closed Sa.

Municipal Police: Av. de la Legión (☎952 70 81 04).

Pharmacy: Farmacia Villodres, on the corner of C. Calzada and C. Diego Ponce on Pl. de San Francisco. Open M-F 9:30am-1:30pm and 5-8:30pm, Sa 10:30am-1:30pm.

Hospital: Comarcal, C. Polígono Industrial, 67 (☎952 84 62 63, urgent 06 11 50).

Internet Access: No Problem (NP), C. Merecillas, 17B (☎952 73 90 78). €1.50 per hr. Open M-F 9:30am-2:30pm and 4:30-11pm, Sa same but from 10am, Su 4-11pm.

Post Office: C. Nájera (☎952 84 20 83). Open M-F 8:30am-2:30pm, Sa 9:30am-1pm. **Postal Code:** 29200.

ACCOMMODATIONS

For its size, Antequera offers a good range of accommodation options, many of which are located near the center of the city.

Hotel Residencia Colón, C. Infante Don Fernando, 31 (☎952 84 00 10; www.castelcolon.com). Wicker mirrors, huge windows and showers, friendly English- and French-speaking staff, and a central location make this hotel the best deal in town. Did we mention the A/C, TVs, elevator, and free internet access? Singles €15, with bath €25; doubles €30/40; triples with bath €55; quads with bath €70. AmEx/MC/V. ❶

Hotel Plaza San Sebastián, Pl. San Sebastián, 4 (☎952 84 42 39; www.hotelplazasansebastian.com). Founded in 1898, this hotel boasts understated, spacious rooms with A/C, TV, and bath, and a lounge with cushy leather chairs. English and French spoken. Internet access €1.20 per hr. Singles €25; doubles €40; triples €54. In Aug. €31/45/60 and during *Semana Santa* €36/55/65. AmEx/MC/V. ❷

FOOD AND NIGHTLIFE

Restaurant and nightlife options in Antequera are limited. The restaurants at local hotels are a good bet for an authentic *menú*, as are those lining **C. Calzada.** Get fresh produce, fish, and meat at the indoor **market** in **Pl. San Francisco.** (Open M-Sa 8am-3pm.) **Mercadona,** C. Calzada, 18, and C. Infante Don Fernando, 17, provides the basics. (Open M-Sa 9:15am-9:15pm. MC/V.)

La Guagua Café, C. Diego Ponce, 6 (☎952 70 21 06; www.barlaguaguaturincon.com). The best family-style eatery in Antequera, this diner is a gaming spot during the day and a bar at night. *Antequeranos* flock to these wooden booths for a full deli menu of baguettes (€2.30-2.80), crepes (€2.10-2.80), and sandwiches (€2.20), as well as teas (€1-2), and an amazing selection of juices and tropical smoothies (€2.70). Beer €2. Mixed drinks €4.20. Open M-Tu and Th 3pm-midnight, F-Sa 3pm-2am. Cash only. ❶

La Espuela, C. San Agustín, 1 (☎952 70 30 31). Excellent fusion of Andalucian and Italian cuisine; the menu accommodates most tastes and has a good vegetarian selection.

Try the *porra antequera*, a cold cream soup with ham and tomatoes (€5). Great appetizers €5-14. Entrees €12-16. *Menú* €14-16. Open daily 8am-midnight. MC/V. ❸

Ambigú Cafe, C. Calzada, 17. This intimate bar boasts funky red, black, and silver decor and an eclectic mix of Spanish pop, smooth rock, and R&B. Linger for darts or to watch the game on their large-screen TV. Beer €2.Mixed drinks €4.50. Open M-F 3:30pm-10:30pm, Sa-Su 3:30pm-1am. Cash only. ❶

SIGHTS

LOS DÓLMENES. Antequera's three ancient caves are some of the oldest in Europe. Once burial chambers with storerooms for the riches of the dead, they illustrate the fascinating process of human cultural evolution from the Stone Age on. Although they were looted long ago, the caves are still worth visiting. The 200-ton roof of the **Cueva de Menga** (2500 BC), considered the most important cave of the three, was hauled five miles to its present location. The **Cueva de Viera** (2000 BC), uncovered in 1905, begins with a narrow passageway leading deep into the darkness of the earth. Somewhat farther afield, **Cueva del Romeral** (1800 BC) consists of a long corridor leading to two round chambers; the second was used for funerary offerings. *(1km to the Cuevas de Menga and Viera; follow signs toward Granada from the town center (15-20min.) and look for a small sign past the gas station. To reach Cueva del Romeral from the other caves, continue on the highway to Granada another 3km. After the 4th rotary, across from Mercadona, a gravel road leads to a narrow path bordered by cypress trees; take this across the tracks. Open Tu-Sa 9am-6pm, Su 9:30am-2:30pm. Free.)*

OTHER SIGHTS. Antequera's Alcazaba, built in AD 1000, is testament to seven centuries of Moorish occupation. From the top, visitors get an unparalleled **view** of the city and surrounding countryside. Next door, the elegant **Real Colegiata de Santa María la Mayor** was the first church in Andalucía to incorporate Renaissance style. *(Pl. de Santa María ☎952 84 61 43. Open July to mid-Sept. Tu-F 10:30am-2pm, W-F also 8:30-10:30pm, Sa 10:30am-2pm, Su 11:30am-2pm; mid-Sept. to June Tu-F 10:30am-1:30pm and 4:30-6:30pm, Sa 10:30am-1:30pm, Su 11am-1:30pm. Free.)* Downhill, one block from the tourist office in the Palacio de Nájera, the **Museo Municipal** includes *Efebo*, a rare bronze statue of a Roman page and the pride of the city. *(☎952 70 40 21. Open Tu 10:30am-2pm, W-F 10:30am-2pm and 8:30-10:30pm, Sa 10:30am-2pm, Su 11:30am-2pm. Mandatory tours leave the entrance every 30min. €3.10.)*

DAYTRIP FROM ANTEQUERA

EL TORCAL DE ANTEQUERA

Casado buses (☎952 84 19 57) leave from Antequera (M-F 1pm, €2.40); the return bus leaves from the turn-off (M-F 4:15pm). Ask the driver to drop you at the turn-off for El Torcal, then it's a 3km walk. Free buses also run from Pl. del Coso Viejo, one block downhill from the tourist office (W-Su 11:30am, return at 1:30pm. ☎952 70 25 05. Reservations recommended.) The standard round-trip taxi price is €30 with a 1hr. wait; for an all-day visit, the fare is €36. Double check taxi fares at the tourist office so you don't get overcharged.

A garden of wind-sculpted boulders, the Sierra de Torcal glows like the surface of a barren and distant planet. The central peak, **El Torcal** (1410m), dominates the horizon, but the surrounding clumps of eroded rocks are even more extraordinary. Declared a natural park in 1978, the Sierra stretches for 11.7km, with trails circling the summit. The well-traveled green arrow path (1.5km) takes about 45min., while the red arrow path (4km) takes over 2hr. All but the green path require a guided tour; call the **Centro de Información** for details. (☎952 03 13 89. Open daily 10am-5pm.) Each path begins and ends at the *refugio* (lodge) at the mountain base. Bring binoculars for the best nature experience and try to catch a spectacular sunset from the striking **Mirador de las "Ventanillas."**

GRANADA ☎958

The splendors of the Alhambra, the magnificent fortress that crowns the city, have entranced princes, paupers, and poets for centuries. The golden hill-sides, white rooftops, and vistas of the Sierra Nevada still bless Granada (pop. 238,000) today, but the city first blossomed into one of Europe's wealthiest, most culturally advanced cities after being conquered by Muslim armies in AD 711. As Christian armies turned back the tide of Moorish conquest in the 13th century, the city became the last Muslim outpost in Iberia. Fernando and Isabel capitalized on the chaos, capturing Boabdil—Granada's last Moorish ruler—and the Alhambra on the momentous night of January 1, 1492. As Boabdil fled, his mother berated him for casting a longing look back at the Alhambra, saying, "You do well to weep as a woman for what you could not defend as a man."

Although the Christians torched all the mosques and the lower city, embers of Granada's Muslim past still linger. The Albaicín, a maze of Moorish houses and twisting alleys, is Spain's best-preserved Arab quarter and the only part of the Muslim city to survive the Reconquista intact. Since then, Granada has grown into a university town, reveling in throngs of backpackers and Spanish youth. Granada's huge student population gives rise to spirited graffiti, lively tapas bars, and a thriving hippie subculture. A few days will give you a taste of Moorish Spain and Granada's vibrant nightlife, wonderfully rich in tapas and *teterías*—smoky, aromatic Arabic tea rooms. But do not be surprised if, like Boabdil, you leave longing for more days in this Andalucian gem.

TRANSPORTATION

Flights: Airport (☎958 24 52 00), 17km west of the city. **Autocares J. Gonzales** (☎958 49 01 64) runs a bus from Gran Vía, in front of the cathedral, to the airport (25min., 5 per day 6:50am-9:30pm, €3). A taxi costs about €25.

Trains: RENFE, Av. Andaluces (☎902 24 02 02. www.renfe.es). Take bus #3-6, 9, or 11 from Gran Vía to the Constitución 3 stops and turn left onto Av. Andaluces. To: **Algeciras** (4-5hr., 3 per day 7:15am-5pm, €18.35); **Almería** (2hr., 4 per day 10:03am-9:06pm, €14.45); **Barcelona** (12hr., 9:45pm, €52.10-57.40); **Madrid** (5-6hr.; 6:42am, 6pm; €61.80); **Sevilla** (4-5hr., 4 per day 8:18am-8:24pm, €21.65).

Buses: All major intercity bus routes start at the bus station (☎958 18 54 80) on the outskirts of Granada on Ctra. de Madrid, near C. Arzobispo Pedro de Castro. Take bus #3 or 33 from Gran Vía de Colón or a **taxi** (€6-7). Services reduced on Sundays.

ALSA (☎902 42 22 42 or 958 15 75 57; www.alsa.es.) to: **Alicante** (6hr., 6 per day 2:31am-11:30pm, €26.69); **Barcelona** (14hr., 5 per day 2:31am-11:30pm, €65.96); and **Valencia** (9hr., 5 per day 2:31am-11:30pm, €40.23). **Algeciras** (3hr., 6 per day 9am-8:15pm, €20.20); **Almería** (2hr., 8 per day 6:45am-7:30pm, €11.50); **Antequera** (1hr., 4 per day 9am-7pm, €7.20); **Cádiz** (5hr., 4 per day 3am-6:30pm, €29.52); **Córdoba** (3hr., 8 per day 7:30am-7pm, €12.04); Madrid (5-6hr., 15 per day 7am-1:30am, €15.66); **Málaga** (2hr., 16 per day 7am-9pm, €9.38); **Marbella** (2hr., 8 per day 8am-8:15pm, €14.35); **Sevilla** (3hr., 7 per day 8am-8pm, €18.57).

Public Transportation: Local buses (☎900 71 09 00). Pick up the bus map at the tourist office. Important buses include: "Bus Alhambra" #30 from Gran Vía de Cólon or Pl. Nueva to the Alhambra; #31 from Gran Vía or Pl. Nueva to the Albaicín; #10 from the bus station to the youth hostel, C. de Ronda, C. Recogidas, and C. Acera de Darro; #3 from the bus station to Av. de la Constitución, Gran Vía, and Pl. Isabel la Católica. €1.10, *bonobus* (9 tickets) €5.45.

Taxis: Teletaxi (☎958 28 06 54 or 958 13 23 23), with service throughout Granada and its environs. Taxi stands in Pl. Nueva and Pl. de la Trinidad 24hr.

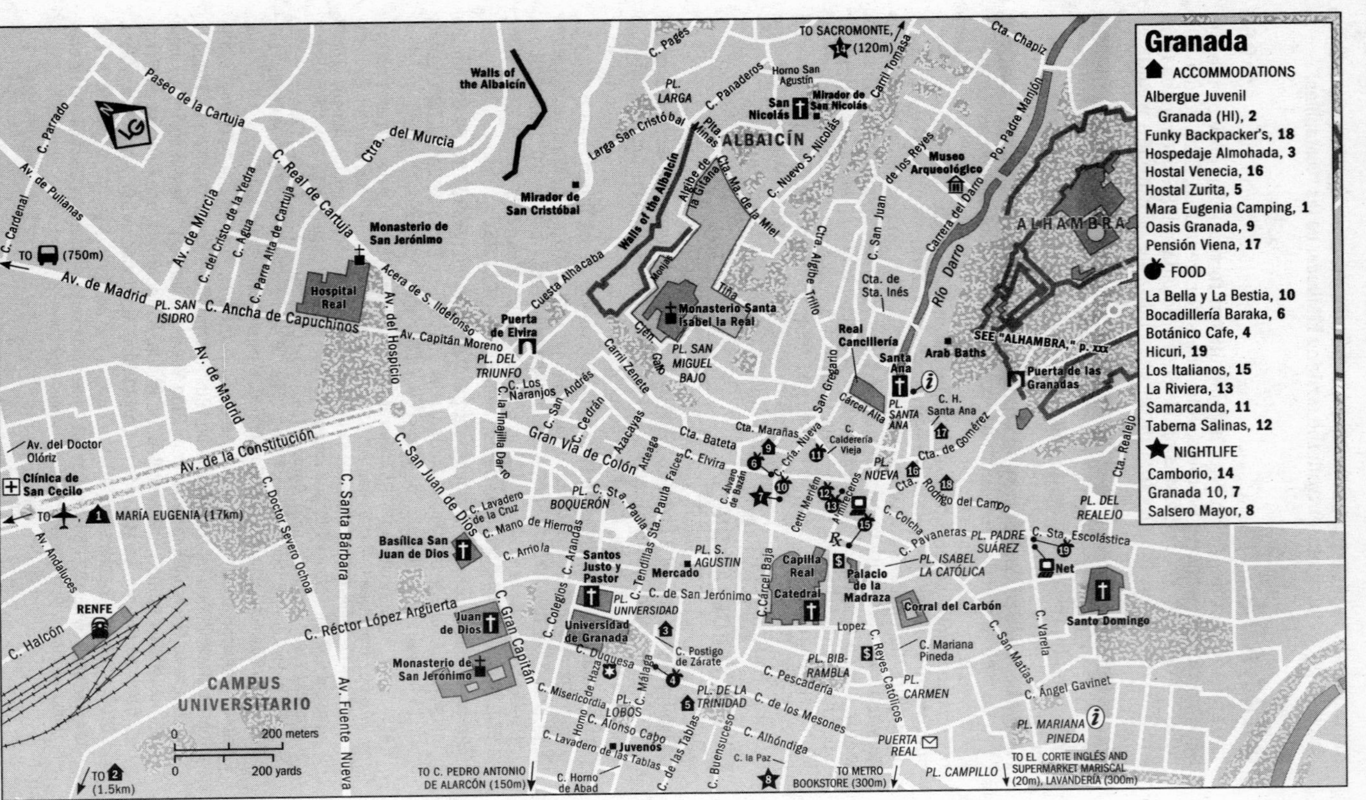
Granada
ACCOMMODATIONS
Albergue Juvenil
Granada (HI), 2
Funky Backpacker's, 18
Hospedaje Almohada, 3
Hostal Venecia, 16
Hostal Zurita, 5
Mara Eugenia Camping, 1
Oasis Granada, 9
Pensión Viena, 17
FOOD
La Bella y La Bestia, 10
Bocadillería Baraka, 6
Botánico Cafe, 4
Hicuri, 19
Los Italianos, 15
La Riviera, 13
Samarcanda, 11
Taberna Salinas, 12
NIGHTLIFE
Camborio, 14
Granada 10, 7
Salsero Mayor, 8
ALBAICÍN
ALHAMBRA
SEE "ALHAMBRA," p. xxx
CAMPUS UNIVERSITARIO
Gran Vía de Colón
Av. de la Constitución
Río Darro
TO SACROMONTE, (120m)
TO (750m)
TO MARÍA EUGENIA (17km)
TO (1.5km)
TO C. PEDRO ANTONIO DE ALARCÓN (150m)
TO METRO BOOKSTORE (300m)
TO EL CORTE INGLÉS AND SUPERMARKET MARISCAL (20m), LAVANDERÍA (300m)
200 meters
200 yards

Car Rental: Hertz, EuropCar, and **Avis** in the airport. Hertz has an office in the lobby of Hotel Central Granada, Av. Fuentenueva (☎902 40 24 05). Reservation line open 8am-11pm. Office open 9am-1:30pm and 3:30-8:30pm.)

ORIENTATION AND PRACTICAL INFORMATION

The center of Granada is small **Plaza Isabel la Católica,** at the intersection of the city's two main arteries, **Calle de los Reyes Católicos** and **Gran Vía de Colón.** Just off Gran Vía, you'll find the cathedral; farther down Gran Vía by Pl. de la Trinidad is the university area. Uphill from Pl. Isabel la Católica on C. Reyes Católicos sits **Plaza Nueva,** and the **Alhambra** rises on the hill above. From Pl. Nueva, **Calle Elvira,** lined with bars and eateries, runs parallel to Gran Vía. Downhill, the pedestrian streets off C. de los Reyes Católicos comprise the shopping district.

Tourist Offices: Junta de Andalucía, C. Santa Ana, 2 (☎958 57 52 02). Open M-F 9am-7:30pm, Sa 9:30am-3pm, Su 10am-2pm. Posts bus and train schedules and provides a list of accommodations. **Oficina Provincial,** Pl. Mariana Pineda, 10 (☎958 24 71 28). Walk up to the left past plaza Isabel and make a right on Pineda. Walk until the square. English spoken. Open M-F 9am-8pm, Sa 10am-7pm, Su 10am-3pm.

Currency Exchange: Banco Santander Central Hispano, Gran Vía, 3 (☎902 24 24 24). Open Apr.-Sept. M-F 8:30am-2pm.

Luggage Storage: 24hr. storage at the train and bus stations (€3). Frequently sold out.

English-Language Bookstore: Metro, C. Gracia, 31, off Veronica de la Magdalena, off C. Recogidas, which begins where Reyes Católicos hits Puerta Real. (☎958 26 15 65). Vast foreign language section. Open M-F 10am-2pm and 5-8:30pm, Sa 11am-2pm.

Gay and Lesbian Resources: Información Homosexual Hotline (☎958 20 06 02).

Laundromat: C. de la Paz, 19., off Veronica de la Magdelena. Wash €8, dry €2 per 10min.; detergent included. Open M-F 10am-2pm and 5-8pm.

Police: C. Duquesa, 21 (☎091). English spoken.

Pharmacy: Farmacia Gran Vía, Gran Vía, 6 (☎958 22 29 90). Open M-F 9:30am-1:30pm and 5-8:30pm, Sa 9:30am-1:30pm and 5:30-9pm.

Medical Services: Hospital Universitario de San Cecilio, C. Dr. Olóriz, 16, near the Plaza de Toros (☎958 02 30 00).

Internet Access: Locutorio Cyber Alhambra, C. Joaquin Costa, 4 (☎958 22 43 96). €1.20 per hour; €5 *bono* for 6hr., €10 *bono* for 13hr. Open daily 9:30am-10:30pm. Second alley to left on Reyes Católicos walking away from Plaza Isabel.

Post Office: Pta. Real (☎958 22 48 35). Lista de Correos and fax service. Open M-F 8:30am-8:30pm, Sa 9:30am-2pm. **Postal Code:** 18009.

ACCOMMODATIONS

NEAR PLAZA NUEVA

Hostels line Cuesta de Gomérez, the street off Pl. Nueva leading up to the Alhambra. Crashing in this area is wise for those planning to spend serious time in the Alhambra complex, but these spots tend to fill up very quickly.

Oasis Granada, Placeta Correo Viejo, 3 (☎958 21 58 48; from Spain free at ☎9001 OASIS; www.hostelsoasis.com). Free internet, common kitchen, ping-pong table on outdoor patio, rooftop lounge. Frequented by the under-30 crowd. Weekly parties and daily activities like tapas tours and pub crawls. Breakfast included. Dinner *menús,* all-you-can-eat €4. If hostel is "full," try showing up early in the morning for a spot as they usually hold about 10 beds for walk-ins. Dorms €18; doubles €40. MC/V. ❷

Funky Backpacker's, Cuesta de Rodrigo del Campo, 13 (☎958 22 14 62; funky@alternativeacc.com). From Pl. Nueva, go uphill on Cuchilleros 20m to find Cuesta de Rodrigo on the right. Sizable dorms surround a central atrium over the funky lobby. Take in the view of the Alhambra, mountains, and rooftops from the bar atop the hostel. The friendly staff hangs out with travelers. Outings to nearby thermal baths (€10), tapas bars and *flamenco* shows (€21). A/C, breakfast, and lockers included. Laundry (wash, dry and fold) €7. Free internet. Dinner €4.50-6. Dorms €16.50-17; doubles €40. MC/V. ❶

Hostal Venecia, Cuesta de Gomérez, 2, 3rd fl. (☎958 22 39 87). Eccentrically decorated with bright colors and Granada paraphernalia, this small, homey hostel has the most character per square meter in town. Homemade herbal tea and conversation available any time of day. Reserve early, especially in summer, since the secret is out. Dorms €19; doubles €34; triples €45. MC/V. ❶

Pensión Viena, C. Hospital Santa Ana, 2 (☎958 22 18 59; www.hostalviena.com). The greatest selling points of this hostel, with simple white walls and blinds, are A/C and proximity to central Granada. Singles €25, with bath €30-38; doubles €37/48; triples €50/65; quads €60/75; quint €65/95. MC/V. ❷

NEAR THE CATHEDRAL AND UNIVERSITY

Hostels surround Pl. de la Trinidad, and *pensiones* around C. de los Mesones cater to students during the year but free up in summer, offering excellent deals to the diligent stair-climber. The ones listed below are open year-round.

Hospedaje Almohada, C. Postigo de Zárate, 4 (☎958 20 74 46; www.laalmohada.com). Follow C. Trinidad out of Pl. Trinidad to the T-intersection, then make a right and walk down the short street ahead. Look for double red doors with hand-shaped knockers. Lounge in the TV area, use the kitchen to cook your own meal, and peruse the communal music collection and travel guides. Laundry (wash and hang-dry) €5 for 8kg. 4-bed dorms €15; singles €19; doubles €35; triples €50. Cash only. ❶

Hostal Zurita, Pl. de la Trinidad, 7 (☎958 27 50 20; www.pensionzurita.com). Soundproof balcony doors are a blessing in this busy student-dominated neighborhood and above one of Granada's most pleasant plazas. Doubles are spacious, singles are small but adequate; all have TV and A/C. Notice some of the pieces of art are actually completed puzzles. Singles €21; doubles €34, with bath €42; triples €51/63. MC/V. ❷

ELSEWHERE

Hostels are sprinkled along Gran Vía de Colón, though many are expensive.

Albergue Juvenil Granada (HI), C. Ramón y Cajal, 2 (☎958 00 29 00). From the bus station, take bus #10; from the train station, #11. Ask the driver to stop at "El Estadio de la Juventud," across the field on the left. From the end of Gran Vía away from Pl. Isabela, continue down Ave. Constitución, make a left on Dr. Severo Ochoa, then eventually a right on Ronda, and look for a narrow street on the left just before a run-down sports complex. English-speaking staff available 24hr., but a trek from all of the sights. Dorm-style rooms and common baths. Dorms €19.5 for guests under 26, €23.5 over 26. HI discount €3.50 per night. ❶

CAMPING

Buses serve all campgrounds within 5km of Granada, albeit irregularly. Check schedules at the bus station or tourist office, and ask the driver to alert you at your stop. While camping is most convenient for those with their own transportation, the tourist office can provide a list of further camping options.

María Eugenia, Av. Andalucía (☎958 20 06 06; fax 20 94 10), at km 436 on the road to Málaga. Take the Santa Fé or Chauchina bus from the train station (every 30min.). Open year-round. Popular with families. €4.85 per person, €3.50 per child. ❶

FOOD

Though Granada offers a variety of traditional Spanish fare and ethnic restaurants, the best way to eat on a budget is to take advantage of the free tapas by ordering drinks. North African cuisine and vegetarian options can be found around the **Albaicín,** while more typical menus await in Pl. Nueva and Pl. de la Trinidad. The adventurous eat well in Granada—*tortilla sacromonte* (omelette with calf's brains and bull testicles) and *sesos a la romana* (batter-fried calf's brains) are traditional dishes. Picnickers can gather fresh fruit, vegetables, and meat at the large indoor **market** on Pl. San Agustín. (Open M-Sa 9am-3pm.)

NEAR PLAZA NUEVA

Pl. Nueva abounds with outdoor cafes. Those seeking more authentic fare would do better to comb the small side streets that lead out of the plaza.

GRANADA FOR POCKET CHANGE. Let's face it, you came to Granada for the Alhambra and complimentary tapas, so why not enjoy both for less than a train ride to Sevilla? Haggle vendors along **C. Cría Nueva** for souvenirs, clothing, and jewelry or get your name painted in Arabic. Refuel at **Oasis Granada** by chowing down at a weekly all-you-can-eat dinner for €4 with an €18 bed to match. If you're still feeling hungry, stock up on some late-night tapas at **La Riviera** and other bars around **C. Elvira** for the price of a drink, or grab a €1 treat at **Bocadillería Baraka.** Walk off the calories with a 15min. walk up to the *mirador* near Iglesia de San Nicolás for an unparalleled view of the Alhambra amidst the echoes of *flamenco.* Back in the city, dance away the night at **Salsero Mayor,** where the only cover is the timbered roof aglow with colored lights and undulating shadows.

La Riviera, C. Cetti Meriem, 7 (☎958 22 79 69), off C. Elvira. The best place to score delicious, free tapas. You can't go wrong with the extensive list of traditional fare. Beer or *tinto de verano* €1.80. Open daily 12:30-4pm and 8pm-midnight. ❶

Hicuri, C. Santa Escolástica, 12 (☎653 78 34 22), on corner of Pl. de los Girones. Walk uphill past Pl. Isabela about 200m. Your search for healthy, affordable cuisine stops here. This popular eatery's huge selection of vegetarian and vegan dishes will satisfy any tofu craving. Entrees €5.80-6.50. *Menú* €12. Open M-F 8:30am-4:30pm, Sa-Su 8:30am-4:30pm and 8:30-11:30pm. Cash only. ❷

La Bella y La Bestia, Carcel Bajo, 14. (☎958 32 55 69). Huge complimentary tapas proportionate to the number in your party, complete with fries, pasta salad, and *bocadillos.* Mixed drinks €1.40-2. Open M-Th and Su noon-2am, F-Su 11am-3am. ❶

ALBAICÍN

Wander the winding streets of the Albaicín and you'll discover many budget bars and restaurants above Pl. Nueva. This is a veritable paradise for fans of Middle Eastern cuisine; cheap falafel sandwiches abound. C. Calderería Nueva, off C. Elvira leading from the plaza, is crammed with teahouses and cafes.

Bocadillería Baraka, C. Elvira, 20 (☎958 22 97 60). Stands out among many Middle Eastern eateries for being the cheapest and the tastiest. Proud that their meat is home prepared and never frozen, Baraka serves delicious traditional pitas (€2.50-4) and addictive homemade lemonade infused with *hierba buena* (€1). Hedi, the owner and formerly in the travel business, also organizes week long, all-inclusive excursions through Morocco (☎649 11 41 71). Open daily 1pm-2am. Cash only. ❶

Taberna Salinas, C. Elvira, 13 (☎958 22 14 11). For a light but authentic dinner in this modern take on a rustic tavern, order a *tabla Salinas surtida* (plate of cheeses and *pâté;* €13.90) to complement a glass of wine. The menu also offers a wide selection of grilled meats and seafood (€11-24). Or enjoy tapas that vary with the day's *menú*. Wine €2.80. Beer €1.80. Open M-Th and F-Sa 12:30pm-2am, Su 12:30pm-1am. MC/V. ❸

Samarcanda, C. Calderería Vieja, 3 (☎958 21 00 04), walking away from Pl. Nueva down C. Elvira, up to the right where the road forks around a kiosk. Outdoor seating in a small, quiet plaza; interior is a calm Middle Eastern setting. For €43, you can order a huge *Mesa Libanesa* platter to share, complete with a bottle of Lebanese wine. English-language menu available. Entrees €8-12.50. Open M-Tu and Th-Su 1-4:30pm and 7:30pm-11:30pm. MC/V. ❸

GRAN VÍA AND ELSEWHERE

Filled with little bars and *pastelerías*, Gran Vía is great for breakfasts on a budget. Busy, student-filled cafes surround Pl. de la Trinidad and nearby Pl. Bib-Rambla. Restaurants right next to the cathedral tend to be overpriced; generally, the restaurants becomes less touristy farther down Gran Vía.

Botánico Café, C. Málaga, 3 (☎958 27 15 98), on the corner of Calle Trinidad. Serving self-described "fusion" cuisine, this trendy restaurant throws everything from Italian, Chinese, Spanish, and Mexican into the mix. Converts into a pub Sa-Su nights, but the kitchen stays open until midnight. Main dishes €8-16.95. *Menú* changes daily (served 1:30pm-4pm; €11.50); drink not included. Also serves tapas. Beer €1.75. Open Su-Th 1pm-1am, F-Sa 1pm-2am. MC/V. ❸

Los Italianos, Gran Vía, 4 (☎958 22 40 34). Don't just gape at the ridiculously cheap ice-cream prices; get in line and try another flavor. No seating. *Barquillos* (cones) €1-2; *tarrinas* (cups) from €1. Mar.-Oct. open daily 9am-2am. Cash only. ❶

SIGHTS

A *bono turístico* pass, which is good for one week and provides direct access to the Alhambra and several other sights throughout Granada, can be useful if you're going to be in the city for several days and are looking to tour the included monuments. The pass also includes nine free trips on local bus lines to destinations within the city. For reservations, call the **Caja Granada** information and booking office (☎902 10 00 95); tickets are available for direct sale at the Parque de las Ciencias. (€30. Cash only. Caja Granada also makes reservations in advance for €32.50. MC/V.)

THE ALHAMBRA

Take Cuesta de Gomérez off Pl. Nueva and be prepared to pant (20min.; no unauthorized cars 9am-9pm), or take the quick Alhambra minibus from Pl. Nueva (every 5min., €1.10). ☎902 44 12 21; www.alhambra-patronato.es; reservations for entrance ☎902 22 44 60; www.alhambra-tickets.es. Open daily Apr.-Sept. 8:30am-8pm; Oct.-Mar. 8:30am-6pm. Also open June-Sept. Tu-Sa 10-11:30pm; Oct.-May F-Sa 8-9:30pm. Audio tours are worth the expense and are available in English, French, German, Italian, and Spanish (€5). €12, under 12 and the handicapped free. €13 if purchased online. EU students with ID and EU seniors €9. Gardens only, €6. Limited to 7700 visitors per day, so get there early or reserve in advance. You must enter the Palace of the Nasrids (Alcázar) during the half-hour time slot specified on your ticket, but you can stay as long as desired. It is possible to reserve tickets in advance at banks for a €1 charge; recommended July-Aug. and Semana Santa. BBVA branches will also book tickets. Hotels can book tickets, but often take a larger commission.

From the streets of Granada, the Alhambra, meaning "the red one" in Arabic, appears blocky and purely practical—a military base planted in the foothills of the Sierra Nevada. This deceptive appearance conceals a universe of aesthetic and symbolic grandeur born of profound spirituality, artistic skill, and precision. The age-old saying holds true: *"Si mueres sin ver la Alhambra, no has vivido"* ("If you die without seeing the Alhambra, you have not lived").

ALCAZABA. The Christians drove the first Nasrid King Alhamar from the Albaicín to this more strategic hill, where he built the series of rust-colored brick towers that form the Alcazaba, or fortress. A dark, spiraling staircase leads to the **Torre de la Vela** (watchtower), where visitors can see all of Granada and the surrounding mountains. The tower's bells were rung to warn of impending danger and to coordinate the Moorish irrigation system. During the annual New Year commemoration of the Christian conquest of Granada, legend holds that local girls who scramble up the tower and ring the bell by hand before January 1st will receive a wedding proposal within a year. Compared to the rest of the Alhambra, the Alcazaba is the most utilitarian and bare-boned structure. Exit through the **Puerta del Vino,** the original entrance to the *medina* (city), where inhabitants of the Alhambra once bought tax-free wine (alas, no more).

ALCÁZAR. Follow signs to the Palacio Nazaríes to see the Alcázar, a royal palace finished by Moorish ruler Mohammed V (1354-1391) after his father, Yusuf I (1333-1354), was murdered by a political enemy in the palace's isolated basement. Throughout the palace, astonishingly intricate carvings and engravings mark every room. In the **Mexuar,** the first pillared council chamber after the entrance, the glazed tile arrangements reiterate the Nasrid dynasty mantra, "There is no victor but Allah," variations of which you'll see repeated throughout the entire palace. Attached to the Mexuar is a small prayer hall with an intricately decorated *mihrab*, marking the direction of prayer to Mecca. The Mexuar adjoins the **Patio del Cuarto Dorado** (Patio of the Gilded Room). The magnificently carved walls are topped by the shielded windows of the harem, so that the women could see out but no one could see in. The *hammams* (Arab baths) are behind an iron-grilled door but have been permanently closed for preservation. Off the far side of the patio, leafy horseshoe archways lead to the Cuarto Dorado, decorated by Mohammed V. Its carved wooden ceiling, inlaid with ivory and mother-of-pearl, displays colorful, geometric ceramic figures.

Next is the **Patio de los Arrayanes** (Courtyard of Myrtles), an expanse of water filled with goldfish. From there, glimpse the 14th-century **Fachada de Serallo,** the palace's elaborate facade. Flanking the courtyard is the **Sala de la Barca** (Hall of the Ship) named not for its inverted boat-hull ceiling, but for the Arabic word *"baraka,"* or blessing. The walls are covered with the 99 names of Allah.

Granada was formally surrendered to the Reyes Católicos in the elaborate **Sala de los Embajadores** (Hall of Ambassadors), adjoining the Sala de la Barca to the north. It was also here that Fernando and Columbus discussed his new route to India. The *mozárabe* dome, carved of more than 8000 pieces of wood and inlaid with cedar, forms its own system of constellations, and a section of the original floor remains in the center. From the **Patio de los Arrayanes,** the Sala de los Mozárabes leads to the **Patio de los Leones** (Courtyard of the Lions), the grandest display of Nasrid art in the palace. An arcade of marble columns borders the courtyard, which centers on a fountain supported by 12 marble lions (under restoration). Some believe that this fountain originally belonged to one of the sultan's Jewish advisors, but was later redecorated with Muslim motifs.

The adjoining **Sala de los Abencerrajes** tells one of the bloodiest chapters in the palace's history. Here, Boabdil, the last Arab king to rule from the Alhambra, slit the throats of 16 sons of the Abencerrajes family after one of them

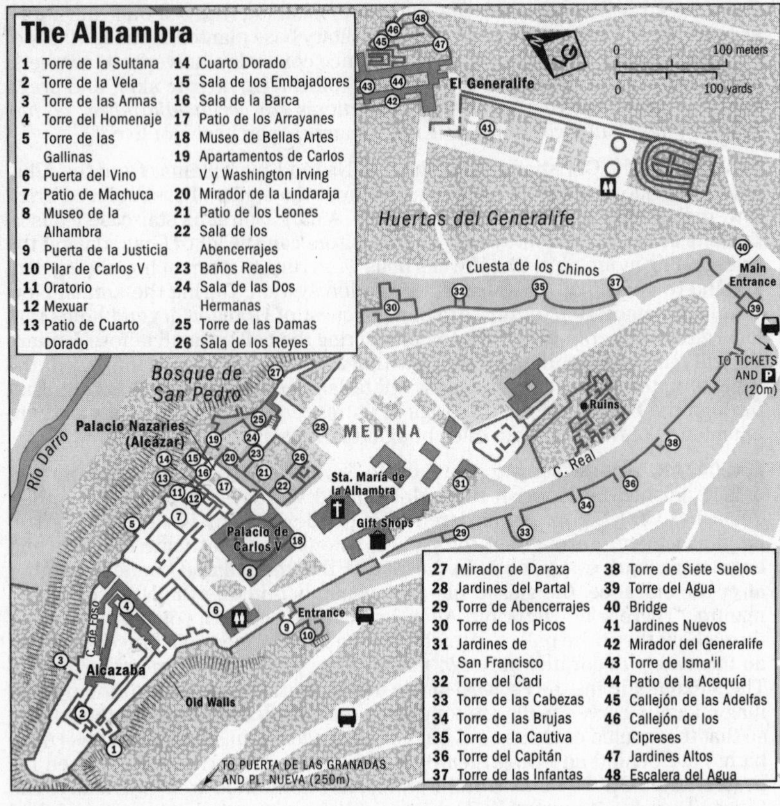

allegedly had amorous encounters with his concubine, Zorahayda. The rust-colored stains in the basin are said to mark the indelible traces of the butchery. Holy Roman Emperor Charles V was unfazed, however, dining here throughout the construction of his palace. Light filters in through the domed ceiling, which features an eight-pointed star representing terrestrial and celestial harmony.

Through archways at the far end of the Patio de los Leones lies the **Sala de los Reyes** (Hall of Kings). The only human figures in the entire palace—the 21 sultans who ruled from the Alhambra, important assemblies, and hunting parties—are depicted on detailed sheepskin paintings fixed to the walls with bamboo pins, but are currently covered for restoration. On the final side of the courtyard, the resplendent **Sala de las Dos Hermanas** (Chamber of the Two Sisters) is named for the matching slabs of marble that comprise most of the floor. It has a *muqarnas* (honeycombed) dome composed of thousands of tiny cells. This stalactite-like structure, typical of Islamic architecture, represents an ascension and the doors of heaven opening. From here, the secluded **Mirador de Daraxa** overlooks the **Jardines de Daraxa** (Gardens of the Sultana).

Passing the room where American author **Washington Irving** resided in 1829 and wrote the famous *Tales of the Alhambra* (1832), a courtyard leads to the Baños Reales, a less ornate 14th-century addition, toward the royal gardens and the exit. Do not leave the Nasrid Palace unless you are satisfied with your visit, because like Boabdil, you will not be allowed to return.

TOWERS AND GARDENS. Just outside the eastern wall of the Alcázar, lily-studded pools stand beside rose-laden terraces in the **Jardines del Partal**. The **Torre de las Damas** (Ladies' Tower) soars above it all. A series of six additional towers fills out the area between the Alcazaba and El Generalife.

EL GENERALIFE. Over a bridge, across the Callejón de los Cipreses and the shady Callejón de las Adelfas are the lively blossoms, towering cypresses, and streaming waterways of **El Generalife,** the sultan's vacation retreat. In 1313 Arab engineers changed the Darro's flow by 18km and employed dams and channels to prepare the soil for Aben Walid Ismail's design of El Generalife. Over the centuries, the estate passed through private hands until it was finally nationalized in 1931. The two buildings of El Generalife, the Palacio and the Sala Regia, connect across the **Patio de la Acequia** (Courtyard of the Irrigation Channel), embellished with a narrow pool fed by fountains that form an aquatic archway. Honeysuckle vines scale the back wall, and shady benches invite long rests. A dead cypress tree stands at the place where the sultana Zorahayda supposedly had amorous encounters with a nobleman from the Abencerrajes tribe.

PALACIO DE CARLOS V. Although Emperor Charles V's *palazzo* is incongruous with the surrounding Alhambra, scholars concede that it is one of the most beautiful Renaissance buildings in Spain. Designed by Michelangelo's disciple Pedro Machuca, the palace has a circular inner courtyard with two stories of Doric colonnades. Inside, the Museo de la Alhambra contains the only remaining original furnishings from the Alhambra, including old doors and the well-preserved *azulejo* tiles. *(☎958 22 75 27. Open Tu-Sa 9am-2:30pm. Free with admission to the Alhambra; free guided visits Tu-Sa 11am-1pm. €1.50. E.U. citizens free.)* Upstairs, the **Museo de Bellas Artes** has recently been renovated to better display its religious sculptures and paintings of the Granada School dating from the 16th century. *(☎958 22 48 43. Open Mar-Oct. Tu 2:30-8pm, W-Sa 9am-8pm, Su 9am-2:30pm.;Nov.-Feb. Tu 2:30-6pm, W-Sa 9am-6pm, Su 9am-2:30pm; €1.50. E.U. citizens free.)*

ALBAICÍN

Although generally safe, the Albaicín is disorienting, so use caution at night. Bus #32 runs from beside the cathedral to C. Pagés at the top of the Albaicín. Bus #31 goes from Gran Vía and Pl. Nueva through the neighborhood.

A labyrinth of steep, narrow alleys, the Albaicín was the only Moorish neighborhood to escape the torches of the Reconquista. After the fall of the Alhambra, a small Muslim population remained here until they were expelled in the 17th century. Today, the Albaicín attests to the persistence of Islamic influence in Andalucía—the mosque near Pl. San Nicolás and resurgence of North African cuisine, outdoor bazaars blasting Arabic music, and teahouses will leave you wondering if you're in Morocco. The best way to explore this maze is to proceed along **Carrera del Darro** off Pl. Santa Ana, climb the **Cuesta del Chapiz** on the left, then wander through the Moorish ramparts, cisterns, and gates. On Pl. Santa Ana, the 16th-century **Real Cancillería,** with its beautiful arcaded patio and stalactite ceiling, was the Christians' town hall. Farther uphill are the 11th-century Arab baths. *(Carrera del Darro, 31. ☎958 22 97 38. Call ☎958 22 56 03 to confirm hours. Free.)* The **Museo Arqueológico** showcases funerary urns, classical sculpture, Carthaginian vases, Muslim lamps, and ceramics. *(Carrera del Darro, 43. ☎958 22 56 03. Open Tu 2:30-8:30pm, W-Sa 9:30am-8:30pm, Su 9:30am-2:30pm. €1.50, EU citizens free.)* The **mirador** adjacent to **Iglesia de San Nicolás** affords the city's best view of the Alhambra. From C. de Elvira, go up C. Calderería Nueva to C.

OF LORCA AND LEMONS

World-famous poet and dramatist, Granada's Federico García Lorca is finally receiving his due. His poetry, full of olive groves, lemons, gypsies, Moors, and bullfighters, brought images of passionate Andalucía to the world. But upon the outbreak of civil war in 1936, Lorca was arrested by Franco's Nationalist forces and killed near the hilltop town of Alfácar, just northeast of Granada. As Lorca was both a known homosexual and a socialist-leaning public figure, the motivations for his murder—social, political, or personal—remain controversial to this day.

Since the fall of Franco, Lorca's childhood homes in the neighboring towns of Fuente Vaqueros and Valderrubio have both become museums honoring his legacy. And in an olive orchard in Alfácar, the alleged site of his execution, a quiet park now shelters a memorial wall engraved with his poetry. Meanwhile, Granada's literary pilgrims visit the blooming Huerta de San Vicente in what is now the Parque García Lorca. The poet wrote some of his best work here in this summer house, shaded by oranges trees and poplars.

(To reach the Parque García Lorca, walk down C. Recogidas from Puerta Real. Take a right when you hit Camino de Ronda, then a left on C. Virgen Blanca. Tours organized through the Granada tourist office in Pl. Mariana Pineda run on F and Sa to each of these sites. For more information, call ☎902 11 46 66.)

San Gregorio and continue uphill past Pl. Algibe de Trillo, where it becomes Cta. Algibe de Trillo. At Pl. Camino, make a left onto Cta. Tomasa and another left onto Atarazana Cta. Cabras. The *mirador* is on the right.

SACROMONTE

If you're not up for the 20min. climb from Pl. Nueva, take bus #34 (€1.10). Ask at the tourist office for schedules and check with the driver that Sacromonte is the destination. Avoid isolated streets and corners in the neighborhood, as they are somewhat unsafe at night.

Above the Albaicín stands Sacromonte, home to a gypsy community ever since they took shelter here during the Inquisition. Cave dwellings plaster the hillside, still inhabited but updated with TVs and satellite dishes. The **Museo Cuevas del Sacromonte,** also called the Centro de Interpretación del Sacromonte, at the top of the hill, has an informative display of model caves, from a house and kitchen to a stable and caves for iron-working, basket-weaving, and pottery-making. The museum also enjoys an impressive view over the Sacromonte back towards the Alhambra and much of Granada. *(☎958 21 51 20; www.sacromontegranada.com. Open Apr.-Oct. Tu-F 10am-2pm and 5-9pm; Nov.-Mar. Tu-F 10am-2pm and 4-7pm. Museum €5.)* In summer, some caves host impromptu flamenco. Ask at the tourist office or the museum.

THE CATHEDRAL QUARTER

CAPILLA REAL. Downhill from the Alhambra, off Gran Vía de Colón on C. Oficios, stands Fernando and Isabel's private chapel. The Catholic monarchs funneled almost a quarter of their royal income into building a proper burial place. Intricate Gothic masonry and **La Reja,** the gilded grille of Maestro Bartolomé, grace the couple's resting place. Behind La Reja lie the lifelike marble figures of the storied royals themselves. Fernando and Isabel are on the right when facing the altar; beside them sleep their daughter, Juana la Loca, and her husband, Felipe el Hermoso. In the adjacent **Sacristía,** Isabel's private art collection favors Flemish and German artists of the 15th century. The glittering royal jewels—including the queen's golden crown and scepter and the king's sword—shine in the middle. *(☎958 22 92 39. Capilla Real and Sacristía both open Apr.-Sept M-Sa 10:30am-12:45pm and 4-7pm, Su 11am-12:45pm and 4-7pm; Oct.-May M-Sa 10:30am-12:45pm and 3:30-6:15pm, Su 11am-12:45pm and 3:30-6:15pm. Both sights €3.50.)*

CATEDRAL. Behind the Capilla Real and the Sacristía is Granada's cathedral. Construction began after the Reconquista, upon the smoldering embers of Granada's largest mosque, and was not completed until 1704. The first Renaissance cathedral in Spain, its massive Corinthian pillars support a 45m nave. While the eclectic side chapels and fanning pipes of its gilded organ are beautiful, this cathedral may not impress those who have seen a number of Spanish cathedrals. *(☎958 22 29 59. Open Apr.-Sept. M-Sa 10:45am-1:30pm and 4-8pm, Su 4-8pm; Oct.-Mar. M-Sa 10:30am-1:30pm and 4-7pm, Su 11am-1:30pm and 4-7pm. €3.50.)*

NIGHTLIFE

Granada's "free tapas with a drink" tradition lures crowds to its many pubs and bars. Some great tapas bars are found on the side streets off Pl. Nueva. The most boisterous crowds hang out on C. Pedro Antonio de Alarcón, between Pl. Albert Einstein and Ancha de Gracia, while hip new bars and clubs line C. de Elvira from C. Cárcel to C. Cedrán. Gay bars can be found by Carrera del Darro. Check the *Pocketguía* (€1), sold at newsstands and available for free at the Pineda Tourist Office; it lists clubs, pubs, and cafes. Clubs in Granada usually aren't lively until around 3am.

Camborio, Camino del Sacromonte, 48 (☎958 22 12 15), a quick taxi ride or 20min. walk uphill from Pl. Nueva; bus #34 stops at midnight. DJ-spun pop music echoes through dance floors to the rooftop patio above. Striking view of the Alhambra. Beer €4. Mixed drinks €5. Cover €6, includes 1 drink. Open Tu-Sa midnight-7am. Cash only.

Salsero Mayor, C. la Paz, 20 (☎958 52 27 41). An ageless group of locals and tourists alike flocks here for crowded nights of salsa, bachata, and merengue. Beer €2-3. Mixed drinks €5. Open M-Th and Su 10pm-3am, F-Sa 1pm-4am. Cash only.

Granada 10, C. Cárcel Baja 3 (☎958 22 40 01). Movie theater by evening (shows Sept.-June at 8, 10pm), raging dance club by night. Flashy and opulent. No sneakers or sportswear. Open M-Th and Su 12:30-4am, F-Sa 12:30-6am. Cover €10. MC/V.

ENTERTAINMENT AND FESTIVALS

The daily paper, *Ideal*, lists entertainment venues in the back under *"Cine y Espectáculos;"* the Friday supplement highlights bars and special events.

FLAMENCO AND JAZZ. The most "authentic" flamenco performances change monthly; shows are advertised on posters around town. The tourist office also provides a list of nightly *tablaos* (flamenco shows), often more expensive and heavily touristed. A smoky, intimate setting awaits at **Eshavira,** C. Postigo de la Cuna, in a secluded alley off C. Azacayas, between C. de Elvira and Gran Vía. This joint is the place to go for flamenco, jazz, or a fusion of the two. Photos of Nat King Cole and other jazz greats plaster the walls. Those with musical talent can pick up a guitar or sit right down at the piano to stage their own impromptu concert. *(☎958 29 41 25. Min. consumption €8. Su night flamenco. M-Th and Su 9 or 9:30pm-3:30am, F-Sa 9 or 9:30 pm-4am; call for schedule.)*

FESTIVALS. Parties sweep Granada in the summer. The **Corpus Cristi** celebrations and bullfights in May/June are world-famous. That same month, avant-garde theater groups from around the world make a pilgrimage to Granada for the **International Theater Festival** (☎958 22 93 44). The **Festival Internacional de Música y Danza** (mid-June to early July) sponsors performances of classical music, ballet, and flamenco in the Palacio de Carlos V and other venues. *(☎958 22 18 44; www.granadafestival.org. Prices vary. Senior and youth discounts available.)*

DAYTRIP FROM GRANADA

NERJA

ALSA buses leave from Granada (7 per day 7am-8pm, €8.84; return 6 per day 6:30am-7:15pm). All buses stop and depart on Av. de la Pescia, just before a roundabout and across the street from the ticket kiosk (☎952 52 15 04).

A 2hr. bus journey from Granada, Nerja is the most popular beach destination on the Costa Tropical. While the tourist presence is undeniable, the city more than makes up for it in sunny plazas, winding streets, palm trees, and dramatic Mediterranean vistas. Much of the town stands 15 to 20m above the water, allowing for brilliant ocean views from seaside cafes, while beaches are framed by rugged cliffs and outcroppings plunging down to clear, sparkling water. Three kilometers east of Nerja are the **Cuevas de Nerja,** Spain's third most popular tourist attraction after the Prado and the Alhambra. Featuring the world's widest column formed by a stalactite meeting a stalagmite, guests will also find the skeleton of an ancient Nerjan in caverns that go back at least 5 kilometers. Concerts are occasionally held in one of the cave's massive caverns. (Buses depart for the caves from the Av. de la Pescia stop. 12+ per day 8:30am-8pm, return 8:45am-7:30pm, €0.90 each way. Caves open daily Sept.-June 10am-2pm and 4pm-6:30pm; July-Aug. 10am-7:30pm. €7, ages 6-12 €3.50.)

Accommodations and eateries are found in abundance throughout town. If you're staying the night, **Nerjasol ❷,** Pintada, 54, is a great deal, with 21 elegant and comfortable rooms, all with A/C, TV, and bath, and a well-furnished terrace with mountain and ocean views. (☎952 52 21 21; www.hostalnerjasol.com. Singles €20-25; doubles €33-50.) To get to the **tourist office,** Puerta del Mar, 2, walk towards the circle, make a right into the triangular park and cross it to the far leg, C. Pintada, which runs down to the **Balcón de Europa,** a dramatic plaza looking over the Mediterranean. The tourist office is on the left just before the road meets the plaza. (☎95 252 15 31. Open daily in summer. English spoken.)

GUADIX

What distinguishes Guadix (pop. 20,000) from other cities in Spain, and the rest of the world, is that almost half its residents still live in caves. The town was founded centuries ago as a Roman outpost, though its distinctive *casas cuevas* (cave houses) were only later inhabited and turned into houses by Moors fleeing the Spanish *reconquista.* Featuring a walled old town and the ruins of a Moorish place, Guadix is a fascinating town set in a dramatic landscape. Indeed, the reddish, rocky terrain surrounding the town appears so similar to the arid land made famous in the first Star Wars movie that local legend often proclaims that parts of the movie were filmed here (filming actually took place in Tunisia). Famous or not, Guadix does not fail to impress.

TRANSPORTATION AND PRACTICAL INFORMATION

Buses to Guadix from **Granada** (1hr., 8-14 per day 6:30am-8:15pm, €4.56.) Buy tickets at station, as the schedule does not appear on the ALSA website. Get off in Guadix just before the large rotary at Pl. de las Américas on **Avenida Mariana Pineda.** The cathedral will be to the right. The bus station is several blocks straight ahead and to the left. From the station on C. Santa Rosa, (☎958 66 06 57) buses depart for: **Almería, Granada,** and **Jaén;** Schedules are subject to frequent change. The **tourist office,** on Av. Mariana Pineda, is several blocks to the left when your back is to the cathedral. (☎958 69 95 74. Open M-F 8:30am-3:30pm.)

The residential area made up of caves, **Barriada de Cuevas,** is behind the *casco antiguo*. Signs point the way to the *barriada*, starting in front of the cathedral and on C. San Miguel (15-20min. walk to the caves).

ACCOMMODATIONS

Despite its proximity to Granada, Guadix remains relatively untouristed—but there are few places you could spend a more memorable night. The tourist office has a complete listing of cave "hotels" and apartments for rent. **Chez Jean & Julia ❹,** Ermita Nueva, 67 (☎958 66 91 91), in the Barriada de Cuevas offers rooms in caves or in the main house. Groups (up to 10) can rent cave apartments with kitchen and bath. Breakfast is included. Reserve a day ahead for July-Aug. Doubles €38; triples €41. 4-person apartments €66-80; increasing approx. €8 with each guest. **Cuevas de María ❷,** Ermita Nueva, 52 (☎958 66 07 16; www.cuevasdemaria.es), next to the Cueva Museo in Pl. Padre Poveda, has hotel-like rooms with TV and heating. Singles €30-40; doubles €45; triples €72; quads €92; 5-person €108; 6-person €125.

FOOD

Walk along **Avenida Mariana Pineda** for bars and cafeterias by day, then take advantage of the Granada tradition of free tapas by wandering to C. Tribuna and nearby side streets by the **Plaza de la Constitución** and the *Ayuntamiento*. **Calatrava Bodega ❷,** C. Tribuna (☎609 91 23 45), is one of the most celebrated bars in town. Locals flock here at night, so claim a seat at the bar or outside before 9:15pm. Order some of the cheapest and most delicious drinks (€1.20-2) around, then choose from an extensive tapas list. Open M-Sa 1-4pm and 10pm-midnight. **Café-Bar Los Arcos ❸** (☎958 66 66 29), in the Pl. de la Constitución, is a great place to take in the bustle of the plaza while enjoying free tapas with each drink. (*Tinto de verano* and beer €1.50. Open daily 9am-2am.)

SIGHTS

Take a break from the climb up to the *barrio de cuevas* in the natural coolness of **Cueva Museo de Alfarería La Alcazaba,** C. San Miguel, 47, underneath the Alcazaba. The museum displays earthenware artifacts and a 17th-century well inside an authentic cave dwelling, along with a large collection of local decorative and domestic pottery. (☎958 66 47 67. Open M-F in summer 10am-1:30pm and 5-8:30pm; in winter 4-7pm. €2, children €1.) In Pl. Padre Poveda, the main square of the Barriada de Cuevas, is the **Cueva Museo de Costumbres Populares.** Also known as just "Cueva Museo," this old cave home was abandoned in the 70s and now pays tribute to the modern-day cave-dweller's life. (☎958 66 55 69. Ermita Nueva 56. Open Apr.-Sept. M-F 10am-2pm and 5-7pm; May-Oct. M-F 10am-2pm and 4-6pm. €2.50, seniors €1.50. Under 14 free.) To truly get a sense of the *barriada*, head to **Mirador Cerro de la Bala.** From the Cueva Museo, continue uphill from the opposite end of the plaza; follow signs or ask a local. From here, the Sierra Nevadas tower over a valley full of chimneys rising out of the surrounding rock.

LAS ALPUJARRAS

Although Andalucía is known for its stretches of sunflowers and grazing cattle, the Sierra Nevada mountains that peek above the rolling fields are an equally stunning sight. In the summer, their white slopes give way to green gorges, hidden streams, and the *pueblos blancos* (white villages) of Las Alpujarras, which blanket the southern slopes in an area known as *La Falda* (the skirt). Although the roads are now paved and the towns more touristed, this is a region blessed with a rare sense of tranquility.

TRANSPORTATION

Las Alpujarras are most easily traversed by car, but for those without wheels, ALSA **buses** (☎958 18 54 80; www.alsa.es) travel from Granada to many of the high-altitude towns, though service is infrequent and not always punctual. The buses trace switchback after unnerving switchback, hugging the scenic road—sick bags are often available at the front for squeamish riders. Bus drivers often stop to let travelers off at intermediate points. Buses (3 per day 10am-5pm) run from **Granada,** stopping in: **Pampaneira** (2hr., €5.12); **Bubion** (2hr., €5.60); **Capileira** (2hr., €5.60); **Trevélez** (3hr., €6.57). Ask in each town for the return schedule. Some hard-core visitors hike from place to place, and locals often sympathize with hitchhikers. *Let's Go* does not recommend hitchhiking.

WATER, WATER EVERYWHERE. All throughout the villages in the Alpujarras, locals drink from fountains of ice-cold mountain spring water. Always check the fountain before imbibing.

OUTDOOR ACTIVITIES

Las Alpujarras is an ideal base for outdoor activities in Spain's highest mountain range, the **Sierra Nevada.** Opportunities for climbing, biking, horseback riding, and hiking abound. The park boasts 19 trails, each heavily marked and totaling over 300km in a circuit around the protected area. If you're planning a long stay in the mountains, don't forget a good map, compass, warm clothes, cooking and camping equipment, and possibly even a GPS system. Whether you're a novice or pro, research trails before starting out; getting lost in the mountains is never fun. Check out **Discovery Walking Guides'** guidebook for blow-by-blow accounts of every trail in Las Alpujarras (www.walking.demon.co.uk), or simply admire the beauty of the peaks from the comfort of a park bench.

For **skiing,** head to the Sierra Nevada resort town, **Estación de Esquí,** a 50min. bus ride from Granada (€5; €8 round-trip). Sierra Nevada has Spain's premier ski resorts in the upper mountains above Granada, offering views of the city, and even to the Mediterranean and Africa on clear days. The ski season lasts from December through April, although due to the mountains' relatively warm climate, artificial snow machines are heavily utilized. (Day pass €32-40, ½-day pass €27-34; under 14 €19-24/16-21. Ski classes offered.) In the summer, the resort town stays open for those wishing to get away to the mountains in luxury and comfort, while the **Club Sierra Nevada** organizes various biking, horse back riding, and trekking excursions, including a bike trip that goes from the mountains to the beach in the same day, passing through all of the province's various microclimates. (☎902 70 80 90; www.sierranevadaski.com.)

PAMPANEIRA ☎958

Pampaneira (1059m) is the first of a trio of picturesque hamlets featuring white mountain houses overlooking the **Poqueira Gorge,** a massive ravine cut by the Río Poqueira. The town makes a great springboard for climbing to Bubión (30min.) and Capileira (40min.). Catch the steep but manageable trail to the higher towns by taking any combination of uphill streets to the top of Pampaneira; sporadic signs point the way. Bear right at any fork in the trail, continuing upwards towards the white village—the path ends in a small plaza around

Bubión's church. Hiking boots are recommended for this often muddy path. Located in the main square, Pl. de la Libertad, **Nevadensis** offers hiking tours of the Sierra Nevada, provides a few maps, sells gear, and arranges accommodations for group tours. They also serve as the town's tourist office. (☎958 76 31 27; www.nevadensis.com. Open M-Sa 10am-2pm and Su 10am-3pm, and most afternoons from 4-6pm; hours vary.) **Hostal Pampaneira ❷**, Av. de la Alpujarra, 1, off Pl. de la Libertad to the left when facing the church, has a terrace and large, simple rooms with private baths, TV, and comfortable beds. (☎958 76 30 02; www.hostalpampaneira.com. Breakfast included at downstairs bar. Singles €28; doubles €40; triples €46. AmEx/MC/V.) A few doors down, **Restaurante Casa Diego "El Alpujarreño" ❷**, Pl. de la Libertad, 3, draws hikers with its cuisine and shady roof terrace. For a pre-trek protein boost, try the *sopa alpujarreña* (€4.50), a yellow broth with fried bread, hard-boiled eggs, and pork. (☎958 76 30 15. Entrees €6.50-13. *Menú* €9. Open daily 12:30-4:30pm and 8-11pm. MC/V.)

BUBIÓN ☎958

Bubión, a steep (30min.) hike on a dirt trail from Pampaneira, is known for its Berber architecture and traditional *artesanía* (craftwork). While it lacks the variety of food and lodging options of its lower neighbor and the higher altitude of its upper neighbor, Capileira (about 200m up a paved road), Bubión enjoys particularly breathtaking views down the valley to the Mediterranean Sea and even, some days, to the Rif mountains of Morocco. Those not up for the steep hike to Bubión can catch the "early" bus from Pampaneira at 12:35pm. The town has no tourist office, but locals are glad to assist when they can. **Rustic Blue,** Barrio La Ermita, is a great resource for action-seekers; the intrepid staff specializes in rentals but has been organizing excursions, guided hikes, and horseback rides into the mountains for a decade. (☎958 76 33 81; www.rusticblue.com. Open M-F 10am-7pm, Sa 11am-2pm.) With its central location and affordable accommodations, Bubión is the best anchor for traveling within the Alpujarras. **Las Terrazas de la Alpujarra ❷**, Pl. del Sol, 7, offers rooms with private baths and breathtaking views of the valley from multiple terraces available to guests. (☎958 76 30 34; www.terrazasalpujarra.com. Free internet access. Trail guides available in English. Breakfast €2.50. Singles €20; doubles €31; apartments for 2-10 people €45-150. Discounts of up to 10% for groups of 10. MC/V.) The *menú* (€8) at **Teide ❷** is limited but generous. (☎958 76 30 37. Entrees €6-14. Open daily 10am-noon, 1:30-4pm, and 8-10:30pm. MC/V.)

CAPILEIRA ☎958

In Capileira (1436m), looming peaks tower over cobblestone alleys. This whitewashed town perches atop the **Poqueira Gorge** (2hr. from Granada, a 1hr. hike on the trail from Bubión or a 10min. walk on the road) and makes a good base for exploring the neighboring villages and the back of *La Falda*. The ascent to **Mulhacén** (3479m), the highest peak of the Iberian peninsula, is possible from Capileira via the *refugio* (shelter); however, novice climbers might prefer to start from the commonly used base town of Trevélez. The **Centro de Información,** on the left side of the main road as you enter Capileira, offers plenty of information about trekking around Capileira and in the Sierra Nevada, organizes tours, and in summer provides a mini-bus service up the old mountain roads closed to the public to Puerto Molina and Mirador Trevélez, a nice boost on any assault of the upper peaks. (☎958 76 34 86 or 671 56 44 066. Open daily 10am-2pm and 5-8pm. Shuttle €4.80, round-trip €8. Reservations required.) This town, while tiny, is full of similar beautiful places to stay, all with character-filled rooms and great views of the gorge and mountains. New rooms, a large pool, and a filling traditional *menú* (€10-11) can be found at **Mesón Poqueira**

❷, C. Dr. Castillo, 11, and its adjacent hostel. Each room has beds covered with traditional Alpujarran blankets, as well as large wooden furniture and a balcony. (☎958 76 30 48; www.hotelpoqueira.com. Open daily 1-4pm and 8-11:30pm. Singles €20; doubles €36; triples €45. MC/V.)

TREVÉLEZ ☎958

Jamón serrano (mountain-cured ham), and lots of it, distinguishes Trevélez, continental Spain's highest permanent community (1476m). The only "houses" you'll find above this tiny town are the shepherds' lean-tos used in the summer when sheep are led to the top of the peaks. Steep roads weave through three *barrios*, and water rushes through Moorish irrigation systems still intact after 1000 years of use. Above all, Trevélez is a logical base for the ascent to **Mulhacén** (3479m). Every August, throngs of locals visit Mulhacén to pay homage to the **Virgen de las Nieves** (Virgin of the Snows), who is carried to the summit during the festival. Summit-bound travelers should prepare with proper equipment and head north on the trail leaving the from the top of the *barrio medio*, across on the other side of town from the road to Granada, leaving behind the Hermita de San Antonio (although hikers should follow signs for "Camino de Siete Lagunas"; avoid the trail that follows the swampy Río Trevélez.) Continue past the Cresta de los Postreros for a good 3-4hr. until you reach a waterfall. Cross the waterfall and climb up its right side until the top of ridge; on the other side, you should see the **Cañada de Siete Lagunas** (the largest lake, Laguna Hondera, should be directly in front of you); go right to see the **Cueva del Cura** (the Priest's Cave), a famous refuge. To reach Mulhacén, go up the ridge south of the *refugio* (3-4hr. farther). Note that no buses from Granada arrive in Trevélez before 1pm, making same-day assaults on Mulhacén an unnecessary challenge. Budget beds aren't hard to find in Trevélez, and are especially prominent in the *barrio bajo*, by the paved plaza where buses depart for Granada.

VALENCIA AND MURCIA

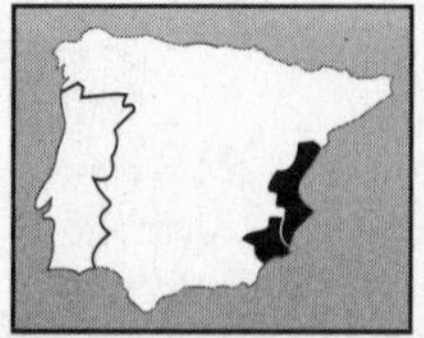

The whimsical southeast corner of Spain proudly boasts a little bit of everything. From the sun-drenched, silky beaches of the Costa Blanca and the unabashed friendliness of Murcia to the cosmopolitan buzz of Valencia, this area is sure to enchant and impress. Its history is rife with power struggles among a cast of usual suspects: Phoenicians, Carthaginians, Greeks, Romans, and Moors, who all contributed to the region's varied architectural influences. The region first fell under Castilian control when El Cid expelled the Moors in 1094; he ruled in the name of Alfonso VI until his death in 1099. Without El Cid's powerful influence, Valencia and Murcia again fell to the Moors, remaining an Arab stronghold until 1238. After the expulsion of the Moors, Valencia established itself as a frontrunner in cultural and technological innovation; in 1492, the *valencianos* were the first bankers to lend funds to Queen Isabel for her patronage of Christopher Columbus. The region was besieged again in the 1930s, this time by Franco's troops. *Valencianos* resisted with strength—it was the last region incorporated into Franco's Spain and regained autonomy in 1977.

HIGHLIGHTS OF VALENCIA AND MURCIA

LIGHT 15 ft. puppets on fire in **Valencia** during the festival of **Las Fallas** (p. 300).

GO MEDIEVAL by visiting the castle in tiny **Morella** (p. 303).

BURN the midnight oil in sleepless **Alicante** (p. 306).

WHIP OUT your toga at the Roman ruins in **Cartagena** (p. 320).

VALENCIA

The region of Valencia is home to layers of history, each of which has left a visible cultural and aesthetic imprint on the region's development. Blue-roofed church domes battle new resort developments for skyline prominence, while pristine beaches, quaint coastal towns, and maze-like inland gardens offer a wealth of refuge for weary travelers. Crowded nightlife challenges even the most nocturnal adventurers on the hectic coastline, but it is worth venturing inland for a bit, if only for the unbeatable taste of local oranges. *Paella* also reaches culinary perfection here in its birthplace, especially the renowned *paella con mariscos* (seafood *paella*) and the hearty *paella valenciana* (chicken and rabbit). The commonly used regional dialect, *valencià*, is the legacy of Moorish invaders and Catalan crusaders who clashed in the northwest hundreds of years ago, and a recent mandate that all students enroll in one course of *valencià* reflects a resurgence of regional pride.

VALENCIA ☎963

Valencia (pop. 805,000) inherited the best genes of its sister cities: the clamoring energy of Madrid, the youthful and quirky sophistication of Barcelona, and the friendly warmth of Sevilla. Ancient traditions remain strong despite increasing modernity and commercialism. An evening glance around the central Pl. del Ajuntament reveals a merry mix of classic Spanish architecture, opulent 19th-century palaces, umbrella-crammed cafe patios, Art Deco movie theaters, and modern towers. After a deadly flood in 1957 drowned the streets in almost two meters of water, Valencia drained and diverted the Río Turia southward; now, the dry riverbed that surrounds the city is a lush, winding

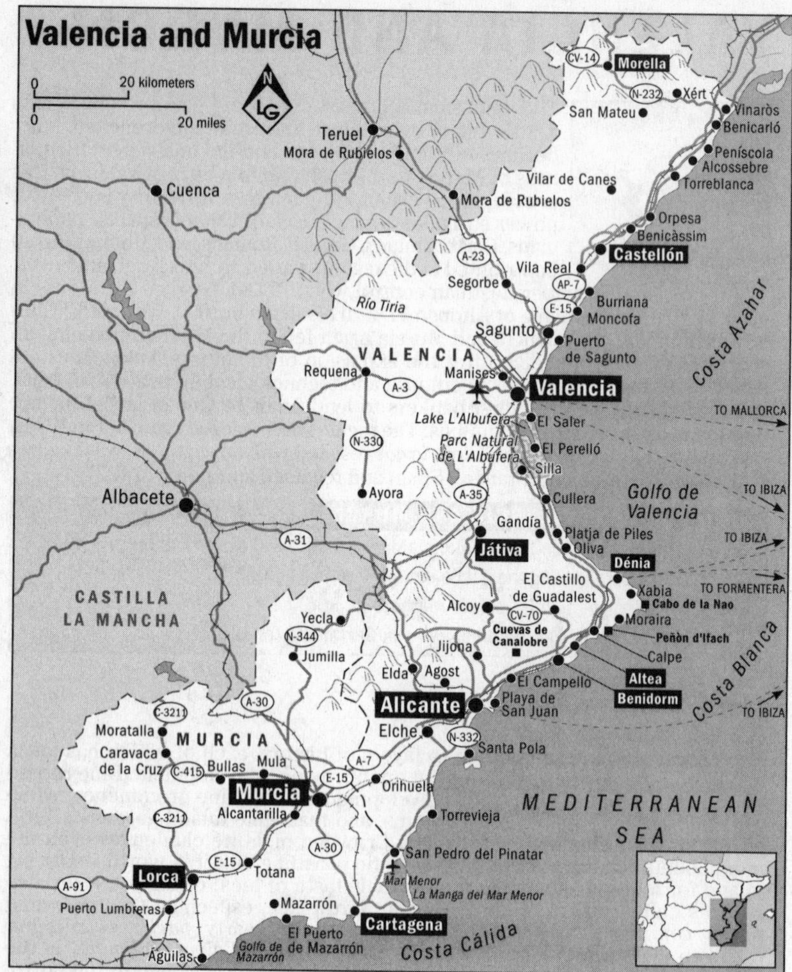

park that offers views of the city's standing fortifications. Beyond these older facades, toward the sea, the riverbed meets the Ciudad de las Artes y las Ciencias, a grandiose scientific complex and architectural marvel. The sudden transition from ancient to avant-garde reflects the city's eagerness to modernize competitively. The city's beaches and palm tree-studded plazas have fewer tourists than Spain's other large cities, so plan on using your Spanish here.

TRANSPORTATION

INTERCITY TRANSPORTATION

Flights: Aena, Aeropuerto de Manises/Airport of Valencia (☎961 59 85 00; www.aena.es), 8km from the city. **Aero-Bus** buses run between the airport and train station (35min.

daily every 20min., €2.50). Stops: Airport, Av. del Cid, Bailén, Angel Guimerá. Subway line #3 or 5 goes straight to C. Xàtiva, on the outskirts of Valencia by the *Ajuntament* (€1.80). Taxis from airport to city about €15. **Iberia,** C. La Paz, 14 (☎963 52 05 00; www.iberia.com). Open M-F 9am-2pm and 4-7:30pm.

Trains: Estación del Norte, C. Xàtiva, 24 (☎963 52 02 02; www.renfe.es). Ticket windows open daily 7am-9pm. 1- to 6-zone distances range €1.15-3.95. **RENFE** (☎902 24 02 02) to: **Alicante** (2-3hr., 12 per day 7:04am-11pm, €23.60-31.30; Su differs by week); **Barcelona** (3hr., every 1-2hr. 5:50am-8:45pm, €29-37); **Madrid** (3hr., 12 per day 6:45am-9:15pm, €19.75-39; Su differs by week); **Sevilla** (8hr., 11:20am, €48.90). Cercanías trains run at least 2 per hr. to **Gandía** (1hr., €3.65), **Sagunt** (23min., €2.40), and **Xàtiva** (45min., €2.85). Allot time to go through security.

Buses: Estación Terminal d'Autobuses, Av. Menéndez Pidal, 11 (☎963 46 62 66), across the riverbed, a 20min. walk from the city center. Municipal bus #8 runs between Pl. del Ajuntament and the bus station (€1.10). **ALSA** (☎902 42 22 42) to: **Alicante** (4hr., 1-3 per hr. 4:45am-9:45pm, €17.70-18.20) via the **Costa Blanca; Barcelona** (4hr., 20 per day, 1-2 every 2hr., €25.14-33); **Granada** (8hr., 8 per day 2:45am-12:30am, €41.55-47.91); **Málaga** (11hr., 8 per day 2:45am-12:30am, €51.07-59.05); **Sevilla** (11hr., 10 per day 8am-4:45am, €49.86-74.69). **Auto Res** (☎963 49 22 30) goes to **Madrid** (4hr., 16-18 per day 1am-11pm, €23.64-25.15).

Ferries: Trasmediterránea, Muelle de Poniente (☎902 45 46 45; www.trasmediterranea.es). Take bus #4 from Pl. del Ajuntament or #1 or 2 from the bus station. To: **Mallorca** (5hr., 7:45pm, in summer €85) and **Ibiza** (3hr., 12:15pm, in summer €85). 1 13hr. ferry to **Menorca** per week. (Sa 11:30pm; in summer overnight €56.50, with cot €111.50.) Reserve through a travel agency or risk inconvenience by buying tickets at the port on the day of departure.

LOCAL TRANSPORTATION

EMT Office, Pl. Correo Viejo, 5 (☎963 15 85 15, handicapped hotline 963 15 85 25; www.emtvalencia.es). Open M-F 9am-2pm and 4:30-7:30pm. Bus schedules depend on route and day. Tourist routes 5, 5B, 35, 95. Bus #8 (every 9-11min. 6am-10:30pm) runs to the bus station. Buses #20, 21,and 22 (every 10-20min. 9am-8:40pm) go to Las Arenas and Malvarrosa along Pg. Marítim. Buy tickets (€1.50) on board; combination bus and metro monthly ticket (€35.60, student €26.70), or 1-day pass (€3.10) available at newsstands. No service 10:30-11:30pm. **Late-night buses** N1, N2, N3, N4, N5, N6, and N7 go through Pl. del Ajuntament (every 45min. M-W and Su 11pm-1am, Th-Sa 11pm-3am). **Metro,** P. de Xirivelleta (☎963 97 40 40; www.metrovalencia.com) service loops around the *casco antiguo* (old quarter) and into the outskirts. The most central stop is on C. Xàtiva across the street from the train station or C. Colón by El Corte Inglés. Buy tickets from machines in any station (€1.20-1.60 depending on distance, 10-ride pass €5.60-8).

Taxis: Onda Taxi (☎963 47 52 52), **Radio Taxi** (☎963 70 33 33), **Tele Taxi** (☎963 57 13 13), and **Buscataxi** (☎902 74 77 47).

Car Rental: C. Xàtiva, 24 (at the Estació del Nord train station). **Europcar** (☎963 51 90 55; www.europcar.es). Open M-Sa 8am-10pm, Su 8am-9pm. **Avis** (train station ☎963 52 42 64, airport 961 52 18 72; www.avis.es). **Hertz** (☎963 52 42 64; www.hertz.com) Car prices vary with season, type, and length of rental, but a medium-size car for 1 week costs around €200.

Bike Rental: Orange Bikes, C. Santa Teresa, 8 (☎963 91 75 51; www.orangebikes.net). From the main entrance of the Mercado Central, walk down Av. María Cristina away from Pl. *Ajuntamiento* and turn down the 2nd street, continuing on to the end. From Pl. de la Virgen, take C. Caballeros until it turns into C. Santa Teresa. Bikes €9-15 per day, €45-55 per week. Open M-F 9:30am-2:30pm and 4:30-8pm, Sa 10am-2pm and 7-7:30pm. **Douyoubike,**

Valencia
ACCOMMODATIONS
Home Youth Hostel, 7
Hostal El Cid, 10
Pensión Alicante, 13
Pensión Paris, 17
Purple Nest Hostel, 19
Red Nest Hostel, 18
Home Backpackers, 3
FOOD
La Lluna, 1
La Pappardella, 11
El Rall, 9
Sagardi, 12
Sol i Lluna, 15
Zumería Naturalia, 14
NIGHTLIFE
Akuarela, 2
Bolsería Café, 5
Cafe Negrito, 8
Fox Congo, 6
Murray Club, 20
Radio City, 4
L'umbracle, 16
Campo de Beisbol
Jardín del Turia
Jardines del Real
EL CARME
CIUTAT VELLA
Torres de Serranos
Real Monasterio de la Trinidad
Museo de Bellas Artes
Palau de la Generalitat
Basílica Virgen dels Desamparats
Santa Iglesia Catedral de Valencia
Miguelete Tower
San Nicolás
San Juan del Hospital
Palacio del Templo
Iglesia de los Santos Juanes
Lonja de la Seda
Iglesia Santa Catalona
MERCAT CENTRAL
Palacio Marqués de Dos Aguas
Museu de Cerámicas
Colegia de Patriarcha
Universidad
Iglesia de San Juan de la Cruz
El Corte Inglés
Ayuntamiento
PL. DEL AJUNTAMENT
Estación del Norte (RENFE)
Plaza de Toros
Museo Taurino
Sorlano Librerías
Work Station
L@undry Stop
Do You Bike
Orange Bikes
Ono
TO AV. PRIMADO REIG (300m)
TO CIUTAT UNIVERSITARIA, AV. BLASCO IBAÑEZ (500m), (1km)
CUIDAD DE LAS ARTES Y LAS CIENCIAS (3km), PALAU DE MÚSICA (700m)
TO IVAM (800m)
TO JARDÍN BOTÀNIC (1.5km)
TO CALLE GUIEM CASTRO (100m)
TO AVE. DEL PUERTO (300m), DUNA VIAJES (50m)
ESTACIÓ MARÍTIMA (5km)
TO EL SALÉR AND L'ABUFERA (100m)
200 meters
200 yards

Corner C. Musico Magenti and Puebla Larga (☎963 15 55 51, Movil ☎675 73 02 18; www.doyoubike.com). Also Av. Puerto, 21 (☎963 37 40 24), and C. Puebla Larga, 13, at Guardia Civil (☎963 38 70 08). M-Th rates from €2 per hour and €10 per day; F-Su rates shoot up to €4 per hr. and €15 per day. Open daily 10am-2pm and 5-8pm.

ORIENTATION AND PRACTICAL INFORMATION

The most convenient way to enter the city is via the new metro line to Xàtiva or C. Colón. Xàtiva is a central stop near the **Museo Taurino de Valencia** (the giant bullfighting arena and museum). **Estación del Norte** is also close to the city center, so entrance by train is convenient. **Avenida Marqués de Sotelo** runs from the train station to **Plaça del Ajuntament (Plaza Ayuntamiento),** in the center of town. At the opposite end of the plaza runs **San Vincente Martir,** which leads to some of the town's most vibrant areas. Take **La Avenida de María Cristina** to **El Mercado,** a bustling fresh-food market, or continue past shop-laden **Calle La Paz** into the **Plaza de la Reina,** central to food, lodging, architecture, and nightlife. To the north of the plaza, streets lead to the bend of the now-diverted **Río Turia,** known today as the **Jardín del Turia,** a verdant park ideal for biking and sightseeing along the way to the port or beaches. Other sights and museums are across the river or on the outskirts of the city. The *casco antiguo* (old quarter) is best explored on foot, but the sidestreets can get confusing—keep a map handy.

Tourist Office: Regional office, C. de la Paz, 48 (☎963 98 64 22; www.comunitatvalenciana.com). Open M-F 9am-8pm, Sa 10am-8pm, Su 10am-2pm. Branches at **Estación del Nord,** C. Xàtiva, 24 (☎963 52 85 73; open M-Sa 9am-7pm, Su 10am-2pm), and Pl. de la Reina, 19 (☎963 15 39 31; www.turisvalencia.es; open M-Sa 9am-7pm, Su 10am-2pm).

Currency Exchange: Banks are easy to find. All have a min. commission of €6, and some will take a small percentage of any money exchanged. Banks are clustered around Pl. del Ajuntament and transportation hubs and are usually open 8am-2:30pm.

Luggage Storage: 24hr. storage at the **bus station** (€2.40-4.50) and **train station** (€2.40-4.50), depending on the size of your luggage. Open daily 5am-1am.

Bookstore: Librería Soriano, C. Xàtiva, 15 (☎963 51 03 78; www.libreriasoriano.com). Across the street from the train station. One of the most historic bookstores in Valencia. Small section of novels in English as well as maps and a few magazines. Open M-Sa 9:30am-9:30pm, Su 10:30am-12:30pm and 5:30-8:30pm. MC/V.

Laundromat: The L@undry Stop, C. Baja, 17 (☎963 91 35 28). This cyber laundromat offers internet while that laundry tumbles. Wash €4, dry €3, soap €0.50. Internet €0.50 for 20min. Wi-Fi available. Open daily 9:30am-10pm.

Emergency: ☎112.

Police: Po. de Alameda, 17 (☎963 60 03 50), or C. Maestre, 2 (☎963 15 56 90). Local police also reachable at ☎092.

Late-Night Pharmacy: Rotates daily, check listing in local paper *Levante* (€1) or the *farmacias de guardia* schedule posted outside any pharmacy around the Pl. de la Reina and Pl. de la Virgen (☎963 91 68 21). **Info Salud** (health info ☎900 20 22 02).

Hospital: Hospital Clínico Universitario, Av. Blasco Ibáñez, 17 (☎963 86 29 00). Take bus #81 from Pl. del Ajuntament or take the metro (line 3) at C. Xàtiva to Facultades. **Ambulance:** ☎112 or 96 152 51 59. **Red Cross Ambulances:** ☎96 367 73 75.

Internet Access: Ono, C. San Vicente Mártir, 22 (☎963 28 19 02; www.ono.com). Close to the *Ajuntament,* this 2-story complex is a high-ceilinged technological haven that was the 1st broadband internet center in Europe. Laptop stations, printing services, Skype, and more. 9am-2pm €2 per 45min., 2-10pm €2 per 30min., 10pm-1am €2 per hr. Cashier closes at 12:30am. Open M-F 9am-1am; Sa-Su and holidays 10am-1am. **Work Center,** C. Xàtiva, 19 (☎961 12 08 30; www.workcenter.es). 24hr. work station across the street from the train station offers office supplies, photocopying, and print services as well as DHL Express. €3 per hr. Open M-Th 24hr., F 7am-11pm, Sa 10am-2pm and 5-9pm, Su noon-2pm and 5-11pm. AmEx/MC/V.

Post Office: Pl. del Ajuntament, 24 (☎963 512 370; www.correos.es). This palatial building is a temple to the mail gods. **Western Union** and call center. Open M-F 8:30am-8:30pm, Sa 9:30am-2pm. **Postal Code:** Center: 46002; Renfe: 46007; Ruzafa: 46005.

ACCOMMODATIONS

Well-run youth hostels and *pensiones* for decent fares abound in Valencia, but finding a room can be a difficult task during travel-heavy summer months or the festival of Las Fallas (Mar. 12-19). The best deals are around **Plaça del Ajuntament** and **Plaça del Mercat,** both in the *casco antiguo.*

Red Nest Hostel, C. La Paz, 36 (☎963 42 71 68; www.nesthostelsvalencia.com). A classic, 16th-century Spanish building with a youthful, bright interior. Centrally located, with a busy atmosphere. Free luggage storage. Huge guest kitchen, lounge area, and terrace. Internet €1 per hr. Wash €2, dry €2. Open year-round. 12-person dorms in winter €14, in summer €18-20; 6-person dorm €16.50/20-22; 4-person dorm €17.50/23-25; doubles €50/58, economy double €37/42; quad €84. In summer months, prices rise on F=Sa. **Purple Nest Hostel** branch with lounge and bar at P. Tetuan, 5 (☎963 53 25 61). AmEx/MC/V. ❶

Home Backpackers, at Pl. Vicente Iborra (☎963 91 37 97; www.likeathome.net). Though slightly farther from the center of the action, this branch of Home Youth Hostel has more beds per room and a more boisterous atmosphere. The bustling kitchen and roof terrace (closes at 11pm) are popular nightime hangouts. Open year-round. Beds in summer from €15 per night. MC/V. ❶

Home Youth Hostel, C. de la Lonja, 4 (☎963 91 62 29; www.likeathome.net). 20 rooms surround a lively, funky lobby. Reading room and kitchen. Hall baths co-ed, free towels. Internet €0.50 per 15min. Singles €23; doubles €40; triples in summer €63-69, in winter €45; qauds €84-92/60. 10% ISIC discount. ❷

Hostal El Cid, C. Cerrajeros, 13 (☎/fax 963 92 23 23). Off C. San Vicente Mártir near the Plaza de la Reina. In an unassuming, tiled building with 12 airy rooms. Antique artwork lines the hallways. Some rooms with balcony. English and French spoken. Book well in advance. Open year-round. Doubles with sink, shower, and TV €40-45. MC/V. ❹

Pensión Alicante, C. de Ribera, 8 (☎963 51 22 96). On a lively, cafe-lined street off the Pl. del Ajuntament in the direction of the train station. Rooms are clean; they vary in size, decoration, and amenities. Rooms facing the street are considerably brighter, with balcony. Common area and library. Open year-round. Singles €24, with bath and A/C €35; doubles for single use €30-35; doubles €35/45; triples €52 with bath. MC/V. ❷

Pensión Paris, C. Salvá, 12 (☎963 52 67 66; www.pensionparis.com). By Universidad de Valencia. 15 simple rooms, most with sink, minute balcony, and hall bath. Open year-round. Singles €22; doubles €32, with shower €38; triples €48. MC/V. ❷

 FOOD

Valencia is renowned as the birthplace of *paella*, and a turn down any side-street will often reveal huge crowds of locals sharing this sticky dish from mammoth skillets. *Valencianos* buy heaps of fresh fish, produce, vegetables, snacks, and fruits in the bustling **Mercat Central,** the largest food market in Europe since 1928, located in an Art Nouveau building on Pl. del Mercat (☎963 82 91 00; open M-Sa 6am-2:30pm). For **groceries,** stop by **El Corte Inglés** on C. Pintor Sorolla (☎963 15 95 00). For a smaller market, try **Mercadona**, C. el Poeta, (open M-Sa 9:15am-9:15pm).

El Rall, C. Tundidores, 2 (☎963 92 20 90). This cheerful restaurant spills into an intimate, serene courtyard. Lucky customers may be serenaded by passing accordion players. *Paella* served in skillets according to party size. €12-21 per person, 2-person min. daily 1:30-3:30pm and 8:30-11:30pm. Reserve ahead. MC/V. ❸

Zumeria Naturalia, C. del Mar, 12 (☎963 91 12 11). This sherbet-colored gem is hidden steps below the cobblestone street outside. Hanging lamps dangle over low tables crammed with cushioned wicker chairs. Offers over 50 fruit drinks (€3.40-4.20 without alcohol, €5.50-6.50 smoothie mixed drinks). Delicious crepes and *bocadillos.* Open M-W 5pm-12:30am, Th 5pm-1am, F-Sa 5pm-2am, Su 5-10:30pm. Cash only. ❶

Sagardi, San Vincente Martir, 6 (☎963 91 06 68; www.sagardi.com). Basque-inspired tapas bar and restaurant with a bustling atmosphere. Lunchtime brings a steady stream of professionals to the tapas bar (tapas €1.60), while dinner and cocktails attract a varied crowd. Open daily, 11:30am-3:30pm and 7:30pm-1:30am. MC/V. ❶

Sol I Lluna, C. del Mar, 29 (☎963 92 22 16; www.solilluna.net). Relaxed bohemian hangout, with tapas bar, salads, and lighter entrees. Go for the set *menú* at midday or the inventive tapas served late into the night (€3.40-9). An eclectic ambience bar and ample open-air seating on a slow street just off Pl. de la Reina. Lots of regulars make for lively evenings. Open M 2-4pm, Tu-Sa 2-4pm and 9pm-last customer. MC/V. ❷

La Pappardella, C. Bordadores, 5 (☎963 91 89 15; www.viciositalianos.com). Chic and charismatic 2-story restaurant with some outdoor seating and a serene view of the plaza. Delicious Italian meals from pizza to spaghetti bolognese and vegetable dishes (€6-14). Ask to sit upstairs. Open daily 2-4pm and 9pm-midnight. AmEx/MC/V. ❷

La Lluna, C. Sant Ramón, 23 (☎963 92 21 46). Dark wood beams and low-hanging lamps characterize this quiet, tucked-away vegetarian restaurant. Serves a wide variety of traditional Valencian dishes, modified and embellished with fresh fruits and veggies. Appetizers and entrees €3.50-7. 4-course lunch *menú* (€6.50) on weekdays. Open M-Sa 1:30-3:30pm and 8:30-11pm. MC/V. ❶

SIGHTS

The older sights cluster around charming streets around **Plaza de la Reina** and **Plaza del Mercado.** Most museums, gardens, and notable landmarks are east along the Turia Riverbed. Though streets bordering the riverbed are high-speed thoroughfares, strolling through or above the riverbed is still a great way to take in the natural beauty and cultural activities that Valencia has to offer. EMT bus #5 drops off at most of the major sights, but, for a full informational tour, the double-decker **Bus Turístic** (☎963 41 44 00; www.valenciabusturistic.com) begins in Pl. de la Reina and loops around the old-town sights and along the riverbed toward the **Ciudad de las Artes y Ciencias** (€12 for a day pass).

CIUDAD DE LAS ARTES Y LAS CIENCIAS. This overwhelming urban citadel, dedicated to the arts and sciences, is a far cry from the blue-tiled church roofs that dominate most of the city skyline. This 350,000 sq. m. mini-city is Spain's largest museum, divided into four buildings covered with over 4000 panes of glass, all surrounding a vast reflecting pool. **L'Hemisfèric,** built to resemble an eye, hypnotizes onlookers with laser shows, a planetarium, and an IMAX theater. **L'Oceanogràfic** showcases 45,500 aquatic creatures in water channeled from the nearby Malvarossa beach. The enormous, glinting **Palau de les Arts** stages opera, theater, and dance performance. The **Museu de Les Ciències Príncipe Felipe,** the insect-like centerpiece, has hands-on exhibits. The garden running alongside L'Hemisfèric turns into a swanky club after dark. See **Nightlife, p. 298**. *(Bus #35 runs from Pl. del Ajuntament. ☎902 10 00 31; www.cac.es. Museum open daily 10am-7pm, high season 10am-9pm. €7.50, students and children €5.80. L'Oceanogràfic open high season daily 10am-midnight. Closed on certain holidays. €23.30, students and children €17.20. L'Hemisferic open M-Th 10am-7pm. €7.50, students and children €5.80. Combination tickets €19-30.50; can be bought at the train station through Cercanias trains.)*

INSTITUT VALENCIÀ D'ART MODERN (IVAM). This avant-garde museum features 20th- and 21st-century art. Its permanent collection on the first floor is famed for abstract works by 20th-century sculptor Julio González and artist Ignacio Pinazo. Temporary exhibits change frequently. *(C. Guillém de Castro, 118. Leaving the Basilica, take C. Caballeros until it turns into C. Quart. Walk under the Torres de Quart and take a right down C. Guillem de Castro; the museum is on the right. Bus #5 from the Pl. del Ajuntament. ☎963 86 30 00; www.ivam.es. Open Tu-Su 10am-10pm. €2, students €1. Su free.)*

SANTA IGLESIA CATEDRAL DE VALENCIA. The original cathedral was replaced by a mosque during Muslim rule in the eighth century, but the first stone of the present cathedral was laid after the conquest of Valencia under James I in 1238. The steep 202-step climb up the **Miguelete** (cathedral tower) is worth the sweat; novelist Victor Hugo once counted 300 bell towers in the city from this vantage point. The Gothic **Capilla de Santo Cáliz** is home to a wealth of treasures, from the Crucifijo de Márfil statues, which depict "man's passions," to a chalice which was once claimed to be the Holy Grail used by Christ at the Last Supper. *(Pl. de la Reina. Cathedral ☎963 91 01 89. Open daily 7:30am-1pm and 4:30-8:30pm. Closes* *earlier in winter. Free. Tower open daily 10am-1pm and 4:30-7pm. €2. Museum ☎963 92 43 02. Open Mar.-Nov. M-Sa 10am-1pm and 4:30-7pm, Su 10am-1pm and 4:30-5:30pm. €4 includes multilingual audio tour. €2.70 for children and seniors. After 6:30pm free.)* Be certain to visit the grandiose gold altar at the neighboring **Basílica Virgen dels Desamparats.** *(In the Pl. de la Virgen, 6, right behind the Catedral. Open for mass M-F 7am-1pm and 4:45-8:30pm, Su 8:30am-1:30pm and 4:45-8:30pm. Free.)*

MUSEU DE CERÁMICA Y DE LAS ARTES SUNTUARIAS "GONZOLEZ MARTI" EN EL PALACIO DE LOS MARQUESES DE DOS AGUAS. This stunning museum packs two of Valencia's finest attractions into one. The museum, which traces the history of ceramics with special Valencian exhibits, did not move into El Palacio de los Marquese de Dos Aguas until 1954. This building is spectacular, lavish, and unlike anything else to be found in Valencia. The alabaster entrance itself is worth the trip. The first two floors have recreated the palace as it appeared during the 14th century. Ornate mirrors and marble work adorn each grandiose and breathtaking room. Though the contemporary exhibits, located on the first and third floors, bear no actual connection to the palace, they are nonetheless particularly innovative and round out the draw of this special museum. *(C. Porta Querol, 2, off C. de la Paz. ☎963 51 63 92; www.mnceramica.mcu.es. Open Tu-Sa 10am-2pm and 4-8pm. €2.40, students €1.40. Sa free.)*

MUSEO DE BELLAS ARTES. This museum features a manageable array of some of Spain's most important. Gothic, Renaissance, Baroque, and 19th- and 20th-century paintings. One floor is dedicated to 14th- to 16th-century Valencian art taken from the area's convents in the 19th century, while other floors feature **El Greco's** *San Juan Bautista*, **Velázquez's** self-portrait, **Ribera's** *Santa Teresa*, and a slew of **Goyas.** *(C. Sant Pío V, 9, near the Jardines del Real. Walk toward the riverbed from Plaza de la Reina and cross Puente de la Trinidad; the museum is just right of this bridge and is easily visible. Bus #8 from the Pl. del Ajuntament drops you off across the river; ☎963 60 57 93; www.cult.gva.es/mbav. Open Tu-Su 10am-8pm. Free. Cafetería, ☎963 69 15 99, serves creative traditional food in large portions for reasonable prices. Entrees €9.)*

LONJA DE LA SEDA (SILK EXCHANGE). This Gothic building was once the financial and commercial center of Valencia. The old silk exchange is composed of three distinct parts: the Contract Hall, the tower (used as both chapel and prison), and the Pavilion of the Consolat de Mar. The building became a provisional hospital when waves of cholera hit the city in the 1800s and was declared an UNESCO World Heritage Site in 1996. Look for the 28 gargoyles surrounding the highest parts of the building. *(Pl. del Mercat. ☎963 52 54 78. Open Tu-Sa 10am-2pm and 4:30-8:30pm, Su 10am-3pm. Free.)*

PARKS. On the other side of the river, next to the Museo de Bellas Artes, off C. Sant Pío, are the **Jardines del Real,** home to oddly shaped ponds, modern sculptures, a small aviary, and even a kitschy duck-shaped fountain dedicated to Walt Disney. Everyone can enjoy a stroll through these labyrinthine paths and ivy-covered arches. The garden also features an aviary and a small zoo. *(C. San Pío V. Walk to the river, take a left, pass the museum, and enter on C. Sant Pío V. Gardens open every day.)* You don't have to be a horticulturist to appreciate the **Jardín Botànic,** a botanical garden that cultivates 43,000 plants of 300 international species, including cacti and tropical palm trees. Benches and friendly felines line the winding paths. *(C. Quart, 80, on the western end of Río Turia near Gran Vía Fernando el Católico. M: Turia. Go left out of the Po. de Pechina, exit down Gran Vía, and take a left onto C. Quart. ☎963 15 68 17; www.uv.es/jardibotanic. Open Tu-Su May-Aug. 10am-9pm; Sept. and Apr. 10am-8pm; Oct. and Mar. 10am-7pm; Nov.-Feb. 10am-6pm. Closed Dec. 25 and Jan. 1. €0.60.)*

STRUMMING SAVVY

I am a musician, but it was not an easy decision to bring my guitar to Spain. Would it look like a Picasso by the end of the trip? But I decided to take my chances. If you too want to make a musical pilgrimage, here's how to travel like the minstrel you truly are.

Spare change? You know you're going to play anyway, so stake out a spot on the sidewalk and plop down a hat for tips. American pop and jazz standards are popular in Spain, and if you sing in English people will stop to listen.

Get help from hostels. Almost all hostels allow luggage storage after check-out—use it.

Buses. Several times, I could almost hear my guitar gently weeping under a mountain of carelessly heaped luggage in the underbelly of the bus. If there's an extra seat, see if the driver will let you bring it onboard. If not, wait until everyone else has loaded their heavy suitcases, then gently place your guitar on top for a safe ride.

Flamenco. While you're in Spain, learn about its musical traditions. Most major cities offer flamenco guitar lessons—take a little Spanish rhythm home with you.

I have spent eight weeks in Las Islas Baleares, the Costa Blanca, and the Costa del Sol, playing in clubs and on the street. Luckily, my guitar has survived like a champ—and the sounds of my spicy Spanish adventure have been incorporated into its strings.

—Jessica Righthand

OTHER SIGHTS. The **Museo Taurino de Valencia** offers a permanent exhibition of Valencian *tauromachia* and a peek inside the formidable 13,000-seat bullfighting arena, the **Plaza de Toros.** *(C. Xàtiva, Open Tu-Su 10am-8pm.)* Valencia's **Palau de Música** is one of the world's premier concert halls, hosting local orchestras, national and international soloists, and jazz bands. *(Bus #35 runs from Pl. del Ajuntament. Po. de la Alameda, 30. ☎963 37 50 20; www.palauvalencia.com. Ticket window open daily 10:30am-1:30pm and 5:30-9pm.)*

NIGHTLIFE

Use your *siesta* wisely; Valencia's nightlife is rigorous. Bars, pubs, and courtyards start to fill up around midnight around **Plaza de la Virgen and Calle de Caballeros,** which hosts veritable tides of gung-ho club-hoppers into the wee hours. Follow the street to **Plazas Tossal** and **Collado,** where outdoor terraces, tall-windowed pubs, upbeat music, and *Agua de Valencia* (the region's famed alcoholic beverage) energize the masses. A lively local crowd frequents bars along C. Quart. The gay and lesbian scene centers on **Calle Quart** and **Plaza Vicente Iborra.**

Discotecas, which are quite empty until at least 1:30 or 2am, dominate the university area, particularly on **Avinguda Blasco Ibáñez.** There are a few calmer pubs with dancing around most of the main plazas. For more info, consult the *Qué y Dónde* weekly magazine (€0.50) or the weekly entertainment supplement, Valencia City (€0.50), both available at newsstands and tourist offices. Check out the free monthly *24/7 Valencia*, available in most internet cafes and tourist booths, for new hot spots.

L'umbracle Terraza, Av. de Saler, 5 (☎963 31 97 45; www.umbracleterraza.com). Located outside in the garden parallel to the Ciudad de las Artes y las Ciencias, this is the perfect setting to view Valencia's newest architectural gems in their illuminated splendor. Giant pink bubbles and couch-beds line the garden paths. 4 different bars, dancing, and hookah make this a truly luxe experience. If it gets chilly, head down to **Mya,** the discoteca below. Cover €15. Open April-Sept. M-Sa 11:30pm-late.

Akuarela, Pub: C. Juan Llorens, 49, disco: Eugenia Viñes, 152 (☎963 85 93 85), in Pl. Malvarossa; you'll probably need to take a moped, car, or taxi. Giant, but remarkably tasteful, discoteca. 4 rooms, each with own bar, and an enormous terrace replete with plush VIP seating. Salsa, top 40, and Valencia's own music from the 80s and 90s echo until dawn in these glam halls. Cover free with purchase of €7 or more at the pub; otherwise Th-Sa €13, 3am €16. Pub open daily 6pm-3:30am. Discoteca open daily midnight-7:30am.

Cafe Negrito, Pl. Negrito, 1 (☎963 91 42 33). A bold little cafe in a charming courtyard a few blocks from the Basilica. Dozens of silver tables, inside and out, fill quickly with revelers starting off the night right. Wide selection of reasonably priced drinks. Jar of *Agua de Valencia* €7. Open daily 3pm-3am. Cash only.

Radio City, C. Santa Teresa, 19 (☎963 91 41 51; www.radiocityvalencia.com). Popular bar and discoteca well suited for casual barhopping or wild dancing on the dark dance floor. Psychedelic lighting effects. Young, high-energy crowd. Order a beer (€2) or mixed drink (€6 and up) from 1 of 3 different bars. Tu flamenco at 11pm. New music and dance/theater performances M-F. Open daily 7:30pm-3:30am.

Bolsería Café, C. Bolsería, 41 (☎963 91 89 03; www.bolseriavalencia.com). Boisterous, beautiful people of all ages pack into this upscale, creatively constructed cafe-bar with floor-to-ceiling windows. Smaller terraces upstairs. Drinks €4-6. Free *Agua de Valencia* before 12:30am. M salsa, 1 drink minimum consumption; W "Americana." Cover Sa €8; includes 1 drink. Open daily 7:30pm-3:30am. MC/V.

Fox Congo, C. Caballeros, 35 (☎963 91 85 67). Walls and poles of welded metal glint under the light of the bar. Draws large crowds of hostel-dwellers and trendy locals. As in all places known to be frequented by travelers, stay alert for theft. T hip-hop nights. Beer €4. Mixed drinks €7. Cover Sa €10; includes 1 drink. Open Tu-Sa 8pm-3:30am.

Murray Club, Av. Blasco Ibáñez, 111 (☎963 71 65 96). An eclectic crowd of students and locals with impressive stamina rock out to a mix of house, 80s, and rock. Pop-art-decorated walls. Plan to stay a while if you make the trek. Festa Brasileira Tu night; Murray Rock Night Th. Cover M-Th and Su €6, F-Sa €9; includes 1 drink. Open daily 1:30-7am.

H_2ORANGE. *Agua de Valencia* is Valencia's ubiquitous drink. Any bartender will make you a pitcher, but each concoction is a slightly different mix of orange juice, *cava,* and various other liquids and liquors, usually rum or champagne. The result can be very potent, and at many clubs it's the cheapest mixed drink on the menu. Go easy!

BEACHES

On sunny weekends in Valencia, azure waters meet a sea of beach umbrellas planted in the fine, cream-colored sand. A wide boardwalk connecting the enormous beach is ideal for sun-drenched walks and bike rides. **Avenida del Puerto** has a direct bike path from the riverbed to the port, site of the 2007 America's Cup. From here, the beach is only a few blocks north. Buses #20, 21, and 22 all stop nearby and take about 15min. from the center of town. The boardwalk connects the most heavily populated beach, **Las Arenas,** to the popular **La Malvarossa.** Equally crowded but more attractive is Salér, a smooth stretch of pebbled beach 14km from the city that divides a lagoon from the sea. Cafeterias and snack bars line the shore. The **Autocares Herca** (☎963 49 12 50) bus goes to **Salér** (on the way to El Perello; 30min., every hr. 7am-9pm, €1-1.10 depending on destination) from the intersection of Gran Vía de Germanías and C. Sueca. To get to the bus stop, exit the train station and take a right down C. Xàtiva, then turn right onto C. Ruzafa to Gran Vía. Look for a yellow MetroBus post. The ride to Salér can be jammed on weekends. Plan on a day for a worthwhile trip. For a better beach experience, hop the bus or train to **Dénia** (p. 314).

FESTIVALS

Valencia's most famous festival is **Las Fallas** (Mar. 12-19), which features *ninots* (gigantic puppets), gunpowder, and bonfires. During **Semana Santa** in April, monks reenact biblical scenes and children perform the plays of Sant Vicent Ferrer. **Our Lady of the Forsaken** (May 11) entails masses of worshippers bearing a famous effigy of the Virgin Mary from the basilica to Valencia's main cathedral. **Corpus Christi,** usually held in June, is a week-long parade of *valencianos* dressing as religious characters to reenact scenes from the Old and New Testament. The **Festiu de Juliol,** in July, brings fireworks, concerts, bullfights, and a *batalla dels flors* (battle of flowers), when young girls in carriages blanket the streets with flowers. October 9 celebrates both lovers and the conquest of Valencia by James I in 1238. On that day, Valencia's coat of arms is paraded and hoisted outside the *Ajuntament.*

DAYTRIPS FROM VALENCIA

L'ALBUFERA

The park is a 40min. (17km) bus ride from Valencia on either the tourist bus, which picks up in Pl. de la Reina, or Autocares Herca (☎963 49 12 50), which leaves from Gran Vía Germanías at the intersection of C. Sueca every hr. 7am-9pm. It is the same bus that goes to Saler. To get to the bus stop, exit the train station, take a right down C. Xativa, and turn right onto C. Ruzafa. Follow it until you reach Gran Via de Germanias. Cross to the other side of the road and walk down to C. Sueca on your right hand side. The bus stop is marked with a yellow post that reads "Metro Bus" (€1). To catch the return bus, walk with your back to the lagoon and cross the bridge on your right. The bus stop is outside the local high school. If you turn left out of the park and catch a bus going the other way, it will continue to El Palmar and then turn around; this route will afford a short tour of the countryside and surrounding towns. Buses don't come very often. Flag down the bus driver at the Herca sign.

Spain's largest lagoon, L'Albufera, and the surrounding Parc Natural de L'Albufera are a nature-lover's paradise. Approved as a natural reserve in 1986, trails for biking and hiking ring the lake (6km in diameter) while small fishing boats hide amid tall wetland reeds. L'Albufera is a prime spot for birdwatching—over 250 migratory species make temporary camps along its shores and, and it was declared a special protection zone for birds (ZEPA) due to its importance to their nesting habits. The three central components of the park are the lake, the marsh and rice paddies, and the dunes, which are of special concern with regard to environmental preservation. Make sure to inquire about water levels before you go—in summer months or periods of drought, the lagoon can look underwhelming and attracts many more mosquitoes. Take a small wood boat out into the calm waters and relax your tired limbs as a glorious sunset settles over the lagoon. Ask at a Valencia tourist office (p. 294) for information on boat tours and excursions.

JÁTIVA (XÀTIVA)

Cercanías (☎902 24 02 02; www.renfe.com/empresa/cercanias) runs from Valencia to Xàtiva (47min., every 30min. 5:38am-10:33pm, €3.05; return 1-4 per hr. 5:38am-10:28pm). To reach the old village and the tourist office from the train station, walk up Baixada de l'Estació and follow signs to the left when it ends at Av. Jaime.

Xàtiva bears few marks of tourism and brings a unique splash of color and culture to the region. It hosts a slew of churches and ruins that date from 30,000 BC and was also the birthplace of Pope Alexander VI (1431-1503). Xàtiva was burned to the ground by Felipe V in 1707, and reconstruction began the year after. Save time to explore the impeccably restored **castle,** which has seen a host of occupants and incorporates Moorish and Roman influences. A patio near the entrance booth provides an impressive panorama over the town to the mountains of Grossa beyond and divides the two sections of the castle: the **castell machor** and **castell chicotet.** The former, used from the 13th through the 16th centuries, bears the scars of sieges and earthquakes. Its vaulted **prison** has held famous wrongdoers, including Fernando el Católico and the Comte d'Urgell, a would-be usurper of the Aragonese throne who is buried in the castle. The prison's garden also contains the shields and histories of its prisoners. Streets become narrower, steeper, and more residential closer to the castle. (Castle open Tu-Su Apr.-Oct. 10am-7pm; Tu-Su Nov.-Mar. 10am-6pm. €2.10, under 18 €1.10. Tu afternoons free.) The spectacular vistas from the walk up to the castle are worth the 30min. walk. For those who didn't bring your walking shoes, a small four-car train chugs up the road from the tourist office. (1:30, 4:30pm; €4). To navigate the town, use the **Basilica de Santa Maria,** also labeled the Iglesia Colegial, as a landmark. This behemoth was begun in 1612, but not finished until the early 20th century. (Mass M-Sa 10am, 8pm, Su 10:30am, 1, 8pm. Museum open Tu-Sa 10:30am-1pm, Su 11:30am-1pm. €1.)

Budget accommodations are difficult to come by in this quiet and untouristed town. **Hotel Murta ❹,** Angel Lacalle, close to the *casco antiguo* on the other side of Av. Jaime, has lovely views and large, clean rooms. (☎962 27 66 11; www.hotelmurta.com. Open year-round. Doubles €43. MC/V.) Streets in the *casco antiguo* are poorly marked, so have plenty of Spanish phrases handy and plan on getting lost once or twice. To relax, have a drink outside at the marble tables of **El Tiradoret ❷,** Pl. del Mercat, 10, or get out of the heat and take a seat at one of the many indoor tables, each with its own—albeit purely ornamental—beer fountain. (☎962 27 63 54. Beer €1.20. Open daily 8am-2am. MC/V.) Since 1250, the **Fira de Xàtiva** festival has stormed the city from August 14-20, featuring live music, theater, bullfights, and huge ceramics and livestock fairs. The **tourist office** is at Alameda Jaume I, 50. (☎962 27 33 46; www.xativa.es. English spoken. Open Tu-F 10am-2:30pm, Sa-Su 10am-2pm.)

CASTELLÓN (CASTELLÓ) ☎964

As the halfway point between Valencia and Barcelona, Castelló (pop. 162,000) can easily seem like little more than a transportation hub or stopover. But set foot in its peaceful parks, chic shops, bustling plazas, and expansive beaches, and you might begin to think otherwise. Home to the large Universidad de Jaime I, this fast-paced and fast-growing city is popular with budget travelers and students; many enjoy Castelló without making a dent in their wallet.

TRANSPORTATION. The combined **train** and **bus** station is on Av. Pintor Oliet, between the university and a 20min. walk to the center of the town. Castelló is most easily reached by train from Valencia, as RENFE **Cercanías** trains run there frequently (1hr., 1-4 per hr. 6:10am-10:30pm, €4). **RENFE** (☎902 24 02 02; www.renfe.es) trains run to: **Barcelona** (2hr., 16 per day 6:06am-9:35pm, €28-34); **Granada** (9hr.; 10:36am, 11:59pm; €49.30); **Málaga** (11hr.; 10:36am, 11:59pm; €54-73.50); Murcia (3hr., 3 per day 2:30pm-7:41pm, €30.20). **ALSA** (☎902 42 22 42) sends buses to: **Alicante** (5hr., 4 per day 3:35am-5pm, €20); **Almería** (9-10hr.; 11:20am, 1pm, 10:50pm; €39-47); **Barcelona** (4-5hr., 6 per day 2:45am-6:20pm, €19-37); **Gandía** (3-4hr.; 9:40, 10:50pm; €10); **Murcia** (6-7hr., 5 per day 11:35am-10:50pm, €22.46); **Sevilla** (11hr., 10:50pm, €61). **Auto-Res** (☎902 02 09 99) goes to **Madrid** (5hr., 5 per day 6:45am-11:45pm, €27). **Autos Mediterráneo** (☎964 22 00 54) departs for **Morella** (2hr.; M-F 8:15am, 3:15pm, Sa 1:15pm; €8) and other towns in the Castellón province. Bus times and pickup locations change throughout the year. Municipal **bus #9** runs from the train station to Pl. Borrul in the center every

10min. (€0.85). For **taxis,** call **Radio Taxi** (☎964 22 74 74) or **Tele Taxi** (☎964 25 46 46). **Bikes** can be rented from the university (☎964 73 08 30).

ORIENTATION AND PRACTICAL INFORMATION. The city center is the Pl. Mayor, and contains the orange-colored **Ayuntamiento,** the **Catedral de Santa María,** and the **Mercado Central.** Po. Morella is a straight shot from the train station, through the tranquil, shady paths of **Parque Ribalt,** and becomes the plaza's northern border when it turns into C. Colon. C. Trinidad and C. Enmedio are excellent options for exploring the town, finding a place to stay, or shopping. **Avenida Mar** and **Avenida Hermanos Bou** both have bike lanes and run to the port, 4km east of the town center. Just north of the port stretches the **Parque del Pinar.** Most services, including **banks** and **ATMs,** can be found in and around the Pl. Mayor. The **tourist office** is a few blocks north from Pl. Mayor at the tip of the **Plaza de María Agustina.** (☎964 35 86 88; www.castellonturismo.com. Open July-Aug. M-F 9am-7pm, Sa 10am-2pm; Sept.-June M-F 9am-2pm and 4-7pm, Sa 10am-2pm.) There is another **branch** at the port on Po. Buenavista, 28. (☎902 20 31 30. Open Tu-Th 10:30am-2:30pm, F-Sa 10:30am-2:30pm and 5-7pm.) The **Hospital General** can be reached at ☎964 72 65 00 or www.gva.es. (**24hr. health- care** assistance ☎900 16 11 61.) The **post office,** in Pl. Tetuán, can be reached at ☎900 50 60 70 or 964 34 03 87. (Open M-F 8:30am-8:30pm, Sa 9:30am-1pm.) **Postal Code:** 12003.

ACCOMMODATIONS AND FOOD. Budget accommodations are hard to come by in Castelló; still, there are other options available besides the expensive hotels across from the train station. **Hostal Corte ❸,** C. Trinidad 23, is a new establishment. Each room has TV, air-conditioning, and a full bathroom. (☎964 22 96 07. Open year-round. Singles €35; doubles €45. MC/V.)

Buy fresh fruit and snacks at the **Mercat Central,** and enjoy the orange groves of the Parque de Ribalta. Around dinner, activity shifts to the **Grau** (port), where seafood restaurants line Pl. de la Mar. For those who opt to stay in the main city, the busy **Avenida Rey Don Jaime** is the best bet for restaurants. Tapas bars and a youthful crowd center around Pl. Santa Clara. Around the port, **Meduse ❷,** Po. Buenavista, 31, has a funky, modern atmosphere and a creative selection of *valenciano* seafood and vegetarian dishes. Try the delicious moussaka. (☎964 06 34 40. Salads and tapas €1-8. Entrees €6-12. Music and art shows every Sa night at midnight; ask for a schedule. Open summer daily 7pm-last customer. Cash only.) C. Lagasca is lined with late-night bars and hangout spots.

SIGHTS. Castelló's cultural hub is the Pl. Mayor, where the freestanding belltower **Torre Campanario de Fadrií,** built between the 15th and 18th centuries and exhibiting both Gothic and Renaissance features, stands 58m tall. (Free.) Next door is the **Concatedral de Santa Maria,** a towering Gothic site built in the 12th century and reconstructed after a fire left it in ruins in the 14th. (☎964 22 34 63. Open daily 7:30am-1pm and 5-8pm. Free.) About 2km northeast of the city center, on Partida la Plana, is the **Basilica Santa Maria de Lledo,** dedicated to the patron saint of the city. (☎ 964 22 04 82. Free.) The lush **Parque de Ribalta** and the neighboring **Plaza de Toros,** which still hosts bullfights during festivals, are worth a mid-afternoon stroll. Toward the port, the avant-garde **Espai D'Art Contemporani de Castelló,** C. Prim, features rotating exhibits of contemporary artists. (☎964 72 35 40. Open Tu-Su 10am-8pm. Guided tours Sa 7pm. Free.) One of Castelló's most attractive modern buildings is the **Museu de Bellas Artes,** C. Hermanos Bou, 28, a 7min. walk from the city center. Bus #4 also runs there from Pl. Bou. The museum offers two floors of 16th- to 19th-century sculptures, ceramics, and paintings, including an impressive collection of works by Castilian painter Gabriel Puig Roda. (☎964 72 75 00; www.culturalcas.com. Open Tu-Sa 10am-8pm, Su 10am-2pm. Free.)

BEACHES. Castelló's **Grau** (port), 4km east of the city between the Ave. del Mar and Av. Hermanos Bou, is a unique, self-contained scene. Buses run from Pl. Borrul to the port and the beaches (every 15min. in summer, €0.80). Surrounding the port is the **Plaça del Mar,** which houses dozens of restaurants and pubs, as well as a small shopping center. A 10-15min. walk north (left when facing the ocean) along Ave. Ferrandis Salvador leads to **El Pinar,** a giant park filled with pines and picnic tables, parallel to the soft sands of **Playa del Pinar.** Farther north are **Playa del Gurugú, Playa del Serradal,** and the family-friendly **Benicassim.** All are fairly crowded, and for good reason, considering their impressive breadth of smooth sands, sparkling waters, and sports facilities. **Playa del Gurugú** was a 2006 recipient of the EU's Bandera Azul, for outstanding beach quality. The **Paseo Buena Vista** runs from the port to the border of El Pinar, while the **Paseo Marítimo** hugs the shoreline. If you're hungry, check out **Dunes Beach Club,** a small snack shack close to the Planetarium on Playa del Pinar. Tapas, *bocadillos,* salads, and combo plates (€3-5) are available as well as alcoholic and non-alcoholic drinks for only €2-5. (Open daily. Cash only.)

MORELLA ☎964

Rising majestically above a fertile valley below, the medieval fortress town of Morella (pop. 2800) is an isolated and idyllic find in the northernmost extremes of the Comunitat Valenciana. The ride to Morella is an experience unto itself, as trees filled with cherries and small, clustered *pueblos* dot the hills along the serpentine highway. With cobblestone streets, medieval walls, and a castle crowning its highest point, Morella draws in visitors with romantic vistas and small-town charm. The people you see here are likely to be residents, and prices are generally low enough to allow for a guilt-free and enjoyable stay.

TRANSPORTATION AND PRACTICAL INFORMATION. Morella is hard to reach. Most visitors arrive via Valencia, though the city is also accessible from Barcelona. Travelers coming from Valencia on the **Cercanías** train line must make a bus connection at **Castelló** (Cercanías to Castelló 1hr., 1-4 per hr. 5:11am-9:30pm, €4). From Barcelona, the **RENFE** Mediterranean goes to Castelló (2hr., 16 per day 7am-9:30pm, €17.50-33). Autos Mediterráneo (☎964 22 05 36) departs from the bus stop outside of Castelló's train station for Morella (2hr.; M-F 8:30am, 3:30pm, Sa 1:30pm; return M-F 8:05am, 3:45pm, Sa 8:15am; €7.15.) Always call the day before to confirm bus schedules, as they change frequently and often unexpectedly. Arrive at the bus station at least 10min. before the expected departure time. In Morella, the bus drops you off either at the Pta. de San Miguel or at the Torre Beneito, on C. Muralla. Morella's **tourist office,** Pl. San Miguel, is through the archway. (☎964 17 30 32; www.morella.net. Open Tu-Sa 10am-2pm and 4-7pm, Su 10am-2pm.) For **medical assistance,** call ☎964 16 09 62. **Internet** access is at **Ciberlocutori Nou,** C. Sant Juliá, 2. (☎964 16 05 11; €0.50 per 15min. Open daily 10am-2pm and 5:30-9:30pm.)

ACCOMMODATIONS AND FOOD. Once you pass through the Gothic archways of Morella, you may never want to leave. Fortunately, most lodgings here offers luxury standards at budget prices. Live royally at **Hotel El Cid ❸,** Portal Sant Mateu, 3, a block to the right of the bus stop when facing the city wall. Gigantic, gleaming rooms come with a colorful plush bedspread, TV, phone, and full bath, and some have balconies with phenomenal views of the countryside. (☎964 16 01 25; www.hotelelcidmorella.com. Breakfast €4. Singles from €29.50; doubles from €50.50. MC/V.) **Hostal La Muralla ❷,** C. Muralla, 12, has large, bright rooms with TV, private bath, and charming Spanish decor. (☎964 16 02 43; www.hostalmuralla.com. TV lounge. Breakfast included. Doubles in high season €46; low season €40. MC/V.)

The town's local specialty is *trufas* (truffles) dug out of the local turf. Specialties include *paté de trufas* and *cordero relleno trufado* (truffle-stuffed lamb). Most eateries are located on C. Don Blasco de Alagón, Morella's main street, with outdoor seating areas enclosed by ancient columns and looming overhangs. Pastries from Castellón's excellent bakeries are a cheap morning option if you are catching a bus from there to Morella (around €1.50). At **Restaurante Casa Roque ❸,** Cuesta San Juan, 1, a giant boar's head watches over the sophisticated dining room. It's not the cheapest option, but definitely worth it. (☎964 16 03 36; www.casaroque.com. Entrees €9-19. *Menú del día* €10.70. Fixed dinner *menú* €26. Open Apr.-Dec. Tu-Sa 1:30-3:30pm and 9-10:30pm, Su 1:30-4pm; Jan.-Mar. closed Tu and W nights. AmEx/D/MC/V.)

SIGHTS. Perched atop a massive rocky plateau, the **Castell de Morella** impresses with its rich history and lovely pathways. Celts, Romans, and Moors have all defended Morella's walls as their own. El Cid stormed the summit in 1084, and Don Blasco de Alagón took the town in the name of Jaume I in 1232. Civil wars in the 19th century damaged the castle but added to its intrigue. Inspect the **Cadro guardhouse** and the eerie **Catxo dungeon,** where the prince of Viana was imprisoned in the 15th century. The highest point, the **Patio de Armas,** provides chilling views of the ancient city through perfectly preserved stone arches. (Entrance at the end of C. Hospital, uphill from the basílica. Open June-Sept. 11am-7pm; Oct.-May 11am-5pm. €2, students and seniors €1.50.) In Pl. Arciprestal, on the way to the castle, the ceiling of the Gothic **Basílica Santa María la Mayor** hovers over an intricate stairwell, a gilded organ installed in 1717, and the ghostly statue of Nuestra Señora de la Asunción. Bracketed by gold-plated chandeliers, the altar is just as breathtaking as the basilica's stained-glass windows. The adjoining museum has the same schedule as the basilica and houses a collection of religious paintings. (Open June-Aug. M-Sa 11am-2pm and 4-6pm; Sept.-May Tu-Su noon-2pm and 4-6pm. Mass M-F 7pm, Sa 8:15pm; Su 10am, 5, 6:30pm. Free. Museum €1.70.) For great views of both the countryside and the castle, stop by the **Mirador de la Plaza Colón** at the end of C. Blasco de Alagón. To see the remnants of the Gothic **aqueduct,** exit the city through the enormous **Portal de San Miguel,** turn left, and walk straight for 5min.

COSTA BLANCA

The "White Coast," named for the color of the fine sand and smooth pebbles that cover its shores, extends from Dénia to Alicante. Jagged mountains, jutting piers, pine forests, cactus-studded rock, and hills covered with cherry trees provide the backdrop for the towns of the Costa Blanca, all of which attract their fair share of tourists. The slower-paced towns of Altea and Dénia, visited primarily for sparkling beaches, each have a small *casco antiguo* surrounded by supermarkets, resort hotels, and construction sites. Nevertheless, they may offer relief from the disco droves that energize Alicante and Benidorm, making them ideal for families or travelers seeking more tranquil locales. These smaller towns are fast becoming havens for those seeking classy beach vacations, and waterfront hotels come at steep prices; many prefer to spend the night in Ali-

Alicante
ACCOMMODATIONS
Hostal Les Monges Palace, 10
Hostal Pensión La Milagrosa, 15
Pensión Alicante San Nicolas, 7
Pensión Versalles, 14
FOOD
El Buen Comer, 3
Kebap, 12
Taberna Ibérica, 9
La Tagliatella, 13
Restaurant Villahelmy, 11
NIGHTLIFE
Artespiritu, 1
Astrónomo, 6
Café de la Sal, 2
Café Directo, 16
Celestial Copas, 5
El Coscorrón, 4
Glass Club, 8
Casco Antiguo
MEDITERRANEAN SEA
Puerto
SANTA CRUZ
SAN ROQUE
Parque de la Ereta
Castell de Santa Bárbara
Castillo de San Fernando
Ermita de Santa Cruz
Museu de Arte del Siglo XX La Asegurada
Museo de Bellas Artes
Santa María
Concatedral de San Nicolás
Mercado Central
Teatro Principale
Portal de Elche
Estación Marina
Estación Término
El Corte Inglés
Palacio Provincial
Mercadona
Deshoras
IVAJ
Elevator to Castell
SEE INSET
Rambla Méndez Núñez
Av. de la Constitución
Av. Alfonso X el Sabio
Av. Federico Soto
Av. Dr. Gadea
Av. Maisonnave
Av. de la Estación
Av. de Salamanca
Av. Oscar Esplá
Av. Jovellanos
Av. Juan Bautista la Fora
Playa del Postiguet
P. Explanada d'Espanya
P. Conde Vallellano
TO BENIDORM (31km), DÉNIA (91km), PLAYA MUTXAVISTA (4km), PLAYA SAN JUAN (3km), VALENCIA (166km)
TO HOSPITAL GENERAL DE ALICANTE (200m)
TO MARQ (100m)
TO MARINA DEPORTIVA (50m).
TO ISLA TABARCA
TO (11km)
0 200 meters
0 200 yards

cante or Benidorm and daytrip all over the coast. Fortunately, cheap, efficient modes of transportation make this an easy option.

TRANSPORTATION

Trains: Ferrocarrils de la Generalitat Valenciana (☎965 92 02 02, in Alicante 26 27 31), also known as the "Costa Blanca Express," hits almost every town and beach along the coast on its Alicante-Dénia line. Switch from train to tram (or vice versa) at the **El Campello** station. From the central TRAM Mercado stop in Alicante, trains run to: **Altea** (1½hr., every hr. 5:44am-8:44pm, €4.20); **Benidorm** (1¼hr.; every hr. 5:44am-8:44pm, €3.40); **Calpe** (1hr., every hr. 5:44am-7:44pm, €4.90); **Dénia** (2½hr., every hr. 5:44am-7:44pm, €7.30). Trains return to: **Alicante** from **Dénia** (every hr., 6:20am-8:20pm); **Calpe** (every hr., 6:59am-8:59pm); **Altea** (every hr., 6:16am-9:16pm); and **Benidorm** (every hr. 6:29am-9:29pm). **Tramsnochador** (☎965 26 27 31), the night train from Alicante, runs in July and Aug. to **Dénia** and **Benidorm.**

Buses: ALSA (☎902 42 22 42) runs between **Alicante** and **Valencia,** stopping in towns along the Costa Blanca. From Valencia buses run to: **Alicante** (2-4hr., 12-20 per day 4:45am-9:45pm, €17.15-20); **Benidorm** (2-4hr., 15-18 per day 4:45am-9:45pm, €13.35-15.75); **Calpe/Altea** (2-4hr., 8-10 per day 6am-5pm, €11); **Dénia** (2-3hr., 11-12 per day 6am-10:45pm, €10.10); **Gandía** (1hr., 9-15 per day 6am-9:45pm, €6.10); **Xàbia/Javea** (2-3hr., 6 per day 6:30am-8pm, €9.45). From Alicante buses run to: **Benidorm** (1hr., 1-4 per hr., €3.80); **Altea** (1hr.; 10 per day 7am-7pm, Sa 6 per day 7am-8pm, Su 8 per day 7am-7pm; €4.50); **Calpe** (1hr.; M-F 10 per day 7am-7pm, Sa 6 per day 7am-8pm, Su 8 per day 7am-7pm; €6); **Dénia** (2½-3hr.; M-F 12 per day 7am-8:10pm, Sa 9 per day 7am-9pm, Su 11 per day 7am-8pm, €9.35); **Valencia** (2½hr., 1-3 per hr. 6:30am-9pm, €17.15-20);

ALICANTE (ALACANT) ☎965

Alicante (pop. 322,000) is a city with verve. Though its wild bars, crowded beaches, and busy streets seem decidedly modern, the looming castle-topped crag, 14th-century churches, and marble esplanades declare otherwise. Alicante, once the Roman city Lucentum, is home to the remains of a fifth-century Iberian settlement. Though it is undoubtedly a traditional Spanish city, it has that extra spark of energy—the locals are friendly, and the nightlife is lively.

TRANSPORTATION

Flights: Aeroport Internacional de El Altet (☎966 91 91 00 or 966 91 94 00; www.aena.es), 11km south of the city center. **Iberia** (☎902 40 05 00) and **Air Europa** (☎902 40 15 01) have daily flights to **Madrid, Barcelona,** and the **Islas Baleares,** among other destinations. **British Midland Airways** (☎902 11 13 33) flies to **London. Alcoyana** (☎965 26 84 00) bus #C-6 runs to the airport from Pl. Luceros (every 40min., €1.10). Buses also leave from Pl. Puerta Mar.

Trains: RENFE, Estación Término (☎902 24 02 02; www.renfe.es), on Av. de Salamanca. Info open daily 7am-midnight. To: **Barcelona** (4-6hr., 5-6 per day 6:55am-6:20pm, €44.50-49.30); **Elx** (30min., every hr. 6:05am-10:05pm, €1.85); **Madrid** (4hr., 4-8 per day 7am-8pm, €39.90 and up); **Valencia** (1hr., 3-4 per day 6:55am-8:45pm, €12.25-25.60). **Cercanías** runs to **Murcia** (1hr., every hr. 6:05am-10:05pm, €4.30). **Ferrocarrils de la Generalitat Valenciana (TRAM),** Estació Marina, Av. Villajoyosa, 2 (☎900 72 04 72; www.fgvalicante.com), by the Mercado Central, has service along the Costa Blanca. In summer, the **Tramsnochador** runs to beaches including **Altea** and **Benidorm,** with some continuing to **Dénia** (every hr. 11:25pm-4:55am, €1.20-5.55).

Buses: C. Portugal, 17 (☎965 13 07 00; www.alicante-ayto.es/trafico). **ALSA** (☎902 42 22 42 or 965 98 50 03 for booking; www.alsa.es) sends buses to: **Altea** (1hr., 10 per day 7am-7pm, Sa 6 per day 7am-8pm, Su 8 per day 7am-7pm, €4.50); **Barcelona** (9hr., 8 per day 4:30am-11:30pm, €39.27-44.44); **Benidorm** (1hr., 1-4 per hr. 6:30am-10:30pm, €3.80); **Calp** (2-3hr.; M-F 10 per day 7am-7pm, Sa 6 per day 7am-8pm, Su 8 per day 7am-7pm; €6); **Dénia** (2½-3hr.; M-F 12 per day 7am-8:10pm, Sa 9 per day 7am-9pm, Su 11 per day 7am-8pm; €9.35); **Granada** (6hr., 7 per day 11:36am-3am, €26.69-32.55); **Madrid** (5hr., 12-15 per day 8:45am-1:45am, €26.27-36); **Málaga** (7hr., 7 per day 2:20am-11:45pm, €35.90-43.60); **Sevilla** (10hr., 11:45pm, €46.49); **Valencia** (2½hr., 1-3 per hr. 6:30am-9pm, €17.15-20); **Xàbia/Javea** (2½hr., 5-8 per day 7am-8pm, €8.35). **Mollá** (☎965 26 84 00) runs buses to **Elx** (30min.; M-F 2 per hr. 6:45am-10:15pm, Sa every hr. 8am-10pm, Su 8 per day 9am-9:30pm; €1.70).

Public Transportation: TAM-Alicante Metropolitan Transport (☎965 14 09 36 or 900 72 04 72; www.subus.es). Buses #21 and 22 run from near the train station in Alicante to Playa San Juan (€1.10).

Taxis: Teletaxi (☎965 10 16 11), **RadioTaxi** (☎965 25 25 11).

VALENCIA AND MURCIA

ORIENTATION AND PRACTICAL INFORMATION

Trains to Alicante from the Costa Blanca arrive at the **TRAM station,** located next to the Mercado Central at the top of Rambla Méndez Núñez. This street, affectionately known as La Rambla, borders the *casco antiguo* and is full of **ATMs,** bus stops, and restaurants. All other trains arrive at the train station, which is toward the city outskirts at the end of **Avenida de la Estación,** which becomes Pl. Luceros. **Avenida Federico Soto** runs toward the beach, perpendicular to Pl. Luceros, which turns into Av. Doctor Gadea. Continuing through Pl. Luceros to **Avenida Alfonso X el Sabio** brings you to the TRAM station, and a right turn just beyond the market puts you on **La Rambla.** The *casco antiguo* is charming; its restaurant-filled plazas and quirky, hidden nooks provide a pleasant contrast to the city's expansive, crowded beaches. Nearly 2km in length and decorated with brilliant red marble only found near Alicante, the **Explanada d'Espanya** traverses the port and links the **Parque de las Canalejas** to the beach.

Tourist Office: Municipal office, C. Portugal, 17, by the bus station (☎965 92 98 02; www.alicanteturismo.com). English spoken. Open M-F 9am-2pm and 5-8pm, Sa 10am-2pm. **Regional office,** Rambla Méndez Núñez, 23 (☎965 20 00 00). Open M-F 9am-8pm, Sa 10am-8pm, Su 10am-2pm. **Branch** at Playa San Juan, on Av. de Niza, open in summer. **Airport branch** (☎965 28 50 11) open M 9am-3pm, Tu-F 9am-8pm, Sa 10am-8pm. Other branches by the train station and on the Explanada d'Espanya.

Budget Travel: IVAJ (Institut Valencia de la Juventud), Rambla Méndez Núñez, 41 (☎966 47 81 09; www.ivaj.es.) HI card €10.80. Open M-F 9am-2pm.

Luggage Storage: At the **bus station** €4-8 per bag. Open 8am-9pm).

English-Language Bookstore: FNAC (☎96 601 01 06), just by the train station on Ave. de la Estacion, 5. Open M-Sa 10am-10pm, Su noon-10pm.

Police: Av. Julian Bestero 15. Open 8am-3pm. **Comisaría,** C. Médico Pascual Pérez, 27 (☎965 10 72 00 or 092).

Hospital: Hospital General, C. Maestro Alonso, 109 (☎965 93 83 00).

Red Cross: ☎965 25 25 25.

Internet Access: Well-equipped internet centers are surprisingly hard to come by in Alicante. Though there are a few *locutorios* near Pl. Portal de Elche, one of the best options is the **Internet Cafe Xplorer,** C. San Vicente, 47, (☎965 21 46 24) with 30 computers, printing, fax, Skype, and breakfast. Internet €0.70 per 30min. 1hr. internet, *bocadillo,* and drink €2.90. Open daily 10am-2am. To get there, continue on La Rambla until it turns into San Vicente after the Mercado TRAM stop.

Post Office: Bono Guarner, 2 (☎965 22 78 71). Open M-F 8:30am-8:30pm, Sa 9:30am-1pm. **Branch** on the corner of C. Arzobispo Loaces and C. Alemania (☎965 13 18 87). Open M-F 8:30am-8:30pm, Sa 9:30am-1pm. **Postal Code:** 03002.

CULTURE COMES FREE. With the exception of Alicante's outstanding archaeological museum, the MARQ, all of the major sights in Alicante—the Castell de Santa Barbara, the Concatedral de San Nicolas, the *Ayuntamiento*, the Basilica de Santa Maria, and more—are free. So store your beach bag for an afternoon and check out the views from the castle or the ornate *Ayuntamiento* without putting a dent in your wallet.

ACCOMMODATIONS

The best budget accommodations in Alicante are in the *casco antiguo*. Though quality hostels abound in this area, ensuring a room requires an early arrival or reservation. If you're not particular, finding a cheap and safe room elsewhere in Alicante is fairly easy, except during **Fogueres de Sant Joan** (June 18-25), when accommodations are booked well in advance.

Hostal Les Monges Palace, corner of C. San Agustín, 4, and C. Monjas (☎965 21 50 46; www.lesmonges.es). Ornate green exterior, equally palatial interior. A/C €5. Breakfast €4. Internet €3 per hr. Singles €30, with bath €40, with hot tub €51; doubles €42/50/66; triples €53, with bath €64. AmEx/MC/V. ❸

Hostal-Pensión La Milagrosa, C. Villavieja, 8 (☎965 21 69 18; www.hostallamilagrosa.com). Soft-colored, spacious rooms in the center of the *casco antiguo* and easy walking distance from the beach and TRAM. Some rooms have balconies with amazing views of the castle or the Iglesia de Santa Maria. Shared baths and A/C. Internet €1.70 per 30min. Laundry €2. Communal kitchen on 3rd floor. Towels and room cleaning available upon request. June-Aug. singles from €20; doubles from €30. MC/V. ❷

Pensión Alicante San Nicolás, C. San Nicolás, 14 (☎965 21 70 39, www.alicantesanicolas.com). A new, polished establishment. 7 elegant rooms in natural pinks and greens. Full English breakfast. A/C. In summer singles €30, with bath €35; doubles €42/48. In winter singles €25/30; doubles €35/42. Extra bed €15. MC/V. ❸

Pensión Versalles, C. Villavieja, 3 (☎965 21 47 93, 965 32 98 00). 12 small, quirky rooms. Fun, communal atmosphere encouraged by a casual outdoor courtyard/kitchen. Great for easygoing groups who want a place to crash. €18 per person. Cash only. ❶

FOOD

Restaurants and *kebap* stops are everywhere, though many are overpriced and on busy streets. Smaller bar/restaurants in the *casco antiguo* are often superior in atmosphere, authenticity, and value. On average, a four-course *menú del día* in the *casco antiguo* costs €9, though often a few extra euro will buy a meal of considerably higher quality. **Rambla Méndez Núñez** is full of chic, popular eateries. The port, which becomes a raucous nightlife hub as midnight nears, is littered with expensive *marisquerías*, generally of average quality. The enormous **central market** is on Av. Alfonso X el Sabio. (Open M-Sa 9am-2pm.) Buy groceries at **Mercadona,** C. Álvarez Sereix, 5 (☎965 21 58 94; open M-Sa 9am-9pm) or at **El Corte Inglés,** Av. Maisonnave, 53 (☎965 92 50 01; open daily 10am-10pm). There are smaller markets across from the **Playa de Postiguet. Deshoras** shops dot the city, a good option for late-night snacks and basic groceries; there's one at C. Bailén, 29. (☎965 21 11 42. Open 24hr.)

Restaurante Villahelmy, C. Mayor, 37 (☎965 21 25 29; www.villahelmy.com) With 2 lone tables amid a sea of patio seating in the Pl. Mayor, Villahelmy can easily go undetected. But its outrageous blue and orange interior, folkloric murals, and decorative birdcages are a far cry from ordinary. Mediterranean and Spanish cuisine, with staples like *paella* and tapas. Salads €5-9, entrees €9-14. *Menú del día* €11. Open Tu-Sa 1-4pm and 8pm-midnight, Su 1-4pm. MC/V. ❷

Kebap, Av. Dr. Gadea, 5 (☎965 14 10 20). Not all *kebaps* are created equal. This shop uses fresh ingredients and is located next to a charming plaza. For lunch, take your food to go and eat outside—a cheap alternative to *bocadillos*. Mouthwatering pitas €3.50. Entrees €5.70-9. Open daily 1pm-1am. 2nd location at C. San Fernando, 12. MC/V. ❷

El Buen Comer, C. Mayor, 8 (☎965 21 31 03; www.elbuencomer.info). A tourist favorite with an old-town, traditional ambience and patio seating. Wide selection of tapas and fresh seafood. Tapas €3.75-9.10, entrees €7.80-30. *Menú del día* €9.50. Tapas fixed menu with drink €16.60 (min. 2 people). Open daily 10am-midnight. MC/V. ❸

La Taberna Ibérica, C. Toledo, 18, at Pedro Sebastia (☎965 21 62 58; www.tabernaiberica.com), 4 blocks behind the *Ayuntamiento* in the *casco antiguo*. Owned and run by an older local couple, this cozy *bodega* and restaurant allows you to sample some of the absolute best of traditional Spanish cooking. Though the menu is fairly standard, ingredients and preparation are top-notch. Tapas €4-10. *Menú del día* €14. Cash only. ❷

La Tagliatella, C. Castaños (☎965 20 87 97; www.latagliatella.es), parallels Rambla Méndez Núñez, a few blocks from the port. A romantically decorated Italian restaurant with warm colors and an upscale ambience; outdoor seating also available on the pedestrian C. Castaños. Serves exquisite variety of gourmet salads, pastas (€11-13), risottos, scallops, and pizza (€10-12). Open daily 1pm-midnight. MC/V. ❷

SIGHTS AND BEACHES

MUSEO ARQUEOLÓGICO PROVINCIAL DE ALICANTE. The ultramodern Museo Arqueológico Provincial de Alicante (MARQ), Pl. Dr. Gomez Ulla, won European Museum of the Year in 2004, and for good reason. Impeccably lit and arranged, the museum showcases remains from the Paleolithic, Iberian, Roman, Islamic, and modern periods. Be sure to ask for the audio tour, which provides a highly dramatic musical soundtrack to accompany your visit. There are always two seasonal exhibits in addition to the permanent collection, and a sizable portion of the museum is dedicated to archaeological methods and techniques. *(Take the TRAM to the Marq stop. ☎965 14 90 00; www.marqalicante.com. Open Tu-Sa 10am-7pm, Su and festivals 10am-2pm; July-Aug Tu-Sa 11am-2pm and 6pm-midnight, Su 11am-2pm. €3, students and seniors €1.50, children and handicapped free.)*

CASTELL DE SANTA BÁRBARA. The Castell de Santa Bárbara keeps guard over Alicante's shores and provides an awe-inspiring backdrop to the *casco antiguo* (old town). The castle's drawbridges, dark passageways, and hidden tunnels date from the ninth to 17th centuries, allowing a glimpse at the many layers of history that characterize the origins of the city. At 166m tall, Santa Barbara is one of Europe's most sizeable medieval fortresses, and it boasts a dry moat, dungeon, and ammunitions storeroom. The **Albacar Vell,** constructed during the Middle Ages, holds a sculpture garden with pieces by Spanish greats. A road from the northern border of the old section of Alicante provides a walk up that is much easier than it looks; otherwise, an elevator is accessible by a tunnel on Av. Jovellanos, across from Playa Postiguet near the white pedestrian overpass. *(☎965 16 21 28 or 26 31 31. Castle open daily until* *sunset. Free. Elevator €2.40, though the elevator has been in and out of service within the past year; the Turibus, which leaves from the elevator, serves as a €2 substitute.)*

BASÍLICA DE SANTA MARIA. In the old town, the Gothic-style Basílica de Santa Maria, Alicante's oldest church, stands over the ruins of an old mosque. The neighboring **Concatedral de San Nicolas de Bari** boasts a different flavor of Baroque architecture; a 45m dome allows light to flutter into the dim enclaves of this church. The **Ayuntamiento** on the edge of the *casco antiguo* (near the port) has a stunning 18th-century facade with twisted columns and stone sculptures. The interior, decorated originally to welcome the Queen to Alicante, is, well, palatial. Portraits of all former (and current) governors are displayed on the second floor, and at the bottom of the stairs, just next to the outrageous golden Gaudí sculpture is the official marker of sea level for the nation.

BEACHES. Alicante's **Playa del Postiguet,** near the *Ayuntamiento*, is a crowded stretch of sand. Sunbathers, ice-cream stands, and small cafes dot the wide adjacent boardwalk. For a more local scene and peaceful shores, the 6km of **Playa de Sant Joan** and **Playa del Mutxavista** are the nearest options, accessible by the tram station at the joint linking the Explanada and the Playa del Postiguet. *(The Alicante-Dénia train, TRAM, leaves the main station every 20min. in the summer, every hr. in winter, and stops at Playa del Muxtavista and Playa de San Juan; €0.95. To Sant Joan, take TAM bus #21, 22, or 31. For Mutxavista, take #21. Every 15min., €0.95.)*

NIGHTLIFE

Alicante's raucous nightlife can be somewhat capricious: bars that overflow one night are often closed or embarrassingly empty the next. Many of the hit locales are only open weekends. It's often best to follow the sound of chattering crowds. The most concentrated nightlife areas are the discotecas along the port and the bizarre pubs that spring to life in the *casco antiguo*.

PARTY ON. Given its long hours and disco destinations, the Tramsnochador is a godsend for all-night partiers. The bus runs to cities like Altea, Benidorm, and Dénia, with service until 5am.

CASCO ANTIGUO

The *casco antiguo* is the perfect place to start off the night while the dance floors along the port fill up. Though there are plenty of watering holes around **Plaza San Cristóbal** and **Calle Mayor,** the older part of town, referred to by most as *el barrio*, has the youngest crowd and the quirkiest bars. The cramped patios outside these hot spots accumulate crowds rapidly: the barhopping mentality in Alicante is unabashedly follow-the-leader.

- **Celestial Copas,** C. San Pascual, 1 (☎663 50 26 32). Fills up later than surrounding bars, but the decor alone makes it worth a visit anytime. The garish bar drips with opulence and is sinfully offset by kitschy religious artwork. Red velvet curtains, decadent colors, and glinting gold chandeliers overwhelm tiny rooms. Spanish, flamenco, and Latin grooves. Outdoor seating also available. Beer €3, mixed drinks from €5. Open winter Th 10pm-3am, F-Sa 10pm-4am; summer daily 10pm-3am. Cash only.
- **Artespiritu,** C. Labradores, 26 (☎675 01 99 94). As you walk along C. Labradores at night, you will inevitably stumble over the crowd at this corner bar, sitting outside, as a steady reggae-groove-electric mix provides the background for conversation and,

later, dancing. Mixed drinks €5. Happy hour 10pm-midnight; €1 beer pints. Open daily 10am-4am, serves juices for breakfast. Cash only.

Astrónomo, C. Virgen de Belén, at C. Padre Maltés (☎965 14 35 22). 2 heavenly floors of dancing and drinking to Spanish pop, house, and everything in between. Escape across the street to their lush, gated outdoor terrace. Beer €3. Mixed drinks from €5. Happy hour midnight-2am. Open Th-Sa 11pm-4am. Cash only.

El Coscorrón, C. Tarifa, 2 (☎965 21 27 27). Named after the bump on the head you might receive from the 4 ft. door frame. Open since 1936, it claims to be the oldest bar in Alicante; from the looks of it, that just might be true. Beer €2. Mixed drinks €4-6. Open daily 7pm-last customer. Cash only.

Glass Club, C. de Montegon. Cool medical lab colors and blank mirrored walls let off icy steam in this large air-conditioned, space-age club. Techno and house music reverberate off of every shiny surface. Beer €4. Mixed drinks €5.50. Open 11pm-4am.

Directo, C. Virgen de Belén, 19. With 2 floors and popular international jams, this bar and dance club keeps everyone feeling good. Dark wood bars and plenty of space to salsa. Mixed drinks €6.50. Open Th-Sa 11:30pm-4am. Cash only.

Café de la Sal, C. Labradores, 5 (☎965 20 50 68; www.cafedelasal.com). You won't find locals here, but you will find great hiphop, crowds of expats and young people from all over the world, and great mixed drinks. Tu beer pong, Sa international guest DJs. Mixed drinks €6. Ask about special promotions/VIP cards, which give discounts on drinks. Open daily 8pm-4am. MC/V.

NEAR THE PORT

Alicante's main port houses a complex of cavernous bars and discotecas pumping music over the water. Though the music starts early, these bars fill up late, and some are only open on weekends. Revelers crowd the many huge discotecas on the port, to the left when facing the water. None of these has a cover charge, though there is sometimes a drink minimum. Beer is almost universally €3.50 and mixed drinks €6. The liveliest spots differ depending on the day of the week, but all have a fairly good crowd any night.

Havana Cafe, Rambla Méndez Núñez, 26 (☎965 21 69 26; www.havana.es). On the way from the old town to the port. Bohemian interior and huge crowds make for a lively feel. Open M-Th 7am-2:30am, F-Sa 3pm-4am. Beer €1.50, €2 outside. Cash only.

Coyote Ugly (☎618 38 00 09; coyoteuglypuerto.com). A popular, scandalous option, complete with poles on the bar. Early-morning breakfast served in the room next to the dance floor. Beer €2, mixed drinks from €6. Open daily 9:30am-6:30am. Cash only.

FESTIVALS

From June 20-24, the **Fogueres de Sant Joan** (Bonfires of St. John) and St. John's feast day celebrate the summer solstice in a hedonistic inferno. This rollicking, fire-worshipping blast kicks off with a citywide parade in traditional garb, and, by the third day, every district in the city has its incredible *foguera* (giant papier-mâché structure) on display. Temporary festival halls are erected and feasts take place in open air, punctuated by daily firework shows in the Plaza de los Luceros at 2pm. Parades, flower-offerings, and wild celebrations fill the hours until the festival culminates in a midnight display of fireworks atop Mt. Benacantil and a huge bonfire in the Pl. de Ayuntamiento. In June, the **Moors and Christians** festival pays costumed tribute to the Christian battles for Valencian reconquest. The city honors its patron saint, **La Virgen del Remedio,** from August 3 to 5 through choral concerts and processions. During late July and early August, Playa de San Juan becomes a stage for ballet and musical performances for the **Plataforma Cultural** series. (Events on Playa de San Juan free.) Monthly schedules for these festivals can be found on the tourist office website (www.alicanteturismo.com).

BENIDORM ☎965

Many believe the name Benidorm (pop. 67,000) means "good sleep" or "come and sleep"; visitors may sleep well, but they certainly won't sleep long. The never-ending beams of light over the 5.5km beach boardwalk are the first indication that no one is deterred by the setting sun. Visitors from all over Europe crowd Benidorm's modern, skyscraper-studded streets, some to sunbathe on the city's hot sands, others to engage in raucous revelry until dawn. If it's the tranquility of the Costa Blanca you seek, you may find it here among secluded coves. If you're eager to be swept away by a tidal wave of energy, look no further than the crazy carnival that lights the summer sands of Benidorm.

TRANSPORTATION. The **train station** (☎965 85 18 95) is atop a hill above the city on Av. de l'Estacio. The walk down to the city is at least 15min. and not pedestrian-friendly—it's best to take a bus or cab. Local bus #7 departs from the train station for the city center. (☎965 85 43 22. Every 30min. 6:30am-9:50pm, €1.) The **ALSA bus station** is on Av. de Europa, at the corner of Av. Gerona about four blocks inland from the beach, close to the city center. For **taxis,** call ☎965 86 26 26 (€3-5 to the city center). **Avenida Ruzafa** is near the *casco antiguo* (old town) and is full of internet cafes, banks, accommodations, and taxis. The *casco antiguo* divides Benidorm into two sections: to the north, the boardwalk **Avenida d'Alcoi** runs through the main beach, **Playa de Levante,** site of most big hotels, restaurants, and bars. On the other side of the *casco antiguo* is the seaside **Parque de Elche** and a more secluded beach, **Playa de Poniente.**

PRACTICAL INFORMATION. The **tourist office** is off the beach at Av. de Martínez Alejos, 16. Signs lead to it from Av. Ruzafa. From the bus stop, continue down Av. de Europa toward the beach, take a right at Av. del Mediterráneo, and continue to **Plaza de la Hispanidad,** also called **Plaza Triangular.** Veer left onto C. Dr. Pérez Llorca and take a left onto Av. de Martínez Alejos. (☎965 85 32 24; www.benidorm.org. Open July-Sept. M-F 9am-9pm, Sa 10am-1pm; Oct.-June M-F 9am-8pm, Sa 10am-1pm.) **Banks** and **ATMs** line C. Dr. Pérez Llorca. **Internet** is at **Cybercat Café,** in the bottom floor of El Otro Mundo de Jaime, Av. Ruzafa, 2, near the *casco antiguo*. (☎965 86 79 04. €1 per 20min. Open daily 9am-2am.) The **post office** is at Av. de Aiguera, 5, next to the Parque Aiguera, next to the *casco antiguo* and a 10min. walk from the water. (☎965 85 34 34. Open M-F 8am-8pm, Sa 8:30am-2pm.) **Postal Code:** 03501 or 03502 (depending on zone).

ACCOMMODATIONS AND FOOD. Benidorm's shoreline is a metallic bouquet of upscale hotels (including the tallest hotel in Europe, the **Gran Hotel Bali** at 186m), making affordable lodging difficult to find. Close to the beach on Av. Ruzafa is **Hostal Tabarca ❷,** Av. Ruzafa, 9, with tiled floors and clean hallway bathrooms. Rooms have large beds, enormous windows, TV, fan, and sink. (☎965 85 77 08. June-Sept. singles €20; doubles €37; triples €42. Oct.-May €18/32/35. Cash only.)

The shoreline is an explosion of *gelaterias*, pizzerias, and cafes, loud music, and blinking lights. These cafes are often packed well into the night by an older crowd. **Restaurante L'Albufera ❷,** on the corner of C. Gerona and Av. del Dr. Orts Llorca, offers 14 different *menús del día* (€12) and hearty portions of Italian and Spanish fare at reasonable prices. (☎965 86 56 61. Entrees €8-12.

Open daily 11am-midnight.) For a quieter atmosphere, walk through the *casco antiguo* to the restaurants along *el mirador* (below). The **produce market** (W and F 8am-3pm) is just outside the *casco antiguo* on Vía de Emilio Ortuño and C. Mercado. The main supermarket, **Mercadona,** is on C. Invierno, one block up C. Mirador, off Vía de Emilio Ortuño. (Open M-Sa 9:15am-9:15pm.)

SIGHTS AND FESTIVALS. Remnants of the old city have been almost totally engulfed by high-rises and roadways, and most of the ocean is obscured by an vast sea of blue-and-white umbrellas standing guard over sunbathers. A bit of a walk to either end of Playa de Levante yields the best views and, farther down the road, more secluded lagoons. The hillside panorama of the clear waters of **Tumbona** beach is unforgettable; if you decide to make the trek down, be warned that access costs €3, and most sunbathers are nude. At the end of **El Carrer del Gats,** one of the area's most picturesque streets, protrudes the gleaming *mirador*, also known as "The Balcony of the Mediterranean." This gabled blue-and-white promenade spans the rocky perimeter of the neighborhood and offers overwhelming views of the Playa del Levante to the north, the Playa de Poniente to the south, and the rocky sea floor below. Straight ahead juts **Benidorm Island,** an enormous slanted-rock formation. The balcony almost entirely conceals the ruins of the **Castillo-Mirador de Benidorm,** built in the 14th century to protect the city from Berber pirates. If it is rowdy beach enjoyment you want, a visit to Benidorm is not complete without a stroll along the 2km long **Paseo Marítimo de la Playa de Levante.** This enormous boardwalk is packed nearly 24hr. a day; the place to see and be seen.

In early summer, Benidorm hosts a world-renowned international music festival, **Festival de la Canción de Benidorm.** Though the festival has changed over the years, beginning in 1959 to promote Spanish music and since taking an international turn, many artists have gotten their start on the shores of Benidorm.

NIGHTLIFE. Day or night, Benidorm is one massive party. The club scene is not for the faint of heart. Partygoers follow an exhausting but hedonistically fulfilling routine every night in July and August, and on weekends during the rest of the year. Beachside locales start to brim as soon as the esplanade floodlights are lit. The crowd is easy to follow as it moves inland through the night (or morning). Covers at clubs are around €12 but usually include a drink (€6). Promoters outside sometimes offer free admission or deals on drinks. Close to the *Ayuntamiento* in the *casco antiguo* is **La Sal,** C. Costera del Barco, 5. This local favorite is busy on the weekends with an ultra-hip crowd. (☎966 87 34 94. Beer €3-5. Open F-Su 11pm-5am.) **Carrer del Gats** is full of other great places to start the night. Beachside cafes close to the *casco antiguo* promise stiffer prices but great atmosphere. After a few drinks, partygoers usually head to disco-pubs along Av. de Mallorca, though some travelers find this area to be more lowbrow and a bit lackluster.

If all you want to do is dance, head to **Penelope,** one of the trendiest venues on the beach. (☎629 69 40 90; www.penelopebeach.com. Mixed drinks €8. Open daily 11pm-5am.) An eclectic crowd grooves to house music at **Ku** (see below for disco), Av. Alcoy, 6, a lounge and club, replete with palm trees and tiki torches. (☎965 86 94 83; http://kubenidorm.es. Mixed drinks €8. Open daily 10pm-5am.) Dance the night away at **KM,** right next to Penelope on the corner of Av. Bilbao and Av. Alcoy. (☎965 86 35 23; www.kmdisco.com. Mixed drinks €8. Open daily 11am-late.)

Around 5am, the party shifts from the beach to the disco gardens on Ave. de la Comunitat Valenciana. It's a good 15min. on foot, but it's best to take a taxi (€4). To get to Av. Valenciana from the beach, walk to Av. del Mediterráneo and head towards the *casco antiguo*. Turn right onto C. Esperanto and follow it for about 7min. Turn left on C. Juan Llorca; Av. Com. Valencia is a block ahead. At **Ku (Disco),** Av. Com. Valenciana, 121, a giant double helix guards imposingly outside. Inside, white walls and red lamps, surrounding a dance floor, outdoor terrace, and pool. (☎965 86 07 11. Mixed drinks €6. Open midnight-6am.) Finally, visit **Pachá,** C. Tomás Ortuño, 5, Spain's largest discoteca chain. (☎965 85 77 96. Mixed drinks €6-8. Open midnight-6am.)

ALTEA ☎965

Altea's yawning coastline is unique on the Costa Blanca for its absence of skyscraper hotels and tourist staples. Though apartment complexes and private homes are clustered toward the sea, Altea retains a pristine quality and small-town modesty. A long jetty with a charming walkway protects Altea's stretch of shoreline from large waves, while egg-size white stones contrast with the turquoise water. Bus #10 runs from Altea to **Altea la Vella** every hour (€1.10). **Comte d'Altea,** which runs into C. La Mar and Pl. del Convent, is the main thoroughfare in Altea. **Carrer Sant Pere** parallels the rocky beach. The walk past the Port d'Altea leads to clearer waters and vistas of **Cap Blanch.** Continuing this walk through a residential area eventually leads to a path that climbs the **Faro de l'Albir,** the peninsula-like peak of the Serra Gelada. The trek takes about an hour but is not taxing. At the top is an unforgettable vista of the entire shoreline. If there's no time for a hike, be sure to climb the steep steps into the old town behind C. del Mar, where the blue dome of the **Plaza de la Iglesia** beckons.

Though Altea isn't touristy, it certainly won't help you recoup. Among the cheapest accommodations is **Habitaciones La Mar ❷,** C. La Mar, 82, close to the train station and beach, with 40 decently sized, simple rooms with bathrooms, air-conditioning, and TV in a concrete building about 10m from the beach. Look for the blue sign as you enter town. (☎965 84 30 16. Singles €27; doubles and triples €43. Cash only.) Past the Port d'Altea is **Camping Cap-Blanch ❶,** Playa Cap Blanch 25, just 2km from downtown Altea and 5km from Benidorm. (☎96 5 84 59 46; www.camping-capblanch.com. €6 per car, tent, and person.) For typical Spanish fare and delicious gazpacho in a cozy setting, try **La Liebre ❷,** Po. Mediterráneo, 39. (☎965 84 45 79. *Menú* €9. Open M-Sa 10am-5pm.) Most bars on the waterfront cater to an older crowd and close early; night owls can be found on the beach toward **Faro de l'Albir.** Check out the oceanfront lounges and bohemian flair of **Cafe del Mar** along Cap Blanch (Drinks only. Open until 5am.) Many partygoers head to Benidorm and Alicante for nightlife.

Both **trains** and **buses** stop at the foot of C. La Mar. The **tourist office** is on C. Sant Pere, 9, on the water. (☎965 84 41 14. Open June-Aug. M-F 10am-2pm and 5-8pm; Sept.-May M-Sa 9:30am-2pm and 5-7:30pm.) **Taxis** can be reached at ☎966 81 00 10. Rent bikes from **Bici Altea.** (☎966 88 09 87. Open M-F 10am-2pm and 5-8:30pm, Sa 10am-2pm.) Local services include the **police,** C. La Mar, 91 (☎965 84 55 11), and **ambulances** (☎965 84 31 83).

DÉNIA ☎966

Dénia is an ideal family resort destination, featuring a 17km ribbon of smooth beaches with silken sands, a thriving fishing port, great watersports, and a harbor that connects ferries to the Islas Baleares. Predictably, restaurants and hotels on the water look pretty but tend to be expensive; you'll find the best deals a bit farther inland, often even beyond the town center. Fortunately, the infinite stretches of groomed beaches, which are truly the town's main attraction, are available free of charge.

TRANSPORTION. The local **train station** (☎900 72 04 72; www.fgvalicante.com) is on C. Calderón de la Barca, just off C. Patricio Ferrándiz and close to the tourist office. The **bus station** is an **ALSA** office on Pl. Arxiduc Carlos and Po. del Saladar, a 10min. walk to the beaches. For train and bus schedules, see p. 306. Local **buses** (☎966 42 14 08) pick up on the **Explanada Cervantes;** to get there, head toward the water from the tourist office and take a left at the Red Cross building. The stop is about 5min. down from the traffic circle, at the port. Take the bus marked "Marina" or "Calma" for the more secluded beaches; the bus marked "Rotas" heads toward great scuba-diving sites, including a shipwreck from the late 19th century. To reach the Baleares by sea, consult **Baleária Eurolínes Marítimes** (☎902 16 01 80; www.balearia.com) in Pl. Oculista Buigues. Ferries run from Dénia to Palma and Ibiza (€49-66). For **taxis,** call ☎966 42 44 44 or 965 78 10 11. **Bike** and **scooter** rental is available from **Motos Luís** on C. Abu-Zeyán, 8. (☎965 78 36 02. Open M-F 9am-1pm and 4-8pm, Sa 11am-1pm. Bikes €7.50 per day €14.50 per 3 days; scooters €39 per day, €24 per day after 3 days.) Another option for bikes is **Desnivell Bicicletes** on Ave. Alicante, 18, where you can pick up information on coastal and mountain excursions. (☎966 425 230. Open M-F 9:30am-2pm and 4:30-8:30pm, Sa 9:30am-2pm.)

ORIENTATION AND PRACTICAL INFORMATION. Local services, including **buses, trains,** and **ferries,** are on **Calle Patricio Ferrándiz,** which runs to the port from the bus station. Orient yourself on the Calle Marqués de Campo, the main tourist strip. The **tourist office** is on Pl. Oculista Buígues, 9, 30m inland from **Estació Marítima,** at the end of C. Patricio Ferrándiz. Follow the signs to the port from the bus station. (☎966 42 23 67; www.denia.net. Open July-Aug. daily 9:30am-1:30pm and 5-8pm; Sept.-June M-Sa 9:30am-1:30pm and 4-7pm, Su 9:30am-1:30pm.) Contact the police at ☎092. **Internet** access is available at **Cyber Mon,** on C. Carlos Sentí in the Mon Blau complex, upstairs in the blue building next to the market on the block between C. de la Mar and C. Magallanes. (€1.50 per hr. Open daily 9am-midnight.) Also available at **Locutorio Dianense,** C. Loreto 52 (☎966 42 68 79. Open M-F, 9:30am-3pm and 4-11pm, Sa 9:30-11pm.) The **post office** is on C. Patricio Ferrándiz, 38. (☎965 78 15 33. Open M-F 8:30am-8:30pm, Sa 9:30am-1pm.)

ACCOMMODATIONS AND FOOD. Dénia's plush hostels fill quickly and don't cater to budget travelers. Be prepared to shell out €30 or more for a single room in the summer, and book in advance, especially during festivals in July. **Hostal L'Anfora ❸,** Explanada de Cervantes, 8, ideally located right on the port, straddles the old and new towns. This spotless find has some of the cheapest rooms in town, all with bath, TV, and air-conditioning. (☎966 43 01 01; www.hostallanfora.com. July-Sept. singles €33, doubles €56; Oct.-June €27/44. AmEx/MC/V.) **Hostal Comerc ❸,** C. La Via, 43, is a giant, spotless hotel-like establishment paralleling Avda. Marques de Campo. A standard, cement facade leads to rooms with balconies, A/C, TV, full bath, and lots of space. (☎965 78 00 71; www.hostalcomerc.com. Singles €33. MC/V). The **market** is on C. Carlos Sentí, 6 (open M-Sa 7am-2pm). Eateries line C. Marqués de Campo and surrounding streets. For breakfast or lunch, **Pastisseria Tano ❶,** C. Marqués de Campo, 54, serves delicious coffees and baked goods. For lunch, fresh, pie-style sandwiches filled with everything from ham and cheese to anchovies and eggplant are ready to take away in gigantic wedges for only €2-3.20. (☎966 42 40 95. Open Tu-Su 8:30am-10pm. MC/V.) Try the compact Pl. San Antoni or Pl. del Convento for more intimate dining establishments. During the month of June, a series of live jazz concerts takes place in Pl. del Convento during dinner time; ask at the tourist office for a calendar. In Pl. San Antoni, try the refreshing cuisine offered at **La Menta ❷,** where rarities like monkfish carpaccio with lime sauce (€7.50) and salmon ragou pasta (€10.50) are served outside, just far enough away from the crazy port. (Open Tu-Su 7-11pm. MC/V.) At night, crowds move to beachside bars and restaurants. But don't pass up a trip to **Casa Francisca,** C. La Mar, 16, a Cuban bar with killer mojitos (€6) and live salsa music and dancing every Saturday at 11pm. (☎966 42 51 33. Open M and Su 8pm-3am, T-Sa 4pm-3am. MC/V.)

SIGHTS AND BEACHES. Away from the beaches, Dénia is best enjoyed in the maze of colorful streets leading up to the **castle;** the walk is steep but short and passes through the most charming part of town. Access the stairway directly from the *Ayuntamiento*. Dénia's castle offers amazing panoramas on all sides. The ruins sprawl across the hilltop and exhibit Moorish relics from the 11th and 12th centuries. Within the walls is a small **museum** of archaeology located in what was once the governor's palace. (☎966 42 06 56. Open daily June 10am-1:30pm and 4-7:30pm; July-Aug. 10am-1:30pm and 5-8:30pm; Sept. 10am-1:30pm and 4-8pm; Oct. 10am-1pm and 3-6:30pm; Nov.-Mar. 10am-1pm and 3-6pm; Apr.-May 10am-1:30pm and 3:30-6pm. Night hours on weekends, July to mid-Sept. weekends 10pm-12:30am. €3.) A **tourist train** chugs to the castle from the tourist office. (☎699 46 88 66. M-F and Su 5, 6:30pm; schedule subject to frequent change. Train ticket includes admission to castle; €6. Min. 4 passengers.) Dénia's biggest draw is its pristine stretch of beaches. Beach bars and volleyball courts are in constant use, and the 17km breadth of coastline rarely gets crowded. Those who crave a beach for relaxation have plenty of options—**Platja Les Marines, Platja Les Bovetes,** and **Platja Punta Raset** are all close to the center of town and well within walking distance from the port. Windsurfers skip over the waves off **Platja Els Molins** (north of the port on the "Marina" bus), while scuba divers explore the depths off **Las Platjas Area de Las Rotes** (south of the port on the "Rotas" bus). The tourist office provides a pamphlet detailing trails in nearby **Montgó Natural Park** (☎966 42 32 05).

FESTIVALS. Dénia holds a miniature **Fallas Festival** March 16-20, burning puppet effigies at midnight on the final day. During **Festa Major,** or **Las Fiestas de la Santisima Sangre** (first 15 days in July), dances, floats, and fireworks explode by the harbor while locals prove they are as gutsy as their countrymen in Pamplona during **Bous a la Mar,** when bulls and fans dive together into the water.

MURCIA ☎968

Though Murcia is becoming increasingly urban and fashionable to accommodate its large university, it maintains deep respect for tradition. The old quarter's quiet lanes reveal the Moorish heart of the historic city of Mursiya, founded by Abderramán II in AD 825, but the city's soul rests in its Gothic and Neoclassical plazas. Though the streets connecting these marbled arenas are lined with chic shops and young crowds, daily life in Murcia unfolds to the steady rhythm of the church bells clanging from its many cathedrals. Be warned that the city bakes in the summer heat and may leave you yearning for the beach. *Murcianos* will tell you that their city is most pleasant to visit from September to June, from the start of the new school year to the explosion of spring festivals.

TRANSPORTATION

Aeropuerto de San Javier (☎968 17 20 00), about 30km to the southeast, has flights to Madrid and London. **RENFE trains** (☎902 24 02 02), at Pl. Industria, across the river from the *casco antiguo*, head to: **Alicante** (1½hr., 1-2 per hr. 5:55am-10:05pm, €4.30); **Barcelona** (6-8hr., 4 per day, €48.10); **Lorca** (1hr., 1-2 per hr. 6:45am-10:05pm, €4.30); **Madrid** (4-6hr., 5 per day, €40.20); **Valencia** (3½hr., 6 per day, €17.10-28.20). **Buses** (☎968 29 22 11) leave from the station on C. Bolos (on the western perimeter of the *casco antiguo*) to: **Alicante** (1hr., 12 per day 7am-9pm, €5.20); **Almería** (4hr., 7-9 per day 5:15am-10pm, €16.59); **Barcelona** (9hr., 10 per day 12:30am-10:15pm, €44.64-50.89); **Dénia** (3hr., 7 per day 2am-8:50pm, €12.31); **Granada** (3½-6hr., 6-8 per day 8:30am-10pm, €19.16); **Mojácar** (4-5 per day, 5am-8:30pm; €10.17); **Lorca** (1½hr., 6-17 per day 7am-9pm, €5); **Madrid** (5-6hr., 1-3 per hr. 9am-1am, €25.02-42); **Málaga** (6-7hr., 9 per day 9:30am-3:50am, €30.54-37.17); **Sevilla** (7-9hr., 4 per day 11:15am-10pm, €36.36); **Valencia** (3-4hr., 4-11 per day 5:30am-3:15am, €11.50). **Municipal buses** (€1.10) cover the city; bus #9 runs past the bus and train stations.

ORIENTATION AND PRACTICAL INFORMATION

The **Río Segura** is a lateral divide, separating the city sights north of the train station, cheap accommodations, and mini-markets in the south (take bus #9, 17, or 39 between the two). Take **Avenida Canalejas** to the Puente Viejo (Old Bridge) across the river to **Gran Vía Escultor Salzillo,** one of the two main streets that cut through the center of town (the other is **Gran Vía Alfonso X El Sabio**), to the Pl. Circular (the former Av. de la Constitución), a giant traffic circle in the city center. G. V. Salzillo is strewn with banks—these may become important once you've stumbled upon the shopping districts. An immediate right off G. V. Salzillo leads to **Plaza Belluga,** a spectacular grouping of the 14th-century cathedral, Palacio Episcopal, and *Ayuntamiento*. The **tourist office** is amid this congress of striking architecture, one of the most important (and beautiful) orienting points in the city. (☎968 35 87 49; www.murciaciudad.com. Open daily Apr.-Sept. 10am-2pm and 5-9pm; Oct.-Mar. 10am-2pm and 4:30-8:30pm.)

The regional **tourist office** is in Palacio González Campuzano, C. Santa Clara, the red building in Pl. Julián Romea. (☎968 22 06 59. Open M-Sa 10am-2pm and 4:30-8:30pm, Su 10am-2pm.) Local services include the **police,** Av. San Juan de la Cruz (☎968 26 66 00 or 092), and **Hospital de la Cruz Roja,** along the river past the *Ayuntamiento* and the Pl. de la Cruz Roja. A 24hr. **pharmacy** is just across the Puente Viejo in the Pl. Martinez Tornel. The primary **post office** is at on G. V. Salzillo and Pl. Circular, near the intersection with Av. Primo de Rivera. (☎968 27 13 13. Open M-F 8:30am-2:30pm.) **Postal Code:** 30008.

ACCOMMODATIONS

In Murcia, finding a room without a reservation, especially in summer, is tricky. Accommodations tend to be budget hotels instead of *pensiones*, often resulting in more amenities but a less personal feel.

Pensión Segura, Pl. Camachos, 14 (☎968 21 12 81; www.pensionsegura.com). Above a small courtyard and 2 blocks from the river, Segura has rooms with small balconies, TV, A/C, and private bath, complemented by a cordial staff and an outstanding breakfast (€1.50) in the cafe downstairs. Singles €39; doubles €50. MC/V. ❹

Hotel Universal Pacoche, C. Cartagena, 21 (☎968 21 76 05). Just blocks from both the train station and the *casco antiguo*. Has simple rooms off slightly dark hallways. Rooms have TV and a tiny private bath. Friendly hotel/restaurant next door serves breakfast to go and gives a 10% discount to those staying in Pacoche. June-Aug. singles €28; doubles €43; triples €60. MC/V. ❷

FOOD

Enjoy breakfast in the Pl. de Flores, a block left of G. V. Salzillo, where tranquil cafes are interspersed with flower shops. Sample the venerated Murcian harvest at the Mercado Verónicas, behind its namesake cathedral on C. de Verónicas (open M-Sa 9am-2pm). A 24hr. walk-through **market** is on C. Puxmanna, paralleling G. V. Salzillo. For other needs, try **El Corte Inglés** at G. V. Salzillo, 42. (☎968 29 80 50. Open M-Sa 10am-10pm. MC/V.) **Plaza Apostoles** (☎968 216 869), behind the cathedral, has outdoor eateries away from tourist traffic. The **Plaza de Santo Domingo,** bordered by an enormous church, offers shaded seating, ice cream shops, and cafes. The smaller **Plaza J. Romea** is lit beautifully at night, bedecked with elegant tapas bars by the imposing Teatro de Romea.

Meson de Jesus, Pl. Romea, 6 (☎968 216 869). Patio seating is great for people-watching, while the wood-paneled indoor restaurant has a warm, tavern-like ambience. Tapas €1.50-6. Open M-Sa 8am-midnight. MC/V. ❶

Casa Carmelina, Pl. Puxmarina, 2 (☎968 22 10 17; www.casacarmelina.com). A more elegant option, with silk and gold decor, heavy drapes, and carefully prepared Italian cuisine. Entrees €9-20. Open M-Sa 1:30-4:30pm and 7:30-11:30pm. MC/V. ❷

Mr. Esmuti, C. Azucaque (☎968 22 38 68; www.misteresmuti.com). An appropriately (and phonetically) named juice bar and cafe. Serves refreshing smoothies to go (€2.90-5.50) as well as a variety of salads and snacks. A left turn from the cathedral leads straight there. Wi-Fi. Open M-F 9am-11pm, Sa 10am-11pm. Cash only. ❶

SIGHTS

The intricate, Castilian Gothic facade of the 14th-century cathedral in **Plaza Belluga** is one of the city's most unforgettable sights. For a schedule of guided visits of the cathedral, consult the tourist office. For *aficionados*, at the opposite end of town, but well worth the walk, is the unassuming **Museo Taurino,** located in the breezy **Jardín El Salitre** just north of the bus station. This nondescript enclave displays bullfighting memorabilia, matador costumes, and mounted bulls' heads that pay homage to particularly exceptional bulls and those who did them in. Shrines to Spain's best toreros exhibit the shredded, bloody shirts they wore when they were gored to death by their 1000lb. opponents. (☎968 28 59 76. Open June-Aug. M-F 10am-2pm and 5-8pm; Sept.-May also Su 11am-2pm. Free.) From the cathedral, walk through the breezy Jardín El Salitre and cut across town on C. Acisclo Díaz to the palatial **Casino de Murcia,** C. Trapería, 18, which served as a gentlemen's club for the city's 19th- and 20th-century bourgeoisie. (☎968 21 22 55. Closed indefinitely for renovations.) Continue up C. Trapería away from the river and take a right onto C. Andres Bacquero, which becomes C. Dr. Fleming. Take a right onto C. Obispo Frutos, and you'll come to Murcia's **Museo de Bellas Artes,** C. Obispo Frutos, 8, containing over 1000 works and a collection of *murciano* art from the 16th to 19th centuries. *(☎968 23 93 46; www.museobellasartesmurcia.com. Open July-Aug Tu-Sa 10am-9pm, Su 10am-2pm.; Sept-June. Tu-Su 10am-8:30pm, Su 10am-2pm.)* Further along is the **Plaza de Toros**, Murcia's bull ring and concert venue.

NIGHTLIFE AND FESTIVALS

Though a very young crowd is the lifeblood of Murcia's nightlife, the overall scene is quite calm. Most partygoers congregate in the city's plazas and the main streets connecting them, migrating later on to the discotecas in nearby Atalayas. Avoid the darker back alleys—unless you're looking for **La General,** C. Mariano Padilla, 15, which sits on an otherwise quiet street. The heavy, industrial-looking door to this hopping bar will fool any passersby not in the know. A steady stream of funky, underground music and retro design provides a sort of conspiratorial ambience. (☎657 21 25 68; www.myspace.com/lageneral. Beer €1.50. Mixed drinks €2-6. Open W-Sa 10pm-last customer; summer open Tu-Sa.) For an energetic club scene, the university area near C. Dr. Fleming and Pl. Universidad does the trick on weekends. The trendy bar/dance club **Fleming, 12,** located predictably at C. Dr. Fleming, 12, spins a variety of hits from different genres for a well-dressed crowd. (☎661 677 654. Beer €3. Mixed drinks €5-6. Cash only. Open from Sept to mid-July Th-Sa 8:30pm-4:30am.)

After **Semana Santa,** the six-day **Fiesta de Primavera** descends upon the city, bringing band processions, flower parades, and theater performances. Every June and July, the **Festival Belluga** draws dance and classical music acts from all over Europe to perform outside the cathedral. All events are free. Check at the tourist office for schedules.

DAYTRIPS FROM MURCIA

LORCA

RENFE Cercanías trains (☎902 24 02 02) run to Lorca's Estación Satullena (the 2nd Lorca stop), Ex. de la Estación (1hr., every hr. 6:45am-10:05pm, €4.30). The bus station (☎968 46 92 70), next to the train station, sends buses to Murcia (1hr., every hr. 7am-9pm, €4.90) and Águilas (30min.; M-F 9 per day, Sa-Su 2-3 per day; €2).

Though the dry hills surrounding Lorca (pop. 84,000) are blanketed with orchards and cropland, ancient battles stripped the actual town of its foliage and left a host of architectural imprints. Medieval ghettos, Renaissance artistry, post-Franco urbanism, and contemporary elitism all dot the town's terrain. Atop the rocky hillside is the **Castillo Fortaleza del Sol,** a Moorish fortress with two preserved Christian towers constructed in the 13th and 15th centuries. During the month of July, the **Espirelia** festival brings international musicians and films to the castle; for more info, see www.espirelia.lorca.es. (☎902 40 00 47. Open Tu-F 10am-2pm, Sa-Su 10:30am-6:30pm. Tu-F €7, Sa-Su and holidays €10, students €7.) The awe-inspiring 16th-century **Ex-Colegiata de San Patricio** was built to commemorate the Lorcan battle against the Muslims in 1492—the same year that Moorish Granada fell. At the bottom of the slope are three churches: **Santa María, San Juan,** and **San Pedro,** all of which stand in ruin beneath the castle. The trek up to the castle is a grueling 20min. climb through a maze of beige, boxy homes, followed by paved roads that wind around the desiccated,

H2... UH-OH.

As one strolls through the ros gardens and trickling fountain outside Murcia's *Ayuntamient* a certain banner hanging belov the Spanish flag is impossible t ignore. *"AGUA PARA TODOS!"* i states in bold, blue lettering. Whil water shortage is a country-wid problem, the region of Murcia ha it the worst. The water supply her has decreased dramatically, jus as use has skyrocketed, and th result is not all roses.

Historically, Murcia has alway been farmland. but in recen years, farmers have begun plantin water-intensive crops like lettuce corn, and tomatoes, rather tha the figs and date palms that use to be so common. Simultaneousl resorts and golf courses hav sprouted up all over the coast creating a much higher deman for water. Today, Murcia consume 2½ times more water than it current supply can provide. An climate change only exacerbate problems—the southern half o Spain is looking increasingly lik the Sahara Desert.

People are quick to ask que tions and point fingers, but answe are slow to come. This past yea Spain hosted a European confe ence on water concerns, issuin a new plan to fight desertifica tion. But until these initiative begin to show their effects, wate will remain a top concern for th country, and especially in Murci The blue banner will continue t wave over the region, reminding a *murcianos* of this dire situation.

cactus-strewn rock. If all else fails, just keep walking uphill. A tourist train makes its way up every 40min. or so and is well worth the €2.

The family-owned and run **Pensión del Carmen ❶**, Rincón de los Valientes, is a great option. Directly across from the Iglesia del Carmen, the *pensión* offers cute, inexpensive rooms with TV, full bath, and air-conditioning. (☎968 46 64 59. Singles €18. MC/V.) It is difficult to find a decent meal here, so stock up on snacks at the market in the plaza directly next to the train station (open daily 9am-2pm, cash only) or the nearby **Mercadona** off Alameda de la Constitucion (open M-Sa 9am-9pm; MC/V). Though you may stumble upon the occasional hole-in-the-wall bar in the old part of town, most streets here are residential or historical. Your best bet for a meal is away from the town cultural center near Ave. de Juan Carlos I. Pl. de Colon, C. Nogalte, and C. Lope Gisbert have quieter cafes.

The **train** and **bus** stations are a block below the town center on Explanada de la Estación. Take Av. Periodista Lopez Barnes from the train station to Av. de Juan Carlos I, which traverses the busiest part of town and contains most bank offices. Most cafes and pharmacies are left on Av. de Juan Carlos I, and a right turn leads to the cultural center. From Av. de Juan Carlos I, take **C. Presbitero Emilio Garcia Navarro** past lovely churches and the town cultural center; a right turn from there onto C. Lope Gisbert leads to the **tourist office,** inside the **Palacio Guevara.** (☎968 44 19 14. Open M-F 9:30am-2pm and 5:30-7:30pm, Sa 10am-3pm and 5:30-7:30pm, Su 10am-3pm.) The **post office** is on the corner of C. Alamo and C. Corredera (☎968 46 71 12).

CARTAGENA

RENFE trains (☎902 24 02 02) head to: Barcelona (8-10hr., 1pm, €50.50) via Alicante; Madrid (5hr., 5 per day 5:30am-6:25pm, €41.70); Murcia (1hr., 9 per day 7:35am-9:10pm, €4.20); Valencia (4hr., 4:43pm, €32.20). They leave from the train station in Pl. de México, several blocks north of the port. Ticket office open 5am-9pm, though tickets for later buses can be bought from the driver. Autocares Costa Azul (☎968 50 15 43) runs to Alicante (3hr., 8 per day 7am-8pm, €7.05). ALSA buses go to: Cádiz (10-12hr.; 10:15am, 9pm; €50.67); Granada (5hr., 5-6 per day 8:30am-9pm, €22.52); Málaga (7-8hr.; 8:30am, 3:30pm; €31.73); Sevilla (9hr., 4 per day 10:15am-9pm, €39.72).

Cartagena's portside area is an oasis of dynamic architecture interspersed with ruins dating back to the third century BC. Though the newer part of the city sprawls to accommodate its 200,000 inhabitants, the historical enclave by the port, embraced by five rolling hills, is a refreshing getaway for art and history aficionados. Founded in 227 BC by the Carthaginian general Asdrubal, the city of Qart Hadast ("New City"), now Cartagena, was modeled after Carthage itself. The city served as the main Punic metropolis in Iberia, rich in natural resources and privileged by its protected interior port. Streets such as C. Mayor, C. Canon, and C. Cuatro Santos brim with marbled, *modernista* buildings with intricate ironwork in light colors. The **Ayuntamiento,** 19th-century **Iglesia de la Caridad,** and 17th-century **Iglesia de Santo Domingo** are standout highlights. The climb up C. Jara tenders close-up views of the **Teatro Romano, Byzantine wall,** and 13th-century **Catedral de Santa Maria la Vieja.**

Architecture aside, the modern and informative museums are arguably the best part of the city. The **Centro de Interpretación de la Muralla Púnica (CIMP),** C. San Diego, 25, just across from the tourist office, provides detailed information about the Punic history of the city, and displays the only remnants of the original defensive wall of Qart Hadast. (Open daily 10am-2pm and 4-8:30pm. €3.50, students and under 16 €2.50.) Continue past Pl. Bastarreche on C. San Diego, which becomes C. Duque and C. Cuatro Santos. This street forms the upper border of the *casco antiguo*, leading past a Byzantine wall, ruins of the Teatro Romano (finished in AD 1), and the **Centre d'Interpretation**

de la Historie de Carthagene. The cross-street C. Caridad, which becomes C. Gisbert, is a lovely walk to the eastern end of the port wall. C. Cuatro Santos ends at C. Aire; from here, the parallel C. Canon leads to the sun-drenched port-side Pl. del Ayuntamiento, a central locale for restaurants, sightseeing, and access to the port. The **Paseo de Alfonso XII** runs along the port, and bus and taxi stops line the way. Perpendicular to the port are the yellowed walls of the **Arsenal Militar,** constructed in the 18th century. Though ruins of the *casco antiguo* are primarily concentrated near the port, Cartagena's sprawl beyond does not feel small or self-contained.

Hostal Rosa ❷, Pl. San Agustín, 61, just behind the *Ayuntamiento,* offers 14 minimalist rooms off long carpeted and mirrored hallways. (☎968 52 02 31. Singles €20; doubles €35, with bath €40; triples €45. MC/V.) There is a **market** on C. Gisbert toward the port. Otherwise, relax in the shady terrace and stone archways of **La Taperia ❷,** C. del Parque, 2, which offers an extensive, high quality tapas menu. (☎968 52 86 14. Open M-Sa 1-4pm, 8:30-midnight. Tapas and starters €1.50-7. *Menú del día* €16. MC/V.) Near the Ronda San Juan in a small square is **Entretapas y Vinos ❷,** Portales de la Lonja, 7, which offers creative Spanish fare for reasonable prices served amid chic black-and-white decor. (☎968 50 22 56. Tapas and starters €2.50-6.50. Huge wine selection. Open M-Sa 8:30am-4pm and 8pm-midnight and Su 8:30am-4pm. MC/V.)

To get to the city center and **tourist office,** walk straight on the tree-lined Av. de América to reach Pl. Bastarreche. The **bus station** is next to the tourist office in Pl. Bastarreche. The **tourist office** (☎968 50 64 83; www.cartagena.es) has free walking tours of the city, maps, and an accommodations list. (Open M-F 10am-2pm, Sa 10am-1pm.) The tourist office on the port, next to the *Ayuntamiento,* has a more extensive schedule (open May-Aug. M-Sa 10am-1:30pm and 5-7pm, Su 10:30am-1:30pm; Sept.-Apr. M-Sa 10am-1:30pm and 4-6pm). For **taxis,** call ☎968 311 515.

A WALK IN THE PARK. Elche (Elx), Alicante's sister city, is home to one of the largest palm tree parks in the world. Only a 30min. bus ride from Alicante, with the park and a number of museums and cultural activities, Elche is a worthwhile and off-the-beaten-path daytrip.

LAS ISLAS BALEARES

While all four islands—Mallorca, Menorca, Ibiza, and Formentera—share the crowds, each has a unique style and character that separates it from the rest. Mallorca, home to the bustling port city of Palma, absorbs the bulk of high-class, package-tour invaders and reigns as the commercial hub of the Baleares. Ibiza, a haven for counter-culture since the 1960s, entices bohemians and fashionistas alike with its outlandish parties, transforming crowds into glittering masses grooving to a deafening techno beat. Menorca, wrapped in green fields, staggering sandstone walls, and placid natural harbors, offers tranquility that the other islands do not, with secluded white beaches, fabulous hidden coves, and mysterious Bronze Age megaliths. Formentera, the smallest and most distant island, is sprinkled with a few fishing villages and boutique resorts, and boasts some of the calmest and most majestic beaches in the Mediterranean.

Summer, the best time to visit any of the islands, is hot, crowded, and fun, while winter tends to be chilly and slow, as nightlife does not hit full swing until around early July. Most hours, schedules, and prices listed are for summer only. Low-season prices at hostels and hotels can drop by up to half, and hours for sights and attractions are often limited.

HIGHLIGHTS OF LAS ISLAS BALEARES

GOSSIP about Chopin's love life in his home in **Mallorca** (p. 324).

GIGGLE in a laughing gas booth at a discoteca in party town **Ibiza** (p. 343).

PEDAL through the wooden walkways of lovely **Formentera** (p. 351).

CAVE IN to the natural wonders of **Ciutadella** (p. 339).

INTERCITY TRANSPORTATION

Flying to the islands is cheap and much faster than taking a ferry. Those under 26 can get discounts with **Iberia Airlines** (in Barcelona ☎902 40 05 00; www.iberia.com). Many travel agencies in Barcelona and Valencia book special airfare packages that include entrance to nightlife hot spots throughout the islands.

BY PLANE

Scheduled flights are the easiest to book, and flights from Spain to the islands won't break the bank as long as you reserve early. Frequent flights leave from cities throughout Spain and Europe (including Frankfurt, London, Paris, and Rome). Many daily Iberia flights connect Palma and Ibiza to Barcelona, Madrid, and Valencia. The cheapest way to get to Menorca is from Barcelona. Flights from the other cities are more expensive. Service from Alicante, Almería, and Bilbao also exists, but is less frequent and sometimes only available during peak summer months.

Iberia offers flights from Barcelona to Ibiza (55min.) and Madrid (1hr.). Prices for these flights can range from €30 to several hundred euro. **Air Europa** (☎902 40 15 01; www.air-europa.com), **Spanair** (☎902 13 14 15; www.spanair.com), and **Vueling** (☎902 33 39 33; www.vueling.com) also offer inexpensive flights to the islands through special *ofertas* if booked well in advance. Schedules and prices are highly variable and subject to change. Another option is a charter

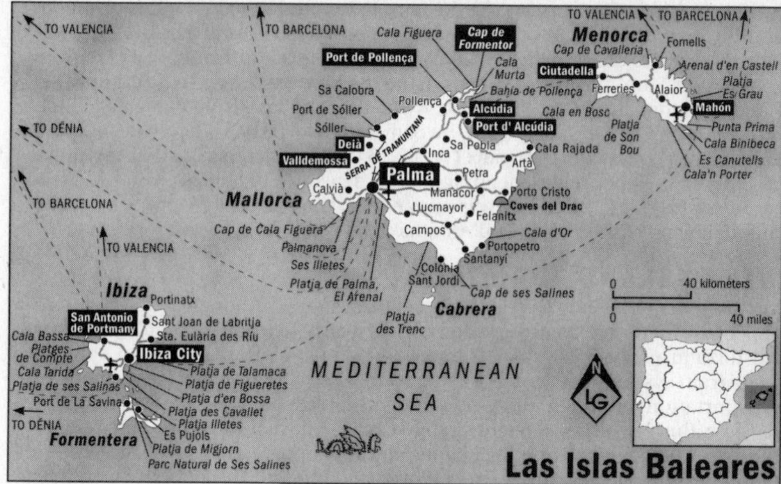

flight, sometimes offered as a division of scheduled airline companies. Most deals entail a stay in a hotel, but some companies (called *mayoristas*) sell unoccupied seats on package-tour flights. Prices during summer, San Juan, and *Semana Santa* are higher than in low season (Oct.-May), when tickets are fairly easy to get not long before departure. Those traveling in July or August should reserve at least a month in advance, especially to Ibiza and Palma.

BY BOAT

Ferry service is not always cheaper than flying, and it takes longer. Discotecas and small swimming pools on some boats ease the ride, but beware that not all boats run at the same speed. Try to book the high-speed ferry options that take only 2-4hr. Ferries run from Barcelona and Valencia to Palma and Ibiza, and from Dénia (in Alicante) to Ibiza. Seats may be available up to an hour before departure, but reserve tickets a few days in advance to be sure.

Balearia (☎902 16 01 80; www.balearia.com) ferries run from **Dénia's** Estació Marítima, Valencia, or **Barcelona** to **Ibiza** (2-4hr., 2 per day, from €48), also with service to **Palma, Port d'Alcudia,** and **Formentera** (from €48).

Buquebus (☎902 41 42 42; www.buquebus.com) has super-fast catamaran service between **Barcelona** and **Palma** (3hr., 2 per day, €30-150).

Acciona Trasmediterránea (☎902 45 46 45; www.trasmediterranea.com) boats depart daily from **Barcelona's** Estació Marítima Moll, **Alicante,** and **Valencia's** Estació Marítima to **Ibiza, Mallorca,** and **Menorca.** Fares from the mainland are €30-150, depending on speed and distance. Fares between the islands range €28-75.

LOCAL TRANSPORTATION

INTER-ISLAND TRANSPORT

Iberia flies between Palma and Ibiza (40min., 11 per day, €72-85) and between Palma and Maó, Menorca (35min., 11 per day, from €84). **Air Europa, Spanair,** and **Vueling** (see **By Plane,** p. 25) connect the islands at similar prices.

Another viable option is to take the **ferry.** Prices and schedules change almost monthly, and can be infrequent depending on the season. It's best to consult with the tourist office or a travel agent. Ferries to and from Mahón can be lengthy (4hr.), but "fast ferries" now make the journey between the other three islands in under 2hr. **Trasmediterránea** (☎902 45 46 45) sails from Palma to Mahón (5hr., Su 8am, €41) and Ibiza (2hr., Su 8am and 8pm, €31-48). There is no direct Mahón-Ibiza connection. **Trasmapi** (☎902 16 01 80) links Ibiza and Formentera (25-35min., 6-10 per day depending on the season 7:10am-8pm, €15-21). **Iscomar Ferries** (☎902 11 91 28; www.iscomar.com) run between Menorca's Port de Ciutadella and Mallorca's Port d'Alcúdia for daytrips.

INTRA-ISLAND TRANSPORT

The three major islands have extensive bus systems, although in quieter areas (especially Menorca) transportation comes nearly to a halt on Sundays. Palma and Ibiza are especially easy to navigate by bus. Mallorca has two narrow-gauge train systems that are more of a tourist attraction than a major mode of transportation, although many recommend taking the train at least once for the view. Bus fares between cities range €1.20-7.50 each way. Cars and mopeds (the latter being substantially cheaper and riskier) are great ways to explore remote or inaccessible areas. On Mallorca and Menorca, roads can be confusing and dangerous, so cars are the best option, while in Ibiza and Formentera, a moped is adequate. Always ride mopeds with extreme caution. A tiny, standard transmission car costs around €45 per day, including insurance. Mopeds cost around €35, and bicycles a mere €8-15.

MALLORCA (MAJORCA)

Mallorca has long attracted the rich and the famous. Pianist Frédéric Chopin and novelist George Sand had a passionate (and scandalous) affair here in the mid-19th century, and Mallorca is also a choice vacation spot for Spain's royal family and the world's most glamorous jetsetters. To the northwest, white sand and olive trees adorn the jagged Sierra de Tramontana, where writers and artists have created some of their most impressive work. To the east, expansive beaches sink into calm bays, while to the southeast, phenomenal caves hide natural wonders. Inland, creaking windmills power a thriving agricultural economy in towns that have managed to maintain a distinct character.

PALMA ☎971

After visiting the designer stores near Plaça d'Espanya and the raucous bars and restaurants along the port of Palma (pop. 375,000), it becomes hard to imagine that the city was once a humble devotional retreat for Fernando and Isabel. Today's devotions are to the sun gods, and the droves of Germans and Brits in Palma certainly participate. Despite the tourist invasion and urban growth, the city retains a local flavor. In its many cafes and tapas bars, where the native dialect of *mallorquí* is the only language heard, it's clear why Palma reigns as the cultural capital of the Baleares.

TRANSPORTATION

Flights: Aeroport Son San Juan (☎971 78 90 00), 8km from downtown Palma. Bus #1 runs between airport and port, stopping along the way in Pl. d'Espanya (every 20min.

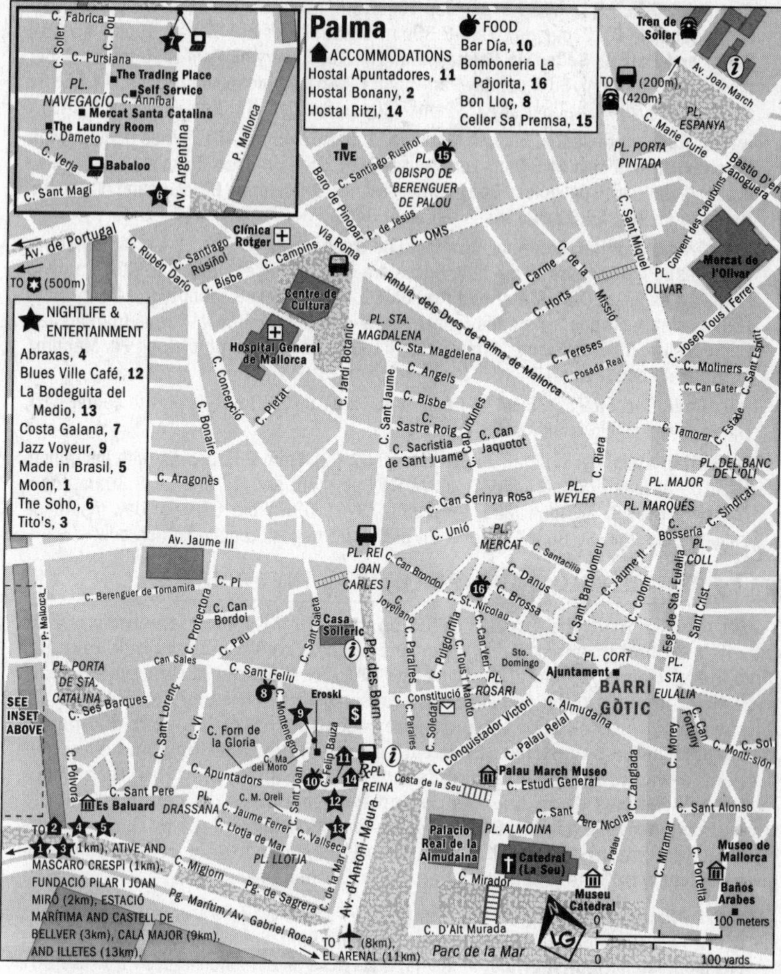

5:50am-2:30am, €1.85). **Air Europa** (☎902 40 15 01), **Iberia** (☎902 40 05 00), and others offer service to Palma. See **By Plane,** p. 25, or **Inter-Island Transport,** p. 323.

Trains: Estacion Plaça Espanya (☎971 752 051), **Ferrocarril de Sóller** (☎971 63 01 30; www.trendesoller.com), **Pl. d'Espanya.** To: **Sóller** (1hr.; 7 per day 8am-7:30pm; €9, round-trip €14). To **Port Sóller** via a tramway from Sóller (20 per day, €3). **Servicios Ferroviarios de Mallorca (SFM),** Pl. d'Espanya (☎971 17 77 77), departs to **Inca** (30min., 34 per day 5:50am-10pm, €1.80) and **Sa Pobla** (35min., 16 per day 5:50am-9:25pm, €2.65).

Buses: Palma is a convenient base for bus travel. Nearly all buses stop at the main stop on C. Eusebi Estada, several blocks down from Pl. d'Espanya; buy tickets on the bus. The tourist office has a bus schedule. Popular destinations include: **Alcúdia** and **Port d'Alcúdia** (45min.; M-Sa 16 per day 8am-9pm, Su 5 per day 9:30am-9pm; €4.50);

Coves del Drac (1hr.; M-Sa 3 per day 10, 11am, noon, Su 10am; €7.30); **Port Pollença** (1hr.; M-F 12 per day 7am-8:30pm, Sa-Su 7 per day 7am-8:30pm; €5.25); **Sóller and Port de Sóller via Palmanyola** (1hr..; M-F every hr. 7am-8:30pm, Sa 7 per day 8:30am-6:30pm, Su 4 per day 9am-5pm; €2.85); **Valldemossa** (30min.; M-F 8 per day 7:30am-7pm, Sa 7 per day 7:30am-7:30pm, Su 5 per day 8am-6:30pm; €1.45).

Ferries: Trasmediterránea, Estació Marítima, 2 (☎902 45 46 45). Ferries dock at **Moll Pelaires.** Tickets sold M-F 9am-1pm and 5-7pm, Sa 9am-noon. Tickets and info also available at travel agencies. Daily ferries run to **Barcelona, Eivissa,** and **Valencia. Balearia** (☎902 16 01 80) sends ferries to **Dénia.**

Public Transportation: Empresa Municipal de Transportes (☎971 21 44 44; www.emt-palma.es). Pl. d'Espanya is the hub. Buses are easy, clean, and efficient. Stops around town and as far as **Cala Major and Arenal.** €1.10 (buy tickets on board), 10-ride pass (€8) available at tobacco stands (only in inner-city Palma). Bus #15 runs from Arenal-Can Pastilla-Pl. Reina (every 15min.). Bus #1 goes from the airport, along Pg. Marítim/ Av. Gabriel Roca (every 15min. 6:10am-2:15am, €1.85).

Taxis: Radio Taxi (☎971 75 54 40) and **Fono** (☎971 72 80 81). Airport to center €15. Old town to Estació Marítima €8-10.

Car Rental: Ative, Pg. Marítim, 28 (☎971 45 62 62). From €35 per day with insurance. Must be at least 23 years old. Open M-Sa 8am-1pm and 4-7pm, Su 8:30am-noon. **Mascaro Crespi,** Av. Joan Miró, 9 (☎971 73 61 03). From €26 per day, insurance included. Open M-Su 8am-1pm and 3-7pm. €157 deposit required. Cash only.

ORIENTATION AND PRACTICAL INFORMATION

To get to town from the airport, take bus #1 to Pl. d'Espanya, the busy hub of the city's ground travel (15min., 4 per hr., €1.85). From the ferry dock, take Pg. Marítim/Av. Gabriel Roca (20min.) or bus #1 to Av. d'Antoni Maura, which leads to Pl. de la Reina and Pg. des Born. The busiest part of the city lies between Pl. d'Espanya and Pl. Reina, by the port. The best street to take from Pl. d'Espanya is **C. Sant Miguel,** a pedestrian street with great window shopping and even better people-watching. The street spills into **Pl. Major,** and a right turn from there leads to **Pl. Rei Joan Carlos I,** a roundabout intersection at the center of the old town. From here **Passeig Des Born** leads toward **Pl. Reina** and the port, the town's cultural and culinary nucleus. Pl. Rei Joan Carlos can also be reached by **Avinguda Rei Jaume III,** which runs through Palma's business artery.

Tourist Offices: Palma branch, Pg. des Born, 27 (☎971 22 59 00; www.a-palma.es), in the book shop of Casa Solleric. Open daily 9am-8pm. Branch in Pl. d'Espanya by the bus stop. **Island tourist office,** Pl. Reina, 2 services all of Mallorca (☎971 17 39 90). Ask for a map and the accompanying street index. Open M-F 9am-8pm, Sa 9am-2pm.

Currency Exchange: Banco Santander, Pg. des Born, 17 (☎971 72 51 46). Open M-F 8:30am-2pm, Sa 8:30am-1pm; Apr.-Sept. closed Sa.

English Bookstore: The Trading Place, C. Pou 35 (☎871 941 350). New and used books. Buy, sell, exchange. Open daily 10am-1:30pm and 4:30-8pm.

Laundromat: Self-Press, C. Annibal, 14 (☎971 73 06 43). €10 per load. Open M-F 8am-1:45pm. Cash only. **The Laundry Room,** Pl. Navegació, 9 bajo (☎971 90 39 25). €16 per wash and dry. Ironing €20 per hr. Dry cleaning and collection/delivery to boats. Open M-F 8am-4pm, Sa 8am-1pm. (Both opposite the old town from Av. Argentina, which bisects the port.)

Local Police: Pg. Mallorca and Sant Ferran (☎971 22 55 00 or 092). Dial ☎091 for national police.

Pharmacy: Plaza de la Reina, 11 (☎971 71 53 71). Open 9am-9pm, M-Sa. 24hr pharmacies rotate daily; see the local paper, *Diario de Mallorca,* or check *farmàcia de guardia* postings outside pharmacies.

Medical Services: Clínica Rotger, C. Santiago Russiñol, 9 (☎971 44 85 00), a ways from the port between Pl. Bispe Bereniguer de Palou and Pl. Hospital. 24hr.

Internet Access: Babaloo, C. Verja, 2, a block behind the port off Av. Argentina (☎871 95 77 25). A backpacker-filled haven with fast tech services, espresso (€1), and other beverages. €2 per hr. Open M-Sa 10am-10pm, Su 3-10pm. The nearby *locutorio* at Av. Argentina, 45a charges €1 per hr. for internet and is open daily until 1 am.

Post Office: C. Constitució, 6 (☎971 22 86 10). Just off Pl. Reina. **Fax** service. Open M-F 8:30am-8:30pm, Sa 9:30am-2pm. **Postal Code:** 07013.

ACCOMMODATIONS

LAS ISLAS BALEARES

The ubiquity of ATMs in Palma is a not-so-subtle hint that travelers are expected to empty their pockets. There are a few, cramped hostels close to the port, most run by expats. You won't get much bang for your buck here—rooms offer more character than amenities. Make reservations far in advance.

Hostal Ritzi, C. Apuntadors, 6 (☎971 71 46 10), a block off Pl. de la Reina, flanked by the best bars and eateries of the *casco antiguo*. Tiny rooms above a Victorian sitting room and kitchen. Breakfast included, served at 8:30am. Laundry €7. Singles €30; doubles €50, with shower €55, with bath €65. Open year-round. Cash only. ❸

Hostal Apuntadores, C. Apuntadors, 8 (☎971 71 34 91; www.palma-hostales.com), next door to Hostal Ritzi above the Cafe Art. The undisputed selling point here is the terrace on the top floor, with a spectacular view. Spacious singles and 1 huge 6-person dorm. Wi-Fi. Dorms €20 per bed; singles €35; doubles €50, with bath €68. MC/V. ❷

Hostal Bonany, C. Almirante Cervera, 5 (☎971 73 79 24), 3km from town between the port and Castell de Bellver, close to some of the island's best discotecas. Take bus #3 or 6 from Pl. d'Espanya or Pl. Rei Joan Carles I to the 1st stop on Av. Joan Miró and walk up C. Camilo José Cela. Take the 1st right and then the 1st left. Extremely pleasant staff (but be prepared to use your Spanish). Swimming pool, outdoor tables, rooms with bath, TV, and some with balcony. Singles €32; doubles €40. Cash only. ❸

FOOD

Palma serves up a winning array of ethnic and international foods, as well as vegetarian and new-age fusion cuisines. Make sure to try the *ensaimadas* (pastries smothered in powdered sugar) and the *sopa mallorquina* (stewed vegetables over brown bread). There are two local markets: **Mercat de l'Olivar** in Pl. Olivar by Pl. d'Espanya, and **Mercat Santa Catalina,** across town at the corner of C. Pou and C. Dameto. For groceries, try **AProp** on C. Felip Bauza, just off C. Apuntadors (☎900 70 30 70; open M-F 8:30am-8:30pm, Sa 9am-2pm).

Celler Sa Premsa, Pl. Obispo Berenguer de Palou, 8 (☎971 72 35 29; www.cellersapremsa.com). An ivy-covered, dimly lit, stone entrance opens into a cavernous restaurant with small, cheery tables dwarfed by floor-to-ceiling wine barrels. Filling half-*raciones* €3.70-6.40. Open M-Sa noon-4pm and 7:30-11:30pm. MC/V. ❶

Bon Lloc Restaurant Vegetaria, C. Sant Feliu, 7 (☎971 71 86 17). A reprieve for vegetarians tired of bread and cheese, this warmly lit, wholesome lunch spot has been the top choice of health-conscious foodies for the past 20 years. The *Menú del Día* (€12.50) promises fresh juices, salads, soups, and excellent desserts. Open M-Sa 1-4pm. ❸

Bar Dia, C. Apuntadors, 18 (☎971 71 62 64). One of the oldest bars in Mallorca, this hole-in-the-wall *taperia* remains perennially popular. Devour delicious tapas (€2-5) and huge *raciones* (€6-7) at the chaotic standing bar or among the raucous maze of tiny tables. Open Tu-Th and Su noon-midnight, F-Sa noon-1:30am. Cash only. ❶

Bomboneria, La Pajarita, C. San Nicolau 2 (☎971 71 69 86). If the flourishing, sweet-filled window displays aren't enough to entice you, the to-go cappuccinos (€1) certainly will be. Leaving without gorging yourself on chocolate truffles or more traditional *mallorquinas* will take some serious willpower. There are no seats here, but the sweets make a stop worthwhile. Open M-F 9:30am-2pm and 4:30-8pm, Sa 9:30am-2pm. MC/V. ❶

SIGHTS

Palma's architecture melds Arabic, Christian, and *Modernista* styles in a vibrant reflection of the island's multicultural past and present. A visit to Mallorca would be incomplete without a stroll along D'Alt Murada, a fortified boardwalk that links many of Palma's landmakrs and museums.

LAS ISLAS BALEARES

CATEDRAL (LA SEU). This Gothic cathedral is Palma's undisputed architectural gem. The cathedral, dedicated to Palma's patron saint San Sebastián, bears the stamp of many centuries—begun in the 1300s, finished in 1601, and then restored by Gaudí in unmistakable Modernista fashion in 1902. The southern facade overlooks a reflecting pool and the ocean, making La Seu the only cathedral in Europe reflected in water. A small museum next to the cathedral explores the church's role in Palma's history. *(C. Palau Reial, 29. ☎971 71 31 33. Cathedral and museum open June-Sept. M-F 10am-6:15pm; Apr.-May and Oct. M-F 10am-5:15pm; Nov.-Mar. M-F 10am-3:15pm; year-round Sa 10am-2:15pm. €4. Video guide €4.)*

ES BALUARD. Palma's contemporary art museum, formerly a 17th-century military fortress, opened in 2004. An impressive collection features three floors of 20th- and 21st-century paintings, sculptures, and installation pieces with a loyal emphasis on work by local artists. Even modern art skeptics will appreciate the portside walk and a tour of the grassy courtyards accented by bizarre outdoor sculptures. *(At intersection of Av. Gabriel Roca and Pg. Mallorca. Enter through Pl. Santa Catalina. ☎971 90 82 00; www.esbaluard.org. Open Tu-Su June-Sept. 10am-10pm; Oct.-May 10am-8pm. Occasional free concerts June-Oct. F 10pm. €6, students €4.50. Tu adult €4.50.)*

FUNDACIÓ PILAR I JOAN MIRÓ. Inaugurated in 1992, this small estate hosts rotating exhibitions on the life and work of Surrealist Joan Miró, a collection of his paintings and sculptures, and his preserved studio, which houses works in progress at the time of his death. *(Av. Joan Saridakis, 29. Take bus #6 from Pl. Progres to Av. Joan Saridakis. ☎971 70 14 20. Open May 16-Sept. 14 Tu-Sa 10am-7pm, Su 10am-3pm; Sept. 15-May 15 Tu-Sa 10am-6pm, Su 10am-3pm. €4.80, students €2.60.)*

CASTELL DE BELLVER. With austere Gothic turrets rising amid groves of trees at the end of town, the circular Castell de Bellver offers a wonderful view of bustling Palma and its sparkling bay. Built in 1300, it served as a summer residence for 14th-century royalty before becoming the prison of Mallorca's most distinguished law breakers. The castle now contains a comprehensive municipal museum and models of archaeological sites. During the summer, the Castell also hosts concerts and theatrical performances. *(Bus #3 from Pl. d'Espanya or #6 from Pl. Rei Joan Carlos I, €1.10. Both drop you off in Pl. Gomila. Walk downhill to C. Bellver and take a left, then a right on C. Drecera. Follow the signs up to the massive staircase. Also accessible by car. Tourist bus #50 drives to the top from Pl. de la Reina or Pl. Gomila, €13. ☎971 73 06 57. Open Apr.-Sept. M-Sa 8:30am-9pm, Su 10am-6:30pm; Oct.-Mar. M-Sa 8am-7:15pm, Su 10am-5pm. €2, students €1. Free on Saturday morning and Sunday.)*

PALACIO REAL DE LA ALMUDAINA. Built as a Moorish fortress, the palace was once a stronghold of Fernando and Isabel. King Jaime II is credited with transforming the Muslim castle into a Christian bastion in the 14th century, with a courtyard surrounded by a chapel, queen's quarters, Arab baths, and great hall. *(C. Palau Reial. ☎971 21 41 34; www.patrimonionacional.es. Open Apr.-Sept. M-F 10am-5:45pm, Sa 10am-1:15pm; Oct.-Mar. M-F 10am-1:15pm and 4-5:15pm, Sa 10am-1:15pm. Guided visits €4, unguided €3.20; students and children €2.30. EU citizens free W. Audio tour €2.)*

BEACHES

The biggest island of the Baleares, Mallorca contains an almost inexhaustable roster of great beaches. Though many are a long haul from Palma, several picturesque (though highly touristed) stretches of sand are accessible by city bus. The beach at **El Arenal** (S'Arenal; Platja de Palma; bus #15), 11km to the southeast (toward the airport), is the prime stomping ground of Mallorca's German and British tourists. With scores of German-owned restaurants, bars, and hotels, the waterfront is practically Frankfurt on the Mediterranean. While still gorgeous, the beach suffers from the onslaught of often rowdy vacationers. Other beaches close to Palma include **Cala Major,** 15km southwest, and Illetes, 9km southwest, which are smaller than El Arenal but equally popular (both accessible by bus #3 from Pl. d'Espanya, leaves every 10min.). The tourist office distributes a list of various nearby beaches.

NIGHTLIFE AND ENTERTAINMENT

Entertainment in Mallorca has that Spanish vim and vigor sometimes lacking on the other islands. The tourist office keeps a list of sporting activities, concerts, and exhibits. There is also *cine a la fresca,* an outdoor movie showing held a few nights per week during summer in the **Parc de la Mar.** For info and events, *El Día del Mundo* (€0.75) has an entertainment supplement every Friday that lists bars and discos, and *La Calle* (€1) offers a monthly review of hot nightspots. Also check out the free youth guide (*Guias de Ocio*) available in cafes, stores, and restaurants.

BARS

At dusk, the crooked streets between Pl. de la Reina and Pl. Llotja are enlivened by foot traffic and hordes of bar-hoppers. Elegant eateries and cozy bars fill fast, but a law requiring downtown bars to close by 1am during the week and 3am on weekends has shifted the late-night action to the waterfront, as many port establishments don't have these restrictions.

The Soho, Av. Argentina, 5 (☎971 45 47 19). This hip "urban vintage" bar has patterned walls and a funky, Warhol-esque interior with black-and-white TV screens. The red-lit den plays alternative music, including 80s hits, classic rock, and underground techno. Beer €2. Mixed drinks from €5. Open daily 6:30pm-2:30am. MC/V with €5 min.

Costa Galana, Av. Argentina, 45 (☎695 16 86 40). This swanky bar has white leather chairs and a combo of surfing videos and electro-jazz music. Daytime cafe vibe upstairs, lounge vibe downstairs. Beer €1.80-2.50. Mixed drinks €5-6. Open M-Th and Su 8am-2am, F-Sa 8am-4am. MC/V.

Jazz Voyeur, C. Apuntadors, 5 (☎971 90 52 92; www.jazzvoyeur.com). This intimate jazz venue hosts some of the biggest names in jazz, as well as the annual Jazz Voyeur Jazz Festival in Palma. €1 cover, with a drink min. of €10 for live concerts. Beer €4. Mixed drinks €8-10. Open June W, Th, and Su 8pm-1am, F-Sa 8pm-3am; July Tu-Su from 8pm. Schedule subject to change. MC/V.

La Bodeguita del Medio, C. Vallseca, 18, plays great Cuban rhythms in a local tavern. The bar boasts a shrine to Ernest Hemingway's alleged drink of choice: the mojito. Mixed drinks €5. Open M-Th and Su 8pm-1am, F-Sa 8pm-3am. MC/V.

Blues Ville Cafe Bar, C. Ma d'es Moro, 3 (www.bluesvillebar.com). This blues and jazz club packs in locals nightly from 11:30pm onward, with live music and a comfortable atmosphere. Beer €1-2. Mixed drinks €3-5. Open daily 10:30pm-4am. Cash only.

DISCOTECAS

The center of the club scene is the **Passeig Marítim/Avinguda Gabriel Roca** strip that runs along the water from Av. d'Antoni Maura to the ferry station. Clubbers start the night in *bares-musicales* a little closer to town. Later, the party moves down the block to the giant discotecas. Look for promoters offering reduced cover prices and drink deals. It's a 20min. walk from Pl. de la Reina, or you can hop on bus #1 from Pl. d'Espanya. (Bus service stops around 2:30am.) There is also the Bus de Nit (night bus; #41), which runs from the Pl. Rei Joan Carles I, stopping at key points along the strip (11:40pm-7am, €1.10). Several clubs and bars are centered on Plaça Gomila and along Avinguda Joan Miró. The bars and clubs around the beach at El Arenal are German-owned, German-filled, and German-centric, but can make for a good *nacht.* The last bus back to Palma leaves at 1:35am, though, so plan to take a cab home.

Abraxas, Pg. Marítim, 42 (☎971 45 59 08). One of the most popular nightspots in Mallorca, complete with 2 dance floors, 3 bars, and a terrace. Cover €15. In winter open Th-Sa 11pm-6am; open daily in summer 11pm-6am. MC/V.

Tito's, Pg. Marítim, s/n (☎971 73 00 17; www.titosmallorca.com). Themed fetish parties, go-go dancers, the works. Cover €15. In summer open daily 10pm-6am. MC/V.

Made in Brasil, Pg. Marítim, 27. Takes you right to Río with Brazilian music and crowd and tropical decor. Try their specialty *caipirinha* (€5.50), a mix of sugar, lime, and the Brazilian liqueur *cachaça,* blended in a sweet, icy slush. Open daily 8:30pm-4am.

Moon, Pg. Marítim, 29, offers a slightly larger venue than the *bares-musicales* and cheaper covers than the big discos. Sleek white interior with flashing neon lights. Cover €6, includes 1 drink. Open daily 10pm-6am.

WESTERN MALLORCA

Ten minutes beyond the urban lifestyle and high-rises of Palma, the road enters a ravine where the island's first cave-dwellers lived, then begins to climb in tight, narrow curves amid steeply terraced mountainsides. This is western Mallorca, one of the most beautiful landscapes in the Mediterranean.

VALLDEMOSSA

TIB buses to Valldemossa leave Palma from the bus station (30min.; M-F 8 per day 7:30am-7pm, Sa 6 per day 7:30am-7:30pm, Su 5 per day 8am-6:30pm; €1.45).

Valldemossa is a tiny web of antique streets in the shadow of the Sierra de Tramontana's rising slopes. Little in this peaceful village hints at the passion that scandalized townsfolk during the winter of 1838, when Frédéric Chopin and George Sand stayed in the 14th-century monastery **Cartoixa Reial.** The Chopin memorabilia now housed in the monastery includes the *Playel* piano that he carried up the mountain. A ticket (€8.50, €7.50 for groups of more than 5) includes access to the both the **monastery** and the **Palau del Rei Sancho,** the two primary sights in this small town. The former has a brief history of the city, an 18th-century Cartusian pharmacy, and a contemporary art room with works by Miró and Picasso. The latter, located just around the corner from the monastery, was commissioned by King Jaime II in 1309 for his asthmatic son. It later became a retreat of Nicaraguan poet Rubén Darío, who wrote some of his best work here. Shady trees and arched doorways line the open courtyard outside, where folk dances take place during the week (M and Th 11am-1:30pm); the music room also hosts piano recitals. (☎971 61 21 06; www.valldemossa.com. Open Su year-round 10am-1pm; June-Sept. M-Sa 9:30am-6:30pm; Nov.-Jan. M-Sa 9:30am-4pm; Feb. 9:30am-4:30pm; Mar.-May and Oct. M-Sa 9:30am-5:30pm. Recitals six per day, 10:30am-5pm in summer., 3 per day 11:30am-1:15pm Nov.-Feb. Church attire.)

Stop by the **Centro Cultural Costa Nord,** Av. Palma, 6, established in 2004 by Michael Douglas, whose summer house can be glimpsed from the hillside. The **Fundación Balears Sostenible,** which owns and manages the Centro, strives to promote sustainable living and tourism on the islands. World renowned musicians have come to this unimposing building every year to perform in the concert series called *Noches Mediterraneas.* A short documentary made by Douglas and the foundation provides historical information about the islands, and is available in several languages. (☎971 61 24 25; www.costanord.com. Open daily 9am-5pm.) For an off-the-beaten path taste of contemporary art, the **Fundació Cultural Coll Bardolet** displays the painting collection of Catalan artist, Coll Bardolet, whose primary subjects are the island's landscapes and traditional dances. (☎971 61 29 83. Open Nov.-Dec. Tu-Sa 10am-4pm; March-Oct. Tu-Sa 10am-6pm; July-Sept. M-Sa 10am-7pm. Free.)

DEIÀ

Buses heading for Port Sóller from Palma stop in Deià after Valldemossa (45min.; M-F 7per day 7:30am-7pm, Sa 7 per day 7:30am-7:30pm, Su 3 per day 8am-6:30pm; €2.45).

Historically a secluded artists' colony, the mountain village and peaceful cove of **Deià** now attracts a ritzy, upscale sect of Europe's most fashionable *nouveau riche.* Besides the occasional bus or moped, the vast silence that envelopes this particular fold of the Mallorcan mountains is enchanting. To get to the small, rocky beach, **Cala Deià,** by car, continue along the highway until the second bus stop, then take a left. There is also a stony path for walking to the beach, which starts from the center of town; use caution, though, as its steep slope is not for the flip-flop clad. The flowery **Cementari Municipal** behind the church atop the hill offers a unique insight into Deià's past, as well as one of its best views. English poet Robert Graves, the community's favorite self-exiled expat, is buried here among a few other early 20th-century artists. Graves' hilltop home was recently converted into a **museum,** preserved exactly as it was when the illustrious poet lived there until his death in 1985. The house, which he named Ca n'Alluny, is just past the center of town, on the main road. (☎971 63 61 85. Open M-F 10am-5pm, Sa 10am-3pm.)

There are two hostels in Deià, both situated on hilltops on opposite sides of town. One is **Hostal Miramar ❸,** on C. Can Oliver. (☎971 63 90 84; www.pensionmiramar.com. Singles €37; doubles €72, with bath €89.) The other option for lodging is the **Hostal Villa Verde ❺,** on C. Ramón Llull, 19, a hilltop retreat with spectacular, antique-laden rooms and views. Breakfast is served on a flower-filled patio that overlooks terraced hills and the menacing rocky peaks above them. (☎971 63 90 37. Singles €50; doubles €68, with terrace €83. MC/V.)

Expensive restaurants dot the lower town, but **Font Fresca ❶,** at the entrance to town, offers moderate prices and a lovely view from its terrace. (*Bocadillos* €3.20-3.60. Salads €6-8. Open 10:30am-7pm for drinks and snacks. Kitchen open noon-5pm.) End your day on another Deià terrace, this time at **Café Sa Fora ❶,** C. Archiduque Luis Salvador, 5, right on the main road. This is the undisputed late-night hangout for everyone in town. (Beer €1.50-2. Mixed drinks €5. Tapas €4. Live Music Sa. Open Mar.-Nov. daily 10am-3am. Cash only.)

NORTHERN MALLORCA

The northern gulfs of Mallorca contain droves of older, package-tour masses in some areas and quieter, family-friendly coves in others. If you don't mind a bit of competition for sun spots, don't miss this region—these jagged coves and long beaches are among the most beautiful on the island.

PORT POLLENÇA

Transunion buses connect Palma and Pollença (1hr.; M-F 12 per day 7am-8:30pm, Sa-Su 7 per day 7am-8:30pm; €5.25). Bus/train combo: take train from Palmato Inca and catch a bus from Inca to Port Pollença (1hr.; 7 trains per day M-F 7:20am-6:25pm, 7 buses per day M-F 8:05am-7:10pm; €5.10). There is also one bus at 9am every morning from Sóller, which stops in Pollença before heading on to Alcudia and Port d'Alcudia. Buses stop along the strip and at the end of Pg. Saralegui.

Port Pollença's tranquil coastline, which features a thin manmade beach along a crescent-shaped bay, lures a calm, classy crowd of tourists, mostly British. The area hosts an extensive **music festival** in July and August, with concerts every Wednesday and Saturday night. A complete schedule of events and list of ticket vendors is available beginning in mid-June at the tourist office (tickets €15-45). Summer also brings plenty of free events such as the much anticipated **Sons de Nit,** free concerts held throughout the island; in Pollença these concerts take place either near the water or in the central plaza. Right next to the *Ayuntamiento*, **Hostal Borrás ❸,** Pl. Miquel Capllonch, 14, which is attached to the Bar Cultural, offers huge rooms with private bath and old red leather chairs. (☎971 866 647. Open June-Aug. Singles €30; doubles €40, with balcony €50. Cash only.) There is an open market in this plaza every Wednesday (9am-2pm). Vendors set out colorful displays of produce, traditional island foods, crafts, and the occasional faux handbag. The **tourist office,** Pg. Saralegui, is next to the bus station, a block from the port, and has lists of all the restaurants and accommodations in town. (☎971 86 54 67. Open M-F 8am-8pm, Sa 10am-5pm.) There is also a **taxi** stand next to the bus station, or call ☎971 86 62 13. **Rent March,** C. Joan XXIII, 89, rents bikes and mopeds. (☎971 86 47 84. Bikes €5.50-12 per day, also available for half-days; mopeds €25-130 per day. Open Mar.-Nov. M-Sa 9am-1pm and 3-8pm, Su 9am-12:30pm.) The **police** can be reached at ☎971 86 62 67.

CAP DE FORMENTOR

Buses stop 11km away from the end of Cap de Formentor. Autocares Mallorca (TIB), sends one bus from Palma (1hr.; 10:15am, return 3:30pm; €5.60). Autocares Mallorca (☎971 54 56 96) leaves Port Pollença (4 per day 10am-4:30pm, 5:30pm last return; €1.30). A boat (☎971 86 40 14) goes to Platja Formentor from Pollença's Estació Marítima (30min.; hourly 10am-3pm except 2pm; returns every hr. 11:30am-6pm except 2:30, 4:30, and 5:30pm; round-trip €8.30).

A trek to Cap de Formentor, 15km northeast of Port Pollença, leads to dramatic seaside cliffs, a lighthouse, and pristine ocean views. The road is peppered with landings perfect for photo-ops, and all are crowded with cars. Eleven kilometers before the lighthouse, the road drops to **Platja Formentor,** where a canopy of evergreens seems to sink into the shore. Just beyond the beach is **Hotel Formentor,** which has been frequented by an astounding list of European celebrities, politicians, and royalty. If you have your own transportation, head to the lighthouse at the top of the steep, winding hill and make a quick stop along the way for two of the most beautiful coves in Mallorca. On the left is the small dirt parking lot for **Cala Figuera,** accessible via a practically vertical dirt path. Across the road to your right is a small wooden sign pointing in the direction of **Cala Murta,** perhaps the most secluded cove on the island. On the trek down, keep your ears open for the tinkling bells of roaming mules. From the road, enter through a small wooden gate on your right, then bear left on the dirt path. After a 25min. (2km) walk, you will stumble upon the cove's tiny pebbly beach, a few scattered picnic tables, and crystal-clear water lapping at jagged cliffs.

ALCÚDIA AND PORT D'ALCÚDIA

Buses (☎971 54 56 96) run to Alcúdia (€4.35) and Port d'Alcúdi (€4.50) from the bus station in Palma (1hr.; M-Sa 16 per day 8am-9pm, Su 5 per day 9:30am-9pm). The bus to Port Pollença and Cap de Formentor leaves from the corner of C. del Coral and Pg. Marítim. Municipal buses run between the port and the town every 15min.

Alcúdia and its nearby port are far from undiscovered, but within the city's fortified walls awaits an ancient intimacy lacking in Alcúdia's southern sister, Palma. The beach is the main attraction here, but the old town has 14th-century ramparts, and **Roman ruins** dating from 2 BC. **Parc de s'Albufera,** within walking distance of the beach, is filled with marshes, flowers, and over 60 species of birds. The interior of the park is only accessible by bike or foot, and the reception is a 1km hike inland. (Open daily in summer 9am-6pm; in winter 9am-5pm. Free, but visitor's permit from reception required.) If you have a car, take the road toward **Artà** and then **Capdepera** from town. About 20km from Port d'Alcúdia, you will see signs leading to **Cala Torta** along a dirt road. If you hike from this beach over the cliffs to the west, you come to **Cala Mitjana,** a cove with crashing waves and tide pools. Past Cala Mitjana is **Es Matzoc,** a white-sand beach that is somewhat tourist-free. Summer brings music, dance, and culture to Alcúdia. The famed **Fiestas de Alcúdia** celebrate the Día de San Jaime (July 25), in honor of the local patron saint.

The recently renovated **Hostal Calma ❸,** C. de Teodoro Canet, 25, offers rooms with A/C, TV, and private bath, as well as a communal kitchen. (☎971 54 84 85; www.hostalcalma.com. Breakfast €4. July-Aug. singles €32, doubles €48, triples €59; Apr.-June and Oct.-Mar. €22/40/53. Prices decrease with longer stays. MC/V.) Port-front restaurants tend to be expensive, so for a budget option try **Oceano ❶,** C. dels Mariners, 18B, a British-owned bar and restaurant that has sandwiches and salads (€4-5.50) served outside facing the port or inside at the shell-adorned bar. (☎971 54 74 14. Open all day. Cash only.) Head to **Supermercats Aprop,** C. dels Mariners, 14, for groceries. (Open M-Sa 9am-9pm.) There are three **tourist offices,** two at the port, one in town. One is on Pg. Marítim in a plaza at the end

"EL CLUB DE POETAS" OF HOTEL FORMENTOR

One auspicious day in 1929, the Hotel Formentor opened its elegant doors on the northern shores of Mallorca. By the 1950s, the hotel's guest list included the who's who of Western Europe: everyone from Churchill to the royalty of Monaco paid a visit.

Soon enough, the Formentor also attracted a young group of intellectuals who were seeking cultural freedom during a period of oppression. Fifty years ago, in 1959, writer Camilo José Cela, together with editor Carlos Barral, hosted a revolutionary meeting of international poets. Participants gathered together in a tiny room of the Hotel Formentor now known as the "Club de Poetas." It was an immediate success.

The next year's meeting drew such literary moguls as Octavio Paz, Henry Miller, and Italo Calvino. With support from his colleagues, Barral established two literary prizes of $10,000: the Prix International des Editeurs, for the most innovative work of literature, and the Premio Formentor, awarded for the best work by an up-and-coming, unpublished author. These prizes have since led to the publication of works that may never have seen the light of day, due to their controversial subject matter and their "subversive" ideologies.

Hotel Formentor–the haunt of these groundbreaking writers–is close to Port d'Alcudia and accessible by bus from Palma.

of the beach, on the left facing the water. (☎971 54 72 5. Open in summer M-Sa 9:30am-8:30pm.) **Police** can be reached at ☎971 54 50 66.

SOUTHEASTERN MALLORCA

Mallorca's southeastern coast is perpetually inundated with tourists, all vying for prime spots on its beautiful beaches and collectively descending into its gaping caves. But if the crowds don't phase you, this region of the island does contain a few natural gems and relaxed port towns that merit a visit.

CUEVAS DEL DRACH. Despite its classification as a bona fide tourist attraction, the **Cuevas del Drach** (Dragon's Caves), just south of Porto Cristo, are among the island's unique natural wonders. The long, artfully lit walkway winds through a dizzying maze of stalactites and stalagmites reflected in crystal-clear saltwater pools. The tour then descends into Lake Martel, one of the largest underground lakes in the world. On the edge of the vast lake, classical musicians play soft, sultry music from illuminated rowboats. The tour and concert last about an hour and are worth the trip and price. A 10min. walk down the main road, across the bridge, and to the right leads to the quiet shores of **Porto Cristo,** a calm port and bay lined with cafes and shops. *(A bus to the caves runs from the bus station in Palma; 1hr.; M-Sa 3 per day 11:10am-1:30pm, Su 10am; one way, €7.35, roundtrip €12. If you're driving, head toward Manacor from Palma and then toward Porto Cristo. Follow the signs through town. Daily tours run every hr. 10am-5pm. Line up early. €10.50, cash only; tickets purchased for entrance at a specific hour are good for 75min. For more information, call ☎971 82 07 53, or visit www.cuevasdeldrach.com.)*

LAS ISLAS BALEARES

MENORCA

Menorca's fantastic beaches, rustic landscapes, and picturesque towns draw sun-worshippers, photographers, and ecologists alike. When UNESCO declared the island a biosphere reserve in 1993, the government took important strides to emphasize preservation of Menorca's natural harbors, pristine beaches, rocky northern coast, and network of farmlands. Menorca's main cities, Mahón and Ciutadella, located at the east and west ends of the island respectively, serve as gateways to the real attraction: crystal-clear aquamarine water that laps stretches of velvety sand and hidden rocky coves (see Beaches, p. 341).

MAHÓN (MAÓ) ☎971

Mahón (pop. 22,000) exudes authentic energy remarkably unspoiled by its spot on the tourist-heavy island itinerary. Many use Mahón as a launching pad to nearby beaches (via scooters or public buses) but return to candle-lit restaurants in the evening to watch the red sun dip behind the harbor.

TRANSPORTATION

Flights: Airport (☎971 15 70 00), 4.5km out of town. The **Aerobús** (operated by Torres ☎902 07 50 66; www.e-torres.net) runs in a loop between the airport, the Pl. de s'Esplanada, and the port (every 30min., 5am-11:15pm, €1.50). Airport **taxis** are €11 to town. **Iberia/Aviaco** (☎971 36 90 15), **Air Europa** (☎971 15 70 31), and **SpanAir**

(☎971 15 70 98) all fly out of Mahón. Advance booking is essential in summer. See **By Plane,** p. 25, and **Inter-Island Transport,** p. 323.

Buses: The bus station is at the far end of Pl. de s'Esplanada, up C. Vasallo and on the left. The station is the hub for buses to and from Mahón, and also houses a tourist information booth. Check the tourist office or newspapers *Menorca Diario Insular* and *Menorca* for schedules (infomenorcamao@cime.es). **Transportes Menorca (TMSA;** ☎971 36 04 75; www.transportesmenorca.net) to: **Ciutadella** via **Es Mercadal** and **Ferreries** (1hr., M-F every hr. 6:45am-11:15pm, F only also 12:15am, Sa 8 per day 8am-9:30pm, Su 6 per day 8am-7pm; €5); **Es Castell** (20min.; every 30min. M-Sa 7:20am-8:45pm, Su 9:15am-1:45pm and 3:45-8:45pm; €2); **Punta Prima** (20min.; M-Sa hourly 7am-11pm, Su 9 per day 9am-1pm and 4-7pm; €1.30); **Son Bou** (30min., every hr. 7:15am-10pm, €1.80). Schedules change every 6 months. **Autobuses Fornells Roca Triay** (☎686 93 92 46; www.autosfornells.com) go to: **Arenal d'en Castell** (30min.; M-Sa 5 per day 9:30am-7pm, Su 11am and 6pm; €1.90); **Fornells** (40min.; M-Sa 4 per day 10:30am-7pm, Su 11am and 6pm; €2.80); **Cala Tirant** (40min., M-Sa 4 per day 10:30am-7pm); **Son Parc** (30min., M-Sa 4 per day 10:30am-7pm, €2.20). Buy tickets on board.

Ferries: AccionTrasmediterránea, Moll de Ponent (☎971 36 60 50 or 902 45 46 45; www.trasmediterranea.es; ticket booth open M and W 9am-1pm and 5-8pm; Tu, Th and F 8am-1pm and 5-7pm; Sa 7-10am; Su 3-5:30pm) sends ferries daily to **Barcelona** and weekly (Su) to **Palma** and **Valencia. Balearia** (☎902 16 01 80; www.balearia.com; ticket booth open M 8:30am-1:30pm and 5-7pm, Tu-F 8am-2:30pm and 5-7pm, Sa 10:30am-12:30pm) sends ferries to **Alcúdia, Barcelona,** and **Palma. Iscomar** provides service to **Valencia** and **Barcelona** from Mahón, and **Port d'Alcudia** from Ciutadella. (☎902 11 91 28; ticket booth open M-F 9am-1pm and 4-7pm, Sa 10am-1pm and 4-7pm, Su 9am-1pm.) For more info, see **Inter-Island Transport,** p. 323.

Taxis: Main stand at **Pl. de s'Esplanada** (☎971 36 71 11), or **Radio Taxi** (☎971 36 71 11). To: **airport** (€11); **Cala Mesquida** (€15); **Cala'n Porter** (€17); **Es Castell** (€10).

Car Rental: Morcamps, C. Gobernador Ramírez, 29 (☎971 36 95 94). Fully equipped cars (4 doors, A/C, radio, and CD player) for as little as €25 per day. Tourist office provides a comprehensive list of all car rental agencies in the city.

Moped Rental: Autos Valls, Pl. de España, 3 (☎971 35 42 44; www.autosvalls.com). Rents both cars and mopeds. Mopeds €25 per day, cars €35 per day or €75 for 3 days. Open M-F 9am-8pm, Sa 9am-1pm and 4-8pm.

ORIENTATION AND PRACTICAL INFORMATION

Plaça de s'Esplanada, a square once used as a parade ground and now lined with chic shops and tapas bars, is the city's transportation hub. **Calle de Ses Moreres** connects the plaza to the five downward-sloping blocks, pedestrian streets at the heart of the old city, that eventually lead to the port. Areas on the other side of the port beyond **Plaça Princep** are quieter and more residential. Various serpentine paths lead down to the port, but the central point of access is a set of steps that wind from the **Plaça Espanya** and end between the **ferry station** and tourist office. To the right of the port is the Moll de Llevant, and to the left is **Moll de Ponent,** which turns into **S'Hort Nou** after Costa des General.

Tourist Office: Moll de Levant, 2, in the Port Authorities Building (☎971 35 59 52; open T-Sa 8am-2:30pm, M and Su 8am-1pm). **Branch** inside the bus station (same hours) and at the airport (☎971 15 71 15).

Currency Exchange: Banks with 24hr. **ATMs** line C. Hannóver and C. Nou, and dot all the pedestrian streets.

Laundromat: Lavandería Marin, Cami des Castell, 64 (☎971 36 23 79). Wash and dry €15.75 for up to 5kg. Open M-F 9am-1pm and 4-7:30pm.

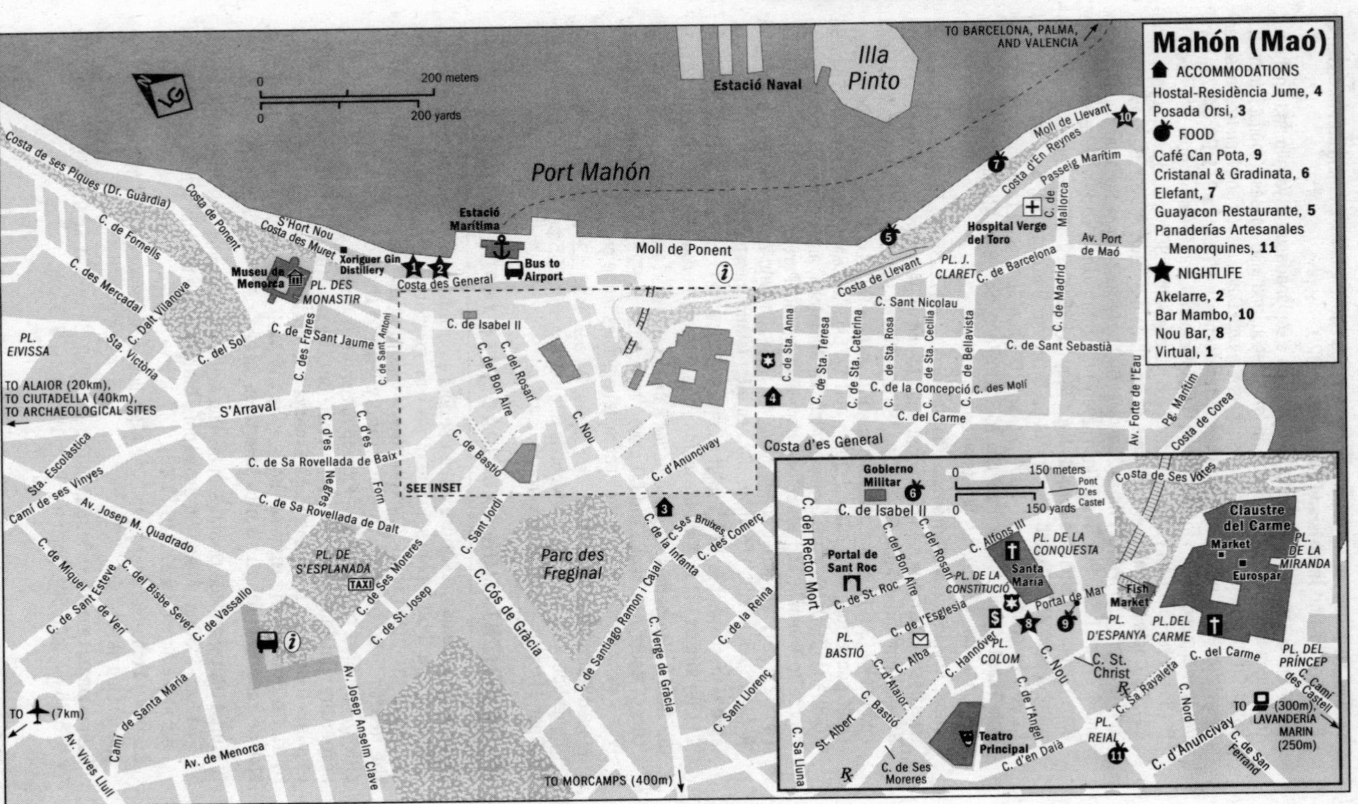
Mahón (Maó)
ACCOMMODATIONS
Hostal-Residència Jume, 4
Posada Orsi, 3
FOOD
Café Can Pota, 9
Cristanal & Gradinata, 6
Elefant, 7
Guayacon Restaurante, 5
Panaderías Artesanales
Menorquines, 11
NIGHTLIFE
Akelarre, 2
Bar Mambo, 10
Nou Bar, 8
Virtual, 1
Port Mahón
Illa Pinto
Estació Naval
Moll de Ponent
Moll de Llevant
Estació Marítima
Bus to Airport
Xoriguer Gin Distillery
Museu de Menorca
PL. DES MONASTIR
Hospital Verge del Toro
Parc des Freginal
PL. DE S'ESPLANADA
SEE INSET
TO BARCELONA, PALMA, AND VALENCIA
TO ALAIOR (20km), TO CIUTADELLA (40km), TO ARCHAEOLOGICAL SITES
TO MORCAMPS (400m)
TO (7km)
Claustre del Carme
Market
Eurospar
Fish Market
Santa Maria
Teatro Principal
Gobierno Militar
Portal de Sant Roc
PL. DE LA CONQUESTA
PL. DE LA CONSTITUCIÓ
PL. D'ESPANYA
PL. COLOM
PL. BASTIÓ
PL. REIAL
PL. DEL PRÍNCEP
PL. DE LA MIRANDA
TO (300m), LAVANDERÍA MARIN (250m)
150 meters
150 yards
200 meters
200 yards

Police: Municipal, Pl. de la Constitució (☎971 37 37 12) and Pl. de la Miranda.

Pharmacy: Check the list outside any pharmacy for the *farmàcia de guardia* (all-night pharmacy), which changes every night. Close to Pl. de s'Esplanada is **Landino Pons,** C. Ses Moreres (☎971 36 05 94); another central pharmacy can be found on C. Sa Ravaleta, 5, right next to Pl. Reial (☎971 36 29 61).

Medical Services: Hospital Verge del Toro, C. Barcelona, 3 (☎971 15 77 00). English spoken. Open 24hr. for emergencies.

Internet Access: Locutorio Velita, C. San Paolo, 1, at C. Cami des Castell (☎971 36 75 71). €3 per hr. Open daily 11am-2pm and 5-11pm.

Post Office: C. del Bon Aire, 11-13 (☎971 36 66 29), at C. de l'Església. Open M-F 8:30am-8:30pm, Sa 9:30am-2pm. **Postal Code:** 07700.

ACCOMMODATIONS

It's easier to find a room in Menorca than on the other islands, but it's still a good idea to call ahead, especially in July and August. **Hostal-Residència Jume ❸**, C. de la Concepció, 6, is meters from Pl. de la Miranda and Pl. Princep. It offers spacious, white-walled rooms with minimal decor and large beds, all with bathrooms. All rooms have TV and A/C. (☎971 36 32 66. July 21-Sept. 10 singles €30.50; doubles €58. Extra bed €26.60. Sept. 22-July 20 €34/63. MC/V.) **Posada Orsi ❷**, C. de la Infanta, 19, is centrally located and has brilliantly colored rooms, each with its own unique character. The residence has a TV room, sitting room, and a friendly staff. Fans are available upon request. (☎971 36 47 51. Breakfast €2-4. Singles €20-25; doubles €30-40, with shower €40-50. Cash only.)

FOOD

Cafes and bars spilling into Pl. de la Constitución, Pl. de Reial, and Pl. de s'Esplanada serve *platos combinados* and *bocadillos* (€2.70-5.10) to throngs of hungry customers during the hot midday hours. Regional specialties include *sobrassada* (a soft sausage and bacon spread) and *camot* (a dark sausage spread made with blood and flavored with fennel). *Mahonesa* (mayonnaise), which was invented in Mahón, and *queso mahon* (strong and savory cheese) are two gastronomic treasures of the island, steeped in pride and tradition. The produce **market** is in the **Claustre del Carme,** a Neoclassical 18th-century building affixed to a church that once housed the town's prison and justice courts. (Open M-Sa 6am-2pm and 5pm-7pm.) Groceries are sold below the produce market at **Eurospar.** (☎971 36 93 80. Open M-F 9am-9pm, Sa 8am-9pm.)

Panaderias Artesanales Menorquines. For the best breads and baked goods, head here, where the best of everything from Menorcan *ensaimadas* to whole-grain croissants to small pizzas cost only €1-3. Booths just off Plaza Reial, on C. de la Infanta, and in many other locations throughout the city. Open daily 8am-9pm. ❶

Elefant, Moll de Llevant, 106. A bohemian nook with tiny outdoor tables and idyllic sunset views, serving deliciously creative tapas to satisfy any craving. Lunches are €7.50 and tapas run €4.50-5. Open M and W-Su noon-4pm and 7pm-late. Cash only. ❷

Cristanal & Gradinata, C. Isabel II, 1 (☎971 36 33 16). An elegant, tucked-away wine-and-tapas bar with 20s jazz tunes, gleaming wood floors, warm lighting, and outdoor tables. While the owner changes the menu every day, the *bocadillos* stuffed with the freshest meat, veggies, and a dab of *mahonesa* are a staple. Open daily 6-11pm. MC/V. ❶

Guayacón Restaurante, Moll de Llevant, 139 (☎971 36 05 28). Another affordable option on the port is this Argentine-owned restaurant, which serves abundant heaps of steaming *patatas bravas,* chicken breast with rosemary, and other half-*raciones* (€2.80-7). Open M-Su 7pm-midnight. Cash only. ❶

Café Can Pota, Portal de Mar, 11 (☎971 36 23 63). An upscale cafe with comfy seating areas (and Wi-Fi) that has been serving delicious coffee, ice cream, and *bocadillos* (€1.50-3) since 1881. Open M-Sa 8am-midnight. MC/V. ❶

SIGHTS

Though the best sights in Menorca lie outside its cities, Mahón's attractions reflect the island's tumultuous history and frequent changes of nationality.

ESGLÉSIA DE SANTA MARÍA. Reconstructed between 1748 and 1772, it offers services in both Spanish and Catalan. The interior trembles with the sound of the 3006 pipes of its über-organ. *(La Major, Pl. de la Constitución. Organ concerts M-Sa 11:30am. Open for visiting M-Sa, 7:30am-12:30pm and 6-8:30pm. Suggested donation €4 for concerts.)*

MUSEU DE MENORCA. This old Baroque Franciscan monastery houses a permanent collection of Menorcan artwork and archaeological relics. *(Av. Dr. Guàrdia. ☎971 35 09 55. Open in summer Tu-Sa 10am-2pm and 6-8:30pm, Su 10am-2pm; in winter M-F 10am-2pm, Sa-Su 10am-2pm. €2.40, groups of more 5 €1.80, students €1.20, children under 12 free. Admission free.)*

PL. DEL CARME. Adjoining the **Pl. Espanya,** the **Pl. del Carme** houses the **Claustre del Carme** (today the public market), **Carme Church,** and **Fish Market.** You can enjoy free liquor samples at the **Xoriguer Gin Distillery,** Moll de Ponent, 93, at the port. Through glass windows at the back of the store, visitors can watch gin bubble and froth in copper vats. *(☎971 36 21 97. Open M-F 8am-7pm, Sa 10am-2pm. Free, tastings offered only after midday.)*

ARCHAEOLOGICAL SITES. Access to the island's numerous **archaeological sites,** some dating back to 3000 BC, is made simple by Menorca's small size and Mahón's efficient bus system. Highlights include prehistoric caves, tombs, settlements, and Paleochristian basilicas—most are accessible only by car or scooter. See the tourist office for information on a self-guided driving tour. The most famous of the monuments is **Torre d'en Galmes,** off the road to Platges de Son Bou from Alaior. This is the second largest settlement on Menorca, and portions date between 1300 and 1500 BC. Atop a hill overlooking the island's interior are three *talayots* (megalithic towers) and a sanctuary that served as both a religious and commercial center for Menorca's megalithic denizens.

OTHER SITES. Pont de Sant Roc is the last fragment of the medieval defensive wall, built nearly a century before the pirate Barbarossa sacked the city in 1535. *(Up C. Sant Roc from Pl. de la Constitución.)* The **Ayuntamiento** has existed in some form since the 17th century and exhibits a Neoclassical interior, complete with portraits of famous Menorcans. *(Next to Església de Santa María. Open M-Sa 8am-2pm.)* **Fort Marlborough,** at the mouth of the harbour by Es Castell, is a remnant of 18th-century British occupation and was one of three fortifications used to protect the city. Across the harbour is **La Mola Fortalessa Isabel II,** another example of 19th-century British military architecture.

NIGHTLIFE

Mahón's nightlife continues the gentle daytime pace of the city. A string of hip bars and clubs line the **Costa d'els General,** a small street that slopes upwards from the start of Moll de Ponent.

Akelarre, Moll de Ponent, 41-43 (☎971 36 85 20; www.akelarre.com.). One of the more fashionable places on the strip, with a cavernous bar and dance floor beneath stone archways and bronze art. Th night jazz jam sessions and occasional live concerts are popular and draw local crowds and musicians. Beer €3. Mixed drinks €7. Open daily June-Oct. 8am-5am; Nov.-May 3pm-3am.

Virtual, Moll de Ponent, 46. A few doors down from Akelarre is Virtual, where standing crowds are illuminated by two small floors of neon lights, lasers, and rows of TV screens. Mixed drinks €3-7. Open in summer M-Th and Su 7pm-4am, F-Sa midnight-4am.

Bar Mambo, Moll Levante 209 (☎971 35 67 82). At the opposite end of the port, this recent addition to the port's bar scene is a sophisticated bar with elegant outdoor seating lit by giant candles and enlivened by New Age music. Open daily noon-4pm and 6pm-4am. Beer (€2.50), wine (€2), *bocadillos,* and ice cream until 11pm. MC/V.

Nou Bar, C. Nou, 1, 2nd fl. (☎971 36 55 00). Away from the port, this establishment overlooks Pl. de la Constitución and serves drinks (€4-6) and beer (€2.50) to a calm crowd of older locals. Wicker chairs outside are popular seats for late-afternoon drinks or *café con leche.* Wi-Fi. Open daily 6pm-3:30am.

FESTIVALS

From May to September, merchants sell shoes, clothing, and bizarre trinkets in *mercadillos* located in the Pl. de s'Esplanada on Tuesday and Saturday. On July 16, Mahón's **Verge del Carme** celebration brings a colorful armada into the harbor and an equestrian procession into the streets. The **Festival de Música de Maó** in July and August showcases Església Santa María's Swiss organ and brings renowned classical musicians to the city's **Teatro Principal,** Costa d'en Deià, 40, built in 1829. Check the tourist office or the box office of the theater for schedules and prices. (Box office ☎971 35 57 76; www.teatremao.org. Open Tu-Sa 11:30am-1:30pm, Th-F also 6:30-8:30pm, and 1hr. before performances.)

CIUTADELLA (CIUDADELA) ☎971

Ciutadella's (pop. 21,000) narrow, cobblestoned paths weave between neighborhoods nearly undisturbed by tourists, while only blocks away, restaurants, shops, and postcard vendors compete for attention in the crowded plazas. Below, a narrow, glassy harbour reflects the tourist traffic of private boats and ferries, as well as a string of bars carved into russet rock. There's a seductive charm in the city's ancient streets, broad plazas, and hectic port. The beauty of the surrounding countryside and beaches only adds to the city's appeal.

TRANSPORTATION

Buses: Estación Mahón (☎971 36 04 75). **Transportes Menorca (TMSA)** runs from Pl. dels Pins (☎971 38 03 93), to: **Mahón** (1hr.; every hr. M-F 6:40am-11:40pm, Sa 8am-9:30pm, Su 8am-7pm; €4.75); **Cala Galdana** (M-Sa 3 per day; 10:40am-4:50pm, Su 3 per day 9:50am-4:45pm); **Cala Tomàs** via Ferreries and Es Mercadal (M-Sa 6 per day, 8am-7:45pm, Su 4 per day 8:10am-6:30pm).

Autocares Torres (☎971 38 64 61) offers daily service from the ticket **booth** in Pl. de los Pinos to surrounding beaches: **Cala Blanca** and **Santandria** (15min.; 1-2 per hr. M-Sa 7am-12:15am, Su 7am-8:55pm; €2); **Cala Blanes, Los Delfines,** and **Cala Forcat** (10-20min.; 1-2 per hr. M-Sa 7:15am-11:30pm, Su 8:40am-9:45pm; €2); **Sa Caleta** and **Cala En Bosc** (25-30min.; 1-3 per hr. M-Sa 7am-12:15am, Su 7am-10:30pm; €2); **Cala Morell** (15min.; 3 per day 8:45, 11am, 6:30pm; €2).

Ferries: Balearia (☎902 16 01 80; www.balearia.com) runs from Alcudia, Mallorca to **Ciutadella** (1hr.; daily 8am; €71). **Iscomar** (☎902 11 91 28; www.iscomar.com) offers the same route at cheaper prices (2½hr.; daily 8:30am and 5pm; €42). **Cape**

Balear (☎902 10 04 44) links Ciutadella to **Cala Ratjada,** Menorca (55min., May-Oct. 4-5 per day 7:30am-7:30pm, €50-60).

Taxis: (☎971 38 28 96). Pl. de s'Explanada is a prime hailing spot.

Car Rental: Europcar, Dragonera, 17, at Av. de Jaume I (☎971 38 29 98; www.europcar.es). 21+. From €45 per day and €210 per week. Open daily 9am-8pm. The tourist office provides an extensive list of all rental car agencies in the city.

ORIENTATION AND PRACTICAL INFORMATION

The bus stop is at the head of Pl. dels Pins (also called Pl. de s'Explanada), which leads directly into the city's harbor-side nucleus, Pl. d'es Born, where the **tourist office** can be found. The port and its accompanying street, C. Marina, lie below the rest of the city and are reached via the stone steps just off the corner of Pl. d'es Born. The *casco viejo* begins in line with the harbor's end and winds several blocks away from the port.

The **tourist office,** at Pl. de la Catedral, 5, provides maps and information on archaeological sights. (☎971 38 26 93; www.ciutadella.org. English spoken. Open M-F 9am-1pm and 5-7pm, Sa 9am-1pm.) There is also a **branch** at the port, inside the ferry terminal on the opposite side of the water from the rest of the city. (☎971 48 09 35. Open Tu-Sa 10:30am-2pm and 6:30pm-9pm, Su 8am-2:30pm.) **BBVA,** at Pl. d'es Born, 14, has **currency exchange.** (☎902 22 44 66. Open M-F 8:30am-2:15pm, Oct.-Mar. also open Sa 8:30am-1pm.) Other **banks** with **24hr. ATMs** can be found around the Pl. dels Pins and Pl. d'es Born. Other services include: **police** (☎971 38 07 87), in Pl. d'es Born; **Clínica Menorca** (☎971 48 05 05; open 24hr.), C. Canonge Moll; and the **post office,** Pl. d'es Born (☎971 38 00 81; open May-Oct. M-F 8:30am-8:30pm, Sa 9:30am-1pm). **Postal Code:** 07760.

ACCOMMODATIONS

Hostels here are few and far between, and some are only open during peak season (June 15-early Sept.). Always reserve ahead in the summer.

Hostal Residència Oasis, C. Sant Isidre, 33 (☎971 38 21 97). From Pl. dels Pins, take Av. del Capità Negrito, take the 3rd left onto Av. Alcantara, and turn right onto C. Sant Isidre. Relax in the quiet courtyard. Open June-Oct. Doubles with bath €50, doubles for single use €25; triples €75. Cash only. ❷

Hostal-Residencia Ciutadella, C. San Eloy, 10 (☎971 38 34 62; www.alojarseenmenorca.com). Offers simple singles and doubles attached to its restaurant. Open year-round. Singles from €29. ❷

Hostal Sa Prensa C. Madrid, (☎971 38 26 98; www.saprensa.com). A bit of a trek, but an excellent choice. By the harbor's mouth, it offers simple and spacious rooms on a phenomenal stretch of coastline. Internet €2 per 30min. Singles €30; doubles €48, with terrace €55. ❸

FOOD

There's a **market** (open M-F 9am-2pm) on Pl. de la Libertat, and a **Supermarket Super Avui** in C. Sant Onofre, 12. (☎971 38 27 28. Open M-Sa 8am-2pm and 5-8pm.) For traditional island cuisine in a hidden nook of the old town, descend into the cavernous **La Guitarra** ❸, C. Dolors, 1, a warmly lit establishment full of old wine racks and tasteful decor. Sample the *sopa mallorquina* (a traditional meat and veggie stew), the stuffed eggplant, or the *caldereta de langosta* (lobster stew). (*Menú* €15. Entrees €6.60-24. Open June-Sept. M-Sa 12:30-5:30pm and 7:15-10:15pm. MC/V.) Get in touch with your Don Quixote side at **Es Molí** ❶, C. de Maó, 1. A bar inside a giant windmill across from the Pl. de ses Palmeres, it is one of the local hangouts away from the water. (☎971 38 00 00. Open M-Th and Su 6am-1:30am, F-Sa 6am-3am. Cash only.) The **cafe** next door has Wi-Fi and attracts younger, artsy types, chatting over glasses of wine.

SIGHTS AND ENTERTAINMENT

Pl. des Born and the *casco viejo*'s churches offer an exemplary array of Spanish architecture and stonework. Past the mouth of the port and to the left stands the hexagonal **Castel San Nicolau,** a watchtower with channels chiseled into the stone. Though the tower is temporarily closed to the public, its architectural innovations can still be admired from outside. Dating from the Bronze Age, the ancient settlement of **Naveta des Tudons** (near the 40km marker from Maó) was built in 1500 BC. (Open daily, free Nov.-March; Apr.-Oct. guided tours with admission fee.) A mere 4km from the city, these perfectly preserved ruins of communal tombs contain the remains of over 100 people. The archaeological sites of **Torre Trencada** and **Torrellafuda** display the ruins of prehistoric settlements. Both protect Stonehenge-like formations that have stood for over 3000 years. If you don't have a car, consider **hiking** (about 8km, 3hr.) along C. Vell de Mahón, the old road to Mahón, or **biking** along the highway (at least 1hr. one-way). An archaeological guide to Menorca is available at the tourist office.

Nightlife in Ciutadella is spirited, with an intimate vibe that emphasizes socializing in smaller groups over drinks. Funky bars cluster near the port's end and a few *discotecas* around the parking lot attract small crowds. There is free live music near the port almost every night in summer, and couples enjoy romantic candlelit dinners by the water. For local jazz right, stop at **Bar Sa Clau,** where island ensembles play every Friday. (☎971 38 48 63; www.saclau.com. Open nightly from 7pm.) From the first week in July to the start of September, Ciutadella hosts the **Festival de Música d'Estiu,** featuring some of the world's top classical musicians. Tickets (€10-24) are sold in various locations throughout town; contact the tourist office for ticket information.

BEACHES

Even the most enticing postcards can't do Menorca's beaches justice. The island has over 80 beaches—most of which are clothing optional. Many are accessible by bus from Mahón and Ciutadella (situated around harbors, not beaches), a fairly comprehensive and reliable transportation system. With beauty comes popularity: in addition to attracting crowds of tourists, many of the most beautiful and accessible beaches are overrun by condominium complexes and resorts, hokey bars, restaurants, and postcard shops. Other beaches are located in more secluded coves that are best explored with a car or **scooter** and the *Let's Go to the Beach* map (not affiliated with *Let's Go* guides) available at any tourist office. You may discover your own hidden beach gems by choosing at random from the map or by taking spontaneous jaunts off the highway.

NORTH SHORE BEACHES

PLATGES D'ALGAIARENS. This stretch east of Cala Morell is home to some of the best beaches on the island, including Cala en Carabó, Penyal de l'Anticrist, Sa Falconera, and Cala Pilar Ets Alocs, all in a lush valley accessible via a path through the woods and over the rocks. Though not as secluded as they used to be, these beaches allow swimmers and sunbathers to forget the outside world for a few hours. The huge waves are great for surfers, but less so for waders. *(Beaches only accessible by car, moped, or a long bike ride from Ciutadella. Parking €5. A taxi from Ciutadella costs €16, but there are no pay phones, and cell phones may lose service.)*

ALBUFERA ES GRAU. Extending 2km in length and covering a surface of over 70 hectares, this lagoon consists mainly of the island of Colom, the Cabo de Favaritx, and the Natural Park, which must be explored via the designated pathways to prevent excessive environmental damage. It contains a network of dunes and small islands that shifts with changing tides and seasons. Activities include biking and hiking to the coves across the bay. Some of the best swimming areas are across from the main lagoon and uphill from town. *(☎971 35 63 02. Albufera Es Grau access by car or moped. Taxi from Maó €17.)*

ARENAL D'EN CASTELL. This deep, yawning cove is one of the north shore's largest, most beautiful, and most accessible, filled with daytrippers from Mahón and vacationing families in the upscale resorts and cheesy bars dotting the steep slope above the beach. A tourist train, "Arenal Na Macaret Express" (€4), makes the short trip from the bus stop in Arenal across a narrow strip of land to Macaret, a tiny fishing village with an even tinier beach. *(Autocares Fornells leaves from Maó. 30min.; M-Sa 5 per day 10:30am-7pm, Su 11am and 6pm; €1.85.)*

FORNELLS. This whitewashed fishing village, known primarily for its lobster farms (and lobster dinners), attracts a hardy crowd of adventurous tourists. Windsurfers and kayakers careen about Fornells's shallow port, and a walk along the town's hushed boardwalk leads to a rocky oasis with unspoiled vistas of the Torre de Fornells, a massive British watchtower built in 1801. True beach gurus make excursions to the deserted golden sands of Cala Tirant, only a few kilometers to the west of the town's center. *(Autobuses Fornells leaves from Maó to Fornells. 30min.; M-Sa 5 per day 10:30am-7pm, Su 11am and 6pm; €2.65. Buses directly to Cala Tirant leave Maó M-Sa 4 per day 10:30am-7pm; €2.85.)*

SOUTH SHORE BEACHES

CALA MITJANA. Thirty minutes by car or moped from Mahón, this small beach overlooks a dramatic cove bordered by limestone cliffs that plunge into the turquoise sea. Climb the staircase on your right upon entering the cove and head down the dirt path for about 5min. to reach **Cala Mitjaneta,** a smaller cove with a tiny beach and even more astounding views. While some visitors wade into the water here, others prove their bravery (or recklessness, as the case may be) by diving from the rocks. *(On the main highway from Maó to Ciutadella, head toward Ferreries, and then take the road to Santa Galdana. Directly on the left before reaching the roundabout above the town is the dirt road that leads to Cala Mitjana. Park in the small dirt lot and continue on foot.)*

CALA BINIBECA. Cala Binibeca is arguably the southern coast's most stunning cove, a tiny beach overlooking hidden underwater caves exposed with the tide. Near the cove is Pueblo Pescadores, a housing development built in 1972 to simulate an old fishing village, with corridors that wind in all directions around white Mediterranean-style houses. The restaurant-bar next to the beach offers free shady picnic tables and €2 beers. Beach chairs and parasols are €5 each for the day. Cash only. To get to Cala Binibeca, take the bus past the Binibequer stop, around a roundabout, and past the big, white sign for the Binibeca Vell houses. Get off right after you see the first beach umbrella down on your right. A small dirt path leads down to the cove. Kiddies and titties are welcome. *(From Maó, take the bus to Sant Lluis, and get off at Pueblo Pescadores. 20min., every hr. 8:10am-8:15pm, €1.20.)*

ELS CANUTELLS. Situated near Cala'n Porter (a 15min. drive from Mahón), Es Canutells is a secluded cove with azure waters, good for swimming and snorkeling and dotted with the boats of faithful returning visitors. Directly next to the beach proper is a narrow, more secluded beach. To get to Es Canutells, follow signs downhill to the beach from the bus stop. *(TMSA buses run to and from Maó. 15min., 4 per day 8:45am-7pm, €1.40.)*

CALA'N PORTER. Cala'n Porter greets thousands of visitors each summer, and caters to a wild, young crowd. *(TMSA buses run to and from Maó. M-Sa 7 per day 9:30am-7:40pm, €1.80.)* Its whitewashed houses, orange stucco roofs, and red sidewalks (a 15min. walk away, following the clearly marked signs) lead to the main attraction: the pristine blue beach and the unbelievable Covas d'en Xoroi, a series of caves etched into the cliffs hundreds of feet above the sea. These natural caves have been turned into an amazing network of bars, chill-out areas, and phenomenal discos that come alive night. *(☎971 37 72 36; www.covadenxoroi.com. Cover for bars before 6:30pm €5.80; 6:30-10:30pm €8.90, includes 1 drink. Children €3.50. Cover for disco F €17, Sa €21-25. Th foam parties. Bars open Apr.-Oct. daily 10:30am-10:30pm. Disco open daily 11pm-late.)*

PLATGES DE SON BOU. Son Bou offers an arrow-straight, 4km expanse of sand, the longest and silkiest stretch on the island. As one of Menorca's most popular beaches, it is frequently filled to capacity with throngs of sunburned tourists. Frequent bus service to and from Maó and Ciutadella, ample parking, beach chairs, and umbrellas for rent (€5 and €6). Cafes make it visitor-friendly, and *discotecas* are only two blocks from the sand. *(TMSA buses to the beaches leave from Maó. 30min., 7 per day 8:45am-7pm, €1.80.)* For those who choose to stay late, **Disco Pub Copacabana,** in the Nuevo Centro Comercial, on the left when heading away from the water, has a huge dance floor, pool tables, and a full arcade, all with a great view of the water. *(Beer €3.50. Mixed drinks €6. Open daily May-Oct. 11pm-3:30am.)* After 7pm, there is a 'Bus de Nit' with service back to Mahón on weekends, but it comes infrequently: only three times throughout the entire night.

IBIZA (EIVISSA)

Nowhere on Earth are decadence, debauchery, and downright hedonism celebrated as religiously as on the turquoise shores of the island of Ibiza (pop. 84,000). Traces of Ibiza's 1960s hippie days still remain amongst the locals and expat populations. In many ways, however, the island has strayed from its bohemian roots towards an extravagant, techno-fueled party mecca. Disco fiends, movie stars, and party-hungry backpackers arrive in droves over the summer to be swept up in the island's outrageous party culture and to bake on its warm sands. Despite Ibiza's wild spirit, the island is a safe and accepting place, where anyone can come to let their hair down.

IBIZA CITY (EIVISSA) ☎971

During the day, Ibiza City (pop. 40,000) is a boutique-laden portside town beneath a 16th-century walled city; it would seem like any seaside village in Spain. At night, however, you couldn't possibly mistake this town for any other. Come sunset, flashy bars and a flashier crowd seem to appear out of nowhere, flooding the port with neon lights, drag queens, pumping music, street stands, and fast-talking promoters. At 3am the scene migrates to the colossal discotecas outside of town, where parties last until dawn (and often well beyond).

TRANSPORTATION

Flights: Airport (☎971 80 90 00), 7.5km southwest of the city, near Ses Salinas. Bus #10 runs between airport and Av. d'Isidor Macabich, 20 (30min.; summer 2 per hr.

6:50am-11:50pm, winter every hr. 7:30am-11:35pm; €1.35). Taxis cost around €14-15. **Iberia,** Pg. Vara de Rey, 15 (☎902 40 05 00), flies to **Alicante, Barcelona, Madrid, Palma,** and **Valencia. Air Europa** (☎902 40 15 01), **Vueling** (☎971 80 90 00), and **Spanair** (☎902 13 14 15) offer similar options. See **By Plane**, p. 25, or **Inter-Island Transport**, p. 323.

Ferries: Estació Marítima and **Estació Marítima Formentera.** Trasmediterránea (☎902 45 46 45) sells tickets for ferries to **Barcelona, Palma,** and **Valencia.** Office open M-F 9am-1pm and 4:30-7:30pm, and 2hr. before departures. **Trasmapi-Balearia** (☎971 31 07 11) runs daily to **Dénia,** near **Alicante, Palma,** and **Formentera.** Office open M-F 9am-2:15pm, 4:30-8pm, and midnight-1:15am; Sa 9am-2:15pm and 6-8pm; Su 9am-2:15pm and midnight-1:15am. **Umafisa Lines** (☎971 19 10 88) sends boats to **Barcelona** 3-4 times per week. For more info., see **Inter-Island Transport,** p. 323.

Buses: Ibiza City has an extensive bus system, but buses to remote areas run only a few times per day. The **bus station** is on Av. d'Isidor Macabich, past Pl. d'Enric Fajarnés i Tur walking away from the port. For an exact schedule, check the tourist office, though sometimes schedules posted at the bus stops themselves are more reliable. **Intercity buses** leave from Av. d'Isidor Macabich, 42 (☎971 31 21 17), to **Sant Antoni** (M-Sa every 15min., Su every 30min. 7:30am-midnight; €1.60) and **Santa Eulària des Riu** (#13 M-F 2 per hr., Sa-Su every hr.; €1.60). Buses to the beaches (☎971 34 03 82) cost €1.35 and leave from Av. d'Isidor Macabich, 20, and Av. d'Espanya to: **Cala Tarida** (5 per day 10:10am-6:45pm); **Cap Martinet** (in summer every hr. M-F 8:15am-11:15pm; in winter M-Sa 9 per day 8:15am-7:30pm); **Platja d'en Bossa** (7:45am and every 30min. 8:30am-11pm); **Ses Salinas** (#11; in summer 3:45 pm and every hr. 9:30am-1:30pm and 4:30pm-7:30pm, in winter M, W, F 10am and 1pm).

Taxis: ☎971 39 84 83 (listed in the *Diario de Ibiza*)

Car and Moped Rental: Casa Valentín, Av. B.V. Ramón, 19 (☎971 31 08 22 or 30 35 31 for the branch on C. Galicia 35; www.welcome.to/casavalentin). Mopeds €25-46 per day. Cars from €36-60 per day. Open daily 9am-1pm and 4-8pm.

ORIENTATION AND PRACTICAL INFORMATION

Ibiza City's energy flourishes in the three small districts clustered to the south of the port. **Sa Penya** and **La Marina** are situated side-by-side on the port and are crammed with bars, restaurants, boutiques, and trinket stands. Rising steeply behind this packed grid of streets is **D'alt Vila,** the historic walled town overlooking the sea. There are four available entrances to D'alt Vila, but the easiest and most central is **Portal de Ses Taules,** the cobblestone pedestrian ramp, just behind the Mercat Vell off Antoni Palau. **Pg. Vara de Rey** leads to La Marina and D'alt Vila from **Avinguda d'Espanya,** which runs to **Platja Figuretas** and boardwalk restaurants. The local paper, *Diario de Ibiza* (€1; www.diariodeibiza.es) has an *Agenda* page with essential information, including water and weather forecasts, and information on the island's 24hr. pharmacies and gas stations, hours for popular museums, and important phone numbers.

Tourist Office: Pg. Vara de Rey (☎971 30 19 00). Open M-F 9am-8pm, Sa 9am-7pm, Su 9am-3pm. Winter schedule subject to change. Second location at airport (☎971 19 43 93). Open May-Oct. Tu-Su 10am-2pm and 5-8pm.

Currency Exchange: *Casas de cambio* do exist in town, but banks and ATMs offer better rates. Major banks like **La Caixa, BBVA, Sa Nostra,** and **Deutsche Bank** huddle around the intersection of Av. d'Espanya and Av. D'Ignasi Wallis, at the end of Pg. Vara de Rey.

Laundromat: Wash and Dry, Av. d'Espanya, 53 (☎971 39 48 22). Self-service wash and dry €13, with service €15, ironing €1.50-3.50 per article.

Police: C. Vicent Serra (☎971 39 88 31 or 092).

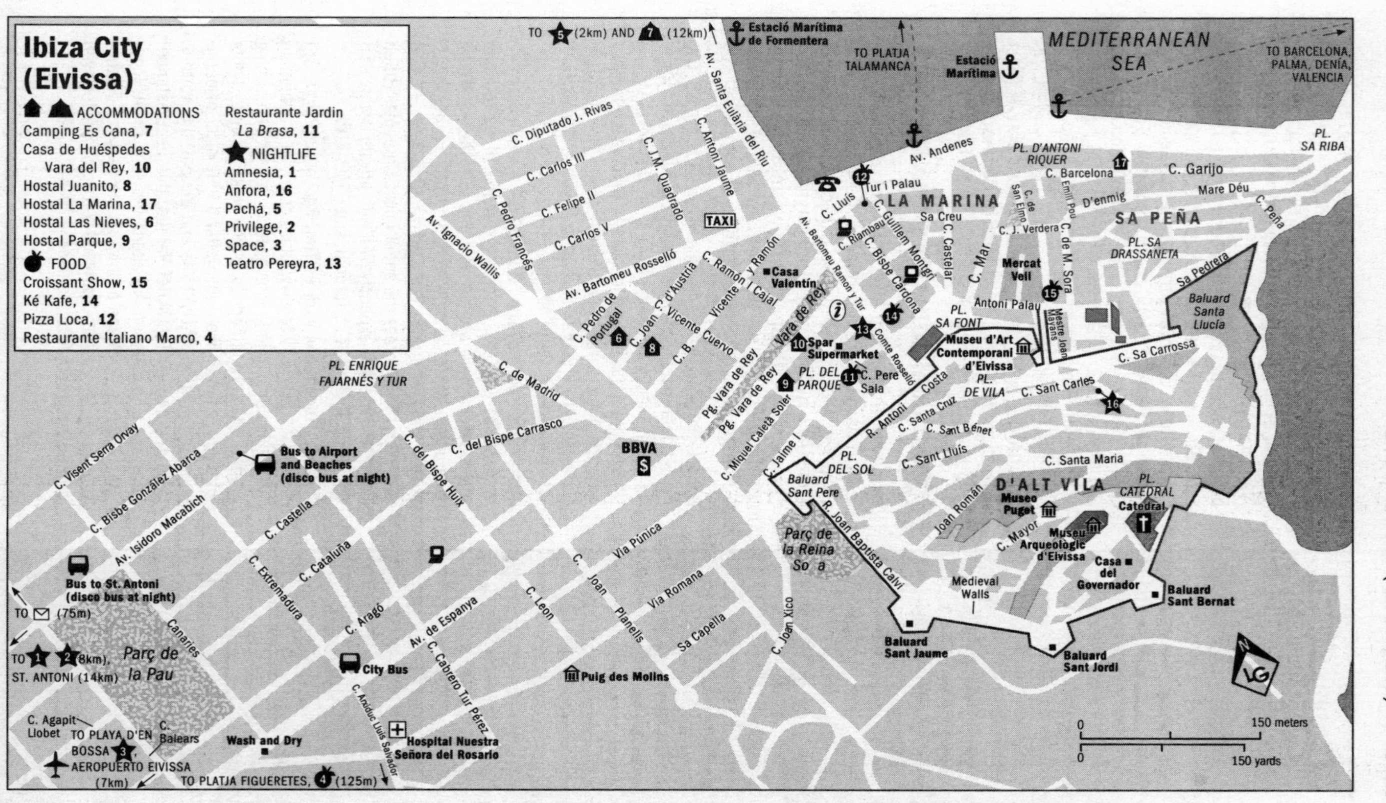

LAS ISLAS BALEARES

IZA'S FLOWER POWER

Famous rock stars, including Mick Jagger and Jim Morrison, ran rampant in this bohemian paradise during the 60s and 70s, earning Ibiza its unofficial nickname, "Ecstasy Island." Bob Dylan set up house in a windmill and Nico, eventually the lead singer for The Velvet Underground, apparently frequented the island's party scene. The island became notorious for its free-wheeling Saturday afternoon jam sessions, when famous rock 'n' rollers would indulge listeners with impromptu concerts while free spirits in the audience passed joints and marinated in good vibes.

Though the turbulent 60s are long behind the island, Ibiza still retains much of the era's bohemian charm. "Hippy markets" like Es Canar and Las Dalias still dot the island, selling organic produce and macramé trinkets. Las Dalias is known for its Saturday drumming circles, an energizing backdrop for shoppers looking to partake in the island's rock culture.

True, today is a new day—Bob Dylan's windmill, which later appeared on a Pink Floyd album cover, is now a popular pilgrimage for latter-day hippies and backpackers. Jade Jagger, Mick Jagger's daughter, owns a villa on the island, and U2's Bono has been seen beneath large sunglasses on several occasions. The 60s may be over, but travelers to Ibiza can still "turn on, tune in, and drop out" on this little island of peace, love, and rock 'n' roll.

Medical Services: Barrio Can Misses (☎971 39 70 00), a **hospital** west of town, and the large **Hospital Nuestra Señora del Rosario,** C. de Vía Romana, s/n (☎971 30 19 16), near the corner of C. Juan Ramón Jiménez. **Ambulance:** ☎971 39 32 32.

Internet Access: *Locutorios* abound by Platja Figueretes and among the streets behind the Estació Marítima de Formentera. Otherwise, try **Euro Ibiza Locutorio,** Av. Espanya, 91 (☎971 39 25 29). €.50 per 15min., €1 per hr. Open daily 10am-11pm. Also at **Touba Khelkom,** Av. Espanya, 32 (☎971 39 84 54). €0.50 per 15min., €2 per hr. Open daily 10am-midnight. Also at **Wash and Dry** (see above).

Post Office: (☎971 19 71 97). At the end of Av. d' Isidor Macabich away from the port. **Lista de Correos**. Open M-F 8:30am-8:30pm, Sa 9:30am-2pm. **Postal Code:** 07800.

ACCOMMODATIONS AND CAMPING

Hostels abound in the city, but few have it all. The best and safest accommodations are by the port, most off of Vara de Rey. The letters "CH" *(casa de huéspedes)* mark many doorways, and although these are often cheaper and have more character than *hostales*, prices still remain above €30 and reservations are often more difficult to make.

Hostel Parque, Pl. del Parque 4 (☎971 30 13 58; www.hostalparque.com). The most well-known hostel in town, ideally located below D'Alt Vila in the lively Plaza del Parque, where locals and tourists sip mojitos into the night. Large, airy rooms overlook the city. Mar.-June singles €45, doubles €110; July-Aug. singles €60, doubles €110. MC/V. ❹

Hostal La Marina/Los Caracoles, C. Barcelona 7 (☎971 31 01 72). Rooms are some of the best in town—each single, double, and mini suite has individual character, with royal blue walls and tidy, inviting beds. Rooms in La Marina (open year-round) have TV and A/C, but those across the street in Loc Caracoles (open Apr.-Oct.) are less expensive. All with private baths. €58 for basic single; €175 for mini suite. MC/V. ❺

Casa de Huespedes Vara de Rey, Pg. Vara e Rey, 7, 3rd fl. (☎971 30 13 76; www.hibiza.com). This bohemian hostel has truly unique rooms, decorated with everything from Tibetan prayer flags to fishing nets. The three flights of stairs can feel like a mile after a long night of partying, but the views of D'Alt Vila and the port are worth it. Also situated on Plaza del Parque, this establishment provides a less expensive alternative in a prime location. Reserve by phone or through the web site. Reception open M-Sa 9am-2pm and 7-10pm. Singles with shared bathroom €35; doubles, €70. MC/V. ❸

Hostal Juanito/Hostal Las Nieves, C. Joan d'Austria, 17-18 (☎971 19 03 19; www.hostalesibiza.com). Across the street from each other and under the same ownership, both hostels offer reasonably priced housing in a central area. All rooms come equipped with cheery yellow-and-blue tiled sinks and large windows. Juanito open year-round; Las Nieves (cheapest rooms with shared bath) open June-Sept. Singles €30; doubles €45, with bath €75. MC/V. ❸

Camping Es Cana (☎971 33 21 17; www.ibiza-spotlight.com/campescana). Pool and clubhouse. Close to restaurants and bars by the beach Des Canar, but a fair distance from Ibiza City. Reserve by phone. €6.50 per person, €7-12 per tent (depending on size). Bungalows €30-75, cabins €30. MC/V. ❶

FOOD

Ibizan dishes include *sofrit pagès*, a deep-fried lamb and chicken dish, *flao*, a lush lemon- and mint-tinged cheesecake, and *graxonera*, cinnamon-dusted pudding made from eggs and bits of *ensaimada* (sugar-coated bread). *Hierbas Ibicencas*, the island's strong, spicy favorite liqueur, often comes complimentary after restaurant meals. The small Mercat Vell, at the mouth of the Portal de ses Taules leading to D'Alt Vila, sells meat, fruit, and vegetables, among many other non-food products (open M-Sa 7am-7pm). For groceries, try **Spar Supermarket,** near Pl. del Parc (open M-Sa 9am-9pm).

Ke Kafe, C. Bisbe Azara, 5 (☎971 19 40 04; www.kekafe.com). Rough stone walls are decorated with local art, and orange globe lights bob from the ceilings of this new-age Middle Eastern restaurant. Try the 7 Pekados salad, with fresh strawberries, goat cheese, walnuts, and baby spinach (€7). MC/V.❷

Croissant Show, Mercat Vell (☎971 31 76 65), on C. Antoni Palau. Bright cafe serves creative sandwiches (€4.50-6), quiches, salads, pastries, and *platos del dia* (€7.50). Popular for breakfast after a night of clubbing. Open daily 6am-2am (closes early for rain). MC/V. ❶

Pizza Loca, C. Lluís Tur i Palau, 15. Oven-heated pizza in all varieties is popular among young bar-hoppers at this happy hole-in-the-wall right on the port. Try the spinach, tomato, and mozzarella with a bit of cumin. Slices €2.70-4. Open daily 11am-4:30am. Cash only. ❶

Restaurante Jardin La Brasa, C. Pere Sala, 3 (☎971 30 12 02). Amongst a maze of candlelit white tables and walls covered with brilliant pink flowers, customers enjoy innovative food in an intimate atmosphere. Try the mussels in almond sauce (€10.50), or the rabbit (€18). Kitchen closes at 11pm, bar open later. MC/V. ❸

Restaurante Italiano Marco, Po. de ses Pitiuses (☎971 30 10 69). This elegant boardwalk establishment, especially popular among tourists, offers candlelit patio seating and friendly service above the sea on Platja Figuretas. Traditional *spaghetti bolognese* (€7.50), soups (€4.50), and pizzas (€5.50-12), with a separate vegetarian menu. Open 8pm-midnight. MC/V. ❷

SIGHTS

Ibiza City's best known sites are portside—the drag queens, disco publicity stunts, and vacationers-gone-wild make people-watching a competitive sport. Rising just behind is another group of sights, enclosed in the 16th-century walls of **D'alt Vila** (Old Town), declared a UNESCO World Heritage site in 1999.

14TH-CENTURY CATHEDRAL. Originally a Carthaginian temple, this cathedral is in the center of town near a small castle. *(Open M-Sa 9:30am-1:30pm).*

MUSEU ARQUELÒGIC D'EIVISSA. This museum houses a variety of artifacts dating from the Phoenician and Carthaginian days of the island. *(Across the small plaza before*

ON THE BIG SCREEN

Ibiza has always drawn international attention, first as a trading hub in the seventh century BC, then as a hippie haven in the 1960s, and recently as one of the most lavish parties in the world. Last year, the time the island made a move toward multicultural advocacy with the genesis of the Ibiza and Formentera International Film Festival, now in its second year.

From May 23-30, 2008, films from England, Russia, the United States, Italy, and even Ibiza itself were shown at various theaters throughout the island. In 2008, when actress Mira Sorvino arrived on the red carpet outside the Cine Serra on Pg. Vara de Rey to promote her film "Leningrad," people truly started to take notice of what has become competition for the film festivals of Cannes and Rome.

In truth, the festival strives to fill a different niche from its European counterparts. The 2008 festival included several special events, such as "Ibiza Spirit," a cycle of movies from the island, "Ciclo Tibet," with multiple showings of Tibetan documentaries, and "Ciclo Green," a film series dealing with environmental issues. A far cry from the artistic stagnation of the Franco regime, this annual film festival celebrates Ibiza's spirit of multiculturalism and *joie de vivre.*

Visit www.ibizaiff.org. for more information on the festival.

the cathedral. ☎971 30 12 31. Open Tu-Sa 10am-2pm and 6-8pm, Su 10am-2pm; in winter Tu-Sa 9am-3pm. €2.40, students €1.20, under 18 and 65+ free.)

MUSEU D'ART CONTEMPORANI D'EIVISSA. The small museum displays art exhibitions ranging from video installations to photography, including a wide array of work by local artists and traveling international collections. *(Ronda de Narcís Puget, at the base of the old city. ☎971 30 27 23. Open Tu-F 10am-1:30pm and 5-8pm, Sa-Su 10am-1:30pm. €1.20, students free.)*

THE MUSEO PUGET. A building on the descent from the cathedral, this museum contains contemporary art by local artists like Antoni Pomar. *(☎971 39 21 47. Open Tu-F 10:30am-1:30pm and 4-6pm. Free.)*

PUIG DES MOLINS. This archaeological museum displays Punic, Roman, and Iberian artifacts. *(Vía Romana, 31 between Platja Figueretes and D'Alt Vila. ☎971 30 17 71. Open Tu-Sa 9am-3pm, Su 10am-2pm. €1.20.)*

BEACHES

In Ibiza City, if you're not at a disco, you're at the beach. Beaches feature satin sands, pale shores, and seas of shading umbrellas. More private coastal stretches lie along the northern and southwestern shores of the island and are accessible by car or moped. Still, there will be crowds everywhere you go. If you're looking for abandoned sands, you're better off heading to Formentera.

PLATJA DE SES SALINAS. A constant party, this beach is reflective of modern Ibiza. Masses of beautiful bodies groove to the New Age music pulsating from the Sa Trincha bar at the end of the beach. Reserve a beach chair for €6 in front of **The Jockey Club** (☎971 39 57 88; www.jockeyclubibiza.com) and receive full bar and restaurant service right from the sand as top DJs warm up for their club gigs. *(Bus #11 runs every hr. to Salinas from Av. d'Isidor Macabich, but not between 1:30pm and 4pm.)*

PLATJA FIGUERETES. This beach is just a short stretch of sand connected by a pedestrian boardwalk lined by large hotels, restaurants, and street-stands. *(Take a 15min. walk from Pl. Vera Rey down Av. d'Espanya and a left on Ramon Muntaner.)*

PLATJA D'EN BOSSA. The longest and liveliest of Ibiza's beaches, the Platja d'en Bossa has thumping bars and throngs of sun-seeking tourists. After tanning all day, take a dance break at the famous open club **Bora Bora** right on the beach. With an outside platform, a beachside bar, and blasting techno, this spot attracts half-naked dancers ready to party all day and into the night. *(Most efficiently reached by bus or ferry. Bus #14 runs every 30min. from Av. d'Isidor Macabich.)*

PLATJA DE TALAMANCA. This beach is a calm stretch of sand where a laid-back clientele enjoys the few bars and restaurants. *(On the opposite side of the port from town. 30min. walk or ferry from the port.)*

CALA DE SANT VINCENT. Among the more private coastal stretches, the German enclave at Cala de Sant Vincent offers white sands and breathtaking views. *(Past Santa Eulària des Riu on the road to St. Carles de Peralta.)*

CALA CARBÓ. This beach is small but beautiful, with awe-inspiring cliffs and a fantastic beachfront seafood restaurant. *(South of St. Antoni and west of St. Josep.)*

NIGHTLIFE

Bars in Ibiza City are crowded between 11pm and 3am and are the place to meet, greet, see, and be seen. The scene centers on **Carrer de Barcelona** and spills into the side streets, which can be jammed to the point of immobility, especially around midnight, when the area is flooded with discotecas promoters. All discos are outside of town, except for **Eden** and **Es Paradis** in St. Antoni which are accessible by foot. The **Discobus** runs to most of the hot spots but can be slow and unpredictable (leaves Ibiza City from Av. d'Isidor Macabich every hour in summer 12:30am-6:30am, schedule for other stops available at tourist office and hotels; €1.75). The main taxi line to the discos is at the end of the port on Av. Bartolome de Rosello—the line is usually long but moves quickly.

DON'T PANIC—GO TO THE DISCO! That's right—even the budget traveler can partake of the opulence that defines Ibiza's discos. By going down to C. Barcelona and talking up club promoters around midnight, you can often get a much better deal on club tickets. Stores and bars in town also sell tickets for cheaper than what you'll find at the door.

The island's **discos** are unbelievable, unequaled, and full of the unexpected; veterans claim that you will never experience anything half as wild. Drinks at Ibiza City's clubs are outrageously expensive—beers generally run €10 and mixed drinks €18, while cover runs €27-65. Most clubs open in early June.

Amnesia (☎971 19 80 41), on the road to Sant Antoni. This former warehouse has a phenomenal sound system, often accented by a live electric violinist. The central dance floor is flooded with psychedelic lights, vents spewing liquid nitrogen, acrobatic go-go dancers, and lasers. This club is also famous for its mobbed annual foam parties. Cover from €20-50. Opens daily 11pm-8am.

Space, Platja d'en Bossa (☎971 39 67 93; www.space-ibiza.es). Hopping party at virtually all hours. "We Love Space 08 Sundays" rocks out nonstop Su 4pm to M 6am, June 15-Sept. 28. Sa mornings "Matinee Group," W "La Troya," and Tu after-parties with Carl Cox are also popular. Cover €30-60. Open at midnight every night.

Pachá (☎971 31 36 00; www.pacha.com), 15min. from the port by foot. The most famous club chain in Spain, and the most elegant of Ibiza City's discos—complete with go-go dancers and all. Cocktails from €10. "Release Yourself" on M brings out the best up-and-coming DJs, and fabulous parties on F attract a rowdy crowd. Only club open year-round. Cover €35-60. Open daily midnight-7:30am.

Privilege (☎971 19 80 86; www.privilegeibiza.com), in the Urbanización San Rafael. On the Discobus to Sant Antoni, near Amnesia. There is a free Privilege bus that leaves from the Estació Marítima every 30min. Taxi €9. One of the world's largest clubs, filled with laughing gas booths and erotic dancers. The absence of a dress code translates to lots of bare skin. Cover from €30-50. Open June-Sept. daily midnight-7am. MC/V.

Anfora, C. Sant Carles, 7, in the D'alt Vila. A gay disco built into the hillside of the old city, the club's sunken dance floor sits beneath a small maze of bohemian lounges, tiled bars, and terraces. Don't miss Th "Night Fever" and Tu "Madonna." Cover €10, after 2am €15; includes 1 drink. Open daily midnight-6am.

Teatro Pereyra, C. Conde Rosello, 3 (☎871 30 44 32; www.teatropereyra.com). Despite Ibiza's roots in rock n' roll, this is the only true live music venue left in the city, where a smokin' blues band plays jaw-dropping solos. A converted theater lobby, Pereyra draws a somewhat older fun-loving crowd and many visiting musical artists. Music starts at 11pm every night and doesn't stop until late. Minimum consumption €7. MC/V.

SAN ANTONIO DE PORTMANY (SANT ANTONI) ☎971

Every summer, masses of youths migrate from the British Isles to Sant Antoni in search of fun in the sun. The rowdy nightlife, easy-going pace, and glam boardwalks with wide ocean vistas have turned the town into a flashy 20-something enclave. Quieter streets and tranquil, sunny spots aren't difficult to find, though, providing an alternative to the island's fast-moving atmosphere.

TRANSPORTATION. **Buses** run from the **Estació D'Autobusos** at the end of C. Paris in Sant Antoni to **Cala Bassa** (#7; 30min., 8 per day 9:30am-6:30pm, €1.35); **Platges de Compte** (20min., 7 per day 9:10am-6pm, €1.35); **Cala Tarida** (10min., 8 per day 9:15am-7:05pm, €1.35); **Eivissa** (30min.; every 15min. M-Sa 7am-9:30pm, Su every 30min. 7:30am-11pm; €1.65); **Santa Eulària** (35min., M-Sa 5 per day 10:15am-6:45pm). **Ferries** leave Sant Antoni for **Dénia** (see **Inter-Island Transport,** p. 323). Prices for these ferries should be available at travel agencies. Smaller companies run daily ferries to nearby beaches, such as **Cala Grassió** and **Cala Bassa;** prices average €5.50-9 round-trip. Signs posted along the port have schedules. Where **Passeig de la Mar** turns into **Passeig de Ses Fonts,** there is a **taxi** stand for *parada* cabs (☎971 34 00 74). You can also call ☎971 34 37 64 for a radio taxi. Try **Moto Luis** for **car** and **moped** rental, which has five locations throughout the city, and a primary office on Av. de Portmany. (☎971 34 05 21. Mopeds from €32. Cars from €58. Note that these prices are for August 2008 and will change; moped rental tends to be the most expensive in August. Open M-Sa 9am-2pm and 5-8pm, Su 9am-2pm.)

ORIENTATION AND PRACTICAL INFORMATION. Sant Antoni's flashy, shop-laden streets lie on a grid behind **Passeig de la Mar**, which crosses the port, eventually becoming **Passeig de Ses Fonts.** A boardwalk beyond the port leads to rocky coves and luxe lounges, while **Av. Dr. Fleming,** a stretch of beach bars and discos, runs perpendicular to the grid, away from the city's center.

The **tourist office** is a tiny white building in Pg. de ses Fonts, on the small plaza between the port and C. Ramón y Cajal. (☎971 34 33 63. Open M-F 9:30am-8:30pm, Sa-Su 9am-1pm.) Local services include: **police,** Av. Portmany, between Bibe Torres and Bisbe Cardona (☎971 34 08 30); a **health center,** C. d'Alacant, at the corner of Av. d'Isidor Macabich (☎971 34 51 21); a **pharmacy** on C. Barcelona (☎971 34 12 23); and **Internet** access at **Surf@net,** C. B.V. Ramón, 5, bajo (☎971 80 39 47; €1 per 15min., €1.20 per 30min.; open daily 10am-midnight).

BEWARE THE HOSTEL SHUFFLE. Many of the hostels in San Antonio are connected to each other; if occupancy is low, owners may close one or more of their hostels, regardless of preexisting reservations. If your trip will take place between seasons, call your hostel to make sure it will be open.

ACCOMMODATIONS. Hostels in Sant Antoni are numerous, highly variable in terms of amenities and seasonal pricing, and full of Brits. **Hostal Roca ❷**, C. Sant Mateu, 7, is in a great location close to the port. The hostal offers plain doubles with TV and private baths. (☎971 34 00 67, roca@hotelgransol.net. €12-33 per person depending on the season. Reception open 24hr. MC/V.) **Hostal Mari ❹**, C. Progrés, 42, has spic-and-span doubles and singles with TV, small desk, and private bath. Prices variable. (☎971 34 19 74; www.hostalmari.com. Also has adjoining restaurant. Singles €40; doubles €70.)

FOOD. Restaurants are almost as numerous as bars in Sant Antoni, and each part of the city has its own flavor. **Passeig de la Mar** runs along the port and connects the two most frequented culinary areas: the winding boardwalk traversing the rocky coves beyond the port, and **Avenida Dr. Fleming**, the garish disco strip along the sandy S'Arenal. The former consists of chic poolside lounges with equally chic customers, the latter a rowdier, disco-esque cluster of beach bars. An epicenter for the Av. Dr. Fleming scene is **Itaca Beach Bar ❷**, which offers breakfast, standard Mediterranean fare, and a few Tex-Mex options. Complete with free Wi-Fi, mojito bar, and live DJ, this popular restauarant and bar also hosts pre-club parties and is an official ticket outlet for the biggest clubs in Ibiza. (☎971 34 41 43; www.itacaibiza.com. Entrees €6.50-12.50. Nachos €9. Bocadillos €3.20-4.50. Open daily early-late.)

BEACHES AND NIGHTLIFE. The town and **Passeig de la Mar** are between the port and the disco-lined sands of Av. Dr. Fleming. The boardwalk at the end of Pg. de la Mar leads to slanted, rocky coves where pretty young things spend hours basking on rocks or lazing about in poolside lounges. Check out **Cala Bassa**, a popular tanning spot, for a gorgeous (and often nude) beach accessible by bus and ferry. **Cala Grassió**, a calm, sun-soaked cove, 1.5km from Sant Antoni, is easily reached on foot or by ferry. **Santa Eulària des Riu**, the third largest city on Ibiza, has a more urbanized but substantially larger beach. Just north, accessible by car or moped, the beautiful **Cala Salada** boasts calm waters.

Like its restaurants, the nightlife in San Antonio is evenly segmented by Pg. de la Marand its continuation, Pg. de Ses Fonts. The smooth boardwalk beyond Pg. de la Mar is full of swanky lounges with sunset vistas and room for dancing. Breezy **Café Mambo**, a seductive poolside bar with blue mosaic decor, is packed morning until night and is the unofficial pre-Pachá stop. Note that the pool is only available to customers staying here. (☎971 34 66 38. Beer €5. Mixed drinks €7-9. Open daily 11am-3am.) A bit closer to town along the boardwalk, **Spacious Savannah** attracts a well-dressed, older crowd with its pale elegance, calm music, and chic liquor list. (☎971 34 80 31.) Near the end of the boardwalk is **Kanya**, C. Soletat, 53, a bright poolside lounge with an energetic, young crowd day and night. (☎971 80 57 89; www.ibiza-kanya.com.) **C. Santa Agnes** and the neighboring streets in the middle of town comprise what is known as the West End, a district packed to the brim with flashy dance clubs that are popular preludes to the two extravagant discos along Av. Dr. Fleming, **Eden** and **Es Paradis.**

FORMENTERA ☎971

Whether you're a beach bum, a cyclist, or a boutique shopper, Formentera will welcome you with open arms. Those looking for a slower pace and a breath of pure sea breeze need look no further than the silky sands, crystal clear waters, and small towns that pepper the island.

TRANSPORTATION AND PRACTICAL INFORMATION. Formentera is easily visited as a daytrip, and the **tourist office,** located in the port complex and in the town of **Es Pujols,** offers a list of **Green Tours** for hikers and cyclists. (☎971 32 20 57; www.formentera.es. Open M-F 10am-2pm and 5-7pm, Sa 10am-2pm.) **Ferries** drop travelers off at **Port de la Savina** (25-35min., depending on the boat), a simple town with a wealth of transportation rental agencies. Inexpensive charters also leave in the morning from **Platja Figueretas** as well as the port of Sant Antoni. Though **buses** run to all of the beaches, they leave infrequently (4-7 buses per day between **La Savina, Es Calo, San Francisco, Es Pujols,** and **San Fernando,** the biggest towns on the island). The easiest way to travel is by **scooter** (€22-40) or **bike** (€8-16). For more info on transportation to Formentera, see **Inter-Island Transport,** p. 323.

Services in Es Pujols include a **supermarket** on Av. Miramar, less than a block from the beach and several scooter/bicycle rental services; signs all over town point to the **pharmacy,** which is in a small plaza off the main streets. **24hr medical care** is available in the nearby town of San Francisco (☎971 32 28 91).

FOOD AND ACCOMMODATIONS. Look for a room in **Es Pujols,** the most popular and lively town on the island. Try **Hostal Alemania ❷**, Av. Miramar, 60, located two steps from the Platja des Pujols (☎971 32 84 36. Single rooms with two beds and bath from €25. MC/V). Es Pujols is full of restaurants that serve tapas and bratwurst, an odd pairing that nevertheless satiates the many Germans who frequent the island. A stroll along the wood boardwalk reveals a series of bars and discos, followed by several small beaches, abandoned dinghies, and sand dunes that the island is trying desperately to preserve.

BEACHES. Some of the most beautiful beaches around Formentera are **Platja Migjorn,** a long stretch where clear water laps velvety white sands, and **Es Calo,** a fisherman's village with wooden walkways and cerulean waves. Popular beaches include **Platja des Illetes** (30min. walk from the port), with golden sands and shallow shores, as well as the nearby **Platja des Pujols,** a protected expanse with deeper waters and a restaurant-filled town.

BARCELONA

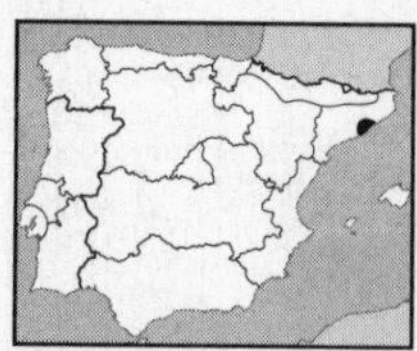

Nobody owns Barcelona. Home to innumerable expats from the US, South America, and a host of other countries, this is a vibrant city in which there are no outsiders. In the 17 years since the Olympics on the waterfront, Barcelona has rocketed to prominence as a hotspot for travelers drawn to sun-soaked beaches, bass-thumping clubs, and first-rate cuisine. Between the urban carnival of La Rambla, the mad, melting buildings of La Manzana de la Discórdia, and Gaudí's towering Sagrada Família cathedral in l'Eixample, the city pushes the limits of style in every medium—and gets away with it.

The center of the whimsical and daring *Modernista* architectural movement and once home to Pablo Picasso and Joan Miró, Barcelona still lives up to its reputation as a mecca for fearless creativity. In the quarter-century since the end of Franco's oppressive regime, Barcelona has led the autonomous region of Cataluña in a cultural resurgence. The result is a vanguard city squeezed between the mesmerizing blue waters of the Mediterranean and the green Tibidabo hills, flashing with such electric colors and shapes that you'll see Barcelona long after you've closed your eyes.

HIGHLIGHTS OF BARCELONA

RAMBLE along La Rambla and revel in the exuberant Barri Gòtic (p. 357).

CHILL at an outdoor jazz concert on the roof of the fantastical Casa Milà (p. 381).

IMAGINE what the future will bring to the unfinished La Sagrada Família (p. 380).

SIP to a speedy return at the Font de les Canaletes (p. 376).

INTERCITY TRANSPORTATION

Flights: Aeroport El Prat de Llobregat (**BCN;** ☎902 40 47 04; www.aena.es), 13km southwest of Barcelona. To get to Pl. Catalunya, take the **Aerobus** (☎934 15 60 20) in front of terminals A, B, or C (approx. 40min.; every 6-13min.; to Pl. Catalunya M-F 6am-1am, Sa-Su 6:30am-1am; to the airport M-F 5:30am-12:15am, Sa-Su 6am-12:30am; €3.90, round-trip €6.45). For early-morning flights, the Nitbus **N17** runs from Pl. Catalunya to all three terminals (from Pl. Catalunya hourly 11pm-5am; returns from airport hourly 10:05pm-5:05am; €1.20). The cheaper, faster option is the new **RENFE train** (L10; 20min. to Estació Sants, 25min. to Pg. de Gràcia; every 30min., from airport 6am-11:44pm, from Estació Sants to airport 5:25am-10:55pm; €2.40). To reach the train, take the pedestrian overpass in front of the airport, on the left with your back to the entrance. **Taxis** (☎933 033 033) are in front of terminals A, B, and C; €25-30 to Pl. Espanya and Pl. Catalunya; €35 to Sagrada Familia.

Trains: Barcelona has 2 main train stations. For general info call ☎902 24 02 02. **Estació Barcelona-Sants,** in Pl. Països Catalans (M: Sants Estació), is the main terminal for domestic and international traffic. **Estació de França,** on Av. Marquès de l'Argentera (M: Barceloneta), services regional destinations, including Tarragona, Zaragoza, and a limited number of international locations. Note that trains often stop before the main stations; check the schedule. **RENFE** (reservations ☎902 24 02 02, general info 902 24 34 02, international 24 34 02) to: **Bilbao** (9-10hr.; 12:30, 11pm; €39.70-52.20); **Madrid** (5-9hr., 14-21 per

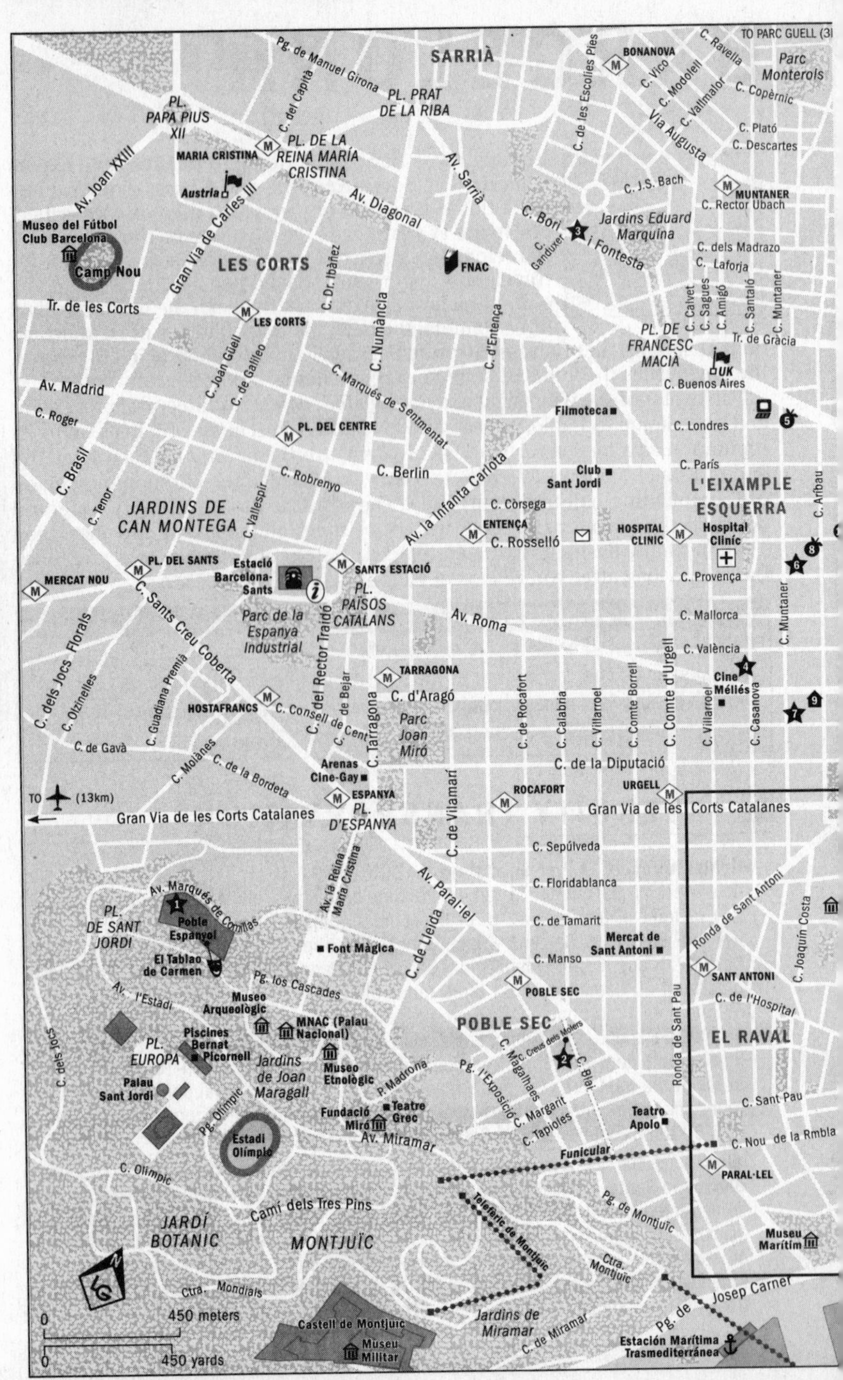

TO PARC GUELL
SARRIÀ
Pg. de Manuel Girona
PL. PRAT DE LA RIBA
BONANOVA
C. Ravella
Parc Monterols
C. Copèrnic
C. Vico
C. Modolell
C. Vallmalor
Via Augusta
C. Plató
C. Descartes
C. de les Escolies Pies
PL. PAPA PIUS XII
C. del Capità
PL. DE LA REINA MARÍA CRISTINA
MARIA CRISTINA
Av. Sarrià
Av. Joan XXIII
Austria
Av. Diagonal
C. J.S. Bach
MUNTANER
C. Rector Ubach
C. Bori i Fontesta
Jardins Eduard Marquina
C. Ganduxer
Museo del Fútbol Club Barcelona
Camp Nou
Gran Via de Carles III
LES CORTS
C. Dr. Ibàñez
FNAC
C. dels Madrazo
C. Laforja
C. Calvet
C. Sagues
C. Amigó
C. Santaló
C. Muntaner
Tr. de les Corts
LES CORTS
C. Numància
C. d'Entença
PL. DE FRANCESC MACIÀ
Tr. de Gràcia
UK
C. Buenos Aires
C. Joan Güell
C. de Galileo
C. Marqués de Sentmenat
Av. Madrid
C. Roger
Filmoteca
C. Londres
PL. DEL CENTRE
C. Berlin
C. París
C. Brasil
C. Robrenyo
Av. la Infanta Carlota
Club Sant Jordi
L'EIXAMPLE ESQUERRA
C. Tenor
JARDINS DE CAN MONTEGA
C. Vallespir
C. Còrsega
ENTENÇA
C. Rosselló
HOSPITAL CLINIC
Hospital Clinic
C. Aribau
PL. DEL SANTS
MERCAT NOU
Estació Barcelona-Sants
SANTS ESTACIÓ
PL. PAÏSOS CATALANS
C. Provença
C. Sants Creu Coberta
Parc de la Espanya Industrial
C. del Rector Traidó
Av. Roma
C. Mallorca
C. dels Jocs Florals
C. València
C. Muntaner
TARRAGONA
Cine Méliés
C. Olzinelles
C. Guadiana Premia
HOSTAFRANCS
C. Consell de Cent
C. de Bejar
C. Tarragona
C. d'Aragó
Parc Joan Miró
C. de Rocafort
C. Calabria
C. Villarroel
C. Comte Borrell
C. Comte d'Urgell
C. Villarroel
C. Casanova
C. de Gavà
C. Moianes
C. de la Bordeta
Arenas Cine-Gay
C. de la Diputació
TO (13km)
ESPANYA
PL. D'ESPANYA
ROCAFORT
URGELL
Gran Via de les Corts Catalanes
C. de Vilamarí
C. Sepúlveda
Av. la Reina Maria Cristina
Av. Paral·lel
C. Floridablanca
Av. Marqués de Comillas
PL. DE SANT JORDI
Poble Espanyol
C. de Tamarit
Ronda de Sant Antoni
C. Joaquín Costa
Font Màgica
Mercat de Sant Antoni
El Tablao de Carmen
C. de Lleida
C. Manso
SANT ANTONI
Pg. los Cascades
POBLE SEC
Av. l'Estadi
Museo Arqueològic
MNAC (Palau Nacional)
C. de l'Hospital
POBLE SEC
Ronda de Sant Pau
EL RAVAL
C. dels Jocs
Piscines Bernat Picornell
PL. EUROPA
Jardins de Joan Maragall
Museo Etnològic
C. Creus dels Molers
C. Magalhaes
C. Blai
Pg. l'Exposició
P. Madrona
Palau Sant Jordi
Pg. Olímpic
Fundació Miró
Teatre Grec
C. Margarit
C. Tapioles
Teatro Apolo
C. Sant Pau
Estadi Olímpic
Av. Miramar
Funicular
C. Nou de la Rmbla
PARAL·LEL
C. Olímpic
Teleferic de Montjuïc
Pg. de Montjuïc
JARDÍ BOTANIC
Camí dels Tres Pins
MONTJUÏC
Museu Marítim
Ctra. Montjuïc
Ctra. Mondials
Pg. de Josep Carner
0
450 meters
0
450 yards
Castell de Montjuïc
Museu Militar
Jardins de Miramar
C. de Miramar
Estación Marítima Trasmediterránea

BARCELONA

Barcelona
ACCOMMODATIONS
Alberg Residència la Ciutat, 29
Hostal Lesseps, 20
Hostal Qué Tal, 26
Hostal Residència Oliva, 19
Pensión Aribau, 9
Pensión San Medín, 18
Somnio Hostel, 14
FOOD
Acalia, 10
Agappe, 16
Agua, 30
La Rita, 24
Ikastola, 25
Jai-Ca Bar, 27
Kirin, 12
Racó d'en Baltá, 8
Restaurant Illa de Gràcia, 21
Sushi Itto, 5
Tenorio, 17
Zahara, 28
NIGHTLIFE
Casa Quimet, 15
Catwalk, 31
Dietrich, 7
La Fira, 6
Les Gents que J'aime, 23
Mojito Club, 11
Otto Zutz, 13
L'Ovella Negra, 32
Pippermint, 3
Razzmatazz, 33
La Terrazza, 1
Tinta Roja, 2
Vinil(), 22
Z:eltas, 4
TO HOSPITAL VALL D'HEBRON (2.3km)
TO PARC GÜELL (100m)
TO 29 (50m)
PÀDUA
C. Pàdua
Av. de la República
Travessera de Dalt
LESSEPS
PL. DE LESSEPS
SAN GERVASI
Canada
PL. MOLINA
C. Sanjoanistes
C. Guillem Tell
Av. Princep d'Asturies
C. Gran de Gràcia
C. Torrent de l'Olla
C. Sant Salvador
C. de Martí
C. Providència
C. Robí
FONTANA
Centre Artesa Tradicionarius
Teatre Lliure
C. de l'Or
C. Sant Lluís
C. Terol Bruniguer
C. Ramón y Cajal
C. Escorial
JOANIC
C. Pi i Margall
GRÀCIA
C. de Marià Cubí
C. de l'Avenir
C. Sant Marc
C. Montseny
C. Perla
C. Ros de Olano
PL. DEL SOL
Tr. de Gràcia
C. Sant Domènec
C. Siracusa
C. de Tordera
DIR Fitness Center
Hertz
C. Tusset
Via Augusta
C. Riera de S. Miquel
Av. Diagonal
C. Bonavista
C. de la Libertat
C. Sant Antoni Maria Claret
C. Indústria
L'EIXAMPLE DRETA
Hospital de la Santa Creu i Sant Pau
TO HOSPITAL DE LA SANTA CREU I SANT PAU (200m)
PL. JOAN CARLES I
C. Còrsega
Cine Casablanca
DIAGONAL
Casa Milà (La Pedrera)
PROVENÇA
Happy Books
La Central
Pg. de Sant Joan
C. Roger de Flor
C. Nàpols
C. Sicília
C. Sardenya
C. de la Marina
Av. de Gaudí
LA SAGRADA FAMÍLIA
La Sagrada Família
ENCANTS
C. Castillejos
C. Rosselló
C. Provença
C. Mallorca
C. València
C. Lepant
C. Padilla
C. Cartagena
VERDAGUER
PL. JACINT VERDAGUER
C. Granados
C. Balmes
Rambla de Catalunya
Pg. de Gràcia
C. Pau Claris
C. Roger Llúria
Fundació Tàpies
PL. DR. LETAMENDI
PG. DE GRÀCIA
La Manzana de la Discòrdia
C. d'Aragó
C. Consell de Cent
C. de la Diputació
C. Bruc
C. Girona
GIRONA
C. Bailèn
PL. PABLO NERUDA
PL. UNIVERSITAT
UNIVERSITAT
PL. DE LES GLÒRIES CATALANES
SEE "CIUTAT VELLA," p. 358-359
TETUÁN
Gran Via de les Corts Catalanes
Plaza de Toros
MONUMENTAL
GLÒRIES
(Pg. de Carles I)
Ronda Universitat
C. Pelai
PL. DE CATALUNYA
CATALUNYA
C. Casp
C. d'Ausiàs Marc
Teatre Nacional de Catalunya
Torre Agbar
Museu d'Art Contemporani
C. Fontanella
URQUINAONA
Ronda de Sant Pere
C. Ribes
L' Auditori
TO PARC DIAGONAL MAR (2.5km)
C. Tànger
CIUTAT VELLA
Av. Portal de l'Angel
Palau de la Música Catalana
C. S. Pere Més Alt
ARC DE TRIOMF
Estació Nord
C. Sancho d'Àvila
C. Carme
La Rambla
C. S. Pere Més Baix
MARINA
Av. Meridiana
C. dels Almogàvers
La Boqueria
LA RIBERA
C. Zamora
C. Pamplona
C. d'Alaba
C. d'Àvila
LICEU
C. Pujades
BOGATELL
AmEx Office
PL. DE ST. JAUME
JAUME I
C. Princesa
C. Commerç
C. Llull
Ajuntament
Museu Picasso
POBLE NOU
PL. REIAL
Còmplices
C. Ciutat
Via Laietana
Pg. Born
Pg. de Picasso
Parc de la Ciutadella
C. Ramon Turró
Palau Güell
Santa Maria del Mar
C. Wellington
C. del Doctor Trueta
BARRI GÒTIC
DRASSANES
Av. Marquès de l'Argentera
Estació de França
Parc Zoològic
Av. Bogatell
Antinous
Pg. de Colom
Av. d'Icària
Monument a Colom
Ronda del Litoral
Pg. Circumval·lació
Vila Olímpica
Museu d'Historia de Catalunya
CIUTADELLA-VILA OLÍMPICA
C. de Ginebra
C. Ramón Trias Fargas
Centre de la Vila
IMAX Port Vell
BARCELONETA
Hospital del Mar
PORT OLÍMPIC
Moll d'Espanya
Cinesa Maremàgnum
Aquàrium de Barcelona
Pg. de Joan de Borbó
TO 28, COOLTRA (500m) AND TORRE SAN SEBASTIÀN (800m)
Pg. Marítim de Barceloneta
BARCELONA

day 6am-11:20pm, €39.70-123.30); **Sevilla** (10-12hr., 3 per day 8am-10:30pm, €57.10-127.30); **Valencia** (3-5hr., 14 per day, €32.40-39.60). International destinations include **Milan, Italy** (via Figueres and Nice) and **Montpellier, France** with connections to Geneva, Paris, and the French Riviera. 20% discount on round-trip tickets.

Buses: Arrive at the **Barcelona Nord Estació d'Autobusos,** C. Alí-bei, 80 (☎902 26 06 06; www.barcelonanord.com). M: Arc de Triomf or #54 bus. Info booth open 7am-9pm. Buses also depart from Estació Sants and the airport. **Sarfa** (☎902 30 20 25; www.sarfa.es). Bus stop and ticket office also at Ronda Sant Pere, 21 (☎933 02 52 23). To: **Cadaqués** (2hr.; 2 per day M-F 11:15am and 8:15pm, Sa-Sun 9:30am and 8:15pm; €19.90); **Palafrugell** (2hr., 10-12 per day 8:15am-9pm, €15:05); **Tossa de Mar** via **Lloret de Mar** (1hr., 11 per day, €9.85). **Eurolines** (☎933 67 44 00; www.eurolines.es) goes to **Paris** via Lyon (15hr., M-Sa 9:30pm, €69); 10% discount under 26 or over 60. **ALSA/Enatcar** (☎902 42 22 42; www.alsa.es) goes to: **Alicante** (8-9hr., 9 per day, €39.27-44.44); **Bilbao** (7-8hr., 4-5 per day, €40.59); Madrid (8hr., 18 per day 7am-1am, €27.08); **Sevilla** (14-16hr., 4:30, €85.48); **Valencia** (4-5hr., 14 per day, €24.35-37.68); **Zaragoza** (3hr., 25-29 per day, €13.18-18.36).

Ferries: Trasmediterránea (☎902 45 46 45; www.transmediterranea.es), in Terminal Drassanes, Moll Sant Bertran. **Catamaran** €75; round-trip €142. **"Superferry"** €46/88 June-Aug. to **Ibiza** (5-9hr., 1 per day M-Th, 2 per day F-Sa); **Mahón** (3-9hr., 1 per day at 9:30pm); and **Palma** (3-7hr., 1-2 per day).

ORIENTATION

Barcelona's layout is easy to visualize if you imagine yourself perched on Columbus's head at the **Monument a Colom** (on Pg. de Colom, along the shore), viewing the city with the sea at your back. From the harbor, the city slopes upward to the mountains. From the Columbus monument, **La Rambla,** the main thoroughfare, runs up to **Plaça de Catalunya** (M: Catalunya), the city center. The heavily touristed historic neighborhood, **Ciutat Vella,** is anchored by La Rambla and encompasses the Barri Gòtic, La Ribera, and El Raval. The **Barri Gòtic** is east of La Rambla (to the right, with your back to the sea), enclosed on the other side by **Via Laietana.** East of Via Laietana lies the maze-like neighborhood of **La Ribera,** bordered by Parc de la Ciutadella and Estació de França. To the west of La Rambla is **El Raval,** Barcelona's most multicultural neighborhood, with a growing number of museums and hip bars.

Beyond La Ribera—farther east, outside Ciutat Vella and curving out into the water—are **Poble Nou** and **Port Olímpic,** which boast the two tallest buildings in Barcelona, not to mention an assortment of discotecas and restaurants on the beach. To the west, beyond El Raval, rises **Montjuïc,** a hill crammed with sprawling gardens, museums, the 1992 Olympic grounds, and a fortress. Directly behind your perch on the Monument a Colom is the **Port Vell** (Old Port) development, where a wavy bridge leads to the ultra-modern (and tourist-packed) shopping and entertainment complexes **Moll d'Espanya** and **Maremàgnum.** North of Ciutat Vella is upscale **l'Eixample,** a gridded neighborhood created during the expansion of the 1860s that sprawls from Pl. de Catalunya toward the mountains. **Gran Via de les Corts Catalanes** defines its lower edge, and the **Passeig de Gràcia,** l'Eixample's main tree- and boutique-lined avenue, bisects this chic neighborhood. **Avinguda Diagonal,** the expansion's largest non-gridded street, marks the border between l'Eixample and the **Zona Alta** ("Uptown"), which includes Pedralbes, Gràcia, and other older neighborhoods in the foothills. The peak of **Tibidabo,** the northwest border of the city, offers the most comprehensive view of Barcelona.

THE BARRIS (NEIGHBORHOODS) OF BARCELONA

BARRI GÒTIC AND LA RAMBLA

The oldest sections of Barcelona—the Barri Gòtic and La Rambla—are the city's tourist centers. Originally settled by the Romans in the 3rd century BC, the Barri Gòtic is built on top of the original Roman city, Barcino. Subsequent periods of medieval Catholic rule and design covered Barcino in a maze of narrow, cobblestone streets, dense with historic and artistic landmarks. The modern tourist industry has added shops, hostels, and bars to these *barris* of medieval monuments. Stroll down **Carrer d'Avinyó** and you'll see some of Barcelona's most treasured architectural landmarks, just meters away from the area's most popular nightlife hotspots.

LA RIBERA

As the stomping ground of Barcelona's many fishermen and merchants, La Ribera has always had a working-class feel. Its confines bore witness to some of the most important events to shape Barcelona's history; in the 18th century, Felipe V demolished much of La Ribera, then the city's commercial hub, to make space for the impressive Ciutadella fortress. Originally the center of Madrid's stringent control, the area is now the site of a beautiful park. The city government has cleaned up La Ribera in the last few years, even demolishing many of the area's legendary haunts (and putting an end to their legendary parties). The result is a neighborhood that locals still love for its intimate restaurants and bars, its free art galleries, and its nightly transformation, come sunset, back to its exciting old self.

EL RAVAL

Located next to La Rambla and the Barri Gòtic, the northern part of El Raval tends to be a favorite of Barcelona's natives rather than its tourists. The southern portion, meanwhile, is home to many immigrants from India and the Middle East. This diverse and mostly working-class neighborhood has a special charm, with small shops and eateries, quirky bars, and hidden historical attractions. In the late 19th and early 20th centuries, overcrowding led to an urban nightmare of rampant crime, prostitution, and drug use. Revitalization efforts, especially since the 1992 Olympic Games, have worked wonders; new museums and cultural centers—not to mention plenty of bars and restaurants—now spatter El Raval, making the neighborhood more accessible to travelers.

L'EIXAMPLE

Barcelona's l'Eixample (luh-SHOMP-luh; "Enlargement") is notable for the unusual circumstances that led to its development. Around the time when the oppressive Bourbon walls of the old city were demolished in 1854, the Catalan cultural *Renaixença* (Renaissance) was picking up. As industries prospered, utopian socialist theories spread like wildfire through philosophical circles, including those of l'Eixample urban planner Ildefons Cerdà i Sunyer. The gridded streets wound up filled with relatively wealthy residents (not a blending of classes as he'd imagined), designer shops, corporate buildings, and great eateries from around the world. Most tourists only see the Pg. de Gràcia and Sagrada Família areas, but you'll be rewarded if you stray; L'Eixample is a lesson in Modernism and a treasure trove of small bars, cafés, and museums.

MONTJUÏC

Montjuïc (mon-joo-EEK), the hill at the southwest end of the city, is one of the oldest sections of Barcelona. Throughout Barcelona's history, whoever controlled Montjuïc's peak controlled the city. Dozens of despotic rulers have

Ciutat Vella
SEE MAP KEY, p. 360
A
B
C
Universitat de Barcelona
Gran Via de les Corts Catalanes
PL. DE LA UNIVERSITAT
UNIVERSITAT
VIPS
Rambla de Catalunya
Ronda Universitat
C. Balmes
C. Comte d' Urgel
C. Villarroel
C. Casanova
C. Muntaner
C. Sepúlveda
PL. DE CASTELLA
C. Torres i Amat
C. Gravina
C. Pelai
C. Bergara
Triangle Shopping Center
C. Tallers
C. Floridablanca
C. Valldonzella
C. Tigre
Centre de Cultura Contemporània de Barcelona
C. Paloma
C. Montalegre
Museu d'Art Contemporani
C. Ferlandina
C. Tamarit
Ronda de Sant Antoni
C. Nou de Dulce
C. Sant Gil
C. Sant Vicenç
C. de la Lluna
C. Joaquín Costa
PL. DELS ÀNGELS
La Central del Raval
C. Elisabets
C. Bonsucces
PL. BONSUCCES
La Rambla
C. Santa
Mercat de St. Antony
SANT ANTONI
C. Príncep de Biana
C. la Cendra
C. Bisbe Laguarda
C. la Riera Alta
C. d'Erasme de Janer
C. Sant Antoni Abat
C. Peu de la Creu
C. dels Àngels
C. Dr. Dou
C. d'en Xuclà
Champion Supermarket
PL. VILA DE MADRID
EL RAVAL
C. Salvador
C. Sanclimient
C. Botella
C. Carme
C. Pintor Fortuny
C. d'en Bot
C. Cera
C. de l'Hospital
C. de la Riera Baixa
C. d'en Roig
C. Egipcíaques
Biblioteca Sant Pau
C. Floristes de la Rambla
Palau de la Virreina
C. de la Portaferrissa
C. d'En Roca
C. Petritxol
C. de Vistalegre
C. la Reina Amàlia
C. les Carretes
PL. DE LA GARDUÑA
La Boqueria
Museu de l'Eròtica
Ronda de Sant Pau
C. de l'Aurora
C. la Cadena
C. Sant Pacià
C. Sant Rafael
C. Leialtat
PL. JOSEP M. FOLCH I TORRES
C. d'en Robador
C. Junta de Comerç
Navegaweb
C. Casañas
PL. DEL PI
C. Pi
Església del Pi
LICEU
EL CALL
C. la Riereta
C. Sant Jeroni
Rambla del Raval
C. Sant Josep Oriol
C. la Boqueria
C. Banys Nous
C. Sta. Elena
PL. SALVADOR SEGUÍ
C. de Sant Pau
Gran Teatre del Liceu
C. Quintana
C. les Flors
Tintorería Ferran
C. Ferran
Tintorería San Pablo
C. de Sant Pau
C. de les Penedides
C. la Unió
Església de Sant Jaume
C. Sant Oleguer
C. Sant Ramón
C. Marqués del Barbera
Budget Bikes
PL. REIAL
C. la Lleona
C. Bda. de S. Miguel
PARAL·LEL (FUNICULAR)
C. Abat Safont
C. Tàpies
Tourist Police
C. Nou de la Rambla
Palau Güell
C. d'Aglà
Cómplices
PL. GEORGE ORWELL (PL. "TRIPPY")
Av. del Paral·lel
C. Santa Madrona
C. de l'Om
C. l'Est
C. Guàrdia
C. Lancaster
Easy Internet
C. Escudellers
Av. de les Drassanes
Institut Català de la Salut
C. Arc del Teatre
PL. DEL TEATRE
C. Cabanes
C. Rull
C. Nou de Sant Francesc
C. Còdols
C. Serra
C. Montserrat
Santa Mònica
Lavomatic
PL. J. XIRAU
Pge. dels Escudellers
C. Cervelló
Centre d'Art de Santa Mónica
C. Cid
C. Peracamps
C. Vila i Vilà
Jardins de les Tres Xemeneies
DRASSANES
Museu de Cera
PL. DE LA MERCÈ
C. Portal Santa Madrona
Pg. de la Banca
Antinous
C. Ample
C. Piquer
C. Palaudaries
C. Josep Anselm Clavé
C. Parc
PL. DUC DE MEDINACELI
TO MONTJUÏC (100m)
C. Puigxuriger
Museu Marítim
Pg. de Colom
Pg. de Montjuïc
C. Albareda
C. Carrera
PL. PORTAL DE LA PAU
Monumenta a Colom
Ronda del Litoral
TO MAREMÀGNUM (80m)

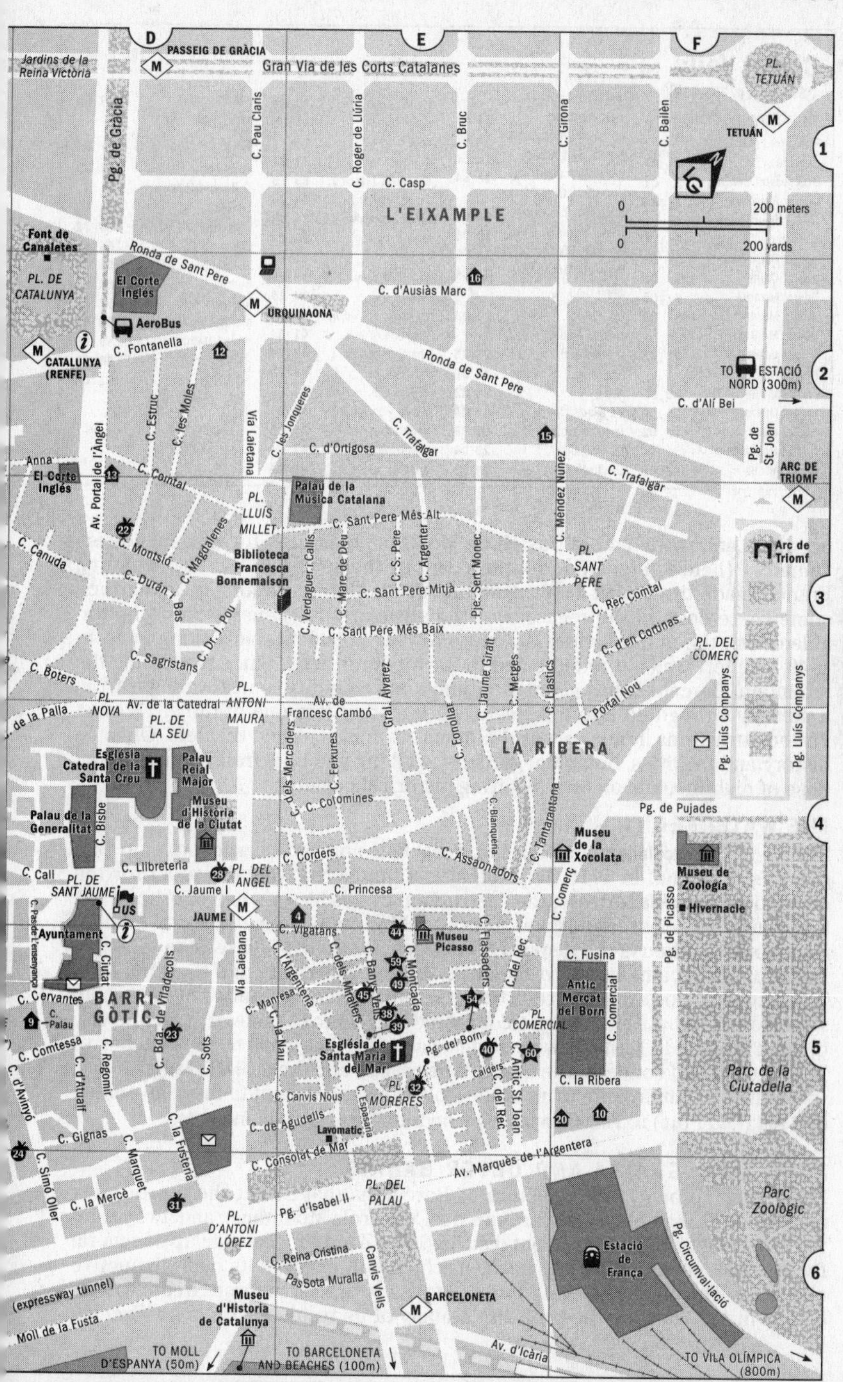
PASSEIG DE GRÀCIA
Jardins de la Reina Victòria
Gran Via de les Corts Catalanes
PL. TETUÁN
TETUÁN
L'EIXAMPLE
200 meters
200 yards
Font de Canaletes
PL. DE CATALUNYA
El Corte Inglés
AeroBus
URQUINAONA
CATALUNYA (RENFE)
Ronda de Sant Pere
C. d'Ausiàs Marc
TO ESTACIÓ NORD (300m)
C. d'Alí Bei
ARC DE TRIOMF
Arc de Triomf
Palau de la Música Catalana
PL. LLUÍS MILLET
Biblioteca Francesca Bonnemaison
PL. SANT PERE
PL. DEL COMERÇ
PL. NOVA
PL. ANTONI MAURA
PL. DE LA SEU
LA RIBERA
Església Catedral de la Santa Creu
Palau Reial Major
Museu d'Història de la Ciutat
Palau de la Generalitat
Museu de la Xocolata
Museu de Zoologia
Hivernacle
PL. DE SANT JAUME
PL. DEL ANGEL
JAUME I
Ayuntament
Museu Picasso
BARRI GÒTIC
Antic Mercat del Born
PL. COMERCIAL
Església de Santa Maria del Mar
PL. MORERES
Parc de la Ciutadella
Lavomatic
Parc Zoològic
PL. DEL PALAU
PL. D'ANTONI LÓPEZ
Estació de França
BARCELONETA
Museu d'Historia de Catalunya
TO MOLL D'ESPANYA (50m)
TO BARCELONETA AND BEACHES (100m)
TO VILA OLÍMPICA (800m)
BARCELONA

Ciutat Vella

SEE MAP, p. 358-359

ACCOMMODATIONS

Name	No.	Map
Barcelona Mar Youth Hostel,	1	A4
BCN Hostal Central,	2	C1
Center Ramblas,	3	B4
Gothic Point Youth Hostel,	4	E4
Hostal Benidorm,	5	C5
Hostal Campi,	6	C3
Hostal Levante,	7	C5
Hostal Maldà,	8	C4
Hostal Mariluz Youngsters,	9	D5
Hostal Nuevo Colón,	10	F5
Hostal Ópera,	11	C4
Hostal Plaza,	12	D2
Hostal-Residència Lausanne,	13	D2
Hostal Residència Rembrandt,	14	C3
Hostal de Ribagorza,	15	E2
Hostal San Remo,	16	E2
Hotel Peninsular,	17	B4
Hotel Toledano/Hostal Residència Capitol,	18	C2
Kabul Youth Hostel,	19	C5
Pensión Ciudadela,	20	F5
Pensión Fernando,	21	C4

FOOD

Name	No.	Map
Els 4 Gats,	22	D3
L'Antic Bocoi del Gòtic,	23	D5
Arc Café,	24	D6
Attic,	25	C3
Café de l'Ópera,	26	C4
Los Caracoles,	27	C5
La Colmena,	28	D4
DosTrece,	29	B3
Hello Sushi,	30	B4
Kaitensushi,	31	D6
La Llavor dels Origens,	32	B4
Madame Jasmine,	33	E5
Maoz Vegetarian (a),	34	C4
Maoz Vegetarian (b),	35	C3
Mendizabal,	36	B4
Organic,	37	B4
El Pebre Blau,	38	E5
Petra,	39	E5
La Pizza del Born,	40	E5
Pla dels Àngels,	41	B2
Les Quinze Nits,	42	C5
Rita Rouge,	43	C3
Tèxtil Cafè,	44	E5
Va de Vi,	45	E5
Vegetalia,	46	C5
Vildsvin,	47	C4
Xaloc,	48	C4
El Xampanyet,	49	E5

NIGHTLIFE

Name	No.	Map
68,	50	B4
Betty Ford,	51	B2
El Bosq de les Fades,	52	C6
Casa Almirall,	53	B2
El Copetín,	54	E5
Jamboree,	55	C5
Karma,	56	C5
Marsella Bar,	57	B4
Moog,	58	B5
Palau Dalmases,	59	E5
Ribborn,	60	E5
Schilling,	61	C4

occupied and modified the Castell de Montjuïc, built atop the ancient Jewish cemetery (hence the name Montjuïc, Hill of the Jews). In the 20th century, Franco made the **Castell de Montjuïc** one of his "interrogation" headquarters; somewhere deep in the recesses of the structure, his *beneméritos* ("honorable ones"; the militia) shot Cataluña's former president, Lluís Companys, in 1940. The fort was not rededicated to the city until 1960. Since reclaiming the mountain, Barcelona has given Montjuïc a new identity, transforming it from a military stronghold into a peaceful park. Today, it is one of the city's most visited attractions, home to world-famous art museums and theaters, Olympic history and facilities, botanical gardens, walking and bike trails, a substantial dose of nightlife, and an awe-inspiring historical cemetery.

THE WATERFRONT

The piers of **Barceloneta** and **Port Vell, Poble Nou,** and **Port Olímpic** make up Barcelona's coastline. In 1718, La Ribera was butchered to make room for the enormous **Ciutadella** fortress; the destruction of this historic neighborhood left thousands homeless, and it was not until 30 years later that the city created Barceloneta to house the displaced refugees. Because of its seaside location, Barceloneta became home to the city's sailors, fishermen, and their families. The neighborhood's drive to refurbish its waterfront also resulted in the expansion of Port Vell. After moving a congested coastal road underground, the city opened Moll de la Fusta, a wide pedestrian zone that leads to the beaches of Barceloneta and connects the bright **Maremàgnum** and the **Moll d'Espanya.** Today, the entire stretch, from in front of the Columbus monument to the rejuvenated **Port Vell** (Old Port) to **Port Olímpic,** is as hedonistic as Barcelona gets.

ZONA ALTA: GRÀCIA AND OUTER BARRIS

Zona Alta (uptown) is the section of Barcelona that lies at the top of most maps: past l'Eixample, in and around the Collserola Mountains, and away from the low-lying historic waterfront districts. The Zona Alta is made up of several formerly independent towns, each of which still exhibits its own distinctive character. The most visited part of Zona Alta is Gràcia, incorporated into Barcelona in 1897 despite the protests of many of its residents. Calls for Gràcian independence continue even today, albeit with less frequency, and the area has always had a political streak, evident in names like Mercat de Llibertat ("Liberty Market") and Pl. de la Revolució ("Revolution Plaza"). After incorporation, the area continued to be a center of left-wing activism and resistance, even during the oppressive Franco regime. Gràcia packs a surprising number of *Modernista* buildings and parks, international cuisine, and chic shops into a relatively small area, making it a fascinating district to explore. Since most tourists don't venture out to Gràcia, the neighborhood still has a local flavor; a stay here is worth the short commute to the center of the city.

MAPS

El Corte Inglés distributes an informative free map, as do a variety of guide/map companies, such as **CitySpy** and **BCN Guide**; check out hotel lobbies to find one you like. The Barcelona **tourist office** (Pl. de Catalunya and Pl. Sant Jaume; p. 363) has maps with an enlarged inset of the Barri Gòtic, although the better ones (which will have street numbers and one-way streets marked, and may include a full index of the city) will cost you between €1-4. There are also maps for almost every theme: **Bici I Vainants** with bicycle lanes marked, an official gay and lesbian tourist guide, a hotel map, an ethnic food map, a shopping map, an art gallery map, and perhaps most importantly, an excellent *plànol turístic ciutat vella* (map of the old city), stretching from Gran Via out past Barceloneta, with Metro stops, services, museums, landmarks, a street index, and more. Bus and Metro maps, one with tourist sights and landmarks (the **metro&bus touristmapbcn**), and one with hours for each bus line (the **plànolbusbcn**), are both free at tourist offices and metro stations.

LOCAL TRANSPORTATION

METRO AND BUS

Barcelona's public transportation (info ☎010) is quick and cheap. If you plan to use public transportation extensively, there are several Autoritat del Transport Metropolità or ATM (www.atm.cat) *abonos* (passes) available, which work interchangeably for the Metro, bus, and urban lines of the FGC commuter trains, RENFE Cercanías, Trams, and Nitbus. The **T-10 pass** (€7.20) is valid for 10 rides and saves you nearly 50% off single tickets. The **T-Dia pass** (€5.50) is good for a full day of unlimited travel, and the **T-mes** (€46.25) is good for a month. If you just plan to use the Metro and daytime buses, there are 2-5 day passes at **Transports Metropolitans de Barcelona** (**TMB;** ☎933 18 70 74; www.tmb.net; **2 days** €10, **5 days** €21.70). These will save you money if you plan to ride the Metro more than three times per day, but they don't work on the Nitbus.

Metro: (☎932 98 70 00; www.tmb.net). Vending machines and ticket windows sell passes. Red diamonds with the white letter "M" mark stations. Hold on to your ticket—riding without one can incur a fine of €40. Trains run M-Th, Su, and holidays 5am-midnight, F 5am-2am, Sa non-stop service. Extended holiday hours. €1.30 per *senzill/sencillo* (1-way ticket). Switching lines may involve a considerable walk.

Ferrocarrils de la Generalitat de Catalunya (FGC): (☎932 05 15 15; www.fgc.es). Commuter trains to local destinations with main stations at Pl. de Catalunya and Pl. d'Espanya. Note that some destinations within the city (parts of Gràcia and beyond) require taking the FGC. Blue symbols resembling 2 interlocking "V"s mark Metro connections. The commuter line costs the same as the Metro (€1.30) until Tibidabo. After that, rates go up by zone: Zone 2 €1.95, Zone 3 €2.70, etc. Metro passes are valid on FGC trains. Info office at the Pl. de Catalunya station open M-F 7am-9pm.

RENFE Cercanías (Rodalies): (☎902 24 02 02; www.renfe.es/cercanias). The L10 to the **airport** (Zone 4; €2.60) is the most popular. Destinations include **Sitges** (Zone 4; €2.60 line C2) and **Blanes** (Zone 6; €4.10; line C1). Main connections at Sants and Pg. de Gràcia, marked by either the RENFE double arrows or a funny-looking red circle with a backwards C.

Buses: Go almost anywhere, usually from 5am-10pm (many leave for the last round at 9:30pm). Most stops have maps, and you can easily figure out which bus to take. Many run on natural gas. Most buses come every 10-15min. in central locations. €1.30.

Nitbus: (www.emt-amb.cat/links/cat/cnitbus.htm). 18 different lines run every 20-30min. 10:30pm-4:30am, depending on the line; a few run until 5:30am. All buses depart from around Pl. de Catalunya, stop in front of most club complexes, and work their way through Ciutat Vella and the Zona Alta. Maps are available at *estancos* (tobacco shops), at some bus stops, online, and in Metro stations.

Bus Turístic: Hop-on, hop-off tours of the city. Passes sold for 1-2 days (€20, €26).

TAXIS

About 11,000 taxis swarm the city. A *"lliure"* or *"libre"* sign or a green light on the roof means vacant; yellow means occupied. On weekend nights, you may wait up to 30min. for a ride; long lines form at popular spots like the Port Olímpic. To call a cab, try **RadioTaxi033** (☎933 033 033; www.radiotaxi033.com; AmEx/MC/V) or **Servi Taxi** (☎933 30 03 00). **Disabled travelers** should call for Taxi Amic's adapted vehicles (☎934 20 80 88).

BARCELONA

CAR AND MOPED RENTAL

Avis, C. Corcega, 293-295 (☎932 37 56 80). Open M-F 9am-9pm, Sa 8am-8pm, Su 8am-1pm. 3 other locations. **Branches** at airport (☎932 98 36 00; open M-Sa 7am-12:30am, Su 7am-midnight), and **Estació Sants,** Pl. dels Països Catalans, s/n. (☎933 30 41 93; fax 91 41 07. Open M-F 7:30am-10:30pm, Sa 8am-7pm, Su 9am-7pm.)

Budget, in El Prat de Llobregat airport (☎932 98 36 38; fax 98 36 42). Open daily 7am-midnight.

Cooltra, Ptge. de Vilaret, 6 (☎932 47 28 34; www.cooltra.com). M: Encants. Mopeds from €25 per day and €230 per month. Open daily 9am-8pm.

Europcar, Pl. Países Catalanes, s/n (☎934 91 48 22; www.europcar.es), near Sants. Open M-F 7am-midnight, Sa-Su 8am-8pm. Branch at El Prat de Llobregat airport (☎902 10 50 55). Open 24hr.

Hertz, C. Tuset, 10 (☎932 17 80 76; www.hertz.es). M: Diagonal or FCG: Gràcia. Open M-F 9am-2pm and 4-7pm, Sa 9am-2pm. **Branch** at airport (☎932 98 36 38), open daily 7am-midnight and by Estació Sants, C. Viriat, 45 (☎934 19 61 56), open M-F 8am-9:30pm, Sa-Su 8:30am-8pm.

BIKE RENTAL

Budget Bikes, C. Marquès de Barberà, 15 (☎933 04 18 85; www.budgetbikes.eu), down C. Unió from La Rambla. €6 for 2 hr., €15 for one day, €25 for 2nd day, extra days €7. Open daily 7am-8pm.

Barcelona Bici (☎932 85 38 32). Offers 10hr. rentals. Customized. 3 rental points: Pl. Catalunya, Mirador de Colom, and Pg. Joan de Borbó.

Fat Tire, C. Escudellers, 48 (☎933 01 36 12; www.fattirebiketoursbarcelona.com). 1-3 hr. rental €7, 6+ hr. rental €15. Shop open daily Mar. 1-Dec. 15 10am-7pm. Famous bike tours include a break at the beach (€22, includes bike rental. Reservations not neccessary. Meet in Pl. St. Jaume. Tours Apr. 16-Oct. 31 at 11am and 4pm, Feb. 1-Apr. 15 and Nov. 1-Dec. 14 at 11am.)

PRACTICAL INFORMATION

TOURIST AND FINANCIAL SERVICES

Tourist Offices:

Plaça de Catalunya, Pl. de Catalunya, 17S, underground on the bottom left-hand corner facing south (toward La Rambla). M: Catalunya. The main office, along with Pl. de Sant Jaume, has free maps, brochures on sights and transportation, booking service for last-minute accommodations, a gift shop, money exchange, and a box office (Caixa de Catalunya). Open daily 9am-9pm.

Plaça de Sant Jaume, C. Ciutat, 2. M: Jaume I. Open M-F 9am-8pm, Sa 10am-8pm, Su and holidays 10am-2pm.

Oficina de Turisme de Catalunya, Pg. de Gràcia, 107 (☎932 38 40 00; www.gencat.es/probert). M: Diagonal. Open M-Sa 10am-7pm, Su 10am-2pm.

Institut de Cultura de Barcelona (ICUB), Palau de la Virreina, La Rambla, 99 (☎933 16 10 00; www.bcn.cat/cultura). Info office open M-Sa 10am-8pm, Su 11am-3pm.

Estació Barcelona-Sants, Pl. Països Catalans. M: Sants-Estació. Info and last-minute accommodation booking. Open June 24-Nov. 24 daily 8am-8pm; Nov. 25-June 23 M-F 8am-8pm, Sa-Su 8am-2pm.

Aeroport del Prat de Llobregat, terminals A and B. Info and last-minute accommodation booking. Open daily 9am-9pm

Tourist Office Representatives booths dot the city in the summer. Open daily July-Sept.; hours vary; many open weekends and shorter hours in winter.

Tours: In addition to the Bus Turístic (p. 361), the Pl. de Catalunya tourist office offers 2hr. **walking tours** of the Barri Gòtic daily at 10am (English) and Sa at noon (Catalan and Spanish). Group size limited; buy tickets in advance. (☎932 85 38 32 for info. €11, ages 4-12 €4.50.) 2hr. **Picasso tour** of Barcelona Tu-Su 10:30am (English) and Sa 11:30am (Catalan and Spanish). €15, ages 4-12 €6.50, includes entrance to the **Museu Picasso.** 2hr. *Modernisme* tour through L'Eixample's Quadrat d'Or F-Sa 4pm (English) and Sa 4pm (Catalan and Spanish). €11, ages 4-12 €4.50. Self-guided tours of Gothic, Romanesque, *Modernista,* and Contemporary Barcelona available; pick up pamphlets with maps at the tourist office. **Bike tours** abound; see **Bike Rental** (p. 362). **Barcelona Segway Glides** offers 2hr. tours ("glides") for €60, Mar. 1-Nov. 30 M-F 10am and 5pm, Dec. 1-Feb. 28 11am. Call for reservations. (☎678 77 73 71; www.barcelonasegwayglides.com. Cash only.)

Currency Exchange: ATMs give the best rates. The very best are those marked **Telebanco;** they report the exchange rate on the receipt and on-screen rather than leaving you guessing. Banks are your next best option. General banking hours M-F 8:30am-2pm. La Rambla has many exchange stations open late, but the rates are not as good and they will take a commission.

American Express: La Rambla, 74 (☎933 42 73 11). M: Liceu. Open M-F 9am-9pm, Sa 9am-2pm.

LOCAL SERVICES

Luggage Storage: Estació Barcelona-Sants, M: Sants-Estació. Lockers €3-4.50 per day. Open daily 5:30am-11pm. **Estació Nord,** M: Arc de Triomf. Lockers €3/4.50/5 per day, 90-day limit. Also at the **El Prat Airport,** €4.60 per day.

Libraries: Biblioteca Francesca Bonnemaison, C. Sant Pere més Baix, 7 (☎932 68 73 60). M: Urquinaona. Walk toward the water, then turn left past the Palau de Música Catalana and C. Sant Pere més Alt. Open M and Th 4-9pm, Tu and F 10am-2pm and 4-9pm, W 10am-9pm, Sa 10am-2pm. **Biblioteca Barceloneta-La Fraternitat,** C. Comte de Santa Clara, 8-10 (☎932 25 35 74), 2 blocks from the beach in Port Vell. Open Aug. 16-Sept. 30 M-Tu and F 4-9pm, W 10am-2pm and 4-9pm, Th 10am-9pm, Sa 10am-2pm. Longer hours during academic year.

Religious Services: Comunidad Israelita de Barcelona (Jewish services), C. Avenir, 24 (☎932 09 31 47; www.cibonline.org; info@cibonline.org). **Comunidad Musulmana** (Muslim services), Mosque Tarek Ben Ziad, C. de l'Hospital, 91 (☎934 41 91 49). Services daily at prayer times. **Església Catedral de la Santa Creu** (Catholic services), Pl. de la Seu, 3 (☎933 42 82 60; www.catedralbcn.org). M: Jaume I. Cloister open daily 9am-1pm and 5-7pm. Mass at 9, 10, 11am, noon, 7pm; Su 9, 10:30am, noon, 1, 6, 7pm (in Spanish or Catalan). **Parròquia María Reina,** Av. d'Esplugues, 103 (☎932 03 55 39). Mass offered in English. **Iglesia Evangélica Pablo Nuevo,** C. Llull, 161 (☎934 85 48 41; www.iepoble9.org). **Testigos de Jehová: Salón Reino,** Consell de cent, 83 (☎934 23 26 68). **Casa del Tíbet,** C. Rosselló, 181 (☎932 07 59 66; www.casadeltibetbcn.org). **Hare Krishna,** Pl. Reial, 12 (☎933 02 51 94; www.iskcon.org). Contact the tourist office or visit www.bcn.es for info on other services.

Gay and Lesbian Resources: Pick up the official **LGBT tourist guide** at the Pl. de Catalunya, 17S, tourist office, which includes a section on LGBT bars, discotecas, publications, and more. Barcelona's gay neighborhood is called **Gaixample**, within L'Eixample. **GAYBARCELONA** (www.gaybarcelona.net) and **Infogai** (www.colectiugai.org) are useful websites in Catalan. Other resources include **Associació de Famílies Lésbianes i Gais** (☎645 31 88 60; www. familieslg.org) and **Associació de Mares i Pares de Gais i Lesbianes** (www.ampgil.org). **Antinous,** C. Josep Anselm Clavé, 6 (☎933 01 90 70; antinouslibros.com). M: Drassanes. Specializes in gay and lesbian books and films. Decent selection in English. Open M-F 11am-2pm and 5-9pm, Sa noon-2pm and 5-9pm. AmEx/MC/V. **Cómplices,** C. Cervantes, 2 (☎934 12 72 83). M: Liceu. A small bookstore with gay and lesbian books in English and Spanish, as well as an adequate selection of films. Also provides a map of Barcelona's gay bars and discotecas. Open M-F 10:30am-8pm, Sa noon-8pm. AmEx/MC/V.

Laundromats:

Lavomatic, Pl. Joaquim Xirau, 1, a block off La Rambla and 1 block below C. Escudellers; branch at C. Consolat del Mar, 43-45 (☎932 68 47 68), 1 block north of Pg. Colon and 2 blocks off Via Laietana. Wash €4.75, dry €0.85 per 5min. Both open M-Sa 9am-9pm.

Wash@Net, C. les Carretes, 56, in El Raval (☎934 42 29 15). Wash €4-6, dry €1 per 10min. Internet €1 per hour. Open 10am-11pm.

Lavamax, C. Junta de Comerç, 14, in El Raval (☎933 01 59 32). Wash €5 for 8kg, dry €1 per 8min. Self-service open daily 9:30am-9pm. Drop-off service M-Sa 9:30am-1:30pm, M-F also 5-9pm.

Orange Laundry, Pl. del Sol, 11-12 (☎934 15 03 61). Wash €4, dry €4. Open 7am-11pm.

"HI. THIS IS BARCELONA." California native, eight year Barcelona resident, and expert on local lore, Jordan Susselman offers a "Hi. This Is Barcelona" tour that shouldn't be missed. He and his team of passionate guides offer private tours and weekly student group tours (7-15 students, 2-3hr., €25 per person). Susselman promises to tell the truth—and only the truth—about a city he's come to know better than some of its locals. Email jordan@hithisisbarcelona.com well in advance for private or student tours, and check out www.hithisisbarcelona.com for more information.

EMERGENCY AND COMMUNICATIONS

Local police: ☎092. **National police:** ☎091. **Mossos d'Esquadra:** ☎088.

Medical Emergency: ☎061.

Tourist Police: La Rambla, 43 (☎932 56 24 30). M: Liceu. Multilingual officers. This is where to go if you've been pickpocketed. Open 24hr.

Late-Night Pharmacy: Rotates; check any pharmacy window for the nearest on duty, or contact the police. Or call **Información de Farmacias de Guardia** (☎93 481 00 60).

Hospital: Hospital Clínic i Provincal, C. Villarroel, 170 (☎932 27 54 00). M: Hospital Clínic. Main entrance at C. Roselló and C. Casanova. **Hospital de la Santa Creu i Sant Pau** (☎932 91 90 00, emergency 91 91 91). M: Hospital de Sant Pau. **Hospital General de la Vall d'Hebron** (☎932 74 61 00). M: Vall d'Hebron. **Hospital del Mar,** Pg. Marítim, 25-29 (☎932 48 30 00), before Port Olímpic. M: Ciutadella or Vila Olímpica.

Telephones: Buy phone cards at tobacco stores and newsstands; the lowest denomination is usually €6, which promises 45min. of international calling, though rates sometimes require you to use all your minutes in a single call. A much better option is to use **Locotorios** (international call centers), which dot the streets on either side of La Rambla. A short call to the US will cost only a few cents. Purchase cell phones in El Corte Inglés in Pl. Catalunya; pre-pay phones with SIM card from €29. **Directory Assistance:** ☎1003 within Spain, 1008 within Europe, 1005 outside Europe.

Internet Access:

Easy Internet Café, La Rambla, 31 (☎933 01 7507; www.easyinternetcafe.com). M: Liceu. Fairly reasonable prices and over 200 terminals in a bright, modern center. CD burning (€3.50), faxing (€.50-1.50), copying, and scanning (€1.30). €2.10 per hour, min. €2, 1-day unlimited pass €7, 1 week €15, 1 month €30. Open 8am-2:30am. Branch at Ronda Universitat, 35. M: Catalunya. €2 per hour, 1-day pass €3, 1 week €7, 1 month €15. Open 8am-2am.

Navegaweb, La Rambla, 88-94 (☎933 17 90 26; navegabarcelona@terra.es). M: Liceu. In the basement of a video arcade. Good rates for international calls ($0.20 per min. to USA). Internet €2 per hour. Open M-Th and Su 9am-midnight, F 9am-1am, Sa 9am-2am.

Bcnet (Internet Gallery Café), C. Barra de Ferro, 3 (☎932 68 15 07; www.bornet-bcn.com), down the street from the Museu Picasso. M: Jaume I. €0.95 for 15 min; €2.90 per hour; 10hr. ticket €19. Open M-F 10am-11pm, Sa-Su noon-11pm.

MS Internet, C. Pintor Fortuny, 30 (☎933 17 55 62), 3 blocks off La Rambla in El Raval. M: Liceu or Catalunya. €1 per hour. Open M-Sa 10am-midnight.

Contacta, Gran Via, 600 (☎933 18 73 51). M: Universitat. €1 per hour. Open M-F 9am-11pm, Sa-Su noon-11pm. Branch at C. Villarroel, 199 (☎934 19 35 39).

Interspace, C. San Miguel, 41-43 (☎932 21 40 58), right off Pl. la Barceloneta. €1.50 per hour. Open M-F 11am-11pm, Sa-Su 3-11pm.

Post Office: Pl. d'Antoni López (☎902 197 197). M: Jaume I or Barceloneta. **Fax** and **Lista de Correos.** Open M-F 8:30am-9:30pm, Su (access on side street) noon-10pm. Dozens of branches; consult www.correos.es. **Postal Code:** 08001.

ACCOMMODATIONS

While accommodations in Barcelona are easy to spot, finding an affordable bed or room can be more difficult. During one of the busier months (June-Sept. or Dec.), wandering up and down La Rambla looking for a place can be a recipe for anxiety and frustration. If you want to stay in a touristy area, reserve weeks ahead. Consider staying outside heavily trafficked Ciutat Vella; there are plenty of hostels in the Zona Alta, particularly in Gràcia, that have more vacancies. For the best rooms, l'Eixample has good deals and is also quiet at night. La Ribera and El Raval are smart alternatives to the hectic Barri Gòtic; they're just as close to the action and often cheaper. There are some less reputable parts of El Raval on the side streets farther from La Rambla, so choose wisely.

ALTERNATIVE ACCOMMODATIONS. Barcelona is not a cheap city, and a decent hostel will cost at least €23 a night. Those passing through for only a short time, and carrying no valuables, sometimes turn to another option: the so-called "illegal hostels" that offer rooms at significantly reduced prices (€15-18). Backpackers looking to stay illegally sometimes ask around at Travel Bar (C. Boqueria, 27). Illegal hostels can be dangerous and unpredictable, and Let's Go does not recommend them.

CAMPING

A handful of sites lie in the outskirts of the city, accessible by intercity buses (20-45min.; €1.50). The **Associació de Càmpings de Barcelona,** Gran Via de les Corts Catalanes, 608 (☎934 12 59 55; www.campingsbcn.com), has more info. A good choice is **Càmping Tres Estrellas ❶,** Autovía de Castelldefells, km 13.2. Take bus L95 (€1.60) from Pl. de Catalunya to the stop just 300m from the campsite, 13km south. (☎936 33 06 37; www.camping3estrellas.com. €5-7 per person, €7-8 per 2-person tent, €6-8 per car. Equipped with internet access, BBQ, pool, ATM, supermarket, and more. Open Mar. 15-Oct.15. AmEx/MC/V.)

BARRI GÒTIC AND LA RAMBLA

LOWER BARRI GÒTIC

The following hostels lie between C. Ferran and the water. Backpackers flock here to be close to the late-night revelry at the popular, heavily touristed La Rambla. Beware of the cheapest options if you want breathing room.

Hostal Mariluz Youngsters, C. Palau, 4 (☎933 17 34 63; www.pensionmariluz.com), up 3 flights. M: Liceu or Jaume I. Gorgeous renovations turned this hostel into a modern and natural light-filled space around a historic courtyard. Offers short-term apartments nearby. Free Wi-Fi. A/C. Dorms €18-24; singles €25-35; doubles €45-58; triples €57-75; quads €68-88, with bath €92. MC/V. ❶

Hostal Levante, Baixada de San Miquel, 2 (☎933 17 95 65; www.hostallevante.com). M: Liceu. New rooms are large and tasteful, with light wood furnishings and fans; some have balconies. TV lounge. Ask for a newly renovated room. Apartments have kitchen, living room, and laundry machine. Spacious doubles. A/C. Singles €33-45; doubles €60-70; 4-person apartments €30 per person per night. MC/V. ❸

Pensión Fernando, C. Ferran, 31 (☎933 01 79 93; www.hfernando.com). M: Liceu. Clean and conveniently located. Dorms with A/C and lockers. Common kitchen with dining room and TV on 3rd fl. Private rooms have TV. Towels €1.50. Internet €1 per 30min. Dorms with lockers €17-21; singles €32-36, with bath €45-50; doubles with bath €55-70; triples with bath €70-85. MC/V. ❶

Kabul Youth Hostel, Pl. Reial, 17 (☎933 18 51 90; www.kabul.es). M: Liceu. Legendary among backpackers; holds up to 200 travelers in rooms of 4-20. Lounge and terrace. Breakfast included. Laundry €3 to wash, €3 to dry. Key deposit €15. Reservations only on website with credit card. Check-out 11am. Free Wi-Fi. Dorms €25-31. MC/V. ❷

Hostal Benidorm, La Rambla, 37 (☎933 02 20 54; www.hostalbenidorm.com). M: Drassanes or Liceu. One of the best values on La Rambla. Phone, A/C, and balconies overlooking the street. Internet €1 per 15min, free Wi-Fi. Singles €40-45; doubles €60-69; triples €85-89; quads €100-110; quints €115-120. MC/V. ❹

UPPER BARRI GÒTIC

This section of the Barri Gòtic is between C. Fontanella and C. Ferran. Portal de l'Àngel, a chic pedestrian avenue, runs through the middle. Rooms can be pricier here; those farther from La Rambla are generally more serene. Reservations are advised in summer.

Hostal Plaza, C. Fontanella, 18 (☎933 01 01 39; www.plazahostal.com). M: Urquinaona. Super-friendly owners, brightly painted rooms decorated with colorful art, many with A/C. Free internet access in the lobby and a great location. Singles €35, with bath €45; doubles €55-65/65-80; triples €75-80/90-95. AmEx/MC/V. ❸

Hostal Maldà, C. Pi, 5 (☎933 17 30 02). M: Liceu. Enter inside the small shopping center and follow the signs upstairs. The friendly owner keeps the hostel occupied year-round. There are 26 rooms with shared baths at rock-bottom prices. No reservations; claim your space the morning of. Returning guests can call ahead. Doubles €30; triples with shower €45. Cash only. ❸

Hostal-Residència Rembrandt, C. de la Portaferrissa, 23 (☎933 18 10 11; www.hostrembrandt.com). M: Liceu. Rooms superior to others in the area; all unique, some with large bath, patio, and sitting area. TV in common area. Breakfast (€5). Fans. Reception 9am-11pm. Reservations require credit card. Singles €25-30, €35-40 with bath; doubles €40-50/45-55; triples €60-65/65-75. MC/V. ❷

Hostal Campi, C. Canuda, 4 (☎933 01 35 45; www.hostalcampi.com). Central location and helpful staff. Most rooms have balconies. Some have TV. Internet €1 per hour. Prices vary, but generally singles €29; doubles €52, with bath €60; triples €72/82. MC/V. ❷

Hostal Residència Lausanne, Av. Portal de l'Àngel, 24 (☎933 02 11 39). M: Catalunya. Great central location. Go up 2 flights at the back of the entrance foyer. White walls, posh lounge with marble staircase, and TV. Free internet. Doubles €50-55, with bath €70-65, for 1 person €30-35; quads with balcony €100. Cash only. ❷

Hotel Toledano/Hostal Residència Capitol, La Rambla, 138 (☎933 01 08 72; www.hoteltoledano.com). M: Catalunya. Rooms with cable TV and phones; outer rooms with balcony, interior with A/C. Free internet access in lobby; free Wi-Fi throughout. 4th fl. hotel (all but cheapest singles have bath): singles €44; doubles €72; triples €95; quads €112. 5th-fl. hostel: €30/49/69/84, shared bath. AmEx/MC/V. ❹

LA RIBERA

Less tourist activity in this neighborhood translates to fewer lodging choices. Still, consider La Ribera for a quieter, but more authentic, alternative.

Gothic Point Youth Hostel, C. Vigatans, 5 (☎932 68 78 08; www.gothicpoint.com). M: Jaume I. Colorful lounge area has free internet and TV. Most beds with curtains and personal lockers in jungle-gym rooms with A/C. Rooftop terrace. Highly social, with lots of events, including a weekly DJ jam and free concerts. Breakfast included. Lockers free, locks cost €3. Sheets €2. Towels €2. Refrigerator and kitchen access. High-season dorms €23; mid-season €19.50; low-season €17.50. €1 credit card fee per person per night. AmEx/MC/V. ❷

Hostal de Ribagorza, C. Trafalgar, 39 (☎933 19 19 68; www.hostalribagorza.com). M: Urquinaona. Rooms in a *Modernista* building complete with marble staircase and tile floors. TV, A/C, and homey decorations. Doubles €45-60; triples €60-75. MC/V. ❹

Pensión Ciudadela, C. Comerç, 33 (☎933 19 62 03; www.pension-ciudadela.com). M: Barceloneta. Climb 5 flights of stairs to this small hostel with 10 spacious, freshly painted rooms. All have A/C, TV, and balcony. Doubles €45, with bath €56; triples €60, with bath €72. AmEx/MC/V. ❹

Hostal Nuevo Colón, Av. Marquès de l'Argentera, 19 (☎933 19 50 77; www.hostalnuevocolon.com). M: Barceloneta. 26 modern rooms in a hotel-quality building with common area and TV. Reservations recommended in high season. Singles €35, with bath €49; doubles €47/67; triples €67/87; quads with bath €87. 3- to 6-person apartments with bunk-beds and kitchenettes €90-155 per day. MC/V. ❹

EL RAVAL

Be careful as you go further from La Rambla towards the park, as streets can be eerily deserted late at night. This relative lack of bustling tourism, however, makes El Raval a good lodging alternative to the more crowded zones.

Hotel Peninsular, C. de Sant Pau, 34 (☎933 02 31 38; http://hotelpeninsular.net). M: Liceu. This *Modernista* building has 80 rooms with green doors, phone, and A/C around its beautiful 4-story interior courtyard festooned with hanging plants. Excellent breakfast included. Free internet and Wi-Fi. Singles €30, with bath €55; doubles with bath €78, triples €95, quads €120, quints €140. MC/V. ❸

Barcelona Mar Youth Hostel, C. de Sant Pau, 80 (☎933 24 85 30; www.barcelonamar.es). M: Paral·lel. Crams in 120 dorm-style beds amid ocean-themed decor; 4-16 per room. A/C; free internet access in the lounge area. Breakfast and locker included. Sheets €2.50, towels €2.50, both €3.50. Self-serve laundry €4.50. Dorms in summer €26, in winter €16-19; Double beds €46-58, F-Sa add €2 per person. AmEx/MC/V. ❷

Center Ramblas (HI), C. de l'Hospital, 63 (☎934 12 40 69; www.center-ramblas.com). M: Liceu. Young staff and cheap beds—though the ambience leaves something to be desired. Breakfast and sheets included. Free internet access. Laundry €5. Towels €2. Lockers €2 each use. Dorms in summer €24; in winter €17-21. MC/V. ❷

Hostal Ópera, C. de Sant Pau, 20 (☎933 18 82 01; www.hostalopera.com). M: Liceu. Renovated rooms feel new; bath, phone, and A/C. Cafe downstairs. Internet access in the small common room, €1 per 15min. Singles €49; doubles €69. MC/V. ❹

L'EIXAMPLE

While pricier than those of other *barris*, l'Eixample's lodgings are usually elegant and nicely equipped. At night, the wide streets tend to be much quieter than those of the Ciutat Vella.

Somnio Hostel, C. Diputació 251. (☎932 72 53 08, www.somniohostels.com) M: Pg. de Gràcia. This brand-new, immaculately clean bargain sports chic decor and is just blocks from Pl. de Catalunya. A/C throughout, free internet and Wi-Fi, TV in common area. Breakfast €5; drinks available at the front desk. Same-sex dorms, complete with sheets, towel, comforter, pillow, and locker €23; Singles €40, with sink and large mirror. Doubles €72, with bath €80. MC/V. ❷

Hostal Residència Oliva, Pg. de Gràcia, 32, 4th fl. (☎934 88 01 62; www.lasguias.com/hostaloliva). M: Pg. de Gràcia. Classy ambience; elegant wooden bureaus, mirrors, and a light marble floor. All rooms have high ceilings, TV, and A/C, some with a view. Singles €37; doubles €62, with bath €80; triples with bath €111. Cash only. ❸

Hostal Qué Tal, C. Mallorca, 290 (☎934 59 23 66; www.quetalbarcelona.com), near C. Bruc. M: Pg. de Gràcia or Verdaguer. This high-quality gay- and lesbian-friendly hostel has one of the best interiors in the city, with a plant-filled terrace and snazzy decor in all 13 rooms. Free internet. Singles €45; doubles €65, with bath €84. Cash only. ❹

BCN Hostal Central, Ronda Universitat, 11, 1st fl. (☎933 02 24 20; www.hostal-central.net). M: Universitat. Some rooms with balconies and inviting nooks. Breakfast (small pastries, coffee, and fruit) included. Free internet. Reception 24hr. Some rooms with TV. Singles with shared bath €25-45; doubles €35-40, with bath €55-60; triples €65-75; quads €85-90. MC/V. ❷

Hostal San Remo, Ausiàs Marc, 19 (☎933 02 19 89; www.hostalsanremo.com). M: Urquinaona. 8 spacious rooms have TV, A/C, and windows; 4 have terraces, and some have stained-glass windows. Free internet. Reserve early. Singles with bath €34-40; doubles €60; triples €75. Nov. and Jan.-Feb. reduced prices. MC/V. ❸

Pensión Aribau, C. Aribau, 37, 1st fl. (☎934 53 11 06; www.hostalaribau.com). M: Pg. de Grácia. Most of the hostel's 11 rooms have TV and A/C. Ask for one of the balconies overlooking a terrace. Reserve at least a month ahead in summer. Singles and doubles €50, with bath €65, triples €65, with bath €80. AmEx/MC/V. ❺

ZONA ALTA: GRÀCIA AND OUTER BARRIS

Gràcia is Barcelona's "undiscovered" quarter, so last-minute arrivals may find vacancies here, even though options are limited. Still, it's best to reserve ahead in the summer. Hostels in Montjuïc are extremely rare.

Hostal Lesseps, C. Gran de Gràcia, 239 (☎932 18 44 34; www.hostallesseps.com). M: Lesseps. The 16 rooms have TV and bath; 4 have A/C (€5 extra). Rooms facing the street are a bit noisy. Cats and dogs allowed. Free internet and Wi-Fi. Singles €40; doubles €75; triples €80, with extra bed €90. MC/V. ❹

Pensión San Medín, C. Gran de Gràcia, 125 (☎932 17 30 68; www.sanmedin.com). M: Fontana. This family-run *pensión* has 12 rooms, 4 with balcony, all with TV. Small common room with TV. Reception 8am-midnight. Free Wi-Fi. Singles €32-35, with bath €42-54; doubles €58-65, with bath 65-78. MC/V. ❸

Alberg Residència La Ciutat, C. L'Alegre de Dalt, 66 (☎932 13 03 00; http://laciutat.nnhotels.es). M: Joanic. Follow C. Escorial for 5 blocks, then cross to C. L'Alegre de Dalt. Lounge areas with TV and kitchen. Private rooms have TV, phone, and bath. Some rooms with A/C. Breakfast included. Sheets €1.80. Laundry €5.40. Free internet. Reception 24hr. 4- to 10-bed dorms €16.50-20; singles €35-50; doubles €52-60. MC/V. ❶

FOOD

Barcelona offers every kind of food and ambience imaginable. Whether Basque, Chinese, Indian, or American, restaurants here will exceed your culinary expectations. However, beware of touristy restaurants offering "traditional" dishes—good authentic food can be hard to find. Our best advice is to look to the Catalan option: *fideuà* unseats *paella*, *cava* champagne complements every meal, and *crema catalana* satisfies the local sweet tooth. Barcelona's tapas (sometimes called *pintxos*) bars, concentrated in La Ribera and Gràcia, often serve *montaditos*, thick slices of bread topped with all sorts of delectables from sausage to *tortilla* (omelette) to anchovies. Hopping from one tapas bar to another can be a fun, social, and often cheap way to pass the evening. Most tapas bars are self-serve and standing room only. Plates in hand, ravenous customers help themselves to the toothpick-skewered goodies that line the bars. The bartender calculates the bill by tallying up the toothpicks on the way out, and then it's on to another bar. Though vegetarian options in general have never been easier to find, vegetarians consult the extensive *Guía del Ocio* (€1) at newsstands for a list of available options.

Markets: La Boqueria (Mercat de Sant Josep), off La Rambla. M: Liceu. Wholesale prices for vegetables, fruit, cheese, meat, and wine. Open M-Sa 8am-8pm. **Mercat de la Concepi,** C. València, between C. Bruc and C. Girona. M: Girona. Open M-Sa 8am-3pm. **Mercat Santa Caterina,** Av. Francesc Cambó, s/n, just off Via Laietana. Newly remodeled; with Wi-Fi to accompany your anchovies (€1 per hour). Open M-Sa 7:30am-2pm.

Supermarkets: Champion, La Rambla, 113. M: Liceu. Open M-Sa 10am-10pm. MC/V. **El Corte Inglés,** Pl. de Catalunya, 14. M: Catalunya. Supermarket in basement. Open M-Sa and occasionally Su 10am-10pm. AmEx/MC/V.

FOOD BY TYPE

B Barri Gòtic **G** Gràcia **L** La Ribera **M** Montjuïc **R** El Raval **W** Waterfront **X** l'Eixample

Restaurant	Area/Price
ASIAN	
Hello Sushi (p. 373)	R ❷
Kaitensushi (p. 370)	B ❷
Kirin (p. 373)	X ❷
Rita Rouge (p. 372)	R ❷
Sushi Itto (p. 374)	G ❸
CAFES AND PASTRY SHOPS	
Arc Café (p. 370)	B ❷
Café de l'Ópera (p. 371)	B ❶
La Colmena (p. 371)	B ❶
Mendizabal (p. 373)	R ❶
Zahara (p. 374)	W ❷
CATALAN AND SPANISH	
Acalia (p. 373)	X ❸
Agua (p. 374)	W ❸
DosTrece (p. 373)	R ❸
Els 4 Gats (p. 371)	B ❹
Ikastola (p. 374)	G ❶
La Rita (p. 373)	E ❷
L'Antic Bocoi del Gòtic (p. 370)	B ❷
Les Quinze Nits (p. 370)	B ❷
Los Caracoles (p. 370)	B ❸
Madame Jasmine (p. 373)	R ❶
Xaloc (p. 371)	B ❷
INTERNATIONAL	
Attic (p. 371)	B ❸
El Pebre Blau (p. 372)	L ❸
La Llavor dels Origens (p. 371)	L ❶
Racó d'en Baltà (p. 373)	X ❸
Tenorio (p. 373)	X ❸
Vildsvin (p. 371)	B ❸
La Pizza del Born (p. 372)	L ❶
Petra (p. 372)	L ❷
TAPAS	
Jai-Ca Bar (p. 374)	W ❶
Tèxtil Cafè (p. 372)	L ❸
Va de Vi (p. 372)	L ❸
El Xampanyet (p. 372)	L ❶
VEGETARIAN	
Maoz Vegetarian (p. 371)	B ❶
Organic (p. 372)	R ❷
Pla dels Àngels (p. 373)	R ❷
Vegetalia (p. 371)	B ❷

BARCELONA

BARRI GÒTIC AND LA RAMBLA

Barcelona's nucleus contains all types of eateries. Classic Catalan cuisine is juxtaposed with fast-food options and every species of bar imaginable. Choose carefully; anything along La Rambla is likely to be overpriced.

LOWER BARRI GÒTIC

Les Quinze Nits, Pl. Reial, 6 (☎933 17 30 75; www.lesquinzenits.com). M: Liceu. Popular restaurant with lines halfway through the plaza every night; arrive early for a classy dinner in this happening setting. Catalan entrees at shockingly low prices. Pasta and rice €4-7. Fish €7-9. Meat €6-10. Open daily 1-3:45pm and 8:30-11:30pm. MC/V. ❷

L'Antic Bocoi del Gòtic, Baixada de Viladecols, 3 (☎933 10 50 67; www.bocoi.net). M: Jaume I. Formed in part by an ancient 1st-century Roman wall. Excellent salads (€7.20-9), *coques de recapte* (open-faced toasted sandwiches, a Catalan speciality, €6.95-8.50), and cheese platters (€13-18.50) feature *jamón ibérico* and local produce. Open M-Sa 8:30pm-midnight. Reserve in advance. AmEx/MC/V. ❷

Arc Café, C. Carabassa, 19 (☎933 02 52 04; www.arccafe.com). M: Drassanes. This secluded cafe serves curries (€9.25-10.25), soups (€4), and salads €4-6.90). Entrees €8-16.50. *Menú del mediodía* €9. Thai menu Th-F. Open M-Th 1pm-1am, F-Sa 1pm-2am. AmEx/MC/V. ❷

Los Caracoles, C.Escudellers, 14 (☎933 02 31 85). M: Drassanes. Once a 19th-century snail shop, now a bustling restaurant with Old World charm. Specialties include *caracoles* (snails; €10.50) and rabbit. Open daily 1:15pm-midnight. AmEx/MC/V. ❸

Kaitensushi, Pg. Colon, 4 (☎933 19 24 58) M: Barceloneta. Locals revel in all-you-can-eat sushi, grabbing whatever delicate sashimi or colorful roll suits their fancy as choices pass by each table on a moving conveyor belt. All-you-can-eat fixed prices; weekday lunch with desert and drink €8.58, dinner and weekends €12.88, less than 10 years old lunch €4.88, dinner and weekends €6.98. Popular, so consider making a reservation. Open daily noon-4pm and 8pm-midnight. MC/V. ❷

Vildsvin, C. Ferran, 38 (☎933 17 94 07, reservations 902 52 05 22; reservas@sagardi.es). M: Liceu. Oysters (€9.50 for half dozen) and international beers (€3-4) are this Central European bar's specialties. Chic restaurant downstairs has salads, salmon, and homemade cheese and sausage. Entrees €13.70-17.50. Desserts €3.50-6.52. Open M-F 8:30am-1am, F-Sa 9am-2am, Su 9am-1am. AmEx/MC/V. ❸

Vegetalia, Escudellers, 54 (☎933 17 33 31; www.vegetalia.es). M: Drassanes. Hardcore veggie protein options based on tofu, *seitan,* and *tempe,* with 7 killer veggieburgers that even meat-eaters can't resist. All dishes made from scratch to order, incorporating organic ingredients when possible. Also a small natural foods store in the back. Entrees €6.50-9.50. Open M-F and Su 1:30-11pm, Fr-Sa 1:30pm-midnight. Cash only. ❷

Maoz Vegetarian, 2 locations: at C. Ferran, 13 and La Rambla, 95 (www.maozvegetarian.com). Falafel haven and Barcelona institution with a bountiful toppings bar. Falafel €3.80-5.20. Open M-Th and Su 11am-2:30am, F-Sa 11am-3am. MC/V. ❶

UPPER BARRI GÒTIC

Els 4 Gats, C. Montsió, 3 (☎933 02 41 40; www.4gats.com). M: Catalunya. Picasso's old Modernista hangout, and the site of his first art exhibit (of portraits and caricatures). Exudes bohemia. Cuisine includes Mediterranean salad (€10.48) and Iberian pork with king prawns and hazelnuts (€18.90). Entrees €16-27. M-F lunch *menú* 1-4pm (€11.97) is the best deal and comes with epic desserts; try the *crema catalana.* Live piano daily 9pm-1am. Open daily 1pm-1am. AmEx/MC/V. ❹

Attic, La Rambla, 120 (☎933 02 48 66; www.angrup.com). M: Liceu. This chic restaurant promises reasonable prices right on touristy La Rambla, in addition to a modern design. Dangling silverware in the stairwell serves as an interesting piece of art. Mediterranean fusion cuisine, including fish (€10-13), meat (€7-15), and their specialty ox burger (€10.35). Open daily 1-4:30pm and 7pm-12:30am. AmEx/MC/V. ❸

Xaloc, C. de la Palla, 13-17 (☎933 01 19 90). M: Liceu. Classy, local-favorite. Features a friendly staff, grown-up ambience, and a butcher counter with pig legs hanging from the ceiling. Meat and poultry sandwiches on tasty baguettes or Catalan bread (€3-6.50). Lunch *menú* €10.50. Open M-F 9am-midnight, Sa-Su 10am-midnight. AmEx/MC/V. ❷

La Colmena, Pl. de l'Àngel, 12 (☎933 15 13 56). M: Jaume I. A busy dessert shop appropriately named "the Beehive," this place is hard to resist. Take a number and don't walk in unless you're prepared to satisfy your sweet tooth. Small pastries €1-3. Open daily 9am-9pm. AmEx/MC/V. ❶

Café de l'Ópera, La Rambla, 74 (☎933 17 75 85; www.cafeoperabcn.com). M: Liceu. Antique mirror-covered cafe used to be a post-opera bourgeois tradition; now it's a hidden favorite. Hot chocolate (€2.10) thick as a melted candy bar. Churros €1.40. Tapas €1.50-8. Salads €6-10. Open M-Th 8am-2am, F-Sun 8am-3am. Cash only. ❶

LA RIBERA

The eclectic gourmet restaurants of La Ribera cater to a young crowd. There is a relatively high concentration of Asian restaurants, tapas bars, and wineries.

La Llavor dels Origens, C. Enric Granados, 9 (☎934 53 11 20; www.lallavordelsorigens.com), C. Vidrieria, 6-8 (☎933 10 75 31), Pg. de Born, 4 (☎932 95 66 90), and C. Ramón y Cajal, 12 (☎932 13 60 31). Check out delectable entrees such as the beef-stuffed onion (€6.36) and the rabbit with chocolate and almonds (€6.36) in the restaurant's magazine-menu. Modeled on traditional markets where villagers saw exactly what

BARCELONA

they were buying. A hip dining room adds a new-school twist. Small soups, meat dishes, and some vegetarian dishes €4.22-6.90. Open daily 12:30pm-1am. AmEx/MC/V. ❷

Petra, C. Sombrerers, 13 (☎933 19 91 99). M: Jaume I. Serves some of the best food in the area at amazingly low prices. Quirky details, like menus printed on wine bottles and lights made of dangling silverware. Try the duck with brie, apple, and pork with banana salsa. Entrees €7.80. Salads €4.85. Pasta €5.15 Open Tu-Th 1:30-4pm and 9-11:30pm; F-Sa 1:30-4pm and 9pm-midnight; Su 1:30-4pm. MC/V. ❷

El Pebre Blau, C. Banys Vells, 21 (☎933 19 13 08). M: Jaume I. *Nouveau* gourmet restaurant serves unique Mediterranean and Middle Eastern fusion dishes under starry lanterns. Attentive waitstaff. Salads €9-17 (for 2). Pastas €10. Kitchen open daily 8:30pm-midnight. Reserve ahead. MC/V. ❸

La Pizza del Born, Pg. del Born, 22 (☎933 10 62 46). M: Jaume I. The best of Argentine thick-crust meets the best of Spain, with toppings like artichoke hearts, *jamón serrano,* or goat cheese. You can take anything to go. Slices €1.80. Lunch *menú:* 2 slices and drink €3.90. Open M-Th and Su 12:30pm-1am, F-Sa 12:30pm-2am. Cash only. ❶

El Xampanyet, C. Montcada, 22 (☎933 19 70 03). M: Jaume I. Near the Museu Picasso. Overflows with a crowd that spills onto the street, drinks in hand. House special, *xampanyet,* is served with anchovies and *pa amb tomàquet* (bread with tomato; €1.80). Offers *cava* (champagne) in over 25 varieties. Less crowded weekday afternoons. Bottles from €8. Open Sept.-July Tu-Sa noon-4pm and 7-11pm, Su noon-3:30pm. MC/V. ❷

Tèxtil Cafè, C. Montcada, 12-14 (☎932 68 25 98; www.textilcafe.com). M: Jaume I. Terrace cafe, nestled in old stone courtyard and surrounded by art and flowers, serves salads, tapas, and entrees with *cava* and wine. Live music in summer: W 8:30-11pm DJ, Su 9-11pm jazz. Lunch *menú* €11; dinner €17.50. Tapas €5.30. Salads €7.50-7.90. Entrees €8.50-10.50. Good vegetarian selection. Wheelchair-accessible. Open mid-Mar. to Nov. Tu-Th and Su 10am-midnight, F-Sa 10am-1am; Nov to mid-March Tu-W 10am-8:30pm, Th and Su 10am-midnight, F-Sa 10am-1am. MC/V. ❷

Va de Vi, C. Banys Vells, 16 (☎933 19 29 00). M: Jaume I. A romantic spot for tapas and drinks in a candlelit 16th-century stone tavern. This hidden gem is easy to miss from the street. Choose from over 300 varieties of wine and *cava* (€1.85-7.65). Wide selection of cheeses €4.60-19.80. Tapas €.90-18.50. Wheelchair-accessible. Open M-Th 6pm-1am, F-Sa 6pm-3am. MC/V. ❸

EL RAVAL

Trendy fusion spots and authentic Catalan mainstays contrast with the many Middle Eastern restaurants and a growing number of vegetarian-friendly alternatives. The Rambla del Raval is a promising place to hunt for food or to stop for tea under the white tents that spring up in summer.

Rita Rouge, Pl. Gardunya (☎934 81 36 86; ritarouge@ritablue.com). M: Liceu. Savor a healthy, delicious, and high-quality lunch *menú* (€11) full of creative offerings and vegetarian choices on a shady, black-and-red terrace just behind La Boqueria, or hop inside for a cocktail in style (€4.50-8). Entrees, like chicken tandoori with yogurt and *basmati* rice, €9.50-22. Salads and wok dishes €6-12. Open daily 9am-2am. Kitchen open 1pm-10pm. Sister restaurant Rita Blue, Pl. Sant Augustí, 3 (☎933 42 40 86; www.ritablue.com) serves a similar *menù.* ❷

Organic, C. Junta de Comerç, 11 (☎933 01 09 02). This vegan-friendly eatery provides wholesome, healthy dishes—starting with the filtered water used to prepare the food. Vegan salad bar and lunch *menú* (€10) served under exposed ceiling and candlelight.

Second location in La Boqueria market also has a €10 *menú* and *bocadillos;* take-out only. Open daily 12:30-11:30pm. MC/V. ❷

Pla dels Àngels, C. Ferlandina, 23 (☎933 49 40 47). M: Universitat. The inspired decor of this colorful, inexpensive eatery is fit for its proximity to the contemporary art museum. Creative, healthy dishes and a large vegetarian selection served on a terrace. Entrees €5-8. Open daily 1:30-4pm and 9-11:30pm. MC/V. ❷

DosTrece, C. Carme, 40 (☎933 01 73 06; www.dostrece.net). M: Catalunya. Young locals dine in this artsy bar with a retro diner feel. Lunch *menú* €11. Entrees €6-17. Open Tu-Su 10am-3am; kitchen open 10am-4pm and 6pm-midnight; terrace open until 1am. AmEx/MC/V. ❸

Madame Jasmine, Rbla. del Raval, 22. Eclectic decorations, a spirited staff, and an array of wonderfully mismatched chairs overlook Fernando Botero's fat cat sculpture in the middle of Rambla de Raval. Delicious *bocadillos* (€4.75) and the best salads in El Raval (€6). Kitchen open daily 1pm-midnight. Bar open until 2:30am. Cash only. ❶

Hello Sushi, C. Junta de Comerç, 14 (☎934 12 08 30; www.hello-sushi.com). M: Universitat. Zen red-and-blue decor and small tea area with floor cushions. Entrees €9. Lunch *menú* €8.50, students €4 during school year. Open Tu-Sa 12:30-4:30pm and 8:30pm-12:30am, Su 8:30pm-12:30am. Reservations required F-Su nights. AmEx/MC/V. ❷

Mendizabal, Junta de Comerç, 2. Try the *zumo del día* (juice of the day) at this colorful student favorite, right near the school of fine arts. Need something to wash down all that juice? No problem: beer is cheap (€2), as are the *bocadillos:* serano ham, brie, tomato (€3.50), mozarella, mango, avocado (€3.80), which are grilled behind the counter. No seating—either stand at the counter or order to go. Open daily 8am-1am. Cash only. ❶

L'EIXAMPLE

Sweet (and savory) deals on *bocadillos* and tapas are found at every corner.

La Rita, C. Aragó, 279 (☎934 87 23 76; www.laritarestaurant.com). A killer afternoon lunch *menú* has made Rita a local favorite for a cheap but quality mid-day meal. Their bright red awning draws crowds to booths of the same color, where they enjoy everything from gazpacho to salmon carpaccio in orange-and-dill sauce. *Menú* M-F €9.70. Entrees €6-10. Open daily 1-3:45pm and 8:30-11:30pm. MC/V. ❷

Racó d'en Baltá, C. Aribau, 125 (☎934 53 10 44; www.racodenbalta.com). M: Hospital Clínic. Founded in 1900, this treasure offers innovative Mediterranean dishes like duck sirloin with rosemary caramel (€13). Entrees €9-17. Lunch *menú* €9.90. Open M-Th 9am-11:30pm, Th-Sa 9am-3am. Kitchen closed M, open 1-4pm and 9-11:30pm. AmEx/MC/V. ❸

Kirin, C. Aragó, 231 (☎934 88 29 19; www.restaurantjaponeskirin.com). All-you-can-eat sushi, edamame, and other Asian delicacies rolls by on a conveyer belt—take your pick. Buffet €9.20-13.90. Children €5.50. Open daily 1-4pm and 8pm-midnight. MC/V. ❷

Acalia, C. Rosselló, 197 (☎932 37 05 15). Sculptural light fixtures inside and a terrace outside complement the *nouveau*-cuisine offerings from this sparkling restaurant. Meat entrees and green salads with fresh fruit. Lunch *menú* €10.19. Dinner entrees €9-17. Open Tu-Sa 1-5pm and 8:30pm-1am. MC/V. ❸

Tenorio, Pg. de Gràcia, 37 (☎932 72 05 92; www.grupcacheiro.com). M: Pg. de Gràcia. International fusion cuisine at reasonable prices, located right in the midst of the *"Manzana de la Discordia."* Grill specialities include baby rabbit (€10.75), and *turrine* of couscous with ratatouille and squid (€8.35). Entrees €6-24. Reserve ahead for inside or line up for patio seating. Open daily 7am-1am. Kitchen open for lunch and dinner 12:30pm-1am. AmEx/MC/V. ❸

MONTJUÏC

Dining options are not as plentiful in Montjuïc as elsewhere in the city, but the Fundació Miró, MNAC, Castell de Montjuïc, and Teatre Grec all have pleasant cafes. **Poble Espanyol,** an artisan village set in a 1929 World Expo castle, has a number of more substantial restaurants (entrance €8, students and seniors €6, 4-12 €5, under 4 free). *Menús* run €10-15. An up-and-coming neighborhood, **Poble Sec** has lots of restaurants, bars, and grocery stores lining Av. Lleida and Av. Paral·lel, but the real hot spot is the pedestrian zone around C. Blai.

THE WATERFRONT

Aside from the dozens of raucous beach bars, there are a handful of tamer establishments for a meal. Stop by **Spar Express,** P. Juan de Borbon, 74 (☎932 21 83 15) for beachside groceries (open daily 9am-11pm, MC/V).

Jai-Ca Bar, C. Ginebra, 13 (☎932 68 32 65), 2 blocks down Pg. Joan de Borbó and 3 blocks toward the beach, on the corner with C. Baluard. Hugely popular tapas bar centered around 2 things: Fútbol Club Barcelona and Estrella Damm. Most tapas—like *patatas bravas*—€3-5. Open Tu and Su 9am-10:30pm, W-Sa 9am-11:30pm. MC/V. ❶

Agua, Pg. Marítim de la Barceloneta, 30 (☎932 25 12 72; www.grupotragaluz.com), the last building on the ocean side of Pg. Marítim before Barceloneta. Tourists, trendy *barceloneses*, and GQ business-types enjoy seafood and rice dishes from the beachfront terrace. Vegetarian options. Entrees €7-21. Wheelchair accessible. Open daily 1-3:45pm and 8-11:30pm, later on weekends. Absolutely reserve ahead. AmEx/MC/V. ❸

Zahara, Pg. Joan de Borbó, 69 (☎932 21 37 65; www.zaharacocktails.com). This hip-and-loud bar is a diamond in the rough of mainstream bar-cafes. The menu uses color-coding and icons to show the contents and potency of each cocktail. Try a "shocktail" (€7-12). Beer €2-5. Salads €10. Sandwiches €5-6. Open daily 1pm-3am. MC/V. ❷

BARCELONA

ZONA ALTA: GRÀCIA AND OUTER BARRIS

Gràcia's restaurants typically serve fresh food amid hip decor, and most of their *menús* run below €10. Veggie options abound, as do places for *bokatas* (big, cheap sandwiches with thinly sliced meat, cheese, or veggies) and beer.

Ikastola, C. Perla, 22, has the best *bokatas* in the city, and all the locals know it; the young hip crowd overflows into the street and onto the small backroom terrace every night. Try the fresh pesto/goat cheese/tomato/basil combination. *Bokatas* €4.50, salads €7, beer €2.30. Open M-Th and Su 7pm-midnight, F-Sa 7pm-1am. Cash only. ❶

Restaurant Illa de Gràcia, C. Sant Domènec, 19 (☎932 38 02 29). M: Diagonal. Follow Gran de Gràcia for 5 blocks and turn right onto C. Sant Domènec. Huge number of vegetarian options, like *seitan* in romanesco sauce (€7.50), served in a fresh and simple dining room. Nothing over €7.50. Open Tu 8pm-1am, W-Th and Su 1pm-1am, F-Sa 1pm-2am. Closed last 2 weeks of Aug. MC/V. ❶

Agappe, C. Riera de Sant Miquel, 19 (☎932 37 86 01). M: Diagonal. Healthy fusion cuisine in an airy, elegant space. Lunch *menú* M-F €12. Entrees €9.75-17. Thai chicken salad (€6.85). Wheelchair-accessible. Open M-Sa 2:30pm-midnight. AmEx/MC/V. ❸

Sushi Itto, C. Londres, 103 (☎932 41 21 99). A classy sushi place combining Japanese cuisine with Western flavors in eclectic roll options. Nigiri €2.10-2.90. Entrees €7-19. Eight-piece rolls (combine 2 half rolls of your choice) €13.40. Delivery €2. Open daily 1:30-4pm and 8:30-11pm. AmEx/MC/V. ❸

SIGHTS

Barcelona has always been on the cutting edge of the art world. Visitors cross continents not only to see the paintings hanging in fantastic museums, but also to admire imaginative modern architecture and parks designed by world-renowned visonaries. The streets are the galleries for Barcelona's artistic spirit; intricate lampposts and murals light up even the most drab neighborhoods. You'll find the classics—Picasso, Miró, Mir, etc.—but also modern shows at museums like the Tàpies. Concentrated in l'Eixample, the *Modernista* treasures draw architeture afficionados from the far reaches of the world. Parc Güell and Parc Diagonal Mar allow for contemplation surrounded by innovative designs and sculptures. Sprinkled throughout the entire city lie plazas, tree-lined avenues, and corner parks, each with their own character to explore and discover.

RUTA DEL MODERNISME

For those with a few days in the city and an interest in seeing some of the most popular sights, the **Ruta del Modernisme** is the cheapest and most flexible option. The pass provides discount admission to dozens of *Modernista* buildings in the city, and comes with the purchase of a guidebook (€12); additional adult passes are €5, though an adult accompanying someone under 18 is free. Passes provide a 25-30% discount on the Palau de la Música Catalana, Fundació Antoni Tàpies, the Museu de Zoologia, tours of l'Hospital de la Santa Creu i Sant Pau and the facades of La Manzana de la Discordia (Amatller, Lleó i Morera, and Batlló), and map tours of Gaudí, Domènech i Montaner, and Puig i Cadafalch buildings, among other attractions. The pass comes with a map and a pamphlet giving the history of different sights, which is helpful for prioritizing visits. Purchase passes at the Pl. Catalunya tourist office, the Modernisme Centre at **Hospital Santa Creu i Sant Pau,** C. Sant Antoni Maria Claret, 167, or **Pavellons Güell,** Av. de Pedralbes, 7. Centralized info can be found at ☎902 07 66 21, 933 17 76 52, and www.rutadelmodernisme.com. Many sights have tour times and length restrictions; visiting all of them on the same day is virtually impossible.

BARCELONA

BARCELONA CARD

Another discount option is the **Barcelona Card.** The card is good for 2-5 days and includes free public transportation (on the Metro, daytime buses, and trains to the airport) and nearly 80 discounts (and sometimes free admission) at museums, cultural venues, theaters, and a few bars and clubs, shops, and restaurants. They are sold at tourist offices, Casa Batlló, El Corte Inglés, the Aquarium, and Poble Espanyol. Prices for 2-5 days range €24-36 for adults and €20-31 for ages 4-12. For students (usually with ISIC card; ISOS accepted less often), it may be cheaper to use student discounts to get into attractions.

BUS TURÍSTIC

Sit back and let the sights come to you. The Bus Turístic stops at 44 points of interest along three different routes (red for the north, blue for the south, and green for the eastern waterfront). Tickets come with an eight-language brochure with information on each sight. A full ride on the red or blue route takes about 2hr., green takes 40min., but the idea is to get off at any place of interest and use the bus (as many times as you want in your allotted days) as a convenient means of transportation. Multilingual guides stationed in every bus help orient travelers and answer questions. You can buy tickets once on board, or ahead of time at **Turisme de Catalunya,** Pl. de Catalunya, 17, in front of El Corte Inglés, and at www.barcelonaturisme.com. Many of the museums and sights covered by the bus offer discounts with the bus ticket; some are closed on

Mondays. (Buses run daily every 5-25min. First departure 9-9:30am; no service Dec. 25 and Jan. 1. 1-day pass €20, ages 4-12 €12; 2-day pass €26.)

BARRI GÒTIC AND LA RAMBLA

BARRI GÒTIC

Brimming with cathedrals, palaces, and unabashed tourism, Barcelona's oldest neighborhood masks its old age with 24hr. energy. The heart of the Barri Gòtic took shape during Roman times, and continued to develop during the medieval period as new ruling powers built on top of old structures and roads. Today it is the political and historical center of the city, with a split personality that is alternately quaint and overwhelming. Catalan commercialism persists in all its glory with store-lined streets and fine restaurants, but the soul of the neighborhood lies deeper than these attractions, down its tiny, twisting alleyways.

MUSEU D'HISTÒRIA DE LA CIUTAT. Buried some 20m below a seemingly innocuous old plaza lies one of the two components of the Museu d'Història de la Ciutat: the subterranean excavations of the Roman city of Barcino. This **archaeological exhibit** displays incredibly well-preserved first- to sixth-century ruins; through glass sections, you can see huge ceramic wine casks, intricate Roman floor mosaics, and reused cornerstones forming part of the Roman walls. Built on top of the 4th-century walls, the **Palau Reial Major** served as the residence of the Catalan-Aragonese monarchs. The Gothic **Saló de Tinell** (Throne Room) is supposedly the place where Fernando and Isabel received Columbus after his journey to America. *(Pl. del Rei. M: Jaume I. ☎ 932 56 21 00; www.museuhistoria.bcn.cat. Wheelchair-accessible. Open Apr.-Sept. Tu-Sa 10am-8pm, Su 10am-3pm; Oct.-Mar. Tu-Sa 10am-2pm and 4-7pm, Su 10am-3pm. Pamphlets available in English. Museum €6, students €4. Exhibition €1.50/1. Museum and exhibition €6.50/4.50.)*

ESGLÉSIA CATEDRAL DE LA SANTA CREU I SANTA EULALIA. This must-see cathedral, referred to in Barcelona as "La Seu," is one of the city's most popular monuments. The 14th-century cloister (home to a clique of white geese) overlooks an arcaded garden, with a fountain and pond. Beneath the cathedral lies the Crypt of Santa Eulàlia. The museum in **La Sala Capitular** holds Bartolomé Bermejo's *Pietà*. *(In Pl. Seu, up C. Bisbe from Pl. St. Jaume. M: Jaume I. Cathedral open daily 8am-12:45pm and 5:15-7:30pm. Cloister open 9am-12:30pm and 5:15-7pm. Elevator to the roof open M-Sa 10:30am-6pm; €2. Choir area open M-F 9am-12:30pm and 5:15-7pm, Sa-Su 9am-12:30pm; €1. Special guided tours daily 1-5pm include everything for €4.)*

PLAÇA DE SANT JAUME. Pl. de Sant Jaume has served as Barcelona's political center since Roman times. Two of Cataluña's most significant buildings have dominated the square since 1823: the **Palau de la Generalitat,** headquarters of Cataluña's government, and the **Ajuntament,** or city hall. *(Generalitat open 2nd and 4th Su of the month 10:30am-1:30pm. Closed Aug. Mandatory tours in Catalan, English, and Spanish every 30min. starting at 10:30am. Free. Ajuntament open 2nd and 4th Su 10am-1:30pm. Free.)*

EL CALL (JEWISH QUARTER). For centuries El Call was Barcelona's center of intellectual and financial activity. Now, one of the synagogues has been transformed into a church, the **Església de Sant Jaume,** C. Ferran, 28. The only tangible remaining evidence of Jewish inhabitants is the ancient **Hebrew plaque** on tiny C. Marlet; the rest of the area has been commercialized. *(M: Liceu.)*

PLAÇA REIAL. This is the most crowded, happening *plaça* in the Barri Gòtic; tourists and locals congregate to eat and drink at night, and to buy and sell at the Sunday morning flea market. Near the fountain in the center of the square are two street lamps designed by Antoni Gaudí—if only he could have witnessed the antics of the drunk backpackers that flood the plaza until sunrise. *(M: Liceu or Drassanes.)*

LA RAMBLA

La Rambla, a pedestrian strip roughly 1km long, is a world-famous cornucopia of street performers, fortune-tellers, pet and flower stands, and artists. No shortage of tourists has led to a ton of restaurants and shops that cater to them. Watch your wallet; this is a pickpocketer's paradise. The tree-lined thoroughfare consists of five distinct *ramblas* (promenades). Each boasts its own specialty—one stretch is lined by cages of exotic birds. Together, the Ramblas form one boulevard starting at the Pl. de Catalunya and the **Font de Canaletes**—legend has it that visitors who sample the fountain's water will itch for Barcelona evermore, and someday return. Halfway down La Rambla, **Joan Miró's** pavement mosaic brightens up the already colorful street. Pass the **Mirador de Colom** on the way to Rambla del Mar for a grand view of the Mediterranean.

GRAN TEATRE DEL LICEU. After burning down for the second time in 1994, the Liceu was rebuilt and expanded dramatically; a tour of the building includes not just the original 1847 **Sala de Espejos** (Hall of Mirrors), but also the 1999 **Foyer** (a curvaceous bar/lecture hall/small theater). The five-level, 2292-seat **theater** is considered one of Europe's top stages, adorned with palatial ornamentation, gold facades, and sculptures. *(La Rambla, 51-59, by C. Sant Pau. M: Liceu, L3. ☎934 85 99 13, for tours 85 99 14; www.liceubarcelona.com. Box office open M-F 1:30-8pm and Sa 1hr. before show or by ServiCaixa. Short 20min. non-guided visits daily 11:30am-1pm every 30min, €4. 1hr. tours 10am by reservation only; call 9am-2pm or email visites@liceubarcelona.com; €8.50.)*

LA BOQUERIA (MERCAT DE SANT JOSEP). Just the place to pick up that hard-to-find animal part you've been looking for, plus any other delicacies you've been craving. A traditional Catalan *mercat*—and the largest outdoor market in Spain—located in a giant, all-steel *Modernista* structure, La Boqueria is a sight in itself. Specialized vendors sell produce, fish, meat, cheese, nuts, wine, and sweets from a seemingly infinite number of independent stands inside. A number of excellent cafes have terraces outside and serve dishes incorporating fresh ingredients from the market. *(La Rambla, 89. M: Liceu. Open M-Sa 8am-8pm.)*

CENTRE D'ART DE SANTA MÓNICA. Once a nunnery, this museum now houses rotating and contemporary, edgy exhibitions. Because it rebuilds its space between shows, call and make sure the galleries are open before you visit. *(La Rambla, 7. M: Drassanes. ☎933 16 28 10. Open Tu-Sa 11am-8pm, Su 11am-3pm. Free.)*

MONUMENT A COLOM. Ruis i Taulet's monument to Columbus towers at the port end of La Rambla. Nineteenth-century *Renaixença* enthusiasts convinced themselves that Columbus was Catalan, not Italian. The statue points proudly in a mysterious direction—not to the Americas, but out over the horizon toward Libya—which some take as error, and others as directions to what would have been Columbus's first refueling point. Take the elevator for a view of the city, including the cathedral, Sagrada Família, and the even more futuristic-looking Torre Agbar. *(Portal de la Pau. M: Drassanes. Elevator open May-Oct. 9am-8:30pm; Nov.-Apr. 10am-6:30pm. €2.30, children and over 65 €1.50, large groups €1.90 per person.)*

MUSEU DE L'ERÒTICA. This stimulating museum has an odd assortment of pictures and figurines that spans human history and depicts a variety of sexual acrobatics that seem to defy the limits of human flexibility. The 7 ft. wooden phallus is a tempting photo-op. *(La Rambla, 96. M: Liceu, L1/3. ☎933 18 98 65. Open daily in summer 10am-10pm; in winter 10am-9pm. €8, students €7.)*

PALAU DE LA VIRREINA. Once the residence of a Peruvian viceroy, this 18th-century palace now houses the Institute of Culture, which displays contemporary photography, music, and graphics exhibits. The ground floor is the perma-

GAUDÍ'S L'EIXAMPLE

DISTANCE: 2.5km/1.6 mi.

DURATION: 3-4hr.

WHEN TO GO: Anytime, but if you want to tour the buildings, visit during the day.

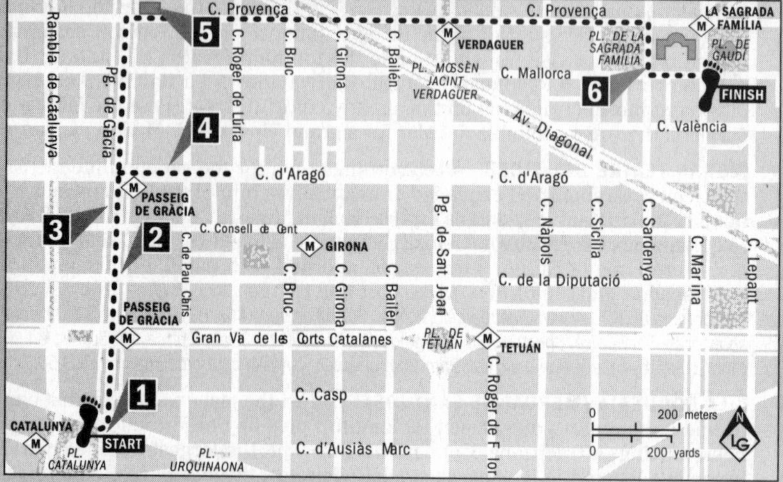

The spacious, right-angled streets of L'Eixample ("expansion" in Catalan) hold a wealth of 19th-century Modernista treasures, full of color and playful curves.

1. PL. CATALUNYA. Start off in Pl. Catalunya, on the lower border of L'Eixample. Make sure to get your **free map** at El Corte Inglés.

2. PG. DE GRÀCIA. Walk along the wide, tree-lined Pg. de Gràcia and resist the temptation to enter (or at least spend money in) the endless array of **designer boutiques.** You may notice that the cramped, old streets of the Barri Gòtic give way to sidewalks that are airy and bright.

3. LA MANZANA DE LA DISCÒRDIA. The block between C. Aragó and C. Consell de Cent is known as *La Manzana de la Discòrdia* ("block of discord"), due to the designs of three prominent structures that vibrantly clash: **Casa Amatller, Casa Lleó,** and Casa Batlló. In Casa Amatller, you can buy a **Ruta del Modernisme** pass.

4. C. ARAGÓ. C. Aragó, to the east of Pg. de Gràcia, has affordable quality restaurants and is a great spot to admire the parade of perfectly dressed *barceloneses*.

5. CASA MILÀ (LA PEDRERA). Three long blocks up Pg. de Gràcia is one of Gaudí's best-known works. This building, designed to mimic the ocean's waves and seaweed, and its **whimsical rooftop** are definitely worth a visit.

6. LA SAGRADA FAMÍLIA. The last stop is well worth the walk. Take a right on C. Provença and follow it for 11 blocks (stay straight and don't turn on Av. Diagonal). You simply cannot miss Gaudí's masterpiece: after 119 years and counting, it is still nowhere near finished.

Metro lines L5 and L2 will transport you back to the city center. Other Gaudí works not in the immediate area include Parc Güell, the Calvet House, the Teresianes Order School, the Bellesguard Tower, the Güell Pavillions, and the Vicenç House.

nent residence of several *gigantes* (giant floats). *(La Rambla, 99. M: Liceu. ☎933 16 10 00. Open daily 10am-8pm. Ground fl. free, exhibits €4 and up.)*

MUSEU DE CERA (WAX MUSEUM). Over 300 wax figures form an endless parade of celebrities, fictional characters, and rather obscure European historical figures. The most recognizable ones have distinctive facial hair, like Fidel Castro and Chewbacca from Star Wars. Picasso's there, too. *(La Rambla, 4-6 or Passage de la Vanca, 7. M: Drassanes. ☎933 17 26 49, www.museocerabcn.com. Open July-Sept. daily 10am-8pm; Oct.-June M-F 10am-1:30pm and 4-7:30pm, Sa-Su and holidays 11am-2pm and 4:30-8:30pm. Last entrance 30min. before closing. €10, ages 5-11 and seniors €6, under 5 free.)*

LA RIBERA

PALAU DE LA MÚSICA CATALANA. This structure is the veritable Graceland of Barcelona. The Orfeó Catalan choir society commissioned *Modernista* master Lluís Domènech i Montaner to design this must-see concert venue, built in the early 20th century. By day, the music hall glows with tall stained-glass windows and an ornate stained-glass skylight, which comes alive again after dark with electric lights. Sculptures of winged horses and busts of the muses come out of the walls flanking the stage. Don't miss the Sala de Luis Millet, with an up-close view of the intricately decorated *"trencadís"* pillars of the breathtaking facade. *(C. Sant Francesc de Paula, 2. ☎932 95 72 00; www.palaumusica.org. M: Jaume I. Mandatory 50min. tours in English hourly Open daily 9am-3:30pm, Aug. and Semana Santa 9am-7pm. €10, students and seniors €9. Check the Guía del Ocio for concert listings. Concert tickets €8-175. Box office open 9am-9pm. MC/V.)*

MUSEU PICASSO. The most visited museum in Barcelona traces Picasso's development as an artist with the world's best collection of work from his early Barcelona period. He donated over 1700 works to the museum himself, and it now boasts 3800 pieces of his collage, painting, sculpture, and engraving. The pieces display the transition from his classical techniques to the stylistic developments that made him an icon. Crucial works include *Portrait of Aunt Pepa*, the most important from his formative period; *First Communion*, his first large exhibited piece; and the 57 canvases of the *Las Meninas* series. Complementing the main attraction are rotating supplemental exhibitions. *(C. Montcada, 15-23. ☎932 56 30 00; www.museupicasso.bcn.cat. M: Jaume I. Open Tu-Su 10am-8pm. Last entrance 30min. before closing. €9, 16-25 and seniors €6, under 16 free. Temporary exhibit €2.90-5.80. 1st Su of the month free.)*

PARC DE LA CIUTADELLA. Host of the 1888 Universal Exposition, the beautiful park contains several museums, well-labeled horticulture, wacky fountains, a pond, and a zoo. Buildings of note include Domènech i Montaner's *Modernista* work *Castell dels Tres Dracs* (Castle of the Three Dragons, now the Museu de Zoología), which houses a large dinosaur exhibit, the geological museum, and Josep Amergós's Hivernacle. The kid-friendly *Parc Zoològic* (zoo) has all kinds of animals and even dolphin shows. *(M: Ciutadella or Marina. Park open daily 8am-9pm. Zoo open daily June-Sept. 10am-8pm; Jan.-Mar. 15 and Oct. 16-Dec. 10am-5:30pm; Mar. 16-May and Oct. 1-25 10am-7pm. Park €15.40, children 3-12 €9.30, over 65 €8.15.)*

MUSEU DE LA XOCOLATA. You won't be able to halt the salivation for a second—this chocolate museum presents gobs of information about the history, production, and ingestion of the sensuous treat. Don't miss the chocolate sculptures, including the Sagrada Família. The cafe offers workshops on chocolate sculpting for children up to 12 years old, and chocolate tasting (€7.70) for the rest of us. *(Pl. Pons i Clerch, C. Comerç 26. ☎932 68 78 78; www.museudelaxocolata.com. M:*

BARCELONA

Jaume I. Open M and W-Sa 10am-7pm, Su 10am-3pm. Workshops for kids from €5.40; reservations required. €4.30, students and seniors €3.70, with Barcelona Card €3, under 7 free.)

ESGLÉSIA DE SANTA MARIA DEL MAR. This 14th-century Gothic church is truly an architectural wonder. The impossibly high ceiling's supporting columns are set a whopping 13m apart—farther than in any other medieval building in the world. *(Pl. Santa María, 1. M: Jaume I. Open M-Sa 9am-1:30pm and 4:30-8:30pm, Su 9:30am-1:45pm and 4:30-8:45pm. Free.)*

EL RAVAL

MUSEU D'ART CONTEMPORANI (MACBA). The MACBA has received worldwide acclaim for its focus on post-avant-garde art and contemporary works. The main attractions are the rotating exhibits and the "Nits de MACBA," which keep the museum open until midnight with concerts and guided tours. *(Pl. dels Àngels, 1. M: Catalunya. ☎934 12 08 10; www.macba.es. Open in summer M-Sa 10am-8pm, Su 10am-3pm; in winter M-Sa 10am-7:30pm, Su 10am-3pm. Th-F open until midnight for Nits de MACBA in summer. Tours in English M 6pm, in Spanish F 6pm. €7.50, students €6, under 14 and over 65 free; single exhibition floor €4/3/free. Nits de MACBA €3.50 after 8pm, guided tour included.)*

BARCELONA

PALAU GÜELL. Gaudí's recently renovated 1889 Palau Güell—the *Modernista* residence built for wealthy patron Eusebi Güell (of Parc Güell fame)—has one of Barcelona's most spectacular interiors. Güell spared no expense on this house, which is considered to be one of the first true representations of Gaudí's revolutionary style. *(C. Nou de La Rambla, 3-5. M: Liceu. ☎933 17 39 74. Partial entrance permitted. Open Tu-Sa 10am-2:30pm. Free.)*

CENTRE DE CULTURA CONTEMPORÀNIA DE BARCELONA (CCCB). The center's striking architecture incorporates an early 20th-century theater with its 1994 addition, a sleek wing of black glass. CCCB now has a cafe, gallery space, screening room, and bookstore, and is also the main daytime venue for the Sonar music festival. Check the *Guía del Ocio* for scheduled events. *(Casa de Caritat. C. Montalegre, 5. M: Catalunya or Universitat. ☎933 06 41 00; www.cccb.org. Open Tu-Su 11am-8pm, Th until 10pm. €4.70, students €3.60, under 16 free. First W of the month free.)*

L'EIXAMPLE

When Cerdà drew up his designs for the expansion of Barcelona, he envisioned city blocks where people of all social classes could live side by side. While Cerdà's utopian ideals lost out to bourgeoisie gentrification, l'Eixample remains Barcelona's most innovative and classy neighborhood. Among the seemingly endless square blocks and wide-open plazas that were the bedrock of this planned community, *Modernista* oddities sit side-by-side with recent additions like **Torre Agbar,** Jean Nouvel's spaceship-like blue- and red-lit glass tower that's visible from just about everywhere.

LA SAGRADA FAMÍLIA. Antoni Gaudí's masterpiece is far from finished, which makes La Sagrada Família the world's most visited construction site. Only the shortest eight of the 18 planned towers have been completed, and the church still doesn't have an "interior," yet millions of tourists make the pilgrimage to witness this work-in-progress. Of the three facades, only the Nativity Facade was finished under Gaudí. A new team of architects, led by Jordi Bonet, hopes to lay the last stone by 2026 (the 100th anniversary of Gaudí's death), and the affiliated museum displays plans and computer models of the fully realized structure. *(C. Mallorca, 401. ☎932 07 30 31; www.sagradafamilia.org. M: Sagrada Família. Open daily Apr.-Sept. 9am-8pm, elevator open 9am-7:45pm; Oct.-Mar. 9am-5:45pm. Guided tours 11am and 1pm in English, noon in Spanish. In summer, also at 3pm and 5pm in English, 4pm in*

Spanish. Tours €4. Entrance €10; over 65, with ISIC , or in a group of 20 or more €8. Under 10 free. Elevator €2. Combined ticket with Casa-Museu Gaudí €12, student and senior €10.)

LA MANZANA DE LA DISCORDIA. A short walk from Pl. de Catalunya, the odd-numbered side of Pg. de Gràcia between C. Aragó and C. Consell de Cent has been leaving passersby scratching their heads for a century. The Spanish nickname, which translates to the "block of discord," comes from the stylistic clash of its three most extravagant buildings. **Casa Lleó i Morera,** 35, by Domènech i Montaner, lies on the far left corner of the block. Sprouting flowers, stained glass, and legendary doorway sculptures adorn the interior (admire from the outside, as entrance is not permited). Two buildings down is Puig i Cadafalch's **Casa Amatller,** 41, perhaps the most beautiful building on the block, with its geometric, Moorish-influenced pattern on the facade, is currently under construction. *(Guided tour with chocolate tasting, M-F 4 per day 11am-6pm, Su at noon; €8.)* The real discord comes next door at Gaudí's **Casa Batlló,** 43, where greenish sparkle and an off-center cross are trumped only by rippling balconies. The most popular interpretation of Casa Batlló is that it represents Cataluña's patron Sant Jordi (St. George) slaying a dragon; the chimney plays the lance, the scaly roof is the dragon's back, and the bony balconies are the remains of his victims. *(☎932 16 03 06; www.casabatllo.cat. Open daily 9am-8pm. €16.50, students €13.20. Call for group discounts for more than 20 people. Free multilingual audio tour.)*

BARCELONA

FUNDACIÓ ANTONI TÀPIES. Less than 30 years old, this contemporary museum has a whole floor devoted to Tàpies, Barcelona's most famous late 20th-century sculptor and painter. The real attractions are the rotating exhibitions on the two lower floors—some of the best modern photography and video art in the city, as well as film screenings and lectures. In summer, check out DJ nights on the terrace, with free drinks and after-hours gallery access. *(C. Aragó, 255. ☎934 87 03 15. M: Pg. de Gràcia. Closed for renovation as of summer 2008. Call for more information.)*

CASA MILÀ (LA PEDRERA). From the outside, this Gaudí creation looks like the sea—the undulating walls are the waves and the iron balconies are seaweed. Chimneys resembling armored soldiers sprout from the roof, blessed with views of every corner of Barcelona. The entrance fee entitles visitors to tour one well-equipped apartment, the roof, and the winding brick attic, now functioning as the **Espai Gaudí,** a multimedia presentation of Gaudí's life and works. The summer concert series—*La Nit de Pedrera*—transforms the roof into a jazz cabaret on weekend nights. *(Pg. de Gràcia, 92. ☎902 40 09 73. Open daily Mar.-Oct. 9am-8pm, last admission 7:30pm; Nov.-Feb. 9am-6:30pm. €9.50, students and seniors €5.50. Free audio tour. Concerts last weekend of June-July F-Sa 9pm-midnight. €12, glass of cava included. Tickets only through Tel Entrada.)*

HOSPITAL DE LA SANTA CREU I SANT PAU. This is not your ordinary hospital. Designated an UNESCO monument in 1997, this is Europe's second-oldest functioning hospital and Domènech i Montaner's lifetime *Modernista* masterpiece. The entire complex, with its whimsical pavilions, covers nine l'Eixample blocks. *(Sant Antoni M. Claret, 167. ☎932 91 90 00; www.santpau.es. M: Hospital de St. Pau, L5. Hospital open 24hr. Free. Guided tours daily, English 10:15am and 12:15pm, Spanish at 1:15pm, €5, under 18 €2.50. Info open daily 10am-2pm.)*

MONTJUÏC

FUNDACIÓ MIRÓ. An extensive collection of sculptures, drawings, and paintings from Miró's career, ranging from sketches to wall-sized canvases, immerses visitors in the work of this Barcelona-born artist. His best-known pieces here include *El Carnival de Arlequín*, *La Masia*, and *L'or de l'Azuz*, and special treats like Calder's Mercury Fountain. The downstairs gallery displays experimental work by young artists and a few famous contributors. The Fundació also sponsors music and film festivals. *(Take the funicular from M: Paral·lel or catch the Park Montjuïc bus from Pl. Espanya. ☎934 43 94 70; www.bcn.fjmiro.es. Open July-Sept. Tu-W and F-Sa 10am-8pm, Th 10am-9:30pm, Su and holidays 10am-2:30 pm; Oct.-June Tu-W and F-Sa 10am-7pm, Th 10am-9:30pm, Su and holidays 10am-2:30pm. Doors close 15min. before closing time. Library open Tu-F 10am-2pm and 3-6pm, M and Sa 10am-2pm. €7.50, students and seniors €5, under 15 free. Temporary exhibitions €4/3/free. Concert tickets €10.)*

MUSEU NACIONAL D'ART DE CATALUNYA (PALAU NACIONAL). Designed by Enric Catà and Pedro Cendoya for the 1929 International Exposition, the magnificent Palau Nacional has housed the Museu Nacional d'Art de Catalunya (MNAC) since 1934. Its main hall is a public event space, while the wings are home to the world's finest collection of Catalan Romanesque art and a wide variety of Gothic pieces. Highlights include works by Joaqim Mir, a second-generation *Modernista* known for color-saturated landscapes, Miró's giant "Gorg Bleu" stained glass, and the gallery of Romanesque cathedral apses. The museum also recently acquired the entire holdings of the Museu d'Art Modern, formerly located in the Parc de la Ciutadella—MNAC is now the principal art museum of Cataluña. In front, the **Fonts Luminoses** (Illuminated Fountains) and the central **Font Màgica** (Magical Fountain) come alive during weekend laser shows. *(From M: Espanya, walk up Av. Reina María Cristina, away from the twin brick towers, and take the escalators to the top. ☎936 22 03 76; www.mnac.es. Open Tu-Sa 10am-7pm, Su and holidays 10am-2:30pm. Temporary exhibits €3-5; both temporary exhibits €6; all exhibits €8.50. 30% discount for students and seniors. Under 14 free. First Su of the month free. Combo ticket with Poble Espanyol €12. Audio tour included.)*

BARCELONA

CASTELL DE MONTJUÏC. This historic fortress and its **Museu Militar** sit high on the hill, and from the external **mirador,** guests can enjoy a multitude of panoramic jaw-droppers and photo-ops. The *telefèric*—an airborne cable-car—to and from the castle is usually half the fun. Even if military history isn't your thing, the view from the roof of the castle makes it well worth entering. *(From M: Paral·lel, take the funicular to Parc de Montjuïc and then the cable car to the castle. ☎933 29 86 13. Telefèric de Montjuïc open in high season M-Sa 10am-9pm; in low season 10am-6pm. €5.70, round-trip €7.90; children €4.50/6. Parc de Montjuïc bus runs up the mountain, leaving from in front of the telefèric, or you can walk up the steep slope on C. Foc from the same spot. Castle open Mar.-Oct. Tu-Su 9:30am-8pm; Nov. Tu-F 9:30am-6:30pm, Sa-Su 9:30am-8pm; Dec.-Mar. Tu-F 9:30am-5pm, Sa-Su 9:30am-7pm. Museum open Tu-Sa Mar.-Nov. 9:30am-8pm; Dec.-Feb. 9:30am-5pm. €3 for museum, fortress, Plaza de Armas, and mirador. Free without the museum.)*

POBLE ESPANYOL. Lower Montjuïc is where you'll find Poble Espanyol, a recreation of famous buildings and sights from all regions of Spain. The courtyards sometimes host performances, and the entire complex is filled with interesting craft shops. *(Av. Marquès de Comillas, 13. M: Espanya or bus #13 or 50. ☎935 08 63 00. Open M 9am-8pm, Tu-Th 9am-2am, F-Sa 9am-4am, Su 9am-midnight. Ticket booth closes 1hr. before park. €8, students and seniors €6, 4-12 €5, after 8pm €4. Prices may vary when there are concerts. Audio tours available 9am-8pm. €3.)*

THE WATERFRONT

MUSEU D'HISTÒRIA DE CATALUNYA. The last gasp of the old city before entering the tourist trap of Barceloneta, the Museu provides a patriotic introduction to Catalan history, politics, and culture. There is a particularly good section devoted to Franco. Recreations of a 1930s Spanish bar, an 8th-century Islamic prayer tent, and other dioramas make the museum a full sensory experience. *(Pl. Pau Vila, 3. Near entrance to the Moll d'Espanya; left walk out toward Barceloneta.*

☎932 25 47 00; mhc.cultura@gencat.net. Open Tu and Th-Sa 10am-7pm, W 10am-8pm, Su 10am-2:30pm. €7; university students, under 7, and over 65 free. Free 1st Su of the month.)

TORRE SAN SEBASTIÀ. An easy way to see the city from (high) above is from these cable cars, which connect beachy Barceloneta with mountainous Montjuïc. *(From Port Vell, walk down Joan de Borbó and see the beaches to the left, stay right and look for the high tower. ☎934 41 50 71; Pg. Joan de Borbó. M: Barceloneta. Open daily 11am-8pm. To Montjuïc one-way €9, round-trip €12.50; just the elevator to the top €4.)*

L'AQUÀRIUM DE BARCELONA. Barely a decade old, this aquarium features sharks, exhibits on marine creatures, and a cafeteria. Kids are definitely welcome. *(Moll d'Espanya. M: Drassanes or Barceloneta. Advance tickets ☎932 21 74 74; www.aquariumbcn.com. Open daily July-Aug. 9:30am-11pm; June and Sept. 9:30am-9:30pm; Oct.-May M-F 9:30am-9pm, Sa-Su 9am-9:30pm. €16.50, students with ISIC €14.50, 4-12 €11.50, over 60 €13. Mini-guide available in English. AmEx/MC/V.)*

VILA OLÍMPICA. The Vila Olímpica, beyond the east side of the zoo, was built to house 15,000 athletes and entertain millions of tourists for the 1992 Summer Olympics. It is home to several public parks, a shopping center, and offices. In Barceloneta, beaches stretch out from the old port. *(Walk along the water on Ronda Litoral toward the 2 towers. M: Ciutadella or Vila Olímpica.)*

MUSEU MARÍTIM. The **Drassanes Reiales de Barcelona** (Royal Shipyards of Barcelona) consists of a series of huge indoor bays in which entire ships could be constructed and stored over the winter. The Maritime Museum traces (a bit dryly) the evolution of shipbuilding and life on the high seas. Make sure you look in the portside window of the submarine in the courtyard. *(Av. Drassanes, s/n, off the rotary around the Monument a Colom. M: Drassanes. ☎933 42 99 20; www.museumaritimbarcelona.org. Open daily 10am-8pm. Free audio tour and entrance to a small museum. €6.50; 11-16, students, and seniors €3.25; under 7 free. Museum and 1hr. ride on TriMar beyond the harbor €13.60/9.50/free. Temporary exhibitions €6, with museum €9.75.)*

PARC DIAGONAL MAR. Enric Miralles's innovative design weaves a sprawling gray sculpture around high-rise apartment buildings and labyrinthine gardens; the park is perfect for relaxing and escaping the masses. *(At the end of Av. Diagonal, where it meets the sea. Walk 1 block toward the water. M: Selva de Mar.)*

ZONA ALTA: GRÀCIA AND OUTER BARRIS

PARC GÜELL. This fantastical park was designed entirely by Gaudí, but—in typical Gaudí fashion—not completed until after his death. Gaudí intended Parc Güell to be a garden city, with dwarfish buildings and sparkling ceramic-mosaic stairways designed for the city's elite. However, only one house, now known as the **Casa-Museu Gaudí,** was built. Two staircases lead to a towering *Modernista* pavilion originally designed as an open-air market but now occasionally used as a stage by street musicians. The longest park bench in the world, a multicolored serpentine wonder made of tile shards, decorates the top of the pavilion. *(Bus #24 from Pl. Catalunya stops at the upper entrance. Open daily 10am-dusk. Park free. Museum open daily Apr.-Sept. 10am-8pm; Oct.-Mar. 10am-6pm. €5; with ISIC, seniors, or under 18 €4; under 10 free.)*

MUSEU DEL FÚTBOL CLUB BARCELONA. A close second to the Picasso Museum as Barcelona's most visited museum, the FCB merits all the attention it gets from soccer fanatics. Sports fans will appreciate the storied history of the team. The high point is the chance to enter the stadium and take in the enormity of 100,000-seat Camp Nou. *(Next to the stadium. M: Collblanc. Enter through* *access gate 7 or 9. ☎934 96 36 08. Open M-Sa 10am-6:15pm, Su and holidays 10am-2pm. €8.50, students and 13 or under €6.80. Museum and Camp Nou tour €13/10.40. Free parking.)*

ENTERTAINMENT

MUSIC, THEATER, AND DANCE

Barcelona offers many options for theater aficionados, though most performances are in Catalan (*Guía del Ocio* lists the language of the performance). Reserve tickets through **TelEntrada** (24hr. ☎902 10 12 12; www.telentrada.com), **ServiCaixa** at any branch of the Caixa Catalunya bank (24hr. ☎902 33 22 11, for groups 88 80 90; www.servicaixa.com; open M-F 8am-2:30pm), or www.ticktackticket.com—the Spanish Ticketmaster. The **Grec** summer festival turns Barcelona into an international theater, music, and dance extravaganza. For information about the festival, ask at the tourist office, check out www.barcelonafestival.com, or, during the festival, stop by the booth at the bottom of Pl. de Catalunya, on Portal de Angel. The **Sónar** music festival comes to town in mid-June, attracting renowned DJs and electronica enthusiasts from all over the world for three days of concerts and partying. Besides Sónar, major music festivals include **Summercase** (indie and pop) and **Jazzaldia.** Check www.mondosonoro.com or pick up the *Mondo Sonoro* festival guide at hostels and bars. For information on cultural activities in the city, swing by the **Institut de Cultura de Barcelona** (ICUB), Palau de la Virreina, La Rambla, 99. (☎933 16 10 00; www.bcn.es/cultura. Info office open M-Sa 10am-8pm, Su 11am-3pm. Ticket sales Tu-F 11am-1:30pm and 4-8pm, Sa 11am-8pm, Su 11am-2:30pm. Most performances around €18-30.) Check www.barcelonaturisme.com for occasional 10% discounts. **Palau de la Música Catalana,** C. Sant Francese de Paula, 2 (☎932 95 72 00; www.palaumusica.org; M: Urquinaona), to the right off Via Laietana near the level of Pl. Urquinaona, also sells concert tickets. (Concert tickets €8-175. Box office open M-Sa 9am-9pm, Su from 1hr. prior to the concert. No concerts in Aug.; check the *Guía del Ocio* for listings. MC/V.)

HIGH CULTURE, LOW BUDGET. The Gran Teatre del Liceu sells nosebleed seats at low prices. Beware of the cheapest tickets (€7-9) unless you want to sit behind an obstruction. Students with ID can arrive at the theater 2hr. before showtime (1hr. on weekends) and pick up remainder seats at a 30% discount. This is best attempted on weekdays, when seats more frequently go unsold. On weekends, arrive exactly 1hr. before curtain.

Centre Artesà Tradicionàrius, Tr. de Sant Antoni, 6-8 (☎932 18 44 85; www.tradicionarius.com), in Gràcia. M: Fontana. Catalana folk music concerts Sept.-June. Tickets €6-12, frequent free concerts. Also dance, music workshops, and summer festivals; ask for details. Open Sept.-July. M-F 11am-2pm and 5-9pm. Cash only.

Gran Teatre del Liceu, La Rambla, 51-59 (☎934 85 99 13; www.liceubarcelona.com). M: Liceu. Founded in 1847, destroyed by fire in 1994, and recently reopened, Liceu has regained its status as the city's premier venue for opera and popular music. Reserve tickets in advance. Box office open M-F 2-8:30pm, Sa and holidays 1hr. before showtime. 24hr. ticket sales at ServiCaixa. AmEx/MC/V.

L'Auditori, C. Lepanto, 150 (☎932 47 93 00; www.auditori.com), in L'Eixample between M: Marina and Glòries. Home to the city orchestra (the BOC) and host to visiting chamber, choral, and jazz groups. Concerts from late Sept. to mid-July. Tickets €6-50; special performances up to €120. Available by phone, through ServiCaixa or TelEntrada, or at ticket windows (open M-Sa noon-9pm, Su 1hr. before show starts). MC/V.

For cheaper rock, pop, and jazz, there are three major venues that invite foreign and local artists. **Apolo,** Nou de la Rambla, 113 (☎934 42 40 02), in Poble Sec, hosts major indie shows. **Jamboree,** Plaça Reial, 17 (☎933 19 17 89, www.masimas.com), has a jazz series that's been active since the 60s and still brings relevant musicians. **Sidecar,** Plaça Reial, 7 (www.sidecarfactoryclub.com) hosts American and European rock and roll. Tickets for Apolo and Jamboree through TelEntrada (www.telentrada.com). Sidecar tickets generally cost €5-8 at the door on the night of the performance.

BEYOND THE GUÍA DEL OCIO. For the lowdown on both mainstream and underground shows in Barcelona, check out the following helpful sites: **www.infoconcerts.cat/ca** for concert listings from ASACC, an umbrella organization for Catalan venues; **http://www.maumaunderground.com** for local music news, reviews, and a daily agenda of shows and other happenings; and **www.lecool.com** to register to receive weekly arts updates.

FILM

Most screens show the latest Hollywood features, some in English. The Cine section in the *Guía del Ocio* denotes subtitled films with **V.O.** (original version) *subtitulada*; other foreign films are dubbed *(doblado)*, usually in Spanish. Many theaters have a discount day (usually Monday or Wednesday). **Filmoteca** (Cine Aquitania), Av. Sarrià, 31-33, screens classic, cult, and other films in V.O. with subtitles in Spanish or Catalan. (M: Hospital Clínic. ☎934 10 75 90. €2.70, students and seniors €2.) **Méliès Cinemas,** C. de Villarroel, 102 (www.cinesmelies.net), shows classics. (M: Urgell. ☎934 51 00 51. M €3, Tu-Su €4.50.) **Icària-Yelmo,** C. Salvador Espriu, 61, in the Olympic Village, boasts 15 screens and V.O. (☎932 21 75 85; www.yelmocineplex.es. M matinees €5, Tu-Su €6.50.) **Casablanca-Kaplan** shows foreign films in V.O., and **Casablanca-Gracias** shows contemporary independent cinema. (☎934 59 03 26. €4.50-6.) The massive **Cinesa Maremàgnum,** Port Vell, in Moll d'Espanya next to the Aquàrium, has eight screens. (M: Drassanes. Tickets by phone ☎902 33 32 31 or ServiCaixa. €7, W €5.50.) Next door, the new **IMAX Port Vell** has an IMAX screen, an Omnimax 30m in diameter, and 3D projection. Get tickets at the door, through ServiCaixa, or by phone. (☎932 25 11 11. Showtimes 10:30am-12:30am. €12, matinees €8.) **Arenas Cine-Gay,** C. Disputació, 5, off of C. Tarragona just below Princep Jorgi, shows contemporary gay-themed films. (M: Espanya. ☎934 23 11 69. €7.)

A MOVIE UNDER THE STARS. Head up the hill to Sala Montjuïc, an annual 5-week film series in the moat of Castell de Montjuïc. Bring a picnic, settle down on the lawn, and listen to live music before the show. Summer (end of June to early Aug) M, W, F at 8:30pm; buy tickets at the castle the day of (€4, deckchair rental €3) or online at www.servicaixa.com.

FÚTBOL

For the record, the lunatics covered from head to toe in red and blue stripes didn't just escape from an asylum—they are **F.C. Barcelona (Barça)** fans. Grab some face paint and join them in the 120,000-seat **Camp Nou,** Europe's largest *fútbol* arena. On game days, the stadium is packed with thousands of passionate fans cheering one of the world's most popular teams. The box office is on

C. Arístedes Maillol, 12-18 (☎902 18 99 00; www.fcbarcelona.com). Get tickets (€30-60) early; Barça is a true Catalan institution. Its motto, *El Barça és més que un club*, "Barça is more than a club," says it all. **R.C. Deportivo Espanyol,** a.k.a. *los periquitos* (parakeets), Barcelona's second professional soccer team, spreads its wings in blue-and-white stripes at **Estadi Olímpic,** Pg. Olímpic, 17-19 (☎932 927 700; www.rcdespanyol.es). This team isn't as renowned as Barça, but the games are fun and cheaper (€20-45). Get tickets from Banca Catalana or call ServiCaixa (☎902 33 22 11; www.servicaixa.com).

BEACHES

The entire strip between Vila Olímpica and Barceloneta is a long, public beach accessible from M: Ciutadella or Barceloneta. The closest and most popular is **Platja Barceloneta,** off Pg. Marítim. Don't be surprised by nudity on **Platja San Sebastià;** however, the only official nude beach is **Platja de la Nova Mar Bella.** Barcelona's beaches are crowded at almost any time of day. Less crowded beaches can be found past the Mapfre tower to the east, or take the commuter rail along the coast and get off when you see one you like.

RECREATIONAL SPORTS

The tourist offices or the online directory (www.barcelonaturisme.com) can provide info about swimming, cycling, tennis, squash, sailing, hiking, scuba diving, whitewater rafting, kayaking, and most other sports.

DiR Fitness Club, 12 branches throughout Barcelona, including one at C. Gran de Gràcia, 37 (branch ☎934 15 55 50; central ☎902 10 19 79; www.dir.es). A popular Barcelona gym chain with every amenity imaginable, from steam bath, solarium, and personalized fitness programs to fingerprint-scan entrance; 13 locations. Prices depend on time of day, age, and number of days per week, but generally €4.25 per day (plus €2 membership card, purchased once); monthly passes range €40-200 depending on location and services. Open M-F 7am-10:15pm, Sa-Su and holidays 9am-7:15pm. MC/V.

Piscines Bernat Picornell, Av. Estadi, 30-40 (☎934 23 40 41; www.picornell.com), to the right when facing the stadium. Test your backstroke in the Olympic pools with stadium seating overlooking the city. €4.80 for outdoor pool (long-term passes available); €9.20 for workout facilities including sauna, massage parlor, and gym. Sa 9pm-11pm and winter M 4:15pm-6pm are nude days. Outdoor pool open June-Sept. M-Sa 9am-9pm, Su 9am-8pm; Sept.-May daily 7:30am-4pm. Workout facilities open M-F 8:45am-11:30pm, Sa 7am-8:45pm, Su 7:30am-3pm. MC/V.

SHOPPING

A shopaholic's paradise, cosmopolitan Barcelona is littered with trendy stores for all audiences and price ranges. Those on the prowl for typical European women's clothing—and if you're lucky, big discounts—should check out C. Portaferrissa, C. Pelai in front of Pl. Catalunya, and Av. Portal de l'Àngel. A stroll down C. d'Avinyó and its smaller side streets will prove beneficial for anyone into underground fashion, as will a trip to La Ribera's hip boutiques. Less expensive jewelry, accessories, and other knick-knacks can be found on C. Boqueria. For more legitimate jewelry, meander into one of the treasure chests on C. Call. The fashionista mecca is still **Passeig de Gràcia** in l'Eixample. One place for bargains is **Carrer Girona,** between C. Casp and Gran Via, in l'Eixample, home to a small string of discount shops offering clothing, shoes, bags, and accessories. (M: Tetuán. Walk 2 blocks down Gran Via and take a left on C. Girona.) **Carrer Bruc,** one street over, offers more retail delights for bargain hunters. Be aware that stores marked "Venta al Mejor" are wholesalers who don't take kindly to browsing. Another area to try for discounts is the **Mercat Alternatiu (Alternative Market)** on C. Riera Baixa in El Raval. (M: Liceu. Take C. de l'Hospital—a right off La Rambla facing the ocean—and follow it to C. Riera Baixa, the 7th right, shortly after the stone hospital.) This short street is crammed with second-hand and thrift stores. For a department store, **El Corte Inglés** by Pl. Catalunya holds anything and everything between its massive walls (including a supermarket in the basement).

BOOKS

Come in Librería Anglesa, C. Balmes, 129 (☎934 53 12 04; www.libreriainglesa.com). English books and a selection of classic novels. Bulletin boards feature ads for travel partners or language instructors. Open M-Sa 9:45am-2pm and 4:30-8:15pm. MC/V.

Documenta, C. Cardenal Casañas, 4 (☎933 17 25 27; www.documenta-bcn.com), just steps off La Rambla, located in the old Cu-Cut! publishing house, forcibly shut down by the army in the 1930s. Decent selection of English novels and travel guides. Open M-Sa 9:30am-8:30pm, Su and holidays 11am-2:30pm and 5-8:30pm. AmEx/MC/V.

FNAC, (www.fnac.es) has 3 locations: Triangle mall in Pl. Catalunya, M: Catalunya (☎933 44 18 00; open M-Sa 10am-10pm); Av. Diagonal, 3-35, M: Besòs Mar (☎935 02 99 00; open M-Sa 10am-10pm); L'Illa Centre Comercial, Av. Diagonal, 557, M: María Cristina (☎934 44 59 00; open M-Sa 10am-9:30pm). AmEx/MC/V.

La Central del Raval, C. Elisabets, 6 (☎902 884 990; www.lacentral.com), off La Rambla in El Raval. M: Catalunya. Literature and nonfiction in 7 languages in a spacious bookstore and cafe, born in 1693 as the Gothic-style Església de la Misericòrdia. Pocket Catalan/English and Catalan/Spanish dictionaries (€12). Open M-F 10am-9:30pm, Sa 10am-9pm. AmEx/MC/V.

Hibernian Secondhand English Bookshop, C. Montseny, 7 (☎932 17 47 96; www.hibernian-books.com). M: Fontana. Small shop in Gràcia selling used English books. Open M 4-8:30pm, Tu-Sa 10am-8:30pm.

NIGHTLIFE

Barcelona truly lives by night (and all the way until early morning). Its wild and varied nightlife treads the precarious line between slick and kitschy. In many ways, the city is a tourist's clubbing heaven: things don't get going until late (don't bother showing up at a club before 1am) and keep going for as long as you can handle it—frequently 6am. Yet for every full-blown dance club, there are a hundred more relaxed bars, from Irish pubs to gay clubs to absinthe dens. Check the *Guía del Ocio*, available at newsstands, for even more up-to-date listings of nighttime fun, as the hot spots change often. *Barcelona Week*, the English arts weekly, also has listings.

BARRI GÒTIC AND LA RAMBLA

Countless *cervecería*s and bar-restaurants can be found on main streets like C. Ferran. C. Escudellers is a lively post-bar location, and Pl. Reial remains busy until early morning. La Rambla becomes questionable late at night, as prostitutes and the homeless emerge where families roam in daylight.

Jamboree, Pl. Reial, 17 (☎933 19 17 89; www.masimas.com). M: Liceu. A disorienting maze of stone arches and swirling lights thumps with hip-hop; 2nd floor plays 80s and 90s music. Drinks €8-9. Jazz 9-11pm €10. Cover €10; look for flyers with discounts.

Difficult to get in on nights with lists. Open daily 9pm-1am; nightclub open 12:30-5am. Upstairs, Tarantos hosts flamenco shows (€6). Open daily 8-11pm.

Schilling, C. Ferran, 23 (☎933 17 67 87). M: Liceu, L3. One of the more laid-back and spacious wine bars in the area, with dim lighting, velvet seat cushions, and bottles climbing the walls. Often attracts British and gay crowds. Excellent sangria (pitcher €17). Wine €2-3, bottle €11-13. Serves breakfast and sandwiches (€2-6) during the day. Open M-W 10am-2:30am, Th-Sa 10am-3am, Su noon-2am.

Karma, Pl. Reial, 10 (☎933 02 56 80; www.karmadisco.com). M: Liceu. Quite a change from the dive upstairs and the airy terrace outside, this multicolored tunnel of a club and bar with fountain view keeps a Pl. Reial crowd dancing and drinking. Beer (€4.50) and mixed drinks (€6) are less expensive than at other clubs. Club cover €10. Bar open Tu-Su 6pm-2:30am; club open Tu-Su midnight-5am.

El Bosq de les Fades, Pg. de la Banca, 16 (☎933 17 26 49), near the Wax Museum. M: Drassanes. This spooky bar/cafe used to be the horror section of the Wax Museum; it's now a great pre-club hangout, if the groves don't scare you away with their grotesque faces and gnarled branches. Beer €2.80. Champagne €3, Tequila Sunrise €7.20. Open M-Th 10am-1am, F 10am-1:30am, Sa 11am-1:30am, Su 11am-1am. MC/V.

LA RIBERA

Besides its wealth of intriguing dinner options, La Ribera has a nightlife scene that is both more local and more varied than the scene on La Rambla. When the gas lantern goes on in front of Eglesia de Santa Maria every night, people begin the migrations from small backstreet bars to second-floor sheesha lounges.

El Copetín, Pg. del Born, 19 (☎607 20 21 76). M: Jaume I. Cuban rhythm invades this casual, dimly-lit nightspot full of young and old alike. Copetín fills up before some places open, making it a good place to start the night. Awe-inspiring mojitos ("cócktail de la casa") €7. Open M-Th and Su 7pm-2:30am, F-Sa 7pm-3am. Cash only.

Palau Dalmases, C. Montcada, 20 (☎933 10 06 73). M: Jaume I. A 17th-century palace filled with lavish paintings and ornate statues. Its large wooden doors, watched over by a guard, make it all the more exclusive. It's whispered that *"quisiera cenar"* (I'd like to have dinner) is the password sometimes required to get in. Mixed drinks €12. Live opera Th 11pm; €20, includes 1 drink. Open Tu-Sa 8pm-2am, Su 6-10pm. MC/V.

Ribborn, Antic de Sant Joan, 3 (☎933 10 71 48; www.ribborn.com). M: Barceloneta. Get drenched in deep crimson light and snap along to the ecclectic music selection—from jazz to funk to soul. Beer €2.50. Mixed drinks €7. Open Tu-Su 10pm-3am.

EL RAVAL

El Raval's specialty is a hip, creatively decorated, colorful bar with a young, laid-back crowd, true to the artsy nature of the area—but establishments of every flavor dot these narrow streets. Be sure to check out C. Joaquim Costa, which packs in numerous distinctive and happening locales in just a few short blocks, near the Museum of Contemporary Art. Keep in mind that the depths of El Raval see less tourism, and wandering there late at night is not advised.

Marsella Bar, C. de Sant Pau, 65. M: Liceu. Don't be deterred by the tarnished mirrors and blackened bottles of Barcelona's oldest bar (built in 1820)—they add to its charm. Religious figurines grace the walls of the bar, famous among locals for its *ansenta* (absinthe; €5). Beer €3.20. Mixed drinks €5-6. Open M-Sa 10pm-2am. Cash only.

Betty Ford, Joaquin Costa, 56 (☎933 04 13 68). This hip, new local favorite is the place to be and be seen—amid chic and simple decor and raucous conversation. Happy hour

8-10pm offers fancy mixed drinks for €3.50; try a Manhattan or sugar-sweet mojito. Beer €2.50-4. Open daily 2pm-2:30am.

Casa Almirall, C. Joaquín Costa, 33 (☎933 18 99 17, casalmirall@telefonica.net). M: Universitat. Cavernous space with weathered couches, cool, dim lights, and equally laid-back clientele. It's house policy to stop you after your third absinthe (€5-7), but the staff is fond of saying that you won't make it there anyway. Beer €2-4. Mixed drinks €76. Free Wi-Fi. Open M-Th 5pm-2:30am, F-Sa 7pm-3am, Su 7pm-2am. Cash only.

68, C. de Sant Pau, 68 (☎934 41 31 15). M: Liceu. Floral wallpaper contrasts with painted black silhouettes and hanging bottle lights, perfectly mixing smooth and gritty. Drinks €2-6. Open M-Th and Su 8pm-2:30am, F-Sa 8pm-3am. MC/V.

Moog, C. Arc del Teatre, 3 (☎933 01 72 82; www.masimas.com/moog). M: Liceu or Drassanes. Industrial metal walls and swirling green lights betray this as the techno headquarters of Barcelona, though the upstairs dance floor blasts music from the 80s and 90s. Look for discount flyers on the street. Cover €10. Open daily midnight-5am, weekends until 6am. W especially popular. MC/V at bar.

L'EIXAMPLE

L'Eixample has upscale bars and some of the best—though not exclusively—gay nightlife in Europe, as evident in the area's nickname, "Gaixample." Some clubs can be difficult to get to, and get back from; you may want to check ahead of time which NitBus route will take you home.

Mojito Club, C. Rosselló, 217 (☎932 37 65 28; www.mojitobcn.com). M: Diagonal. This club lures a fun-loving crowd with Latin beats. Brazilian party W with free samba lessons at 11:30pm and R&B all night. Salsa lessons Th 11:30pm and Su 9pm, free with one drink minimum; also F-Sa 11pm-1am, €10 cover including drink; full courses and intensives available, call for information. Open Tu-Sun 11pm-4:30am. MC/V.

Z:eltas, C. Casanova, 75 (☎934 50 84 69 , www.zeltas.net) Complete with shimmering cloth hangings, feathered boas, and low white couches, this exotic bar welcomes classy clientele–usually gay–to sip a drink and enjoy the ambience. Wine €3. Beer €4.50. Mixed drinks €7. Open daily 10:30pm-3am. MC/V.

La Fira, C. Provença, 171 (☎650 85 53 84). M: Hospital Clínic or FGC: Provença. A hip crowd surrounded by carousel swings, carnival mirrors, and a fortune teller–not to mention eerie clowns painted on the walls. Variety of shows and parties, often with entrance fee. Open M-Th 7pm-2:30am, F-Sa 7pm-3am. MC/V.

Les Gents que J'aime, C. València, 286, downstairs (☎932 15 68 79). M: Pg. de Gràcia. Background soul, funk, and jazz soothe patrons enjoying drinks like Les Gents (kiwi, lime, and pineapple juice; €7) and lounging in red velvet armchairs. Beer €4. Bottles of wine €12.50. Open M-Th and Su 7pm-2:30am, F-Sa 7pm-3am. AmEx/MC/V.

Dietrich, C. Consell de Cent, 255 (☎934 51 77 07; www.dietrichcafe.com). M: Pg. de Gràcia. An unflattering caricature of a semi-nude Marlene Dietrich greets patrons at this inclusive gay bar. Beer €3.50. Mixed drinks €6. Trapeze shows 1:30am, drag shows some weekends. Open M-Th and Su 10:30pm-2:30am, F-Sa 10:30pm-3am. MC/V.

MONTJUÏC

Lower Montjuïc is home to **Poble Espanyol** ("Spanish Village"), a reacreation of famous buildings and sights from all regions of Spain. A number of clubs open once night falls. When La Terrazza closes, buses take the most serious party animals to *"los afters"*—clubs open 6am-7pm. Merci and Souvenir are the most popular, but ask around when La Terrazza lets out. The *barrio* Poble Sec also offers some off-the beaten-path late-night hangouts.

Tinta Roja, C. Creus dels Molers, 17 (☎934 43 32 43; www.tintaroja.net). Located just off Av. Paral·lel in a newly pedestrian section of Poble Sec. The best combination bar and dance floor in the city. Tango classes W 9-10:30pm, basic couse 2 months (call for prices). Specialties include tropical mixed drinks and Argentine *yerba-mate.* Open Th 8:30pm-2am, F-Sa 8:30pm-3am. Cash only.

La Terrazza, Avda. Marquès de Comillas, s/n (☎934 23 12 85). An outdoor madhouse and the undisputed king of Poble Espanyol nightlife. Cover €10; €3 with flyer. Open June-Oct. Th-Sa midnight-6am.

THE WATERFRONT

Every night Barcelona's biggest mall, **Maremàgnum,** opens one rooftop terrace with a half-dozen clubs, attracting throngs of tourists and the occasional Spaniard. Though these clubs are not the most authentic experience in Barcelona, crowds are guaranteed all week. None of the Maremàgnum clubs charge cover; they profit from their exorbitant drink prices (beer €6, mixed drinks €9-11).

L'Ovella Negra (Megataverna del Poble Nou), C. Zamora, 78, (☎933 09 59 38; www.ovellanegra.com). M: Bogatell or Marina. On the corner of C. Pallars. What was once a warehouse is now the place to come for the first few beers of the night. Large beers €2.50, 2L pitchers €9. Mixed drinks €4-5. Open M-W 7am-5pm, Th 7am-5pm and 10pm-2:30am, F 7-3am, Sa 5pm-3am. Kitchen open all night, serving *panzzas* (pizza) and *creptilles* (crepes) among other snacks. Cash only.

Razzmatazz, C. Pamplona, 88, and Almogàvers, 122 (☎932 72 09 10; www.salarazzmatazz.com). M: Marina. A warehouse complex that houses 5 clubs: Pop Bar, The Loft, Razz Club, Lo*Li*Ta, and Rex Room, each with its own live music specialty. Concert prices vary; call ahead or check website. Beer €4. Mixed drinks €8. Cover €12-15, includes access to all 5 clubs. Open F-Sa and holidays 1-5am. AmEx/MC/V.

Catwalk, C. Ramón Trias Fargas, 2-4 (☎932 24 07 40; www.clubcatwalk.net). M: Port Olímpic. Sleek interior, with hanging red couches and a crowd dressed to the nines—this is one of the hottest places in town. Cover €18. Open W-Su midnight-6am. MC/V.

ZONA ALTA: GRÀCIA AND OUTER BARRIS

The area around C. Marià Cubí has great nightlife, but you'll have to take a taxi (or the NitBus). For more accessible fun in Gràcia, head to Pl. del Sol to find the **Eldorado,** Pl. del Sol, 4 (☎932 10 59 00; www.eldoradobcn.com; open daily 10pm-2:30am; terrace from 7pm), or the more relaxed **Café del Sol,** Pl. del Sol, 16 (☎934 15 56 63; open M-Th and Su 12:30pm-2:30am, F-Sa 12:30pm-3am).

Otto Zutz, C. Lincoln, 15 (☎932 38 07 22). FGC: Gracia or M: Fontana. Japanimation lighting and three dance floors make this one of Barcelona's most famous clubs. Beer €6. Mixed drinks €6-12. Cover €10-15, includes 1 drink; look for flyers at bars and hotels to get in free before 2am. Open Tu-Sa midnight-6am. AmEx/MC/V.

Vinil(), C. Matilde, 2 (☎669 17 79 45; www.vinilus.blogspot.com). Between this bar's plethora of mismatched pillows, mellow pop, rock and soul background music, and a different movie (sometimes black and white) screened silently on one wall each night, you'll never want to leave. Beer and wine €2.50, mixed drinks €6. Open in summer M-Th and Su 8pm-1am, F-Sa 8pm-2am; in winter, M-Th and Su 7pm-1am, F-Sa 7pm-2am.

Pippermint, C. Bori i Fontestà, 20 (☎932 08 00 00, www.pippermintbcn.com), has the largest drinks you'll ever see. Cuba libre (6L) €37.40. Beer (13L) €70—really. Also has normal-sized drinks for tamer, or smaller, groups. 1L €10-12. University Bar every Th. Open daily 4pm-about 3am. MC/V.

Casa Quimet, Rambla de Prat, 9 (☎932 17 53 27). Don't be deceived: what looks like a music store from the outside is actually the best place around to hear jazz, surrounded by hanging instruments. Beer €2.50. Wine €2.50. Open Th and Su 6:30-11pm, F-Sa 6:30pm-1:30am. Cash only.

FESTIVALS

While Barcelona works hard to distinguish itself from the rest of Spain, the city shares at least one thing in common with the rest of the country: it knows how to have fun. For information on all festivals, call the tourist office (☎933 01 77 75; open M-F 10am-2pm and 4-8pm) or check the "Agenda" or "Diary" on www.bcn.es. Double-check sight and museum hours during festival times, as well as during the Christmas season and *Semana Santa.* The streets fill with book vendors and rose sellers on the **Festa de Sant Jordi** (St. George; Apr. 23), the Catalan take on Valentine's Day; the day officially celebrates Cataluña's patron saint with a feast. Men give women roses, and women give men books. In the last two weeks of August, city folk jam at Gràcia's **Festa Mayor;** lights blaze in *plaças* and music plays all night as two dozen streets compete to be the best decorated. On September 11, the **Festa Nacional de Cataluña** brings out traditional costumes, dancing, and Catalan flags hanging from balconies. Barcelona's main festival, the **Festa de Sant Joan,** takes place the night of June 23. You might as well surrender to the all-night beachside partying (and erratic nightclub hours); ceaseless fireworks and bonfires in the street will keep your eyes wide open anyway. The largest Barcelona celebration, however, is the **Festa de Mercè,** the weeks before and after September 24. To honor the patron saint of the city, *barceloneses* revel with fireworks, *sardana* dancing, and concerts. **Santa Eulàlia,** the city's female patron saint, is celebrated February 12-13.

DAYTRIP FROM BARCELONA

MONTSERRAT ☎938

A 1235m peak of limestone, quartz, and slate protruding from the Río Llobregat Valley, Montserrat (Sawed Mountain) is an inspiration to its 2.5 million annual visitors. A millennium ago, one wandering mountaineer claimed to have spotted the Virgin Mary; as the story spread, pilgrims flocked to the mountain. The Monastery of the Virgin, founded in 1025 by the opportunistic Bishop Oliba, is tended today by 80 Benedictine monks. The site attracts those who come to see the Black Virgin of Montserrat, her ornate basilica, the complex's art museum, and panoramic views of Cataluña from the mountain's stunning rocks.

TRANSPORTATION AND PRACTICAL INFORMATION

FGC (☎932 05 15 15) line R5 runs to Montserrat from M: Espanya (1hr.; every hr. 8:36am-5:36pm; return from Montserrat 10:33am-10:33pm; round-trip including cable car €13.70); get off at Montserrat-Aeri. From there, catch the **Aeri cable car** right by the station, the coolest way to ascend to the monastery. (Runs daily Mar.-Oct. every 15min. 9:40am-2pm and 2:35-7pm. Price included in bus combo fare or €8 round-trip by itself, one way €5, ages 4-13 €4.50. Additional times in summer; call ☎938 77 77 01.) Another option is to take the FGC's train, the **Cremallera de Montserrat.** (☎902 31 20 20; www.cremalleratdemontserrat.com.) From Barcelona, this requires a combined R5 train plus the Cremallera (Rack Railway) instead of the cable car (Cremallera €6.50-7.30, children €3.60-4, retired €5.85-6.55; combined, including train from Pl. Espanya, €13.70-14.40/10.80-11.20/13.05-13.75). Get off the FGC one station later, at Monistrol de

BARCELONA

Montserrat, and take the railway up (every 20-30min.). **Autocars Julià buses** run to the monastery, from near Estació Sants. (Leave Barcelona daily 9:15am and return June-Sept. at 6pm, Oct.-May at 5pm. Call ☎934 90 40 00 for reservations. €10. MC/V.) If you plan to use the funiculars, consider buying the **Tot Montserrat** (€28.60, children €17, retired €25) at tourist offices or in M: Espanya; it includes tickets for the FGC, cable car, funiculars, Museu de Montserrat, and a meal. Also available is the **Trans Montserrat** (€13.85/7.95/12.55), same as the Tot but without the Museu and the meal. Beyond the first 30 min., there is car parking fee. Call ☎938 35 03 84 for a **taxi** (from Barcelona €85).

Visitor services are in Pl. Creu, the area straight ahead from the top of the Aeri cable car steps and the Cremallera station. The **Info booth** in Pl. Creu provides free maps, schedules of religious services, and advice on mountain navigation. An audioguide with a booklet on Montserrat is €5, and an audio guide with headphones for two is €6.50. (☎938 77 77 77. Opens daily 9am, closes 5:45-8pm depending on season). For more information, buy the *Official Guide to Montserrat* (€7.50) or the museum guide (€4). Services include: **ATMs** and **bank** at La Caixa, next to the **Info booth** (open M-F 9:15am-2pm; Oct.-May M-F 9:15am-2pm, Sa 9:15am-1:30pm); **public bathrooms** to the right up the stairs if you're facing the tourist office; **ambulance** (inquire at info booth); the **Patronat del Parc Natural** (☎938 35 05 91); and the **post office** (open M-F 10am-1:30pm, Sa 10am-noon).

ACCOMMODATIONS AND FOOD

Cel·les Abat Marcet ❶ has beautiful apartments with bath, kitchen, and heating. (☎938 77 77 01; ask for Cel·les. Reception daily 9am-1pm and 2-6pm. From €15-29.50 for one person, €27.50-44 for two. Min. 2 nights; discounts for longer stays.) **Camping Montserrat ❶** is a 5min. walk past the funiculars on the road that goes uphill. Its library has out-of-print climbing books for Montserrat, and the mountain-savvy staff can put you in touch with climbing guides. (☎938 77 77 77; ask for camping. No parking on the site but available near Pl. Creu, €5 for 3 days. Open Apr. 1-Oct. 31. €3 per person, €2 for kids under 12, €2.50 per tent. Reception open 8am-2pm and 5pm-9pm Cash only.)

Food options in Montserrat are limited and aimed entirely at tourists trapped on a mountainside with no other alternatives. Pack food for your hike before coming or else descend into buffet hell. You can pick up some snacks at the small **Queviures supermarket** in Pl. Creu (open daily 9am-6:30pm). For a quick meal, **Bar de la Plaça ❶** is an option. (*Bocadillos* and hamburgers €3-4.50. Open M-F 9:30am-5pm, Sa-Su 9:30am-6:40pm. Cash only.) A new **cafetería ❶**, in Pl. Creu, has limited self-service food options. (Sandwiches €3.50-4.20. Salads €3.45-4.50. Steak and fries €5.80. Open M-F 8:45am-7pm, Sa-Su 8am-8pm. MC/V.) There's a very popular **self-service cafetería ❷** up the hill to the right from the cable car steps (in the building with the red "Mirador" sign), with wider selection and included in the price of the Lucky Tot Montserrat card. (With card, 2 dishes, chosen from *paella*, pasta, and meat, plus dessert and bread, drinks not included; otherwise, *paella* €6.60, meat and fish €4-7, salads €4-5. Open daily noon-4pm.) A fancier alternative, **Restaurant de Montserrat ❹**, is located in the same building. (*Menú* €23; children's dishes available. Open Mar. 15-Nov. 15 daily noon-4pm. AmEx/MC/V.)

SIGHTS

Above Pl. Creu (facing the info booth, take the stairs up and to the right), the beautiful **basilica** looks onto Pl. Santa Noría. Inside the courtyard, next to the main chapel entrance, a marble hallway through side chapels leads to an elevated shrine with the 12th-century Romanesque **La Moreneta** (the Black

Virgin), an icon of Mary. (Hallway open daily 8-10:30am and noon-6:30pm; in summer also Sa-Su 7:30-8:15pm. Expect a line in summer.) For many years it was revered as a Black Virgin, until it was discovered that the statue was merely very dirty; the custom stuck, however, and it was subsequently painted black. The **Escalonia boys' choir** performs in the basilica (Aug. 21-June 29 M-F 1pm; Su noon and 7:30pm; schedules may change; check www.escalonia.net). Also in Pl. Santa María, closer to the stairs up from Pl. Creu, the small **Museo de Montserrat** has art ranging from a mummy to Picasso's *Old Fisherman* and Dalí's *El Mariner*, as well as works by Degas, Renoir, and Monet. (Open daily June 26-Sept. 15 10am-7pm; Sept. 16-June 25 10am-5:45pm. €6.50, students and over 65 €5.50, ages 6-12 €3.50, under 8 free, temporary exhibits €3.)

HIKES

Some of the most beautiful areas of the mountain are accessible only by foot. The steep **Santa Cova funicular** descends from Pl. Creu to the **Rosario Monumental,** which winds along the face of the mountain past 15 religious sculptures by notable Catalan artists, culminating at the ancient hermitage **Santa Cova** where the Virgin Mary sighting took place. (Funicular daily every 20min. 10am-1pm and 2-5:45pm. Round-trip €2.70, students and over 65 €2.45, ages 3-14 €1.50. Santa Cova chapel open Apr.-Oct. daily 10:30am-5:15pm; Nov.-Mar. M-F 11:30am-4:15pm, Sa-Su 10:30am-4:30pm.) Take the **Sant Joan funicular** up the hill for inspirational views of Montserrat, the monastery, and surrounding towns. (Daily every 20min. in summer 10am-6pm. Check the signs for the last return. Round-trip €6.60, students and over 65 €5.95, ages 10-14 €3.60; joint round-trip ticket with the Santa Cova funicular €7.45/6.70/4.10.) Upstairs in the upper station you'll find an exhibit on the funiculars and the **Nature Hall,** containing a model of Montserrat and some of the mountain's history. The **Sant Joan monastery** and **shrine** are only a 20min. tromp from here, and **Sant Jerónim** (the area's highest peak at 1236m), with its views of Montserrat's jagged, mystical rocks, is worth the 1hr. trek from Pl. Creu (1hr. from the terminus of the Sant Joan funicular). The paths are long and winding but not difficult—after all, they were made for guys wearing very long robes.

CATALUÑA (CATALUNYA)

Cataluña is the most prosperous region in Iberia—and one of the proudest. The region's linguistic identity, rich natural resources, and cultural tradition have set it apart from the rest of Spain. Colonized first by the Greeks and then the Carthaginians, Cataluña later became one of Rome's favored provinces. It was briefly subdued by the Moors, and then fell into Charlemagne's domain for a short time. Cataluña declared independence in 989, growing more powerful after it united with the throne of Aragón in 1137. Still, while this pact allowed Cataluña to pursue her own empire for a time, it ultimately meant one thing: surrender to Spanish rule. The Catalan Nationalist Movement that resulted from the subjugation has been a contentious political issue for centuries.

Cataluña's achievements have lent credence to the region's fierce sense of autonomy. In the late 18th century, the region became one of Europe's premier textile manufacturers and pursued a robust trade with the Americas. Nineteenth-century industrial expansion nourished the arts and sciences, ushering in an age known as the Catalan *Renaixença* (Renaissance). The turn of the century gave birth to the *Modernista* movement and an all-star list of wildly innovative artists and architects including Picasso, Miró, Dalí, Gaudí, Domènech i Montaner, and Puig i Cadafalch. Despite all of its achievements, it was also the site of merciless persecution under Franco's dictatorship. Many *catalaneses* were imprisoned or killed, and dictatorship brought suppression of Catalan language instruction and publications, degrading the very foundation of the population's identity: its beloved tongue, a Romance language—not a dialect—closely related to Spanish and French. There is no "Spanish" here, only *castellano*, (literally, "language spoken in Castilla"), a distinction that allows *catalaneses* to differentiate themselves from a historically dominant culture. Since receiving full autonomy in 1979, Cataluña's media and arts have flourished; Catalan is once again the official language. After you've been to Cataluña, you may understand why many here call it "A Nation of Europe"—it isn't quite like anywhere else in Spain.

HIGHLIGHTS OF CATALUÑA

IMMERSE yourself in the Mediterranean on the **Costa Brava** (p. 406)

UNCOVER the secrets of the Kabbala at its birthplace in **Girona's** El Call (p. 413).

SURRENDER to Dalí's egotism at the Teatre-Museu Dalí in **Figueres** (p. 415).

COME OUT of your culinary shell at **Lleida's** snail festival in May (p. 421).

COSTA DORADA

SITGES ☎938

Forty kilometers south of Barcelona, the beach town of Sitges (pop. 27,000) just might deserve its self-proclaimed title as the "jewel of the Mediterranean." Composed of crystalline water, sweeping bays, and beautiful tanning grounds baked by 300 sunny days per year, Sitges gained prominence in the late 19th

century as one of the principal centers of the *Modernista* art movement. Today, it's swarmed with young and fun-loving tourists who come for the thriving gay community and pulsating nightlife. Sitges makes an ideal daytrip along the coast, but it also merits a few nights' stay.

TRANSPORTATION

Trains: Cercanías trains (a.k.a. Rodalies; RENFE ☎902 24 02 02, www.renfe.es/cercanias) run from **Estació Barcelona-Sants** to **Sitges** (Line 2 toward St. Vicenç de Calders or Vilanova; 45min., every 15-30min. 5:40am-1:06am, €2.50). Trains also run from **Sitges** to **Cambrils** (1hr., €4.40) via **Tarragona** (€3.60).

Buses: Mon Bus (☎938 93 70 60; www.monbus.cat; info@monbus.org) connects the Barcelona **airport** to Pg. de Villafranca in **Sitges** (M-F every hr. from airport 7:40am-11:40pm, from Sitges 5:55am-11:55pm, Sa-Su every 2hr. from airport 8:40am-10:40pm, from Sitges 7:25am-8:55pm; €2.85). Late-night buses operate from Pg. de Villafranca to Rambla de Catalunya in Barcelona and back (12:11-4am, €2.85). **Bus Urbà** (☎938 14 49 89) runs 3 local bus lines (all leave from the train station; every 30min. M-F 8am-9pm, Sa-Su 9:30am-9pm; earlier in winter; €0.90-0.95).

Taxis: ☎938 94 13 29. Run between **Barcelona** and **Sitges** (€60-65).

Car Rental: ☎938 11 19 96. To reach the beaches and the *cales* (caves), rent a car in Barcelona or Sitges at **Europcar,** on the 1st fl. of the Mercat to the right from the train station. Open daily 7am-9pm. AmEx/MC/V.

ORIENTATION AND PRACTICAL INFORMATION

Most people arrive at the train station on **Carrer Carbonell** in the northern part of town. From there, the town center is 5min. by foot, and the beach 10min. To reach either, take a right as you leave the station and the third left onto **Carrer Sant Francesc.** This leads to the old town and intersects **Carrer de les Parellades,** the main strip of stores and restaurants running parallel to the ocean. Any street off Parellades will lead to the waterfront. **Passeig de la Ribera** runs along the central and most crowded beaches.

Tourist Office: C. Sinia Morera, 1 (☎938 10 93 40; www.sitgestur.com). From the station, turn right on C. Carbonell and take the next right at the roundabout, onto Pg. de Vilafranca. The office is 1 block up on the left. Free maps and monthly bulletin of events, **Sitges Agenda.** Open from mid-June to mid-Sept. M-Sa 9am-8pm; from late Sept. to early June M-F 9am-2pm and 4-6:30pm. **Branches** at the train station and near the beach, below the church. **Agis** offers **guided tours** of the city (☎619 79 31 99; www.sitges.com/agis; €8), while **Jafra Natura** takes visitors through the bordering Garraf Natural Park (☎938 96 84 65; www.jafranatura.com; €4, children €3).

Police: Pl. Ajuntament (☎704 10 10 92).

Medical Services: Hospital Sant Camil (☎938 96 00 25).

Internet Access: Cafe Cappuchino, C. Sant Francesc, 44. €1 per 15min. Open daily 9am-11pm.

Post Office: Pl. d'Espanya (☎938 94 12 47). Open M-F 8:30am-2:30pm, Sa 9:30am-1pm; no package pickup Sa. **Postal Code:** 08870.

ACCOMMODATIONS

Accommodations are difficult to find on summer weekends (especially F-Sa). Be sure to call well in advance for a room (although the nightlife is crazy enough that you may not need a bed of your own).

Hostal Parellades, C. de les Parellades, 11 (☎938 94 08 01; hostalparellades@hotmail.com), 1 block from the beach. Well-kept rooms, a terrace, and a piano. Easily accessible after late nights, as customers are given a key to the main door. Singles €30; doubles with bath €60; triples with bath €75. MC/V (but cash preferred). ❸

Hostal Bonaire, C. Bonaire, 31 (☎938 94 53 26 www.bonairehostalsitges.com). 12 cozy rooms a block from the beach. Ask for one of the rooms with a terrace overlooking party-prone C. Bonaire. Reception 24hr. All with TV, some with A/C. In summer singles with bath €40; doubles €55-65. In winter €35/45-50. MC/V. ❹

Hotel El Cid, C. Sant Joesp, 39 (☎938 94 18 42; www.hotelsitges.com). From the train station, take a right, pass the rotunda, and take the 4th left off C. Carbonell. One of the best deals in town and popular with young travelers. All rooms come with bath, safe, and fan. Small pool, bar, and garden in back. Reserve more than a month ahead. Breakfast included. Singles €48-82; doubles €71-107; triples €103-156, depending on season. Deals for stays of 6 nights or longer. Closed Nov.-Mar. MC/V. ❹

FOOD

Many of the restaurants in Sitges are tourist traps, especially on the beachfront, but the food here is world-class. Venture far down C. de les Parellades or on the pleasant side streets to escape the generic scene. Sitges isn't cheap by any means, however. You'll generally pay at least €20 for dinner, but expect to get your money's worth. Groceries are available at **Suma,** C. Carbonell, 24, across from the train station. (☎938 94 12 00. Open M-Sa 9am-9pm, Su 10am-2pm. MC/V.) Alternatively, swing by the **Mercat de Sitges,** C. Carbonell, 26, next door to the train station, which has fruit and vegetables, meat, fish, and cheese vendors as well as several cafes and bakeries and even a clothing store. (Open M-Th 8am-2pm, F-Sa 8am-2pm and 5-8:30pm.)

Izarra, C. Major, 24 (☎938 94 73 70), behind the museum area. Basque tapas bar good for a quick fix or a leisurely meal. Ask for a *plato* and grab whatever looks tasty, from Basque seafood concoctions to more traditional Spanish *croquetas.* Big entrees (€6.50-15) and great *sidra* (cider; €1.50). Bar open daily 8:30am-midnight, *menú* available 1:30-4pm and 8:30-11pm. MC/V. ❷

Ma Maison, C. Bonaire, 28 (☎938 94 60 54). This vast restaurant (which is gay-friendly) has outdoor seating and intricately detailed walls. It serves Mediterranean entrees from a different menu every 2 months. Su is *paella* day in winter. Dinner entrees €20. Open daily 8:30pm-midnight. MC/V. ❹

Alfresco Cafè, C. Mayor, 33 (☎938 11 33 07, www.alfrescorestaurante.com). Healthful, gourmet choices found on chalkboard menus that change regularly, with relaxing music and white, modern decor. Check out mouthwatering desserts in the glass case at the bar or admire the creative presentation of the mixed green salmon salad with sesame seeds, caramelized onions, and garnish (€10) or the pita filled with chicken, tomato, mango sauce and sweet chile (€7). Free Wi-Fi. Open daily 9am-11pm. MC/V. ❷

SIGHTS

Tourists flock to shop, eat, and drink on the pedestrian walkway Carrer de les Parellades, but wise locals stick to the side streets and the peaceful beaches that are located farther up the coast.

PALAU MARICEL. Across the street from the waterfront museums, fragments of Spanish artistic culture unite with *Modernista* ceramics here, on C. Fonollar, built in 1910 for the American millionaire Charles Deering. Prepare to be wowed by its sumptuous halls and rooftop terraces. Guided tours are available on some summer nights (July-Sept.) and include a glass of *cava* (sparkling wine) and a castanet concert in the rooftop *claustro. (☎938 94 03 64. Days and times vary; call ahead for reservations. €10.)*

MORELL'S MODERNISTA CLOCK TOWER. As soon as you come into the Plaça at the intersection of C. de les Parellades and C. Sant Francesc, stop and look high up above the Òptica store for this whimsical clock tower. It's easy to miss but worth ogling for a while. *(Pl. Cap de la Vila, 2.)*

MUSEUMS. Sitges has neatly united all of its museums under one consortium; they all have the same hours and prices, and combo tickets are available. Seven blocks from the clock on C. Fonollar, the **Museu Cau Ferrat** hangs high over the water's edge. Once the home of a driving force of *Modernista* architecture, Santiago Rusiñol (1861-1931), and a meeting place for the young Pablo Picasso and Ramón Casas, the building is a shrine to *Modernista* iron and glass work, sculpture, ceramics, and painting, featuring pieces by El Greco and Picasso. Farther into town, the **Museu Romàntic,** C. Sant Gaudenci, 1, off C. de les Parellades, is an immaculately preserved 19th-century house filled with period pieces like music boxes and two surprising collections: over 400 antique dolls from all over the world, and over 25 intricate dioramas of 19th-century life in Sitges. *(General info ☎938 94 03 64; www.diba.es/museus/sitges.asp. All museums open July-Sept. Tu-Sa 9:30am-2pm and 4-7pm, Su 10am-3pm; Oct.-June Tu-Sa 9:30am-2pm and*

3:30-6:30pm, Su 10am-3pm. Hourly guided tours in summer in Museu Romàntic €3.50, students and seniors €1.75; combo ticket for several museums €6.40/3.50.)

BEACHES

Sitges's sky-blue waters and proximity to Barcelona make it a viable alternative to the crowded sands of Barceloneta and Port Olímpic. At **Platja de la Fragata,** the main beach farthest to the left as you face the sea, sand sculptors create new masterpieces every summer day. By midday, the beaches close to downtown can become almost unbearably crowded; the best beaches, with calmer waters and more open space, like **Platja de la Barra** and **Platja de Terramar,** are a 1-2km walk away (or catch the L2 bus from the train station to the stop next to Hotel Terramar, and walk a bit back toward town; every 30min. 9am-9pm, €0.95). If you decide to walk, you will pass several small beaches, including **Platja de la Bassa Rodona,** popular with gay sunbathers. Rocks partly shield these beaches from waves, creating a shallow ocean swimming pool that extends far into the water and is ideal for children. Farther down, the water is bluer and there's more open sand to claim. Sitges is also well known for its peaceful nude beaches. **Platja de l'Home Mort** can be reached by walking past Terramar until you hit a golf course at the end of the sidewalk. Walk on the beach past the golf course, and **l'Home Mort** is in a small cove behind the hills where the train tracks run by the coast. Alternately, flaunt your birthday suit at **Cala Morisca,** on the opposite side of the city, past **Platja d'Alguadolç.** To reach **Platja del Balmins,** with clear water ideal for snorkeling, walk past the church and **Platja de Sant Sebastià,** go around the first restaurant you come to, and then take the dirt walkway between the coast and the high white walls of the cemetery. The path will go up and down a slope; the beach is a quiet cove before the port.

NIGHTLIFE

Sitges makes an easy daytrip and an (arguably) better night-trip. The wild clubs are the perfect escape from the confines of Barcelona's decidedly more cosmopolitan atmosphere. The places to be at sundown are **Carrer Primer de Maig** (which runs directly from the beach and Pg. de la Ribera) and its continuation, **Carrer Marquès Montroig,** off C. de les Parellades. Bars and clubs line both sides of the small streets, overflowing onto the roads and blasting pop and house music from 10pm until 3am. The clubs here are wide open and accepting, with a vibrant mixed crowd of people, gay and straight. Other popular spots can be found on C. Bonaire and C. Sant Pau, but most open only on weekends. The tourist office has copies of **Gay Life,** a gay map of Sitges including a guide to gay hotels, restaurants, bars, clubs, and sex shops.

Atlàntida, Platja les Coves, s/n (☎934 53 05 82; www.clubatlantida.com). For a crowded and sweaty (even shirtless) "disco-beach" scene, check out this club. It's about 3km from the city, and buses run from the Calipolis Hotel. On busier nights they may stop a 10min. walk from the club. Cover €10-20. Open Tu-Su midnight-6am. MC/V.

Pachá, C. de Sant Didac (☎938 94 22 98; www.pachasitges.com). A legendary club, the 1st of a chain in Spain. Cover €15-20; includes 1 drink.

Trailer, C. Àngel Vidal, 36 (☎693 55 94 40). Among the gay cafes and clubs of the town. Cover €15 with drink; flyer/invitation grants free admission. Open daily June-Sept. 1-6am; in winter only F, Sa, and holidays. MC/V.

Bar Perfil, C. Espalter, 7 (☎656 376 791). A gay-friendly discoteca with infamous W and Su foam parties, half a block from C. Sant Francesc. Open daily 10:30pm-3:30am.

FESTIVALS

When celebrating holidays, Sitges pushes the boundaries of style and spares no extravagance. During the **Festa de Corpus Cristi** (late May or early June), townspeople collaborate to create intricate carpets of fresh flowers in the **Concurs de Catifes de Flors.** To see papier-mâché dragons, devils, and giants dancing in the streets, visit during the **Festa Major,** held August 21-27 in honor of the town's patron saint, Bartolomé (fireworks on Aug. 23). Nothing compares to **Carnaval,** a preparation for fasting during the first week of Lent. Spaniards crash the town for a frenzy of parades, dancing, costumes, and vats of alcohol. Saturday and Tuesday nights are the wildest. A pistol shot starts the **Rallye de Coches de Época** in late March, an antique-car race from Barcelona to Sitges. July or August brings the **Festival Sitges Jazz Internacional** (part of the larger Sitges Music Festival; €10 per concert). In September, competitors tread on fresh grapes on the beach for the annual **Festa de la Verema,** or grape harvest, and September 22-23 brings the **Festivitat de Santa Tecla.** The famous **Festival Internacional de Cinema de Catalunya** runs through October and is perhaps Sitges's biggest event.

TARRAGONA ☎977

The strategic position of Tarragona (pop. 130,670) on the Mediterranean coast made the city a provincial Roman capital under Augustus; today, an amphitheater and other ruins hark back to its imperial days. Down the hill from the old city, wider avenues host the best in shopping and dining. Less overwhelming than Barcelona, less sleepy than many coastal towns, and both more sophisticated and kid-friendly than its beachy neighbors, Tarragona is the perfect anchor of a Costa Dorada vacation.

TRANSPORTATION

Trains: ☎902 24 02 02, on Pl. de la Pedrera by the water, downhill from the old city. Wheelchair accessible. Ticket booth open daily 4:30am-midnight. Customer service open daily 6am-8pm. The best transportation option. Trains run to: **Alicante** (4hr., 8 per day 7:54am-6:54pm, €41.30-46); **Barcelona** (1hr., 54 per day 5:20am-11:05pm, €5.15-18.40); **Bilbao** (8hr.; 1:27, 11pm; €37.20); **Madrid** (8hr., 9:41pm, €36.90-80.50); **Pamplona** (5-6hr.; 1:27, 11pm; €31); **Salou** (15min., 19 per day 7:07am-10:24pm, €1.40-10.90); **Sitges** (4 per day 5:52am-10:25pm, €3.15); **Valencia** (2-3hr., 15 per day 7:54am-10:24pm, €17.10-33.60); **Zaragoza** (2-4hr., 5 per day 10:09am-9pm, €17.10-37.40).

Buses: Pl. Imperial Tarraco (☎977 22 91 26). Follow Rambla Nova away from the water; the station is to the left of the roundabout. **ALSA/Enatcar** (☎902 42 22 42) goes to **Valencia** (4hr., 8 per day, €17.25). **HIFE** (☎977 38 10 44; www.hife.es) and Plana (☎977 21 44 75; www.autocarsplana.com) to **Barcelona** (1hr., 17 per day, €6.91-8.55) also leave from the station.

Public Transportation: EMT Buses (☎977 54 94 80; www.tinet.org/~emt) run daily 7:30am-10pm. Convenient for trips to beaches and ruins in the outskirts. €1.10, 10-ride *abono* ticket €5.40.

Taxis: Radio Taxi (☎977 22 14 14).

Car Rental: Avis (☎977 23 47 72), by the train station at Pl. de la Pedrera, 2. Open M-F 9am-1pm and 4-7:30pm, Sa 10am-12:30pm.

ORIENTATION AND PRACTICAL INFORMATION

Most sights are clustered above the train station on a hill surrounded by remnants of Roman walls. On the hill, **Rambla Vella** and **Rambla Nova** (parallel to each other and perpendicular to the sea) are the main thoroughfares of the new city. Rambla Nova runs from **Passeig de les Palmeres,** a walkway overlooking the sea, to **Plaça Imperial Tarraco,** the largest rotunda and home of the bus station. To reach the **Pl. de la Font** in the old quarter, or *casc antic*, from the train station, turn right and follow the shoreline up the hill. At the roundabout, turn left onto Rambla Vella, then right at the first stoplight.

Tourist Office: C. Major, 39 (☎977 25 07 95; www.tarragonaturisme.cat), half a block downhill from the bottom of the cathedral steps, in the center of the old quarter. Open June 21-Sept. M-Sa 9am-9pm, Su 10am-2pm; Oct.-June 20 M-Sa 10am-2pm and 4-7pm, Su and holidays 10am-2pm. English spoken. **Cataluña Regional Tourist Office,** C. Fortuny, 4 (☎977 23 34 15; www.catalunyaturisme.com). 1 block off Rambla Nova. Info on the whole Cataluña region. Open M-F 9am-2pm and 4-6:30pm, Sa 9am-2pm. Summer branches at L'Imperi Romà, Rambla Nova, and Unió with same hours.

Tourist Information Booths: Glass-and-steel kiosks at 3 locations: Pl. Imperial Tarraco, at the end of Rambla Nova by the bus station, and the end of Rambla Vella where Av. de Catalunya meets Via de l'Imperi Romà. Open June 21-Sept. 26 daily 10am-1:30pm and 5-8:30pm; Sept. 27-June 20 Sa 10am-2pm and 4-7pm, Su 10am-2pm.

Police: Comissaria de Policia, Pl. Orleans (☎977 24 98 44). From Pl. Imperial Tarraco, walk down Av. President Lluís Companys and take the 3rd left to the station.

Hospital: Hospital de Sant Pau i Santa Tecla, Rambla Vella, 14 (☎977 25 99 00).

Internet Access: Tarraconet@, C. Cós del Bou, 9 (☎977 23 98 18). Half a block from Pl. de la Font. €1.50 per hr. Open M-Sa 11am-2pm, 5-10:30pm, Sun 5-10:30pm. **Netgaming Tarragona,** C. Méndez Núñez, 7 (☎977 23 45 52). Half a block down from Rambla Nova. €1.80 per hr. Open daily 11am-10pm.

Post Office: Pl. Corsini, 12 (☎902 197 197), 6 blocks from the coast and 2 blocks below Rambla Nova, off C. Cañellas. Open M-F 8:30am-8:30pm, Sa 9:30am-2pm. **Postal Code:** 43001.

CATALUÑA

ACCOMMODATIONS AND CAMPING

Most of the city's accommodations are two- to four-star hotels. Charismatic **Pl. de la Font,** in the *casc antic* (old city) by the *Ajuntament* (a long plaza parallel to Rambla Vella), and the area around **Pl. Imperial Tarraco** uptown are filled with cheaper lodgings. Several campsites line the road toward Barcelona (Via Augusta or CN-340) along the northern beaches, around km 1. Take bus #9 (every 20min., €1) from Pl. Imperial Tarraco.

Hostal Noria, Pl. de la Font, 53 (☎977 23 87 17, info@hostalnoria.com), in the heart of the historic town. Enter through the restaurant on the plaza. 29 rooms with bath, some with balconies. June-Sept. singles €30; doubles €48. Oct.-May €22/36. MC/V. ❸

Pensión Forum, Pl. de la Font, 37 (☎977 23 17 18), upstairs from the restaurant of same name. 21 rooms with ceiling fans and pink or blue bathrooms at great prices. Exterior rooms overlook plaza. Singles €21; doubles €34-37. Cash only. ❷

Platja Llarga (☎977 20 79 52; www.campingplatjallarga.com), is the closest campsite, along the beach. Open *Semana Santa*-Sept. €4.50-5.90 per adult, per tent, and per car; €4.10-5.25 per child. 2- to 8-person. Bungalows €55-120. MC/V. ❶

FOOD

Ramblas Nova and Vella and the streets in between, especially **C. Mendéz Nuñez,** are full of restaurants serving cheap *menús del día* and *platos combinados* (€5.50-8). The narrow streets of the *casc antic,* especially in and around Pl. de la Font, have higher-end restaurants. Tarragona's **Mercat Central** is in Pl. Corsini next to the post office. (☎977 23 15 51. Open M-Th and Sa 7:30am-2pm, F 7:30am-2pm and 5:30-830pm. Flea market Tu and Th.) For regular **groceries,** head to **Opencor,** Pl. Imperial Tarraco, 2. (☎977 24 91 37. Open daily 8am-2pm. AmEx/MC/V). **El Serrallo,** the fishermen's quarter, next to the harbor, has excellent seafood. Try your fish with Tarragona's typical **romesco sauce,** made with red peppers, garlic, toasted almonds, and hazelnuts simmered in olive oil.

El Apapacho, C. Major, 13 (☎977 24 95 57), on the steep main street of the old quarter, near the cathedral. Fresh, flavorful authentic Mexican food awaits you amids colorful place mats, masks and sombreros. The fajitas and enchiladas (€7) are favorites of locals and travelers alike. Open Tu-Th 8-11pm, F-Sa 8pm-midnight. MC/V. ❷

La Teula, C. Merceria, 16 (☎977 24 86 00), half a block in the direction of the cathedral from Pl. del Fòrum in the old city. Superb salads (€7-8.50) and tapas, including toasted *entrepans* with vegetarian and meat combos (€4.90-10.90). Lunch *menú* Tu-F €9.90 Sa-Su €12.90. Open Tu and Su 1-4pm, W-F 1-4pm and 8pm-midnight. MC/V. ❷

Giuseppe, C. St. Domènec, 28 (☎659 79 81 49), behind Pl. de la Font. Outdoor tables under a giant mural and next to Roman ruins are the perfect setting for delicious flat-bread pizzas, salads, and beer. *Menú* €8. Open Tu-Su 7pm-12:30am. Cash only. ❷

SIGHTS AND BEACHES

Tarragona's status as a Roman provincial capital transformed the small military enclosure into a glorious imperial port. Countless Roman ruins stand amid the 20th-century hustle and bustle, all just minutes uphill from the beach.

ROMAN RUINS. Below Pg. de les Palmeres between Ramblas Vella and Nova, set in the gardens above Platja del Miracle, is the **Amfiteatre Romà.** Gladiators once killed wild animals for captivated audiences in this massive structure. It was also a site for public executions; in AD 259, the Christian bishop Fructuosus and his two deacons were burned alive here. In the AD sixth century, these martyrs were honored with a basilica built in the arena.

Up the hill from here, between the theater and the city, is the entrance to a double-shot attraction: the **Pretori Romà,** former administrative center of the region, and the **Circ Romà,** built in the AD first century for chariot races and other spectacles. The only part of the praetorium still standing is this stair tower, which connects the level of the commoners (the circ) to that of the politicians (the praetorium). Visitors descend into the dark tunnels that led fans to their seats and marvel at medieval houses built in the center of the circus.

The heavily weathered **Fòrum Romà,** with reconstructed Corinthian columns, is near the post office on C. Lleida, three blocks below Rambla Nova and six from the coast. Remember that this forum was the center of town; its distance from the other ruins demonstrates how far the walls of the ancient city extended. To see the remnants of the second-century-BC walls that stretched all the way to the sea, stroll through the **Passeig Arqueològic** in the inland part of the city, near the cathedral. *(Amphitheater ☎977 24 25 79, praetorium 22 17 36, circ 23 01 71, forum 24 25 01, passeig 24 57 96. All ruins open May-Sept. Tu-Sa 9am-9pm, Su 9am-3pm; Oct.-Apr. Tu-Sa 9am-7pm, Su 7am-3pm. Admission to each €2.45, students and seniors €1.25, all ruins plus the Museu Casa Castellarnau €9.25, under 16 free.)*

MUSEUMS. The **Museu Nacional Arqueològic,** at Pl. del Rei just above the praetorium, displays ancient Roman architecture, sculptures, bronze tools, and mosaics (including the famous *Head of Medusa*) and offers insight into daily life in the Roman Empire. It is considered the most important collection of Roman artifacts in Cataluña. *(Pl. del Rei, 5. ☎977 23 62 09. Wheelchair-accessible. Open June-Sept. Tu-Sa 9:30am-8:30pm, Su 10am-2pm; Oct.-May Tu-Sa 9:30am-1:30pm and 3:30-7pm. €2.40, students and seniors €1.20, under 18 or over 65 free. Tu free. Includes entrance to the necropolis.)* If you'd prefer to get a feel for the Tarragona of recent years, there is the small but interesting **Museu d'Art Modern de Tarragona,** featuring 20th-century photography, painting, and sculpture from famous and local artists. One exhibit includes a Miró/Josep Royo textile, the *Tapís de Tarragona*, accompanied by photos of Miró weaving it in his studio. *(C. Santa Anna, 8. Between Pl. del Fòrum and Pl. del Rei. ☎977 23 50 32; www.altanet.org/MAMT. Open Tu-F 10am-8pm, Sa 10am-2pm and 5-8pm, Su and holidays 11am-2pm. Free.)*

BEACHES. The hidden access to **Platja del Miracle,** the main beach visible from the hill, is along Baixada del Miracle, starting from Pl. Arce Ochotorena. Walk left from the amphitheater until the underpass. Then continue under the train tracks to the beach. Perhaps not on par with the region's other beaches, this secluded spot (with generous sand space) is not bad for a few hours of relaxation. A bit farther away are the larger beaches: **Platja Llarga** and the favorites for those in the know, **Platja de l'Arrabassada** and **Platja de la Mora.** *(Take bus #1 or 9 from Pl. Imperial Tarraco or any of the other stops.)*

OTHER SIGHTS. Located in the center of the old quarter and lit by octagonal windows flanking the transept, the gigantic Romanesque-Gothic **cathedral,** dating back to 1171, is one of the most magnificent buildings in Cataluña. The dark interior of this former mosque holds the tomb of Joan d'Aragón and the adjoining **Museu Diocesà** showcases religious relics from the last 700 years. *(Entrance to both hidden on C. Claustre; follow signs at the bottom of the Pl. La Seu. Open M-Sa Mar. 16-May 30 10am-6pm; June-Oct. 15 10am-7pm; Oct. 16-Nov. 15 10am-5pm; Nov. 16-Mar. 15 10am-2pm. €3.50, students and seniors €2.50, ages 7-16 €1, under 7 free.)* The **Pont del Diable** (Devil's Bridge), a Roman aqueduct, is visible on the way out of town. Take municipal bus #75 (every 20min., €1.10) from the corner of C. Cristòfor Colom and Av. Prat de la Riba or from Pl. Imperial Tarraco.

CATALUÑA

NIGHTLIFE AND FESTIVALS

Weekend nightlife in Tarragona takes place on a much smaller scale than in Sitges or Barcelona. After 10pm, the pedestrian streets liven up and fireworks brighten the sky, especially during the first week of July. Even later, the place to be is **Port Esportiu,** a seaside plaza near the train station and loading docks that is full of restaurant-bars and little discos. Heading up Rambla Nova away from the beach, take a left onto C. la Unió; bear left at Pl. de General Prim and follow C. Apodaca six blocks. Cross the tracks; the fun awaits on the port to the left.

The unique **Festa de Sant Magí** for the town's minor patron saint brings waterfront processions, music, and human *castells* (towers) to Tarragona in mid-July. Pyromaniacs shouldn't miss the end of the first week of July, when fireworks light up the beach in the **Concurs Internacional de Focs Artificials** (International Fireworks Display Contest; www.piroart.com). In even-numbered years, the first Sunday in October brings the **Concurs de Castells,** a competition of tall human towers, as high as seven to nine "stories," called *castells*. More *castells* appear during the annual **Fiesta de Santa Tecla** (Sept. 14-24), Tarragona's *festa major*, featuring *gigantes* (giant dancing puppets), medieval treats, "spoken dances," *dracs* (dragons), and much more.

REUS

☎977

Reus (pop. 107,000) lacks the splendid coastlines of nearby towns but still attracts visitors looking to learn more about the birthplace of Antoni Gaudí, the iconic Catalan architect. Before Gaudí, a period of industrial growth in the 19th century put Reus on the map as a major trader of *aguardent* (firewater). Around the turn of the century, the *Modernistas* swept its city blocks, and the architectural fruits of that period remain. Reus is Catalan Modernism at its most refined and a subdued alternative to Cataluña's wilder coastal havens.

TRANSPORTATION

Flights: Aeroport de Reus (☎977 77 98 32), Autovia Reus, km 3. Reus Transport Públic runs 8 buses per day from the airport to the train and bus stations 8:35am-10:10pm.

Trains: Pl. de l'Estació (☎902 24 02 02). Customer service open 9am-2pm and 4-7pm. Station open 24hr. By far the best method of transportation to Reus. Trains to **Barcelona** (1hr., 15 per day 4:51am-9:18pm, €5.90-13.70) via **Tarragona** (15min., €1.40-8.40), **Madrid** (7hr., 11:56pm, €36.10), and **Pamplona** (5hr.; 1:41, 9:14pm; €29.70-38.80).

Buses: Stations at Av. Jaume I and Av. President Macià Fortuny. **Hispano Igualadina** (☎977 77 06 98) goes to **Tarragona** every 30min. during the day on weekdays and hourly on weekends. **Autocars Plana** (☎977 54 72 90; www.autocarsplana.com) runs to **Salou** (July-Aug. every 30min. 6:30am-11pm; Sept.-June every hr). **Nocturn** service runs (7 per night July-Aug. daily 10:45pm-5:15am; Sept.-June F-Sa and nights before festivals) to **Cambrils** (2-6 per day). Buses leave from the station but stop at Pl. de les Oques in the city before leaving town.

Public Transportation: Reus Transport Públic (☎977 30 00 06; www.reustransport.com) runs 5 bus lines daily 6am-10pm; some every 10-20min., others 1 per hr. Visit the tourist office and pick up the **Nova Guia Transport Urbà,** which has routes and schedules. €1, 10-ride *abono* €6.

Taxis: Radio Taxi (☎977 34 50 50).

ORIENTATION AND PRACTICAL INFORMATION

Reus's sights are concentrated in the city center anchored by **Plaça Prim** and **Plaça Mercadal.** From the train station, walk straight out past the small **Plaça Joan Rebull** onto **Passeig Sunyer,** a wide tree-lined promenade, and follow it for four blocks until **Plaça de les Oques.** Then, turn left on **Carrer de Sant Joan,** one of the city's main streets, which leads to the tourist office and the center of town.

Tourist Office: Plaça Mercadal, 3 (☎977 01 16 70; www.reus.net/turisme). Next to the *Ayuntamiento* in the central plaza. Provides free map and *Guia del Modernisme.* Guided **walking tours** of the city daily July-Sept. 6pm in Catalan and English, noon in French and Spanish. Contact office for more info or group reservations. €5 Ruta Modernista tour, €5 IPM tour, €6 Gaudí Centre tour, €14 combined. Open M-Sa July-Sept. 9:30-8pm; Oct.-June 9:30am-2pm and 4-8pm.

Police: Comissaria de Policia, C. General Moragues, 54 (☎977 32 80 00), a block from Pl. Llibertat.

Medical Services: Hospital de Sant Joan, C. Sant Joan (☎977 32 04 24).

Internet Access: Biblioteca Publica Central, C. Escorxador, 1 (☎977 01 00 25). Free, reserve up to 1hr. Open July-Sept. M-F 10am-2:30pm; Oct.-June M-F 10am-8pm, Sa 10am-2pm and 4-8pm. Closer to the city center is **Cyber Cafe,** C. Batan, 2 (☎619 18 14 60). €1.20 per hr. Also offers cell phone charges. Open daily 10am-11pm.

Post Office: Pl. Llibertat, 12 (☎977 31 46 62). Open M-F 8:30am-8:30pm, Sa 9:30am-2pm. **Postal Code:** 43201.

ACCOMMODATIONS

Reus boasts a wide variety of accommodations, most of which are within the city center and cover a wide range of prices and amenities.

Hostal Santa Teresa, C. Santa Teresa, 1 (☎977 31 62 97). For a younger feel, check out this student residence next to Pl. Prim, with 15 tastefully decorated rooms with fans, wood desk, and large, clean baths (some with tub). Laundry €2, terrace with clotheslines; public phone. Singles €21, otherwise €20 per person. Cash only. ❷

Hotel Ollé, Pg. de Prim, 45 (☎977 31 10 90; www.hotelolle.com). By Pl. La Pastoreta. Has 30 hotel-quality rooms at hostel prices. Rooms have big windows, TV, A/C, and bath. Wheelchair-accessible. Singles €28; doubles €48; triples €65; quads €72. MC/V. ❷

FOOD

The narrow streets around Pl. Prim and Pl. Mercadal are filled with bakeries and small tapas bars sandwiched between classy boutiques and *perfumerías*. Reus prides itself on its Siurana olive oil, a special oil extracted from the *arbequina*, a small olive of concentrated flavor very typical of the region. For a delicious local dessert, try the *menjablanc* (almonds and sugar). The **Mercat Central,** in the center of the city, offers a colorful array of fresh produce as well as other delicacies. (Open M-Th 8am-2pm, F 7:30am-2:30pm and 5:30-8:30pm, Sa 7:30am-2pm.) Outrageously popular flea markets shut down this part of the city Mondays and Saturdays 9am-2pm.

La Ferreteria, Pl. de la Farinera, 10 (☎977 34 03 26), behind the *Ayuntamiento.* Has a delicious lunchtime *menú* as well as large servings of local tapas (€3.22-8.83) in a gorgeous old iron-working shop with an outdoor patio. Order a single tapa per person, like the marinated smoked salmon with toast (€6.40), or share one for a snack. *Menú* (€13) M-F 1-4pm. Open M-Th and Su 10am-1am, F-Sa 10am-2am. AmEx/MC/V. ❷

La Bajoqueta, C. de la Mar, 5 (☎977 34 54 53), right off Pl. Mercadal. One of the best-priced restaurants among the shopping streets. The *Bajoqueta* salad consists of artfully displayed tomato slices, green beans, olives, and eggs, and the *pa amb tomàquet* (tomato-rubbed bread) drips with flavor. Entrees generally €12-13, salads €7-8. *Menú* M-F €10, Sa €11. Open M-Sa 9am-4pm and 8:30-11pm. MC/V. ❷

Le Bon Profit, C. Cristófor Colom, 5, on a side street walking to town from the train station. Serves snails cooked on a flaming open grill in the middle of a packed dining room. Snail entrees €12.50. Appetizers €5-17. Open M-Tu and Th-Su 1-3pm and 8:30pm-midnight. Reservations recommended. MC/V. ❸

SIGHTS

Reus attracts visitors for two reasons: Gaudí's legacy and the insane amount of shopping. The entire **Tomb de Reus** is packed with shops, but the block along **Carrer Monterols** leading down from Pl. Prim is particularly chic and crowded. The tourist office provides the **Guia Comercial**, a color-coded map of Reus's modern boutiques selling everything from clothes and shoes to wedding dresses.

LA RUTA DEL MODERNISME DE REUS. A visit to Reus is not complete without walking this route, which runs past the beautiful and uniquely detailed *Modernista* buildings scattered throughout the old town. It starts and ends near the tourist office and conveniently passes through the main shopping streets. One highlight is the **Casa Navàs** (1901), Pl. Mercadal at the corner with C. de Jesús,

CATALUÑA

by Lluís Domènech i Montaner, one of the most significant *Modernista* architects and figurehead of Reus's movement. Casa Navàs was inhabited until 1999 and retains the character of its past: all furniture and fixtures are original and untouched. *(Privately owned; occasional guided tours. Contact the tourist office ☎977 01 16 70.)* Domènech i Montaner's biggest work in town is the **l'Institut Psiquiàtric Pere Mata,** a multi-pavilion complex that recalls his hospital project in Barcelona and is also still a functional hospital. *(2km west of the city. Guided tours daily July-Sept. 11:30am in Catalan and English, 5:30pm in French and Spanish; €14 for combined IPM, Modernista, and Dalí Centre tours, €5 for individual tickets. Bus #32 runs there and back 22 per day; for the tour catch the 11:14am bus from Pl. Oques and the 12:51pm bus back.)* The greatest number of buildings on the trail belong to **Pere Caselles i Tarrats,** a local star who received less international attention than his peers. Most of the rest of the *Modernista* buildings on the trail are privately held and closed to the public. Some, such as the **Casa Natal de Gaudí** (C. Sant Vicenç 4 and C. Amargura, between 7 and 9) have sculptures like the "Gaudí adolescent," erected in 2002 to commemorate the 150th anniversary of his birth here. The new **Gaudí Centre museum,** in the tourist office, satisfies your appetite for interactive Gaudí models as well as childhood notebooks and other Gaudinian curiosities. *(Plaça Mercadal, 3. Open June 15-Sept. 15 M-F 10am-8pm, Sa-Su 10-2pm; Sept. 16-June 14 M-F 10am-2pm and 4-8pm, Sa-Su 10-2pm. €6, ages 7-14 and seniors €4, under 7 free.)*

NIGHTLIFE AND FESTIVALS

Reus has more quiet plazas than crazy parties; however, an increasing number of entertaining pubs dot the city, most of which surround Pl. Prim, Pl. del Mercadal, and Pl. de les Peixeteries Velles in the center of the shopping district. Sip wine or tea at **Portia,** C. de Rosich 10-14, among pink barstools, rose walls, and live musical performances. (☎977 34 33 40. Open Tu-F from 5pm, Sa-Su from 6pm.) A couple of others line the Pg. de Mata in front of the train station, including **La Fàbrica,** Pg. de Mata 32-34, with ballroom dancing, disco music, and an older crowd (www.lafabricareus.com. Open Tu-Sa 11pm-5am, Su 6:30-11pm.) But many of the real partiers, locals and tourists alike, prefer to hop on the bus and head to **Salou** (bus leaves daily and regularly from the Pl. de les Oques and takes approx. 15min.), where discotecas groove all night.

"CAT" GOT YOUR TONGUE?

Catalunya is home to a people defined by a shared mother tongue. Many *catalaneses* (Catalonians) consider themselves an independent nation, and not without reason. The language we call Spanish, or *español,* doesn't exist in Cataluña. It's termed *castellano*—that which is spoken in Castilla, the region around Madrid.

Catalan, like *castellano,* French, Italian, and Portuguese, harkens back to Latin—but that's where the similarities end. Like countless oppressors before him, dictator General Francisco Franco spent 36 years insisting that Spain had only one true language (besides *euskera,* which he conveniently overlooked). Franco proclaimed Catalan a "dialect" of *castellano*—an outright untruth—and banned its use. Printing in the language halted almost entirely, but speaking continued to flourish. In fact, every Catalan utterance became a tiny rebellion, an act of cultural pride. When Franco died in 1975, the language blossomed, as Catalans from Cadaqués to Barcelona celebrated newfound freedom.

With an increasingly global community, living solely in a Catalan bubble has become nearly impossible. Still, most natives raise their children, read menus, and speak to passersby using the words of their ancestors. To them, Catalan is more than just grammar and vocabulary—its brisk melody defines their cultural identity.

COSTA BRAVA ☎975

Skirting the Mediterranean Sea from Barcelona to the French border, the Costa Brava's cliffs and beaches draw throngs of European visitors—especially French—in July and August. Early June and late September can be remarkably peaceful; the water is warm and the beaches are much less crowded. In winter, the "Wild Coast" lives up to its name, as fierce winds batter quiet, practically empty beach towns. These rocky shores have long attracted romantics and artists like Marc Chagall and Salvador Dalí, a Costa Brava native. No wonder, then, that the Costa Brava is so distinctively Catalan—this is a region that prides itself on its history and on the architectural and artistic treasures it holds. Among these are Dalí's house in Port Lligat and his museum in Figueres. Certain towns have survived the summer-tourist onslaught better than others (Cadaqués has fared well), but there are still clear waters and pine-covered cliffs almost everywhere you turn.

TOSSA DE MAR ☎972

"Tossa," with 12th-century medieval ruins abutting long stretches of beach, has been a magnet for artists and romantics since French artist Marc Chagall fell in love with it in 1934. Shortly after in 1951, actress Ava Gardner fell for Spanish bullfighter Mario Cabrera during the filming of *The Flying Dutchman* here, much to the chagrin of her then-husband, Frank Sinatra. Like many coastal towns, Tossa (pop. 5893) suffers from the blemishes of tourism, but the beaches, Vila Vella (old quarter), and good Catalan food leave no doubt as to why Chagall called Tossa "blue paradise."

TRANSPORTATION

Buses: On Av. Pelegrí at Pl. de les Nacions Sense Estat. Ticket booth open daily 7:15am-12:40pm and 3:30-7:40pm. **Pujol** (☎972 34 03 36) takes the scenic route to **Lloret del Mar** (20min.; June-Aug. every 30min. 8am-9:10pm; Sept.-May every hr. 7:40am-8:40pm; €1.40). **Sarfa** (☎972 34 09 03; www.sarfa.com) goes to **Barcelona** (2hr., daily 11 per day 7:40am-7:40pm, €9.70), **Girona** (1hr., 7:15am, €4.85), and **Aeroport Girona** (May-June 24 11:25am, 3:40pm; €8).

Boats: Slow service to towns and otherwise inaccessible *cales* (coves) along the coast, including Lloret and Sant Feliu. **Viajes Marítimos** (☎972 36 90 95; www.viajesmaritimos.com) and **DofiJet Boats** (☎972 37 19 39; www.dofijetboats.com) depart every hr. 9:35am-5:30pm (€10-15.30). 30min. to Lloret; 1hr. to Blanes. Buy tickets and board on Pg. de Mar, on the beach in front of the first-aid stand.

Car Rental: Viajes Tramontana, Av. Costa Brava, 23 (☎972 34 28 29). Rentals provided by **Olimpia** and **SACAR.** 21+. Credit card, driver's license, and passport required. From €42 per day. Open daily July-Aug. 9am-9pm; Sept.-Nov. and Apr.-June 9am-1pm and 4-8pm. AmEx/MC/V. Also **Viajes Internacional,** C. Peixaterias, 1 (☎972 34 02 41).

Taxis: Taxi stand outside the bus station (☎972 34 05 49).

ORIENTATION AND PRACTICAL INFORMATION

Buses arrive at **Plaça de les Nacions Sense Estat** where Avinguda del Pelegrí and Avinguda Ferran Agulló meet; the town slopes down to the waterfront. From the station, make a right onto Av. del Pelegrí, then a left onto C. La Guardia. The street narrows, curving around to become C. Socors and then **Carrer Portal;** any street downhill to the left will lead to the beach, while staying on C. Portal will take you to the old quarter, known as the **Vila Vella** (5min.). Running back along Tossa's main beach, the Platja Gran, is the hyper-touristy Passeig del Mar.

Tourist Office: Av. del Pelegrí, 25 (☎972 34 01 08; www.infotossa.com), by the bus terminal at Av. Ferran Agulló and Av. del Pelegrí. English spoken. Hiking info and a posted schedule of upcoming events. Weekend guided hikes and walks (usually Sa-Su 8am). Open June-Sept. M-Sa 9am-9pm, Su and holidays 10am-2pm and 5-8pm; Oct. and Apr.-May M-Sa 10am-2pm and 4-8pm; Nov.-Mar. M-Sa 10am-2pm and 5-8pm. **Branch** at Av. Palma, s/n, right on Platja Gran. Open June-Sept. daily 10am-2pm and 4-8pm; Oct. and Apr.-May Tu-Su 10:30am-1:30pm and 4-7pm.

Currency Exchange: Banco Santander Central Hispano, Av. Ferran Agulló, 2 (☎972 34 10 65). **ATM** on the street. Open M-F 8:30am-2pm, Oct.-May also Sa 8:30am-1pm.

Police: Municipal Police, Av. del Pelegrí, 14 (☎972 34 01 35). English spoken. At night, they'll escort you to a 24hr. pharmacy if necessary.

Pharmacy: Farmàcia Castelló, Av. Ferran Agulló, 12 (☎972 34 13 03). Open daily 9:30am-1:30pm and 4:30-9pm; Oct.-June closes at 8pm.

Medical Services: Casa del Mar, Av. de Catalunya s/n (☎972 34 18 28). Primary care and immediate attention. The nearest hospital is in **Blanes,** 30min. south.

Internet Access: Tossa Bar Playa, C. Socors, 6, off the main beach. €1 per 20min. Open daily July-Aug. 9:30am-10pm; Sept. and May-June 9:30am-7pm.

Post Office: C. María Auxiliadora, 4 (☎972 34 04 57), down Av. del Pelegrí from the tourist office. Open M-F 8:30am-2:30pm, Sa 9:30am-1pm. **Postal Code:** 17320.

ACCOMMODATIONS AND CAMPING

Tossa de Mar is a seasonal town; many accommodations, restaurants, and bars are open only from May to October.

Fonda Lluna, C. Roqueta, 20 (☎972 34 03 65; www.fondalluna.com). From Pg. del Mar, turn right onto C. Peixeteries, veer left onto C. Estolt, walk uphill, and go left. Its tidy singles, doubles, and triples sport summery prints and come with bath and roof access (with a sweeping view). Breakfast included. Lunch €10. Dinner €5-9. Free internet. June-July €21 per person; Aug. €25; Sept.-May €19. Book ahead in summer. MC/V. ❷

L'Hostalet de Tossa, Pl. de l'Església, 3 (☎972 34 18 53; www.hostalettossa.com), in front of the Església de Sant Vicenç. 32 hotel-quality doubles with bath (some with TV and fan), plus foosball and pool tables. Breakfast buffet included. July 15-Aug. and *Semana Santa* singles with balcony €44-46; doubles €69-78. Sept. and June-July 14 €33-35/54-62. May €28-30/46-54. MC/V. ❹

Camping Can Martí (☎972 34 08 51), at the end of Rambla Pau Casals, off Av. Ferran Agulló. A popular, friendly campground near a wildlife reserve. Hot showers, telephones, pool, and restaurant. June 25-Aug. 9 €9 per person; €9 per tent; €5 per car; €6 per child. Sept. 1-19 and May 14-June 19. €6/6/4/4. Cash and travelers checks only. ❶

FOOD

Most restaurants in Tossa specialize in seafood and have reasonably priced *menús*, but the best food and ambience is found in the old quarter. For groceries, head to **Can Palou,** C. La Guardia, 25.

La Lluna, C. Abat Oliva, 10 (☎972 34 25 23). Resting on the roughly cut stone path running up the the Vila Vella. Offers flavorful Catalan specialties served in the coziest of dining rooms (or on the flower drenched terraces). Whet your appetite with one of the fruit *pâtés,* from the mountain region of Cataluña (€4.30), and follow with a large farmer's bread toast covered in caramelized onion, artichoke, mushroom, asparagus, and melted

CATALUÑA

Brie (€6.70). Finish with the *crema catalana* (€3.65). Tapas €1.35-9.40. Open daily in summer 11am-4pm and 7-11pm. Closed Tu from late Sept.-June. Cash only. ❶

Restaurant Santa Marta, C. Francesc Aromi, 2 (☎972 34 04 72), in a medieval dwelling inside the old fortress, just 20m up from C. Portal. Innovative cuisine, including dishes like salmon with raspberry and kiwi sauce. Entrees €10-31. *Menú* €15.50. Open from *Semana Santa* to Sept. daily 12:30-3:30pm and 7:30-11pm. AmEx/MC/V. ❸

SIGHTS AND BEACHES

CENTRE D'INTERPRETACIÓ DELS FARS DE LA MEDITERRÀNIA. Inside the walled fortress of the Vila Vella, an escalating spiral of medieval alleys and steep stairways lead all the way to a picture-perfect view of the city and the surrounding *cales* (small coves) as well as this recently opened museum, where an audio-visual exhibit depicts the history and culture of lighthouses. *(☎972 34 33 59. Open daily June 15-Sept. 15 10am-10pm; Sept. 16-Semana Santa 10am-6pm; Semana Santa-June 14 10am-7pm. €3, students €1.50, under 12 free.)*

MUSEU MUNICIPAL. At the tiny Pl. Pintor J. Roig y Soler, this museum has a collection of 1920s and 30s modern art. The room dedicated to Marc Chagall holds *El violinista celest*, one of his only remaining works in Spain, as well as letters he wrote to the mayor of Tossa. *(☎972 34 07 09. Open June 16-Sept. 15 M-Su 10am-8pm; Sept. 16-Sept. 30 and June 1-June 15 M-F 11am-1pm and 3-5pm, Sa-Su 11am-6pm; Oct.-May Tu-F 11am-1pm and 3-5pm, Sa-Su 12am-5pm.)*

FORMER 14TH-CENTURY PALACE. Tossa's Roman mosaics (dating from the AD 4th to 5th centuries) and other astonishingly well-preserved artifacts from the ancient Villa dels Ametllers are displayed in a former 14th-century palace. *(☎972 34 07 09. Open Semana Santa-Sept. Tu-Su 10am-1pm and 5-8pm; Oct.-Semana Santa hours vary. €2, students and seniors €1, under 12 free. Guided tours available M 10:30am in Catalan, W 10:30am in Spanish; €3.)*

BEACHES. Tossa's main beach, surrounded by cliffs and the Vila Vella, draws the majority of beachgoers. To escape the crowds, visit some of the neighboring coves, accessible by foot. The tiny **Es Codolar** rests under the tower of Vila Vella, hugged by wooded cliffs.

CATALUÑA

NIGHTLIFE

Bars line the narrow streets near the old quarter, packed closely together, so you can stroll down C. Portal and Pg. del Mar and take your pick.

Bar del Far del Mar (☎972 34 12 97). If you don't mind a bit of an uphill walk, then check out this new establishment, nestled romantically at the foot of the functioning lighthouse on the peak of the Vila Vella. The bar offers tart mojitos and a sweet, sweeping view. Mixed drinks about €6. Appetizers €2-6.50. Open daily June 10am-11:30pm; July-Sept. Tu-Su 10am-11:30pm; Oct.-May Tu-Su 10am-6pm. MC/V.

Bar El Pirat, C. Portal, 32 (☎972 34 14 43). Don an eye patch to blend in at this small establishment and its companion bar **Piratín,** C. Portal, 30, with ship-worthy skull and crossbones decor inside and a tranquil view from tables overlooking the sea below at Es Codolar. House sangria €4. Open Apr.-Oct. daily 1pm-3am. Cash only.

Mar i Cel, C. Estolt, 4 (☎655 83 43 50). If you're in the mood for some *Modernisme*-inspired decor and want to schmooze with a younger, local crowd, this place—complete with brightly colored mosaic tiles and billiard tables—is just for you (€1.50 per game). Beer €2.40. Open daily *Semana Santa*-Nov. 9:30pm-3:30am; Dec.-*Semana Santa* Sa-Su 9:30pm-3:30am.

CALELLA DE PALAFRUGELL

Like Llafranc, Calella de Palafrugell harbors beautiful stretches of beach and coastline, drawing vacationers to bask in the Mediterranean sunlight and admire the boat-filled bay. Though locals refer to it simply as "Calella," it is not to be confused with the town of Calella on the Costa del Maresme, nor with the nearby Palafrugell, about a 15min. bus ride from Calella de Palafrugell.

TRANSPORTATION AND PRACTICAL INFORMATION. **Buses** run from Palafrugell to Calella de Palafrugell and Llafranc (15-20min.; July-Aug. 24 per day; Sept. and June 14-16 per day; Oct.-May 4-5 per day 7:40am-4pm; €1.30). For **taxi** service, call the 24hr. **Rádio Taxi** (☎972 61 00 00) or **Parada de Taxi** (☎972 30 07 61). The Calella de Palafrugell **tourist office** is located at C. de las Voltes, 2. (☎972 61 44 75. Open daily June 10am-1pm and 5-8pm; July-Aug. 10am-8pm.) The **hospital, CAP Alsina i Bofill,** is in Palafrugell on C. d'Angel Guimerá, 6 (☎972 61 06 07). **Internet** access is at **Pizzeria La Chispita,** C. de Chopitea at C. del Pintor Joan Serra, where 14min. costs €1. (☎972 614 735. Open from Mar. to mid-Sept. 11am-12:30am.) The **post office** of Calella de Palafrugell is on Pl. de las Escoles s/n. (Open M-F 9am-11:30am, Sa 9:30-11am.) **Postal Code** (Palafrugell): 17200.

ACCOMMODATIONS AND FOOD. Hotel prices in Calella de Palafrugell range from expensive to outrageous—many budget travelers choose to stay in neighboring Llafranc, which offers some hostels at more reasonable rates. **The Hotel Mediterrani ❺**, C. Francesc Estrabau, 40, is, believe it or not, the most reasonable in Calella de Palafrugell. More affordable rooms are simply furnished, and a comfortable lounge area and dining room feature beautiful views of the bay. (May-Oct. ☎972 61 45 00, Nov.-Apr. 932 09 91 13; www.hotelmediterrani.com. Breakfast included. All rooms have private bath and TV. MC/V. Singles €55-69; doubles usually €80-139.) For camping, go to **Moby Dick ❶**, C. Costa Verda, 16-28. Look for the white whale made of ship's line to find this convenient campground close to the water. (☎972 61 43 07; www.campingmobydick.com. Open Apr.-Sept. Also offers bungalows (€49-96.30). Reception July-Aug. 8am-midnight; Sept.-June 10am-1pm. €3.21-5.35 per adult, tent, and car; €1.76-3.21 per child. Cash only.) At **Restaurant-Pizzeria Sol Ixent ❷,** C. dels Canyers, 24, on the rightmost end of the bay facing the water, a modest outdoor patio boasts a magnificent view away from the touristed section of the boardwalk. Fresh salads, *tostas* (open-faced sandwiches), and other items run €6.50-15, with good vegetarian options. Try the arugula salad with mixed greens, pear, shredded Manchego cheese, and a peppery vinaigrette for €7. (☎972 61 50 51. Open daily 11am-4pm and 7pm-midnight, closed M Oct-May. MC/V.)

NIGHTLIFE AND FESTIVALS. Nightlife in Calella de Palafrugell consists mostly of pubs that close relatively early. There are some festivals, such as **Festival Jardins de Cap Roig,** held in July and August, which features a series of concerts by big-name international artists like Pink Martini and Julio Iglesias. (For more information, contact Fundació Caixa de Girona, ☎972 20 98 36 or visit www.caixagirona.com. General admission tickets €25-60.) The **Costa Brava Jazz Festival** also brings music to Calella de Palafrugell in July. The **Festa de Sant Pere** takes place mainly in Calella de Palafrugell; the **Cantada de Havaneres** is celebrated the first Saturday in July in Calella de Palafrugell and the first Saturday in August in Llafranc. Llafranc holds its **Festa Major de Santa Rosa** with dances and activities around August 30. If you are here the first Saturday of September, check out the **Mercat Boig** in Pl. del Promontori, where practically anything and everything is sold (but mostly crafts and antiques).

GIRONA (GERONA) ☎972

Modern Girona (pop. 92,000) is Catalan through and through, but it's been almost everything else over the course of history. A Roman *municipium* and then an important medieval center, the "city of four rivers" was an exemplar of the Spanish settlements where Christians, Jews, and a small number of Arabs were able to coexist in peace. Girona was the home of the renowned *cabalistas de Girona*, a group of 12th-century rabbis credited with founding the school of mystic thought called the Kabbala. Although they, and other Jews, were banned from the city in 1492, you can still walk the streets (or, more accurately, the staircases) of El Call, the old Jewish quarter. In more recent years, the *Ajuntament* of Gerona returned to the city's roots by changing its name back to the original Catalan—Girona—in 1980. Now, this many-splendored metropolis enjoys international recognition as a cyclist's paradise—former Tour de France hero Lance Armstrong called the city home during training season.

TRANSPORTATION

Flights: Aeropuerto de Girona-Costa Brava, Termino Municipal de Vilobi d'Onyar (☎972 18 66 00; www.aena.es, choose Girona from the dropdown menu), is small and services a few regular flights on **Iberia** (☎902 40 05 00; www.iberia.com) and **Ryanair** (☎972 47 36 50; www.ryanair.com). **Barcelona Bus** (☎902 36 15 50; www.sagales.com) runs shuttles from Girona, Barcelona, and the Costa Brava to the airport (from the Girona bus station every hr. 5am-10pm, return every hr. 5:30am-12:30am; €2; from Barcelona 23+ per day 3:45am-7:30pm, return 28 per day 8:30am-12:10am; €12). A taxi to Girona's old city is roughly €35 (12km).

Trains: RENFE (☎902 24 02 02; www.renfe.es), in Pl. d'Espanya to the southwest of the city center. Open M-Sa 5:30am-11pm, Su 6:30am-11pm, info 6:30am-10pm. Trains to: **Barcelona** (1¼-1½hr.; M-F 23 per day 5:56am-9:40pm, Sa-Su 17 per day; €7), change at Maçanet for coastal train; **Figueres** (30-40min.; M-F 22 per day 7:25am-10:10pm, Sa 14 per day 8:28am-9:42pm, Su 15 per day 10:06am-10:10pm; €2.60) via **Flaçà** (15min., €1.70); **Milan,** ITA (11hr.; Tu, Th, Su 10:15pm, €168, under 26, over 60, and students with ISIC €118); **Zurich,** DEU (13 hr., Tu, Th, Sun 9:25pm, €170; under 26, over 60 and students with ISIC €119); and **Paris,** FRA (10½hr.; 10:17pm; €175, under 26, over 60, and students with ISIC €123).

Buses: Next to train station, 5min. from city center. **Sarfa** (☎902 30 20 25). Info open M-F 7:30am-8:30pm, Sa-Su 8:45am-noon and 4:30-8:30pm. Buses to: **Cadaqués** (2hr., M-F 6:30pm, €9); **Palafrugell** (1hr., M-F 14 per day 7:45am-8:30pm, €5) for connections to **Calella** and **Llafranc; Tossa de Mar** (40min., July-Aug. 6:30pm, €4.85). **Teisa** (☎972 20 02 75; www.teisa-bus.com) info open M-F 9am-7:15pm with 20min. breaks, Sa-Su 9am-1pm, Su 4:30-5:30pm. Buses to: **Lérida** (3hr.; M-F 3 per day 7:30am-7:15pm, Sa-Su 8:30am, 5:30pm; €20.05); **Ripoll** (2hr.; M-F 4:15pm, 8:15pm; €9.30). **Barcelona Bus** (☎902 36 15 50; www.barcelonabus.com). Express buses to **Barcelona** (1hr.; M-F 5 per day 7am-7:15pm, Sa-Su 3 per day; €11) and **Figueres** (50min.; M-F 4 per day 7:45am-6:15pm, Sa 2 per day, Su 3 per day; €4.65).

ORIENTATION AND PRACTICAL INFORMATION

The Riu Onyar divides the city into old and new sections. Eleven bridges, mostly pedestrian, connect the two banks. The **Pont de Pedra** leads into the **Barri Vell** (old quarter) by way of C. dels Ciutadans, one block off the bridge, which turns into C. Bonaventura Carreras i Peralta and then C. Força, leading to the cathedral and **El Call,** the historic Jewish neighborhood. The **train** and **bus terminals** are situated off **Calle Barcelona,** in the modern neighborhood. To get to the old city from a bus, walk through the terminal, across the parking lot and Pl. Espanya, turn left onto C. Barcelona and go straight (a bit more than three blocks) until you reach a plaza, then bear right on the plaza and right again onto the small C. Nou; it will take you across Pont de Pedra to the historic area. The iron bridge to your right was built by the Eiffel Company of Paris, France.

Tourist Offices: Rambla de la Llibertat, 1 (☎972 22 65 75; www.ajuntament.gi/turisme), by Pont de Pedra in the old town. English spoken. Pick up the biweekly *La Guia,* in Catalan but with clear listings of events. Also has listings of hotels, hostels, pharmacies, art galleries, theaters, libraries, and classes with addresses and phone numbers. Open M-F 8am-8pm, Sa 8am-2pm and 4-8pm, Su 9am-2pm. The **Punt de Benvinguda** office, C. Berenguer Carnicer, 3 (☎972 21 16 78) is 7 blocks up on the other side of the river. Open M-Sa 9am-2pm and 3-5pm, Su 9am-2pm.

Police: Policia Municipal, C. Bacià, 4 (☎972 41 90 92). To report a pickpocketing, contact the Mossos d'Esquadra, C. Vista Alegre (☎972 18 16 00).

Hospital: Hospital de Girona "Josep Trueta," Av. França, 60 (☎972 94 02 00).

Internet Access: Alberg de Joventut Cerverí de Girona (HI), C. dels Ciutadans, 9 (☎972 21 80 03; www.xanascat.net;alberg_girona@tujuca.com). This youth hostel offers unlimited internet access for €1 regardless of whether you choose to stay (see below). Cafes that line C. Coitadans often offer internet, many at reasonable prices.

Post Office: Av. Ramón Folch, 2 (☎902 19 71 97), a brick building with the golden dome. Open M-F 8:30am-8:30pm, Sa 9:30am-2pm. **Postal Code:** 17001.

ACCOMMODATIONS

There are enough hostels in Girona to find a room without much trouble, but some are no less expensive than the hotels in the new city. The best locations are within a couple of blocks of the river on either bank. If you have your heart set on a specific lodging, call ahead in the summer.

Pensión Residència Bellmirall, C. Bellmirall, 3 (☎972 20 40 09; email bellmirall1@telefonica.net for availability). To your right when facing the Museu d'Art. Pricey but well worth it. Delightful rooms, all with private bath, in a 14th-century house by the main cathedral. Included breakfast is served on the flowering garden patio. Closed Jan.-Feb. Singles €35; doubles €65; triples €80. €10 more in high season. Cash only. ❸

Pensión Viladomat, C. Ciutadans, 5 (☎972 20 31 76). Many rooms with balconies, some with high ceilings and large windows. Even if your room isn't the lap of luxury, the price is right. Quiet at night and at the center of the action during the day. All rooms have heaters. Singles with shared bath €22; doubles €40, with bath and TV €60; triples and small quads with bath and TV €85-100. Cash only. ❷

Alberg de Joventut Cerverí de Girona (HI), C. dels Ciutadans, 9 (☎972 21 80 03; www.xanascat.net; alberg_girona@tujuca.com). Plain walls and metal bunks, but good price, location, and amenities. Sitting rooms with TV/VCR, board games, videos, and ping-pong. Rooms of 2-8 or 10 beds with lockers (€2 each use). Breakfast included; lunch €5.90-7.75; dinner €7.50-10.55. Sheets included. Wash €2.50, dry €1.50. Unlimited internet access. Reception 8:30am-2:30pm, 3:30-9pm, and 10-11:30pm. Check-in 24hr. Dorms end of June-Sept. €19.25-21.90; Oct.-June €15.40-17.90. Non-HI members €2 more. AmEx/MC/V. ❷

FOOD

Girona boasts exciting local cuisine, both savory and sweet. Local specialties are *botifarra dolça* (sweet sausage made with pork, lemon, cinnamon, and sugar) and *xuixo* (sugar-sprinkled pastries filled with cream). A good place

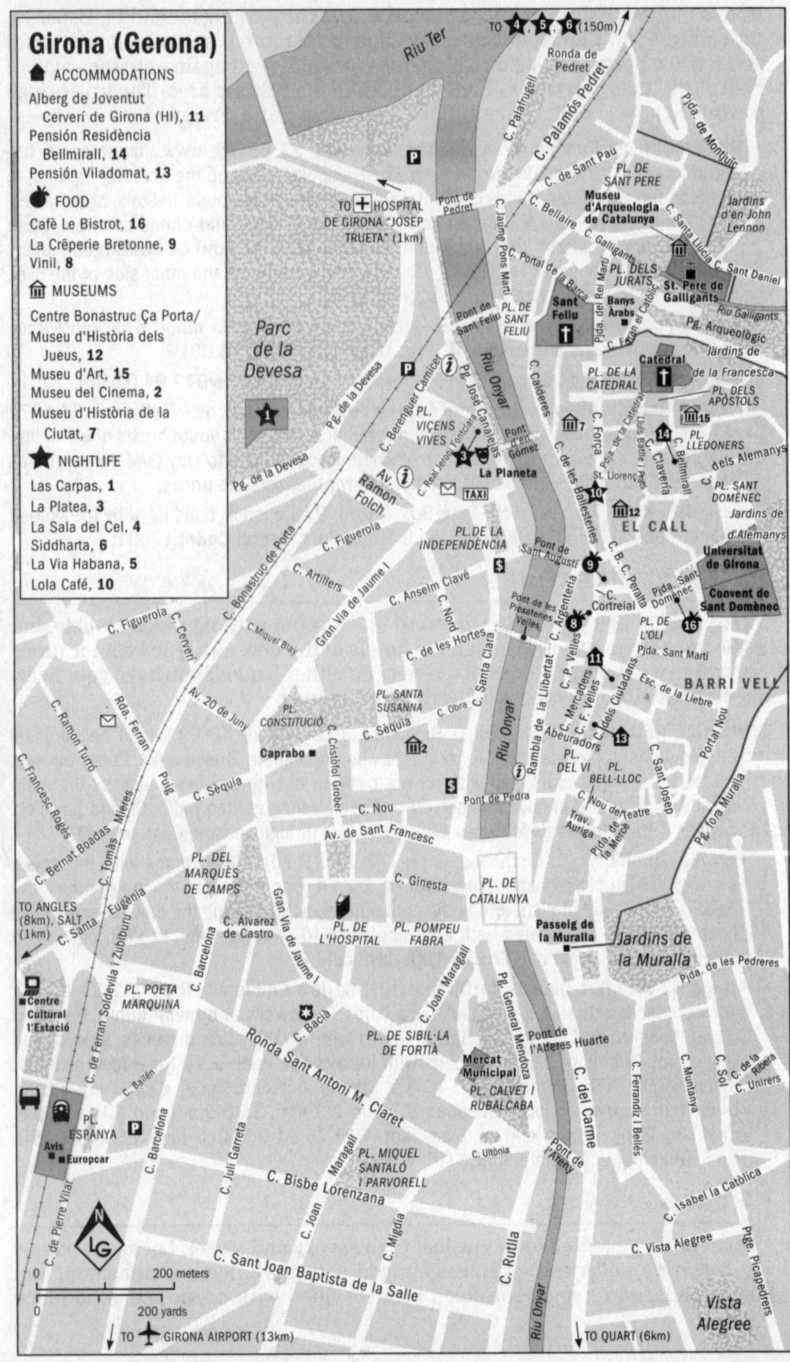
Girona (Gerona)
ACCOMMODATIONS
Alberg de Joventut Cerverí de Girona (HI), 11
Pensión Residència Bellmirall, 14
Pensión Viladomat, 13
FOOD
Cafè Le Bistrot, 16
La Crêperie Bretonne, 9
Vinil, 8
MUSEUMS
Centre Bonastruc Ça Porta/ Museu d'Història dels Jueus, 12
Museu d'Art, 15
Museu del Cinema, 2
Museu d'Història de la Ciutat, 7
NIGHTLIFE
Las Carpas, 1
La Platea, 3
La Sala del Cel, 4
Siddharta, 6
La Via Habana, 5
Lola Café, 10
TO 4, 5, 6 (150m)
Riu Ter
Ronda de Pedret
C. Palafrugell
C. Palamós Pedret
Pjda. de Montjuïc
C. de Sant Pau
PL. DE SANT PERE
Museu d'Arqueologia de Catalunya
Jardins d'en John Lennon
TO HOSPITAL DE GIRONA "JOSEP TRUETA" (1km)
Pont de Pedret
C. Bellaire
C. Galligants
C. Santa Llúcia
C. Sant Daniel
C. Jaume Pons Martí
C. Portal de la Barca
PL. DELS JURATS
St. Pere de Galligants
Riu Galligants
Sant Feliu
Banys Àrabs
Pg. Arqueològic
Pont de Sant Feliu
PL. DE SANT FELIU
Parc de la Devesa
Jardins de la Francesca
Catedral
PL. DE LA CATEDRAL
PL. DELS APÒSTOLS
Pg. de la Devesa
C. Berenguer Carnicer
Pg. José Canalejas
Riu Onyar
C. Calderes
C. Força
PL. VIÇENS VIVES
Pont d'en Gómez
PL. LLEDONERS
La Planeta
C. dels Alemanys
PL. SANT DOMÈNEC
Av. Ramon Folch
TAXI
C. de les Ballesteries
St. Llorenç
EL CALL
Jardins de d'Alemanys
C. Figuerola
PL.DE LA INDEPENDÈNCIA
Pont de Sant Agustí
Universitat de Girona
Convent de Sant Domènec
C. Artillers
C. Anselm Clavé
C. Bonastruc de Porta
Gran Via de Jaume I
C. Nord
Pont de les Peixateries Velles
C. Cortreial
PL. DE L'OLI
Pjda. Sant Martí
C. Argenteria
C. Figuerola
C. Cerverí
C. de les Hortes
C. Santa Clara
BARRI VELL
Esc. de la Llebre
Av. 20 de Juny
PL. SANTA SUSANNA
Rda. Ferran
C. Ramon Turró
PL. CONSTITUCIÓ
C. Sèquia
Rambla de la Llibertat
Abeuradors
PL. DEL VI
PL. BELL-LLOC
C. Sant Josep
Portal Nou
C. Francesc Rogès
Caprabo
C. Cristòfol Grober
Puig
C. Sèquia
Pont de Pedra
C. Nou del Teatre
Pg. fora Muralla
C. Nou
Av. de Sant Francesc
C. Bernat Boadas
C. Tomàs Mieres
PL. DEL MARQUÈS DE CAMPS
C. Ginesta
PL. DE CATALUNYA
Gran Via de Jaume I
TO ANGLES (8km), SALT (1km)
C. Santa Eugènia
C. Àlvarez de Castro
PL. DE L'HOSPITAL
PL. POMPEU FABRA
Passeig de la Muralla
Jardins de la Muralla
Pjda. de les Pedreres
C. Barcelona
PL. POETA MARQUINA
C. Joan Maragall
Centre Cultural l'Estació
C. de Ferran Soldevila i Zubiburu
C. Bacià
Ronda Sant Antoni M. Claret
PL. DE SIBIL·LA DE FORTIÀ
Pont de l'Alferes Huarte
Mercat Municipal
PL. CALVET I RUBALCABA
C. del Carme
C. Ferrandiz I Bellés
C. Muntanya
C. Sol
C. Unirers
PL. ESPANYA
Avis
Europcar
C. Barcelona
C. Juli Garreta
C. Maragall
PL. MIQUEL SANTALÓ I PARVORELL
C. Ultònia
Pont de l'Areny
C. Bisbe Lorenzana
C. Isabel la Catòlica
C. de Pierre Vilar
C. Joan
C. Migdia
C. Rutlla
C. Vista Alegree
Ptge. Picapedrers
C. Sant Joan Baptista de la Salle
0 200 meters
0 200 yards
Riu Onyar
Vista Alegree
TO GIRONA AIRPORT (13km)
TO QUART (6km)

CATALUÑA

for moderately priced food is on **Calle Cort-Reial** at the top of C. Argenteria. **Rambla de la Llibertat** has several tourist cafes with terrace seating, and Pl. de la Independència, Girona's restaurant hub, offers both high-end and cheaper options, most of which have tables on the square. Join locals at the covered **mercat municipal** located in Pl. Salvador Espriu. (From the tourist office facing Pont de Pedra, walk left past Pl. Cataluña and cross the river at Pont de l'Areny. (☎972 20 19 00. Open M-Sa 6am-2pm. Cash only.) Get your **groceries** at **Caprabo,** C. Sèquia, 9, a block off the Gran Viade Juame 1. (☎972 21 45 16. Open M-Sa July-Aug. 9am-9pm; Sept.-June 9am-2pm and 5-9pm. MC/V.)

Cafè Le Bistrot, Pjda. Sant Domènec, 4 (☎972 21 88 03). Eat on the stone steps of the Convent de Sant Domènec, with a view of the old city below, or inside amidst Art Nouveau posters. Specialty creations are the *pizzas de pagès* (farmer's bread pizzas) made on typical Catalan round bread (€6-8, only offered for dinner). Lunch *menú* M-F €12-14, Sa-Su €17-20. Open daily 1-4pm and 8pm-1am. MC/V. ❸

La Crêperie Bretonne, C. Cort-Reial, 14 (☎972 21 81 20; www.creperiebretonne.com). Proof of Girona's proximity to France, this popular crepe joint brings a youthful atmosphere and tasty eats to the historic district. The food is cooked in a small bus bound for the town of Cerbère, but you can eat it on the cozy alley terrace or in the train-themed interior while it's fresh (never reheated). Lunch *menú* €8.50-11 Crepes €2.75-8.60. Unusual salads (fig, duck) €9-10. Vegetarian options available. Open Tu-Sa 1:30-3:30pm and 8-11:30pm. MC/V. ❷

Vinil, C. Cort Reial, 17 (☎972 21 64 40). If you took Vinil's mantra, *"som el que mengem,"* (you are what you eat) to heart, then you'd be a salad with honey-soy dressing and thin slices of ham, a knockout hamburger, or a potato purée drizzled in raspberry sauce. Green chairs and walls, with renowned comics hanging from the walls. Lunch *menú* varies daily (€10.40). Open M-F 9am-1am, Sa 1pm-2am, Su 7pm-1am. MC/V. ❷

SIGHTS

Start your self-guided historical tour of the city at the **Pont de Pedra** and turn left down the tree-lined **Rambla de la Llibertat.** Continue on C. Argenteria, bearing right across C. Cort-Reial. C. Força begins on the left up a flight of stairs.

EL CALL. The part of the old town around C. Força and C. Sant Llorenç was once the center of Girona's thriving medieval Jewish community ("call" comes from *kahal*, Hebrew for "community"). The site of the last synagogue in Girona now serves as the Centre Bonastruc Ça Porta. The center includes the prominent **Museu d'Història dels Jueus,** with an excellent audio tour that explains the old Hebrew tombstones and text, as well as the story of the Jews in Girona before and after the Inquisition. Be sure to lose yourself (quite literally) in the narrow, winding stone staircases that surround the museum. *(C. Força, 8, halfway up the hill. ☎972 21 67 61; ajgirona.org/call. Center and museum open June-Oct. M-Sa 10am-8pm, Su 10am-3pm; Nov.-May M-Sa 10am-6pm, Su 10am-3pm. Wheelchair-accessible. Museum €2, students and over 65 €1.50, under 16 free. Guided walking tours of the Barri Vell, including El Call, are available through Ajuntament de Girona i Patronat Call de Girona (☎972 21 16 78; puntb@girona-net.com); tours leave from C. Berenguer Carnicer, 3, Tu-Su at 10:30am, June 15-Sept.15 €15, Sept. 16-June 14 €10, under 16 free. Tour price includes museum entrance.)*

CATHEDRAL COMPLEX. The breathtaking Gothic **Catedral de Girona** rises 90 steps from the *plaça*. Its tower, along with that of **Sant Feliu,** defines the Girona skyline. The **Torre de Charlemany** and **cloister** are the only structures left from the 11th and 12th centuries; the rest of the building dates from the 14th-17th centuries. Look at the keystone of the world's widest Gothic **nave** (23m); the builders eschewed solid stone in favor of a hollow rock with a wood "cork" for fear of weighing the structure down and collapsing it. A door on the left leads to the trapezoidal cloister and the **Tresor Capitular** museum, which holds some of Girona's most precious paintings, sculptures, and decorated Bibles. Its most famous piece is the **Tapis de la Creació**, an 11th-century tapestry depicting the events of Genesis. *(Museum ☎972 21 44 26; www.catedraldegirona.com. Open Apr.-Oct. M-F 10am-8pm, Sa 10am-4:30pm, Su 2-8pm; Nov.-Mar. M-F 10am-7pm, Sa 10am-4:30pm, Su 2-7pm. Wheelchair-accessible with advance notice. Cathedral, tresor, and cloister €5, students and over 65 €2, ages 7-16 €0.90, under 7 free. Free to all on Su.)*

SCENIC WALKS. Girona's renowned **Passeig de la Muralla,** a 2km trail along the fortified walls of the old city, can be accessed at several points: at the **Jardins de la Francesa** (behind the cathedral), the **Jardins d'Alemanys** (behind the Museu d'Art), and the main entrance at the bottom of the Rambla in Pl. de la Marvà. *(Open daily 8am-10pm.)* Behind the St. Pere de Galligants church (by the Museu d'Arqueologia), you can go up on a *mirador* for great views of the city. Behind the cathedral, the walk coincides with the equally beautiful **Passeig Arqueològic.** This path skirts the northeastern medieval wall and also overlooks the city. For the less athletically inclined, a small green train offers a 30min. guided tour of the main sights of the old town, including the town hall, cathedral, Església de Sant Feliu, El Call, and the walls. *(In summer tour leaves daily from the Pont de Pedra every 40-45min. 10am-1pm and 3-6pm. Less frequently in the winter; check at the tourist office. Available in English. €4, children under 10 €3.50.)* Alternatively, relax in the flower-filled Jardins del la Francesa or the shady and tranquil Jardins d'Alemanys.

CATALUÑA

MUSEU DEL CINEMA. This unusual collection of artifacts, clips, and heavy machinery documents the rise of cinema from the mid-17th to 20th centuries, interspersed with a few Asian shadow theater pieces from as early as the 11th century. The exhibit chronicles the invention of the *camera obscura* (9th-12th centuries), the "magic lantern," and eventually daguerreotypes, 35mm, Edison, and TV, as well as the viewing culture that developed around each advance. A must for movie buffs, given Cataluña's central role in the early Spanish cinema. *(C. Sèquia, 1. ☎972 41 27 77; www.museudelcinema.org. Open May-Sept. Tu-Su 10am-8pm; Oct.-Apr. Tu-F 10am-6pm, Sa 10am-8pm, Su 11am-3pm. Wheelchair-accessible. €4, students and over 65 €2, under 16 free. AmEx/MC/V.)*

OTHER MUSEUMS. The **Museu d'Art** has enchanting pieces spanning the Romantic to the modern; look for the Saints' Day book, the pregnant virgin, and the temporary exhibition space in an old prison cell. *(Pujada de la Catedral, 12. ☎972 20 38 34; www.museuart.com. Open Mar.-Sept. Tu-Sa 10am-7pm, Su and holidays 10am-2pm; Oct.-Feb. Tu-Sa 10am-6pm, Su 10am-2pm. Wheelchair-accessible. €2, students, under 19, and over 65 €1.50.)* The **Museu d'Història de la Ciutat** showcases 2000 years of Girona's history and prominent figures. The exhibit on the *sardana*, Cataluña's national dance, features old musical instruments once used in a *cobla* (the band that traditionally plays for the *sardana*) and a how-to of *sardana* steps. *(C. La Força, 27. ☎972 22 22 29; www.ajuntament.gi/museuciutat/eng/index. Open Tu-Sa 10am-2pm and 5-7pm, Su and holidays 10am-2pm. Some descriptions in English. €3, students €2, under 16 free.)* The small **Banys Àrabs,** inspired by Muslim and Roman bathhouses, once contained saunas and baths of varying temperatures; now the graceful 12th-century structure hosts outdoor art exhibits in the summer. With no descriptive placards on the walls, you'll want to use an audio tour (€3) to appreciate the architecture and history of the space, or just rely on the free, basic pamphlet provided. *(C. Ferran el Catòlic, s/n ☎972 19 07 97; www.banysarabs.org. Open Apr.-Sept. M-Sa 10am-7pm, Su 10am-2pm; Oct.-Mar. daily 10am-2pm. €1.80, students €1.)*

NIGHTLIFE

Nightlife in Girona ranges from finger-snapping coffeehouses to rock bars and crowded discotecas. In the summer there is really only one nightlife alternative, and that is **Las Carpas** (the tents), an outdoor circus of dance floors, bars, and swirling lights in the middle of the **Parc de la Devesa.** Many clubs close in summer and operate only from their *carpa*, though some morph a bit and remain open in both guises. Las Carpas is so dazzling, though, that locals don't head inside until the park shuts down. (Drinks start at €4. Open May-Sept. 15 M-Th and Su 11pm-3:30am, F-Sa 11pm-4am.) The artsy bars and cafes in the old quarter are particularly mellow and a great place to start the evening.

Lola Café, C. Forca, 7 (☎972 22 88 24; www.lola-cafe.com). Patrons wait outside to crowd in and enjoy the sophisticated ambience (mood lighting, stone walls). Mixed drinks €6. Open daily 6pm-3am.

La Platea, C. Fontclara (☎972 22 72 88; www.localplatea.com), next to the Pont d'en Gomez. Flashing neon green stairs, white leather stools, mock-Gothic chandeliers, and pop music to boot. Mixed drinks €8-10. Open W-Sa midnight-6am.

La Sala del Cel, C. Pedret, 118 (☎972 21 46 64; www.lasaladelcel.cat). A 10min. walk down the Riu Ter, this popular nighttime destination is known as La Pedret. Its labyrinthine dance floors, massage parlor, game room, pool-side terrace, and, yes, **pool** are worth the walk. Cover €12 and up; drink included. Open F-Sa and nights before fiestas midnight-6am. Cash only.

Siddharta, C. Pedret, 116 (☎972 22 04 20). Siddharta specializes in pitchers of Tisane and fruity concoctions with cognac and other liquors, served in a maze of old stone arches. 1.5Lpitchers €16. Open daily 8pm-3am. Cash only.

La Via Habana, C. Pedret (www.viahabana.net). Drink mojitos (€7) and stumble your way to salsa prowess with a local crowd. Open Th-Su 11pm-5am. Cash only.

FESTIVALS

Starting on the second Saturday in May and lasting through the following two weeks, government-sponsored **Temps de Flors** (www.gironatempsdeflors.net) exhibitions spring up all over the city; local monuments and pedestrian streets swim in blossoms, and the courtyards of Girona's finest old buildings are open to the public (ask for the "*mapa de flors*" from the tourist office). Summer evenings often inspire spontaneous *sardana* dancing in the *plaça*. Girona, along with the rest of Cataluña, lights up for the **Focs de Sant Joan** on the night of June 23, featuring fireworks and bonfires. Try the traditional Coca de Sant Joan dessert with a glass of *cava*, of course. For *Viernes Santo*, the Friday of **Semana Santa,** *Cofrarías*, or church groups, dress up in Old World costumes. Keep an eye out for the men from San Luc decked out in full Roman soldier gear, including horses and weapons. From the end of June into July, the **Festival de Músiques Religioses del Món** (☎872 08 07 09; www.ajuntament.gi/musiques-religioses) draws choirs and artists from all over the world to perform in the cathedral and on its grand steps, while local restaurants cater from stands. The patron saint, **Sant Narcís,** is celebrated for five days at the end of October.

CATALUÑA

FIGUERAS (FIGUERES) ☎972

Sprawling Figueres (pop. 42,000) is functional, not beautiful. Outside of the touristed area, parts of the city seem to have fallen into disrepair. Nevertheless, it is the capital of Alt Empordà county and a major gateway city to France and the rest of Europe. In 1974, the mayor of Figueres asked native

Salvador Dalí to donate a painting to an art museum the town was planning. Dalí saw his chance and ran with it, donating an entire museum. The construction of the Teatre-Museu Dalí in Figueres further catapulted the artist to international renown. To this day, a multilingual parade of Surrealism fans are entranced by Dalí's mind-bending and erotic works.

TRANSPORTATION AND PRACTICAL INFORMATION

Trains: Pl. de l'Estació (☎902 24 02 02). To **Barcelona** (2hr.; M-F 22 per day, Sa-Su 17 per day; €10) via **Girona** (30-40min., €2.60).

Buses: All buses leave from the **Estació d'Autobusos** (☎972 67 33 54), on the left side of Pl. de l'Estació if your back is to the train station. Sarfa (☎972 67 42 98; www.sarfa.com) is open 6am-9pm. If closed, buy tickets on bus. To: **Cadaqués** (1hr.; July-Aug. 7 per day 9am-8pm; Sept.-June M-F 3 per day, Sa-Su 4 per day; €4.50) and **Palafrugell** (1hr.; M-F 6 per day 8:30am-8pm, Sa 2 per day 12:15, 6pm, Su 12:30pm, 6pm; €7.50). Barcelona Bus (www.barcelonabus.com) runs to **Barcelona** (2hr.; M-F 4 per day 7:45am-8:15pm, Sa 2 per day 11am-4:15pm, Su 3 per day 7:45am-6:15pm; €15.50) via **Girona** (1hr., €5). Buy tickets on bus, platform 4.

Taxis: Taxis line La Rambla (☎972 50 00 08) and the train station (☎972 50 50 43).

Car Rental: Hertz, Pl. de l'Estació, 9 (☎972 67 02 39). 25+; must have had driver's license for 1 year. All-inclusive rental from €59 per day. Open M-F 9am-1pm and 4-7pm, Sa 9am-1pm. AmEx/MC/V. **Avis,** Pl. de l'Estació s/n (☎972 51 31 82), in the train station. 23+; credit card only. Rental from €50 per day (underage surcharge varies; approx. €30). Open M-Sa 9am-1:30pm and 4-7pm. AmEx/MC/V.

CATALUÑA

ORIENTATION AND PRACTICAL INFORMATION

From the tip of **Plaça de l'Estació** with your back to the train station, bear left on C. Sant Llàtzer, walk six blocks to C. Nou (the third main road), and take a right to get to Figueres's tree-lined **Rambla.** To reach the **tourist office,** walk all the way up La Rambla and continue on C. Lasauca straight out from the left corner. The blue, all-knowing "i" beckons across the rather treacherous intersection with Avinguda Salvador Dalí.

Tourist Offices: Main Office, Pl. Sol s/n. (☎972 50 31 55; www.figueresciutat.com, English spoken). Dalí-themed tours M-Sa 11am, noon, 2, 3, 5pm. €16; includes Teatre-Museu Dalí. Open July-Sept. M-Sa 8am-8pm, Su 10am-3pm; Oct. and Apr.-June M-F 8:30am-3pm and 4:30-7pm, Sa 9:30am-1:30pm and 3-6pm; Nov.-Mar. M-F 8am-3pm. 2 additional summer **branches**, in the train station (open July-Sept. 15 M-Sa 10am-2pm and 3-6pm) and in front of the Teatre-Museu Dalí (open July-Sept. 15 M-Sa 9am-7pm, Su 10am-3pm).

Currency Exchange: Banco Santander Central Hispano, La Rambla, 21. Open M-F 8:30am-2pm, Sa 8:30am-1pm. **ATMs** on La Rambla, Pl.

Police: Av. Salvador Dalí, 107 (☎972 51 01 11). To report a crime, contact the **Mossos d'Esquadra,** C. Ter s/n (☎972 54 18 00).

Hospital: Hospital Comarcal de Figueres, Ronda Rector Arolas s/n (☎972 50 14 00), behind and to the left of the Dalí museum.

Internet Access: Biblioteca Fages de Climent, Pl. Sol, 11 (☎972 67 70 84) Offers free 15min. internet access. Open M-F 10am-8:30pm, Sa 10am-1:30pm. **Café de Nit** offers free **Wi-Fi** to customers (see **Nightlife**).

Post Office: C. Santa Llogaia, 60-62 (☎972 50 54 31). Open M-F 8:30am-8:30pm, Sa 9:30am-1:30pm. **Postal Code:** 17600.

ACCOMMODATIONS

Many visitors to Figueres make the journey a daytrip from Barcelona, but quality, affordable accommodations in Figueres are easy to find. Many hostels are on upper floors above bars or restaurants. Others are closer to La Rambla and Carrer Pep Ventura. Inquire at the tourist office about hostels and pensions.

Hostal La Barretina, C. Lasauca, 13 (☎972 67 64 12; www.hostalbarretina.com). From the train station, walk up La Rambla to its end; take a left on C. Lasauca; the hostel is a block up on the left. Hotel-like luxury—each room has TV, A/C, heat, and bath. Reception in the restaurant downstairs. Breakfast €3, other meals €10. Wheelchair-accessible. Reservations recommended. Singles €30; doubles €45. AmEx/MC/V. ❸

Hostal San Mar, C. Rec Arnau, 31 (☎972 50 98 13). From the beginning of La Rambla, follow C. Girona and continue as it becomes C. Jonquera; take the 5th right onto C. Isabel II (the plaza with trees after Museu Dalí), then the 2nd left on C. Cadaqués. Follow to end of street. Clean rooms with bath and TV, but removed from city center in an area that is not well trafficked. Singles €17; doubles €34; triples €51; quads €68. Cash only. ❶

FOOD

The restaurants surrounding La Rambla on the small side streets tend to be of higher quality than those near the Teatre-Museu Dalí that serve *paella* to the masses. The extensive outdoor **market,** at Pl. del Gra, has an amazing fruit and vegetable selection. (Open Tu, Th, Sa 5am-2pm.) Another option is to buy groceries at **Bonpreu,** Pl. Sol. (☎972 51 00 19. Open M-Sa 9am-9pm. MC/V.)

Cafè Hotel París, La Rambla, 10 (☎972 50 07 13). This chic, thoroughly modern spot is a great deal if you opt for the combination plates (€8-14). Chicken with sesame salad (€8.70), salmon with ratatouille, and spaghetti with clams (€8.20). All natural and homemade, down to the coffee ice cubes for iced coffee. Desserts €3.10. By day, the outdoor patio's wicker chairs attract those seeking the breeze and a chat, while by night red leather chairs lend the establishment a low-key but sophisticated feel. Open daily 8am-midnight. MC/V. ❷

Restaurant Hotel Duran, C. Lasauca, 5 (☎972 50 12 50; www.hotelduran.com). Walk up La Rambla to the end and look for C. Lasauca on the left. One of Dalí's haunts; you can eat in the dining room—complete with arches and green chandeliers—where he once held court. Delicious *canelones* (cannelloni; €9.75). Most meat and seafood entrees €10.50-26. *Menú* €17. Open daily 12:45-4pm and 8:30-11pm. AmEx/MC/V. ❸

CATALUÑA

SIGHTS

TEATRE-MUSEU DALÍ. Welcome to the world of the definitive Surrealist master. This site, home of the self-proclaimed "largest surrealistic object in the world," held the municipal theater for the town of Figueres before it was destroyed at the end of the Spanish Civil War. Dalí's personal mausoleum/museum/monument is ego worship at its finest. Naughty cartoons, trippy sculptures, a dramatic, traditional tomb, and a pantheon of paintings of Gala, his wife and muse, immerse the audience in his world. The collection includes *Soft Self-Portrait with a Slice of Bacon*, *Poetry of America*, *Galarina*, *Meditating Rose*, and *Galatea of the Spheres*. A small number of hand-selected works by other artists, including El Greco, Marcel Duchamp, and architect Peres Piñero, round out the collection. The museum is large and takes at least an hour to see regardless of your chosen route. *(Pl. Gala i Salvador Dalí, 5. ☎972 67 75 00; www.salvador-dali.org. From La Rambla, take C. Sant Pere 3 blocks up. Or just follow the crowds and signs at every street corner. Open July-Sept. daily 9am-7:45pm; Oct.. and March-May Tu-Su*

9:30am-5:45pm; Nov.-Feb. 10:30am-7:45pm; June daily 9:30am-5:45pm. Last entry 30min. before close. €11, students and seniors €8, groups over 25 €7 per person, under 8 free.)

OTHER SIGHTS. Museu Empordà, La Rambla, 2, features works varying from archaeological objects of the region to medieval, Baroque, and contemporary Catalan art. Look for canvases by Modest Cuixart and Ramon Pujol Boira. Temporary exhibitions vary widely. "Un Art que Perviu" in 2008 showcased sculptures of the female body by a deceased Catalan artist, while in 2007 the exhibit "Recto-Verso" displayed the backs of famous canvases. *(☎972 50 23 05; www.museuemporda.org. Open Tu-Sa 11am-7pm, Su and holidays 11am-2pm. Free with entrance to Dalí Museum, temporary exhibitions always free. €2, students €1, under 18 and seniors free.)* Up the street, delight in the wonders of your favorite childhood toys at the **Museu del Joguet de Cataluña,** winner of Spain's 1999 National Prize of Popular Culture. *(Sant Pere, 1, off La Rambla. ☎972 50 45 85; www.mjc.cat. Open June-Sept. M-Sa 10am-7pm, Su 11am-6pm; Oct.-May Tu-Sa 10am-6pm, Su 11am-2pm. €5, students and under 12 €4.)*

NIGHTLIFE

A bit removed from touristy Rambla, **Plaça del Sol,** behind the tourist office, contains nearly all of the town's nightlife. **Cafè de Nit,** Pl. del Sol, n/a, offers pool in the back (€2 per game) and mixed drinks for €5.50. Crowd onto the terrace out front or enjoy your sweet *caipirinha* under the artistic lights inside. (☎972 50 12 25. Free Wi-Fi. Open daily 5pm-3am. Cash only.) The popular dance club **La Serradora,** Pl. del Sol, 6, features a disco ball, long twisting bar, and maze-like dance floor. (Open W-Su 11pm-3:30am. Cash only.)

CADAQUÉS AND PORT LLIGAT ☎972

Forty years ago, Cadaqués (pop. 2900) was a well-kept Catalan secret. Only a trickle of French tourists visited every summer, and the town had closer diplomatic relations with Cuba than with the rest of Cataluña. The distinctive variety of Catalan spoken here is a testament to the enduring individuality of this drop-dead gorgeous beach town. The whitewashed houses with terracotta roofs and the azure bay have attracted artists, writers, and musicians ever since Dalí built his summer home on the neighboring beach, Port Lligat, in the 1930s. From September to May, the town is best experienced as a daytrip, as many food and entertainment establishments close in the low season; however, keep in mind the limited transportation options for a same-day return.

TRANSPORTATION

Buses: Sarfa buses (☎972 25 87 13; ticket office open July-Aug. daily 7-8:30pm; Sept.-June opens 15min. before every departure) run to **Barcelona** (2hr.; July-Aug. 4-5 per day 7:45am-8:45pm; Sept.-June M-F 7am, 4pm, Sa-Su 7am, 7pm; €20), **Figueres** (1hr.; July-Aug. 7 per day 9am-8pm, Sept.-June 3 per day 7:15am-5pm, weekends 4 per day 8:25am-7:10pm; €4.50), and **Girona** (2hr.; July-Aug. daily 8:40am, 5:10pm; Sept.-June M-F 7am; €8.70). The **bus stop** is in the parking lot across from the ticket office. On your way there, stop at the indexed map on the wall to your right to orient yourself. Then head left past the ticket office and turn right onto Av. Caritat Serinyana; the waterfront Plaça Frederic Rahola (known to locals as Ses Herbes) is 4 blocks from this roundabout.

Taxis: Taxi Josep Giró (☎696 61 17 84) and **Olé Taxi** (☎626 52 68 32).

Bike Rental: Rent@Bit, Av. Caritat Serinyana, 9 (☎972 25 82 26; www.rentabit.net). Rents scooters and bikes for exploring the remote areas around Cadaqués. Open daily 9:30am-8pm. Bikes €20 per day, €75 per week; scooters €38 per day, €220 per week; hourly rates available. Internet access €0.50 per 5min., €4 per 1hr. MC/V.

Bikes & Boats Cadaqués, Pl. Dr. Trèmols, 8 in Platja es Portal (☎972 25 80 27) rents—you guessed it—bikes and boats. Electric bikes from €10 per 2hr., €25 per day, €142 per week. Simple boats from €115 per 4hr. (more complex are more expensive). Shop open Apr.-Sept. 9am-8pm; to rent in winter call ☎615 41 91 99. MC/V. Taxi services available, although many will not transport within the city center due to short distances.

PRACTICAL INFORMATION

Tourist Office: C. Cotxe, 2 (☎972 25 83 15). Off Pl. Frederic Rahola, on a small street running alongside the beach. They have an excellent *plànol turistic* as well as a listing of hotels and hostels. Open from late June to mid Sept. M-Sa 9am-9pm, Su 10am-1pm 5-8pm; from Sept. to mid-June M-Sa 10am-1pm and 3-6pm, Su 10am-1pm.

Bank: Banco Santander Central Hispano is at Av. Caritat Serinyana, 4 (☎972 25 83 62). Open M-F 8am-2pm. ATMs line the last few blocks of Av. Caritat Serinyana and the Passeig.

Police: C. Carles Rahola, 9 (☎972 15 93 43).

Medical Services: C. Nou, 6 (☎972 25 88 07).

Internet Access: Telecomunicaciones Cadaqués, Riera de Sant Vicenç, 4, a block off Pl. Frederic Rahola (☎972 25 92 48). €2.50 per hr. Open daily 9am-1pm and 3:30-11pm, closed W in low season. At **Casino,** Pl. Frederic Rahola, s/n, €2 per 30min., pay with coins. Open daily 7am-12:30am. Internet also available at **Rent@Bit** (see **Bike Rental**). **Hostal Cristina** offers free internet access to guests; €1 for 20min. for non-guests (see **Accommodations,** p. 417).

Post Office: On Av. Rierassa off Av. Caritat Serinyana, 2 blocks from the bus station (☎972 25 87 98). Open M-F 9am-2pm, Sa 9:30am-1pm. **Postal Code:** 17488.

ACCOMMODATIONS AND CAMPING

As Cadaqués is a beach town, many accommodations only open during the summer and often require reservations.

Hostal Cristina, Riera de Sant Vicenç (☎972 25 81 38). By the water, to the right of Av. Caritat Serinyana on the plaza. Cristina offers cheerful, renovated rooms with private baths. Rooms with plaza views also have A/C and TV. Reception 8am-10pm. Summer prices include breakfast. June-Sept. singles €40; doubles €66-76. Oct.-May. €35/56-66. Free internet for guests; otherwise, €1 for 20min. Dogs allowed. MC/V. ❹

Hostal Vehí, C. de l'Església, 6 (☎972 25 84 70). Across from the tall white church and a short walk from the water, amid narrow cobblestone streets and hanging ivy. Follow signs from bus stop or Pl. dr. Trémols. Breakfast €6. Reserve ahead. A/C and TV. Singles with shared bath €30; doubles with shared bath €35-45, with bath €45-90 (depending on season and view); triples with bath €75; quads with bath €80-100. AmEx/MC/V. ❸

Camping Cadaqués, Ctra. Port Lligat, 17 (☎972 25 81 26). 100m from the beach on the way to Dalí's house; follow the signs for Hotel Port Lligat. The campground is crowded, but it's clean and not far from the beach or the center of town. Showers with hot water, pool, restaurant, supermarket. Open Apr.-Sept. Reception 8am-10pm, quiet hours midnight-8am. €6.70 per person; €8.45 per tent; €6.80 per car. MC/V. ❶

FOOD

Cadaqués tourists (many of them French) expect only the best. Even seaside restaurants in the town serve respectable food, but you may find more interesting choices in the back streets. C. Miquel Rosset, off Pl. Frederic Rahola, has some great options for filling your cavity. **Valvi,** on Riera de Sant Vicenç, is only a block from Pl. Frederic Rahola. Groceries can be purchased here for beachside picnics, which are always a good idea. (☎972 25 86 33. Open June-Sept.

MUSE OF A MASTER

While Dalí's presence still permeates the landscape of Cadaques years after his death, tourists rarely pay homage to a lesser known name—yet her face has grown famous, thanks to the artist she loved.

Gala, Dalí's muse and wife, lived with him for a time in their coastal home of Port Lligat, known now as the Casa-Museu Salvador Dalí. His model and manager, Gala lives on eternally through some of her husband's most famous pieces, including La Galarina and Galatea of the Spheres. While Port Lligat seemed like the setting for a fairy tale, however, the Dalís' relationship was far from simple. Gala met Salvador in 1929 while traveling with her first husband, Paul Éluard. When Dalí admitted he adored Gala, who was ten years his elder, she divorced Éluard and they married. While Dalí often commented on the perfection of Gala's body, their relationship was said to lack physical intimacy. In fact, Gala and her first husband allegedly continued to sleep together after she re-married—which allegedly did not bother Dalí. The Dalís spent time apart in the summer, when Gala lived alone in a castle Dalí had bought for her in Púbol; her passion for young artists lead to numerous extramarital affairs before she died in 1982. Still, she remained the guiding light of his work, and to this day, there is a small boat in Port Lligat that Dalí named in Gala's honor.

M-Sa 8:30am-9pm, Su 9am-2pm; Oct.-May M-Sa 8:30am-3pm and 4-8:15pm, Su and holidays closed in the evening. MC/V.)

Canshelabi, C. Riera, 9 (☎972 25 89 00). Like its name, this restaurant is a fusion of Cataluña and Morocco ("can" is "house" in Catalan, "Shelabi" is the owner's Moroccan nickname). *Tajine* (couscous stew with beef or chicken cooked in a ceramic pot; €13.50-16) is the house specialty. Stop by in the afternoons to enjoy the sweet mint tea and vibrant decor. Entrees €11-17; fixed *menú* (€13.50) includes appetizer, entree, drink, and dessert or coffee. Open daily 11am-2am. MC/V. ❸

Algianni, C. Riera s/n (☎972 25 83 71). The owner has been preparing the freshest food by hand for 15 years. A terrace with climbing greenery invites diners to enjoy pastas with shellfish, colorful risottos, and fresh fish. Entrees €7-11, meat and fish €11.50-17.50. Open in summer daily 1:30-4pm and 7:30pm-2am; in winter M and W-Su, 7pm-2am. MC/V. ❸

SIGHTS

Església de Santa María, the defining feature of the Cadaqués landscape, is a small 16th-century Gothic church featuring an enormous Baroque altar with 365 carved faces. Listen for the organist, who practices in the afternoons from his special elevated cabin. (Open during mass, Sa 8pm and Su 10:30am.) Two blocks up, down cobblestone stairs and to the right, the **Museu de Cadaqués,** C. d'en Narcis Monturiol, 15, displays rotating exhibits that are usually centered on Dalí. (☎972 25 88 77. Open July-Sept. daily 10am-8pm, except Su closed 1:30-3pm; Oct.-June M-Sa 10:30am-1:30pm and 4-7pm. €4, in summer can rise to €6.) From the museum, it's a pleasant walk (20min.) to **Casa-Museu Salvador Dalí,** in Port Lligat, the house where Dalí and his wife Gala lived until her death in 1982. Follow the signs at C. Miranda or take the trolley that leaves from Pl. Frederic Rahola for the scenic 10km route to Port Lligat. (1hr.; 6 per day 11am-6pm; €7, children €5; the trolley also offers 1 ride per day to Cap de Creus, the farthest point on the peninsula: 2hr.; leaves at noon; €14, children €10.) The house is actually seven fishermen's houses that Dalí bought and transformed one by one. While lacking in original Dalí paintings, the house is overflowing with esoteric trinkets like a stuffed bear and lip-shaped sofas. The pool—inspired by the Alhambra—is inexplicably guarded by a plastic Michelin Man. (☎972 25 10 15. Open from mid-June to mid-Sept. daily 9:30am-9pm, last entry 8:10pm; mid-Sept. to Jan. and from mid-Mar. to mid-June Tu-Su 10:30am-6pm, last tour 5:10pm.

Visits are supervised and space is limited: call 4-5 days in advance to reserve. €10, students and seniors €8, under 9 free.) **Boat rides** in Dalí's own *Gala* depart from the dock in front of the house on the hour for a 55min. trip to Cap de Creus. (☎617 46 57 57. Open daily 10am-8pm, depending on weather. Min. 2 people. €10, children €5.)

NIGHTLIFE

Nightlife in Cadaqués is vibrant in summer but limited to weekends in winter, and focused on C. Miguel Rosset, off Pl. Frederic Rahola. A local and international crowd of all ages heads to **Café Tropical,** C. Miguel Rosset, 19, for mouthwatering mojitos and dancing in a jungle-like atmosphere—plants hang from the ceiling, and the terrace roof is made of tree branches. (☎972 25 88 01. Open M-Th and Su 10:30pm-2:30am, F-Sa 10:30pm-3am. Beer €4. Mixed drinks €8. MC/V.) Also popular is the **L'Hostal,** at the Passeig, 8, right by the plaza, with a Dalí-designed logo and delicious tequila sunrises (€10). 36 years of candle burning have created the massive wax statues adorning the bar, and live music is featured daily in summer (midnight-2am), ranging from rumba to rock. (☎972 25 80 00. Open May-Dec. daily 5pm-5am; Jan.-Apr. F-Sa 5pm-5am. Cash only.)

OUTDOOR ACTIVITIES

Diving Center Cadaqués, C. de la Miranda (☎652 31 77 97; www.divingccadaques.com, info@divingccadaques.com), offers 45min. dives at 9 and 11am for €30 (including tank, air, and weights). Certain routes depend on wind direction and weather: call for information on special offers. Reservations suggested. The first weekend in September brings dozens of old-fashioned sailboats to the harbor for the renowned **Trobada de Barques de Vela Llatina.** On the weekend before September 11, the **Festa Major d'Estiu** fills the streets with *sardanas*, *fútbol*, dances, concerts, and more. December 18 brings more of the same at the **Festa Major d'Hivern.** From late June through August, the **Festival Internacional de Música de Cadaqués** attracts big-name international classical musicians.

INLAND CATALUNYA

LÉRIDA (LLEIDA) ☎973

Lleida (pop. 130,000) lives in the constant presence of history; trendy boutiques are framed by old churches and palaces, and well-kept parks and plazas compete with the fashion retail frenzy of C. Major. Founded in the sixth century BC by the Llergete tribe, Lleida's strategic location has produced a legacy defined by struggle. The city was destroyed by Germanic tribes in the third century but, by the 15th century, had recovered enough to produce great architectural works. In the 16th and 17th centuries, unrest returned with Catalan peasant uprisings, then with Napoleon's invasion in the early 1800s. The Spanish Civil War nearly leveled it again, but Lleida is currently undergoing a cultural renovation, with new galleries, a new theater, and a modern art center set to open in 2012. Catalan roots are deep: do not expect to find many menus in *castellano*. The area is not heavily touristed, and streets tend to be deserted at night.

TRANSPORTATION

RENFE trains, Pl. Berenguer IV (☎902 24 02 02). **Trains** to: **Barcelona** (3hr., 9 per day 6:14am-9:14pm, €11-21); **Tarragona** (1½hr., 3 per day 6:14, 8:03am, 4:51pm,

€12.20-16.40); **Zaragoza** (2hr., 5 per day 8:57am-12:15am, €12-21). **AVE** or **Altaria high-speed trains** run to: **Barcelona** (1½hr., 8 per day 9:40am-9:40pm, €42); **Calatayud** (1hr., 4 per day 9:05am-9:05pm, €37); **Guadalajara** (2hr., 4 per day 7:05am-7:05pm, €61); **Madrid** (2½hr., 9 per day 7:05am-9:05pm, €71-106); **Zaragoza** (1hr., 9 per day 7:05am-11:05pm, €25.30). **Central Bus Station** (☎973 26 85 00; open daily 6am-10pm), on Av. Catalunya half a block up from the river, sends buses to: **Andorra** (2-3hr., 4 per day 9:30am-7:30pm, €17); **Barcelona** (2hr.; M-F 5 per day 6am-7:30pm, Sa-Su 3 per day starting at 6:30am; €17.50); **Girona** (3hr.; M-F 3 per day 6:15am-5:30pm, Sa-Su 2 per day after 8:30am; €18.15); Tarragona (2hr.; M-F 6 per day 7:30am-9pm, Sa-Su 9:30am, 9:15pm; €5); **Zaragoza** (2hr.; M-F 5 per day 8am-6pm, Sa 4 per day, Su only 6pm; €9.48). Yellow **city buses** (☎973 27 29 99; www.autobusoslleida.com) run throughout the city; the tourist office has a map/schedule. For a taxi, call **Radio Taxi** (☎973 20 30 50).

ORIENTATION

There is a **map** posted on C. Cardenal Remolins (to the right of the traffic circle in front of the train station) to help you navigate to the main tourist office. Bordered by the **Río Segre,** Lleida sprawls up the hill toward Seu Vella, the imposing cathedral. **Rambla de Ferran,** the wide street that heads straight out from the train station, runs parallel to the river and changes its name every few blocks, becoming Av. de Francesc Macià/Av. de Blondel/Av. de Madrid. **Carrer Major,** the main, pedestrian commercial street, runs parallel to Ferran, one block inland. The city center stretches from Av. de Madrid/Blondel/Francesc to Rambla d'Aragó, and is bordered on the west by Av. de Catalunya and on the east by Seu Vella massif. Tourism centers on **Plaça Sant Joan,** at the end of C. Major, with several hostels and cafes right at the foot of the stairs to the cathedral. From the **bus station,** take Av. de Blondel to C. Cavallers, go one block away from the river (to your left), and you'll be on C. Major; alternatively, go four blocks straight from the train station (starting on C. Cardenal Remolins, which becomes C. Sant Joan).

PRACTICAL INFORMATION

Lleida has two **tourist offices.** The main one is at C. Major, 31, three blocks past Pl. Sant Joan coming from the train station. Make sure to get a free map and the very useful *Guía de Turismo*, with information on museums and festivals. (☎902 25 00 50; www.turismedelleida.com. English spoken. Open M-Sa 10am-2pm and 4-7pm, Su and holidays 10am-1:30pm.) The Catalunya tourist office outpost in front of the train station (Pl. Berenguer) has both local and regional information. Banks with 24hr. **ATMs** line Rambla de Ferran and C. Major. Other services include: **police,** Gran Passeig de Ronda, 52 (☎088); **Arnan de Vilanova Hospital,** Av. de l'Alcalde Rovira Roure, 80 (☎973 24 81 00); **Internet** access at **Cafetó Internet,** C. del Bonaire, 8 (☎973 72 51 48; €2 per hr.; open M-Sa 9am-2pm and 4pm-midnight, Su 4pm-midnight), and at the public **library,** Rambla d'Aragó, 10 (☎973 27 90 70; http://cultura.gencat.net/bpl; drop by to reserve up to 1hr.; open M-F 10am-8pm, Sa 10am-2pm); and the **post office,** Rambla de Ferran, 16, four blocks toward town from the train station. (☎976 24 87 20. Open M-F 8:30am-8:30pm, Sa 9:30am-2pm.) **Postal Codes:** 25001-25007.

ACCOMMODATIONS AND FOOD

Most budget accommodations double as student housing, so term-time (Oct.-June) space is limited. **Hostal Mundial ❷,** Pl. Sant Joan, 4, has rooms with abundant floor space, shower or bath, sink, and desk. The best rooms have balconies overlooking the plaza. (☎973 24 27 00. Breakfast €2. M-F *menú* €9.

Free Wi-Fi. Singles with bath or shower €20; doubles with bath and TV €34. AmEx/MC/V.) Lleida's local specialty is *caragoles* (snails), and the city consumes over 12 slimy tons of them each year, most notably during their popular food festival, the **Aplec del Caragol.** Held after the Festival Mayor, usually the third weekend in May (F-Su night), the festival features **feasting** and **snail races** in the Parque dels Camps Elisis. The tourist office has a list of restaurants that serve snail-based dishes—some of the more popular ones include snails cooked on a *llauna* (metal sheet), served with *allioli* (mayonnaise and garlic), *a la vinagreta* (cooked with veggies on a stone tile), and *a la gormanta* (fried with seasonings). For those who would rather chop off a finger than eat a snail, the area surrounding C. del Bonaire Av. de l'Alcalde Rovira and Pl. de Ricard Vinyes has the majority of Lleida's restaurants. The area east of Seu Vella has several establishments serving African cuisine. Across from the bus station on Av. de Catalunya, the supermarket **Esclat** meets all your grocery needs.

SIGHTS

SEU VELLA. Perched atop the hill above the city, **Seu Vella,** nicknamed *el castillo* by *leridanos* because of its fortress-like appearance, was used as a military barracks until 1948. For a historical and architectural account of the 14th-century cathedral and cloister, get the audio tour for €1. The long climb up to the **bell tower** is worth each of the steep 238 steps; two of the seven bells are Gothic originals from the 15th century, and the view is incomparable. To reach the cathedral, ride the escalator up from Pl. Sant Joan, then the elevator (€0.20 each way), or take the path and stairs to the left of it. *(☎973 23 06 53. Open Tu-Su June-Sept. 10am-1:30pm and 4-7:30pm; Oct.-May 10am-1:30pm and 3-5:30pm. Bell tower closes 30min. before the rest of complex. Guided tours in Spanish July 15-Sept. 15 Sa-Su noon; brochures available in English. €3, students and ages 6-19 €2, under 6, over 65, and teachers free. Tu free.)* You can still reach several beautiful churches without climbing the hill, most notably the 19th-century **Església de Sant Joan** in Pl. Sant Joan and the 18th-century **Catedral Nova,** in the Pl. de la Catedral at the end of C. Major.

CENTRE D'ART DE LA PANERA. The new Centre d'Art de la Panera, Pl. de la Panera, 2, was created in the 13th-century market building and houses rotating temporary exhibitions of edgy contemporary and mixed-media art. It will be the site of Lleida's modern art complex, scheduled for completion in 2012. *(It's easy to get lost finding the Panera: from Plaza Sant Joan, walk down C. Mayor with the river on your left, make a right on C. Cavallers, another right at C. Universitat, a left on C. Sant Martí, and the 2nd left. Panera is the grey building with the staircase. Exhibits on both floors. ☎973 26 21 85. Open in summer Tu-F 10am-2pm and 4-8pm, Sa 11am-2pm and 4-8pm, Su 11am-2pm; winter Tu-F 10am-2pm and 5-8pm, Sa 11am-2pm and 5-8pm, Su 11am-2pm. Free tours Sa at noon, 6pm, Su at noon, or by appointment. Generally in Catalan, but English can be arranged. Free.)*

MUSEU D'ART JAUME MORERA. In a temporary space until it joins the Panera complex in 2012, the Museu d'Art Jaume Morera houses a rotating display of 19th- and 20th-century work: painting, sculpture, and photography, with works by Morera himself. *(2 exhibit spaces; enter at Avda. Blondel, 40, or at C. Mayor, 31, 2nd fl. ☎973 70 04 19. Open Tu-Sa 11am-2pm and 5-8pm, Su 11am-2pm. Free.)*

THE PYRENEES

Nowhere in Spain is the wear of time more marked than along the sprawling stretch of the Pyrenees. Throughout the region, antique cobbled towns rest quietly among steep, snow-capped mountains and gently eroded green valleys. Vast nature preserves welcome travelers fleeing the throngs of tourists and manic pace of nearby Pamplona, San Sebastián, and Barcelona. In many of the hills and valleys, Catalan is spoken more frequently than Spanish. The French portion of the Camino de Santiago crosses into Spain at Roncesvalles, and pilgrims on their way to Santiago de Compostela in Galicia rest in mountainside refugios. A calm, tempered pace governs life throughout the day, leaving ample time to take in the splendor of the surroundings. For those seeking adventure, vast national parks teeming with natural beauty beg to be explored, and the dramatic landscape provides endless opportunities for excursions and adventure sports of all kinds. During the summer, the mountain air and breezes offer welcome respite from Spain's sweltering heat, and come winter, skiers of all kinds fill world-class ski resorts in the high mountains of Aragón and Cataluña. Early June to late September is the best time for trekking—any earlier and avalanches are a potential danger, and any later the harsh Pyrenean winter sets in. The Pyrenees are best explored by car, as public transportation is as common as the area's endangered bears. If you must resort to public transportation, be aware that train and bus schedules can be quite erratic.

HIGHLIGHTS OF THE PYRENEES

RAFT down **La Seu d'Urgell's** Olympic park rapids (p. 439).

TRIPLE your fun by skiing in three countries at **Puigcerdà** (p. 429).

VISIT the Monasterio de San Juan de la Pena, hidden near Jaca (p. 444).

ROUGH IT in the glorious **Parque Nacional de Ordesa** on the French border (p. 447).

CATALAN PYRENEES

While beachgoers and city-lovers flock to Barcelona and the Costa Brava, Cataluña's Pyrenees draw a different breed of traveler. Bikinis are tossed aside for wool socks, as hikers and skiers, mostly from Spain and France, migrate to the region's refined ski resorts, with some of Spain's wildest mountain scenery. Meanwhile, history and architecture buffs, notebooks in hand, eagerly explore the tranquil mountain towns filled with well-preserved Romanesque buildings and bridges. Unless you happen upon some of the few visiting teachers brought into the region, do not expect to hear much English around here. Foreign tourists can be extremely rare in some parts, and Spanish is a second language for many locals. Nonetheless, do not let this deter you. The grandeur of this mountain sanctuary should not be missed.

RIPOLL ☎972

About two hours by train from Barcelona, Ripoll (pop. over 10,800) marks the beginning of Pyrenean escape, where carefully preserved, thousand-year-

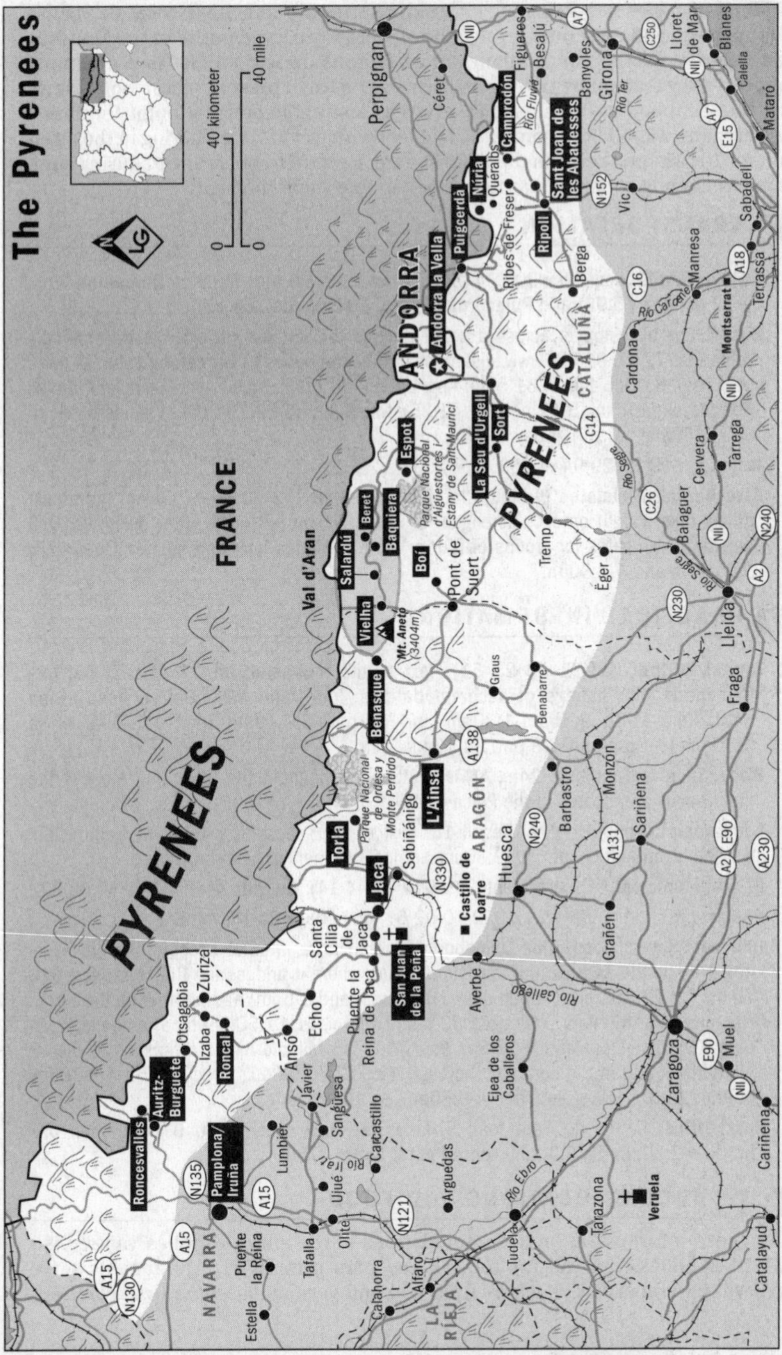

The Pyrenees

old monasteries nestle among chic ski resorts. Ripoll is a guardian of Spain's Romanesque architectural legacy; the elaborately carved portal of the Monestir de Santa María is one of Spain's most famous doorways. Set in a charming green valley framed by two rivers, this serene town present picturesque views of snow-capped mountains and serves as a suitable starting point for alpine excursions. Ripoll holds onto its local feel with townfolk gathering in the afternoons to chat and relax in the main square. Be sure to book ahead during summer weekends, when *catalaneses* flock in to escape the heat.

TRANSPORTATION

Trains: RENFE, Progres (☎902 24 02 02; www.renfe.es) runs trains to **Barcelona** (2hr., 9-12 per day, €5.90) and **Puigcerdà** (1.5hr., 7-12 per day, €3.15).

Buses: The bus stop is across a small park to the left as you exit the train station. **Teisa** (☎972 26 01 96; www.teisa-bus.com) sends buses to **Barcelona** (1hr. 35 min.; M-F 7am, Su Oct. 1-Mar. 31 5pm; Apr. 1-Sept. 30 6pm; €7.50) and Sant Joan de les Abadesses (15min., 8-12 per day, €1.25). **Mir S.A.** (☎972 70 30 12) sends buses to Ribes (30min., 4-15 per day, €1.60).

Taxis: (☎609 33 29 94 or 659 43 74 30).

Bike Rental: Bicicletes Pirineu, Ctra. Ribes, 11B (☎972 70 36 30). From the tourist office, take a right onto C. Berenguer El Vell and then left on to Ctra. De Ribes. €10 per day, lower rates for groups of four or more. Includes lock and helmet. Open daily 9am-1pm and 4-8:30pm.

PRACTICAL INFORMATION

Tourist Office: (☎972 70 23 51) Next to the monastery on Pl. Abat Oliba, has free maps with listings of accommodations, food, and essential services. Open Sept.-June M-Sa 9:30am-1:30pm and 4-7pm, Su 10am-2pm; July-Aug. M-Sa 9:30am-1:30pm and 4-8 pm, Su 10am-2pm.

Bank: There are multiple 24hr. **ATMs** scattered throughout the town, and most of the main banks are located in the Plaça Gran.

Laundromat: Limpid, Pg. el Regull 10, next to the gas station. Open M 5-8pm, Tu-F 9:30am-1pm and 5-8pm, Sa 9:30am-1pm; €3.65 per kg, next-day pickup.

Police: Municipal, Pl. Ajuntament, 3 (☎972 71 44 14); **Guardia Civil** (☎972 70 00 82).

Pharmacy: Pl. St. Eudald 2 (☎972 70 02 61; open daily 9am-10pm).

Internet: Several **locutorios** (telephone centers) have internet access: one on Pg. el Regull 2, on the right side of the Pont l'Arquer where it bridges the Riu Fresser (☎972 70 42 70; €1.50 per hr.; open daily 10am-2pm and 3-5pm) and another on the tiny C. Llupions, near the Pont D'Olot (€1.80 per hr. mornings, €1.50 per hr. afternoons; open daily 10:30am-2pm and 4-10pm). Free Wi-Fi is available in the civic zone in the Pl. Ajuntament and in the library C. Vinyes, 6. (☎972 70 07 11; open M-Tu,Th 4-8:30pm, W 9am-2pm, F 10am-2pm and 4-8:30pm, Sa 10am-2pm.)

Post Office: C. Pg. de Sant Joan 5, faces the park. (☎972 70 07 60; open M-F 8:30am-2:30pm, Sa 9:30am-1pm.) **Postal Code:** 17500.

ACCOMMODATIONS AND FOOD

For more information on accommodations in the entire Ripolles valley, visit www.elripolles.com. As for food, many bars around Pl. Ajuntament serve everyday Catalan fare, such as fried cod and various *boccatas* (sandwiches).

Pick up groceries at **Condis** on C. Progrés, 33-37, across from the bus station. (☎972 70 31 69. Open M-Sa 9am-9pm, Su 10am-3pm. AmEx/MC/V.)

Habitaciones Paula: C. Pirineus, 6, on Pl. Abat Oliba (☎972 70 00 11). Just past the tourist office. All rooms have an adjoining bathroom and shower, as well as a small TV. Doubles €42.80; triples €59.92. MC/V. ❹

Hostal del Ripolles: Pl.Nova, 11 (☎972 70 02 15). Rooms with TV and private baths overlooking Pl. Nova. The restaurant downstairs, **La Plazetta** provides some of the best food in town (past dishes and pizza €7-12), but can be fairly noisy for the rooms on the first floor until around midnight. Restaurant open M-Th 1-3:15pm and 8-10pm, F 1-3:15pm and 8-11pm, Sa 1:30-3:15pm and 8-11pm. MC/V. Breakfast included. Singles €36; doubles €26.75 per person; triples €23.75 per person. AmEx/MC/V. ❸

Bar El Punt: Pl. Civica 10, right across from the monastery, also offers hamburgers and pizza (€5-7). Locals take their afternoon coffee there, but there are menus in several languages to accommodate travelers. ❷

SIGHTS

Most visitors to Ripoll come to see the intricate 12th-century portal of the **Monasterio de Santa María.** Founded in AD 880 by Count Guifré el Pelós (Wilfred the Hairy), the Santa María monastery was once one of the most important cultural centers in all of medieval Europe. The curved doorway, nicknamed the "Stone Bible," depicts scenes from the Old and New Testaments as well as a hierarchy of the Christian universe. The portal leads to the **church** that contains the tomb of the Count and several other important figures from the monastery's past. Adjoining the church is a peaceful two-story Romanesque and Gothic **cloister,** built between the 12th and 16th centuries. Take a left on C. Progrés toward town from the train and bus stations, following it to the Pont d'Olot on the left, cross the river, then continue straight on C. Bisbe Morgades to Pl. Ajuntament and Pl. Abat Oliba. (Church open daily 10am-1pm and 3-7pm. €3, students €2. Free information in English available at the nearby tourist information office.) Check out the **Scriptorium** on the Raval de L'Hospital, which houses an exhibit of the daily works of the scrivening monks who once lived in the town. Ripoll also has some great **hiking** and **biking** options that start right inside town. Ask the tourist information office for the green *El Nostre Entorn* brochure that has a map and information about all trails in the area.

DAYTRIPS FROM RIPOLL

CAMPRODON

Camprodon is accessible by Teisa bus (☎972 74 71 81) from Ripoll (35min.; M-F 12 per day 8:15am-9:15pm, Sa-Su 7 per day 9:05am-9:05pm; return M-F 14 per day 7am-8pm, Sa-Su 7 per day 8:15am-7:55pm; €2.80.) Be aware that these times are approximate, as bus schedules tend to change monthly.

In friendly Camprodon (pop. 2500), narrow streets meander around a 12th-century monastery, **Monestir de Sant Pere,** and the picturesque Pont Nou, a bridge constructed in the Romanesque style. There is a small **museum** dedicated to renowned Spanish musician Isaac Albéniz, who was born in Camprodon. (C. Sant Roc, 22, near the Pont Nou. ☎972 74 11 66. Open M, W-F 11am-2pm and 4-7pm, Sa-Su 11am-2pm, Closed Tu. €2.40, Students €1.50. €1.50 per person in groups larger than 20.) During July and Aug., the town hosts the **Isaac Albéniz music festival,** which features local musicians in classical and jazz concerts. For well-priced pizza or sandwiches (€5-7) and a welcoming atmosphere, try **Bar Canigo** ❷, in the Pl. del Carme 16B, the first plaza off C. Catalunya on the way to the tourist office (open 9am-12am). **Cook Robin ❸**, on the Pl. Dr. Robert, serves up brick-oven pizza. (☎972 74 04 49. Pizzas €8-12.) The **Vall de Camprodon** is a pastoral paradise for outdoor lovers of all kinds. The **tourist office** offers a comprehensive selection of maps detailing the hiking routes throughout the region. There are also many mountain biking trails in the valley; **bike rental** is available at **Esports VIVAC,** Ctra. C-38, across from the tourist office along the highway at the entrance to the town. (☎972 13 04 26. Open M-F 10am-1pm and 5-8pm, Sa 10am-2pm and 4:30-8:30pm, Su 10am-2pm and 4:30-7pm. Half-day €10, full-day €15.) **Bastiments Aventura,** located at C. San Antoni, 13, provides outdoor options like archery, climbing, and snowboarding. (☎972 74 08 71; www.bastimentsaventura.com.) Find **skiing** information at ☎972 13 60 57.

A twenty minute walk outside of the city (following the highway towards Llanars and the ski resort Vallter 2000), **L'hipic Hotel ❹** is reminiscent of a Western dude ranch, offering horseback excursions into the local mountains. In the hotel's restaurant, you can enjoy a three-course meal for €17. (☎639 36 19 78, www.lhipichotel.com. Double €45 per night; triple or quad €70 per night. Offers horseback excursions. 1-4 hr. €20-60, full day €90.) There are two tourist offices in Camprodon. The **regional office** for the Vall de Camprodon area is located by the highway at the entrance to town nearest Ripoll, in the middle of a traffic rotary. The staff offers extensive information on outdoor activities for the entire valley. (☎972 74 09 36. Open Tu-Sa 10am-2pm and 4-7pm, Su 10am-2pm.) The second office in Camprodon is located in the Pl. D'Espanya. From the bus station, follow the C. Catalunya straight to the the Pl. D'Espanya; the **tourist office** is located in the building with the ornate cast iron grates over the windows. (☎972 74 00 10. Open T-Sa 10am-2pm and 4-7pm, Su 10am-2pm.) Free Wi-Fi in the civic zone in the Pl. D'Espanya.

VALLE DE NÚRIA ☎972

Tucked in a high-altitude valley surrounded by mountain peaks and mist, Núria attracts tourists from both sides of the Pyrenees. Legend has it that around AD 700, Sant Gil lived in the **Valle de Núria,** preaching the gospel to mountain shepherds. Before he left to avoid the persecution of a Gothic king, he carefully hid several items that would become hallmark symbols of the valley: the bell he used to call the shepherds, the pot in which he kept his dinner, his cross, and a wooden statue he had carved, known as the Virgen de Núria. The remote sanctuary has become a full-blown ski resort and summer hiking base, the church and hermitage now overshadowed by restaurants and hordes of tourists.

TRANSPORTATION AND PRACTICAL INFORMATION. **RENFE** trains run to Ribes from **Puigcerdà** (90min.; 6 per day 5:49am-6:13pm, return 9:16am-9:16pm) and **Ripoll** (20min.; 7 per day 8:55am-8:53pm, return 7:24am-7:48pm; €2.40). **Mir** buses also run to Ribes from Ripoll (30min.; M-Sa 10 per day 7:45am-7:55pm, Su 4 per day 9:10am-4:10pm, return M-Sa 16 per day 7:25am-6:45pm, Su 4 per day 9:45am-4:45pm). Be sure to check both bus and train schedules, as they change frequently. **Taxis** can be reached at ☎616 64 48 84. Núria is accessible only by foot or by the rail known as the **Cremallera,** or "Zipper," which starts in Ribes de Freser and stops in Queralbs. The 40min. ride up the mountainside costs a hefty €19.50 (round-trip) from Ribes, but the awe-inspiring cliffside ride and pastoral valley above are worth the price. (Open high season and weekends 8:30am-5:40pm, return 8:30am-6:30pm; low season, M-F 7 per day 7:30am-5:40pm, return 8:30am-6:30pm, €16.30. Includes cable car ride at the top.) The Cremallera station in Ribes is next to the train station. To get to the center of town, pass behind the Cremallera station and follow C. Pedrera, which becomes C. St. Quinti. As the road crosses the river, veer right into the

Pl. Ajuntament (about 60m). The Ribes **tourist office,** with info on accommodations, transportation, and local sights, is to the left. (☎972 72 77 28. Open Tu-Sa 10am-2pm and 5-8pm, Su 10am-1pm; July and Aug. 10am-2pm and 5-8pm.) Local services in Ribes include: **police** (☎627 41 75 35); **medical services** at **Centro Assisténcia Primaria** (☎970 72 77 09). **Internet** access is at Televall, C. Major 26, about one block from the tourist office past the church. (€3 per hr. Open M-Sa 10am-2pm and 4-8pm, Su 10am-2pm.) The **post office** is on C. St. Quinti between the train station and tourist office. (☎902 19 71 97. Open M-F 8:30am-2:30pm, Sa 9:30am-1pm.) **Postal Code:** 17534.

ACCOMMODATIONS. Núria itself has few accommodations. Families and individuals are welcome at the **Albergue Pic de l'Áliga (HI) ❶,** reached by a 20min. walk up the hill from the upper Cremallera station, or by a free cable car ride. (☎972 73 20 48. Reception 9am-1pm and 5-8pm. 4- to 18-bed dorms €16.55-22.25, over 26 €20.25-24.30. All rooms with shower and bathroom. Non HI members €2 extra. Breakfast included. Closed Nov. AmEx/MC/V.) Also offers a snack bar and a broad veranda for those passing through. Limited **camping ❶** is available behind the sanctuary complex. (☎972 73 20 30. €2.10 per person, per day, per tent, per night. Register at the reservations desk inside the main building before pitching your tent. Advance reservations accepted.) One of the best budget options for food on weekends is **Finestrelles ❶,** which serves delicious sandwiches for under €5. (Open Sa-Su 8:30am-6pm.) Dish up your own cafeteria fare at the **Autoservei ❷,** under the hotel restaurant. (Open daily 1-3:30pm; €6-10, three-course meal €14.)

OUTDOOR ACTIVITIES. The intrepid lot who choose not to take the Cremellera can hike up to Núria from **Queralbs,** which is accessible by car, or from Ribes via the Cremallera train. The 3hr. hike is somewhat difficult, with a 731m elevation gain, but those who brave it will be rewarded with dazzling vistas and refreshing waterfalls. The Núria **tourist office** (information desk), located in the lobby of the hotel in the main sanctuary complex, gives out basic hiking information and sells a map (€2.50) with descriptions of over 40 hiking routes in the valley of all difficulty levels. (☎972 73 20 20; www.valldenuria.cat. Open daily 8:30am-5:45pm.) During winter, full **ski equipment rental** is available toward the back of the tourist office in the main building. (☎972 73 20 30. As of June 2008, ski rental €16.55, children €13.55. Snowboard €24.95; all with boots per day. Snowshoes €7.00. Prices subject to go up.) On weekends in the winter, ski passes cost €17.50; €27.50 includes Cremallera ticket; winter weekdays, €14.70/€22.60. Lockers are available down the stairs opposite the tourist office, next to Finestrelles. Obtain the key at the information desk. (€4 for 24 hr. with €5 key deposit.) Ski rental is also available at **Ski & Mountain,** next to Condis on C. Pedrera. (☎972 72 73 39, www.skimountain.net. Full ski equipment €17, snowboard €26, snowshoes €8, crampons €5.) Also sells a variety of outdoor and hiking equipment. **Condis Supermarket** is a few minutes walk from the train station on the way into town on C. Pedrera. (M-Th 9am-1:30pm 4:30pm-8:30pm, F-Sa 9am-9pm, Su 9am-2pm)

PUIGCERDÀ ☎972

Puigcerdá (pooh-chair-DAH; pop. 7000) lies in a broad valley surrounded by flourishing wheat fields and mountains decorated in snow. By bus or by train, the ride to Puigcerdà boasts some of the most awe-inspiring views in the Pyrenees. Puigcerdà's location along both the French and Andorran borders also makes it a cheap base for hiking, biking, or skiing in three different countries.

TRANSPORTATION

Trains: RENFE (☎972 88 01 65; www.renfe.es) sends trains to **Barcelona** (3hr.; 6 per day 5:49 am-6:13pm) and Ripoll (2hr., 6 per day 8:55am-8:53pm, €3.15).

Buses: Alsina Graells (☎973 35 00 20) sends buses to **Barcelona** via **Lleida** (3hr.; M-F 5:15am and 1:15pm, Sat 7:26am and Su 4:11pm; €15) and **La Seu d'Urgell** (1hr.; M-F 5 per day 7:30am-5:30pm, Sa-Su 9:15am, 12:15, 7pm; €5.30). **Teisa** buses (☎972 20 02 75) run to **Girona** (3½hr.; M-F 6:05am, return at 4:15pm). Buses leave from Pl. Barcelona and then stop outside the train station; buy tickets onboard. Schedules are at Bar Estació, in the station and in Pl. Barcelona.

Taxis: (☎972 88 00 11). Can be found on Pl. Cabrinetty.

ORIENTATION AND PRACTICAL INFORMATION

Puigcerdà's center is at the top of the hill. The train station is at the foot of the western slope. Buses stop at the train station and then Pl. Barcelona; get off at the second stop if you wish to arrive within the town itself. To reach Plaça Ajuntament from the **train station,** walk past the stairs in the station's plaça until you reach the first flight of stairs between two buildings. To save your legs, take the free **cable car,** which leaves from a station about 50m straight in front of the train station (runs 5:30 am-12am, July and Aug. 5:30am-1am). At the top, take the elevator (in front of the station and to the left), up to level 2, the Pl. Ajuntament. From the plaça, walk one block on C. Alfons I to **Carrer Major.** Turn left on C. Major to Pl. Santa María. Reach Pl. Barcelona through the Pl. dels Herois, the end of Pl. Santa María farthest from the bell tower. If you are traveling outside of the month of August, note that most services and stores shut down on M (and Su, as in much of Spain).

Tourist Offices: C. Querol, 1 (☎972 88 05 42 or 14 15 22). Off Pl. Ajuntament, ahead and to the right as you step off the elevator. English, Spanish, and French are spoken. Open Tu-Sa 10am-1pm and 4-7pm. Regional Comarcal tourist office (☎972 14 06 65) on the junction of the N-152 and N-160, about a 10min. walk down the highway towards Barcelona from the train station. Turn right as you exit the station. Walk this route with caution, especially during times of heavy traffic, as parts of the road have no sidewalk. Open M-Sa 9am-1pm and 4-7pm, Su 10am-1pm.

Bank: Banco Santander Central Hispano, on Pl. Cabrinetty, 15, has a 24hr. **ATM** (open M-F 8:30am-2pm, Sa 8:30am-1pm); other ATMs throughout the city.

Police: Municipal police on Pl. Ajuntament, 1 (☎972 88 19 72).

Hospital: Hospital de Puigcerdà in Pl. Santa María (☎972 88 01 50/54), behind the bell tower.

Library: Pg. 10 d'Ábril, 2 (☎972 88 03 04). Next to Eglésia de Sant Domènech, around the back of the building. Free **Internet** access, and lots of helpful tourist info. Open M, W, F 3:30-8:30pm, Tu 10am-1:30pm and 3:30-8:30, Th 10am-1:30pm.

Internet Access: Locutorio Corami, Pl. Cabrinetty, 10 (☎972 14 16 72). Open daily 10:30am-1pm and 5-10:30pm; €2 per hr.

Post Office: Av. Coronel Molera, 11, 1 block down from Pl. Barcelona. (☎972 88 08 14; open M-F 8:30am-2:30pm, Sa 9:30am-1pm.) **Postal Code:** 17520.

ACCOMMODATIONS

Many *pensiones* can be found around Pl. Santa María in the old town.

Hostal Cerdanya: C. Ramon Cosp, 7 (☎972 88 00 10). Has basic rooms with all the essentials, including a small TV. Friendly owner. Singles €19-34. Cash only. ❷

THE PYRENEES

Hotel Alfonso: C. D'Espanya, 5 (☎972 88 02 46.). Main advantage is its location in the streets below Pl. Santa Maria. Singles €25; doubles €45; triples €60. Cash only. ❷

Mare de Déu de les Neu: Ctra. de Font Canaleta (☎934 83 83 63 for reservations). Not too far from the RENFE station and the slopes, and offers discounted dorms for patrons under 25 (€16.45-20.35), as well as dorms for those over 25 (€20.25-24.30). ❶

Camping Stel: (☎972 88 23 61). 2km from Puigcerdà on the road to Llivia, offers full-service camping with a chalet-style restaurant, bar, and lounge, as well as a supermarket. €5.50 per person, site with tent €11.50, with car €22.30. Open daily June 1- Sept. 28, weekends only during ski season. MC/V. ❶

FOOD

Buy cheap produce at the weekly farmer's **market** at Pl. 10 d'Ábril. (Open Su 6am-2pm.) Or grab groceries at **Bonpreu,** Av. Coronel Molera, 12, diagonally across from the post office. (Open M-Sa 9am-9pm, Su 10am-2:30pm. MC/V.)

Central, Pl. Santa Maria, 6 (☎972 88 25 53). Serves a great selection of tapas and pizzas. Free Wi-Fi. Entrees €8. Open daily 10am-2:30am. MC/V. ❷

El Pati de la Tieta, C. Ferrers, 20 (☎972 88 01 56). Rustic and secluded. A good restaurant to visit with your special someone. Serves delicious fresh homemade pasta (€10-12) and pizzas (€8-12) within thick stone walls or out on their ivy-covered patio. Fish and meat entrees €15-22. 1pm-4:30pm, 8pm-midnight. MC/V. ❸

Kennedy Restaurant, Pl. Herois 2. Exemplifies the lingering Spanish affinity for the former American President. Offers large portions and an attentive waitstaff. Entrees €8-17, Kennedy Rib of Beef €29.50. ❸

SIGHTS AND SLOPES

Just above the Pl. Barcelona (follow the C. Pons Gash) the lake and the **Parc Schierbeck** offer a bit of calm respite, as swans glide over reflections of the snow-covered mountains. **Cercle Aventura** offers a formidable list of outdoor activities in the summer and winter. (☎902 17 05 93; www.cercleaventure.com. Open daily 9am-2pm and 4-8pm. Canyoneering €45-55. Rock climbing €65. Paintball €30. Canoe Rental €30. Snowshoe rental €10. Bike rental €10 half-day, €16 full day.) **Ski** in your country of choice (Spain, France, or Andorra) at one of 19 ski areas within a 50km radius. The closest on the Spanish side is **Alp 2500,** a conglomerate of **La Molina** (☎972 89 20 31, ski school 978 89 21 57; www.lamolina.cat) and nearby **Masella** (☎972 14 40 00; www.masella.com), which offers the longest run in the eastern Pyrenees. For cross-country skiing, a close site is **Guils-Fontanera** (☎972 19 70 47; www.guils.com/esqui). Also try **Lles** (☎973 29 30 49) or **Aránsa** (☎973 29 30 51). In the spring and summer, the Puigcerdà area is also popular for **biking;** the tourist office has a map detailing several routes. The town of **Llívia,** a Spanish enclave surrounded by France, can make for a pleasant pastoral afternoon excursion. Some travelers also stop by **Rigolisa** on the way back for a view of the wheat fields at sunset. **Sports Iris,** Av. de França, 16, rents bikes and skis. (☎972 88 23 98. Open 9:30am-2pm, 4pm-8pm daily. Bike rental €15 half day, €20 full day.) For horseback riding, call **Hípica Sant Marc** (C. de Sant Marc; ☎972 88 00 07). Try piloting or ballooning at **Globus de Pirineu** (☎972 14 08 52; www.globospi.com) or **Cerdanya Globus** (☎609 83 29 74; www.osonaglobus.com). Other adventure sports such as 4X4 and motorbike rental can be arranged with La Molina or Alp 2500 Viatges (☎972 89 20 29) and at **Turing Cerdanya,** Escoles Pies 19 (☎972 88 06 02; www.turingcerdanya.com).

PARC NACIONAL D'AIGÜESTORTES I ESTANY DE SANT MAURICI

Cataluña has only one national park, and its snow-capped peaks and lush valleys merit a visit at some point in your itinerary. The **Estany de Sant Maurici,** the park's largest lake, in the east and the winding cascades of the **Ribera de Sant Nicolau** in the west have earned the park the nickname *"Aigües Tortes"* (Twisted Waters). With more than 200 glacial lakes and over 102,300 acres to explore, the park and its surrounding protected reserves deserve at least two days on your itinerary. Be sure to bring warm clothes and appropriate trekking gear. Winters are long in the higher altitudes, and even some of the lowest passes can be snowbound until mid-June—seriously.

ORIENTATION AND PRACTICAL INFORMATION

The two main gateway towns to the park are **Boí** to the west and **Espot** to the east. To drive from Boí, take the main highway (L-500) north for about 2km, then turn right in to the park. The public **taxi** service (office ☎973 69 63 14) runs from the main plaza in Boí to the last information booth 6km past the official park entrance. (20min.; office open daily July 1-Sept. 15 8am-1pm and 3-7pm. In winter call for service. Taxis leave when there are groups of four or more and arrangements are made for return service. One-way €4.40.) From the Espot side, drive up the main road that goes through Espot to the park entrance (50min. hike to Estany de Sant Maurici) or take a **jeep taxi** into the park, leaving from the plaza next to the park office. (☎973 62 41 05; www.taxisespot.com. Taxis run July-Sept. 15 9am-8pm; June 9am-6pm. Call for service in winter.) Espot taxis go to: **Estany de Sant Maurici** (20min., €4.85); Estany de Ratera (40min., €14.80); Estany d'Amitges (50min., €19.50); **Estany Negre** (1hr., €21.50). There is a four-person minimum.

ACCOMMODATIONS

Since camping is not permitted within park borders, *refugios* (mountain cabins with bunks, a kitchen, and bathrooms) are the only option for wilderness adventurers planning to stay more than one day. Mattresses are provided, but make sure to bring your own sheets or a sleeping bag. Reserve several days (or months for July-Aug.) in advance for a spot. Note that not all *refugios* are open year-round; check their status with the park office. Hot showers generally cost about €2 for 5min. Contact the Central de Refugios for more info. (☎902 73 41 64; www.lacentralderefugis.com.)

INSIDE THE PARK

Refugio de Ernest Mallafré (refuge ☎973 25 01 18, in winter 973 25 01 05), a 15min. walk from the information point near the Estany de Sant Maurici. One of the more popular *refugios* because of its proximity to the lake. Be prepared to squeeze in. 28-person capacity. Offers pillows, blankets, toilets, showers. Breakfast €6.20, lunch or dinner €17. €13.50 per night. Cash only. ❶

Refugio d'Amitges (refuge ☎973 25 01 09, in winter 973 25 00 07; www.amitges.com), near Estany de Amitges, just over 1hr. away from Estany St. Maurici trailhead. 74-person capacity. Offers blankets, WiFi, public telephone, showers. Breakfast €6, lunch or dinner €15.50. €13.50 per night. V. ❶

Refugio de Josep María Blanc (☎973 25 01 08, in winter 934 23 23 45; www.jmblanc.com), recently renovated, near Estany Tort de Peguera. 60-person capacity. Breakfast €6, lunch or dinner €16. €14 per night. V. ❶

Refugio de Estany Llong (☎973 29 95 45, 629 37 46 52), next to Estany Llong, a 45min. walk from the park taxi stop on the Boí side. Spacious *refugio* with 47-person capacity. Breakfast €4.80, lunch or dinner €13.50. Lunch available from 2-4pm. Open June 1-Oct. 15. €6.70 per night. Cash only. ❶

Refugio de Ventosa i Calvell (refuge ☎973 29 70 90), in winter 973 64 18 09; www.refugiventosa.com), in the northern portion of the park on the Boí side, next to Estany Negre de Boí. 70-person capacity. Breakfast €6, lunch or dinner €16. €14. ❶

OUTSIDE THE PARK

These *refugios* are in the areas surrounding the national park. Though not officially part of the park, they are still somewhat-protected natural reserves.

Refugio de Colomers (refuge ☎973 25 30 08, in winter 973 64 05 92, www.refugiocolomers.com), on the north side of the park by Lac Major de Colomers. 40-person capacity. No showers. Breakfast €6, lunch or dinner €16. €13.50 per night. ❶

Refugio dera Restanca (☎608 03 65 59; www.restanca.com), north of Refugio de Ventosa i Calvell next to Lac dera Restanca. 80-person capacity. €13.50 per night. Breakfast €6, lunch or dinner €16. ❶

Refugio de Saboredo (refuge ☎973 25 30 15, in winter 665 28 98 96 www.refugisaboredo.com), north of Refugio d'Amitges across the Serra de Crabes. 21-person capacity. €13.50 per night. Breakfast €6, lunch or dinner €16. ❶

Refugio de Colomina (refuge ☎973 25 20 00, in winter 973 68 10 42; www.colomina.casacota.net), south of the park, near the Estany de Mar 50-person capacity. €13.50 per night. Breakfast €6.20, lunch or dinner €17. ❶

Refugio del Gerdar (☎973 25 01 70, in winter 973 60 74 40 50; www.refugigerdar.com), located to the north of the park. 25-person capacity. With breakfast €19, with breakfast and dinner €29.50. ❶

FREE REFUGIOS (OUTSIDE THE PARK)

These *refugios* are unguarded, unattended, and free throughout the year. Check with the park office before you leave to make sure they're open.

Refugio Gerber "Mataró," above the Estany Gerber. It can be reached in about 3hr. from C-28. 16-person capacity. ❶

Refugio Besiberri, just northeast of Besiberri Nord. It can be reached in about 2hr. from N-230 at La Contesa, 2km south of the Vielha tunnel. 16-person capacity. ❶

HIKING

Free maps from the park information offices in Espot and Boí list well-defined itineraries, but explorers may want to drop the extra cash to buy the more detailed *Editorial Alpina* map (€10) or the topographical survey (€8). For more detailed hiking info, contact the park **tourist offices** (Espot ☎973 62 40 36, Boí ☎973 69 61 89). Check trail conditions and weather with a park office before heading out, as both are subject to significant and immediate change.

BOÍ SIDE (ALTA RIBAGORZA/VALLE DE ARÁN)

El Valle de Dellui (4-5hr., moderate difficulty). A more difficult trail to Estany Llong. Beautiful hike among alpine meadows and glacial lakes. For the best views of both sides of the park, climb the 450m. up to the pass of Portarró de Espot (2424m). From the Portarró pass, a side trail leads up the Pic del Portarró (2736m), with a 360° panorama (3hr. from parking lot, moderate difficulty due to elevation gain).

Ruta de la Nutria (1¾hr., low difficulty). Leaves from the main public parking lot and park taxi stop, heading along the Ribera de Sant Nicolau and its waterfalls to the last information booth at the Aigüestortes, passing Estany de Llebreta on the way.

Camino de Estany Llong (45min., low difficulty). Heads from Aigüestortes to Estany Llong and its *refugio.*

ESPOT SIDE (PALLARS SOBIRÁ/PALLARS JUSSÁ)

Hike across the park (5hr., moderate difficulty due to length and elevation gain). From Estany de Sant Maurici to Aigüestortes. A good day's hike, leading over the Portarró. Stunning views on both sides of the park; make sure to reserve a bed for the night at the Refugio de Mallafré or Refugio de Estany Llong, depending on your direction.

Ruta del Isard (1¼hr., low difficulty). Well-traveled trail leads from the last parking lot before the park entrance to the Estany de Sant Maurici. A pleasant hike through flowery meadows and evergreen forests.

El Mirador del Estany de Sant Maurici (2½hr., low difficulty). Circular route with great view of the lake and valley. Runs around the lake to the Cascada de Ratera (waterfall) and the Estany de Ratera before looping back. To get to the **Estany de Amitges** and the popular **Refugio d'Amitges** (Ruta #3; 1hr., 45 min., low difficulty to Estany de Ratera, moderate difficulty continuing on to Amitges), start at the Estany de Sant Maurici and continue up the trail past Estany de Ratera. **The Portarró de Espot** (2hr., 30 min. moderate difficulty due to elevation gain) is accessible from Estany de Sant Maurici.

Carros De Foc (Chariots of Fire) trail is a famous multi-day, circular route through the whole park. Stops at all the park's *refugios* along the way. Reserve beds in advance. (Trail open mid-June to late Sept. Visit www.carrosdefoc.com for more information.)

ESPOT ☎973

The gateway to the eastern half of the park and the best point of entrance coming from Barcelona, the tiny town of Espot is comprised mostly of rustic restaurants and quiet accommodations for the weary hiker. Espot also boasts the Torre dels Moros, a medieval defense tower. Those with cars can park at the last parking lot, just outside the park entrance. The hike up to Estany Sant Maurici takes around 50-60 mins.

TRANSPORTATION AND PRACTICAL INFORMATION. Buses stop within 7km of Espot, on highway C-13 at the La Torrassa crossing. The nearest stop from La Seu d'Urgell is at **La Guingueta d'Aneu** (via Sort), about 9km from Espot, with service to **Barcelona** (5hr.; July 1-Sept. 15 1:44pm, Sept. 16-June 30 2:34pm; €26) and **Lleida** (3hr., M-F 5:33am and 2:34 pm, Sa 5:33am). From La Guingueta you can either walk to Espot (2hr.) or call the jeep service. (☎973 62 41 05 or 62 41 32. €10-12 to Espot. €20 if returning to the stop for the 5:33 am bus to Lleida.) The extremely helpful **park information** office (on the right as you enter Espot) provides brochures on accommodations around Espot, itineraries, maps, and trekking advice. (☎973 62 40 36. Open June-Sept. daily 9am-1pm and 3:30-7pm; Oct.-Apr. M-Sa 9am-2pm and 3:30-6pm.) The local **bank,** with 24hr. **ATM,** is **La Caixa,** next to the park office. (Open M-F 11am-2pm.) The **police** can be reached at ☎088; **firemen** ☎085. There is a **supermarket** just past the bank on your way into town past the tourist office.

ACCOMMODATIONS AND FOOD. **Casa Peret de Peretó ❶** and **Camping Solau ❷** run a joint establishment, offering sunny rooms with private baths. Solau also features 22 campsites. From the center of town, walk uphill; follow the sign at the arched stone bridge. (☎973 62 40 68. Singles €17.50; doubles €35; Aug. add €7; kitchen add €4; campsites €4.75 per person, per tent, and per car. Cash only.) **Residència Casa de Pagés Felip ❷** has comfortable rooms and private baths. From the park office, follow the main road for two blocks and then take a left; the residencia is up the hill behind Hotel Roya. (☎973 62 40 93. Laundry available. Singles, doubles, and triples €20 per person. Breakfast €6). Located 1km down the park entrance road on the right, **Camping Vora Parc ❶** offers the closest camping to the park, with secluded campsites along the riverbank and a swimming pool. (☎973 62 41 05; www.voraparc.com. Electricity €4.25. Reception open daily 8am-11pm. €5.15 per person, tent, and car. Children 5-14 €4.75, under 5 free. MC/V.) For fresh food made from local ingredients, try **Grill L'Avet de St. Maurici ❷**, near the Hotel Saurat. (☎973 62 41 62; www.hotelsaurat.com. *Menú del dia* with appetizer, main course, dessert, and bottle of wine €15. Sandwiches and burgers €3-6. Open daily 1-11pm, closed Oct. MC/V.) Gourmet diners will appreciate **Restaurant Juquim ❷**, on Pl. Sant Marti, which serves *jabalí* (warthog) and shepherd's egg soup on a €17 *menú del día* that includes plenty of wine and a dessert. (☎973 62 40 09. Entrees €8-12. Sandwiches €3-6. Open daily 1pm-4:30pm; in winter closed Su. MC/V.)

BOÍ ☎973

Despite the nearby ski resort in **Taüll,** tiny Boí hasn't lost its country charm. The village's cobblestone streets wind their way through low arches and plazas, and the town's Romanesque church has been awarded UNESCO World Heritage Site status. Boí is the most convenient base for exploring the western half of the park, and its main road is full of stores and accommodations.

TRANSPORTATION AND PRACTICAL INFORMATION. Public transportation from the east to Boí is inconvenient but possible. From **Vielha,** take the bus (M-F 1pm) to Boí via Pont de Suert (1hr., returns to Vielha between 8:30-9am, €4.21). Taxis run from Boí to the park and other nearby towns. (☎973 69 63 14 or ☎629 20 54 89, www.taxisvalldeboi.com to Aigüestortes €4.85, to Pont de Suert €23.) The **Casa del Parc de Boí,** Ca de Simamet, is on C. de les Graieres 2. (☎973 69 61 89; www.parcsdecatalunya.net. Open daily June-Sept. 9am-1pm and 3:30-6:45pm; Oct.-May 9am-2pm and 3:30-6pm.) Call the **Mossos d'Esquadra** (*català* police) at ☎973 69 08 15 (in Pont de Suert); emergencies ☎088.

ACCOMMODATIONS AND FOOD. Green RCPs (Residèncias Casa de Pagés) indicate local residences offering lodging for travelers. **Casa Rural Marco ❶**, on C. de les Graieres s/n (on same street as the Casa del Parc de Boí) has four rooms and shared bathrooms. (☎973 69 61 61; www.ribagorcarural.com. Singles €15. Doubles €30. Cash only.) **Hostal Fondevila ❷**, to the right of the main road through Boí, has well-kept rooms with baths and plenty of social space. (☎973 69 60 11. Breakfast €5. Dinner €12. Reception 8am-midnight. Wheelchair-accessible. Singles €25; doubles €45; triples €65. MC/V.) **Camping Taüll ❶**, is uphill 4km on the main road just before Taüll. (☎973 69 61 74; www.campingtaull.com Reception daily 9am-2pm and 5-8pm. Electricity €6.50. €5.50 per person, per car, and per tent; €4.90 per child. Bungalows for 2 people €65; 4-5 people €80; 6 people €135; 8 people €145; all with private bathrooms and kitchen, some with shower. In Aug. min. stay 5 nights; closed Oct. 15-Nov. 15.) **Restaurante Pey**

❷, Pl. Treijo, 3, has tasty entrees like roasted chicken. (☎973 69 60 36. *Menú* with bottle of wine €13. Open daily 1-4pm and 8-10pm. AmEx/MC/V.)

VAL D'ARAN

Roughly translated as "valley of the valley," the Val d'Aran is anything but redundant. Cut off from the rest of Spain by some of the Pyrenees' highest mountains, the verdant Val D'Aran has a rich history of self-government and cultural independence, notable especially within a region as autonomous as Cataluña. Today it contains some of the best skiing in Spain, as well as a multitude of other outdoor activities during the rest of the year. Bear in mind that the Val D'Aran's high season is the ski season, so don't be surprised to find signs reading *"cerrado por vacaciones"* ("closed for vacation") filling the windows of restaurants and accomodations throughout the summer months.

VIELHA ☎973

The capital and biggest town of Val d'Aran, Vielha (pop. 4500) demonstrates just how small and remote this *val* truly is. Whether you sit to relax in its small old quarter or stroll down its main thoroughfares, Vielha feels more like a small ski resort town than a regional capitol.

TRANSPORTATION AND PRACTICAL INFORMATION. **Alsina Graells** (Lleida office ☎973 27 14 70) runs buses from Vielha to **Barcelona** (6hr.; M-F 4:12am, 5:30am, 1:30pm, Sa 5:30am and 1:30pm, Su 5:59am and 1:30pm; €28-33) via **Lleida** (3hr.); **Baqueira** via **Salardú** (20-30min.; 9-13 daily 8:10am-8:30pm, return 5-13 daily 7:55am-9:40pm; all intercity shuttles within Val D'Aran €0.90.) To get to Boi you must go through Pont de Suert. For a **taxi,** call ☎973 64 01 95. The **tourist office,** C. Sarriulèra, 10, is one block upriver from Pl. de Gléisa and gives out free maps and pamphlets, including hiking and biking maps for the entire valley. (☎973 64 01 10; www.torismearan.org. Open daily 9am-9pm.) **ATMs** pepper the main thoroughfare, Av. Castièro. Local services include: a drop-off **laundromat, Jonerik Elurra,** in the Complejo Elurra commercial building, a 10min. walk down Av. Pas d'Arró towards Baqueira, on the left (☎973 64 09 54; €13.90 for up to 4kg; open M-Sa 8am-8pm); **Mossos d'Esquadra** (local police; ☎973 35 72 85) and **Guardia Civil** (☎973 64 00 05); **Farmàcia Palá,** C. de Sentin, 2, across the river from Pl. de Gléisa one street down on the left before the traffic rotary (☎973 64 25 85; open daily 9am-9pm); **Hospital Val d'Aran** (☎973 64 00 06); **internet** access at **Biblioteca Generau de Vielha,** Av. Garona, 33, on the left side of the Riu Garona facing Baqueira, inside the gigantic Palai de Geu (☎973 64 07 68; 30min. free, €0.50 every 15min. thereafter; open M, W, F 3-9pm, Tu and Th 9am-3pm, Sa 5-9pm); the **post office,** C. Sarriuléra, 6, by the tourist office (☎973 64 09 12; open M-F 8:30am-2:30pm, Sa 9:30am-1pm). **Postal Code:** 25530.

ACCOMMODATIONS AND FOOD. Several inexpensive *pensiones* fill the end of C. Reiau, off Pg. Libertat. One option is the **Pensión Casa Vicenta ❷**, C. Reiau, 3. (☎973 64 08 19; casavincenta@teleline.es. Closed parts of the off-season, so call ahead. Breakfast €12. High-season singles €31; doubles €49; triples €76. Low-season singles €21; doubles €37; triples €48. Cash only.) **Eth Breç ❶**, Av. Castièro, 5, beneath Hotel d'Aran, serves incredible, filling pastries (€1-3) and teas (€1.50) and has free internet access. (☎973 64 00 50. Open daily 8:30am-1:30pm and 4-8:30pm. MC/V.) You can find breakfast and dessert all day at **Restaurant Era Placa ❷**, as well as a selection of pizzas (€6-8) and entrees

(€8-10). Those with a true sweet tooth should try their fresh *churros* served with thick hot chocolate (€3.75). Snag some groceries at **Bona Compra Supermarket,** C. Major 10 or **Pas d'Arro,** 46, on the road towards Baqueira. (Open daily 9:30am-1:30pm and 4:30-8:30pm. MC/V.)

SIGHTS AND OUTDOOR ACTIVITIES. Vielha welcomes many hikers and skiers to its lively streets. In Pl. d'Era Gléisa, the **Gléisa de Sant Miquéu de Vielha,** a simple 12th- to 13th-century Romanesque church facing the tourist office, contains the famous carved statue Crist de Mijaran. (Open daily 11am-8pm.) The **Muséu dera Val d'Aran,** C. Mayor, 26, explains the Aranese culture and language. (☎973 64 18 15. Open Tu-Sa 10am-1pm and 5-8pm, Su 11am-2pm. €2, students €1.) **Camins del Pirineu,** Av. Pas d'Arró, 5, is a great place to go for organized outdoor activities. The staff leads hikes and multi-day treks into the nearby mountains, including the Parc Nacional Aigüestortes i Estany Sant Maurici (€20-26 for a full-day hike) as well as rafting, horseback-riding, canyoning, and paragliding trips. They also rent mountain bikes (half day €15, full day €22). Ask about the Turismo Activo combinations (€100-140), which include hiking, rafting, and horseback riding. (☎973 64 24 44; www.camins.net.) **Palai De Geu,** Av. Garona 33, has a swimming pool, sauna, and sizable ice skating rink. (☎973 64 28 64. Ice rink open M-F 5:30-8:45pm, Sa 4:30-9pm, Su noon-2pm and 4:30-8pm. €6.40, skate rental €4. Pool and sauna open M-F 8:30am-9:30pm, Sa 11am-2pm and 4:30-9pm, Su 11am-2pm and 4:30-8pm. €6.20. MC/V.)

BAQUEIRA-BERET AND SALARDÚ ☎973

Baqueira-Beret is Spain's most fashionable ski resort and a favorite of the Spanish royal family. Currently, about 80 alpine trails and a few cross-country ones wind down the peaks at four different *estaciones*. For skiing info and reservations, contact the office of **Baqueira-Beret.** (☎973 63 90 00; www.baqueira.es. €42 per day for over 2000 hectares of mountain terrain, including the most off-trail terrain in the Pyrenees.) While in this part of the Val, don't miss the recently restored 16th-century murals on the ceiling of Salardú's 13th-century **Església de Sant Andreu,** just off the C. Sant Andreu. During the summer and the skiing off-season, Baqueira-Beret is mostly shut down.

While Baqueira and Beret themselves don't have much in the way of budget accommodations, a few reasonably priced options can be found along the streets of picturesque Salardú, just 4km down the highway from Baqueira. **The Auberja Era Garona (HI) ❶,** Ctra. de Vielha, is a 5min. walk up the highway from the bus stop in Salardú towards Baqueira. The enormous Auberja has plenty of dorm rooms and boasts a gigantic patio and a game room/discoteca. (☎973 64 52 71; www.eragarona.com. Breakfast included. Private bath €6. Laundry €4.50. Internet €3 per hr. Reception 8am-11:30pm. Door locked at midnight, but opened every hour on the hour. €15.15-24.30 per person, under 25 €13.80-26.30. MC/V.) The rooms of **Pensión Montanha ❷,** C. Major, 8, amplify the area's rustic setting with wooden beds. (☎973 64 41 08. Doubles €28-45; triples €35-51. Breakfast available at the bar/restaurant downstairs for about €4. Cash only.)

Salardú's **tourist info office** is uphill from the bus stop on and to the right on C. des Estudis. (☎973 64 01 10. Open M-Sa 9am-2pm. Closed June-July 3.) If arriving by public bus, take the stairs next to Refugi Rosta to get to the main plaça, on C. Major. Both Baqueira and Salardú have 24hr. **ATMs** scattered throughout town. Salardú has a **pharmacy,** C. Major, 4 (open M and W-F 11:30am-2pm). For **medical emergencies,** call ☎973 64 00 46. Wi-Fi available at the public library tucked up on the street behind the Auberja. (☎973 64 55 32. Open M-T, Th-F 4:30-7:30pm and W 11am-2pm.)

SORT

The town of Sort (pop. 2000), tucked away in the heart of the Catalan Pyrenees, is a mecca for lovers of whitewater rafting and canyoning. Sort's relative accessibility makes it a practical gateway to the nearby Parc Nacional d'Aigüestortes i Estany de Sant Maurici in the summer and to various ski resorts in winter.

TRANSPORTATION AND PRACTICAL INFORMATION. To get to La Seu d'Urgell, reserve a spot on the shuttle (☎689 49 57 77 for the morning bus or 610 47 71 57 for the afternoon bus; leaves Sort at 8am and 5:30 pm, returns leaving La Seu d'Urgell at 10:30 and 7:30). **Alsina Graells** buses leave **Barcelona** for Sort. (4-5hr.; 7:30am year-round. Return July-Sept. 15 2:10pm, Sept. 16-June 3pm.) Another way to get to the Parc Nacional d'Aigüestortes i Estany de Sant Maurici is the Alsina Graells bus towards Esterri d'Aneu. Get off at the turnoff to Espot, at the La Crossarra gas station (M-F 12:11, 2:51 pm, also 7:10 pm in summer). From there, you can call a jeep taxi (☎973 62 41 05; 9am-6pm, €10).

Buses to Sort deliver travelers to the bus station at the junction between Av. de la Verge Montserrat and Av. Comtes del Pallars. Both feed into Av. de la Generalitat, which follows the river. Most shops and services are on Av. de Pallars or Generalitat, some on the C. Major. The town's **tourist office** is in a new building across from the police station on the Cami de la Cabanera. From the bus stop, follow C. del Profesor Fassman which becomes Av. de la Disputacio, which then becomes Cami de la Cabanera. (☎973 62 10 02. Open July-Sept. 5 M-Sa 9am-3pm, 4pm-7pm; rest of year M-Th 9am-3pm). Other services include **emergency medical care** (☎973 62 01 63; emergencies to the fire department ☎085); **police,** Mossos d'Esquadra (☎088). There are several 24hr. **ATMs** throughout town. The **post office** is at the corner of C. del Doctor Muxi i Monroset and Av. de la Disputacio, across from the Hotel Pessets. (☎973 62 02 41. Open M-F 8:30am-2:30pm, Sa 9:10am-1pm.) **Postal Code:** 25560.

ACCOMMODATIONS AND FOOD. Sort's popularity can make cheap lodging hard to come by, so reserve well in advance for weekends in June and during July and August. Certainly check for inexpensive rooms at the **Can Josep** ❷, Ctr. La Seu d'Urgell, 12, a friendly *residencia* across the river from town on the road to La Seu. Rooms include bathroom and shower. (☎973 62 01 76. Breakfast included. High-season singles €29, doubles €52, triples €61; low-season singles €26; doubles €45; triples €55. MC/V.) Another option is **Hospedatge Les Collades** ❸, C. Major, 5, which has new hotel-style rooms with adjoining bathrooms. (☎973 62 11 80. Full-board double €40. MC/V.) Camping is available at **Noguera Pallaresa** ❶, with wooden furniture and grassy sites on Av. de la Generalitat on the way out of town, but reservations are highly recommended (☎973 62 08 20; info@noguera_pallaresa.com, €5.15 per person/car/tent, discounts in the low season.) Sort is home to a string of bars and cafes along Av. del Pallars. **Restaurante Les Brases** ❸, Av. Generalitat, 27, offers Catalan entrees (€8-19, *menú* €15-19) in an elegant and family friendly environment. (☎973 62 10 71. Open daily 7-10:30am, 1-4pm, and 8-11pm.) If you prefer to prepare your own meals, there is a **supermarket** at C. Major, 15, **Can Kiko** (open M-Sa 10am-2pm and 5-9pm), as well as several other small markets throughout town.

OUTDOOR ACTIVITIES. Sort's gushing river is regulated for optimal rafting conditions, and numerous companies offer excursions on its waters. **Alta Ruta,** Av. de la Pallars, 15, leads guided rafting, climbing, canyoning, horseback riding, and mountain biking trips. (☎973 62 08 09; www.altaruta.com. Rafting €20-69 depending on length. Canyoning €32-60. Package excursions with rafting, hiking, and horseback trek from €57.) **Rafting Sort,** C. Disputacio, 14, offers canoe, kayak, and rafting excursions (€35-60) as well as a 3-day kayak course for €70. (☎973 62 02 20; www.rubber-river.com. Open daily 9am-2pm and 5pm-8pm.) The company also has rustic lodging just outside of Sort at **Hotel Florido ❹**, Pl. Carles Dulcet (☎973 62 02 37; www.hotelflorido.com. High-season singles €58, doubles €44, triples €42 per person; low-season €46/38/35) A popular nearby ski resort is **Port Ainé**, accessible by taxi from the Rialp bus stop (10min. from Sort). It features 44km of trails and €31 per day lift passes (☎973 62 03 25, reservations ☎902 19 01 92; www.port-aine.com. Trails open Dec.-Apr.) Backcountry and cross-country skiers can find a mix of steep and flat trails at **Tavascan**, accessible from the Llavorsí bus stop. A ski pass costs €20, or €12 for children. (☎973 62 30 79, ski school/activities ☎902 45 78 94. Trails open Dec.-Mar.)

LA SEU D'URGELL ☎973

La Seu (pop. 12,200), a peaceful town on a Pyrenean plain between two rivers, was an important political center in the Middle Ages and still retains its religious significance today. More recently, it hosted the 1992 Summer Olympics canoe and kayak events. La Seu also serves as Spain's gateway to the tiny country of Andorra, just a few kilometers to the north. Budget accommodations, a relaxed atmosphere, and a very pleasant series of parks make this a good place to rest between excursions throughout the region.

TRANSPORTATION. The **bus station** (☎973 35 00 20) is located on Av. de J. Garriga i Massó at the end of town nearest to Andorra, about 400m from the town center. To get to the main plaza from the bus station, walk left down Av. de J. Garriga i Massó until you come to the traffic rotary at the intersection with Av. de Pau Claris, where both become C. De Sant Ot. Continue two blocks to the main plaza, Pl. de Catalunya. (Bus information desk open M-F 9am-1pm and 3-7pm, Sa 9am-12:15pm and 3-7pm, Su 3-7pm.) **Buses** run to: **Andorra la Vella** (40min.; M-Sa hourly 7am-8pm, Su 5 per day 7:45am-6:30pm; €2.65 on Hispano Andorra); **Barcelona** (3hr., 1 per day, upwards of €20); **Puigcerdà** (1hr., M-F 7:30, 9:15am, 12:15, and 7pm; Sa-Su 9:15am, 12:15, and 7pm; €5.60.) A shuttle runs to **Sort** (1hr., 10:30am and 7:30pm, €3.20; call in advance to reserve, morning van ☎689 49 57 77, afternoon van ☎610 47 71 57).

ORIENTATION AND PRACTICAL INFORMATION. The main road in La Seu is **Avinguda de Pau Claris**, which runs north to the highway toward Andorra and becomes C. de Sant Ot to the south, leading to the main plaza **Passeig de Joan Brudieu** and to Parc Olímpic del Segre. The historic district is to the left of Av. de Pau Claris facing the Passeig, the new center of town. The main **tourist office**, Av. de les Valls d'Andorra, 33, is inconveniently located at the very edge of town, just before the start of the highway to Andorra; ask your bus driver to drop you off here so you don't have to backtrack uphill from the bus station. From the center of town, head up Av. de Pau Claris, veering left at the fork onto Av. de les Valls d'Andorra. (☎973 35 15 11; www.turismeseu.com for info on accommodations and outdoor activities. Open July-Aug. M-F 9am-8pm, Sa 10am-2pm, 4-8pm, Su 10am-2pm; Sept.-June M-Sa 10am-2pm and 4-6pm.) More convenient (but less helpful) guidance is available at the **Oficina Comarcal de Tourisme**, Pg. Joan Brudieu, 15 (☎ 973 35 31 12. Wheelchair accessible. Open M-F 10am-2pm and 5-8pm, Sa 11am-2pm and 5-8pm.) They also have **Internet** access downstairs (first 15min. free, €0.40 every 30min. thereafter, €0.30 for students). Local services include: **banks** and 24hr. **ATMs** lining C. de Sant Ot; municipal police (emergencies ☎010 or 092; non-emergencies ☎973 35 04 26); **Mossos d'Esquadra** (emergencies ☎088, non-emergencies 973 36 00 73); and the **hospital**

on C. de Sant Ot, beyond the Pg. Brudieu (☎973 35 00 50). Find inexpensive **Internet** access at the civic **Telecentre de l'Alt Urgell** on C. Capdevila, 29, just off Av. J. Garriga i Masso. (Open M-F 9am-2pm and 5pm-8pm, Sa 10am-2pm.) Purchase a host of regional maps at **Llibreria i Papereria Ex Libris** on C. St. Josep de Calassanc, 8 just off of C. de Sant Ot. (Open daily 9am-2pm and 5pm-8pm.) The **post office** is on C. de Josep Zulueta at Av. del Salória. (☎973 35 07 24. Open M-F 8:30am-2:30pm, Sa 9:30am-1pm.) **Postal Code:** 25700.

ACCOMMODATIONS. The **Alberg de la Seu d'Urgell (HI)** ❶ (also known as La Valira) at C. Joaquim Viola, 57, has a beautiful tree-bound location in a residential area on the edge of town with well kept dorms, a cafeteria, and a game room in the basement. Head toward town from the bus station on Av. de J. Garriga Massó, and take a right at the traffic rotary. (☎973 35 38 97. High season €19.25, over 26 €21.90; low season €15.40/17.90. . Lunch and dinner available €5.90/€7, €2 extra for non HI members. Cash only.) Conveniently located in the town center is **Alberg Centre Residencial i de Serveis** ❶, C. Sant Joan de La Salle, 51, on the corner of C. Zulueta, in a building originally built for the Olympics in 1992. Today, it houses both a school and a youth hostel. Utilitarian dorm-style rooms on long hallways with large communal bathrooms. (☎973 35 38 16. Breakfast €2; full board €13. Sept.-June dorms €14; July-Aug. €16. Cash only.)

FOOD. La Seu has plenty of fairly priced eating options, most of them concentrated around C. de Sant Ot and Pg. Brudieu and down along the C. Major in the old part of town. The town has an open air **market** that has continued since the 11th century every Tu and Sa from 8am-2pm on the C. Major and C. Canonges. **El Celler** ❷, Llorenc Tomas i Costa, 35, offers some of the best tapas in town for between €3 and €9. (☎973 35 32 39. Open Tu-Su 1pm-midnight, closed Su afternoon.) The popular **Bar El Plano** ❶, Pl. de la Carme, dominates local nightlife. It serves tapas (€3-6), beer, and other Spanish bar food in a cheerful, smoky atmosphere. (☎973 35 41 04. Free Wi-Fi. Open daily 9am-1am, F later. Cash only.) For a hip dining experience, head to **Miscela** ❷, Av. Claris, 24, which has ornate dishes and a creative menu. Try some homemade pasta (€10) with the blissfully flavorful *porcini ceps* sauce, and finish it off with the absurdly rich warm chocolate souffl e (€5.75). Gluten-free and vegetarian options available. (☎973 35 46 20. Open daily 1-3:45pm and 9-10:45pm. MC/V.)

SIGHTS. The 12th-century **Catedral d'Urgell** is the only strictly Romanesque cathedral in Cataluña with a preserved Romanesque cloister to match. The oldest piece in the connected **Museu Diocesá d'Urgell** is a codex of 10th-century illustrations of the apocalypse, known as Beatus. Museum offers a 15min. captioned slide show on the Codex, complete with resounding classical music. (☎973 35 32 42. Information desk inside the museum has a very informative pamphlet. Cathedral and museum open June-Sept. M-Sa 10am-1pm and 4-7pm, Su 10am-1pm; Oct.-May daily 10am-1pm, cathedral only 4-6pm. €3.) Inquire at the tourist office for details on other workshops, including a number of popular cheese tours (☎973 36 05 52). Diehard whitewater fans and novices alike converge on the **Parc Olímpic del Segre** (open summer 8am-8pm, winter 8am-7pm), which was constructed to host the canoe and kayak events for the 1992 Barcelona Olympic Games and now serves as a pleasant riverside park. (Trips €11-35 per person per hr., including canoe or kayak, equipment, and drinking water; classes €37 per hr.) The park also rents mountain bikes. (☎973 36 00 92; www.parcolimpic.com. Open M-F 10am-7pm, Sa 10am-2pm and 4-7pm, Su 10am-2pm. Half-day €19, full day €25.)

ANDORRA

The tiny Principat d'Andorra (pop. 72,400) bills itself as *El País dels Pirineus*, the country of the Pyrenees. The natural beauty of its towering and dramatic mountainous surroundings is closely rivaled by the artificial glitz, busy highways, and gaudy billboards of its flashy capital, Andorra la Vella. According to legend, Charlemagne founded Andorra in AD 784 as a reward to the valley's inhabitants for having led his army against the Moors. For the next 12 centuries, the country was the rope in a four-sided tug-of-war between the Spanish counts of Urgell, the French counts of Foix, the Spanish bishop of Urgell, and the king of France. Not until 1990 did the country create a commission to draft a democratic constitution, adopted on March 14, 1993.

TRANSPORTATION

The only way to get directly to Andorra is by car or bus. There are multiple ways to get from France to Andorra by car. For instance, both Foix and Perpignan are possible starting points (55km and 128 km from Andorra, respectively). A bus runs regularly between Toulouse and Andorra, as well. Driving in Andorra la Vella is an adventure for some. Road signs can be confusing, and navigating the crowded, twisting streets can prove a difficult chore.

International Buses: Catch international buses to destinations other than La Seu d'Urgell at either of the 2 offices (separated by a fence) at **Estació Central d'Autobusos,** C. Bonaventura Riberaygua, in Andorra la Vella. **Autocars Julia\Nadal** (☎902 40 50 40; www.autocaresjulia.es) goes to **Barcelona** (3hr.; daily 8 per day, 6:15am-10:15pm; €24.50/42 round trip; also stops at Barcelona Airport, €30/52). **Novatel** (☎376 35 20 13) has service to **Barcelona** (3hr.; daily 5, 8, 10am, 12:30, 3:15pm; €28/€48 round-trip). **Alsina Graells** has buses to downtown **Barcelona** (3hr., daily 9 per day 6am-7:15pm, €23). **La Seu d'Urgell** is accessible every hr. on a **La Hispano-Andorra** bus (☎376 82 13 72, www.andorrabus.com; 30min.; M-Sa every hr. 8am-9pm, Su 5 per day 8:15am-7:15pm; €2.65) departing 200m from Pl. de la Rotonda.

Intercity Buses: Efficient intercity buses connect the villages along the 3 major highways that converge in Andorra la Vella. The tourist office provides a helpful bus schedule. Since most towns are only 10min. apart, the outlying cities can be seen in a day via public transportation (€1-5.50).

ANDORRA LA VELLA ☎376

Andorra la Vella (pop. just over 20,000), the capital, is anything but *vella* (old). Remnants of the city's past, however, make for quirky contrasts to shiny new electronics and sporting goods stores. After doing a little shopping, escape to the countryside for a walk in the mountains.

ORIENTATION AND PRACTICAL INFORMATION. Coming from Spain, visitors first pass through Sant Julía de Lòria and then reach the tiny road, Santa Coloma, that runs directly into Andorra la Vella. The main thoroughfare, **Avinguda Santa Coloma,** becomes **Avinguda Príncep Benlloch** several blocks into the city, becoming **Avinguda Meritxell** at Pl. Príncep Benlloch before continuing on as the highway to the northeast. There are several **tourist offices** scattered throughout Andorra la Vella, including the National Tourism Office at the junction of C. Dr. Vilanova and C. Prat de la Creu (☎376 87 57 00; open M-Sa 10am-1:30pm and 3pm-7pm) and the **Oficina d'Informacio i Turisme** located on the Pl. de la Rotonda (☎376 82 71 17; open Sept. 10-June 30 M-F 9am-1pm and

3-7pm, Sa 9am-1pm and 3-8pm, Su 8am-1pm). Andorra La Vella connects with the next town, Escaldes, but if you can't walk between them, the information office there will direct you to bus stops. At any one of the tourist offices, the multilingual staff offers free *Sports Activities* and *Hotels i Restaurants* guides. Local services include: 24hr. **ATMs** located directly across from the information office on Pl. Rotonda; weather and ski conditions from **Ski Andorra** (☎376 80 52 00); **taxi** service (☎376 86 30 00 or 376 82 80 00); **medical emergency** (☎116); **police** (emergencies ☎110, non-emergencies 376 87 20 00); and **Hospital Nostra Senyora de Meritxell** (☎376 87 10 00). **Internet** access is available at the public library, in the Edifici Prada Casadet on the C. Prat de Creu and C. Prada Casadet (☎376 82 87 50; open M-F 10am-8:30pm, Sa 10am-1pm; July-Aug. M-F 8:30am-7pm; €1.50 per hr.) and at **E-Cafe,** on the corner of C. Marfany and C. la Llacuna (walk C. Marfany from the Pl. Guillemó; open daily 8am-12:30am; €1.35 per 30min.) The Spanish post office is at C. Joan Maragall, 10. (☎376 82 02 57. Open M-F 8:30am-2:30pm, Sa 9:30am-1pm.)

PHONE CALLS FROM ANDORRA. Collect calls to most countries—including the US—are not possible. Buy an STA (Servei Telefonica Andorra) teletarjecta (telecard) at the tourist office for calls within the country (€3-6). Ask for an international calling card for calls out of the country, since the domestic STA card will only get you a few minutes. To call Andorra from Spain or France, you must dial the international code (☎376) first. For directory assistance, dial ☎111 or 119 (international).

ACCOMMODATIONS. For a bargain, the quiet **Pensión Rosa ❶,** Antic C. Major 18, offers well-kept rooms with shared bathrooms. (☎376 82 18 10. Breakfast €4. Singles €18; doubles €29.50; triples €45; quads €58. MC/V.) **Hotel Viena ❸,** C. de la Vall, 32, has an open ground-floor lounge with a bar, pool table, and foosball table beneath a television. Their big rooms include bathroom, shower, TV, and telephone. (☎376 82 34 46; internet access €0.50 per 20min. Singles €30; doubles €36; triples €45; quads €50. Cash only). You don't exactly rough it at shaded **Camping Valira ❶,** Av. de Salou, behind the Estadi Comunal d'Andorra la Vella, which has satellite TV, showers, a restaurant, laundry, and a pool, as well as a supermarket. (☎376 72 23 84; www.campvalira.com. Wheelchair-accessible. €5.50 per person, €11.50 for a tent and a car).

FOOD. **Casa Teresa ❷,** C. Bonaventura Armengol, 11, has phenomenal spaghetti (€6.75) and a variety of delicious dishes, including large, creative pizzas (€6-7) and fish and meat entrees (€9-17). Try the sweet red sangria (€2.75). (☎376 82 64 76. *Menú* €9. Open daily 8am-10pm. Kitchen open 12:30-3:30pm and 8-11pm. Bar open 8am-10pm. MC/V.) **Les Alpi ❸,** is convenient and distinctly modern. (☎376 80 81 00. Open daily noon-3:30pm and 8-10:30pm. Catalán meat dishes €8-18. MC/V.) For herbivores itching to try *paella*, **La Cantina ❷,** on Pl. Gulliemó, has a delicious vegetarian version (€12), and also serves pastas and pizzas, for €7-8. (☎376 82 30 65. MC/V.)

SIGHTS. Tourists often head to the **Santauri de Meritxell,** a modern building that incorporates disparate elements of Andorra's past. The original Romanesque chapel was completely remodeled in the 17th century, only to burn down in 1972. The new chapel was designed by Catalán architect Ricardo Bofill.(☎376 85 12 53. Open M and W-Su 9am-1pm and 3-6pm. Inquire about summer guided tours. Free.)

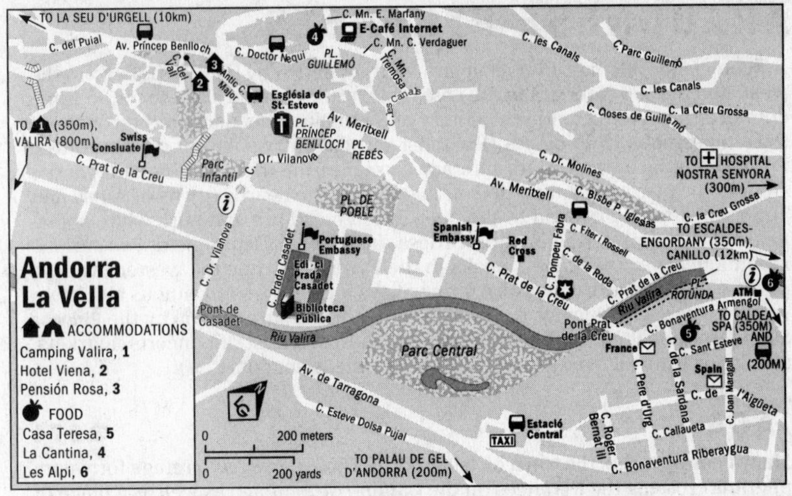

HIKING AND THE OUTDOORS. An extensive network of hiking trails traverses Andorra. The multilingual and extremely helpful tourist office brochure *Mountain Activities* includes 41 hiking routes, 9 mountain biking itineraries, and several rock-climbing routes, as well as bike rentals and cabin and refuge locations. Most trailheads can be reached by Andorra's public transportation system. La Massana is home to Andorra's tallest peak, **Pic Alt de la Coma Pedrosa** (2942m). For organized hiking trips, try the **La Rabassa Sports and Nature Center** (☎376 32 38 68; www.naturlandia.ad), in the parish of Sant Julía de Lòria. Vertical enthusiasts may want to try **Bosc Aventura's** treetop activities, closed in summer 2008 for renovations. Activities are €22. Call for summer 2009 hours (☎376 385 077). The **Canillo Tourist** Office, Av. Sant Joan de Caselles, offers half-day canyoneering (€31) and hiking (€17) excursions, from 8:30am-3pm (☎376 75 36 00). **Natura I Aventura** (376 34 95 42) offers excursions for groups of 5-10 (€25-20), as well as trips for individuals with a single guide (€120 per day).

SKIING. With five outstanding resorts, Andorra offers skiing opportunities galore from December to April. Lift ticket prices range €38-55, and **Ski Andorra** provides a 5-day pass to all sites (€157-168). Vall Nord is composed of resorts: **Pal** (☎376 878 000), 10km from La Massana, is accessible by bus from La Massana (5 per day, 8:45am-7:45pm, return 9:10am-5:05pm; €1) and nearby **Arinsal** (☎376 73 70 20), which is also accessible from Andorra la Vella by bus (every hr.; 8:15am-8:45pm, return 8:25am-8:45pm; €1). On the French border, **Grand Valire** (☎376 80 10 60) is the valley's highest resort at 2050m, with 53 slopes, totaling 100km—more than any other resort. It is accessible by bus from Andorra la Vella (4 per day 9am-6:45pm, return 9:30am-7:45pm; €4.70). The more horizontal **La Rabassa** (☎376 75 97 98 or 38 75 58) is Andorra's only cross-country ski resort. If you want someone else to propel you, try taking the **sled dogs.** More recently added winter activities include snowshoeing, snowmobiling, and heli-tours. Andorra's tourist office publishes a winter edition of *Ski Andorra*, a guide to all things skiing-related. Call **SKI Andorra** (☎376 80 52 00; www.skiandorra.ad) or the tourist offices for information on reservations, prices, and transportation. Prices at ski resorts are subject to change.

ARAGONESE PYRENEES

Aragón claims 90km of Pyrenean grandeur, bounded by the Río Gallego in the west, and the Río Nobuera in the east. This fertile region gave rise to the Kingdom of Aragón in the mid-9th century and remained unconquered throughout the tempestuous Middle Ages. The most popular entry point for the Aragonese Pyrenees is Jaca, the former military capital of the medieval kingdom and a stop on the historic Camino de Santiago. From the nearby towns of Aínsa and Torla, most travelers head to the deep green meadows and pure white snowfields of the Parque Nacional de Ordesa. In the east, Benasque draws serious mountaineers to the highest peaks in the Pyrenees, while the western valleys of Ansó and Hecho are peaceful farm valleys ideal for less strenuous mountain rambling or scenic bicycle tours. In summer, make sure to stop by the **Pirineos Sur** international cultural festival, which features a host of concerts, markets, and foods from all over the world (www.pirineos-sur.com).

JACA ☎974

Many centuries ago, the town of Jaca (pop. 12,553) served as a refuge for weary pilgrims crossing the Pyrenees on the Camino de Santiago as well as a place of great strategic military importance. Today, you can begin your own excursions on the Camino or plan your attacks on the nearby ski slopes amid the medieval religious and military wonders of Jaca's old city.

TRANSPORTATION

Trains: RENFE trains leave from the station, 1km from the *ciudadela* (fortress) at the end of Av. Juan XXIII (☎902 24 02 02; open daily 9am-1pm and 4-8pm) to **Zaragoza** (3hr.; 3 per day 7:20am, 3:35 pm, 5:25 pm; €10.65-13.75) via **Huesca** (2hr., €5.90-6.70).

Buses: Alosa buses (☎902 21 07 00; www.alosa.es) run to **Pamplona** (2hr.; M-Sa 8:45am, F also 1:45pm; €6.79), **Sabiñánigo** (20min., 6-9 per day 8:15am-7:15pm, €1.45), **Huesca** (6-8 per day 8:15am-7:15pm, €6.55) and **Zaragoza** (2hr., 6-9 per day 8:15am-7:15pm, €12.60). From Sabiñánigo, **Empresa Hudebus** (☎974 21 32 77) goes to **Torla** (1hr.; July-Aug. 11am and 6:30pm, Sept.-June 11am; €2.85), near **Ordesa** and **Aínsa. Josefa Escartín** buses (☎974 36 05 08) go to **Ansó** (1hr., M-Sa 6:30pm, €3.74) via **Hecho** (45min., €2.91) and **Siresa** (1hr., €3.05).

Taxis: Get a taxi (central station ☎974 36 28 48 or individual driver 609 34 44 66) on the Plaza Cortes de Aragón, where Av. Regimento Galicia becomes Primer Viernes de Mayo or on the Av. Escuela Militar right next to the bus station.

ORIENTATION AND PRACTICAL INFORMATION

The bus station is located on Av. Jacetania, facing the Pl. Bizcos and the **parte viejo.** To get to the cathedral, walk through the **Pl. Biscos** and bear right through the **Pl. Ripa** into the **Pl. Catedral.** To get to the **ciudadela** from the **bus station,** facing the Pl. Biscos, turn right along **Av. Jacetania** and follow it until it bears gently left and becomes **Av. Primer Viernes de Mayo.** Follow this avenue straight to get to the **Calle Mayor** and the Pl. Cortes de Aragón, where Av. Primer Viernes de Mayo becomes Av. Regimiento "Galicia 19."

Alcorce Aventura, Av. Regimiento de Galicia, 1 organizes **hiking, rock climbing, canyoning,** and **rafting** trips. (☎974 35 64 37; www.alcorceaventura.com. Guided hiking from €28 per day; rafting from €29. Bike rentals €15 per half-day, €25 per full day. Also has **ski** and **snowboard rentals.** Open daily June-Sept. 10am-1:30pm

THE PYRENEES

and 5-8:30pm; Oct.-May M-Sa 10am-1:30pm. MC/V.) For ski conditions, call **Nieve de Aragón** (☎976 20 11 12; www.nievedearagon.es) or the **tourist office.**

Tourist Office: Plaza de San Pedro 11-13 (☎974 36 00 98; www.jaca.es). Near the cathedral. Staff speaks English, French, and Spanish, and will give you more tourist literature than you can carry. Open July-Aug. M-Sa 9am-9pm, Su 9am-3pm; Sept.-June 9am-1:30pm and 4:30-7:30pm.

Bank: Barclay's (UK) has a 24hr. **ATM** at the corner of C. Mayor and C. del Carmen, one block down C. Mayor from Av. Primer Viernes de Mayo. Bank of America customers do not pay fees, as Barclay's is an affiliate. (Mon-Fri 8:30am-2:30pm). Various local banks (also with 24hr. **ATMs**) concentrated around the Pl. Cortes de Aragón and the C. Mayor. Police, C. Mayor, 24 (☎974 35 57 58)

Medical Services: Centro de Salud, Pl. de la Constitución, 6 (☎974 36 07 95).

Internet Access: Ciber Civa, on Av. Regimiento de Galicia (☎974 35 67 75). €2 per hr. Open M-Sa 11am-1:30pm and 5-10pm, Su 5:30-9:30pm. **Biblioteca Municipal,** C. Levante 4 (☎974 35 55 76). Free Wi-Fi and internet. Open M 5-9pm, Tu-F 11am-1pm and 5-9pm, Sa 10:30am-1:30pm; July-Sept. also M 11am-1pm.

Post Office: C. Pirineos, 8 (☎974 35 58 86). Open M-F 8:30am-2:30pm, Sa 9:30am-1pm. **Postal Code:** 22700.

ACCOMMODATIONS

Jaca's hostels and pensiones cluster around C. Mayor and the cathedral.

La Casa del Arco, C. San Nicolás, 4 (☎974 36 44 48or 616 86 31 96). This eccentrically decorated old stone house provides cozy rooms with balcony views of the cathedral. Reserve ahead. Breakfast €4. Singles €18-20 with shared bath; doubles €36, with private bath €50. Cash only. ❶

Hostal Alpina, C. Mayor, 57 (☎974 36 07 00). A quiet, more conventional budget option with basic, spacious rooms, TV, and bathrooms. Reception at the nearby Hotel La Paz, C. Mayor 41. Closed parts of Nov. Singles €24-32; doubles €41-45. MC/V. ❷

Hostal Paris, Pl. San Pedro, 5 (☎974 36 10 20; www.jaca.com/hostalparis). From the front door of the cathedral, head across the square to the right. Conservative, dim rooms. Breakfast €2.75. Reception open 7am-midnight. Closed May and Nov. Rooms with sinks and hallway bathrooms. Singles €28-30; doubles €38-41; triples €52-56. Prices are subject to change. MC/V. ❷

FOOD

Bocadillos fill the menus on Av. Primer Viernes de Mayo, and locals fill the cafes on Pl. de la Catedral. You can stop at **Supermercado ALVI,** C. Correos, 9, and Av. Francia (a quick right off Av. Jacetania) to pick up groceries. (Open M-Sa 9:30am-2pm and 5:30-8:30pm. MC/V.)

Restaurante Vegetariano El Arco, C. San Nicolás, 4. On the 2nd floor of the Casa del Arco, this restaurant serves a refreshingly original all-vegetarian *menú* (€12-15) with ingredients from the owners' orchards 15km outside of Jaca. Try the *cebolla asada con pisto y roquefort* (roasted onions with mixed vegetables in Roquefort sauce). Open 1-3pm and 8:30-11:30pm. Appetizers €6. Entrees €8. Cash only. ❸

Bar Restaurante La Paz, C. Mayor 41. Serves a breakfast of fresh-squeezed orange juice, toast or croissant, and *café con leche* for just €3.50. Opens at 8am. ❶

Cafetería Burnao, Av. Primer de Mayo, 14 (☎666 66 01 04). Boasts an inexpensive *menú* (€10) as well as standard Aragón entrees (€6-9), and gluten-free options. Their sidewalk terrace has the perfect location for views of the Ciudadela and the hills beyond. Small surcharge for terrace service. Open 9am-1am. ❷

SIGHTS

16TH-CENTURY CIUDADELA. The whole western side of Jaca is dominated by the pentagonal *ciudadela* (fortress), a military fortification from the 16th century constructed during the reign of Felipe II. Though a tourist attraction, today the complex is still the site of the Command and Headquarters of the 64th Galicia High Mountain Regiment, the oldest regiment in the Spanish military. The only time the fortification saw battle was when the Spanish reclaimed it after the Napoleonic invasion. The surrounding park is free and open at all times, but to get inside the *ciudadela*, you must take a guided tour. *(☎974 36 37 46. Open Tu-Su 11am-2pm and 5-8pm. Group reservations available. €10, students €8, price includes entry to military miniatures museum; www.museominiaturasjaca.es.)*

OTHER SIGHTS. A number of sights preserve Jaca's medieval grandeur, notably the **Catedral de Jaca,** begun in the 11th century and one of the first Romanesque buildings of its kind in Spain. The adjoining **Museo Diocesano** houses one of the most important collections of medieval art in Europe. *(Pl. de la Catedral, across the street from the bus station. Museum currently undergoing renovations; cathedral open daily 8am-1:30pm and 4-8pm. Group visits M-F 9:30-10am noon-1:30pm, 4-6:30pm Su 4-6:30pm.)*

FESTIVALS

If you arrive in Jaca during the spring and summer months, you're almost certain to stumble across a fiesta of some sort. The biggest celebrations are the **Primer Viernes de Mayo,** held on the first Friday in May to celebrate the 8th century triumph of the Christian army over the Moors, and the week-long **Fiestas de Santa Orosia y San Pedro,** held annually from June 24-29 in honor of the city's patron saints. During the festival, religious ceremonies, cultural performances, and concerts run through the day and late into the night.

DAYTRIP FROM JACA

MONASTERIO DE SAN JUAN DE LA PEÑA. Finding the monastery today requires only that you follow signs up a narrow mountain road, but this monastery's remote location protected an alleged Holy Grail for three centuries. On the side of a canyon 22km from Jaca, and invisible even from the other side of the same valley, the extreme isolation of this hermitage protected both the church and the chalice from centuries of Moorish invasion. The monastery gained so much importance and power that the first king of Aragón, Ramiro I, was buried there. The building displays a veritable timeline of Spanish architecture, with Mozarabic and Romanesque yielding to Renaissance Baroque, carved into the rock such that it seems the entire cliff rests on its roof. The 17th-century *monasterio* alto (upper monastery) sits 1.5km uphill and has just reopened. It includes a cultural and historical museum with a 45min. audiovisual presentation on the history and origins of Aragón, as well as a look into the daily lives of Aragonese monks. *(☎974 35 51 19; www.monasteriosanjuan.com. Open June 1-July 14 10am-2pm and 3-8pm; July 15-Aug. 31 daily 10am-8pm; Sept.-Oct. 10am-2pm and 3:30-7pm; Nov.-March 15 11am-2pm and 3:30-6pm; March 16-May 31 daily 10am-2pm and 3:30-7pm. €10, €8 for students, includes entrance to church in Santa Cruz de la Seró, both monasteries, and parking lot shuttle. Taxis (☎974 36 28 48 or 609 34 44 66) will make the journey for €26 each way, or will add €15 for every hour they wait for you. In July or August, park at the lot above the monastery. A shuttle transports visitors every 30min. from the monasterio alto to* *the monasterio viejo (1.5km), though the hike between the two offers expansive views of the entire Jaca valley. The adventurous can catch a bus from Jaca to Pamplona and ask to be dropped at the intersection with the monastery road (CN 240, km 295). From there, it's a 14km hike.)*

PARQUE NACIONAL DE ORDESA

The well-maintained trails, sheer canyons, and impressive waterfalls of **Parque Nacional de Ordesa y Monte Perdido** draw hikers out of crowded *refugios* and through the park. If you're lucky, you might just catch a glimpse of an endangered *quebrantehueso*, or bearded vulture, the largest bird of prey in the Pyrenees. The park is located just south of the French border, and includes the canyons and valleys of Ordesa, Añisclo, Escuaín, and Pineta. Huge crowds ascend into Ordesa through the village of Torla in July and August, and traipse along the park's diverse trails all year.

TRANSPORTATION

Trains: All trains along the Zaragoza-Huesca-Jaca line stop in Sabiñánigo.

Buses: Alosa (☎974 48 00 45; www.alosa.es) runs a bus between **Sabiñánigo** and **Jaca** (20min.; M-Sa 8 per day 8am-9:20pm, Su 8 per day 10:20am-10:35pm; €1.35) From Sabiñánigo, buses run to **Torla** (55min.; July-Aug. 11am, 6:30pm; Sept.-June M-Sa 11am, Su 5pm; €3.10). Torla, 8 km from the Ordesa, is the closest outpost of civilization to the park. From July 1-Sept. 14 and from Oct. 11-13, a **shuttle** runs between **Torla** and **Ordesa** (15min.; every 15-20min.; July 1-Aug. 30 6am-7pm, returning until 10pm; Sept. 1-Sept. 14 6am-6pm, returning until 9pm; Oct 11-13 7am-6pm, returning until 8:30pm; €4.50, one-way €3). When the shuttle is running, cars are prohibited from entering the park. (Parking lot in Torla €0.72 per hr. 9am-8pm; overnight parking free; 20% discount after first 24hr.; free in the low season.) In the low season, those without a car will have to either hike the 8km from Torla to the park entrance or catch a **jeep taxi** (☎630 418 918; www.ordesataxi.com; €20). The company also offers narrated van **tours** into the higher altitudes for up to 8 people. Buses leave Torla for **Sabiñánigo** (1hr.; daily 3:30pm, Su also 6:25pm, July-Aug. also daily 8pm; €2.88) and **Aínsa** (1hr., daily at noon, €3.03).

STREET SMARTS. Don't drive off the main road in any of the towns near the park, especially Torla. The narrow, steep streets were not designed with cars in mind. Just park and walk; your car's suspension will thank you.

ORIENTATION AND PRACTICAL INFORMATION

C. A Ruata is the main cobblestone road that passes through Torla. This will bring you to the Pl. Ayuntamiento and the Pl. Aragón.There you can find the Torla **tourist office,** in the Pl. Aragón. Torla has a park **information center** across the *carretera* from the bus stop (☎974 48 64 72; open M-Th 8am-3pm and 4-6pm, F 8am-3pm, Sa-Su 9am-2pm and 4-7pm). The park visitors center is 1.8km beyond the park entrance. The shuttle stops here on the way to the *pradera*, an area of the park with a parking lot, 3km farther on. (Open daily Mar.-Dec. 9am-2pm and 4-7pm.) This year or next year, however, this separate office is going to be removed; there will be just one inclusive park information office in Torla. You can pick up free maps and the *Senderos Sector Ordesa* trail guide from the park info center, or the indispensable *Editorial Alpina* guide (€8) in town.

Across from the pharmacy on C. Ruata, **Compañía Guías de Torla** organizes rafting (from €39), canyoneering (€38-60), and year-round mountaineering (€30-70), expeditions including mountains **Perdido** and **Aneto.** (☎974 48 64 22;

www.guiasdetorla.com. Open daily 9am-2pm and 5-8pm; extended hours July-Aug. MC/V.) In neighboring **Broto** (4km from Torla), **Aventuras Pirenaicas,** Av. de Ordesa, 13, offers **rafting** (€43) and **canyoneering** (starting at €42, depending on experience) trips (☎974 48 63 92. Open daily 10am-2pm and 5-7:30pm. Closed.) **Wi-Fi** is free at the Torla tourist office. Local services include: **Guardia Civil** (☎974 48 61 60); a **pharmacy,** between Restaurant la Brecha and Refugio l'Atalaya (☎974 48 62 06; open M-F 10am-1:30pm and 5-8pm); and the **post office,** Pl. de la Constitución (open M-Sa 9-11am). **Postal Code:** 22376.

ACCOMMODATIONS

Torla has budget accommodations close to the park, but they fill up fast in July and August—reserve ahead. There is a **free campsite** behind the *refugio*, though tents must be taken down in the morning. Otherwise, **free overnight camping** is available in the park above certain altitudes depending on which sector you are in. Contact the park info office for more details. Obtain a map with details from the park office before camping.

Refugio Lucien Briet, C. Ruata (☎974 48 62 21; www.refugiolucienbriet.com). Named for Ordesa's best-known poet, this *refugio* has dorm-style rooms with bunks, a double with bath and TV (€40), and smaller rooms with bunks, bath and TV. Reception across the street at Restaurant La Brecha. Sheets and towels €4. Breakfast €4.50. Basic kitchen with sink and tables available. Dorms €10; doubles with bath and TV €40; triples €36; quads €48. Cash only. ❶

La Casa de Laly, C. Fatas (☎974 48 61 68). Across from the tourist office, La Casa de Laly has a cozy B&B atmosphere and friendly owners. Breakfast €3.50. Curfew 12:30am. Oct.-June singles or doubles €25, with bath €30; July-Aug. €30/35. Note that prices are approximate and subject to change. Cash only. ❷

Refugio Góriz, (☎974 34 12 01.; www.goriz.es). The only option within the park, a 5hr. hike from the *pradera* past the Cola de Caballo. Be sure to reserve ahead. Bunks €13; Breakfast €5; dinner €14.60. ❶

Camping San Antón (☎974 48 60 63), closest to the park, rents 4-person bungalows (€93) and 4-6-person apartments (€75-90), open-year round. Camping open *Semana Santa*-Sept. Electricity €4.20. €4.20 per person, per car and per tent, €4 per child. ❶

FOOD

Most accommodations serve dinner (€13-15) and include a simple breakfast. For groceries, visit **Supermercado Torla** close to the end of C. Ruata furthest from the tourist office. (☎974 48 61 63. Open daily 9am-2pm and 5-8:30pm. MC/V.)

Restaurant La Brecha, C. Ruata (☎974 48 62 21). For the cheapest *menú* in town (€13.90), check out this restaurant. Hours vary. Cash only. ❸

Pizzeria-Bocatería Santa Elena, C. Furquieto (☎974 48 63 59). Offers a friendly, casual setting and cheap, hearty eats. In addition to pizzas both individual (€5.50-7) and family sized (€9.50-12), the pizzeria offers a selection of salads (€3-3.50) and *bocadillos* (€3-4), as well as huge *jarros* of beer for (€3). Open daily 1:30-3pm and 8-11pm. July-Sept. extended hours. Cash only. ❷

Bar Frankfurt La Gruta, Pl. Aragón (☎666 60 34 76). Serves cheap sandwiches (€3.50-4.50) and its specialty, hot dogs (€3.50), at your stool in its cozy eating space. Open June-Oct. 9am-midnight. ❶

Pub Arco Iris, C. Fatas (☎974 48 64 52). If loud dance music until the wee morning hours suits your tastes, Pub Arco Iris' 2 smoky bars reign over the night in Torla. Mixed drinks start at €4.50. Open 10pm-5am, weeknights until 4am. ❶

HIKES

A main trail runs up the Río Arazas to the foot of Monte Perdido and Refugio Góriz. Passing through evergreen forests and a spectacular open valley, and with three spectacular waterfalls within 1hr. of the trailhead, it's the most practical and rewarding hike, especially for inexperienced hikers who don't mind crowded pathways. The full round-trip hike from the *pradera* to the *refugio* takes about 8-9hr., but many worthwhile points lie between the two for hikers interested in a shorter excursion. A 6-7hr. round-trip hike leads to the busy **Cola de Caballo** (horse tail), one of the most photographed waterfalls in the park, with an excellent view of the open valley and snow-capped Monte Perdido in the distance. A trek to the **Gradas de Soasa** waterfall is about 5hr. round-trip. The **Cascadas de Estrecho,** a breathtaking waterfall that drops 30m through a narrow chute, has viewing platforms both at the base and above, and makes for a 2hr. round-trip hike. For experienced hikers, **Sendero Faja Pelay,** along the ridge above the main valley path, is a good day hike that also reaches the Cola de Caballo. From the parking lot at the Pradera de Ordesa, take the trail right, across the Río Arazas, and follow the signs for Senda de los Cazadores. The trail includes the steep snake-like path, **Senda de los Cazadores,** and the beautiful lookout point at **Calcilarruego.** Return via the main valley path along the Río Arazas (7-8hr. round-trip). Don't be surprised to see snow on the highest peaks even in the middle of June.

WINTRY WEATHER. Check for weather conditions at the park office (☎974 48 64 72 or 24 33 61). The park can be dangerous in the snow or rain and wintry conditions can last at higher altitudes well into June. The descent of the Senda de los Cazadores is treacherously steep, so returning to the Pradera on the Faja Pelay path is not encouraged.

To see the impressive **Cascada de Cotatuero,** which drops nearly 200m from the Cotatuero glacier, it's a more difficult 4hr. round-trip hike. Take the left-hand trail that breaks away from the main trail at the Virgen de Pilar monument. If you still have time and energy, the best way back to get to Torla on a clear afternoon is by trekking the **Torla por Turieto** path (2 hr. from the *pradera*) which curves down past three waterfalls and a monument to Lucien Briet, who explored the Pyrenees and advocated the establishment of the national park. If you want any sort of tranquility, regardless of the trail, arrive early, especially July-August, as the park is flooded with visitors by noon.

L'AINSA (AÍNSA) ☎974

A thousand years ago, romantic Aínsa (pop. 1700) was the capital of the Kingdom of Sobrarbe (later incorporated into Aragón). Aínsa's hilltop old neighborhood (*casco antiguo*) offers visitors the nobility of medieval charm and the grandeur of panoramic views.

TRANSPORTATION. **Alosa** (☎974 21 32 77; www.alosa.es) runs daily buses from Sabiñánigo to **Aínsa** (2hr.; 11am, return 2:30pm; €6.06) stopping in **Torla** (1hr., €3.10), and from Aínsa to **Barbastro** (1hr.; M-Sa 7am, returns 7:45pm; July-Aug. also 2:45pm from Aínsa and 11am from Barbastro; €4.88), where buses connect to Benasque (2hr.; M-F 11, 11:30am and 5:20pm; €7.24). Buses stop in front of Hotel Sanchez on Av. Sobrarbe.

ORIENTATION AND PRACTICAL INFORMATION. To get to the *casco antiguo* from the bus stop, take a left onto Av. Ordessa past the post office and go up the stone stairs on your right. (Ready your legs—it's a substantial trek up.) The regional **tourist office** can be found within the castle's walls. (☎974 500 512. www.turismosobrarbe.com; English spoken; Open M-Th 9:30am-1:30pm and 4:30-8pm; F-Su 9:30am-1pm and 4-8pm.) The Aínsa **tourist office** is on Av. Pirenáica, 1, at the highway crossroads visible from the bus stop. (☎974 50 07 67. English spoken. Open daily 10am-2pm and 4-8pm.) For the **Guardia Civil**, call ☎974 500 174. For **ambulances**, call ☎061. In case of emergencies call ☎112. A **pharmacy** is on Av. Sobrarbe just before the bridge. (☎974 50 00 23; open M-Sa 9:30am-2pm and 4:30-8:30pm, Su 10am-2pm.) **Internet** access is at the library, C. los Murros, 2, on the top floor of the big stone building at the entry to the old quarter. (☎974 50 03 88. €1.50 per hr., free Wi-Fi. Open M-F 10am-1:30pm and 4-8pm.) The **post office** is on Av. Sobrarbe, down the street from the tourist office towards the old town. (☎974 50 00 71; open M-F 8:30am-2:30pm, Sa 9:30am-1pm.) **Postal Code:** 22330.

ACCOMMODATIONS AND FOOD. In the old part of town up the hill, the brand new **Albergue Mora de Nuei** ❶ on C. Mayor offers brightly hand-painted dorms with 6-10 bunks (€15-17) and doubles (€50-60). Doubles and dorms have bath. As of June 2008, this hostel was still under construction, but they plan to include Wi-Fi, washer and dryer, and kitchen. (☎974 51 06 14; www.alberguemoredenuei.com.) **Casa El Hospital** ❷, C. Arco del Hospital, 1, occupies a centuries-old stone building right next to the Iglesia. (☎608 39 97 90 or 974 50 07 50; www.casaelhospital.com; Singles €24-29; doubles €33-55.) For a more elegant stay, the traditional **Hotel Villa Romanica** ❹ (operated by the same family) offers modern amenities under exposed wood beams. First floor enjoys a sunlit dining room and common space, with broad windows overlooking the valley and river. (☎608 39 97 90 or 974 50 07 50; www.hotelvillaromanica.com. All rooms with bath and television, Wi-Fi, and parking. Doubles €45-75; apartments (with kitchen) for 4 €85; for 6 to 8 €120-€150.) For a budget hotel in the new part of town, try **Hostal Pirineos** ❸, C. Sobrarbe, 15, near the bus stop, which has large rooms with a view and private bath. (☎974 50 02 71; www.pirineo.com/hostal_pirineos. Breakfast €4.50, lunch or dinner €10.70. Singles €27.50-38.50; doubles €38.50-53. MC/V.) Across from the tourist office, **Cafetería Dos Ríos** ❷, Av. Central, 4, offers stone-oven pizzas and Spanish classics in the bar or under sidewalk canopies. Its *platos combinados* (€8-10) are a great deal. (☎974 50 09 61. Open daily 8am-12:30am. MC/V). Some of the best dining in town can be had along the cobblestone streets and the Pl. Mayor of the *casco viejo*. For groceries, head to **Supermercado Alvi,** Av. de la Sobrarbe, 15. (☎974 50 00 18. Open daily 9am-2pm and 4-8:30pm; Oct.-June closed Su. MC/V.)

SIGHTS. In 1181, priests consecrated the **Iglesia de Santa María,** at the lowest part of Plaza Mayor. The church and adjoining **cloister** are free and open to the public. Across the plaza lies the 11th-century **Castillo de Aínsa,** which houses a museum with teaching demonstrations of the geology, flora and fauna of the Central Pyrenees in English, French, and Spanish. (☎974 50 05 97. Open W-F 11am-2pm, Sa and Su 10:30am-2pm and 4-7pm. Wheelchair accessible. €3.50 per person, €3 for people in groups of 20 or more.) The castle in Aínsa is host to a series of outdoor concerts and festivals throughout the summer that draw artists from all over the continent. (For info., call the Aínsa tourist office ☎974 50 07 67; www.festivales.aragon.es.)

VALLE DE BENASQUE ☎974

The Valle de Benasque is a haven for hard-core hikers, climbers, and skiers. Countless trails wind through the mountains, and the area teems with *refugios*, allowing for longer expeditions. With many excursion companies and nearby trailheads, the mellow town of Benasque (pop. 2160) is a great place to drop your luggage and take to the mountains. Casual hikers are often scared off by the valley's reputation for serious mountaineering—the Pyrenees' highest peaks, including awe-inspiring Mt. Aneto (3404m), are here—but relaxing walks are within every visitor's reach.

TRANSPORTATION. **Alosa** (☎974 21 07 00; www.alosa.es) runs buses to **Zaragoza** (4 hr.; M-Sa 6:45am and 3pm, Su 3pm, return M-Sa 9am and 3:30pm, Su 9am; €17.18); to **Lleida** (4-5 hr.; M-Sa 6:45am and 3pm, Su 3, return M-Sa 9:30am and 4pm, Su 9:30am; €12.50); and **Barcelona** (6hr.; M-Sa 6:45 and 3pm, Su 3pm, return M-Sa 7:30am and 1pm, Su 7:30am; €20.11). From June 28-Sept. 7, the shuttle bus **Pirineos 3000** makes runs from the town to the trailhead parking lots of **Senarta** (3 per day; 5, 7am, 3pm. 15 min. €2.95; round-trip €4.60) and **La Besurta** (6 per day, 4:30 am, 7:30, 9, 11am, 2:30, 6pm; €6.80, round-trip €10.50). During the rest of the year, call **4X4 Taxis** (☎608 93 04 50).

ORIENTATION AND PRACTICAL INFORMATION. To get to the **tourist office,** C. San Sebastián, 5, face Hotel Aragüells at the main bus stop and walk one block down the alley between the BBVA **bank** and the building with the KHURP sign. The office has a map of the town, and basic hiking maps for the area. (☎974 55 12 89; www.turismobenasque.com. Open daily 9:30am-1:30pm and 4:30-8:30pm.) Several banks along Av. los Tilos, past Hotel Aragüells, have 24hr. **ATMs**. The bank, on the Av. los Tilos, next to Hotel Aragüells, has a 24hr. ATM. (☎902 24 24 24. Open M-F 8:30am-2pm, Sa 8:30am-1pm.) In case of a **medical emergency,** call ☎974 55 21 38. For the **Guardia Civil,** call ☎974 55 10 08. A **pharmacy** is at Av. de Francia, 38, about 2 blocks past the BBVA. (☎974 55 28 10. Open M-F 10am-2:30pm and 5-8:30pm, Sa 10am-2pm and 5-9pm.) Find Wi-Fi in the cafeteria of the Gran Hotel Benasque on the corner of Av. de Los Tilos and Av. de Francia. The **post office,** Pl. del Ayuntamiento, is on the first floor of the *Ayuntamiento* across from the church. (☎974 55 20 71. Open M-F 8:30am-2:30pm, Sa 9:30am-1pm.) **Postal Code:** 22440.

ACCOMMODATIONS. What Benasque lacks in cheap hostels, it makes up for in reasonably priced modern hotels on the main road. The centrally located **Hotel Avenida ❸**, Av. de Los Tilos, 14, is one of the cheapest options in town. Its comfortable rooms (complete with TV and private bath) and a common room with wooden floors, a mounted goat head, and classic literature make for a cozy stay. (☎974 55 11 26; www.h-avenida.com. From the bus station, cross the street towards town, and walk past Hotel Aragüells. Wi-Fi available on lower floors and in common room. Singles €30-50; doubles €39-65. MC/V.) **Hotel El Pilar ❸**, on Av. de Francia past the C. del Castillo, offers modern rooms with private bathrooms and showers, the best of which provide beautiful mountain views. (☎974 55 12 63. Singles €32-39; doubles with complete bath €50-68). **Apartamentos Les Arkades ❶**, C. Ministro Cornell, 2 just off the Pl. Ayuntamiento, offers newly remodeled apartments with kitchens and private baths off a sunlit courtyard garden. (☎974 55 20 92, €15-20 per person, group discounts). Those with strong legs can head 3km up the highway toward France, where **Camping Aneto ❶** serves as a convenient starting point for a day's hike, with a mountain setting complete with, playground, TV lounge, and bar-restaurant. (☎974 55 11 41; www.campinganeto.com. Heated pool and supermarket July-Aug. Rooms with shared kitchen, living room, and bath €17.20 per person year-round. Camping €5.60 per person, per car, and per tent; electricity €5.60; 2-person bungalows €70-82. MC/V.) **Free camping** is also available inside the park in Senarta. Inquire at the park office about current regulations. (☎974 55 20 66.)

FOOD. Newly opened **Puzzle ❶** on Av. Luchón serves up an assortment of inexpensive yet delicious sandwiches and burgers (€3.60-4.40) always in the spirit of "*simpatía and alegría.*" (☎974 55 10 48. Open daily 9am-11:30 pm.) Signs from C. Ministro Cornel off Pl. del Ayuntamiento will lead you to **Pub-Terraza Les Arkades ❸**, a stone building built in 1647 attached to the apartments. (☎974 55 20 92. *Menú* €14. Restaurant open daily 1-4pm and 8-11pm; bar open 5:30pm-3:30am.) Stock up at **Supermercado Aro Rojo,** C. Molino. From the main road, take Av. de los Tilos one block and then left onto C. Molino. (☎974 55 28 79. Open M-Sa 9:30am-2:30pm and 5-9pm, Su 10-2pm.)

OUTDOOR ACTIVITIES. For updated information on each season's mountain guide companies in Benasque, contact the tourist office (☎974 55 12 89). A number of forest trails lead from Benasque, including an easy hike to the nearby village of **Cerler** (1hr.) and a longer hike to the **Valle de Estos** (3hr. by foot, 1hr. by bike; moderate difficulty.) The park info office and the tourist office have free maps of excursions by foot and bike, but serious hikers should buy an additional guide at one of the bookstores in town. (Note that hours may vary by season.) Benasque serves as the entry point to the **Parque Natural de Posets-Maladeta,** with numerous snow-covered peaks above 3000m, and 13 of the southernmost glaciers in Europe. The **Centro de Visitantes** is about 1km down the road to Anciles from Benasque. (☎974 55 20 66. Open Sa-Su spring and early summer 10am-2pm and 4-8pm; fall and winter 10am-2pm and 3pm-6pm.)

Experienced hikers can take the 4hr. hike to the Lago de Cregüeña, the highest lake in the area at 2657m. Start out early from Benasque and hike 8km uphill on the valley road toward France, or take a shuttle to Senarta. From Senarta, turn right onto the trail off the main road and climb up, following the falls of the Río Cregüeña. The ascent twists through glens, but never strays far from the river's edge. Another longer, though less strenuous route (5hr. one-way from Senarta) leads to the **Lagos de Vallibierna** (2432m and 2484m) from Senarta. Take the GR-11 along the river up the Valle de Vallibierna to the **Refugio de Vallibierna.** From there, look for the signs to the lakes, which lie another 2hr. up. Those wishing to scale **Mount Aneto** (3404m), the highest of the Pyrenees, can pick up gear at El Ribagorza on the corner of Av. Luchón and Av. Francia (open 10am-1:30pm and 4:30-9pm) and head out at 5am from the **Refugio de la Renclusa ❶.** To reach the *refugio*, take the main road (follow the signs to France) north 14km until the paved road ends at Besurta, or take a shuttle; from there it is a 30min. hike to the *refugio*. (☎974 34 46 46. Open Apr.-Sept. Bunks €14; breakfast €5; dinner €14.70. Reserve ahead.) Hiking in the Benasque valley does not require a permit, but the park office encourages all who wish to ascend peaks above 3000m to bring proper equipment (crampons, rope, winter garments). In case of accidents, call ☎112 or **Mountain Rescue** ☎974 55 10 08. For less-strenuous wandering, head in the opposite direction down the main road and follow signs to **Forau de Aigualluts,** a lovely pond at the base of a waterfall (40min.). Trails can be impassable in winter, so ask at the tourist office in advance for details on trail conditions.

NAVARRAN PYRENEES

The Navarran Pyrenees mark the peaceful transition from bare mountaintops to forested slopes, pastoral farmlands, and a maritime landscape. The many hamlets scattered throughout the mountains and the impressive Selva de Irati forest make for a good escape from the craziness of Pamplona during *San Fermín*. Mist obscures visibility at high altitudes to create a dreamy ambience (or nerve-racking driving conditions). The Navarran Pyrenees are difficult to traverse using public transportation, but daytrips to Roncal, Ochagavía, and Roncesvalles from Pamplona are possible.

RONCESVALLES ☎948

The first stop on one of the main routes into Spain on the Camino de Santiago, the town of Roncesvalles is an enclave amidst miles of thickly wooded mountains and acres of wheat. Folklore buffs come to this tiny town (pop. 25) in search of French hero Roland (known here as Roldán), Charlemagne's favorite soldier, who died nearby with the French rearguard in the Battle of Roncevaux, fought against the Basques in AD 778. The remains of the troops supposedly rest in the 12th-century Capilla de Sancti Spiritus (Silo de Carlomagno), with the bones of pilgrims who died en route to Santiago de Compostela.

TRANSPORTATION AND PRACTICAL INFORMATION. **Autobus Artieda** buses (☎948 30 02 87) run between **Pamplona** and Roncesvalles via **Burguete.** (1hr.; Sept.-June M-F 6pm, Sa 9:30am; €5.40; return buses M-F 9:20am, Sa noon. July-Aug. buses run from Pamplona M-F 10am and 6pm, returning 8:30am and 11:30am; Sa 9:30am and 4pm, returning 8am and noon.) **Taxis** available from Burguete. The **tourist office,** uphill from Casa Sabina Hostería, provides information on the sights of Roncesvalles and the Camino de Santiago. (☎948 76 03 01. Open *Semana Santa*-Oct. 12 M-Sa 10am-2pm and 4-7pm, Su 10am-2pm; otherwise M-F 10am-2pm and 2:30-5pm, Sa-Su 10am-2pm.) An **ATM** is inside the lobby of **La Posada,** as well as internet access (€1 per 20min.). Enter the **Oficina de Peregrinos** adjoining the monastery to obtain your "official pilgrim" status (€1); it is disrespectful to do so simply for cheap lodging. (☎948 76 00 00. Reception M-F 10am-1:30pm and 4-7:30pm, Sa-Su 10am-1:30pm and 4-6pm.)

ACCOMMODATIONS AND FOOD. **Albergue de Peregrinos ❶,** the first building on the left across from the Silo, provides basic *refugio*-style lodging for pilgrims. (Reception 4-10pm. Sheets and blanket €5. Curfew 11pm. Check-out by 8am.) Because the Albergue Juvenil is closed for renovation as of summer 2008, your only non-pilgrim options in town are the two hostels. **La Posada ❹,** the first building on your right entering town from the Spanish side, has basic rooms with private bath. For pilgrim meals, reserve ahead at the bar by 7pm. (☎948 76 02 25. Restaurant open 1-3:30pm and 8:30-10:30pm. *Menú* €16, for pilgrims €9. Bar open 8:30am-10:30pm. Closed Nov. Doubles €45-50; triples €60-65. MC/V.) **Casa Sabina ❹,** across the street from the Albergue de Peregrinos, offers rooms with private baths (€50) and apartments (€64-75). Their restaurant serves a *menú* (€14, €9 for pilgrims) from 1-3:30pm and 7-10pm, but combo plates and *cruji* (pizza served with a heavy metal tool to dash it apart yourself) are available at the bar from 8:30am-10pm. (☎948 76 01 05, www.casadebeneficiados.com). Accommodations are more plentiful and cheaper in nearby **Burguete,** 3km away and accessible by car or a 20min. walk on the first part of the Camino de Santiago.

SIGHTS. The church buildings known as the **Colegiata** include the 13th-century French Gothic **Iglesia Colegial** and the adjoining cloister and museum. Behind the cloister, King Sancho El Fuerte (the Strong) rests in solitary splendor in his tomb, lit by the stained-glass windows of the Capilla de San Agustín. (☎948 79 04 80. Church of St. Mary open daily 9am-9pm. Free. Chapel, cloister, museum, Silo, and Church of St. James open April-Oct. daily 10am-2pm and 3:30-7pm; Nov.-March daily 10am-2pm and 3:30-5:30pm; Jan.-Feb. 15 M-T and Th-Su 10am-2:30 pm. €3.90 for entire complex, €3 for retired, pilgrims, students, and families with 3 or more children. Includes a guided tour (in Spanish) of museum, chapel, and Silo.)

BURGUETE (AURITZ-BURGUETE) ☎948

Just 2km. below Roncesvalles on the Camino de Santiago, Burguete was a favorite of Ernest Hemingway for his trout fishing expeditions into the Navarran Pyrenees. Here you will find a quieter, more serene ambience than in the higher peaks to the west, with wheat fields that stretch out towards the hills on either side of the town. You can see why one might choose Burguete as a a refuge to relax, think, and maybe even write a novel.

ORIENTATION AND PRACTICAL INFORMATION. Burguete has no tourist office, but its layout is simple. The main road through town is the C. San Nicolás, which runs in the direction from Pamplona and towards Roncesvalles. Everything in town is located on C. San Nicolás or just off of it. A **pharmacy** is located on Pl. de Hermilio de Oloriz, 3, directly across from Hostal Burguete (☎948 76 00 39; open M-F 9:30am-1:30pm and 4:30-7pm, Sa 10am-1pm). Caja Navarra on C. San Nicolás has a 24hr. **ATM** (bank open M-F 8:30am-2:15pm). **Post office** on C. Roncesvalles (open M-F 9-10am). **Postal Code:** 31640.

ACCOMMODATIONS. Not much has changed at **Hostel Burguete ❸**, C. San Nikolás, 71 (founded in 1880), since **Hemingway** rested in room 23; the hostel is still owned and run by the same family. Hemingway immortalized the hostel in *The Sun Also Rises*. (☎948 76 00 05, www.hotelburguete.com. *Menú* €14. Restaurant open daily 1:30-3pm and 8:30-10pm. All rooms with bathroom. Breakfast included all year except Aug. Curfew 11:30pm. Wheelchair-accessible. Singles €33.17-39.59; doubles €48.15-54.15; triples €67.41-74.90. MC/V.) For cheaper accommodations, **C. San Nicolás** has several **casas rurales,** marked with the green "CR" sign. **Casa Loperena ❷**, C. San Nicolás, 25, has 2 doubles (€27) and a single (€20) with shared bath during the warmer seasons (☎948 76 00 68). Tasty Navarran dishes (vegetarian options available) are served up nightly at **Restaurante Loizu ❸**, C. San Nikolas, 13. (☎948 76 00 08. *Menú* €15.50. Open daily 1-3:30pm and 8:30-11pm. Closed Jan. MC/V.)

VALLE DE RONCAL

Carved by the Río Esca, the Valle de Roncal (pop. 1500) is a handsome valley covered by dark pine groves and winding trails, stretching south from the French border. White beech forests and ochre tiled roofs balance out the color palette. Open pastures ensure that the area's sheep continue to produce top-quality milk used to make the valley's famous cheese. Livestock aside, the Valle de Roncal offers travelers intimate towns, cozy *casas rurales*, and prime hiking trails. Visit www.vallederoncal.es for more information.

RONCAL ☎948

Smack in the center of the Valle de Roncal, tiny Roncal (pop. 400) prides itself on two things: its famed *queso Roncal*, a sharp, sheep's milk cheese, and its world-renowned tenor, Julián Gayarre (1844-1889). **Casa Museo Julián Gayarre,** on C. Arana, which occupies the singer's birthplace, showcases the tenor's preserved larynx. (☎948 47 51 80. Open Tu-Su 11:30am-1:30pm and 4-6pm. €1.80; seniors and children under 12 €0.90.) After the tour, walk out to the town cemetery to see the carved sculptures of Mr. Gayarre's mausoleum. (Take the left after crossing the bridge from Pamplona and walk 0.8 km. Stay on the paved road.) **Casa Villa Pepita ❶**, Po. Julián Gayarre, 4, to the left after crossing the bridge from Pamplona feels more like your grandparents' home than temporary lodgings. (☎948 47 51 33. Breakfast €3.50, other meals €11.50. Singles €13.50; doubles €29, with bath €40. Cash only.) **Zaltua ❺**, C. Castillo, 23, right across the river, offers comfortable rooms with private bath and TV. (☎948 47 50 08. Doubles €50. MC/V.) Their restaurant offers an appetizing *menú* with standard Navarran fare for €13. Go to **Panadería Lus ❷**, C. Iriondoa, 3, down the path next to Caja Navarra, for wine and a taste of one of the five varieties of the lauded Roncal cheese. (☎948 47 50 10. Open daily 9:30am-1:30pm and 5-7:30pm. MC/V.) Find groceries at **Autoservicio a Mano.** (☎978 47 51 82. Open M-Sa 9:30am-1:30pm and 4:30-7pm, Su 9:30-11am.)

La Tafallesa buses (☎948 22 28 86) run to Pamplona (2hr., M-F 7am, €7.67). The **tourist office** on Roncal's main road, Po. Julián Gayarre, near the exit towards Izaba, has English-speaking staff and **Internet** access for €1 the first 15min. and €0.50 each additional 15min. (☎948 47 53 17. Open June 15-Sept. 15 M-Sa 10am-2pm and 4:30-8:30pm, Su 10am-2pm; Sept. 16-June 14 M-Th 10am-2pm, F-Sa 10am-2pm and 4:30-7:30pm.) A **museum** displaying the valley's impressive wildlife occupies the top floors (€1.20 admission). Local services include the **Guardia Civil** (☎948 47 50 05) and a **pharmacy,** next to the tourist office (☎948 22 77 18; open M-F 10am-2pm and 5-7:30pm, Sa 10am-2pm).

ARAGÓN, LA RIOJA, AND NAVARRA (NAVARRE)

To the south of the Pyrenees lie the provinces of Aragón, La Rioja, and Navarra, a collage of semi-desert and lush countryside, Mediterranean and Continental climates. Regional delights lie in every direction. To the south, a collection of sun-baked towns and flaxen plains are scattered with fine examples of ornate *mudéjar* architecture. In the center, prosperous Zaragoza reigns as Aragón's capital and the fifth largest city in Spain. Out west, Logroño offers travelers a taste of urbanism infused with Santiago's pilgrim culture—and the chance to taste La Rioja's famed wines. Pamplona, the capital of Navarra, is preceded by its reputation thanks to Ernest Hemingway's famous novel *The Sun Also Rises*. The Ebro, Spain's largest river, ties these three distinct regions together.

HIGHLIGHTS OF ARAGÓN, LA RIOJA, AND NAVARRA

TOAST yourself for a week at **Teruel's** liquor fest (p. 465).

CAVE in to the temptation of the grottoes at the **Parque de la Piedra** (p. 463).

SOAK in **Logroño's** wine culture at one of its many *bodegas*. (p. 468).

ABANDON your sanity and run with the bulls in **Pamplona** (p. 478).

ARAGÓN

Aragón's harsh climate, coupled with the region's strategic location, has lent it a martial history. Established as a kingdom in AD 1035 and united with enterprising Cataluña in 1137, Aragón forged a Mediterranean empire. But when Felipe II marched into Zaragoza in 1591, he brought the region to its knees. Economic decline followed political humiliation, and as eyes turned to the New World, Aragón's people moved to the coast in search of wealth. Aragón gained state autonomy in 1982 and is now back on its feet. The region continues to expand its political influence, along with its appeal for travelers and Spaniards alike. When the Mediterranean coast and wild Barcelona are flooded by summer crowds, Aragón is a relaxing getaway.

ZARAGOZA ☎976

As host of the 2008 World Expo, lively Zaragoza (pop. 700,000), once relatively obscure as the political and cultural center of Aragón, is now finally getting the recognition it deserves. Augustus founded the city in 24 BC as a retirement colony for Roman veterans (ruins of the public baths still remain) and lovingly named it Caesaraugusta, after himself; the name was eventually blurred to Zaragoza. Many of the major plazas and leafy boulevards have been converted into modern, tourist-friendly sights with luxury shopping, but take heart: there are still plenty of establishments unaffected by tourism. With the "Water and Sustainable Design"-themed World Expo site, mostly free museums, and awe-inspiring cathedrals, Zaragoza provides a more intimate

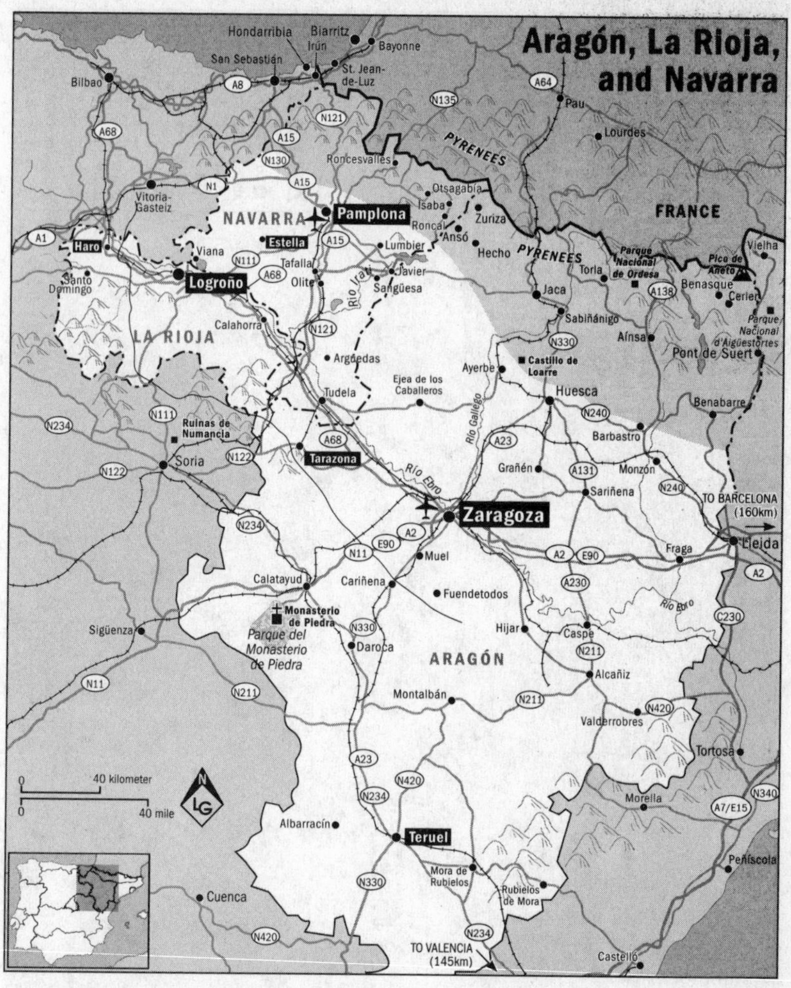

alternative to Spain's well-traversed famous cities. For the best place to perfect that Spanish lisp, look no further than "Tharagotha."

TRANSPORTATION

Flights: Zaragoza Airport (☎976 71 23 00). **Iberia** (www.iberia.com) has flights to other parts of Spain and nearby international destinations. Buses run between the **Delicias** train/bus station and airport (25min.; from Delicias station M-Sa every 30 min. 6:45am-10:30pm, Su every hr.; return M-Sa every 30min. 6:45am-11:15pm, Su every hr.; €1.50). Taxi to the airport €23.

Trains: Estación Zaragoza-Delicias, Av. de Navarra, 80 (☎902 24 02 02). Open daily 5:30am-midnight; if closed, entrance only with pre-purchased ticket (booth open daily

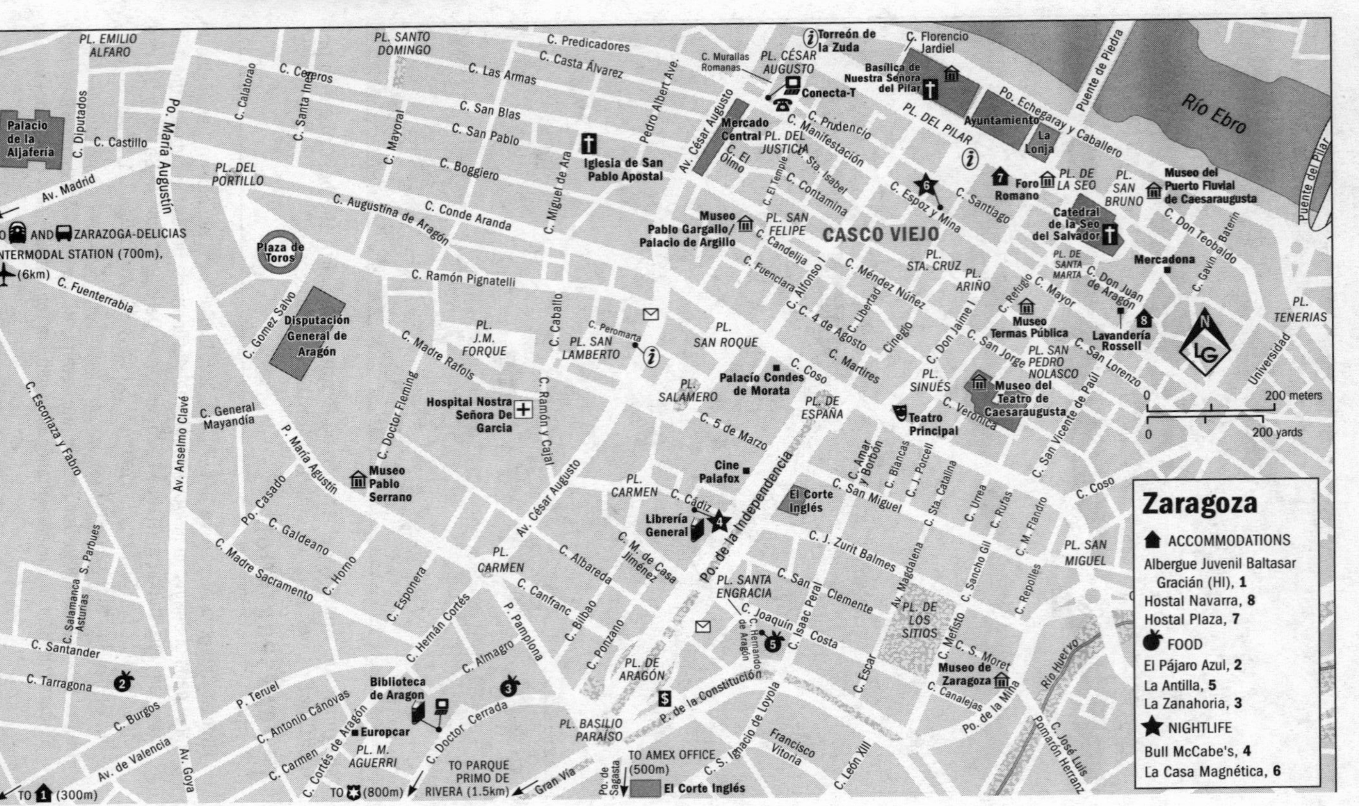
Zaragoza
ACCOMMODATIONS
Albergue Juvenil Baltasar Gracián (HI), 1
Hostal Navarra, 8
Hostal Plaza, 7
FOOD
El Pájaro Azul, 2
La Antilla, 5
La Zanahoria, 3
NIGHTLIFE
Bull McCabe's, 4
La Casa Magnética, 6
200 meters
200 yards
Río Ebro
Puente del Pilar
Puente de Piedra
CASCO VIEJO
Torreón de la Zuda
Basílica de Nuestra Señora del Pilar
Ayuntamiento
La Lonja
Foro Romano
Catedral de la Seo del Salvador
Museo del Puerto Fluvial de Caesaraugusta
Mercadona
Lavandería Rossell
Museo Termas Pública
Museo del Teatro de Caesaraugusta
Teatro Principal
Conecta-T
Mercado Central
Museo Pablo Gargallo/ Palacio de Argillo
Palacío Condes de Morata
Iglesia de San Pablo Apostal
El Corte Inglés
Cine Palafox
Librería General
Hospital Nostra Señora De Garcia
Museo Pablo Serrano
Disputación General de Aragón
Plaza de Toros
Palacio de la Aljafería
Museo de Zaragoza
Biblioteca de Aragon
Europcar
PL. EMILIO ALFARO
PL. SANTO DOMINGO
PL. CÉSAR AUGUSTO
PL. DEL PILAR
PL. DEL JUSTICIA
PL. DE LA SEO
PL. SAN BRUNO
PL. DEL PORTILLO
PL. SAN FELIPE
PL. STA. CRUZ
PL. ARIÑO
PL. DE SANTA MARTA
PL. TENERIAS
PL. J.M. FORQUE
PL. SAN LAMBERTO
PL. SAN ROQUE
PL. SALAMERO
PL. DE ESPAÑA
PL. SINUÉS
PL. SAN PEDRO NOLASCO
PL. CARMEN
PL. SANTA ENGRACIA
PL. DE LOS SITIOS
PL. SAN MIGUEL
PL. DE ARAGÓN
PL. BASILIO PARAÍSO
PL. M. AGUERRI
C. Predicadores
C. Casta Álvarez
C. Las Armas
C. San Blas
C. San Pablo
C. Boggiero
C. Cerros
C. Santa Inés
C. Calatorao
C. Mayoral
C. Diputados
C. Castillo
C. Murallas Romanas
C. Florencio Jardiel
Po. Echegaray y Caballero
Pedro Albert Ave.
Av. César Augusto
C. Miguel de Ara
C. Prudencio
C. Manifestación
C. El Olmo
C. El Temple
C. Sta. Isabel
C. Contamina
C. Espoz y Mina
C. Santiago
C. Don Teobaldo
C. Gavín
Baterín
Av. Madrid
Po. María Augustín
C. Augustina de Aragón
C. Conde Aranda
C. Candelija
C. Fuenciara
C. Alfonso I
C. Méndez Núñez
C. Libertad
C. 4 de Agosto
Cinegio
C. Don Jaime I
C. Refugio
C. Mayor
C. Don Juan de Aragón
C. San Jorge
C. San Lorenzo
Universidad
C. Ramón Pignatelli
C. Fuenterrabia
C. Gomez Salvo
C. Madre Rafols
C. Caballo
C. Peromarta
C. Coso
C. Martires
C. Veronica
C. San Vicente de Paúl
C. Escoriaza y Fabro
Av. Anselmo Clavé
C. General Mayandía
P. María Augustín
C. Doctor Fleming
C. Ramón y Cajal
C. 5 de Marzo
Po. de la Independencia
C. Cádiz
C. Amar y Borbón
C. Blancas
C. J. Porcell
C. Sta. Catalina
C. Urrea
C. Rufas
C. M. Flandro
C. San Miguel
Po. Casado
C. Galdeano
C. Horno
C. Madre Sacramento
C. Esponera
C. Albareda
C. M. de Casa Jimenez
C. J. Zurit Balmes
C. San Clemente
Av. Magdalena
C. Sancho Gil
C. Repolles
C. Salamanca
S. Parbues
Asturias
C. Santander
C. Tarragona
C. Burgos
Av. de Valencia
Av. Goya
P. Teruel
C. Antonio Cánovas
C. Carmen
C. Cortés de Aragón
C. Hernán Cortés
C. Almagro
C. Doctor Cerrada
P. Pamplona
C. Canfranc
C. Bilbao
C. Ponzano
C. Joaquín Costa
C. Hernando de Aragón
C. Isaac Peral
C. Escar
C. Mefisto
C. S. Moret
C. Canalejas
Po. de la Mina
Río Huervo
C. José Luis Pomarón Herranz
P. de la Constitución
C. S. Ignacio de Loyola
Francisco Vitoria
C. León XIII
Gran Vía
Po. de Sagasta
TO AMEX OFFICE (500m)
El Corte Inglés
TO PARQUE PRIMO DE RIVERA (1.5km)
TO (800m)
TO 1 (300m)
TO AND ZARAZOGA-DELICIAS INTERMODAL STATION (700m),
(6km)

5:30am-11pm, advance tickets sold 8am-10pm). Trains to: **Barcelona** (4-6hr. 5 per day 6am-3:17am, €26-35); **Logroño** (2hr.; 6 per day, M-F 6:38am-2:15am, Sa-Su 2:25pm-2:15am; €11-17.30); **Madrid** (3hr.; 2 per day 12:48am-10pm, 5:25pm, 3:05am; €22-26); **Pamplona** (2hr.; 4 per day 10:50am-2:15am; €11-23); **San Sebastián** (4-5hr., 2 per day 4:48pm and 2:15am, €24-31); **Teruel** (2½hr.; 3 per day 8:12-7:12pm; €10.65-12.25); **Valencia** (4½hr., 2 per day 8:12am and 4:03pm, €22). **AVE** or **Altair** high-speed trains go to: Barcelona (2hr., 13 per day 6:57am-9:49pm, €59); **Guadalajara** (1hr.; 5-6 per day 7am-7:54pm; €40-60); **Lérida** (1hr.; 7-9 per day 6:57am-11pm; €25-37.50); **Madrid** (2hr.; 21 per day 7am-10:32pm; €51-75).

Buses: Bus companies run from the **Estación Central** in the Zaragoza-Delicias Station, Av. de Navarra, 80 (☎902 49 06 90, www.estacion-zaragoza.es). Confirm schedule details using excellent, centralized website. **ALSA** runs to **Barcelona** (3hr., 25 per day 5-4:30am, €13.17) and **Madrid** (3hr., 29 per day 5:45-4:45am, €13.90); **Therapsa** and **Linecar** run to **Soria** (2hr.; 6-12 per day 7:30am-8:30pm; €9.60).

Public Transportation: TUZSA buses, Po. Independencia 24-26. (☎902 39 20 08; www.tuzsa.es. Open M-F 9:30am-2pm and 5-8pm; phone information daily 6am-11pm) cover the city (approx. 6am-midnight, depending on line; €0.90, 10-ride pass €4.65; tickets available at the office or on the bus). Nighttime service (Búho) limited to 7 lines with up to 45min. waits. Bus #51 runs from the train/bus station to Pl. Basilio Paraíso on Po. de la Constitución. Bus #23 runs down Av. César Augusto past Pl. Pilar, through Pl. España, then south of Po. Constitución.Bus #21 runs down C. San Vicente de Paúl to Pl. España, Pl. Paraíso, and then toward Palacio de la Aljaferia.

Taxis: Radio-Taxi Aragón (☎976 38 38 38) and **Cooperative** (☎976 75 15 15 or 976 42 42 42).Train station to Pl. del Pilar €12-15.

Car Rental: Europcar, C. Hernán Cortés, 31 (☎976 23 23 63). Second location in RENFE station. From €52 per day or €180 per week. Many discounts offered. 21+. Under 25 fee €6 per day. Open M-F 8am-1:30pm and 4-8pm, Sa 9am-1pm.

ORIENTATION AND PRACTICAL INFORMATION

Catch one of two city buses (€0.90) right outside of **Estación Zaragoza-Delicias** to take you towards the *casco viejo* (old quarter), where most tourist attractions are located. Get off #51 at the **Plaza Basilio Paraíso;** five spokes radiate from it. Facing the center of the plaza with the IberCaja bank building at your back, the spokes (moving clockwise) are: Po. de Sagasta; Po. Gran Vía, which becomes Po. Fernando el Católico; Po. Pamplona, which leads to Po. María Agustín and the **train/bus station;** Po. de la Independencia, which ends at **Plaza de España** (at the bottom of the *casco viejo*); and Po. de la Constitución, (the top border of La Zona). Alternately, take the #142 to Plaza Europa; from there, walk left (with your back to the river) on Po. Echegaray y Caballero, towards **Plaza de Pilar,** the tourist hub a block from the water. The areas around the university (corner of Pamplona and Gran Vía), as well as **C. Espoz y Mina,** are full of small cafes and bars where students and locals sip drinks and eat one *bocadillo* after another.

Tourist Office: Pl. del Pilar (☎976 39 35 37; www.turismozaragoza.com). Friendly, multilingual staff offer a free **map** and brochures. The *Guía de Servicios Turísticos de Aragón* has information on services for the whole region. The Zaragoza Card (€14) waives all museum admission fees for 24hr. Open daily Sept.-Mar. 10am-8pm; Apr.-Oct. 9am-9pm. **Branches** in the train station (☎976 32 44 68; same hours) and in the Torreón de la Zuda (☎976 20 12 00; open daily Apr-Oct. 9am-9pm, Nov.-Mar M-Sa 10am-2pm and 4:30-8pm, Su 10am-2pm). **Tourist bus** (☎902 14 20 08 or 976 20 12 00. 1hr.; daily July-Sept. 14. every 15min. 10am-8pm; Sept.-Oct. Sa-Su every 15min. 10am-8pm. Night tours July 9:30 and 11pm, Aug. also 10pm; Sept.-Oct. 17 9:30pm; day €6, over

65 half-price, night €10; children under 5 free). Tickets on sale on the bus and in tourist offices; night bus tickets at the Pl. de Pilar office before 7pm.

Currency Exchange: Banks line Po. de la Independencia, and **ATMs are** easy to spot. **Banco Santander Central Hispano,** Pl. de Aragón, 6 (24hr. ☎902 24 24 24) has good rates on traveler's checks, with no commission on AmEx Traveler's Cheques. Open M-F 8:30am-2pm, Sa 8:30am-1pm.

Luggage Storage: Train station (small €3, large €4.50 per 24hr.). Open 7am-11pm.

English-Language Bookstore: Librería General, Po. de la Independencia, 22 (☎976 22 44 83). 5 levels with modest English selection in the basement. Open M-Sa 10am-1;30pm and 5-8:30pm.

Laundromat: Lavandería Rossell, C. San Vicente de Paúl, 29 (☎976 29 90 34). Wash and dry small load €7, large €13. Open M-F 8:30am-1:15pm and 4:45-8pm.

Police: Emergency ☎092, all other calls (☎ 976 72 41 11), on C. Domingo Miral and in train station lobby.

Medical Services: Emergency (☎112). **Hospital Universitario Miguel Servet, Av. Isabel la Católica,** 1 (☎976 76 55 00). **Ambulancias Cruz Roja,** C. Sancho y Gil, 8 (☎976 22 48 80).

Internet Access: Conecta-T, C. Murallas Romanas, 4 (☎976 20 59 79). €0.80 per 30min. Flat screens. International calls €0.13 per min. to US. Open M-F 10am-11pm, Sa-Su 11am-11pm; **Biblioteca de Aragón,** C. Doctor Cerrada, 22 (☎976 71 50 26). Has free internet, but expect a wait. Open M-F 8:30am-8:30pm, Sa 9:30am-2pm.

Post Office: Po. de la Independencia, 33 (☎902 19 71 97). **Faxes** upstairs; **locutorio** (cheap long-distance calls) downstairs. Open M-F 8:30am-8:30pm, Sa 9:30am-2pm. **Postal Code:** 50001.

ACCOMMODATIONS

Small hostels and *pensiones* line the narrow streets of the central *casco viejo* (old town), especially within the rectangle bounded by C. Alfonso I, C. Don Jaime I, Pl. de España, and Pl. del Pilar. Be wary the week of October 12, when Zaragoza celebrates the *Fiesta de la Virgen del Pilar.* Make reservations as early as possible and expect to pay up to double the rates listed below. Reservations are essential during *Ferias* (trade shows; Feb.-Apr.).

Hostal Navarra, C. San Vicente de Paúl, 30 (☎976 29 16 84). Comfortable rooms with sink, some with balconies. TV lounge. Convenient location near nightlife in La Zona and close to Pl. del Pilar. Singles €23, with bath €30; doubles €40; triples €60. MC/V. ❷

Hostal Plaza, Pl. del Pilar, 14 (☎976 29 48 30). Upstairs from the Plaza in a prime location. TV and phone in the 13 cozy rooms; 2 interior rooms have A/C. Shared shower leaves something to be desired. Singles with shower and sink or toilet €30, larger with full bath €40; doubles €48. AmEx/MC/V. ❸

Albergue Juvenil Baltasar Gracián (HI), C. Franco y López, 4 (☎976 71 68 80; central reservation line 902 08 89 05). From Pl. de España, take bus #38 to Av. Valencia and turn right on C. Franco y López. Quite out of the way, but a real deal. Sheets and breakfast included. Reception 7am-3am; after that, it opens on the hour at 4am, 5am, and 6am. Free Wi-Fi. HI card required. Dorms €12-17. MC/V. ❶

FOOD

Zaragoza is the self-proclaimed tapas capital of Spain. Check out the tourist-office pamphlet, *Guía de Tapas,* for details and information on this tasty tradition. The staple food of Zaragoza are *bocadillos,* and visitors are never far from a salty snack and a cold *tubo* (beer on tap). The side streets between C. Don

Jaime I and C. Alfonso I, above C. Coso (called the "Tubo"), and Pl. de Santa Marta positively brim with tapas bars, restaurants, and *cervecerías* (breweries, such as El Lino and Cervecería Marpyi). **Domino** (☎976 39 80 51), in particular, boasts an authentic tapas bar—with a napkin-covered floor to prove it. Most tapas €2-3. Open daily 7pm-midnight. Cash only. Fresh fruits, meats, cheeses, and vegetables are stashed in the **Mercado Central,** a long green building on Av. César Augusto off Pl. del Pilar. (Open M-F 9am-2pm and 5-8pm, Sa 9am-2pm.) Stock up on groceries at **Mercadona,** C. San Vicente de Paúl, 42 (☎976 20 57 83. Open M-Sa 9:30am-9:30pm. MC/V.) The **supermarket** is located in El Corte Inglés, Po. de Sagasta, 3. (☎976 21 11 21. Open M-Sa 10am-10pm. AmEx/MC/V.)

La Zanahoria, C. Tarragona, 4 (☎976 35 87 94). One of a handful of vegetarian restaurants in all of Aragón, Zanahoria has dished up fresh salads (€4-5), quiches (€8.50), and soup (€4-6) for over 25 years. Food served in the multi-colored, homey dining room. *Menú* €11. Open Tu-Sa 1:30-4pm and 9-11:30pm, Su 1:30-4pm. MC/V. ❷

La Antilla, C. Hernando de Aragón, 1 (☎976 23 87 83), off Pl. Santa Engracia just across the street from the church when walking from Po. Independencia. Look for the orange sign. Serves tasty *bocadillos* (€3.90) and *tostadas* (€2.30) with smoked ham, egg, peppers, and cheeses. Slightly upscale crowd packs in for lunch, but space at the bar turns over quickly. Open M-Sa 7am-1am. AmEx/MC/V. ❶

El Pájaro Azul, C. Doctor Cerrado, 8 (☎976 23 93 83). The perfect place for a beer (€1.20) and *bocadillos* (€1.30-2.90). The Pájaro sports retro blue and yellow tiled floors, salty *jamón serrano,* and a diverse crowd of students and locals. Like any *bocadillo* place worthy of the name, this one's cheap, so try anything that catches your eye from the clear glass case on the bar. Open M-Sa 7am-11pm. Cash only. ❶

SIGHTS

AROUND PLAZA DEL PILAR. A sweeping square bordered by buildings that range from Baroque to ultramodern, Pl. del Pilar is a striking urban center. The ornate, soaring-ceilinged **Basílica de Nuestra Señora del Pilar,** flanked on one side by a dignified Goya statue-fountain and on the other by a modernist angular fountain, presides over the square. It is the perfect place to begin a city tour or simply sit and feed pigeons all day.

BASÍLICA DE NUESTRA SEÑORA DEL PILAR. Zaragoza's defining landmark was built to replace temples destroyed by fires in 1443 and again in 1515. The structure was built around the **Sacred Pillar of the Virgin,** which has remained in its original location and now supports a statue of the Virgin Mary. Numerous walls feature frescoes by Goya, who was commissioned to paint the church's cupolas. Three bombs (two of which are now on display) were dropped on the basilica during the Spanish Civil War in 1936, but they failed to explode, purportedly due to divine intervention ("low-flying planes" to skeptics). The **Museo del Pilar** inside the basilica exhibits the glittering **Joyero de la Virgen** (Virgin's jewels), including a gold crown inlaid with jewels from every region of Spain and preliminary paintings of the ceiling frescoes. The one absolute must-see is the breathtaking **panorama** of Zaragoza from one of the towers (access from rear). The view, which includes everything from Roman ruins and 10th-century farms to the towering IberCaja building, harkens back to Zaragoza's past and offers a taste of its future. *(Pl. del Pilar. Basílica open daily in summer 6:45am-end of 9pm mass; in winter 6:45am-end of 8pm mass. Free. Museum ☎976 29 95 64. Open Tu-Su 9am-2pm and 4-6pm. €2. Elevator open June-Aug. M-Th and Sa-Su 9:30am-2pm and 4-7pm; Sept.-May M-Th and Sa-Su 9:30am-2pm and 4-6pm. €2.)*

SUSTAINABLE SPAIN

Vhen it comes to preserving the planet, Spain means business. As a tourist, you can also take on a significant role in preserving the country's natural resources.

Using the Baños: Flushing a toilet in Spain is an act of environmental protection. Choose either the smaller round button or the big one, depending on how much water your business requires. Don't be alarmed if the light goes off while you're washing your hands—it's on a timer to prevent unconscientious patrons from leaving without turning it off. Once you're finished, you probably won't find paper towels to dry your hands. Instead, use the noisy but effective automatic hand dryers.

Getting Around: Travelers tend o agree that Spain's train, bus, and metro systems are reliable, safe, and convenient. But only Barça locals know the whole story: many make use of a free bike-rental system with huge environmental benefits. Anyone with a permanent address in Barcelona qualifies for a Biking card, usable at 372 bike racks located throughout the city.

Spreading the Word: Zaragoza hosted the World Expo 2008 themed "Water and Sustainable Design," which garnered attention throughout Spain and around the world. The city greeted visitors from all over Europe with calls to preserve the world's water supply.

CATEDRAL DE LA SEO DEL SALVADOR. This intricate Romanesque cathedral was constructed in the latter half of the 12th century, and reworked in Gothic style between 1316 and 1319. Inside, the jaw-dropping alabaster high altarpiece (1434) has the tomb of the first Archbishop of Aragón embedded in it. *(Pl. de la Seo, to the right when facing the Basílica. Entrance through the back, on C. Palafox. ☎976 20 07 52. Open June 15-Sept. M-F 10am-6:30pm, Sa 10am-12:30pm and 3-6:30pm, Su 10am-noon and 2:30-6:30pm; Oct-June 14 M-F 10am, 2pm, and 4-6:30pm, Sa 10am-12:30pm and 4-6:30pm, Su 10am-noon and 4-6:30pm. Last entrance 30min. before closing. €2.50, over 65 and under 18 €1.50.)*

BEYOND PLAZA DEL PILAR

MUSEO PABLO GARGALLO. Dedicated to one of the most influential Aragonese sculptors (1881-1934) of the 1920s, the Museo Pablo Gargallo houses 170 of his works in the graceful Palacio de los Condes de Argillo, built in 1670. The building's layout and bright interior reinforce Gargallo's commitment to space as a sculptural medium. The collection also holds drawings, jewelry, and pieces shaped for use in sculptures, providing insight into Gargallo's artistic process. *(Pl. San Felipe, 3. ☎976 72 49 22. Closed indefinitely for renovations. Free.)*

PALACIO DE LA ALJAFERÍA. The turrets, towers, and great halls of this impressive palace are an architectural documentary of the history of Aragón and Spain. In its long history, Aljafería was host to Muslims, Catholics, and various monarchs. The palace's oldest standing structure, the **Troubador Tower,** is emblematic of the palace's original defensive purposes. Sheltered within this site is the exquisitely detailed **Taifal Palace,** built in the Omeya style, an influence of 9th-century Muslim palaces. When Alfonso I el Batallador (The Warrior) took Zaragoza from the Muslims in 1118, the Aljafería was Christianized, but the influence of Islamic art and architecture still lingers. In 1492, **El Palacio de los Reyes Católicos** was erected by Fernando and Isabel. Visitors are free to go upstairs into the palace and enjoy room after immaculate room. *(C. Diputados. Take bus #21, 51, or 33 until you reach the massive compound. ☎976 28 96 85. Open all year M-W and Sa-Su 10am-2pm and April-Oct. M-W and Sa-Su 4:30-8pm, Nov-Mar M-W and Sa 4-6:30pm. Guided tours in English. €3, students and seniors €1, under 12 and on Su. Free.)*

MUSEO PABLO SERRANO. This modern building houses 150 bronze sculptures by the rhythm-and-space-obsessed *aragonés* Pablo Serrano (1908-1985). Look for *Gran pan partido* (Big Sliced Bread) and sculptures influenced by some of the greats: Picasso, Velázquez, and Goya. Serrano's distorted busts of famous writers make parts of the exhibit a "who's who" of Spanish literature, with Machado, Cela, Velázquez, and others all in attendance. *(Po. María Agustín, 20. Catch #21 bus from Pl. España. ☎976 28 06 59. Open July-Sept. W-Sa 10-2pm and 6-9pm, Oct.-June W-Sa 10-2pm and 5-8pm; year-round Su and holidays 10-2pm. Free.)*

MUSEO DEL TEATRO DE CAESARAGUSTA. The ruins of this 1st-century Roman theater were dug up unexpectedly by Zaragozans in 1972. To protect the archaeologically important structure, it has been covered by a trussed hemispherical roof and interlaced with suspended footpaths. The theater is accompanied by a museum. Those interested in the Christian and Jewish history of Zaragoza shouldn't miss exhibits that recount practices such as the system of locking doors that kept the city's Jewish population out of the Christian neighborhoods during Easter in the 13th century. *(Calle San Jorge 12. ☎976 20 50 88. Open Tu-Sa 10am-9pm, Su 10am-2pm. Last entrance 30min. before closing. €4.)*

NIGHTLIFE AND FESTIVALS

The nightlife scene in Zaragoza is limited almost entirely to weekends—many bars don't open until Thursday or even Friday. Most locals begin their nights in swanky **La Zona,** the streets bounded by Po. de la Constitución, C. León XIII, Po. de las Damas, and Camino de las Torres, between Plaza Del Pilar and downtown. Partiers craving flashing lights and thumping music should head over to C. Espoz y Mina near Pl. del Pilar, or small streets north of Pl. San Felipe like C. Temple, C Contamina, and C. Santa Isabel, for a variety of venues. Party the night away at **La Casa Magnética,** a part-time dance club with black lights and a bar suspended from the ceiling. (Beer €2.50. Mixed drinks €4.50. Open Tu-Su 9pm-late. Cash only.) For a taste of home, stop by **Bull McCabe's,** C. Cádiz, 7. This old-fashioned Irish pub has two floors, pizza, and five TVs. (☎976 22 50 16. Beer €4.40. Open F-Sa 10am-2:30am, Su-W until 1am, Th until 2am, food until 10:30pm. MC/V.) Gay bars and discotecas can be found in and around the west side of the *casco viejo.*

DAYTRIPS FROM ZARAGOZA

Ask at the Zaragoza tourist office for information on excursions like the Ruta de Goya. Students of the Romanesque should inquire at the regional tourist office about visits to the *Cinco Villas* (Five Villages).

PARQUE DEL MONASTERIO DE PIEDRA

Autocares Zaragoza, Estación Delicias (☎976 21 93 20), leave from Zaragoza (2hr.; July to mid-Oct. daily 9am, return 5pm; mid-Oct. to June M, Th, and Sa-Su only; round-trip €17.16). Park open daily Apr.-Nov. 9am-8pm (or until dark); Dec.-March 9am-6pm. ☎976 84 90 11; www.monasteriopiedra.com. Monument open April-Nov. 10am-1:15pm and 3-7pm; Dec.-Mar. 10am-1:15pm and 3-6pm. Park, monument, museum, and presentation €12, 4-12 and seniors €8.50; monument only €6.50.

In the heart of semi-arid central Spain, 100km southwest of Zaragoza, the Parque del Monasterio de Piedra seems like a mirage: a blur of greenery, waterfalls, and ponds fill the park. At the orders of Alfonso II of Aragón, who sought to extend the influence of Catholicism in this region, the monastery was constructed in the late 12th century by Cistercian monks over 23 years from remnants of a Moorish wall and castle. After 700 years and many wars, a state order forced its abandonment in 1835. The monastery is still privately owned, currently serving as a three-star hotel and a wine museum (once the monastery's cellar). A tour through the monastery takes you past translucent alabaster windows (which admitted light but prevented views of the tempting world outside the monastery) and other ingenious architectural ploys. Don't miss the park's highlight, **La Gruta Iris** (Iris Grotto), the narrow, dripping system of caverns behind the 53m **Cascada Iris** (Iris Waterfall). The waterfall is part of the Río Piedra, a calcium-rich stream that, according to legend, once turned everything it touched into stone. For a special treat, visit at sunset.

TARAZONA

Therpasa (☎976 22 57 23, at Delicias Station) runs buses from Zaragoza (1hr., 9 per day 7am-8:30pm, €6.26) and Soria (1hr., 8 per day 7:30am-9pm, €4.90). Tarazona station (☎976 64 11 00) is on Av. Navarra, near Pl. San Francisco.

Low-key Tarazona (pop. 11,000) is a wanderer's paradise. The hilly, winding streets at the base of this ancient Roman city are lined with one-room *panaderías* (bakeries), cafes, and markets. In the old Jewish Quarter, iron lanterns hang from the walls, and the streets open onto small green plazas just waiting to be explored. Known as the "*Mudéjar* City," Tarazona was ruled by Romans, Visigoths, and Muslims. Legend has it that Hercules himself helped build it.

The town makes an easy daytrip from Zaragoza, especially worthwhile during **Las Fiestas de Cipotegato** (Aug. 27-Sept. 1). The festivities begin at noon on the 27th, when a jester, clad in a harlequin suit, is released into the crowd from the **Ayuntamiento.** After being pelted with tomatoes, he makes his way through the city. Once he completes his route, the jester's identity is triumphantly revealed before the townsfolk. The next six days are ablaze with activities, including *encierros*, bullfights, concerts, and dances honoring San Atilano, Tarazona's patron saint. At other times of the year, you can visit the *Ayuntamiento* (Pl. de España) and admire its beautiful 16th-century facade.

Tarazona's centerpiece is its hulking 15th- and 16-century **cathedral,** dedicated to "Nuestra Señora de la Huerta" (Our Lady of the Garden), which is under renovation until spring 2009. The brick towers, belfry, lantern, and plasterwork in the inner cloister and ceiling are fine examples of *mudéjar* work. From the cathedral, follow signs for Soria and Zaragoza down C. De Los Laureles, then take your first right and enter the yellow, octagonal **Plaza de Toros Vieja.** Erected in 1792, the bullring included private residences with built-in balconies for watching *corridas* (bullfights). Now renovated, it houses offices and a *taberna* (bar/restaurant). Exit the bullring on the side opposite the entrance, cross the river, and climb the stairs to explore the *casco viejo* (signs indicate a walking route). It begins with the current **Palacio Episcopal,** the occasional residence of Aragón's kings until the 15th century; before that, it was a Muslim palace. Opposite the Palacio Episcopal, in the heart of **El Cinto** (the medieval quarter), rises the 12th-century **Iglesia de Santa Magdalena,** with its *mudéjar* tower. (Open in summer M-F 8pm, Sa 7pm, Su 11:30am; in winter M-F 7pm.) Entrance across from the Palacio, on the Plaza del Palacio. From Santa Magdalena's stairs, there is a wonderful panoramic view of the cathedral and the bullring. Many travelers with cars drive the 10min. to the nearby **Monasterio de Veruela,** while those without take a Therpasa bus to Vera and follow the signs.

The **tourist office,** Pl. de San Francisco, 1, is on the opposite side of the river from most of the *casco viejo.* English is spoken here, and make sure to stop by and get their excellent *Plano-Guía,* a combination map and guide. (☎976 64 00 74. Open M-F 9am-1:30pm and 4:30-7pm, Sa-Su 10am-1:30pm and 4:30-7pm; Sept.-June Sa-Su closes at 7pm. Tours by reservation. €5.) **Banco Santander Central Hispano,** in Pl. San Francisco, charges no commission and has a 24hr. **ATM.** The **police station** is on Pl. de San Francisco (☎976 64 16 91).

TERUEL ☎978

Teruel (pop. 31,000), the small capital of southern Aragón, seduces visitors with its history of tragic love and rich cultural exchange. Muslims, Jews, and Christians lived and worked here together between the 12th and 15th centuries, and this pluralism is still evident today: the city's ubiquitous *mudéjar* architecture mixes Arabic patterns with Gothic and Romanesque styles. The town's welcoming narrow streets and tucked-away plazas belie its cosmopolitan past, while the modern city is the busier counterpart to the winding streets of the *casco antiguo*. An easy stopover between Valencia and Zaragoza, Teruel doesn't reach its prime until July, when citizens celebrate the resilience of their *torico* (iron bull) in an insane, seven-day liquor fest.

TRANSPORTATION

Trains depart from Camino de la Estación, 1 (☎902 24 02 02), downstairs from Po. del Óvalo, to **Valencia** (2-3hr.; 3, 8am, 6:45pm; €9.20-10.60) and **Zaragoza** (2hr.; 6:45, 11:52am, 6:17pm; €11.25). **Buses** depart from the station on Ronda de Ambeles (☎978 61 07 89; www.estacionbus-teruel.com), opposite the casco antiguo from the train station. **Abasa** (☎978 83 08 71) goes to **Barcelona** (5-6hr., M-Sa 8am, €25). **Tezasa** runs to **Zaragoza** (3hr.; M-Sa 6-7 per day 7am-10:40pm, Su 3 per day 2:15-7pm; €9). **Samar** (☎978 60 34 50) goes to **Cuenca** (2hr.; M-Sa noon, Su 7:45pm; €8.20) and **Madrid** (4-5hr.; M-F 4 per day 6:30am-5pm, Sa-Su 7:30am, 1:30, 5pm; €16.50). Schedules change frequently, so be sure to call ahead. For a **taxi**, call ☎978 61 75 77.

ORIENTATION AND PRACTICAL INFORMATION

With your back to the train station, the *casco antiguo* lies at the top of a postcard-worthy staircase, perched on a hilltop. Modern Teruel is to the right over the bridges joining two hills; most of the city's charm, however, is concentrated in the old town. The center of the *casco antiguo* is affectionately known as **Plaza del Torico** for the tiny bull statue perched atop a column in the street. The plaza, C. Nueva, and Pl. de Tomás Bretón also house a handful of *Modernista* buildings by Pablo Monguió, a Gaudí follower. To reach Pl. del Torico from the **train station,** go up the staircase from the park in front and walk down C. Nueva, the street that runs straight from the stairs; it ends in Pl. del Torico. From the **bus station,** a purple sign to your left points to a small street. Take it, and make a right at the intersection with the blue "Sony" sign.

There are two **tourist offices** in Teruel: one is hidden in the tiny Pl. de los Amantes, between Pl. del Torico and the Mausoleo de los Amantes. The other is on C. San Francisco in a large, modern Gobierno de Aragón building. To get there from the train, turn left immediately after scaling the stairs. From Pl. del Torico, follow C. Salvador and turn right on C. San Francisco. Most useful are their *itinerarios*, walking routes through the *casco antiguo*, which feature guides to *Modernista* buildings and the *mudéjar* towers throughout the city. (Free guided tour in Spanish or English; www.turismoaragon.com. Open M-Sa 10am-2pm and 4-8pm; Aug. M-Sa 10am-8pm, Su 10am-2pm and 4-7pm.) **Banco Santander Central Hispano** is at Pl. del Torico, 15. (Open M-F 8:30am-2:30pm; Oct.-May also Sa 8:30am-1pm.) **Internet, international calls, fax,** and **Western Union** money transfers are available at CiberTozal, Joaquín Costa, 8B, just off Pl. del Torico. (☎978 60 25 24. Internet €1.80 per hr. Open M-Sa 10:30am-2pm and 5-10pm, Su 5-10pm.) The **post office,** C. Yagüe de Salas, 19, can send faxes. (☎978 61 84 75. Open M-F 8:30am-8:30pm, Sa 9:30am-2pm.) **Postal Code:** 44001.

ACCOMMODATIONS

Lodgings are scarce during August and Semana Santa and impossible during the fiesta in early July—reserve months in advance. One of the oldest hostels in all of Spain, **Fonda del Tozal ❶,** C. Rincón, 5, promises the rustic charm and comfort of a *casa rural* complete with tiled floors, flowered bedspreads, and skeleton keys. Guests will enjoy the impressive stable-turned-bar downstairs. (☎978 60 10 22. Doubles with bath and balcony €48; triples €55. Extra bed €9. Cash only.) To get to **Hostal Aragón ❷,** C. Santa María, 4, head in the direction the *torico* statue faces and take the first left as you leave Pl. del Torico. Friendly owners keep spacious rooms, some with TV. (☎978 61 18 77; hostalaragon.org. Singles €25; doubles €44; triples with bath €51. MC/V.)

FOOD

Teruel is famous for its cured ham, *jamón de Teruel,* featured in tapas bars, Rokelín ham stores, and restaurants; there are several in town (C. Comandante Foreta, 9, C. Rincón, 2, and C. Joaquin Costa, 33). During the summer, Thursdays bring heaps of fresh fruit and vegetable stands to **Los Arcos** 9am-2pm; follow Ronda Damaso Torán a few blocks downhill to the left. Prepare a gourmet picnic at **Martin Martin,** Pl. Domingo Gascón. Baskets of olives, onions, and peppers are just waiting to be scooped up and layered on top of fresh-baked breads (2 rolls for €1.50). (☎978 61 72 94. Open M-Sa 9am-9pm, Su 10am-9pm. MC/V.)

Rokelín, C. Ramón y Cajal, 7 (☎978 60 93 63; www.rokelin.com). Tapas bar off Pl. del Torico serves trays of fresh ham, cheese, salads, and sandwiches (€3-12). Open daily, 9am-1am. MC/V. ❷

Bar Gregory, Po. del Ovalo, 6 (☎978 60 05 80). For a quick bite in a prime location (albeit a slightly touristy one), check out the giant *bocadillos* (€3.90-7), *patatas bravas,* and salads (€4-10) at this restaurant. Overlooks the city staircase. Liters of beer or sangria €5-7. Open daily 7-1am. MC/V. If you're looking for a little something more, head next door to **Bar Gregory Plus,** which has a full *menú del día* for €12. Try the pork loin with honey sauce (€9.50). Open daily 1:15-4pm and 8pm-midnight. ❷

Los Caprichos, C. Caracol, 1 (☎978 60 03 30). From Pl. del Torico, two blocks up C. Hartzenbusch on the right. Lovers of all things Italian will appreciate the pastas (€5.40-7.20) and crisp specialty pizzas (€7-10), along with local wines. Takeout available. Open Tu-Su 1:30-3:30pm and 8:30-11:30pm. MC/V. ❷

Pastelería Sanz, C. Ramón y Cajal, 4 (☎978 61 78 48). Half a block from the plaza, has flawless croissants and *ensaimadas* for under €1. Open M-F 8am-2:30pm and 5-8:30pm, Sa 9am-2pm and 5:30-8:30pm, Su 10am-2pm. MC/V, €10 minimum. ❷

SIGHTS

CATEDRAL DE SANTA MARÍA DE MEDIAVILLA. The mother of all Teruel's *mudéjar* monuments is the 13th-century Catedral de Santa María de Mediavilla. The vast aesthetic difference between the two chapels is noteworthy—the gilding of the Baroque **Capilla de la Inmaculada,** dating from the 18th century, is brilliant compared to the more subdued, though intricately detailed, wooden carvings of the 16th-century *retablo mayor* (altar). What brings the cathedral fame, however, is the intricate *techumbre mudéjar,* a decorative red-and-blue ceiling displaying Islamic influence in depictions of religious scenes, animals, and even vegetables. Behind the cathedral in the Episcopal Palace is the **Museo de Arte Sacro,** exhibiting paintings by local artists, carvings, and sculptures from medieval to Baroque origin. *(☎978 61 80 16. Cathedral open daily 11am-2pm and 4-7pm;*

May-Sept. open until 8pm. Call ahead for guided tours in Spanish, at no extra charge. Museum open M-Sa 10am-2pm and 4-8pm. Cathedral and museum €3, students and seniors €2.)

TORRES MUDÉJARES. Muslim artisans built the brick-and-glazed-tile Torres Mudéjares between the 12th and 15th centuries. The most intricately designed of the towers is the 14th-century Torre del Salvador, which rises above C. del Salvador and literally straddles the street, a striking green and white welcome to the city. Climb 122 steps through several chambers, packed with intricate model cities, to the bell tower and its panoramic views. Also, the tourist office offers a full walking tour. *(☎978 60 20 61; www.teruelmudejar.com. Open Tu-Su 11am-2pm and 4:30-7pm, M 11-2pm. Closed July 10-13. €2.50, ages 6-12 and seniors €1.80.)*

MAUSOLEO DE LOS AMANTES. According to local legend, in 1217 Teruel's Diego Marcilla died from heartache after his lover, Isabel Segura, was married off to a wealthy nobleman. After his funeral, Isabel gave her dead lover a kiss and collapsed dead on top of his body. It is rumored that Cervantes himself recorded this history, and it may have even fallen into the hands of a certain British bard. Teruel's famous love story is kept alive at the colorful **Mausoleo de los Amantes,** C. Matias Abad, 3, where the bodies of the two lovers are eerily preserved and displayed in a recently renovated tomb connected to the *mudéjar* **Iglesia de San Pedro.** The church has a 14th century structure, but was designed by 20th-century local artist Salvador Gisbert. It accompanies the **Torre San Pedro,** Teruel's first *mudéjar* tower. Ask at the museum about guided tours of the Tower and especially the Ándito, a tiny path around the outside of the church providing close-up views of the magnificent 19th century stained glass windows. *(☎978 61 83 98; www.amantesteruel.com. Open daily 10am-2pm and 4-8pm; last entry 30min. before closing. €7 for the Conjunto Amantes: San Pedro, its tower, and the tomb/museum. Less expensive packages are also available for those who feel the urge to pick and choose.)*

FESTIVALS

Teruel's many celebrations manifest the hearty, passionate spirit of the city. Perhaps most renowned is *La Vaquilla* (or heifer) *del Ángel.* The 10-day celebration takes place from the weekend closest to the **Fiesta del San Cristóbal** (July 10), usually the second weekend of July. The festivities are in loving honor of the town square's little *torico* (he wears an honorary red handkerchief for the week). The second guest of honor is Santa Emerenciana, the patron saint of Teruel. Participants dress in white with a red handkerchief for the *corridas,* puppet parades, public picnics, fireworks, and, of course, the continuous liquored-up nighttime festivities (Su-Tu dawn). Teruel's population quadruples for this celebration, so plan accordingly. In the month of August, the **Festival Folklórico,** a recent addition to Teruel's festivities, infuses the city with international flair, bringing folk dance companies from all over the world to perform their traditional dances. Sept. 10-17 brings the **Feria del Jamón,** when ham producers set up stands to advertise their mouthwatering delicacies.The **Festivales Medievales,** in the second weekend of February, cover the streets of Teruel with straw and convert the town into an ancient market, complete with reenactments of the story of Los Amantes for **El Día de Los Amantes** (Valentine's Day).

LA RIOJA

La Rioja is synonymous with great wine. The Ebro tributary Río Oja, from which the region's name is derived, trickles through the countless vineyards and wineries that characterize the region. "Rioja" is an internationally acclaimed family of wines with an 800-year-old tradition; the '94, '95, '01, and '02 grapes received the highest ratings possible, and since 1991, it has been the only Spanish wine to earn the coveted *Calificada* rating. The best *bodegas* (wine cellars) draw from the lands in western Rioja Alta. The region also welcomes countless *"peregrinos"*—pilgrims—passing through as they hike the long Camino de Santiago. The Camino towns take great pride in their role in the pilgrimage and show hospitality to pilgrims and tourists alike. The smallest of Spain's provinces, La Rioja offers a relaxed atmosphere and varying terrain—the Sierra mountains, with tranquil fields at the feet of their towering peaks, line the region's southern border.

LOGROÑO ☎941

Logroño (pop. 150,000), the capital city of La Rioja and an official stop on the Camino de Santiago, is the best place to enter the region's vineyard towns, loosely known as the *"Ruta de Vino,"* or wine route. The city's first priority has always been its *bodegas*: in 1635, the mayor banned carts from streets next to wineries "for fear that the vibration caused by these vehicles might affect the wine." But Logroño offers more than just wine; it calls itself Spain's first commercial city, boasting a long tradition of arts, theater, and food. The mayor himself wrote the city's best tapas guide. Logroño's name dates as far back as the 10th century and comes from *"illo Gronio"* (the passageway), the gate-like rock elevations along the Río Ebro. Many castles guarded the crucial *puente de piedra* (stone bridge) over the Ebro, as Logroño was a prized target for conquest. Though the town is home to several stops on the Camino de Santiago, these days Logroño offers little but commerce for the culture-hungry tourist. Delicious local specialties, however, are sure to satisfy the heartiest appetite.

TRANSPORTATION

Trains: RENFE, Pl. de Europa (☎902 24 02 02), off Av. de España on the south side of town, southeast of the bus station. Info open daily 7am-11pm, advance tickets 9am-9pm. To: **Barcelona** (7hr., 5 per day 12:46pm-4:04am, €34.10-44.60); **Bilbao** (4hr., 2 per day 4:20am-6:48pm, €17.10-23.30); **Burgos** (2hr., 4 per day 4:20am-1:58am, €11-17.40); **Madrid** (4hr., M-Sa 7:52am, €51.80); **Vitoria-Gasteiz** (1hr., M-F 7pm, €7.50); **Zaragoza** (2hr., 5-6 per day 1:41am-8:05pm, €11-23).

Buses: Av. de España, 1 (☎941 23 59 83), on the corner of C. del General Vara de Rey and Av. de Pío XII. More convenient than trains for nearby destinations. Info M-Sa 6am-11pm, Su 7am-11pm. To: **Barcelona** (6hr., 6 per day 1am-3:30pm, €26); **Burgos** (2hr.; M-Sa 6-7 per day 8:30am-7:30pm, Su 3 per day 11am-9:45pm; €12); Madrid (4-4½hr.; M-Th and Sa 8 per day 6:45am-1:30am, F and Su 11 per day €20-30); **Pamplona** (1-2hr.; M-Sa 8 per day 7am-8pm, Su 4 per day 10am-8pm; €8-10); **Santo Domingo de la Calzada** (1hr.; M-F 11 per day 7:15am-8pm, Sa 7 per day 8:30am-7:30pm, Su 3 per day 11am-9:45pm; €3); **Soria** (1½hr., departure times same as **Madrid,** €7-12); **Vitoria-Gasteiz** (1½-2hr.; M-F 6 per day 7am-8pm, Sa 4 per day 10am-8pm, Su 5 per day 10am-9:30pm; €8-10); **Zaragoza** (2-3hr.; M-F and Sa 6-7 per day 7am-6:30pm, Su 4 per day 10:30am-9pm; €12).

Public Transportation: All local buses (☎941 20 27 77) run to Gran Vía del Rey Juan Carlos I at the intersection with C. del General Vara de Rey, 1 block from Parque del Espolón. **Info booth** at the bus station. Buses #1 and 3 pass the bus station. €0.56.

Taxis: Stands at the bus station (☎941 23 75 29) and Parque del Espolón (☎941 22 42 99). **Radio Taxi** (☎941 50 50 50). **ENO-Taxi** offers fixed prices on round trips.

Car Rental: Europcar, Pl.de Europa (☎941 51 23 41), to the left in the same building when exiting the train station.

ORIENTATION AND PRACTICAL INFORMATION

Gran Vía del Rey Juan Carlos I is Logroño's main east-west road. The token border between the old and new towns, **Paseo del Espolón,** also the city's central park, runs one block north of Gran Vía. The *casco antiguo* (old quarter) lies between the park and the Río Ebro on the far north side of the city. To reach the park (and the regional tourist office, located in the park behind a dome-shaped stage by C. del General Vara de Rey) from the **train station,** angle left on Av. de España, which runs from the train station, a bit to your left with your back to the station. This will lead to the **bus station** (the next major intersection), where you turn right on **C. del General Vara de Rey,** which leads north to the park and the *casco antiguo* on your left (10min.).

Tourist Office: C. Portales, 50(☎941 27 33 53; www.logroturismo.org). Next to Pl. Alférez Provisional, near Avda. Portugal and C. Portales intersection. Call for information on *casco antiguo tours*. English, French, and German spoken. Open July-Sept. daily 9am-2pm and 5-8pm; Oct.-June M-Sa 10am-2pm and 4:30-7:30pm, Su 10am-2pm.

Currency Exchange: Banco Santander Central Hispano, Muro Francisco de la Mata, at Parque del Espolón. **ATM** inside. Open Apr.-Sept. M-F 8:30am-2pm; Oct.-Mar. M-F 8:30am-2pm, Sa 8:30am-1pm.

Luggage Storage: At **bus station.** €2 per locker. Open M-Sa 6am-11pm, Su 7am-11pm. At train station; €3. Open 24hr.

English-Language Bookstore: Santos Ochoa, C. de Sagasta, 3 (☎941 25 86 22; www.santosochoa.es). Books in English, coffee, and free Wi-Fi in a comfortable room upstairs. Open M-F 10am-1:45pm and 5-8:30pm, Sa 10:30am-2pm. MC/V.

Police: C. Ruavieja (☎092), near Iglesia de Palacio. Walk up C. Sagasta toward the river, make a right on C. Ruavieja and walk 2 blocks.

Medical Services: Hospital San Pedro, Pl. de San Pedro s/n (☎941 29 75 00). Follow Av. de La Paz away from the *casco antiguo;* go right 5 blocks after the *Ayuntamiento.*

Library, C. Merced, 1 (☎941 21 13 82; www.blr.larioja.org). La Rioja **public library** has 2 computer terminals for public use on the top floor; 1 hr. max.

Post Office: C. Pérez Galdós, 40. From the bus station, turn left and walk 5 blocks. Open M-F 8:30am-8:30pm, Sa 8:30am-2pm. **Postal Code:** 26001.

ACCOMMODATIONS

The *casco antiguo*, brimming with hostels and *pensiones*, is your best bet for budget accommodations. Try C. San Juan, the second left past Parque del Espolón from the stations, or C. San Agustín and C. Laurel. Reservations are crucial for fiesta week near September 21.

Fonda Bilbaína, C. Capitán Eduardo Gallarza, 10, 2nd fl. (☎941 25 42 26). Take C. de Sagasta into the *casco antiguo,* turn left onto C. Hermanos Moroy and then right onto C. Capitán Eduardo Gallarza. Has bright rooms with high ceilings, tiled floors, TVs, and big beds. Many rooms have private bath and Wi-Fi. Ask for a room with a balcony. Singles €25-30; doubles €36-40 MC/V. ❷

Pensión Sebastián, C. San Juan, 21 (☎941 24 28 00). Accessible from C. Muro del Carmen or C. Hermanos Moroy. This social, family-owned pension has colorfully decorated rooms with shared bath. Singles €20; doubles €30. Cash only. ❷

Hostal Niza, C. Capitán Eduardo Gallarza, 13 (☎941 20 60 44; www.hostalniza.com), a block before Bilbaína. 16 rooms with TV, A/C, bath, coffee and cookies, hair dryers, and (in some) DVD players. Doubles €64.20, for individual use €40-42.80; for 3 with extra bed €79.20. AmEx/MC/V. ❹

Asociación Riojana, Ruavieja, 32 (☎941 26 02 34; www.asantiago.org). Enter on Travesado Palacio. Exclusively for *"peregrinos"*—pilgrims hiking the Camino de Santiago. Provides 88 beds in rooms of 24. Patio and fountain. Laundry, free internet, and overnight bike storage available. Lights out 10pm. Check-out by 8am. €3. Cash only. ❶

FOOD

Logroñeses take their grapes seriously—wine is the beverage of choice. C. Laurel and C. San Juan brim with bars and cafes. The **Mercado de Abastos** offers meat, fresh fruit, and vegetables in a building on C. Capitán Eduardo Gallarza. (Open M-F 7:30am-1:30pm and 4-7:30pm, Sa 7:30am-1:30pm.) For groceries, head to **Champion,** Av. La Rioja 14-16, at C. Miguel Villanueva. (☎941 22 99 00. Open M-Sa 9am-9:30pm. AmEx/MC/V.)

Juan & Juan, C. Albornoz, 5 (☎941 22 99 83). Brothers Juan Marcos and Juan Manuel opened this intimate restaurant 2 years ago as a quality, budget alternative to high-priced neighboring establishments. The lunch *menú* (€9) includes table wine, creative fries, and clever takes on local specialties like *lomo a la plancha* (pork loin). Salads €4, most entrees €7. Lots of vegetarian options. Open Tu-Sa 1:30-4pm and 9pm-late, Su 1:30-4:30pm. MC/V. ❷

Bar De La Tortilla "Mere," Travesía de San Juan, 2 (☎941 23 07 16). Family-owned bar known for a variety of tapas, often involving tortillas in creative guises. Adventurous diners order the fried lamb's ears, then offer a toast with a local Rioja wine. Standing room only. Tapas generally €1.60. Open Tu-Su 10am-3pm and 7pm-midnight. Cash only. ❷

En Ascuas, C. Hermanos Moroy, 22 (☎941 24 68 67; www.enascuas.com). White tablecloths and rustic decor offset large black-and-white pictures and a window into the grill. Great appetizers, like homemade red peppers (€3.35-13.85) and salads (€4.75-7.75). Fish entrees €8-14. Open Tu-Su 1:30-3:30pm and 8:30-11:30pm. D/MC/V. ❷

SIGHTS

In addition to the aesthetic draw of Logroño's beautiful **Parque del Espolón** and the people-watching pleasure of its *casco antiguo*'s numerous shop and cafe-lined walkways, Logroño also offers historically significant attractions. In an 18th-century Baroque palace, the **Museo Provincial de La Rioja** has a collection of art, mostly religious works, spanning the last eight centuries. The museum also hosts a rotating contemporary art exhibit. *(Pl. San Agustín, 23, along C. Portales. ☎941 29 12 59. Closed indefinitely for renovations. Free.)* The twin towers of the 19th-century **Catedral de Santa María de La Redonda,** that hide a well-protected Michelangelo inside (*Calvario*, €0.50 to view), dominate Pl. del Mercado in the *casco antiguo.* (Open daily 9am-1pm and 6-9pm. Free.) To get to **Iglesia de Santiago El Rea,** take C. Sagasta towards the river and make a left on C. Barriocepo. A mandatory stop on the Camino de Santiago, it is home to the Virgen de la Esperanza and a gleaming gold altar. (Open daily 8am-1:30pm and 6-8pm. Free.) To walk a small stretch of the Camino de Santiago, face the river and make a right on C. Ruavieja (the oldest street in the city and part of the Camino) then follow it to the water and over the bridge. Walk through **Parque del Ebro** along the river for a view of the *casco antiguo* and the Ebro.

NIGHTLIFE AND FESTIVALS

Logroño nightlife begins in the densely packed bars along C. Laurel in the *casco antiguo.* Alternatively, check out C. Portales along Pl. del Mercado, C.

de Sagasta, and C. Carnicerías, which get busy early and stays that way until after midnight. The central blocks of C. Herreros are packed with bars with outside tables. Two of the best spots are the elegant, artsy **Tras Luz,** C. Portales, 71 (☎947 21 41 94; open M-Th 9am-10pm, F-Sa 5:30pm-3am; cash only) and the sophisticated but inviting **Noche y Día,** C. Portales, 63. (☎941 20 64 06; www.nochedia.com. Open M-Th 7am-2am, F-Sa 8:30am-2:30am. Cash only.) Head down to the stylish and slick **Casablanca,** Av. de Portugal, 30. Flowered walls, hanging chandeliers, and curving gold booths lend this cafe-bar an elegant air. (☎941 22 09 45. Beer €2. *Pinchos* €1.50. Coffee €1. Open M-Th 8am-2am, F-Sa 8am-2:30am, Su 3pm-2am. Cash only.) The **Fiestas de San Bernabé** (June 8-11) feature the procession of the Virgen Esperanza from Iglesia Santiago to the cathedral, along with revelry and fireworks. The biggest party in town begins the week of September 21 for the **Fiestas de San Mateo,** and that same week, locals celebrate the grape harvest with the **Fiestas de la Vendimia,** when they make an offering of wine to the Virgin of Valvanera, patron saint of La Rioja; the event is accompanied by bullfights and plenty of regional street food.

DAYTRIP FROM LOGROÑO

HARO

RENFE trains (☎947 34 80 52) connect Logroño to Haro. (40min.; daily 7:36am and 6:48pm, also M, W, F 7pm; €3.65-11. Return trains run daily 8:55am, 9:47pm, M-F also 8:55am; €3.65-11.) Jimenez (☎941 23 12 34) runs buses from Logroño to Haro. (1hr.; M-F 7 per day 7:30am-7:15pm, Sa 2 per day 10:15am and 5pm, Su 3 per day 10:15am-8:30pm; €2.73. Return buses M-F 8 per day 7:45am-8:45pm, Sa 2 per day 8:45am and 2:45pm, Su 3 per day 8:45am-7pm.)

Haro (pop. 12,000) is the heart of La Rioja's wine industry, thanks to its grape varieties, climate, and soil. No fewer than nineteen *bodegas* (wineries) occupy a fertile stretch of land just across the River Tirón. Haro gets festive on June 29, the day of San Pedro, when participants spray wine at innocent bystanders during the **Batalla del Vino.** Most *bodegas* offer tours of their facilities between 9am and 2pm, but you can pick up a complete list of their schedules at the tourist office. Tours typically include a tasting, and reservations are almost always required. The large **Bodegas Muga,** which produces the most popular Spanish wine in the US, offers a detailed, enjoyable tour (max. 12 people per tour) of its facility, including its 14,000 barrel cellar. They also sell bottles from €4.50 to €70. The *bodega* is a 10min. walk across the Río Tirón: cross the bridge and bear right, then go under the train tracks and they're straight ahead. (☎941 31 04 98. Call for tour times and reservations. €5 (including 2 wine samples. MC/V.) **Bodegas C.V.N.E. (Compañía Vinícola del Norte de España)** also offers tours in English, including two wine tastings. (☎941 30 48 09; visitas@cvne.com. Call ahead. Closed in Aug.) If the samples just aren't enough, hit up the numerous **wine shops** on C. Santo Tomás and find a quiet spot back on the winery side of the river, or take a bottle to the flower-filled **Jardines de la Vega,** on C. Virgen de la Vega, three blocks up from the tourist office. Most shops charge €1.75-3 (and *way* up) per bottle, but *jarreros* (Haro locals) insist that any bottle less than €2.90 isn't worth drinking. The government-run **Centro de Interpretación del Vino de La Rioja,** Av. Bretón de los Herreros, 4, has sleek exhibits with multimedia, detailing everything you could possibly want to know about the production and tasting of wine. (☎941 30 05 47. Open Tu-F 10am-2:30pm and 3:30-7pm, Sa 10am-7pm, Su 10am-2pm. €3, seniors/under 16 €2, children under 6 free.)

Most food options are fairly similar. For large portions of salads, pizzas, pastas, and *platos combinados* (€g-14), try **Popy's ❷,** C. Arrabal, 3, right off Pl. de la Paz. (☎941 30 35 74. Open Tu-Th 7:30-11:15pm, F 7:30-11:45pm, Sa-Su 1-3:30pm and 7:30-11:45pm.)

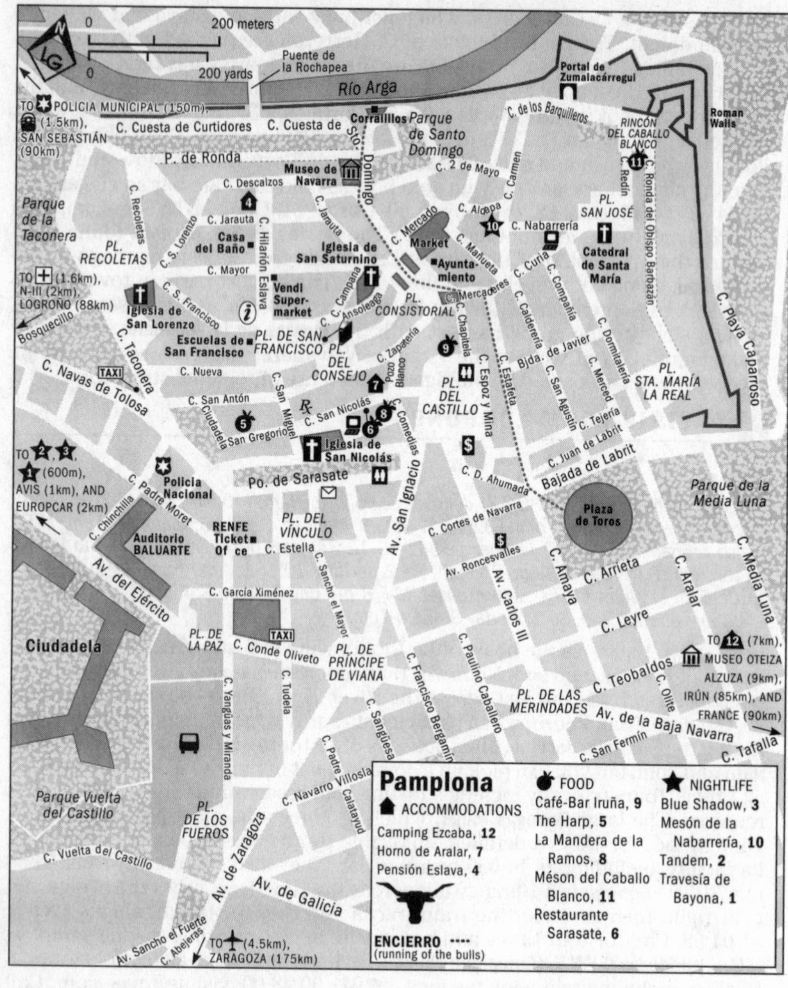

To reach **Plaza de la Paz** from the **train station,** turn left and take the road downhill, bear right for a while and then left across the river, and follow C. Navarra uphill to the plaza (15min.); look for white signs to *"centro ciudad."* From the **bus station,** follow signs to *"centro ciudad"* along C. la Ventilla, around the corner to the left from where the bus leaves you. You will reach Pl. de la Cruz six blocks from the station; there, veer left on C. Arrabal, which leads straight into Pl. de la Paz. The **tourist office,** in Pl. Florentino Rodríguez on C. de la Vega, provides a list in English of all the *bodegas* and tours. Take curving C. Virgen de la Vega from the corner of Pl. de la Paz; the office is in the plaza to the left around the bend, in the stone building. (☎941 30 33 66. Open M-Sa 10am-2pm and 4-7pm.) Other services include: **municipal police** (☎941 31 01 25); **Guardia Civil** (☎941 31 09 99); **Cruz Roja** (Red Cross) (☎941 31 18 38); **Centro de Salud** (☎941 31 05 39); and **taxis** (☎941 31 01 07).

NAVARRA (NAVARRE)

Navarra is a historically independent kingdom that formed in the Middle Ages from eastern segments of the Basque country as a wedge against aggressive neighbors. The religiously and politically conservative region sided with the fiercely Catholic Nationalist forces in the Spanish Civil War, but Navarrans also throw the country's wildest parties—Pamplona's **Fiestas de San Fermín** (July 6-14) are undoubtedly the most (in)famous. Aside from summer partying, Navarra is the entry point to Spain on the **Camino de Santiago** and home to pastoral mountain villages famed for cheese-making and quality hiking and cycling.

PAMPLONA (IRUÑA) ☎948

El encierro, la Fiesta de San Fermín, the Running of the Bulls, utter debauchery—call it what you will, the outrageous festival of the city's patron saint is the principal attraction that gained Pamplona (pop. 200,000) international notoriety. *San Fermín* is rightly touted as the biggest and craziest festival in all of Europe. The famous *encierro*, the daily running of the bulls from July 7 to 14, draws visitors from around the world. Ever since Ernest Hemingway immortalized the chaos of *San Fermín* in *The Sun Also Rises*, visitors have come to experience the legendary spectacle, and drink themselves silly while they're at it. At the bull ring, Hemingway's bust welcomes fans to the eight-day extravaganza of dancing, dashing, and drinking—no sleeping allowed.

Although *San Fermín* may be the city's most irresistible attraction, Pamplona's lush parks, Gothic cathedral, massive citadel, and winding *casco antiguo* merit a visit at any time of the year. However, beware of the post-*San Fermín* recovery period, when many establishments close for one to two weeks. Despite being the capital of Navarra, Pamplona has Basque roots; the area was settled by the early shepherds and nomads of this distinct culture long before the Roman "founders" arrived and named the city after Pompey.

TRANSPORTATION

Flights: Aeropuerto de Noaín (☎948 16 87 00; www.aena.es), 6km from town. Accessible only by **taxi** (€10-12). **Iberia** (☎948 31 71 82) to **Barcelona** and **Madrid. Spanair** (☎902 13 14 15; www.spanair.com) flies to **Palma** and **Tenerife. TAP-Air Portugal** (☎902 10 01 45; www.flytap.com) flies to **Lisboa.**

Trains: Estación **RENFE,** Av. de San Jorge (☎902 24 02 02). Bus #9 from Po. Sarasate (20min., every 15 min., €1). Info daily 6am-10pm. **Ticket office,** C. Estella, 8 (☎948 24 02 02). Open M-F 9am-1:30pm and 4:30-7:30pm, Sa 9:30am-1pm. Trains are not the best option, as Pamplona is not well connected by rail and the station is far from the city center. To: **Barcelona** (6-8hr., 3 per day 12:31pm-12:57am, €33-45); **Madrid** (3hr., 4 per day 6:45am-7:34pm, €50.20); **Olite** (35min.; M-Sa 4 per day 9:22am-8:10pm, Su 7:05pm; €2.50); **San Sebastián** (1hr.; 5 per day 5:36am-6:42pm, Su 3 per day 10:55am-6:42pm; €14.20-19.65); **Vitoria-Gasteiz** (1hr., M-Sa 3 per day 8:45am-7:40pm, €4-11); **Zaragoza** (2hr., 2 direct per day 4:45 pm and 7:03pm; 3 others connect through Castejon de Ebro).

Buses: Estación de Autobuses on C. Yangüas y Mirandaby the Ciudadela. **La Burundesa** (☎948 22 17 66; www.laburundesa.com) to **Bilbao** (2hr.; M-Sa 6 per day 7am-8:30pm, Su 5 per day 9am-8pm; €12.85) and **Vitoria-Gasteiz** (1.5hr.; M-F 11 per day 7am-9pm, Sa 8 per day 7am-8:30pm, Su 6 per day 9am-9pm; €6.85-7.50). **Conda** (☎948 22 10 26; www.conda.es) to **Madrid** (5hr.; M-Sa 6 per day 1:30am-6:30pm, Falso midnight-9:30pm, Su 10 per day 1:30am-9:30pm; €25.24) and **Zaragoza** (2-3hr., M-Sa9-12 per day 7am-10pm, €11-12). **La Estellesa** (☎948 22 22 23; www.laestellesa.com) to **Estella** (1hr.; M-Sa 12 per day 7:30am-8:30pm, Su 4 per day 10am-7pm; €3.69) and **Logroño** (1hr.; M-Sa 5 per day 7:30am-7pm, Su 4 per day 10am-7pm; €7.69). **La Tafallesa** (☎948 22 28 86) to **Olite** (50min.; M-F 3 per day 8:15am-9pm, Sa 6 per day 9:30am-8:30pm, Su 1 and 8:30pm; €2.84) and **Roncal** (leaves 5pm, returns 7am, €7.67). **La Veloz Sangüesina** (☎948 87 02 09) to **Sangüesa** (M-Sa 3 per day 1-8pm, Su 8:15pm; €3.30). **Vibasa** (☎948 10 13 63) to **Barcelona** (6-8hr., 4-5 per day 8:05am-5:15pm, €26). **La Roncalesa** (☎948 22 10 26) to **San Sebastián** (M-F 14 per day 7am-10:45pm, Sa-Su 11 per day 8:15am-10:45pm; €6.50).

Taxis: Teletaxi (☎948 23 23 00) or **Radiotaxi** (☎948 22 12 12). Taxi stand at Parque de la Taconera at the intersection of C. Navas de Tolosa and C. Taconera; another at C. Conde Olivio and C. Tudela near the bus station.

Car Rental: Europcar, Hotel Blanca Navarra, Av. de Pío XII, 43 (☎948 17 25 23). Take bus #4-1, 4-2, or 15 from Po. Sarasate and get off after the traffic circle past the Ciudadela. 21+. Open M-F 8:30am-1pm and 4-7:30pm, Sa 9am-1pm. Airport office open M-F 8:30am-3:30pm and 4-10pm, Sa 10am-1pm, Su 5-10pm. (☎948 31 27 98). AmEx/MC/V. **AVIS,** C. Monasterio de la Oliva, 29 (☎948 17 00 36) and at airport (☎948 16 87 63). Open M-F 8am-1pm and 4-7pm, Sa 9am-1pm. Airport hours coincide with arrivals (M-F morning and evening, Sa morning, Su evening). AmEx/MC/V. **Hertz** at airport (☎948 31 15 95) open M-F 8am-12pm and 3-10pm, Sa 10am-1pm, Su 5:10-8:10pm.

ORIENTATION AND PRACTICAL INFORMATION

Pamplona is a relatively small city, and most sites are generally accessible on foot. The **casco antiguo,** in the northeast quarter of the city, contains most major attractions. The wide-open **Plaza del Castillo** is Pamplona's center. To reach it from the **bus station,** take Av. Conde Oliveto, then turn left after two blocks at Pl. Príncipe de Viana onto Av. de San Ignacio (second from the left), which runs into the plaza. From the **train station,** take bus #9 to Pl. de las Merindades and head up Av. Carlos III until the plaza at the end. North of Pl. del Castillo, the Baroque **Ayuntamiento** is a helpful marker in the swirl of medieval streets, but it is still easy to get lost—pick up a free map at the tourist office. The **ciudadela** is outside of the *casco antiguo*, just 5min. up Av. del Ejercito from the bus stop. The **Río Arga** runs along the high northern walls of the casco antiguo.

Tourist Office: C. Hilarión Eslava, on Pl. San Francisco (☎848 420 420; www.turismo.navarra.es). Aside from maps and info on the region, accommodations, food, and culture, the staff offers a crucial minute-by-minute **San Fermín Fiesta Programme** guide that lists every event and another guide to the encierro with relevant bank schedules in addition to info on transportation, internet access, laundry, showers, and luggage storage. Info also available at www.pamplona.net. Ask about private guided tours. English and French spoken. Open during San Fermín daily 8am-8pm; July-Aug. M-F 9am-8pm,Sa 10am-8pm, Su 10am-2pm; Sept.-June M-Sa 10am-2pm and 4-7pm, Su 10am-2pm.

Currency Exchange: Banco Santander Central Hispano, Pl. del Castillo, 21 (☎948 20 86 00), has a 24hr. **ATM** and will exchange American Express travelers checks commission-free. During *San Fermín* open M-F 9:30am-noon; April-Sept. M-F 8:30am-2pm; Oct.-Apr. M-F 8:30am-2pm, Sa 8:30am-1pm. Note that hours are reduced right after *San Fermín*—make sure to get money before the weekend.

Luggage Storage: At the **bus station.** Bags €5.10 per day, large packs €3 per day. Open M-Sa 6:15am-9:30pm, Su 6:30am-1:30pm and 2-9:30pm. Closes for *San Fermín*, when the **Escuelas de San Francisco,** the stone building at the end of Pl. San Francisco, opens instead from July 4 at 8am to July 16 at 2pm. Lines are long, and you must have passport or ID. €3.40 per day and each time you check on luggage. Open 24hr.

Laundromat and Public Baths: Casa del Baño, C. Eslava, 9, (☎948 22 17 38). Drop-off laundry service (€10.60 wash and dry). Open M-Sa 8:30am-8pm and Sunday 9am-2pm. Showers €1.05, full bath €3.10. No laundry service during *San Fermín*. Showers open daily 8am-9pm.

Municipal Police: C. Monasterio de Irache, 2 (☎092 or 948 42 06 40). **National Police,** C. General Chinchilla, 3 (☎091).

Pharmacy: FarPlus, C. San Nicolás, 74 (☎948 21 07 04). Open M-F 9am-1:30pm and 4:30-7:30pm, Sa 9:30am-1:30pm. Late-night pharmacy on some nights, rotates daily. All pharmacies post location for that evening.

Medical Services: Hospital de Navarra, C. Irunlarrea 3 (☎848 42 22 22, medical emergencies 112), at the corner with Av. de Pío XII. The **Red Cross** sets up stands at the bus station and along the *corrida* during *San Fermín*.

Internet Access: At the **library** on Pl. San Francisco. Free **Internet** access for up to an hour with a sign-up sheet, and free Wi-Fi, accessible in parts of the plaza close to library. Open Sept.-June M-F 8:30am-8:45pm, Sa 8:30am-1:45pm; July-Aug. M-F 8:30am-2:45pm. **Kuria.net,** C. Curia, 15 (☎948 22 30 77). Look for the big yellow sign. First 10min. €0.50, 1hr. €2.50. During *San Fermín* €4.50 per hr. English-speaking staff. Open July-Aug. daily 10am-10pm; Sept.-June 10am-2:30pm and 4-10pm closed Su. **Locutorio San Nicolás,** C. San Nicolás, 37. €2 per hr. Open daily 11am-11pm (☎948 21 24 61).

Post Office: Po. de Sarasate, 9 (☎948 20 68 40). Open M-F 8:30am-8:30pm, Sa 9:30am-2pm; July 6th 9am-2pm; closed July 7th. **Postal Code:** 31001.

ACCOMMODATIONS AND CAMPING

If you think you're going to get a good night's sleep on a budget during *San Fermín*, think again. Unless you've booked a hotel room at least five months in advance, start fluffing up your sweatshirt: it's going be your pillow on the park grass or a *pensión* floor. Some early birds may be lucky enough to secure space at campgrounds or the few hostels that don't take reservations. Expect to pay rates up to four times the listed prices in most budget hotels. Many who can't find rooms (or never planned on finding them at all) sleep outside on the lawns of the park around the Ciudadela, Pl. de los Fueros, and Pl. del Castillo, or along the banks of the river. Those who choose this risky option should store their luggage, or, at the very least, sleep on top of it. Try to stay in a large group or near other tourists.

HOSTEL HASSLES? During *San Fermín*, the tourist office offers a real-time list of available official accommodations in the city, but don't expect to find much during the first 2 or 3 days. Check the newspaper *Diario de Navarra* for unofficial *casas particulares* (guest homes), though some advertisers are hesitant to let non-Spanish speakers into their home; look for advertisements posted on the streets in the days leading up to the festival.

During the rest of the year, finding a room in Pamplona is no problem. Hostels line busy C. San Nicolás and C. San Gregorio, off Pl. del Castillo, as well as the parallel C. Zapatería and C. Nueva, off Pl. de San Francisco. On weekends, expect plenty of noise on these streets; rabble-rousing (and open drinking) in Pl. del Castillo and the surrounding streets may make it difficult to sleep. Most hostels have different prices for *temporada alta* (before, after, and during *San Fermín*), *temporada media* (usually only July and Aug., but sometimes June or Sept.), and *temporada baja* (the rest of the year). The price icons below reflect *temporada media* prices.

Pensión Eslava, C. Hilarión Eslava, 13, 2nd fl. (☎948 22 15 58). Although inside the *casco antiguo,* it is not as crowded as other *pensiónes* and relatively quiet. Big, very basic rooms, some with balconies. Shared baths. Doubles for *San Fermín* €100. Otherwise singles €15; doubles €20-30. Cash only. ❶

Horno de Aralar, C. San Nicolás, 12 (☎948 22 11 16). Five fresh, sunny, spotless rooms with TV, fan, and full bath above an upscale, homey restaurant. During *San Fermín* all rooms €200-300. Otherwise singles €40; doubles €50; triples €55. MC/V. ❹

Camping Ezcaba (☎948 33 03 15; www.campingezcaba.com), in Eusa, 7km down the road to Irún. Take city bus line 4-V (dir.: Oricaín) from Pl. de las Merindades (4 per day, during *San Fermín* 26 per day). Hop off at the final stop; ask the driver or follow other backpackers on the moderate walk (500m) to the campground. The taxi ride costs around €15. Fills fast during *San Fermín*. *San Fermín* prices €10.59 per person, €11.68 per tent, €10.59 per car and €9.31 for electricity. Otherwise €4.90 per person, €5.35 per tent, and €4.90 per car; electricity €4.28. MC/V. ❶

FOOD

Tiny neighborhood cafe-bars advertise their hearty *menús* on their doors or on placards outside: try the side streets near C. Jarauta, C. Descalzos, near Po. de Ronda, and the area above Pl. San Francisco. C. Navarrería and Po. de Sarasate are lined with numerous *bocadillo* bars. Many cafes and restaurants raise their prices during *San Fermín* and then close for one to two weeks to recover. The nicely renovated city market, **Mercado de Santo Domingo,** C. Mercado, is to the right of the Casa Consistorial, down the stairs, and hosts hordes of the butchers and produce-sellers. (Open M-Th 8am-2pm, F 8am-2:30pm and 4:30-7:30pm, Sa 8am-2:30pm.) **Vendi Supermarket** is at the corner of C. Hilarión Eslava and C. Mayor. (☎948 22 15 55. Open during *San Fermín* M-Sa 9am-2pm; otherwise M-F 9am-2pm and 5:30-7:30pm, Sa 9am-2pm. MC/V.)

Café-Bar Iruña, Pl. del Castillo (☎948 22 20 64). This former casino that Hemingway made famous in *The Sun Also Rises* serves up typical Navarran dishes in classic form. From the antique decor of the elegant interior and the bust of Hemingway at the attached bar, you'll be reminded that this cafe (dating back to 1888) is fully conscious of its robust history. Reasonably-priced *menú* (€13). Otherwise tranquil interior becomes a roaring banquet hall around 10pm. Drinks and *bocadillos* at the bar, terrace seating on the famed plaza. During *San Fermín* bar only. Open M-Th and Su 8am-11pm, F 8am-2am, Sa 9am-2am. MC/V. ❸

The Harp, C. San Gregorio. Come for a lively dose of English language and Irish breakfasts, along with moderately priced imported beers and a welcoming atmosphere. The only authentic (i.e. owned by an Irishman) Irish bar in Pamplona. Often open late nights when everything else is closed. *Menú* €9-13. Sandwiches €5. Open M-Th and Su 10am-1am, F-Sa 10am-3am. MC/V. ❷

Mesón del Caballo Blanco, C. del Redín, at the Ricón del Caballo Blanco along the Roman walls past the cathedral. (☎948 21 15 04). Take a break for a few drinks and *pinchos,* like *tostadas* (toasted bread with various toppings, €5), or salads (€5.50-7). Grab a seat on the old stone terrace along the high northeast corner of the city. A local favorite on summer afternoons. Open daily noon-midnight, weekends until 1:30. ❶

Restaurante Sarasate, C. San Nicolás, 19 (☎948 22 57 27), above a seafood store. Mellow atmosphere. Organic, flavorful vegetarian dishes, both typical and innovative options. Vegan and gluten-free dishes available. Try one of the delicious mixed fresh fruit juices (€1.30). Lunchtime *menú* €10.50, F-Sa night and Su *menú* €16. During *San Fermín*, pure capitalism and culinary tradition prevail, and the restaurant serves typical meat and fish dishes. Open M-Th and Su 1-4pm, F-Sa 1-4pm and 8:30-11pm. V. ❸

La Mandera de la Ramos, C. San Nicolás, 9, is a mark of the new, hip, modern Pamplona. Subdued purple lounge lighting reveals original stone walls, dark wood beams, and a glass-covered stone wine vat beneath the floor. Gleaming legs of pork for *Jamón Ibérica* (a traditional Spanish snack) hang over a bar bearing images of Pamplona's storied past. Serves *pinchos* (tapas) and *tostadas* (€5-8), as well as a selection of *bocadillos* (€5). On weekend nights, tables are put away to make way for a dance floor. ❷

SIGHTS

CATHEDRAL AND CHURCHES. Carlos III and his wife Queen Leonor are entombed here, in an alabaster mausoleum in the recently restored 16th to 18th-century Gothic **Catedral de Santa María**. *(Pl. San José. ☎948 22 29 90. Open during San Fermín 10am-2pm; closed July 7 and 11; otherwise M-F 10am-2pm and 4-7pm, Sa 10am-2pm. Guided tours, including church, cloister, and Museo Diocesano; for groups, call ahead. €4.40, groups €3.35 per person, children €2.60.)* The 13th-century Gothic **Iglesia de San Saturnino,** C. Ansoleaga, 4, which served both religious and defensive purposes in the city's past, is near the *Ayuntamiento*. *(☎948 22 11 94. Open 9:30am-12:30pm and 6-8pm; July 6, 7, and 13 9:30am-1:30pm and 6:30-8pm. Free.)* The Romanesque 12th-century **Iglesia de San Nicolás,** in Pl. San Nicolás, is also close by. It too once served as a fortress; its turrets were removed after the Castilian conquest of Navarra. *(C. San Miguel, 15. ☎948 22 12 81. Open daily 9am-12:30pm and 6-8:30pm. Free.)* For a peek at *San Fermín*, head to **Iglesia de San Lorenzo,** also known as Capilla San Fermín, and follow the C. San Francisco past the tourist office. *(C. Mayor, 74. ☎948 22 87 90. Open M-F 8am-12:30pm and 6:30-8pm, Sa 8am-1pm. Free.)* All churches in Pamplona have modified visiting hours during *San Fermín*. Check with tourist office for more information.

MUSEO DE NAVARRA. This museum, atop Pamplona's highest hill, showcases art and artifacts from prehistoric to present. The museum's four floors contain Iron-Age relics, Roman mosaics, medieval pieces, and a collection of 14th- to 20th-century works, including Goya's portrait of the Marqués de San Adrián. Ask for an information leaflet in English. *(Up C. Santo Domingo from Pl. Consistorial. ☎848 42 64 92. Open Tu-Sa 9:30am-2pm and 5-7pm, Su 11am-2pm; San Fermín open 11am-2pm. €2, students €1, under 18 and retired free, Sa afternoons and Su mornings free.)*

MUSEO OTEIZA. Although it is accessible only by car or bus, this unique, modern museum is worth the short drive. It houses Basque sculptor Jorge

THE LOCAL STORY

HEMINGWAY: PUTO OR PAPA?

Ernest Hemingway first came to Pamplona in the early 1920s. His 1926 novel, *The Sun Also Rises* gave this city and its fanatical fiesta the international fame that it now enjoys. However, for many of Pamplona's residents, this international fame was not so welcome—hundreds, even thousands, of drunk and wild tourists began to descend upon their city year after year. For those who remembered the old days of San Fermín, that "*puto* Hemingway" brought the ruin of their fiesta. Still, some appreciated the notoriety that "Papa," as he is known on both sides of the Atlantic, brought to their little city—suddenly cast into the limelight.

Today, the city openly expresses its appreciation for Ernest Hemingway. The waiters at the Café Bar Iruña on the Pl. del Castillo will quickly tell you that this was, in fact, Hemingway's favorite restaurant in Pamplona, as a bust of the man leans casually against the bar. Bars throughout the *casco antiguo* bear his name, and street signs for the walkway around the Plaza de Toros proudly read Av. de Hemingway. As you approach the Plaza de Toros, a large stone structure rises up, a bust of Hemingway at its top. It reads, "Ernest Hemingway, Nobel Laureate for Literature, friend of this town, admirer of its fiestas, who knew best how to describe and promote the city of Pamplona. San Fermín, 1968."

Oteiza's 1650 sculptures and 2000 "experimental" pieces, along with sketches and handwritten manifestos of his artistic theory. *(C. de la Cuesta, 7, in Alzuza, 9km northeast of Pamplona. Río Irati buses go to Alzuza M-Sa 8:45am and 1:30pm, Su 4 and 7:30pm; return buses M-Sa 9:30am and 2:15pm, Su 4:20 and 7:55pm; €1.20. ☎948 33 20 74; www.museooteiza.org. Open June-Sept. Tu-Su 11am-7pm; Oct.-May Tu-F 10am-3pm, Sa-Su 11am-7pm. €4, students and retired €2, under 12 free. Free.)*

CIUDADELA. Felipe II built the pentagonal Ciudadela in an effort to secure the city from attack. Its impressive **walls** reputedly discouraged even Napoleon from invading. Today, it is part of a grassy park that hosts a *San Fermín* fireworks display and free exhibits and concerts during the summer. For a scenic walk to the Ciudadela from the *casco antiguo*, find C. Redín at the far end of the cathedral plaza. A left turn follows the walls past the Portal de Zumalacárregui and along the Río Arga. Bear left through the gardens of the **Parque de la Taconera**—where deer, swans, and peacocks roam—until reaching the Ciudadela. If you're in the city during *San Fermín*, you can get a glimpse of the bulls in their corrals from the lookout point at **Portal Nuevo,** at the northern end of the park. *(Located right next to the bus station. To get to the walls directly from Pl. del Castillo, follow Po. de Sarasate to its end, then take a right onto C. Navas de Tolosa. Take the next left on C. Chinchilla; you'll see the entrance at the end of the street, 2 blocks down Av. del Ejército. ☎948 22 82 37. Park open M-Sa 7:30am-9:30pm, Su 9:30am-9:30pm. Exhibits open M-Sa 6:30-9pm, Su noon-2pm. Entire ciudadela closed July 6-14. Free.)*

NIGHTLIFE

There is (night)life after *San Fermín*, and it is not difficult to find. **Plaza del Castillo** is the social heart of Pamplona, with outdoor seating all around the beautifully lit plaza. Revelers of all ages gather at bars in the *casco antiguo* to demonstrate their vocal abilities: singing, shouting, and any other type of loud carousing are the norm. Barhopping down C. San Nicolás and C. San Gregorio is a favorite nighttime activity (check out The Harp and La Mandarra de la Ramos on p. 476), as is drinking at the bars on C. Calderería, C. San Agustín, and C. Jarauta. On summer weekend nights, the drinking and partying pours out onto the streets and sidewalks. **Mesón de la Nabarrería,** C. Nabarrería, 15, a down-to-earth establishment near the cathedral, draws crowds day and night to dance to a funky mix of Spanish and American music and enjoy cheap beer. (☎948 21 31 63. Open July-Aug. M-Th and Su 10am-2am, F-Sa noon-4pm and 6:30pm-2:30am; Sept.-June M-Th and Su noon-4pm and 6:30pm-midnight, F-Sa noon-4pm and 6:30pm-2:30am. Open all night during *San Fermín.*)

If you don't mind the trek, follow the example of claustrophobes and college students who escape the cramped streets of the *casco antiguo* to the bars in Barrio San Juan on Av. de Bayona. You'll find more dancing and partying at **Travesía de Bayona,** a small plaza of bars and discotecas off Av. de Bayona, just before it forks into Monasterio de Velate. The most popular clubs are **Blue Shadow** (☎948 27 51 09) and **Tandem** (☎948 26 92 85), Tr. de Bayona, 3 and 4, both of which have good dancing, big crowds, and friendly bartenders. (Beer €3.50. Mixed drinks €6. Both open Th-Sa 10pm-4am.) Av. de Bayona also boasts a great number of stylish and pricey nightspots.

FIESTA DE SAN FERMÍN (JULY 6-14)

No limits, no lethargy, and no liability make Pamplona's **Fiesta de San Fermín**—known to English-speakers as "The Running of the Bulls"—Europe's premier party. At no other festival will you witness mayhem quite like this 9-day frenzy of parades, bullfights, dancing, fireworks, concerts, champagne-spraying, and wine. *Pamploneses*, clad in white with *fajas* (red sashes, about

€5) and *pañuelos* (handkerchiefs, €1.50-5) display impossible levels of physical stamina and alcohol tolerance envied by even the hardiest of partiers. From the moment the fiesta starts on July 6th until the moment it ends on July 14th, the party doesn't let up for even a second.

FERMÍN FAUX PAS. Don't commit the faux pas of wearing your *pañuelo* before the first *chupinazo* (rocket blast); tie it around your wrist to keep it safe. The plaza gets unbearably packed; wear closed-toed shoes and prepare to get up close and personal with fellow revelers; be wary of pickpckets. Other potential dangers include suffocation and injury from broken glass. Claustrophobics and agoraphobics should avoid the square.

Around 10am on July 6th, the whole city crowds around the **Casa Ayuntamiento** and the adjacent streets in anticipation of the mayor's noontime appearance. If you plan to get in to the square, arrive no later than 10:45am. While they wait, the people in the square spray each other with various alcoholic drinks, sing fiesta chants, and have massive food fights. The residents who live in the buildings above the square also join in the fun, throwing down buckets of water and other goodies, like giant beach balls, on the masses below. If you're planning to be in the plaza, don't expect to remain dry or clean by the end. As the midday hour approaches, the crowd sings and chants *"San Fermín!"* raising *pañuelos* high above their heads. As the mayor emerges, he fires the awaited rocket blast from the balcony and screams, "People of Pamplona! Long live *San Fermín!*" in Spanish and *Euskera* (Basque), a roar erupts from the sea of waving red triangles in the plaza below. Champagne and corks rain down along with eggs, ketchup, mustard, wine, flour, and yellow *pimiento.* Within minutes, the streets of the *casco antiguo* flood with improvised singing and dancing troupes, and the streets stay crowded for the remainder of the fiesta. The *peñas*, Pamplona's celebrated social clubs, lead the hysteria. Several times throughout the festival, they are joined by the *Comparsa de Gigantes y Cabezudos*, a troupe of beloved *gigantes* (giant wooden monarchs) and *zaldikos* (courtiers on horseback). *Kilikis* (swollen-headed buffoons) run around chasing little children and hitting them with fake clubs. These misfits, together with the city band and church and town officials, escort a 15th-century statue of *San Fermín* on his triumphant procession through the *casco antiguo*, serenading him with the *jota*, a local folk song. The statue is brought from the Iglesia de San Lorenzo at 10am on July 7, the actual *Día de San Fermín;* in exchange for this promenade, he is asked to protect the runners of the *encierro*, who sing to him before their fateful sprint.

THE RUNNING OF THE BULLS

The *encierro* (running of the bulls) is the highlight of *San Fermín.* The ritual dates back to the 14th century. It served the practical function of getting the bulls from their corrals to the bullring until someone decided it would be fun to run in front of—not behind—the bulls. The city authorities originally tried to ban the dangerous practice, but eventually decided that if they couldn't beat the masses, they should join them, and made the *encierro* an official part of *San Fermín.* These days, the first and grandest *encierro* of the festival is at 8am on July 7 and is repeated every day for the next week. Hundreds of bleary-eyed, adrenaline-charged runners flee from large, horned bulls, as bystanders cheer from barricades, windows, and balconies.

One rocket marks the release of the bulls; another announces that all the bulls have left the enclosure into the course. Both the bulls and the mob scurrying ahead of them are dangerous: in recent years, overcrowding has resulted in the bulls getting blockaded by the masses. The course has three sharp turns, which the bulls often have difficulty navigating; when their legs slide out from under them, they falter, creating a heaping pile of bull. Avoid outside corners to prevent getting crushed under said pile, and be especially careful at the Mercaderes-Estafeta corner. Bulls that are separated from the herd tend to be more nervous and aggressive, often turning against the flow of the crowd and attacking runners. After the final, dangerous, downward-sloping stretch, the run cascades through a perilously narrow opening (where a large proportion of injuries occur) and pours into the bullring amid shouts and cries from spectators. After the bulls have been rounded into their pens inside the Pl. de Toros, young bulls with protective padding on their horns are released into the ring to "play" with the mass of people.

NO BULL. Some of the more sober participants walk the course the night before. If you're planning to run, don't bring anything except for your rolled-up newspaper. Those with backpacks, cameras, or anything of the sort will be thrown out of the course by the police.

The safer alternative is to watch the *encierro* from the bullring or the sidelines. Music, waves, chanting, and dancing pump up spectators until the headline entertainment arrives. Bullring spectators should arrive at 6:45am at the latest. Tickets for the *grada* (free) section are available at 7am in the bullring box office (July 7, 8, and 14, €5.50; July 9-13, €4.50). You can watch for free, but the free section is overcrowded, and it can be hard to see and breathe. To watch from the sidelines, arrive by 6:15am or earlier, as the fences get unbearably packed. One of the best places to sit is the wall over C. Santo Domingo, right near the beginning of the run.

Tickets to the daily **bullfights,** every evening at 6:30pm, are incredibly hard to get, as over 90% of the tickets belong to season ticket-holders. The remaining few are sold every evening for the next day's fight. You can try your luck by lining up at the bullring ticket office before 8:30pm every evening, from the 7th of July onwards, or just buy scalped tickets (€40 and up). For prices of face-value tickets, if you're lucky enough to get them, check www.feriadeltoro.com.

TICKET TIP. Don't get ripped off by the scalpers outside the bull ring! Your best bet is to wait until right before the fight starts and then bargain tough with them. You may be able to cut the asking price in half.

THE PARTYING OF THE PARTICIPANTS

Right after the first rocket goes up on July 6th, the insanity spills over to the streets, gathering steam until nightfall, when it explodes with singing in bars, dancing in alleys, spontaneous parades, and a no-holds-barred party in **Pl. del Castillo,** which quickly becomes a huge open-air dance floor. If you don't want to stick out like a sore thumb, the attire for this dance-a-thon includes sturdy, closed-toed shoes (there's glass everywhere), a white T-shirt and pants or skirt (soon to be wine-soaked), a red *pañuelo* (handkerchief), and a cheap bottle of champagne (to spray—don't pay more than €3). Cheap white clothes are available at countless stands throughout the city.

After each night's hedonistic carnival, the new day's party begins (or ends) each day at 6am, when bands with shrill trumpets march down the streets. The city eases the transition with tamer concerts, outdoor dances, a mule-and-horse procession, a rural sports festival, fun fairs, bull leaping and swerving demonstrations in the bullring, and other such performances. To catch an important event that doesn't involve binge drinking, check out the Pamplona Cathedral Choir's performance of the Vespers, a religious song for the occasion, at 8pm on July 6 in the chapel of *San Fermín.* Also, don't miss the fireworks competition that takes place every night at 11pm over the *Ciudadela.* After the first few days of *San Fermín*, crowds thin out, and the atmosphere goes from Olympic-level citywide debauchery to a more distilled, experts and locals-only flavor of insanity. The festivities culminate at midnight on July 14 with the singing of *Pobre de mí: "Pobre de mí, pobre de mí, que se han acabado las Fiestas de San Fermín."* (Poor me, poor me, the festivals of *San Fermín* have ended.)

ESTELLA ☎948

Hiding between Logroño and Pamplona, charming Estella (pop. 14,000) lies nestled in a bend of the Río Ega, surrounded by mountains. With walking sticks and backpacks, *peregrinos* have been descending on Estella since the town's founding in 1090. Sancho Ramírez reworked the route to include this historic town because the medieval pilgrim found "good bread, excellent wine, and an abundance in meat and fish" when he arrived in Estella. The city's cathedrals still remain largely untainted by tourism, and the town is a great alternative if you can't find accommodations in Pamplona for *San Fermín.*

TRANSPORTATION. **La Estellesa buses** (☎948 55 01 27) leave from the station (☎948 32 65 09) on Pl. de la Coronación to: **Logroño** (1hr.; M-Sa 8-12 per day 8:30am-8:30pm, Su 9 per day 10:15am-8:30pm; €4.18); **Pamplona** (1hr.; M-F 13 per day 6:45am-8pm, Sa 4 per day 11am-8pm, Su 5 per day 11am-7:35pm; €3.69); **San Sebastián** (1-2hr., 3-6 per day 11am-8pm, €9.29); **Zaragoza** (2hr., M-Sa 8:30am, €12.71); **Vitoria-Gasteiz** (1hr.; M-F 3 per day 8:30am-8:45pm, Sa 4 per day 8:30am-8:45pm, Su 2 per day 4:15-9pm; €3.20). Check the second page of the local newspaper (€1) for daily schedules and destinations or ask for a schedule at the tourist office. **Teletaxi Estella** can be reached 24hr. at ☎948 55 00 01.

ORIENTATION. **Calle San Andrés/Baja Navarra** runs north-south from the back of the bus station on Pl. de la Coronación to the Plaza de los Fueros, while **Paseo de la Inmaculada** runs east-west from C. Dr. Huarte de San Juan/Avenida de Yerri to the Puente del Azucarero. **Calle Mayor/Zapatería/Ruiz de Alda/eEpoz y Mina** runs parallel to Po. de la Inmaculada and is the main commercial hub. Estella is unusual in that its historic neighborhood lies outside the city center. The river divides the city disproportionately; the older sites and the tourist office are on the smaller south side. To reach the bridge to the tourist office and old city from the bus station, turn your back to the front of the station and walk left across the parking lot. Then follow C. Sancho el Sabio to the river and cross the bridge. Make a left at the rotary, walk one block, and the **Plaza de San Martín** and the Renaissance **Fuente de los Chorros** will be on the right.

PRACTICAL INFORMATION. To reach the **tourist office,** C. San Nicolás, 1, walk across Pl. de San Martín toward the building with the wooden doors and flags. Turn right onto the street just in front of it—the tourist office is the fifth archway on your right. Pick up a good town map and information on local services. English, French, and *euskera* spoken. (☎948 55 63 01; oit.estella@cfnavarra.es. Open in summer M-Sa 10am-2pm and 4-7pm, Su 10am-2pm; in winter M-F 10am-5pm, Sa-Su 10am-2pm.) The **police,** Po. de la Inmaculada, 1 (☎092), are in the red building with wooden doors. The entrance is on C. Sancho el Fuerte, around the corner to your left when facing the station. **Medical**

services (☎948 55 63 50) are at the opposite end of Po. de la Inmaculada, near C Dr. Huarte de San Juan, and at the **Hospital Comarcal** (☎848 43 50 00). Call ☎**112** (only valid in Navarra) to reach **police, fire,** and **ambulance services** and for information on late-night pharmacies. The **library,** C. Ruiz de Alda, 34-36, provides free **internet** to patient patrons; drop by to reserve a 30min. slot. (☎948 55 64 19. Open June-Sept. M-F 8:30am-2:30pm; Oct.-May M-F 9am-9pm.) **Locutorio Internet Latina,** Pl. de los Fueros, 52 (☎948 55 53 84) offers internet at €2 per hr. (Open daily in summer 11am-1:30pm and 5-11:30pm; in winter daily 11am-1:30pm and 5:30-9:30pm.) The **post office** is at Po. de la Inmaculada, 5. (☎948 55 17 92. Open in summer M-F 8:30am-2:30pm, in winter 8am-8:30pm.) **Postal Code:** 31200.

ACCOMMODATIONS. Estella is a good place to catch some shut-eye during *San Fermín.* Reservations are advisable then and during Estella's own *encierro* (running of the bulls) the first week of August and the first few weeks of September. Many bars offer upstairs rooms for the night—check around Pl. de los Fueros and Pl. de Santiago, or consult the map in the pedestrian zone of C. Baja Navarra. Straight out from the back of the bus station, follow C. San Andrés to C. Mayor, found at the end of the pedestrian zone of C. Baja Navarra, and go left two blocks to **Pensión San Andrés ❷,** C. Mayor, 1. Clean rooms have TVs, and some have refrigerators and microwaves. Balconies overlook the peaceful plaza and become exhilarating lookout points during the *encierro.* (☎948 55 41 58. Singles €20, with half bath €32; doubles €32/40; triples with half bath €50; quads with half bath €60. MC/V.) Turning to the left after visiting the tourist office, it's 1km (20min.) Follow the river past the factory to **Camping Lizarra ❶,** C. Ordoiz; let the Pamplona bus driver know where to stop. The grounds include a supermarket, pool, laundry, playground, money exchange, horseback riding, fishing, a 300-bed hostel, and a bar. (☎948 55 17 33; www.campinglizarra.com. Open year-round. €5 per person, €4.43 per child; €5 per tent; €13.42 per *parcela* (site), €8.60 per smaller site; hostel bunks €9.03. MC/V.)

FOOD. Estella is known throughout the region for its *gorrín asado* (roast piglet, also called *gorrín de Estella*). The huge portions of juicy regional food served upstairs at **Restaurante Casanova ❸,** C. Nueva s/n, are sure to slow any pilgrim's progress. Entering Pl. de los Fueros from C. Baja Navarra, take the immediate left and find the black and yellow sign. Ask to sit upstairs. (☎948 55 28 09. *Menú* M-F €11.50, Sa-Su €19. Fish and meat entrees €6-22. Tu-Su 1-3:30pm and 8-11pm. MC/V.) **Asador Astarriaga ❸,** Pl. de los Fueros, 12, offers Navarran fare such as *gorrín* (€13.80) and other meat entrees (€11.80-16.60). The idyllic outdoor setting is worth the price of the food. (☎948 55 08 02. Fish entrees €12-20. *Menú* M-F €13.30, F-Sa €24.40. Open M-Th 1-4pm and 8-10pm, F 1-4pm and 9-11pm, Sa 1:30-4pm and 9-11pm, Th and Su 1:30-4pm. MC/V.)

SIGHTS AND ENTERTAINMENT. Next to the tourist office, a representation of the medieval French hero Roland jousts with Farragut the Moor on the columns of the 12th-century **Palacio de los Reyes de Navarra,** the city's self-proclaimed "architectural jewel" and now the **Museo Gustavo de Maetzu.** Inside, nine galleries of the works of painter Gustavo de Maetzu, who spent his last years in Estella, accompany rotating modern exhibitions. *(☎948 54 60 37; fax 948 55 32 57. Open Tu-Sa 11am-1pm and 5-7pm, Su 11am-1:30pm. Free.)* The 12th-century **Iglesia de San Miguel** commands a view of Estella from the hilltop Pl. de San Miguel, to the right after crossing the Puente del Azucarero from the tourist office. Its ornate stone portal depicts San Miguel fighting dragons, weighing souls, and taking care of celestial business. Exit at the door opposite the entrance to catch some more dazzling stone arches. Opposite the tourist office, the late Romanesque-early Gothic **Iglesia de San Pedro de la Rúa,** with its picturesque, half-destroyed cloister garden, towers above Calle de la Rúa. This church retains an authentic, undiscovered feel that is rare at more touristed spots. Tours of the San Pedro de la Rúa and San Miguel churches leave from the tourist office *(45min.; about 5 per day, after masses; €3.50, both churches €4.80; pilgrims €2.70/3.85; children €2.50/3.50, under 8 free.)* as well as a general monuments visit. *(☎948 55 00 70. Tours daily noon and 5pm; €5.50, pilgrims €4.50, children €4, under 8 free).*

During the third week of July, the city's more enthusiastic residents dress up in medieval garb for **Semana Medieval,** featuring parades, concerts, an Arab Market with food and crafts in Pl. de Santiago, theater performances, a roaming storyteller, and even a jousting match. The week-long **Fiestas de la Virgen del Puy y San Andrés** kick off the Friday before the first Sunday in August, featuring an *encierro* of baby bulls (less ferocious than Pamplona's), kiddie entertainment, a fair, Navarrese dancing, and *gaitas* (traditional instruments of northern Spain: like bagpipes, but without the bags).

PAÍS VASCO (EUSKADI)

As the Basque saying goes, "Before God was God and the rocks were rocks, the Basques were Basques." The País Vasco is officially composed of the provinces Gipuzkoa, Álava, and Vizcaya, but the Basque homeland, *Euskal Herria*, extends into Navarra and southwestern France. The region boasts one of the most varied landscapes in Spain, from verdant hills to industrial wastelands and quaint fishing villages to the glittering coastal cities of Bilbao and San Sebastián. The people are marked by their deep attachment to the land and immense cultural and national pride. However, it is *euskera*, a language unrelated to any other in Europe, that binds and literally defines them. Even the Basque name for themselves, *Euskaldinuak*, means "speakers of *euskera*."

The Basques are thought to have descended from the first Europeans, whose arrival predated that of the Indo-European tribes. Their culture and genes have gone relatively undiluted despite Roman incursions, medieval interference, and finally the Spanish abolition of the *fueros*, medieval grants of semi-autonomy. The Basques enjoyed a brief return to independence under the Second Spanish Republic, but the Republican defeat in the Spanish Civil War ushered in the Fascist rule of General Francisco Franco, who oppressed the Basques and banned *euskera* and other forms of cultural self-expression. In 1968, in response to such injustices, the organization *Euskadi ta Askatasuna* (ETA; "Basque Country and Freedom") began a terrorist movement that persists today. Anti-ETA sentiment is now quite strong among Basques, but many also argue that the methods employed to suppress ETA undermine free speech and disregard human rights either way. Street protests and graffiti continue to call for amnesty for political prisoners.

Today, most Basques share a desire to preserve their cultural identity. Although *castellano* is the predominant language, *euskera* has enjoyed a resurgence since Franco's death. Traditions like *cesta punta* or *pelota vasca* (known outside Spain as the deathly fast sport of *jai alai*) continue to thrive. Basque cuisine is some of Iberia's finest, including *bacalao a la vizcaína* (salt cod in tomato sauce) and dishes *a la vasca* (in parsley steeped white wine sauce). Tapas, considered a regional specialty, are called *pintxos* (PEEN-chos); locals wash them down with *sidra* (cider) and the local white sparkling wine, *txakoli*. Several famous chefs, including Juan Mari Arzak, hail from this region.

HIGHLIGHTS OF PAÍS VASCO

BASQUE in the seaside splendor of **San Sebastián** (p. 484).
ADMIRE your reflection (and the art) at the **Museo Guggenheim** in Bilbao (p. 497).
PAVE the road to peace in resilient **Guernica** (p. 498).
IMPROVE your groove at Vitoria-Gasteiz's **International Jazz Festival** (p. 505).

SAN SEBASTIÁN (DONOSTIA) ☎943

San Sebastián (pop. 180,000) glitters on the shores of the Bay of Biscay. An elaborate, Romantic-style boardwalk, elegant waterfront palaces, and wide golden beaches give the city an air of gentility masking the 21st-century edge found in its boutiques, surf shops, and nightclubs. Ever since Queen Isabel

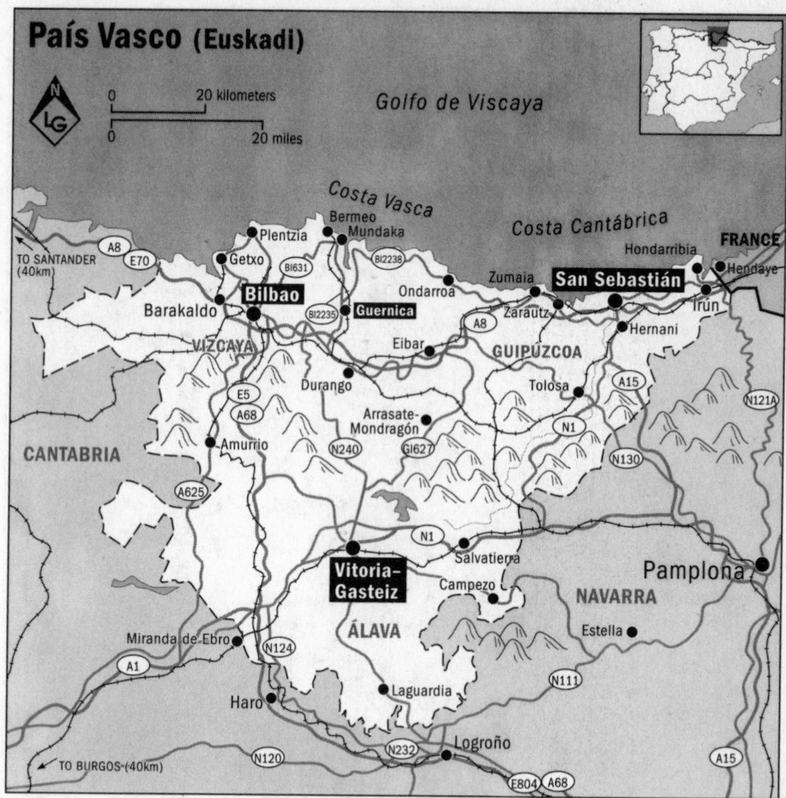

II made Playa de la Concha popular in the mid-19th century, the city has been a fashionable vacation venue for much of Europe's aristocracy. Still, its cosmopolitan air doesn't interfere with its strong sense of regional culture. San Sebastián once stood as one of Spain's great ports, but much of it was destroyed during the 1813 Peninsular War, when an invading Anglo-Portuguese force dislodged Napoleon in the process of setting fire to the city. The ruined walls were finally torn down in 1864, amid the construction of a more modern city replete with French architectural influences. Today, San Sebastián draws tourists old and young to bathe and surf along its beaches, hike its mountains, and enjoy its lively and friendly atmosphere.

TRANSPORTATION

Flights: Airport in Hondarribia (☎943 66 85 00; www.aena.es), 22km east of the city. **Iberia** (☎943 66 85 21; www.iberia.es) flies to **Madrid. Air Nostrum** (☎902 40 05 00; www.airnostrum.es) flies to **Barcelona, Málaga, Palma di Mallorca,** and **Sevilla. Interbus** service to Hondarribia stops at airport (45min.; every 20-30min. M-Sa 7:35am-9:45pm, July-Aug. also Su 8:45am-9:45pm; €1.75). A new airport shuttle goes to and from the bus platform at Pio XIII with each flight (€2). A **taxi** to the airport costs €27.

Trains: San Sebastián has 2 train stations.

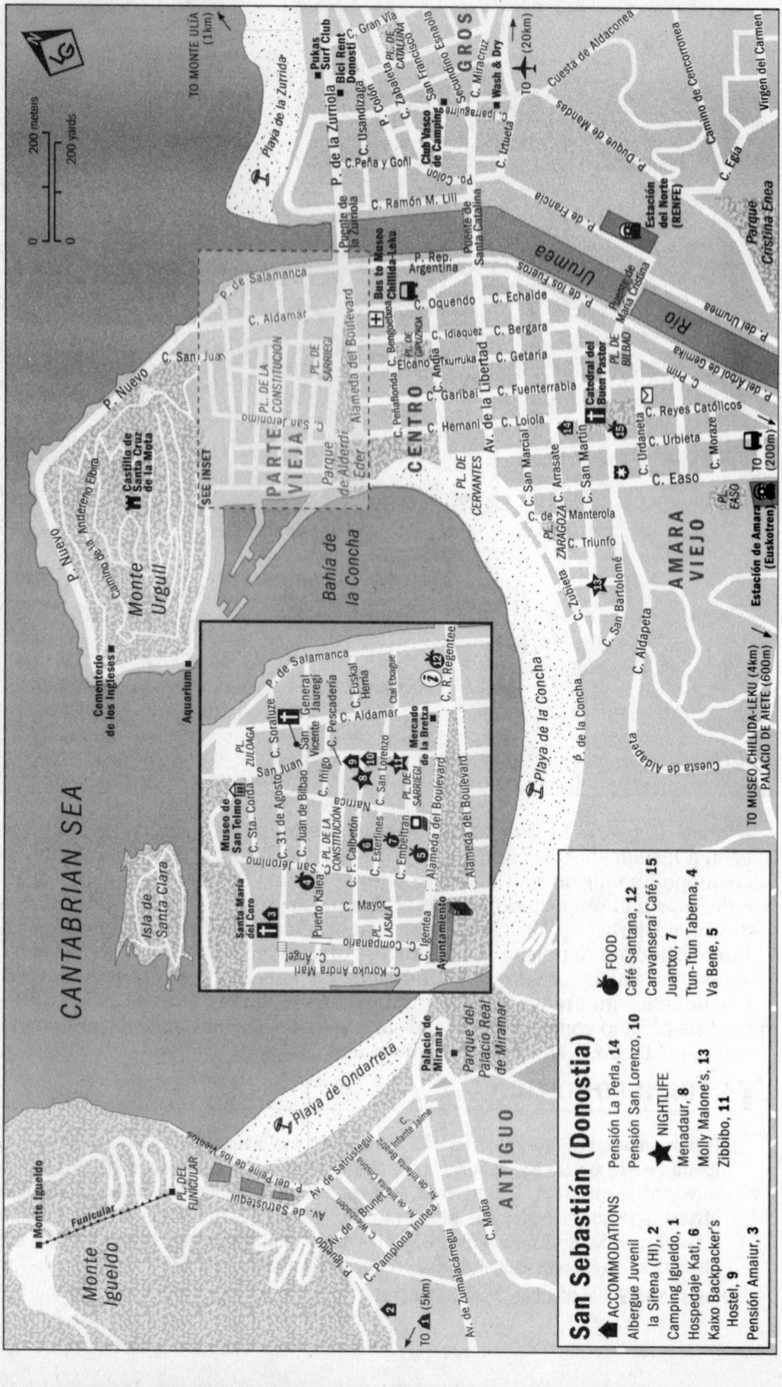

San Sebastián (Donostia)

ACCOMMODATIONS
- Albergue Juvenil la Sirena (HI), 2
- Camping Igueldo, 1
- Hospedaje Kati, 6
- Kaixo Backpacker's Hostel, 9
- Pensión Amaiur, 3
- Pensión La Perla, 14
- Pensión San Lorenzo, 10

NIGHTLIFE
- Menadaur, 8
- Molly Malone's, 13
- Zibbibo, 11

FOOD
- Café Santana, 12
- Caravanserai Café, 15
- Juantxo, 7
- Ttun-Ttun Taberna, 4
- Va Bene, 5

Estación de Amara, Euskotren (www.euskotren.es), runs to: **Bilbao** (2hr., hourly 5:47am-8:47pm, €6); and **Hendaye, France** (every 30min., €1.35).

Estación del Norte, RENFE (☎902 24 02 02; www.renfe.es), Po. de Francia. across the river over Puente María Christina. Info open daily 7:30am-11pm. To: **Barcelona** (8hr.; daily 10:45am, M-F and Su 10:59pm; €37.10-48.70); **Burgos** (3hr., 6 per day 8:32am-10:20pm, €21); **Hendaye, France** (45min., 4 per day 6:34am-8:43pm, €9.90-11.20); **Madrid** (7-8hr.; 8:32am, 2:37pm; €37.20-56.70. Express train 5hr., 8:32am, 2:37pm and 5:51pm; €55); **Salamanca** (6hr.; M-F and Su 8:32am, 1:37pm, 10:20pm; €30.70-39.90); **Tarragona** (7½hr.; 10:45am and 10:59 pm, €47) and **Vitoria-Gasteiz** (1hr.; M-Sa 8 per day 6:57am-10:20pm, Su 7 per day 8:32am-10:37pm; €8.85-17.20).

Buses: San Sebastián has a bus platform and a series of ticket windows around the corner, though not all under 1 roof. Av. de Sancho el Sabio, 31-33, and Po. de Vizcaya, 16. Most open June-Aug. daily 8am-9pm.

ALSA, Po. de Vizcaya, 16 (☎902 42 22 42), to **Santander** (3hr., 8 per day 8:10am-12:20am, €12.48).

Continental Auto, Av. de Sancho el Sabio, 31 (☎943 46 90 74; www.continental-auto.es) to: **Madrid** (6hr., 7-10 per day 7:15am-12:30am, €30-42) and **Vitoria-Gasteiz** (1hr., 8 per day 7:15am-12:30am, €7.50).

Interbus, Pl. Gipuzkoa (☎943 64 13 02; www.interbus.es) to **Hondarribia** (45min.; every 20-30min. 7:45am-10:05pm, July-Aug. also Su 8:45am-10pm; €1.75.) and **Irún** (35min., every 15-30min., €1.60).

La Burundesa, Av. de Sancho el Sabio, 31 (☎943 46 23 60; www.laburundesa.com), to **Vitoria-Gasteiz** (1hr., 7-8 per day 8:30am-8:30pm, €7.50).

La Estellesa, Po. de Vizcaya, 17 (☎943 47 01 15; www.laestellesa.com), to **Logroño** (2hr., 4 per day 8:30am-8:15pm, €11.97-13.66).

La Roncalesa, Po. de Vizcaya, 16 (☎943 46 10 64), to **Pamplona** (1hr., 6-10 per day 7am-9:15pm, €6.50).

Transportes PESA, Av. de Sancho el Sabio, 33 (☎902 10 12 10; www.pesa.net), to **Bilbao** (1hr.; M-F every 30min. 6:30am-10pm, Sa every hr. 7:30am-10pm, Su every hr. 8:30am-10pm; €9.20).

Public Transportation: Local buses (☎943 00 02 00; www.dbus.es). Maps and schedule at the tourist office. **Bus #16** goes from Alameda del Boulevard to campground past Mt. Igueldo and beaches (€1.25).

Taxis: Vallina Teletaxi (☎943 40 40 40; www.vallinagrupo.com) and **Radiotaxi Donosti** (☎943 46 46 46; www.taxidonosti.com).

Bike Rental: Bici Rent Donosti, Po. de la Zurriola, 22 (☎639 01 60 39). Provides bike trail maps. Bikes €13 per 4hr., €17 per day. Tandem bikes €6 per hr., €20 per 4hr., €30 per day. Also sells second-hand bikes. Call ahead for mopeds. Open July-Sept. daily 10am-8:30pm; Oct.-June 10am-2pm and 4-8:30pm.

ORIENTATION AND PRACTICAL INFORMATION

The **Río Urumea** splits San Sebastián down the middle, with the **parte vieja** (old town) to the east, and **El Centro** (the new downtown) to the west, separated by the wide pedestrian **Alameda del Boulevard.** The famed **Playa de la Concha** is to the west of El Centro, starting just beneath the end of Alameda del Boulevard. The **RENFE train station** and the neighborhood **Gros** lie on the east side. Intercity **buses** stop in the south of the city on the west side of the river.

Tourist Office: Centro Municipal de Atracción y Turismo, C. Reina Regente, 3 (☎943 48 11 66; www.sansebastianturismo.com), on the river edge of the *parte vieja.* English, French, and German spoken. Open June 15-Aug. M-Sa 9am-8pm, Su 10am-2pm; July-Aug. also Su 3:30-7pm; Oct.-May M-Sa 9am-1:30pm and 3:30-7pm, Su 10am-2pm.

Hiking Information: Club Vasco de Camping, C. Iparraguirre, 8 (☎943 27 18 66; www.vascodecamping.org). Local mountaineering and hiking club organizes and coordinates excursions. Info on hiking opportunities in País Vasco. Open M-F 6-8:30pm.

Luggage Storage: At the **Continental Auto** ticket office, Av. de Sancho el Sabio, 31 (€2, open 7am-2pm and 3-8:30pm); also at **Wash & Dry** (€3 per day, free with drop-off and pickup wash.)

Laundromat: Wash & Dry, C. Iparraguirre, 6 (☎943 29 31 50). On the east side of the river, over Puente de Santa Catalina. Lines are long in high season. Coin-operated washer and dryer available daily 8am-10pm. €6 wash, €6 dry, €0.50 detergent. Drop-off and pickup service available M-F 9:30am-1pm and 4-8pm, €20.

Police: Policia Municipal, C. Easo, 41 (☎092).

Medical Services: Casa de Socorro, C. Bengoetxea, 4 (☎943 44 06 33). Provides services to EU citizens only, but will redirect others to a private clinic.

English-Language Book Store: Elkar, C. Fermín Calbetón, 30, (☎943 42 26 96, www.elkar.com). Sells a wide selection of novels, as well as travel guides, maps, and Spanish-English dictionaries. (Open M-Sa 10am-2pm and 4-8pm, July and Aug. until 9pm)

Internet Access: You can find a *locutorio* offering internet access, phones, and calling cards all over the place in the *parte vieja,* though prices tend to be better outside of the busy center. Also at the **Biblioteca Central,** Pl. Ayuntamiento, at the front of the huge Casa Consistorial. Free Wi-Fi; free internet access up to 45min.; sign up at front desk. Open M-F 10am-8:30pm, Sa 10am-2pm and 4:30-8pm.

Post Office: C. Urdaneta (☎902 19 71 97), behind the cathedral. Open M-F 8:30am-8:30pm, Sa 9:30am-2pm. **Postal Code:** 20006.

ACCOMMODATIONS AND CAMPING

Small *pensiones* are scattered throughout the noisy *parte vieja.* For a more restful night's sleep farther from the action, look for *hostales* and *pensiones* on the outskirts of El Centro. Many *pensiones* and *hostales* in San Sebastian offer great low prices during the off-season, but when the high season hits in early-mid June (depending on the establishment), prices jump way up, some as much as double the low season cost. In July and August, *completo* (no vacancy) signs appear in many doorways. Particularly tight times are during *San Fermín* (July 6-14), the International Jazz Festival (July 22-27), and *Semana Grande* (week of Aug. 15); September's film festival is not much better. To make matters worse, many *pensiones* don't take reservations in summer. Come early in the day and be prepared to shop around, as finding a room may take some time. Solo travelers should be prepared to barter for a double; single rooms are virtually impossible to come by. The tourist office has a list of all registered accommodations in the city and a booking service for a charge, though many of the cheapest *pensiones* are not registered with the office.

PARTE VIEJA

Brimming with reasonably priced *pensiones* and restaurants, the *parte vieja* is where backpackers go for a night's rest (or more accurately, a night's partying). Its proximity to Playa de la Concha and the port makes this area a prime night-spot; scores of places offer a night's sleep above loud *pintxos* (tapas) bars. Call in advance for reservations, and expect to deal with some noise.

Pensión Amaiur, C. 31 de Agosto, 44, 2nd fl. (☎943 42 96 54; www.pensionamaiur.com). Facing the Iglesia de Santa María, look for the flower-filled balconies to your right. The owners are passionate about operating this beautiful *pensión.* After Virginia, the owner, greets you like a family member, choose from 13 bright rooms in a historic, warmly decorated house. 7 common baths and 2 tidy kitchens with microwave and toaster. Study room with travel info, public phone, and internet access (€1 per 18min.) Free Wi-Fi. English spoken. Singles €24-37; doubles €35-50, with balcony €42-60; triples €54-80; quads €65-95. AmEx/MC/V. ❷

Pensión San Lorenzo, C. San Lorenzo, 2 (☎627 34 32 06; www.pensionsanlorenzo.com), off C. San Juan by the *mercado.* This hostel's helpful owner offers rooms with kettle, toaster, fridge, TV, and private bath. Internet access €1.50 per hr. Free Wi-Fi. Doubles June €40, July-Sept. €55, Oct.-May €28. Cash only. ❷

Kaixo Backpacker's Hostel, C. San Juan, 9, 2nd fl. (☎659 39 38 42; reservations ☎943 42 06 51). This hostel is ideal for the budget traveler. Dorms and shared baths with free laundry, free internet, and kitchen access. Insider tapas tours of the city on weekend nights, as well as hiking and surfing. Bike rentals €2 per hr. and surfboard rentals €20 per day for guests. Dorms €25, Sept.-May €20. ❷

Hospedaje Kati, C. Fermín Calbetón 21, (☎943 43 04 87 or 677 06 69 00; www.hospedajekati.com). This *hostal* lets beds in homey shared rooms on the 5th fl. of their building in the heart of the *parte vieja.* Owners treat guests like beloved grandchildren. Elevator and outdoor terrace. Shared bathrooms with shower. Beds €20, July €25, Aug. €30. Also offers a private double and single (€50, Aug. €60). Cash only. ❷

OUTSIDE THE PARTE VIEJA

These accommodations tend to be quieter than those in the *parte vieja*, but are still close to the port, beach, bus, and train stations, with most accommodations no more than 10min. from the old city by foot. This area is also home to some of the city's most elegant boulevards and buildings.

Pensión La Perla, C. Loiola, 10, 2nd fl. (☎943 42 81 23; www.pensionlaperla.com), on the street directly in front of the cathedral. English spoken. Rooms come with private bath with bathtub, beautiful wooden floor, and balcony. Free internet and Wi-Fi. Quiet, central location. Singles €25-35; doubles €35-55. Cash only. ❷

Albergue Juvenil la Sirena (HI), Po. Igueldo, 25 (☎943 31 02 68), 3min. from the beach. Bus #16 runs to Po. Igueldo, right in front of the albergue, from Alameda del Boulevard (every hr. 7:30am-10pm, €1). Clean, large dorms as well as 2- to 4-person rooms. Multilingual staff. Laundry and kitchen available. Library and free internet. Breakfast included. Sheets €3. Max. 3-night stay if full. Curfew 2am, 4am on weekends. May-Sept. €16-19, 26+ €18-20. €2 extra without HI or ISIC card. MC/V. ❶

Camping Igueldo, (☎943 21 45 02; www.campingigueldo.com), 5km west of town atop Monte Igueldo. Bus #16 ("Barrio de Igueldo-Camping") runs between site and Alameda del Boulevard (every hr. 7:30am-10pm, €1). *Parcelas* (spot for 2 people with room for car and tent, includes water and electricity) June 16-Sept. 15 and *Semana Santa* €29.10, extra person €4.60; electricity €3.60. Sept. 16-June 15 *parcelas* €19-26. Fully equipped family-size bungalows €69-101. Min. 5-night stay in high season. MC/V. ❷

FOOD

Pintxos (tapas), chased down with local *sidra,* are a religion here. Bars line the streets in the *parte vieja,* where arrays of enticing tidbits on toothpicks cover countertops everywhere. The modern **Mercado de la Bretxa,** in an underground shopping center, sells everything from fresh produce and meat to *pintxos.* The huge supermarket inside offers a choice of groceries (open M-Sa 8am-9pm, though most vendors take lunch 3-5pm).

PARTE VIEJA

Juantxo, C. Esterlines, 6 (☎943 42 74 05), main entrance off C. Embeltran, 6. An authentic *pintxos* experience in a warm, friendly setting (some local *pintxos* bars can be surprisingly intimidating). Juantxo serves up the delicious little snacks (€1.35) in larger *ración* portions (€3.25-4.50) too, as well as sandwiches (€3-3.50) and *tortillas* (€3-3.50). Open daily 9am-11:30pm. Cash only. ❶

Ttun-Ttun Taberna, C. San Jeronimo, 25. (☎943 68 82). Painted with the red, green, and blue of the Basque flag and decorated with photographs of local festivals and *pelota* *vasca*. For lunch, they offer one choice: a superb and inexpensive *menú* (€9) with an assortment of authentic Basque options. Open daily 1-4pm. ❷

Café Santana, C. Reina Regente, half a block toward the river from the tourist office. *Pintxos* (€1.40-2.40) all nicely labeled. *Bocadillos* €4-6. Open July-Sept. daily 7am-10pm; Oct.-June M-Sa 7am-10pm, Su 7am-3pm. MC/V. ❶

Va Bene, Alameda del Boulevard, 14 (☎943 42 24 16). Frequented by tourists and locals alike for high-quality, low-price hamburgers and hot dogs served in the tradition of the best American diners. Norman Rockwell prints and an English-speaking staff lay on the Americana unoppressively. Burgers €2.95-4.95, sandwiches (ham, chicken, etc.) €3.15-4.95. Open daily June-Sept. 11:30am-1am, F-Sa until 2:15; Oct.-May 11am-12:15am, F-Sa 11:30am-1:45am. Cash only. ❶

OUTSIDE THE PARTE VIEJA

C. Reyes Católicos, outside the *parte vieja* just below the cathedral, is lined with popular bars and restaurants. If you wish to have a nice, quiet restaurant meal either out on a terrace or inside, this is the place to go.

Caravanseraí Café, Pl. del Buen Pastor (☎943 47 54 18), near the cathedral. Chic and artsy, without pretentious prices. Fabulous vegetarian appetizers and entrees (€4-10). Entrees €6-10. €0.60 surcharge for patio dining. Open M-Th 8am-midnight, Sa-Su 10:30am-11:30pm. AmEx/MC/V. ❷

SIGHTS

San Sebastián has enough sights and attractions to keep you running from one end of the bay to the other for days. After enjoying them one by one, the best way to absorb it all is an evening stroll along *Playa de la Concha*, which has breathtaking views of both mountains. Santa Clara, the Estatua del Sagrado Corazón, and the city's skyline are all within view from here.

MUSEO CHILLIDA-LEKU. The Museo Chillida-Leku houses a large collection of the works of Eduardo Chillida, San Sebastián's contemporary art guru and former Harvard University professor. His stone and steel sculptures are spread over peaceful, spacious outdoor lawns; pieces are hidden around every turn of the path. The 16th-century farmhouse at the center, a spectacular construction of huge wood beams and arching stone restored by the sculptor himself (and considered a work of art on its own), now houses some of Chillida's earliest pieces. *(Bo. Jauregui, 66. 15min. from the town center. Autobuses Garayar, line G2, leave from C. Oquendo every 30min. daily 7am-10pm, €1.25. By car, take N-1 out of San Sebastián south toward Vitoria-Gasteiz. Turn toward Hernani on GI-131. Museum is on the left. ☎943 33 60 06; www.museochillidaleku.com. Open July-Aug. M-Sa 10:30am-8pm, Su 10:30am-3pm; Sept.-June Tu-Su 10:30am-3pm. Daily tours and audioguides. €8.50, students and retired €6.50, under 12 free.)*

MONTE IGUELDO. San Sebastián's mountains afford spectacular views, but those from Monte Igueldo win hands down if you can bear (or if you seek) the noise of the amusement park atop the mountain. Monte Igueldo is located across the bay from the *parte vieja*. The sidewalk toward the mountain ends just before the base of Monte Igueldo, next to Eduardo Chillida's spectacular sculpture, *El Peine de los Vientos* (Wind Comb) by the raging sea. The best way to the summit is the #16 bus, then the funicular to the top. If you choose to walk, be careful; the only way up is along a narrow *carretera* (road/highway) with no sidewalks. On top of the hill you'll find an 18th-century tower with a dazzling **panoramic view** of the sea, mountains, and city. *(☎943 21 02 11. Open July-Sept. daily 10am-10pm; Oct. and Jan.-May M-F 11am-6pm, Sa-Su 11am-8pm; Apr.-June M-F*

11am-8pm, Sa 11am-10pm, Su 10am-10pm. €2, children €1. Funicular runs every 15min. €1.30, round-trip €2.30. Tower open daily 10am-9pm. €2. Mar.-Oct. opening hours depend on weather.)

MONTE URGULL. Across the bay from Monte Igueldo and just above the *parte vieja*, the paths on Monte Urgull wind through shady woods and monuments, providing stunning vistas of the old town and fishing port below. The fortified hills served as a major defense base for the city until the 19th century; today, visitors can absorb its history, as well as some local art, at the **Castillo de Santa Cruz de la Mota,** which tops the summit with 12 cannons, a chapel, a museum of San Sebastian's military and maritime history, and the statue of the **Sagrado Corazón de Jesús** that towers, watchful, over the city. *(Paths lead to the summit from Po. Nuevo; the official Subido al Castillo (Ascent to the Castle) starts at the end of Pl. de Kaimingaintxo, past the Iglesia de Santa María toward Santa Clara. Entire park open May-Sept. 8am-9pm; Oct.-Apr. 8am-7pm. Castillo and exhibitions open daily in summer 8am-8pm, in winter 8am-6pm. Free.)*

MUSEO DE SAN TELMO. The Museo de San Telmo resides in a former Dominican monastery and houses magnificent collections of Basque art, funerary relics, prehistoric Basque artifacts, dinosaur skeletons, and more recent anthropological exhibits. Especially impressive is the converted church, hung with monumental tapestries of Basque traditions like whaling and navigation in Republican style. *(Pl. Zuloaga, 1. ☎943 48 15 80; www.donostiakultura.com. Currently under renovations, expected to reopen in 2010.)*

PALACES. When Queen Isabel II started vacationing here in the mid-19th century, fancy buildings sprang up like wildflowers. The **Palacio de Miramar** has passed through the hands of the Spanish court, Napoleon III, and Bismarck. *(Between Playa de la Concha and Playa de Ondarreta. Open daily June-Aug. 8am-9pm; Sept.-May 8am-7pm. Free.)* The other royal residence, Palacio de Aiete, is also closed to the public, but surrounding trails in the adjacent garden are not. *(Follow Cuesta de Aldapeta or take bus #19 or 31. Grounds open daily June-Sept. 8am-9pm, Oct.-May 8am-7pm. Free.)*

AQUARIUM. If you can't stand to eat any more of your finned friends, come see thousands of them on display. The second floor holds a coral and conch collection. Come Monday, Thursday, or Sunday at noon to see the feeding. *(Po. del Muelle, 34, on Pl. de Carlos Blasco de Imaz. Arrows point the way from the port. Look for the big "Aquarium" sign. ☎943 44 00 99; www.aquariumss.com. Open July-Aug. daily 10am-9pm; Apr. 8-June 30 and Sept. M-F 10am-8pm, Sa-Su 10am-9pm; Mar. 1-Apr. 7 M-F 10am-7pm, Sa-Su 10am-8pm. €10, students and seniors €8, children €6.)*

BEACHES

The gorgeous **Playa de la Concha** curves from the port to **Pico del Loro,** the promontory home of the **Palacio de Miramar.** The flat beach, popular among families with children, virtually disappears during high tide. Sunbathers jam onto the smaller and steeper **Playa de Ondarreta,** beyond Miramar, and surfers flock to the bigger waves of more exposed **Playa de la Zurrida,** across the river from Mt. Urgull. Picnickers head for the alluring **Isla de Santa Clara** in the bay. (☎943 00 04 50. Motorboat ferry (5min.) departs from docks behind the *Ayuntamiento* June-Sept. every 30min. Round-trip €3.25.)

Several sports-related groups offer a variety of activities and lessons. For kayaking, call the **Federación Gipuzkoaka de Piragüismo,** Po. de la Concha, 18. (☎943 44 51 03. €7 per hr. Open July-Aug. M-F 10am-1pm and 4-7pm.) Surfers should check out the **Pukas Surf Club,** Av. de la Zurriola, 24, or the hut on the beach, for expert info, lessons, and rentals. The store manufactures its own surfboards and offers 5hr. courses at various levels for €65. (☎943 32 00 68; www.pukassurfeskola.com and www.pukassurf.com. Surfboard rental €25 per day, fins €3 per hour, wetsuits €20 per 2 days. Guided surfing €49 per hr. Open

M-Sa 9am-9pm. MC/V.) For general information on all sports, pick up a copy of the **UDA-Actividades Deportivas** brochure at the tourist office.

NIGHTLIFE AND FESTIVALS

The *parte vieja* pulls out all the stops in July and August, particularly on C. Fermín Calbetón, three blocks in from Alameda del Boulevard. During the year, when students outnumber backpackers, nightlife tends to move beyond the *parte vieja.* Keep an eye out for coupons, but beware—some deals are phony.

San Sebastián is a great city for cultural events and festivals. Highlights of the year are the renowned, week-long **Jazzaldia** jazz festival in late July and the equally prestigious San Sebastián **International Film Festival** in late September. During both, ticketed events take place alongside free street performances. For more traditional celebrations, come for **Semana Grande,** held annually the week around August 15th, when the entire city heads to the streets for shows, parades, concerts, and a nightly international fireworks competition over the Concha beach. Reserve ahead if you plan to visit during any of these events.

Molly Malone's, C. San Martin, 55, (☎943 46 98 22). San Sebastian's popular Irish bar fills with a crowd of Spaniards and travelers. A popular pregame spot before hitting the discotecas, the bar also draws the college-age crowd on Thursdays for international music night. Open 4pm-4am, weekends until 5am.

Mendaur, C. Fermín Calbetón, 8, (☎943 42 22 68; www.mendaur.es). Mendaur pumps dance music until the wee hours of the morning. Drink deals for the night posted on the chalkboard outside. Beer €3. Mixed drinks €6. Open 5pm-3:30am.

Zibbibo, Pl. de Sarriegi, 8, (☎943 42 53 34). In the *parte vieja* and packed with young tourists, Zibbibo is practically a disco, just on a smaller scale. Blend of Top 40 and Euro-techno. "Grande" sangria €5.50. 2-pint Heineken €5.50. Happy hour daily 7-9pm and 10:30-11:30pm. Open M-W 4pm-2:30am, Th-Sa 4pm-3:30am. AmEx/MC/V.

BILBAO (BILBO) ☎944

Over the last decade, Bilbao (pop. 354,000) has made a technological, cultural, and aesthetic turnaround. The economic engine of the Basque country and a major shipbuilding center since the 1700s, Bilbao, known as "Botxo" to Basques, was an important trade link between Castilla and Flanders. Bilbao has diversified from its industrial roots by appealing to tourists with its forward-thinking architecture, busy shopping streets in the *casco viejo,* and pleasant green spaces. Its incredibly efficient public transportation, built around a futuristic subway system and the recently overhauled international airport, remains the envy of other big cities. Frank Gehry's Guggenheim Museum, whose graceful gleaming curves embody the spirit of the new Bilbao, has powerfully fueled the city's rise to international cultural prominence. Enjoy Basque cuisine, summer festivals, and unforgettable art in this booming tourist destination.

TRANSPORTATION

Flights: Airport (☎944 86 96 64; www.aena.es), 12km from Bilbao. Serviced by many European budget airlines flying to different cities in Spain and Europe. To reach the airport take **BizkaiBus** (☎902 22 22 65) marked *Aeropuerto* from Termibus, or Pl. Moyúa in front of the Hacienda building (line A-3247; 25min., every 30min. 5:25am-9:55pm; €1.10). Buses return from airport to Pl. Moyúa (2 per hr. 6:15am-midnight). **Taxis** from airport to Pl. Moyúa cost approx. €18-20.

Trains: Bilbao has 3 train stations.

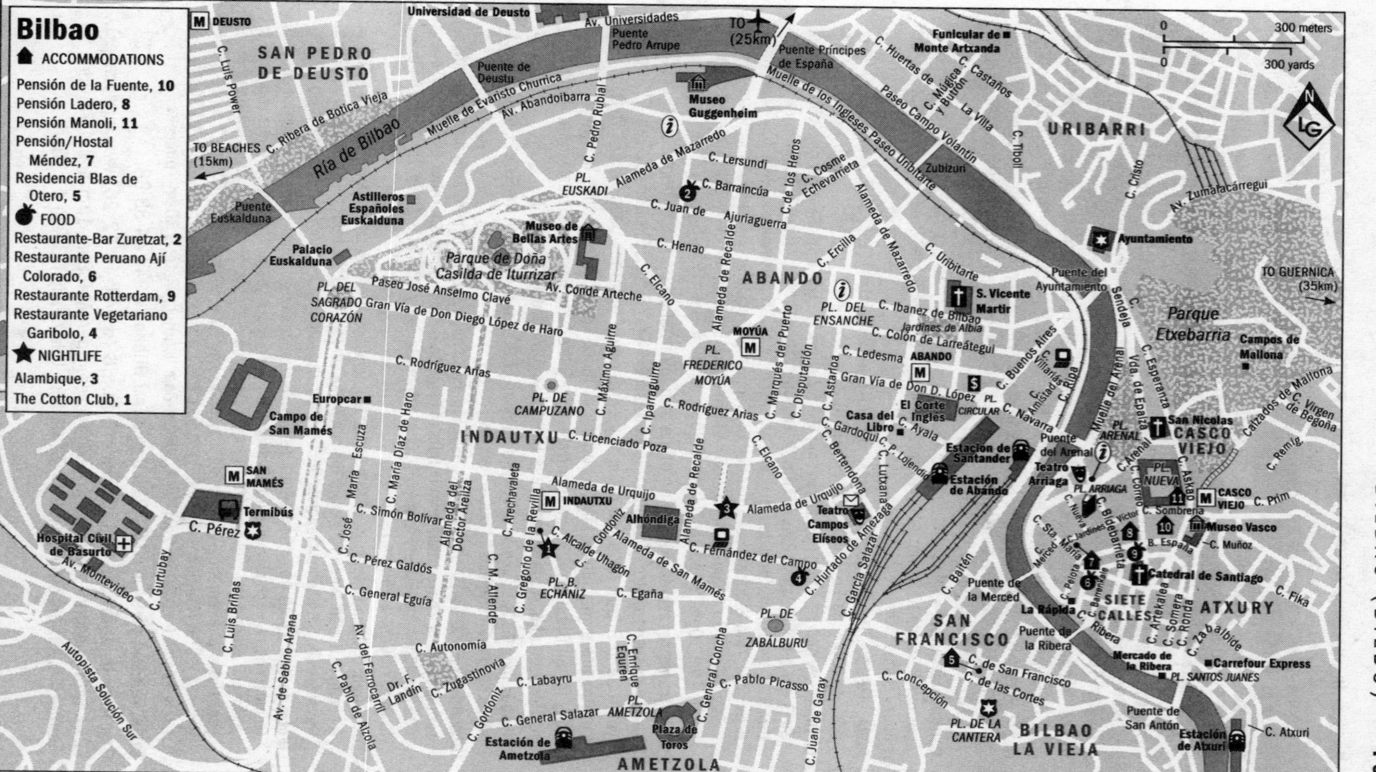
Bilbao
ACCOMMODATIONS
Pensión de la Fuente, 10
Pensión Ladero, 8
Pensión Manoli, 11
Pensión/Hostal Méndez, 7
Residencia Blas de Otero, 5
FOOD
Restaurante-Bar Zuretzat, 2
Restaurante Peruano Ají Colorado, 6
Restaurante Rotterdam, 9
Restaurante Vegetariano Garibolo, 4
NIGHTLIFE
Alambique, 3
The Cotton Club, 1
SAN PEDRO DE DEUSTO
URIBARRI
ABANDO
INDAUTXU
CASCO VIEJO
SIETE CALLES
ATXURY
SAN FRANCISCO
BILBAO LA VIEJA
AMETZOLA
Ría de Bilbao
Museo Guggenheim
Museo de Bellas Artes
Parque de Doña Casilda de Iturrizar
Parque Etxebarria
Campo de San Mamés
Catedral de Santiago
Museo Vasco
Estación de Abando
Estación de Santander
Teatro Arriaga
Ayuntamiento
TO BEACHES (15km)
TO GUERNICA (35km)
0 300 meters
0 300 yards

Ferrocarriles Vascongados/Eusko Trenbideak (FV/ET): Estación de Atxuri, Cl. Atxuri, 8 (☎902 54 32 10; www.euskotren.es). Trains to **San Sebastián** (2hr.; 17-18 per day M-F 5:57am-8:34pm, Sa-Su 6:57am-8:34pm; €6.20), **Guernica** (every 15 min., 5:57am-10:27pm, €2.40). Also connects to Hendaye, France.

FEVE: Estación de Santander, C. Bailén, 2 (☎944 25 06 15; www.feve.es). To: **León** (7hr., 2:30pm, €20.55) and **Santander** (3hr.; 8am, 1, 7:30pm; €7.25). Also offers extensive local service.

RENFE: Estación de Abando, Pl. Circular, 2 (☎902 24 02 02). M: Abando. To: **Barcelona** (9-10hr.; July-Aug. daily 10:05am, 10:25pm; Sept.-June daily 10:05am, M-F 10:25pm; €38.40-50.50); **Madrid** (5-6hr., daily 8:55am and 5:10pm, €40.10-45.20); **Salamanca** (5hr., 2pm, €28.20); **Burgos** (2½ hr.; 6 per day, 8:55am-11pm; €17-30). Info booth open in summer daily 7:30am-10:30pm; in winter 9:30am-1:30pm and 4:30-8pm.

Buses: The following companies are based at the **Termibús terminal,** C. Gurtubay, 1 (☎944 39 52 05). M: San Mamés. **Info booth** open M-F 7am-10pm, Sa 8am-9pm, Su 9am-10pm.

ALSA: (☎902 42 22 42; www.alsa.es). To: **Barcelona** (7hr.; 4 per day 7:15am-10:30pm, F and Su also 11:30pm; €40.59); **Santander** (1hr.; every 30-60min. 6am-11:30pm, also 1:45am; €6.44-11.80); **Zaragoza** (4hr.; 7 per day 6:30am-8:45pm, F and Su also 4:30 and 9:30pm; €19.10).

Continental Auto: (☎944 27 42 00). To: **Burgos** (2hr.; M-Sa 7-10 per day 6:30am-8:30pm, Su 7 per day 8:30am-10:30pm; €10.49) and **Madrid** (4-5hr.; M-F 10-18 per day 7am-1:30am, Su hourly 8am-1:30am; €26.11).

PESA: (☎902 10 12 10; www.pesa.net). To **San Sebastián** (1hr.; M-F every 30-60 min. 6:30am-10pm, Sa-Su 7:30am-10pm; €9.20).

La Unión: (☎944 27 11 11). To: **Haro** (1hr.; M-F 5 per day 7:30am-8pm, Sa 4 per day 8:30am-8pm, Su 3 per day 8:30am-7:30pm; €8.55); **Logroño** (1hr.; M-F 6 per day 7:30am-8pm Sa 4 per day 8:30am-10pm, Su 4 per day 8:30am-11pm; €11.05); **Pamplona** (2hr.; July-Sept. M-Sa 6 per day 7am-8:30pm, Su 5 per day 8:30am-8pm; Oct.-June M-Th and Sa 7:30am-7pm, F 7:30am-8pm, Su 11am-8pm; €12.85); **Vitoria-Gasteiz** (1hr.; M-F every 30min. 6am-10pm, Sa hourly 7am-10pm, Su hourly 7:45am-9:30pm except 9:30am; €5.45).

Public Transportation: There is an office with information on public transportation in the San Mames metro stop just below Termibus. (☎944 76 61 50; open 8:30am-7:30pm). If you'll be in Bilbao for a few days, buy a pre-paid Creditrans pass for €5, €10, or €15 at metro ticket machines, ONCE booths, or most kiosks. The card is a convenient way to pay for all Bilbao public transportation on Bilbobús, BizkaiBus, EuskoTran, the metro, and the funicular. All fares on these lines discounted with the card.

Bilbobús runs 23 lines across the city (daily 6am-11:30pm; M-F €0.90, Sa-Su €1). Signs at most stops have extensive lists of bus schedules.

BizkaiBus (☎902 22 22 65) connects Bilbao to the suburbs and the airport. 20% discount on fares with Creditrans. Leaves daily from in front of Estación de Abando to **Guernica** (lines A-3514 and A3515; 45min.; M-F every 15min. 6:15am-10pm, Sa every 30min. 6:30am-10:30pm, Su every 30min. 7:30am-10:30pm.)

EuskoTran, C. Buenos Aires, 9 (☎902 54 32 10), runs brand-new, fast, comfortable tram-trains on a circuit in Bilbao. When walking in the city, make sure to avoid the tracks, which often run next to the sidewalk. Service now reaches from the Termibus station to Atxuri (€1; Creditrans €0.40).

Metro (☎944 25 40 00 or 944 25 40 25; www.metrobilbao.net). Ultra-modern. Though it only has 2 lines, one on each side of Bilbao's river, it will quickly get you just about anywhere you need to go in and around the city. Look for 3 interlocking red circles to find entrances, and **hang on to your ticket** after entering—you'll need it again to exit. Travel within 1 zone €1.30, 2 zones €1.45, 3 zones €1.55 (Creditrans €.68/€.81, €.91). Trains run daily every 15min. 6am-10:30pm, also every 30min. F 10:30pm-2am, Sa 10:30pm-6am hourly, in winter 8:30am-7pm.

Taxis: Teletaxi (☎944 10 21 21). **Radio Taxi Bilbao** (☎944 44 88 88).

Car Rental: Europcar, C. Licenciado Poza, 56 (☎944 42 22 26; www.europcar.es). 21+ with passport and valid driver's license. Open M-F 8am-1pm and 4-7:30pm, Sa 9am-1pm. Airport branch (☎944 71 01 33). Open daily 7:30am-11:30pm.

ORIENTATION AND PRACTICAL INFORMATION

The Ría de Bilbao runs through the city, separating the historic **casco viejo** to the east from the newer parts of town to the west. The train stations are directly across the river from the **casco viejo,** while the bus station is considerably farther west. **Gran Vía de Don Diego López de Haro** connects three of Bilbao's main plazas, heading east from **Pl. del Sagrado Corazón,** through central **Pl. Federico Moyúa,** and ending at **Plaza Circular.** The **Guggenheim Museum** is in the mid-northern part of the newer, western bank, about a 20min. walk from the *casco viejo.*

Tourist Office: Oficina de Turismo de Bilbao, central branch at Pl. Ensanche, 11 (☎944 79 57 60; www.bilbao.net/bilbaoturismo). Provides information on city transportation, accommodations, museums, and restaurants. Open M-F 9am-2pm and 4-7:30pm; Semana Grande (mid-Aug.), Sa-Su 9am-2pm and 4-7:30pm. **Branch** at **Teatro Arriaga** (open July-Aug. M-Sa 9:30am-2pm and 4-7:30pm, Su 9:30am-2pm; Sept.-June Tu-F 11am-6pm, Sa 11am-7pm, Su 11am-2pm), and another near the **Guggenheim,** Abandoibarra Etorbidea, 2. English spoken. Open Tu-F 11am-6pm, Sa 11am-7pm, Su 11am-2pm; July-Sept. M-Sa 10am-7pm, Su 10am-6pm. All 3 offices offer guided walking tours of the old quarter and of the newer Ensanche-Abandoibarra (Sa-Su 10am for old quarter, noon for newer neighborhood, €4.) The tourist office also runs an accommodations booking service for a fee, call for information.

Currency Exchange: Caja Laboral, Pl. Circular. 24hr. ATM. Open M-F 8:30am-2:15pm and 4:15-7:45pm; Oct-Mar. Sa 8:30am-1:15pm; June 15-Sept. 30 closed F afternoons.

Luggage Storage: In **Termibús terminal** by information booth, lockers €1; inside €1 per bag. Open M-F 7am-10pm, Sa-Su 8am-9pm.

English-Language Bookstore: Casa del Libro, Alameda de Urquijo, 9 (☎944 15 32 00), next to New Inn Urrestarazu. English, French, and Italian best-sellers and classics; find Grisham next to Gogol. Open M-Sa 9:30am-9pm. AmEx/MC/V.

Municipal Police: C. Luis Briñas, 14 (☎092).

Medical Services: Hospital de Basurto, Av. Montevideo, 18 (☎944 00 60 00). For **emergencies** call ☎112.

Internet Access: Biblioteca Municipal, C. Bidebarrieta, 4 (☎944 15 09 15) has part-time free Wi-Fi, internet access, and library card with sign-up. Open Sept. 16-May 31 M 2:30-8pm, Tu-F 8:30am-8:30pm, Sa 10am-1pm; June Tu-F 8:30am-7:30pm, Sa 10am-2pm.; July M-F 8:30am-7:30pm; Aug. M-F 8:30am-1:45pm.

Post Office: Alameda de Urquijo, 19 (☎944 70 93 38). Open M-F 8:30am-8:30pm, Sa 9:30am-2pm. **Postal Code:** 48008.

ACCOMMODATIONS

During **Semana Grande** (Aug. 17-25), rates are higher than those listed below. **Plaza de Arriaga** and **Calle Arenal,** near the *casco viejo,* have budget accommodations, while upscale options pepper the river and new city off **Gran Vía.**

Pensión Méndez, C. Sta. María, 13, 4th fl.(☎944 16 03 64). Bright, very cheerful rooms with firm beds and spacious balconies. Singles €25; doubles €35; triples €50. MC/V. ❷. The affiliated **Hostal Méndez,** 1st. fl. is pricier, but has newly renovated rooms with windows, full bath, and TV. Many have balconies. Singles €38-40; doubles €50-55; triples €65-70. MC/V. ❹

Residencia Blas de Otero, C. de las Cortes, 38 (☎944 34 32 00). A university dorm that rents out rooms in summer. All rooms come with desk, full kitchenette and private bathroom. Free internet in lobby and connection in rooms, and 24hr. guard. Laundry machines (€3 wash and dry) and game room in basement. Location can be somewhat

A PEACE POSTPONED

After nearly 40 years of violence ınd 8000 deaths, the Basque ;eparatist movement, ETA ("Basque Homeland and Freedom" n *euskara*), announced a perma-ıent ceasefire in early 2006 and ɔegan negotiations with the Span-sh government. As discussions ɔrogressed, there was hope that he organization's bloody cam-ɔaign for an independent Basque state was nearing an end.

That optimism vanished in December 2006, when ETA claimed responsibility for a ɔombing in Madrid's Barajas Airport. Though the organization ınnounced that it was still com-nitted to the ceasefire, the Span-sh government announced that ETA had clearly violated the terms of the truce, and declared the ɔeace process as unquestionably over. In June 2007, the ceasefire officially came to an end. In an nterview with El País in June of 2008, Prime Minister Jose Luis Rodriguez Zapatero stated that he vas no longer willing to negotiate vith ETA, noting that dialogue had hus far proven useless.

Meanwhile, in the Plaza de España in Vitoria-Gasteiz, a ban-ıer bears the message "No to ETA," vhile the *Ayuntamiento* in San Sebastian proclaims: "No to ETA; Human Rights and Co-Existence in Peace." The sight of such slogans s a powerful sign that political dialogue has its place. Though ETA continues to be a significant orce, not all advocates of Basque iberation are with them.

dangerous at night; travel in a group. Singles €31.50-38; doubles €46-55.50. MC/V. ❸

Pensión Ladero, C. Lotería, 1, 4th fl. (☎944 15 09 32). Recently renovated shared baths, rooms with TV, some with balcony. Two extremely large triples, and several considerably smaller doubles, though all well-appointed. Singles €24; doubles €36; triples €53. No reservations. Cash only. ❷

Pensión Manoli, C. Libertad, 2, 4th fl. (☎944 15 56 36). Tucked on the tiny C. Libertad just outside the Pl. Nueva by the *casco viejo* metro stop with small but tidy rooms and shared baths. Rooms with balconies over the street. Free Wi-Fi. Singles €25; doubles €30. ❷

Pensión de la Fuente, C. Sombrerería, 2 (☎944 16 99 89). Quiet, comfortable rooms with basic amenities. Doubles differ in size, some include porches. TV €2. Wi-Fi available. Singles €24; doubles €33-36, with private bath €45. Extra bed €12. Cash only. ❷

FOOD

Restaurants and bars in the *casco viejo* offer a wide selection of local dishes, *pintxos*, and *bocadillos.* The new city has even more variety. **Mercado de la Ribera,** on the riverbank at the end of C. Somera and C. Ronda, is the biggest indoor market in Spain; it's worth a trip just to see the endless counters of freshly caught fish and the rows of equally fresh vegetables (open M-Th and Sa 8am-2pm, F 8am-2:30pm and 4:30-7:30pm). **Carrefour Express,** Pl. Santos Juanes, has groceries and is just past Mercado de la Ribera. (Open M-Sa 9am-9pm. AmEx/MC/V.) **El Corte Inglés,** Gran Vía, 7-9, in Pl. Circular, has a supermarket on the sixth floor. (☎944 25 35 00. Open M-Sa 10am-9pm. AmEx/MC/V.)

Restaurante Peruano Ají Colorado, C. Barrenkale, 5 (☎944 15 22 09). This intimate restaurant specializes in traditional Andean ceviche (marinated raw fish salad; €9.95-12.75), and serves up a full menu of excellent, filling Peruvian mountain dishes. M-F lunch *menú* €12. Open Tu-Sa 1:30-4pm and 9-11pm, Su 1:30-4pm. MC/V. ❷

Restaurante Vegetariano Garibolo, C. Fernández del Campo, 7 (☎944 22 32 55). Bright white walls and delicious, creative vegetarian fare, but get here early; seating is limited and the line is long. *Menú* M-F and Su €12; Sa €15, F and Sa night €25. Open M-Th 1-4pm, F-Sa 1-4pm and 9-11pm. MC/V. ❸

Restaurante Rotterdam, C. del Perro, 6 (☎944 16 21 65). The first owner opened this restaurant after retiring from the sea, naming it after his favorite city abroad. Serves authentic Basque dishes (entrees €9-14) in a cozy restaurant decorated with pictures of Bilbao's historic past. For dessert, don't miss the *Goxua*, a local dessert layering whipped cream, cake, and *crema catalana* (€3). Menu in *euskera*, Spanish, English, and French. Open 11am-4pm and 7-10:30pm. ❷

Restaurante-Bar Zuretzat, C. Iparraguirre, 7 (☎944 24 85 05), near the Guggenheim. The walls are lined with helmets signed by the workmen who built the Guggenheim from 1993 to 1997. High-quality seafood. Don't miss the incredibly sweet cinnamon rice pudding (€3.20). *Menú* €10-12. Open daily 7:30am-11:30pm. MC/V. ❷

SIGHTS

MUSEO GUGGENHEIM BILBAO. Lauded in the international press with every superlative imaginable, Frank Gehry's Guggenheim, opened in 1997, has catapulted Bilbao straight into cultural stardom. Visitors are greeted by Jeff Koons's *Puppy*, a dog composed of 70,000 live flowers standing almost as tall as the museum. The undulating shapes and flowing forms of the building itself are undoubtedly its main attraction. Sheathed in mute titanium, tan limestone, and fluid glass, the US$122 million building is said to resemble an iridescent fish, ship, or a blossoming flower. The dramatically spacious interior features a towering atrium and a series of unconventional exhibition spaces, including a colossal 130m by 30m hall with *The Matter of Time*, a massive permanent installation of curving steel plates by Richard Serra. Especially endearing is the mammoth 30 ft. high metal spider lovingly called *"Maman,"* (mommy) on the walkway by the river. Don't be surprised if you are asked to take your shoes off, lie on the floor, walk through mazes, or even sing during your visit to the eccentric exhibits. For those who find modern art hard to swallow, a handy (and free) multilingual audioguide provides good commentary and explanations, some by the artists themselves. *(Av. Abandoibarra, 2. Easily reached by Euskotran, Guggenheim stop. ☎944 35 90 80; www.guggenheim-bilbao.es. Open July-Aug. daily 10am-8pm; Sept.-June Tu-Su 10am-8pm. Free guided tours Tu-Su 11am, 12:30, 4:30, 6:30pm. Sign up 30min. before tour at the info desk. Restaurant open Tu-Su 1-3:15pm, W and Sa also 9-10:30pm. Menú €19-24. Adjacent cafeteria open Tu-Su 9am-9pm, July-Aug. also M. First-floor cafe open Tu-Su 9am-9pm. Wheelchair-accessible. Museum €12.50, students and seniors €7.50, under 12 accompanied by adult free. Audio tour included in admission price.)*

MUSEO DE BELLAS ARTES. Although it can't boast the name recognition of the Guggenheim, the Museo de Bellas Artes wins the favor of locals. The museum has an impressive collection of 12th- to 20th-century art, featuring excellent 15th- to 17th-century Flemish paintings and works by El Greco, Zurbarán, Goya, Gauguin, Francis Bacon, Velázquez, and Mary Cassatt, as well as canvases by Basque artists. A separate section showcases contemporary art, with works by Basque sculptors Chillida and Oteiza. *(Pl. del Museo, 2. Take C. Elcano to Pl. del Museo or bus #10 from Pte. del Arenal. ☎944 39 60 60. Guided visit every Sunday at noon with reservations; call ahead ☎944 39 61 47. Open Tu-Sa 10am-8pm, Su 10am-2pm. €5.50, students and seniors €4, under 12 free. W free. Guided visit €4.)*

OTHER SIGHTS. The best view of the Guggenheim, the city, the surrounding landscape, and the perfect place for a picnic is atop Monte Artxanda, north of the old town and equidistant from the *casco viejo* and the Guggenheim. Topside park features sculptures, snack stands, and a playground for children. *(Funicular 3min., every 15min. M-F 7:15am-10pm; additional service June-Sept. Sa 7:15am-11pm, holidays 8:15am-11pm. €0.86, with Creditrans €0.52. Wheelchair-accessible lift.)*

NIGHTLIFE AND ENTERTAINMENT

Bilbao has a thriving bar scene. In the *casco viejo*, revelers spill out into the streets to sip their *txikitos* (chee-KEE-tos; small glasses of wine), especially off of Barrenkale, one of the seven original streets from which the city of Bilbao has grown. The action in the *casco viejo* tends to die down around 2am. Then, teenagers and 20-somethings fill C. Licenciado Poza on the west side of town, especially between C. General Concha and Alameda de Recalde, where a covered alleyway connecting C. Licenciado Poza and Alameda de Urquijo teems with bars and loud, flashy discotecas. Laid-back **Alambique,** Alda. Urquijo, 37, provides elegant seating and chance for conversation under chandeliers and photos of old Bilbao. (☎944 43 41 88. Beer €2-3. Open M-Th 8am-2am, F-Sa 8am-3am, Su 5pm-3am.) **The Cotton Club,** C. Gregorio de la Revilla, 25 (entrance on C. Simón Bolívar, around the corner from the metro stop), decorated with over 30,000 beer bottle caps, draws a huge crowd on Friday and Saturday nights, while the rest of the week draws a more lowkey 30-something crowd. A DJ spins Friday and Saturday at 1am; occasional live concerts with notable Spanish artists. (☎944 10 49 51. Beer €3. Over 100 choices of whiskey; mixed drinks €6. Rum €6. Open M-Th 5pm-3:30am, F-Sa 5pm-6am, Su 6:30pm-3:30am.)

FESTIVALS

The massive fiesta in honor of *Nuestra Señora de Begoña* takes place during **Aste Nagusia,** a nine-day party in late August, with fireworks, concerts, theater, bullfighting—you name it. Pick up a *Bilbao Guide* from the tourist office for event listings. Street theater takes over the Pl. Arriaga in mid-July. Documentary and fantasy filmmakers from all over the world gather for a week in December for the **Festival Internacional de Cine Documental y Cortometraje de Bilbao.** Contact the tourist office for specific information and ticket sales, or visit www.zinebi.com/fant. Each January, Bilbao hosts **Zinegoak,** an international festival of gay, lesbian, and transgender film (www.zinegoak.com). During the summer, the municipal band offers free **concerts** every other Sunday morning at the bandstand in Pl. Arriaga, Parque del Arenal in winter. Bilbao is also the home of a world-class opera season (www.abao.org, tickets range from €53-169). Catch some *fútbol* at an Athletic de Bilbao match at **Campo de San Mamés.**

GUERNICA (GERNIKA)

Founded in 1366, Guernica (pop. 16,000) long served as the ceremonial seat of the Basque country. Representatives from all seven Basque provinces met in Guernica's *Casa de Juntas*, and under a nearby oak tree, Castilian monarchs ritually swore to uphold the *fueros*, ancient laws guaranteeing Basque autonomy. Guernica is currently home of the parliament of Bizkai and occasionally hosts ceremonial meetings of the entire Basque parliament. Since suffering almost total destruction under Franco-ordered bombs in 1937, the town has since been revived, yet remains a symbol of the atrocities of war.

TRANSPORTATION AND PRACTICAL INFORMATION. Trains (☎902 54 32 10; www.euskotren.es) connect Guernica to **Bilbao** (45min.; M-F every 30min. 6:15am-10:56pm except 9:45pm, Sa-Su every hr. 7:15am-10:15, last at 10:56pm; €2.40, round-trip €4). **BizkaiBus** (☎902 22 22 65) sends more convenient and more frequent **buses** from Bilbao's Estación Abando (RENFE) to **Bermeo** and **Lekeitio** via Guernica. (Lines A-3514 and A3515. 45min.; buses leave from Hdo. Amezaga in front of RENFE station M-F every 15min. 6:15am-10pm, Sa every 30min. 6:30am-10:30pm, Su every 30min. 7:30am-10:30pm. Return buses M-F every 30min. 6:15am-9:45pm; €2.15, Creditrans €1.65.) **Taxi** services include **Tele-Taxi** (☎944 10 21 21) and **Radio Taxi Bizkai** (☎944 44 88 88). There is free **internet** access at the former waiting lounge next to the bus stop (open M-F 9am-1pm and 4-8pm). To reach Guernica's multilingual **tourist office,** Artekalea, 8, from the train or bus station, cross the street and head right onto Geltoki Pl. Then walk up C. Adolfo Urioste, past C. 8 de Enero, and turn right onto Barrenkalea. Turn left at the alley marked by yellow "i" signs. The office is at Artekalea, 8. (☎946 25 58 92; www.gernika-lumo.net. Rents historical audioguides of the city and sells booklets on Guernica's history (€3). Open July-Aug. M-Sa 10am-7pm, Su 10am-2pm; Sept.-June M-Sa 10am-2pm and 4-7pm, Su 10am-2pm.) Several banks with 24hr. **ATMs** are located along C. Pablo Picasso by the intersection with C. Adolfo Urioste. **Farmacia Ledo R. Boyra Navea,** is at Artekalea, 1. (☎946 25 11 76. Open M-F 9am-1:30pm and 4:30-8pm, Sa 9am-1:30pm.) The **post office,** C. Iparragirre, 26, is two blocks to the left of the main bus stop on C. Iparragirre; turn right at C. Alhóndiga. (☎946 25 03 87. Open M-F 8:30am-2:30pm, Sa 9:30am-1pm.) **Postal Code:** 48300.

ACCOMMODATIONS AND FOOD. Although Guernica's main attractions can be seen in a daytrip from Bilbao, accommodations are available for those looking to spend a relaxing night away from the big city. Sit on the terraces at **Akelarre Ostatua Pensión ❸**, Barrenkalea, 5, and enjoy the panoramic views of Guernica. The new rooms are clean and large, with TV, phone, and private bath. From the train station, walk up C. Adolfo Urioste and take a right onto Barrenkalea. (☎946 27 01 97; www.hotelakelarre.com. Free internet and Wi-Fi. Breakfast €4.50. Reception 9am-1pm and 6-9pm, automated check-in machine at front door. Wheelchair accessible. Singles €32-40.50; doubles €42-54. MC/V.) Alternatively, head next door to **Hotel Boliña ❸**, Barrenkalea, 3, for rooms with bath, phone, and TV. (☎946 25 03 00; www.hotelbolina.com. Breakfast included. Singles €35-48; doubles €41-51, extra bed €12.86. AmEx/MC/V.) Downstairs from the hotel is **Restaurante Boliña ❷**, which draws a large local crowd with a classy low-key vibe, friendly waitstaff, and huge portions of delicious food. (☎946 25 03 00. *Menú* M-F 1-3:30pm €10. Open daily 9am-10:30pm. AmEx/MC/V.) For lunch, step away from the shopping streets to **Bar Gernika ❷**, C. Industria, 12, which serves €10 lunch *menús*, €18 on the weekends, including exquisite Basque fish dishes, and original *pintxos*. From the train station, walk up C. Adolfo Urioste and take C. Pablo Picasso left until it becomes C. Industria. (☎946 25 07 78. Open M-Sa noon-midnight, Su 1-4pm. MC/V.)

DAYTRIPPIN'. Plan your daytrip to Guernica around the opening hours of the museums. It may be best to see the Museo de Euskal Herria or the Casa de Juntas first, since both close during the siesta. Then check out the Peace Museum and get lunch while they take their afternoon break.

SIGHTS AND FESTIVALS. In January 2003, after a complete overhaul, the modest Gernika Museoa reopened its doors as the **Guernica Peace Museum,** in Pl. Foru, 1, across from the town hall. From the train station, walk two blocks up C. Adolfo Urioste and turn right onto Artekalea. A sign near the entrance displays a quote from Gandhi's dictum: "There is no road to peace, peace is the road." *(☎946 27 02 13. Free guided tours at noon and 5pm. Open July-Aug. Tu-Sa 10am-8pm, Su 10am-3pm; Sept.-June Tu-Sa 10am-2pm and 4-7pm, Su 10am-2pm. €4, students and seniors €2. First Su of every month free.)* The historical focus of Guernica is **El Árbol,** inside the gates of the **Casa de Juntas,** up C. Adolfo Urioste from the train station and on the left, past the Museo de Euskal Herria. Encased in stone columns, the 300-year-old oak trunk is the most important symbol for Basques and marks the former political center of the País Vasco. The old tree is not the original Árbol, but its oldest preserved descendant. Today, the Vizkaya General Assembly meets in the Casa, which is open to the public. (☎946 25 11 38; www.bizkaia.net. Open daily June-Sept. 10am-2pm and 4-7pm; Oct.-

THE LOCAL STORY

RAGEDY OF GUERNICA

Billing itself today as a "City of Peace," Guernica was once the ite of one of the most horrifying isplays of absolute warfare. The istoric Basque town was almost ntirely wiped out on April 26, 937, as bomb after bomb was ropped on the town for more han 3hr., until over 100,000 lb. of explosives had been unloaded n the battered buildings.

The bombardment was carried ut at the behest of Generalissimo rancisco Franco by the German ondor Legion, eager to test its ew strategy of carpet-bombing ivilian populations to achieve uick military victories. The Spansh leader-to-be wanted to make n example out of Guernica and o prevent any potential Basque prising. While the town itself had o strategic military significance, oth Franco and the Germans had omething to gain from its utterly emoralizing destruction

Survivors from that Monday, a arket day, recall being chased n the fields and forced into their omes by machine-gun fire, only o have the buildings above them orn apart by bombs moments ater. One woman recalled fires urning in the town for three days fter the bombardment. When it as all over, over three quarters of the town had been destroyed, eaving only the Casa de Juntas the Biscayan assembly chamber), he church of Santa Maria, and he symbolic oak tree of Guernica ntouched. Hundreds were killed n the attack and many thousands

May 10am-2pm and 4-6pm. Free.) Nearby is the **Parque de los Pueblos de Europa.** Eduardo Chillida's dramatic sculpture **Gure aitaren etxea** (Our Father's House), a monument commissioned for the 50th anniversary of the city's bombing, stands in a quiet corner of the park. To get to the park from the bus station, follow C. Adolfo Urioste; at the top, follow the arrow to the right. *(Open daily June-Aug. 10am-9pm; Sept.-May 10am-7pm. Free.)* At the park's entrance, paintings and artifacts on display inside the **Museo de Euskal Herria,** C. Allende Salazar, 5, document Basque history, culture, language and folklore. The extensive collection of historical maps of the Basque country, the oldest dating from the 16th century, is not to be missed. The building itself, the Palacio Alegra, is an impressive 18th-century mansion that survived the 1937 air raid. *(☎946 25 54 51. Audio tour included. Open Tu-Sa 10am-2pm and 4-7pm, Su 11am-3pm. €3, under 26 and over 65 €1.50.)*

The biggest fiesta of the year honors **San Roque** (Aug. 14-18). From June-October, a special **market day** is held the first Saturday of every month in the Pl. del Mercado; there are also two major market days the first and last Mondays of October. On these days, as well as at smaller weekly markets every Monday morning, vendors sell everything from fine chocolates to freshly grilled emu.

VITORIA-GASTEIZ ☎945

While most tourists flock to San Sebastián and Pamplona, the hidden cosmopolitan gem of Vitoria-Gasteiz (pop. 229,000) lies only an hour away. This city, the capital of Basque Country, is threaded with green lines of trees and long pedestrian walkways, and the music of street performers drifts about the elegant avenues on many a summer night. The relaxing pace of the city nurtures a thriving arts scene; numerous posters advertise live shows and jams, and one of the most prestigious jazz festivals in the world is held here every summer. Plenty of hiking and biking await visitors here as well. The city has a progressive and feisty attitude, evident in everything from the politically charged graffiti art to its public bicycles, free for all to use. Vitoria-Gasteiz's hyphenated name testifies to its regional ties; founded as Villa de Nueva Victoria by King Sancho VI of Navarra in 1181 over the small Basque village of Gasteiz, the city regained its original name centuries later when the Basques recovered regional autonomy in 1979. Spray-painted road signs with "Vitoria" crossed out are evidence of continuing loyalty to Basque roots today.

TRANSPORTATION

Flights: Aeropuerto Vitoria-Foronda (☎902 40 47 04; www.aena.es), 9km outside town. Airport info open M-F 8am-2:15pm. Flights to Dublin, London, and Mallorca. Accessible May-Oct. by **La Union** bus from the bus station (☎944 76 50 07; www.laburundesa.com. €3). Otherwise, the airport is accessible only by car or taxi (approx. €17-20). **Iberia** (☎902 40 05 00). Info open daily 6am-midnight.

Trains: RENFE, Pl. de la Estación (☎902 24 02 02). Info open daily 7am-10pm. To: **Barcelona** (7hr., 4:23pm, €42.60); **Burgos** (1hr., 10 per day 7:20am-1:15am, €7.85-18.80); **Logroño** (1hr., 8:10am, €7.60); **Madrid** (5-7hr., 5-6 per day 7:20am-5:55pm, €30.55-43.20); **Pamplona** (1hr., 4 per day 7:40am-7:05pm, €4.30-14); **San Sebastián** (1hr., 8 per day 4:24am-7:53pm, €8.18-16).

Buses: C. los Herrán, 50 (☎945 25 84 00). Bus #2 goes from the bus station to C. Florida, but it is probably easier to walk, as buses come infrequently and stops are poorly marked. Open M-F 8am-8pm, Sa-Su 9am-7pm. ALSA (☎945 42 22 42; www.alsa.es) to: **Barcelona** (6-7hr.; 3 per day 7:15am, 3:15pm, 11:25pm; €36.48) and **Zaragoza** (3hr.; M-Th and Sa 5 per day 7:30am-9:45pm, F and Su 7 per day 7:30am-10:30pm; €15.17). **Burundesa** (☎948 26 46 26; www.laburundesa.com) to **Pamplona** (1hr.; M-F 11 per day 7am-9pm, Sa 8 per day 7am-9pm, Su 6 per day 9am-9pm; €7.50). **Continental Auto** (☎945 28 64 66) to **Burgos** (1hr., 8 per day 6:45am-2:05am, €7.37); **Madrid** (4-5hr.; M-Sa 9 per day 6:45am-2:05am, Su 11 per day 8:45am-2:05am; €23.04-36); and **San Sebastián** (1hr.; M-Th and Sa 6 per day 5am-11:30pm, F and Su 7 per day 5am-1:30am; €7.50). **La Unión** (☎945 26 46 26; www.laburundesa.com) to **Bilbao** (1hr.; M-F every 30min. 6am-10pm, Sa every 45min. 7:30am-10pm, Su 16 per day 9am-9:30pm; €5.45).

Public Transportation: Tuvisa Buses (☎945 16 10 54) cover the city and suburbs (7am-10pm, €0.80). A **tourist train** makes a loop of major landmarks, departing from Pl. de la Virgen Blanca (July-Sept. hourly 11:30am-1:30pm and 5-8pm; €4, children €3).

Taxis: Radio Taxi (☎945 27 35 00). 24hr. service to Vitoria and surrounding areas.

Car Rental: Europcar, C. Adriano VI, 29 (☎945 20 04 33). 21+. Open daily 9am-1pm and 4-7:30pm, Sa 9am-1pm. Airport **branch** (☎94516 36 44). Open M-F 1:30-2:45pm. **Avis,** Av. Gasteiz, 53 (☎945 24 46 12, airport office ☎945 27 65 39; www.avis.es). **Hertz,** Portal de Betoño, 11 (☎945 26 55 90, airport office ☎945 26 55 90, reservations ☎902 40 24 05; www.hertz.es).

more injured. In just a few hours, Guernica was transformed into a smoldering shell of its former self.

Guernica was rebuilt over the following five years, and it has since remained a universal symbol for the atrocities of warfare and indiscriminate killing. Many pictures, sketches, and paintings have attempted to capture this nightmarish day. In a painting now at the Guernica Peace Museum (p. 499), Sofía Gandarias depicts women holding dead children underneath the words *"y del cielo llovía sangre"* (and from the sky rained blood). Picasso's famous masterpiece, *Guernica,* which now hangs in Madrid's Reina Sofia (p. 111), chillingly captures the unspeakable horror of that day, and tries to bring Guernica's tragedy international recognition. When asked by a German ambassador, "Did you do this?" Picasso answered simply, "No, you did."

Today, Guernica is looking to move beyond its devastating past, and to become a herald of peace and reconciliation throughout the world. In 1989, the town received a public apology from the president of Germany for his country's role in the attack, and it has since adopted the motto *"renunciar a olvidar, renunciar a la venganza"* (not forgetting, not seeking vengeance). Once the setting for one of humanity's darkest moments, Guernica is now looking to light the way for the rest of the world.

Bike Rental: Free from tourist office and civic centers. Open July-Sept. daily 10am-7pm; Oct.-June M-Sa 10am-7pm, Su 11am-2pm. 4hr. limit.

ORIENTATION AND PRACTICAL INFORMATION

The medieval *casco viejo* is the almond-shaped core of Vitoria-Gasteiz, and shelters its three oldest streets: **Fray Zacarias Martinez, Santa Maria** and **Las Escuelas** in the highest and most central part of town. **Plaza de la Virgen Blanca,** which is directly beneath this area, is the focal point of the town and is filled with fountains, restaurants, and bustling activity.

Tourist Office: Pl. del General Loma, 1 (☎945 16 15 98; www.turismo.vitoria-gasteiz.org). **Guided tours** of the *casco viejo* (11:30am) and other sights (5:30pm) leave from the office. July-Sept. daily; €5, min. 2 people. For tours in languages other than Spanish reserve in advance with the tourist office. **Bike tours** are also available (2-3 per month, inquire at tourist office for details; €7). Open July-Sept. daily 9:30am-7:30pm; Oct.-June M-Sa 10am-7pm, Su 11am-2pm.

Currency Exchange: Banco Santander Central Hispano, Pl. del Arca, 1-3 (☎945 14 24 00). 24hr. ATM. Open May-Sept. M-F 8:30am-2pm; Oct.-Apr. also Sa 8:30am-1pm.

Luggage storage: At the **bus station.** €2 per item per day, €3 large items. Open M-Sa 8am-8pm, Su 9am-7pm.

Laundromat: Autoservicio Lavandería Rico Valle, C. Luis Heinz, across from the Parque de Florida. Open daily 7am-10pm, holidays 9am-10pm. 8kg wash €5; 30min. dry €2.

Police: Municipal Police, C. Aguirrelanda, 8 (☎092).

Medical Services: Osakidetza Servicio Vasco de Salud, Av. de Santiago, 7 (☎945 24 44 44), off C. de la Paz. Open M-F 5pm-midnight, Sa 2pm-midnight, Su 9am-midnight. **Hospital General de Santiago,** C. Olaguíbel, 29 (☎945 00 76 00). **Pharmacy College** (pharmacy information) ☎945 23 07 21.

Internet Access: Casa de Cultura (library) Po. de la Florida along the park has free internet access. (Open M-F 9am-2pm and 4-8pm; www.bibliotecaspublicas.es/vitoria).

Post Office: C. Postas, 9 (☎902 19 71 97). Open M-F 8:30am-8:30pm, Sa 9:30am-2pm. **Lista de Correos** on C. Nuestra Señora del Cabello. **Postal Code:** 01001.

ACCOMMODATIONS AND CAMPING

Vitoria-Gasteiz is loaded with deluxe options, but a growing number of budget accommodations are beginning to appear along the main streets of C. Francia and C. de la Paz, leading away from the bus station. If you plan to come during the Jazz Festival (July 16-21) or the *Fiestas de la Virgen Blanca* (Aug. 4-9), make reservations at least one week in advance.

Hotel Dato, C. Dato, 28 (☎947 14 73 05; www.hoteldato.com). An impressive stone sculpture greets you at the entrance to this luxurious establishment, an art museum of its own. Rooms with large crown wall-pieces and curtains set over every bed make you feel like royalty without spending a kingly amount. Free Wi-Fi. Singles €33.17-36.48; doubles €51.78, with glassed-in terrace €58.05; triples €79.44. AmEx/MC/V. ❸

Hotel Iradier, C. Florida, 49 (☎945 27 90 66; www.hoteliradier.com). Big blue and yellow modern rooms with new mattresses. Some with balconies, all with private bath, TV, and phone. Free Wi-Fi. Singles €35; doubles €56; triples €70. AmEx/MC/V. ❸

Pensión Araba, C. Florida, 25, 1st fl. (☎945 23 25 88). Attractive rooms, thoughtfully decorated with TV, some with VCR. Parking available. Apartments available at a separate location on C. Iradier and C. Independencia; all reception at C. Florida. Wi-Fi available. Singles €28; doubles with bath €40-42; triples €55. Cash only. ❷

Pensión Amaia, C. La Paz, 15 (☎945 25 54 97). Conveniently located between the bus station and the *casco viejo.* Well-maintained, clean rooms come with TV and private bath. Parking available. Singles €27, with private bath €32; doubles €36/€42. ❷

Camping Ibaya, Ctra. Nacional, 102 (☎945 14 76 20), 4km from town toward Madrid. Follow Portal de Castilla west from the new cathedral. Restaurant, hot showers. Electricity €3. Open year-round. €3.50 per person, per tent, and per car. MC/V. ❶

FOOD

You can't go wrong in the *casco viejo.* The area around Pl. de España has *pintxos* (tapas) galore, many marked with "*pintxos* €1" signs. Get your groceries at **Carrefour Express,** C. General Álava, 10. (☎945 14 45 30. Open M-Sa 9:15am-9:15pm. AmEx/MC/V.) **El Corte Inglés,** on C. de la Paz, has a supermarket downstairs. (☎945 26 63 33. Open M-Sa 10am-10pm. AmEx/MC/V.)

Museo del Órgano, C. Manuel Iradier, 80 (☎945 26 40 48), on the corner just before the Pl. de Toros. Locals line up at lunch for fresh, filling vegetarian cuisine. 4-course *menú* €12 includes unlimited tasty salad bar. Open M-F 1-4pm. MC/V. ❸

El Siete, C. Cuchillería, 3 (☎945 27 22 98). Popular with locals in search of traditional food—and lots of it. Offers an astounding 38 varieties of sandwiches (€2.50-3.60). *Pintxos* €1.35-1.50. *Menú* 1-4pm €10, weekends €15. Open M-Th and Su 9:30am-12:30am, F-Sa 10:30am-3am or later. Cash only. ❷

La Taberna de Los Mundos, C. de la Independencia, 14 (☎945 13 93 42). Serves affordable, mouth-watering sandwiches (€4-4.50) in a friendly, neighborhood-haunt atmosphere. Free Wi-Fi. Perhaps the best deal is the personalized individual salad (base of lettuce and tomato €3, €0.60 each added ingredient). *Menú* €10. Open M-Th 8:30am-midnight, F 8:30am-1am, Sa 10:30am-1am, Su 11:30am-midnight. MC/V. ❷

SIGHTS

Both the tree-lined pedestrian walkways of the new city and steep narrow streets of the *casco viejo* make for pleasant strolls. **Plaza de la Virgen Blanca** is the focal point of the *casco viejo* and site of Vitoria-Gasteiz's fiestas. Beside Pl. de la Virgen Blanca is the broad, arcaded **Plaza de España,** which marks the division between the old and new towns. **Los Arquillos,** a series of arches that rise above Pl. de España, were designed by architect Justo Antonio de Olaguíbel and constructed from 1787 to 1802 to connect the *casco viejo* with the growing new town below. **El Anillo Verde,** a ring of parks and promenades encircling the city, makes for a beautiful afternoon walk, bike ride, or bird-watching sojourn.

VITORIA-GASTEIZ FOR POCKET CHANGE. The capital of Basque Country may have its share of fancy accommodations and ritzy restaurants, but it can also be a delight for budget travelers. Start your day off with a satisfying combo breakfast at the **Taberna de Los Mundos** (€3.30), then head over to the tourist office and rent a **free bike.** Go for a spin down the shady **Po. de la Senda** and stop in for a free visit at the grand **Museo de Bellas Artes.** Then, head back towards town, buy a picnic lunch at the supermarket, and spend the rest of the afternoon in the peaceful **Salburua park.**

ARTIUM. The rotating permanent collection at Artium, the city's contemporary art museum, boasts multimedia works and paintings by 20th-century greats such as Dalí, Picasso, and Miró. You're nearly guaranteed to see something shocking as you walk through the unconventional exhibits. The two galleries on the bottom floor feature regular multimedia exhibitions by prominent contemporary artists. *(C. de Francia, 24. ☎945 20 90 00; www.artium.org. Open Tu-Su 11am-8pm. €4.50; students, seniors, and ages 14-17 €2.20; under 14 free. W by donation, proceeds from which are used to make annual acquisitions.)*

PALACIO DE AUGUSTI AND MUSEO DE BELLAS ARTES. Many of the *casco viejo*'s Renaissance palacios are open to the public as museums. The gorgeous Palacio de Augusti houses the Museo de Bellas Artes, with works by regional artists. The permanent collection contains Spanish art from the 17th to 19th centuries and marvellous Basque art from the mid-19th to the mid-20th centuries. *(Po. Fray Francisco de Vitoria, 18. ☎945 18 19 18. Open Tu-F 10am-2pm and 4-6:30pm, Sa 10am-2pm and 5-8pm, Su 11am-2pm. Free.)*

CENTRO CULTURAL MONTEHERMOSO. At the other end of town, the spacious, modern Centro Cultural Montehermoso sits in the stately 16th-century **Aguirre Palace,** C. Fray Zacarias Martinez, 2, at the highest point of the *casco viejo* and overlooking the city. Rotating exhibits, cinematic events, and courses on visual art are held throughout the year. Extensive modern and experimental art exhibits. Free concerts are held during the jazz festival. From Pl. de la Virgen Blanca, walk up the stairs to C. Correría, and follow the street until you see stairs on your right. The Centro Cultural is at the end of the stairs. *(Open Tu-F 11am-2pm and 6-9pm, Sa 11am-2pm and 5-9pm, and Su 11am-2pm.)*

MUSEO FOURNIER DEL NAIPE. The **world's largest deck of playing cards,** recognized by the *Guinness Book of World Records,* weighs 10kg and measures 94 by 61.5cm, and you'll find it (along with 23,000 other decks of cards and a ton of information on their production) at the unusual and magnificent museum of playing cards, the Museo Fournier del Naipe. *(C. de la Cuchillería, 54. ☎945 18 19 18. Closed for renovations until mid-late 2009. Call tourist office for information.)*

CATEDRAL NUEVA. The apse of the 20th-century neo-Gothic Catedral Nueva, in the *casco viejo,* hosts the **Museo Diocesano de Arte Sagrado,** an extensive collection of religious artifacts from Basque churches, including canvases by El Greco and Ribera. *(C. Monseñor Cadena y Eleta. ☎945 15 06 31.)*

NIGHTLIFE AND FESTIVALS

After nightfall, the *casco viejo* lights up. Bars line C. Cuchillería ("La Cuchi"), C. Herrería ("La Herre"), C. Zapatería ("La Zapa"), and C. San Francisco, where university and high school students revel on the weekends. A slightly older crowd gathers in the bars along C. Dato. For a chance to catch a conversation in English and converse with an international crowd, try **The Man in the Moon,** C. Manuel Iradier, 7. (☎945 15 71 80. W Pop Quiz night in English, Th jazz night. Open M-Th 8am-11pm, F 8am-2am, Sa 11am-3am, Su 4-11pm.)

Vitoria-Gasteiz hosts countless cultural, music, and sports festivals throughout the year. For info on **theater** and special events, pick up the free monthly guide *Gidatu* at the tourist office or check out the official city website, www.vitoria-gasteiz.org. The city grooves to jazz the third week of July at the **Festival de Jazz de Vitoria-Gasteiz.** Tickets cost €10-40, but there are free street performances. Call or visit the **Asociación Festival de Jazz de Vitoria,** Po. Florida, 3, for more specific information. (☎945 14 19 19; www.jazzvitoria.com) Rockets and a massive gathering in the square mark the start of Vitoria's biggest, craziest party of the year, the **Fiesta de la Virgen Blanca** (Aug. 4-9), at 6pm on August 4th in Pl. de la Virgen Blanca. After the rockets go off, one of the greatest spectacles of the fiesta takes place: **El Celedón,** a doll of a Basque child in traditional garb, holding an open umbrella, descends *à la* Mary Poppins from the top of the tower of the church of San Miguel towards the crowd in the square.

ASTURIAS AND CANTABRIA

Asturias and Cantabria are a far cry from familiar sun-and-tapas Spain. These tiny northern regions, tucked between País Vasco and Galicia, are distinguished by endless greenery, precipitous ravines, and jagged cliffs. The impassable peaks of the Cordillera Cantábrica halted the advance of the Moors, making Asturias and Cantabria the stronghold of the Visigoth Christians, who left behind a trail of pre-Romanesque churches. Cut off from the rest of Spain during Moorish rule of the country, today the Asturians and Cantabrians take pride in their states' preservation of "true Spain." It was the Asturian hero Don Pelayo who officially launched the *Reconquista* in AD 722 from the Picos hamlet of Covadonga, a campaign that lasted until the fall of Granada in 1492. Today the heir to the Spanish throne is titled the Príncipe de Asturias. Asturias and Cantabria remain somewhat isolated from Spain proper—the endless, rough terrain has limited the number of rail lines through the regions, leaving lone roads to wind along the steep mountain sides and scalloped shore. These two little territories also maintain cultures that differ from the rest of Spain—they have their own dialects, drinking customs, and way of life.

Despite their shared landscape and location, Asturias and Cantabria have distinct personalities from one another as well. Asturias draws hearty mountaineers looking to reach new heights in its national parks, while Cantabria—with the world-class resort towns of Santander and Comillas—appeals to Spain's vacationing elite. Cuisine also distinguishes the two regions. Asturias is famous for its apples, strong cheeses, wholesome fresh fruit, and *arroz con leche* (rice pudding); true Asturians can be recognized by the way they take their cider, poured from several feet above and downed immediately. Cantabrian cuisine comes from the mountains and the sea, with *cocido montanés* (bean stew) and *marmita* (tuna, potato, and green pepper stew) as popular delicacies. No matter what's on the menu, portions are always hearty and filling.

HIGHLIGHTS OF ASTURIAS AND CANTABRIA

RELAX on the renowned Península de Magdalena in **Santander** (p. 527).

PARQUE yourself on the peaks of the **Picos de Europa** (p. 517).

SWIG some of Asturias's famous cidra in **Oviedo** (p. 507).

BURY your feet in the silky sand of **Comillas** (p. 535).

ASTURIAS

Mountain ranges and dense alpine forests define the Asturian landscape. Though Asturias never fell to the marauding Moors, today visitors invade to take advantage of the booming adventure tourism industry in the Parque Nacional Picos de Europa. The wide swaths of sand and lively waves of Gijón draw swarms of beachgoers, but plenty of quiet, cliff-lined coves lie just off the beaten path, where tropical and alpine vegetation mingle.

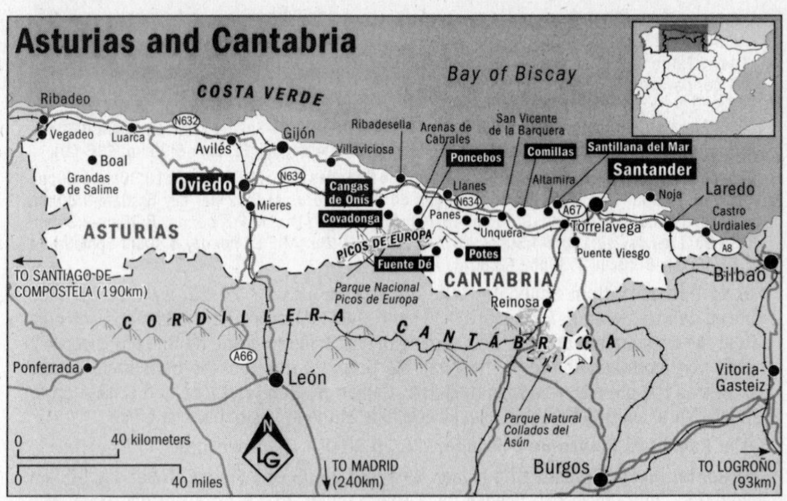

OVIEDO

☎958

Although the city of Oviedo (pop. 200,000) has faded into the background of Spanish political life, its bustling old quarter, immense park, spectacular art museum, and endless shopping are more than enough to keep visitors busy for several days. Oviedo's name comes from the Latin *urbis* (city), and for a few centuries, it was the most important city in Spain. As a haven from Moorish attacks, Oviedo became the epicenter of the *Reconquista* and was made the capital of the Kingdom of Asturias around AD 810. If the urban scene isn't for you, the mountains on the horizon, with majestic Monte Naranco minutes away and the Picos de Europa beyond, allow you to explore the countryside.

TRANSPORTATION

Flights: Aeropuerto de Ranón/Aeropuerto Nacional de Asturias (☎985 12 75 00), in Avilés, 28km from Oviedo. **ALSA** runs buses from the station to the airport M-F every hour 6am-11pm, €5.80. **Aviaco** (☎985 12 76 03) and **Iberia** (☎985 12 76 07) fly to **Barcelona, London,** and **Madrid.**

Trains: Both **RENFE** and **FEVE** serve Oviedo from **Estación del Norte,** Av. de Santander.

FEVE (☎985 29 76 56), 3rd fl. Info open daily 7am-9:30pm. To: **Bilbao** (7-8hr.; 9am, 3:35pm €20.55); **El Ferrol** (6hr.; 7:47am, 2:47pm; €19.35) via **Ribadeo** (4hr., €10); **Llanes** (2hr., 5 per day 9:05am-6:55pm, €6.95); **Santander** (4hr.; 9:05am, 3:35pm; €13.20).

RENFE (☎902 24 02 02), 1st fl. Pay attention to the type of train; a slow local train through the mountains can double your travel time. Info open daily 8am-9pm. To: **Barcelona** (12-13hr.; daily 10:57am, 7:34pm; €48-56) via **Burgos** (5-6hr., €25-29); **Gijón** (30min.; daily 3-4 11:10am-10:05pm, Sa-Su also at 10:29pm; €2.60-10.80); **León** (2hr.; M-F 7 per day 7:29am-7:24pm, Sa-Su 7 per day 7:43am-8:50pm; €7-18); **Madrid** (6-9hr., 3 per day 7:43am-6:43pm, €45.30) via **Valladolid** (4hr., €28).

Buses: Information open daily 7am-10:30pm. **ALSA** (national) and **Económicos/EASA** (regional) buses run out of the station on C. Pepe Cosmen (☎902 49 99 49). Open daily 6:30am-12:30am.

ALSA (☎902 422 242). To: **Barcelona** (12hr.; 8:30am, 7:30pm; €51); **Burgos** (3hr.; 8:30am, 7:30pm; €16.67); **La Coruña** (4-6hr.; M-Sa 6 per day 6:30am-6:30pm, Su 6 per day

6:30am-7pm; €21-35); **León** (1½hr., 9-12 per day 12:30am-10:30pm, €8.30); **Logroño** (6hr.; 8:30am, 7:30pm; €23-25). **Madrid** (5hr.; M-Sa 11-13 per day 12:30am-7:30pm, Su 14 per day 12:30am-7:30pm; €31-49); **San Sebastián** (6-8hr.; M-Sa 6-8 per day 1am-5:45pm, Su 8 per day 1am-9:45pm; €25-45); **Santander** (3-4hr.; M-Th, Sa 10-12 per day 1am-8:45pm, F, Su 12-13 per day 1am-9:45pm; €13-22); **Santiago de Compostela** (5-7hr.; 6 per day M-Sa 6:30am-6:30pm, Su until 7pm; €26-38); **Valladolid** (3-4hr.; M-Sa 5 per day 12:30am-6:30pm, Su 6 per day 12:30am-7:30pm; €17.63); **Vigo** (7-9hr.; 4 per day 6:30am-6:30pm; €36-59).

Económicos/EASA (☎985 29 00 39). To: **Arenas de Cabrales** (2hr.; M-F 3 per day 10:30am-6:30pm, Sa-Su 10:30am, 6:30pm; €8.10); **Cangas de Onís** (1½hr.; M-F 12 per day 6:30am-9:30pm, Sa-Su 7-8 per day 8:30am-9:30pm; €5.70); **Covadonga** (1hr.; M-F 3 per day 8:30am-3:30pm, Sa-Su 3 per day 12:15pm-4:30pm; €6.70); **Llanes** (1-2hr.; M-F 14 per day 8:30am-9pm, Sa-Su 11 per day 8:30am- 7:30pm; €8.80).

Public Transportation: Schedules vary, but **TUA** (☎985 22 24 22, www.tua.es) runs buses daily between 6-7am until 10-11pm (€0.85). All stops have bus maps. #4 runs from the train station down C. Uría, turning off just before Campo de San Francisco. #2 goes from both stations to the hospital. #2, 5, and 7 run from the train station along C. Uría to the old city. #10 also runs from Campo de San Francisco and C. Uría up to Monte Naranco. Bus schedule usually available at the municipal tourist office.

Taxis: Radio Taxi Ciudad de Oviedo (☎985 25 00 00). 24hr. service.

Car Rental: Hertz, C. Ventura Rodríguez, 4 (☎985 26 39 05). From €45 per day. 200km limit. 23+, must have had license for 2 years; under 25 €8 extra per day. Open M-F 9am-1pm and 4-7:30pm, Sa 9:30am-noon. AmEx/MC/V.

ORIENTATION AND PRACTICAL INFORMATION

The train station is at the top of **Calle Uría,** the city's main passage. Follow it downhill from the station to the city center and *casco viejo,* with the park, **Campo de San Francisco,** on your right. The cathedral is down C. San Francisco from C. Uría. From the bus station, turn right out of the main entrance and walk up the road, which will bring you C. Uria in front of the train station.

Tourist Office: Regional Office, C. Cimadevilla, 4 (☎985 21 33 85). Open Sept.-June daily 10am-7pm, July-Aug. 1am-8pm. **Municipal Office,** C. Marqués de Santa Cruz, 1 (☎985 22 75 86). Open Sept.-June daily 10am-2pm and 4:30-7pm, July-Aug. 9:30am-2pm and 4:30-7:30pm. Branch in *Ayuntamiento* stays open through siesta.

Currency Exchange: Banco Santander Central Hispano, C. Pelayo Esq. Alonso Quintanilla (☎985 24 24 24). Branch, C. Uría, 1 (☎985 10 60 00), across the street from the park. Both open Apr.-Sept. M-F 8:30am-2pm; Oct.-Mar. M-F 8:30am-2pm, Sa 8:30am-1pm.

Luggage Storage: Lockers at the train station (open daily 7am-11pm; medium bags €3 per day, large €4.50) and the bus station (open daily 6:30-12:30am; €2 per day).

English-Language Bookstore: Librería Cervantes, C. Dr. Casal, 9 (☎985 20 77 61). The English-language book section is on the 2nd floor. Open M-Sa 10am-1:30pm and 4:15-8:15pm. Closed the last two Sa of July and the first two Sa of Aug. MC/V.

Laundromat: C. Emilio Alarcos Llorach, 1. (☎985 08 88 66). Open daily 9am-10pm.

Police: Municipal, C. General Yague (☎985 11 34 77), across the street from Hotel Reconquista. Main office located on the Carretera del Rubín. **Guardia Civil** (☎985 28 02 04), also located on the Carreterra del Rubín, next door to the municipal office.

Pharmacy: Farmacia Dr. Luis Gómez Prado, C. Magdalena, 17 (☎985 20 30 84).

Medical Services: Hospital Central de Asturias, C. Calvo Sotelo. (☎985 10 61 00) **Emergencies:** ☎112.

Internet Access: Free internet at **Biblioteca de Asturias Ramon Perez Ayala,** Pl. Daoíz y Velarde, 11. Max. 30min. Open M-F 8:30am-8:50pm, Sa 10pm-1am and 4-8:50pm, Su

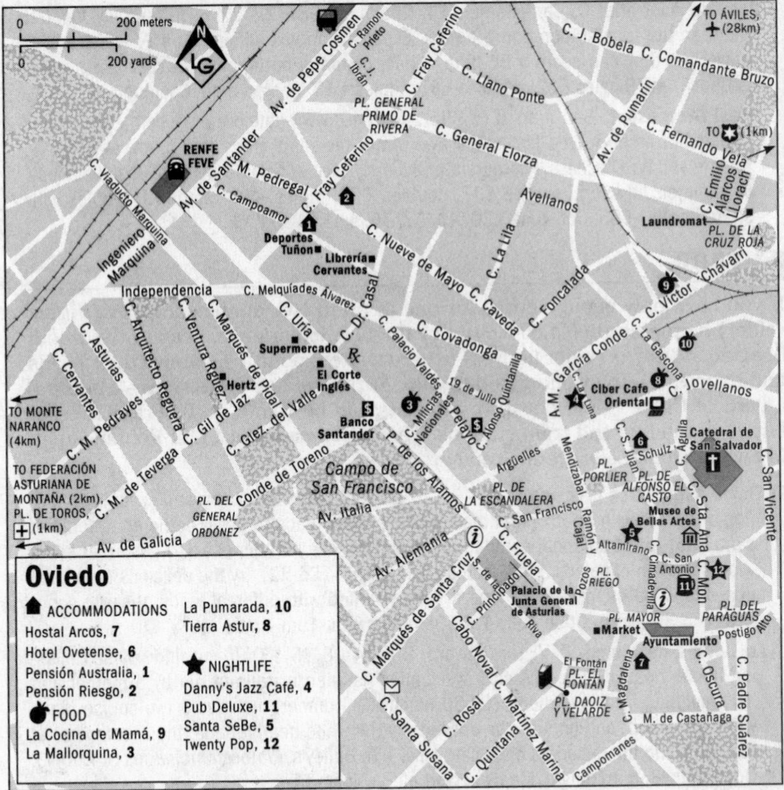

10am-1pm. **Ciber Cafe Oriental,** C. Jovellanos, 8 (☎985 20 28 97). €1.50 per 30min., €2.20 per hr., €3.90 per 2hr. Free Wi-Fi. Open M-F 8am-1am, Sa-Su 9am-3am.

Post Office: C. Santa Susana, 18 (☎985 20 88 62). **Lista de Correos,** fax, and photocopying. Open M-F 8:30am-8:30pm, Sa 9:30am-2pm. **Postal Code:** 33007.

ACCOMMODATIONS

Although *pensiones*, *hostales*, and hotels pack the new city on C. Uría, C. Campoamor, and C. Nueve de Mayo, cheap accommodations can be scarce in July and August. Most rooms are clean and many are in restored buildings, offering comfort and convenience at a higher price than nearby cities.

Hostal Arcos, C. Magdalena, 3, 2nd fl. (☎985 21 47 73). Minutes away from the grand cathedral. Vibrant paint colors and photos of Oviedo at its finest adorn the walls of this romantic, friendly hostel. All rooms have TVs and free Wi-Fi, and a few come with chandeliers. Singles €30-35; doubles €40-55, depending on the season. Cash only. ❸

Pensión Riesgo, C. Nueve de Mayo, 16 (☎985 21 89 45). Doilies, heavy curtains, and mismatched bedspreads decorate this *pensión*. Wheelchair-accessible. Singles €15; doubles €26-28, with shower €28-30; summer prices average €3 more. Cash only. ❶

Pensión Australia, C. Campoamor, 14, 2nd fl. (☎985 22 22 67). Centrally located between the train station and the park. Expansive rooms come with a TV and big windows, but they can seem a bit bare. Clean, common bathroom and cozy living room. Laundry free. Singles €22; doubles €35; triples €40. Shared bath. Cash only. ❷

Hotel Ovetense, C. San Juan, 6 (☎985 22 08 40; www.hotelovetense.com). Well-maintained but small rooms just steps away from the main plaza. Full bath, satellite TV, phone, and Wi-Fi access. Restaurant and *sidrería* (cider bar) downstairs. Reserve ahead in summer. July-Sept. singles €37, doubles €53, triples €63, quads (2 doubles with shared bath.) €85. Oct.-June €30/45/57/75. AmEx/MC/V. ❹

FOOD

If you have only enough euros for one drink in Oviedo, be sure to try **sidra** (cider) by the bottle (€1.50-3.60). For the best experience, head to the wood-beamed *sidrerías* (cider houses), where waiters pour from above their heads and expect you to swallow in one gulp. *Sidrerías* line **C. Gaconga**—"The Boulevard of Cider"—and cheap restaurants can be found on C. Fray Ceferino between the bus and train stations. The **indoor market** at Pl. el Fontán (open M-Sa 8am-8pm) sells produce and groceries.

Tierra Astur, C. La Gascona, 1 (☎985 20 25 02). Wooden *terraza* and cavernous interior, complete with a faux meat market. The perfect place to down bottle after bottle of *sidra* (€5) with traditional Asturian meat and cheese platters (€5-14). Also features a wide selection of salads and generous fish entrees (€5-22). Try the delicious traditional desserts, such as *frixuelos,* a type of crepe stuffed with different kinds of sweet goodness (€3.30-4.80). Open daily 1-4:30pm and 8pm-1am. AmEx/MC/V. ❸

La Cocina de Mamá, C. Victor Chavarri, 9 (984 08 35 13). If you find yourself missing home, head over to this cozy, welcoming Asturian restaurant run by a mother and her daughter. Delicious *menú* (€8.50 lunch, €10 dinner) includes a two-course meal, wine and bread, and homemade dessert. Try the white bean *fabada,* the *escalopines al cabrales*, and the decadent chocolate cake with Bailey's. *Platos combinados* (€4.50-7). Open daily 8am-midnight. Meals served all day long. ❷

La Mallorquina, C. Milicias Nacionales, 5 (☎985 22 40 75; www.la-mallorquina.net). This restaurant has a glass terrace and the feel of a Parisian cafe. Magnificent range of cakes, pastries, and chocolates. Salads (€8-14), sandwiches (€3-7), and entrees (€10-18). Open M-F 7am-11pm, Sa 7:30am-11pm, Su 8am-11pm. AmEx/MC/V. ❷

La Pumarada, C. Gascona, 8 (☎985 20 02 79). Down the street from Tierra Astur. Popular for its Asturian entrees and *sidra*-soaked atmosphere. Waiters pour cider from bottles high over their heads, and every table has a bucket to catch the spills. Tapas €6-15. Entrees €8-22. Sidra €2.50. Open daily 9am-1:30am. MC/V. ❸

SIGHTS

MUSEO DE BELLAS ARTES. The three beautifully maintained buildings of the Museo de Bellas Artes in the Palacio de Velarde display one of the best public art collections in Spain. In addition to the Klimt-esque work of Hermen Anglada Camarasa, highlights include 18 pieces of the original *Retablo de Santa Marina* and works by Goya, Velázquez, Sorolla, Dalí and Picasso—there is also an entire room on the first floor full of saint portraits by El Greco. *(C. Santa Ana, 1, just up from Pl. de Alfonso II. ☎985 21 30 61. Open July-Aug. Tu-Sa 10:30am-2pm and 4-8pm, Su 10:30am-2:30pm; Sept.-June Tu-F 10:30am-2pm and 4:30-8:30pm, Sa 11:30am-2pm and 5-8pm, Su 11:30am-2:30pm. Free.)*

CATEDRAL DE SAN SALVADOR. A recent renovation restored Oviedo's 14th-century Gothic cathedral to its original splendor. The **Capilla de Santa María del Rey Casto,** which contains the royal pantheon, was chosen by Alfonso II el Casto in AD 802 to house the remains of Asturian monarchs and Christian relics rescued from the Moors. In this chapel, also look for the statue of San Pedro holding a metal key in his hand. According to legend, if you make three wishes and turn the key around three times, one of the wishes will come true. The cathedral complex includes pristine cloisters, the famous crypt of **Santa Leocadia,** which holds the remains of the martyrs Eulogio and Leocadia, and a *cámara santa* (holy chamber) containing several enormous golden and jeweled crosses. The highlights of the church museum, a Bible from the 12th century and a modern painting of Mother Teresa, warrant the entrance fee. *(Pl. de Alfonso II. ☎985 22 10 33. Open July-Sept. daily 10:15am-8pm. Last entry 7:15. Oct.-June 10:15am-1pm and 4-6pm. Cathedral free. Cámara Santa €1.50. Museum, including cloisters and crypt, €3; children €1.50. Th evening free.)*

MONTE NARANCO. Take an afternoon away from the hustle and bustle of Oviedo and venture into the Picos by way of Monte Naranco. Not only does the mountain make for a pleasant half-day hike, but it also showcases some of Asturias' oldest sites. The recreational palace **Santa María del Naranco** and the royal church of **San Miguel de Lillo,** located on the side of Monte Naranco, both built in the 9th century, represent some of the first European attempts to blend architecture, sculpture, and murals after the fall of the Roman Empire. A guided tour around the two ancient buildings will tell you all about how the two buildings were utilized when Asturias was the last defense against the Moors. The top of Monte Naranco is approximately a 4km hike from the center of Oviedo. Bus #10 takes you near the top, but the walk up the mountain should take no more than two hours; the municipal tourist office has maps. Although the main trail is a bit steep, the path brings you through some of the beautiful greenery around Oviedo and allows you a glimpse of the majestic mountains surrounding the city. *(From C. Uría, take bus #10 toward the train station. Daily 7:50am, then hourly 8:30am-7:30pm, 8:15pm, 9:40pm.; €0.75. ☎676 03 20 87. Both structures open Apr.-Sept. Tu-Sa 9:30am-1pm; 3:30-7pm, M-Su 9:30am-1pm; Oct.-March M 10am-1pm, Tu-Sa 10am-12:30pm, 3-4:30pm, Su 10am-12:30pm. €3, children €2. M free, but no guide.)*

NIGHTLIFE

The streets south of the cathedral, especially C. Mon and around Pl. Riego, Pl. el Fontán, and Pl. el Paraguas, teem with noisy *sidrerías* and clubs. Midweek nightlife in Oviedo is pretty tame, and some clubs and pubs close despite official weekday hours. But from Thursday to Saturday, the discotecas and bars keep the music pumping all night long. **Pub Deluxe,** C. Mon 15, has both a laid-back bar and disco-dance club feel, and is popular with younger crowd. (Beer €2.50-3. Drinks €4.50. Open M-W and Su 11pm-3:30am, Th 11pm-4:30am, F-Sa 11pm-5:30am.) After a few *chupitos* (shots) and *copas* (mixed drinks), most students head to one of the clubs near the Pl. Riesgo. **Twenty Pop,** C. Mon, 12, features pop music and 70s decor, while **Santa SeBe,** C. Altamirano, 6, has a vaguely psychedelic feel. Both clubs pick up after 2am and are popular with locals. (Beer €2.20-2.50. Mixed drinks €3.50-5. Open weekends 11pm-5:30am.) At **Danny's Jazz Café,** C. La Luna, 11, between C. Alcalde M. García Conde and C. Jovellanos, Nat King Cole and Miles Davis LPs fill the walls. A lively spot even mid-week. Live music is an occasional treat. (☎985 21 14 83. Beer €2.80. Mixed drinks €5.50. Open M-Th, Su 11pm-3:30am, F-Sa 11pm-4:30am.) Wine connoisseurs follow *la ruta de los vinos* (the wine route) from bar to bar along **C. El**

Rosal. For about 10 days around Sept. 21, Oviedo throws a fiesta with concerts and processions in honor of its patron saint, San Mateo.

OUTDOOR ACTIVITIES

Though not the best base for hiking in the **Parque Nacional Picos de Europa** (p. 517), Oviedo is definitely the place to stock up on gear and supplies, as shops within the park and in gateway towns can be prohibitively expensive. A good first stop is the **Federación Asturiana de Montaña,** Av. de Julián Clavería, 11, near the bullring and university, a 30min. walk from the city center, or take bus #2 (dir.: Hospital) from C. Uría. From the bus stop, go into green gate for the **Federación Deportivos del Principado de Asturia,** enter the building through the second door on the right, and go up to the second floor. This office is in charge of all outdoor activities in the national park and can direct visitors to branches throughout the area. It organizes excursions and provides guides and advice on weather and the best hiking routes. Instructors for everything from paragliding to kayaking are available, and the office also provides guidance on gear suppliers in Oviedo. (☎985 25 23 62; www.fempa.net. Open M-Th 10am-2pm.)

GIJÓN ☎985

Gijón (pop. 275,000) may harbor nine beaches along its shoreline, but sand, sun, and sea are not the only reasons to visit this lively coastal city. Both an industrial port and a seaside resort, Gijón (*Xixón* in the local dialect) has made the transition to a modern city while remaining solidly connected to its history. The reconstructed Roman wall still stands, and the name of Gijón's most famous citizen, Gaspar Melchor de Jovellanos, an illustrious 18th-century thinker and close friend of Diego Velázquez, adorns many of the city's main buildings. Old cobblestone streets wind up from the Plaza del Marques and the Plaza Mayor to the Cimadevilla—once the site of the Roman city and today a hotbed of fantastic restaurants and booming nightlife.

TRANSPORTATION

Airport: Aeropuerto de Asturias (☎985 127 500 or 902 400 500) is 14km from Gijón toward Avilés. ALSA **buses** (☎985 12 76 00) run from the bus station to the airport (45min.; M-F hourly 6am-11pm, Sa-Su 9 per day 6am-10pm; €11).

Trains: Gijón has 2 train stations, **Estación FEVE-RENFE,** C. Álvarez Juárez and **Estación Jovellanos RENFE,** C. Sanz Crespo (☎985 17 02 02). **RENFE:** (☎985 98 13 63). To **Barcelona** (13hr.; daily 10:30am, 7:05pm; €48-56), **Madrid** (6-7hr.; 7:15am, 2, 6:15pm; €46.50), and **Oviedo** (35min.; M-F 7 per day 6:50am-7:05pm, Sa-Su 7 per day 7:15-8:20pm; €2.60-10.80). **FEVE:** (☎985 34 24 15). To **Avilés** (40min., 2 per hr. 6:20am-10pm, €1.45) and **Cudillero** (1hr.; M-F 18 per day 6:22am-7:32pm, Sa-Su 7 per day 7:32am-6:32pm; €2.60).

Buses: (☎985 35 75 82), Av. Magnus Blikstad at Av. Llanes. Info open daily 9am-2pm, 4-8pm. Runs **ALSA** buses to: **Barcelona** (12-13hr.; 8am, 7pm; €52.56); **Bilbao** (5hr.; 9-11 per day M-Th 12:14am-7:15pm, F-Su until 9:15pm, Sa until 5:15pm; €21-36); **Madrid** (5hr., 11-14 per day 1am-11:59pm, €33-49); **Oviedo** (30min.; M-Sa 2 oer hr. 6:30am-10:30pm, Sa night also hourly, Su 2 per hr. 7am-10:30pm; €1.95); **Ribadesella** (1hr., 8-11 per day 12:14am-8pm, €5.60-6.78); **San Sebastián** (6hr.; 6-8 per day M-Sa 12:14am-5:15pm, Su 12:14am-9:15pm; €27-42); **Santander** (2-3hr.; 9-11 per day M-Th 12:14am-7:15pm, F-Su 12:14am-9:15pm, Sa until 12:14am-5:15pm; €13-22); **Villaviciosa** (1hr.; M-F every hr. 6:30am-10:30pm, Sa-Su 13 per day 8am-10:30pm; €2.45).

Taxis: Radio Taxi, Antolín de la Fuente Cla, 4 (☎985 14 11 11).

ORIENTATION AND PRACTICAL INFORMATION

The high headland of the peninsula known as Cimadevella marks the edge of the old town, which centers around the **Plaza Mayor.** The main beach to the east (Playa de San Lorenzo) and the Puerto Deportivo dock to the west sandwich the more modern downtown; the **Jardines de Begoña,** public gardens, lie to the south. To reach the municipal **tourist office** from the train station, exit through the main entrance directly in front of the ticket gates and head straight onto C. Álvarez Garaya. Take the first left onto C. de Felipe Menéndez and follow the street to the ocean—the tourist office is on the dock in front of you.

Tourist Offices: Municipal office (☎985 34 17 71, www.gijon.info), on the big dock in the Puerto Deportivo. Listings of accommodations, restaurants, attractions, and festivals. Open daily July-Sept. 9am-10pm; Oct.-June 9am-8pm. Two smaller summer offices at **Playa de San Lorenzo** (open July-Sept. 10am-2pm and 4-8pm) and **Pl. de los Campinos** (open July-Sept. 10am-2pm and 4-8pm), next to the Jardines de Begoña.

Laundromat: Lavarama, C. Dindurra, 5. Open M-F 9am-1:30pm and 4:30-8pm.

Police: Municipal station, San Jose, 2 (☎985 18 11 00).

24hr. Pharmacy: Farmacia Begoña (☎985 34 25 18), Po. de Begoña, 7,next to the Teatro de Jovellanos.

Medical Services: Health center at C. Donato Argüellas (☎985 14 30 30), 300m east of the Teatro Jovellanos. The nearest hospitals are **Hospital de Jove** (☎985 32 00 50) and **Hospital de Cabueñes** (☎985 18 55 00). **Ambulance:** ☎1006.

Internet access: InterMedia, C. Salustio Regueral, 4 (☎985 17 50 13), near Jardines de la Reina. From main tourist office, cross the street and follow C. Felipe Mendez until 3rd left (C. Cervantes). Turn onto C. Cervantes and follow until right turn, followed immediately by a left turn onto C. Salustio Regueral–the shop will be up the street on your left. €1.80 per hour. Open M-F 10:30am-8:30pm. The library, **Biblioteca Pública Jovellanos,** C. Jovellanos, 21 (985 34 32 66) has free internet access on the second floor. 1hr. time slots. Open M-F 9am-9pm, Sa 10am-2pm and 4-9pm, Su 10am-2pm.

Post Office: Pl. Seis de Agosto, s/n. (☎985 17 68 06). Open M-F 8:30am-8:30pm, Sa 9:30am-2pm. **Postal Code:** 33206.

ACCOMMODATIONS AND CAMPING

Expensive hotels fill the streets near the stations and along the beach, while a few reasonably priced hostels are scattered through town. Book in advance in the summer, as hostels tend to fill up quickly. If you are staying only one night, it might be cheaper and more convenient to book a room in Oviedo, since the two cities are only a 30min. bus ride away.

Hospedaje Don Pelayo, San Bernardo, 22 (☎985 34 44 50; www.hostaldonpelayo.com). 17 spacious, colorful rooms with TV and free Wi-Fi just 1 block from the beach. 2 comfortable common lounges with couch and flowers. Shared bath. Doubles €50; triples €65; in winter €30/40. MC/V. ❷

Hostal Covadonga, C. La Libertad, 10, 3rd fl. (☎985 34 16 85; www.hostalpensioncovadonga.com). Salmon-pink walls, modern rooms, and friendly staff lend a welcoming vibe. Rooms have TV and free Wi-Fi, and some have balconies. Singles €20-35; doubles €33-55. All doubles have private bath. AmEx/MC/V. ❷

Hostal Manjon, Pl. de Marques, 1, 1st fl. (☎985 35 23 78), between Playa de San Lorenzo and Playa de Poriente overlooking the plaza. Rooms are spacious, though the linoleum floors and mismatched furniture leave something to be desired. In summer, singles €36, doubles €45-49. In winter, €20-28/€30-36. Cash only. ❸

Camping Deva-Gijón (☎985 13 38 48, www.campingdeva-gijon.com), exit A-66 Salida Deva from Cta. N-632, 4km east of the city. Complete with pools, tennis court, restaurant, and lounge, making this campground seem like a hotel. €5.50 per person, €5.40 per tent, €5.50 per car. Cash only. ❶

FOOD

The tourist office hands out the **Guía de Empresas,** which lists restaurants, *sidrerías*, and bars in city. Local specialties include delicious seafood dishes such as clam and mussel *paella.* In restaurants, *sidra* is sold by the bottle (€2-8). For groceries, try **Mercados Oblanca,** C. Corrida, 3. (Open M-F 9am-2pm and 5-8:30pm, Sa 9am-2pm. AmEx/MC/V.)

La Zamorana, Hermanos Felgueroso, 38-40 (☎985 38 06 32). Located south of the Jardines de Begoña, La Zamora is one of the best *sidrerías* in town. Excellent seafood, including trout and *paella.* Entrees €11-29, special plate of the day €12-15. Open Tu-Su noon-5pm and 7:30pm-12:30am. MC/V. ❸

Café Dindurra, Paseo Begoña, 11 (☎985 35 26 14), next to the Teatro Jovellanos. One of the snazzier cafes in the Jardines de Begoña, with over 18 different specialty coffees (€3.75-5.25) to savor under big umbrellas. Sandwiches €3-6. *Raciones* €2.50-15. Open Su-Th 8-12:30am, F-Sa until 2am. Cash only. ❷

La Casona, Pl. de Jovellanos, 1 (☎985 34 18 20). Situated in the center of old Gijón at the center of the plaza up the hill from the water. Delicious seafood as well as a selection of salads and cheeses. Terrace with beautiful view of the ocean. *Menú* €10. Entrees €5-13. Open daily in summer 1-3pm and 8-11pm. MC/V. ❷

La Farándula, C. Marques de San Esteben, 7 (☎984 29 63 33). This cross between sexy wine bar and fancy restaurant is pricey, but has the sensual ambience and popularity to back it up. Entrees €10-20, traditional and more experimental gourmet meat and fish dishes €12-22. Open daily noon-4pm and 7pm-12am. MC/V. ❸

SALUD! The quality of an establishment's *sidra* can be measured by the server's style of pouring. Generally, the higher they hold the bottle over their heads and the farther down and more horizontally they hold the glass, the better the *sidra* is. Remember to down your glass quickly, in true Asturian style, to get all the good fizz at the top. Watch your shoes, as servers often care more about the height of their pour than the amount they spill.

SIGHTS AND BEACHES

MUSEO EVARISTO VALLE. The museum houses the works—and conch collection—of Asturian painter Evaristo Valle (1873-1951), a major Spanish post-Impressionist, in the former residence of Valle's niece, María Rodríguez. The mansion's century-old garden, with some 16,000 sq. mi. of greenery, 120 species of fauna, and scattered sculptures, is no less impressive than the artist's works. *(On Camino de Cabueñes, 261, in the nearby town of Somio. Take bus #10 from Gijón. ☎985 33 40 00; www.evaristovalle.com. Open Apr-Oct. Tu-Sa 5-8pm, Su noon-2pm; Nov.-Mar. Tu-Sa 4-6pm, Su noon-2pm. €3, students €1.80, children free.)*

TERMAS ROMANAS. Located directly under the Campo Valdés, the 1st-2nd century Roman baths, discovered in 1903 and opened as a museum in 1990, are the most impressive remains of the fortified Roman city that originally sat on the Cimadevilla. Other parts of this ancient city include sections of the old wall that have been reconstructed. *(Campo Valdés, underground at the old town end of* *the Playa de San Lorenzo. ☎985 18 51 51. Open July-Aug. Tu-Sa 11am-1:30pm and 5-9pm, Su and holidays 11am-2pm and 5-8pm; Sept.-June Tu-Sa 10am-1pm and 5-8pm, Su and holidays 11am-2pm and 5-7pm. €2.40, students and seniors €1.40.)*

MUSEO DEL FERROCARRIL DE ASTURIAS. Situated in the late 19th-century North Station, this museum is dedicated the history of trains and railways in Asturias. Explore the old station, and step inside some of the old-fashioned train cars scattered all over the museum. *(In the old Estación del Norte, in front of the Playa de Poniente. ☎985 30 85 75. Open July-Aug. Tu-Sa 10am-2pm and 5-9pm, Su and holidays 11am-2pm and 5-9pm; Sept.-June Tu-Sa 10am-2pm and 4-8pm, Su 11am-2pm and 4-8pm. €2.40, students, retirees and under than 16 €1.40.)*

CENTRO CULTURAL CAJASTUR AND PALACIO REVILLAGIGEDO. This *sala de exposiciones* has contemporary exhibitions that rotate monthly—with free admission, it's worth a visit. *(Plaza del Marqués, 2. ☎985 34 69 21; www.cajastur.es. Open July-Aug. Tu-Sa 11am-1:30pm and 4-9pm, Su and holidays noon-2:30pm; Sept.-June Tu-Sa 10:30am-1:30pm and 4-8pm, Su noon-2:30pm. Free.)*

BEACHES. When the sun is shining, the beaches are the place to be in Gijón. Decidedly warmer that the frigid beaches of the Atlantic, these Cantabrian stretches of sand and sea overflow with eager bathers during the summer months. The city's main beach, **Playa San Lorenzo,** located to the east of the old quarter, attracts hordes of eager sunbathers, but it virtually disappears at high tide. On the other side of the Puerto Deportivo, the **Playa de Poniente** is sheltered by breakwaters, making for gentler waves. To reach the Playa de Poniente, simply walk past the dock where the tourist office is, with the old quarter behind you; the sand is up ahead. Past **San Lorenzo,** a series of beaches string out at the foot of the cliffs, isolated from the hustle above. While rougher and rockier, these beaches still offer a serene break. At the top of the day, hike up the hills of the **Cimadevilla** for a view of the coastline and city at sunset; at the top of the hill, the majestic *Elogio del Horizonte*, created by Basque sculptor **Eduardo Chillida** in 1990, looks out to the Atlantic's endless horizon.

CANGAS DE ONÍS ☎985

Compared to the other hamlets and villages in the Picos, Cangas de Onís seems almost urban and cosmopolitan. Restaurants, book stores, and gift shops line its paved and sidewalked streets, and children play in the main square while diners look on from the cafes. Cangas is very well connected by bus to much of the northern and western Picos and is used as a base for mountaineering and adventure tourism of all kinds. With all the hiking hullabaloo, the historical significance of this mountain town is often overlooked. For 50 years, it was the first capital of what would become the country of Spain—founded in AD 718 when Don Pelayo defeated the Moors, marking the beginning of the *Reconquista*. Between outdoor excursions, take a break to explore the legacies left behind by Pelayo and the previous Paleolithic, Celtic, and Roman inhabitants.

TRANSPORTATION. ALSA (☎985 84 81 33), in the new bus station across the river from the main part of town, has **buses** to: **Arenas de Cabrales** (35min.; M-F 4 per day noon-8pm, Sa-Su noon, 8pm; €2.40); **Covadonga** (20min.; M-F 5 per day 8:45am-5pm, Sa-Su 4 per day 10am-6pm; last bus back daily 8pm; €1.20); Gijón (1½hr., daily 8:15pm, €6.35); **Madrid** (7-8hr.; M-Sa 9:05am, Su 1:50, 3:20pm; €29.75); Oviedo (1-2hr.; M-F every 1-2hr. 6:15am-10pm, Sa-Su 7 per day 8:15am-8:15pm; €5.35); **Valladolid** (5hr., 9:05am, €15.93). Better connections to the rest of Spain through Oviedo. For a taxi, call **Taxitur** (☎985 84 87 97). Taxis are also near the *Ayuntamiento*. Rent cars at **EuropCar,** C. San Pelayo, 17. (☎985 94 75 02. Open Tu-Sa 9:30am-1:30pm and 4:30-7:30pm, Su 10am-2pm. MC/V.)

ORIENTATION AND PRACTICAL INFORMATION. The main street in Cangas de Onís is Avenida de Covadonga. Head through the bus stop and out across the footbridge over the river, then up one block. The **tourist office,** Jardines del Ayuntamiento, 2, is in the Plaza del Ayuntamiento and has information about the town, accommodations, and adventure tourism offices located in other park border towns. (☎985 84 80 05. English spoken. Open *Semana Santa*-Oct. daily 9am-9pm; Nov.-*Semana Santa* M-Sa 10am-2pm and 4-8pm, Su 10am-3pm.) There is also a **park information office,** Casa Dago, Av. Covadonga, 43, with maps, regulations, and a host of information on the flora and fauna of the Picos (☎985 84 86 14; Open M-F 9am-2pm, Sa-Su 9am-2pm and 4-7pm). Local services include: **ATMs** all along Av. Covadonga; **library,** Casa de Cultura, C. La Carcel, 13, with **internet access,** art exhibitions, and evening concerts (☎985 84 86 01. Open M-F 11am-1pm and 5-8pm); **laundromat,** HigienEc Tintorería, C. Rey Fruela, 1-B (☎985 94 74 71; open Tu-Sa 10am-2pm and 4-8pm, Su 10am-2pm; €14 wash and dry, 24hr. pickup); the **municipal police** at Av. de Covadonga, 21, in the *Ayuntamiento* (☎985 84 85 58); health center, adjoining the Casa de Cultura at C. de la Cárcel, 13 (☎985 84 85 71; regularly open 3-8pm; **Emergencies** call ☎112); **Red Cross** on Av. Contraquil across the river (open M-F 11am-3pm) and internet access in the Telecentro (Open M-F 4-9pm, Tu-Th also 11am-1:30pm, in the same building as the **post office,** Av. Constantino González, to the right off Av. de Covadonga heading toward the bridge. (☎985 84 81 96. Open M-F 8:30am-2:30pm, Sa 9:30am-1pm.) **Postal Code:** 33550.

ACCOMMODATIONS. There are many mid-range hotels in Cangas, and cheaper *pensiones* abound along Av. Covadonga. **Pension Principado ❶,** Av. Covadonga, 6, 4th fl., has comfortable rooms with TV and hall bath. (☎985 84 83 50 or 667 983 185. Singles €15-18; doubles €25-36; with private bath €30-45. Cash only.) **Pensión El Gijonés ❷,** C. El Mercado, 18 offers tiny but impeccably neat singles (€20 year round) and doubles (€35-50), all with private bath. (☎945 84 81 37. Reception in Bar Gijonés on C. El Mercado behind Iglesia Santa Maria).

FOOD. At **Sidreria Lo de Fidel ❷,** C. San Pelayo, 9, waiters serve tapas while pouring local *sidra* from high above their heads. (☎985 84 87 58. Sidra €2.20. Entrees €8-14. Open in summer daily 9am-11pm; in winter closed M.) Find local fare in the orange, white, and black modern setting of **Restaurante Río Grande ❷,** Av. Covadonga, 16. The *ciervo estofado* (deer) melts tenderly off the bone. (☎985 84 83 17. *Menú* €10. Open daily 7am-midnight, winter M-F and Su 7am-10pm.) The hidden local secret for mountainous plates of tapas is **El Monarca ❸,** Cangas de Arriba, 22 (follow C. Emilio Laria off Av. Covadonga all the way to the top of the hill, then go around the big Aula del Reino de Asturias). This restaurant offers meat selections (€11-19), salads (€7.50-11), tapas (€4.50-15), huge portions well worth the price. (☎985 84 94 72. Reservation necessary for dinner. Open daily 1-3:30pm and 9-11:30pm.) At **La Parolaccia ❷,** C. Constantio Gonzalez 27, fill your stomach with hearty Italian food, all made from scratch. Indulge in the creative pizzas (€7.50) or lasagna (€6.80) served still sizzling in the pan. (☎985 84 86 11. Open 1-4:30pm, 7-noon.) For a do-it-yourself-meal, stop by **Alimerka Supermercado's,** Av. de Covadonga, 13 and Av. de Castillo, 16. (☎985 84 94 13. Both open M and Su 9am-2pm, Tu-Sa 9am-9:30pm. MC/V.)

SIGHTS AND EXCURSIONS. At the far end of Av. de Covadonga you will see the **Puente Romano,** an ancient bridge with an ornate golden cross hanging from the main arch, particularly beautiful at night. From the bridge, follow Av. de Covadonga into town, turn left onto C. Constantino González, and cross the river to reach the **Capilla de Santa Cruz.** This Romanesque chapel, built in AD 737, sits atop the town's oldest monument, a Celtic dolmen (stone tomb) dating from 3000 BC, which can be seen from the chapel's cave. (☎985 84 80 05. Open M-F 10am-2pm and 4-7pm, Sa-Su 11am-2pm and 4-7pm. €1, visit includes audio-visual presentation of chapel's history.) **Cueva del "Buxu"** (BOO-shoo) offers an intimate glimpse into the lives of Cangas's Paleolithic residents, whose few preserved drawings depicting deer and horses date from over 15,000 years ago. To reach the cave, follow the main road to Covadonga for 3km until the signs for the Cueva del Buxu and Cardes, the closest town, direct you left. Cardes is up the hill about 600m, and the path to the cave starts in front of Bar Buxu. From the bar, it's about 1km to the actual cave. Buses to Arenas de Cabrales, Covadonga, and Llanes run near the cave; ask to be dropped off at the **Cruce de Susierra.** Tours W-Su every hr. 10:15am-1:15pm limited to 6 people, make sure to reserve ahead. (☎608 17 54 67, line open 3-5pm. €3, children €1.50, W free.) At **La Grandera Zoo,** up highway AS-114 about 4km toward Soto, visitors can get up close and personal with gray bears *(osos sardos)*, Iberian wolves *(lobos)*, wild boars *(jabalí)*, Iberian lynx, and 200 other native species. (☎985 94 00 17; www.zoolagrandera.com. Open daily 11am-8pm; Nov.-Mar. closed M. €9, children €6.) Those with wheels will want to head south from Cangas on highway N-625, which winds along the Río Sella. This route heads through Santillán and Sames, finally coming to the awe-inducing **Desfiladero de los Beyos,** an 11km gorge with wet rocks and blossoming beech trees.

OUTDOOR ACTIVITIES. Cangas de Onís is the perfect place to arrange outdoor activities. As a rule, reserve at least two days ahead, or three to five days from June to August. There are several outfitters in town, but all are closed from December to February. **Cangas Aventura,** Av. de Covadonga, 17, sets up expeditions, including *barranquismo* (canyoneering; €36), canoeing (€23), horseback riding (€15 per 1hr., €25 per 2hr.), and hiking. Prices include equipment, a guide, transportation to and from Cangas, and sometimes a bagged lunch. (☎985 84 92 61; www.cangasaventura.com. Open daily 9:30am-10pm. MC/V.) The **Centro de Aventura,** C. Puente Romano, 6, is also the site of **Escuela Asturiana de Piraguismo.** Paragliding courses run €270, but a single tandem flight is only €42. Kayaking, whitewater rafting, canyoneering, and hydrospeed are also available, starting at a reasonable €23. (☎985 84 12 82; www.piraguismo.com. Open daily 10am-1pm and 3:30-8:30pm. MC/V.) **Centro Multiaventura Los Cauces,** Av. Covadonga, 23, offers horseback riding (from €15), spelunking (€25), as well as mountain bike rental (€6 per hr., €18 per day). **Deportes Tuñon,** C. San Pelayo, 31, sells hiking boots (€38-129), backpacks (€20-180), as well as maps and other gear for conquering the Picos. (☎985 94 70 61. Open daily 10:30am-4:30pm, July and Aug. 10:30am-8:30pm. MC/V.)

PARQUE NACIONAL PICOS DE EUROPA

The twisted limestone folds of the Picos de Europa emerged 300 million years ago, creating a mountain range of chaotic beauty and a formidable border separating the Asturias and Cantabria regions from the rest of Spain. Founded in 1918 as the Parque Nacional de Covadonga, Spain's first national park grew into the second largest national park in Europe, spanning three *macizos* (groups of mountains) and three provinces. The ancient crags and summits of the Picos

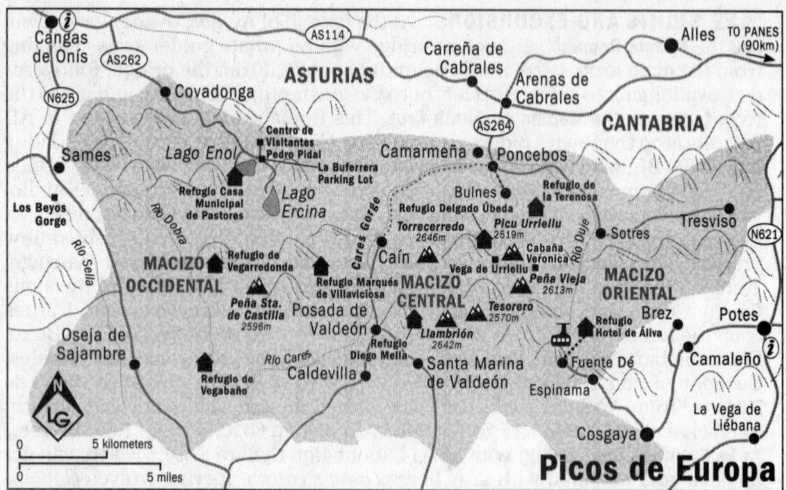

de Europa shelter some of Europe's most elusive endangered species. The scrub-spotted peaks also lure thousands of outdoor enthusiasts to the caves and caverns carved by centuries of glacial activity and to the backcountry trails that trace the contours of the mountains. Highlights include the remote and regal **Naranjo de Bulnes** (p. 518), the sparkling **Lagos de Covadonga** (p. 521), and the astounding but crowded 13km walk along the **Cares Gorge** (p. 518).

TRANSPORTATION

Getting to the Picos is certainly easier than getting around them. The most important towns within the park are **Covadonga** (accessible from Cangas by bus or car), **Posada de Valdeón** (accessible only by car from Potes through Portilla de la Reina), and **Poncebos** (accessible from Arenas by bus or car). **ALSA buses** connect Cangas de Onís (p. 515) and **Arenas de Cabrales**, the gateways in the west and the north, to towns just inside the borders of the park. In summer, these buses run from Arenas to Panes, as well. **La Palomera buses** connect Potes, the gateway in the east, with Panes to the north, and during July and August, with Fuente Dé to the south. It is much more efficient to travel by car, as buses run infrequently and irregularly and make many stops. By car, approach from either Oviedo or Santander via the **E70** (A8), which connects to the N625 (to Cangas de Onís) and the N621 (to Potes). Route **AS-114** runs along the northern edge of the Picos from Cangas de Onís through Arenas de Cabrales and on to Panes, where it intersects Route N-621. N-621 runs 50km south and west to Potes, where a branch (CA-185) leads to Fuente Dé. If you don't plan on hiking the dusty roads and mountains, it is sensible to visit the base towns as daytrips for a day or so; otherwise, the many *refugios* and *albergues* within the park provide adequate stops for multi-day treks into the interior.

ORIENTATION AND PRACTICAL INFORMATION

Part of the larger Cordillera Cantábrica, the Picos de Europa consist of three macizos (massifs): the **Occidental (Cornión),** the **Central (Urrieles),** and the **Oriental (Ándara).** The highest peak, Torre Cerredo (2648m), rises out of the Central *macizos.* Several rivers wind through the park; the four largest, which mark the borders between the different *macizos*, are the Sella, Dobra, Cares, and Duje.

The **Garganta del Cares** (Cares Gorge) cuts a line between the Macizo Oriental and Macizo Central, the latter of which holds the park's most popular trails and famous peaks: the treacherous **Peña Vieja** (2613m) and **Pico Tesorero** (2570m), the stark **Llambrión** (2642m), and the epic **Naranjo de Bulnes** (Picu Urriellu; 2519m). Part of the Picos's allure is that many of the highest areas are relatively easily accessible for the average hiker, with well-marked trails and plenty of *refugios*. There are also many guided hiking options for more difficult ascents and lengthier excursions. For more information, visit www.picoseuropa.net.

ACCOMMODATIONS

The most convenient accommodations are in Cangas de Onís, Arenas de Cabrales, and Potes. For multi-day hikes, the **refugios** and the **albergues** in the towns within the park are the best option for staying overnight in the backcountry. *Refugios* provide shelter in the mountains in the form of dorm-style bunks (sometimes mattresses or sheets; a few rent blankets or sleeping bags) and most cost €8-10 per night and accept cash only. They are often known by several names, and the larger ones, such as Vegarredonda and Vega de Urriellu, tend to have better amenities. All of the park offices have lists of the *refugios*. Before embarking on any hikes in the park, consult the list of *refugios* below, many of which also double as **ranger stations** in spring and fall. The stations are often unmanned in the winter, though there is at least one building per region open for winter hikers. For more information, inquire at the park info office.

There are only four private **campgrounds** ❶ inside the park (at Caín, Santa Marina, Soto de Valdeón, and Fuente Dé), and they are all in the southern half. In addition, many towns close to the park borders, including Cangas and Arenas de Cabrales, have campsites. Prices for camping are €3-5 per person, car and tent; call in advance to see if sites are open and spots are available, though reservations are generally not accepted. Other lodging options include **albergues** (dorm-style hostels, usually in ancient buildings with several basic services, shared bathrooms and beds with sheets; towels are not included) and **casas** (buildings with bunks, hot water, and stoves); these, however, are also only in or near towns, and nonexistent farther out in the mountains. In all cases, bring a sleeping bag. Towns within the park also have **pensiones, hostels, hotels,** and **rooms** in private homes; look for *camas* and *habitaciones* signs (typically €35-45 per double). For information on the *refugios* in Asturias, check www.fempa.net/refugios or www.refugiopicos.com.

MACIZO OCCIDENTAL

Casa Municipal de Pastores/Vega de Enol (telephone line available Oct. 15-June 1 ☎985 94 42 12; alt. 1100m). Overlooking Lago Enol, accessible from the Lagos de Covadonga road by car. Shower and meals. Breakfast €2.50, dinner €10-11. 10 beds. Open year-round. Bunks €8. Cash only. ❶

Vegarredonda (☎985 92 29 52; alt. 1410m), south of Lake Enol. Accessible from Lake Enol via Mirador del Rey and Pozo del Aleman (1½hr.). Blankets and meals. Dinner €14, breakfast €5.20. 68 spots. Open year-round. Bunks €10. Cash only. ❶

Marqués de Villaviciosa/Vega de Ario (☎650 90 07 60; alt. 1630m), by Vega de Ario southeast of Lago Enol. Open year-round. 40 bunks. Little water in winter. Breakfast €5.20, dinner €14. Accessible from Lago Ercina (2hr.). Open May-Oct. Bunks €10. Cash only. ❶

Vegabaño (☎699 63 32 44; alt. 1340m), in the southwest corner of the park. Shower and meals. Breakfast €4, dinner €11. 25 bunks. Accessible from Soto de Sajambre (1hr.). Open year-round. Bunks €10. Cash only. ❶

Ordiales (alt. 1750m), at the Ordiales lookout, 30-45min. from Vegarredonda. No rangers in residence. Houses the remains of the Marques de Villaviciosa, who was instrumental in founding the park. 4 bunks. Free access. Cash only. ❶

El Frade (alt. 1700m), near the Pico del Frade in the southwest of the park. Accessible from Posada de Valdeón or Refugio Vegabaño. 8 bunks. Unattended, free access. ❶

MACIZO CENTRAL

Delgado Úbeda/Vega de Urriellu (☎985 92 52 00; www.picuurriellu.com; alt. 1953m), by Vega de Urriellu. 96 spots, open year-round with rangers in residence. Accessible from Sotres via Pandebano and Vallejo (3hr.), from Fuente Dé's teleférico via Collado Horcados Rojos and Jou de los Boches (4hr.). Also accessible from Poncebos via Bulnes and Camburero by foot (5hr.). Reservations recommended in peak summer months. €10 per night, half-board €29.20. Cash only. ❶

Hotel de Áliva (☎942 73 09 99; alt. 1670), in the Puertos de Áliva. 24 hotel-style doubles with private bath in a beautiful valley where goats, donkeys and horses roam free. A 2-star hotel masquerading as a *refugio*. Open June-Sept. Doubles €75, cheaper for larger groups. Breakfast €4, full board €28. MC/V. ❺

Cabaña Verónica (☎942 73 00 07; alt. 2325m), near Pico Tesorero. The highest *refugio* in Spain, this tiny igloo-shaped cabin (made from parts of a US WWII aircraft carrier) is placed right on the edge of the ridge looking southeast. 4-6 spots. Guarded all year. No water in vicinity, but bottles and other drinks for sale, as well as basic meals. Accessible from Espinama via Aliva and Covarrobles (5-6hr.) and from the upper Fuente Dé teleférico station (2hr.). €8 per person, dinner €10. Cash only. ❶

El Redondo/Fuente Dé (☎942 73 66 99; alt. 1085m), 100m above the *teleférico* parking lot. 16 bunks. No reservations. Open May-Oct. €9 per night. Cash only. ❶

Diego Mella/Collado Jermoso (☎636 99 87 27; www.colladojermoso.com; alt. 2060m), next to Collado Jermoso, in the southern central part of the park. 28 bunks. Guarded May-Oct. Sleeping bags for rent. Accessible from Fuente Dé via Tornos de Liordes; also from Cabana Veronica via Tiro Callejo or via Tiros de Casares (4hr., difficult). Open May-Oct. Breakfast €5, dinner €14. Bunks €6. Cash only. ❶

José Ramón Lueja/Jou de Los Cabrones (☎985 92 52 00; alt. 2034m), by Jou de los Cabrones. 24 bunks. Open year-round. Blankets for rent. Accessible from Poncebos via Bulnes, Amuesa, and Cuesta de Trave (5hr.); from Vega de Urriello via Collada Arenera (3hr.); from Cabana Veronica via Horcada de Don Juan and Jou Cerredo (2-3hr.). Bunks €10. Dinner €14, breakfast €5.20 Cash only. ❶

La Terenosa (alt. 1315m), near the Collado Pandébano en route to Vega de Urriellu. 30 spots. Open May-Oct. No meals. Accessible from Poncebos via Sotres and Collado Pandebano, or from Picu Uriellu. No rangers in residence. Free access, keys are in first cabin coming from Pandebano. ❶

MACIZO ORIENTAL

Casetón de Andara (☎671 404 277; alt. 1725m), by Vegas de Andara and Pica del Mancondiú. Accessible from Bejes (3hr.), as well as from Potes via Hito de Escarand via Ctra. Sotres-Treviso (1hr.). 18 bunks. Meals available. Be aware that there is no water in the vicinity. Open July-Oct. Sa-Su. ❶

OUTDOORS

While many visitors opt for organized bus tours and adventure sports from the base towns, the beauty of the Picos and the variety of the landscape are best appreciated on foot. The many *refugios* scattered throughout the park facilitate long treks, and a decent network of roads allows good access for day-hikes. For multi-day routes, consult one of the Picos de Europa park offices. These offices also arrange **free, guided day hikes** (min. 3 people) departing from various base towns in the park from July-Sept. Simply show up at the departure point at the listed time to participate; consult the park office for the most up-to-date schedule. The hikes listed at the end of this section are arranged according to the nearest trailhead or town. Before embarking on any hike, get a map that has all trails clearly marked. Locals use the *Ediciones Adrados* maps (1:25,000), available in bookstores and some tourist offices. The Asturias government prints a *Sin Miedo Con Seguridad* ("Without Fear, With Safety") pamphlet, a good resource for hiking safety information.

Note that while the gateway towns may appear well developed in tourism, much of the Picos remains untamed, and few amenities are available within the park proper. Non-technical hiking is possible from May to September, and the best times to visit the Picos are July and August. In spring, it is colder, and storms and snow are still a real possibility. September weather can be equally unpredictable. However, the Picos are particularly popular during July and August, so make reservations at least a week in advance if you plan to stay in the gateway cities to the park (Cangas de Onís, Arenas de Cabrales, and Potes). For information on adventure tourism outings, see **Cangas de Onís** (p. 515), **Arenas de Cabrales**, and **Potes** (p. 524).

WATERWISE. Don't drink the water from springs and streams in the Picos that aren't clearly labeled as potable. Many water sources in the mountains here, even those that appear perfectly clean and safe, are tainted with E. coli and other contaminants from agricultural runoff. Likewise, swimming in lakes and rivers in the Picos is prohibited unless clearly indicated otherwise.

HIKING

LAGOS DE COVADONGA

These mountain lakes are accessible from Cangas de Onís and Covadonga. ALSA buses (☎902 42 22 42) run from Covadonga to Lago Enol in the summer (30min.; July 8 per day 10am-6pm, Aug., 1st half of Sept. every 10-15min. 10am-6:30pm; returns July 8 per day 11am-7pm, Aug., 1st half of Sept. every 10-15min. 10am-7pm; €1.85, €3.55 round trip.) During Semana Santa, Aug., and early Sept., it is prohibited to drive up with private cars to the lakes. Visitors need to park in one of the many parking lots between Cangas and Covadonga and take the ALSA bus from there. Find a complete schedule with all parking lots and bus stops at any tourist or park information office. During the rest of the year, access to the lakes is open. From Lago Enol (alt. 1060m), it is a 1km walk or 5min. drive to Lago Ercina (alt. 1108m). In Covadonga, buses leave from the basilica to follow a road lined with pastures and precipitous cliffs; the right side of the bus has the best views en route. Alternatively, Turataxis runs tours several times daily between the lakes and the basilica. (20min., schedule varies, €10 per person depending on group size.)

The **Lagos de Enol y Ercina** sparkle between the peaks of the mountains past Covadonga. An information point in the Buferrera parking lot by Lago Enol is open daily, from July to September 9am-5pm. The **Centro de Visitantes Pedro Pidal,** a short climb up from the lower parking lot, has an exhibit recreating the natural conditions in the park, laden with sound and water effects. Extensive info on the Lagos region and on the entire park, including geology, flora, and fauna, is available. The center also provides info on hikes and *refugios* in the entire park. (Open from *Semana Santa* to Dec. daily 10am-6pm. Free.) Free **guided hikes** around the lakes depart from the Buferrera parking lot. Just below Lago Ercina is a path through the former **Minas de Buferrera,** still equipped with rails and mining implements. In August, the pastures surrounding the lakes feel like a crowded beach with picnicking families. Hit the trails to ditch the crowds. To see both lakes in all of their splendor, head to the aptly named **Mirador de Entrelagos** ("between the lakes"). A short climb up from the Lago Ercina parking lot, the lookout has great views of both lakes and of the mountains surrounding them. Don't forget your camera. Each of the lakes harbors a restaurant for the hordes of hungry hikers. At Lago Enol, **Bar Restaurante El Casin** crafts traditional Asturian entrees (€8-12) in its cozy dining room while serving up salads (€4-6) and sandwiches (€4-5) at the outdoor bar on its stone terrace. (☎985 92 29 27. Open daily 10am-8pm). Head to **Bar Maria Rosa on Lago Ercina** for the full lunch *menú* (€11). (☎985 92 20 09. Open 8:30am-late.)

Two especially good hikes, at a slightly higher level of difficulty, take travelers east from the lakes to the **Vega de Ario,** which offers a panoramic view of the Urrieles Mountains (7hr. round-trip, medium-high difficulty), or south to the **Mirador de Ordiales,** a vantage point overlooking the Pico de las Vidriosas, Río Dobra, and a terrifying gorge (7-8hr. round-trip, high difficulty). Alternatively, head west 2km to the **Mirador del Rey** lookout point (1hr. round-trip), where you can see the **Bosque de Pome.** The **Casa Municipal de Pastores ❶,** just past Lago Enol on the road to the Mirador del Rey in the Vega de Enol, has 10 spots year-round and provides meals, hall bath, and bunks, as well as a view of the lake. Bring your own sleeping bag. (Accessible by car. Breakfast €2.50; dinner €10-11. €8.) Note that cars are generally not allowed in the park in high season.

COVADONGA

The sanctuary of Covadonga is accessible only through Cangas, on the Bustio-Arriondas route. ALSA buses (☎902 42 22 42; www.alsa.es) run from Cangas (20min.; M-F 5 per day 8:45am-5pm, Sa-Su 3 per day 10:35am-6pm; €1.20) and back (20min.; M-F 5 per day 9am-5:30pm, Sa-Su 4 per day 10am-6pm; €1.20). Buses stop at the Hospedería, uphill at the basilica, and at the bus station in Cangas.

"This little mountain will be the salvation of Spain," Don Pelayo, the first King of Asturias, prophesied to his Christian army in AD 722, gesturing to the rocky promontory above what is now Covadonga. The mountain soon became the site of the first successful battle in the *Reconquista*, although legend claims that it was not geography but the intervention of the Virgin Mary that made victory over the Moors possible. Today, Covadonga is one of Asturias's most important historical and religious sites. At its center, the candlelit **Santa Cueva grotto,** where the Virgin appeared to Pelayo, contains the King's remains. (Open daily in summer 9am-8pm; in winter 9am-7pm. Free.) Under the cave, to the right of the water, is the **Fountain of Seven Spouts,** which blesses young girls with marriage and fertility. Below the Grand Hotel is the **San Fernando Collegiate Church** (constructed 1585-1599), the oldest building in town, which houses the tombs of two abbots from the 11th century. Visitors are not allowed inside. The **Museo de Covadonga,** next to the bus stop above the cave, has explanations in Spanish on the history of Covadonga, and displays the treasures—including royal paintings, swords, books, and jewelry—donated to the Virgin over the years. Make sure to see the sparkling crowns of Our Lady of Covadonga and the baby Jesus, encrusted with gold, platinum, pearls, sapphires, and rubies. (☎985 84 60 96. Open in summer daily 10:30am-2pm and 4-7pm; in winter 10:30am-2pm and 4-6:30pm. €3, children €2.) Lockers available in museum foyer. (Open during museum hours. €0.50.) From there, head to the **Basílica de Covadonga,** a neo-Romanesque basilica built in 1901, whose red and white marble towers provide a marvelous contrast against the lush backdrop of the mountains; the best view is from the road up. (Open daily in summer

9am-8pm; in winter 9am-7pm. Free.) A **monument** to King Pelayo, built in 1964 and inscribed with his prophetic declaration, stands in the basilica square.

Cangas offers cheaper accommodations, but it's hard to resist the friendly atmosphere and stunning views of the mountains at the **Hospedería del Peregrino ❸**, on the main road next to the bus stop below the basilica. All rooms are carpeted and have sinks; bathrooms are shared. The **restaurant ❷** downstairs offers an €12.50 *menú* that includes half a bottle of Rioja wine served in a spacious dining room. (☎985 84 60 47. Singles €23.54-39.59; doubles €36.38-55.10. Breakfast included. Reserve ahead in summer. Closed Nov.-Mar. MC/V.) At **El Huerto del Ermitaño ❹**, savor local dishes like baked *jabali* (wild boar, €17) to the tune of the Cueva's waterfall just across the road. (Halfway up the hill to the basilica. ☎985 84 60 97. Entrees €17-32. *Menú* €15. July-Sept. open daily 11am-11pm; Oct.-June M-W and F-Su 11am-4pm.) Covadonga's **info booth,** at the top of the hill, has details in English on local accommodations and the sanctuary. (☎985 84 60 35. Open W-Su 10am-2pm and 3:30-7:30pm. Closed Jan. and first half of Feb. When closed, info available in museum.)

CAMPING CORRECTLY. Though you may come across travelers setting up camp along trails in the Picos, camping is not officially allowed within the park. Tents can be pitched, according to a set of rules available at park offices, only above 1600 m. at night and must be taken down at dawn. Your best option to avoid embarrassment and fines is to stick to the official campsites or arrange for *refugio* accommodations.

PONCEBOS

Poncebos is accessible from Arenas de Cabrales and Cangas de Onís. ALSA buses run from Arenas (15min., end of July to early Sept. 6 per day 9:30am-7pm, €1.15) to the Hotel-Restaurante-Bar Garganta del Cares. Return 9 per day 10am-7:30pm. From Cangas, there is 1 bus per day (1hr.; 10am, returns to Cangas at 7pm; €3.60). By car, take AS-114 from Panes to Las Arenas; cross the river where signs point to Poncebos onto AS-264. Taxis (☎985 84 64 87 or 985 84 67 98) go to Poncebos at almost any time of day (€5-6).

Poncebos, a cluster of buildings just within the park's borders, about 6km from Arenas, is the starting point for many of Arenas's hiking trails. The walk to the main trailhead from Arenas threads through the feet of surrounding mountains; tight, winding roads make some corners dangerous. To stay overnight in Poncebos, try **Hostal Poncebos ❷,** downhill through the tunnel from the main intersection. (☎985 84 64 47. Singles €23-33; doubles €45-65. MC/V.) Otherwise, head to **Hotel-Restaurante-Bar Garganta del Cares ❷.** (☎985 84 64 63. Singles €25-38; doubles with TV and bath €40-62. MC/V.)

The famous 12km **Ruta del Cares,** perhaps the park's most popular trail, is an easy 3hr. one-way hike along a trail that can be done in either direction from Caín to Poncebos. The trail itself is carved along a water canal straight into the cliffside, which drops 200m from the trail down to the Río Cares below. It was constructed between the 1920s and 1950s as workers built a canal from Caín to the hydroelectric plant in Poncebos. A longer alternative is to include the stretch from **La Posada del Valdeón** to Caín. Stay overnight in Caín at Albergue "El Diablo de la Peña," whose friendly owners let out bunks in rooms of 4-8 (€12-15). Before you hit the trails, grab breakfast for only €2.50. (☎696 89 51 21). For more private accommodations, try **Hostal La Ruta ❸** (☎987 74 27 02; www.hostallaruta.com; closed Oct. 1 to *Semana Santa.* Doubles with shared bath €37; doubles with bath and TV €50), or **La Posada del Montañero ❹** (☎987 74 27 11; doubles €40-50). The **Poncebos-Bulnes** route, a medium difficulty 1hr. hike, follows the Río Tejo to **Bulnes,** a small village seemingly frozen in time, except for the Coca Cola signs and plastic beer-logo bar chairs. An underground funicular also connects Bulnes with Poncebos. The ride takes 7min. (☎985 84 68 00. Runs every 30min. Open daily July-Sept. and Easter week 10am-8pm, otherwise 10am-6pm. €14.42, round-trip €18.03.) Pamper yourself at **La Casa del Chiflón ❸**, which has 14 beds, a bar, hot showers, guides, weather reports, and meals in a century-old, recently renovated stone house. (☎985 84 59 43; www.casadelchiflon.com. One-week advance reservations suggested. Breakfast included. Open from *Semana Santa* to Nov., and around Christmas. Singles €30-40; doubles €50-59; triples €61-70; quads €72-80. MC/V.)

The park service offers free **guided hikes** to Bulnes on Saturdays at 9:30am (4hr.; departs from the small information hut by Poncebos's funicular). The **Poncebos-Collado Pandébano-Naranjo de Bulnes (Mt. Urriellu)** route, a spectacular 17km hike (8-10hr. round-trip), showcases the park's mountain streams and peaceful green pastures and leads to the saddleback Collado Pandébano, and eventually to the foot of the Picos's most famous mountain, **Naranjo de Bulnes**, named for its sunburnt orange face.

EXPERTS ONLY. From Bulnes, make sure to take the path marked to Pandébano; the other path to Urriellu through the Canal de Balcosin is not well-marked and is treacherously steep. This second option should only be attempted by experienced hikers looking for a challenge.

Most climbers choose to start the Urriellu hike in Sotres, the highest town in the Picos, and continue from there (5hr. round-trip). For accommodations in Sotres itself, try the friendly **Albergue Peña de Castil ❶**, which has dorm-style bunks (€14, breakfast €3) or private rooms of four bunks (€20 per person, breakfast included). Each bed also has a personal light and electric socket, and there is plenty of hot water for showers. (☎985 94 50 70 or 629 82 02 26. Curfew midnight. Quiet hours 11pm-7am. MC/V.)

If you have a car and are coming from **Sotres**, consider driving up part of the way to Pandebano, as the first part of the path is a wide dirt road.There are two *refugios* in the Naranjo de Bulnes area: **Refugio Vega de Urriellu/Ubeda ❶** (☎985 92 52 00), at the foot of the Naranjo, and **Refugio Jou de Los Cabrones/Lueje ❶** (☎985 92 52 00 or 650 78 03 81). It's worth going beyond the Poncebos-Camareña path to Puertos de Ondón, where the view is gorgeous.

POTES

Potes (pop. 2000) has an unbeatable location for access to the heart of the Picos. Although the streets crowd with tourists, travelers, and mountaineers in summer, the town's ancient cobblestone streets, arcades, and hidden wine *bodegas* maintain the desirable charm of a Spanish mountain town.

TRANSPORTATION. La Palomera **buses** (☎942 88 06 11 or 50 30 80) travel to **Fuente Dé** July-Aug. (45min.; M-F 8:30am; 1pm, July 14-Aug. 14 also 8pm; Sa-Su 1pm; €1.50) and back (M-F 9:15am, 5pm, mid-July-mid-Aug. also 8:45pm; Sa-Su 5pm). During the rest of the year, buses run to **Espinama**, 4km below Fuente Dé (40min., M-F 1pm, €1.10) and back (M-F 9am and 2:10pm). Buses also go to **Santander** (2¼hr.; July-Aug. M-F 7, 10am, 5:30pm; Sa-Su 10am, 5:30pm; Sept.-June M-F 7, 10am, 5:30pm; Sa 10am, 5:30pm, Su 5:30pm; €7.05) via **Panes** (40min., connection available to Cangas de Onis and Arenas de Cabrales) and **Unquera** (1hr.). There are two **taxi** stops in town, one about 100m toward the town center from the tourist office on Pl. de la Serna and the other across town on C. Dr. Encinas (☎942 73 04 00 or 942 73 04 52).

PRACTICAL INFORMATION. The **tourist office,** in the bus station, has info on adventure tourism, local hikes, *refugios*, and accommodations. (☎942 73 07 87. Open daily 10am-2pm and 4-8pm. Hours can be irregular.) The **Sotama** park office and visitor's center, Av. Luis Cuevas, 2A, in nearby Tama (3km) on the road to Panes, has more extensive information on the national park, as well as an extensive exhibit on the geology, flora and fauna of the park with signs in English. (☎942 73 81 09. Open daily July-Sept. 9am-8pm; Oct.-June 9am-6pm.) Local services include: **Banco Santander Central Hispano,** C. Dr. Encinas, with a 24hr. **ATM** (☎902 24 24 24; open M-F 8:30am-2pm, Oct.-Mar. Sa 8:30am-1pm); **Guardia Civil** (☎942 73 00 07), on C. Obispo off C. Dr. Encinas; **Farmacia F. Soberón,** C. Palacios, 2 (☎942 73 00 08; open daily 9:30am-9:30pm); **Centro de Salud** (☎942 73 03 60) on C. Eduardo García de Enterría; **Internet access** at **CyberLiebana,** C. Roque, 1 (☎942 73 01 03; €2 per hr.; open daily noon-2am) or at the **Biblioteca Municipal,** C. Independencia, 22, across the park from the church (free; open M-F 8am-2pm); **post office,** Pl. de la Serna, a block from the tourist office on the main road toward the bridge (☎942 73 03 34. Open M-F 8:30am-2:30pm, Sa 9:30am-1pm). **Postal Code:** 39570.

ACCOMMODATIONS. Several hostels are scattered on C. Dr. Encinas and on C. Cántabra, a side street. The beautiful **Casa Cayo ❸,** C. Cántabra, 6, a right off C. Dr. Encinas when walking into town from the bus stop, has the feel of a country cottage in the middle of town. All the rooms are spacious and immaculate with TV, phone, and bath. There's also a cozy lounge with a big TV. (☎942 73 01 50. Open Mar. 1-Dec. 22. Singles €35; doubles €50; triples €60; quads €40. MC/V.) The **restaurant ❷** downstairs serves delicious meat and fish dishes; try the incredibly tender veal cutlet (€11) with a shot of *urquijo*, the Spanish version of grappa, distilled with herbs. (Open M-Sa 1-4pm and 8-11pm.) If you're looking for a clean, relatively cheap place to stay, try **Hostal Lombraña ❷,** right in the center of town, next to the bridge over the river. Most of the rooms have private bathrooms, while several share a hall bath. (☎942 73 05 19. Doubles €21-25, with bath €25-29. Cash only.) The closest campsite is **Camping La Viorna ❶,** about 1km up Hwy. 885 toward Monasterio Santo Toribio, which has a restaurant-bar, supermarket, and pool. The campsite also offers organized hiking, mountain biking, and spelunking excursions. (☎942 73 20 21. Open from Apr. 1 to Oct. 30. €4-4.40 per person, per car, and per tent. MC/V.) **La Isla,** N621, on the way to Fuente Dé, is a shadier campsite with a flatter, if slightly longer (3km), walk from town, and a pleasant bar/restaurant with a terrace right on the Rio Deva's edge. (☎942 730 896. Pool, hot showers, and market. Hiking maps sold at reception. In summer €4 per person, per car, and per tent. In winter €3.65. Bungalows for 4 people €55-68; for 6 €65-78.

FOOD. **Supermarket El Árbol** is across the street from the bus station and tourist office. (☎942 73 05 26. Open in summer daily 9am-9pm; in winter M 9:30am-8:30pm, Tu-Sa 9:30am-2pm and 5-8:30pm. MC/V.) Potes feeds plenty of hungry hikers, and despite its touristic popularity, it does so cheaply. C. Dr. Encinas, C. Cántabra, and C. San Cayetano are packed with restaurants, tapas bars, and cafeterias. For crispy pizzas made on renowned local bread, try **Cafe de Picos,** C. Palacios, 22 (☎676 86 58 24. Open M and W-Su July-Aug. 9am-11:30pm; Sept.-June 9am-11pm. Cash only.) Tucked up behind the main thoroughfare, **Restaurante El Refugio ❷,** C. Obispo 4, serves a tasty *menú* (€9.50) as well as a large selection of tapas (€2.50-6) on its canopied, grape-vined terrace or in its brick-lined interior. For Picos-specific cuisine, opt for the *Cocido Lebaniego* (€9.50), a meal complete with soup, meats, greens, and dessert. (☎942 73 10 28. Open daily Nov.-Mar. 1-4pm; Apr.-Oct. 1-4pm and 8-11pm). Ditch the crowds of tourists taking their drinks at the overpopulated bars along the arcade and sneak a glass of *tostadillo*, the local sweet wine, at the nearly hidden **Bodega de las Teleranas** ❶ (first door on the left on C. Independencia heading up towards the library). Look one door before the large arched door for cobwebbed bottles and old wine casks in the cool, dark *bodega*. (Glasses €0.80. Bottles €3.50. Open in summer M-F noon-8pm; in winter Sa-Su noon-6pm. Cash only.)

SIGHTS AND OUTDOOR ACTIVITIES. **Urdón,** 15km north of Potes on the road to Panes, is the start of a challenging 6km (2hr.) hike to **Tresviso,** a tiny town where chickens outnumber humans. A 3km uphill hike from the tourist office toward Fuente Dé and left at the intersection with the Hwy. 885 is the **Monasterio de Santo Toribio de Liébana,** which protects the Lignum Crucis, reportedly the largest surviving piece of the cross. *(☎942 73 05 50. Open daily in summer 10am-1pm and 4-7pm. Free.)* In town, the recently restored **Molino del Palacio,** behind the library, offers a look at a functional flour mill dating to at least 1468. The tourist office has a list of the outfitters in town. **EuroPicos,** San Roque, 6, a couple of blocks past the bridge on the main road toward Panes, leads trips on horseback (€20 per 1½hr., €30 per 3hr.), canyon descents (€36), 2-seater paragliding (€100), and other activities. *(☎942 73 07 24; www.europicos.com. Open daily July-Aug. 8:30am-9pm; Sept.-June 10am-1pm and 5-8pm. AmEx/MC/V.)* **Extreme Factory,** C. Sol, 1, by the bridge in the middle of town, offers paragliding (€95, includes transportation) and bungee jumping in addition to the other outdoor activities. Call ahead. *(☎942 73 06 19; www.extremefactoryliebana.com. Open daily Aug. 10am-10pm; Mar.-July and Sept.-Nov. 10am-2pm and 4:30-8:30pm. MC/V.)*

FUENTE DÉ

Fuente Dé is only accessible July-Aug. from Potes on La Palomera buses (☎942 88 06 11 or 50 30 80; 30min.; M-F 8:30am, 1pm, mid-July-mid-August also 8pm, Sa-Su 1pm; €1.40; return M-F 9:15am, 5pm, mid-July-mid-August 8:45pm, Sa-Su 5pm). The bus stops in front of the Parador de Fuente Dé, just below the teleférico (cable car) base. During other months, take the bus to Espinama and walk the rest of the way to Fuente Dé (4km).

Only 23km from Potes, the **Teleférico de Fuente Dé** is well worth an excursion. The goosebump-inducing *teleférico*, the third-largest cable car system in the world, jets 800m to the mountain top (1834m) in less than 4min., at some points going up along an almost vertical rock-face. Many hikes are possible from Fuente Dé itself. From the cable car's lower station, the **Somo Waterfall Route** (11.5km, 4hr.) swings through the Berrugas cattle sheds, the soft Bustantivo meadows, and on to the Somo waterfall. The upper station is ideally located for hikes into the heart of the central *macizo* (massif). (☎942 73 66 10; www.cantur.com. Open daily July-Aug. 9am-8pm; Sept.-June M-F 10am-6pm, Sa-Su 10am-8pm. €8, round-trip €14.) A zig-zagging trail ascends just left of the cable car (3hr.) for those up for a brutal but dramatic hike, but the path is not well-marked along the entire route. At the top, there are also many hikes along 4WD tracks and trails toward *refugios* and the high peaks of the eastern macizo. From the upper station, follow the main path until the first fork. From there, you can head left (north) to **Monte Urriellu, Naranjo de Bulnes,** via the tiny Cabaña Veronica and Horcados Rojos; (5hr., medium to high difficulty), or turn right to get to the Hotel-Refugio de Áliva (40min., low difficulty) and continue to **Poncebos** via **Sotres** (3hr. from Hotel-Refugio de Áliva to Sotres and 5-6hr. descending from Sotres to Poncebos, low difficulty). The path from **Hotel-Refugio de Áliva to Sotres** winds through gorgeous alpine valleys, passing through the abandoned stone walls and ruins of Las Vegas del Toro. **Sotres** itself, a 1km detour from the main walking path, is a town frozen in time at the foot of the mythic peaks. Hikers wearied by a day's descent can find rustic lodging with spectacular views at Fuente Dé's **El Redondo Camping ❶**, just above the base of the *teleférico*. A small garden at the entrance sets the relaxed tone for the campsite. Their 16-bunk *refugio* has a common space with tables and sink with potable water. (☎942 73 66 99; www.elredondopicosdeeuropa.com. Open May-Oct. Bar, market, and hot showers. Reception daily 9am-9pm. No reservations. €5 per person, €7 per site. Electricity €3. Cash only.) Their **restaurant** serves hearty *platos combinados* (€6-10) and salads (€3), amid wooden furniture under old-fashioned hiking implements and antique decor. A higher, more expensive option is to spend the night at **Hotel-Refugio de Áliva ❺** (1666m), the most expensive and luxurious *refugio* in the park, located 3km from the top of the *teleférico* (40min., all-terrain jeep ride €3 each way). All 24 doubles come with full bath and heat in winter; there is also a restaurant and cafeteria on site. (☎942 73 09 99. Breakfast €4. Full board €28. Doubles €75; triples €92. MC/V.)

CANTABRIA

From the spectacle of Santander's El Sardinero beaches to the provincial park of Oyambre, it's the coast that makes Cantabria famous. Though it has yet to see the resort build-up of Spain's southern shores, the region's beach towns, declared by some to have the world's cleanest surfing water, are by no means untouched or secluded. Cantabria also has hiking in the Picos de Europa, Paleolithic cave drawings, and renowned architecture, including Gaudí's **El Capricho** and the 12th-century **Colegiata de Santa Juliana** in Santillana del Mar.

SANTANDER ☎942

Every summer in Santander (pop. 185,000), beautiful coastline and miles of spotless, sandy beaches play host to thousands of tourists looking to catch up on their tans. Palm trees rub shoulders with pines, pasty Brits bake next to bronzed Spaniards, and the hustle and bustle of the city center is easily forgotten on a stroll down El Sardinero's vine-filled boardwalks. Santander became fashionable thanks to royal attention; King Alfonso XIII summered in the early 20th century on Peninsula La Magdalena, and hotels now occupy the summer palaces of his court in El Sardinero. Santander is well-visited, yet far more relaxed than the frenetic beaches in the Costa del Sol, and in the weeks between its big summer festivals, the crowds thin a little. With a mountainous horizon and cliff-top lighthouses, Santander is the Bay of Biscay at its best.

TRANSPORTATION

Flights: Aeropuerto de Santander, Av. de Parayas (☎942 20 21 00; www.aena.es), in nearby Camargo (5km away). Serviced by many European budget airlines, including **Ryanair.** Accessible by taxi (€15-17); buses run from bus station to airport every 15-30min. 6:30am-10:45pm (€1.50).

Trains: FEVE (☎942 20 95 22; www.feve.es) and **RENFE** (☎902 24 02 02; www.renfe.es), Pl. de las Estaciones. RENFE serves distant destinations to the south, as Santander is the terminus of a national rail line; take a regional FEVE train to cities east or west of Santander. RENFE info open daily 8:30am-1pm and 3:30-9pm; station open 5am-12:30am. RENFE goes to **Madrid** (5-6hr.; M-F 3 per day 7:05am-7:20pm, Sa 2 per day 7:05am, 2:05pm, Su 4 per day 7:05-7:20pm; €31.75-44.20), **Valladolid** (3-4hr., 5-8 per day 7:05am-8:10pm, €14.90-26.40) and **Palencia** (2-3hr.; 5-7 per day 7:05am-7:20pm, Su 7:05am-8:10pm; €11.75-23.20) as well as **Barcelona** to

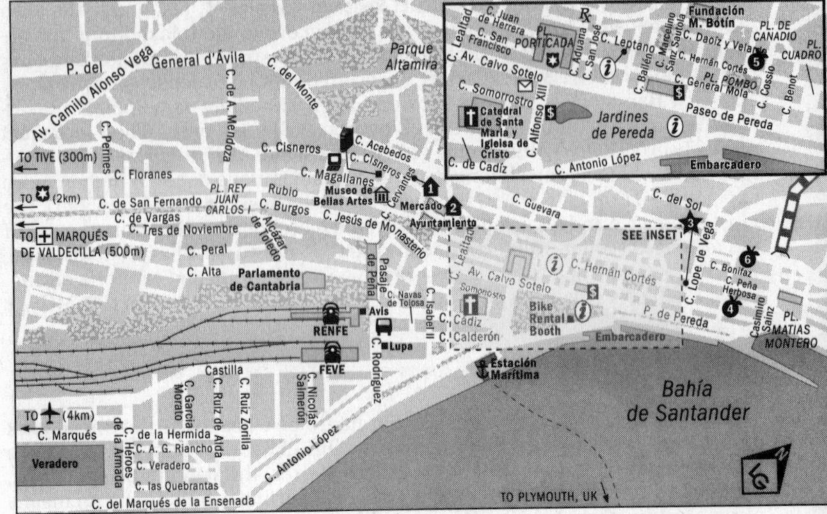

the west (9-10hr.; daily 10:05am, Su-F 12:25pm; €40-52.90, overnight bunk €50.90. FEVE goes to: **Bilbao** (2¾hr., 3 per day 8am- 2pm,7pm, €7.35) and **Oviedo** (4hr.; 9:10am, 4:10pm; €13.50), as well as several local destinations.

Buses: C. Navas de Tolosa directly in front of train stations (☎942 21 19 95; www.santandereabus.com). Info open daily 8am-10pm.

ALSA (☎902 42 22 02; www.alsa.es) goes to: **Barcelona** (8-9hr.; 9am, 9pm; €47.31) via Lleida (8hr., 9pm only, €36.86); **Bilbao** (1hr., every 30min.-1hr. 3:45am-11:59pm, €6.44-11.80); **Oviedo** (3hr.; 8-12 per day 7:15am-8pm and 3:30am, F, Su also 10:15pm; €12.59-21.70); **San Sebastián** (2-3hr.; 9-11 per day 3:45am-8:30pm, Su also 11:55pm; €12.48-23.71); **Salamanca** (6hr.; 8:30am, 5pm.; €16.05) and **Vitoria-Gasteiz** (2½hr., 4-5 per day 8am-9pm, €10.33).

Continental Auto (☎902 33 04 00; www.continental-auto.es) goes to: **Madrid** (6hr.; M-Sa 6 per day 12:30am-7pm, Su 8 per day 12:30am-11:59pm; €26.43-39); and **Burgos** (4hr.; M-Sa 6 per day 8am-12:30am, Su 8 per day 12:30am-8pm; €10.12-18.50).

La Cantabrica (☎942 72 08 22) runs buses to **Comillas** (1hr., €3.40) through **Santillana del Mar** (40min., €2.15; Sept.-June M-F 4 per day 10:30am-7:15pm, Sa-Su 3 per day 11:30am-8:30pm; July-Aug. M-F 7 per day 8:30am-9:30pm, Sa-Su 5 per day 10:30am-9:30pm). Buy tickets onboard.

Palomera (☎942 88 06 11) runs buses to the town of **Potes** in the **Picos de Europa** during July-Aug. (2hr.; M-F 3 per day 10:30am-5pm, Sa 10:30am, 3:15pm, Su 10:30am). Call in advance for groups larger than 6 people. Continuing service also available to **Fuente Dé** during July and Aug.

Ferries: Brittany Ferries, Estación Marítima (☎942 36 06 11; www.brittany-ferries.com), by the Jardines de Pereda. Reserve 2 weeks ahead in summer. Info open M-F 9am-7pm. To **Plymouth, UK** (18-22hr., 2 per week, €45-73, car with 2 passengers €225-363 plus €10 for a seat). **Los Reginas,** C. Embarcadero (☎942 21 67 53; www.losreginas.com), by the **Jardines de Pereda,** runs to **Pedreña, Somo,** and the **Playas del Puntal** (15min., every 30min. leaving from 8:30am, returning until 8:25pm, round-trip €3.90), and runs **tours** of the bay (1hr., July-Oct. 13 per day 11:15am-8:30pm per day, €8).

Public Transportation: Transportes Urbanos buses (☎942 20 07 71) run throughout the city (July-Aug. roughly 6am-11pm, Sept.-June 6am-10:30pm; night buses hourly midnight-6am; €1). Buses #1, 4, 7, 9, 13, and 14 run from the *Ayuntamiento* to El Sardinero on Po. de Pereda and Av. de la Reina Victoria, stopping at Pl. de Italia and Jardines de Piquío. #15 runs from the RENFE station to El Sardinero and out to

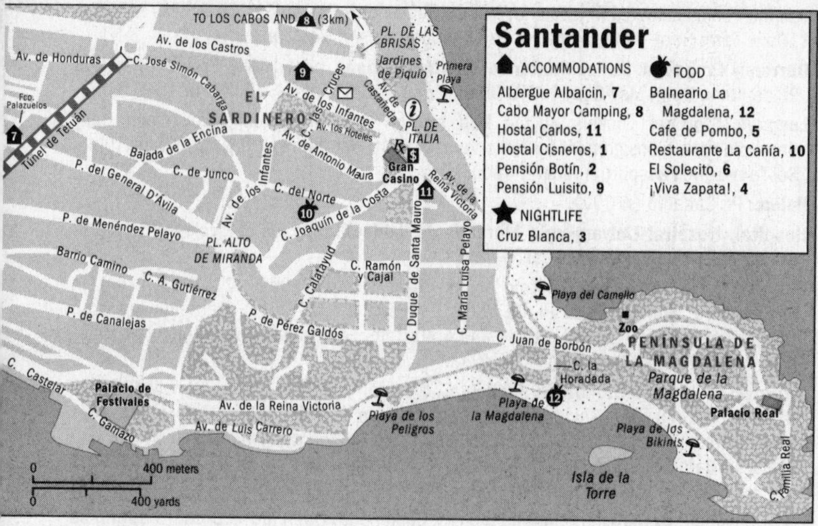

the Cabo Mayor campground. The tourist office gives out free schedules, and maps are posted at every stop.

Taxis: (☎942 33 33 33 or 36 91 91). 24hr. service to greater Santander. Taxis wait outside the train and bus stations, on C. Vargas, and near the *Ayuntamiento* as well as by the Gran Casino in El Sardinero. The tourist office has a map with all taxi stops throughout the city.

Car Rental: Avis (☎942 22 0 25), in the RENFE parking lot, Pl. de los Estaciones. 21+, must have had license for 1 year. Open M-F 8:30am-1pm and 4-7:30pm, Sa 9am-1pm. **National** (☎942 22 29 26), right next to Avis. Open M-F 9am-1pm and 4-7pm, Sa 9am-1pm, Su 10am-1pm.

ORIENTATION AND PRACTICAL INFORMATION

Santander sits on a peninsula in the Bay of Biscay, and its southern shores form the Bahía de Santander. There are two main sections of the city: **El Centro,** around the train and bus stations and the Jardines de Pereda, and **El Sardinero,** along the beach to the east. El Centro and El Sardinero are separated by a hill. The main roads connecting them are the **Túnel de Tetuán** and the main thoroughfare, which starts at the *Ayuntamiento* as **Avenida Calvo Sotelo** and runs along the shore to the Jardines de Piquío in El Sardinero, changing its name to **Paseo de Pereda** and **Avenida de la Reina Victoria** along the way. Santander's famed park, **La Península de la Magdalena,** sits at the eastern tip of Santander. The best way to get around is by bus on one of the free bikes loaned out by the tourist office.

Tourist Office: Regional office inside Mercado del Este (☎942 31 07 08; www.turismocantabria.com), open July-Sept. daily 9am-9pm; Oct.-June daily 9:30am-1:30pm and 4-7pm. Santander tourism office in Jardines de Pereda (☎942 20 30 00; www.ayto-santander.es). Open daily July-Aug. 9am-9pm; Sept.-June M-F 8:30am-7pm, Sa 10am-2pm. **Branch** in El Sardinero, across from the grand casino, open July-Aug. daily 10am-9pm; June M-F 10am-7pm, Sa-Su 10am-2pm. Both branches, as well as a booth on the Península de La Magdalena, rent out **free bicycles** for 4hr. Open daily July-Aug. 10am-7pm; Sept.-June 10am-2pm and 4-6pm. Closed Nov.-Jan.

Currency Exchange: Banco Santander Central Hispano, on Av. Calvo Sotelo. **Branch** at Pl. de Italia. Open May-Sept. M-F 8:30am-2pm, Oct.-Apr. also Sa 8:30am-1pm. 24hr.

Luggage Storage: Lockers at the **bus station** on the bottom level. Open daily 6am-midnight. Consignment for large items (€2.40 per item per day) M-F 7am-10pm, Sa 7am-1am. Passport or local ID required.

Police: Pl. Canadio (☎092).

Hospital: Hospital Universitario Marqués de Valdecilla, Av. de Valdecilla, 25 (☎942 20 25 20). For **emergencies** call ☎061.

Pharmacy: Farmacia Calvo Sotelo on Av. Calvo Sotelo (☎942 22 43 15). 24hr. In El Sardinero, **Somacarrera,** Pl. de Italia, 1 (☎942 27 05 96), underneath the Gran Casino. Open daily 9:30am-1:30pm and 4:30-8pm. For locations of late-night pharmacies, check the schedule at any pharmacy.

Internet: Free at the **Biblioteca Pública,** C. Gravina 4 (☎942 24 15 50) July-Aug. M-F 8:15am-1:45pm, Sept.-June daily 8:15am-1:45pm and 4-9:30pm. Also at **Divernet Informática,** C. Cisneros, 29 (☎942 24 14 25). English spoken. €2 per hour. Open M-Sa 9:30am-2pm and 3:30-8:30pm, Su 4-9:30pm.

Post Office: Av. Alfonso XIII (☎942 36 55 19). Open M-F 8:30am-8:30pm, Sa 9:30am-2pm. **Branch** in El Sardinero on Av. Castaneda. Open M-F 8:30am-8:30pm, Sa 9:30am-1pm. **Lista de Correos** and fax. **Postal Code:** 39080.

ACCOMMODATIONS AND CAMPING

Accommodations fill quickly in July and August, especially during the big festivals, so reserve ahead. For a complete list of *pensiones* and *hostales* along with their prices, contact the tourist office or visit its website.

EL SARDINERO

Lodging in El Sardinero is available along the busy Reina Victoria, overlooking the bay and close to the beaches and promenade. There are also a few quieter *pensiones* along Av. de las Castros. From the *Ayuntamiento* in El Centro, ask bus drivers to drop you off at El Piquío (Hotel Colón).

Pensión Luisito, Av. de los Castros, 11 (☎942 27 19 71). Well-kept rooms and an incredibly friendly owner will make you feel right at home. Many have spacious balconies, and some overlook the garden and a slice of the sea. Room sinks, hall baths. Breakfast €2.82 Open July-mid-Sept. Singles €26; doubles €44. Cash only. ❷

Hostal Carlos, Av. de la Reina Victoria, 135 (☎942 27 16 16). Stay in the wood-floored and marble-sculptured palace where King Alfonso XIII put up his favorite barons at the beginning of the 1900s. English and French spoken. Breakfast €3.60. Singles €37-56; doubles €53-76. AmEx/MC/V. ❹

Cabo Mayor Camping, Av. del Faro (☎942 39 15 42; www.cabomayor.com). On the scenic bluff of Cabo Mayor, 3km from Playas Primera and Segunda. From the *Ayuntamiento,* take bus #15 to "Camping." By car, follow Av. del Faro north out of El Sardinero. Pool, currency exchange, supermarket, bar, and tennis courts. Reception 8am-11pm. Electricity €3. Open Apr.-Oct. €5 per adult and per tent, €4.50 per car. Cash only. ❶

EL CENTRO

The city center has the advantage of being near cheap food, convenient transportation, a pleasant portside *paseo,* and busy nightlife. North of the *Ayuntamiento* and Av. de Calvo Sotelo is a tranquil collection of restaurants, shops, and bars. Pl. Santa Lucia is the nucleus of several blocks of bars and nightclubs that spill into the streets on weekends.

Pensión Botín, C. Isabel II, 1, 1st fl. (☎942 21 00 94; www.pensionbotin.com). The committed owners have over 20 years' experience keeping guests happy. Immaculate, homey rooms, some with balconies overlooking the market behind the *Ayuntamiento*. All rooms have TV, brand-new private showers, and sink. Singles €27-40; doubles €36-58; ask about rates for rooms of up to 5 people. ❸

Hostal Cisneros, C. Cisneros, 8, 1st fl. (☎942 21 16 13). Cozy rooms have clean wooden floors overlooking the nearby streets. Some have a covered balcony. Shared baths, TV, free Wi-Fi. Sept-June singles €25; doubles €35. July-Aug. all rooms €51. Cash only. ❷

Albergue Albaícin, C. Francisco Palazuelos 21-23, (☎942 21 77 53). A school that converts classrooms into dorm-style rooms in the summer; probably your only chance to write on a blackboard from your bed. On the hill above El Centro, it has stunning views of the bay, but be prepared for a steep climb. Coin-operated laundry machines. Breakfast included. Open July-Aug. Bunks in 10-bed mixed or single-sex dorm €18. ❶

FOOD

EL SARDINERO

El Sardinero is packed with ice cream stands and expensive restaurants, though the better values may be found in El Centro. One of the best grocery options is **Diferente,** C. Joaquín de la Costa, 28, in the Hotel Santemar shopping complex. (☎942 281 782. Open M-F 9am-2:30pm and 5:30-9:30pm, Sa 9am-2:45pm and 5:45-9:30pm, Su 9:30am-3pm. AmEx/MC/V.)

Balneario La Magdalena, C. la Horadada (☎942 03 21 07), on Playa de la Magdalena. Bar and restaurant perched above the beach, with a delectable menu of meat (€12-17) and fish (€13-17). Lunch *menú* €15.50. Open daily 9am-midnight. MC/V. ❸

Restaurante La Cañia, Joaquín Costa, 45 (☎942 27 04 91). Popular among tourists and reasonably priced. A variety of seafood and helpful waitstaff. *Pintxos* €1-1.50. Fish €7.50-15. Su *menú* €13. Open daily 1-4pm and 8pm-midnight. ❸

EL CENTRO

Many restaurants in and on the streets surrounding Pl. Cañadio serve entrees until drinks and dancing take over. In the Barrio Pesquero (Fisherman's Neighborhood), the day's catch is grilled within sight of the docks. For fresh meat and vegetables, roam the aisles of the **Mercado de la Esperanza** behind the *Ayuntamiento.* (Open Su-F 8am-2pm, Sa 8am-2pm and 5-7:30pm.)

El Solecito, C. Bonifaz, 19 (☎942 36 06 33, takeout 32 51 18). The plates are the only square things in this artsy hole-in-the-wall bistro. Autumn leaves, African masks, and intimate booths make for a unique dining experience. Try the incredibly tender *croquetas de solomillo* (sirloin croquettes; €7.50) or their large selection of pastas (€8.50-10). Pizzas €6.50-10. Reservations recommended for weekend dinner. Open M-Th and Su 1-4pm and 8-11:30pm, F-Sa 1-4pm and 8pm-12:30am. MC/V. ❷

Café de Pombo, C. Hernán Cortés, 21 (☎942 22 32 24). On Pl. de Pombó, behind the central Banco de Santander, in a building once home to Cuban national hero José Martí. Coffee, pastries, ice cream, crepes, sandwiches—all delicious, all huge, all between €1-5, served out on the square or in an elegant dining area that conjures up the feel of a literary haunt. Open daily 8am-1am. Cash only. ❶

¡Viva Zapata!, C. Hernán Cortés, 47 (☎942 21 20 31). Dine to the tune of Mexican *corridos* alongside Diego Rivera prints and indigenous tapestries. Mexican entrees (€9.75-

12.75) made from authentic ingredients are served with true Mexican beers and a selection of delicious tequilas. Open daily 12-4pm and 8pm-12:30am. ❷

SIGHTS

Assuming you're not fast asleep on the beach, the best way to experience Santander is to wander the beaches and peninsulas. The tourist office has a list of 1-2hr. walking tours; they are definitely a good way to get to know the city itself. On a rainy day, head indoors to the free museums and churches.

PENÍNSULA DE LA MAGDALENA. Although more like an amusement park than a palace grounds, La Magdalena is Santander's prime attraction and one of the most beautiful parts of the city. The entire peninsula is filled with palms and pines, and is ringed by bluffs plunging into the sea. **Playa de la Bikini** is, according to local lore, the first place where the two-piece bathing suit was ever worn in Spain. Crowds of people line the main walkways, but you can find peace and quiet among the paths or in a secluded, romantic cliffside nook. The park's crowning landmark is the **palacio,** a neo-Gothic mansion that Alfonso XIII used as a summer home. Today, the palace hosts the elite Universidad Internacional Menéndez Pelayo's summer sessions on oceanography. You may find tourists exchanging grunts with the sea lions at the mini-zoo, which also houses penguins and seals. A **tourist train** runs past the zoo, an adjacent display of historic ships, and through the rest of the peninsula. *(☎942 29 10 44 or 639 51 36 72. Open 9:15am-9:15pm. €2.10, children €1.40)* You can also rent Segway scooters at a booth near the park entrance. *(☎630 32 32 30. Open 11am-2:30pm and 4-9pm. Peninsula tours €8-15, 2hr. city tour €35.)* Walking, however, is the best way to explore, and the 2km path ends with tasty incentives: snack stands and bars flank the park's entrance. *(☎942 27 25 04. Park open daily June-Sept. 8am-10pm; Oct.-May 9am-8:30pm. The palace has no scheduled visiting hours, during winter months inquire at tourist office.)*

LOS CABOS. More peninsular parks lie just north of the El Sardinero beaches. While Cabos Menor and Mayor lack the manmade attractions and action of La Magdalena, their bluffs and secluded beaches make for a more peaceful setting. Cabo Menor, the southernmost of the two, houses Santander's golf course and another mini-zoo; it also has postcard-worthy views of Cabo Mayor's 19th-century lighthouse. From Pl. de Italia, walk up Av. de Castañeda past Glorieta del Dr. Fleming, and turn right onto Av. de Pontejos, which turns into Av. del Faro and takes you toward the capes. There are great views from the path around the cliffs encircling the Cabos. To reach it, follow Av. García Lago to the end of Playa la Segunda and look for stairs that lead up to the top of the peninsula. *(Parque Municipal de Mataleñas on Cabo Menor open 9am-9pm.)*

CATEDRAL DE SANTA MARÍA DE LA ASUNCIÓN. Santander's Gothic cathedral is composed of two churches, built one on top of the other. The lower temple was built to guard the heads of martyred Roman soldiers Emeterio and Celedonio, now held in silver reliquaries there. After dropping into the guillotine basket in AD 300 in La Rioja, the heads were brought to Santander in the 8th century for safekeeping during the Moorish invasion, where they were kept in the ruins of an oven. These ruins have now been excavated, and you can see them through a section of glass flooring below the church. The upper cathedral, built after the XII century, was partially rebuilt after the fire of 1941 that leveled much of Santander. *(Pl. del Obispo José E. Eguino, behind the post office and Banco España. ☎942 22 60 24. Open M-F 10am-1pm and 4:30-7:30pm, except during mass. July-Aug. free tours in Spanish at 10:30am, 11:30am, 12:45pm, 4:30pm, 5:30pm, 6:30pm, 7:30pm, departing from the entrance to the lower church.)*

MUSEO DE BELLAS ARTES. Devoted to the eclectic works of local artists, Santander's Museo de Bellas Artes houses an impressive permanent collection, including an original Goya. Modern photographs share wall space with canvases from classic artists, but the majority of the works are by local artists, featured in rotating exhibitions on the ground floor. Art history buffs will enjoy the collection 20th-century pieces, and even the amateur art-lover will appreciate the multimedia demonstrations and rotating galleries. *(C. Rubio, 6. ☎942 20 31 20. From the Ayuntamiento, walk up C. Jesús de Monasterio and turn right onto C. Cervantes. Open June 16-Sept. 14 M-F 10:45am-1pm and 6-9pm, Sa 10:30am-1pm; Sept. 15-June 15 M-F 10:15am-1pm and 5:30-9pm, Sa 10am-1pm. Free.)*

BEACHES

In Santander, every day is a beach day: rain or shine, locals flock to the beach as soon as work gets out and spend the late afternoon and evening soaking up the sun. Whichever beach you choose, it is hard to go wrong in Santander, where the sand is always silky, soft, and clean. The waves, however, can get very rough, and with the raging wind, it is not uncommon for five-foot breakers to crash onto the beach. Calmer water and rockier beaches can be found on the bay side. The best and most popular beaches are undoubtedly **Playas Primera y Segunda** in El Sardinero. Not only does the sand go on forever, but the EU has declared these one of its "blue flag" cleanest beaches. Primera and Segunda are also hangouts for Santander's surfing crowd, which emerges during and after rain. Crowds rush to the calmer waters on the southern shore of La Magdalena. Rock-framed **Playa de Bikinis** is the secluded haunt of Santander's guitar-strumming teens. To escape the beach-going hordes, either head across the bay by ferry to **Playas Puntal, Somo,** and **Loredo,** which line a narrow peninsula of dunes, or hike up to the remote beaches of Los Cabos where **Playa de Mataleñas** and **Playa de los Molinucos** await you without throngs of people (or lifeguards).

NIGHTLIFE AND FESTIVALS

Santander's nightlife revolves around multiple epicenters and has a definite schedule. Dinner lasts roughly from 10pm until midnight or 1am at places like **Cruz Blanca,** C. Lope de Vega, 5, where you can have a table with its own beer tap (€6 per liter) to warm up for the evening. (☎942 08 47 00. Open M-Th and Su 9am-11:30pm, F-Sa 9am-1:30am. MC/V.) After that, people begin to carry drinks from bars into outdoor spaces like the **Pl. Santa Lucia.** Pl. Cañadio fills to the brim with drink-bearing locals. Try nearby Australian-themed **El Dorado,** C. Hernan Cortes, 18 (open daily noon-5am). In El Sardinero, visit Pl. de Italia, which also hosts the **Gran Casino** (18 to gamble, long pants and shoes required). By 2am on a weekend, Pl. Santa Lucia, C. Rio de la Pila, and C. Casimior Sainz are filled with waiters desperately trying to recover glasses before patrons flock to nightclubs for the last stops of the night. The night isn't dead until you've had **chocolate con churros** (€3), a traditional Spanish breakfast of hot chocolate so thick, that it's more of a dipping sauce than a drink. Treat that early morning hangover at **Chocolateria Aliva ❶, C.** Daoiz y Velarde, 7, which starts serving churros at 5am on weekends. (☎942 22 20 49. Open M-F 7am-12:30pm and 5:30-10pm, Sa-Su 5am-12:30pm and 5:30-10pm. Cash only.)

The huge, month-long **Festival Internacional de Santander** in August brings crowds of people and myriad classical music and dance performances to town, many held in the city's historic churches. For more info, contact the office in the Mercado del Este (☎942 22 34 34. Open M-F 11am-2pm and 5-8pm, Sa 11am-1pm in the months leading up to the festival.) For a younger, more contemporary scene, try the **Santander Summer Festival** (mid-August), which brings rock, pop and techno to the beaches (www.santandersummerfestival.com). The **Semana Grande** festival takes place the third week of July on the El Sardinero promenades, with bathers clad in swimsuits. That same week, the *barrio pesquero* celebrates the **Virgen del Carmen,** patron saint of men of the sea.

DAYTRIPS FROM SANTANDER

SANTILLANA DEL MAR

La Cantábrica (☎942 72 08 22) buses depart from the main bus station in Santander. (45min.; July-Aug. M-F 7 per day 8:30am-9:30pm, Sa-Su 5 per day 10:30am-9:30pm; Oct.-June M-F 4 per day 10:30am-7:15pm, Sa-Su 3 per day 11:30am-8:30pm; €2.15. Return to Santander July-Aug. M-F 7 per day 7:30am-8:15pm, Sa-Su 5 per day Sa-Su 10:20am-8:15pm; Oct.-June M-F 4 per day 7:30am-6pm, Sa-Su 3 per day 10:20am-7:30pm.) The bus stop is at the foot of the town near the park.

The layout of the stone streets and medieval palaces in Santillana del Mar remain practically unchanged since the 16th century. Some say the city's name contains three lies; the town was never home to a saint (*sant*), is not flat (*llana*) and it does not lie on the sea (*mar*). In fact, the name is derived from the name of Saint Juliana, whose relics were housed in the *Colegiata* there. Beyond striking architecture, the town has several worthwhile museums and lies within walking distance of the famed Altamira cave drawings.

Although the caves housing the Altamira cave drawings are closed indefinitely to preserve the prehistoric artwork, the **Museo de Altamira** (2km from Santillana) seeks to bring information about the **caves** and Spanish prehistory to the public. The museum includes a reproduction of the caves modeled using precise digital topographical surveys. Call ☎942 84 01 57 to inquire about seeing the real thing; a limited number of people who book ahead are allowed to see the caves on designated days. (☎942 81 80 05. Open June-Sept. Tu-Sa 9am-8pm, Su 9:30am-3pm; Oct.-May Tu-Sa 9:30am-6pm, Su 9:30am-3pm. €2.40, students with ID €1.20, under 18 and retired free. Su free. Follow purple signs off of the highway as it enters town from the south. 25min. walking; ALSA buses run to the museum on the way to Torrelavega, 12 per day 8am-10:15pm.) The **Museo de la Inquisición** does not limit its catalog of torture instruments to Spain but covers all of Europe's gruesome past (and present). Sardonic notes in English explain the uses of lovely tools such as the rack, the iron maiden, and the bull of Phalaris. (C. Jesus Otero, 1. Open daily in summer 10am-9pm, winter 10:30am-8pm. €3.60, students €2.40.) The **Museo de Jesus Otero** is located at the upper end of C. Jesus Otero, and contains many of the famous local sculptor's works in the yard and in the building, which also contains a library (Open Tu-Sa 10am-1:30pm and 4-8pm. Free.) The town's religious centerpiece is the **Colegiata de Santa Juliana,** whose 12th-century ivy and moss-covered **cloister** leads to a Romanesque **church.** (Follow C. de la Carrera as it becomes C. Canton and then C. Rio to the top of the town. Open daily 10am-1:30pm and 4-7:30pm. €3.) The **Museo Diocesano** has its own cloister, as well as exhibits from local archaelogical digs and a display of religious art from former Spanish holdings in the Americas and Philipines. (Corner of C. Jesus de Tagle and Av. le Dorat, just up from the bus stop. Open in summer 10am-1:30pm, 4-7:30pm; in winter 10am-1:30pm and 4-6:30pm. €3.) The tourist office gives out a pamphlet with a guide to the town's historic architecture. Many of these centuries-old buildings are closed to the public, but their outer grandeur is on display to all.

Santillana is small, so orientation is simple with the help of the tourist office's map. From the bus stop, head uphill across Av. le Dorat to entier the city. C. Santo Domingo branches into C. Juan Infanta (which leads into the Pl. Mayor) and C. de la Carrerea which becomes C. Canton and leads up towards the

Colegiata at the northern end of town. Parallel to that runs C. Jesus Otero. The **tourist office** is located at C. Jesus Otero, 20. From the bus stop, walk up to Av. le Dorat, take a right and then your first left onto C. Jesus Otero. (☎942 81 82 5. Open in summer 9am-9pm; winter closes at midday for siesta.) The **post office** is at Pl. Mayor, 3. (☎942 81 80 40. Open M-F 8:30am-2:30pm, Sa 9:30am-1pm.)

COMILLAS

Note that Santillana del Mar and Comillas are on the same bus line. La Cantábrica (☎942 72 08 22) buses depart from the main bus station in Santander. (1hr.; July-Aug. M-F 7 per day 8:30am-9:30pm, Sa-Su 5 per day 10:30am-9:30pm; Oct.-June M-F 4 per day 10:30am-7:15pm, Sa-Su 3 per day 11:30am-8:30pm; €3.40. Return to Santander July-Aug. M-F 7 per day 7:15am-8pm, Sa-Su 5 per day Sa-Su 10am-8pm; Oct.-June M-F 4 per day 7am-5:30pm, Sa-Su 3 per day 10am-7:15pm.) The bus stop is at the bottom of the hill across from the Palacio de Sobrellano.

The coast of Comillas (pop. 2500), with gorgeous green hills rolling into the sea, boasts an intoxicating landscape. Whether you choose the tranquil inlets or the wind-swept swaths of sand on the Bay of Biscay, the beaches of Comillas are the main attraction, drawing everyone from Spanish nobles to foreign visitors to its shores. This small resort town's central beach, **Playa Comillas,** is an expanse of silky sand; on windy days, 10-foot breakers pound the shores.

Comillas is also known for its architectural attractions. Most notable, and amusing, is **El Capricho,** Gaudí's summer palace, built between 1883-1885. While it is not open to tourists, most visitors are content to see the swirling turrets, sunflower facades, and gingerbread-esque windows from outside. Behind the palace, a quiet corner contains a statue of a sitting Gaudí, looking up and admiring his whimsical work. From the bus stop, you can see the colorful palace on the hill; follow the footpath across the street for a closer view. One way to get a look inside El Capricho is to eat in its **restaurant ❹.** (Reservations ☎924 72 03 65. Entrees €16-20. *Menú* €21-25. Open Tu-Sa 1-3:30pm and 9-11pm, Su 1-3:30pm; in August 1-4pm and 9-11:30pm. MC/V). Next to it on the same hill are the neo-Gothic **Palacio de Sobrellano,** designed by Catalan architect Joan Martorell, and the **Capilla-Panteón,** containing furniture designed by Gaudí. (Open May-Sept. daily 10:30am-8:30pm; Oct.-Apr. 10:30am-2pm, 4-7:30pm. Entrance to both only by guided tours. Tickets sold 5min. before each tour; €3 each for the *capilla* and *palacio*. Tours run every 30min., *palacio* lasts 20min., *capilla* lasts 15min.) From the lawn of the *palacio*, you can see the impressive facade of the **Universidad Pontificia** (closed to the public). Comillas goes up in a blaze of fireworks, goose-chasing, and dancing during the town's **Fiesta de Cristo del Amparo** in the days surrounding July 15th.

Comillas Aventura's booth by the bus stop will take care of all your active sporting needs, with bike rentals, surf rentals and lessons, canyoning, and horseback riding. (☎625 61 14 49. Open daily 9:30am-1:30pm and 6-9pm). The **tourist office** is at Pl. Joaquín de Piélago, 1, two blocks from main bus stop. (☎942 72 25 91. Open July-Aug. daily 9am-9pm; Sept.-June daily 9am-2pm and 4-6pm.)

GALICIA (GALIZA)

If, as the Galician saying goes, "rain is art," then there is no area more artistic than northwestern Spain. Often veiled in a silvery mist, this province of fern-laden woods, slate-roofed fishing villages, and endless beaches has earned a reputation as a land of magic with tales filled with witches, fairies, and buried treasure. The Celts stopped by during their voyage to Ireland around 900 BC, and ancient *castros* (fortress-villages), inscriptions, and *gaitas* (bagpipes) attest to this Celtiberian past. The rough terrain has historically hampered trade, but ship building, auto manufacturing, and even renowned fashion labels are contributing to the region's gradual modernization and development. Tourists have begun to visit even Galicia's smallest towns, and Santiago de Compostela, the terminus of the Camino de Santiago, continues to be one of the world's most popular destinations for backpackers and religious pilgrims.

Galicians speak *gallego*, the linguistic link between Castilian Spanish and Portuguese. Newspapers and street signs alternate *gallego* and *castellano*, but most conversations are conducted in the latter. Regional cuisine features *caldo gallego* (a vegetable broth), *vieiras* (scallops), *empanadas* (stuffed turnovers), and *pulpo a gallego* (boiled octopus). While regionalism in Galicia certainly doesn't cause the well-publicized political stir that it does in the País Vasco or Cataluña, you still may see graffiti calling for *"liberdade"* (liberty).

HIGHLIGHTS OF GALICIA

PROGRESS with other pilgrims on the way to **Santiago de Compostela** (p. 536).

WATCH your step at the edge of the world, **Cabo Finisterre** (p. 543).

GULP down the fiery local concoction during the Fiesta de San Xuan in **Vigo** (p. 549).

MARVEL at Hercules' strength in his lighthouse in **A Coruña** (p. 560).

SANTIAGO DE COMPOSTELA ☎981

For hundreds of years, visitors to Santiago de Compostela (pop. 94,000) have arrived with sore feet, aching shoulders, and tears of joy. As the final stop on the Camino de Santiago, an 800km pilgrimage through northern Spain that ends in the cathedral housing the remains of St. James, this bewitching city brims with life. The city, which developed parallel to the Camino, is rich with symbols honoring the pilgrims' presence, from cross-emblazoned pastries to scallop-shell jewelry. But the city is not merely a pilgrims' post—Santiago is a rich and rewarding destination for all who pass through its streets. The contagious excitement of pilgrims and students gathering in countless tapas bars, the smell of sweet almond cakes, and the eerie strains of Celtic bagpipes and flutes fill the city's crooked Baroque streets from night 'til the dawn light.

TRANSPORTATION

Flights: Aeropuerto Lavacolla (☎981 54 75 00), 10km toward Lugo. Buses leave for the airport from the bus station and the C. Doutor Teixeiro (6:40am-10:30pm, €1.55).

Schedule in the daily *El Correo Gallego* (€0.75) and at the tourist office. **Iberia,** R. do Xeneral Pardiñas, 36 (☎981 57 20 24). Open M-F 9:30am-2pm and 4-7pm.

Trains: R. do Hórreo (☎902 24 02 02). Info open daily 7am-11pm. To: **Bilbao** (10hr., 9:04am, €41) via **León** (6hr., €29) and **Burgos** (8hr., €36); **A Coruña** (1hr.; M-F 20 per day 6:55am-10:54pm, Sa 18 per day 6:55am-10:34pm, Su 17 per day 7:23am-10:34pm; €3.90-13.80); **Madrid** (8hr.; M-F and Su 1:57, 10:35pm, Sa 9:54am, 10:35pm; €45); **Vigo** (2hr., M-F 17 per day 5:35am-9:22pm, €5.90-8) via **Pontevedra** (1hr., €3.90-5.25).

Buses: Estación Central de Autobuses, R. de Rodríguez (☎981 54 24 16), 20min. walk from downtown. **Bus #5** goes to Pr. de Galicia (10min.; M-F every 20 min. 6:40am-10:40pm, Sa every 20min. 7am-3pm, every 30min. 3-10:30pm, Su every 30min. 7:30am-10:30pm; €0.90). Info open daily 6am-10pm. **ALSA** (☎981 58 61 33, reservations 902 42 22 42, www.alsa.es). Open daily 6:30am-9pm. To **Madrid** (8-9hr.; M-Sa 4-5 per day 7am-9:30pm, Su 4 per day 9:45am-9:30pm; €40-57, round-trip €67-108), **San Sebastián** (13hr.; 8:30am, 4pm on Fr, 6pm; €55.66, round-trip €102), and **Bilbao** (11hr.; 8:30am, Fr and Su at 4pm, 6, 11:15pm; €48.79, round-trip €67). **Castromil** (☎981 58 97 00). To: **Finisterre** (2hr.; M-F 4 per day 8am-7:30pm, Sa 4 per day 9am-3:20pm, Su 3 per day 9am and 10am; €11.75); **A Coruña** (1hr.; M-F 6:50am, hourly 8am-10:30pm, Sa 12 per day 9am-10:30pm, Su 11 per day 10am-10:30pm; €5.75); **El Ferrol** (2hr.; M-F 7 per day

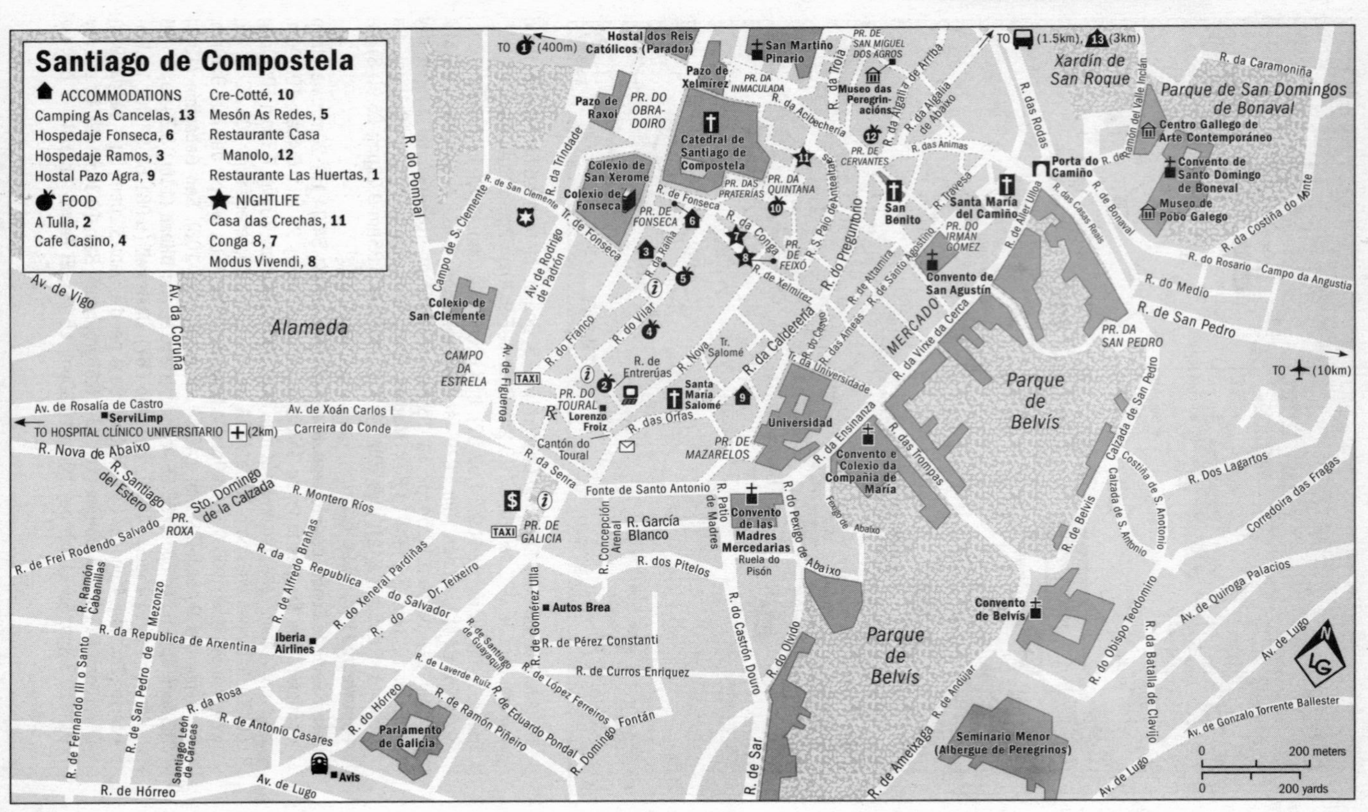
Santiago de Compostela
ACCOMMODATIONS
Camping As Cancelas, 13
Hospedaje Fonseca, 6
Hospedaje Ramos, 3
Hostal Pazo Agra, 9
FOOD
A Tulla, 2
Cafe Casino, 4
Cre-Cotté, 10
Mesón As Redes, 5
Restaurante Casa Manolo, 12
Restaurante Las Huertas, 1
NIGHTLIFE
Casa das Crechas, 11
Conga 8, 7
Modus Vivendi, 8
TO (400m)
Hostal dos Reis Católicos (Parador)
San Martiño Pinario
PR. DE SAN MIGUEL DOS AGROS
TO (1.5km), (3km)
Xardín de San Roque
Parque de San Domingos de Bonaval
Centro Gallego de Arte Contemporáneo
Convento de Santo Domingo de Boneval
Museo de Pobo Galego
Pazo de Xelmírez
Pazo de Raxoi
PR. DO OBRADOIRO
PR. DA INMACULADA
Catedral de Santiago de Compostela
Museo das Peregrinacións
PR. DE CERVANTES
Colexio de San Xerome
Colexio de Fonseca
PR. DE FONSECA
PR. DAS PRATERÍAS
PR. DA QUINTANA
San Benito
Santa María del Camiño
PR. DO IRMÁN GÓMEZ
Convento de San Agustín
Porta do Camiño
PR. DE FEIXÓ
MERCADO
PR. DA SAN PEDRO
Parque de Belvís
Colexio de San Clemente
Alameda
CAMPO DA ESTRELA
PR. DO TOURAL
Lorenzo Froiz
Cantón do Toural
Santa María Salomé
Universidad
PR. DE MAZARELOS
Convento e Colexio da Compañía de María
Convento de las Madres Mercedarias
Ruela do Pisón
PR. DE GALICIA
PR. ROXA
Autos Brea
Iberia Airlines
Parlamento de Galicia
Avis
Convento de Belvís
Seminario Menor (Albergue de Peregrinos)
ServiLimp
TO HOSPITAL CLÍNICO UNIVERSITARIO (2km)
TO (10km)
TAXI
0 200 meters
0 200 yards
Av. de Vigo
Av. da Coruña
Av. de Rosalía de Castro
Av. de Xoán Carlos I
Carreira do Conde
R. Nova de Abaixo
R. Santiago del Estero
Sto. Domingo de la Calzada
R. Montero Ríos
R. de Frei Rodendo Salvado
R. Ramón Cabanillas
R. da Republica de Arxentina
R. de Fernando III o Santo
R. de San Pedro de Mezonzo
Santiago León de Caracas
R. da Rosa
R. de Antonio Casares
R. de Hórreo
Av. de Lugo
R. do Pombal
Campo de S. Clemente
R. de San Clemente
R. da Trindade
Tr. de Fonseca
Av. de Rodrigo de Padrón
Av. de Figueroa
R. do Franco
R. do Vilar
R. da Raíña
R. de Fonseca
R. da Conga
R. de Xelmírez
R. de Entreruas
R. Nova
Tr. Salomé
R. das Orfas
R. da Caldereria
Tr. da Universidade
R. da Senra
Fonte de Santo Antonio
R. Concepción Arenal
R. García Blanco
R. Patio de Madres
R. do Pexigo de Abaixo
Fexigo de Abaixo
R. dos Pitelos
R. do Castrón Douro
R. de Sar
R. do Olvido
R. de Alfredo Brañas
R. do Xeneral Pardiñas
R. do Dr. Teixeiro
R. do Salvador
R. de Gomérez Ulla
R. de Pérez Constanti
R. de Curros Enriquez
R. de Santiago de Guayaquil
R. de Laverde Ruiz
R. de López Ferreiros
R. de Ramón Piñeiro
R. de Eduardo Pondal
R. Domingo Fontán
R. do Hórreo
R. da Acibechería
R. da Troia
R. da Algalia de Arriba
R. da Algalia de Abaixo
R. das Animas
R. S. Paio de Antealtares
R. do Preguntoiro
R. de Altamira
R. de Santo Agostiño
R. das Ameas
R. do Castro
R. da Virxe da Cerca
R. da Ensinanza
R. das Trompas
R. Travesa
R. de Aller Ulloa
R. das Casas Reais
R. de Bonaval
R. das Rodas
R. Ramón del Valle Inclán
R. da Caramoniña
R. da Costiña do Monte
R. do Rosario
Campo da Angustia
R. do Medio
R. de San Pedro
Calzada de San Pedro
Costiña de S. Antonio
Calzada de S. Antonio
R. Dos Lagartos
Corredoira das Fragas
R. de Belvís
R. do Obispo Teodomiro
Av. de Quiroga Palacios
R. da Batalla de Clavijo
Av. de Gonzalo Torrente Ballester
R. de Andújar
R. de Ameixaga

9:15am-9pm, Sa-Su 6 per day 9:15am-9pm, Su until 10pm; €9.60); **Noia** (1hr.; M-F 12 per day 9am-9:30pm, Sa 8 per day 10am-10pm, Su 6 per day 10am-8pm; €3.20); **Vigo** (2hr.; M-F hourly 9am-10pm, Sa hourly 9am-1pm and 5-9pm, Su 9 per day 10am-9pm; €8) via **Pontevedra** (1hr., €5.50).

Public Transportation: Local buses (☎981 58 18 15). **Bus #6** goes to the train station (7:20am-11pm), **#4** to the campgrounds (7am-10:30pm), and **#5** to the bus station. In the city center, almost all buses stop at Pr. de Galicia, where there are 2 stops, one on the R. do Dr. Teixeiro side and one along R. de Montero Ríos. Except for #6, buses run daily 7:30am-10:30pm every 20-30min. €0.90.

Taxis: Radio Taxi, (☎981 569 292) at the bus station and Pr. de Galicia. Stand outside Zara in Pr. de Galicia. 24hr. Late-night service near clubs in Pl. Roxa.

Car Rental: Avis (☎981 59 04 09), at the train station. 23+, must have had license for 1 yr. Open M-F 9am-1:15pm and 4-7pm, Sa 9am-12:45pm, Su 9:30am-12:30pm. From €47.86 per day, plus €0.19 extra per kilometer, €396.41 per week, 25 and under €12 extra per day. Discounts are available for longer rentals. **Autos Brea,** Gomez Ulla, 8 (☎981 56 26 70), 23+, must have had license for 2 yr. Open M-F 9am-1:30pm and 4-8pm, Sa 9am-1pm and 4-7pm, Su 10am-1pm. Cars from €63 per day, with insurance included. Deposit required for all rentals.

GALICIA

ORIENTATION AND PRACTICAL INFORMATION

Santiago centers around **Pr. de Obradoiro** and the **Catedral de Santiago de Compostela.** The cathedral marks the center of the old city, on a hill above the new city. The train station is at the southern end of town. To reach the old city from the station, take bus #6 to **Praza de Galicia** or walk up the stairs across the parking lot from the main entrance, cross the street, bear right onto R. do Hórreo, and continue uphill for 10min. The **bus station** is at the town's northern end, a 20min. walk; exit the bus station, walk up R. de Anxel Casal and turn left at the roundabout onto R. da Pastoriza, which becomes R. dos Basquinos, R. de Santa Clara, and then R. de San Roque. Follow the road left on R. das Rodas, which becomes R. de Aller Ulloa, R. da Virxe da Cerca, and R. da Ensinanza, which leads to Pr. de Galicia; or take bus #5 to Pr. de Galicia (5min.). In the old city, three streets lead to the cathedral: **Rúa do Franco, Rúa do Vilar,** and **Rúa Nova.**

Tourist Office: Municipal Office, R. do Vilar, 63 (☎981 55 51 29; www.santiagoturismo.com). English, French, German, Portuguese, Italian, and other languages spoken. Open June-Sept. 9am-9pm; Oct.-May 9am-2pm, 4-7pm. **Regional Office,** R. do Vilar, 30 (☎981 58 40 81), provides information about Galicia and daytrips from Santiago. Open M-F 10am-8pm, Sa 11am-2pm and 5-7pm, Su 11am-2pm. Info about guided tours of Santiago. **Oficina Xacobeo,** (☎981 58 40 81) also at R. do Vilar, 30, provides information on the Camino de Santiago. Open M-F 10am-8pm. There is another tourist office located closer to the train station at Pr. de Galicia. Open M-F 10:30am-1:30pm.

Currency Exchange: Banco Santander Central Hispano, Pr. de Galicia, 1 (☎981 58 61 11). Open Apr.-Sept. M-F 8:30am-2pm; Oct.-Mar. M-F 8:30am-2pm, Sa 8:30am-1pm. **Western Union** services and 24hr. **ATM** outside.

Religious Services: Mass in the cathedral (p. 541) M-F 9:30am, noon, and 7:30pm vespers; Sa 9:30am, noon, 6, 6:30pm (vespers) Su 10am, noon, 1, 6, and 7:30pm vespers. Special pilgrim's mass at noon featuring the *botafumeiro* (huge incense burner).

Laundromat: ServiLimp, C. Rosalía de Castro, 33 (☎981 59 24 08). 4kg of laundry €7.80. Open M-F 9:30am-1:30pm and 4-8pm, Sa 10am-2pm. Jul-Aug closed on Sa.

Police: Pr. do Obradoiro, 1 (☎981 54 23 23).

24hr. Pharmacy: Farmacia R. Bescanses, Pr. do Toural, 1 (☎981 58 59 90).

Hospital: Hospital Clínico Universitario, Tr. da Chupana (☎981 95 00 00).

Internet Access: CyberNova, R. Nova, 50 (☎981 56 41 33). 23 fast computers. €1.90 per hr. Open daily 8:30am-1am.

Post Office: R. Orfas, 17. (☎981 58 12 52). **Lista de Correos** and fax. Open M-F 8:30am-8:30pm, Sa 9am-2pm. **Postal Code:** 15703.

ACCOMMODATIONS AND CAMPING

The liveliest and most popular rooms are on R. do Vilar and R. da Raíña. Youthful celebration may filter up into your room if you are staying in the old city, so consider staying in another part of the city if you need quiet.

Hospedaje Ramos, R. da Raíña, 18, 2nd fl. (☎981 58 18 59), above **O Papa Una** restaurant. In the center of the old city, these well-lit, modern rooms have private baths and sound-proof windows. Some rooms have views of the cathedral. Reserve 2 weeks ahead in summer. Singles €23; doubles €36. Cash only. ❷

Hospedaje Fonseca, R. de Fonseca, 1, 2nd fl. (☎646 937 765). Colorful rooms with floor-to-ceiling windows that let in lots of sun. Shared baths. Sept. 16-June singles, doubles; and triples €15 per person. July-Aug. singles €20, doubles €30. Cash only. ❷

Hostal Pazo Agra, R. da Caldereria, 37 (☎981 58 35 17). Rich colors, beautiful fixtures, and an old-fashioned feel, as well as an extremely friendly family ownership, characterize this *hostal*. Rooms have high ceilings and glass doors opening onto balconies. Exterior bathrooms are private. Reception in *hostal* or in **Restaurante Zingara,** Cardenal Payá, 2, just around the block. Grandma cooks breakfast everyday for €4. May-Oct. singles €28; doubles €38. Nov.-Apr. €25/36. MC/V. ❸

Camping As Cancelas, R. 25 de Xullo, 35 (☎981 58 02 66). 3km north of the cathedral. Take #4 from R. da Senra, 1 block off Pr. de Galicia as you head toward it. Laundry, supermarket, and pool. Reception 8am-11pm. July-Aug. €5.90 per person, €6.15 per car and tent; Sept.-June €4.50 per person, car, and tent. Electricity €4.10. MC/V. ❶

FOOD

Santiago's restaurants are worth the trek, but be wary of exorbitant prices. **Rúa da Raíña** is the best street for delicious, affordable meals, and **Rúa do Franco** has excellent tapas bars. **Rúa do Vilar** and **Rúa Nova** are also good options. In the new city, look near Pr. Roxa. Santiago is famous for its seafood, so be sure to try *paella* or *mejillones* (mussels) before you leave. End your meal with a *tarta de Santiago*, a rich almond cake emblazoned with a sugary St. James cross. The best bakery in town, **Confitería El Coral,** R. Dr. Teixeiro, 32, has a tantalizing selection of homemade chocolate, ice cream, and pastries. (☎981 56 20 10. Open M-Sa 9:30am-2:30pm and 4:30-9pm, Su 9:30am-3pm and 5-10:30pm, Jun-Sept closed during Su afternoons.) The **market** near the **Convento de San Agustín** is a sight in its own right. (Open M-Sa 8am-2pm.) **Supermercado Lorenzo Froiz,** Pr. do Toural, is one block from Pr. de Galicia. (Open M-Sa 9am-10pm. MC/V.)

Restaurante Casa Manolo, Pl. Cervantes, s/n (981 58 29 50). Extremely popular among pilgrims and locals alike, this restaurant becomes packed with hungry voyagers who come for the hearty portions and great prices. Delight in the sizable *menú* (€8), while lounging to laid-back music. Open M-Sa 1pm-4pm and 8-11:30pm, Su open only during early afternoon. MC/V. ❷

A Tulla, R. de Entrerúas, 1 (☎981 58 08 89). This family restaurant is hidden behind a tiny, easy-to-miss alley between R. do Vilar and R. Nova. To get there from R. do Vilar, look for the alley to the right of Consorcio de Santiago, underneath the overhang labeled "Casa del Doctor." Entrees €6.50-8.50. *Menú* €11.80, vegetarian *menú* €9.50. Open M-Sa 1-4pm and 8:30pm-midnight. MC/V. ❷

Restaurante Las Huertas, R. das Hortas, 16 (☎981 561 979). Right down the street from the cathedral, Las Huertas is an intimate, elegant nook that offers delicious food at reasonable prices. Excellent *paella* for 2 with a bottle of *albariño* (a local white wine) €26. *Menú del día* €9. Entrees €9-12. Open daily 1-4pm and 9-11:30pm. MC/V. ❷

Café Casino, Rúa de Vilar, 35 (☎981 57 75 03). With deep armchairs, dark wood, and stained glass, this coffee shop wouldn't be out of place on a Parisian boulevard. Delicious coffees (€2.50-4) and rich desserts (€3.20-5). Open daily 8:30am-1:30am. ❶

Cre-Cotté, Pr. de Quintana, 1 (☎981 57 76 43). Rich crepes (€5.80-8.50) and an extensive selection of salads (€7.80-8.80) served on the beautiful terrace next to the cathedral or in the lemon-colored, welcoming dining room. *Menú* €11. Open July-Aug. 1pm-midnight; Sept.-June 1-4:30pm and 8:30pm-midnight. AmEx/MC/V. ❷

Mesón As Redes, R. da Raiña, 17 (☎981 576 822). Over half the options at this laid-back restaurant are under €6 and can serve as a full meal—Spanish tortillas, pastas, seafood, hamburgers, sandwiches, and even heaping *platos combinados.* Open M-Th noon-4:30pm and 8pm-midnight, F-Su noon-4:30pm and 7pm-1am. Cash only. ❶

GALICIA

SIGHTS

CATEDRAL DE SANTIAGO DE COMPOSTELA. This Romanesque masterpiece has been the terminus Christian pilgrimages for close to a millenium. The 9th-century discovery of James the Apostle's relics gave rise to a small chapel, then two pre-Romanesque churches, followed by the development and flourishing of the entire city. The current cathedral, which faces east into Pr. do Obradoiro, was erected in 1075. Pilgrims unburdened of their backpacks fill the plaza, gazing for hours upon the cathedral's magnificent moss-covered walls and ornate spires. The Baroque **Obradoiro Facade** dominates the square of the same name, which means "workshop" in *gallego;* it was here that stonemasons worked during its construction. Many consider Maestro Mateo's **Pórtico de la Gloria,** set in the Obradoiro facade, the crowning work of Spanish Romanesque sculpture. This apocalyptic 12th-century amalgam of angels, prophets, saints, sinners, demons, and monsters is a veritable compendium of Christian theology.

From the southern **Praza das Praterías,** recognizable by the sea horse, enter the cathedral through the Romanesque arched double doors. To the west of the cathedral, the **Pórtico Real** and **Porta Santa** face **Praza da Quintana.** To the north, a blend of Doric and Ionic columns, rebuilt after a fire in the 18th century, grace **Praza da Inmaculada,** which mixes Romanesque and Neoclassical styles. Inside the cathedral, the revered remains of **Saint James** (Santiago) lie beneath the high altar in a silver coffer, while his bejeweled bust, polished by the embraces of thousands of pilgrims, rests above it. The **botafumeiro,** a silver censer used in religious rituals, swings during High Mass and liturgical ceremonies. Older than the towers that house them, the bells of Santiago were stolen in 997 by Moorish invaders and transported to Córdoba. When Spaniards later conquered Córdoba, they had their revenge when they forced Moors to carry the bells back. *(☎981 58 35 48. Open daily 7am-9pm. Free.)*

MUSEUM AND CLOISTERS. The cathedral's museum gives access to the treasury and relics, cloister, tapestry room, archaeology rooms, chapter house, crypt, library, and archives. The museum also has an extensive collection of coins from Santiago, dating as far back as the 1300s. The 12th-century Codex, five volumes of manuscripts of the stories of the Apostle James, includes travel information for early pilgrims. *(☎981 56 93 27. Museum open June-Sept. M-Sa 10am-2pm and 4-8pm, Su and holidays 10am-2pm; Oct.-May M-Sa 10am-1:30pm and 4-6:30pm, Su and holidays 10am-1:30pm. €5, students, seniors, and pilgrims €3; includes entrance to crypt. Pamphlets for tour of the museum available in German, English, French, Italian, and Portuguese.)*

MUSEO DAS PEREGRINACIÓNS. This three-story 14th-century Gothic building is full of creatively displayed historical tidbits about the Camino and other worldwide pilgrimages. It also includes statues of the Virgin as a pilgrim carrying the baby Jesus, illustrations of the different routes to Santiago, and exhibits on the rituals of pilgrimage and the iconography of Santiago. *(R. de San Miguel, 4. ☎981 58 15 58; www.mdperegrinacions.com. Open Tu-F 10am-8pm, Sa 10:30am-1:30pm and 5-8pm, Su 10:30am-1:30pm. €2.40, students, seniors and children €1.20, pilgrims free. Special expositions and most of the summer free.)*

PAZO DE RAXOI. Facing the cathedral, the facade of the Pazo de Raxoi majestically completes the square. Once a royal palace, it now houses the *Ayuntamiento* and the office of the president of the *Xunta de Galicia* (Galician government). At night, floodlights illuminate the remarkable bas-relief of the 844 AD Battle of Clavijo, during which, according to legend, St. James helped to fight off the Moors. *(Across Pr. do Obradoiro, facing the cathedral.)*

CENTRO GALLEGO DE ARTE CONTEMPORÁNEO. The expansive galleries and rooftop *terraza* of the sparkling Centro Gallego de Arte Contemporáneo (CGAC) house cutting-edge exhibitions of boundary-bending artists from around the world, including photo exhibitions, sculptures, and paintings. The *terraza* has incredible views of all of Santiago. *(R. de Ramón del Valle Inclán. Next to the Museo de Pobo Gallego. ☎981 54 69 29; www.cgac.org. Open Tu-Su 11am-8pm. Free.)*

NIGHTLIFE

Many begin the night by hopping from one tapas bar to another. The best street for tapas is **Rúa do Franco,** with popular options including **A Taberna do Bispo** (Franco, 37), **Casa Rosalía** (Franco, 10), and **Xantares** (Franco, 40). If you'd rather boogie with local students, try the bars and clubs off **Pr. Roxa.**

Casa das Crechas, Vía Sacra, 3 (☎981 57 61 08). A cavernous, witchcraft-themed drinking hole, alive with good cheer and bonhomie. Renowned for its live jazz and Galician folk concerts, as well as the spontaneous *foliadas* that erupt when celebrants arrive with instruments to improvise raucous music and dance unrestrainedly. Call ahead for schedule. Beer €2. Open daily in summer noon-4am; in winter 4pm-3am.

Modus Vivendi, Pr. Feixóo, 1 (☎981 57 61 09; www.pubmodusvivendi.net). Welcome to bohemia. A hot spot on the Santiago scene, with a darkened interior and psychedelic decoration. Indie music and cool art set the tone at this pub, as locals and foreigners chat in the cramped but cozy interior. Events listed on the website and cultural magazine, *Revista Move.* Beer €2. Mixed drinks €4.50. Open Jul-Sept M-W 6:30pm-3am, Th-Su until 4:30am; Oct.-June M-W 4:30pm-3am, Th-Su 6:30pm-4:30am.

Conga 8, R. da Conga, 8 (☎981 58 34 07). Salsa, merengue, and Spanish pop music mix keep the basement dance floor crowded. Popular hangout for locals around 3am. Beer €2. Mixed drinks €4.50. Open daily 10pm-5am.

ENTERTAINMENT AND FESTIVALS

The local newspaper *El Correo Gallego* (€0.75) and the free monthly *Compostela Capital* list art exhibits and concert information. Consult any of three local monthlies, *Santiago Días Guía Imprescindible*, *Compostelán*, or *Modus Vivendi*, for updates on the live music scene. One of the city's biggest festivals, **Fiestas de la Ascensión,** 40 days after Easter Sunday, features concerts, a famous cattle market, and the consumption of many an octopi in the *Santa Susana* oak grove. The city celebrates the **Día de Santiago** (July 25, 2009) for a full two weeks (July 15-31, 2009), in a celebration called **Apóstolo;** on the night of the 24th, a Pontifical Mass is held in the cathedral during **Las Vísperas de Santiago.**

DAYTRIPS FROM SANTIAGO DE COMPOSTELA

The northern part of the Rías Baixas hides undiscovered hamlets frequented only by pilgrims. These small towns make good daytrips from Santiago, although buses in this area tend to make frequent stops, so travel can be slow.

CABO FINISTERRE (CABO FISTERRA)

Arriva/Finisterre buses run from Santiago to Fisterra (2½hr.; M-F 9am, 10am, 12pm and 7pm, Sa 9 and 10am, 12 and 3:20pm, Su 9 and 10am; €11.75, round-trip €21.40) and back (M-F 8:20 and 11:45am, 2:45, 4:45 and 7pm; Sa 11:45am, 1:45, 4:45 and 7pm; Su 11:45am, 4:45 and 7pm.). The bus stop is near the Albergue de Peregrinos, 50m uphill from the water.

After arriving in Santiago, many pilgrims decide to continue as far as their feet and the land will take them; the windswept shores of Fisterra, once believed to be the end of the world, are their final stop. Jutting out precariously from the infamously rocky **Costa de la Muerte** ("Coast of Death"; Costa da Morte in Gallego), **Cabo Fisterra** was, for centuries, a crucial port for all naval trade along the Atlantic. Today, the isolated town, Spain's last stop before the "New World," still feels like the end of the earth. The 45min. trail up to the lighthouse from the center of town reveals a truly breathtaking view. The best beach in the town is on the flat isthmus that connects the peninsula with the mainland. The beaches are powdery and wide, the waters calm but frigid. To get there, either walk 4km along the road to Santiago or take the bus and ask to stop. The 1hr. hike from the port up **Monte San Guillermo** cuts through heather-covered mountainside and commands incredible views of the sea. At the top of the cliffs, pilgrims burn their clothes and throw the ashes into the wind, as a ritual for cleansing their souls after the long journey. The mountain also hosts Fisterra's famous bed-shaped fertility rocks. Couples having problems conceiving are advised to make a go of it on the rocks under a full moon (harvest moons give best results). On another hill on San Guillermo are **As Pedras Santas,** two large boulders that slide effortlessly side-to-side when you press the right spot.

If you miss the last bus back to Santiago, you can stay at **Hospedaje López ❷**, R. de Carrasqueira, 4. The clean, inexpensive rooms with shared baths all have views of the coast, and some have balconies. From the bus stop, cross the street and walk uphill; when you reach the post office turn left onto the

ROADTRIPPING

What do the Camino de Santiag and LSD have in common? Well... more than one might think. During the Middle Ages, thousands o pilgrims all over Europe trekke across Spain for more than enlightenment: they were afflicted by St Anthony's Fire, a convulsive condition characterized by gangren hallucinations, and "possession Along the Camino, monks woul touch the afflicted with sacre scepters, which were believed t be the only cure for the illnes As they approached Santiag pilgrims would progressively los the symptoms of the illness an become "cured," due to the magical powers of the scepter.

Lo and behold, what seeme like a spiritual high turned ou to have a rather more mundan explanation. Turns out, their condition has a name: ergotism, kind of intoxication brought on b consuming rye infected with ergot a parasitic fungus that produce the same alkaloids found in th hallucinogen LSD. The illnes was prevalent in Europe in thos years, especially in France, wher rye was abundant. As pilgrims se out on the Camino from the field of France to the plains of Spai they would encounter less an less rye and progressively mor wheat, which was—miraculously— not susceptible to ergot. So whil St. Anthony's sparks are unlikely t burn Spanish pilgrims today, don' forget to send him some love th next time you're roadtripping.

narrow street, C. Carrasqueira; you'll be greeted by welcoming lawn gnomes. (☎981 74 04 49. Singles €20; doubles €25.) For delicious and inexpensive seafood, try the numerous cafes and restaurants lining the Paseo del Puerto, right on the ocean. **Bodegón O Casón ❷,** Paseo del Puerto s/n, is the cheapest of the restaurants along the Paseo Marítimo, offering fresh seafood on fantastic terraces, with views of the harbor and cove. (☎981 74 02 86. *Menú del día* €8 Open daily noon-4:30pm and 7:30-11pm.) The **Albergue de Peregrinos,** C. Real, 2, has brochures and tourist info. From the bus stop, facing the water, turn right. (☎981 74 07 81. Open Sept.-May M-F 11am-2pm and 5-10pm; June-Aug. 1-10pm.) Nearby, **Bazar de Artesanía da Costa da Morte** has maps and information on bike rentals and tours. (☎981 74 00 74. Bikes €4 per hr., €12 per day. Open daily 10am-1:30pm and 5-9pm.)

O CASTRO DE BAROÑA AND PORTO DO SON

To reach these two towns, you'll need to make a connection in Noia. Castromil (☎981 58 90 90) runs buses from Santiago to Noia (1hr.; M-F 13 per day 8:15am-10pm, Sa 8 per day 10am-10pm, Su every 2hr. 10am-8pm; €3). From Noia, Hefsel buses stop at Porto do Son and O Castro de Baroña (in front of Café-Bar O Castro) en route to Riveira (30min.; M-F 14 per day 6:50am-9:30pm, Sa 7 per day 8am-9pm, Su 10 per day 9am-10pm; €1.60). Be sure to tell the bus driver where you're going, as the stop for Castro is easy to miss. From the bus stop at Castro, follow signs to the fortress, downhill toward the water. Catch the bus home across the road from Café-Bar O Castro.

One of Galicia's best-preserved coastal Celtic villages, **O Castro de Baroña** lies 19km south of Noia. The remains of a fifth-century Celtic fortress cover the neck of the isthmus, ascending to a rocky promontory above the sea; circular foundations are all that remain of the 1500-year old structures, but they make for a tangled, snaky vista from the area's highest point. Waves crash against the sides of the little peninsula, giving the remains of the fortress a lonely, peaceful feeling. The bluff descends to the soft sands of an excellent crescent beach, where clothing is "*prohibido*," but don't be intimidated by the hostile graffiti denouncing those who don swimsuits; beachgoers are friendly and some cover their bodies as well. **Hotel Villa del Sol ❷,** Tr. 13 de Septiembre, 4, has clean rooms with white-curtained windows, closet, bath, and TV. (☎981 85 30 49. Singles €25; doubles €30.)Stop for coffee or a bite at **Café-Bar O Castro ❶,** Lugar Castro de Baroña, 18, in the Castro de Baroña bus stop. Neighboring Porto do Son has inexpensive accommodations scattered around the bus stop.

MUROS AND LOURO

Castromil runs buses between Santiago and Muros (2hr.; M-F 11 per day 9am-9:15pm, Sa 8 per day 10am-10pm, Su every 2hr. 10am-8pm; €5.90) via Noia. Arriva buses run from Muros to Cee via Louro—make sure to tell the bus driver where you are going (M-F 8 per day 7:30am-7pm, Sa 6 per day 8am-9pm, Su 5 per day 8:30am-5:30pm; €1). The bus stop is to the right of the Hotel Muradana (when facing the ocean), across the street from the harbor.

Tucked into the arm of a large cove, Muros is a small but lively fishing village. The town is recognized as a historical site for its traditional Gothic architectural design, sailors' houses, and diminutive plazas. The main road in town is **Av. de Castelao,** which runs along the coast from the *Ayuntamiento* to the town's outskirts. In Louro, 4km away, are some of the most secluded soft sand beaches in all Galicia. The two towns make an ideal daytrip—Muros, with its transportation facilities, accommodations, and restaurants, provides the amenities necessary for a day in the surf at Louro. After roaming Muros's winding streets, visitors can take the **Paseo Marítimo** (to the right, facing the water) to Louro, with views of cobalt waters on the way. The first beach in Louro, **Playa San Francisco,** is less than 3km from Muros.

Stay right on the beach at **A Vouga Camping ❶**, which has a restaurant, bar, hot showers, and a small market. (☎981 82 61 15. Reception 9am-2pm and 5-8pm. Reserve a few days ahead. €3.53 per person, €3.75 per tent. Electricity €2.67. AmEx/MC/V.) If you'd like to stay in Muros, try **Hospedaje A Vianda ❷**, Av. de Castelao, 47. White-washed walls, linen sheets, and ceiling lanterns make up this plain but pleasant *hospedaje*. Some rooms have ocean views, and all have bath and TV. Book ahead in the summer months. (☎981 82 63 22. Reserve a month ahead for Aug. stays. Doubles €35, with view €40; triples with shared bath €35. Prices subject to change; call to confirm rates. Cash only.) Cheap cafes can be found off Pl. de Pescadería or along the harbor on Av. de Castelao. Ship-themed restaurant **A Darsena ❷**, Av. Castelao, 11, offers huge pizzas (€6), salads (€2.50-6), and sandwiches. (☎981 82 68 64. Open daily noon-5pm and 8pm-1am.) Another tasty option is **Bar Encontos ❷**, Pl. Pescadería, 15, with a plasma TV for *fútbol* nights (☎981 76 20 26. *Bocadillos* €2.80-4.50, *raciones* €4-10. Open daily 10am-midnight.) For bike rentals, visit **Muradana** (☎981 82 68 85) on R. Castelao, 99, a hotel that rents mountain bikes for €2.50 per hr. and €10 for a half-day. The **police,** C. Curro de Praza, 1, can be reached at ☎981 82 72 66. The *Ayuntamiento* at the end of the Av. de Castelao has **tourist information** (☎981 82 60 50. Open M-F 10am-2pm and 4-7pm, Sa-Su 11am-2pm.)

RÍAS BAJAS (RÍAS BAIXAS)

According to Galician lore, the Rías Baixas (Low Estuaries) were formed by God's tremendous handprint, with each river stretching like a finger through the land. Their deep bays, sandy coves, and calm, cool waters have lured vacationing Spaniards for decades. While not nearly as cool or rainy as their Galician neighbors, the Baixas are blessed with an ocean wind that provides a refreshing respite from the scorching heat (and hordes of tourists) of central and southern Spain. Due to its proximity to Portugal, there's also greater cultural fluidity in this part of Spain. Here, the *gallego* is stronger, the accents thicker, and the people more diverse; it all adds to the Baixa's allure.

VIGO ☎986

Spanish poet José María Álvarez once wrote that "Vigo does not end, it goes on into the sea." Sure enough, the downward sloping streets are packed with restaurants, shops, and people right up to the waterfront. Often called Spain's door to the Atlantic, Vigo (pop. 300,000) began as an unobtrusive fishing port. With the arrival of the Citröen manufacturing plant, it exploded into the biggest city in Galicia, putting its neighbors to shame with its liveliness and nightlife; Vigo's countless and diverse bars and clubs keep thumping into the wee hours of the morning. Its increasing popularity among European travelers has prompted extensive construction projects to expand pedestrian space near the city center and the marina. Vigo is also a good launching pad for exploring the many beach towns and rocky islands that surround the city.

TRANSPORTATION

Flights: Aeropuerto de Vigo, Av. del Aeropuerto (☎986 26 82 00), 15km from the city center. The local bus #9 runs regularly from R. Urzáiz, near R. Colón, to the airport (€1). **Iberia** (☎986 26 82 28) and **Air Europa** (☎986 26 83 10) have offices at the airport. Daily flights to **Barcelona, Bilbao, Madrid,** and **Valencia.**

Trains: RENFE, Pr. de la Estación (☎902 24 02 02), off R. Urzáiz. Open daily 7am-11pm. To: **A Coruña** (2hr.; M-F 15 per day 6:30am-9:05pm, Sa-Su 13 per day 6:30am-9:05pm; €9.60-13); **Madrid** (8-9hr.; M-F and Su 1:37, 10:20pm; Sa 9:30am, 10:20pm; €44); **Pontevedra** (30min.; M-F 21 per day 5:50am-10:30pm, Sa 14 per day 5:50am-9:59pm, Su 14 per day 5:50am-10:09pm; €2.70); **Santiago de Compostela** (2hr.; M-F 11 per day 5:40am-9pm, Sa-Su 13-14 per day Sa until 9:05pm, Su 5:50am-10:30pm; €5.90-8); **TUY** (Tui) (35min.; 7:40am, 7:40pm; €2.50).

Buses: Estación de Autobuses, Av. de Madrid (☎986 37 34 11), on the corner of R. Alcalde Gregorio Espino. Info daily 6:30am-10pm. ATSA (☎986 61 02 55) to: **Bayona** (Baiona) (50min.; Sept-June M-F every 30min.-1hr. 7am-1:45pm, every 15-30min.; Sa-Su every 15-45min. Sa 7:30am-11pm, Su 8am-11pm; July-Aug every 30min.-1hr. 7am-1:30pm, every 15-30 min. 2pm-10:15pm; Sa-Su every 15-45 min. Sa 7:30am-10:30pm, Su 8am-11pm €2.10); **La Guardia** (A Guardia) (1hr.; July-Aug M-F every 30min.-1hr. 7:30am-9:30pm; Sa 12 per day 8:30am-9:30pm, Su 6 per day 10am-9:30pm; Sept.-June M-F 7:30am-9pm; Sa 11 per day 8:30am-10:30pm; Su 6 per day 10am-9pm; €4.80); **TUY** (45min.; M-F every 30min.-1hr. 7:30am-9:30pm, Sa 10 per day 8:30am-9:30pm, Su 4 per day 10am-9:30pm;Sept-Jun M-F 7:30am-9pm; Sa 9 per day 8:30am-10:30pm; Su 4 per day 10am-9pm; €2.80). Buy tickets onboard. **Auto-Res** (☎902 02 09 99; www.auto-res.net) to: **Madrid** (6-8hr.; 6-7per day 8:30am-11:30pm; €32-39, round-trip €57-68).

Ferries: Estación Marítima de Ría, R. As Avenidas (☎986 22 52 72; www.mardeons.com), past nautical club on harborside walkway. To: **Cangas** (20min.; M-F every 30min. 6:30am-10:30pm, Sa-Su hourly 6:30am-10:30pm; €4.20 round-trip); **Islas Cíes** (45min.; July-Aug. 8 per day 9:45am-7pm (weather dependent, call ahead), Sept.-June 4 per day 11am-7pm; round-trip €17.50, children €6); **Moaña** (30min.; M-Sa every 30min.-1hr. 6:30am-10:30pm, Su hourly 8:30am-10:30pm; €3.70 round-trip).

Taxis: Central Radio Taxi, at Porta do Sol (☎986 47 00 00). About €0.50 per km.

Car Rental: Europcar Ibérica, Pl. de la Estación, s/n, (☎986 22 91 61; www.europcar.es) at the train station. 21+, must have had license at least 1 yr. Open M-F 8am-1:30pm and 4-7:30pm, Sa 9am-1pm. From €79 per day.

ORIENTATION AND PRACTICAL INFORMATION

Gran Vía, the main thoroughfare, stretches south to north from **Pr. de América** through **Pr. de España** and ends on the very steep slope of **R. Urzáiz.** A left turn downhill onto R. Urzáiz leads to C. Príncipe, Pta. do Sol, and into the **casco antiguo.** As you exit the train station onto R. Urzáiz (upstairs from the main entrance), go right for two blocks to reach Gran Vía. Keep walking on R. Urzáiz for 10min. and bear right at the fork onto C. Colón to reach the **waterfront.** To get to the municipal **tourist office,** bear left at the fork with C. Colón to stay on R. Urzáiz, which becomes R. Príncipe. At the Porto do Sol, continue up the street. Turn right directly after the Pr. de Princesa and pass through the Pr. de la Constitución onto R. do Triunfo. Make a left onto R. da Palma and then a right to pass through Pr. a Pedra. Go down the stairs in front of you to street level and the office is on your right. The **city center** is a 25min. walk from the **bus station.** Exit right uphill along Av. de Madrid. When you arrive at a large rotary, make a right on Gran Vía at Pr. de España, leading to the intersection with R. Urzáiz. It's easier to take bus #12a, or 12b from Av. de Madrid in front of the bus station to Gran Vía, R. Urzáiz, or R. Colón (€1). You can also take the C4C bus (€1.80) between the train station and the center.

Tourist Office: Regional branch, R. Cánovas de Castillo, 22 (☎986 43 05 77; www.turgalicia.es). Open July-Aug. M-F 9:30am-2pm and 4:30-7:30pm, Sa 10am-2pm and 4:30-7:30pm, Su 10am-1:30pm; Sept.-June M-F 9:30am-2pm and 4:30-6:30pm, Sa

10am-1:30pm. Vigo branch, Teofilo Llorente, 5 (☎986 22 47 57; www.turismodevigo.org). Open M-Sa 10am-2pm, and 4-7:30pm, Su 10am-2pm. There are also tourist info stands scattered throughout the city, including locations at the Porto do Sol and train station, most open June-Oct. daily 10am-2pm and 4-7:30pm.

Currency Exchange: Banco Santander Central Hispano, R. Urzáiz, 2 (☎902 24 24 24). Open Apr.-Sept. M-F 8:30am-2pm; Oct.-Mar. M-F 8:30am-2pm, Sa 8:30am-1pm. There is an **ATM** outside the bank.

Luggage Storage: At the bus station (€2 per day; self-service storage open daily 6:30am-midnight, buy tokens at the information stand (open daily 8am-10pm). Storage also available at the information booth from 10am-1pm and 4-7pm; €0.66 per bag.

English-Language Bookstore: Casa del Libro, C. Velázquez Moreno, 27 (☎902 02 64 12), downhill off C. Príncipe. Open M-Sa 9:30am-9:30pm. Books in English on 2nd fl.

Police: Pr. do Rei (☎092).

Pharmacy: Jose Luis Charro Pharmacy, R. Urzaia, 176 (☎986 27 29 86).

Medical Services: Hospital Xeral, R. Pizarro, s/n (☎986 81 60 00).

Internet Access: Sereo Cyber's, Pr. de Princesa, 3 (☎986 22 36 35), by the bus stop. €1.80 per hour. Calls to the USA €2 per 15min. Open M-F 9am-midnight, Sa 10am-midnight, Su 11am-midnight.

Post Office: C. Garcia Barbon, 50-52 (☎986 43 81 44). Lista de Correos and fax. Open M-F 8:30am-8:30pm, Sa 9:30am-2pm. **Postal Code:** 36201.

GALICIA

ACCOMMODATIONS

Most accommodations are near the train station on R. Alfonso XIII. Reserve ahead in summer and visit an ATM before checking in, as some places ask for payment upon arrival instead of departure.

Ancla Dorada Hostal-Residencia, C. Irmandiños, 2 (☎986 43 66 07; www.ancladorada.com), near the train station off R. Cervantes. Yellow walls, photos of old Vigo, and wrought-iron beds make this hostel homey. Free internet access in the lounge. Rooms have Wi-Fi and TV. Laundry €6. July-Aug. singles €34; doubles €38; triples €59; with bath €41/48/69; Sept.-June €26/30/50, with bath €32/35/59. MC/V. ❸

Hostal Ría de Arosa, R. Cervantes, 4, 2nd fl. (☎986 43 50 96). At the very end of R. Cervantes, so the noise of nightlife is less noticeable. Beautiful rooms with white fixtures and lemon-colored walls. All have TV, some have balconies. Spotless hall baths. July-Aug. singles €20; doubles €28. Sept.-June €15/22. Cash only. ❷

Hostal Ría de Vigo, R. Cervantes, 14, 1st fl. (☎986 43 72 40), a left off R. Alfonso XIII, 4 blocks down from the station. Wooden-framed beds in cheerful rooms with private bath, TV, some with balconies over R. Cervantes. July-Sept. singles €21; doubles €31. Oct.-June €19/26. Cash only. ❷

Hospedaje La Estrella, C. Martín Codax, 5 (☎986 22 50 35), a left off R. Alfonso XIII, 3 blocks down from the station. Basic but large rooms in this antique apartment building come complete with TV and clean bath. Reserve at least 2 weeks ahead in summer. Singles €20; doubles €25-35. Cash only. ❷

FOOD

Gran Vía and **C. Venezuela,** four streets uphill from R. Urzáiz off Gran Vía, brim with bright cafeterias and *terrazas*. Many seafood restaurants and *pulperías* (octopus stands) lie around the As Avenidas boardwalk by the water, near the touristy *casco antiguo*. On late nights, visit **Ecos Cafetería**, R. Urzáiz, 25. (☎986 22 34 81. *Platos combinados* €6-12, sandwiches €2.50-4. Open 24hr.) For groceries, hit up **Supermercado Froiz,** R. do Uruguai, 14 (open M-Sa 9:30am-9:30pm).

Restaurante Don Quijote, C. Laxe, 4 (☎986 22 93 46). Enjoy savory *pulpo* (octopus; €10) cooked in a steaming cauldron while sitting on outdoor terrace overlooking the harbor below. *Menú del día* €10. Open daily 1-4pm and 8pm-midnight. MC/V. ❷

Estrella de Galicia, Pl. de Compostela, 17, (☎886 11 72 67) near the harbor. Doubles as a warehouse-style bar. Inexpensive dishes including a variety of tapas-style *bocados* (€1.50 each, €7.50 sampler), and *filloas,* crepe pockets stuffed with deliciousness (€4.60-7.30). Kitchen open daily 12:30-4pm and 8pm-midnight. ❶

Restaurante Lamari, Pl. de la Piedra (☎986 22 32 43). The seafood is so fresh you can see the boats pulling in their nets from the restaurant's terrace. Low-key ambience and high-quality food. Entrees €4-12 (market price varies), mostly fish and shellfish. Open M-Sa 1-4pm and 8pm-midnight, Su 1-4pm. Closed Su in summer. MC/V. ❷

Cafetería El Coral, R. Ecuador, 71 (☎986 41 07 19), on the corner of C. Ecuador and C. Cuba. This relaxed cafeteria is a good spot for a cup of coffee or a cheap meal. *Platos combinados* €6.10-8.85. Open daily 7am-midnight. Cash only. ❶

NIGHTLIFE

Vigo loves to party. The area around R. Areal and R. Concepción Arenal is jam-packed with discotecas, nightclubs, and bars playing the latest Spanish hits for trendy crowds. Near the train station—on R. Cervantes, R. Lepanto, and R. Churruca, in particular—are dark, smoky bars and clubs with great music, decor, dancing, and a curiously prevalent 70s theme.

Black Ball, R. Churruca, 8. A throwback complete with disco balls, life-size Star Trek posters, and psychedelic lighting. Black Ball is the spot for an alternative music scene, a hipster crowd, and cheap mixed drinks (€5). Beer €3. Open July-Aug., Dec. Tu-Sa 11:30-3:30am; Sept.-Nov., Jan.-June Th-Sa 11:30-3:30am.

El Monstruo de un Solo Ojo, C. Cervantes, 18 (www.myspace.com/elmonstruodeunsoloojo). A funky club that stays true to its name, with one-eyed monster cartoons strewn all over the walls. Regular summer concerts/promotional parties with mostly indie and alternative bands. Beer €3. Drinks €5. July-Aug. open M-W 11:30pm-3am, Th-Sa until 4:30am; Sept.-June open Th-Sa 11:30pm-4:30am.

Kenzo Café, R. Arenal, 40 (www.kenzocafe.com). A dark pub right off the wharf decorated with African masks and gin bottles. Beer €1.90. Open daily 7:30am-3:30am.

SIGHTS AND FESTIVALS

The original settlement of Vigo was founded on the slopes of Mt. Castro. At the top lie the remains of a massive fortress (now an expensive restaurant). You'll forget you're in the confines of the city when you reach the very top of the *monte.* The view is definitely worth the climb and gives an idea of the city's gradual expansion. To get to the park, walk up the Gran Via from R. Uzaia and turn right at R. Venezuela. Continue for six blocks; the park is on the left. The **Museo Municipal de Vigo** "Quiñones de León," Parque de Castrelos, s/n, is also worth visiting. The museum houses a large variety of art and an impressive archaeological collection. If art isn't enough to draw you in, visit just to explore the *pazo* (palace), which dates from the 18th century. Getting to the museum is a 45min.-1hr. walk from city center; head up the Gran Vía from R. Urzaíz, straight through the rotary at the Pr. España and downhill to the Pr. America. Turn left onto Av. de Castrelos, and after the stone entrance to the Parque Municipal, turn left onto Carretera O Pazo. The museum is up the hill on your right. (☎986 29 50 70; www.museodevigo.org. Open Tu and Th-F 10am-1:30pm and 5-8pm, W 10am-8pm, Sa 5-8pm, Su 10am-1:30pm. Temporary exhibitions open Tu-Sa 5-8pm, Su 10am-1:30pm. Free.) Popular museums include the

Museo de Arte Contemporáneo de Vigo (C. del Príncipe, 54; open Tu-Sa 11am-9pm, Su 11am-3pm; free.) and the **Museo del Mar de Galicia,** which has an aquarium and exhibitions on the social history of the fishing industry. (☎986 24 76 95; www.museodomar.com, Av. Atlántida, 160. Open June-Sept. Tu-Th 10am-2pm and 5-10pm, F-Sa 10am-2pm and 5-11:30pm, Su 10am-10pm; Oct.-May Tu-Th 11am-8pm, F-Sa 11am-11:30pm, Su 10am-9pm. €6, students €3.)

Watch for the magical **Fiesta de San Xuan** on June 23, when neighborhoods light huge cauldrons of *aguardiente* (firewater) to concoct an infusion called **la queimada,** made of aguardiente, coffee, lemon, and sugar. Revelers pass around the sweet mixture while dancing among bonfires on the beach or in the streets. You can catch a similar display, as well as concerts and processions, during the **Fiestas del Cristo de la Victoria** in the end of July and beginning of August.

DAYTRIPS FROM VIGO

ISLAS CÍES (ILLAS CÍES)

Ferries make the 14km trip between Estación Marítima in Vigo and the islands. (45min.; July-Aug. 8 per day 9:45am-7pm, Sept.-June 4 per day 11am-7pm; ferries return to Vigo July-Aug. 7 per day 12-10pm, Sept.-June 4 per day 12-10pm; round-trip €17.50, children €6.) Ferries also run from Cangas and Moaña. Book round-trip tickets early in the day, as tickets to the islands sell out quickly.

The Romans called them the "Islands of the Gods," and it is easy to believe that the deities happily left Olympus to spend their weekends in the Illas Cíes. Guarding the mouth of the Ría de Vigo, two connected islands—**Illa de Monte Agudo** (a.k.a. Illa del Norte) and **Illa do Medio** (a.k.a. Illa del Faro)—offer gorgeous beaches and cliffside hiking trails. The islands were declared a national park in 1980; only 2200 visitors are allowed per day, ensuring wide stretches of uncrowded beach. The ferry drops off at **Playa de Rodas,** a pristine beach with fine white sand. For smaller, more secluded spots, head right on the trail from the tourist office juncture to **Area de Figueiras** (300m), another white-sand beach with sheltered, crystal-clear waters. Four main trails traverse the two islands, passing beaches, coves, and rocky cliffs. A 4km hike to the left of the dock on the main path leads to a bird observatory and two lighthouses with breathtaking views. The park campground lies along this trail, and visitors can stop for picnic essentials at the **market** here before a hike to the **Faro de Cíes,** the big lighthouse on the southern tip of the island.

Facilities at the campground include a small market, bar, baths, and hot showers. (Reservations ☎986 43 83 58. Reception 10am-10pm. Market 10am-9pm. Open June-Sept. and *Semana Santa*. Camping €7.15 per person, €5.56 per child 3-12, €7.45 per tent. IVA not included.) Before leaving Vigo to camp on the islands, be sure to make reservations for a **Tarjeta de Acampado** in the Camping Office (☎986 43 83 58; open daily 8:30am-1pm and 2:30pm-7pm) at the Estación Marítima. If you plan on staying, stock up on food in Vigo, as prices on the island are higher. To get to the **tourist office** (open June daily 11:30am-2:15pm and 5-8pm; July-Sept. 10am-8pm), just follow the trail from the dock (50m). The tourist office has information on hikes around the island and beach locations.

LA GUARDIA (A GUARDA)

ATSA Buses (☎986 61 02 55) go to Vigo (1hr.; M-F every 30min.-1hr. 5:45am-8pm, Sa 12 per day 7am-8pm, Su 6 per day 8:30am-8pm; €5.20) or Tui from bus stop at the corner of C. Domínguez Fontela and C. Concepcíon Arenal (45min., M-F every 30min.-1hr., 5:45am-8pm, Sa 9 per day 7am-8pm, Su 4 per day 8:30am-8pm; €2.80). Buy tickets on the bus.

A Guarda (pop. 10,000), between the mouth of the Río Miño and the Atlantic Ocean, thrives on an active fishing industry and the 500,000 tourists who annually make their way up its mountain, **Monte Santa Tecla.** The town itself does not have much to offer; most visitors skip it and head off to scale the majestic peaks. From the bus stop, turn right onto C. Domínguez Fontela and right again onto C. José Antonio. From C. José Antonio, bear right uphill onto C. Rosalía de Castro, which continues to the top (3.5km). Alternatively, 5min. up the road, take the steps off to the left that mark the start of a shorter, steeper pedestrian pathway through the woods (3km). The highlight of the climb is the ruins of a pre-Roman Celtic fortress located about three quarters of the way up the mountain. Originally occupied between 600-200 BC, it was a walled town with gates; the foundations of houses, ovens, water canals, and circular dwellings are still visible today. A chapel dedicated to Santa Tecla, the patron saint of headaches and heart disease, is near the peak of the mountain. A small archeological museum displaying Celtic objects from the excavations is near the chapel. Cured worshippers gave the wax body parts inside the church (hearts, heads, and feet) as gifts. (Open Mar.-Nov. daily 11am-2pm and 4-7:30pm. Free.) For a bite to eat in town, there are a number of decent, albeit expensive, restaurants along the harbor next to the tourist office. For a little pick-me-up after the climb up Monte Santa Tecla, head to the funky **Art Cafe,** in the Plaza do Relo, where you can plop yourself on a plush sofa, read a magazine, and listen to chill music while you drink a coffee—or something a bit stronger. (☎986 61 20 40. Open M-Sa 9am-7pm, Su 10am-7pm. Cash only.) A Guarda's main **tourist office** is by the harbor on the left side of the crescent (☎986 61 45 46. Open daily noon-3pm and 5-8pm.) with a second office at C. Rosalia de Castro, 13 (☎986 61 18 50; open 10am-3pm, 7:30-9:30pm.)

TUI (TUY)

The train station (☎986 60 08 13) on Av. Concordia sends trains to Vigo (40min.; 11:08am, 10:28pm; €2.35), but it's much more convenient to travel by bus. An ATSA bus (☎986 61 02 55) from Vigo stops on C. Calvo Sotelo at Hostal Generosa and returns on the other side of the street (45min.; M-F every 30min.-1hr. 6:30am-8:45pm, Sa 9 per day 7:45am-8:45pm, Su 4 per day 9:15am-8:45pm; €2.75).

The medieval town of Tui (pop. 16,000), on the Portuguese border by the Río Miño, is notable for its *casco antiguo* and views of the Río Miño valley. It has also been, historically, a stop on the Camino de Santiago. The old city's centerpiece is the **cathedral,** constructed in 1120, which houses the first Gothic portico in Iberia and the relics of San Telmo, patron saint of fishermen. Constructed in 1756, the building was originally a hospital for pilgrims and now shelters regional religious art. (☎986 60 31 07. Cathedral open July-Sept. daily 11am-2pm and 4-9pm; Apr.-June 11am-2pm and 4-8pm; Oct.-Mar. 11am-1:30pm and 4-7pm. Museum same hours, but closed Nov-Mar. Cathedral €2, museum €1.)

To spend a night in Tui, head to the bright, high-ceilinged rooms at **Hostal La Generosa ❶,** P. Calvo Sotelo, 37. (☎986 60 00 55. Singles €15; doubles €25. Cash only.) **Pizzeria di Marco ❷,** C. Seijas, serves pizza and pasta (€5.50-10) on a quaint patio. *Menú* €10.20. (☎986 60 36 85. Open daily noon-4pm and 8pm-midnight. MC/V.) **Supermercado Froiz,** on Po. Calvo Sotelo, has groceries. (Open M-Sa 9:30am-9:30pm. MC/V.) To get to the regional tourist office on R. Colón, continue on Po. de Calvo Stelo from the bus stop and turn right onto R. Augusto González Besada (☎986 60 17 89. Open July-Aug. M-F 10am-2pm and 5-7pm, Sa-Su 10am-2pm and 5-6:30pm; Sept.-June M-F 9:30am-1:30pm and 4:30-6:30pm, Sa 10am-2pm.) The municipal **tourist office** (open July-Sept.) is in Pl. de la Inmaculada. Local services include: **Banco Santander Central Hispano,** R. Augusto Gonzales Besada, 7 (open Apr-Sept. M-F 8:30am-2pm; Oct.-Mar M-F 8:30am-2pm, Sa 8:30am-1pm), with a 24hr. **ATM** outside; the **police** in the *Ayuntamiento* in Pl. de la Inmaculada (☎986 60 36 77); **medical services** at Centro

GALICIA

Salud on R. Lugo (☎986 60 18 00); **Internet access** at Infortui Cafe, Tr. Foxo, 1 (☎986 60 41 90, €2 per hr; open M-F 10am-midnight, Sa 10:30am-midnight); and the **post office,** R. Martínez Padín, 12 (Lista de Correos and **Western Union;** open M-F 8:30am-2:30pm, Sa 9:30am-1pm). **Postal Code:** 36700.

BAYONA (BAIONA)

ATSA buses run to Vigo (50min.; 2 per hr. July-Aug. M-F 6am-9:15pm, Sa 6:30am-9:30pm, Su 7am-10pm; Sept-June M-F 6am-9pm, Sa 6:30am-9pm, Su 7am-10pm €2.20).

In March 1493, Columbus returned from the New World to Bayona (pop. 10,000), making it the first Iberian town to receive word of the Americas. A small beach town with exquisite views of the Islas Cíes, the town boasts a reconstructed version of the famous globe-trotting ship, **La Caravela Pinta,** which sits in the harbor, reenacting the landing every March. (Open daily 10am-8:30pm. €1.) The entire town is surrounded by blustery Atlantic beaches, and the golden sand is perfect for lounging. The 2km pedestrian Av. Monterreal loops along the shore. As you get off the bus, walk along Av. Moterreal to your right for 15-20min. to get to the enormous crescent-shaped stretch of sand at **Praia Ladeira.** To your left, the path leads to the shell-filled **Praia Concheira** and loops around the fortress to the rocky and quieter **Praia de los Frailes.** The path goes along the water around the 16th-century **Fortaleza de Monterreal,** a fortress that is now a *parador* sitting just above the beaches and offering a great view of the islands. Inquire at the tourist office about guided tours of local monuments, the *Caravela*, or the fortress of Monterreal.

Excellent seafood restaurants are on the marina front in Pl. Pedro de Castro and on the parallel street behind it, Ventura Misa. For a good, fresh bite to eat and sea views, check out **Cafe Cerchas ❷**, C. Eiduayen, 11. This cafe/restaurant offers several reasonably priced and tasty dishes, a variety of *raciones* (€3.30-9.60) and *platos combinados* (€5.50-6.50) with seafood or meat options. (☎936 35 53 22. Kitchen open 11am-4pm and 7:30pm-11pm. MC/V.) For internet access, head to **Euris Cyber Cafe** (☎986 35 54 63. €1.50 per 30min. Open daily 10:30am-2:30pm and 5:30-9:30pm.) The **tourist office** provides maps and walking routes. Once off the bus, with your back to the water, head right on Av. Monterreal until the road bends; it's in a small glass building. (☎986 68 70 67; www.baiona.org. Open Nov.-Mar. M-Sa 10am-2pm and 3-7pm, Su 11am-2pm and 4-8pm; Apr.-June and Sept.-Oct.M-Sa 10am-2pm and 4-8pm, Su 11am-2pm and 4-8pm; July-Aug. 10am-3pm and 4-9pm.)

RIBADAVIA

The train station is on R. Estación (☎988 47 03 08). Trains run to Ribadavia from Vigo (4 per day 9:09am-10:45pm). Trains from Vigo to Ribadavia (1hr., 3 per day 6:40am-7:23pm, €5.65). The bus station is on R. San Francisco (☎988 21 32 40). Buses from Vigo to Ribadavia (M-F 4 per day 8:30am-7pm, Sa-Su 4 per day 8:30am-6:30pm). Buses to Vigo leave from the bus stop just across the bridge, Ponte de San Francisco, in front of "Auto Industrial" (M-F 6 per day 9:30am-9pm, Sa 9:30, 1:45pm, Su 9:30am, 1:45pm; €7.15).

Ribadavia (pop. 5700), capital of the kingdom of Galicia from 1065-1701, is most famous for its remarkable Jewish history, exquisite wines, and international theater festival in mid-July. Festivals in the area include the **Fiesta del Pulpo** (octopus-fest) in mid-August, a spectacular gastronomic adventure, the **Feria del Vino** during the last week of April and first week of May, and the **Festa da Istoria,** on the last Saturday of August, a medieval celebration. During the 11th century, the town's Jewish population blossomed, only to disperse and flee to Portugal during the 15th-century Inquisition. The **old synagogue** stood in Pl. de la Magdalena; the beautiful **Iglesia de Santa María Magdalena** now sits in its place at the intersection of C. Puerta Nueva de Arriba and C. Puerta Nueva de Abajo.

The **Jewish Information Center of Galicia** is located above the tourist office in Pr. Maior and houses a fascinating museum outlining the history of the Jewish population of the area, as well as an interactive model of a beautiful Galician Bible found in A Coruña (museum hours same as tourist office) or visit the **Museo Etnolóxico,** R. de Santiago, 10 (☎988 47 18 43; open Tu-F 10am-2:30pm and 4-8pm, Sa-Su 11am-2:30pm. Free.) The tourist office provides information about guided tours and hikes. Possible routes include monastery-hopping, bodega visits, and visiting nearby *balnearias* and thermal waters. Other highlights of historic Ribadavia include the 15th-century **castle,** immediately above Pr. Maior, which has an auditorium for summer theater and music.

To spend the night, seek out **Hostal Plaza ❷,** Pr. Maior, 15. Rooms have fans, TV, phone, and bath, and most face the square. (☎988 47 05 76. Ground fl. restaurant. Singles €25; doubles €35; triples €45. Cash only.) For groceries, head to **Supermercado Froiz,** R. Progreso, near the old quarter opposite Sergy's Hair Design. (Open M-Sa 9am-2:30pm and 4:30-9pm. MC/V.) For a more substantial meal, head to **Latino Restaurante ❷,** C. García Penedo, 5, which has a bar downstairs. (☎988 47 22 37. *Menú* €9. Open daily 1-5pm and 9pm-midnight.) The **tourist office** is on Pr. Maior, 7. (☎988 47 12 75; www.ribadavia.com. Open July-Sept. M-Sa 10am-3pm and 5-8pm, Su 10:30am-3pm; Oct.-June M-F 9:30am-2:30pm and 4:30-7pm, Sa 10:30am-2:30pm and 4:30-7pm, Su 10:30am-2:30pm.) Local services include: **Banco Santander Central Hispano** on the corner of R. Progreso and R. Salgado Moscoso (☎902 24 24 24; open Apr.-Sept. M-F 8:30am-2pm; Oct.-Mar. M-F 8:30am-2pm, Sa 8:30am-1pm), with a 24hr. **ATM** outside; the **police,** on R. Redondela (☎650 45 00 70); a **pharmacy,** García Carrera, on R. Progreso (☎988 47 00 77; open M-F in summer 9am-1:30pm and 4-8pm, in winter 9am-1:30pm and 4-7:30pm) and the **post office,** next to the police station on R. Redondela (open M-F 9:30am-2:30pm, Sa 9:30am-1pm). **Postal Code:** 32400.

CANGAS

Ferries run between Vigo's Estación Marítimo and Cangas approximately every 30min. (20min., daily 6:30am-10:30pm, round-trip €4.20). Cangas also sends ferries to Islas Cíes and back. Departs Cangas (July-Sept. 10:15am, 12:15, 4:15, and 6:15pm; returns 1, 5, and 7pm; round-trip €17.50). Confirm departures, as frequency depends on weather.

Cangas is a quiet coastal town with an uncrowded beach, a charming *casco antiguo*, and traditional dance festivals throughout the year. The town is speckled with churches, statues, crosses, and *gallego* architecture, of which the **Casa de Patín,** in the old city, is a perfect example. The *patin*, or exterior staircase, was traditionally a place for people to gather and fishermen to hang their nets to dry. The **Excolegiata de Santiago** dates from the sixteenth century and exhibits a mix of Renaissance, Gothic and Baroque styles. The **Paseo Marítimo,** a refreshing stroll along the coast of Cangas, beginning at the port and ending in the golden-sand beach, **Praia de Rodeira,** also allows for views of the reconstructed **Capilla del Hospital.** During July and August, open-air markets and many small festivals fill the streets. If you wish to spend the night, **Camping Limens ❶,** Praia de Limens, is a good option. (☎986 30 46 45; www.campinglimens.com. Sept-June electricity €3.69. €5.18 per person, €4.38 per child, and €5.18 per tent. July-Aug. electricity €4.20, €5.75 per person, €4.80 per child, and €6.20 per tent.) For a bed, seek out the **Hostal Belén ❹,** C. Antonio Nores, 12. (☎986 30 00 15. July-Aug. all rooms €42. Sept.-June €30.) Inquire at the **tourist office,** on the port with the bus station and Estación Marítima (Jul-Aug. M-F 10am-2pm and 4:30-8:30pm, Sept-June 10am-2pm and 4-8pm.) about current festivals. The tourist office also offers free guided tours (M-F 11am) through the **casco antiguo.** Inquire about ecological hikes and routes, such as the coastal **Senda Aramilla,** the **Senda de Molinos de Ardán,** and the **Senda de Molinos de Coiro.** Local services include: **Banco Santander Central Hispano,** across the street from the bus/ferry stations (☎986 30 07 36; Nov.-Mar. M-F 8:30am-2pm, Sa 8:30am-1pm, Apr.-Sept. M-F 8:30am-2pm); **police,** Av. da Castelao, s/n (☎986 30 30 31); **youth information center,** C. Real, with **internet access** (☎986 39 21 71); **women's information center,** R. Andalucía, 3, in the Xoia building (☎986 39 22 68).

PONTEVEDRA ☎986

According to legend, Pontevedra (pop. 80,000) was founded by the Greek archer Teucro as a place to convalesce after his Trojan War exploits. Greek origins notwithstanding, Pontevedra is a typical Galician city. The old town—filled with palm trees, flowering balconies, stately cathedrals, and squares lined with traditional arcaded *gallego* buildings (along with the occasional graffiti)—is calm and inviting. At night, plazas and countless outdoor cafes fill with people enjoying wine and tapas. There isn't too much to see in Pontevedra itself, but it makes a good base for exploring nearby beach towns.

GALICIA

TRANSPORTATION

Trains: R. de Estación (☎902 24 02 02), a 20min. walk southeast of the old city. Info open daily 7:30am-10pm. To: **A Coruña** (2-3hr.; M-F 15 per day 7am-9:21pm, Sa-Su 12 per day 7am-9:21pm; €8:55-11:55) via **Santiago** (1-1hr., €5.05); **Madrid** (11hr.; M-F and Su 12:50, 9:30pm, Sa 8:45am, 9:30pm; €46.10); **Vigo** (20-35min.; M-F 20-21 per day 6:50am-10:21pm, Sa-Su 15-16 per day Sa 6:50am-10:21pm, Su 8:40am-10:21pm; €2-10.70).

Buses: Av. Alféreces Provisionales (☎986 85 24 08). Info open daily 8am-10pm. To: **A Coruña** (2hr.; M-F 9-10 per day 6:45am-9:30pm, Sa 8 per day 9am-9pm, Su 7 per day 9am-9:30pm; €11.35); **Cambados** (1hr.; M-F 10 per day 8:15am-8:35pm, Sa 4 per day 9:30am-8:35pm, Su 3 per day 12:15-8:35pm; €2.60); **Madrid** (8hr., 6-7 per day 9am-11pm, €31-39); **Santiago** (1hr.; M-F every hr. 6:45am-9pm, Fr until 9:30pm, Sa 11 per day 8am-8pm, Su 9 per day 9am-9pm; €5); **Vigo** (1hr.; M-F every 20min.-1hr. 7am-10:50pm, Sa 16 per day 9:30am-10pm, Su 14 per day 10:50am-10pm; €2.40).

Taxis: Radio Taxi (☎986 86 85 85). 24hr. From the stations to town €3-4.

Car Rental: Avis, Plaza Estacion Renfe, Avenida Eduardo Pondal s/n (☎986 860 129). 23+, must have had license for 1 yr. From €49 per day. Ages 23-25 add €12 per day for insurance. Discounts for longer rentals. Open M-F 9am-1:30pm and 4-7:30pm, Sa 9am-1pm.

ORIENTATION AND PRACTICAL INFORMATION

Six streets branch out from **Praza da Peregrina,** the main plaza connecting the new city and the old city, or *casco antiguo*. The main streets are **R. Oliva, R. Michelena, R. Benito Corbal,** and **R. da Peregrina. Pr. de Galicia** is a 5min. walk from Pr. da Peregrina; from Pr. da Peregrina, head down R. da Peregrina and veer right at the first fork on R. Andrés Muruais. **Pr. de España** is a 5min. walk up R. Michelena from the Pr. da Peregrina. The **train** and **bus stations,** located across from each other, are about 1km from Pr. da Peregrina. From the train station, walk straight out of the station to the rotary and continue straight onto C. Calvo Soleto. From the bus station, turn left out of the station onto C. Calvo Soleto. Follow the road straight to the intersection and continue straight through the rotary onto Av. de Vigo, which will become R. da Peregrina. Stay on this road until the Pr. da Peregrina—you will see a church on your right when you have reached the plaza.

Tourist Office: R. General Gutiérrez Mellado, 1 (☎986 85 08 14). From Pr. da Peregrina, get on R. Michelena and take the first left onto R. General Gutiérrez Mellado. English spoken. Open July-Sept. M-F 10am-2pm and 4:30-7:30pm, Sa 10am-2pm and 4:30-7:30pm; Oct.-June M-F 10am-2pm and 4-6pm. **Branch** in a wooden kiosk on Pr. de España. Open June-Nov. daily 10am-8pm.

Currency Exchange: Banco Santander Central Hispano, R. Michelena, 26. (☎986 85 61 50). Open M-F 8:30am-2pm; Oct.-Mar. also Sa 8:30am-1pm. 24hr. **ATM** outside.

Luggage storage: At the bus station, on the top floor. Lockers €2 per day.

Police: C. Ingeneiro Rafael Aresas s/n, under the Pazo Cultura (☎986 83 30 80).

Pharmacy: Farmacia C. Carballo, R. Oliva, 30 (☎986 85 13 69). Open daily 9:30am-10pm.

Hospital: Provincial, C. Loeiro Crespo, 2(☎986 80 70 00). **Emergencies** ☎061.

Internet Access: Avalon, R. Sta. Clara, 29 (986 86 65 66), right next to Pension Santa Clara. €2 per hr., has Wi-Fi. Open daily 9am-1am, Su 5pm-1am.

Post Office: R. Oliva, 19 (☎986 85 16 77, 986 86 81 60). Lista de Correos, fax, and **Western Union.** Open M-F 8:30am-8:30pm, Sa 9:30am-2pm. **Postal Code:** 36001.

GALICIA

ACCOMMODATIONS

The most reasonably priced accommodations are in the *casco antiguo*. Reservations are necessary in August, when coastal towns and cities fill up.

Pensión Santa Clara, R. de Santa Clara, 31, 1st fl. (☎986 84 68 20). A few blocks away from the Pr. da Peregrina, this *pensión* has friendly management and huge, bright, wood-floored rooms, some with TV. Shared bathroom. Ask the staff to use the kitchen and washing machine. June-Aug. singles €20; doubles €30. Sept.-May €18/25. ❷

Casa Maruja, Av. de Santa María, 12 (☎986 85 49 01). From Pr. da Peregrina, walk up R. Michelena through Pr. de España and turn right onto R. Mestre Mateo. Most rooms in this very friendly family-run *pensión* have pleasant views of the old city. Rooms are sparsely decorated, but spacious. Private bath and TV. June-Sept. 15 singles €20-30; doubles €38; triples €46;. Sept. 16-May €15-20/30/36. MC/V. ❷

FOOD

Pontevedra prides itself on seafood. Tiny bars crowd the streets around Pr. da Peregrina. C. Figueroa, Pr. da Leña, Pr. de Verdura and C. San Sebastián harbor some of the most popular *marisquerías* and tapas bars. For groceries, try **Gadis Supermercado,** Av. de Vigo, 8. (Open M-Sa 9:30am-3pm and 5-9:30pm. MC/V.)

A Casa do Lado, Pr. da Leña, 3 (☎986 86 02 25). Directly across from the Museo de Pontevedra in the pleasant and secluded Pr. da Leña, this tapas joint keeps the customers happy with new spins on typical Spanish cuisine. Serves food on a beautiful terrace, alive with locals unwinding. Creative *croquetas* (€5-8). *Menú del dia* €11. Kitchen open M-Sa 1:30-4pm and 8-midnight, Su 1:30-4pm. MC/V. ❷

La Algueria Mudéjar, C. Churruchaos, 2 (☎986 85 12 58). On the other side of the *Ayuntamiento* from Pr. de España. Rowdy Spanish tapas bar meets the Middle East. Extensive wine selection. Entrees €8-11. Glass of wine €1-2.80. Open daily 1:30-4pm and 8:30pm-midnight, F and Sa later. MC/V. ❷

Bodegón Micota, R. da Peregrina, 4 (☎986 85 59 17). This basement *bodega* serves Spanish renditions of global classics like fajitas (€10.90), kebabs (€13.50-16.50), omelettes (€8.90-10.50), and fondue (€17.50-19.80). The tables are filled with locals and the walls are decorated with wine bottles in true *bodega* fashion. Open daily noon-4:30pm and 7:30pm-midnight. MC/V. ❸

SIGHTS

Pontevedra's primary sight is the extensive **Museo de Pontevedra,** R. Pasantería, 10. From Pr. da Peregrina, walk up Po. de Antonio Odriozola, which runs between the gardens and Pr. da Ferrería. Bear left at the fork; this road eventually curves into R. Pasantería and leads to the museum right on the Pr. da Leña. The *museo* exhibits religious sculptures, models of a traditional Galician structures, contemporary art, and a renowned collection of the mineral *azabache*, culturally significant in Galicia. (☎986 85 14 55. Open June-Sept. Tu-Sa 10am-2pm and 4:30-8:30pm, Su 11am-2pm; Oct.-May Tu-Sa 10am-2pm and 4-7pm, Su 11am-2pm. Free.) The moss-covered 14th through 15th-century Gothic **Ruinas do Convento de Santo Domingos** are in Pr. de España. (Opens for visits by request; call ☎986 85 14 55. Free.) The **Basílica de Santa María a Maior,** Av. de Santa María, 24, features a 16th-century door that depicts versions of Mary. From Pr. de España take Av. de Santa María, 24, downhill to the left of the *Ayuntamiento*. (☎986 86 61 85. Open daily 10am-1pm and 5-9pm.)

NIGHTLIFE AND BEACHES

Sunny days bring crowds to the white-sand beaches and coves of nearby Marín. **Monbus** buses make the journey from the outer corner of Pr. de Galicia on Av. Augusto García Sánchez (30min., every 15min., €1.90). Buses leaving from the bus station to **Cangas** also stop in **Marín** (M-F 7:35am and hourly 9:15am-9:30pm, Sa 11 per day 9:15am-9:30pm, Su 9 per day 10:10am-9:30pm; €1.90). From the bus stop in Marín, facing the water, head left on C. Angusto Miranda around the military school and up the hill. To reach the beaches, turn right on C. Tiro Naval Janer, continue for 15min., and exit right at the turn-off. The first beach is **Playa Porticelo;** another 10min. along the path is the larger **Playa Mogor.**

At night, you'll find bar after pub after *taparía* on the triangle of streets made by R Princesa, R. Paio Gómez Charino, and R. Tetuán. Pr. de Vendura also hosts a crowd of pleasant terraced bars. A local crowd chows on late night tapas and drinks at the popular **Café Universo,** in the neighboring Pr. Méndez Núñez, 1. (☎986 86 59 53. Mixed drinks €6. Beer €2. Wine €2. Open daily 7am-2am.) The festival of **Santiaguiño del Burgo** (July 25) is marked by religious processions throughout Pontevedra, and **La Peregrina** (the second week of August, peaking on Su) brings films, concerts, loads of honey, and bullfights to the city.

DAYTRIPS FROM PONTEVEDRA

Buses run frequently to all nearby towns. The towns can also be reached easily from Santiago de Compostela.

CAMBADOS

26km from Pontevedra. Plus Ultra buses run from Pontevedra to the bus station in Cambados near Pr. Concello (1hr.; M-F 10 per day 8:15am-8:35pm, Sa 4 per day 9:30am-8:35pm, Su 3 per day 12:15-8:35pm; €2.60). Return schedule is posted on the bus station window.

Visitors to harborside Cambados (pop. 15,000) will enjoy views of sweeping vineyards, orchards, and a glass of renowned *albariño* wine accompanying a platter of fresh shellfish. Begin at the **Palacio de Fefiñanes,** a 16th-century palace-turned-*bodega* that brims with giant, sweet-smelling barrels of *albariño*. Although the majority of the palace is closed due to reconstruction, you can still tour the *bodega* and sample some of the vineyard's wine (€3). With your back to the tourist office, turn left and head for the park to your right. At the end of the park, bear right onto C. Príncipe. At the plaza bear right onto R. Real, which will bring you to the Pl. de Fefiñanes and the palace. (☎986 54 22 04.

Open for visits Apr.-Oct. Tu-Su 10am-2pm and 4-8pm.) To reach the river, walk straight down Po. os Olmos (on the right facing the museum gate), cross the main street, and continue walking until you hit the water and see the **Torre de San Sadorniño.** The remains of this 12th-century fortification stand on a seemingly dissolving island connected to the mainland by a tiny bridge. The **Museo Etnográfico do Vino** on Avenida da Pastora, 104, was the first wine museum in Galicia. (☎986 52 61 19. Open Tu-Su 10am-2pm and 5-8pm.) From the tourist office, walk straight up Av. de Villarino and then take your first right onto R. San Francisco. Stay straight onto Av. da Pastora.

The first weekend in August brings in famous poets and politicians for the town's well-known **wine festival.** The culinary specialities, including shellfish and cheese, are just an excuse to keep sampling the *albariño*—its vines peek out from backyard fences and porch rooftops throughout Cambados. Most of the celebrations take place on Paseo de la Calzada, with additional feasts in the courtyard behind the Fefiñanes *bodega.* Otherwise, try **Raxeria Martinez Mariscos ❷,** at C. Real, 16, which serves traditional Galician fare and delicious seafood and salad options for those who have overdosed on tentacles. Be sure to try some of the local wine. (☎676 33 01 34. *Menú* €10. Open daily 1pm-2am. AmEx/MC/V.) **Moldes Supermercado,** Pr. Ramon Cabanillas, will meet your grocery needs. (Open M-Sa 9:30am-2pm and 5-9:30pm.)

Visitors may find it helpful to start at the **tourist office** at Praza do Concello, s/n. Inquire here about **La Ruta del Vino** as well as local festivals, events, and beaches. (☎986 52 07 86. Open daily July-Sept. 10am-2pm and 5-8pm; Oct.-June 10am-2pm and 4:30-7:30pm.) Three **ATMs** are across the street from the tourist office. The **police** can be reached at ☎986 52 40 92.

EL GROVE (O GROVE) AND LA TOJA (A TOXA)

Monbus (☎902 29 29 00) runs buses from Pontevedra to O Grove (1hr.; M-F every 30min.-1hr. 7:45am-10pm, Sa-Su 9-11 per day 9:30am-10pm; €3.60); an equal number return (20-22 per day 6:30am-8pm). Buses also run from Santiago (€6) via Cambados (M-F 4 per day 11:30am-8:30pm, Sa-Su 11:30am, 8:30pm; €2.05). Schedules are posted in the O Grove bus station (☎986 680 411).

The self-proclaimed *"Paraíso de Marisco"* (Shellfish Paradise), O Grove, a tranquil fishing wharf west of Pontevedra, offers access to pleasant hiking trails and secluded white sand beaches. Incidentally, it is also a paradise of sorts for drug traffickers; cocaine and hash are smuggled from Latin America and North Africa to the secluded coves of the northwest, though you'd never know it. The island of **A Toxa,** O Grove's fancy neighbor across the bridge, is dotted with elegant summer homes, a country club, a golf course, and a casino, and all watched over by an army of security guards. Besides worldwide acclaim for its soap production (made from native salts in the spas), A Toxa is a popular destination for couples looking to tie the knot. A fish auction is held in O Grove weekdays from 5-6:30pm in the Lonja building, directly behind the **market** (next to the tourist office). The market sells fresh fish, fine cheeses, organic breads, and honey (open M-Sa 9am-2pm). Fridays also provide a chance to peruse clothing, local food, and crafts at the **waterside moving market** (9am-2pm)—like a traveling circus, the market moves from town to town each day of the week. The town's popular **seafood festival** draws flocks of visitors during the first two weeks of October. For a night's rest in O Grove, look on **C. Castelao** or **Av. Teniente Domínguez,** but most accommodations are expensive (€30-40 per night). The **tourist office,** Pl. de Corgo, 1, has information on boat rides and beaches. (☎986 73 14 15. June-July 15 10am-2pm and 4-7pm; July 16-Oct. 10am-8pm; Nov.-Dec. 10am-2pm and 4-7pm.) Ask here about **Pescanatur** to spend the day fishing with the *marineros* (☎986 73 35 90; www.pescanatur.es).

LA LANZADA (A LANZADA)

Buses run frequently between Pontevedra and O Grove on Transportes La Unión (1hr.; M-F 18 per day 7:45am-10pm, Sa-Su 9-11 per day 9:30am-10pm; €3.60) via either A Lanzada (45min-1hr., €2.90) or Villalonga—check schedule for buses stopping in A Lanzada. Schedule and prices subject to change after July 2008.

A Lanzada, between Pontevedra and O Grove, is best known for its magnificent beaches, which ancient legends claim have the virtue of increasing women's fertility. As beach towns in Spain go, it has another virtue for travelers: the backdrop to the sands isn't high-rises and schlocky beach stalls, but beautiful, government-protected sand dunes. The **Torre de la Lanzada, Castro de la Lanzada,** or the **Ermita de Nuestra Señora de la Lanzada** could also be of interest to monument-seeking beachgoers. The bus drops off across the street from **Playa de La Lanzada,** and there is really no reason to walk much further—the beach is a massive stretch of soft sand sheltered by cliffs and dunes. (Lifeguards are on duty daily July-Sept. 11am-8pm.) Summer weekends are quite crowded, but the massive beach is relatively empty on weekdays. If you walk left for 1km (facing the water) along the highway by the beach, you will arrive at **Capilla de La Lanzada,** a Roman chapel that offers spectacular views of the beach and sea. Continue walking to find many more less crowded, beautiful beaches. The only **cafe** on the beach serves up cheap sandwiches, tapas, and drinks. (Open daily July-Sept. 10am-9pm.) The bus route from La Lanzada to Pontevedra is lined with beaches, most of which are public; look out the window as you travel, and ask to stop when you see a beach you like. Beware of the undertow, which locals report is strong. The last Sunday of August brings **Nueve Olas,** a festival of fertility; people gather by the beach for food, drink, bonfires, and festivity.

RÍAS ALTAS

If you're one to fall asleep during train rides, make the effort to stay awake during the trek through the breathtaking valleys and magical pine forests of Rías Altas. Thick fogs and misty mornings do a good job of keeping the Rías Altas hidden from most visitors. With the exception of A Coruña, the area's busy capital, the Rías Altas seem to have been nearly forgotten by tourism, but that's the most compelling reason to visit: residents of the tiniest of coastal towns heartily welcome travelers, and visitors who make it here will find miles of green estuaries and secluded beaches all to themselves.

LA CORUÑA (A CORUÑA) ☎981

Unlike most of its Galician neighbors, A Coruña (pop. 260,000) is a big city, complete with high-rises, expressways, and urban sprawl. At the same time, A Coruña maintains natural beauty and quirky charm. The city center is a maze of narrow alleys that teem with raucous bars and popular *marisquerías* (seafood restaurants). The miles of harborside walks echo with Galician legend and lore: Hercules supposedly built the lighthouse here, and the city's nickname, the Crystal City, refers to the blinding sunset reflected on rows of tightly packed windows. As any *coruñese* will tell you, Santiago might be the northwest's most popular city, but A Coruña has its own Galician pride.

TRANSPORTATION

Flights: Aeropuerto de Alvedro (☎981 18 72 00), 8km south of the city. **Air Europa** (☎981 18 73 08), **ERA** (☎981 18 72 86), **Spanair** (☎902 13 14 15), and **Iberia**

(☎981 18 72 54). Daily flights to **Madrid, Lisboa,** and **Paris** via **Barcelona** and **London.** Bus from the airport to the bus station is run by **ASICASA** (☎981 231 234) from 6:45am-10:45pm.

Trains: Estación San Cristóbal, Av. Joaquín Planells Ríera s/n (☎902 24 02 02). Info open daily 7am-10:30pm. **RENFE** to: **Madrid** (8-11hr.; daily 9:45pm, M-F and Su also 1:10pm, Sa also 9am; €47.70); **Santiago** (1hr.; M-F 20 per day 5:36am-10:25pm, Sa-Su 17-18 per day, Sa 6:50am-9:45pm, Su 6:50am-10:25pm; €3.90-13.80); **Vigo** (2hr.; M-F 15 per day 5:36-8:36pm, Sa-Su 13 per day 6:50am-8:36pm; €9.60-13) via **Pontevedra** (€8.55-11.55).

Buses: C. Caballeros (☎981 23 96 44).

ALSA/Enatcar (☎902 42 22 42) to: **Madrid** (8hr.; M-Sa 5-6 per day 7am-10:30pm, Su 6 per day 7am-11:30pm; €39); **Oviedo** (4-6hr., 3-4 per day 9:30am-7pm, €21); **San Sebastián** (14hr., 2 per day 9:30am and 7pm, €50) via **Santander** (10hr., €35).

Castromil (☎902 29 29 00) to: **Santiago** (50min.-1½hr..; M-F 6:35am, and every hr. 8am-10:20pm, Sa 6:35am and hourly 8am-10:20pm, Su 6:30am and hourly 11am-10pm; €6.70) and **Vigo** (2-2hr.; M-F 9 per day 8am-8:15pm, Sa 8 per day 8am-8:15pm, Su 6 per day 11am-8:15pm; €14.20) via **Pontevedra** (1-2hr., €12).

IASA-Arriva (☎902 27 74 82) to: **Betanzos** (40min.; M-F every 30min. 6:30am-10:30pm, Sa-Su hourly 6:30am-10:30pm, Su until 11pm; €2.15); **El Ferrol** (45min.; M-F hourly 7:20am-9:20pm, Sa 6 per day 9:20am-6:20pm, Su 8 per day 11:20am-9:20pm; €6.40); **Ribadeo** (4hr.; M-F 4 per day 8am-4pm, Sa 3 per day 8am-4pm, Su 8, 11am; €16.50); **Viveiro** (3hr.; M-Sa 4-6 per day 6:30am-7pm, Su 3 per day 11:30am-7pm; €13.70) via **Betanzos.**

Public Transportation: Red Compañía de Tranvías de La Coruña buses (☎981 25 01 00) run frequently (6:15am-midnight, €1). Buy tickets on board. The night bus, **Búho,** runs F-Sa hourly 12:30am-4:30am.

Taxis: Radio Taxi (☎981 24 33 33) and **TeleTaxi** (☎981 28 77 77). Both operate 24hr. Train and bus stations to the *ciudad vieja* €5.

Car Rental: Autos Brea, Av. Fernández Latorre, 110 (☎981 23 86 45). 21+, and must have had license for 1 yr. From €63 per day with unlimited mileage. Open M-Sa 9am-1pm and 4-7pm.

ORIENTATION AND PRACTICAL INFORMATION

A Coruña sits on a narrow peninsula between the Atlantic Ocean and the Ría de A Coruña. The new city stretches across the mainland; the peninsula encompasses the *ciudad vieja* (old city). Beaches are on the Atlantic side and the harbor is on the river. **Avenida de la Marina** runs along the harbor and leads past the obelisk and the tourist office to Puerta Real, the entry into **Plaza de María Pita** and the *ciudad vieja.* From the **bus station,** take bus #1 or 1A to the tourist office at Puerta Real. For buses from the train station to the *ciudad vieja*, exit from the main entrance of the train station on Pr. San Cristóbal, cross the plaza, and walk right on R. de Outeiro. At the rotary, turn left onto R. Estaciones and follow the pedestrian paths over the highway. The bus station and stop for buses #1 and 1A are across the parking lot from the pedestrian stairs. Bus #14 connects the center with the monuments along Paseo Marítimo.

Tourist Office: Regional Office, Av. de la Marina (☎981 22 18 22; www.turgalicia.es). English spoken. Info on regional travel and daytrips from A Coruña. Open M-F 10am-2pm and 4-7pm, Sa 11am-2pm and 5-7pm, Su 11am-2pm. **Turismo A Coruña** (☎981 18 43 43; www.turismocoruna.com), in a glass building in a corner of Pl. María Pita, offer extensive maps and helpful local guidance. Feb.-Oct. Open M-F 9am-8:30pm,

Sa 10am-2pm and 4-8pm, Su 10am-3pm. Nov.-Jan. M-F 9am-2:30pm and 4-8:30pm, Sa 10am-2pm and 4-8pm, Su 10am-3pm.

Currency Exchange: There are many banks throughout the city. **Banco Santander Central Hispano,** C. Cantón Grande, 4 (☎981 18 88 44), next to **Banco Popular.** Open M-F 8:30am-2pm; Oct.-Mar Sa 8:30am-1pm.

English-Language Book Store: Librería Universal, Galerias Centro Real, 86-1a (☎981 22 96 45). In a small shopping center right off the C. Real, it's the only all-English book store in town. Open Sept.-June M-F 10am-1:30pm and 5-8pm, Sa 10am-1:30pm; July-Aug. M-F 10am-1:30pm. MC/V.

Laundromat: Surf, C. Hospital San Roque, 35 (☎987 20 44 20). Wash and dry up to 6kg for €12. Open M-F 9:30am-1:30pm and 4:30-8pm.

Police: Municipal, C. Tui, s/n (☎981 18 42 25).

Pharmacy: C. del Torre, 54 (☎981 20 38 42). Open 24hr.

Medical Services: Ambulatorio San José, C. Comandante Fontanes, 8 (☎981 22 60 74 or 22 63 35).

Internet Access: One of the cheaper cafes is **Cyber,** C. Zalaeta, 7, near the Museo de Bellas Artes. (☎981 92 30 45). Speedy connections. €1 per 30min., €1.50 per hr. Open M-Sa 10am-midnight,Su from 3pm-12:30am.

Post Office: C. Alcalde Manuel Casas (☎981 22 51 75). **Lista de Correos** and fax service. Open M-F 8:30am-8:30pm, Sa 9:30am-2pm. **Postal Code:** 15071.

ACCOMMODATIONS

Most accommodations are in or near the *ciudad vieja*, on **C. Riego de Agua** and **R. Nueva.** Make reservations for August visits due to the month-long festival.

Pensión Roma, R. Nueva, 3 (☎981 22 80 75; www.pensionroma.com). Spotless, sunny rooms with TV, phone, and bath. Very clean and comfortable. 24hr. reception. Internet access. Rooms usually completely rented by students Sept.-June. July singles €27; doubles €42; triples €62; quads €68; Aug. €37/52/74/83. MC/V. ❸

Pensión la Alianza, C. Riego de Agua, 8, 1st fl. (☎981 22 81 14), next to Pl. María Pita. An eclectic assortment of paintings cover the hallways and smallish rooms of this old-fashioned but charming *residencia.* Staff is very friendly. Be sure to request a room with a window. Singles €20; doubles €35. MC/V. ❷

Pensión Las Rías, C. San Andrés, 141, 2nd fl. (☎981 22 68 79). With private bath, TV, and phone, these spacious rooms are comfortable, but a pricier option for solo travelers. The owner is happy to help with plans and directions. July-Aug. doubles €40; Sept.-June €25, weekends €30. Cash only. ❹

FOOD

The streets around C. Estrella, C. de la Franja, and C. la Galera teem with cheap seafood restaurants and cafes. The area around Av. Rubine off Playa de Riazor is fancier. If you're looking for something cheaper, **Pl. María Pita** is full of inexpensive tapas bars with glass-enclosed outdoor terraces. The **Mercado San Agustín** is in the oval building on Pr. San Agustín, near the old town. (Open M-Sa 8am-3pm.) For groceries, stop by **Supermercado Gadis,** just off C. del Orzán. (Open daily M-Sa 9am-4:30pm and 5:30-10pm.)

Kismet, C. Galera, 16 (981 87 89 29). After days of eating *pulpo a feira,* no matter how delicious, Kismet's subtle spice is a welcome break. This beautifully decorated establishment sells delicious Turkish fare at reasonable prices. The vegetable dishes, like eggplant with tomatoes and pepper (€3.80-6) and meat dishes (€4.20-6.80) are more

than enough for one, and perfect for sharing. Delicious complimentary tea. Open M-Sa 1-4:30pm and 7:30pm-12:30am, Su 7:30pm-12:30am. AmEx/MC/V. ❷

La Casa de las Tortillas, C. del Orzán, 5 (☎981 22 67 18). A cross between a cave and odd clock shop, quirky evening spot La Casa de las Tortillas offers sangria (€10) and dozens of creative varieties of *tortilla española* (€6-10), the Spanish everyman's meal. Open M and Th-Su 8:30pm-12:30am, F-Sa until 1:30pm. AmEx/MC/V. ❸

Créperie Petite Bretagne, C. Riego de Agua, 13-15 (☎981 22 48 71). A romantic, subtly-lit restaurant with a seaside terrace off the Pl. de María Pita. Specializes in crepes, stuffed with everything from mozzarella and sausage to decadent chocolate (€2.50-10). *Menú* €10. Open daily 1:30-4:30pm and 8:30pm-12:30am. AmEx/MC/V. ❷

La Bottega, C. Olmos, 25 (☎981 91 46 76, www.labottega.es). An intimate interior, decorated in nautical paintings. Wide variety of crepes (€7-10), salads (€5.90-8.75), creative omelettes, and delicious meat and fish dishes. Most dishes well under €10. Open M-Th 1:30-4:15pm and 8pm-12:15am, F-Sa until 12:45am. AmEx/MC/V. ❷

SIGHTS

A Coruña is not famous for its wealth of historic monuments, but it has phenomenal attractions along Po. Marítimo. To visit them all in one day, start from Playa del Orzán and follow waterside Po. Marítimo to the major museums and Torre de Hércules. The route begins at the start of Po. Marítimo, near Puerta Real, and ends at Pl. del Orzán. *(Trolleys daily every 30min. noon-9:35pm; €2. A €12 bono ticket allows same-day admission to all 3 museums; details at www.casaciencias.org.)*

TORRE DE HÉRCULES. A Coruña's major landmark, the Torre de Hércules, stands on a hill overlooking the city, and looms over rusted ships at the peninsula's end. The tower dates from the second century BC, but was renovated in Neoclassical style in 1790. Legend has it that Hercules erected the tower, the world's oldest working lighthouse, over the remains of his defeated enemy, Geryon. After taking a look at the tower's ancient foundations in the basement of the lighthouse, climb the 234 steps to the top of the tower for stunning views of the city and bay. Note that there is no elevator. A sculpture park, **Hercules's Garden,** surrounds the tower. *(Av. de Navarra, s/n. On Po. Marítimo, a 20min.*

walk from Puerta Real—or a 5min. trolley ride. From C. Millán Astray, turn left onto C. Orillamar, which turns into Av. de Navarra and brings you to the tower. ☎981 22 37 30. Open daily July-Aug. 10am-9:45pm; Sept.-June 10am-6:45pm. €2, children and seniors €1.)

MUSEO DE BELAS ARTES. This superb museum displays classic Spanish, French, Italian, and Flemish art from the Renaissance to the 20th century. Its magnificent new building, lit by a skylight and stone-set windows, is a renovated convent. Includes works by Murilla, Sorolla, Rubens, and Tintoretto, and Goya (an entire room is devoted to his works, including sketches from *Los Caprichos*), and a Picasso. It also houses the work of *gallego* artists. *(Rua Zalaeta. ☎981 22 37 23. Open Tu-F 10am-8pm, Sa 10am-2pm and 4:30-8pm, Su 10am-2pm. Free.)*

AQUARIUM FINISTERRAE. Known as the *Casa de los Peces*, this aquarium is A Coruña's homage to the sea. Over 200 species of local marine life are displayed in vast tanks, while the downstairs room features interactive exhibits on marine ecosystems from all over the world. Don't miss Nautilus, a huge, eerie basement aquarium that recreates Jules Verne's adventure in *20,000 Leagues Under the Sea*. *(On Po. Marítimo at the bottom of the hill from the Torre de Hércules. Bus #14 from the Puerta Real. ☎981 18 98 42. Open July-Aug. daily 10am-9pm; Sept.-June M-F 10am-7pm, Sa-Su 10am-8pm. €10, children, seniors and holders of Carnet Joven or ISIC cards €4.)*

CASA MUSEO PICASSO. Pablo Picasso lived in this house as a child from 1891-1895, while his father was a professor of drawing in A Coruña. This beautiful, simple house is now a museum, with some original furniture and several early works by Picasso. While less famous or extensive than those in Málaga and Barcelona, this museum remains a worthwhile stop on the Picasso trail. *(C. Payo Gomez, 14. ☎981 18 98 54. Open W-Su 10:30am-2pm, Th-Sa also 5:30-8pm. Free.)*

MUSEO DOMUS. The Domus, also called the *Casa del Hombre* (House of Man), is a natural history and science museum in one, with interactive exhibits on human cultures and anatomy. Watch "blood" spurt from a model heart, hear "Hello, I **love** you" in over 30 languages, and spend hours playing with microscopes and other gizmos. Exhibits are in Spanish, but many, like the childbirth video, need no translation. *(C. Santa Teresa, 1, on Po. Marítimo between aquarium and Playa Orzán. ☎981 18 98 40. Open daily July-Aug. 11am-9pm; Sept.-June 10am-7pm. €2, children, seniors and holders of either Carnet Joven or ISIC cards €1.)*

CASA DE LAS CIENCIAS. Located in the beautiful **Parque de Santa Margarita**, the kid-friendly *Casa de las Ciencias* is designed for hands-on learning about physics, geology, and the environment. There are several exhibits about the environment and natural world, including a chicken hatchery and insect-holding geospheres—look out for the *cucarachas* (cockroaches). The four-story building features a giant Foucault's pendulum and a planetarium. *(Parque Santa Margarita. ☎981 18 98 44; www.casaciencias.org. Open daily July-Aug. 11am-9pm; Sept.-June 10am-7pm. Casa €2, children, holders of Carnet Joven, and seniors €1. Planetarium €1. Check show schedules. Sept.-June planetarium open only weekends.)*

BEACHES

A Coruña's best beaches are the long, narrow **Playa del Orzán** and **Playa de Riazor** that flank Po. Marítimo on the Atlantic side of the peninsula. On weekends, the sand along these calm waters is packed with people. Small, secluded beaches, including **Playa del Matadero, Playa de San Amaro,** and **Playa das Lapas,** hide farther down Po. Marítimo near Torre de Hércules, although these tend to be a bit rockier and more seaweed-prone.

NIGHTLIFE

In the early evening, *coruñeses* linger in Celtic pubs throughout the *ciudad vieja*, bar-hopping around **C. del Orzán, C. del Sol,** and the mess of streets near **C. de la Franja** and **C. de la Florida.** Popular Celtic pubs include **Rochester,** C. de la Franja, 61, where posters from Ireland plaster the walls and Irish stouts flow from the taps, though the crowd inside certainly isn't foreign. (Beer €1.20. Open M-Th, Su 7:30pm-1:30am, F-Sa until 2:30am). The tightest squeeze is **Ocacivache** on C. Orzan, 28, a darkened pub/dance bar with a hippie vibe that specializes in **queimada,** the traditional Galician liquor. A reenactment of the ceremony used by medieval witches to ward off evil spirits is performed every Thursday night (☎981 91 47 33). When bars die down around 2am, discotecas pick up along the two beaches and on C. Juan Flórez. **Sol Pirámide,** C. Juan Flórez, 50, plays dance music loud enough to rouse the dead. (Open daily 1-6am.) Locals pack the small dance floor of **Kántaro,** C. del Sol, 21. (Open Th-Sa midnight-5am.) Across the street, **Lautrec** plasters its walls with old movie posters and draws crowds with electronica. (Open M-Th 1am-5am, F-Sa until 5:30am.)

FESTIVALS

Party-hardy *coruñeses* spend the month of August celebrating **Las Fiestas de María Pita,** with concerts, parades, and medieval fairs. To kick off the events, the city holds a mock naval battle in the harbor on July 31 to honor María Pita, the woman who single-handedly rallied a defense against the invading army of Sir Francis Drake in 1589 after the townsmen allegedly fled the port in fear. Although **La Noche de San Juan** (June 23) is celebrated in many parts of Europe, A Coruña greets the occasion with particular fervor, since it coincides with the opening of sardine season. Locals light bonfires with *aguardiente* (firewater) before spending the night leaping over flames and gorging on sardines. Risks aside, the rite is supposed to ensure fertility. And if you drop an egg white in a glass of water on the night, its shape is supposed to give you some clue to your future spouse's occupation.

LUGO ☎982

Lugo (100,000), founded by the Romans in 15 BC, is the oldest city in Galicia, and is still in the process of uncovering the incredible heritage within its confines. A 2km-long *Muralla Romana* (Roman stone wall), built around 300 BC, surrounds the city center and is one of the few walls that can be entirely traversed on foot. The wall was declared an UNESCO World Heritage Site in 2000, as the finest example of late Roman fortifications in Western Europe. The walls have been left intact by time, and visitors can still see the remains of each of the wall's 85 towers. The modern Lugo, which was built over the remains of the ancient Roman city Lucus, is a constantly evolving archaeological site; construction projects are constantly arrested due to new findings.

TRANSPORTATION. Arriva (☎902 27 74 82) **buses** run from Lugo to **A Coruña** (2hr.; M-F 12 per day 6:40am-9:05pm, Sa 8 per day 8:10am-7pm, Su 7 per day 8:10am-8:40pm), **Ferrol** (2½hr., M-F 8 per day 11am-9:30pm, Sa 3 per day 11:30am-6:30pm, Su 4:15, 7:30pm.), **Viveiro** (2-3 hr. M-F 6 per day 9am-6pm, Sa 4 per day 9:15am-6pm, Su 9:15am, 6, 8pm), and **Ribadeo** (2 hr., M-F 4 per day 10:30am-7:45, Sa 3 per day 9:15am-7:45pm). Call Lugo bus station (☎982 22 39 85) for prices and updated routes.

ACCOMMODATIONS AND FOOD. Hostal Darío II ❷, C. Franco, 12, offers comfortable rooms at about a 15min. walk from the city center. Usually host to visiting Spaniards, the prices are very reasonable and not tourist-inflated. (☎982 20 34 83. Singles €20; doubles €40. Cash only.) Lugo takes pride in its gastronomy, particularly its *pulpo a feira*, bread, and *empanadas*. For a taste of traditional *lucense* cuisine, visit **Curruncho a Nosa Terra ❷,** R. Nova, 8, a restaurant with a tavern-like interior and poetic sensibility, with quotations by famous Galician writers posted on its walls. Meat dishes run €8-18, vegetable and pasta options €7-14. Try the *pimientos de padron* (€7), a Galician staple, or indulge in the octupus dish *pulpo a galega* (€9), a must in Lugo. *Menú* €9.50. (☎982 22 92 35. Open daily 1:15-4pm and 9:15pm-midnight.) In the evening, tapas-hopping is the thing to do.

SIGHTS. The **Museo Provincial de Lugo,** Plaza de la Soledad, s/n, formerly the Convento de San Francisco, contains souvenirs of the city's Roman past, as well as Galician and other contemporary art. (☎982 24 21 12; www.museolugo.org. Open Sept.-June M-F 10:30am-2pm and 4:30-8:30pm, Sa 10:30am-2pm and 4:30-8pm, Su 11am-2pm; July-Aug. M-F 11am-2pm and 5-8pm, Sa 10am-2pm. Free.) The **Casa de los Mosaicos,** C. Dr. Castro, 22, has a small collection of well-preserved Roman mosaics. A video providing historical background is shown every hr., but you'll be set with a quick peek at the one-room museum. (☎982 25 48 15. Open daily July-Aug. 11am-2pm and 5-8pm; Sept.-June 11am-2pm and 5-7pm.) The **Termas Romanas** (thermal baths), built around 15 BC, make for an interesting stop. They lie under what is now the hotel **Balneario de Lugo,** Barrio del Puente, s/n, about a 20min. walk from the town center. (☎982 22 12 28. Call for group reservations. Open year round 8:30am-8:30pm, for large groups open 12:30-1 and 4-6.) For a beach excursion, visit **La Playa de las Catedrales,** situated in the province of Lugo, but about a 1½ hour drive away on the northern coast of Lugo province, 10km west of Ribadeo. This beach, declared a natural monument by the Junta de Galicia, has impressive cliffs and rock formations that, during low tide, possess an eerie resemblance to the arches of a cathedral.

NIGHTLIFE AND FESTIVALS. Tapas bars are plentiful in the *Zona de Vinos*, constituted by the **Plaza de Campo** and adjacent streets. Lugo's inhabitants are a lively crowd; the city and surrounding towns have many festivals year-round, but Lugo is

CELTIC SPIRITS

Every year, thousands of free spirits with nothing but a tent, a love for music, and rugged determination pack up their sleeping bags and their kegs of Estrella de Galicia, and head out to the sands of Ortigueira. Beginning in 1978, this beach town on Galicia's northern coast has hosted the renowned international Celtic Music Festival on a stretch of land between Morouzos Beach, where the lively spirits camp out, and the city center of Ortigueira. While many tend to associate Spanish music with flamenco, the strong tradition of Galician folk music shares more cultural similarities with the Celtic music of Scotland and Ireland than anything you might find in Andalucía or Madrid.

Today, the festival features stellar performances by world-renowned Celtic music artists, as well as theatre shows, street performances, puppet shows, and exhibitions. But it is not just the incredible performances by talented Galician, Irish, and other international artists that give it such life: with beautiful beaches and enthusiastic crowds, this festival is a way of life. Ortigueira evokes the magic of Galicia, with people sitting around a bonfire, laughing to the rise and fall of the music as they toast with a heart-warming gulp of *queimada*.

The 25th annual festival will be held July 9-12, 2009. For more information, visit www.festivalde-ortigueira.com.

especially known for the **Fiestas de San Froilán,** October 5-12, 2009, when the city raises a medieval market complete with traditional Galician music, performances, and of course, an abundant supply of *pulpo a feira.*

THE NORTHERN COAST

If you're looking for unspoilt wilderness, go north. The rainy Rías Altas are quiet treasures—nowhere else will you find such dense forests, dramatic cliffs, and striking beaches all together. Half the enjoyment of the trip is getting there; the rail lines and lonely highways snake past endless forests and majestic ocean views—just make sure you stay awake to see the views. Public transportation is reliable, but renting a car can be more convenient.

VIVEIRO

The FEVE train (☎982 55 07 22; www.feve.es) leaves Viveiro for Ferrol (4 per day 7:53am-7:22pm, €5.40) and Oviedo (10am, 5:10pm, €13.80). Arriva buses (☎982 56 01 03) from Viveiro connect to: A Coruña (4hr.; M-F 5 per day 6:15am-7:45pm, Sa 4 per day 8am-7:45pm, Su 3 per day 11:15am-7:45pm; €12.70); through El Ferrol (2hr.; M-F 8 per day 6:15am-7:45pm, Sa 4 per day 8am-7:45pm, Su 3 per day 11:15am-7:45pm; €8); Ribadeo (1hr.; M-F 6 per day 9:15am-8pm, Sa noon-4:45pm; €5.20); Santiago (3hr.; M-F 5 per day 6:15am-3pm, Sa 11:15am, Su 3pm, 6:15pm, change over in Ferrol; €16.90).

A tranquil old port poised between forest and sea, Viveiro (pop. 16,000) is known for its pristine beaches and fresh seafood—especially octopi. In the historic city center, the Concepcionistas Monastery and the Santa María del Campo Church both exhibit Romanesque urban architecture. For a dose of natural beauty, head 5km away from Viveiro, to **Playa de Area,** which stretches for 1km and forms the only set of sand dunes in the district. The local bus company, **Autobuses de Viveiro** (☎982 55 11 17), runs buses between the towns and beaches. See bus station for details on schedules and costs.

For information on **Camping Viveiro ❶,** next to Playa de Covas, call ☎982 56 00 04. (€4 per person, €4 per tent.) The tourist office has information on popular local hikes. If you choose to stay in town, **Nuevo Mundo ❷,** C. Teodoro de Quirós, one block uphill from Pr. Maior, has wood-paneled rooms, most with sun-filled balconies, and modern, tidy common baths. (☎982 56 00 25. In summer singles €17, doubles €33; in winter €15/30. Cash only.) Also reasonably priced is **Hotel Vila ❷,** C. Cora Montenegro, 57, which has comfortable, spacious rooms with private bath, phone, and free Wi-Fi. (☎982 56 13 31. Breakfast €2.50. Sept.-June singles €25, doubles €32; Jul-Aug. single €40, doubles €50.) Visitors head to popular **Restaurant O Muro ❸,** C. Margarita Pardo de Cela, 28, a pizzeria-*pulpería* combo, for friendly service and delicious food. (☎982 56 08 23. Entrees €7-16. Pizza €8-12. Open daily 1-4 pm and 8pm-midnight. Cash only.) **Mesón Restaurante Xoquín ❷,** C. Irmáns Vilar Ponte, 19, offers traditional dishes for reasonable prices in a cozy atmosphere. *Platos combinados* (€5-12), *paellas* (€8-9).Try the *lomo with pimientos.* (☎982 562 756. Open 1-4:30pm, 8:30pm-midnight.)

Though Viveiro is a beautiful spot throughout the summer, July is a particularly good time to visit. Horses undergo a ritual tail- and mane-cutting ceremony at **Las Rapas das Bestas** festival, which takes place the 1st Sunday of July in the nearby town of Candaoso. The second weekend of July, Galicia's youth pitch tents out on the beaches of **Ortiguera,** 36km from Viveiro, for the town's **Celtic Music Festival.** A special bus runs from A Coruña to Ortiguera Wednesday through Sunday of festival week.

Viveiro's **tourist office,** Av. Ramón Canosa, s/n, has town maps and information. (☎982 56 08 79; www.viveiro.es. Open Sept.-June M-F 11am-2pm and 4:30-7:30pm, Sa 11am-2pm and 5-7pm; July-Aug. M-F 10am-2pm and 4:30-8pm,

Sa 11am-2pm and 5-7pm, Su 11:30am-1:30pm.) Ask for the monthly newspaper, *Qué ver, qué hacer en Viveiro*, for details on festivals, events, and restaurants. Local services include: **banks** along Av. de Marina; **police** (☎982 56 29 22) on Pl. Mayor, 1; **medical services** at the **Centro de Salud** (☎92 56 12 01) on Av. Ramón Canosa; **Internet** access at **Ciberfox,** C. Nicolas Cora Montenegro, 68; and the **post office** on Av. Ramón Canosa, which offers Lista de Correos and fax. (☎982 56 08 23. Open M-F 8:30am-2:30pm, Sa 9:30am-1pm). **Postal Code:** 27850.

VALDOVIÑO AND CEDEIRA

Rialsa buses (☎981 31 59 55) run from El Ferrol to Cedeira (40min.; M-F 9 per day 7:30am-10pm, Sa 6 per day 8:30am-10:30pm, Su 5 per day 11am-10:30pm; €2.60) via Valdoviño. The bus to Cedeira leaves from Plaza de España. In El Ferrol, connections can be made to and from A Coruña (1hr., every hr. 6:30am-9:30pm, €5.70).

Valdoviño, 61km northeast of A Coruña, is home to gorgeous, isolated beaches and incredible fauna, and hosts the **Pantín Classic** surfing competition at its famous Playa de Pantín, located 10km towards Cedeira. The neighboring municipality of **Cedeira** has beautiful beaches as well as one of the most important pilgrimage sites on the Camino de Santiágo. About 12km from Cedeira lies the **Sanctuary of San Andrés de Teixido,** which is situated in the **Sierra da Capelada.** At 140m above sea level, these are some of the highest cliffs in Europe. Legend has it that the ship carrying the remains of San Andres was wrecked near these cliffs, after which God vowed to create a sanctuary every Christian must visit before entering heaven. As the *gallegos* say, to this windy, secluded spot, '*o que non vai de vivo vai de morto*' ('who goes not in life, will go in death'). Every July, Valdeviño's **Plaza Sagrado Corazón** becomes the site of a medieval fair, and on summer afternoons, locals gather in the port to practice their haggling skills over fish fresh off the boats. To reach the port from the Playa Magdalena, walk right, cross the bridge, and continue to follow the path along the coast for 1.5km. In summer, you can pitch a tent in Valdoviño at **Camping A Lagoa ❶,** just off Playa Frouxeira, which features a beautiful lagoon. (☎981 48 71 22. Open June 15-Sept. 15. €3.40 per person and per car, €3.40-4.40 per tent. Electricity €3.40.) Just steps away from the beach in Cedeira, **Hostal Chelsea ❸,** Pl. Sagrado Corazón 9, provides a comfortable night's rest. All 20 rooms have TV and full bath, and some have views overlooking the plaza. (☎981 48 23 40. In summer singles €38, doubles €42. In winter €30/35. Cash only.) **Pizzeria Lanus ❶,** C. Ezequiel Lopéz, 25, is a great place to grab sandwiches (€2.30-3.50), salads (€2.50-4.50), burgers, and 37 varieties of pizza (€4.60). (☎981 482 930. Open M-Sa 1-4pm and 9pm-midnight. Cash only.) **Buses** arrive outside the Caixa Galicia bank and leave from the **Banco de Galicia;** for updated schedules, call the **tourist office** on C. Ezequiel Lopéz, 17. (☎981 48 21 87. Open M-F 10:30am-1:30pm and 5-8pm, Sa 10:30am-2pm, second Su of every month noon-2pm.)

PORTUGAL

Portugal wears the ornaments of modernity and the artifacts of the past with equal elegance. With the oldest established borders in Europe, Portugal broke free from Moorish rule to reach great heights as a superpower during the Golden Age of discovery and imperial expansion, but plummeted to lows as a vassal under Spanish and French dominion. These extremes of fortune have contributed to the Portuguese concept of *saudade*, a yearning for people, places, and times that are gone, an idea that finds its greatest expression in the musical style *fado*. *Saudade* may be stitched into the soul of the nation, but Portugal is a vibrant country with pulsing cities, animated festivals, and a fervent passion for soccer. From the quiet forests of Douro and Minho to the rollicking coastal scene of the Algarve, cosmopolitan Lisboa to the sun-drenched, castle-dotted interior towns, the country is a treasure trove of landscapes, art, and architecture. Portugal has something to offer every traveler, including a sense of *saudade* when it comes time to leave.

HISTORY

In the 14th and 15th centuries, Portugal ruled a wealthy empire that stretched from America to Asia, and was one of the most powerful nations in the world. While the country's international prestige diminished with the Spanish invasion in 1580, the Portuguese people's pride did not, and they regained independence in 1640. Today national pride is as strong as ever: one need look no further than the emotional fanfare surrounding the 2008 European Football Championship and the 2006 World Cup semifinals for evidence. Modern Portugal, a country with a stable democracy, a growing economy, and a vibrant culture, has proven the strength of its national character.

EARLY HISTORY (8000 BC-AD 469). Settlement of Portugal began around 8000 BC when neolithic tribes arrived from Andalucía. The traditions of these hunters and fishermen evolved into the Megalithic culture that emerged in 2000 BC and left its mark in the necropolises scattered across the Beira Alta. During the first millennium BC, several tribes began to enter the Iberian Peninsula, including the **Celts,** who settled in northern Portugal and Galicia in the 9th century BC, and the **Phoenicians,** who founded fishing villages in the Algarve. The **Greeks** and **Carthaginians** soon followed in 600 BC, settling the southern and western coasts. The Romans gained control of Portugal in 140 BC and integrated the region into the Iberian province of Lusitania, which included the whole of Portugal and parts of western Spain. Six centuries of Roman rule ensued.

GIMME MOORS (469-1139). Rome's decline in the AD 3rd and 4th centuries had a heavy impact on the Iberian Peninsula. In the wake of diminished Roman power, the **Visigoths,** a wandering Germanic tribe, crossed the Pyrenees in 469 and dominated the peninsula for the next two centuries. In 711, Muslims (also known as **Moors**) invaded Iberia, toppling the Visigoth monarchy and establishing a foothold along the southern coast, which they called the *al-Gharb* (Algarve). Their 400-year rule left a legacy of agricultural advances, architectural landmarks, and linguistic and cultural trends.

THE RECONQUISTA AND THE BIRTH OF PORTUGAL (1139-1415). Though the Christian *Reconquista* officially began in 718, it didn't pick up steam until the 11th century, when Fernando I united Castilla and León, providing a strong base from which to reclaim territory for the Christians. At the same time, Portugal was fighting for its own sovereignty. The groundwork for this sovereignty was laid in the Battle of São Mamede in 1128, when **Dom Afonso Henriques (Afonso I)** declared independence from Castilla and León. The following year, after the victory over the Muslims in Ourique, Afonso named himself the first king of Portugal. Dom Afonso Henriques' legacy, the boundary between Spain and Portugal, is the oldest established border in Europe.

With the help of Christian military groups like the Knights Templar, the new monarchy battled Muslim forces, capturing Lisboa in 1147. By 1249, the forces of the *Reconquista* under **Afonso III** had defeated the last remnants of Muslim power with campaigns in the Alentejo and the Algarve. The Christian kings, led by **Dinis I** (1279-1325), promoted the Portuguese language above Spanish, and, with the **Treaty of Alcañices** (1297), settled border disputes with neighboring Castilla, asserting Portugal's identity as the first unified and independent nation in Europe.

João I (1385-1433), the first king of the House of Aviz, ushered in a period of unity and prosperity. Dom João increased the power of the crown, establishing a strong base for future Portuguese expansion and economic success. The Anglo-Portuguese alliance, secured with the **Treaty of Windsor** (1386) and João's marriage to Phillipa of Lancaster, influenced Portugal's foreign policy well into the 19th century.

PORTUGAL SAILS THE OCEAN BLUE (1415-1580). The 15th century was one of the greatest eras of imperial expansion in Portuguese history. Under the leadership of João's son, **Prince Henry the Navigator,** Portugal became a world leader in exploration and trade. Portuguese adventurers captured the Moroccan city of Ceuta in 1415, discovered Madeira (and scurvy) in 1419, happened upon the uninhabited Açores in 1427, and began to exploit the African coast for riches. Lagos became Europe's first slave market in 1441. In 1488, **Bartolomeu Dias** opened the route to the East and paved the way for Portuguese entry into the spice trade when he rounded Africa's Cape of Storms, later renamed the Cape of Good Hope.

The Portuguese monarchs may have rejected **Christopher Columbus,** but they funded many other momentous voyages. In 1497, they supported **Vasco da Gama,** who led the first European naval expedition to India. Successive expeditions put numerous East African and Indian colonies under Portuguese control. (The colonies were less than thrilled about this, as revolts would often prove.) Three years after da Gama's voyage, **Pedro Álvares Cabral** claimed Brazil for Portugal, establishing a far-flung empire. Portugal's international power peaked during the reign of **Dom Manuel I the Fortunate** (1495-1521). Under Manuel, known as "the King of Gold,"

8000 BC
Neolithic tribes settle in Portugal.

1000 BC
Portugal's love affair with *bacalhau* (cod) officially begins with the arrival of Phoenician fishermen.

200 BC
Romans invade the Iberian Peninsula, gaining control of Portugal half a century later.

AD 469
Visigoths cross the Pyrenees and invade Iberia.

711
The Moors settle in the area they called the al-Gharb (Algarve).

718
The *Reconquista* begins.

1139
Dom Afonso Henriques declares Portuguese independence from Spain and crowns himself king.

1279-1325
Dinis I reigns and writes copious amounts of poetry in the Portuguese language.

1386
The Treaty of Windsor is signed, assuring centuries of cooperation between Britain and Portugal.

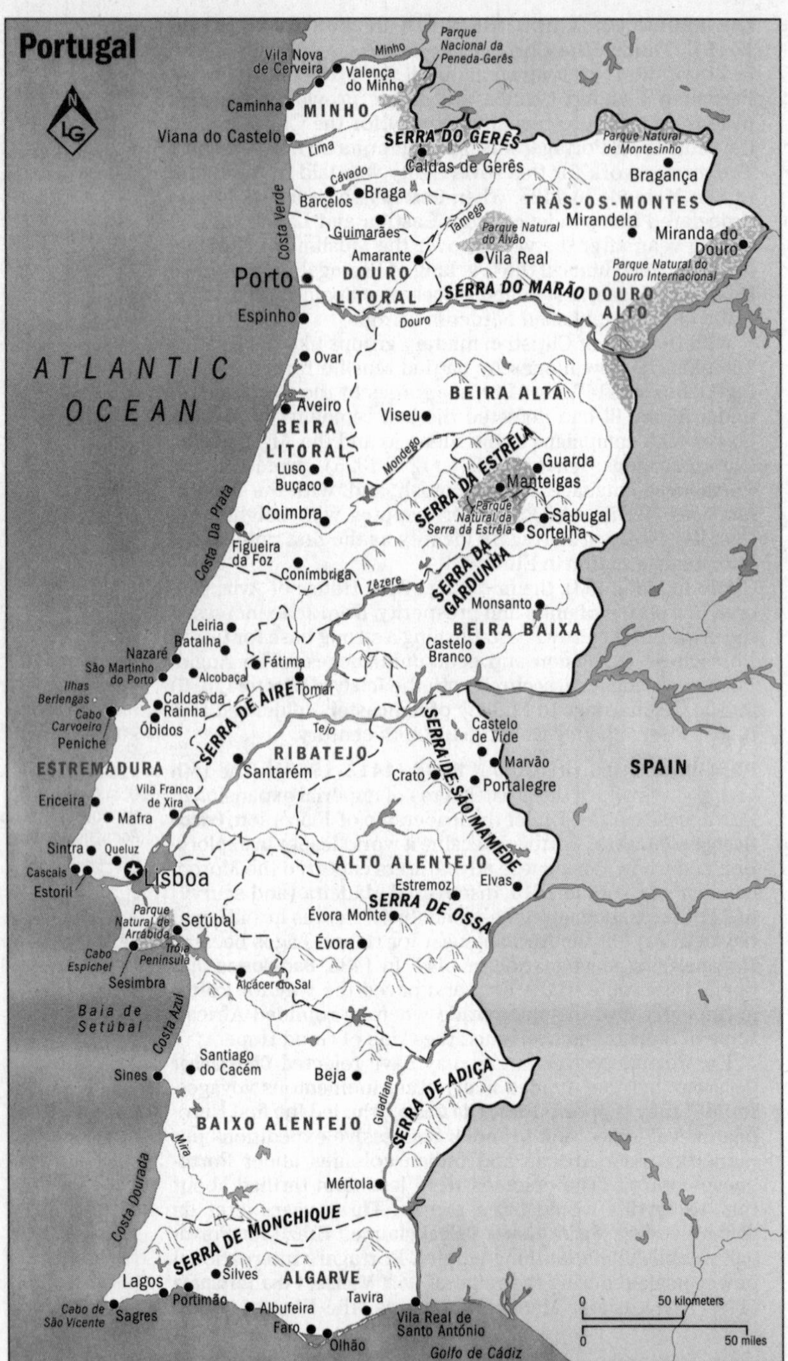
Portugal
ATLANTIC OCEAN
SPAIN
MINHO
TRÁS-OS-MONTES
DOURO LITORAL
DOURO ALTO
BEIRA ALTA
BEIRA LITORAL
BEIRA BAIXA
ESTREMADURA
RIBATEJO
ALTO ALENTEJO
BAIXO ALENTEJO
ALGARVE
SERRA DO GERÊS
SERRA DO MARÃO
SERRA DA ESTRÊLA
SERRA DA GARDUNHA
SERRA DE AIRE
SERRA DE SÃO MAMEDE
SERRA DE OSSA
SERRA DE ADIÇA
SERRA DE MONCHIQUE
Parque Nacional da Peneda-Gerês
Parque Natural de Montesinho
Parque Natural do Alvão
Parque Natural do Douro Internacional
Parque Natural da Serra da Estrêla
Parque Natural de Arrábida
Minho
Lima
Cávado
Tamega
Douro
Mondego
Zêzere
Tejo
Guadiana
Mira
Costa Verde
Costa Da Prata
Costa Azul
Costa Dourada
Vila Nova de Cerveira
Valença do Minho
Caminha
Viana do Castelo
Caldas de Gerês
Bragança
Barcelos
Braga
Guimarães
Mirandela
Miranda do Douro
Amarante
Vila Real
Porto
Espinho
Ovar
Aveiro
Viseu
Guarda
Luso
Buçaco
Manteigas
Coimbra
Sabugal
Sortelha
Figueira da Foz
Conímbriga
Monsanto
Leiria
Batalha
Castelo Branco
Nazaré
São Martinho do Porto
Alcobaça
Fátima
Tomar
Ilhas Berlengas
Caldas da Rainha
Cabo Carvoeiro
Óbidos
Peniche
Castelo de Vide
Santarém
Marvão
Crato
Portalegre
Vila Franca de Xira
Ericeira
Mafra
Sintra
Queluz
Cascais
Lisboa
Estoril
Estremoz
Elvas
Setúbal
Évora Monte
Évora
Cabo Espichel
Tróia Peninsula
Sesimbra
Alcácer do Sal
Baia de Setúbal
Santiago do Cacém
Sines
Beja
Mértola
Silves
Lagos
Portimão
Albufeira
Tavira
Cabo de São Vicente
Sagres
Faro
Olhão
Vila Real de Santo António
Golfo de Cádiz
0
50 kilometers
0
50 miles

Portugal controlled vast tracts of land and the riches these lands contained. One of the greatest feats of Portuguese navigation occurred at the end of Manuel's rule, when Fernão de Magalhães, known as **Magellan,** completed the first circumnavigation of the globe in 1521.

BRING ON THE BRAGANÇA (1580-1801). Competition from other commercial powers with alternative routes to the east eventually took its toll, and the House of Aviz lost its predominance in 1580. After a succession crisis, the Habsburg King of Spain, **Felipe II,** claimed the Portuguese throne, and the Iberian Peninsula was briefly ruled by one monarch. Over the course of the next 60 years, the Habsburgs dragged Portugal into several ill-fated wars, including the Spanish Armada's crushing loss to England in 1588. After initial good relations, King Felipe began to neglect his smaller domain, and Portugal quickly lost much of its once-vast empire. In 1640, however, the **House of Bragança** engineered a nationalist rebellion against the unfortunate monarch. After a brief struggle, the House of Bragança assumed control, asserting Portuguese independence from Spain. To secure sovereignty, the Bragança dynasty went to great lengths to reestablish ties with England. In 1661, Portugal ceded Bombay to England, and the marriage of Catherine of Bragança to England's Charles II cemented the Portuguese-British alliance. Nearly half a century later, **João V** (1706-1750) restored a measure of prosperity for Portugal, if not Brazil, using newly mined gold and diamonds from the colony to finance massive building projects in the mother country, including the construction of extravagant palaces. The bulk of the architecture did not survive the momentous **earthquake of 1755,** which struck during Mass, devastating Lisboa and southern Portugal, not to mention rattling the clergy and intellectuals of Europe. Fires, started by the overturned votive candles in churches, raged throughout the city, ultimately killing over 60,000 people. Dictatorial minister **Marquês de Pombal** was able to rebuild Lisboa, repairing widespread damage and reshaping the royal government while he was at it.

BACK AND FORTH (1807-1910). Napoleon took control of France in 1801 and set his sights on the rest of Europe. When he reached Portugal six years later, his army encountered little resistance. The Portuguese royal family opted for flight over fight and escaped to Brazil. **Dom João VI** returned to Lisboa in 1821, only to face an extremely unstable political climate. Amidst turmoil within the royal family, João's son **Pedro** declared Brazil's independence, becoming the country's first ruler. The Constitution of 1822, drawn up in Portugal during the royal family's absence, severely limited the power of the monarchy. After 1826, the **War of the Two Brothers** (1828-1834) between constitutionalists (supporting Pedro, the new king of Brazil) and monarchists (supporting Miguel, Pedro's younger brother) divided the country over the question of the Portuguese throne. Six gory years later, Pedro's daughter **María II** (1834-1853) ascended the throne at the tender age

1415
Ceuta conquered; Prince Henry the Navigator fosters Portuguese overseas expansion.

1495-1521
Dom Manuel I the Fortunate reigns.

1498
Vasco da Gama lands in India.

1500
Pedro Alvares Cabral claims Brazil for Portugal.

1519
Portuguese-born explorer Magellan sets sail around the globe on Spain's dime.

1580-1598
Spaniard Felipe II reigns as King of Portugal.

1588
Portugal is dragged into Spain's conflict with England; the Iberian armadas are crushed.

1640
The House of Bragança leads the reassertion of independence from Spain.

1706-1750
João V, bolstered by gold extracted from Brazil, builds new palaces and academies in Portugal.

1755
A massive earthquake shakes Portugal, destroying Lisboa and killing up to 100,000.

1807
The royal family flees for Brazil as Napoleon's forces approach the border.

1828-1834
Sibling rivalry and political strife collide in the War of the Two Brothers.

1839
Construction begins on Sintra's Palacio da Pena.

1869
Portugal abolishes slavery.

1916
Portugal joins the Allies in World War I.

1917
Three children claim to see the Virgin Mary in Fatima and receive her secret message.

1932
António de Oliveira Salazar begins his 36-year regime as prime minister and dictator.

1974
Caetano is overthrown in the Carnation Revolution.

1976
Free and open elections are held in Portugal for the first time in history. Mario Soares becomes prime minister.

1986
Portugal joins the European Community.

of 15. The next 75 years were marked by continued tension between liberals and monarchists.

SUPER SALAZAR (1910-1970). Portugal spent the early years of the 20th century trying to recover from the political discord of the 19th century. On October 5, 1910, the king, 20-year-old **Dom Manuel II,** fled to England in search of amnesty; the military officers and middle classes that overthrew him soon set up the **First Republic.** Their aim of a stable, bourgeois democracy was soon derailed by tensions with the Church, and the republic gained worldwide disapproval for its expulsion of the Jesuits and other religious orders. Additionally, conflict between the government and labor movements undermined domestic stability. Portugal's decision to enter **World War I** on the side of the Allies proved economically fatal and internally divisive, despite the eventual victory. The weak republic teetered and eventually fell in a 1926 military coup. General **António Carmona** took over as leader of the provisional military government and, in the face of financial crisis, appointed **António de Oliveira Salazar,** a prominent economics professor, as minister of finance. In 1932, Salazar became prime minister, but soon devolved into a dictator. His *Estado Novo* (New State) granted suffrage to women, but was otherwise rigidly traditionalist and authoritarian. During this period, society was frozen around the ideal of "God, Fatherland, and Family," only opening to the outside world and economic growth near the regime's end. A terrifying secret police, *Polícia Internacional e de Defesa do Estado* (PIDE) crushed all opposition to Salazar's rule, and rebellions in the African colonies were quelled in bloody battles.

YOU SAY YOU WANT A REVOLUTION (1974-2000). The slightly more liberal prime minister **Marcelo Caetano** continued the unpopular African wars after Salazar's death in 1970. In just a few years, international disapproval of Portuguese imperialism and the army's dissatisfaction with colonial entanglements led **General António de Spinola** to call for decolonization. On April 25, 1974, a left-wing military coalition calling itself the Armed Forces Movement overthrew Caetano in a quick coup. This **Carnation Revolution** sent citizens dancing into the streets, and put a "Rua 25 de Abril" in nearly every town in Portugal. The Marxist-dominated armed forces granted civil and political liberties and withdrew claims on the country's African colonies by 1975, resulting in the immigration of over 500,000 refugees.

The socialist government nationalized several industries and seized large estates in the face of substantial opposition, but would soon back off from outright Marxism. The country's first elections, in 1976, put the charismatic socialist prime minister **Mario Soares** into power. When a severe economic crisis hit, Soares instituted "100 measures in 100 days" to shock Portugal into shape. In 1986, Portugal was admitted into the European Community, bringing it into the European fold. Despite losing the premiership to the center-right Social Democratic Party (PSD) in the previous year, Soares then became the nation's first civilian president in 60 years. Soares was eventually replaced by the Socialist former mayor of Lisboa, **Jorge Sampaio,** in 1996.

CURRENT EVENTS

The **European Union** declared Portugal a full member of the EU Economic and Monetary Union (EMU) in 1999, and the nation continues its quest to close the economic gap with the rest of Western Europe. Political integration was furthered during Portugal's tenure as President of the Council of the European Union in 2007. In 1999, Portugal ceded **Macau,** its last overseas territory, to the Chinese. Portugal and Indonesia have agreed to cooperate over the reconstruction of East Timor, formerly a Portuguese colony.

1988
Marathoner Rosa Mota takes the gold for Portugal in the 1988 Olympic Games.

Jorge Sampaio returned to the presidency after the January 2001 parliamentary elections, but Socialist prime minister **António Guterres** resigned in December of 2001, just after overseeing Portugal's successful transition to the euro. President Sampaio then appointed Social Democrat **Jose Manuel Durão Barroso** as prime minister. Barroso resigned the post in July 2004 to accept the Presidency of the European Commission. **Pedro Santana Lopez,** of the same party, took his place but lost the post to **José Sócrates,** the leader of the Socialist party, in March 2005. The presidential elections of 2006 named **Aníbal Cavaco Silva,** who had lost to President Sampaio in the 1996 presidential elections, as the next head of state.

2002
Jose Manuel Durao Barroso becomes prime minister only to leave two years later to become President of the European Commission.

PORTUGAL

In 2004, Portugal hosted the **European Football Championship.** In preparation, local transportation, such as the Lisboa metro system and national rail lines, was vastly improved. On the other hand, Portugal has encountered challenges to its economy. In 2005, a severe drought hit the Algarve region, hampering agriculture and tourism, which together account for more than 60% of Portugal's employment. The drought also resulted in uncontrollable wildfires.

2004
Portugal hosts the European Football Championship; much drunken cheering ensues.

2007
The Africa-EU Summit takes place in Lisboa.

FURTHER READING.

A Concise History of Portugal, by David Birmingham (1993). An amazing amount of historical and cultural information in one volume.

Prince Henry 'the Navigator,' by Peter Russell (2000). A debunking of numerous myths about one of Portugal's most misunderstood leaders.

Journey to Portugal, by José Saramago (1990). A literary examination of Portugal from the Nobel Prize-winning author.

PEOPLE AND CULTURE

LANGUAGE

Although this softer sister of Spanish is closely related to the other Romance languages, modern Portuguese is an amalgamation of diverse influences. The majority of Portuguese is derived from Latin, but the Moorish occupation also left behind Arabic echoes. A close listener will also find hints of English,

LOOKING BACK

Portugal emerged from Antonio de Oliveira Salazar's dictatorship (1932-1974) far behind much of Europe. Although physical results of the dictatorship remain evident in broken windows, unpaved roads, worn-down buildings, and murals of political slogans, the effects on the people are not as easy to see or understand.

Chatting with a senior citizen gave me insight into how life has changed for older generations. Sitting at an oak table in a century-old house with my octogenarian friend, Maria, I was shocked to learn that a mere 15 years ago her town, only an hour's drive from Lisboa, had no running water, no electricity, and no paved roads. Living in the grasp of a harsh dictatorship, she said, was like living in another universe.

Before democracy, many citizens, including Maria, did not realize other religions besides Catholicism existed. The opening of the political sphere has allowed for more religious freedom, but progress has been slow. Even though it has been decades since Salazar ruled, marriages sanctioned by non-Catholic churches were only recently recognized by the state. The process of understanding and accepting others is in many ways just beginning in Portugal. Older generations are curious about how younger generations understand the world and about where they will guide it.

—Illiana Quimbaya

Italian, French, and even Slavic languages. Portugal's global escapades spread the language to other regions, from Brazil in South America to Macau in China. Today, Portuguese (the world's sixth most-spoken language) unites over 200 million people worldwide, most of them in Portugal, Brazil, Mozambique, and Angola. Some travelers may be heartened to know that English, Spanish, and French are widely spoken throughout Portugal, especially in tourist-oriented locales. The *Let's Go* **Phrasebook** (p. 765) contains useful phrases in Portuguese, and the **Glossary** (p. 765) lists terms used in this guide.

RELIGION

Though the constitution mandates that there be no state religion in Portugal, roughly 85% of the Portuguese population identifies as Roman Catholic, though a large number are non-practicing. A major force in shaping Portugal's history, the Catholic Church still influences present-day Portugal; cathedrals dot the cities and *romarias* (festivals honoring patron saints), are celebrated everywhere. Portugal is also home to communities of Protestants, Jehovah's Witnesses, and Mormons, as well as 40,000 Muslims and a few hundred Jews.

FOOD AND DRINK

The Portuguese season their dishes with the basics of Mediterranean cuisine: olive oil, garlic, herbs, and sea salt. Cumin and coriander are especially popular, and dishes can be quite spicy. Pork, potatoes, and pastries are the omnipresent Holy Trinity of Portuguese cuisine, although each region has its own distinctive culinary traditions.

LOCAL FARE

LISBOA AND THE NORTH. The cuisine of Northern Portugal reflects its geography. Open ocean and lush forests provide for delicious seafood, game, and produce. Small farms produce succulent sausages, as well as distinctive *queijos* (cheeses) like Serra da Estrela, which is made in the region of the same name (p. 695). This cheese is so soft that it is typically eaten with a spoon. Excellent produce means that *sopas* (soups) are usually made from local vegetables. Common varieties include *caldo de ovos* (bean soup with hard-boiled eggs), *caldo de verdura* (vegetable soup), and the famous *caldo verde* (a potato and kale mixture with a slice of sausage and olive oil). Portugal's delectable *broa* (cornbread) is at its best in this region. For dessert, dine on *pasteis de nata* (custard tarts) in Belém (p. 604), *queijadas da Sapa* (cheese tarts) in Sintra (p. 609), and egg yolk-based sweets just about everywhere.

ALGARVE. Miles of coastline have established fresh seafood as the core of the cuisine in this area. While *bacalhau* (cod) is undoubtedly the fish of choice for most Portuguese, *choco grelhado* (grilled cuttlefish) and *peixe espada* (swordfish) are also excellent. More adventurous diners should try the *polvo* (boiled or grilled octopus) and *lulas grelhadas* (grilled squid). In Lagos (p. 616), dishes served *em cataplana* (in a clam-shaped steaming dish) are an expensive treat. For the more economically savvy, *caldierada* is a fish stew that is sure to satisfy any traveler. Marzipan made with almonds from local groves are reminders of the region's Moorish legacy. The Algarve is also known for its oranges and figs. For something different, try *pêras* (pears) drenched in sweet port wine and served with raisins and hazelnuts on top. *Pastelarias* (bakeries) are in most towns, and provide a cheap and tasty breakfast.

ALENTEJO. The arid plains of central Portugal lend themselves to ranching rather than farming. Pork, chicken, and beef appear on most menus, often combined in *cozida à portuguesa* (boiled beef, pork, sausage, and vegetables), or served with heavy sauces and other embellishments. True connoisseurs add a drop of *piri-piri* (chili pepper sauce) to their *cozida* (meat and vegetable stew). This sauce also adds a kick to *frango assado* (roast chicken), which competes with *bacalhau* (cod) for the title of Portugal's favorite dish. A more expensive delicacy is roasted *cabrito* (goat). Hearty bread-based soups like *açorda à alentejana* (Alentejan stew) round out the menu, or could be a meal in themselves. No matter what you order, leave room for the *batatas* (potatoes), prepared countless ways, that accompany every meal.

DRINKS

The exact birth date of Portuguese wine is unknown, although 5000 BC is a good estimate. It may not be an international star, but the quality and low cost of Portuguese *vinho* (wine) is truly astounding. The best of them all, *vinho do porto* (port), pressed by foot from the red grapes of the **Douro Valley** (p. 664) and fermented with a touch of brandy, is a dessert in itself. When chilled, white port can be a snappy aperitif, while ruby or tawny port is an after-dinner classic. The island of Madeira produces its own popular wine, heated for six months before bottling. Sparkling *vinho verde* comes in either red or white—its name refers to the wine's age, rather than the color. Excellent local table wines include *Colares*, *Dão*, *Borba*, *Bairrada*, *Bucelas*, and *Periquita*. If you can't decide, experiment with the *vinho de casa* (house wine), either the *tinto* (red) or the *branco* (white). Tangy *sangria* comes filled with fresh orange slices and makes a meal festive at minimal expense. Your Portuguese drinking vocabulary should contain the terms: *claro* (new wine), *espumante* (sparkling wine), *rosado* (rose wine), *vinho de mesa* (table wine), and *vinho verde* (young wine).

Bottled Sagres, Cristal, and Super Bock are excellent beers. If you don't ask for it *fresco* (cool), it may come *natural* (room temperature). A tall, slim glass of draft beer is called a *fino* or an *imperial*, while a larger stein is a *caneca*. To sober up, order a *bica* (espresso), a *galão* (coffee with milk, served in a glass), or a *café com leite* (coffee with milk, served in a cup).

A SWEET GUIDE

You've probably found yourself ogling the glass display case of Portugal's many *pastelarias* wondering which tempting treat to pick. Wonder no more with this quick guide to sugar heaven:

Altreia: a sweet and simple treat from Northern Portugal made of pasta cooked with eggs and sugar topped with cinnamon.

Arroz-doce: sweet rice. There are an infinite number of variations on this simple rice pudding, so try it wherever you go!

Bolinhos: balls of cake filled with cream and/or dried fruit.

Bolinhos de Jerimu: pumpkin, egg, and Port wine fried to sweet perfection. Yum.

Dolce de Ovos: Aveiro's sweet made of egg yolk and sugar.

Pão-de-ló: the Portuguese version of sponge cake.

Pastel de Natas: petit pastries filled with cinnamon cream, also known as *pastel de Belém.*

Pastel de Santa Clara: star-shaped puffs filled with almond cream from the northeast.

Rabanadas: thick slices of bread soaked in milk (or wine), tossed in sugar, and fried.

Pão de Deus: sweet bread topped with a pineapple and coconut concoction. Add butter and the bread melts in your mouth while the shredded coconut gives a slight crunch. God's bread indeed.

MEALS AND DINING HOURS

Portuguese eat their hearty midday meal—*almoço* (lunch)—between noon and 2pm, and *jantar* (dinner) between 8pm and midnight. Breakfast in Portugal is typically a small affair—a pastry from a *pastelaria* (bakery) and *cafezinho* (espresso) from a cafe usually suffice for *pequeno almoço* (literally, "small lunch"). If you get the munchies between 4 and 7pm, snack bars sell *sandes* (sandwiches) and sweet cakes. It is advisable to make reservations when dining in some of the more upscale city restaurants. A full meal costs €6-15, depending on the restaurant's location and quality. *Meia dose* (half-portions) cost more than half-price but are often more than adequate. The ubiquitous *prato do dia* (special of the day) or *ementa* (menu) of appetizer, bread, entree, dessert, and beverage will satisfy even the largest appetite. Standard pre-meal bread, butter, cheese, and *pâté* may be served without your asking, but these pre-meal munchies are not free (€1-3 per person). You may appreciate them, however, since chefs start cooking only after you order, so be prepared to wait. Smoking is somewhat accepted in most establishments, although signs stating "*proibido fumar*" (no smoking) are more and more common. A ban on public smoking was enacted in May 2007 but was revised shortly after and came into effect in January 2008.

CUSTOMS AND ETIQUETTE

The Portuguese are generally friendly, easygoing, and receptive to foreign travelers. Even if your Portuguese is a little rusty, a wholehearted attempt at speaking the native tongue will be appreciated.

TABOOS. Shorts and flip-flops may be seen as disrespectful in some public establishments and rural areas, even during a heat wave. Though dress in Portugal is more casual in the hot summer months than in the cold of winter, strapless tops on women and collarless t-shirts on men are generally unacceptable. Skimpy clothes are always a taboo in churches, as are tourist visits during masses or services. Do not automatically assume that Spanish will be understood by the Portuguese; while many Portuguese do speak Spanish, one of the best ways to offend a local is to tacitly suggest that Portugal is part of Spain.

PUBLIC BEHAVIOR. On any list of Portuguese values, politeness would be at the top. Be sure to address a Portuguese as *senhor* (Mr.), *senhora* (Ms.), or *senhora dona* (Mrs.), followed by the first name. To blend in, it's a good idea to be as formal as possible at first meeting. Introduce yourself in detail, giving more than just your name. You'll be welcomed openly and made to feel at home if you mention who you are, where you're from, and what you are doing in Portugal. Don't be surprised if you get pecked on both cheeks by younger Portuguese, but handshakes are generally the standard introductory gesture.

TIPPING. In restaurants, a service charge *(serviço)* of 10% is usually included in the bill. When service is not included, it is customary to leave 5-10% as a tip. It is also common to barter in markets.

THE ARTS

ARCHITECTURE

PREHISTORIC ARCHITECTURE. The largest prehistoric remains in Portugal are at Valverde, near Évora. These **dolmens,** or ancient tombs, complement the town's later architectural styles manifest in the Celtic round stone houses, Roman forums, and the temple of Diana. Romanesque cathedrals can also be found in Lisboa (p. 579), Porto (p. 664), and Coimbra (p. 684), while Alcobaça (p. 651) and Batalha (p. 655) feature Gothic-style monasteries.

MANUELINE STYLE. Portugal's signature **Manueline** style celebrates the prosperity and imperial expansion of Dom Manuel I's reign (p. 567). Manueline works merge Christian images and maritime motifs, such as shells, coral, waves, fish, anchors, and ropes, with lavish Gothic, Plateresque, and Moorish-influenced ornaments. The **Torre de Belém** (p. 606), an elaborate expression of Manueline style, was built by King João II as a defense fortress. Close seconds are the **Mosteiro dos Jerónimos** (p. 605) in Belém and the **Mosteiro Santa Maria de Vitória** (p. 656) in Batalha, both grand testaments to Portugal's imperial success.

AZULEJOS. Few Moorish structures survived the *Reconquista*, but the style influenced later Portuguese architecture. One of these most beautiful traditions is that of the colorfully painted ceramic tiles **(azulejos)** that grace walls and ceilings. These ornate tiles, originally carved in relief by the Moors, later took on Flemish designs. Contrary to popular belief, their name comes not from the color, *azul* (blue), but rather from the Arabic word *azulayj* (little stone). Lisboa's **Museu Nacional do Azulejo** (p. 599) showcases *azulejo* collections.

PAINTING AND SCULPTURE

THE AGE OF DISCOVERY. The 15th and 16th centuries saw vast cultural exchange with Renaissance Europe and beyond. Flemish masters like **Jan van Eyck** brought their talent to Portugal, and many Portuguese artists polished their skills in Antwerp, Belgium. One result of this exchange was the emergence of a group of painters known as the **Lisbon School,** which included Gregorio Lopes, Garcia Fernandes, and Dom Manuel's favorite artist, **Jorge Afonso.** Afonso stood out for his realistic portrayals of human anatomy, and today his best works hang at the **Convento de Cristo** in Tomar (p. 661) and the **Convento da Madre de Deus** in Lisboa (p. 599). In the late 15th century, the talented **Nuno Gonçalves** led a revival of the primitivist school, which is characterized by simple forms rendered in bold, primary colors.

THE BAROQUE ERA. Portuguese Baroque art featured even more diverse styles and themes. Wood-carving became extremely popular in Portugal during the

PORTUGAL

Baroque period. **Joachim Machado** carved elaborate *crèches* (figurines of the nativity) in the early 1700s. On canvas, portraiture became a hallmark of Portuguese painting. The prolific 19th-century artist **Domingos António de Sequeira** depicted historical, religious, and allegorical subjects using a technique that would later inspire French Impressionists. Many of Sequeira's works can be found in Mafra (p. 606) and throughout palaces and churches in Lisboa. Portugal has also seen its share of sculptors as well as carvers and painters. Porto's prominent **António Soares dos Reis** brought his Romantic sensibility to 19th-century Portuguese sculpture. His work went largely unappreciated in his lifetime, however, and the sculptor ultimately committed suicide.

PRESENT DAY. In the 20th century, Cubism, Expressionism, and Futurism trickled into Portugal despite Salazar-instituted censorship. More recently, the late **Maria Helena Vieira da Silva** won international recognition for her abstract works, and the master **Carlos Botelho** gained international renown for his wonderful vignettes of Lisboa life before his death in 1982.

LITERATURE

THE RENAISSANCE. Portuguese literature blossomed during the Renaissance, most notably in the letters of **Francisco de Sá de Miranda** (1481-1558) and the poetry of **António Ferreira** (1528-1569). **Luís de Camões** (1524-1580) celebrated Vasco da Gama's sea voyages to India in Portugal's greatest epic, *Os Lusíadas (The Lusiads;* 1572), modeled on the *Aeneid.*

NINETEENTH-CENTURY REBIRTH. Portugal's imperial decline was paralleled in the literature of the 17th and 18th centuries. The 19th century, however, saw a dramatic rebirth led by poet **João Baptista de Almeida Garrett** (1799-1854), the leader of the romantic movement in Portugal and a twice-exiled political liberal. Political thinkers dominated the crop of literary intelligentsia in the **Generation of 1870,** shifting the focus literature from the romantic to the realist. The most visible influence on this shift was novelist and life-long diplomat **José Maria Eça de Queiroz.** He conceived a distinctly Portuguese social realism often critical of the bourgeois elements of 19th-century Portugal. His most famous work was *O Crime do Padre Amaro* (*The Sin of Father Amaro;* 1876).

PESSOA AND THE MODERN TRADITION. Fernando Pessoa (1888-1935), Portugal's most famous writer and poet of the late 19th and early 20th centuries, wrote in English and Portuguese under four different names: Pessoa, Alberto Caeiro, Ricardo Reis, and Alvaro de Campos; each alias is associated with a different writing style. His semi-autobiography, *Livro do Desassossego* (*The Book of Disquiet;* 1982) his only prose work, was posthumously compiled and is viewed today as a modernist classic.

RECENT WORKS. Portugal's literary tradition continues to thrive in the contemporary era, as writers like Miguel Torga have gained international fame for their satirical novels. **José Saramago,** winner of the 1998 Nobel Prize for Literature, is Portugal's most important living writer. His work, written in a realist style and laced with irony, has achieved new acclaim in the post-Salazar era, dominating in all genres from the dystopian parable of *Blindness* (1998) to the historical fiction of *Baltasar and Blimunda* (1987). The end of the dictatorship also saw the emergence of female writers. In *Novas Cartas Portuguesas* (1972), collectively written by Maria Barreno, Maria Horta, and Maria Velho da Costa, the three female protagonists expose the mistreatment of women in a patriarchal society. Other acclaimed post-Salazar authors include **António Lobo Antunes** and **José Cardoso Pires.** Antunes is known for his scattered style and psychoanalytic themes. Pires, known for his 'cinematic' style, often commented on the repression of the Salazar regime.

FURTHER READING. For Portuguese classics, check out Literature (p. 576). The more famous works have been translated into English.

Ballad of Dogs' Beach, by Jose Cardoso Pires (1986). Examines the terror of Salazar's secret police.

The Last Kabbalist of Lisbon, by Richard Zimler (1998). A murder mystery that explores the world of Portugal's 16th-century Jewish mystics.

The History of the Siege of Lisbon, by José Saramago (1989). A subversive and allegorical perspective on Portuguese history by the Nobel Laureate.

PORTUGAL

MUSIC

FADO. **Fado** (FAH-doo) is a musical tradition unique to Portugal, identified by a sense of *saudade*, meaning pining or nostalgia. Literally translated as "fate," *fado* is characterized by tragic, romantic lyrics and mournful melodies. Supposedly, these songs of longing were originally sung by fishwives whose husbands were at sea. Lisboa and Coimbra are now the most active centers for this tradition, but the two regional styles differ sharply. Lisboa's singers tend to be female, and the songs are up-tempo, while almost all *fado* singers in Coimbra are male and the tunes are more tearful. Solo ballads, accompanied by the *guitarra portuguesa* (a flat-backed guitar similar to a mandolin), appeal to the romantic side of Portuguese culture. **Amália Rodrigues** (1920-1999) gained international renown as a singer of *fado* and Portuguese folk music. **Mariza,** Portugal's answer to Madonna, continues the tradition today, alongside more conventional pop artists of Portuguese descent, like Nelly Furtado.

CLASSICAL. Apart from its folk tradition, the music of Portugal has yet to achieve international fame. Portuguese opera peaked with **António José da Silva** (1705-1739), a victim of the 1739 Inquisition. The Renaissance in Portugal led to the development of pieces geared for solo instrumentalists and vocals. Coimbra's **Carlos Seixas** thrilled 18th-century Lisboa with his genius, and contributed to the development of the sonata. **João Domingos Bomtempo** (1775-1842) introduced symphonic innovations from abroad and established the *Sociedade Filarmónica*, modeled on the London Philharmonic, in Lisboa in 1822.

In the late 19th century, **Joly Braga Santo** led a modern revival of Portuguese classical music. The Calouste Gulbenkian Foundation in Lisboa has also kept Portuguese music alive, sponsoring a symphony orchestra since 1962 and hosting local folk singers (including Fausto and Sérgio Godinho), ballets, operas, and jazz festivals. The **Teatro Nacional de São Carlos,** with its own orchestra and ballet company, has further bolstered Portuguese music. The Teatro has spawned a group of talented young composers, including **Filipe Pires, Antonio Vitorino d'Almeida,** and **Jorge Peixinho,** all of whom have begun to make their mark in international competitions.

THE MEDIA

Portugal's most widely read daily newspapers are *Público* (www.publico.pt), *Diário de Notícas* (www.dn.sapo.pt), and *Jornal de Notícas* (www.jn.sapo.pt). If you haven't mastered Portuguese, check out *The News* (www.the-news.net), Portugal's only online English-language newspaper. Those interested in international news can also pick up day-old foreign papers at larger newsstands.

Portuguese TV offers four main channels: the state-run Canal 1 and TV2, and the private SIC (Sociedade Independente de Communicação) and TVI (TV Independente). Couch potatoes can also enjoy numerous cable channels, most airing Brazilian and Portuguese soap operas and subtitled foreign sitcoms.

SPORTS

Futebol is the game of choice for just about all Portuguese sports fans. Team Portugal has had its moments in the sun—the national team took second in the 2004 European Championships and garnered a third-place finish in 2000 at the European Championship with the help of Luis Figo and goldenboy Cristiano Ronaldo. However, the team has also fallen short at crucial moments, like at the World Cup 1998 qualifications, the semifinals of the World Cup in 2006, and the 2008 European Championship quarterfinals. Portugal hosted the 2004 European Championship, in which Greece emerged victorious over Portugal in the final match. Lisboa's **Benfica,** with some of the world's best players, including American sensation Freddy Adu, has not only an avid Portuguese fan base but also a substantial international following.

Portuguese athletes have also made names for themselves in long-distance running. Marathon queen **Rosa Mota** dominated her event during the 1980s, and runner **Carlos Lopes** brought home Portugal's first Olympic gold medal at the 1984 games. Besides jogging and pick-up soccer, the Portuguese often turn to the sea. Wind, body, and conventional **surfers** make waves along the northern coast, while **snorkelers** and **scuba divers** set out to the south and west.

NATIONAL HOLIDAYS

The following table lists the national holidays for 2009.

DATE	FESTIVAL
January 1	Dia do Ano Novo (New Year's Day)
January 6	Dia do Reis (Epiphany)
February 24	Carnaval (Carnival)
April 3-12	Semana Santa (Holy Week)
April 9	Senhor Ecce Homo (Maundy Thursday)
April 10	Sexta-feira Santa (Good Friday)
April 12	Páscoa (Easter)
April 25	Dia de 25 Abril (Liberation Day)
May 1	Dia do Trabalhador (Labor Day)
June 10	Dia de Camões (Portugal Day)
June 11	Corpo de Deus (Corpus Christi)
August 15	Assunção (Feast of the Assumption)
October 5	Dia da República (Republic Day)
November 1	Dia de Todos Santos (All Saints' Day)
December 8	A Conceição Imaculada (Feast of the Immaculate Conception)
December 25	Festa de Natal (Christmas)
December 31	Noite Velha (New Year's Eve)

LISBOA

At sunset, the scarlet glow cast over the Rio Tejo is matched by the ruby red shimmer inside your glass of vinho do porto. Welcome to Lisboa. A magnificent history has left its mark upon this ancient city: illustrious bronze figures stand proud in open plazas, Roman arches and columns inspire reverence in visitors, and a towering 12th-century castle keeps watch from atop one of the city's infamous seven hills. Lisboa is quickly becoming one of the most talked-about capitals in Europe, driven by cutting-edge fashion, flourishing art and music scenes, and relentlessly enthusiastic nightlife. Graffiti adorns the time-worn walls of Bairro Alto and Santa Catarina, and at night the cobblestone sidewalks echo with the modern rhythms of local clubs. A monumental past may loom over every corner of the city, but Lisboa is thriving in the present. Immigrants and visitors from all around the world give Lisboa an international feel that is hard to come by anywhere else in Portugal. Crowds of unique people—street performers, break dancers, and peddlers of various sorts—line the streets of Baixa and Bairro Alto, giving the city its diverse and distinctive flavor.

Complexity is not new to Lisboa. Half a dozen civilizations claim parenthood of the city, beginning with the Phoenicians, Greeks, and Carthaginians. The Romans arrived in 205 BC and ruled for 600 years. Under Julius Caesar, Lisboa became one of the most important port cities in Lusitania, and in 1255, Lisboa was made the capital of Portugal. The city, along with the empire, reached its zenith at the end of the 15th century, when Portuguese navigators pioneered explorations of Asia, Africa, and South America during the Age of Discovery. A catastrophic earthquake on November 1, 1755 catalyzed the nation's fall from glory—close to one-fifth of the population died, and two-thirds of Lisboa was destroyed in the resulting fires. Immediately, the Prime Minister Marquês de Pombal began a massive reconstruction effort, an overhaul that explains the contrast between the neat, grid-like layout of Baixa and the hilly mazes of surrounding areas. Twentieth-century Lisboa saw plenty of change, as new technologies complemented the traditions of the past. Temples, castles, and cathedrals left behind by prior civilizations, juxtaposed with crowded plazas, buzzing cafes, and blaring *discotecas*, give Lisboa a life of its own.

INTERCITY TRANSPORTATION

BY PLANE

All flights land at **Aeroporto de Lisboa** (☎218 41 35 00, 41 37 00 for departures and arrivals) near the city's northern edge. Major **airlines** have offices at Pr. Marquês de Pombal and along Av. da Liberdade. The cheapest way into town is by bus: walk out of the terminal, turn right, and go straight across the street to the bus stop, marked by yellow metal posts with arrival times of incoming buses. Take bus #44 or 45 (15-20min., every 12-15min. 6am-midnight, €1.60) to Pr. dos Restauradores; the bus stops in front of the tourist office, located inside the Palácio da Foz. The express AeroBus #91 runs to the same locations (15min.; every 20min. 7am-9pm; €3, TAP passengers free); it's a good option during rush hour. The bus stop is in front of the terminal exit. A **taxi** downtown costs about €10

Lisboa and Vicinity

(plus a €1.60 baggage fee) at low traffic, but you're billed by time, not distance. Beware that some drivers may keep your change or take a longer route.

PRE-PAY YOUR WAY. Ask at the airport tourist office (☎218 45 06 60; open 7am-midnight) about the voucher program, which allows visitors to pre-pay for cab rides from the airport (M-F €15, Sa-Su €18).

BY TRAIN

Train service in and out of Lisboa routinely confuses newcomers, as there are three stations in Lisboa and one across the river in Barreiro, each serving different destinations. Buses, although more expensive and lacking toilets, are faster and more comfortable. The two train lines with service to **Cascais** and **Sintra** (and stops along the way) are most reliable. Contact **Caminhos de Ferro Portugueses** for further info. (☎808 20 82 08; www.cp.pt. Open daily 7am-11pm.)

Estação do Barreiro, across the Rio Tejo. Has southbound trains. Accessible by ferry from the Terreiro do Paço dock off Pr. do Comércio (30min., 2 per hr., €2.10). Trains go to **Pinhal Novo** (25min., every 25min., €1.25) and **Setúbal** (20min., every 40min., €1.75). To get to **Évora** and **Lagos**, take a train to **Pinhal Novo** station and transfer. From Pinhal Novo, trains go to **Lagos** (3hr., 5 per day 9:04am-8:04pm, €18) and **Évora** (1hr., 3 per day, €8.50).

Estação Cais do Sodré, just beyond the end of R. do Alecrim, a 5min. walk from Baixa. M: Cais do Sodré. Take the metro or bus #36, 45, or 91 from Pr. dos Restauradores or tram #28 from Estação Santa Apolónia. The station is across R. 24 de Julho, on the river side. To the monastery in **Belém,** take trains labeled "Cascais Todos" or "Oeiras," which stop in: **Belém** (10min., 4 per hr. 5:30am-1:30am, €1.15); **Cascais** and **Estoril** (40min., 2 per hr. 5:30am-1:30am, €1.65); and the youth hostel in **Oeiras** (20min., 2 per hr. 5:30am-1:30am, €1.30).

Estação Rossio, M: Rossio or Restauradores. Travels west. Its destinations, **Sintra** and **Queluz,** can be reached using metro connections to other stations or the bus system. You can get off at M: Rossio and walk across the *praça* for 2 blocks until you see the station on your right. Alternatively, you can get off at M:Restauradores, and go down Av. da Liberdage, and the station will be on your right. The **Estação de Sete Rios** on the top fl. of M: Jardim Zoológico sends trains every 20min. to **Queluz** (€1.20) and **Sintra** (€1.65).

Estação Santa Apolónia, Av. Infante Dom Henrique. Runs the international, northern, and eastern lines. All trains stop at **Estação Oriente** (M: Oriente) by the **Parque das Nações.** The ticket office is open M-F 5:30am-1030pm and Sa-Su 6am-10:30pm. There is a **currency exchange** station and an **information desk** (English spoken). To go downtown, take bus #9, 46, or 59 to Pr. dos Restauradores. To: **Aveiro** (2½hr., 16 per day 6am-9:30pm, €24-35); **Braga** (3½hr.; 7am, 1:55, 4, 6:55pm; €21.50-30); **Coimbra** (2hr., 24 per day 6am-9:30pm, €15-20.15); **Madrid** (10hr., 10:05pm, €70); **Porto** (3-4hr., 20 per day 5:55am-7:55pm, €19.50-27).

BY BUS

The **bus station** in Lisboa is close to the Jardim Zoológico metro stop, but it can be tricky to find. Once at the metro stop, follow the exit signs to Av. C. Bordalo Pinheiro. Exit the metro and go around the corner. Walk ahead 100m and then cross left in front of Sete Rios station. The stairs to the station are on the left.

Rede Expressos (☎707 223 344; www.rede-expressos.pt). To: **Braga** (5hr., 20 per day 7am-12:15am, €17.50); **Castelo Branco** (2-3hr., 13 per day 8am-10:30pm, €11.50); **Coimbra** (2hr., 25 per day 7am-12:15am, €12); **Évora** (2hr., 22 per day 7am-10:30pm, €11); **Faro** (4hr., 12 per day 7am-1am, €17.50); **Lagos** (4-5hr., 13 per day 7:30am-1am, €17.50-18); **Peniche** (1-2hr., 11 per day 7am-10pm, €7.50); **Portalegre** (4hr., 10 per day 7:30am-8pm, €13); **Porto** (3-4hr., 19 per day 7am-12:15am, €16.50); **Tavira** (5hr., 10 per day 7am-1am, €17.50-18).

ORIENTATION

The city center has three neighborhoods: shop-filled **Baixa** (the low district), nightlife-rich **Bairro Alto** (the high district), and hilly, winding **Alfama.** The latter, Lisboa's famous medieval Moorish neighborhood, was the lone survivor of the 1755 earthquake. The city's oldest district is a labyrinth of narrow alleys, unmarked streets, and *escandinhas*—stairways that only seem to lead to more unmarked streets. Expect to get lost repeatedly without a detailed map. The street-indexed **For Ways** maps (including Sintra, Cascais, and Estoril) are good, though expensive (sold at newsstands; €5). The maps at the tourist offices are also reliable and free. The suburbs extending in both directions along the river are some of the fastest-growing sections of the city. Areas of interest

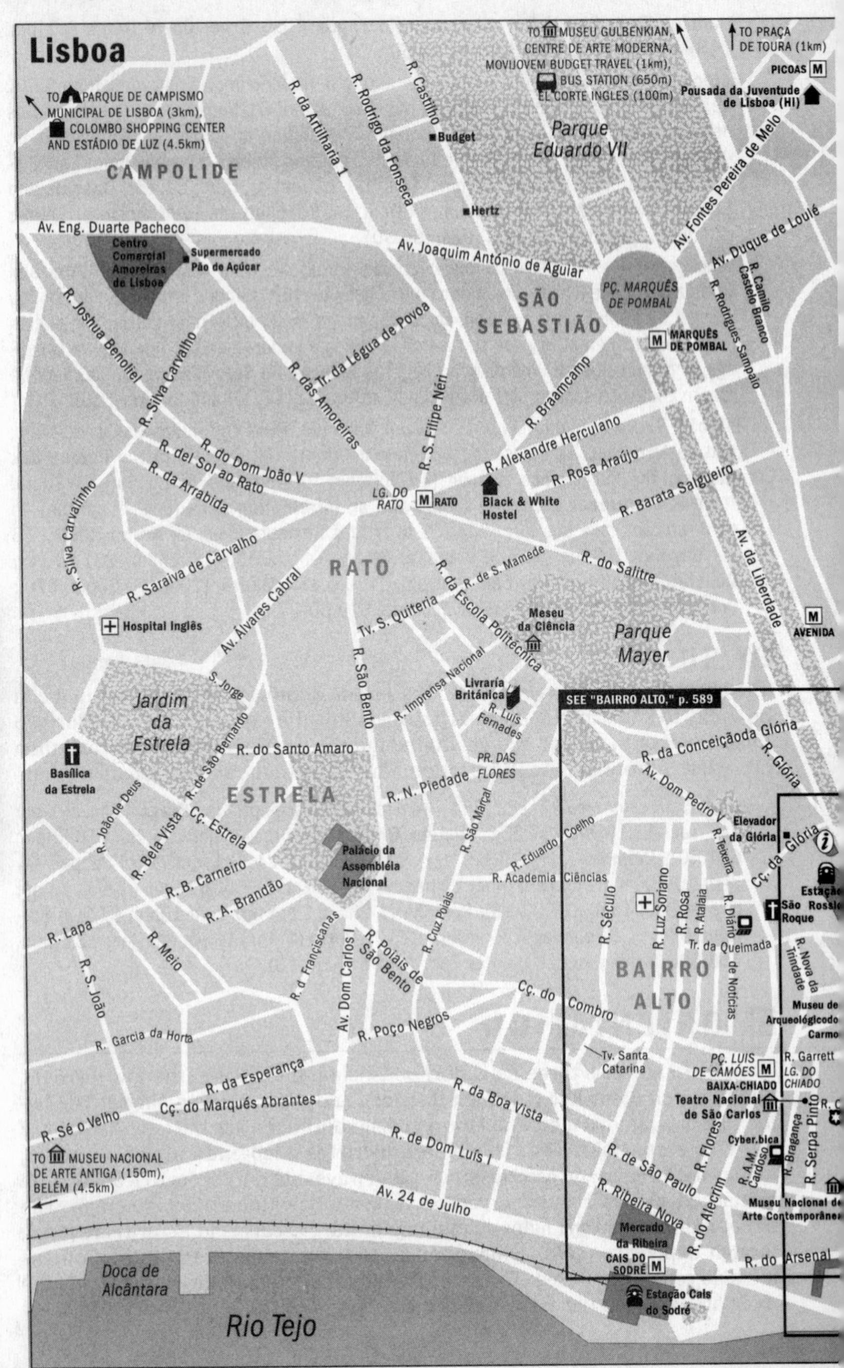
Lisboa
TO PARQUE DE CAMPISMO MUNICIPAL DE LISBOA (3km), COLOMBO SHOPPING CENTER AND ESTÁDIO DE LUZ (4.5km)
CAMPOLIDE
TO MUSEU GULBENKIAN, CENTRE DE ARTE MODERNA, MOVIJOVEM BUDGET TRAVEL (1km), BUS STATION (650m) EL CORTE INGLES (100m)
TO PRAÇA DE TOURA (1km)
PICOAS
Pousada da Juventude de Lisboa (HI)
Parque Eduardo VII
Budget
Hertz
Av. Eng. Duarte Pacheco
Centro Comercial Amoreiras de Lisboa
Supermercado Pão de Açúcar
Av. Joaquim António de Aguiar
PÇ. MARQUÊS DE POMBAL
SÃO SEBASTIÃO
MARQUÊS DE POMBAL
Av. Fontes Pereira de Melo
Av. Duque de Loulé
R. Camilo Castelo Branco
R. Rodrigues Sampaio
R. da Artilharia 1
R. Rodrigo da Fonseca
R. Castilho
R. Joshua Benoliel
R. Silva Carvalho
Tr. da Légua de Povoa
R. das Amoreiras
R. S. Filipe Néri
R. Braamcamp
R. Alexandre Herculano
R. Rosa Araújo
R. Barata Salgueiro
R. do Dom João V
R. del Sol ao Rato
R. da Arrabida
LG. DO RATO
RATO
Black & White Hostel
R. Silva Carvalinho
R. Saraiva de Carvalho
RATO
R. da Escola Politécnica
R. de S. Mamede
R. do Salitre
Av. da Liberdade
AVENIDA
Hospital Inglês
Av. Álvares Cabral
Tv. S. Quiteria
Meseu da Ciência
Parque Mayer
R. São Bento
R. Imprensa Nacional
Livraría Británica
R. Luís Fernades
SEE "BAIRRO ALTO," p. 589
Jardim da Estrela
S. Jorge
R. de São Bernardo
R. do Santo Amaro
Basílica da Estrela
PR. DAS FLORES
R. N. Piedade
ESTRELA
R. São Marçal
R. da Conceiçãoda Glória
R. Glória
Av. Dom Pedro V
Elevador da Glória
R. João de Deus
R. Bela Vista
Cç. Estrela
Palácio da Assembléia Nacional
R. Eduardo Coelho
R. Academia Ciências
R. Teixeira
Cç. da Glória
R. B. Carneiro
R. A. Brandão
R. Século
R. Luz Soriano
R. Rosa
R. Atalaia
R. Diário de Notícias
Estação Rossio
São Roque
R. Lapa
R. Meio
R. S. João
R. d. Franciscanas
Av. Dom Carlos I
R. Poiais de São Bento
R. Cruz Poiais
Tr. da Queimada
R. Nova da Trindade
BAIRRO ALTO
Cç. do Combro
Museu de Arqueológicodo Carmo
R. Garcia da Horta
R. Poço Negros
Tv. Santa Catarina
PÇ. LUIS DE CAMÕES
BAIXA-CHIADO
R. Garrett
LG. DO CHIADO
R. da Esperança
Cç. do Marqués Abrantes
R. da Boa Vista
Teatro Nacional de São Carlos
R. Sé o Velho
R. de Dom Luís I
R. Flores
Cyber.bica
R. A.M. Cardoso
R. Bragança
R. Serpa Pinto
TO MUSEU NACIONAL DE ARTE ANTIGA (150m), BELÉM (4.5km)
R. de São Paulo
Av. 24 de Julho
R. Ribeira Nova
R. do Alecrim
Museu Nacional de Arte Contemporânea
Mercado da Ribeira
CAIS DO SODRÉ
R. do Arsenal
Doca de Alcântara
Estação Cais do Sodré
Rio Tejo

LISBOA

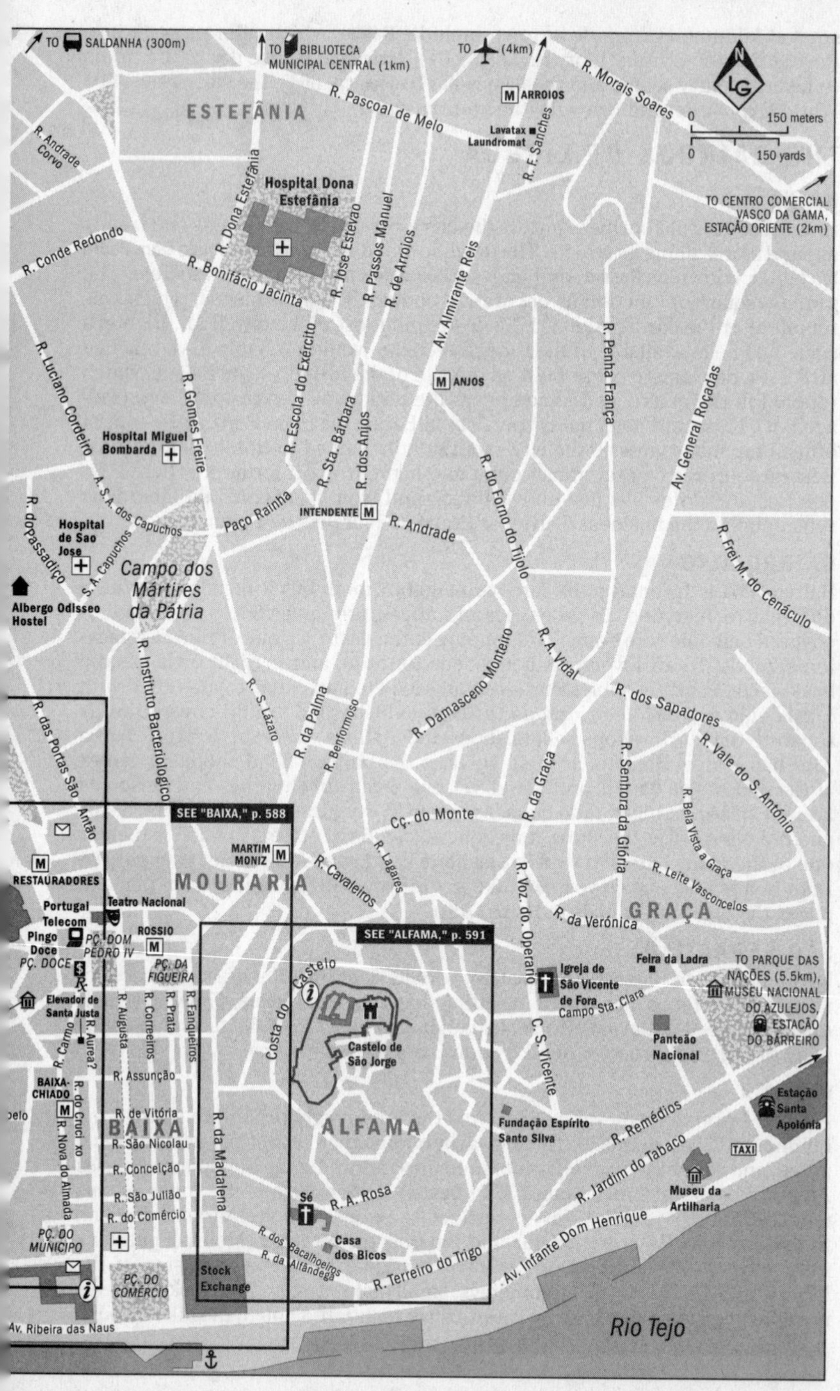

TO SALDANHA (300m)
TO BIBLIOTECA MUNICIPAL CENTRAL (1km)
TO (4km)
R. Morais Soares
ARROIOS
0 150 meters
0 150 yards
ESTEFÂNIA
R. Pascoal de Melo
Lavatax Laundromat
R. F. Sanches
R. Andrade Corvo
R. Dona Estefânia
Hospital Dona Estefânia
TO CENTRO COMERCIAL VASCO DA GAMA, ESTAÇÃO ORIENTE (2km)
R. Conde Redondo
R. Bonifácio Jacinta
R. Jose Estevao
R. Passos Manuel
R. de Arroios
Av. Almirante Reis
R. Penha França
R. Escola do Exército
ANJOS
R. Luciano Cordeiro
R. Gomes Freire
Av. General Roçadas
Hospital Miguel Bombarda
R. Sta. Bárbara
R. dos Anjos
R. do Forno do Tijolo
A. S.A. dos Capuchos
R. doPassadiço
Hospital de Sao Jose
S.A. Capuchos
Paço Rainha
INTENDENTE
R. Andrade
R. Frei M. do Cenáculo
Campo dos Mártires da Pátria
Albergo Odisseo Hostel
R. Instituto Bacteriologico
R. A. Vidal
R. Damasceno Monteiro
R. dos Sapadores
R. das Portas São Antão
R. S. Lázaro
R. da Palma
R. Benformoso
R. Vale do S. António
R. da Graça
R. Senhora da Glória
R. Bela Vista a Graça
SEE "BAIXA," p. 588
Cç. do Monte
MARTIM MONIZ
RESTAURADORES
MOURARIA
R. Cavaleiros
R. Lagares
R. Voz. do. Operario
R. Leite Vasconcelos
Portugal Telecom
Teatro Nacional
R. da Verónica
GRAÇA
Pingo Doce
PÇ. DOM PEDRO IV
ROSSIO
SEE "ALFAMA," p. 591
PÇ. DOCE
PÇ. DA FIGUEIRA
Costa do Castelo
Igreja de São Vicente de Fora
Feira da Ladra
TO PARQUE DAS NAÇÕES (5.5km), MUSEU NACIONAL DO AZULEJOS, ESTAÇÃO DO BÁRREIRO
Elevador de Santa Justa
R. Augusta
R. Correeiros
R. Prata
R. Fanqueiros
Campo Sta. Clara
R. Carmo
R. Aurea?
Castelo de São Jorge
Panteão Nacional
C. S. Vicente
R. Assunção
BAIXA-CHIADO
R. do Cruci xo
R. de Vitória
R. da Madalena
Estação Santa Apolónia
BAIXA
ALFAMA
Fundação Espírito Santo Silva
R. Remédios
R. São Nicolau
R. Nova do Almada
TAXI
R. Conceição
R. Jardim do Tabaco
R. São Julião
Sé
R. A. Rosa
Museu da Artilharia
R. do Comércio
PÇ. DO MUNICIPO
R. dos Bacalhoeiros
Casa dos Bicos
Av. Infante Dom Henrique
R. da Alfândega
R. Terreiro do Trigo
PÇ. DO COMÉRCIO
Stock Exchange
Av. Ribeira das Naus
Rio Tejo

several kilometers from downtown include: **Belém,** which offers a peek into Portugal's 16th-century glory days (p. 604), **Alcântara,** whose docks are home to Lisboa's party scene, and the **Parque das Nações** (p. 604), the site of the 1998 World Exposition and many daytime attractions.

THE BAIRROS OF LISBOA

BAIXA

Baixa, Lisboa's old business hub, is the city's core, with restaurants and trendy apparel stores lining its streets. The neighborhood grid begins at **Praça Dom Pedro IV** (better known as **Rossio**) and ends at **Praça do Comércio** on the Rio Tejo. The *praças* (squares) function as decorative bookends to new Lisboa, which was rebuilt after the earthquake of 1755 destroyed most of the city. If Mr. Richter's scale had been available at the time, the quake would probably have reached an 8.9. Pr. do Comércio was built on the site of the former Royal Palace, which toppled in the quake, and hence bears the nickname Terreiro do Paço (Palace Lot). Expect to meet many travelers in Baixa: the main Portuguese tourist office here makes Rossio the city's tourist hub. Linked to Rossio is Praça dos Restauradores, a central transit point and main drop-off for airport buses. Pr. dos Restauradores lies just above Baixa, and from it, Avenida da Liberdade runs uphill to the business district at Praça do Marquês de Pombal.

BAIRRO ALTO

Bairro Alto is Lisboa's most famous neighborhood, but it means something different to everyone. To thousands of natives, the upper floors and laundry-covered balconies are home. To shopping enthusiasts, it's one of Europe's fashion capitals. To art lovers, it's a must-see for *fado*, and to night owls, it's the best place to party. Cobblestone sidewalks lead to inexpensive cafes filled with locals enjoying *bacalhau assado* (grilled codfish), and graffiti-covered walls separate the quirky shops selling shoes and T-shirts with rare designs. Bairro Alto has budget delights as well, such as the bargain-filled shopping center at the end of **Rua Garrett,** and better yet, the beautiful churches and museums around **Chiado.** At night, *fado* houses present Portuguese songs over fine meals and red wine. After the show, fans congregate in the streets outside and enter one of the many bars between **Rua do Norte** and **Rua da Atalaia.** Get your *caipirinha* in a plastic cup so you can take it with you as you wander from place to place; the night never ends in Bairro Alto.

SÃO SEBASTIÃO

Located north of Baixa, São Sebastião, with its department stores and scores of strip malls, offers a more modern setting than much of Lisboa. Those in search of culture need not avoid São Sebastião; it also has two of the finest museums in all of Portugal, legacies of oil tycoon Calouste Gulbenkian.

ALFAMA

Alfama, Lisboa's medieval quarter, was the lone neighborhood to survive the infamous 1755 earthquake. The fine layer of dust that has settled over the blue, green, and rose-toned *azulejos* (ceramic tiles) adorning the buildings increases Alfama's sense of timelessness. The **Castelo de São Jorge** is the focus of this neighborhood. Around it, layers of houses, shops, and restaurants descend to the Rio Tejo. Between Alfama and Baixa is the **Mouraria** (Moorish quarter), ironically established by Dom Afonso Henriques after the expulsion of the Moors in 1147. This labyrinth of alleys, small stairways, and unmarked streets is a challenge to navigate, so be careful after nightfall. Though the hike through

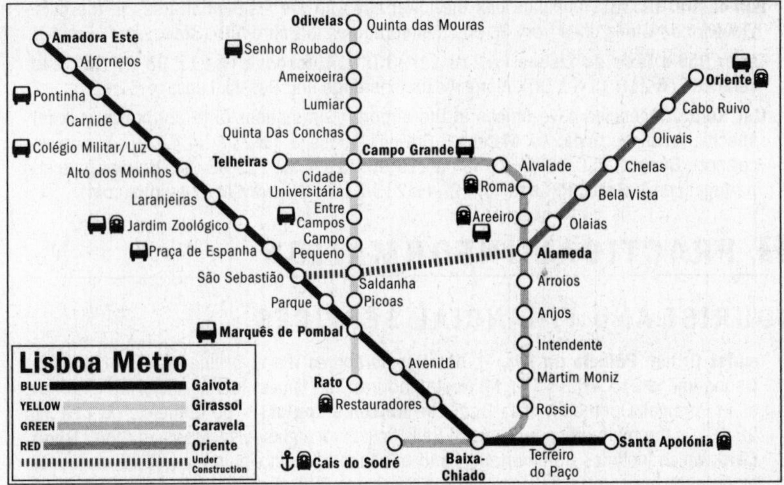

Alfama's streets is half the fun, visitors can also hop on historic tram #28 from Pr. do Comércio (€1.35), which winds past most of the neighborhood's sights.

GRAÇA

If the climb to Graça doesn't take your breath away, the incredible *miradouros* (lookout points) you'll find there will. The neighborhood is one of the oldest in Lisboa, and in addition to great views of the city and river, Graça offers several impressive historical sights that keep tourists trekking up its hilly streets day after day. Graça is a mainly residential area, easily accessible by tram (#28, €1.35), making it a quick and convenient daytrip from Baixa or Bairro Alto. Even if your stay is short, you won't want to leave town without grabbing a bite to eat. Graça is known for its amazing Brazilian cuisine, due to its large population of São Paulo expats.

LOCAL TRANSPORTATION

Lisboa and its surrounding areas have an efficient public transportation system with subways, buses, trams, and funiculars run by **CARRIS** (☎213 61 30 00; www.carris.pt), and therefore no suburb takes longer than 1hr. to reach. If you plan to stay in Lisboa for long, consider a **passe turístico,** good for unlimited travel on all CARRIS transports. Passes are available for one day (€3.50). CARRIS booths, located in most network train stations and the busier metro stations (e.g., M: Restauradores), sell multi-day passes. (Open daily 6:30am-1pm.)

Buses: €1.35 within the city; pay on the bus. Exact change not required.

Metro: (☎213 50 01 00; www.metrolisboa.pt). €0.75 per ride, round-trip €1.40, unlimited daily use ticket €3.50, 10 tickets €9.85. You must purchase a rechargable card for €0.50 to use the subway. 4 lines, crossing downtown and business district. A red "M" marks metro stops. Trains run daily 6:30am-1am, though some stations close earlier.

Trams: €1.35. Many date from before WWI. Line #28 is great for sightseeing in Alfama and Mouraria (stop in Pr. do Comércio). Line #15 heads from Pr. do Comércio and Pr. da Figueira to Belém, Av. 24 de Julho, and Docas de Santo Amaro.

Funiculars: €1.35. Funiculars link the lower city with the residential areas in the hills. Elevador da Glória goes from Pr. dos Restauradores to Bairro Alto (3min., every 5min.).

Taxis: Rádio Táxis de Lisboa (☎218 11 90 00), **Autocoope** (☎217 93 27 56), and **Teletáxis** (☎218 11 11 00). Along Av. da Liberdade and Rossio. Luggage €1.60.

Car Rental: Agencies have offices at the airport, train stations, and downtown; ask for specific locations. **Avis,** Av. Marechal Craveiro Lopes, 2 (☎217 54 78 25; www.avis.com.pt); **Budget,** R. Castilho, 167B (☎213 86 05 16, fax 213 83 09 78; www.budget-portugal.com); **Hertz,** R. Castilho, 72A (☎213 81 24 30; www.hertz-europe.com).

PRACTICAL INFORMATION

TOURIST AND FINANCIAL SERVICES

Tourist Office: Palácio da Foz, Pr. dos Restauradores (Portugal line ☎213 46 63 07, Lisboa line ☎213 46 33 14). M: Restauradores. The largest tourist office, with info for all of Portugal. Open daily 9am-8pm. The **Welcome Center,** Pr. do Comércio (☎210 31 28 10), is the main office for the city. Sells tickets for sightseeing buses and the **Lisboa Card,** which includes transportation and entrance to most sights, as well as discounts at various shops, for a flat fee (1-day €15, 2-day €26, 3-day €32; children age 5-11 €8/13/16). English spoken. Open daily 9am-8pm. An **airport branch** (☎218 45 06 60) is by the airport entrance. English spoken. Open daily 7am-midnight. For info, check kiosks that read "Ask me about Lisboa" in Santa Apolónia, Belém, and other locations.

Budget Travel: Movijovem, R. Lúcio de Azevedo, 29 (☎707 23 32 33; www.pousadasjuventude.pt). M: São Sebastião. Make reservations at **Hostelling International** youth hostels all over Portugal. Open daily 9am-7pm.

Embassies: See **Embassies and Consulates,** p. 10.

Currency Exchange: Banks are open M-F 8:30am-3pm. **Cota Câmbios,** Pr. Dom Pedro IV, 41 (☎213 22 04 80). Open daily 8pm-10pm. Sells 2hr. phone cards to the US and European land lines for €5. **Western Union** inside for money transfers. The main post office, most banks, and travel agencies also change money. Exchanges line the streets of Baixa. Ask about fees first—they can be exorbitant.

LOCAL SERVICES

English-Language Bookstore: FNAVC, Armazéns do Chiado, 4th fl., R. do Carmo, 2 (☎213 22 18 00). Large section just for English books, but they can be found throughout the store in the regular sections, as well. Open daily 10am-10pm.

Libraries: Biblioteca Municipal Central, Palácio Galveias (☎217 80 30 40). M: Campo Pequeno. Open M-F 10am-7pm and Sa 11am-6pm. **Biblioteca Municipal Camões,** Largo do Calhariz, 17 (☎213 42 21 57). Free internet access. Open July 15-Sept. 15 M-F 1-7pm, 2nd and 4th Sa of every month 1-8pm; Sept. 16-July 14 M-F 10am-7pm, 2nd and 4th Sa 11am-6pm.

Shopping Centers:

Armazéns do Chiado, (☎213 21 06 00) R do Carmo 2. Food court at the top. Open daily 10am-10pm, restaurants close at 11pm.

El Corte Inglés, between Av. António Augusto de Agular and Marquês da Fronteira e Sidónio Pais, (☎213 71 17 00; www.elcorteingles.pt). M: São Sebastião. Portugal's first branch of the Spanish department store. Open M-Th 10am-10pm, F-Sa 10am-11:30pm, Su 10am-1pm. MC/V.

Colombo, Av. Lusíada (☎217 11 36 00; www.colombo.pt), in front of Benfica stadium. M: Colégio Militar-Luz. Over 400 shops, a 10-screen cinema (adult ticket €5), and a small amusement park. Open daily 9am-midnight.

Centro Comercial Amoreiras de Lisboa, Av. Eng. Duarte Pacheco (☎213 81 02 00; www.amoreiras.com), near R. Carlos Alberto da Mota Pinto. M: Marquês de Pombal. Towers house 383 shops, including a huge **Pão de Açúcar** supermarket and cinema. Open daily 10am-11pm.

Centro Comercial Vasco da Gama, Av. Dom João II (☎218 93 06 01; www.centrovascodagama.pt). M: Oriente. Open daily 9am-midnight.

Laundromats: Lavatax, R. Francisco Sanches, 65A (☎218 12 33 92). M: Arroios. Wash, dry, and fold €3 per kg. Open M-F 9am-1pm and 3-7pm, Sa 8:30am-1pm. **Lavanderia Clin,** R. de São João da Praça, 5-7 (☎218 86 64 44) in Alfama. Wash, dry, and fold €4.50 per kg. Open M-F 8:30am-7:30pm, Sa 9am-1pm.

EMERGENCY AND COMMUNICATIONS

Police: Tourism Police Station, Palácio Foz in Restauradores (☎213 42 16 24), and at R. Capelo, 13 (☎213 46 61 41 or 42 16 34). English spoken.

Late-Night Pharmacy: ☎118 (directory assistance); 24hr. pharmacy rotates. Look for the green cross at intersections, or check listings at **Farmácia Azevedos,** Pr. Dom Pedro IV, 31 (☎213 43 04 82), at the base of Rossio in front of the metro. Regular hours 8:30am-7:40pm.

Medical Services: ☎112 in case of emergency. **Hospital de Saint Louis,** R. Luz Soriano, 182 (☎213 21 65 00, fax 46 02 21) in Bairro Alto. Open daily 9am-8pm. **Hospital de São José** (☎218 84 10 00 or 261 31 28 57), R. José António Serrano.

Telephones: Portugal Telecom, Pr. Dom Pedro IV, 68 (☎808 21 11 56). M: Rossio. Pay the cashier after your call or use a phone card. Also has internet access. (€2 per hr.) Office open daily 8am-11pm. Portugal Telecom phone cards (50 units €3) available at the office or at bookstores and stationers. Local calls cost at least 2 units. Minutes per unit vary. PT cards should only be purchased for local use; better deals on non-local calls can be found elsewhere.

Internet Access: Portugal Telecom (see above). **The Instituto Portuges da Juventude** has 30 min. of free internet and offer assistance for students (☎213 17 92 00). Av. Liberdade 194. Open Tu-Sa 9am-8pm. 2 fun cyber cafes in Bairro Alto also double as bars: **Web C@fé,** R. Diário de Notícias, 126 (☎213 42 11 81; €0.75 per 15min, open daily 4pm-2am) and **Blue Net Cafe,** R. da Rosa, 165 (☎213 473 095). €1 for 30min. Mixed drinks €3. Beer €1.20. M-F 11am-midnight, Sa-Su 3pm-midnight. Cash only.

Post Office: Main office, Pr. dos Restauradores (☎213 23 89 71). Open M-F 8am-10pm, Sa-Su 9am-6pm. To avoid the lines, go to the **branch,** Pr. do Comércio (☎213 22 09 20). Open M-F 8:30am-6:30pm. Cash only. **Postal Code:** 1100.

LISBOA

ACCOMMODATIONS AND CAMPING

Pensões and budget hotels abound in Lisboa, but room quality varies significantly—ask to see the room before paying. During the summer, expect to pay €20-30 for a single and €35-45 for a double, depending on amenities. You can usually find a room in the summer with little or no notice, but you may want to book in advance during mid-June for the Festa de Santo Antonio. In the low season (Oct.-Apr.), prices generally drop €5 or more, so try bargaining. Many establishments only have rooms with double beds, and charge per person. Backpacking hostels have only recently hit the Lisboa scene, with most opening their doors within the last year or two. Most are found in Bairro Alto, and are very similar in setup: mixed four- to eight-person dorms, shared bathrooms, a common living room, and free internet access. They do differ slightly in amenities, but most are comfortable and run €18-20 in the summer. Due to online booking, they fill up fast, so reserve ahead.

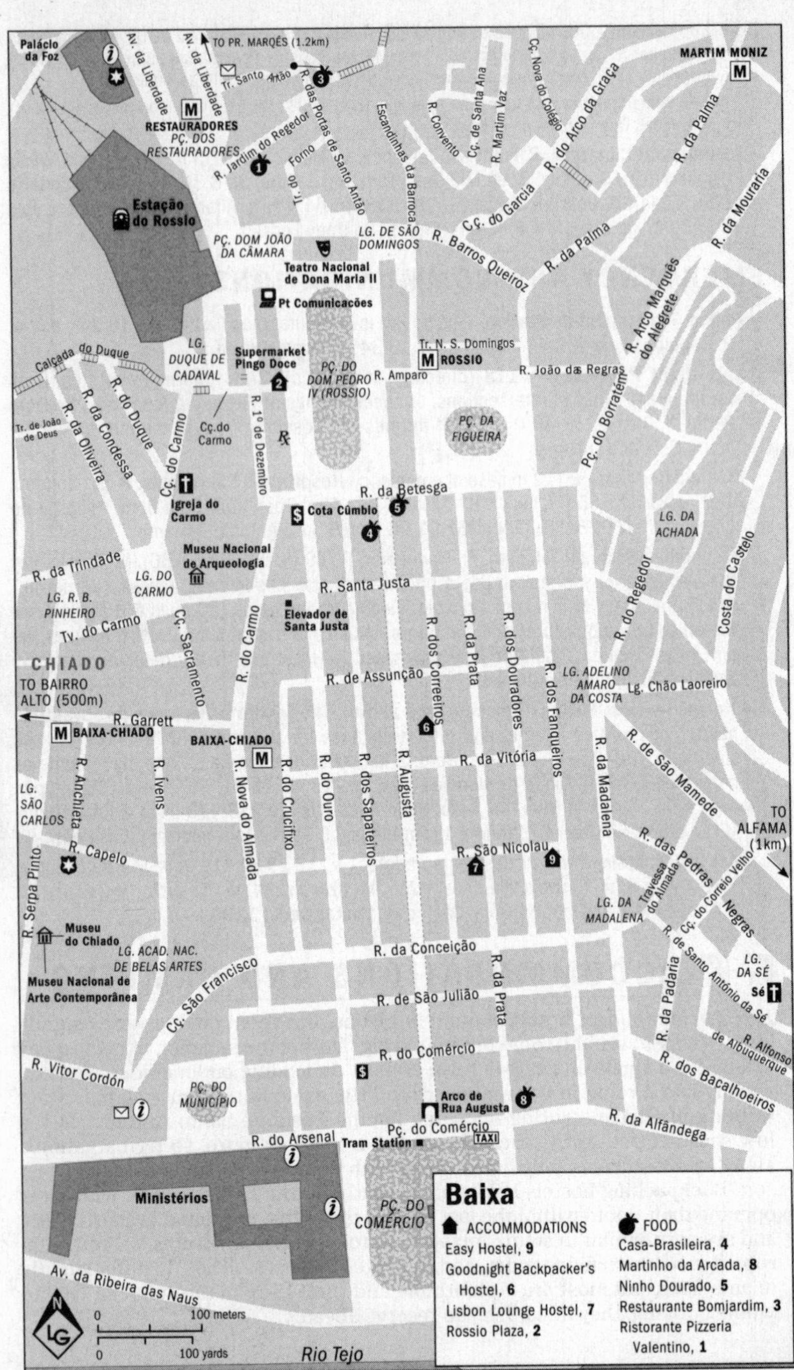
Palácio da Foz
Av. da Liberdade
TO PR. MARQUÊS (1.2km)
Tr. Santo Antão
RESTAURADORES
PÇ. DOS RESTAURADORES
R. Jardim do Regedor
Tr. do Forno
R. das Portas de Santo Antão
Escandinhas da Barroca
R. Convento
Cç. de Santa Ana
R. Martim Vaz
Cç. Nova do Colégio
R. do Arco da Graça
MARTIM MONIZ
R. da Palma
R. da Mouraria
Estação do Rossio
PÇ. DOM JOÃO DA CÂMARA
Teatro Nacional de Dona Maria II
LG. DE SÃO DOMINGOS
R. Barros Queiroz
Cç. do Garcia
Pt Comunicacões
R. Arco Marquês do Alegrete
Calçada do Duque
LG. DUQUE DE CADAVAL
Supermarket Pingo Doce
PÇ. DO DOM PEDRO IV (ROSSIO)
Tr. N. S. Domingos
ROSSIO
R. Amparo
R. João das Regras
Tr. de João de Deus
R. da Oliveira
R. da Condessa
R. do Duque
Cç. do Carmo
Cç.do Carmo
R. 1º de Dezembro
PÇ. DA FIGUEIRA
Pç. do Borratém
Igreja do Carmo
Cota Cûmbio
R. da Betesga
LG. DA ACHADA
Museu Nacional de Arqueologia
R. da Trindade
LG. DO CARMO
R. Santa Justa
LG. R. B. PINHEIRO
Tv. do Carmo
Elevador de Santa Justa
R. dos Correeiros
R. da Prata
R. dos Douradores
R. do Regedor
Costa do Castelo
CHIADO
Cç. Sacramento
R. do Carmo
R. de Assunção
R. dos Fanqueiros
LG. ADELINO AMARO DA COSTA
Lg. Chão Laoreiro
TO BAIRRO ALTO (500m)
R. Garrett
BAIXA-CHIADO
R. de São Mamede
R. Anchieta
R. Ivens
R. Nova do Almada
R. do Crucifixo
R. do Ouro
R. dos Sapateiros
R. Augusta
R. da Vitória
R. da Madalena
LG. SÃO CARLOS
TO ALFAMA (1km)
R. das Pedras Negras
R. Capelo
R. São Nicolau
Travessa do Almada
Cç. do Correio Velho
R. Serpa Pinto
LG. DA MADALENA
Museu do Chiado
LG. ACAD. NAC. DE BELAS ARTES
R. da Conceição
R. de Santo António da Sé
LG. DA SÉ
Sé
Museu Nacional de Arte Contemporânea
Cç. São Francisco
R. de São Julião
R. da Padaria
R. Alfonso de Albuquerque
R. Vitor Cordón
R. do Comércio
R. dos Bacalhoeiros
PÇ. DO MUNICÍPIO
Arco de Rua Augusta
R. da Alfândega
R. do Arsenal
Pç. do Comércio
Tram Station
TAXI
Ministérios
PÇ. DO COMÉRCIO
Av. da Ribeira das Naus
0
100 meters
100 yards
Rio Tejo
Baixa
ACCOMMODATIONS
Easy Hostel, 9
Goodnight Backpacker's Hostel, 6
Lisbon Lounge Hostel, 7
Rossio Plaza, 2
FOOD
Casa-Brasileira, 4
Martinho da Arcada, 8
Ninho Dourado, 5
Restaurante Bomjardim, 3
Ristorante Pizzeria Valentino, 1

LISBOA

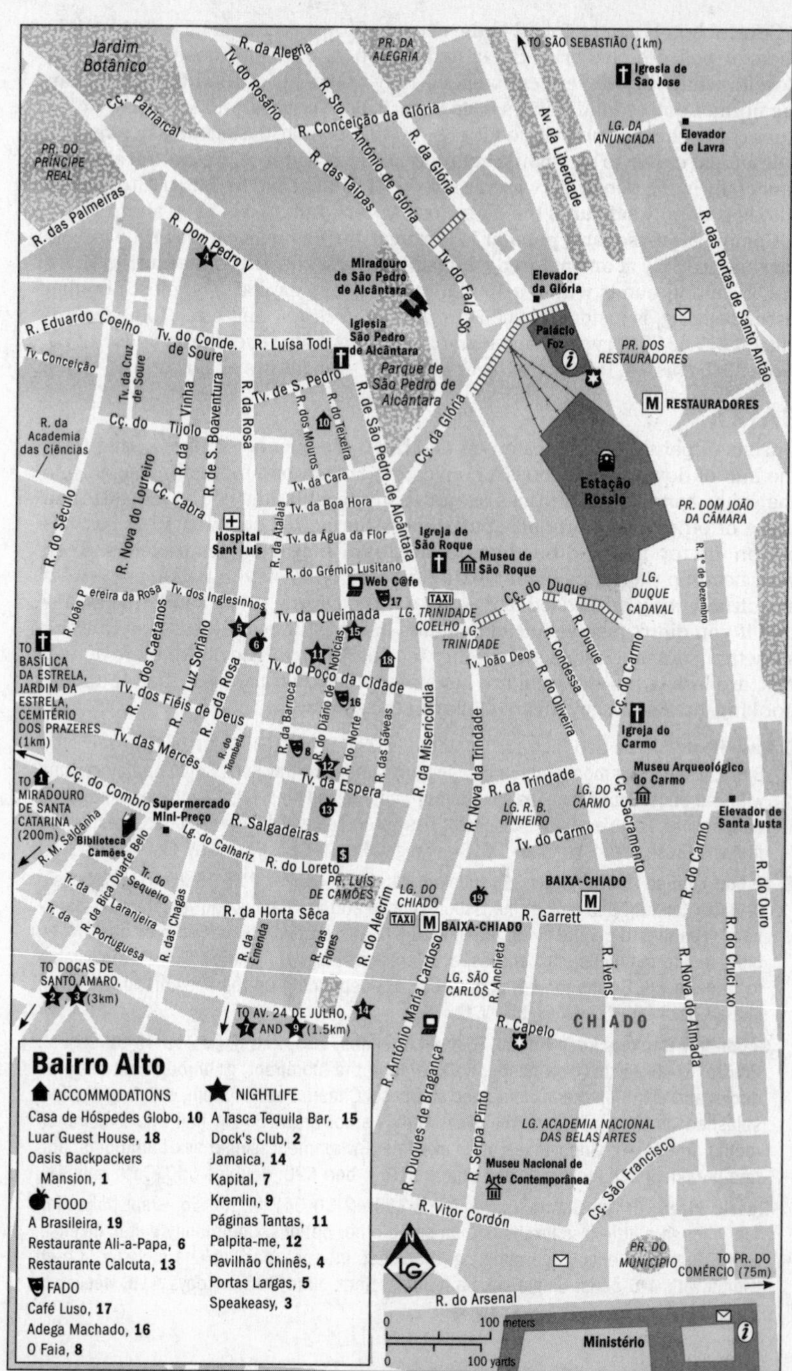
Bairro Alto
ACCOMMODATIONS
Casa de Hóspedes Globo, 10
Luar Guest House, 18
Oasis Backpackers Mansion, 1
FOOD
A Brasileira, 19
Restaurante Ali-a-Papa, 6
Restaurante Calcuta, 13
FADO
Café Luso, 17
Adega Machado, 16
O Faia, 8
NIGHTLIFE
A Tasca Tequila Bar, 15
Dock's Club, 2
Jamaica, 14
Kapital, 7
Kremlin, 9
Páginas Tantas, 11
Palpita-me, 12
Pavilhão Chinês, 4
Portas Largas, 5
Speakeasy, 3
Jardim Botânico
PR. DO PRÍNCIPE REAL
PR. DA ALEGRIA
TO SÃO SEBASTIÃO (1km)
Igresia de Sao Jose
LG. DA ANUNCIADA
Elevador de Lavra
R. da Alegria
Tv. do Rosário
Cç. Patriarcal
R. Sto António de Glória
R. Conceição da Glória
R. da Glória
R. das Taipas
Av. da Liberdade
R. das Portas de Santo Antão
R. das Palmeiras
R. Dom Pedro V
Tv. do Fala Só
Miradouro de São Pedro de Alcântara
Elevador da Glória
Palácio Foz
PR. DOS RESTAURADORES
RESTAURADORES
R. Eduardo Coelho
Tv. do Conde. de Soure
R. Luísa Todi
Iglesia São Pedro de Alcântara
Parque de São Pedro de Alcântara
Tv. Conceição
Tv. da Cruz de Soure
R. da Vinha
R. de S. Boaventura
R. da Rosa
Tv. de S. Pedro
R. dos Mouros
R. do Teixeira
R. de São Pedro de Alcântara
Cç. da Glória
R. da Academia das Ciências
Cç. do Tijolo
Estação Rossio
R. Nova do Loureiro
Cç. Cabra
Tv. da Cara
Tv. da Boa Hora
R. do Século
Hospital Sant Luis
R. da Atalaia
Tv. da Água da Flor
Igreja de São Roque
Museu de São Roque
PR. DOM JOÃO DA CÂMARA
R. do Grémio Lusitano
Web C@fe
LG. DUQUE CADAVAL
R. 1º de Dezembro
R. João Pereira da Rosa
Tv. dos Inglesinhos
Tv. da Queimada
LG. TRINIDADE COELHO
LG. TRINIDADE
Cç. do Duque
R. Duque
R. dos Caetanos
R. Luz Soriano
TO BASÍLICA DA ESTRELA, JARDIM DA ESTRELA, CEMITÉRIO DOS PRAZERES (1km)
Tv. do Poço da Cidade
Tv. João Deos
R. Condessa
R. do Oliveira
Cç. do Carmo
Tv. dos Fiéis de Deus
R. da Barroca
R. do Diário de Notícias
R. do Norte
R. das Gáveas
R. da Misericórdia
R. Nova da Trindade
Igreja do Carmo
Tv. das Mercês
R. do Trombeta
Tv. da Espera
Museu Arqueológico do Carmo
TO MIRADOURO DE SANTA CATARINA (200m)
Cç. do Combro
Supermercado Mini-Preço
R. da Trindade
LG. DO CARMO
LG. R. B. PINHEIRO
Cç. Sacramento
Elevador de Santa Justa
R. M. Saldanha
Biblioteca Camões
Lg. do Calhariz
R. Salgadeiras
Tv. do Carmo
R. da Bica Duarte Belo
R. do Loreto
PR. LUÍS DE CAMÕES
LG. DO CHIADO
BAIXA-CHIADO
R. do Carmo
R. do Ouro
Tr. do Sequeiro
Tr. da Laranjeira
Tr. da Portuguesa
R. das Chagas
R. da Horta Sêca
R. da Emenda
R. das Flores
R. do Alecrim
R. Garrett
R. Ivens
R. Nova do Almada
R. do Crucifixo
TO DOCAS DE SANTO AMARO, (3km)
LG. SÃO CARLOS
R. Anchieta
R. Capelo
CHIADO
TO AV. 24 DE JULHO, AND (1.5km)
R. António Maria Cardoso
R. Duques de Bragança
R. Serpa Pinto
LG. ACADEMIA NACIONAL DAS BELAS ARTES
Museu Nacional de Arte Contemporânea
Cç. São Francisco
R. Vitor Cordón
PR. DO MUNICIPIO
TO PR. DO COMÉRCIO (75m)
R. do Arsenal
Ministério
0 100 meters
0 100 yards
TAXI
LG

LISBOA

Several hotels can be found in the center of town on Av. da Liberdade, while cheaper *pensões* cluster in Baixa and Bairro Alto. Avoid those surrounding Rossio: while they're very convenient, they're usually around €10 more than the norm. Look around Baixa's **R. da Prata, R. dos Correiros,** and **R. do Ouro** (R. de Aurea) for cheaper accommodations. Lodgings near **Castelo de São Jorge** are quieter and closer to the sights, but more difficult to reach. Be careful at night, especially in the poorly-lit, winding streets of Alfama and in Bairro Alto. Bairro Alto is generally safe until the bars close at 4am, but it pays to be alert.

Camping is reasonably popular in Portugal, but campers can be prime targets for thieves. Stay at an enclosed campsite and ask ahead about security. There are 30 campgrounds within a 45min. radius of the capital. The most popular, **Lisboa Camping,** is inside the 900-acre *parque florestal*, and has a four-star rating. (☎217 62 82 00; www.lisboacamping.com. Adults €6, children under 12 €3, tents €6-7, cars €4. Prices are lower in winter. Bungalows available.)

BAIXA

Dozens of pensions are located around the three connected *praças* that form the hub of downtown Lisboa. A convenient launch pad for visiting sights. On the other hand, Baixa's prices are often noticeably higher (by €10-20) than those of other neighborhoods, particularly during the summer. Most *pensões* are on the top floors of buildings, a hassle for luggage-laden travelers. Keep your head up (literally) when looking for a place to stay in Baixa, as *pensões* are often poorly advertised and easy to miss. On the other hand, this means that if you didn't reserve ahead in summer, it is still usually possible to track something down. Hostels are another feasible choice. They have more amenities, are less expensive, and are generally nicer than *pensões.* Due to online booking, however, they fill up quickly in the summer.

LISBOA

Easy Hostel, R. de São Nicolau, 13, 4th fl. (☎218 88 5312). Good location in central Baixa. Great living room area for hanging out with fellow travelers. Bright and airy rooms with 4-6 beds. Each room has soundproof walls, ceiling fans, night lamps, and magnetic card access. The elevator makes life at Easy even easier. Laundry included. Free breakfast with fresh bread. Wi-Fi. M-F €18 per night, Sa-Su €20. Cash only. ❷

Lisbon Lounge Hostel, R. de São Nicolau, 41, 1st fl. (☎/fax 213 46 20 61). M: Rossio or Baixa-Chiado. One look at the Lisbon Lounge and you'll think you've entered a classy hotel. Features a central living room, lounge areas on each floor, free breakfast, Wi-Fi, ultra-secure magnetic card access, and lockers. Hungry for more? Dinner is available for a mere €6. Dorms for 4-8 people €18-22 depending on the season, doubles with shared bath €50-60. AmEx/MC/V. ❷

Goodnight Backpacker's Hostel, R. dos Correeiros, 113, 2nd fl. (☎213 43 01 39). M: Rossio. To get to this new hostel, walk through the storefront, go through the mirrored doors, and climb up the *azulejo*-lined staircase. Cheerful atmosphere, with bright colors splashed on the walls and whimsical Andy Warhol art. A dining hall and 2 common rooms, free Wi-Fi, videogames, a smoke-free environment, single sex bathrooms, and free breakfast and lockers. 8-bed dorms €19; 4-bed €20; doubles €50. Cash only. ❶

Rossio Plaza, Cç. do Carmo, 6, 2nd fl. (☎213 42 60 04). M: Rossio. Great bohemian feel, though a little less luxurious than some other options. Community guitar, incense, and living room encourage mingling. Breakfast, internet, and lockers included. Co-ed rooms with 4-6 beds. Single sex bathrooms. Sept.-June 30 weekdays €18, weekends €20; July-Aug. €20/22. Cash only. ❷

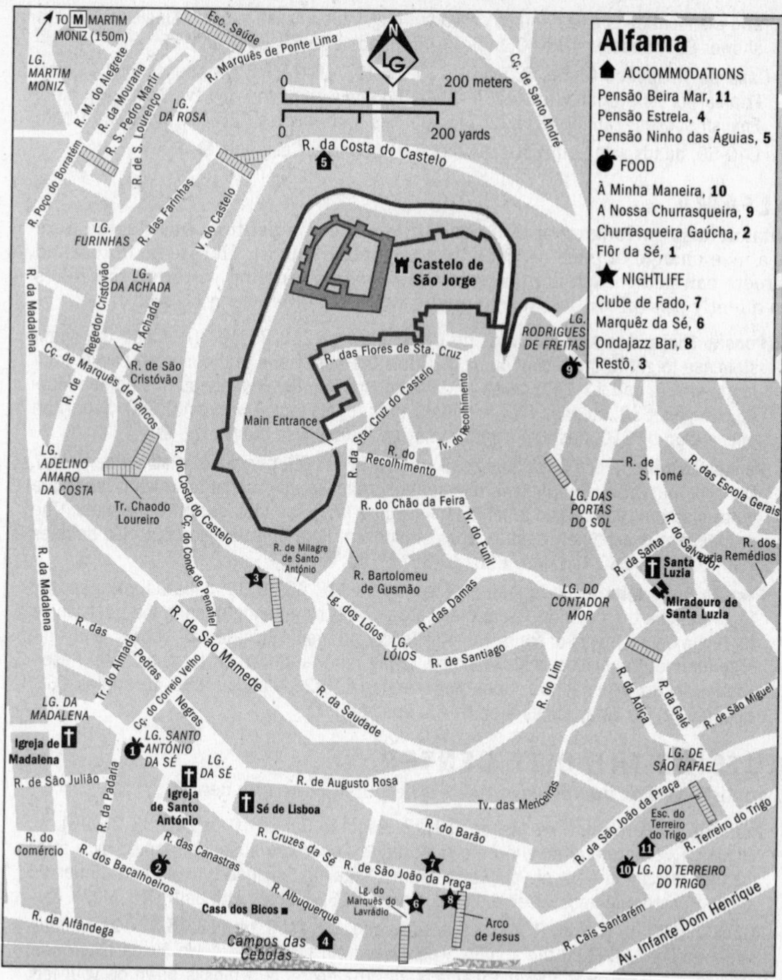

LISBOA

BAIRRO ALTO

If you're seeking a central location for nightlife and entertainment, there's no better place than Bairro Alto, which has many great budget accommodations where you can meet fellow backpackers and hit the bars and clubs together.

Oasis Backpackers Mansion, R. de Santa Catarina, 24 (☎213 47 80 44; www.oasislisboa.com). M: Baixa-Chiado, exit Largo do Chiado. Perhaps the best place to stay in Lisboa, the gorgeous Oasis is a dream: free internet, free breakfast, spacious living room, and personal safes, all extremely clean. Laundry €6. M-Sa dinner €5. F free Portuguese lessons. €18 for a co-ed dorm; €20 if you book online. AmEx/MC/V. ❷

Luar Guest House, R. das Gáveas, 101 (☎213 46 09 49; www.pensaoluar.com). Follow the beautiful *azulejo*-decorated staircase to Luar's bright rooms. The staff is friendly and the location is great. Laundry €10 per 6kg. Little English spoken. Singles €15, with shower €30; doubles €35-40; triples €45; quads €55-60. Cash only. ❷

Casa de Hóspedes Globo, R. Teixeira, 37 (☎213 46 22 79; www.pensaoglobo.com). Popular for its proximity to great nightlife. Rooms with phone and TV; most have bath. English spoken. Laundry €10 for 6kg. Singles and doubles €25-45; triples with bath €40-50; quads with bath €50; summer €10-15 more. Cash only. ❷

ALFAMA

Alfama has few lodging options and little price competition, but staying here is a nice change of pace (especially after hectic Baixa). The steep, unmarked streets can make each trip back to the *pensão* a grueling workout, but hikes frequently pay off with postcard-quality views of downtown Lisboa.

Pensão Ninho das Águias, Costa do Castelo, 74 (☎218 85 40 70). Climb the spiral staircase to get to the reception desk. Offers the best views of the city, especially from rooms #5, 6, and 12-14. English and French spoken. Reserve ahead in summer. May-Aug. singles €30; doubles €45, with bath €50; triples (some with bath) €60. Sept.-Apr. prices drop by €10. Cash only; prices may be flexible with bargaining. ❸

Pensão Estrela, R. dos Bacalhoeiros, 8 (☎218 86 95 06; pensaoestrela@hotmail.com). Don't be put off by the ancient, dilapidated staircase; the rooms to which it leads are quite nice and have basic amenities, including TV. Some look out onto the water. The proprietress is extremely helpful. Spanish spoken. June-Sept. Singles €20-30; doubles €35-40; triple €60. Oct.-May €20/30-35/45-50. ❷

Pensão Beira Mar, Largo Terreiro do Trigo, 16 (☎218 86 99 33; beira@iol.pt), near the Sta. Apolonia train station. Avoid the 4-story climb by entering through the back where there are only 2 flights of stairs. Brightly decorated rooms include a TV, shower, and sink. Free internet, munchies, and breakfast. Living room and kitchen for guest use. Reservations by fax or email only. June-Aug. singles €20-25; doubles €35-45; triples €60; quads €70; Oct.-May prices drop by €5. Cash only. ❷

OUTSIDE THE CITY CENTER

Two high-quality, inexpensive hostels lie outside the city center.

Pousada de Juventude de Lisboa (HI), R. Andrade Corvo, 46 (☎213 53 26 96). M: Picoas. Exit the metro station onto R. Andrade Corvo; the hostel is marked by a large banner directly in front of you. Large rooms. Breakfast included; lunch and dinner €6 each. HI card required. Reserve ahead. Dorms €16; doubles with bath €43. MC/V. ❶

Black and White Hostel, R. Alexandre Herculano, 39, 1st fl. (☎213 46 22 12). M: Marquês de Pombal. From the station, walk away from the statue down Av. da Liberdade, and take a right on R. Alexandre Herculano. The hostel is 3 blocks down on your left. Rock bottom prices for a stay at one of the most artistic hostels in town—rooms are boldly painted with murals of psychedelic spirals and abstract creatures. 15min. walk to both Baixa and Bairro Alto. Free internet, towels, and breakfast. M-F 4- to 6-person room €17 person. 14-person room €14. Sa-Su all rooms €17. Cash only. ❶

FOOD

Calorie-counters beware: Lisboa has some of the cheapest, most irresistible restaurants of the western European capitals, not to mention the best wine. A full dinner costs about €9-11 per person and the *prato do dia* (daily special) is often only €5-7. Between lunch and dinner, snack on cheap, filling, and addictive Portuguese pastries. Lisboa boasts almost as many *pastelarias* as Spain has tapas bars, and abounds with seafood specialties such as *pratos de caracois* (snail dishes), *creme de mariscos* (seafood chowder with tomatoes), and *bacalhau cozido com grão e batatas* (cod with chickpeas and boiled potatoes, doused in olive oil). For a more diverse selection, head up to the winding streets of Bairro Alto where you'll find many international restaurants.

FOOD BY TYPE

INTERNATIONAL

Restaurante Ali-a-Papa (p. 594)	BA	❸
Restaurante Calcuta (p. 594)	BA	❷
Ristorante-Pizzeria Valentino (p. 593)	B	❷
Restaurante Bomjardim (p. 594)	B	❷

PORTUGUESE

À Minha Maneira (p. 594)	A	❷
A Nossa Churrasqueira (p. 594)	A	❶
Churrasqueira Gaúcha (p. 594)	A	❷
Martinho da Arcada (p. 593)	B	❹

CAFES

A Brasileira (p. 594)	BA	❷
Bar Cerca Moura (p. 595)	G	❶
Casa-Brasileira (p. 593)	B	❶
Esplanada Igreja da Graça (p. 595)	G	❶
Flôr da Sé (p. 594)	A	❶
Ninho Dourado (p. 594)	B	❷
O Pitéu (p. 595)	G	❷
Pastelaria Estrela da Graça (p. 595)	G	❶

A Alfama **B** Baixa **BA** Bairro Alto **G** Graça

SUPERMARKETS

Pingo Doce, R. 1 de Dezembro, 81-83 (☎213 24 73 30). Just outside Pr. do Dom Pedro IV is one location of this very common supermarket chain. Open daily 9am-8:30pm.

Mercado da Ribeira, Av. 24 de Julho (☎213 46 29 66). M: Cais de Sodré. Accessible by bus #40 or tram #15. This vast, picturesque market complex is more than a century old and located inside a warehouse just outside Estação Cais do Sodré. Go early for the freshest selection of fruit, fish, and a variety of other foods. Prices on produce can't be beat. Open Tu-Sa 5am-2pm for produce, M-Sa 5am-7pm for flowers. Cash only.

Supermercado Mini-Preço, R. do Loreto (www.clubeminipreco.website.pt). Open M-Sa 9am-8pm, Su 9:30am-1:30pm and 3:30-7:30pm. Also on R. de São Paulo, 80, and numerous other locations throughout Lisboa. Open M-Sa 9am-8pm.

Supermercado Pão de Açúcar, located in the Amoreiras Shopping Center de Lisboa, Av. Duarte Pacheco (☎213 82 66 80). Take bus #11 from Pr. dos Restauradores or Pr. da Figueira. Open daily 9am-11pm.

BAIXA

There are a ton of restaurants along R. dos Correeiros and on R. das Portas de S. Antão, but the revolving menu stands in nine different languages should tip you off to their tourist orientation. Those with menus in Portuguese tend to serve the more affordable meals.

Ristorante-Pizzeria Valentino, R. Jardim do Regedor, 37-45 (☎213 46 17 27). Portugal's very own Italia in the Pr. do Restauradores. Watch the chefs prepare a variety of dishes in the open kitchen. Keep your eyes peeled for famous Portuguese soccer players; they've been known to frequent Valentino's. Try the crunchy-crusted Pizza Caprese (€8.50). Entrees €7-19. Pizzas €6-10. Open daily noon-midnight. AmEx/MC/V. ❷

Martinho da Arcada, Pr. do Comércio, 3 (☎218 87 92 59). Enjoy the one-of-a-kind ambience at the oldest restaurant in Lisboa, founded in 1782. Guests can read poems on the walls by Portuguese poet Fernando Pessoa, a regular during his lifetime. Outside seating available. Fish options less expensive than grilled meats or chicken, though still pricey. Entrees €17-38. Open M-Sa noon-4pm and 7-11pm. AmEx/MC/V. ❹

Casa-Brasileira, R. Augusta, 267-269 (☎213 46 97 13). A great place to grab some food and a pastry while sightseeing. Cheap sandwiches (€2-3), pizza (€2-4), and fruit smoothies (€1.25-1.75). Menu of the day (sandwich, fries, and a freshly squeezed smoothie or an ice cold beer) for €4.50. Open daily 7am-1am. ❶

Ninho Dourado, R. Augusta, 278 (☎213 46 97 39). Situated in the heart of Baixa. Pleasant outdoor seating, a huge menu, and decent prices. Daily special offers a complete meal (plate of the day, drink, dessert, and coffee) for €6. Sandwiches €3-4. Pizzas for 2 €9.50. Entrees €7-10. Open daily 6am-2am. Cash only. ❷

Restaurante Bomjardim, Tr. Santo Antão, 10 (☎213 42 74 24). The self-proclaimed "king of chicken" serves up hearty portions of scrumptious fried, baked, and roast chicken (€9.20) both indoors and under the umbrellas outside. Other grilled meats €9-12. Open daily noon-11:30pm. AmEx/MC/V. ❷

BAIRRO ALTO

The narrow streets of Bairro Alto are lined with bars, restaurants, and the famous *casas de fado.* Prices range from modest to supremely immodest, as in the *casas.* Budget eaters and those searching for veritable Portuguese food should not be discouraged by Bairro Alto's expensive international eateries; though it may take a grueling search to find the cheap, traditional restaurants, it's worth the extra effort. Here's a hint: you can usually find nicer restaurants on the water in the Docas de Santo Amaro area.

A Brasileira, R. Garrett, 120-122 (☎213 46 95 41). M: Baixa-Chiado. A former stomping ground of early 20th-century poets and intellectuals, this cafe verges on doubling as a tourist mainstay. Poet Fernando Pessoa was once a frequent patron, and his statue now sits at his regular chair. Restaurant downstairs serves up platters of Portuguese food. Entrees €6-13. Sandwiches €2-5. Open daily 8am-2am. AmEx/MC/V. ❷

Restaurante Calcuta, R. do Norte, 17 (☎213 42 82 95; www.calcuta1.pt), near Lg. Camões. Listen to Indian music in a relaxing atmosphere while you enjoy Calcutta favorites like the prawn *masala* (€9.50). Wide selection of vegetarian options (€7.50-10). Open M-Sa 11:30am-3pm and 6:30-11:30pm, Su 6:30-11:30pm. MC/V. ❷

Restaurante Ali-a-Papa, R. da Atalaia, 95 (☎213 47 41 43). Serves generous helpings of Moroccan food in a quiet atmosphere; dishes include couscous and tangine. Vegetarian-friendly. Entrees €9-14.50. Open M, T, Th-Su7pm-12:30am. AmEx/MC/V. ❷

LISBOA

ALFAMA

The winding streets of Alfama conceal a number of small and simple restaurants, often packed with locals. The Rua da Padaria and the area around its intersection with Rua dos Bacalhoeiros offers the cheapest options in Lisboa.

À Minha Maneira, Largo do Terreiro do Trigo 1 (☎218 86 11 12; www.a-minha-maneira.pt). Once a bank, the old vault has been revamped into a wine closet. Various meat and fish dishes with little choice for vegetarians. Free Wi-Fi. Entrees €8-15. Open daily noon-3pm and 7-11:30pm. Cash only. ❷

Churrasqueira Gaúcha, R. dos Bacalhoeiros, 26C-D (☎218 87 06 09). Portuguese food cooked to perfection in a comfortable, cavernous setting. One of the best restaurants on a street already packed with great deals. Incredibly fresh meat, poultry, and fish. No vegetarian options. Entrees €8-12. Open M-Sa 10am-midnight. AmEx/MC/V. ❷

Flôr da Sé, Largo Santo António da Sé, 9-11 (☎218 87 57 42). Next to the Santo Antonio church. This *pastelaria* is extremely clean, brightly lit, and serves quality food at some of the lowest prices in Lisboa. The lunchtime *prato do dia* (€4) is scrumptious, and the varied selection of desserts and candies taste as good as they look. Open M-F and Su 7am-8pm. Cash only. ❶

A Nossa Churrasqueira, Lg. Rodrigues de Freitas, 2 (☎218 86 66 02). A quality budget restaurant in the heart of Alfama. Serves hearty portions. Chickens rotate over flaming coals behind the counter, while diners enjoy the outdoor seating. Entrees €7-9. Open Tu-Su noon-10pm. Cash only. ❷

GRAÇA

Good, cheap eats abound in the alleys of Graça. Things heat up after dark, when churches and markets recede and thumping beats take center stage.

O Pitéu, Lg. da Graça, 95-6 (☎218 87 10 67), next door to Pastelaria Estrela da Graça. *Azulejo*-lined walls and wine-inspired decorations. The restaurant serves a few Brazilian dishes in addition to traditional Portuguese dishes of fish, chicken, pork, and steak. Entrees €8-12. Open M-F noon-3pm and 7-10pm, Sa noon-3pm. Cash only. ❷

Bar Cerca Moura, Largo das Portas do Sol, 4 (☎218 87 48 59). Take the #28 tram up the hill from the stop on R. da Conceição. Hop off when you see the statue and the gorgeous view on the right; the bar is on your left. Cozy, leather-covered interior and airy outdoor seating are perfect for kicking off the night. Snacks €2-4. Beer and wine €2-3. Mixed drinks €5. Open daily noon-2am. Cash only. ❶

Esplanada Igreja da Graça, Lg. da Graça. Walk 1 stop uphill beyond the Panteão Nacional to the Lg. da Graça, then follow the Lg. da Graça to the left. This *miradouro* has a perfect view of Baixa and the Rio Tejo. Two kiosks serve up a variety of snacks. Sandwiches €2-4.25. Tea €1.50. Open daily 10am-3am. ❶

Pastelaria Estrela da Graça, 98 Lg. da Graça (☎218 87 24 38), 1 tram stop above the Panteão Nacional. The mouth-watering pastries, candy, cakes, and lunch entrees, are well worth a stop. *Prato do dia* (€4-5.50). Open daily 7am-10pm. Cash only. ❶

SIGHTS

With 3000 years of history, Lisboa has acquired a fascinating aesthetic pedigree. Moorish *azulejos* (painted tiles) adorn the Alfama district; the 12th-century Sé cathedral maintains a tough Romanesque stone facade, contrasting with the elaborate Manueline monastery in Belém, which features excessive ornamentation reflective of Portugal's glory during the Age of Discovery. The Neoclassical design of Praça do Comércio's triumphal Roman arch marks a return to the simpler forms favored by the Marquês de Pombal's post-earthquake rebuilding. But Lisboa's beauty speaks of the present as well, from the sleek, modern Parque das Nações to the expressive, graffitied streets of Bairro Alto. Those planning to do a lot of sightseeing in a few days should consider purchasing the Welcome Center's **Lisboa Card** for a flat fee (p. 586). Museums and many sites are closed on Mondays and free on Sundays before 2pm.

BAIXA

Although Baixa claims few historical sights, the lively pedestrian traffic and dramatic history surrounding the neighborhood's three main *praças* make it a monument on its own. Beware Baixa's softly cooing pigeons, well-trained by countless statues of distinguished leaders on which they've made their mark.

AROUND ROSSIO. Begin your tour of 18th-century history Lisboa at its heart: **Rossio,** or **Praça Dom Pedro IV** as it is more formally known. The city's main square was once a cattle market, public execution stage, bullring, and carnival ground. Today, it is the fast-paced domain of tourists and ruthless local drivers circling Pedro's enormous statue, and shadier characters by night. Another statue, this one of Gil Vicente, Portugal's first great dramatist (p. 576), peers from atop the **Teatro Nacional de Dona Maria II** (easily recognized by its large, Parthenon-esque columns) at one end of the *praça*.

DISTANCE: 1 mi.

DURATION: 2hr.

WHEN TO GO: Tu or Sa for the Feira da Ladra.

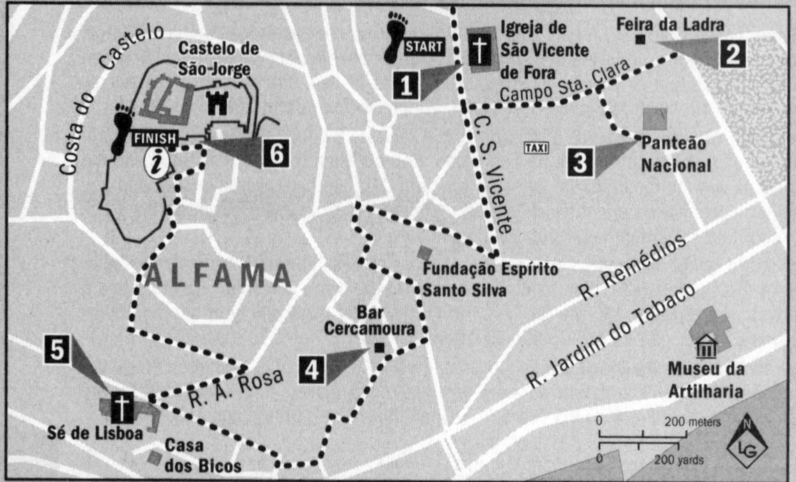

Much of Lisboa was destroyed in the 18th century by a massive earthquake. The most interesting and well-preserved structures are located in the areas of Alfama and Graça. To save yourself the grief of a 2+ hr. hike uphill, start this walking tour of Lisboa with a ride in one of the city's trams. From Praça do Comércio take tram #28 (€1.30) up to the Igreja de São Vicente de Fora.

1. IGREJA DE SÃO VICENTE DE FORA. Built between 1582 and 1629, the Igreja, like many in Portugal, is ornately decorated with gold leafing, large archways, and stained-glass windows. The sacristas, covered with beautiful Sintra marble, are a sight to see. This house of worship is particularly interesting because it's dedicated to Lisboa's real patron saint, St. Vincent.

2. FEIRA DA LADRA. If you happen to be strolling along on a Tuesday or a Saturday between 7am and 4pm you will find a pleasant surprise behind the large church structure: the Feira da Ladra, a flea-market style fair that sells everything from used shoes to African necklaces.

3. PANTEÃO NACIONAL. Around the corner from the feira is the stunning Panteão Nacional. The Panteão was intended to be a church but the town ran out of money before it could be completed. Seized by the government, it was turned into a monument documenting and honoring the forefathers of Portugal.

4. BAR CERCAMOURA. From the Panteão Nacional follow the tram tracks downhill. Window shop or stop at variety of unique antique stores on either side of the street. About ½ mi. downhill there is a great viewpoint from which the skyline of Lisboa, from Alfama, to Baixa, and to the Tejo, can be viewed. Take a break at the Bar Cercamoura before heading onward.

5. SÉ DE LISBOA. The small but impressive Sé lacks the splendor of Lisboa's grander cathedrals, but its sheer age and wonderful location make for an enjoyable visit.

6. CASTELO DE SÃO JORGE. Follow the signs to the castle. At the top of the small hill you'll find the entrance to the Castelo de São Jorge. Constructed during the 5th century by Visigoths, the castle was later dominated by the Moors and finally by the royal family of Portugal. Today, it stands as a series of stone walls with amazing views of Lisboa.

AROUND PRAÇA DOS RESTAURADORES. In Praça dos Restauradores, a giant obelisk celebrates Portugal's hard-earned independence from Spain, achieved in 1640 after 60 years of Spanish rule. The obelisk stands by a bronze sculpture of the "Spirit of Independence," a reminder of the centuries-old Spanish-Portuguese rivalry. The tourist office is housed at Palácio da Foz, and shops line the *praça* and C. da Glória, the hill that leads to Bairro Alto. Pr. dos Restauradores is also the start of Avenida da Liberdade, one of Lisboa's most elegant promenades. Modeled after the boulevards of 19th-century Paris, this mile-long thoroughfare ends at **Praça do Marquês de Pombal.** There, an 18th-century statue of the Marquês still watches over the city he whipped into shape 250 years ago.

AROUND PRAÇA DO COMÉRCIO. After the earthquake of 1755 leveled this section of Lisboa, the Marquês de Pombal designed the new streets to serve as a conduit for goods from the ports on the Rio Tejo to the city center. The grid formed perfect blocks, with streets designated for specific trades: *sapateiros* (shoemakers), *douradores* (gold workers), and *bacalhoeiros* (cod merchants) each had their own avenue. The roads lead to Praça do Comércio, on the banks of the Tejo. Today the *praça*, watched over by a 9400 lb. statue of **Dom João I**, serves as a tourist hub, providing a wide and inviting space between the Tejo's many boats and the city's buzzing crowds.

BAIRRO ALTO

MUSEU ARQUEOLÓGICO DO CARMO. Located under the fantasy-like skeletal arches of an old church destroyed in the catastrophic 1755 earthquake, this partially outdoor museum allows visitors to get up close to historical relics like a 16th-century coat of arms. Check out the two Peruvian mummies and the Egyptian sarcophagus inside. *(On Largo do Carmo. Open M-Sa Oct.-Mar. 10am-6pm; Apr.-Feb. 10am-7pm. €2.50, students €1.50, under 14 free.)*

CEMITÉRIO DOS PRAZERES. At the cemetery, hundreds of small family mausoleums are lined together, forming a genuine city of the dead. Many of these mini-buildings have broken doors or glass pane windows, allowing you to see inside (if you want to). Watch out, as some of the older ones have broken coffins. The easily-frightened may want to visit in the assuring light of day. *(Pr. S. João Bosco. ☎213 96 15 11. Take tram #28 to the end of the line, in the opposite direction as you would for the castle. Open daily Oct.-Apr. 9am-4:30pm; May-Sept. 9am-5:30pm. €1.35.)*

ELEVADOR DE SANTA JUSTA. This historic elevator, built in 1902 inside a Gothic wrought-iron tower, once served as transportation up to Bairro Alto, but now takes tourists up 45m to the top. There is a small cafe where visitors can have a drink while enjoying a view of the city. Avoid the elevator on weekends—there's a huge line. *(Runs daily 7am-8:45pm. €2.80 round-trip.)*

BASÍLICA DA ESTRELA. Directly across from the **Jardim da Estrela**, the Basílica da Estrela dates back to 1796 and casts an imposing presence over the *Praça*. Its dome, poised behind a pair of tall belfries, towers over surrounding buildings to take its place in the Lisboa skyline. The desperate Dona Maria I promised God anything and everything if she were granted a son. When a baby boy was finally born, she built this church, and today, architecture aficionados are grateful. Ask to see the 10th-century nativity. *(Pr. da Estrela. Accessible by metro or tram #28 from Pr. do Comércio. ☎213 96 09 15. Open daily 7:45am-8pm. Free.)*

IGREJA DE SÃO ROQUE. When the Catholic church brought Saint Roque's bones and other relics to Lisboa from Spain in the 1500s, they had not intended to build a church in his name. But when the epidemic-inducing rodents terrorizing Lisboa miraculously vanished upon his arrival, Sr. Roque became a São (saint); a Jesuit church with all the bells and whistles of the era was quickly built in his honor. Inside, the **Capela de São João Baptista** (fourth from the left) blazes with agate, lapis lazuli, and precious metals. Considered a masterpiece of European art, the chapel caused a stir upon its installation in 1747 because it took three ships to transport the church from Rome, where it was built. The ceiling is covered by a magnificent painting portraying scenes from the life of Jesus. *(Lg. Trindade Coelho. ☎213 23 53 80. Open daily 8:30am-5pm, holidays 8:30am-1pm.)*

PARKS. Across from the Basílica on Lg. da Estrela, the wide paths of the **Jardim da Estrela** wind through flocks of pigeons, happily quacking ducks, and lush flora. *(M: Rato. With your back to the metro stop, follow R. Pedro Álvares Cabral, the 2nd road from the left in the traffic circle, for 10min. You can also take tram #28 from Barrio Alto. Open daily 6am-midnight.)* More greenery awaits uphill along **R. Dom Pedro V** at the **Parque Príncipe Real,** which connects to the **Jardim Botánico.** For a good view, head to the **Parque de São Pedro de Alcântara.** The Castelo de São Jorge in Alfama occupies the cliff opposite the park, and Bairro Alto twinkles below.

SÃO SEBASTIÃO

MUSEU CALOUSTE GULBENKIAN. Perhaps Portugal's biggest fan ever, native Armenian Calouste Gulbenkian was so charmed when he visited in 1942 that he stayed in the same hotel in Lisboa for 13 years, until his death in 1955. In his will, the millionaire left his extensive art collection (some of it purchased from the Hermitage in St. Petersburg, Russia) to Portugal. The collection is divided into sections of ancient art—Egyptian, Greek, Roman, Mesopotamian, Islamic, and Oriental—and European pieces from the 15th to 20th centuries. Highlights include the Egyptian room, Rembrandts, Monets, Renoirs, Rodins, Manets, and a collection of ancient coins. *(Av. Berna, 45A. M: São Sebastião. From the main entrance of El Corte Inglés, follow the main road, Av. Augusto Antonio de Aguiar, downhill until you see the sign for the "Fundação Calouste Gulbenkian." Take a right up the staircase, climb another set of stairs, and the Museu is across the parking lot. Bus #16, 26, 31, 46, 56. ☎217 82 30 00; www.gulbenkian.pt. Open Tu-Su 10am-5:45pm. €4, pass for both the Gulbenkian and the CAMJAP €7. 50% discount for students, teachers, and seniors everyday; free on Su.)*

CENTRO DE ARTE MODERNO. Though not as famous as its neighbor, this modern art museum promotes Portuguese talent from the late 19th century to the present. The center also places an emphasis on works originating from Portugal's former colonies across the globe. Don't miss the sculpture gardens that separate the two museums. *(R. Dr. Nicolau Bettencourt. M: São Sebastião. From the main entrance of El Corte Inglés, follow the steep Rua Marquês de Fronteira downhill, take a left before the palace, the Ministério do Exército; the Centro will be on your right about 200m farther. Bus #16, 26, 31, 46, 56. ☎217 82 30 00. Open Tu-Su 10am-6pm. €4. Students, teachers, and seniors get a 50% discount. Su free for general public.)*

ALFAMA

CASTELO DE SÃO JORGE. Built by the Moors in the 11th century, the castle was conquered by Don Alfonso Enriquez, first king of Portugal, then converted into a playground for the royal family between the 14th and 16th centuries. The towers and castle walls allow for a spectacular panoramic view of Lisboa and the Rio Tejo. *(☎218 80 06 20; www.egeac.pt. Open daily Mar.-Oct. 9am-9pm; Nov.-Feb. 9am-6pm. €5, students €2.50, with Lisboa card €3.50, under 10 or over 65 free.)*

LOWER ALFAMA. The small white **Igreja de Santo António** was built in 1812 over the saint's alleged birthplace. The construction was funded with money collected by the city's children, who fashioned altars bearing saintly images to place on doorsteps. The custom is reenacted annually on June 13, the saint's feast day and Lisboa's biggest holiday, which draws out thousands and involves a debaucherous festival the night before. The church is located on R. da Alfândeo, which begins two blocks away from Pr. do Comércio and connects Baixa and lower Alfama. *(Veer right when you see Igreja da Madalena in Lg. da Madalena on the right. Take R. de Santo António da Sé and follow the tram tracks. ☎218 86 91 45. Open daily 8am-7pm. Mass daily 11am, 5, and 7pm.)* In the square beyond the church is the 12th-century **Sé de Lisboa.** The cathedral's interior lacks the ornamentation of the city's other churches, but its age and treasury make it an intriguing visit. *(☎218 86 67 52. Open daily 9am-7pm except during mass, held Tu-Sa 6:30pm, Su 11:30am and 7pm. Free. Treasury open M-Sa 10am-5pm. €2.50, students €1.50. Cloister open daily May-Sept. 2-7pm; Oct.-Apr. M-Sa 10am-6pm, Su 2-6pm. €2.50, students €1.25.)*

GRAÇA

PANTEÃO NACIONAL. The National Pantheon was originally meant to be the Igreja da Santa Engrácia; the citizens of Graça started building the church in 1680 to honor their patron saint. Their ambitions outstripped their finances, however, and they abandoned the project before completing the dome, leaving a massive hole in the top. General Salazar's military regime eventually took over construction, dedicating it as the National Pantheon, a burial ground for important statesmen, in 1966. In a twist of irony, when democracy was restored in 1975, the new government relocated the remains of prominent anti-Fascist opponents to the building and prohibited those who had worked with Salazar from entering. The dome juts out from among the other old buildings of Graça, providing an amazing view of Lisboa from the outdoor terrace. Highlights include the tombs of presidents as well as cenotaphs (honorary tombs for people buried elsewhere) for explorers. The Pantheon houses the remains of Amália Rodrigues, the queen of *fado*, and the cenotaphs of Vasco da Gama, the famous Portuguese explorer, and Luis de Camoes, the legendary poet of Portugal. *(To reach the Panteão, take the #28 tram from R. Do Loreto or R. Garrett. ☎218 85 48 20 ; fax 218 85 48 39. Open Tu-Su 10am-5pm. €2.50, seniors €1.25. Free Su and holidays)*

IGREJA AND MOSTEIRO DE SÃO VICENTE DE FORA. Built between 1582 and 1629, the Igreja is dedicated to St. Vincent, Lisboa's official patron saint, though Lisboa tends to celebrate its adopted patron saint, St. Antony, much more. Ask to see the *sacristia* (chapel) with its inlaid walls of Sintra marble and the Madre de Deus crib. *(From the bottom of R. dos Correeiros in Baixa, take bus #12 or tram #28. You can also go to M: Santa Apolonia and walk upthill. ☎218 82 44 00. Open daily 10am-6pm except for mass. Mass Tu and F 9:30am, Sa-Su 10am. Free. Chapel open Tu-Su 10am-5pm. €2.)*

FEIRA DA LADRA. Every Tuesday and Saturday between the Panteão and Igreja de São Vicente, local vendors hit the streets in the early morning for the Graça "thieves market." Merchants bring piles of goods, from Beatles paraphernalia to African sculptures, and passersby are encouraged to make an offer. Get steals on old wristwatches and cameras, dig through piles of jewelry, or admire handmade chandeliers and crucifixes. *(Tu and Sa 8am-late afternoon.)*

MUSEU NACIONAL DO AZULEJO. Housed within the 16th-century Convento da Madre de Deus, this museum is devoted to the art of the *azulejo* (see **Architecture,** p. 595). A Manueline doorway leads into a Baroque interior embellished with oil paintings and *azulejos*. Don't miss the chorus room on the second floor, and notice the royal skulls on both sides of the room. *(R. Madre de Deus, 4. East of Alfama in Xabregas. From Pr. do Comércio, just next to the giant arch, take bus #104 or 105. From M: Santa Apolonia cross the street and take bus #28 or 754. The museum is next to the Igreja*

Madre de Deus. ☎218 10 03 40; www.mnazulejo-ipmuseus.pt. Open Tu 2-6pm, W-Su 10am-6pm. Last entrance 5:30pm. €4; under 25, seniors, and teachers €2. Free Su before 2pm.)

ENTERTAINMENT

Agenda Cultural and **Follow Me Lisboa,** free at the tourist office and at kiosks in the Rossio on R. Portas de Santo Antão, have information on concerts, *fado*, movies, plays, and bullfights, as well as lists of museums, gardens, and libraries.

FADO

A mandatory experience for visitors, Lisboa's trademark entertainment is the traditional *fado*, an expressive art combining elements of singing and narrative poetry (see Music, p. 577). *Cantadeiras de fado*, cloaked in black dresses and shawls, relate emotional tales of lost loves and faded glory. Numerous *fado* houses lie in the small streets of Bairro Alto and near R. de São João da Praça in Alfama. Some have both *fado* and folk dance performances. To avoid making a tragedy of your budget, explore nearby streets; various bars and small venues often offer free shows with less notable performers. Book in advance, especially on weekends, and arrive at *fado* houses 30-45min. early. Minimum consumption requirements tend to run €10-20, but ask ahead of time as they may only apply to the second show, which starts around 11pm. The following places are quite touristy, but they do feature Portugal's top names in *fado*.

Café Luso, Travessa da Queimada, 10 (☎213 42 22 81; www.cafeluso.pt). Pass below the club's glowing neon-blue sign to reach *fado* nirvana. Open since 1927, Lisboa's premier *fado* club combines the best in Portuguese music, cuisine, and atmosphere. *Menú* €25. Entrees €22-29. Min. €25. Fado 8:30-10pm then folklore dance until 2am. Make reservations for F and Sa nights. Open M-Sa 7:30pm-2am. AmEx/MC/V. ❹

O Faia, R. Barroca, 56 (☎213 42 67 42). Performances by famous *fadistas* like Anita Guerreiro and Lenita Gentil, as well as very fine Portuguese cuisine, make O Faia worth your time and money. 4 singers. Entrees €20-35. Min. €20, includes 2 drinks. *Fado* starts at 9:30pm. 2nd show starts at 11:30pm. Open M-Sa 8pm-2am. AmEx/MC/V. ❹

Adega Machado, R. do Norte, 91 (☎213 22 46 40; fax 46 75 07). Founded in 1937, Machado is one of the larger *fado* restaurants and features some of the best known *cantadeiras* and guitarists. The many portraits and wall decorations make this cavernous bar warm and inviting. Slightly older crowd. A typical meal, including drinks, is €35. Min. drink charge €16. *Fado* starts at 9pm. Open Tu-Su 8pm-3am. AmEx/MC/V. ❹

LISBOA

THEATER, MUSIC, AND FILM

Teatro Nacional de Dona Maria II, Pr. Dom Pedro IV, stages performances of classical and foreign plays. (☎213 25 08 00. Tickets €5-20.) At Lisboa's largest theater, **Teatro Nacional de São Carlos,** R. Serpa Pinto, 9, near the Museu do Chiado in Bairro Alto, opera reigns from late December to mid-June, and the **Orquestra Sinfonica Portuguesa** plays from December to July. (☎213 25 30 45. Tickets €7-60. Open M-F 1-7pm, performance days 1pm until 30min. prior to shows.)

The **São Jorge movie theater,** Av. da Liberdade, 175 (☎213 10 34 00) is one of the oldest in Portugal. Daily shows are held between 2:30 and 9:30pm. Ten-screen cinemas are also located in the **Amoreiras** (☎213 81 02 00; M: Marquês de Pombal), the **Colombo** shopping center (☎217 11 36 00; M: Colegio Militar Luz), and on the top floor of the **Centro Vasco da Gama** (☎218 93 06 01; M: Oriente). The largest theater, with 14 screens, is part of the **El Corte Inglés** shopping complex (☎213 71 17 00; M: São Sebastião). American films are shown with Portuguese subtitles. Movies cost about €7; matinee shows are slightly less.

BULLFIGHTING

Portuguese bullfighting differs from the Spanish variety in that the bull is typically not killed in the ring, but butchered afterwards, a tradition that dates back to the 18th century. These spectacles take place most Thursdays from late June to late September at **Praça de Touros de Lisboa,** Campo Pequeno. (☎217 93 21 43. Open daily 10pm-2am.) The newly renovated *praça* doubles as a shopping center during the day and also features the distinctly Portuguese *toureio equestre*, or horseback bullfighting at night. Aficionados should include **Santarém** (p. 641) in their travel plans—it's the capital of Portuguese bullfighting and hosts the most celebrated *cavaleiros*.

FUTEBOL

Futebol is the lifeblood of many a Portuguese citizen. *Futebol* fever became an epidemic during the 2006 World Cup, and after a month of nail-biting, shop-closing, crowd-gathering soccer mania, the Portuguese team returned from Germany national heroes after reaching the semifinal round for the first time in 40 years. These days, the Portuguese get riled up for the popular Euro Cup and regional games. If you are in Lisboa when Portugal is playing, go to **Marques de Pombal** (M: Marques de Pombal), where you will see hundreds of fans screaming at a giant TV screen. If they win, follow the fans to the main *praça*, where they will stop traffic, clamber onto random cars, and sometimes flip them over. Portugal's two most renowned teams are in Lisboa: **Benfica** and **Sporting,** both of which feature some of the world's finest players. (Benfica at Estádio da Luz. ☎707 200 100; www.slbenfica.pt. M: Colégio Militar-Luz. Ticket office open daily 10am-7pm. Sporting at Alvalade Stadium. ☎707 20 44 44; www.sporting.pt. M: Campo Grande. Ticket office open M-F 10am-7pm.) Benfica made headlines with its magical rise to the semifinal round of the 2006 UEFA Champions League, the most prestigious club tournament in Europe, for the first time in over a decade. Benfica and Sporting are bitter rivals—be careful whom you support, since both have diehard fans who won't care that you're "just a tourist." Check the newspaper **A Bola** for games.

NIGHTLIFE

Bairro Alto is the first place to go for nightlife, especially before 2am. **R. do Norte, R. do Diário de Notícias, R. da Rosa,** and **R. Atalaia**, which run parallel to each other, pack many small bars and clubs into three short blocks, making bar-hopping as easy as crossing the street. Several gay and lesbian establishments lie in this area, as well as in **Rato** near the edge of Bairro Alto, past Pr. Príncipe Real. The options near the water are larger, flashier, and generally more diverse. The **Docas de Santo Amaro** host a strip of waterfront bars, clubs, and restaurants, while the Av. 24 de Julho and the parallel R. das Janelas Verdes (Street of Green Windows), in the **Santos** area, have some of the most popular clubs and discotecas. Newer expansions include the area along the river across from the Santa Apolónia train station, home to glitzy club Lux. The Bairro Alto bar scene is very casual, but at clubs, jeans, sandals, and sneakers are generally not allowed—some places have uptight fashion police at the door. Inside, beer runs €3-5, and it gets more expensive as the night goes by. Some clubs also charge a cover (generally €5-13), which usually gets you two to four free drinks. Usually, entrance is free for girls. There's no reason to show up before midnight; crowds flow in around 2am and stay past dawn.

BAIRRO ALTO

From tiny bars to punk clubs to posh *fado* restaurants, the Bairro Alto and nearby districts can't be beat for nightlife and entertainment.

BAIRRO ALTO AND NORTH TO THE JARDIM BOTÁNICO

A Tasca Tequila Bar, Tr. da Queimada, 13-15 (☎919 40 79 14). A great place to go on a slow weekday night, this Mexican bar is always full. The bartenders don't forget to have a good time themselves while serving up potent mixed drinks at the T-shaped counter. Mixed drinks €5-6. Open M-Sa 6pm-2am.

Pavilhão Chinês, Dom Pedro V, 89 (☎213 42 47 29). Ring the doorbell and a red-vested waiter ushers you into this classy establishment, where the walls and ceilings hang heavy with art pieces. You can chill at one of the leather couches, smoke a cigar, or play pool in the back room, but if you're looking for loud music and dancing, it's not the place for you. Mixed drinks €6. Beers €30. Open daily M-Sa 6pm-2am, Su 9pm-2am.

Palpita-me, R. Diário de Notícias, 40-B (www.palpita-me.com). Sing out of tune to your favorite hits from the 80s and 90s at this karaoke bar smack in the center of it all. Drinks are on the cheaper side (beer €2, whiskey €4) and there is frequently live music. Order a drink, write your name and the song you'll sing in the ballot, and get ready to shine. Go early, as you won't be the only star. Open M-Sa 10pm-4am. Cash only.

Páginas Tantas, R. Diário de Notícias, 85 (☎213 46 54 95). This classical jazz bar provides a quiet and cool retreat from the wild street parties of Bairro Alto. A diverse group of young professionals sips on the bar's specials during happy hour (9-11pm). Open daily 9pm-4am. AmEx/D/MC/V.

Portas Largas, R. da Atalaia, 105 (☎965 24 76 15), at the end of Tr. da Queimada. Located in the heart of Bairro Alto, the recently renovated Portas Largas is one of the district's most popular bars. Diverse crowds keep this place full every night of the week. Open daily July-Sept. 7pm-3:30am; Oct.-June 8pm-3:30am.

SOUTH OF BAIRRO ALTO: AVENIDA 24 DE JULHO AND SANTOS

It is best to take a cab (€6 from Rossio) to these clubs due to their distance and the danger in walking alone at night—the E-15 line stops at 1am.

Jamaica, R. Nova do Carvalho, 6 (☎213 42 18 59). M: Cais do Sodre. This small 40-year old club is famous for playing 80s music, alternative rock, and political protest songs prohibited during the Salazar era. Packed until early morning, and a big line starts forming at 2am. Women get in free, but cover usually €6 for guys (includes 3 free beers). Open Tu-Sa midnight-6am.

Kapital, Av. 24 de Julho, 68 (☎213 95 71 01). One of the classiest clubs in Lisboa, it has a ruthless door policy that makes admission a competitive sport. Don't expect to get in, especially if you're an unaccompanied male or if it's clear you're a tourist. Panoramic view of the Rio Tejo. Drinks €5. For the best chance, go with regulars and dress nicely. Cover €10-20. Open M-Sa 11pm-6am. MC/V.

Kremlin, Escadinhasda Praia, 5 (☎213 95 71 01; www.kremlin-k.com), off Av. 24 de Julho. During the 80s, this discoteque somewhat mystifyingly claimed to be the 3rd best in the world. Run by the same management as Kapital, but has a more mixed crowd, including Kapital rejects and newcomers to Lisboa. Come nicely dressed. Rave music and ambience. Cover usually €7 for women, €12 for men. Open W-Th midnight-7am, F-Sa midnight-9am. MC/V.

WEST OF BAIRRO ALTO: DOCAS DE SANTO AMARO

To get to the Docas, take the E-15 electric car from the Praça do Comércio to the Alcantara-Mar stop and then walk or take a cab from there. It's cheap (€6) to take a cab straight from Rossio. Should you choose to walk, be forewarned that the docks can be dangerous at night and the bars are a long, uncertain walk away. The only way back is a cab, as the E-15 stops at 1am.

Dock's Club, R. da Cintura do Porto de Lisboa, 226 (☎213 95 08 56). A €4-6 cab ride from the taxi station in Bairro Alto. This huge club plays great hip hop, latino, and house music, and starts to fill up around 2am. Two bars inside and one outside if you need to cool off (or dry off). On Tu nights girls get in free with 4 free drinks (men pay €12 and get 2 free drinks). Open Tu, F-Sa midnight-5:30am. AmEx/Mc/V.

Speakeasy, Docas de Santo Amaro (☎213 90 91 66; www.speakeasy-bar.com), between the Santos and Alcântara stops, near the river. More of a concert with waiters and beer than a bar. Live rock, pop, jazz, and blues concerts almost every night. Beer €3.50. M night jazz. Open Tu-Sa 10pm-3am, restaurant 10pm-midnight. Cash only.

ALFAMA

Restô, R. Costa do Castelo, 7 (☎218 86 73 34). Don't be surprised to see a flying trapeze or tightrope act—Restô is on the grounds of a government-funded clown school, Chapitô. Upstairs serves Argentine steaks (€17-30) and Spanish tapas (€4-8). Huge patio. Open daily. Lunch noon-3pm. Dinner 7:30pm-1:30am. Cash only.

Clube de Fado, R. S. João da Praça, 92/94 (☎218 88 26 94; www.clube-de-fado.com). A relaxed alternative to the *fado* scene in Bairro Alto, Clube de Fado's rustic wood and stone parlor takes you back to the days of a less hectic Lisboa. Entrees €20-50. Reserve ahead. Min. €10. Open daily 8pm-2am; *fado* starts at 9:30pm. AmEx/MC/V.

Ondajazz Bar, Arco de Jesus, 7 (☎ 919 18 48 67, www.ondajazz.com). Visit the Ondajazz Bar for a wide selection of performances including jazz, blues, and poetry readings. Tu live Jazz band. W open mic. €6-7 drink min. Sometimes an entrance fee (€5-7) applies, with no drink min. Dinner and concert package (€25-30) includes starter, entree and a drink. Open Tu-Th 9pm-2am, F-Sa 9pm-3am.

Marquês da Sé, Lg. do Marquês do Lavrádio, 1 (☎218 88 02 34). *Fado* under vaulted ceilings and lit by candles perched along the walls. A little on the pricey side (€20 drink min., entrees €17-24) but well worth it. Reservations recommended. Open daily 8pm-2am; *fado* starts at 9:30pm. AmEx/MC/V.

GRAÇA

Lux/Frágil, Av. Infante D. Henrique A, Cais da Pedra a Sta. Apolonia (☎218 82 08 90). Take a taxi (€5 from Chiado) to the area across from the Sta. Apolónia train station to get to this enormous 3-story complex. One-of-a-kind view from the roof of what some fans call "the perfect nightclub." High-tech lighting system and awesome music playing all night long. Bouncers are very selective, so dress well (though stylish hipster works better than suiting up), hide the foreign accent, go in small groups, don't be loud, and say "please." Cover is €12 which includes 2 mixed drinks or 4 beers. Arrive after 2am. Open Tu-Sa 10pm-6am. AmEx/MC/V.

FESTIVALS

Those who love to mingle with locals will want to visit Lisboa in June. Open-air *feiras*—festivals of eating, drinking, live music, and dancing—fill the streets. After savoring *farturas* (huge Portuguese pastries whose name means "abundance") and Sagres beer, join in traditional Portuguese dancing. On the night of June 12, the streets explode into song and dance in honor of St. Anthony during the **Festa de Santo António.** Banners are strung between streetlights and confetti falls in buckets during a parade along Av. da Liberdade. Young crowds pack the streets of Alfama and the neighborhood of Santa Catarina, and grilled *sardinhas* (sardines) and *ginja* (wild cherry liqueur) are sold everywhere. Lisboa also has a number of commercial *feiras*. From late May to early June, bookworms burrow for three weeks in the outdoor **Feira do Livro** in Parque Eduardo VII, behind Pr. Marquês de Pombal. The **Feira Internacional de Lisboa** occurs every few months in the Parque das Nações; in July and August, the **Feira de Mar de Cascais** and **Feira de Artesanato de Estoril** (celebrating famous Portuguese pottery) take place near the casino. Year-round *feiras* include the **Feira de Oeiras** (sells antiques on the fourth Sunday of each month) and the **Feira de Carcanelos** (sells clothes Th 8am-2pm) in Rato. Packrats should catch the **Feira da Ladra,** a large flea market, whose name literally means "thieves' fair" (don't be surprised if your stolen watch turns up there). It's held behind Igreja de São Vicente de Fora in Graça (Tu 7am-1pm and Sa 7am-3pm; take tram #28, €1.30).

OUTER DISTRICTS

PARQUE DAS NAÇÕES

From Lisboa, take the metro to M: Oriente at the end of the red line. The station has escalators to the park's main entrance, through the Centro Vasco da Gama shopping center. (☎218 93 06 01; www.centrovascodagama.pt. Open daily 10am-midnight.) Alternatively, city buses #5, 25, 28, 44, 68, 210, 708, 750, 759, and 79 all stop at the Oriente station (€1.35). Parque das Nações (☎218 91 93 33; www.parquedasnacoes.pt). If you are planing to visit many attractions buy the Cartão do Parque. (€17.50, under 17/ over 65 €9).

Until the mid-1990s, this area was a muddy mess consisting of a few run-down factories and warehouses along the banks of the Tejo. Today, after millions spent preparing for the 1998 World Exposition, the Parque das Nações (Park of Nations) is a masterpiece in civil planning and engineering. Much more than a park, the region is becoming a small city, with residential areas to the north and south. Visitors can find map kiosks outside the **Centro Vasco da Gama** shopping mall across the street, at the information center. On the way in, take a look at the unusual **Estação Oriente.** Santiago Calatrava, Spain's most famous contemporary architect, designed its arches. The park extends along the river, enclosing numerous exhibitions and attractions for kids and adults alike.

OCEANÁRIO. The park's biggest attraction, this enormous oceanarium has interactive sections showcasing the four major oceans, recreating their character right down to their sounds, smells, and climates. All of these connect to the main tank, which has over 470 different species of fish, sharks, and other sea creatures. Visitors can get within arm's length of playful sea otters and penguins. (*☎218 91 70 02/06; www.oceanario.pt. Open daily Apr.-Oct. 10am-7pm; Nov.-Mar. 10am-6pm. €11, under 12 €5.50, over 65 €6. Families with children pay one price of €26.50.*)

CABLE CARS. Gondolas connect the ends of the park and offer visitors a bird's eye view of the park and Rio Tejo. (*☎218 95 61 43. 8min.; M-F 11am-7pm Sa-Su 10am-7pm €3.90 one-way, €6 round-trip; under 14, over 65 €2/€3.30 round-trip.*)

BELÉM

Visitors can reach Belém by tram, bus, or train. By tram, take #15 (toward Algés) and get off at the Mosteiro dos Jerónimos stop, 1 stop beyond the regular Belém stop. You can also take tram #28 or bus #714 from Pr. Figueira or Pr. do Comércio (25min., €1.35) or from Cais do Sodré). Alternatively, take the train from Estação Cais do Sodré. To start at the Padrão dos

Descobrimentos, exit the station by the overpass toward the water. To begin at Mosteiro dos Jerónimos, exit the overpass to the right, then go through the public gardens to R. de Belém.

The Age of Discovery began in Portugal, and there is no greater tribute to its pioneering spirit than the seafront of Belém. Explorers like Vasco da Gama and Prince Henry the Navigator launched their famous 15th-century voyages from its sands. Today, visitors come from around the world to see the embodiments of Portugal's past glories of exploration and faith. But it is not just a rich history that makes Belém worth your while. The town is also famous for its delicious custard-filled pastries, *pasteis de Belém*. These desserts, with a recipe perfected at the nearby monastery, have been served in their original form at the famous **Pastels de Belém ❶**, R. de Belém, 84-92, since the restaurant's 1837 opening. (☎213 637 423; www.pasteisdebelem.pt. Open daily 9am-11pm.) If wandering the shores has left you with an empty stomach, stop in at **Pão Pão Queijo Queijo ❶**, R. de Belém, 124. This small, quaint locale is perfect for a quick bite, serving delicious pitas (€3-4), sandwiches (€3-4), and entrees (€6.55). Exceptionally crowded at peak lunchtime hours (1-3pm). Additional seating upstairs. (☎213 62 33 69. Open M-Sa 8am-midnight, Su 8am-8pm.)

MOSTEIRO DOS JERÓNIMOS. Established in 1502 in commemoration of Vasco da Gama's ground-breaking expedition to India, the Mosteiro dos Jerónimos is a gorgeous cloister designed with minute Renaissance detail and ornate Gothic construction. It was recognized for its beauty in the 1980s, when it was granted UNESCO World Heritage status. Note the anachronism on the main church door: Prince Henry the Navigator mingles with the Twelve Apostles on both sides of the central column. The symbolic tombs of Luís de Camões and navigator Vasco da Gama lie in opposing transepts. *(☎213 62 00 34. Open Tu-Su May-Sept. 10am-6:30pm; Oct.-Apr. 10am-5:30pm. Last admission 30min. before closing. Church free. Cloister €6, students free with ID, seniors over 65 €2.)* Directly across from the church lies the **Museu Nacional de Arqueologia.** This five-room museum explores Portugal's ancient past, including prehistoric ruins and evidence of Roman influence. Check out the treasure room, full of priceless works of gold and silver from thousands of years ago. Also notable is the Egyptian archaeology room that features several sarcophagi. *(☎213 62 00 00. Open Tu-Su 10am-6pm. €4, students, teachers, and seniors €2. LisboaCard holders get in free. Cash only.)*

PADRÃO DOS DESCOBRIMENTOS. Along the river and directly across the highway from the Mosteiro is the Padrão dos Descobrimentos, built in 1960 to celebrate the 500th anniversary of Prince Henry the Navigator's death. The view is better than that from the Torre, and there's an elevator that transports visitors 50m up to the narrow roof top. You can see the 25 of Abril bridge, Lisboa and the Cristo Redentor monument on your left, and the Atlantic Ocean on your right. The Padrão also hosts temporary art exhibits, as well as Lisboa Experience, a 25min. audovisual presentation about the history of Lisboa. *(Across the highway from the Mosteiro. ☎213 03 19 50; www.egeac.pt. Open May-Sept. Tu-Su 10am-7pm; Oct.-Apr. 10am-6pm. Last admission 30min. before closing. €2.50; students and seniors €1.50. Lisboa Experience presentation runs from 10:30am-5pm every 30min.; €4, Students and seniors €3, Lisboa Card €2.80. Narrated in English, Spanish, German, and French)*

CENTRO CULTURAL DE BELÉM. Contemporary art buffs will bask in the glow of this luminous complex, which could best be described as a modern Mayan fortress. With three pavilions holding rotating world-class exhibitions and a huge auditorium for concerts and performances, the center provides the only modern entertainment in a sea of imperial landmarks. The new **Museum Colecção Berardo** of modern and contemporary art has an eclectic and extensive exhibition of surrealist paintings, utopian ideas, and architecture, featuring greats such as Le Corbusier, Miro, and Picasso. The CCB also holds a wide variety of performances, ranging from puppet shows to plays, orchestral music, and even Indonesian music and dance. *(☎213 61 24 00; www.ccb.pt. Ticket office open daily 1-7:30pm. Museu Colecçâo Berardo ☎213 61 28 78. Open M-Th 10am-7pm. F-Sa 10am-10pm. Last entrance 30min. before closing. Free.)*

TORRE DE BELÉM. The best-known tower in all of Portugal, the Torre de Belém is a stone fortress sitting on the banks of the Rio Tejo. Built under Manuel I from 1514-1519 as a military stronghold, the Torre has served several functions, including a stint as Portugal's most famous political prison. The tower is a powerful symbol of Portuguese grandeur and has majestic views in every direction. Images of this UNESCO World Heritage site can be found in just about every postcard stand in Lisboa. *(A 15min. walk from the monastery, with the water on your left. Take the overpass by the gardens to cross the highway. Open Tu-Su May-Sept. 10am-6:30pm; Oct.-Apr. 10am-5:30pm. Last admission 30min. before closing. €4; under 25 and seniors €2.)*

DAYTRIP FROM LISBOA

MAFRA

Mafrense buses run from Lisboa's Campo Grande and stop in the square across from the palace (the "Mafra Convento" stop). Buses from Mafra serve Lisboa (1hr.; hourly M-F 5:26am-9:20pm, Sa 5:30am-8:44pm, Su and national holidays 6:23am-9:56pm; €3.40), Sintra (40 min; every hr. M-F 6:20am-7:35pm, Sa 7:30am-7:30am, Su 9:00am-7:30pm, €2.60),and Ericeira (20min.; every hr. M-F 7:36am-12:32am, Sa 7:36am-12:32pm, Su and national holidays 8:05am-12:33am; €1.70). Don't take the train from Lisboa's Estação Santa Apolónia unless you're up for the 7km walk to Mafra; cabs are rare by the station. To return to Ericeira, walk down Terreiro de D. J. V and veer left. Continue down Av. 25 de Abril. The stop is on the right-hand side of the road about 50 ft. from the gas station.

LISBOA

Mafra is a tiny country village with an enormous claim to fame: the **Palácio Nacional de Mafra**. Built by Dom João V as a "hunting palace," and made famous by Saramago's *Memorial do Convento*, the building took 50,000 workers and 30 years to build. Its unusual monastery has its own hospital-chapel hybrid, where patients' bed curtains were pulled back for mass. There is also the chilling **Sala de Penitência** (Penance Room), where the Franciscan monks performed self-flagellation—notice the four-sided cage for mad monks. The **Sala do Trono** (Throne Room), where the king gave his speeches, is covered with murals representing his eight ideal virtues, starting with *"perfectio"* (perfection). The **Sala da Caça** (Hunting Room) is decorated with antlers and heads of all kinds—the chairs, the tables, and even the chandelier are all made of elk antlers. The most impressive space is the palatial *biblioteca* (library) containing 40,000 volumes from the 16th-18th centuries, many of which were bound by the monks. The monks were fastidious about the preservation of books, bringing a colony of bats into the library to eat insects and other would-be book vandals; a few bats still come out from the ancient bookshelves at night. (☎261 81 75 50. Open M and W-Su 10am-5pm, last entrance at 4:30pm. Daily 1hr. tours in English and Portuguese 11am and 2:30pm. €4, students and seniors €2.50, under 14 free; Su before 1:30pm free. *Palácio* tickets sold in the room to the left of the main palace steps. *Basílica* open daily 10am-1pm and 2-5pm. Free.) For a quality bargain meal, try the cozy, wood-adorned **A Toca da Raposa,** R. 1 de Dezembro, 2B. From the palace entrance, cross the street to the shops, go downhill on R. J. M. Costa one block, and turn right. Serves up a variety of fresh Portuguese dishes, though vegetarian options are limited. (☎261 81 51 22. Entrees €7-14. Open M-Su noon-2:30pm, W-Sa 7-9:30pm.) The **tourist office** is inside the palace compound, to the right of the large church entrance. In addition to maps, the office offers 10min. of free **internet** access. (☎261 81 71 70; www.cm-mafra.pt. Open daily 9:30am-1pm and 2:30-6pm.)

BEYOND LISBOA

CASCAIS

Cascais is a beautiful beach town, serene during the low-season, and brimming with vacationers in the summer. Surfers and beach lovers will find everything they need in this tight-knit community.

TRANSPORTATION. Trains from Lisboa's **Estação Cais do Sodré** (☎213 42 48 93; M: Cais do Sodré) head to **Cascais** (30min., 3 per hr. 5:30am-1:30am, €1.65). **Scott URB** has a bus terminal in downtown Cascais, to the left side of the blue glass tower of the shopping center behind the train station. Buses #418 (40min., every 50min. 6:30am-7:50pm) and the more scenic #403 via Cabo da Roca (60-80min.; every 75min. M-Sa 6:30am-8:40pm, Su 9:10am-8:40pm) go from Cascais to **Sintra** for €3.35. To visit **Praia de Guincho,** a popular windsurfing beach considered by many to be best on the coast, take the circular route bus #405/415 to the Guincho stop (22min., every 1-2hr. 7:15am-7:40pm, €2.60).

PRACTICAL INFORMATION. To get to the **tourist office,** Av. dos Combatentes de Grande Guerra, 25, exit the train station through the ticket office and look for the McDonald's arches across Lg. da Estação. To the right of McDonald's is Av. Valbom; the office is a yellow building with *"turismo"* in big letters at the end of the street. The staff has English, Spanish, French, German, and Russian speakers. (☎214 86 82 04. Open in summer M-Sa 9am-7pm, Su 10am-6pm; in winter M-Sa 9am-7pm, Su 10am-6pm.)

ACCOMMODATIONS AND FOOD. Sleeping in Cascais; most stay in Lisboa or at nearby Oeiras, which has a *pousada da juventude* (HI youth hostel). If you do stay, the best place to crash is **Cascais Beach Hostel ❷,** R. da Vista Alegre, 10, located five blocks away from the beach, and relatively well-located. Green co-ed dorms with 4-8 beds are very clean. Offers shared kitchen, free internet, luxurious common room with TV, swimming pool, and sunbathing deck. (☎309 90 64 21; www.cascaisbeachostel.com. Dorms Apr. 15-Nov. 15 €20; Nov. 16-Apr. 14 €18; doubles €49, with bath €69. Cash only.)

There are several restaurants on Av. dos Combatentes de Grande Guerra. The best is **Restaurante Dom Manolo ❷,** one of the only restaurants that cooks with a charcoal oven. Try their *sardinhas assadas,* mussels, and grilled chicken. (☎214 83 11 26. Entrees €6.5-11. Open daily 10am-midnight. Cash only.) For a rawer taste of the sea, head to **Sushi eXpress ❸,** R. Dra. Iracy Doile, 9A. Located 1 block from the train station, it serves up Japanese favorites to go. (☎214 86 74 28. Rolls €5-10. Sushi/sashimi boxes €7-16. Open daily noon-9pm. Cash only.)

OUTDOOR ACTIVITIES AND ENTERTAINMENT. Praia da Ribeira, Praia da Rainha, and **Praia da Conceição** are especially popular with sunbathers. To reach Praia da Ribeira, take a right upon leaving the tourist office and walk down Av. dos Combatentes de Grande Guerra until you see the water. Facing the water, Praia da Rainha and Praia da Conceição are to your left. Or take advantage of the **free bike rentals** offered at two kiosks in Cascais (one is in front of the train station, by the McDonald's, the other is in the parking lot of the Cidadela fortress, up Av. dos Carlos I). With a passport or driver's license and your hotel information, and you can use the bikes from 8am to 6:30pm. Ride along the coast (to your right if facing the water) and check out the **Boca de Inferno** (Mouth of Hell), a stunning open cave where the crashing waves supposedly whisper the devil's words. Go on a rainy day to really hear the cave roar. (About 1km outside Cascais, a 20min. walk up Av. Rei Humberto de Itália.) Devilry of a different sort starts as the sun sets, as nightlife picks up on **Largo Luís de Camões,** the main pedestrian square.

ERICEIRA ☎261

Ericeira is a pleasant fishing village whose white sand beaches were the departure point of Dom Manuel II, the last king of Portugal, when he was exiled in 1910. Restaurants, bars, and white-washed houses stand on the edge of a cliff that overlooks the Atlantic.

TRANSPORTATION AND PRACTICAL INFORMATION. **Mafrense** buses run from Lisboa's **Campo Grande;** the bus for Ericeira leaves from the middle platform at the left-most part of the waiting area (70min., every hr. 6:30am-11:40pm, €4.70). Get off at the bus station. Buses run from Ericeira to **Lisboa** (70min.; every hr. M-F 5:10am-8:18pm, Sa 5:10am-8:20pm, Su 5:58am-9:33pm; €5.10) via **Mafra** (25min., €1.60) and to **Sintra** (50min., €1.80). To get to the **tourist office,** R. Dr. Eduardo Burnay, 46, from the bus station, cross the road (EN 247-2), turn left, and walk uphill. At the top of the hill, follow the signs for the Centro and go right on R. Prudêncio Franco da Trindade. Go straight downhill until Pr. da República; the tourist office is at the opposite end of the square. (☎261 86 31 22. Open M-F 10am-1pm and 2:30-6:30pm, Sa 10am-1pm and 3-10pm, Su 10am-1pm and 3-7pm.)

ACCOMMODATIONS AND FOOD. You might have trouble finding a cheap room in summer; check with the tourist office for a list of rooms in private homes. **Hospedaria Pedra Dura ❸,** Rua Dr. Eduardo Burnay, 28, has eight renovated rooms with private baths, impeccable decor, and great location. Warm colors adorn the beds and rugs of each room. Facing the tourist office, go up the road on the right-hand side. (☎261 86 21 62. Doubles Sept. 1-June 15 €30-35; June 15-July 15 €40; July 15-Aug. 31 €50. Reservations recommended in the summer. MC/V.) The cheapest option is **Hospedaria Bernardo ❷,** R. Prudêncio Franco da Trindade, 11, a hotel-style *residencial* with amenities. Each has TV, table, and chairs. (☎261 86 23 78; hospedariabernardo@iol.pt. *Residencial* singles €25-30; doubles €35-40; triples €40-45. Prices drop €5-10 Sept.-May. Reservations recommended in Aug.) Seafood restaurants and bars can be found along R. Dr. Eduardo Burnay, which runs south from Pr. da República.

OUTDOOR ACTIVITIES AND NIGHTLIFE. Beachgoers quickly find their way to nearby **Praia do Norte** (a.k.a. Praia do Algodio), a long beach in the northern part of the port, and **Praia do Sul** in the south. Experienced surfers head past Praia do Norte, however, to the more pristine **Praia de São Sebastião, Praia da Ribeira d'Ilhas** (site of a former World Surfing Championship), or **Praia dos Coxos** (Crippled Beach) beyond Ribeira d'Ilhas. There are several shops in town that give surfing lessons and rent out boards. If you've never surfed, contact licensed **NaOnda Surfschool,** whose teachers are lifelong surfers and speak English. It's a 2km walk from Ericeira; head left from the port. (☎916 00 90 04; www.ericeirasurf.com. Lessons 2hr. per day for 3 days €59, children €39. Prices include wetsuit and board rental. Private lessons €25 per hr., max. 3 people.

Board €15 per day, wetsuit €7 per day. Open daily 10am-6pm.) For an adrenaline rush on land, call **Tres Ondas,** for guided mountain bike rides. (☎261 81 98 38. €30 for bike, helmet, and 3hr. tour. Max. 4 people. Rides depart at post office on R. Prudêncio Franco da Trindade. Rides Tu-F 4:30pm, Sa 10am.)

Ericeira is home to the second-oldest discoteca in Portugal, **O Ouriço,** R. Capitão João Lopes, 9, right next to the cliff. This beachfront club, whose name means "hedgehog," opened in 1960 and still packs in locals every night. (☎261 86 21 38. Open F-Sa 11pm-6am.)

SINTRA ☎219

Deep in the misty Serra mountains lies the enchanting city of Sintra, home to ancient castles, fairy-tale palaces, and verdant gardens. For centuries, sultans, kings, and wealthy noblemen were drawn by the area's haunting beauty, and they left a trail of opulence and grandeur behind them. Today, Sintra is Portugal's dreamland. Tourists from around the world explore the mysterious city, eager to absorb every detail and uncover every secret.

TRANSPORTATION

Horse-drawn Carriages: Sintratur, Largo Rainha D. Amélia (☎219 24 12 38; www.sintratur.com). Fixed routes or pay by the hr. Carriages, drivers, and horses for hire wait in the Praça da República. To **Quinta da Regaleira** and back (30min., €30) or **Monserrate** and back, including a 30min. stop on the grounds for a quick picnic (1hr., €70). Prices are for up to 4 people per ride. Carriages available daily Apr.-Sept. 10am-6pm.

Trains: Estação de Caminhos de Ferro, Av. Dr. Miguel Bombarda (☎219 23 26 05). To Estação Sete Rios in **Lisboa** (40min., daily every 20min. 5:06am-12:56am, €1.65). From the train station, take the subway to downtown Lisboa.

Buses: ScottURB buses (☎214 69 91 25; www.scotturb.com), on Av. Dr. Miguel Bombarda. Buses run to **Cascais** (#417; 40min., every hr. M-F 6:30am-9:15pm, Sa 7:20am-7:50 pm, Su 8:10am-7:50pm, €3.25; or #403 Via Cabo da Roca; every hr. M-Sa 6:35am-8:40pm, Su 9:10am-8:40pm). **Mafrense** buses, 500m up the street away from Vila on Av. Dr. D. Cambournac, go to **Ericeira** (50min., daily every hr. 7:15am-8:25pm, €2.60).

ORIENTATION AND PRACTICAL INFORMATION

Situated in the mountains 25km northwest of Lisboa and 12km north of Cascais, Sintra has three main neighborhoods. Excursions to the area by bus or train begin in the modern **Estefânia,** where several banks and budget accommodations can be found. **São Pedro de Sintra,** farther uphill, has more shops and municipal offices. Sintra, famous for its heart, **Sintra-Vila,** better known as the **Historic Center** and home to most of the town's fantastic sights. The 15min. walk from Estefânia is scattered with statues and fountains like bread crumbs for sight-hungry tourists. To get to the Historic Center, take a left out of the train station onto Av. Dr. M. Bombarda and follow it for 150m. At the intersection, take the curving road to the left, **Volta do Duche,** which passes the **Parque da Liberdade** and leads to the edge of the Historic Center, where shops begin to appear again. Stay to the right, and the **Palácio Nacional de Sintra** should be visible on the right. The tourist office is straight ahead. Sintra is navigable by foot, but a few sights lie outside (and uphill from) the town center. The ScottURB bus #434 sells day tickets to most of these sights (€4). Pay on the bus, which departs from in front of the main train station (every 15min. 9:35am-7:05pm) and stops in the Historic Centre. From there, the bus will head to the **Castelo dos Mouros**

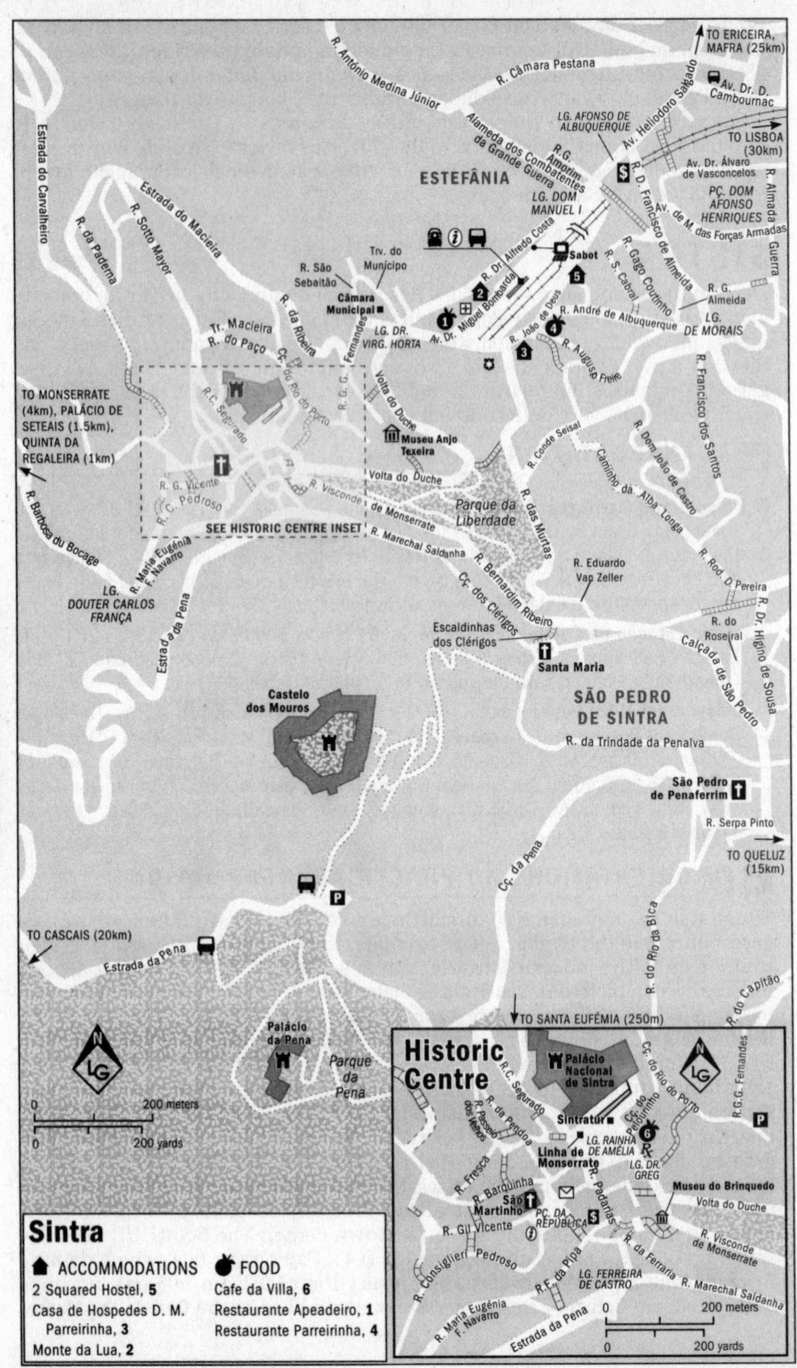
Sintra
ACCOMMODATIONS
2 Squared Hostel, 5
Casa de Hospedes D. M. Parreirinha, 3
Monte da Lua, 2
FOOD
Cafe da Villa, 6
Restaurante Apeadeiro, 1
Restaurante Parreirinha, 4
Historic Centre
ESTEFÂNIA
SÃO PEDRO DE SINTRA
Castelo dos Mouros
Palácio da Pena
Parque da Pena
Parque da Liberdade
Câmara Municipal
Museu Anjo Texeira
Santa Maria
São Pedro de Penaferrim
SEE HISTORIC CENTRE INSET
TO ERICEIRA, MAFRA (25km)
TO LISBOA (30km)
TO QUELUZ (15km)
TO CASCAIS (20km)
TO SANTA EUFÉMIA (250m)
TO MONSERRATE (4km), PALÁCIO DE SETEAIS (1.5km), QUINTA DA REGALEIRA (1km)
Sabot
Palácio Nacional de Sintra
Sintratur
Linha de Monserrate
Museu do Brinquedo
São Martinho
PÇ. DA REPÚBLICA
LG. RAINHA DE AMÉLIA
LG. DR. GREG
LG. FERREIRA DE CASTRO
LG. AFONSO DE ALBUQUERQUE
LG. DOM MANUEL I
PÇ. DOM AFONSO HENRIQUES
LG. DR. VIRG. HORTA
LG. DE MORAIS
LG. DOUTER CARLOS FRANÇA
R. Câmara Pestana
R. António Medina Júnior
Alameda dos Combatentes da Grande Guerra
Av. Heliodoro Salgado
Av. Dr. D. Cambournac
Av. Dr. Álvaro de Vasconcelos
Av. de M. das Forças Armadas
R. Almada Guerra
R. D. Francisco de Almeida
R. Gago Coutinho
R. S. Cabral
R. André de Albuquerque
R. João de Deus
R. Augusto Freire
R. Dr. Alfredo Costa
Av. Dr. Miguel Bombarda
Estrada do Carvalheiro
R. da Paderna
R. Sotto Mayor
Estrada do Macieira
Tr. Macieira
R. do Paço
R. da Ribeira
R. São Sebaitão
Trv. do Município
Volta do Duche
R. Visconde de Monserrate
R. Marechal Saldanha
R. Bernardim Ribeiro
Cç. dos Clérigos
Escaldinhas dos Clérigos
R. das Murtas
R. Conde Seisal
Caminho da Alba Longa
R. Dom João de Castro
R. Francisco dos Santos
R. Eduardo Van Zeller
R. Rod. D. Pereira
R. do Roseiral
R. Dr. Higino de Sousa
Calçada de São Pedro
R. da Trindade da Penalva
R. Serpa Pinto
Cç. da Pena
R. do Rio da Bica
R. do Capitão
Estrada da Pena
R. Barbosa du Bocage
R. Maria Eugénia F. Navarro
R. G. Vicente
R. C. Pedroso
R. C. Segurado
Cç. do Rio do Porto
R. G. G. Fernandes
R. G. Almeida
R. da Pendoa
R. Passeio dos Velhos
R. Fresca
R. Barquinha
R. Gil Vicente
R. Consiglieri Pedroso
R. Padarias
R. da Ferraria
R. F. da Pipa
Cç. do Pelourinho
0 200 meters
0 200 yards

and then **Palácio da Pena.** On the way back down the mountain, the bus stops in front of the **Museu Brinquedo** (Toy Museum).

Tourist Office: Pr. da República, 23 (☎219 23 11 57; fax 210 23 87 87), in the Historic Center. Open daily June-Sept. 9am-8pm; Oct.-May 9am-7pm. **Branch** in the train station (☎219 24 16 23) with the same hours. English, French, and Spanish spoken.

Police: Guarda Nacional Republicana, R. João de Deus, 6 (☎219 24 78 50), next to the train station.

Pharmacy: Pharmazul, Av. Dr. Miguel Bombarda, 37 (☎/fax 219 24 38 77). Open M-F 10am-7pm, Sa 10:30am-7:30pm, Su 10am-2pm.

Medical Services: Centro de Saúde, R. Dr. Alfredo Costa, 34, 1st fl. (☎219 23 62 00). Open M-F 8am-8pm, Sa-Su and holidays 10am-7pm.

Internet Access: Sabot, R. Dr. Alfredo Costa, 74 (☎219 23 08 02), across the street from the main train station, to the right of the Chinese restaurant. €1 per 15min., €1.60 per 30min., €2.50 per hr. CD burning €1.80 (CD included). Open M-Sa 1pm-midnight, Su 7pm-midnight.

Post Office: Pr. da República, 26 (☎219 10 67 91). Open M-F 9:30am-12:30pm and 2:30-6pm. **Postal Code:** 2710.

SAVE YOUR STAMPS. Many post offices in Portugal sell pre-stamped postcards for international postage, saving you up to €0.75 per card.

ACCOMMODATIONS

In Sintra, you can stay at the oldest hotel in Iberia or in an 19th-century palace, but grandeur is matched by price. Most hotels in Sintra are more expensive than in nearby towns or Lisboa, a 45min. train ride away. For those on a budget, the central tourist office has a list of private accommodations, but prices are similar to the *residenciais* (singles €25-60; doubles €40-70).

2 Squared Hostel, R. João de Deus, 68 (☎219 24 61 60). The best budget accommodation in Sintra, this hostel also has a cafe downstairs. Brightly painted rooms are spacious and open, though some face the train station and can be loud. 30min. free internet access and Wi-Fi. Private lockers in each room. Reserve ahead by phone. English spoken. Dorms €15; double with shared bath €20. Cash only. ❶

Casa de Hóspedes Dona Maria Parreirinha, R. João de Deus, 12/14 (☎219 23 24 90; www.dmariaparreirinha.com). Exit the train station and go left around the tracks. *Azulejo*-decorated hallways, immaculate tile floors, and cable TV. Most rooms have private baths. Free parking available. Some English spoken. Singles €30, with bath €35; doubles €35/40; triples €45; quints €70. €5-10 less in winter. Cash only. ❸

Monte da Lua, Av. Miguel Bombarda, 51 (☎219 24 10 29). Across the street from the train station. Excellent location. Offers rooms with heat, TV, and telephone. Singles €25, with private bath €30; high-season doubles €40, low-season €35. Cash only. ❷

FOOD

Pastelarias and restaurants crowd the end of Rua João de Deus and Avenida Heliodoro Salgado. In the old town, Rua das Padarias (near the **Palácio Nacional**) is lined with lunch spots. On the second and fourth Sundays of every month, take bus #433 from the train station to São Pedro (15min.) for the **Feira de São Pedro,** which features local cuisine, music, clothes, flowers, and antiques.

Café da Villa, Calçada do Pelourinho, 8 (☎967 09 13 96), in the main square in front of the Palácio Nacional. Decorated with colorful flags and paintings of famous faces, like the Dalai Lama's. Offers internationally themed meals (€8-15), which include 3 courses and a drink. Great late-night hangout. Open daily noon-2am. AmEx/MC/V. ❷

Restaurante Parreirinha, Rua João de Deus, 43 (☎219 23 12 07), behind the train station. A welcome change from the dark, antiquated café-bars of the city. Stainless-steel appliances, a flat-screen TV, and cinnamon-colored tablecloths make for a modern vibe. Variety of fish and wine. Daily special €6.50. Entrees €7-10. No vegetarian entrees. Open M-Su 10am-4pm and 7-10pm. MC/V. ❷

Restaurante Apeadeiro, Av. Miguel Bombarda, 3A (☎219 23 18 05). From the flag on the wall to the *futebol* (soccer ball) over the bar, this is a classic Portuguese cafe. Entrees €7-13. Open M-W and F-Su 11am-3pm and 7-10pm. AmEx/MC/V. ❷

SIGHTS

QUINTA DA REGALEIRA. A UNESCO World Heritage sight, this turret-studded palace was built in the early 1900s by Brazilian Antonio Monteira and flamboyant Italian architect Luigi Manini. Quinta's gardens, wells, grottoes, and towers form one of the oldest occult gardens of Europe, a true dreamland in fairy tale Sintra. Its design follows mythological and historical themes, rendered in a fascinating amalgam of Manueline (Portuguese late-Gothic) and Renaissance styles. The **Poço Iniciatico** (Initiation Well) was inspired by the secret rituals performed by the famous Knights Templar. Beneath the castle you can explore a fantastic tunnel system. *(To get to the Quinta da Regaleira, turn right out of the tourist office and follow R. Consiglieri Pedroso as it turns into Rua M. E. F. Navarro, a 15min. walk. ☎219 10 66 50. Open daily Oct. and Feb.-Apr. 10am-6:30pm, last entrance 6pm; Apr.-Sept. 10am-8pm, last entrance 7pm; Nov.-Jan. 10am-5:30pm, last entrance 5pm. Unguided visits €6, students and seniors €4. Guided tours at 10:30, 11am, noon, 2:30, 3:30pm; €10, students and seniors €8.)*

PALÁCIO DA PENA. Built in the 1840s by Prince Ferdinand of Bavaria, husband of Portugal's Dona Maria II, this royal retreat embraces romantic and fantastic styles with meticulous detail. The prince, nostalgic for his native country, rebuilt and embellished the ruined monastery with the assistance of a Prussian engineer, combining the artistic heritages of Germany and Portugal. The result is magical: a colorful Bavarian castle decorated with Arabic minarets, Gothic turrets, Manueline windows, and a Renaissance dome. *(Bus #434 runs to the palace from outside the tourist office every 15min. All-day bus pass €4. ☎219 10 53 40; www.parquesdesintra.pt. The area surrounding the palace, Parque da Pena, is open daily June-Aug. 9:30am-8pm, Sept.-May 9am-7pm. €7.50, children and seniors €5.50. Palacio admission Sept.-Apr. €8, children and seniors €6. May-Aug. €11, children and seniors €9. Open daily 9:45 am-5:30pm. Tickets for both attractions are sold until 1hr. before closing. Guided tours in English, Portuguese, and Spanish; €5, €3.50 per person for groups of 10 or more.)*

CASTELO DOS MOUROS. Built in the 8th century by the Moors, this ancient castle rests on the slopes of the Serra mountains. It was abandoned during the Moorish retreat to the south in 1147, but Dom Fernando II made some much-needed repairs in the 19th century. On a clear day, a long, steep climb up the walls will be rewarded with unmatched views of the Ribatejo plains and the clashing natural rock formations and manmade walls. *(1km below the Palácio da Pena. Bus #434 departs from outside the tourist office and stops at the castle. All-day bus pass €4. ☎219 23 73 00; www.parquesdasintra.pt. Open daily June-Sept. 9am-8pm, last entrance 7pm; Oct.-May 10am-6pm, last entrance 5pm. €5, seniors and under 17 €3, family price for 2 children and 2 adults €12. Guided tours €5, €3.50 per person for groups of 10 or more.)*

MONSERRATE. Located 4km from the center of Sintra, Monserrate is well worth a visit for those staying in town for more than a day. This sprawling estate is known for its quiet botanical gardens shaded by towering sequoias and tropical ferns. The garden has more than 3500 species of plants, and its lawn is watered by the oldest irrigation system in Portugal. The Moghul-style mansion, with its burnt-orange roof modeled on Brunelleschi's Dome in Florence, is a classic example of Portuguese Romanticism. Designed by the English architect John T. Knowles in 1858, the estate became a refuge for eccentric English aristocrat William Beckford following scandals regarding his homosexual affairs. *(To get to Monserrate, catch the small green train/roofless bus line, Linha de Monserrate, ☎214 66 26 03, beside the Palácio Nacional in Pr. da República. 20 min., every hr., €6 round trip. Monserrate ☎219 23 73 00 or 10 78 06. Open daily summer 10am-1pm, 2pm-7pm; winter 10:30am-1pm, 2pm-5pm. Last entrance 30min. before closing. €5, children and seniors €3, families of 2 adults and 2 children €12. Guided tours €5, €3.50 for groups of 10 or more.)*

PALÁCIO NACIONAL DE SINTRA. The palace, also known as the Paço Real or Palácio da Vila, dominates Pr. da República. Once a summer residence for Moorish sultans and their harems, the Palácio da Vila was taken over by the Portuguese following the Muslim defeat. The conquest is illustrated in the paintings of Portuguese noblemen gunning down Moorish soldiers. The palace and gardens were built in two stages: Dom João I built the main structure in the 15th century, and Dom Manuel I made it home to the best collection of *azulejos* (glazed tiles) in the world a century later. The palace has over 20 rooms, including the *azulejo*-covered **Sala dos Árabes** and the gilded **Sala dos Brasões.** Some of the palace's greatest treasures are overhead: look up at the ceiling to see the royal coat of arms surrounded by the armorial bearings of 72 noble families, elaborately painted animals, and various other artistic flourishes. The palace is marked by a bird theme: doves symbolizing the Holy Spirit line the walls of the **Capela,** swans grace the **Sala dos Cisnes,** and on the ceiling of the **Sala das Pegas** magpies representing ladies-in-waiting hold a piece of paper proclaiming D. João I's motto—*"por bem,"* or "for good." *(Lg. da Rainha Dona Amélia. ☎219 10 68 40; www.ippar.pt. Open M-Tu and Th-Su 10am-5:30pm. Last entrance 5pm. €5, seniors and students €2.50; Su and holidays before 2pm free.)*

LISBOA

SETÚBAL ☎265

There's no question about it, Setúbal is a city of the sea—you can smell it in the air and see it on the menus. But unlike the coastal developments in the Algarve, Setúbal leaves travelers with more options than just beaches and *bacalhau* (cod). The wild dolphin population in the Reserva Natural do Estuário do Sado offers a relaxing opportunity to commune with some of Mother Nature's perkiest creatures. If you're fleeing from campy tourist traps in a quest to discover the real Portugal, Setúbal will more than oblige, with central city squares full of traditional *lojas* (shops), cobblestone streets, and statues of Portuguese statesmen. Though the trip from Lisboa is lengthy, Setúbal takes no more than a day or two to visit, and it makes a good base for daytrips.

TRANSPORTATION

Trains: leave from **Estação Praça de Quebedo,** which can be reached conveniently from the city center, **Estação de Setúbal** (☎265 52 68 45), in Pr. do Brasil (a 10min. walk down the same street) and **Estação do Barreiro** (50min., 2 per hr. 5am-noon, €1.60), where you transfer to a boat to get to Lisboa.

Buses: leave from Av. 5 de Outubro, 44 (☎265 52 50 51). From the tourist office, walk up R. Santa Maria to Av. 5 de Outubro and turn left; the station is about 2 blocks down on the right, in the building with "Rodoviária" written vertically down the front. Buses go to: **Évora** (2hr.; 10:25am, 5:10pm; €10); **Faro** (4hr., 3:05pm, €15.80);

Lisboa's Praça de Espanha (1hr., 17 per day 6:55am-10pm, €5.20); **Sesimbra** (45min., 9 per day 7:20am-8pm, €2.60).

Ferries: Transado, Doca do Comércio (☎265 23 51 01), off Av. Luísa Todi at the waterfront's end, sends ferries to **Tróia** (15min.; every 30min.; €1.15, ages 5-10 €0.55, under 5 free).

Taxi: Rádio Táxi (☎265 23 33 34) is at Av. Luísa Todi and by the bus and train stations.

ORIENTATION AND PRACTICAL INFORMATION

Setúbal's main artery is **Avenida Luísa Todi,** a wide boulevard parallel to the **Rio Sado.** Farther inland from Luísa Todi is **Avenida 5 de Outubro,** and between the two major roads lies a dense district of shops and restaurants centered around the **Praça de Bocage. Avenida da Portela** runs perpendicular to Av. 5 de Outubro, past the train and bus stations.

Tourist Office: Posto de Turismo da Costa Azul, on Tr. Frei Gaspar, just off Av. Luísa Todi near Lg. da Misericórdia (☎265 53 91 20). English, French, and Spanish spoken. Open May-Sept. M-Su 9:30am-7pm, M and Sa the office closes 12:30pm-3pm. Oct.-Apr. open M-Sa 9:30am-6pm. M and Sa closes 12:30-2pm. There is another municipal **branch** at R. Santa Maria, 2-4.

Currency Exchange: Banks line Av. Luísa Todi. (All open M-F 8:30am-3pm.) **Agência de Cambios Central,** Av. Luísa Todi, 226 (☎265 54 80 40) has currency exchange. Open M-Sa 9am-7pm.

Police: Station at Av. Luísa Todi, 350 (☎265 52 20 22).

Pharmacy: Farmácia Normal do Sul, Pr. de Bocage, 135 (☎265 52 84 50; open M-F 9am-7pm, Sa 9am-7pm).

Hospital: São Bernardo, R. Camilo Castelo Branco (☎265 54 90 00).

Laundromat: Lavanderia Donini, R. Oliveira Martins, 17 (☎265 52 71 54). Open M-F 9am-1pm and 3-7pm, Sa 9am-1pm. €2.25 per kg.

Internet Access: Cybertody, R. São Cristóvão, 7 (☎265 22 12 54). Follow the sign for Residencial Bocage off Av. Luísa Todi. It's in the building in front of the Residencial on the 2nd fl. €1.65 per hr. Open M-F 10:30am-11pm, Sa-Su 2:30pm-11pm.

Post Office: at Ctt Correios, Praça de Bocage (☎213 55 35 05). Open M-F 9am-12:30pm and 2:30-6pm. **Postal Code:** 2900.

ACCOMMODATIONS

There are a few good *pensões* along Av. Luísa Todi and near Pr. de Bocage, or ask at either tourist office for a list of available *quartos* in private houses.

Pousada da Juventude de Setúbal (HI), Lg. José Afonso (☎265 53 44 31; fax 53 29 63). Facing the river, walk right on Av. Luísa Todi until you reach a large plaza on the left with a salmon-colored building in the center. Cut in front of the building to the parking lot; the *pousada* is the building ahead with the 2-story glass tower. The *pousada* has clean, cozy rooms, a common room with TV, and a friendly multilingual staff. Provides 30min free internet access. Reception 8am-noon and 6pm-midnight. Check-out noon. 4-person dorms €9; doubles €18, with bath €22. HI discount 15%. V. ❶

Residencial Bocage, R. São Cristóvão, 14 (☎265 54 30 80), off Av. Luísa Todi, has fully loaded suites without fully loaded prices. Conveniently located near the main avenue and several cafes. Recently renovated rooms include bath, phone, TV, A/C, and breakfast. The front desk staff is helpful and friendly. Jan.-Mar. singles €29, doubles €40; Apr.-July €37/45; Aug. €38/50; Sept. €37/45; Oct.-Dec. €29/40. AmEx/MC/V. ❸

Pensão O Cantinho, Beco do Carmo, 1-9 (☎265 52 38 99), is in an alley off Av. Luísa Todi behind Lg. do Carmo, near the police station. Spacious rooms above the restaurant have private baths and are among the cheapest in town. Reserve ahead in summer. Singles €10-15; doubles €20. Cash only. ❶

FOOD

Seafood places line Av. Luísa Todi, up the street from Doca do Comércio; watch as they cut and fry your fish on sidewalk grills. You can also head to the Barrio das Fontanhas at the end of Av. Luisa Todi, an area frequented by locals.

Duarte Dos Frangos, Av. Luísa Todi, 285 (☎265 52 26 03), across the plaza from the youth hostel. Chatty locals and a friendly staff makes the place warm and welcoming. Ask for a *meia* of pork *portuguesa* (€6). Fish and meat entrees €5.50-14. Open daily noon-3pm and 7-10pm. AmEx/MC/V. ❷

Novo 10, Av. Luísa Todi, 422-426, is one of the best seafood restaurants around. Try Setubal's famed specialty, *choco frito*. Additionally, the beef (€8-12) is among the best in town. Open daily noon-2pm, 7pm-2am. AmEx/MC/V. ❷

Cais 56, Av. Luisa Todi 56, (☎265 23 84 75). A great hangout with good pizza and *choco frito* (€6). Open M-Tu, Th-Su 12pm-3pm, 6:30pm-10:30pm. ❷

SIGHTS AND FESTIVALS

The town's most impressive sight, the 16th-century **Forte de São Filipe,** sits just outside the city. Designed by Italian engineer Filipe Terzi, the fortress was built in 1582 during the Spanish occupation of Portugal and took almost 20 years to finish. The star-shaped fortress is now a luxury *pousada*, but anyone is free to explore it. During the last week of July and first week of August, the **Feira de Santiago,** held in Lg. José Afonso, brings a carnival, folk music, and enormous outdoor market to Setúbal. The fair is accompanied by Portuguese bullfighting at Pr. dos Touros by the train station. Setúbal's best **beaches** are **Praia Figueirinha** and **Praia Galapos** (buses run from the main station to Figueirinha, 20min., round-trip €2.80). **Vertigem Azul,** Edificio Marina Deck Rua Praia da Saude, 11D-Loja 10, near the fisherman harbor (☎265 23 80 00; www.vertigemazul.com), offers dolphin-watching daytrips (€30, children €20) in addition to kayaking, snorkeling, and jeep tours (approx. €15 per hr.). **Planeta Terra,** Praça General Luís Domingues, 9, rents street, hybrid, and mountain bikes from €8 per day. (☎919 47 18 71; www.planetaterra.pt. Delivery available. Reserve ahead.)

ALGARVE AND ALENTEJO

The Algarve and the Alentejo form a striking contrast. The Alentejo's small villages, seemingly stuck in another time, provide an escape from the Algarve's heavily touristed beaches and wild nightlife. Nearly 3000hr. of annual sunshine have transformed the Algarve from a fishermen's backwater town into one of Europe's favorite vacation spots. In July and August, visitors mob its resorts, packing bars and discos from sunset until long after sunrise. Still, the Algarve isn't all about excess. The region between Faro and the Spanish border remains relatively untouched, and, to the west of Lagos, towering cliffs shelter pristine beaches. Life slows down even more as you enter the Alentejo, where arid plains punctuated by olive trees, two-toned cork trees, and fields of wheat and sunflowers stretch to the horizon in a display of endless shades of yellow. This vast region appeals to those in search of relaxation, history, and plenty of wine. The Algarve and Alentejo provide visitors with the best of both worlds.

HIGHLIGHTS OF ALGARVE AND ALENTEJO

SPELUNK among the grottoes and sea cliffs of **Lagos** (p. 616).

CHANNEL the spirit of Prince Henry the Navigator at his outpost in **Sagres** (p. 622).

FEEL it in your bones at Évora's **Capela dos Ossos** (p. 633).

STORM the walls of the 13th-century castle in **Marvão** (p. 635).

ALGARVE

Behold the Algarve: a land where happy campers come to bask in the sun. Off the sands, the geometric designs and minaret-style chimneys of Algarve's old houses reveal a strong Arab influence. While regional crafts specialize in basket-weaving, the Algarve's most perfect craft is its delicious seafood—local favorites include flavorful *sardinhas assadas* (grilled sardines) and the creamy *caldeirada* (seafood chowder). Almonds and figs also make their way into most regional cooking, especially in divine desserts like *figos cheios*. In the winter, the resorts empty and wildlife of a different sort arrives, as roughly one-third of Europe's flamingos migrate to the wetlands surrounding Olhão.

LAGOS ☎282

Lagos (pop. 17,500) has a way of making visitors want to stay forever; just ask any one of city's expatriate bartenders, surf guides, or restaurant owners. As the Algarve's capital for almost 200 years, Lagos launched many of the caravels that brought Portugal power and fortune in the 15th and 16th centuries. Today, the city is immersed in another, equally profitable golden age—tourism. While the 20-somethings recuperate from the previous night, the 40-plus crowd comes out in the morning and lingers until dinner time, perusing storefronts, taking dolphin tours, and relaxing in the sunny plazas.

TRANSPORTATION

To reach Lagos from northern Portugal, you must go through Lisboa; trips originating in the east generally transfer in Faro.

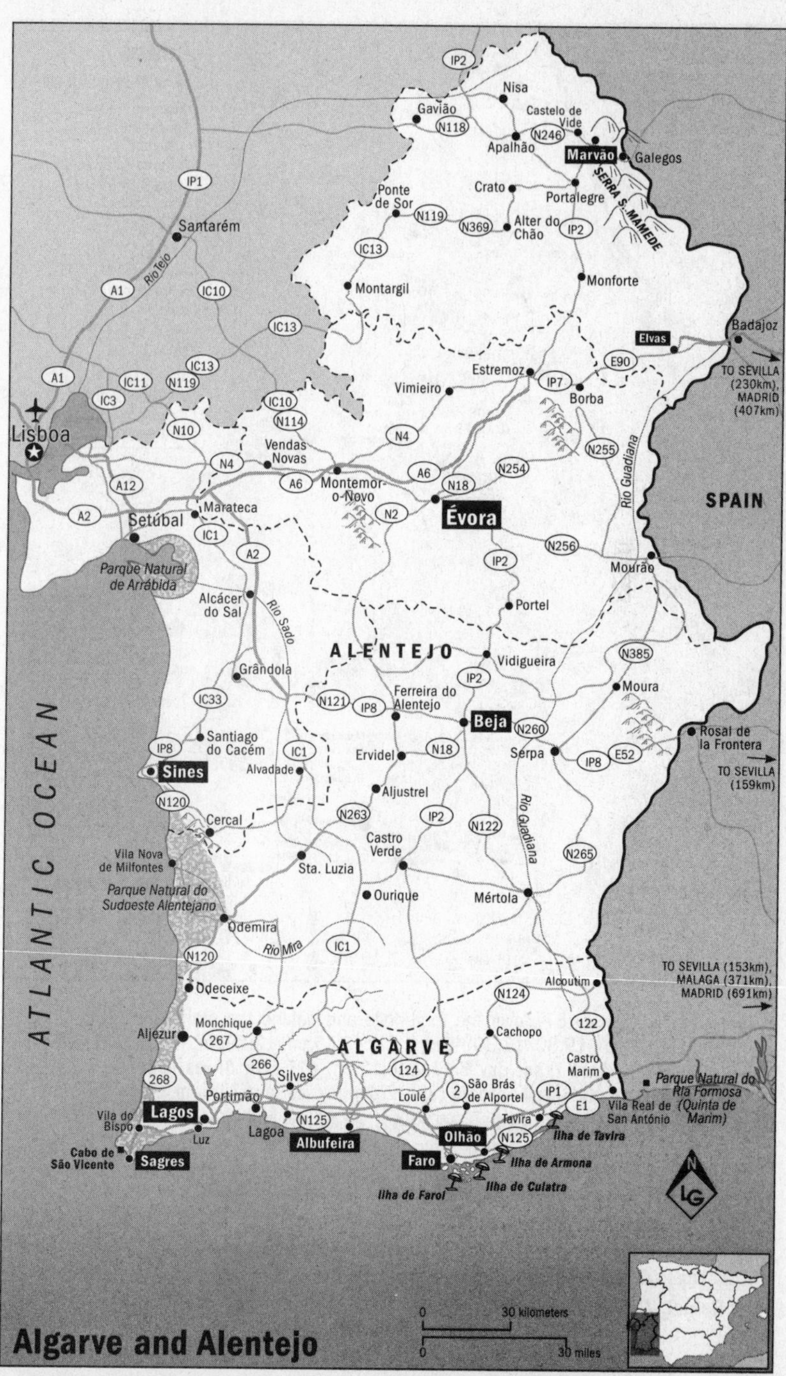

ALGARVE AND ALENTEJO

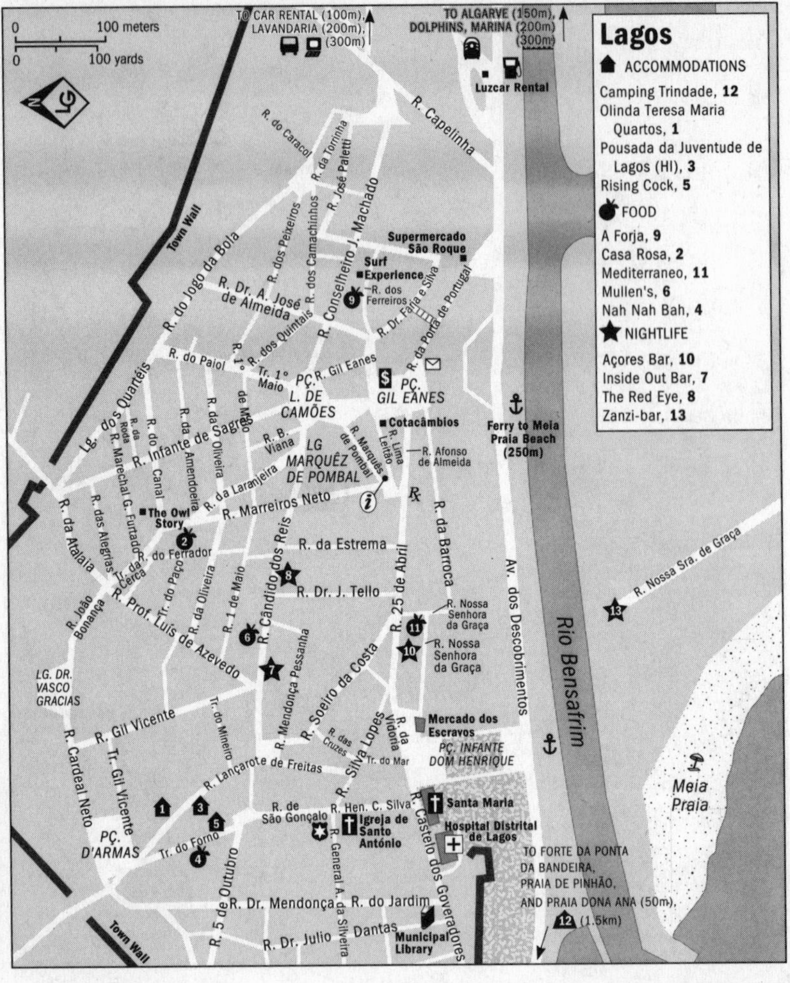

Trains: (☎282 76 29 87), over the footbridge and behind the marina. To: **Beja** (4hr.; 8:19am, 12:19pm; €9.80/17.30); **Évora** (5hr.; 8:19am, 12:19pm; €14.50/21.60) via **Faro; Lisboa** (3-4hr., 7 per day 6:11am-6:12pm, €15.50); **Silves** (40min., 1:39pm, €1.70); **Vila Real de Santo António** (3hr., 7 per day 7:03am-7:04pm, €6.50) via Faro.

Buses: The **EVA** bus station (☎282 76 29 44), off Av. dos Descobrimentos, is just before R. Porta de Portugal (when walking into town) and across the channel from the footbridge to the marina and train station. To: **Albufeira** (13hr., 6 per day 7am-5:15pm, €5); **Faro** (2hr., 6 per day 7am-5:15pm, €5.35); **Lisboa** (5hr., 6 per day 5:30am-6:15pm, €19); **Sagres** (1hr., 16 per day 7:15am-8:30pm, €3.40); **Sines** (2-4hr.; 3:20pm, 4:30pm;€12.30/6.70).

Taxis: Lagos Central Taxi (☎282 76 24 69). 24hr. service to Lagos and environs.

Car Rental: 21+ for cars, 16+ for mopeds.

Auto Jardim, Travessa do Ferro de Engomar (☎282 76 94 86; www.auto-jardim.com). Cars from €91.50 per 3 days, without tax or insurance. Open 8:30am-1pm and 2:30-7pm. AmEx/MC/V.

Luzcar Rent-a-Car, Lg. Portas de Portugal, 10 (☎282 76 10 16; www.luzcar.com). July-Sept. cars from €200 per week including tax and insurance; Apr.-June and Oct. €150; Nov.-Mar. €130. Baby seat and roof rack included. AmEx/D/MC/V.

Motorent, R. Victor Costa Silva, 8B (☎282 76 97 16). Rents bikes (€20 per 3 days, €37), scooters (€63 per 3 days, €120), and motorcycles (€55-110 per 3 days, €100-320). 18+, 25+ for motorcycles; license required. AmEx/MC/V.

ORIENTATION AND PRACTICAL INFORMATION

Running the length of the channel, **Avenida dos Descobrimentos** carries traffic to and from Lagos. From the train station, walk through the marina and cross the pedestrian suspension bridge; turn left onto Av. dos Descobrimentos. From the bus station, walk straight until Av. dos Descobrimentos and turn right. **Praça Gil Eanes** is the center of the old town and extends into Lg. Marquêz de Pombal, where the tourist office is located. Follow R. Silva Lopes to R. General Alberto da Silveira to reach the grotto-lined beach of **Praia Dona Ana.**

Tourist Office: Municipal (☎282 76 41 11), on Lg. Marquêz de Pombal. Open M-Sa 10am-6pm. Open daily in summer 10am-7pm, in winter 10am-6pm.

Currency Exchange: Cotacâmbios, Pr. Gil Eanes, 11 (☎282 76 44 52).

English-Language Bookstore: The Owl Story, Marreiros Neto, 67 (☎282 79 22 89). Large selection of secondhand English novels and travel guides. Comfy chairs available for clients. Open M-F 10am-7pm, Sa 10am-2pm.

Library: R. Dr. Julio Dantas. Open Sept.-July Tu-W and F 10am-6pm, Th 10am-8pm, Sa 10am-1pm. Free internet access upstairs.

Laundromat: Lavanderia Míele, Av. dos Descobrimentos, 27 (☎282 76 39 69). Wash and dry €7 per 5kg. Open M-F 9am-1pm and 3-7pm, Sa 9am-1pm. Some youth hostels and apartments have a laundry service, usually €2-5 per load.

Police: R. General Alberto da Silveira (☎282 76 29 30).

Pharmacy: Farmácia Silva, R. 25 de Abril, 9 (☎282 76 28 59). Ask at any pharmacy for a pamphlet listing the hours and locations of all the pharmacies in Lagos.

Medical Services: Hospital Distrital de Lagos, R. Castelo dos Governadores (☎282 77 01 00).

Internet Access: Snack Bar Ganha Pouco, 1st right after the footbridge coming from the bus station. Internet access and munchies. €2.50 per hr.; €0.50 per fax. Open M-Sa 8am-7:30pm, Su 9am-7:30pm. Several bars in Lagos have computers; check along R. Lançarote de Freitas. Free access also found in the **library** and the **Cultural Center** lobby, just minutes down from all the listed hostels. Open daily 1pm-midnight.

Post Office: R. da Porta de Portugal (☎282 77 02 50), between Pr. Gil Eanes and the river. Fax €4.25 per 2 pages. Open M-F 9am-6pm. **Postal Code:** 8600.

ACCOMMODATIONS AND CAMPING

In July and August, budget spots fill quickly; reserve more than a week in advance. Some places, like the Rising Cock, set aside a limited number of last-minute rooms. Locals trying to rent rooms in their homes will probably greet you at the station or in the streets. Though these rooms may be a little out of the way, they can be the best deals in town at €10-15 per person in summer.

Pousada da Juventude de Lagos (HI), R. Lançarote de Freitas, 50 (☎282 76 19 70. July-Aug; book through Movijovem at ☎217 23 21 00). Social staff and lodgers congregate in the courtyard and barhop at night. Kitchen and TV room with billiards and foosball. Breakfast included. Internet €1 per 15 min. From mid-June to mid-Sept. dorms €16; doubles with bath €43. From mid-Sept. to mid-June €11/32. Cash only. ❶

Rising Cock, Travessa do Forno, 14 (☎968 75 87 85; www.risingcock.com). Legendary among backpackers and spring-breakers. Youthful, gregarious atmosphere. Mrs. Ribeiro, referred to by guests as "Mama," makes breakfast (included). Upstairs patio, kitchen, huge common room with big-screen TV, DVD library, and free internet access and Wi-Fi. Co-ed rooms with lockers; most have baths. Reserve ahead. Prices vary by season. In summer mixed dorms €22-25. AmEx/MC/V. ❷

The Monkey House, R. Gil da Vicente, 23. (☎282 76 03 89; www.themonkeyhouse.eu). Not quite a zoo. 4-room dorms and clean, tiled bathrooms open into a spacious common room with big-screen TV, terrace, kitchen, and free internet. Mountain-bike rental €10 per day. Laundry €5. Breakfast included in the One Fat Monkey Diner (next door). Call for bus/train station pickups. €22-25. AmEx/MC/V. ❷

Camping Trindade (☎282 76 38 93), just outside town. Follow Av. dos Descobrimentos toward Sagres. €3.50 per person; €4.50 per tent; €4.80 per car. ❶

FOOD

The cheapest dining options in Lagos are the local indoor produce **market** on Av. dos Descobrimentos and **Supermercado São Roque,** R. da Porta de Portugal, 61 (☎282 76 28 55; open July-Sept. M-F 9am-8pm, Sa 9am-7pm; Oct.-June M-F 9am-7:30pm, Sa 9am-7pm). Eateries on R. de Silva Lopes and R. 25 de Abril tend to be more expensive.

Casa Rosa, R. do Ferrador, 22 (☎282 18 02 38). The friendly staff at this Australian/American restaurant will engage the daring in an intense game of Connect Four. Various vegetarian options. Entrees €5-7.50. All-you-can-eat spaghetti or vegetarian bolognese €5 daily. The strawberry daiquiris (€4.50) are a sweet start or finish to any meal. Free internet access for diners. Open daily 5pm-midnight. ❶

A Forja, R. dos Ferreiros, 17 (☎282 76 85 88). Few traditional Portuguese restaurants exist in Lagos but locals swear by A Forja, known affectionately as "Blue Door." Serves Algarvian seafood; look for a placard outside listing specials, like the tremendous plate of *pato* (duck). Entrees €7-15. Open daily noon-3pm and 6:30-10pm. Cash only. ❷

Mediterraneo, R. Senhora da Graça, 2 (☎282 18 31 00). Mediterranean and Thai cuisine, including enticing tapas (€2-7.50). Great seafood, and some of the town's most enticing options for vegetarians. Salads €6-8. Pizza €7-8. Entrees €8.50-14.50. Open Tu-Sa 7pm-late. Cash only. ❷

Mullen's, R. Cândido dos Reis, 86 (☎963 50 16 58). A unique combination of great Portuguese and international cuisine, stereotypical Irish pub atmosphere, and live jazz. Try the duck in orange sauce and the spicy *frango grelhado* (grilled chicken). Live music Tu. Tapas €2.50-6. Entrees €8-14. Beer €3.50. Mixed drinks €5. Restaurant open daily 6-10:30pm; bar open daily 11pm-2am. ❷

Nah Nah Bah, Travessa do Forno, 11. Owner personally prepares dishes and chats with customers nightly. Try The Nah Nah Bird (seasoned with Algarvian spices, fresh oranges, and strawberries) with the "legendary" Nah Nah chips (€8.50). Reggae beats (sometimes with live DJ) and cabana-feel keep the relaxed vibe alive well into the night. Entrees €6.50-10. Open 6pm-late. ❷

SIGHTS AND BEACHES

The few sights that Lagos has to offer can be seen on a lazy afternoon walk back from the beach. The **Forte da Ponta da Bandeira,** a 17th-century fortress with maritime exhibitions and tiled chapel, overlooks the marina. It is the site of Lagos's traditional **Banho 29** (Bath 29) festivities; in ancient times, locals traveled to the waters of Lagos and purified themselves in the sea at midnight on August 29. The date has been transformed to an annual celebratory rave. (☎282 76 14 10. Open Tu-Su 9:30am-12:30pm and 2-5pm. €2, students €1, under 13 free.) Also near the waterfront is the former **Mercado dos Escravos** (slave market). Legend has it that the first sale of African slaves in Portugal took place here in 1444. It is currently an art gallery, although one wall bears the arms of the 17th-century Marquis de Nisa. The second floor housed the Lagos Customs Office until 1820. One block from Pr. Infante Dom Henrique is **Igreja de Santo António.** The church is home to a museum containing artifacts ranging from the Neolithic age to the present, along with a magnificient guilded vault and *retablo mayor.* (Open Tu-Su 9:30am-12:30pm and 2-5pm. €2.20; seniors, students, and under 18 €1.) Lagos's beaches are undeniably seductive. A 4km blanket of flat, smooth sands (crowded in summer but bare in the sunny low season) lines the well-known Meia Praia, across the river from town. To get there, hop on the quick ferry near Pr. Infante Dom Henrique (€0.50). For plunging cliffs and smaller coves, follow Av. dos Descobrimentos toward Sagres to **Praia de Pinhão** (20min.). Five minutes farther down the coast lies **Praia Dona Ana,** with sculpted ochre cliffs and grottoes that appear on half of all Algarve postcards.

WATER ACTIVITIES

If you're up for more than lounging, Lagos offers a wide variety of watersports, from scuba diving to surfing to (booze) cruising. For **grotto boat tours,** stroll the various companies on Av. dos Descobrimentos, on the marina side. Most tours last 45min. and start from €10. **Bom Dia** offers a 2hr. tour for €17-21.

The Booze Cruise (☎969 41 11 31). A 4hr. afternoon boat ride around Lagos's coast. You're certain to get vertigo, whether from looking up at the dizzying heights of the cliffs or the all-you-can-drink bar. Not for those looking for a tour—anchor drops about an hour in. €35, all inclusive. Booking available through The Rising Cock and Joe's Garage.

Algarve Dolphins, Marina de Lagos, 10 (☎282 76 46 70; www.bomdia-boattrips.com). 1hr. of dolphin-watching in the ocean in high-speed rescue boats. Tours leave from the Lagos Marina. €30, €35 for guaranteed sightings.

Surf Experience, R. dos Ferreiros, 21 (☎282 76 19 43; www.surf-experience.com). 1- to 2-week surfing trips with lessons, transportation, and accommodations in a Lagos surf house. All levels welcome. Daytrips when space available. Board and wetsuit rental €75/114. Apr.-Nov. 1 week with board €525, 2 weeks €881; Dec.-Mar. €473/836.

NIGHTLIFE

Lagos's young crowd flocks from the beaches to the bars as the sun dips below the horizon. In town, the area between **Praça Gil Eanes** and **Praça Luis de Camões** is filled with cafes. **Rua Cândido dos Reis, Rua do Ferrador,** and the intersection of **Rua 25 de Abril, Rua de Silva Lopes,** and **Rua Soeiro da Costa** are the bar and club scene mecca. The streets get busy around 10pm, and serious pedestrian traffic hits at midnight. Bars boast an abundance of drink specials.

Inside Out Bar, R. Cândido dos Reis, 119 (www.insideoutbar.com). Inside Out is an insomniac's dream come true; things don't pick up until a little after 2am, when most of the other bars close. The house specialty is the barely legal Fishbowl (€25), mixed by feisty bartenders. Outfitted with a pool table, an extensive drink menu, and entertaining staff, it's a shame this bar ever has to close. Beer €3-4.50. Shots €3-3.50. Mixed drinks €5-6.50. Open daily 8pm-4am.

Zanzi-bar, R. 25 de Abril, 93. Another "2 o'clock" stop, Zanzi-bar is always packed. The back room has a few tables for a more intimate setting. Scan the crowd for waiters and waitresses from local restaurants. Beer €3. Shots €2.50-3. Try house specials such as the *morangsca* (with fresh strawberries, 0.5L €8, 1L €15), sangria (€5/9), frozen margarita (€9/18), and kamikazi (€9/12.50). Open daily 7pm-4am.

The Red Eye, R. Cândido dos Reis, 63. Brits and Aussies flood in around midnight for the classic rock, cheap liquor, and casual pool games. Mostly a pickup scene. Free shot with 1st drink. Beer €2-3. Mixed drinks €3.50-5. Shots €2.50. Jug of sangria €10. Happy hour with €5 2-pint mixed drinks 8-10pm. Open daily 8pm-2am.

Açores Bar, R. Sra. da Graça, 12. A Portuguese twist on the mainly Anglophone-run bar scene, owned by a couple from the Açores. Multi-level bar allows for more breathing room than most surrounding establishments can claim, although the population explodes around 1am. Reggae music nightly. €8 for L of sangria. Open daily 6pm-2am.

DAYTRIP FROM LAGOS

PRAIA DA ROCHA

To reach Praia da Rocha from Lagos, take the bus to Portimão (40min., 10 per day 6:11am-8:19pm, €3.75) and get off at the Praia da Rocha stop.

A short jaunt from Lagos, locals and tourists agree that Praia da Rocha is the best beach that the Algarve has to offer. With vast expanses of big surf, red cliffs, and secluded coves, Praia da Rocha's reputation is well deserved, and the crowds attest to this fact. The tourist office at the end of R. Tomás Cabrieira offers maps and lists of accommodations and restaurants. (☎282 41 91 32. Open May-Sept. daily 9:30-7pm; Oct.-Apr. M-F 9:30am-12:30pm and 2-5:30pm, Sa-Su 9:30am-12:30pm.)

SAGRES ☎282

Marooned atop a windy plateau at the southwesternmost point in Europe, Sagres (pop. 3000) was considered the end of the world for centuries and its name ("Sacrum" or "Sacred Place") bears witness to that mystical impact as world's end. It was here that Prince Henry's famous school of navigation organized exploratory voyages to the far reaches of the globe. While large tour groups and upscale vacationers are discouraged by its desolate location and relative lack of recreation, Sagres's picturesque beaches, friendly locals, and lively nightlife make it a perfect destination for travelers in search of a stress-free day. Sagres, with access to both southern and western coasts, is rapidly becoming one of Europe's prime surfing grounds.

TRANSPORTATION AND PRACTICAL INFORMATION. EVA **buses** (☎282 76 29 44) run from Lagos (1hr.; 14 per day M-F 6:10am-7:35pm, Sa 9 per day 6:10am-7:10pm, Su 7 per day 7:15am-7:10pm; €3.40). Buses also run to Lisboa (5hr., July-Sept. daily 4pm, €18). When arriving in Sagres use the **tourist office** on Av. Comandante Matoso as a signpost for when to get off. Schedules are posted to the left of the tourist office door. The office offers practical and recreational pamphlets in English, including maps, regional information, and suggestions for golfing and enjoying the surf. (☎808 78 12 12; www.visitalgarve.pt. Open Tu-Sa 9:30am-12:30pm and 1:30-5:30pm.) The **police** are in Vila do Bispo (☎282 63 91 12). Other local services include: **banks** and **ATMs** along Av. Comandante Matoso and across from the post office and at the supermarket; a **pharmacy** all the way down on R. Comandante Matoso, at the corner of R. Jaime Conde (☎282 62 48 50; open M-F 9am-2pm and 3-7pm, Sa 9am-1pm and 5-7pm, Su 11am-1pm and 5-7pm); and a **post office** on the right-hand side of Av. Comandante Matoso as you walk toward Praia da Baleeira (☎707 26 26 26; open M-F

9am-12:30pm and 2-5:30pm). **Freeride Surfcamp,** or Casa Azul, with a blue-tiled hub on Pr. da República, offers surf lessons and packages from €45 per day (including free pickup from Lagos bus and train stations) for surfers of all levels. (☎282 62 42 45; www.freeridesurfcamp.com). Other bookings are available at **Surf Planet,** Est. Nacional, 268 (☎282 62 48 15; www.surfplanet-pt.com; from €45 per day; open M and Th-Su 9am-8pm, W 9a,-7:30pm; AmEx/MC/V) and **Sagres Natura,** R. Mestre Antonio Galhardo (☎282 62 40 72; www.sagresnatura.com; from €45 per day; open daily 9:30am-8pm, AmEx/MC/V). **Bike rentals** at **Surf Planet** (€5/10/15 for 1/4/8hr.) and **Sagres Natura** (€15 per day). Free internet at Água Salgada and neighbor O Dromedário (see **Entertainment,** p. 624).

ACCOMMODATIONS AND CAMPING. Finding a bed in Sagres is not hard; windows everywhere display multilingual signs advertising rooms. Singles and doubles range €20-30 and triples €30-40, with lower rates in winter. Use caution if considering offers at the bus station; prices tend to run a little higher than those on Av. Comandate Matoso, and rooms could be outside the main city. To stay within city limits, try **Atalaia Apartamentos ❷,** on R. Patrão António Faustino, just off the main drag. The spacious beach-themed rooms match the blue and yellow painted tiles adorning the hallway. The apartments boast full kitchen, bath, living room, and terrace. (☎282 62 46 81. Prices vary; call ahead.) The shop owner at **Oceanus ❷,** R. Comandante Matoso near the pharmacy, offers clean, colorful and mostly spacious rooms with complete bath above the store. (☎282 62 45 58. Small singles €20; doubles €25; triples €30. Larger rooms €30/35/40. Reception open daily 9am-8pm.) Sagres strictly forbids open-air **camping** due to its strong winds. Campers can get their fix at **Orbitur Campground ❶,** 2.5km toward Cabo de São Vicente, just off ER 268 and about a 25min. walk to the lesser-known Praia do Belixe. (☎282 62 43 71. Reception 8am-10pm. June-Aug. €4.30 per person; €4.60 per tent; €3.80 per car. Sept.-May prices €0.20 less.)

FOOD. For groceries, try **Alisuper,** a supermarket on R. Comandante Matoso. (☎282 62 44 87. Open daily 9am-8pm.) **O Dromedário Bistro ❷,** on R. Comandante Matoso, is a Moroccan-inspired haven with an extensive bar, constant stream of American pop/rock, and free internet (ask the bartender for the code). Try the hearty crepes (€2.40-5.30), colorful salads (€3.90-6.80), inventive sandwiches (€2.10-6.70), and fresh fruit juices and shakes (€2-3.50). The bar is a hot nightspot, especially on Karaoke Thursdays. (☎282 62 42 19; www.dromedariosagres.com. Restaurant open daily 10am-midnight. Bar open daily in summer until 3am; in winter until 2am.) The colorful, minimalist decor of **Com Alma Caffé ❷,** right across Atalaia Apartamentos, is inviting. (☎282 62 48 56. Pasta and pizza €6.80-9.30. Beer €1-2.60. Mixed drinks €3.50-5.)

SIGHTS AND BEACHES. Near town, the **Fortaleza de Sagres** divides the famed Ponta de Sagres that grips both coasts of the jutting peninsula with its far-reaching walls. The fort, once home to Prince Henry the Navigator, is an integral part of every visit to Sagres, if only for its sweeping ocean views. (Open daily May-Sept. 9:30am-8pm; Oct.-Apr. 9:30am-5:30pm. Closed May 1 and Dec. 25. €3, under 25 or retired €1.50. Youth cardholders €1.20. Free 30min. guided tours at noon, 4, 5pm. Max. 20 people. Meet near compass.) Several swimmer-friendly **beaches** fringe the peninsula, the most prominent of which is **Mareta,** at the bottom of the road from the town center. Craggy rock formations bookend this sandy crescent. Mareta is popular for its length and isolation, but this beach is not immune to Sagres's infamous wind. Less than a mile up the coast from **Praia da Baleeira** is **Praia de**

Martinhal, widely acclaimed for its windsurfing. Less windy **Praia da Belixe** is located 3km outside of town on the way to Cabo de São Vicente.

ENTERTAINMENT. With the last traces of sunlight snuffed out, rock music and crowds fill the lively **Rosa dos Ventos** in Pr. da República. (☎282 62 44 80. Beer €1-2. Mixed drinks €3-5. Famous sangria €6.50. Happy hour 5-8pm, sangria €4. Open M-Tu and Th-Su 10am-2am.) Another hot spot is **Água Salgada,** on R. Comandante Matoso, pulsing with mixes spun by a live DJ. Free Wi-Fi and PC access, card games, and foosball provide entertainment off the dance floor. (☎282 62 42 97. Beer from €1.70. Mixed drinks €5. Shots €2. Sandwiches, pizza, and salads available. Open June-Aug. daily 10am-4am. Sept.-May M abd W-Su 10am-4am.) Next door is **O Dromedário** (see **Food,** p. 623), where trendy young locals let loose. A projector screen plays surf movies while the DJ keeps the party moving with the likes of Lynyrd Skynyrd and REM. (☎282 62 42 97. Beer €1.70-4. Daiquiris and coladas €4.50-7. Open in summer daily 10pm-3am; in winter Th and Su 10am-2am, F-Sa 10am-4am.)

ALBUFEIRA ☎289

Sandwiched between two hills, Albufeira's landscape is covered in sprawling hotel and condominium developments—get moving early if you want to avoid the madding crowd. The lively international nightlife includes such stellar (impersonation) performances as The Rolling Stones and Neil Diamond. But don't let the hype and glamor of Swedish hotels and English pubs scare you off; you are in the Algarve, and that means fabulous beach space. Soak it up, especially since your hotel is most likely only a 5min. walk from the shore.

TRANSPORTATION. EVA **buses** (10min., every hr. 7:05am-8:20pm, €1.90) connect the train station (☎289 57 26 91) and bus station (☎289 58 97 55) to the town center 6km away. **Trains** to: **Faro** (1hr., 8 per day 7:17am-11:10pm, €2.35); **Lagos** (1hr., 8 per day 7:38am-9:17pm, €3.85); **Lisboa** (3-5hr., 5-7 per day 6:06am-6:28pm, €17); **Olhão** (1hr.; M-F 9 per day 7:17am-10:31pm, Sa-Su 6-7 per day 8:13am-10:31pm; €2.75); **Vila Real de Santo António** (1-2hr., 7-9 per day 8:13am-10:31pm, €6.30). The EVA bus station is in nearby **Caliços. Buses** head to **Faro** (40min., 7 per day 7:05am-6:35pm, €4.20), **Lagos** (1hr., 6 per day 8:50am-6:25pm, €5), and **Lisboa** (6 per day M-F 7:05am-7:50pm, €19). To get between the train or bus stations and the center of town, you can call **Táxi Rádio** (☎298 58 32 30).

ORIENTATION AND PRACTICAL INFORMATION. Albufeira spreads along the Atlantic, with R. Latino Coelho, R. Bernardino Sousa, and R. da Bateria bordering the coast. R. 5 de Outubro and Av. da Liberdade run perpendicular to the ocean and separate the town's busy cafe- and bar-filled section to the east from the slightly calmer area to the west. From the new bus station, it is at least a 25min. trek to the town center. Take the blue or green line (not the 40min. city-sweeping red, or *vermelha*, line) of the **Giro city bus** from the station to Av. da Liberdade (every 20min. 9am-8pm, €1.10). To reach the **tourist office,** R. 5 de Outubro, 8, follow Av. da Liberdade downhill to Tr. 5 de Outubro and take a right. Turn left when this small street intersects R. 5 de Outubro. The staff offers maps and info on watersports, fishing, and scuba diving. (☎289 58 52 79. Open M-F 9:30am-12:30pm and 1:30-5:30pm.) Local services include: **banks,** surrounding the tourist hub Lg. Eng. Duarte Pacheco; **police** (☎289 58 33 10) on Av. 25 de Abril; **Farmácia Piedade** (☎289 51 22 54) on R. João de Deus, open daily until 7:30pm with listings of on-call pharmacies; and **Centro de Saúde** in nearby Caliços (☎289 59 84 00). **Internet** access can be found in the **Shopping**

Center California, R. Cândido dos Reis, 1. (☎289 00 15 33. €1.50 per 30min. Open daily 10am-midnight.) The town's only English-language bookstore is **Julie's Secondhand Book Shop,** R. Igreja Nova, 6, which gives a small refund if you bring the book back. (☎965 12 94 82. Open M-F 10am-4pm, Sa 10am-1pm. The **post office** is next to the tourist office on R. 5 de Outubro. (☎289 58 08 70. Open M-F 9am-12:30pm and 2-6pm.) **Postal Code:** 8200.

ACCOMMODATIONS. Most lodgings in Albufeira are booked solid by package tours from late June through mid-September. To find a room, head to R. Cemitério Velho, R. do Saco, R. Igreja Nova, and R. Igreja Velha; looking expectantly at anyone around and saying *"Quartos?"* will automatically start the process. Some of the rooms can be far away from the city center—make sure to see the room before agreeing on anything, settle on a price, and get a receipt for your stay. **Pensão Dianamar ❺**, R. Latino Coelho, 36, is close to the beach and has a charming courtyard, kitchen, TV lounge, and bright, white rooms with bath. (☎289 58 78 01. Breakfast included. July-Sept. singles €50; doubles €60-65; triples €75. Sept.-Oct and Apr.-June. €40/50-55/65.) Open-air camping is illegal, but travelers can pay for **Parque de Campismo de Albufeira ❶**, 2km outside town on the road to nearby Ferreiras, boasts a moat, three swimming pools, a playground, restaurant, tennis courts, supermarket, and a dance club. From the bus station, take the red *(vermelha)* line and get off at the fourth stop. (☎289 58 76 29; www.campingalbufeira.net. May 16-Sept. €5.20 per person; €4.70 per car; €5.30 per tent. Oct.-May 15 50% discount. AmEx/MC/V.)

FOOD. For fresh produce and seafood, check out the **mercado municipal.** Follow R. Paul Harris from the main bus station and take a right onto Es. Vale Pedras. (Open Tu-Su 8am-1pm, Th offers most variety.) **R. 5 de Outubro** offers ample options with many inexpensive, fast eateries. Alternatively, **O Zuca ❶**, Travessa de Malpique, offers a wide variety of Algarvian entrees (€5-11). Try the cilantro-garnished *carapau.* (☎289 58 87 68. Open M-Tu and Th-Su noon-3pm and 6:30-10:30pm.) For tapas, head to **Rossi Spot ❶**, R. Latino Coelho, 14. This Havana-inspired cafe doubles as a bar at night and serves a variety of tapas (€2-5) against a backdrop of Cuban and reggae beats. (☎915 47 42 45. Sandwiches €2-4. Meat dishes €4-7. Open daily 11am-2pm and 6pm-2am. AmEx/MC/V.) For a cozy and classy spot farther from the bustle, head to **Augusto's ❷**, Av. de Liberdade, 81, which offers meat and fish (€9-15) and specialty (€30) Algarvian dishes. (☎289 51 57 38. Open daily 6pm-midnight. MC/V.)

BEACHES. The constant stream of tourists that flows into Albufeira empties into the city's spectacular spread of beaches, ranging from the popular **Galé** and **São Rafael** (4-8km toward Lagos) to the chic local favorite **Falésia** (10km toward Faro), both accessible by car, taxi, or bus. Check the tourist office for seasonal schedules. To get to the centrally located **Inatel** beach from the main square, Lg. Eng. Duarte Pacheco, follow Av. 25 de Abril to its end and continue down R. Gago Coutinho until you hit sand. Beautiful, but packed, **Praia de Albufeira** awaits through the gate to the tourist office

ENTERTAINMENT. Bars and restaurants line all the town's streets, but all you really need to do for a great night out is head for R. Cândido dos Reis where the young, lively crowd hangs out. Locals recommend **Atrium Bar,** R. Cândido dos Reis, 7, especially for no-holds-barred karaoke. (☎289 58 91 16. Karaoke nightly 9pm-4am. Beer €2.50. Mixed drinks €6-7.50. Light food served until 11pm. Open daily 6pm-4am.) **Bubha Bar,** Tr. Cândido dos Reis, 3, offers a large dance floor and lounge, opening right onto the town square. At midnight, an intimate rooftop bar with chill-out music and spaces for hip-hop beats and popular Spanish rock opens up. (☎289 51 42 60. Open daily 7pm-late.) **Classic Bar,** R. Cândido dos Reis, 10, is a rocking spot with elaborately concocted drinks and a largely anglophone clientele. (☎289 51 20 75. Beer €2-3. Mixed drinks €5-7.50. Open daily June-Sept. noon-4am; Oct.-May noon-midnight.)

FARO ☎289

Step off the bus in Faro (pop. 42,000), and you'll find yourself in the shadow of McDonald's arches and a run-of-the-mill chain sandwich shop. Don't let these sights discourage you, however; a few blocks down, the street spills out into a square overlooking a tightly packed marina, the lifeline of the city for centuries. Visitors can take advantage of a pedestrian shopping district, museums of all sorts, a quiet historical neighborhood in the *cidade velha* (old city), and beaches on the estuary's island.

TRANSPORTATION

Flights: Aeroporto de Faro (☎289 80 08 00, flight info 80 08 01; www.ana.pt/portal/page/portal/ana/aeroporto_faro), 4km west of the city, has car rental, tourist info booth, bank, police station, and post office. Open daily 10am-midnight. Buses #14 and 16 run there from opposite the bus station (20min.; M-F 18 per day 7am-8:40pm, Sa-Su and holidays 12 per day 8am-7:30pm; €1.65).

Trains: Lg. da Estação (☎808 20 82 08), from the bus station, exit left and walk 4min. Not to be confused with a secondary station in Faro 2km away. Free internet access available at 2 kiosks. To: **Albufeira** (30min., 5 per day 6:45am-6:05pm, €2.35); **Beja** (2hr.; M-F 3 per day 9:10am-3:32pm, Sa-Su 9:10am, 2:10pm; €15.35); **Évora** (4-6hr.; M-F and Su 3-4 per day 6:45am-4:04pm, Sa 6:45, 9:10am; €19.80); **Lagos** (1hr., 9 per day 7:12am-8:11pm, €6.15).

Buses: EVA, Av. da República (☎289 89 97 00. Open M-F 6am-11pm, Sa-Su 7am-11pm). To: **Albufeira** (1hr.; M-F 15 per day 6:30am-7:15pm, Sa-Su 9 per day 7:20am-6:45pm; €4.20); **Beja** (3hr., 5 per day 8:30am-5pm, €12.70); **Huelva** (3hr.; 8:20am, 3:35pm; €12); **Lagos** (2hr., 7 per day 8am-5:30pm, €5.35); **Olhão** (20min., 13 per day 7:35am-7:50pm, €1.75); **Vila Real de Santo António** (1hr., 9 per day 7:15am-6:20pm, €5). EVA also provides long-distance service to **Braga** (8hr., 9 per day 5:30am-1:30am, €27) and **Porto** (7hr., 6-13 per day 5:30am-1:30am, €26) via **Lisboa** (4hr., 9 per day, €18-19; 5% ISIC discount).

Taxis: Táxis Rotáxi (☎289 89 57 95). Taxis gather near Jardim Manuel Bívar (by the tourist office) and at the bus and train stations.

ORIENTATION AND PRACTICAL INFORMATION

Faro's center nestles against the **Doca de Recreio,** a marina lined with luxurious ships and bordered by the **Jardim Manuel Bívar** and **Praça Dr. Francisco Gomes.** The lively, walkable shopping district is tucked between Pr. Ferreira de Almeda and R. da Misericórdia, near the entrance to the old city. From the train or bus stations, turn right and follow Av. da República toward the harbor. Enter the *cidade velha*, with its ancient walls and cathedral, through the Arco da Vila, a stone passageway next to the tourist office on the far side of the garden bordering Pr. Dr. Francisco Gomes.

Tourist Office: R. da Misericórdia, 8 (☎289 80 36 04; www.visitalgarve.pt). From the bus or train station, turn right down Av. da República along the harbor, then left at the garden. English and French spoken. Website has guides for download. Open daily

June-Sept. 9:30am-12:30pm and 2-7pm; Oct.-May 9:30am-12:30pm and 2-5:30pm. Regional office, Av. 5 de Outubro, 18-20 (☎289 80 04 00). Open M-F 9am-7pm.

Currency Exchange: Cotacâmbios, R. Dr. Francisco Gomes, 26 (☎289 82 57 35). Open daily June-Sept. 9am-8pm; Oct.-May 9am-7pm.

Luggage Storage: €1.50 per bag per day at the bus station (look for the sign next to the ticket counter). Open 9am-1pm and 4-7pm.

Laundromat: Sólimpa, R. Batista Lopes, 30 (☎289 82 29 81). Wash and dry €7 for 4kg, €1.75 per additional kg. Open M-F 9am-1pm and 3-7pm, Sa 9am-1pm.

Police: R. Polícia da Segurança Pública (☎289 89 98 99).

Pharmacy: Farmácia Caminé, R. Dr. F. Gomes, 14 (☎289 82 22 77). Open M-F 9am-10pm, Sa 9am-10pm.

Hospital: R. Leão Penedo (☎289 89 11 00), just north of town across from the old soccer stadium. **Centro de Saúde** (☎289 83 03 00). Open daily 8am-8pm.

Internet Access: Free at the **Instituto Português de Juventude,** next to the youth hostel (☎289 89 18 20). Max. 30min. Open M-F 9am-8pm.

Post Office: Lg. do Carmo (☎289 89 25 90), across from Igreja do Carmo. Open M-F 8:30am-6:30pm, Sa 9am-12:30pm. **Postal Code:** 8000.

ACCOMMODATIONS

Lodgings surround the bus and train stations as well as the pedestrian streets of R. Vasco de Gama, R. de Santo Antonio, and R. Conselheiro Bivar. Most of the low-end budget *pensões* are plain but adequate.

Pousada da Juventude (HI), R. Polícia de Segurança Pública, PSP (☎289 82 65 21; faro@movijovem.pt). A 15min. walk from the bus station. Take Dr. F. Gomes, which becomes R. de San António. Take a right on R. Bemardo Passos, which becomes R. PSP. Basic, but the best value in town. Rooftop patio and TV common room. Basic, industrial-style interior and shared bathrooms. Breakfast included. July-Aug. dorms €13; doubles €28, with bath €38. Sept.-June €9/22/25. AmEx/MC/V. ❶

Pensão Emilia, R. Reitor Teixeira Guedes, 21 (☎289 80 19 62). Tiled facade, big windows, and dark wood lend the pension Old World charm. Oct.-June singles €15; doubles €25; triples €40. July €20/40/45. Call ahead to verify prices. Cash only. ❷

FOOD

Pizzerias and sandwich shops abound along **Rua Conselheiro Bívar** and **Praça Dr. Francisco Gomes,** but be wary of overpriced fast food. The true Faro flavor comes out a few blocks from the shopping district, where you'll find restaurants that cater to local families. At the **market** in Lg. Dr. Francisco Sá Cameiro, fishermen peddle the day's catches. (Open daily 7am-3pm.) Always a quick, cheap option, the **Alisuper** grocery store, Lg. de Carmo, is to the right when facing the church. (☎289 82 49 20. Open M-Sa 8:30am-8pm, Su 9am-1pm. AmEx/MC/V.)

Restaurante São Domingos, R. da Trindade, 10. Serving local fish and meat dishes, this small restaurant is recommended and frequented by locals. Entrees €5.50-9. Bottle of house wine €4. Open daily noon-2:30pm and 7-10pm. Cash only. ❶

O Ribatejano, R. São Luis, 32A (☎289 81 21 10; www.ribatejano.net). A rarity in carnivorous Portugal. Chef whips up protein-conscious vegetarian platters delicious enough to rival classic fare. Entrees €6-13. Open daily noon-3pm and 7-11pm. Cash only. ❶

SIGHTS

Faro's **Vila-Adentro,** a medley of ornate churches and museums punctuated by shops selling local handicrafts and houses of multi-generational families, is an uncorrupted haven for those looking for a slice of the Old World. As you walk through the **Arco da Vila,** look to the right to see the city's only remaining Moorish door. At the end of a sweltering day, seek refuge in the **Jardim Alameda João de Deus,** next door to the Pousada da Juventude, where you can relax under lush tropical greenery. (Minigolf €0.27. Open daily 8am-8pm.)

CAPELA DOS OSSOS. The Capela dos Ossos (Chapel of Bones) in the courtyard of the **Igreja de Nossa Senhora** was built to commemorate the monks who were formerly buried behind the church. Brace yourself; the walls and ceiling were constructed with over 1245 skulls and countless other bones. *(Lg. do Carmo. ☎289 82 44 90. Open May-Sept. M-F 10am-1pm and 3-6pm, Sa 10am-1pm; Oct.-Apr. M-F 10am-1pm and 3-5pm, Sa 10am-1pm. Su mass 8:30am. Chapel €1, church free.)*

CATEDRAL (SÉ). A narrow road climbs up from the Arco da Vila to a square lined with orange trees and blindingly white buildings, home to Faro's cathedral, a compilation of Roman, Moorish, and Catholic architecture. The tower is easy to climb and provides a fantastic vantage point of the town's seascape and landscape peppered with stork nests. The small museum displays a limited selection of religious artifacts, but Sr. Zacariah, who is often found by the cathedral's gate, will tell you the church's history more comprehensively than any museum. *(Open M-F 10am-6pm, Sa 10am-1pm. Museum €3.)*

CEMITÉRIO DOS JUDEUS. One of a few Jewish cemeteries left in Europe, this cemetery is dedicated to the memory of the courageous Dr. Aristides de Sousa Mendes, who helped Jews escape the Nazis. The scattered marble gravestones were restored in 1952 and serve as symbols of one community's long, often painful, history. *(R. Leão Penedo, between the hospital and the soccer stadium. A 20min. walk from the tourist office. Cemetery and small museum open M-F 9:30am-12:30pm. Free.)*

BEACHES AND NIGHTLIFE

Faro's sandy beach, **Praia de Faro,** hides on an islet off the coast with the **Parque Natural da Ria Formosa** on one side. Take bus #16 from the bus station, the stop in front of the tourist office, or under the blue bus sign near Pousada da Juventude. From Faro, you can also explore Portugal's southernmost point, the beautiful **Ilha Deserta;** boats leave from Faro's central pier. (www.ilha-deserta.com. 30min.; 4 per day 10am-4:15pm, last return from the island at 6pm; €7.) Sidewalk cafes crowd the pedestrian walkways off the garden in the town center, and several bars liven **R. Conselheiro Bívar** and its side streets in July and August (the bar scene is pretty dead for the rest of the year).

OLHÃO ☎289

Olhão (ol-YOWN, pop. 31,000), though it blatantly caters to tourism, takes pride in its status as the largest, most productive fishing port in the Algarve. The port stretches along the coast, paralleled by a strip of pork and fish restaurants nearly as long and twice as welcoming. Buildings are peeling and historical sights are few, but the region's natural beauty, friendly locals, bird sanctuary, and necklace of unspoiled islands make the port town worth a trip.

TRANSPORTATION. The train station is on Av. dos Combatentes da Grande Guerra, one block from Av. da República. (☎289 70 53 78. Open daily 6am-8pm.)

Trains run to **Faro** (10min., 9-16 per day 6:37am-9:40pm, €1), **Tavira** (30min., 6-16 per day 8:16am-12:04am, €1.61), and **Vila Real de Santo António** (1hr., 10-11 per day 8:45am-12:33am, €3.01). The **bus station** is on R. General Humberto Delgado, one block from Av. da República. (☎289 70 21 57. Open M-F 7am-7:30pm, Sa 7:05am-12:40pm and 1:30-6:30pm, Su and holidays 7:45am-12:40pm and 1:30-6:30pm.) **EVA** buses run to **Faro** (20min., 13 per day 7:35am-7:50pm, €1.75) **Tavira** (40min., 11 per day 8:15am-8:30pm, €2.40), and **Vila Real de Santo António** (1hr., 9 per day 8:55am-8pm, €3.90).

ORIENTATION AND PRACTICAL INFORMATION. To reach the **tourist office** from the train station, turn left onto Av. dos Combatentes da Grande Guerra and take a right onto **Avenida da República** past the Palácio da Justiça (5min.). From the bus station, turn right down R. General Humberto Delgado and then take another right onto Av. da República. Once on Av. da República, go straight until you reach Olhão's main church. Here, Av. da República splits into three streets—take the middle path, **R. do Comércio,** which turns into a pedestrian street. Continue as far as possible, following the street right as it turns into **R. da Lagoa.** After a block, the street becomes a little plaza, **Lg. Sebastião Martins Mestre,** and the tourist office (#8A in the plaza) is directly opposite the **Câmara Municipal.** Its English-speaking staff has maps and ferry schedules. (☎289 71 39 36. Open M-F 9:30am-1pm and 2-5:30pm.) **Internet** access is at **Olhão Internet** at the end of R. Téofilo Braga. (☎289 70 10 40. max. 30min. Open M-F 10am-10pm, Sa 10am-8pm.) **Lavanderia Olhanese,** R. Téofilo Braga, 54, across from Pensão Bela Vista, does laundry for €2 per kg, with a 4kg minimum. (☎289 70 26 41. Open M-F 9am-1pm and 3-7pm, Sa 9am-1pm.) Other services include: **police,** R. 5 de Outobro, 178 (☎289 71 07 70); local **Centro de Saúde,** off R. Antero Nobre (☎289 70 02 60; open daily 8am-8pm); **Farmácia Rocha,** R. do Comércio, 120 (☎289 70 30 85), with a list of all of Olhão's pharmacies, their numbers, and their hours; and the **post office** at Av. da República, 17 (☎289 70 06 00; open M-F 9am-7:30pm, Sa 9am-1pm and 3-7pm). **Postal Code:** 8700.

ACCOMMODATIONS AND FOOD. To live like a king on a pauper's budget, head to **Pensão Bicuar ❸,** R. Vasco de Gama, 5, which has dark wood furnishings, chairs upholstered in red velvet, a kitchen, and a terrace with a magnificent view. From the tourist office, retrace back to R. do Comércio. (☎289 71 48 16; www.pension-bicuar.net. Reception 9am-midnight. Singles €30,with bath €35; doubles €40/45, with small child €48; triples €55; quads €65. Discount for longer stays. Cash only.) Olhão's year-round campground is the **Parque de Campismo dos Bancários do Sul e Ilhas ❶,** off the highway outside of town. (☎289 70 03 00; www.sbsi.pt.) The town **market** is housed in two red brick buildings adjacent to the city gardens on R. 5 de Outobro, along the river near Pr. Patrão J. Lopes. (Open daily 9am-12:30pm and 2-5:30pm.) Many eateries on Av. 5 de Outubro, including **Restaurante O Bote ❷,** Av. 5 de Outubro, 122, serve the daily catch fresh off the boat. Although meat is offered, seafood is the star here—try the traditional entrees (€5.75-11), like the scabbard fish. (☎289 72 11 83. Open M-Sa 11am-4pm and 7pm-midnight. Cash only.)

DAYTRIPS FROM OLHÃO

ILHAS ARMONA, CULATRA, AND FAROL

Ferries go to Armona (30min.; July-Aug. 13 per day M-F 7:30am-8pm, Sa-Su 8am-8pm; Sept and June. M-F 9 per day 7:40am-7:30pm, Sa-Su 11 per day 8am-7:30pm; Oct.-May 3 per day 8:30am-5pm; last return July-Aug. 8:30pm, June 8pm; €2.90). Another fleet serves Culatra (45min.; June-Aug. every 2hr. 7am-7:30pm; Sept.-May 4 per day

7am-6:30pm; last return June-Aug. 8pm; €2.90) and Farol (1hr.; June-Aug. every 2hr. 7am-7:30pm; Sept.-May 4 per day 7am-6:30pm; last return June-Aug. 8:20pm; €3.50).

Long expanses of uncrowded, sandy beach and a glistening blue-green surf surround the islands off Olhão's coast. Ilhas Armona and Culatra, the two major islands, and then Farol, trailing the far end of Culatra, are convenient daytrips from Olhão. Armona's and Farol's cottages house mostly vacationers, while Culatra remains a fishermen's village. Farol is easily the most beautiful of the islands, but none of the three has the volume of tourists seen in other sections of the Algarve. The islands and sandbars just offshore fence off the Atlantic, creating the **Parque Natural da Ria Formosa,** an important 80km lagoon and wetland habitat home to an impressive variety of sea creatures and bird life. During the winter, roughly one-third of Europe's flamingo population can be found here. If you'd like to roost in Armona, head to **Camping Orbitur ❶**, on the central path 5min. from the dock, best for a family or group of friends willing to exchange the 30min. ferry for a late-morning sleep-in. (☎289 71 41 73. July-Aug. 4-night min. stay; Sept.-June 2-night min. stay. 4-person bungalow in summer €43-56; in winter €30-41. Cash only.) While in Armona, check out the international **Restaurante Santo António ❷**, at the entrance to the beach 15min. from the dock, down the central path. It's renowned for its specialty: grilled *chocos* (large squid) caught right off the island's coast. (☎289 70 65 49. Meals €8-11. Open Apr. 15-Sept. 15 9am-11pm. Cash only.)

QUINTA DE MARIM

Only local buses stop within walking distance of Quinta de Marim. Rodoviária buses go to the town of Marim but will leave you stranded on the highway, far from the park. Local CircuitOlhão buses drop you at "Parque de Campismo," and then it's a 3min. walk over the train tracks to the park's main gates. Take the green line from the bus station or across from the gardens near the church on Av. 5 de Outubro (10min.; M-F 13 per day 7:15am-7:15pm, Sa 6 per day 8:15am-1:15pm; €0.80). To get back to Olhão, take the yellow line, which stops across the street from the green line in front of the campground (10min.; M-F 13 per day 8:30am-8:30pm, Sa 7 per day 8:30am-2:30pm; €0.80). Reception/front gate open M-F 8am-8pm, Sa-Su 10:30am-6pm (☎289 70 02 10). Visitors center open M-F 9am-12:30 and 2-5:30pm. €1.50 per person, students and under 18 €1.

A serene, isolated escape to nature, **Quinta de Marim** was created in 1987 as a representative sample of the larger **Ria Formosa Natural Park.** An internationally recognized protected wetland, the park provides a haven for many endangered birds and fish. On the 3km walking trail, you'll find salt marshes, sand dunes, fields, and pine forests as well as paths through blooming rhododendron bushes. The park, originally created for conservation and educational purposes, is now suffering from governmental neglect; funds are being diverted to other projects. The bird specialists, however, are not deterred by the decrease in funding. The hospital is still fully functional and, though prolonged human contact tames the birds and is detrimental to their redistribution, the doctors gladly oblige eager visitors looking for a more hands-on experience. Visitors can also play with the two champion Portuguese water dogs in the park's kennel. (Open M-F 11am-1pm and 2-4pm.)

ALENTEJO

Vast golden plains dotted with giant stone castles and tiny red-roofed villages cover the region between the Tagus and the Algarve. A sharp contrast to the commotion of Lisboa or the wilds of the Algarve, the Alentejo graces travelers with a more stately, historical setting. Évora, Elvas, and other remarkably well-preserved towns lie in the Alto Alentejo, while Beja remains the only major town on the seemingly endless Baixo Alentejo plain. The region is known primarily for its cork; more than two-thirds of the world's supply comes from here, and the local villages specialize in cork handicrafts. The area is best in the spring; fiery temperatures can turn the Alentejo into an oven in summer.

ÉVORA ☎266

Évora (pop. 55,000) is the capital and largest city of the Alentejo region, with a wall-enclosed old city of palaces, churches, and Roman ruins at its center. The city is also famous for its unusual medieval approach to recycling (see **Capela dos Ossos,** p. 633). Across the city, mock burials decorate the sidewalks in lieu of benches. During the school year, university students enliven the town, especially during the Queima das Fitas (Burning of the Ribbons), a week-long graduation celebration the last week of May with live music, dancing, and drunken merriment. The town remains surprisingly active in the summer, despite the absence of students and the locals' inclinations to vacation on the coast.

TRANSPORTATION

Trains: Lg. da Estação de CP, at Av. dos Combatentes de Grande Guerra (☎266 70 21 25 or 808 20 82 08; www.cp.pt). Service to: **Beja** (1hr., 5 per day 6:22am-6:44pm, €6.40-11.40), **Faro** (5hr.; 6:22am, 12:44pm; €12.80-19.80), and **Lisboa** (2hr., 3 per day 6:44am-6:44pm, €11.10).

Buses: Av. São Sebastião (☎266 76 94 10), 300m outside the town wall. More frequent schedules than trains. Buses go to: **Beja** (1hr., 7 per day 8:45am-8pm, €7); **Braga** (8-10hr.; M-Sa 8 per day 6am-8:45pm, Su 9 per day 6am-9:30pm; €20) via **Porto** (6-8hr., 6 per day 8:30am-8pm, €16); **Castelo Branco** (2-3hr., 6 per day 6am-5pm, €11.90); **Elvas** (1hr.; 12:15, 1:45, 5pm; €9.50); **Faro** (4hr.; 8:45am, 2:30, 5:15pm; €13.50); **Lisboa** (2hr., 9 per day 7am-8pm, €10.80); **Portalegre** (1hr.; 10:25am, 2, 5:15pm; €10); **Setúbal** (1hr.; 8:30, 10:15am, 2pm; €8.70).

Taxis: ☎266 73 47 34. 24hr. taxis wait in Pr. do Giraldo and Pr. do Sertorio.

ORIENTATION AND PRACTICAL INFORMATION

To reach **Praça do Giraldo** from the **bus station** (15min. walk), turn right up Av. São Sebastião, keeping the small white wall to the right, and continue straight when it turns into R. Serpa Pinto at the city wall. Follow this road into Pr. do Giraldo, the center of the city. All major sights are a short walk from this square. No direct bus connects the train station to the center of town. By foot, go up Av. Dr. Baronha and continue straight as it turns into R. da República at the city wall. To avoid either walk, hail a taxi (€3).

Tourist Office: Pr. do Giraldo, 73 (☎266 77 70 71; www.cm-evora.pt/guiaturistico). Staff speaks English, French, and Spanish and provides maps, lists of restaurants, and public phones. Self-guided audio tours of the city €2, due back before 5:30pm. Wheelchair-accessible. Open daily May-Oct. 9am-7pm; Nov.-Apr. 9am-6pm.

Currency Exchange: 24hr. **ATM** outside the tourist office. Several banks line Pr. do Giraldo, all open M-F 8:30am-3pm.

Police: R. Francisco Soares Lusitano (☎266 70 20 22).

Pharmacy: Farmácia Galeno, R. da República, 34 (☎266 70 32 77). Open M-F 9am-1pm and 3-7pm.

Hospital: Hospital do Espírito Santo, Lg. Senhor Jesus da Pobreza (☎266 74 01 00 or 266 75 84 24), near city wall and the intersection with R. Dr. Augusto Eduardo Nunes.

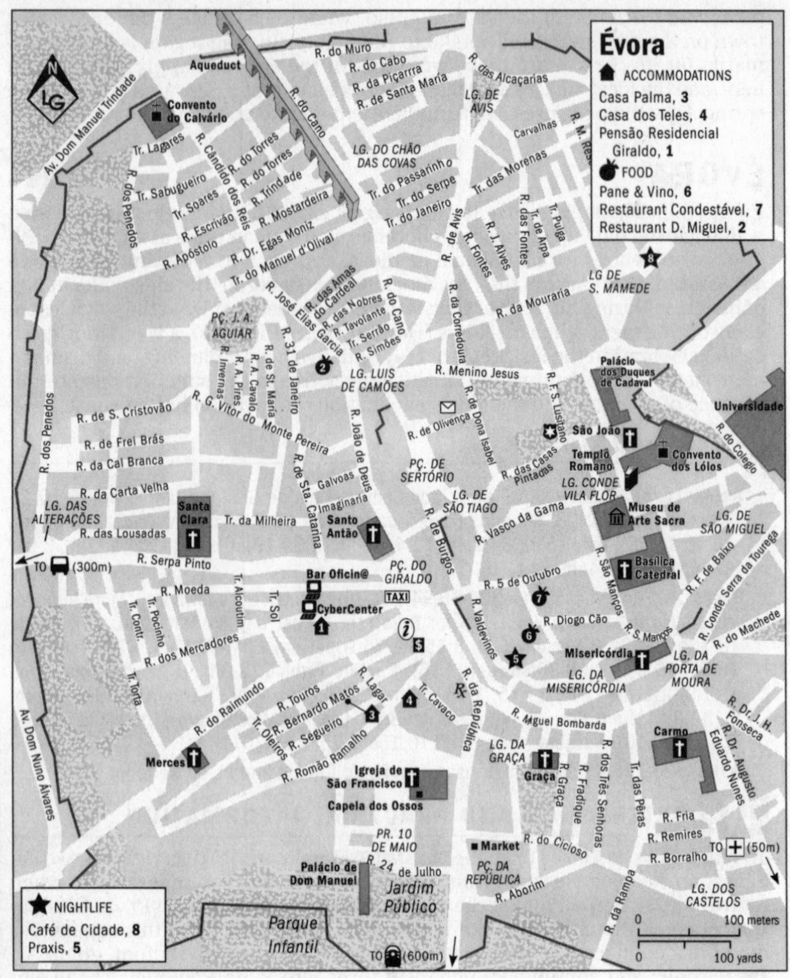

Internet Access: CyberCenter, R. dos Mercadores, 42 (☎266 74 69 23). 20 high-speed computers. €1.50 per hr. Open M-F 10:30am-11pm, Sa-Su 2-10pm. **Bar Oficin@,** R. Moeda, 27 (☎266 70 73 12). Only 1 computer, so expect to wait. €0.50 per 10min., €2.50 per hour. Open Tu-F 8pm-2am, Sa 9pm-2am.

Post Office: R. de Olivença (☎266 74 54 80; fax 74 54 86). **Poste Restante** and fax. Open M-F 8:30am-6pm. Main office on Largo Portas de Moura (☎266 74 98 40). **Postal Code:** 7999.

ACCOMMODATIONS AND CAMPING

Most accommodations cluster on side streets off Pr. do Giraldo and are well advertised. They're crowded in the summer, especially during graduation in May and the Feira de São João, the June celebration of Évora's patron saint.

Private *quartos*, about €25-30 per double, are pleasant summer alternatives to the crowded *pensões;* check with the tourist office for listings.

Casa dos Teles, R. Romão Ramalho, 27 (☎266 70 24 53, casadosteles@planetaelix.pt). 1 block off Pr. do Giraldo. The friendly dog gives this 200-year-old private home a welcoming feel. Spacious, private rooms are decorated with pictures from around town. All with TV, 4 rooms with A/C. The top room serves as a double, triple, or quint with private bath and fridge. Reserve ahead. June-Sept. singles €20-25; doubles €30-35, with bath €40; triple/quad €40. Oct.-May €5 less. Cash only. ❷

Casa Palma, R. Bernardo Matos, 29A (☎266 70 35 60). Located right off Pr. da República. The house is over 100 years old and looks like an antiques market. Its grandmotherly owner keeps it in excellent shape and charges reasonable prices for petite rooms on the top floor. She'll meet you at the door every time you return, as well. All rooms have TV, some a small balcony. Singles €20-25; doubles €30-35. Cash only. ❷

Pensão Residencial Giraldo, R. dos Mercadores, 27 (☎266 70 58 33). Spacious, comfortable rooms have TV and carpeting. Clean rooms with A/C make for a refuge from the streets outside. Reserve ahead. In summer singles €30, with bath €35; doubles €35/45; triples €55. In winter €5-15 less. Cash only. ❸

FOOD

Restaurants are scattered near Pr. do Giraldo, especially along **Rua dos Mercadores** and the small streets off **Rua 5 de Outubro,** but many are tourist-oriented; to find inexpensive local favorites, wander away from the center and the main sights. The **market,** near Pr. da República, sells crafts and regional goods as well as cheese and produce. (Open Tu-Su 7am-1pm.)

Condestável, R. Diogo Cão, 3 (☎266 70 20 08; www.softline.pt/residencial-diana). Cheap, simple, but delicious. Enjoy a two-course meal with soup, fish or meat, drink and coffee for €5.90-7. Also nice for a drink at night. Open daily 8am-midnight. MC/V. ❶

Pane & Vino, R. Diogo Cão, 22 (☎266 74 69 60). This popular corner restaurant's classic, thin-crust pizzas are too good to be missed. Pizzas and pasta €6-9. Open Tu-Su noon-3pm and 7-11pm. AmEx/MC/V. ❷

D. Miguel, Trav. de Cavella (☎ 266 74 14 42) The cheapest Portuguese meal you can find in Évora. The food has a homemade feel with several meat and fish options. Entrees €5-7. Open M-F 8am-10pm. Cash only. ❶

SIGHTS

CAPELA DOS OSSOS. Few places on earth rival the Capela dos Ossos in spookiness. The "Chapel of Bones" warmly welcomes visitors: "*Nós ossos que aqui estamos, pelos vossos esperamos*" ("We bones that are here are waiting for yours"). In order to provide a hallowed space to reflect on the profundity of life and death, three Franciscan monks built this chapel from the remains of over 5000 anonymous bodies buried in surrounding churches. The walls are covered in neatly piled bones and skulls, while the three founders lie enclosed in stone sarcophagi. For thrills and chills, check out the preserved corpse hanging from one of the chapel's walls, then go give Mom a call: legend has it that the body is a son cursed by his mother for disobedience and cruelty. *(Pr. 1 de Maio. Follow R. da República from Pr. do Giraldo, then take a right into Pr. 1 de Maio; next to the Convento de São Francisco to the right of the church steps. ☎266 70 45 21. Open M-Sa May-Sept. 9am-12:50pm and 2:30-5:45pm; Oct.-Apr. 9am-12:50pm and 2:30-5:15pm. Last entrance 5min. before closing. An audio tour plays in several languages inside the chapel. €1.50, students €1, €0.50 more for camera use—well worth it.)*

BASÍLICA CATEDRAL. Built during the 12th century, the Basílica Catedral, also known as the Sé, looms over Évora with its two giant asymmetrical towers like a mad scientist's castle. Inside, however, its ornate carvings and splendid architecture are similar to those of other European cathedrals. Climb the cloisters' stairs to see the view of Évora from the terrace or tour the **Museu de Arte Sacra,** which displays religious ornaments and sculptures from the 17th and 18th centuries. *(From the center of Pr. do Giraldo, head to the end of R. 5 de Outubro. Cathedral open M 9am-12:45pm and 2-4:45pm, Tu-Su 9am-4:45pm. Cloisters open daily 9am-noon and 2-4:30pm. Museum open Tu-Su in summer 9am-4:30pm; in winter 9am-12:30pm and 2-4:30pm. Cloisters and museum €3, students €2.50; cloisters and cathedral €1.50, cathedral only €1.)*

TEMPLO ROMANO. Enormous and well-preserved columns of an ancient Roman temple sit in a spacious square at the highest point of the city, perpetual reminders of Évora's long history. The small temple was built in the AD first century from local granite but walled up in the Middle Ages and used as a slaughter house. It is widely believed, despite scarce historical evidence, that the small temple was built in honor of the goddess Diana.

IGREJA DE SÃO JOÃO DE EVANGELISTA AND PALÁCIO DE DUQUES DE CADAVAL. Also known as the Convento dos Loíos, the Igreja faces the Templo Romano. The church and ducal palace are owned by the Cadaval family, who restored the buildings with their personal fortunes in 1957-58. The interior of the church is covered with dazzling *azulejos,* and a beautiful cloister with an outdoor cafe is open to tourists. The main part of the convent is now used as a luxury *pousada* for guests looking for a unique overnight experience. *(Lg. Conde do Vila Flor. Spring-fall Tu-Su open 10am-12:30pm and 2-6pm; winter 10am-12:30pm and 2-5pm. €3, €5 for church and next-door exhibition hall.)*

NIGHTLIFE

Évora's nightlife is fueled largely by the students from the university, who fill the bars after midnight and then move on to the clubs. Wednesday nights are student nights at most establishments, so expect larger crowds. The cafes in Pr. do Giraldo are great for socializing and stay busy until around midnight. The infamous **Praxis,** R. Valdevinos, is the only nightclub in town, boasting four different bars and two floors for dancing. (☎266 70 81 77. Beer €1.50. Mixed drinks €4-6. Min. consumption €7 for men, €5 for women. Open W-Su until 6am.) A warehouse-like bar/cafe, **Café de Cidade,** R. das Alca Carias, 1, swarms with local crowds. (☎266 78 51 63. Open M-Sa 11am-2am. AmEx/MC/V.)

ELVAS ☎268

Elvas (pop. 25,000) is located 13km from the Spanish border and is surrounded by fields of vineyards and olive trees. The quiet, hilly town has an inviting main square and narrow, steep cobblestone streets leading to the fortified city walls. To walk into the old portion of town is to find a lost time capsule: the traditional architecture is straight out of the 19th century. The city pulses with the vibe of a border town; mixed conversations of Portuguese and Spanish, affectionately referred to by locals as *Portanhol,* fills the streets. Elvas's main sight, the **Aqueduto da Amoreira,** clearly visible from many kilometers away, marks the entrance to the town. Begun in 1498 and not finished until 1622, the colossal structure is Europe's largest aqueduct—its 843 arches extend almost 8km. The **castelo,** above Pr. da República, has a pleasant view of the aqueduct and the infinite rows of olive trees on the horizon; a stairwell to the right of the entrance leads up to the castle walls. (Castle open M-F 9:30am-1pm and 2:30-5:30pm. €1.50, ages 14-25 and seniors €0.75, under 14 free.) The **Igreja de Nossa Senhora da Assunção,** better known as the **antiga Sé,** in Pr. da República, was designed by Francisco de Arruda, who was also the mind behind the great aqueduct. The Igreja features 17th-century *azulejos*. (☎268 62 59 97. Open M-F 10am-12:30pm and 3-6pm. Mass Su 6pm. Free.)

António Mocisso e Garcia Coelho ❷, R. Aires Varela, 15, is one of the most reasonably priced accommodations in town. From the tourist office, take a right out of the *praça* and then the first left; go left at the end of the street and reception is on the right. The small rooms have TV, A/C, fridge, desk, and private baths. Reservations are recommended June-September. (☎268 62 21 26. Breakfast included. Check-in after noon. Singles €20; doubles €30; triples €40; quads €50. Cash only.) For camping, the **Parque de Campismo ❶** is ideal. From the bus station, follow the road that leads toward the aqueduct until the park's sign. (☎268 62 89 97. Reception daily 8am-11pm. €3.50 per person; €3.50 per car; €5 per tent. Cash only.) Fresh fish, fruit, and vegetables abound at the **mercado municipal** on Av. de São Domingos. (Open M-Sa 7am-1pm.) **O Lagar ❷,** R. Nova da Vedoria, 7, is considered by many the best restaurant in Elvas. The *bacalhau*, *bife*, and *espetada à Lagar*, a succulent layering of veal steak with cheese and ham in between, are recommended. (☎966 03 89 95. Entrees €6.50-13.50. Open M-W and F-Su noon-4pm and 7-11pm. AmEx/MC/V.)

Taxis (☎268 62 22 87 or 266 73 06 90) provide the only transportation to town (€5). The bus station (☎268 62 28 75), at the entrance of the city, is the best option, with **buses** going to: **Castelo Branco** (4hr.; 1, 4:30pm; €17.50) via **Estremoz; Évora** (1hr.; 6:40, 8:30am, 6:30pm; €10.50); **Faro** (6hr., 6:40am, €18.50); **Lisboa** (3hr., 8 per day 6:40am-6:30pm, €15); **Portalegre** (1hr.; 7am, 1, 4:30pm; €12.40). Some buses stop at the entrance of town, others leave you at the bus station. To get downtown, exit through the stairs and go right until the rotary, then take a right and you will see the entrance to the walls of the city. The **tourist office** is in **Praça da República.** From the city's entrance, take a right and go through Lg. da Misericórdia; continue up to R. da Cadeia and after a series of fountains take a left into Pr. da República—the office is on the right after a 5min. walk. (☎268 62 22 36. Open May-Oct. M-F 9am-7pm, Sa-Su 10am-12:30pm and 2-5:30pm; Nov.-Apr. M-F 9am-5:30pm, Sa-Su 10am-12:30pm and 2-5:30pm.) The **Banco Espírito Santo** is in Pr. da República, in front of the tourist office, and has a 24hr. **ATM** (☎268 63 92 40; open M-F 8:30am-4:30pm). Other local services include: **police,** R. André Gonçalves (☎268 63 94 70), **Farmácia Moutta,** directly behind the tourist office (☎268 62 21 50; open daily 9am-1pm and 3-7pm), and **Hospital de Santa Luzia,** Estrada Nacional, 4 (☎268 63 76 00). **Centro da Juventude** on Praça da Republica provides free **internet** access for up to 30min., but the limit is only enforced if people are waiting. (☎268 62 30 90. Open M-F 9am-7pm.) Another option is **Espaço Internet,** on the road behind Centro da Juventude off the Praça. (☎268 62 30 90.) The tourist office offers 5min. of free internet access. The **post office,** Lg. da Misericórdia, 1, is one block behind the tourist office to your right. (☎268 63 90 33. Open M-F 9am-6pm.) **Postal Code:** 7350.

MARVÃO ☎245

This Portuguese candidate for UNESCO World Heritage status is one of the Alentejo's best-kept secrets. The ancient walled town of Marvão (pop. 185) floats like an island over the vast expanse of the Alentejo plains; in fact, it is the highest town in Portugal. The hills and meadows of the **Parque Natural de São Mamede** only add to the village's appeal. Almost all of the town's white-washed houses are enclosed by walls that have protected the village for nearly 700 years—before the walls' construction, Marvão was repeatedly seized. Marvão's noteworthy 13th-century **castelo,** atop the ridge at the west end of town, contains a museum of archaic weaponry, but the real highlight is the breathtaking view of the Alentejo's arid plains. Remnants dating as far back as the Paleolithic era are on display at the **Museu Municipal,** near the castle in the **Igreja de Santa Maria.** (☎245 90 91 32. Open daily 9am-12:30pm and 2-5:30pm. €1, students €0.75.) From Elvas, take the train to **Portalegre** (50min.; 5:26am, 2:31pm; €3.10) or a bus from **Castelo Branco** (1hr.; 10:45am, 2:15pm; €10) or from **Évora** (1hr.; 1:30, 5:15, 5:30pm; €11) and then a bus from Portalegre to Marvão (50min.; M-F 10:30am, 5:10, 5:35pm; returning at 7am and 1:10pm; €2.60-3.40). The bus will drop you off outside the town wall. Enter through a gate and walk up R. Cima until you see the stone whipping post in Pr. Pelourinho. From here, R. Espírito Santo leads toward the *castelo* and the **tourist office.** (☎245 90 91 31. Open daily 9am-12:30pm and 2-5:30 pm.)

BEJA ☎284

The stunning landscape alone—seemingly endless stretches of burnt grass punctuated by olive trees, vineyards, cattle, and half-stripped cork trees—makes it worth traveling to Beja (pop. 35,000). The town's winding cobblestone streets bear the footprints of the likes of Julius Caesar and Arab poet Al-Mu'Tamid. Beja has grown into a small, modern town relatively untouched by tourism and still steeped in tradition; the sounds of late-afternoon bocce games echo through the squares. Though Beja can be seen in a day, it is a convenient base for a tour of the villages nearby and can serve as a calm hiatus from the hurried rhythm of traveling.

TRANSPORTATION. **Trains** run from the station (☎284 32 61 35), outside the historical center on Lg. da Estação, to **Évora** (1hr., 7 per day 6:22am-6:44pm, €8.40), **Faro** (3hr.; 8:53am, 1:55pm; €8.50) via **Funcheira,** and **Lisboa** (2-3hr., 5 per day 8:10am-7:10pm, €8.60). Timetables and destinations can be found on the schedules opposite the ticket window. The **bus station** (☎284 31 36 20; open M-F 6:30am-8:30pm, Su 7:30am-8:30pm) is on R. Cidade de São Paulo, across from Av. do Brasil. Most attendants speak English. Buses go to: **Faro** (3hr., 3 per day 10:10am-7pm, €12.70); **Lagos** via **Albufeira** (3hr., 3:30pm, €13.20); **Lisboa** (3hr., 6 per day 7:45am-3pm, €12.75) via **Évora** (3hr., 4 per day 6:45am-6pm, €5.75-7.50); **Portoalegre** (5hr., 3 per day 11:30am-6pm, €7.70-12.70); **Serpa** (35min., 7 per day 6:50am-6:20pm, €2.88); **Sines** via **Santiago de Cacém** (3hr., 4:20pm, €6.05).

ORIENTATION AND PRACTICAL INFORMATION. The **tourist office,** R. Capitão J.F. de Sousa, 25, provides free internet access, comprehensive city and regional maps (also available at most tourist stops in the city), and information pamphlets about Beja and other nearby villages. To get to the tourist office from the train station, take a left out of the station and then a right onto the main road, Lg. da Estação. At the rotary, go straight up R. Pedro Victor and straight again up R. Frei Manuel do Cenáculo. Continue uphill onto R. D. Nuno Álvares Pereira with the park (Jardim Gago Coutinho e S. Cabral) on your left. Take a right at the rotary onto R. Portas de Mertola and a left onto R. de Mertola. Turn right onto the pedestrian street R. J.F. de Sousa; the tourist office is about 200m up the street on the right. (☎284 31 19 13. Open M-Sa 10am-1pm and 2-6pm.) Local services include: **banks** (open M-F 8am-3pm); **ATMs** near the bus station and by the tourist office; **luggage storage** at the bus station on weekdays (€1.50 per day); **laundry** at **Lavanderia Baldeira,** R. Dr. Brito Camacho, 11 (☎284 32 99 57; open M-F 9:30am-1pm and 3-7pm, Sa 9:30am-1pm); **police** on R. D. Nuno Álvares Pereira (☎284 32 20 22 or 32 20 23), a 2min. walk from the tourist office across R. Portas de Mertola; **taxis,** with hubs at the bus station and Lg. Conde de Boavista; several **pharmacies** in the historical center, including **Farmácia J.A. Pacheco,** R. Capitão J.F. de Sousa (☎284 32 25 01; open M-F

9am-8pm, Sa 9am-1pm). Free **internet** can be found at the **Instituto Português da Juventude** (☎284 31 49 00; open M-F 9am-8pm), next to the Pousada de Juventude de Beja on R. Professor Janeiro Acabado, as well as at the **library,** on R. Luís de Camões. (☎284 31 19 00. Open M 2:30-11pm, Tu-F 9:30am-12:30pm and 2:30-11pm, Sa 2:30-8pm). To get to the **post office,** Lg. dos Correios, take a left from the tourist office and a right onto R. Infantaria. **Poste Restante** and fax are available. (☎284 32 21 11. Open M-F 8:30am-6:30pm.) **Postal Code:** 7800.

ACCOMMODATIONS AND CAMPING. Most accommodations are located within a few blocks of the tourist office or the bus station, like the **Pousada de Juventude de Beja (HI) ❶**, R. Professor Janeiro Acabado. From the front of the bus station, turn left at the rotunda on R. Cidade de São Paulo, then right on R. Professor Janeiro Acabado; the hostel is on the left. The government-run inn boasts impeccably clean rooms with lockable cabinets, a laundry room, and a kitchen. Doubles, quads, and six-person rooms are available. (☎284 32 54 58. Breakfast included. Reception 8am-midnight. July-Aug. dorms €11; doubles with bath €26.) Marked by a two-story vine of fuschia flowers, the three-star **Residencial Bejense ❸**, R. Capitão J.F. de Sousa, 57, is just steps from the tourist office. On the other side of a stunning doorway, 24 spotless individually themed rooms await, all with marble bathrooms, TVs, phones, A/C, and tiny balconies. (☎284 31 15 70; www.residencialbejense.com. Breakfast included. Singles €32; doubles €45, with 3rd bed €55. AmEx/MC/V.) The **Parque de Campismo Municipal de Beja ❶**, Av. Vasco da Gama, offers the security of an enclosed campground and modern amenities such as free showers, bathrooms, cheap electricity (€1.75), and a bar. (☎284 31 19 11. Reception 8am-11pm. Oct.-Apr. €1.75 per person; €1.20 per tent; May-Sept. €2.75/1.85. 10% discount with student ID and up to 25% discount for extended stays.)

FOOD. The **Mercado 25 de Abril,** in Lg. do St. Amaro next to the castle at the end of town, has a small selection of local produce. (Open M-Sa 6am-1:30pm.) Head to the **Casa de Pasto O Saiote ❶**, R. de Biscainha, 6, for filling portions of no-frills, classic Alentejano fare amid locals. Leaving the tourist office, turn left and walk nearly to the end of the block; R. de Biscainha is a small side street on the right. Try the *carne de porco à l'Alentejana* (pieces of pork in a light, buttery sauce) and some of the local wine. (☎284 32 92 89. Entrees €5-7.50. Open M-Sa noon-3pm and 7-10pm. MC/V.) For a quick, greasy, and delicious bite of chicken or for

NAUGHTY, NAUGHTY NUN

You are a nun, living a life of piety and devotion—until you have a passionate, scandalous affair with a dashing French army official. What do you do when he leaves, never to return? Establish a genre of literature, of course!

That's what Beja's Mariana Alcofonado did, anyway. While living in the Convento de Nossa Senhora da Conceição in the 17th century, Mariana became enveloped in an illicit romance with the French Marquis of Chamilly, Noel Bouton, who was fighting in the War of Portuguese Restoration (1640-1668). When Bouton was called back to France, Mariana wrote him a series of five love letters, collected and edited in 1669 as *Les Lettres Portugaises.* Since then, the letters have been edited in more than 30 languages and are considered a landmark work of literature.

Besides the steamy details, Mariana's self-reflection and earnestness in expressing her undying love set a precedent for sentimentalism in literature, later reflected in works such as Samuel Richardson's *Pamela* (1740). Although there has always been the question of the letters' authenticity, even today Mariana's story continues to capture readers' imaginations—recently, novelist Katherine Vaz published *Mariana* (2004), yet another attempt to imagine the life of one of the most passionate nuns of all time.

one of the deepest baskets of fries in Portugal (€2), pop by **Restaurante O Frangote ❶**, R. Cidade de São Paulo, 7, right next to the bus station. (☎284 31 04 20. Sandwiches from €1.80. Entrees €4-6. Open M-F 9:30am-10pm, Sa 9:30am-3pm.) One of Beja's few vegetarian options, **Restaurante Sabores do Campo ❶**, R. Professor Bento de Jesus Caraça, 4, is a self-serve, cafeteria-style cafe that features creative offerings, including *tofu de fricassé* and *"bacalhau" com natas*, a meatless take on the traditional codfish plate. (☎284 32 02 67. Open M-Th 9am-8pm, F 9am-5:30pm.)

SIGHTS. At the center of the historic area lies the **Convento de Nossa Senhora da Conceição,** at Lg. de Conceição. Take a right from the tourist office and walk down Pr. Diogo Fernandes de Beja. Go right on R. Dr. Brito Camacho, through Lg. de São João to Lg. da Conceição; the convent is on the right. The convent is known in French and Portuguese literary circles as the site of an illicit love affair between Sister Mariana Alcoforado and Noël Bouton, a French Marquis who enlisted to reorganize the Portuguese army in 1665. The romance is chronicled in the 1669 book *Cartas Portuguesas (Portuguese Letters)*, widely considered a fictional work, though a 2007 book by Myriam Cyr attempted to reassert the authenticity of these five letters of lust and betrayal. (☎284 32 33 51. Open Tu-F 9:30am-12:30pm and 2-5:15pm, Sa-Su 9:30am-12:30pm. €2, students €1, Su free. Closed on holidays. Ticket includes the Museu Regional de Beja, on the 2nd fl. of the convent.) One block downhill from the Convento-Museu is the 13th-century **Igreja de Santa Maria da Feira,** Lg. de Santa Maria. Briefly transformed into a mosque during the Moorish invasion, the church houses heavyset columns that divide three naves. The sobering altars display elaborate *talha dourada* carvings, while the retable within the Chapel of the Blessed Sacrament features Renaissance paintings of the Last Supper. (Open daily for mass 6-6:30pm and Su noon. Free.) Take a right out of the *Igreja*, cross Lg. de Santa Maria, and take R. Dr. Aresta Branco until you see the **Castelo de Beja,** founded by the Celts as a fortified village around 40 BC and later transformed into a Roman fortress. The surrounding ramparts, turrets, and single tower are all that remain. (Closed for renovations through 2009.)

SINES ☎282

Tiny Sines (pop. 16,000) is a seaside town steeped in Portuguese tradition. Its port, which inspired native son Vasco da Gama, remains the lifeline of the city, providing a source of fresh seafood for the local restaurants. Sines is also making a name for itself with its renowned World Music Festival (in late July) and its new Arts Center. From the unmistakably salty air to the impossibly narrow cobblestone streets and the bronze Da Gama overlooking the Atlantic, Sines offers an authentic Portuguese maritime experience.

TRANSPORTATION. The bus station, R. Julio Gomes da Silva (☎269 63 22 68; free public toilets; open M-F 7am-1pm and 3-6:30pm, Sa-Su 7:45-11am and 3-6pm), is an easily missed small, green, shed-like office with *"Rodoviária Alentejo"* written on it. Plan ahead, since most trips out of Sines involve multiple transfers and departures are infrequent. **Buses** are the only way in and out of town and go to: **Beja** (3hr., M-F 8:20am, €6.05) via **Santiago de Cacém; Lagos** (3hr., 10:15am, €12.30); **Lisboa** (2hr.; schedules vary, roughly 3 per day 5:30am-10:30am; €12.50); **Setúbal** (2hr.; 3, 6pm; €11.50).

ORIENTATION AND PRACTICAL INFORMATION. Everything in Sines centers on the castle and its surroundings. A few shops line R. Serpa Pinto and R. Francisco Luís Lopes, both pedestrian walkways a block away from the castle. The **tourist office** is located right next to the castle, at the corner of R. Teófilo Braga, and offers pamphlets, maps, and other essential information in Portuguese, French, and English. From the bus station, go through Pr. da República, take R. Marquês de Pombal, and go straight until Lg. Afonso Albuquerque; there, take a left and go straight until you reach the castle. (☎269 63 44 72. Open daily 10am-1pm and 2-6pm.) Local services include: **banks** and **ATMs** around Pr. da República and the castle; **police,** Av. General Humberto Delgado (☎269 63 22 54 or 269 63 66 11); **hospital (Centro de Saúde),** R. Julio Gomes da Silva, across from the bus station (☎269 63 21 72); **laundry** at **Lavanderia Varanda,** R. Francisco Luís Lopes, 47, (☎269 63 23 88; open M-F 9am-1pm and 3-7pm, Sa 9am-1pm); **Farmácia Atlântico,** on Pr. da República (☎269 63 00 10; open M-F 9am-1pm and 3-7pm). The **library** is found in the **Centro de Arte de Sines,** R. Cándido dos Reis, 49, and offers free **internet** access. From the castle, take R. Teófilo Braga and turn right at Pr. Tomás Ribeiro. Head for the two modern buildings made of pink granite at the end of the street. (☎269 86 00 80. Open M 2-8pm, Tu-F 10am-8pm.) Public internet access is also available at the **post office** in Pr. Tomás Ribeiro. (Open M-F 9am-6pm.) **Postal Code:** 7520.

ACCOMMODATIONS. As word has gotten out about Sines's charm, truly affordable accommodations have become scarcer. Most accommodations in Sines take advantage of the limited tourist season, upping prices by an average of 10% during July and early August. Less than a block away from the castle is **Pensão Carvalho ❷,** R. Gago Coutinho, 27. Guests buzzing into the *pensão* and should take note of the 1am curfew. Ask to use the second-floor terrace for a coastal panorama; the view itself is worth the cost of the stay. (☎269 63 20 19. Singles €22, with bath €32; doubles €35/42. Prices slightly lower Sept.-May. Cash only.) Though a pricier option, **Residencial Veleiro ❺,** R. Sacadura Cabral, 19A, offers sea views from 12 of its 14 rooms, each of which is equipped with full bath and balcony. (☎269 63 47 51; www.residencialveleiro.com. Breakfast included. June-Aug. singles €70 doubles €75. Sept.-May €55/65. MC/V.)

FOOD. Sines offers both typical Alentejano meat-based dishes and an excellent variety of freshly caught seafood. Strict vegetarians beware: you may have to survive on dessert, fruit, and wine during your stay. **Churrasqueira Regional ❶,** R. António Aleixo, 18, serves excellent grilled cuisine, churrasco (gently grilled meat) style. Be prepared to wait around 40min. for the delicious *frango assado* (roast chicken; €5.50) and reward your patience with a slice of the revered *chorlote*, a four-layer chocolate mousse cake soaked in rum and topped with whipped cream. (☎269 08 70 95. Open M-Sa noon-3pm.) Tucked away from the city center, **Restaurante A Nau ❷,** R. Marquês de Pombal, 103B, is a pleasant place to dine alongside local families and seasoned travelers at one of five extra-long picnic tables. Try the grilled sardines—if you don't mind dealing with bones (or fish heads)—and don't miss the true steal: the *prato do dia* (€7.50), which includes an entree, bread, a bottle of wine, and espresso. Outdoor seating and takeout available. (☎269 08 76 51. Open daily 11am-midnight. AmEx/MC/V.) Underneath the wall of the castle is the ever-popular **Ponto d'Encontro ❷** (Point of Encounter), Lg. do Poeta Bocage, 3. Going back and forth between courtyard benches and the spacious two-tiered interior, its young clientele indulge in tapas, crepes (€4.50-6), and fish and meat dishes. (☎269 08 68 14. Beer €1. Mixed drinks €3. Entrees €8-9. Open daily noon-3am.)

SIGHTS. Famous Portuguese navigator Vasco da Gama was born in the keep of the **Castelo de Sines,** but the arresting stature of the *castelo* gives way to a deserted courtyard. Don't let this discourage you; if you cross the courtyard to the right wall and climb the ramparts, you will be rewarded with a breathtaking ocean panorama. (Open daily 10am-noon and 2-6pm. Free.) Turn the corner to find the **Igreja Matriz,** a 14th-century church that was rebuilt during the 18th century. Outside, a bronze Vasco gazes over the open seas. (Open daily 9am-6pm. Summer mass M-Sa 6:30, 7pm, Su 9:30, 11am; winter M-Sa 6:30pm, Su 9:30, 11am.) A recent addition to Sines, the **Centro de Artes de Sines,** located on R. Cândido dos Reis, 49, holds rotating exhibitions and houses the municipal library. It is the only truly modern architecture in town and is worth a visit, if just for its unusual granite and glass composition. (☎269 86 00 80; www.centrodeartesdesines.com.pt. Open daily 2-8pm.) **Praia Sines,** also known as Praia Vasco da Gama, stretches along Av. Vasco da Gama. Lifeguard, bathrooms, and beach bar make for comfortable seaside excursions. The beach's soft sand and indigo waters are undeniably beautiful; still, Sines is a port, and debris and refuse from ships and nearby fisheries collect near the beach wall.

RIBATEJO AND ESTREMADURA

Some of the greatest treasures of Portugal can be found in the region just north of Lisboa. Home to festivals of food, bullfighting, and crafts, the old provinces still maintain a regional character. The Ribatejo is often referred to as the "Heart of Portugal" for its central location and bountiful agricultural production. With the ornate monasteries in Alcobaça and Batalha, the fairy-tale town of Óbidos, and the hallowed sanctuary at Fátima, one of the largest Catholic pilgrimage destinations in the world, Ribatejo boasts some of the country's finest sights. Its beaches are exquisite too: serrated cliffs and whitewashed fishing villages line Estremadura's Costa de Prata (Silver Coast), where majestic palaces overlook the oceanic expanse and the undiscovered alleys of charming villages.

HIGHLIGHTS OF RIBATEJO AND ESTREMADURA

PUSH your limits surfing **Supertubos,** famously unforgiving beach breaks (p. 647).

RECHARGE with a short trip to beautiful and relaxing **Nazaré** (p. 649).

WORSHIP the mysterious ways of the Virgin Mary at **Fátima** (p. 656).

HAUNT the stomping grounds of the Knights Templar at **Convento de Cristo** (p. 661).

SANTARÉM ☎243

Nicknamed the "balcony over the Tagus," Santarém (pop. 60,000) is a 3000-year-old city known for its ancient churches connected to the Knights Templar, traditional farming festivals, and the best view of the Tejo in all of Portugal. From religious *festas* in the winter months, to bike festivals in the fall, to a celebration of national theatre in the spring, this small city is in constant motion. The prime time to visit Santarém is in the first days of June, when the city holds its Feira Nacional de Agricultura, a renowned festival featuring bullfighting, good food, and wild, yet traditional, celebration.

TRANSPORTATION

Trains: The **station,** Estrada da Estação (☎243 32 11 99), 2km outside of town. **Bus** service between the station and town (10min.; M-F every 45min. 6:50am-7:45pm, Sa 4 per day 8am-1:30pm; €1.30). Taxi service from town to the station Su, €4.30. Trains run to: **Faro** via **Lisboa's Estação do Barreiro** (4hr., 5 per day 9:16am-6:09pm, €27); **Lisboa's Sta. Apolónia** (1hr., 15 per day 9:16am-10:16pm, 6.40); **Porto** (2½ hrs., 12 per day 8:14am-10:14pm, €22); **Tomar** (1hr., 17 per day 6:15am-10:20pm, €6.40); **Coimbra** (1½ hr., 12 per day 8:15am-10:15 pm, €11).

Buses: Rodoviária do Tejo, on Av. do Brasil (☎243 33 32 00). To: **Braga** (4 hr., 3 per day 10:45am-6:45pm, €16.10); **Caldas da Rainha** (1hr., 2-3 per day 7:20am-6:20pm, €5.25); **Coimbra** (2hr., 3 per day 10:45am-6:45pm, €11.80); **Faro** (7hr.; M-F 10 per day 7:45am-7pm, Sa 10:30am-4:30pm, Su 10:30am-7pm; €18.50); **Leiria** (1hr., 4 per

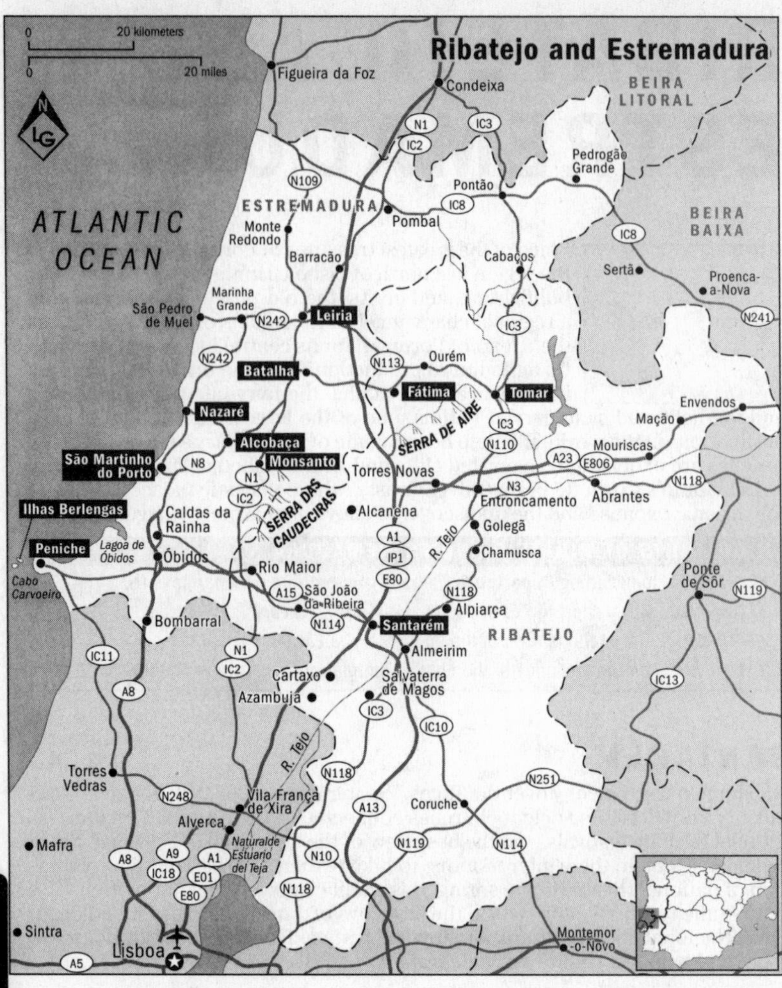

day 10:45am-6:45pm, €10.50); **Lisboa** (1hr.; M-F and Su 7 per day 10:45am-7pm, Sa 7:45am-7pm; €6.70); **Óbidos** (1hr., 4 per day 7:20am-2:45pm, €5.75) via **Caldas Rainha; Porto** (4hr., 5 per day 10:45am-6:45pm, €15); **Nazaré** (2hr., M-F 7:30am, €6.40).

Taxis: Scaltaxis (☎243 33 29 19) has a stand across the park from the bus station. 24hr. service.

ORIENTATION AND PRACTICAL INFORMATION

The historic center consists of narrow grid-like streets typical of old Portuguese cities. The main square is **Praça Sá da Bandeira.** From there, Rua Serpa Pinto and Rua Capelo e Ivans run through the core of old Santarém. Avenida Sá da Bandeira marks the outer edge of the historic center and meets Avenida Afonso Henriques at the "W" shopping center. Av. Afonso Henriques runs to the newer part of the city, and passes the bullfighting stadium in Praça de Touros.

Tourist Office: R. Capelo e Ivens, 63 (☎243 30 44 37). Maps and informative brochures on accommodations and transportation. Helpful, friendly staff speaks English, French, and Spanish. Open M 9am-12:30pm and 2-5:30pm, Tu-F 9am-7pm, Sa-Su and holidays 10am-12:30pm and 2:30-5:30pm.

Currency Exchange: Caixa Geral de Depósitos (☎243 33 30 07), at R. Dr. Texeira Guedes and R. Capelo e Ivens. Open M-F 8:30am-3pm.

Police: Av. do Brasil (☎243 32 20 22), down the street from the bus station.

Pharmacy: Farmácia Veríssimo, R. Capelo e Ivens, 72 (☎243 33 02 30). Open M-F 9am-7:30pm, Sa 9am-1pm.

Hospital: Av. Bernardo Santareno (☎243 30 02 00). Take R. Alexandre Herculano until it becomes Av. Bernardo Santareno. English spoken.

Internet Access: Esp@ço Net (☎243 32 53 11), in the Sala de Leitura Bernardo Santa Reno, a public library by the park between the bus station and the police station. 9 computers, max. 40min. Free. Library open M-F 9am-8pm, Sa 9:30am-1pm, internet access M-F 10am-6:30pm.

Post Office: (☎243 30 97 00), on the corner of Lg. Cândido dos Reis and R. Dr. Texeira Guedes. Open M-F 8:30am-6:30pm, Sa 9am-12:30pm. **Postal Code:** 2000.

ACCOMMODATIONS

Accommodation prices, while never rock-bottom in Santarém, increase during the **Ribatejo** fair in early June.

Residencial Muralha, R. Pedro Canavarro, 12 (☎243 32 23 99, fax 32 94 77). Simple, comfortable, and charming rooms, all with TV and large *azulejo*-covered private bath. Centrally located. Reserve a week ahead in summer. Singles with bath €30; doubles €35-40; quads €50. Cash only. ❸

Residencial Beirante, R. Alexandre Herculano, 5 (☎243 32 25 47, fax 33 38 45). This 42-room mini-hotel has tidy rooms with all the perks: phone, blow-dryers, A/C, TV, breakfast, and a restaurant downstairs. Call ahead in summer. Singles €30; doubles €40. Cash only. ❸

Pensão José Rodrigues, Tr. Do Froes, 14 (☎ 962 83 79 09), marked by a small hanging "Dormidas" sign. Half the price of everything around it. Gigantic footprint rugs mark the way to spotless rooms decorated with pastel-flowered bedspreads. Some doubles are a combined bedroom and bathroom. Singles €15, with shower €20; doubles with shower €25. During the 1st 2 weeks of June, prices might increase by €5. Cash only. ❶

FOOD

Many small eateries reside in the narrow streets around R. Capelo e Ivens and R. Serpa Pinto. The municipal **market,** in the pagoda on Lg. Infante Santo near Jardim da República, sells fresh produce. (Open M-Sa 6am-2pm.) The somewhat pricey **Supermercado Minipreço,** R. Pedro Canavarro, 31, is on the street leading from the bus station to R. Capelo e Ivens. (Open M-Sa 9am-8pm.)

Adiafa, Campo E. Infante da Câmara (☎243 32 40 86), out by the bullfighting stadium. A giant restaurant that looks like a barn on the inside. Try their *sopa de legumes* (€1.50) or pork *portuguesa.* Ask for a half, or *meia,* portion; it is more than enough. Entrees €6-13. Open daily 10am-9:30pm. AmEx/MC/V. ❷

A Caravana, R. Capelo e Ivens, 28. A great place for lunch, with cafeteria-style entrees cooked fresh for takeout. Also a sit-down restaurant, with glass-covered tables showcasing a variety of seeds and beans. Entrees €6-10. Open M-Sa 10am-7pm. Cash only. ❷

O Saloio, Tr. do Montalvo, 11 (☎243 32 76 56), off R. Capelo e Ivens. This local favorite serves a variety of meat and a mean *caldeirada* (monster fish stew). No vegetarian options. Entrees €5-10. Open M-Sa 10am-7pm. Cash only. ❷

SIGHTS

PORTAS DO SOL. Imposing Moorish walls surround this tranquil park of flowers and fountains, high above the Rio Tejo and the Alentejo plains. Climb the stone steps to the top and take in the timeless beauty of the surrounding countryside. Don't be surprised if you're the only one noticing the spectacular view, though; the park serves as Santarém's prime spot for lovers' rendezvous. A quiet cafe, a large birdcage, and a playground are enclosed by the ancient castle walls. *(Take R. Serpa Pinto to R. São Martinho, past the Torre das Cabaças, and stay right as the road becomes Av. 5 de Outubro after the abandoned Art Deco theater. Open daily June-Aug. 9am-10pm, Sept.-May 9am-6:30pm. Free.)*

PRAÇA VISCONDE DE SERRA PILAR. Centuries ago, Christians, Moors, and Jews gathered for social and business affairs in this small *praça*. *(Take R. Serpa Pinto from Pr. Sá da Bandeira.)* The 12th-century **Igreja de Marvila,** off the *praça*, was revamped in the late 17th century with traditional ornamentation of the era, and is undergoing another renovation in 2008. Don't be fooled by the simplicity of the exterior; the *azulejo*-covered interior is dazzling, as is the Manueline entrance. *(Open Tu-Su 9am-12:30pm and 2-5:30pm. Free.)* The early Gothic minimalism of nearby **Igreja da Graça** contrasts with Marvila's exuberance; construction began in 1380 on the orders of the first earls of Ourém, and the cloister dates back to the 16th century. Inside, in the **Capela de São João Evangelista,** lies Pedro Cabral, the explorer who "discovered" Brazil, and one of the few of his crew to live long enough to return home. *(Open Tu-Su 9am-12:30pm and 2pm-5:30pm. Free.)*

TORRE DAS CABAÇAS. The medieval Torre das Cabaças (Tower of the Gourds) was named after the eight earthen bowls installed in the 16th century to amplify the sound of the bell's ring. Today the tower serves as the **Museu de Tempo.** The interior walls of the tower are peppered with clocks and sundials from different eras and civilizations. Buy tickets across the street at the small **Museológio de Arqueologia e Arte Medievais,** which has a hearty collection of medieval cookware and an exhibit comparing Christian and Muslim influences on Santarém. *(Take R. Serpa Pinto to São Martinho, past Pr. Visconde de Serra Pilar. Open W-Su 9am-12:30pm and 2-5:30pm. Tower €1, Archaeology Museum €2, both €2.50; under 25 €0.50/1/1.25.)*

NIGHTLIFE AND FESTIVALS

Most of the fun in Santarém takes place outside the historic center. Every other Sunday, bargain hunters flock to the large market in front of the bullfighting stadium, where they sift through mounds of goods, from clothes to furniture to pets. (Open 7am-2pm.) This is also the location of the annual **Festival Nacional de Gastronomia,** a giant celebration of Portuguese cuisine in late October or early November. Better known is the **Feira Nacional de Agricultura** (a.k.a. Feira do Ribatejo), a 10-day extravaganza of markets, bullfighting, and farmers racing tiny horses. The party starts the first week of June and continues until the 11th or 13th. When there is no BBQing or horseback riding to be done, however, Santarém is a little lethargic, especially in comparison with Lisboa. A few sleepy pubs can be found beside the shopping center, along R. Pedro de Santarém, the road that leads to the bullfighting stadium in Pr. de Touros.

PENICHE ☎262

Whether lured by rolling waves, beautiful beaches, or delicious seafood, vacationers to Peniche (pop. 27,000) have one thing in common: a love for the ocean. From decor to cuisine, natives and visitors alike can't get enough of the sea. Peniche is also home to some fantastic rock formations, a 16th-century fortress, and the pristine Berlengas Islands. After a leisurely, sun-filled day, surfers, nature-lovers, and history buffs mingle in the local cafes and bars. Endowed with the best of it all, Peniche makes the perfect weekend getaway.

TRANSPORTATION

Buses: Peniche is accessible only by bus. The **station** (☎968 90 38 61) is on R. Dr. Ernesto Moureira, on an isthmus outside the town walls. Wait until the bus gets to the station to exit. Although it feels isolated, it is quite close to the center of town. Buses run to: **Alcobaça** (1hr., 2:45pm, €8); **Leiria** (2hr., 3 per day 7am-6pm, €9.70) via **Caldas da Rainha** (1hr., 16 per day 6:55am-7:40pm, €2.80); **Lisboa** (1hr., 6 per day 6am-8:45pm, €7.40); **Nazaré** (1hr.; 7am, 3pm, 6pm; €7.80); **Porto** (6hr., 11 per day 6am-6:30pm, €14); **Santarém** (1hr., 7 per day 6am-6:30pm, €12) via **Caldas da Rainha.**

Taxis: (☎262 78 26 87 or 78 29 10) in Pr. J. Rodrigues Pereira and Lg. Bispo Mariana.

ORIENTATION AND PRACTICAL INFORMATION

A giant wall and a small waterway divide Peniche in half. From the bus station, visitors must cross a small bridge to enter the city center. Tracing the inside of this wall is **Rua Alexandre Herculano,** which passes the tourist office and the central square, **Praça Jacob Rodrigues Pereira.** The wall ends at the restaurant-lined **Avenida do Mar,** which continues along the water toward the docks and the fortress. Parallel to Av. do Mar two streets inland is **Rua José Estévão,** where numerous residenciais can be found. This street and those nearby fill with loud music and bar-hoppers until the morning hours.

Tourist Office: R. Alexandre Herculano s/n (☎262 78 95 71). The office is located in the small park. Reservations for camping and bungalows can be made in the tourist office. Bus schedules also available. English spoken.

Banks: Caixa Geral de Depósitos, on R. Alexandre Herculano across from the tourist office. Open M-F 8:30am-3pm. 24hr. **ATMs** line R. Alexandre Herculano and Av. do Mar.

Police: R. Heróis Ultramar (☎262 790 310). From the tourist office, go right on R. Alexandre Herculano, then left on R. Arquitecto Paulino Montez, past the post office. Turn left on R. Heróis Ultramar.

Pharmacy: Farmácia Higiênica, R. António Conceição Bento, 21 (☎262 78 24 15). From the tourist office, turn onto R. Alexandre Herculano, left onto R. Arquitecto Paulino Montez, and right on R. António da Conceição Bento. Open M-F 9am-8pm.

Hospital: R. Gen. Humberto Delgado (☎262 78 19 00). From the tourist office, turn right and take the first left onto R. Arquitecto Paulino Montez; walk past the post office, then take a right onto R. Gen. Humberto Delgado. English spoken.

Internet Access: 30min. of free internet is available at **Espaço Internet,** R. Dr. João Matos Bilhau 28 (☎969 19 58 95), around the corner from the police station. Call ahead to make sure computers are available for public access. Open M-Sa 10am-1pm and 3-10pm, Su 10am-noon and 3-8pm.

Post Office: R. Arquitecto Paulino Montez, 53 (☎262 78 00 60/61). From the tourist office, turn right on R. Alexandre Herculano, left on R. Arquitecto Paulino Montez, and walk 3 blocks. **Poste Restante** and **fax.** Open M-F 9am-6pm. **Postal Code:** 2520.

CASH WITHDRAWAL. If you're staying in Peniche over the weekend, bring a good amount of cash. The city is popular with foreigners and ATMs usually run out of cash by Saturday afternoon.

ACCOMMODATIONS AND CAMPING

Peniche's budget accommodations are often located above restaurants of the same name; look for signs to find a *residencial* on Av. do Mar. Rooms in private homes are the best budget options, but ask to see them first and inquire about amenities. The tourist office has a listing of several private rooms, but many ladies will offer you rooms as soon as you walk into town.

Pensâo Maria Adelina Bulhôes, R. Salvador Franco 28 (☎262 78 41 34). A hotel-quality room, inside a private home, at a hostel price. Cozy and carefully decorated rooms with TV, closet, and private bath. Communal kitchen. Located 2 blocks away from the beginning of Av. do Mar, the *pensâo* is in a central location. Bargaining is recommended. Singles €15, Doubles €20. Prices might go up by €5 June-Sept. Cash Only. ❶

Residencial Marítimo, R. António Cervantes, 14 (☎262 78 28 50). Colorful hallways and bedrooms add to the atmosphere. Rooms are on the smaller side but come packed with amenities—42-channel TV, private, beautifully tiled bathroom, internet access (€1.50 per hr.), and a great location. Reserve ahead. Sept.-May singles €25, doubles 40; June-Aug. €30/50. Cash only. ❷

Residencial Aviz, Pr. Jacob Rodrigues Pereira, 2 (☎262 78 21 53). Centrally located with unbeatable prices. Singles €12, with bath €20; doubles €20/30. Cash only. ❶

Peniche Praia Municipal Campground, Estrada Marginal Norte (☎262 78 34 60; www.penichepraia.pt). On the opposite side of the peninsula. Located across the street from Peniche's rock formations. Laundry €6. Hot showers and swimming pool free. €3.45, ages 5-9 €1.75, under 5 free; €3.45-4.40 per tent depending on size, €3.10 per car. Bungalow with bathroom and TV for 2 people high/mid/low season €57/42/27. With living room and kitchen €67/51/35. Cash only. ❶

FOOD

The restaurants lining Av. do Mar serve excellent fresh seafood. Despite the multilingual menus, prices are reasonable and plenty of locals mix with tourists. Peniche's *sardinhas* (sardines) are reputedly the best in Portugal, as are the seafood *espetadas* (skewers). The outdoor cafes on Praça Jacob Rodrigues Pereira are lively, even on Sundays when the town is quiet. The **market,** on R. António da Conceição Bento, stocks produce. (Open Tu-Su 7am-1pm.)

Marinheiro, Av. do Mar 64 (☎262 78 38 35). The cheapest you can find along Av. do Mar, this restaurant offers all the gourmet seafood plates essential to the Peniche experience. Try the *pulpo à marinheira* (€8.50), a delicious plate of octupus and potatoes in a homemade sauce. The grilled *calamari* (€7) is also a favorite. Open daily summer 10am-midnight, winter 10am-9pm. MC/V. ❷

Restaurante Kate Kero I, Av. do Mar, 90 (☎262 78 14 80). The bounties of the sea are brought straight to your plate at Kate Kero I. Entrees (€6.50-20) include boiled potatoes and a hearty helping of salad. Save room for a delicious dessert (€1.50-3.25). Summer daily noon-4pm and 6pm-11pm, winter Tu-Su noon-4pm and 6-11pm. MC/V. ❷

Ristorante Il Boccone, Av. do Mar, 4 (☎262 78 24 12). Fantastic pizza (€5-8) and enormous pasta dishes (€6-8.50) provide a welcome reprieve from seafood. Great sangria (€3.50) Open daily 11am-3:30pm 6:30pm-midnight. Cash only. ❷

Java House, Av. do Mar, 14 (☎ 262 18 56 22). Craving a fancy coffee? The frozen *café frappe* (€2.40) and house specialty, the *café moka* (€1.50), are the closest things you'll find in Portugal. Fully stocked bar at night. Shots €1.50, mixed drinks €3. Open daily June-Aug. 8am-4am; Sept.-May M-Th 9:30am-2am, F-Su 9:30am-4am. Cash only. ❷

SIGHTS

FORTALEZA. António Salazar, Portugal's longtime dictator from 1932 to 1968, chose Peniche's formidable 16th-century fortress as one of his four high-security political prisons. Today it houses the **Museu de Peniche,** the highlight of which is a chilling tour of the cells of Salazar's prison, including replicas of the torture room and interrogation chamber. Outside the museum, a small exhibition traces the fascist dictatorship and underground resistance, from the seizure of power in 1926 to the coup that toppled the regime on April 25, 1974. *(Campo da República, near the dock where boats leave for the Ilhas Berlengas. Fortaleza open Tu 2-5:30pm, W-F 9am-12:30pm and 2-5:30pm, Sa-Su 10am-12:30pm and 2-5:30pm. Free. Museum ☎262 78 01 16; www.cm-peniche.pt. Same hours as Fortaleza. Last entrance 30min. before closing. €1.45, under 16 free.)*

BEACHES. For sun and surf, head to any of the town's three beaches. They are within walking distance, but bikes can be rented for the day from several local shops (€4-5 per day). The windy **Praia de Peniche de Cima,** along the north crescent, is the highlight of the three, with beautiful white sand and warm water. *(From the tourist office, take a right on R. Alexandre Herculano, cross the bridge over the river, take a left on R. da Ponte Velha, and continue 10-15min. to the ocean. Once at the water, Praia de Peniche de Cima is 300m to your right.)* About a 30min. walk farther, Praia de Peniche de Cima merges with another beach at Baleal, a small fishing village very popular with tourists, especially surfers and body boarders. The southern **Praia do Molho Leste** marks the entrance to **Supertubos,** also known as the "Portuguese Pipeline" (after the famous Hawaiian break), a perfect spot to watch daring surfers risk bodily injury on the unforgiving beach break. *(Praia do Molho Leste is over the river by the rotary at the end of Av. do Mar; cross the bridge and follow the coastline around the Porto de Pesca (15min.). Praia do Molho Leste is just after the jetty.)* Beyond Molho Leste lies crowded **Praia da Consolação,** a favorite of Portuguese families on weekend getaways. The strange humidity and hot rocks at this beach supposedly cure bone diseases. Watch out for elderly visitors seeking relief from their ailments as they often wear nothing but a hopeful smile.

NIGHTLIFE

Peniche may seem sleepy during the day, but the town's nightlife gets going after dinner and continues into the night, especially during summer. The area by the docks has some great bars, as do the streets around R. José Estévão.

Três Ás, Lg. da Ribeira, 12 (☎262 18 96 77). Wooden nautical decor gives this cafe a classy ambience that's popular with young locals. Três Ás has 2 bars and patio seating, but still manages to stay full every night in the summer. Shots €2-3, mixed drinks €3. Sandwiches €1.20-2. Open M-F 10:30am-2am, Sa-Su 10:30am-4am. Cash only.

Bar No. 1, R. Afonso Albuquerque, 14 (☎919 04 36 22), off R. José Estévão just after the church. After 10pm on Sat, the friendly owner gets on the turntables, turning this big bar into a rocking dance floor. The bar also exhibits local art and karaoke on F. Beer €1, shots €1-1.50, mixed drinks €3. Open daily noon-2am.

FESTIVALS

For daytime party-seekers, Peniche's biggest festival starts the first weekend in August, when boats festooned with flags and flowers parade into the harbor to launch the two-day **Festa de Nossa Senhora da Boa Viagem,** celebrating the protector of sailors and fishermen. The town lets loose with carnival rides, live entertainment, wine, and seafood, continuing the festivities that begin two weeks before the launch. If you're lucky, you'll be in town during early June for the **Sabores do Mar** festival, when Peniche enjoys an eight-day celebration of all things seaworthy and offers discounts on local specialty seafood dishes.

DAYTRIP FROM PENICHE

ILHAS BERLENGAS

Several companies operate boats from Peniche's public dock, near the fort at the end of Av. do Mar. Viamar ferry. (☎262 78 56 46; www.viannas-berlengas.com.) Ticket booth (open 8:30am-noon and 3-5:30pm) offers 1 or 2 crossings per day. (40min.; July-Aug. 9:30am and 4:30pm, returns 11:30am and 6:30pm; May 15-June and Sept. 1-15 departs 10am, returns 4:30pm. Same-day round-trip ticket €18, ages 5-12 €10, under 5 free.) Other companies have smaller boats at the same price, and though they post schedules, they will leave when full. If they don't fill up by the scheduled departure time, they will send you off on the big Viamar boat. Smaller boats have earlier and more frequent return times. To stay overnight, buy an €11 ticket each way. Arrive 15-30min. in advance. Reserve camping 3-4 days in advance at the tourist office in Peniche (☎262 78 95 71; tent for 2 people €9.25, 3 people €13, 4 people €16.50). The crossing is somewhat rough, and you may witness or experience sea sickness.

With its enormous orange cliffs rising off the coast of Peniche, the main island of Berlengas is not easily missed,. The inspiration for the setting of Alfred Hitchcock's *The Birds*, the rugged Ilhas Berlengas (the main island and the smaller surrounding Farilhões, Estelas, and Forcados) are inhabited by thousands of screeching seagulls. The **Reserva Natural da Berlenga** is also home to wild black rabbits, lizards, and a very small fishing community. Unfortunately for visitors, the reserve is off-limits to non-researchers, and hikers risk garnering serious institutional fury by stepping off the paths. Nevertheless, the real prize of the islands is the collection of wild rock formations. Deep gorges, natural tunnels, and pebble-strewn caves carve through Berlenga, begging to be explored. Bring a pair of hiking shoes and a walking stick if you plan to hike, as several of the trails are quite steep and strewn with small rocks. At the docks, kayaks are rented by the hour (single €4, doubles €6). The main path (2km) goes up past the lighthouse to the other side of the island, where the formidable 17th-century fortress **Forte de São João Batista ❶** sits out in the crystal clear water. Accessible by bridge, it now functions as a hostel with a small cafe inside. (☎918 61 41 90. No running water. Reception 11am-2pm and 6-8pm. Singles €11.) The fortress walls have openings that form mini-patios perfect for sunbathing and with unbeatable views of the water. Outside the fortress, small motorboats offer tours of the caves (20min., €4). The main beach lies in a small cove by the landing dock. For those willing to brave the cold, the beach has an accessible cave beside it and a jumping board off the dock.

NAZARÉ ☎262

Home to a beautiful stretch of golden sand and calm turquoise water, Nazaré (pop. 16,000) has become one of the Ribatejo's main tourist attractions. In true postcard fashion, the beaches are lined with hundreds of small colorful tents that help visitors escape the hot summer sun. In Nazaré, tourism is a big business dominated by women dressed in traditional black scarves and aprons who sell snacks and souvenirs and rent rooms or beach tents to tourists. Still, the town's relaxed feel begs tourists to return year after year for a peaceful vacation under the warm Portuguese sun. At night, Nazaré is just as busy as it is during the day. Local bars and cafes stay crowded all night, and the beach comes alive again in the early morning.

TRANSPORTATION

Buses: Av. Vieira Guimarães (☎967 44 98 68), perpendicular to Av. da República. More convenient than trains (6km away). To: **Alcobaça** (20min.; M-F 12 per day 7:10am-7:10pm, Sa 8 per day 7:10am-6:45pm; €1.75); **Batalha** (50min., 6 per day 7:10am-6:50pm, €3.30); **Caldas da Rainha** (1hr.; M-F 10 per day 6:30am-7:25pm, Sa-Su 2-3 per day 8:30am-2:45pm; €3.10); **Coimbra** (2hr.; 4 per day M-Sa 6:25am-7:25pm, Su 8:25am-7:25pm; €10.20); **Fátima** (1hr., 3 per day 7:10am-5:10pm, €4.50); **Leiria** (1hr., 5 per day 7:10am-6:45pm, €3.30); **Lisboa** (2hr.; M-Th 6 per day 6:50am-6:40pm, F and Su 9 per day 6:50am-7:40pm, Sa 5 per day 6:50am-4:40pm; €8.30); **Porto** (3hr.; M-Sa 4 per day 6:25am-7:25pm, Su 7 per day 8:25am-7:25pm; €12.50).

Taxis: Praça de Taxi (☎262 55 13 63).

ORIENTATION AND PRACTICAL INFORMATION

All of the action in Nazaré takes place near the beach, mainly along **Avenida da República,** which follows the coastline. The avenue runs past the two main squares, **Praça Dr. Manuel de Arriaga** and then **Praça Sousa Oliveira,** before ending at the cliffs. From there, the funicular runs up the side of the mountain, connecting the two levels of Nazaré. **Sítio,** the old town, forms the second story of the city, and its position 100m above the water has kept it calmer and more traditional than the beach area below. The downtown area is grid-like and easily navigable by foot. To get to the tourist office from the bus stop, take a right out of the station toward the beach and then another onto Av. da República; the office is a 5min. walk along the shore and lies between the two plazas.

Tourist Office: (☎262 56 11 94), beachside on Av. da República. Provides maps and info. English, French, and Spanish spoken. Open daily July-Aug. 9am-9pm, Sept. and Apr.-June 9:30am-1pm and 2:30-7pm, Oct.-Mar. 9:30am-1pm and 2:30-6pm.

Bank: Major banks lie on and around Av. da República. **Millennium BCP,** Av. Manuel Remígio (☎262 00 11 70), is right on the beach. Open M-F 7:30am-3:30pm.

Laundromat: Lavandaria da Nazaré, Rua Branco Martins, 19 (☎262 55 27 61). Walk away from the cliffs on Av. da Republica, turn left on R. das Traneiras and then take a right on R. Branco Martins. The laundromat will be the 2nd door on your left. Dry-cleaning and laundry available. English spoken. Wash and dry (€3 per kg), ironing (€0.15 per kg). Open M-Sa 9am-1pm 3-7pm. Cash Only.

Police: (☎262 55 00 70) at the corner of R. Sub-Vila and Av. Vieira Guimarães near the bus station.

Pharmacy: Farmácia Sousa on R. Mouzinho de Albuquerque, 30 (☎262 56 12 21). Up the street from Pr. Sousa Oliveira. Open M-Th 9am-7pm, F 9am-8pm, Sa 9am-1pm.

Medical Services: Hospital da Confraria da Nossa Senhora de Nazaré (☎262 55 23 23), in the Sítio district on the cliffs above the town center. **Centro de Saúde** (☎262 56 91 20), Urbanização Caixins, in the new part of town. Go down Av. da República, which becomes Av. Manuel Remígio. Turn left on R. das Hortas, and go almost to the end. Open M-F 9am-1pm and 2-6pm.

Internet Access: Centro Cultural, Av. Manuel Remígio (☎262 56 23 88), on Av. da República. Max. 30min. Free. Open Sept.-July 14 M-F 9:30am-1pm and 2-7pm, Sa 3-7pm. July 15-Aug. M-F 10am-1pm, 3-7pm, and 9pm-midnight, Sa 3pm-7pm and 9pm-midnight.

Post Office: Av. da Independência Nacional, 2 (☎262 56 91 00). From Pr. Sousa Oliveira, walk up R. Mouzinho de Albuquerque. **Posta Restante** and **fax.** Open M-F 9:30am-12:30pm and 2:30-6pm. **Postal Code:** 2450.

ACCOMMODATIONS AND CAMPING

Nazaré is inhabited by the most aggressive room-hawkers in Portugal. They swarm arriving buses at the station and line Av. da República offering their homes to tourists and locals alike. Bargain with the same aggressive attention they use to court you. Agree on a price before seeing the room, but don't settle the deal until afterward. In summer, don't pay over €30 for a rented room.

Hospedaria Ideal, R. Adrião Batalha, 98 (☎262 55 13 79), a block away from Pr. Dr. Manuel. 6 rooms with high ceilings, mirrors, and comfortable beds. Clean shared bathroom with retro linoleum. During the summer, rooms include 3 meals per day without beverages. July-Aug. singles €35-40, doubles €75, triples €100-110; Sept.-June €15/20/25-30 Cash only. ❸

Vila Turística Conde Fidalgo, Av. da Independência Nacional, 21-A (☎262 55 23 61). Choice of rooms with private bathroom TV and mini-fridge or private apartments with TV, kitchen, refrigerator, microwave, and bath. Laundry €5. July-Aug doubles €40-50, apartments for 5 €90; Sept-Jun €30-35/75-80. Cash only. ❹

Vale Paraíso, Estrada Nacional, 242 (☎262 56 18 00; www.valeparaiso.com), 2.5km out of town in a wooded area. Take the buses to Alcobaça or Leiria (10min., 12 per day 7am-7pm, €1.70). This camping complex includes swimming pools, restaurant, supermarket, showers, internet access (€2 per 30min., €3 per hr.), and laundry (€7). June-Sept. 14 €4.50 per person, €4-5.50 per tent, €3.50 per car; Sept. 15-May €3.20/3-4.50/2.90. Bungalows Oct.-Mar. €15.50 for 2 people, €20.50 for 3-4 people; Apr.-May and Sept. €23/31; June-July 14 €33/41; July 15-Aug. €56/65. AmEx/MC/V for purchases over €150. ❶

FOOD

For groceries, check out the municipal market in the huge warehouse across from the bus station. (Open daily 7am-2pm.) Supermarkets, like **Minipreço,** line R. Sub-Vila which is parallel to Av. da República. (Open daily 9am-9pm.)

Pastelaria Batel, R. Mouzinho de Albuquerque, 2 (☎262 55 11 47), and on Av. Vieira Guimarães. The best-known pastry shop in Nazaré, and the place to try sweet local specialties. All pastries €0.80-1.20. Try the *tamares* (little boats with custard filling capped in chocolate), *sardinhas* (flaky pastry, not fish), or the *nazarenos* (almond pastry). Open daily June-Aug. 7am-2am, Sept.-May closed W. Cash only. ❶

O Borgas, R. Mouzinho de Albuquerque, 4 (☎262 56 20 02), near Pr. Sousa Oliveira. *Bife na lage,* seasoned steak grilled on a heated rock at the diner's table, is the house specialty (€10). Complete tourist menu for €11.50 (plate of the day, bread, a drink, dessert, and coffee). Vegetarian options include grilled vegetables, various soups, and salad. Entrees €6-12.50. Open M-W and F-Su noon-4pm and 6pm-2am. MC/V. ❷

BEACHES AND ENTERTAINMENT

Nazaré's main attraction is its beautiful beach, where locals spend their days playing volleyball, racquetball, and, of course, soccer. The colorful tents ornamenting it can be rented from the women sitting in front of them along Av. da República (€6 per day, €35 per week). After catching some rays, take the **funicular** (3min.; every 15min. 7:15am-9:30pm, every 30min. 9:30pm-midnight; €0.90), which runs from R. Elevador off Av. da República, to the **Sítio,** the cliff top area of Nazaré. For centuries, all of Nazaré stood on the Sítio, well above the dangerous tide below. The charming cobbled streets, weathered buildings, and breathtaking views are perfect for a picnic. Consider making the 20min. trip to **São Martinho do Porto,** whose tranquil waters, red-roofed houses and palm-studded hillside give this lagoon a Mediterranean charm unsullied by the hordes of tourists seen in Nazaré. Bus schedules are posted at the tourist office.

On Saturday afternoons in May and June, locals dress in traditional outfits and haul fishing nets out of the water, using an old-fashioned technique in an event known as **Arte Xávega,** named after the style of boat used. An exciting fish auction, open to the public, follows. During the summer, look for late-night **folk music** gatherings on the beach. **Bullfights** are also popular and Nazaré features *corridas* on various summer weekends (usually Sa 10pm; tickets from €10). Bullfights occur the first three Saturdays in July and August and the first week of September. Inquire at the tourist office for exact times, dates, and prices.

DAYTRIPS FROM NAZARÉ

ALCOBAÇA

Buses are the best way to reach Alcobaça. The bus station on Av. Manuel da Silva Carolino (☎262 58 22 21) offers service to: Batalha (30min., 7 per day 7:30am-7:10pm, €2.60); Leiria (1hr., 6 per day 7:30am-7:10pm, €3.25); Lisboa (2hr.; M-F 2 per day, Sa-Su 1 per day 6:30am-3pm; €8.30); and Nazaré (25min.; M-F 11 per day 7:30am-7:40pm, Sa-Su 7-9 per day 8:10am-7:25pm; €1.70).

Visitors from around the world travel to this tranquil hillside town to stand inside the **Mosteiro de Santa Maria de Alcobaça,** the largest church in Portugal. This enormous abbey was founded in 1153 by Portugal's first king, Dom Afonso Henriques, following his removal of the Moors from Santarém. In an attempt to secure Christianity in the region, the king granted the land to Cistercian monks. In gratitude, the monks built a monastery spanning over 200m in length, the largest building of the Cistercian order in all of Europe. It was also the first Portuguese structure constructed using Gothic techniques. Today, all that remains of the original facade are the pointed-arched doorway and the rose window above it. In the sanctuary of the church lie the tombs of Portugal's most famous star-crossed lovers, Dom Pedro I and his wife, Inês de Castro. Note the engravings, which draw a close comparison between the life of Christ and that of Dona Inês. Surrounding the monastery's cloisters are numerous Gothic rooms, most notably the **Sala dos Monges** (Monks' Hall), and the immense *azulejo*-covered kitchen and refectory, where the monks could roast more than six oxen at a time. If you can manage it, time your visit to coincide with the religious opera concerts held M-F at 11am and 3pm, or just wander the halls to their somber accompaniment. *(☎262 50 51 20. Open daily Apr.-Sept. 9am-7pm, Oct.-Mar. 9am-5pm. Last entrance 30min. before closing. €5, seniors over 65 €2.25, students free. Su before 2pm free.)*

To escape the international swarm flowing in and out of the monastery, take a 5min. hike to the **Castelo de Alcobaça** and check out the ruins of a 12th-century castle. The remaining stone walls provide a serene retreat for crowd-weary travelers and an incredible panoramic view of the surrounding area. Be careful, as the climb up the walls is easier than the descent. From R. D. Pedro V, turn right on R. Alexandre Herculano. At the end of the street, go left, following the "*castelo*" sign. Continue through the intersection as the road becomes R. do Castelo, passing Igreja da Misericórdia on the left. About 200m up the hill the road splits, and there will be a dirt trail to the left, marked by a "*castelo*" sign.

Alcobaça makes a great daytrip, but should you spend the night, **Pensão Corações Unidos ❶**, R. Frei António Brandão, 39, off Pr. 25 de Abril, has 35 rooms decorated in a rustic style with private bathrooms. Buffet breakfast is included. (☎262 58 21 42. Reception 8am-midnight in the restaurant below. July-Sept. €17 per person, Oct-June €12.50. AmEx/MC/V.) The **tourist office** is on the corner of Pr. 25 de Abril, across from the hulking monastery. Turn right out of the bus station and right again onto Av. dos Combatentes de Grande Guerra, following the road as it becomes R. D. Pedro V and curves around the monastery. The tourist office is at the end of the strip of shops, across from the monastery. (☎262 58 23 77. English, Spanish, and French spoken. 15min. free internet access provided. Open daily May-July and Sept. 10am-1pm and 3-7pm; Aug. 10am-7pm, Oct.-Apr. 10am-1pm and 2-6pm.)

SÃO MARTINHO DO PORTO

Buses run to Nazaré (20min., M-F 11 per day 7:04am-7:45pm, Sa-Su 2-3 per day 9:54am-6:24pm €1.70). Schedules are posted in the tourist office. The bus stops on the main road leading into São Martinho do Porto, R. Conde de Avelar.

A stroke of geological good fortune for beachgoers, São Martinho do Porto's bay is a lagoon connected to the ocean by only a narrow aperture. Millennia of crashing surf hollowed out the area to form a 2km semi-circle of gorgeous, breezy beach. Rolling hills and steep cliffs extend outward, leaving only a small opening for the sea to enter. São Martinho do Porto's tranquil water, red-roofed houses and palm-studded hillside give it a Mediterranean charm unsullied by the hordes of tourists seen in Nazaré.

If a tiring day at the beach calls for a night of quality relaxation, then **Residencial Atlântica ❹**, R. Miguel Bombarda, 6, just up the road from the tourist office, is your best bet. Spotless rooms decorated in an oceanic theme come complete with cable TV, a small veranda, private bathroom, and a buffet breakfast. Some of the larger rooms also include a mini-fridge. In August, prices rise steeply. (☎262 98 01 51; fax 98 01 63. Reserve ahead for July and Aug. July-Aug. singles €40, doubles €50-60, triples €60-70; Sept.-June €25-30/40-45/45-50. AmEx/MC/V.) For something cheaper, try the **Pensão Americana ❸**, R. D. José de Saldanha, 2, about 20m from the bus stop on the corner of R. Conde de Avelar. While not as nice as the Atlântica, you'll be hard-pressed to find anything cheaper. The 22 rooms are decorated with dark wood furniture and pastel bed linens, which creates an inviting, relaxing environment. All rooms come with a private bathroom and cable TV. Rooms for 3+ persons come with a full-sized bath tub. (☎262 98 91 70. June singles €15, doubles €20,; triples €35, quads €65; July €25/40/50/60; Aug. €30/50/70/85;. Sept.-May €15/30/40/50. AmEx/MC/V.) If you want to finish your day by drinking a *caipirinha* as the moon hangs over the sea, **Pato Barvo,** on Avenida Marginal, offers mixed drinks for €4.39-6 and sangria for €2. (Open daily 1pm-3am. Cash only.)

The bus stop is on R. Conde de Avelar, which runs parallel to the beach. To get to the tourist office, Lg. Vitorino Fróis, stay on this road and head toward the hills (if facing the water, the hills are to the right). The tourist office is on the right. (☎262 98 91 10. English, French, and Spanish spoken. Free internet access for 15min. Open Tu-Su 10am-1pm and 3-7pm.)

LEIRIA ☎244

An ancient castle towers over this city of 120,000, while a *futebol* stadium glistens below. In Leiria, Portugal's two great passions, history and soccer, rival one another for veneration. Situated between Lisboa and Coimbra, Leiria was a strategic point during Dom Afonso Henriques's campaign against the Moors, culminating in its recapture in 1135. Today, the city is one of Portugal's most important economic centers, and it is bedecked with trendy boutiques and cozy restaurants. Leiria has not lost its historic feel, and its population, hailing from across Portugal, makes for a diverse urban center basking in a regal past.

TRANSPORTATION

Trains: The train station is 3km outside town (☎244 88 20 27). Buses run to train station from stop on Av. 25 Abril, the street beside the garden connecting the tourist office and the bus station. The stop is a green post marked "*urbana*." (15min.; every 45min. M-F 7:22am-7:32pm, Sa 7:22am-4:42pm; €1. Ask the tourist office for an exact schedule.) To: **Coimbra** (1-3hr., 5 per day 7:10am-7:59pm, €5-8); **Figueira da Foz** (1hr., 3 per day 9:51am-8pm, €4.90); **Lisboa** (2-4hr., 4 per day 7:11am-8:22pm, €6-14).

Buses: The bus station (☎244 81 57 17), off Pr. Paulo VI, is across the park from the tourist office. Ticket office in back. Most convenient transport out of Leiria. Express buses are usually twice the price of regional buses. To: **Alcobaça** (50min., M-F 10:30am and 5:15pm, €2.60); **Batalha** (20min., 8 per day 7:30-4:50pm, €1.57-2.60); **Coimbra** (1hr., 11 per day 7:15am-2am, €8.50); **Fátima** (1hr., 10 per day 8am-7:25pm, €2.73-5); **Figueira da Foz** (1hr., 12 per day 7:45am-7:25pm, €5); **Lisboa** (2hr., 13 per day M-F 6am-11pm, Sa 7am-11pm, Su 7:45am-11pm; €11); **Nazaré** (1hr., 12 per day 8am-9:30pm, €2.60-6.60); **Porto** (3hr., 10 per day 7:15am-2am, €13.50); **Santarém** (2hr., 3 per day 10:30am-5:15pm, €4.50-11); **Tomar** (1hr., 4:30pm, €8.50).

Taxis: Many gather at the Jardim Luís de Camões (☎244 81 59 00 or 88 15 50).

ORIENTATION AND PRACTICAL INFORMATION

The **Jardim Luís de Camões** is at the center of Leiria, surrounded by *pensões* and restaurants. Just off the garden is **Praça Rodrigues Lobo,** the heart of the historical center, between the Jardim Luís de Camões and the castle. The *praça* is full of cozy cafes and student bars, and the castle is a 10min. climb from here.

Tourist Office: (☎244 84 87 70), in the Jardim Luís de Camões, across the park from the bus station. Has maps, accommodations lists, and a **model of Batalha's monastery** made entirely of sugar, egg whites, and water. Free short-term luggage storage, **internet** access (15min. limit), maps, and other goodies on occasion. English, French, and Spanish spoken. Open daily May-Sept. 10am-1pm and 3-7pm, Oct.-Apr. 10am-1pm and 2-6pm.

Laundromat: Ecosec Lavanderia (☎244 83 36 38), on Beco de São Francisco. From the bus station, walk away from the tourist office on Av. Heróis de Angola, take a left at the theater on Cor. T. Sampaio, and take a right on Beco de São Francisco. €4 per kg, shirts and pants €3.80 per kg. Open M-F 9am-6pm.

Police: Lg. São Pedro (☎244 82 43 00), by the castle.

Hospital: Hospital de Santo André (☎244 81 70 00), on R. Olhalvas, on the way to Fátima. For non-emergencies, go to the closer **Centro Saúde Dr. Arn. Sampaio** (☎244 81 78 20), R. Dr. Egas Moniz, a 10min. walk from the tourist office.

Internet Access: Convenient (and free) service at **Espaço Internet,** Lg. de Santana (☎244 81 50 91), in the Mercado Sant'Ana. 12 computers with fast connections. 1hr. time limit when people are waiting. Gets crowded in the afternoon. Identification (passport, driver's license) required to use a computer. Open M-F 9am-7pm, Sa 2-7pm. Access also free at **Biblioteca Municipal Afonso Lopes Vierira,** Lg. Cândido dos Reis, 6, beside the Pousada de Juventude. Open M 1-6pm, Tu-F 10am-6pm.

Post Office: Downtown office, **Estação Santana** (☎800 20 68 68), Av. dos Combatentes da Grande Guerra, between the tourist office and the youth hostel. Open M-F 8:30am-12:30pm and 2-6pm. **Main office,** Av. Heróis de Angola, 99 (☎244 84 94 00), past the bus station toward the mall. Open M-F 8:30am-12:30pm and 2-6:30pm, Sa 9am-12:30pm. **Postal Code:** 2400.

ACCOMMODATIONS

Pousada da Juventude de Leiria (HI), Lg. Cândido dos Reis, 7 (☎244 83 18 68). From the bus station, walk across the garden and cross the street to the plaza with fountains. Take a right after the Caixa Geral de Depósitos building, and follow to the end. If there is construction going on, follow the metal wall down the street. Take a left on Lg. Cândido dos Reis. The *pousada* is on the left. An old bishop's residence, now with guest kitchen, TV room, and library. Wi-Fi (€5/hr.) Breakfast included. Single-sex dorms €11; doubles €26, with bath €28. HI card required (get it there for €2). AmEx/MC/V. ❶

Pensão Residencial Leiriense, R. Afonso de Albuquerque, 6 (☎244 82 30 54; fax 82 30 73). Off Pr. R. Lobo. Bright, slightly undersized rooms with private bath, A/C, cable TV and phone. Great location for hitting up the bars around the area. Check-out noon. Singles €25; doubles €40. MC. ❷

Residencial Dom Dinis, Tr. Tomar, 2 (☎244 81 53 42; fax 82 35 52). Turn left after exiting the tourist office, cross the bridge, walk 2 blocks, and make a left up the hill at the Residencial's sign. 28 neatly decorated rooms with private bathrooms, phone, and cable TV. In a quiet part of town, but still near the action. Large lounge area with comfy couches. Internet available. Breakfast included (8-10am). July-Aug. singles €27.50, doubles €35, triples €45; Sept.-June €25/35/45. AmEx/MC/V. ❷

FOOD

The **Mercado Municipal,** on Av. Cidade de Maringá, near the stadium and beside the river, sells fresh fish and produce. (Open Tu and Sa 8am-1pm.) Groceries and fresh bread are available at Leiria's convenient **Pingo Doce,** Av. Heróis de Angola, 69, just past the bus station. (Open daily 9am-9pm.)

O Tamoeiro, Rua Barão Viamonte, 48 (☎). Right off Rua Direita. Dine like a king, with the whole *menú* served to your table. Cheese, ham, gourmet seafood, and vegetarian dishes (€1.50-3), and the signature meat plate (€6) come in small plates, and you choose what to eat once everything is served. Add a cup of wine for €1.50. Open M-Sa 7:30pm-2am. Reserve ahead on F. AmEx/MC/V. ❷

Cervejaria Camões, Jardim Luís de Camões (☎961 94 77 08) behind the tourist office. French-inspired steaks, served in a pan with a delicious array of sauces, are the house specialty. Vegetarians can chow down on one of many creative salads. Budget friendly lunch specials for €6. Entrees €5-16. Open daily 10am-2am. MC/V. ❷

Restaurante Monte Carlo, R. Dr. Correia Mateus (☎244 82 54 06). Don't be discouraged by the musty decor; guests at the Monte Carlo get the highest quality seafood for the lowest prices in town. Entrees €5-9. Open M-Sa 9am-midnight. Cash only. ❶

SIGHTS AND BEACHES

Leiria's most significant monument is the giant **Castelo de Leiria,** visible throughout the city and particularly stunning late at night, when it is completely lit up against the dark mountainside. Built by Dom Afonso Henriques after he snatched the town from the Moors, this granite fort presides atop the crest of a volcanic hill on the north edge of town. One of the *castelo's* highlights is the **Torre de Menagem** (Homage Tower), which houses rusty swords, chain mail armor, and artifacts found on-site. The **Sala dos Namorados** (Lovers' Hall) sets the stage for medieval courting—don't miss the beautiful view of the town and river from the terrace, as well as the gigantic, colorful **Estádio Doutor Magalhães Pessoa,** built especially for two Euro Cup 2004 soccer games. From the main square, walk toward the bus station on Lg. 5 de Outubro. Turn left on Lg. das Forças Armadas, just after the Banco de Portugal. Follow the signs past the austere, Sé (cathedral) and zigzag up to the castle. *(☎244 81 39 82. Castle open Apr.-Sept. M-F 9am-6:30pm, Sa-Su 10am-6:30pm; Oct.-Mar. M-F 9am-5:30pm, Sa-Su 10am-5:30pm. Tower open Tu and Su 10am-noon and 1-5pm. €2.50; students, children, and seniors €1.25.)*

Nearby beaches are accessible via buses running from the station to **Praia de Viera** (45min.; 9 per day 7am-7:30pm, last return 6:30pm; July-Sept. 14; €2.60). **Praia Pedrógão,** popular with locals and lined with stately residences (1hr.; 5 per day 9:15am-6pm, last return 7:30pm; €2.60) and the more secluded **São Pedro de Muel** (45min.; 4 per day 8:50am-4:30pm, last return 7:15pm; €2). Check for the exact schedules at the bus station in Leiria, as they are subject to change.

DAYTRIP FROM LEIRIA

BATALHA

Buses run from Leiria to Batalha (20min., 8 per day 7:30-4:50pm, €1.57-2.60), and return to Leiria (20min. M-F 16 per day 7:15am-7:43pm. Sa-Su 3 per day 8:03am-7:43pm, €1.65). The easiest way to get to the caves is by taxi (€30-40 round-trip including waiting time). Be sure to set the price with the taxi driver before you head out. It is possible to take a bus, but the bus schedules from Batalha require careful planning and involve several hours of layover. Check with the tourist office to confirm schedules.

The **Mosteiro Santa Maria da Vitória,** a UNESCO World Heritage site, puts Batalha on the map. Its flamboyant facade soars upward in Gothic and Manueline style, opulently decorated and crowned in dozens of spires. Construction began in 1386 to fulfill Dom João I's covenant to the Virgin Mary: he promised to build a monument in her honor if the Portuguese defeated the Castilian invaders at the Battle of Aljubarrota. The **Capela do Fundador,** the pantheon of João I and the Avis dynasty, lies immediately to the right of the church, housing the sarcophagi of Dom João I, his English-born queen Philippa of Lancaster, and their famous son Prince Henry the Navigator. Just outside the pantheon entrance rests the simpler tomb of Martin Gonçalves, the man who saved Dom João I's life at Aljubarrota. Though the 15th-century **Claustro de Dom Afonso V** is the *mosteiro's* highlight, the **Capelas Imperfeitas** (Unfinished Chapels) are also impressive. Jealous of his predecessor's impressive pantheon, Dom Duarte commissioned the construction of an equally impressive pantheon to house his remains and those of his progeny; unfortunately, construction of the Mosteiro dos Jerónimos in Belém drained resources and interest, leaving the elegant Renaissance chapel roofless. Today the *mosteiro* houses a tomb of unknown soldiers from WWI, and is under constant guard by military officials. There is also a professional school of stone carving that demonstrates how some of the mosteiro's ornate sculptures were made. (Open daily Apr.-Sept. 9am-6pm, Oct.-Mar. 9am-5pm. €5, seniors €2.5, under 14 and students free. Su before 2pm free.)

A 20min. drive outside town brings you to a spelunker's paradise: a series of spectacular underground *grutas* (caves) in Estremadura's natural park. The **Grutas de Mira de Aire,** with a river 110m below ground level, are the deepest and the largest in all of Portugal. They are so popular that 3 million people visited them within the first 10 years of their opening. The nearby **Grutas de Santo António and Alvados,** with their caverns and sandcastle-like limestone formations, are equally impressive. (☎244 44 03 22 or 249 84 18 76. Grutas de Mira de Aire open daily June-Sept. 9:30am-6pm, Oct-May 9:30am-5pm, €5 per person. Grutas de Santo António and Alvados open daily Sept.-May 10am-5pm, June-Aug. 10am-6pm. €5. Last tickets sold 30min. before closing.)

FÁTIMA ☎249

Until May 13, 1917, when the Virgin Mary appeared to three local peasant children, Fátima (pop. 8,000) was just a quiet sheep pasture. Now, every year, over 4 million Catholics make the pilgrimage here to see the stunning Santuário built to honor the miracle. A sign at the entrance of the Santuário complex states, in several languages, "Fátima is a place for adoration; enter as a pilgrim." Only France's Lourdes rivals this site in popularity with Catholic pilgrims; the miracles believed to have occurred here attract an endless international procession of religious groups. The plaza in front of the church, larger than St. Peter's Square in the Vatican, floods with pilgrims on the 12th and 13th of each month. These pilgrims have created a large tourism industry in Fátima—there are over 10,000 beds for visitors in the various hotels and *residenciais.*

TRANSPORTATION

Trains: The **Caxarias** station (☎808 208 208; www.cp.pt), 20km out of town, is closer than the **Fátima** station, 25km away. Caxarias to: **Coimbra** (1hr., 17 per day 5:10am-10:01pm, €6.40-10.10); **Lisboa** (2hr., 12 per day 3:56am-9:43pm, €10-17); **Porto** (2-3hr., 15 per day 5:15am-10:52pm, €13.40-24); **Santarém** (1hr., 16 per day 3:56am-9:43pm, €4.90-7.60). Buses run between Caxarias and Fátima stations (30min., 5 per day 7:40am-5:20pm, €2) and the Fátima train and bus stations (45min., 7 per day 7:40am-6:45pm, €2.67).

Buses: Av. D. José Alves Correia da Silva (☎249 53 16 11). To: **Batalha** (30min., 3 per day 8:07-5:40pm, €1.1.65); **Coimbra** (1hr., 16 per day 7:45am-9:30pm, €8); **Leiria** (35min., 13 per day 7:45am-8pm, €2.67-5); **Lisboa** (1-2hr., 11-19 per day 7am-8pm, €8.70); **Nazaré** (1hr., 8:45am-7:45pm, €3.50-8.70); **Porto** (2-3hr., 4 per day 7:45am-7:40pm, €12); **Santarém** (1hr., 5 per day 7:30am-5:45pm, €10); **Tomar** (1hr.; M-Sa 9:15am and 7:23 pm, Su 8:58pm; €3.20).

Taxis: Next to the bus station (☎49 53 11 93 or 249 53 38 16).

ORIENTATION AND PRACTICAL INFORMATION

Fátima is essentially a religious monument surrounded by souvenir shops, and all activity centers around the basilica complex. The **Santuário de Fátima** is the huge, open *praça* in the middle of everything, which fills with visitors on special occasions and on the 12th and 13th of each month. Directly below it, the new 9000-seat church, inagurated in 2007, stands as the fourth largest church in the world. **Av. Dom José Alves Correia da Silva** is below the Santuário, beginning near the bus station. It runs past the lower end of the complex to the tourist office, which is situated in a stone building with a wooden roof. From the bus station, go right and walk approximately 10min.; the office is on the right.

Tourist Office: The Santuário has its own information **office** (on the left side when facing the basilica; ☎249 53 96 23) with temporary **luggage storage.** Every day at 6:30am it posts the day's schedule of masses. English, French, and Spanish spoken. Open M-Sa 9am-6pm, Su 9am-5pm. The **town office** is at Av. D. José Alves Correia da Silva (☎249 53 11 39). Free **Internet** access (15min. limit). English, French, and Spanish are spoken. Open daily June-July and Sept. 10am-1pm and 3-7pm, Aug. 10am-7pm; Oct.-April 10am-1pm and 2-6pm.

Banks: Several major banks have branches along the commercial center of R. Jacinta Marto. Most open 8:30am-3pm.

Police: Av. D. José Alves Correia da Silva (☎249 53 05 80), past the bus station.

Medical: Centro de Saúde (☎249 53 18 36) on R. Jacinta Marto, near bus station.

Internet: Space Net on the 3rd fl. of the Museu da Vida do Cristo complex has self-service coin-operated internet access. €0.50 per 15min. Open daily 9am-11pm.

Post Office: R. Dr. Jose A Formigão (☎249 53 90 81). Open M-F 8:30am-6pm. **Postal Code:** 2495.

ACCOMMODATIONS AND FOOD

Scores of *residenciais* and hotels surround the basilica complex. Prices vary greatly. Saturday stays are usually €5-10 more than weekday stays, and it's best to reserve a month ahead on summer weekends and holidays and a week ahead otherwise. **Residencial Aleluia ❷**, Av. D. José A. C. Silva, 120, down the street from the bus stop on the lower corner of the complex, has chic rooms with A/C, TV, hardwood floors, suede bedspreads, and leather couches. (☎249 53 15 40; www.residencialaleluia.com. Breakfast €3. Lunch/dinner buffets €11. Singles €25-30, doubles €30-35, triples €42-48. Prices go up €5 on summer weekends and during all of Aug. AmEx/MC/V.) Another option is the new **St. Brigid Hotel ❸**, R. Francisco Marto, 100, two blocks away from the *santuario*. The hotel just opened in 2008 and all rooms have TV, A/C, and private bathrooms. (☎249 53 31 11, fax 249 53 20 28. Singles €30, doubles €40, triples €50. MC/V.)

Restaurants and snack bars cluster between souvenir shops along R. Francisco Marto, R. Santa Isabela, and R. Jacinta Marto. Close to the wax museum

THE MIRACLE

t's October 13th, 1917, and 0,000 people have gathered, xpecting a miracle predicted by hree children. Accordingly, the sun changes in color and starts descending in circles around a panicking crowd. The miracle is seen miles away, but its message will go even further. The three kids ell the world that the Virgin Mary has called for the end of war and he conversion of Russia. She has also predicted the end of WWI, the possibility of WWII, and the assassination attempt suffered by John Paul II in 1981, in prophecies that will be revealed by the church eight decades later.

While the interpretation of he secrets is controversial, their mpact is hard to deny. Catholics adore the image of the Virgin of Fatima, counting the rosary is stronger than ever as a gesture of faith, and the prophecy may have spurred the church to stand against communism, a mission dear to Pope John Paul II. Moreover, the secrets revealed in Fatima were the subject of controversy for decades, especially after he Church decided to delay their evelation by four decades. Truth or not, the happenings of Fatima are still a powerful force within the Catholic faith, and it remains for many the most important miracle of the modern age.

on the left side of the Santuário, the upstairs **O Terminal ❷**, R. Jacinta Marto, 24, offers the biggest portions of traditional Portuguese food for the best prices in town. Entrees €5-9. (☎249 53 19 77. Open daily 10am-3:30pm and 6-9:30pm. Cash only.) On the other side of the Santuário, well-established **Restaurant Alfredo ❷**, R. Francisco Marto, 159 CV, serves huge plates and is always filled with locals. Their *bacalhau no forno* (oven-broiled cod) is a house specialty. Limited vegetarian options. (Down the stairs past the corner Millennium BCP bank. Entrees €6-10. Open daily noon-3pm and 7-10pm. MC/V.) Rock-bottom prices can be found at the **Pingo Doce** supermarket on Av. D. José A. C. da Silva. (From the bus station, go to the left. Open daily 8:30am-9pm.)

SIGHTS

SANTUÁRIO DE FÁTIMA. As soon as you walk into the main *praça*, you'll feel Fátima's overwhelming presence. Many of the devout travel the length of the gigantic plaza on their knees, all the way from the cross to the *capelinha*, praying for divine assistance or giving thanks to the Virgin Mary. During the grand pilgrimages on the 12th and 13th from May to October, the crowds fill the entire plaza.

Uphill, overlooking the plaza, rises the **Basílica do Rosário** (erected in 1928), featuring a crystal cruciform beacon atop the tower's seven-ton bronze crown. Inside are the tombs of the three "seers," or witnesses of the apparitions. Francisco and Jacinta died as children, and lie in opposite naves. Lúcia, the third and oldest child, died in 2005 at the age of 97 after serving as a devout nun for over 70 years. Her tomb was placed beside Jacinta's in February 2006. *(Open daily 7:30am-10:30pm. Mass daily at 7:30, 9, 11am, 3, 4:30, and 6:30pm. Free.)* To the left is the **Capelinha das Aparições,** the first of the buildings to be constructed, where a statue of the Virgin now stands in the exact location where the miracles are said to have taken place. Sheltered beneath a metal and glass canopy, the *capelinha* was built in 1919 and continues to house "Perpetual Adoration," which consists of several masses in various languages during the day and a fire continuously fueled by the candles of visitors. *(International mass Th 9am. Candlelight procession daily Apr.-Oct. 9:30pm.)*

GRUTAS DA MOEDA (MOEDA CAVES). Fátima's caves offer a refreshing change from the religious sites and are easily accessible. Discovered in 1971 by two hunters chasing a fox, the caves lie 45m below the surface and conceal several stunning limestone formations and an underground waterfall. Bring a rain jacket if you go in the winter, as cave showers are frequent. *(☎244 70 43 02 or 244 70 38 38. www.grutasmoeda.com. Call ☎800 20 56 18 from the tourist office to schedule a free pick-up. The number does not work outside of the tourist office. Caves open daily July-Sept. 9am-7pm, April-June. 9am-6pm, Oct.-Mar. 9am-5pm; last tickets sold 30min. before closing. €5, cartão jovem €3.50, children 6-12 €2.50.)*

MUSEUMS. The **Museu de Arte Sacra e Etnologia** exhibits Catholic icons from various cultures, showcasing the interplay between Catholicism and native societies around the world. *(R. Francisco Marto, 52. ☎249 53 94 70; fax 53 94 79. Open Tu-Su Apr.-Oct. 10am-7pm; Nov.-Mar. 10am-5pm. €2.50, seniors and students €1.50.)* Other tackier museums surround Fátima. The **Museu de Cera** (Wax Museum) gives a comprehensive history of Fátima and the miracles that made it famous, taking visitors through 31 unnervingly realistic wax scenes. *(R. Jacinta Marto. ☎249 53 93 00; www.mucefa.pt. Open daily Apr.-Oct. 9:30am-6:30pm; Nov.-Mar. M and Sa 9am-5:30pm, Tu-F and Su 10am-5pm. €6, under 12 €3.50.)* The **Museu Fátima 1917 Aparições,** with its descriptions and visual and sound effects, is a similar but more dramatic (and kitschier) version of the wax museum. The audio guide is available in English, Portuguese, Spanish, French, Italian, and German. *(R. Jacinta Marto below ground level in the J.P. II building. To the left of the basilica, follow the signs to the underground complex across the street from Hotel Fátima. ☎249 53 28 58; www.museuaparicoes.com. Open daily Apr.-Oct. 9am-7pm, Nov.-Mar. 9am-6pm. €3.50, under 12 €1.50.)* Fátima's newest museum, the **Museu do Vida de Cristo,** traces the life of Jesus from conception to resurrection in 33 scenes for those seeking a modernized, commercialized religious experience. The shiny, white-marbled modern complex also houses a mini-shopping center where wine, religious artifacts, and other trinkets can be purchased. *(Rua Francisco Marto. ☎249 53 06 80; www.vidadecristo.pt. Open Apr-Oct M-Sa 9am-7pm, Su 9am-6pm; Nov.-Mar. M-Sa 9am-6pm, Su 9am-5:30pm. €7, children under 12 €4)*

TOMAR ☎249

Visitors come to Tomar (pop. 20,000) to walk wide-eyed through the castle, fortress, convent, and beautiful gardens that make up the Convento de Cristo. In 1160, Dom Afonso Henriques enlisted the Knights Templar to build a fortified castle at Tomar, then the weak spot between Lisboa and Coimbra. When the Knights fell out of favor with the Pope 200 years later, sheepish Portuguese royalty quickly founded a new religious order and gave them the Templar's property, resulting in today's unique collage of menacing medieval walls and ornate architecture. The rest of the town lazes beside the Rio Nabão, but goes into overdrive every four years for the Festival dos Tabuleiros.

TRANSPORTATION

Trains: Av. dos Combatentes da Grande Guerra (☎808 20 82 08; www.cp.pt). Tomar is the northern end of a minor line, so most destinations require a transfer at Entroncamento or Lamarosa; ask about this when purchasing your ticket and pay attention to the stops. Ticket office open M-F and Su 5:30am-8:30pm and 9:30-10:30pm, Sa 5:30am-8:30pm. To: **Coimbra** (2hr., 10 per day 5:15am-8pm, €8.20); **Lisboa** (2hr., 16 per day 5am-10pm, €8.20); **Porto** (4hr., 11 per day 5:15am-8pm, €17.05-23.50); **Santarém** (1hr., 16 per day 5am-10pm, €4.90).

Buses: Rodoviária Tejo, Av. dos Combatentes da Grande Guerra (☎968 94 35 50). Beware: express buses are twice the price of regular buses. To: **Coimbra** (2hr., 7am, €11.80); **Fátima** (30min., 5 per day 7:50am-5:20pm, €2.98-5.20); **Figueira da Foz** (4hr., 7am, €12.50); **Lisboa** (2hr., 5 per day 9:30am-4:45pm, €8.50); **Nazaré** (1hr., 6 per day 7:30am-5:20pm, €5.50); **Porto** (4hr., 7am, €11.60); **Santarém** (1hr., 12:52pm, €4.70).

Taxis: Taxis wait by the bus and train stations and across the river on R. Santa Iria. ☎249 31 23 73 or 917 81 68 19 to schedule a pick up.

ORIENTATION AND PRACTICAL INFORMATION

The Rio Nabão divides Tomar into east and west banks. Almost all travelers need—the train and bus stations, accommodations, and sights—can be found on the western bank around the checkered **Praça da República.** Running from this main square to the river is **Rua Serpa Pinto,** which ends at the ancient **Ponte Velha** (Old Bridge) and becomes **Rua Marquês Pombal** on the other side of the water. **Avenida Dr. Cândido Madureira** parallels R. Serpa Pinto a few streets away, starting at the main **tourist office** and running into the **Ponte Nova** (New Bridge), the second bridge connecting the halves of Tomar. The bus and train stations sit side by side on **Avenida dos Combatentes da Grande Guerra** at the edge of town.

Tourist Office: Av. Dr. Cândido Madureira (☎249 32 24 27; www.tomartourism.com). From the bus/train stations, head down Av. General Bernardo Faria, which runs parallel to the river toward the city past several municipal buildings. Turn left 3 blocks later onto Av. Cândido Madureira. Short-term luggage storage available. English, Spanish, and French spoken. During the winter open daily from 10am-1pm and 2-6pm; summer M-F 10am-7pm, Sa-Su 10am-1pm and 2-6pm.

Laundromat: 5 á Sec (☎249 32 35 31), inside Supermercado Modelo. From Pr. da República, take R. Serpa Pinto and go straight for about 1.5km; the *supermercado* will be on your right after passing the McDonald's. €4 per kg for towels and sheets. Wash, dry, and iron €2.30 for shirts, €2.95 for pants. Next day service. Open daily 9am-9pm.

Police: R. Dr. Sousa (☎249 31 34 44).

Pharmacy: Farmácia Central, R. Marquês de Pombal, 18 (☎249 31 23 29). From Pr. da República, take R. Serpa Pinto and cross the bridge; it will be on your left. Open M-F 9am-7:30pm, Sa 9am-1pm.

Hospital: Hospital Nossa Senhora da Graça, Av. Dona Maria de Lourdes Melo e Castelo (☎249 32 01 00), on the other side of the river (25min. walk).

Internet Access: Espaço Internet, R. Amorim Rosa, 33 (☎249 312 291), across the river. From Ponte Velha, make a right onto R. Amorim Rosa. From Ponte Nova make a left. Free. 30min. limit enforced only if people are waiting. €2 per additional hr. Open M-F 9am-2pm and 2:30-6pm.

Post Office: Av. Marquês de Tomar (☎249 31 04 00, fax 31 04 06), across from Parque Mouchão. **Poste Restante** and fax. Open M-F 8:30am-6pm, Sa 9am-noon. **Postal Code:** 2300.

ACCOMMODATIONS

Finding accommodations is a problem only during the Festival dos Tabuleiros. **R. Serpa Pinto** is lined with great lodging, while budget options lie closer to the bus and train stations.

Residencial União, R. Serpa Pinto, 94 (☎249 32 31 61), halfway between Pr. da República and the bridge. One of the nicest budget accommodations Tomar has to offer, in an elegant 113-year-old house decorated with antique furniture. 28 cozy rooms have satellite TV, phone, regal red carpet, and private bath. Breakfast included. Internet access (first 5min. free, €0.50 per 10min. afterwards). Reserve ahead. Singles €25, doubles €30, triples €45. Cash only. ❷

Residencial Luz, R. Serpa Pinto, 144 (☎249 31 23 17; www.residencialluz.com). 14 tidy, snug rooms, most with small private bath, TV, and phone. Common room with satellite TV and movies in English. Internet €2.40 per hr. May 16-Sept. singles €17.50-19, with bath €19-20; doubles €22.50-32.50; triples €35; quads €40-50; quints €60. Oct.-May 15 €17.50/25/35/45. Cash only. ❶

Residencial Cavaleiros de Cristo, R. Alexandre Herculano, 7 (☎249 32 12 03 or 249 32 10 67; fax 32 11 92). 1 street to the right of Pr. da República (if facing the castle). Rooms decorated in a steel-gray Egyptian motif have satellite TV, minibar, A/C, central heat, phone, and tile bathroom. Breakfast included. In summer singles €36.75, doubles €51.45; in winter €27.80/43. AmEx/MC/V. ❸

FOOD

Tomar is home to some of the cheapest, most delectable restaurants in Portugal. Around Pr. da República, a full meal can be enjoyed for under €5. Still, there is no better place for a picnic than the lush **Parque do Mouchão** in the center of the river near **Ponte Velha.** The **market,** on the corner of Av. Norton de Matos and R. Santa Iria, provides all but the red-checkered blanket. (Open Tu and Th-F 8am-2pm. Flea market on F.) Several mini-markets line the side streets between the tourist office and Pr. da República. Supermarket **Ponto Fresco,** Av. Dr. Cândido Madureira, 56, is on the same street as the tourist office. (Open daily 9am-1:30pm and 3-8pm.)

Piri/Piri, R. dos Moinhos, 54 (☎249 31 34 94). Make a right off R. Serpa Pinta, one street from the river. One of the friendliest places in town. Pick from the list of daily specials of Portuguese cuisine (€5.70; ½-plate €3.95) and add a half-bottle of red wine for €1.50. Entrees €5-10. Open daily noon-3pm and 7-10pm. Cash only. ❶

Salsinha Verde, Pr. da República, 19 (☎249 31 65 63), to the left of town hall. While the *pratos do dia,* like the baked chicken, are only €3.50, the real steal is the *ementa económica,* a full meal consisting of soup, an entree, dessert, and coffee for only €5.50. Other entrees €5-8. Open daily 8:30am-4pm and 7pm-midnight. Cash only. ❶

O Siciliano, R. Voluntários da República, 164 (☎249 32 43 88, www.osiciliano.com), across the river from R. Serpa Pinto; take a left at the first real intersection. This welcoming little restaurant promises a hearty Italian meal. Delicious pasta entrees (€6-10) and massive pizzas (€6.50-10). Open M-Sa noon-3pm and 7:30-11:30pm. Cash only. ❷

SIGHTS AND FESTIVALS

Tomar is known throughout the world for its **Convento de Cristo,** an architectural treasure filled with peaceful cloisters, stunning domes, and beautiful, winding staircases. From the tourist office, take a right and follow the road until you see a steeper stone path to the left. It's a 3min. climb to the convent. Now a UNESCO World Heritage site, the structure was begun by the Moors during the 9th century as a defense from insistent invaders. The attempt failed, and after the defeat of the Moors, the Knights Templar fortified the stronghold in 1160. One of the more impressive aspects of the convent is the area that surrounds its entrance: *azulejo*-covered benches beckon visitors to sit in the garden and admire the views of the nearby national forest. At the entrance to the castle, an ornate canopy protects the high altar of the **Templo dos Templares,** modeled after the Holy Sepulchre in Jerusalem. Below stands the **Janela do Capítulo** (chapter window), a tribute to the Age of Discovery. Further into the complex lies one of Europe's masterpieces of Renaissance architecture: the **Claustro dos Felipes,** or Claustro Principal. The Claustro honors Felipe II of Castilla, crowned here as Felipe I of Portugal during Iberia's unification (1580-1640). Stairs spiral upward to views of the **Terraço da Cera.** The nearby **Charola** (oratory) was built in the second half of the 12th century and was the original Templar church. *(☎249 31 34 81. Open daily June-Sept. 9am-6pm, Oct.-May 9am-5pm. €5, over 65 €2.50. Students free.)*

The **Museu Luso-Hebraico Abraáo Zacuto** is the most significant reminder of Portugal's historical importance to the European Jewish community. This synagogue was built between 1430 and 1460 and abandoned in 1496 when the Jews faced exile or conversion to Christianity. It is the oldest Jewish temple in Portugal, and it became the town prison in 1516. Over the years, it was converted first into a Catholic chapel, then a storehouse, and finally an urban barn. Today, it houses a small museum of Jewish history and a part-time synagogue, with a collection of tombstones, inscriptions, and objects from around the world. *(R. Dr. Joaquim Jaquinto, 73. Open daily 10am-1pm and 2-6pm. Free. Donations welcome.)*

Around the 20th of October, during the **Feira de Santa Iria,** handicrafts, folklore, *fado*, and raisins (for the Raisin Fair) fill Tomar. Since 1984, Tomar has also celebrated the **Feira de Artesanato** (Crafts Fair) during the first half of May. The biggest party in Tomar is the **Festa dos Tabuleiros,** a festival celebrating the Holy Spirit that takes place in mid-June every four years (next scheduled for 2011). Six thousand people swarm the town for a week to watch young girls walk in a 4km procession bearing the traditional 40 lb. *tabuleiro* (tray) stacked on their heads. The *tabuleiro* consists of flowers and 30 loaves of bread, symbolizing the 30 pieces of silver for which Christ was sold to the Romans.

CASTELO BRANCO ☎272

The capital of the Beira Baixa province, Castelo Branco (literally "White Castle") is the largest city for miles, but it is more a transportation hub and a base for daytrips than a tourist destination itself. Nevertheless, in its 700 years, the city has managed to create several worthwhile historical sites. The most popular are the **castle** ruins, of which there are just enough left to determine that the castle was not, in fact, white. It is a steep 10min. climb from the center to the ruins, but visitors are free to climb the 15th-century **walls** and towers for a spectacular view of the surrounding towns (and countries, on a clear day). The nearby **Miradouro de St. Gens** offers magnificent views as well. Down in the city, the highlight is the **Jardim do Paco,** formerly the gardens of the Bishop's estate, now speckled with small allegorical statues, including Death and Hell in the far corners of the main garden. (☎272 34 05 00. Open daily 9am-5:30pm. €2.)

Residencial Arraiana ❷, Av. 1 de Maio, 18, has sparsely decorated, average-sized rooms, with small, clean private bath, TV, A/C, balconies in some rooms, and even a mini-bar. From the tourist office, go left on Al. da Liberdade and continue straight as it becomes Av. 1 de Maio. (☎272 34 16 34, ext. 7. Breakfast included. Singles €25, doubles €40, triples €50. AmEx/MC/V.) For a cheaper stay, go to **Residencial "A Floresta" ❶,** R. Ruivo Rodinho, 11, near the historic center. All rooms have a private bath and TV. (☎ 272 08 17 62. Singles €10, doubles €20.) **Restaurante Kalifa ❷,** R. Cadetes de Toledo, 10, around the corner from the tourist office and down a ramp from Av. Nuno Alvares, has served traditional Portuguese favorites for 25 years. (☎272 34 42 46. Entrees €4-14. Open daily 7am-midnight. AmEx/MC/V.) For groceries, hit **Pingo Doce,** Av. 1 de Maio, 60. (Open daily 8:30am-9pm.)

Rede Expressos buses, R. Rod. Rebelo, are just down the street from the central square. Buses run to: **Coimbra** (2¼hr.; 6:30, 7:30am, 2:30pm; €12.30); **Elvas** via Lisboa or **Estremoz.** (5hr.; M-Sa 10:45am, 2:15pm, Su 10:45am, 2:15 pm, 6pm; €17.50); **Guarda** (2hr.; M-Sa 8 per day 8am-9:34pm, Su 9am-9:34pm; €9.20); **Lisboa** (3hr., 8 per day 5am-6:36pm, €12); **Porto** (4hr., 8 per day 6:30am-4:47pm, €15.80). **Taxis** (☎272 341 539) are on Av. Nuno Alvares, around the corner from the tourist office. Castelo Branco's backbone is a street with several names: the **Alameda da Liberdade** runs the length of the main square, **Praça do Município,** and then becomes **Avenue 1 de Maio** as it leaves the town center. The corner of the square, in front of the municipal building, marks the point of departure for the hike to the hilltop **castle.** In the other direction, Al. de Liberdade becomes **Rue das Olarias** and runs past the cathedral to **Largo da Sé,** then to the **Jardim do Paco.**

The **tourist office** is in a kiosk on the top level of the main square just off of Al. da Liberdade. From the bus station, exit toward the tunnel across the street, take a right onto R. do Saibreiro, take your first left, walk a block, and turn right onto R. S. da Piedade; the office is at the end on the right, across from the white rocks that spell out Castelo Branco. Its multilingual staff provides short-term **luggage storage.** (☎272 33 03 39. Open M-F 9:30am-7:30pm, Sa-Su 9:30am-1pm and 2:30-6pm.) **Banks** and 24hr. **ATMs** line Al. da Liberdade; for currency exchange, go to **Millennium BCP,** Al. da Liberdade, 19. (☎707 50 24 24. Open M-F 8:30am-3pm.) **Farmácia Nuno Alvares** is on Av. 1 de Maio, 83. (☎272 34 14 45; www.farmacianunoalvares.com. Open M-Th 8:30am-7:30pm, F open 24hr. Weekend pharmacy opening schedules available.) The **Hospital Amato Lusitano** (☎272 00 02 72) is on R. da Granja. The **police** (☎272 34 06 22), R. de S. Jorge, are next to the government building at the corner of the main square. **Internet** access at **Cyber Centro,** Pça Municipio, through the courtyard of the yellow building on Av. G. H. Delgado, the street parallel to Al. da Liberdade on the other side of the square. (☎272 34 87 90. Open M-F 9am-11pm. Students €0.70 per hr., others €1.) The **post office,** R. da Se, €30/32, is across from the cathedral. (☎272 34 00 30. Open M-F 8:30am-6:30pm, Sa 9am-12:30pm.) **Postal Code:** 6000.

MONSANTO

A tiny village carved into the peak of a granite mountain, Monsanto would warrant a daytrip even without its amazing **castle ruins.** Deemed "the most Portuguese village in Portugal" in 1938, Monsanto captures the Portuguese spirit with its stone houses, friendly residents, and incredible sweeping views of the countryside. Starting from the town's center, the 15th-century **Igreja de São Salvador,** walk uphill and follow the pedestrian signs to the castle. The ruins are one of the most beautiful sites in Portugal. The castle that once crowned the city was destroyed in a massive explosion of stored munitions in the 19th century. The 12th- and 13th-century Roman-inspired **Capela de São Miguel** and the empty **graves** carved into the rock by its entrance are of particular interest. Cross the short path to the left of the castle, just after the Capela de São Miguel, to see the **Capela de São João,** a ruined chapel overgrown with vegetation. Only a few buses go to Monsanto, and trips usually require overnight stays. **Casa da Maria ❷,** Av. Fernando Ramos Rocha, 11, is on the street leading into town, about 50m down from the bus stop. Dona Maria and her English-speaking husband Erizo rent out the house to visitors. The town is tiny, so just ask around for them or try calling. Breakfast included. (Dona Maria ☎965 62 46 07, Erizo 966 44 36 63. TV, A/C, kitchen, 2 bathrooms. €25 per person per night. Cash only.) **Divino Monsanto ❷,** R. do Arco, 2, is attached to a luxury hotel, and serves typical Portuguese plates, in addtion to some not-so-typical ones, like the vegetable tart (€12.50), in a classy setting. Lunch options, mostly fish or meat dishes with rice and salad, for €8.50 (☎277 31 44 71. Entrees €8-15. Open daily 1-3pm and 7:30-10pm.) The **bus** to Monsanto leaves from Castelo Branco's bus station (1hr.; M-F 12:30pm, returns to Castelo Branco 2:30pm; €4.50). The drop-off and pickup spot is in a small parking lot on top of a steep hill. From there, it's a short walk to anywhere in town, including the tourist office. Just follow the signs up the road, past the church and to the left. Be aware: there is only one bus per day from Monsanto. Alternatively, buses can be taken to Adeia do Bispo, and from there a taxi (€14). There is a **tourist office** uphill from the central church that provides maps and information. English, French, and Spanish are spoken by friendly staff. **Internet** is available. (☎277 31 46 42. Open daily in summer 10am-1pm and 2-6pm, in winter 9:30am-1pm and 2-5:30pm.)

THE NORTH

As new buildings and modern flair come to Europe, many lament the loss of the "old country," as if the last century's big cities and big governments squashed the soul of the continent. This march of progress must have lost its beat when it neared the north of Portugal, where ancient narrow streets, ornately decorated buildings, green mountains, and peaceful vineyards stretch for miles, unaltered by time. The region is not just famous for its sweet wine; history buffs go to the North to retrace the steps of Lusitania's ancestors. With ample opportunities for hiking, camping, and relatively untamed forestry, the region is also paradise for nature-lovers. A visit to the North is indispensable. After all, though wine can be shipped, Portugal's finest countryside cannot.

HIGHLIGHTS OF THE NORTH

CRAWL through Celtic ruins on **Monte de Santa Luzia** in Viana do Castelo (p. 682).

MARVEL at the elaborate **Capela de São Miguel** in Coimbra (p. 688).

SAVOR the brilliant flavors in a glass of port wine at a vineyard in **Porto** (p. 664).

HIKE a misty mountain top in the medieval town of **Sortelha** (p. 694).

DOURO AND MINHO

The region of the Douro and Minho rivers is wine country—the purples, blues, and greens of the stretching vineyards and *quintas* (wine estates) are worthy of a Keats ode. The major cities of this region, Porto and Braga, are enchanting as well. With lively festivals, tall medieval towers, and amazing shopping, these metropolises provide numerous opportunities for adventure.

PORTO (OPORTO) ☎22

Stunning edifices rise up from the bustling city squares of Oporto (pop. 263,000) with an elegance reminiscent of Paris or Prague. Portugal's second largest city, commonly referred to as Porto, is brimming with small shops and residences that seem to be on the brink of toppling into the Rio Douro. Once a magnificent Roman trade center, Porto still retains its thriving commercial industry, focusing predominantly on the production, sale, and most importantly, consumption, of port wine. Visitors to Porto usually come to admire the monuments of its medieval glory days, but it's the warmth of the city that makes them fall in love with it. The charm of its friendly bars and cafes by day, and the yellow lights reflected in the Rio Douro by night, lend Porto an unforgettable romance.

TRANSPORTATION

Flights: Aeroporto Francisco de Sá Carneiro (☎229 43 24 00), 13km from downtown. The recently completed **metro E** (violet line) goes to the airport and is the fastest and cheapest option (25min., €1.35). Buses #601 and 87 run to the airport from R. do Carmo, but make multiple stops (1hr., €1.50). The **aerobus** (☎225 07 10 54) from Av.

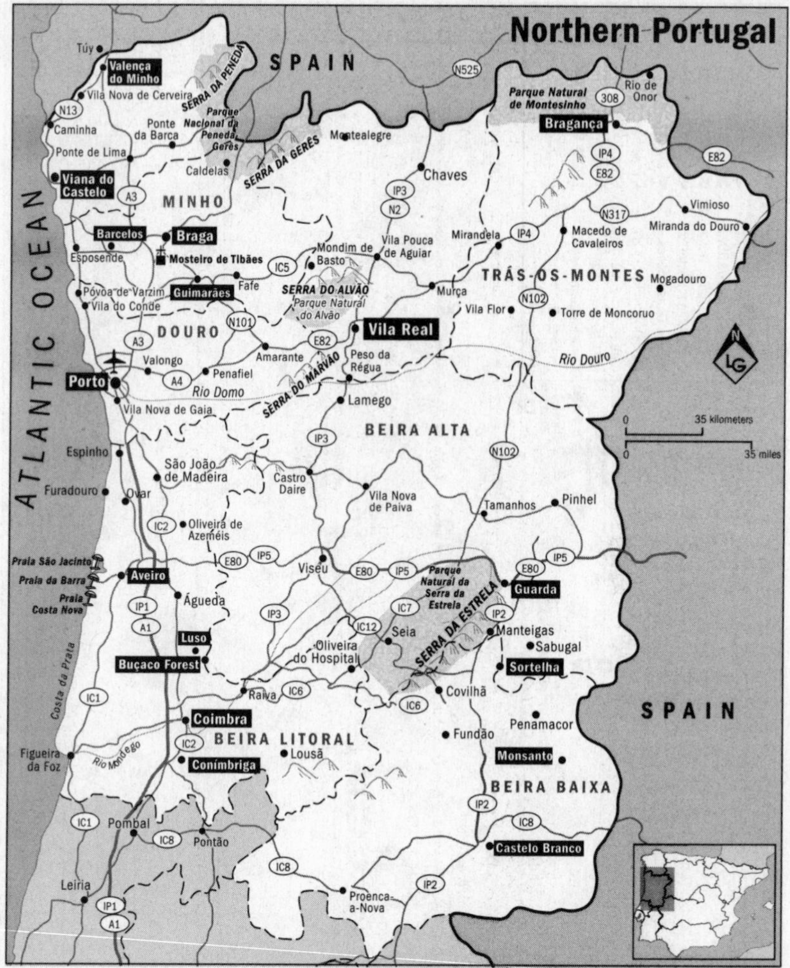

dos Aliados near Pr. da Liberdade is more efficient (40min., every 30min. 7am-7pm, €4, free for TAP passengers). Buy tickets on board. **Taxis** are even quicker (15-20min., €18-20). **TAP Air Portugal,** Pr. Mouzinho de Albuquerque, 105 (☎226 08 02 31), flies to major European cities, with 6 daily shuttles to Lisboa (35min., €100-150).

Trains: Trains arriving in Porto stop at **Estação de Campanhã** (☎808 20 82 08; www.cp.pt), on R. da Estação, before entering the station in the town center, **Estação de São Bento** (☎808 20 82 08), Pr. Almeida Garrett. Trains leaving S. Bento will run to Campanhã first (5min., every 5-10min. 5:35am-12:40am, €1). From Estação de Campanhã trains run to: **Aveiro** (1hr., 47 per day 5:09am-1:23am, €2.10-12.50); **Braga** (1hr., 30 per day 5:55am-10:50pm, €2-12.50); **Coimbra** (1-2hr., 17 per day 6:05am-1:35am, €12-16.10); **Lisboa** (3-4hr., 18 per day 6:15am-1:35am, €15.60-28.60); **Madrid** (11-12hr., 10pm, €64; change at Entroncamento); **Viana do Castelo** (1-2hr., 11 per day 6am-8:35pm, €4.75-7); **Vigo,** Spain (4hr.; 8:05am, 6:05pm; €12.80).

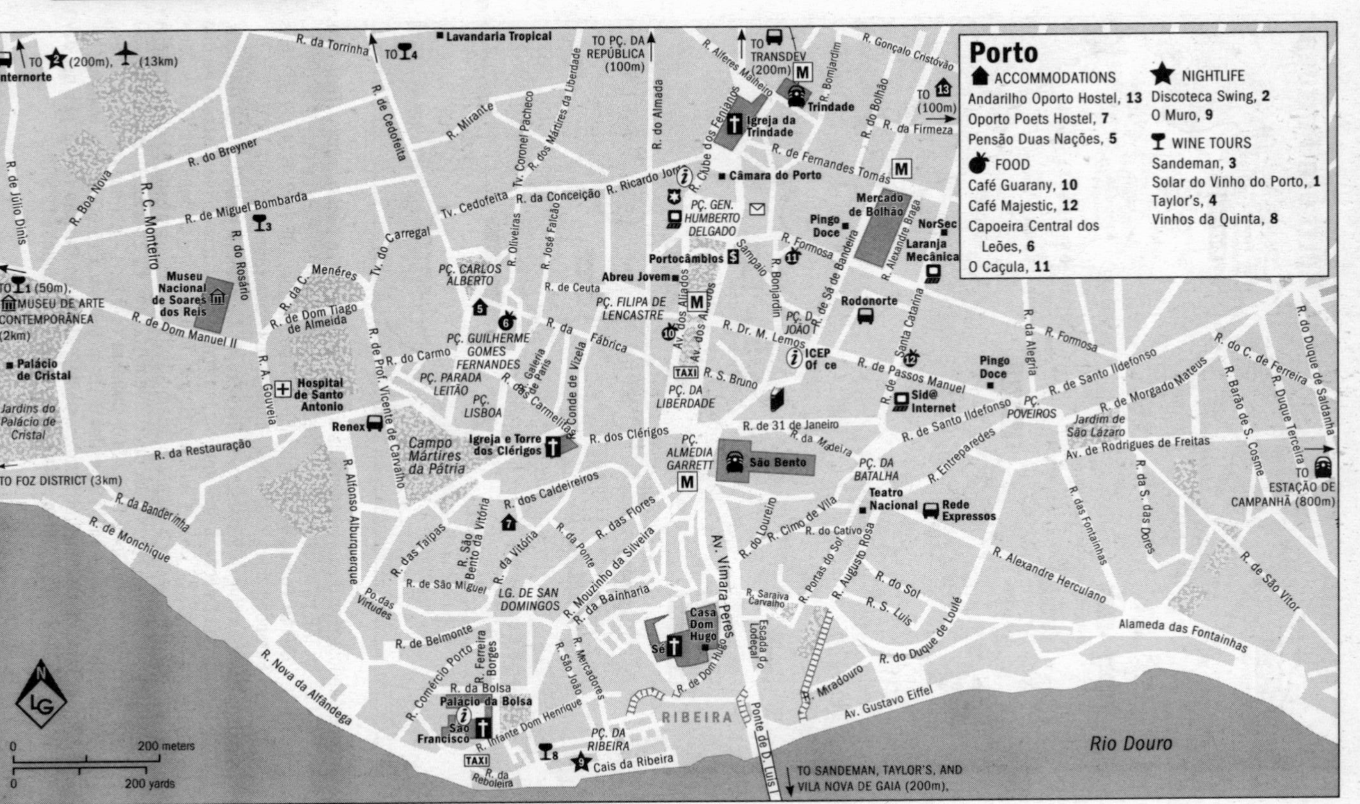
Porto
ACCOMMODATIONS
Andarilho Oporto Hostel, 13
Oporto Poets Hostel, 7
Pensão Duas Nações, 5
FOOD
Café Guarany, 10
Café Majestic, 12
Capoeira Central dos Leões, 6
O Caçula, 11
NIGHTLIFE
Discoteca Swing, 2
O Muro, 9
WINE TOURS
Sandeman, 3
Solar do Vinho do Porto, 1
Taylor's, 4
Vinhos da Quinta, 8
Rio Douro
Av. Vímara Peres
Ponte de D. Luís I
RIBEIRA
Cais da Ribeira
PÇ. DA RIBEIRA
Sé
Casa Dom Hugo
São Bento
PÇ. ALMEIDA GARRETT
PÇ. DA LIBERDADE
PÇ. DA BATALHA
Teatro Nacional
Rede Expressos
Mercado de Bolhão
Câmara do Porto
Igreja da Trindade
Trindade
Igreja e Torre dos Clérigos
Campo Mártires da Pátria
Hospital de Santo Antonio
Museu Nacional de Soares dos Reis
Palácio de Cristal
Jardins do Palácio de Cristal
Palácio da Bolsa
São Francisco
Lavandaria Tropical
Portocâmbios
Abreu Jovem
Pingo Doce
Rodonorte
Renex
Internorte
NorSec
Laranja Mecânica
Sid@ Internet
ICEP Office
TO PÇ. DA REPÚBLICA (100m)
TO TRANSDEV (200m)
TO FOZ DISTRICT (3km)
TO SANDEMAN, TAYLOR'S, AND VILA NOVA DE GAIA (200m).
TO ESTAÇÃO DE CAMPANHÃ (800m)
TO 1 (50m), MUSEU DE ARTE CONTEMPORÂNEA (2km)
R. de Júlio Dinis
R. Boa Nova
R. C. Monteiro
R. do Rosário
R. A. Gouveia
R. de Cedofeita
R. da Restauração
R. de Monchique
R. Nova da Alfândega
R. Alfonso Alburquerque
R. de Prof. Vicente de Carvalho
R. dos Clérigos
R. das Flores
R. Mouzinho da Silveira
R. de 31 de Janeiro
R. de Santa Catarina
R. de Sá da Bandeira
R. Formosa
R. da Alegria
R. Alexandre Herculano
Alameda das Fontainhas
R. das Fontainhas
R. de São Vitor
R. do Duque de Saldanha
R. Duque Terceira
R. Barão de S. Cosme
R. do Almada
R. de Fernandes Tomás
Av. dos Aliados
Av. Gustavo Eiffel
R. Mercadores
R. São João
R. Infante Dom Henrique
200 meters
200 yards

Buses: Several companies operate in the downtown area.

Internorte, Pr. Galiza, 96 (☎226 05 24 20) has service to **Madrid** (10hr., daily 9am and 9:45am,and 8:30pm, €48), as well as other international cities. Book 3 days ahead. Open M-F 9am-12:30pm and 2-6:30pm, Sa 9am-12:30pm and 2-4pm, Su 9am-12:30pm and 2-5:30pm.

Rede Expressos, R. Alexandre Herculano, 366 (☎222 00 69 54; www.rede-expressos.pt). To **Braga** (1hr., 10 per day 10am-4:30am, €5.70); **Bragança** (3-5hr., 7 per day 9:15am-11pm, €12); **Coimbra** (1hr., 11 per day 6:45am-12:45am, €11); **Lisboa** (4hr., 11 per day 6:45am-12:45am, €16); **Viana do Castelo** (1hr., 4 per day 11am-11pm, €7.20).

Renex, Campo Mártires da Pátria, 37 (☎222 00 33 95), has express service to **Lagos** (8hr., 6 per day 7:30am-1:15am, €24) via **Lisboa** (3hr., 12 per day 7:30am-1:15am, €29) and **Vila Real de Santo António** (9hr., 3 per day 9am-5pm, €44).

Rodonorte, R. Ateneu Comercial do Porto, 25 (☎222 00 56 37 or 00 43 98), to **Vila Real** (1hr.; M-F 16 per day 7am-9:20pm, Sa-Su 7 per day 7am-9:20pm; €6.50-7) via **Amarante** (1hr., €5.20).

Transdev, R. Dr. Alfredo Magalhães, 94 (☎222 00 26 60), 2 blocks from Pr. da República, has buses to **Braga** (1hr.; M-F 17 per day 7:30am-8pm, Sa-Su 5-6 per day 10am-6pm; €4.20).

Public Transportation: A €0.50 rechargeable **Andante** card must be purchased before using the metro, trams, and some buses. It can be purchased with an individual ticket or beforehand at the tourist office, at many small kiosks throughout the city, or at the **STCP** office, Pr. Almeida Garrett, 27 (open M-F 8am-7:30pm, Sa 8am-1pm). Transportation ticket prices are determined by a zone system; each zone is an additional fare. Most of Porto is in 1 zone, and 2 trips on the metro or tram are €1.80; €9.50 for 11 trips. A single bus fare is €1.40. The best option for those planning on significant travel is an unlimited Andante tour ticket (1-day €5, 3-day €11; available on board or at the tourist office), which is valid for all STCP buses and trams, the Aerobus, and the metro. All buses operate between 6am-9pm, half operate until 1am, and a handful run 1-5am. Tram operates 8am-8pm every 30 min. Metro 6am-1am.

Taxis: Av. dos Aliados and along the river in Ribeira. Ask for a quote, and only use metered taxis. Luggage €1.60 extra. **Radiotáxis,** R. de Alegria, 1802 (☎225 07 39 00).

ORIENTATION AND PRACTICAL INFORMATION

Porto's heavy traffic and chaotic maze of one-way streets fluster travelers who come by car. The city center is easy to navigate, however: hillside **Praça da Liberdade** is joined to **Praça General Humberto Delgado** by **Avenida dos Aliados,** forming a long, open, and easily recognizable main square. The liveliest part of the city during the day is located around the gigantic **Mercado do Bolhão** and includes the main pedestrian thoroughfare, **R. de Santa Catarina,** packed with stores and cafes as well as a large shopping center. Along the Río Douro, directly below the city center, lies the **Ribeira** district, where much of Porto's sights and nightlife are located on steep sidestreets. The two-level **Ponte de Dom Luís I** spans the river, connecting Ribeira to **Vila Nova de Gaia** and its many port wine cellars. Down the river from Ribeira (5km), the **Foz** district has many popular beaches and venerable nightclubs, but the **industrial area,** 4-5km northwest of the city center, has the best discotecas in Porto.

Tourist Office: Main office, R. Clube dos Fenianos, 25 (☎223 39 34 70; www.portoturismo.pt). Staff speaks English, French, German, Italian, and Spanish. Offers maps and general info about Porto. Open M-F 9am-6:30pm, Sa-Su 9:30am-6:30pm. Ribeira branch, R. Infante Dom Henrique, 63 (☎222 06 04 12); same hours and services. **Turismo de Portugal** office, Pr. Dom João I, 43 (☎222 05 75 14). Open Nov.-Mar. M-F 9am-7pm, Sa-Su 9:30am-3:30pm; Apr.-Oct. M-F 9am-7:30pm,

Sa-Su 9:30am-3:30pm. Airport **branch** (☎229 41 25 34). Open daily Jan.-Mar. 8am-11pm; Apr.-Dec. 8am-11:30pm.

Budget Travel: Abreu Jovem, Av. dos Aliados, 221 (☎222 04 35 80). Between Pr. da Liberdade and the main tourist office. English-speaking staff offers advice and student rates. Open M-F 9am-12:30pm and 2:30-6:30pm.

Currency Exchange: Portocâmbios, R. Rodrigues Sampaio, 193 (☎222 00 02 38). Open M-F 9am-noon and 1-6pm, Sa 9am-12:30pm. ATM on Av. dos Aliados.

Laundromat: NorSec, Via Catarina, 115, 1st fl. (☎222 00 31 32), in the shopping center on R. de Santa Catarina. Go down the stairs, and NorSec is in the back on the left. €5 per kg wash and dry. Open daily 10am-10pm.

Police: R. Clube dos Fenianos, 11 (☎222 08 18 33).

Pharmacy: Farmácia Souza Soares, R. de S. Catarina, 141 (☎222 00 21 45). 3 blocks from Pr. G. H. Delgado at R. Formosa. Posts 24hr. pharmacy schedule. Open M-F 9am-8pm, Sa 9am-7pm.

Hospital: Hospital de Santo António (☎222 07 75 00), on R. Alberto Aires Gouveia.

Internet Access: Laranja Mecânica, in a small shopping center on R. de Santa Catarina, 274; €0.50 per 15min., €1.30 per hr. Open M-Sa 10am-midnight, Su 3pm-8pm. **Sid@Internet,** R. Santa Catarina, 72. 2nd fl. €0.90 per hr. 10am-7pm, €0.50 per hr. 7pm-1am. Open M-F 10am-1am, Sa-Su 2pm-midnight.

Post Office: Pr. Gen. Humberto Delgado (☎223 40 02 00). Fax, phone, and **Poste Restante.** Financial services closed after 6pm. Open M-F 8:30am-7:30pm, Sa 9:30am-3pm. **Postal Code:** 4000.

ACCOMMODATIONS

Expensive *pensões* congregate around Av. dos Aliados. The best deals are around Pr. Filipa de Lancastre or near the *mercado* on R. de Fernandes Tomás and R. Formosa. Prices dip in the low season (Oct-May), so try bargaining.

Oporto Poets Hostel, Tv. do Ferraz, 13 (☎223 32 42 09). The hippest place to stay in Porto, with colorful, 6-to 8-bed co-ed dorm rooms. Check out the nighttime view from the patio with a beer and grilled sausage from the barbecue. Laundry €5, with dry €7. High season dorms €20, doubles €44; low season €18/40. Cash only. ❷

Andarilho Oporto Hostel, R. da Firmeza, 364 (☎222 01 20 73; www.andarilhohostel.com). No sign; look for a red door right on the street. Co-ed rooms of 6, 8, or 10 beds are large enough to do cartwheels in. Bright, huge living area just off the patio garden. Laundry €4, with dry €6. Free breakfast, Wi-Fi and internet access. High season €20 per person; low season €18. Cash only. ❷

Pensão Duas Nações, Pr. Guilherme Gomes Fernandes, 59 (☎222 08 16 16). Bedroom walls painted brightly for an upbeat feel. Well-furnished rooms, though modestly decorated. Reception until 2am. Laundry €7. Internet access €1 per 30min. Singles €14, with bath €22.50-25; doubles €23-25; triples €36; quads €46-53. Cash only. ❶

FOOD

Quality budget meals can be found near Pr. da Batalha on R. Cimo de Vila and R. do Cativo. Try the delicious *bifanas* (small pork sandwiches) on R. Bomjardim and the wide selection of olives in the local *azeitarias* (olive houses). Ribeira is popular for affordable riverside dinners, but for something even cheaper you can try the local *francisinhas* (bread, cheese, ham and meat covered in a secret sauce) at many of the local cafes. **Supermarket Pingo Doce** is on R. de Sa de Bandeira, 387, two blocks from Pr. G. H. Delgado. (Open M-Sa 8:30am-8:30pm,

Su 9am-8pm.) The **Mercado de Bolhão** has an enormous selection of fresh bread, cheese, meat, and olives. (Open M-F 7am-5pm, Sa 7am-1pm.)

O Caçula, R. do Bonjardim, 20 (☎222 05 59 37; www.ocacula.com). The only place in town where a fancy 3-course meal goes for €6.50. Drinks not included. Delicious vegetarian options. Free Wi-Fi. Open M-Sa noon-3pm and 7pm-last customer. MC/V. ❶

Café Majestic, R. de Santa Catarina, 112 (☎222 00 38 87). One of the best replicas of 19th-century bourgeois opulence—it was originally called Elite Café—this Titanic-inspired restaurant is the oldest and best known in the city. Entrees €9-16. Sandwiches €5-13. Elaborate pastries €4-6. Open M-Sa 9:30am-midnight. AmEx/MC/V. ❷

Capoeira Central dos Leões, Pç. Guilherme Gomes Fernandes, 16 (☎222 05 11 85). Large portions for a small budget. Chicken with a generous side of fries goes for €2.30, and a whole chicken is €7.20. Save room for the creative and yummy desserts (layered strawberry ice cream cake €2.50). Delivery available. Open 9am-9pm. Cash only. ❶

Café Guarany, Av. dos Aliados, 85 (☎223 32 12 72; www.cafeguarany.com). On Pr. da Liberdade. Features live weekend entertainment, from *fado* to Cuban music. Best for coffee and dessert (€2-3). Duck with port wine €15. Sandwiches €3.50-9. Salads €6-10, entrees €6-14. Wi-Fi (15min. €1.25). Open daily 9am-midnight. AmEx/MC/V. ❷

SIGHTS

For most travelers, the first brush with Porto's fine artwork is the Estação de São Bento, a monastery-turned-*azulejo* collection, which displays ancient forms of transportation. Up Av. dos Aliados in Pr. Gen. Humberto Delgado, the **Câmara do Porto** (City Hall) attests to Porto's late 19th-century prosperity.

PALÁCIO DA BOLSA. The elegant Palácio da Bolsa (Stock Exchange) is one of Porto's most visited sites, as it is essentially one tremendous work of art. It was built over the ruins of the Convento de São Francisco, after the convent was destroyed by fire in 1832. The construction took 60 years longer than expected due to the painstaking task of making the enormous granite staircase. The pinnacle of embellishment is the golden **Sala Árabe** (Arabian Hall), designed by Portuguese artists with the sole intention of impressing potential foreign investors. The green crests on the ceiling proclaim "Allah above all," and its gold and silver walls are covered with the oddly juxtaposed inscriptions "Glory to Allah" and "Glory to Dona Maria II," the Catholic queen. Only guided tours are allowed, since the building still houses the Commerce Association of Porto. *(R. Ferreira Borges. ☎223 39 90 00. Open daily Apr.-Oct. 9am-7pm, Nov.-Mar. 9am-1pm and 2-6pm. Last tour 30min. before closing. Multilingual tours every 30min. €5, students €3. Tour of palace and wine cellars across the river €6/4. Palace and a bus tour of Porto €12. Palace and a Port wine cruise €12. Palace tour, bus tour, and wine cruise for €20.)*

IGREJA DE SÃO FRANCISCO. The Gothic and Baroque eras of ecclesiastical architecture were known for gilded wood, but they outdid themselves here. At one point, there was between 400-600kg of gold on the chapel's walls and altar, all donated by rich families trying to buy their way into paradise. Check out the giant family tree tracing Christ's genealogy, starting from the loins (literally) of a statue of Jesse of Bethlehem, father of King David. Next door, a museum showcases religious art from the 16th-18th centuries; in the basement of the museum lies the Ossário, the mass burial grounds for Porto's poor. The cavernous catacombs have several individual graves belonging to the benefactors. *(R. Infante Dom Henrique. ☎222 06 21 00. Open daily Feb.-May 9am,-6pm June-Oct. 9am-7pm, Jul.-Aug. 9am-8pm. €3, students €2.50.)*

MUSEU NACIONAL DE SOARES DOS REIS. A former royal residence and Portugal's first art museum (founded in 1833), Soares dos Reis houses a collection of

19th-century Portuguese painting and sculpture, much of it by Soares dos Reis, often called Portugal's Michelangelo. It features works by other greats as well, like Marquês de Oliveira. *(R. Dom Manuel II, 44. ☎223 39 37 70. Open Tu 2-6pm, W-Su 10am-6pm. Last entrance 5:30pm. €3, seniors and students €1.50. Su until 2pm free.)*

IGREJA E TORRE DOS CLÉRIGOS. The 18th-century **Igreja dos Clérigos** is decorated with Baroque and Rococo carvings. The highlight of the church is its **Torre dos Clérigos,** the city's tallest landmark and the tallest tower in Portugal, topping out at over 75m. The spectacular view of the Rio Douro valley doesn't come easily, though: it involves 225 spiraling steps. *(R. S. Filipe de Nery. ☎222 00 17 29. Church open M-Sa 8:45am-12:30pm and 3:30-7pm, Su 10am-1pm and 8:30-10:30pm. Tower open daily Apr.-July and Sept.-Oct. 9:30am-1pm and 2:30-7pm; Aug. 9:30am-7pm; Nov.-Mar. 10am-noon and 2-5pm. Tower €2, church free.)*

JARDINS DO PALÁCIO DE CRISTAL. Beautiful gardens lie outside the Palácio do Cristal (Glass Palace), which is not, in fact, made out of glass. Take a gander at the geese, swans, ducks, peacocks, and fountains, while enjoying a stroll through the lush vegetation. Walk toward the side opposite to the entrance, and you'll get an unmatched view of the Douro and its picturesque bridges. *(R. Dom Manuel II. ☎226 05 70 80. Open daily until dark.)*

SÉ. On the hilltop south of the train station stands Porto's imposing Romanesque Sé (cathedral). The Sé was built in the 12th-13th centuries, and the Gothic, *azulejo*-covered cloister was added in the 14th century. The gold and silver **Capela do Santíssimo Sacramento,** to the left of the altar, was used as the bishop's study. During the Napoleonic invasion, townspeople whitewashed the altar to prevent vandalism. *(Terreiro da Sé. ☎222 05 90 28. Open M-Sa 9am-12:30pm and 2:30-7pm, Su 2:30-6pm. Nov.-Mar closes 1hr. earlier. Cloister €2.)*

MUSEU DE ARTE CONTEMPORÂNEA. This museum houses rotating exhibits of contemporary international paintings, architecture, photography, and sculpture. Its 44 colossal acres of manicured gardens, fountains, and old farmland, tumbling down toward the Douro River, are also easy on the eyes. *(R. D. João de Castro, 210. ☎226 15 65 00. Several kilometers out of town, on the way to the beach. Bus #207 leaves from Av. dos Aliados; ask the driver to stop at the museum. 30min., return buses run until midnight. Museum open Apr.-Sept. Tu-F 10am-7pm, Sa-Su 10am-8pm; Oct.-Mar. Tu-Su 10am-7pm. Park Tu-Su 10am-7pm. Museum and park €5, park only €2.50. Su before 2pm free.)*

NIGHTLIFE

The heart of Porto's nightlife is **Ribeira.** Summer crowds leave outdoor cafes at 2am and head to neighboring bars or more distant clubs. The Ribeira's narrow, poorly lit streets can be unsafe at night, so don't go alone. Nightlife in Porto is tough without a car, as most clubs are along the river in **Foz** and in the industrial zones. Bus #500 runs until 1am from the São Bento train station to the beach at Matosinhos, passing Foz along the way. Bus #200 also runs past Foz to the beach until 1am, but begins at Pr. da Liberdade. A taxi to Foz from downtown costs €4-5. To get to the clubs in the **industrial center,** take the metro to Viso, which runs until 1am, as does bus #201 from Pr. da Liberdade to Viso. A taxi ride will cost €5-6. **Gaia,** on the other side of the Douro River, is safer and better lit. Here, numerous bars, discotheques, wineries, and arcades line up with a beautiful view of Porto's lights. You can cross the D. Luis bridge by foot to get back to Porto and catch a bus or taxi from there.

Discoteca Swing, R. Julio Dinis, 766 (☎226 09 00 19). A staple of Porto's nightlife for over 25 years, Swing is at its most swinging at around 2 or 3am. Beer €2-3. Mixed drinks €6-8. Su ladies' night includes 2 free drinks. W-Th no cover, F-Su €2.50-10, usually €5. Open W-Su midnight-6am. AmEx/MC/V.

O Muro, Muro dos Bacalhoeiros, 87-88 (☎222 08 34 26), upstairs from a pedestrian street along the water off Pr. de Ribeira. A tiny yet remarkable restaurant during the day, O Muro attracts night owls with a great view of the river and complimentary snacks with a beer (€1-4.50) or a glass of port (€2.50). Entrees €7.50-12. Kitchen closes at midnight. Open Tu-Su noon-2am.

WINERIES

No visit to Porto is complete without one of the city's famous wine-tasting tours. They are incredibly cheap (€1-3), if not free, and take about 30min. Wine tasting is most prevalent across the river, in Vila Nova de Gaia and its 17 large port lodges reside. Tours there often include visits to the wine caves below. To get there, walk across the bottom level of the Ponte de D. Luiz I in Ribeira. It's best to visit the wineries from noon-2pm when most tourists head away from the tours for lunch.

Solar do Vinho do Porto, R. Entre Quintas, 220 (☎226 09 47 49). Go around the Palácio de Cristal to the end of R. de Entre Quintas. Enjoy a fine glass of port on the swanky outdoor terrace of a former manor house. Limited snack menu includes cheesecake (€3). Port €1-25. Open M-Sa 4pm-midnight. AmEx/MC/V.

Vinhos de Quinta, R. Fonte Taurina, 89 (☎222 08 92 57). A small, humble, non-profit wine shop dedicated to small, lesser-known port wine producers. The owners serve samples for a fee of €2.50-10. Prices are rock bottom (about half off retail, €2.50-70) and all proceeds go to farmers in the Douro. Open Tu-Su 11am-8pm.

Sandeman, Lg. Miguel Bombarda, 3 (☎233 74 05 00, fax 233 74 05 94), just off Av. Diogo Leite. Founded by a Scottish merchant 2 centuries ago, Sandeman now offers a tourist-friendly dive into the world of port. Lively tours every 20min. €3. Open Mar.-Oct. daily 10am-12:30pm and 2-6pm; Nov.-Feb. M-F 9:30am-12:30pm and 2-5:30pm.

Taylor's, R. do Choupelo, 250 (☎223 74 28 00; www.taylor.pt). Walk along the river and make a left on R. Afonso III. Go right as it splits and take the stairs to R. do Choupelo. Taylor's will be on the left. Offers expert wine knowledge, outdoor gardens (complete with peacocks), and free tours and tasting. Tours every 20-30min., last tour 5pm. Open July-Aug. M-Sa 10am-6pm, Sept.-June M-F 10am-6pm. AmEx/MC/V.

FESTIVALS

For two weeks in February, Porto hosts the **Fantasporto Film Festival,** screening international fantasy, sci-fi, and horror flicks for crowds of film enthusiasts. Early June brings the **Festival Internacional de Teatro de Expressão Ibérica,** which stages free performances of Portuguese and Spanish drama. Porto's biggest party, however, is the **Festa de São João** (June 23-24), when locals storm the streets for free concerts, folklore, *fado*, and (of course) wine. After the fireworks on the first night of the festival, people go to the beach to fulfill superstitious traditions including jumping over bonfires three times for good luck, and for the women, rolling around in the morning dew to ensure fertility.

BRAGA ☎253

Elegant fountains and open plazas welcome visitors to Braga (pop. 166,000), the "Portuguese Rome." Nine centuries ago it was the nation's religious capital and the seat of Portugal's archbishops. Though Braga has lost much of its religious influence over time, it still remains a devout city, and it is home to

Portugal's Catholic University. It was in Braga that the 1926 coup paved Salazar's path to power, and the city retains conservative tendencies. Nonetheless, Braga is on the cultural edge, boasting innovative restaurants, a flourishing art scene, and the best *Semana Santa* celebration in Portugal. Braga also makes a great base for daytrips to the lush natural beauty nearby.

TRANSPORTATION

Trains: The recently renovated train station, Estação da Braga (☎808 20 82 08; www.cp.pt), is 1km from Pr. da República. Take R. do Souto and pass through the town gate; the station is 400m to the left. Trains run to: **Lisboa** (4-5hr., 12 per day 6:04am-9:30pm, €21.50-30), **Porto** (45-60min., M-F 26 per day 5:30am-9:30pm, €2-12.50), and **Vigo, Spain** via **Nine** (4hr., trains leave Nine 8:49am and 7:52pm, €16).

Buses: The bus station is the **Central de Camionagem,** R. General Norton de Matos (☎253 20 94 00; offices open M-Sa 6am-8pm, Su 9am-9pm), a few blocks north of the city center. **Rodoviária** (REDM) runs to **Guimarães** (1hr.; M-F every 30min. 10:35am-8:05pm, Sa every hr. 7:10am-7:10pm, Su 8 per day 8:10am-6:40pm; €2.80). **Rede Expressos** runs to: **Coimbra** (3hr., 11 per day 6am-11:30pm, €12.70); **Faro** (12-15hr.; June-Sept. 6 per day 5am-11:30pm, Oct.-May 3 per day 5am-7pm; €27); **Lisboa** (5hr., 10-11 per day 6am-11:30pm, €18); **Porto** (1hr., 25 per day 5am-11:30pm, €5.70). **Hoteleira do Gerês** runs to **Caldas de Gerês** from terminal #18 (1hr.; M-F 11 per day 7:05am-8pm, Sa 9 per day 8am-8pm, Su 6 per day 8am-7:10pm; €3.90).

Taxis: (☎253 68 32 28 or 61 19 92). Next to the train and bus stations, in Largo de S. Francisco, and next to Pr. da República.

ORIENTATION AND PRACTICAL INFORMATION

Braga's focal point is the **Praça da República,** a large central square. The tourist office is at the corner of the square and marks the start of the large **Avenida da Liberdade.** Across the plaza from the tourist office is the enormous **Braga Shopping** center, where visitors can find a grocery store and even lodgings among the various shops and cafes. Pedestrian thoroughfare **Rua do Souto** begins at the tourist office corner of Pr. da República, eventually becoming R. Dom Diogo de Sousa and then R. Andrade Corvo, before leading to the train station. To get to Pr. da República from the bus station, take a right onto the commercial street with your back to the station. Continue straight under the overpass onto Pr. Alexandre Herculano, then take R. dos Cháos straight into the square.

Tourist Office: Av. da Liberdade, 1 (☎253 26 25 50; www.cm-braga.com.pt/turismo), in Pr. da República. Open June-Sept. M-F 9am-7pm, Sa-Su 9am-12:30pm and 2-5:30pm; Oct.-May M-Sa 9am-12:30pm and 2-6:30pm.

Budget Travel: Tagus, Pr. Municipal, 7 (☎253 21 51 44). Open June-Sept. M-F 9am-7pm, Sa 10am-1pm; Oct.-May M-F 9am-1pm and 2:30-6pm.

Currency Exchange: Caixa General de Depósitos, Pr. da República (☎253 60 01 00), next to Café Astória. Open M-F 8:30am-3pm. **ATM** outside.

Laundromat: Lavandaria Confiança, R. D. Diogo de Sousa, 46 (☎253 21 69 07). Wash, dry, and iron €2.50 per kg. Open M-F 9am-1:30pm and 3-8pm, Sa 9am-2pm.

Police: R. dos Falcões, 12 (☎253 20 04 20).

Pharmacy: Farmácia Cristal, Av. da Liberdade, 571 (☎253 26 23 21). Open M-F 9am-7:30pm, Sa 9am-1pm.

Hospital: Hospital de São Marcos, Lg. Carlos Amarante, 6e (☎253 20 90 00). From the tourist office, walk down Av. da Liberdade away from Pr. da República and make a right onto R. 25 de Abril. The hospital is on the right.

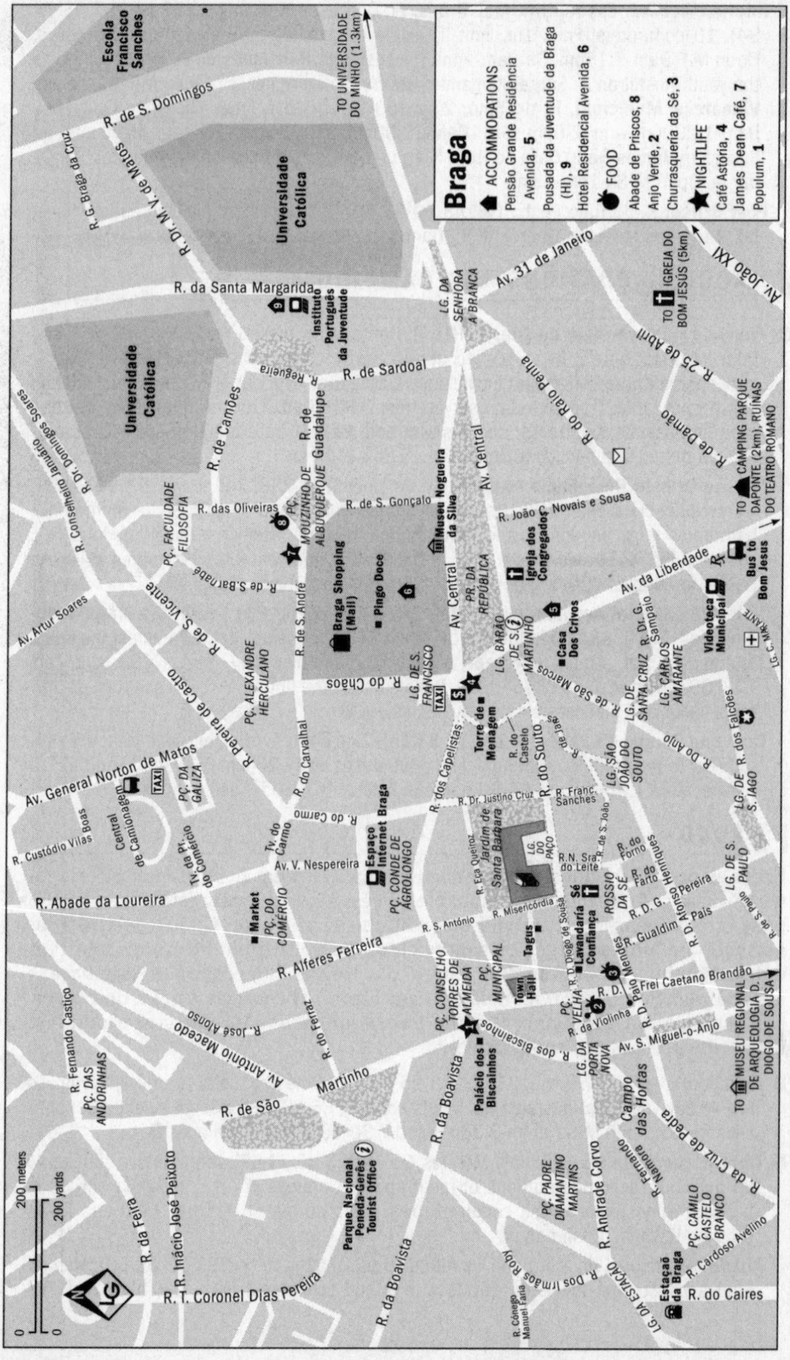

Braga

ACCOMMODATIONS
- Pensão Grande Residência Avenida, **5**
- Pousada da Juventude da Braga (HI), **9**
- Hotel Residencial Avenida, **6**

FOOD
- Abade de Priscos, **8**
- Anjo Verde, **2**
- Churrasquería da Sé, **3**

NIGHTLIFE
- Café Astória, **4**
- James Dean Café, **7**
- Populum, **1**

Internet Access: Espaço Internet Braga, Pr. Conde de Agrolongo, 177 (☎254 26 74 84). 10 computers. Free. 1hr. limit if people are waiting; go early to avoid a crowd. Open M-F 9am-7:15pm, Sa 9am-1pm. The **Instituto Português de Juventude,** next to the youth hostel on R. Santa Margarida, has free internet access. Open M-F 9am-8pm. **Videoteca Municipal,** R. do Raio, 2 (☎253 26 77 93). Free. 1hr. limit. Open M-F 9am-12:30pm and 2-6pm, Sa 10am-12:30pm and 2-5pm. For late night internet access try **James Dean Cafe** on R. de S. André next to Pç. Mouzinho de Albuquerque. €1 per hr. Open M-Sa 1pm-2am.

Post Office: R. do Raio Penha (☎253 20 03 60), 2 blocks from Av. Liberdade. Phone, fax, and other services. Open M-F 8:30am-6pm. **Postal Code:** 4700.

ACCOMMODATIONS AND CAMPING

Pousada da Juventude de Braga (HI), R. Santa Margarida, 6 (☎253 61 61 63). Taxi from train station €5. 8- to 10-bed dorms are on the small side, but have a friendly atmosphere and a convenient locale. Large living area with cable TV, communal kitchen and a pool table. Free breakfast served from 8:30-10am. Lockout noon-6pm, but bag drop-off possible. Dorms €9, doubles with bath €22. HI card required but may be purchased there (€2). AmEx/MC/V. ❶

Pensão Grande Residência Avenida, Av. da Liberdade, 738, 2nd fl. (☎253 60 90 20; www.residencialavenida.net). Handsome rooms with phone and TV. Some rooms have bathrooms large enough for the Brady Bunch to share. Breakfast included. June-Aug. singles €22.50-30, with bath and A/C €30-35; doubles €30/40; triples €40/50. Sept.-May singles €20/25, doubles €25/30, triples €35/40. MC/V. ❷

Hotel Residencial Avenida, Av. Central, 27 (☎253 61 63 63). Inside the Braga Shopping Mall, 3rd fl. 48 comfortable rooms with A/C and private bath. Breakfast included. Internet €1 per 30min. July-Sept. singles €37, doubles €47, triples €60; Oct.-Feb. €28/38/45; Mar.-June €33/40/50. Rooms on the top floor are €5-10 cheaper, as they are smaller and inaccessible by elevator. MC/V. ❸

Camping Parque da Ponte (☎253 27 33 55), 2km down Av. da Liberdade from the center, next to the stadium and municipal pool. Buses every 20min. 6:30am-11pm. €2.15 per person, €1.85 per car, €1.80 per tent. Electricity €1.65. Cash only. ❶

FOOD

Braga is one of the more visitor-friendly places to eat in Portugal, offering a wide variety of cuisines at reasonable prices. Modest local restaurants on the busy streets near the train and bus stations serve cheap €2.50-3 *menús* that normally include a burger or sandwich and a soft drink. More upscale Portuguese dining can be found in Campo das Hortas. Supermarket **Pingo Doce** is inside Braga Shopping. (Open daily 10am-11pm.) The **market** is in Pr. do Comércio. (Open M-Sa 8am-5pm.) Try the *pudim do Abade de Priscos*, a pudding flavored with caramel and port wine.

Anjo Verde, Lg. da Pr. Velha, 21 (☎253 26 40 10). Dine like a star at one of Portugal's few strictly vegetarian restaurants. Meals are only €6.50, with a large selection of specials for €5. Open M-Sa noon-3:30pm and 7:30-10:30pm. Cash only. ❶

Churrasquería da Sé, R. D. Paio Mendes, 25 (☎253 26 33 87). The attentive staff serve up delicious, generous portions of meat and fish entrees (€7-13) to lunch crowds in a classy atmosphere at the center of town. *Prato do dia* €5-7. Open M-Tu and Th-Su 9:30am-9:30pm. Cash only. ❷

Abade de Priscos, Pr. Mouzinho de Albuquerque, 7, 2nd fl. (☎253 27 66 50). Named after a priest from the early 1900s who is still considered Portugal's best chef. The *menú* is small but the food is outstanding. Open M 7:30-10pm, Tu-Sa noon-3pm and 7:30-10pm. Closed last 3 weeks of June and last week of Dec. Cash only. ❷

SIGHTS

IGREJA DO BOM JESUS. Crowning a hillside 5km outside of town stands one of Portugal's most impressive religious sanctuaries and Braga's most famous landmark. The 18th-century church was built in an effort to recreate Jerusalem in Braga, providing Iberian Christians with a pilgrimage site closer to home. The 20-25min. walk up the staircase, which many devout Christians tread on their knees during the May Pilgrimage to Bom Jesus, represents the progression of a spiritual journey and the ascent to heaven. The staircase passes the 14 Stations of the Cross, fountains representing the five senses ("smell" spouts water through a boy's nose), and the staircase of three virtues, "Fé, Esperança, e Caridade" (faith, hope, and charity). Alternatively, the 285m climb can be made in an antique cable car, in use since 1882 (daily 8am-8pm, every 15min., €1.50). From the top, you'll get an unmatched view of Braga and the Tras-os-Montes mountains. Behind the church is a small and peaceful lake where visitors can rent paddle boats (€1.50 per 15min.). *(Buses labeled "#02 Bom Jesus" depart at 10 and 40min. past the hour in front of Farmácia Cristal, Av. da Liberdade, 571. Buses stop at the bottom of the stairway; the last bus from Bom Jesus leaves at 9pm, Su 7pm. €1.40.)*

CATEDRAL. Braga's Sé, Portugal's oldest cathedral, has undergone a series of renovations since its construction in the 11th and 12th centuries. Today, it's a glorified graveyard: the **Capela dos Reis** (Chapel of the Kings) houses the 12th-century stone sarcophagi of the parents of Dom Afonso Henriques, as well as the all-too-accessible mummified remains of the 14th-century archbishop Dom Lourenço Vicente. The cathedral has a collection of *cofres cranianos* (brain boxes), one of which contains the 6th-century cortex of São Martinho Dume, Braga's first bishop. There's no need to pay for the other parts; the treasury showcases a small collection of artifacts, while the chapels and choir are standard Portuguese cathedral fare. *(☎253 26 33 17. Mass daily 5:30pm. Open to visitors Tu-Su 9am-noon and 2-6:30pm. Cathedral free. Treasury €3, chapels and choir €2.)*

MUSEU REGIONAL DE ARQUEOLOGIA DOM DIOGO DE SOUSA. Braga's newest museum focuses on the rich Roman history of the area, and on display are artifacts collected during the excavation of the Roman ruins scattered around the city. Check out the collection of ancient coins and everyday objects (combs, toothpicks, etc.). To get to the museum, walk down R. do Souto away from the tourist office. Take a left on R. do Matadouro and follow it until it becomes R. dos Bombeiros Voluntários just past Lg. Paulo Orósio. The museum will be on your left. *(☎253 27 37 06; www.mdds.ipmuseus.pt. Open Tu-Su 10am-5:30pm. €3.)*

NIGHTLIFE

Locals and travelers of all ages head to **Populum,** off Pr. Conde de Agrolongo. The cavernous bar and discoteca's dance floors are always pumping at full force with Top 40 hits or merengue and salsa. (☎253 61 09 66. Beer €2. Mixed drinks €4. Min. consumption for men €5, after midnight €10; women €5, W free. Open Th-Sa 10pm-5am. Closed Aug.) The upstairs bar of **Café Astória,** Pr. da República, 5, next door to Café Vianna, is a popular student hangout after midnight during the school year. (☎966 08 36 97. Beer €1. Open daily 8am-2am). Another option during the week is **James Dean,** R. Santo André 85, a cafe-bar that offers snacks and burgers in a chill atmosphere. (☎253 6 2 76 02. Open

M-Su untill noon-2am). The area around Pr. do Comércio between Tr. do Carmo and R. Alferes Ferreira is quite dangerous at night; be cautious after dark.

FESTIVALS

Nowhere in Portugal is there a better Easter celebration than in Braga, where endless **Semana Santa** processions trace the city, some somber and hooded, others upbeat and musical. Each parish church brings a cross to the neighborhood doorstops to be kissed by the residents inside. Families signal that the cross is welcome by leaving flowers outside their front door; it doesn't take long before Braga is literally a bed of roses. Another popular festival is the **Festa de São João,** a week-long celebration culminating on the night of June 23. Traditional folk music, good food, colorful lights, and general revelry take over Av. da Liberdade and Lg. São João da Ponte. Don't be surprised to see locals running around beating each other on the head with **toy hammers.** Few seem to remember the bizarre ritual's origin, but older folks relate that it's a tribute to São João, Protector of the Head. The **Festival de Teatro de Braga** takes place in the first week of July and celebrates the art of theatre, putting on shows all across the city's open air plazas. Toward the end of July and the beginning of August the streets of Braga are filled with music as the **Festival de Música Tradicional** takes over the city. 100 per hr.

DAYTRIPS FROM BRAGA

GUIMARÃES

Several lines of buses, including Transdev and REDM (☎253 20 94 01), run from Braga to Guimarães (1hr.; M-F 20 per day 6:35am-8:05pm, Sa 12 per day 7:10am-7:10pm, Su 8 per day 8:10am-6:40pm; €2.55) and return (same schedule, €2.75).

Portugal's original capital, Guimarães (pop. 60,000) claims to be the birthplace of the nation. The city was home to the first king of Portugal, Dom Afonso Henriques, and the site of his first court in the 12th century. Besides its historical significance, Guimarães is famous for its wild and decorative saints celebration, the **Festas Gualterianas,** during the first week of August. Many restaurants and shops gather in the narrow streets of the medieval center, and the Colina Sagrada gardens on the edge of downtown are home to one of the country's most gorgeous medieval estates, the **Paço dos Duques de Bragança** (Ducal Palace). The palace was modeled after the manors of northern Europe, and its numerous brick chimneys makes it easy to distinguish from a distance. The museum inside includes furniture, silverware, tapestries, and weapons. Don't miss the elaborate floor-to-ceiling Pastrana tapestry replicas in the **Sala dos Pasos Perdidos** (Hall of Lost Footsteps), or the large display of archaic weaponry in the **Sala das Armas,** including swords, daggers, and armor nearly 600 years old. (☎253 41 22 73. Palace open M-F 9:30am-6:30pm, Sa-Su 9:30am-7:30pm. Last entrance 30min. before closing. €4, ages 15-25 and seniors €2. Su before 2pm free.)

Near the palace is the **Igreja de S. Miguel do Castelo,** the small Romanesque chapel in which Dom Afonso was baptized. On the floor are the tombs of warriors who fought alongside him at the nation-founding Battle of Ourique. Just up from the church is the **Castelo de Guimarães,** built as a fort in the 10th century under Countess Mumadona Dias, who had been recently widowed and wished to protect her nearby monastery and residence from Moorish attacks. Visitors scramble up the small stairs of the castle's central tower, the **Torre de Menagem,** which works hand in hand with the arduous climb to leave viewers breathless. The outline of this castle appears on the Portuguese coat of arms and flag. (☎253 41 22 73. Church and castle open M-Su 9:30am-12:30pm and 2-6:30pm.

Free. Torre de Menagem open Tu-Su 9:30am-1pm and 2:30-5:30pm. €1.50, ages 14-25 €0.75. Last entry to all sites 30min. before closing.)

Even the view from the Torre can't match the one from the top of **Monte da Penha,** which looms over the city and is home to an excellent campsite, several picnic areas, a mini train, and mini golf. A **teleférico** (cable car) starting from Lg. das Hortas makes the 400m climb to the top, crossing over the city. Take a right out of the tourist office, and at the rotary take the second right (R. José Sampaio). Make another right onto R. Rei do Pegu and follow it to the cable car station. At the top of the mountain, boulders line the pathways leading to *miradouros* (lookouts) at the Santuário de Penha and at the Monumento a Pio IX. (☎253 51 50 85. www.turipenha.pt. Open M-F 10am-7pm, Sa-Su 10am-8pm. Last ticket 30min. before closing. €2.40, round-trip €3.80.)

TELEFÉRICO OR TAXI? If you plan on taking camping equipment up Monte da Penha, it's best to invest in a taxi, as the *teleférico* does not go all the way up to the campsite.

For an authentic Portuguese meal with local company, head off the beaten path to the family-run **Restaurante O Pinguim ❷,** Tr. do Picot. From Av. Conde Magaride, head straight until reaching Lg. Navarros de Andrade. Go around the rotary and up Av. Humberto Delgado. Make a left onto R. Picoto up the hill; the restaurant is off to the left as the street starts to curve right. (☎253 41 81 82. Entrees €6-11. Open Tu-Su 8am-10:30pm. Serves meals 11:30am-3:30pm and 6:30-10:30pm.) A similar option is **Solar do Arco ❷,** R. Sta. Maria below the arch. Entrees €9-11. (☎253 51 30 72. Open daily noon-3pm and 7-11pm). Cheap accommodations can be found at the **Pousada de Juventude de Guimarães (HI) ❶,** Complexo Multifuncional de Couros, Lg. do Cidade. From the tourist office, go right on Alameda S. Dâmaso. Make a right before the "*pousada*" sign and follow the road as it curves down and around to the youth hostel. (Breakfast included. Lockout noon-6pm, but bag drop-off available. Single-sex dorms €13, doubles with bath €32. AmEx/MC/V.)

The main **tourist office** is on Alameda de São Dâmaso, 83, and the staff speaks English, French, and Spanish. (☎253 41 24 50. www.guimaraesturismo.com Open M-F 9:30am-12:30pm and 2-6:30pm.) A second tourist office on Pr.de Santiago has longer hours. (☎253 51 87 90. Open M-F 9:30am-6:30pm, Sa 10am-6pm, Su 10am-1pm.) The **bus station** (☎253 51 62 29) is in the Guimarães Shopping complex, on Alameda Mariano Felgueiras. To get to the main tourist office from the bus station, go right on the large street in front, Av. Conde Margaride. Walk uphill, and turn right at the intersection onto R. Paio Galvão. Follow it past Lg. do Tournal to its end; the tourist office is on the left. From the **train station** (☎253 41 23 51) it is a 10min. walk to the tourist office. Go left on Av. D. João IV from the station, and then right on Av. Afonso Henriques; the office will be on the right. The **police** are on Alameda Alfredo Pimenta (☎253 51 33 34) and the **hospital** is on R. dos Cutileiros (☎253 54 03 30).

BARCELOS

REDM buses (☎253 80 83 00) run from Braga to Barcelos (40-50min.; M-F 14 per day 7:15am-7:10pm, Sa 8 per day 7:15am-7:10pm, Su 6 per day 8:35am-7:10pm; €2.30) and return from Av. Dr. Sidónio Pais, 245, across the street from the marketplace (the Campo da República) near the rotary and outside the REDM office (M-F 15 per day 7am-7:20pm, Sa 8 per day 7:40am-7:20pm, Su 6 per day 7:40am-7:20pm; €2.30).

Trains run from Porto-Campanha to Barcelos (1hr.; M-F 13 per day 5:55am- 8:50pm, Sa-Su 3-4 per day 6:45am-8:45pm).

Barcelos's fame is rooted in a legend dating back to the Middle Ages. A Galician traveler was wrongly accused of theft and taken to the gallows while his rich accuser sat down for dinner. Just before the boy was to be hung, the chicken on the nobleman's plate stood up and crowed, proclaiming the boy's innocence. The legendary "Barcelos cock" has been a national icon ever since, and much of the town's touristic appeal is centered on the famous rooster. Barcelos has also made a name for itself by hosting one of the largest weekly markets in Europe—vendors come on Thursdays to sell everything from produce and ceramics to live animals and furniture. The market, the **Feira de Barcelos,** was inaugurated in 1412 by Dom João I. Vendors begin arriving at the huge **Campo da República** late Wednesday night, and by 8am on Thursday the market is going at full force; the lively vendors don't leave until 5pm (7:30pm in summer). To get to the the market place from the bus station, follow Av. dos Combatentes uphill until you hit Campo da Republica, where the market takes place. To get to the **tourist office,** Lgo. Dr. Jose Novais, 8, turn left on Av. da Liberdade and the office will be next to the church behind Torre da Porta Nova, part of the town's original 15th-century wall and the only remaining tower of the three that once marked the entrance to the ancient city. (☎253 81 18 82. Short-term **luggage storage.** Open Mar. 15-Sept. 30 M-F 9:30am-6pm, Sa 10am-1pm and 2-5pm, Su 10am-1pm and 2-4pm; Oct. 1-Mar. 14 M-F 9:30am-5:30pm, Sa 10am-1pm and 2-5pm.) Local services include the **police** (☎253 80 25 70) on Av.Dr. Sidónio Pais and the **hospital** (☎253 80 92 00) on Lg. Campo da República.

COCK-A-DOODLE-DOO. Bent on buying one of Portugal's national icons? The infamous ceramic cocks generally cost 50% less in Barcelos.

PARQUE NACIONAL DA PENEDA-GERÊS

Portugal's northern border with Spain is a sight to behold: a dark, quiet forest spread over rugged mountains and winding rivers, punctuated by faint hiking trails. A crescent-shaped nature reserve, the **Parque Nacional da Peneda-Gerês,** became Portugal's first protected area in 1971. The park consists of the northern Serra da Peneda and the southern Serra do Gerês, and it provides refuge for the endangered Iberian wolf. Most travelers base themselves in Vila do Gerês (also called Caldas do Gerês), a spa town that draws hordes in late summer. From here, visitors can explore the park's many relaxing villages, turquoise waters, tree-covered mountains, and Iron Age ruins. Activities range from hikes past abandoned monasteries to adrenaline-powered water sports to pampering in the thermal waters.

TRANSPORTATION AND PRACTICAL INFORMATION. Empresa Hoteleira do Gerês (☎253 26 20 33) runs buses between **Braga** and **Gerês,** from terminal #18 in Braga's **bus station.** (to Gerês 1hr.; M-F 11 per day 7:05am-8pm, Sa 7 per day 8am-7:10pm, Su 6 per day 8am-7:10pm; return 1hr.; M-F 11 per day 6:30am-6:30pm, Sa 6 per day, Su 5 per day 7:15am-6:30pm. €3.80.) Gerês is essentially a 500m one-way street loop, running beside the water. The tourist office is at the far end of the loop, uphill from the bus stop. Next to the tourist office is a two-lane highway which continues 13km to Spain. To catch the bus back to Braga, you must be on the side of the loop that leads traffic away from the tourist office downhill.

To get to the **tourist office** from the bus stop, walk uphill along Av. Manuel Francisco da Costa; the office is off the rotary at the end of the mini-shopping center. The staff speaks English, French, Italian, and Spanish and provides information on activities in the park as well as **luggage storage.** (☎253 39 11 33. Open M-W and F-Sa 9am-12:30pm and 2:30-6pm.) The **police** (☎253 39 11 37) are off Av. Manuel Francisco da Costa, and the **Red Cross** (☎253 39 16 60) is on Cha de Ermida. **Espaço Internet** in the Biblioteca Municipal on Av. Manuel Francisco da Costa, across from the spa, has free **Internet.** (☎253 39 17 97. Open M-F 9:30am-1pm and 2-5:30pm, Sa 9am-12:30pm.) The **post office** is off the rotary that leads to the center. (☎253 39 00 10. Open M-F 9am-12:30pm and 2-5:30pm.)

ACCOMMODATIONS AND FOOD. There are plenty of accommodations in Gerês, from fancy hotels to budget *pensões*. Try **Residencial Ribeiro ❷**, R. Miguel Torga, 101, where the kindly owner offers beautiful rooms with private bathrooms and free breakfast. From the bus stop, head down the street until the road splits off at the ice cream shop and goes downhill. Follow the road to the bottom of the hill, then follow the signs left. (☎253 39 19 09. Singles €25, doubles €35, triples €45. Cash only.) A comparable option is **Pensão Residencial o Horizonte de Gerês ❷**, R. de Arnaçó, 19. Go around the loop past the tourist office until the road splits. Take a right uphill for two blocks and the *pensâo* will be on the left. Simply decorated rooms come with a TV and private bath. More expensive rooms have a view of the valley. (☎253 391 260. Breakfast included. Singles €25-30, doubles €35-40, triples €45-50. Cash only.) For camping, try **Camping Vidoeiro ❶**, 1km up the road from the tourist office and 250m beyond the park office. (☎253 39 12 89. Reception 8am-noon and 3-7pm. Open May 15-Oct. 15. €2.20 per person, €3.10-4.20 per tent, €3.10 per car.) Meals are served at the *pensões* throughout town. A small **supermarket** is on the way into town, across from the post office. (Open M-Sa 8am-12:30pm and 2:30-7pm, Su 8am-noon.) Restaurants line Av. Manuel Francisco da Costa, near the bus stop where the buses from Braga arrive. For a filling meal, try **Vai-Vai ❷**, located just down the street from the tourist office, across from the spa. The *menú* (€8) includes a choice of fish, chicken, or pork served with soup, a drink, and dessert. Entrees run €7-12. Cheaper snack menus are available at the cafe next door. Come early for lunch; the place is small and gets packed from 1-2pm. (☎253 39 12 26. Open M-Sa 10am-10pm. Cash only.)

MIND THE SILENCE

"Please mind Lisbon's silence. If you are loud, go to Spain." While the graffiti has been erased from one of the city's *miradoures*, that's a message the Portuguese would like tourists to remember.

At bars, supermarkets, restaurants, and even in celebrating a victory, moderation is key. If you have the chance to watch a Portuguese soccer match, you'll notice the slow, quiet tone of the commentator as he mumbles in the background. Even when they score, he only raises his voice a bit, to say "Gol." That's enough.

It is important to recognize how loud is loud enough, lest you get shushed. After hearing *fado* in a small bar in Alfama, I embarrassed myself by clapping at the end, while the rest of the spectators rubbed their hands in quiet appreciation of the singer. There was an old lady living on the top floor who, in true Portuguese fashion, did not mind the music, but was annoyed by the clapping. The owner asked the audience not to clap any more, and that was that.

While the Portuguese are warm, welcoming, and willing to help you at any point, they will do so in a discreet and quiet way. After all, they appreciate silence.

HIKING AND OUTDOOR ACTIVITIES. The main **park office** is in **Braga,** on Av. António Macedo. (☎253 20 34 80. Open M-F 9:30am-12:30pm and 2:30-5:30pm.) The Gerês **branch,** on Av. Manuel Francisco da Costa, is a white building 1km uphill from the tourist office, near the campgrounds. (☎253 39 01 10. Open in summer daily 9am-noon and 2-5:30pm; in winter M-F 9am-noon and 2-5:30pm.) Casual visitors tend to stick to the gentle, scenic southern trails, while dedicated hikers head north. The popular **Trilha da Preguiça** (Lazy Trail; 5km) begins 3km north of Gerês proper, on the right side of the highway, and follows the Rio Gerês. Another hike follows the road from the tourist office to Spain 10km farther toward **Portela do Homem,** a town with a river pool in the **Minas dos Carris** valley. Other popular longer trails are Trilho da Aguia do Sarilhâo, Trilho dos Currais, and Trilho da Cidade da Calcedonia. The tourist and park offices can recommend additional hikes.

As the name suggests, the main attraction of **Caldas do Gerês** (Gerês hot springs) is its spa, owned by **Empresa das Águas do Gerês,** on Av. Manuel Francisco da Costa, 133, as are the hotel, restaurant, and park by the tourist office. The spa complex (the pink building in the center of town) contains therapeutic waters. (☎253 39 11 13; www.aguasdogeres.com. Open May-Oct. M-Sa 8am-noon and 4-6:40pm.) For a bewildering array of spa services, go to the office, a yellow building across from Hotel das Águas do Gerês. (30min. full-body massage €20. Sauna €7.50. Whirlpool €6. Open M-Sa 8am-noon and 2:30-5:30pm.) To the left of the tourist office, the beautiful **Parque das Termas** has mineral waters, jogging trails, three pools, and canoe rentals. Purchase tickets at the booth inside. (☎253 39 11 13. Park open 9am-7pm. Entrance €1, under 12 €0.50. Free if at hotel. Pool open daily July-Sept. 10am-7pm; M-F €4, Sa-Su €6; May-June 9am-6pm; €4, under 12 €2. Tennis €3 per hr. Canoeing €3 per 30min.)

Geresmont, R. de Arnaçó, 43, has a variety of outdoor activities, including paintballing, rope climbing, canoeing, and off-roading. (☎919 61 77 73; www.geresmont.com.) South of Gerês, the **Miradouro do Gerês** overlooks the **Caniçada** reservoir—beware the mass migrations of weekend picnickers. The village of **Rio Caldo,** at the base of Caniçada reservoir just 8km south of Gerês, is a base for canoeing and waterskiing through **Água Montanha Lazer.** (☎253 39 17 79; www.aguamontanha.com. Single canoe €4.50 per hr, €14 per ½-day, €22 per day. Double canoe €7.50/23/25. 5-person motorboat €35/95/125. Waterskiing boat with driver and equipment included €40 per 20min., €100 per hr.

VIANA DO CASTELO ☎258

The landscape of Viana do Castelo (pop. 37,000), nestled among mountains and overlooking the sea, is a real-life postcard. The surrounding hilltops and the nearby Monte de Santa Luzia offer unparalleled views of the fertile landscape and the sea from this beachside town. Viana is mainly a beach resort, but it also has a lively historic district, unique culinary specialties, and intriguing architecture, including a bridge designed by Gustave Eiffel. The town's buildings, some of the best preserved in all of Portugal, are an intriguing mix of Baroque, Art Deco, and Revivalist styles. The antiquity of the architecture, combined with the tranquility of the sea, make Viana more than worth a visit.

TRANSPORTATION

Trains: The station (☎258 82 13 15) is at the top of Av. dos Combatentes da Grande Guerra, under the Santa Luzia hill. Trains to **Porto** (2hr., 11-14 per day 5:34am-8:23pm, €7), **Valença do Minho** (1hr.; M-F 9 per day 7:33am-9:34pm, Sa-Su 7 per day 8:46am-7:35pm; €2.90), and **Vigo, España** (2hr.; 9:35am, 7:35pm; €8.15).

Buses: The new bus station is next to the train station in the basement of the new mall. Enter the mall to the left of the train station, go up the escalator, across the 1st fl., and then down the escalator on the opposite side of the mall. Transdev runs to **Braga** (1hr.; M-F 8 per day 7am-6:35pm, Sa 6 per day 7am-6:35pm, Su 4 per day 8:20am-6:35pm; €3.70). Linhares also runs to **Braga** (1hr.; M-F 6:30, 9am, 2:25, 5:55pm; €3.70). **A.V. Minho** runs to **Porto** (2hr.; M-F 4 per day 7:15am-5:30pm, Sa 6 per day 7:30am-5:30pm, Su 4 per day 7:30am-6:30pm; €4.60). **Avic** runs to **Lisboa** (5hr.; M-F 8am, 12:30pm, 11:59pm; Sa 7am, 12:30pm; Su 8am, 6:15pm, 11:59pm; €14.50) and **Valença do Minho** (1hr., M-F 5 per day 11:30am-5:30pm; €4).

Taxis: Táxis Vianenses (☎258 82 66 41 or 82 20 61). About €0.75 per km.

ORIENTATION AND PRACTICAL INFORMATION

Av. dos Combatentes da Grande Guerra runs from the train station to the port. Most accommodations and restaurants are on or near the Avenida. Facing the ocean, the historic center stretches left of the avenida around the **Praça da República. Templo de Santa Luzia** is above the town, behind the train station. Beaches, sights, and stations are all within a 10min. walk from Pr. da República.

Tourist Office: Rua Hospital Velho, s/n (☎258 82 26 20). From the train station, walk down the Rua des Combatentes da Grande Guerra, take the 4th left on R. da Picota and then a right. Open May-July, and Sept. M-F 9:30am-1pm and 2-6pm, Sa 9:30am-1pm and 2:30-6pm, Su 9:30am-1pm; Aug. M-F 9:30am-7pm, Sa 9:30am-1pm and 2:30-6pm, Su 9:30am-1pm; Oct.-Apr. M-F 9:30am-1pm and 2-5:30pm, Sa 9:30am-1pm and 2:30-5:30pm, Su 9:30am-1pm.

Currency Exchange: Banco Santander, Av. dos Combatentes da Grande Guerra, 332 (☎258 82 88 97), near the train station. 24hr. **ATM** outside. Open M-F 8:30am-3pm.

Bookstore: Livraria Bertrand, R. Sacadura Cabral, 32 (☎258 82 28 38). English fiction, travel guides, and Portuguese classics. Open M-F 9am-7pm, Sa 9am-3pm. MC/V. The same bookstore has a branch on the 1st fl. of the bus station mall (☎258 82 97 26), open daily 10am-11pm.

Police: R. de Aveiro (☎258 80 98 80).

Pharmacy: Farmácia Almeida, R. João da Costa, 34 (☎258 82 25 20). Open daily June-Aug. 9am-10pm, Sept.-May 9am-8pm. Check the door for a listing of rotating 24hr. pharmacies.

Hospital: Centro Hospitalar Alto Minho, Estrada Sta. Luzia (☎258 80 21 00).

Internet Access: Free at the **Biblioteca Municipal** on Lg. 5 de Outubro, s/n (☎258 80 93 02), right off Av. dos Combatentes da Grande Guerra near the water. 5 computers. ID required. Strict 30min. limit. Open M-Sa 10am-8pm. For later hours, try **Pekim Online,** R. General Luis do Rego, 121. €1 per hr. Open daily noon-midnight.

Post Office: Av. dos Combatentes da Grande Guerra (☎258 80 00 84). Poste Restante, fax, and **Western Union.** Open M-F 9am-6pm, Sa 9am-1pm. **Postal Code:** 4900.

ACCOMMODATIONS AND CAMPING

Pousada de Juventude de Viana do Castelo (HI), R. de Límia (☎258 80 02 60), off R. da Argaçosa and Pr. da Galiza. Dorm-style rooms with spacious communal bathrooms. All rooms have balconies overlooking the marina. Internet €5 per hr. Breakfast included, 8-11am. Laundry €2.50. Reception 8am-midnight. Reserve ahead. July-Aug. and festivals, dorms €13; doubles €30; doubles with bath €38. Sept.-June €11/26/32. ❶

Residencial Viana Mar, Av. dos Combatentes da Grande Guerra, 215 (☎/fax 258 82 89 62), 2min. from the train station. Large antique-styled rooms with cable TV, sink, and mirror. Lounge has bar, TV, and stereo. Breakfast included. June-July rooms with shower €35, with full bathroom €40; Aug.-Sept. €40/60; Oct.-May €25/35. AmEx/MC/V. ❸

Orbitur (☎258 32 21 67; www.orbitur.pt), at Praia do Cabedelo. Catch a **Trans-Cunha** *"Cabedelo"* bus from Lg. 5 de Outubro. See tourist office for details on bus schedule. A well-equipped campsite. Free showers. July-Aug. €4.80 per person, €5.40 per tent, €4.70 per car. Sept.-June €4/5/4.20. ❶

FOOD

Food is more than just fuel in Viana do Castelo. Local specialities include *arroz de sarabulho* (rice cooked with blood and served with sausages and potatoes) and *bacalhau à Gil Eanes* (cod cooked with milk, potato, onion, garlic, and oil). Most budget restaurants lie off Av. dos Combatentes da Grande Guerra. The **municipal market** is on Av. Capitão Gaspar de Castro. With your back to the train station, go left and walk for 3min. (Open M-F 7am-7pm, Sa 7am-1pm.) A weekly market with produce, fresh fish, ceramics, live birds, and flowers is held Fridays from dawn to dusk off Av. Campo do Castelo.

Restaurante Dolce Vianna, R. Poço, 44 (☎258 82 48 60), at the corner of Pr. da Erva, across the square from the tourist office. Italian-style restaurant with brick-oven pizzas made right in front of you (€4.50-6.25) and a variety of pasta dishes (€4.50-6). Delicious gelato (€2-5). Open daily May-Oct. noon-3pm and 7:30-10:30pm; Nov.-Apr. noon-3pm and 7-10pm. MC/V. ❶

Restaurante Glamour, R. da Bandeira, 185 (☎258 82 29 63). Choose from a small menu of fish and meat entrees and an extensive wine menu in this sleek, contemporary restaurant, upstairs from the bar. Entrees €10-13. Open daily 7:30pm-2am. Bar open W-Sa 10pm-4am. MC/V. ❷

Restaurante Camelo, Estação Viana Shopping (☎258 83 90 90), 2nd fl. While located in the mall food court, the gorgeous views of the city, ocean, and mountains from Camelo's outdoor terrace make this a relaxing stop. Try the traditional food, including *arroz de Galo* (€9). Entrees €7-12. Open noon-3pm and 6:45-10:30pm. AmEx/MC/V. ❷

SIGHTS

The **Monte de Santa Luzia,** overlooking the city, is guarded by the monumental **Templo de Santa Luzia.** Conceived of by the same architect who designed the Sacre Coeur in Paris, this early 20th-century church has brilliant views out over the valley and the bay. Behind the *templo* are the ruins of a Celtic village, including circular foundations and a village wall. Although there is an elevator up to the *mirador,* don't shy away from the 30min. hike to the top—the moss-covered stairwells and breathtaking views make the walk more than worth it. (*Templo* open daily June-Aug. 8am-7pm, Sept.-May 8am-5pm. Mass Sa 4pm, Su 11am and 4pm. Free. Elevator every 15min. Open daily June-Sept. 8am-8pm; Oct.-May 8am-6pm. €2, round-trip €3. Mirador, €1.80.) For a less active pursuit, check out the **Museu de Traje** in Pr. da República, which displays traditional attire of the region. (☎258 80 01 71. Open Tu-Sa June-Sept. 10am-1pm and 3-7pm; Oct.-May 10am-1pm and 3-6pm. €2, students €1. Closed for remodeling as of July 2008; inquire at the tourist office for more information.)

BEACHES

Sunbathers, swimmers, and windsurfers fill the beaches of Viana do Castelo and its neighboring towns. **Praia Norte,** at the end of Av. do Atlântico, is an easy 15min. walk to the west edge of town, and has two natural swimming pools (although frigid water and a rocky beach discourage beach activity).

Praia da Argaçosa is a small beach covered with sunbathers on Rio Lima next to the marina. A ferry runs to Praia do Cabedelo, a great beach for surfing and windsurfing (7min.; every hr., ask tourist office for details; €1). A 10min. train ride north of Viana leads to Afife's **Praia do Bico,** frequented by surfers, where the acclaimed surfing school **Escola Zurf** offers lessons and equipment rentals. (☎966 22 10 92; www.surfingviana.com. Lessons June to mid-Sept. €20 per person in group, €40 private. Surfboards €15 per 3hr., €20 per day; bodyboards, wetsuits, and bikes €10 per 3hr., €15 per day; fins €5/10.) The **Pralas de Âncora, Moledo,** and **Caminha** are farther north.

NIGHTLIFE AND FESTIVALS

The cafes and bars around Pr. da República fill up in the evening. The most popular place in Viana is **Bar Glamour,** R. da Bandeira, 183, down the street from the plaza and away from the main avenue. With white-mod furniture, artistically broken mirrors, and a stage set for the next hot band, this lounge bar and concert venue melds the chic and the eclectic. (☎258 82 29 63. www.glamourmusic.com. Open W-Sa 10pm-4am. Drinks €4.) Viana's biggest festival is the annual **Festa de Nossa Senhora da Agonia,** celebrated with processions, parties, and performances in the plaza on August 20 and the weekend closest to August 20th. The **Feira do Livro,** held for most of July in the Jardim Público, promotes literary arts and culture in Viana. Though the focus is on books, the festival also includes nightly musical events, art displays, a merry-go-round and bumper cars for children, and food vendors.

DAYTRIP FROM VIANA DO CASTELO

VALENÇA DO MINHO

The cheapest and most convenient way to reach Valença do Minho is by train. Trains leave from Viana do Castelo (M-F 9 per day 7:33am-9:34pm, Sa-Su 7 per day 8:46am-7:35pm; €3.10). From the train station, walk through the rotary in front and take a right at the end of the street. Up this hill is another rotary with a large fountain; cross it and make your way uphill until you see the fortaleza. The tourist office is at the base of this hill; to get there, continue straight after the rotary until you see the wooden house on your left.

Valença's sizeable **fortaleza,** whose 13th-century walls once kept outsiders out, now brings them in. Wide-eyed tourists, bustling locals, eager vendors, and patient cars jumble together in the *fortaleza*'s streets, infusing the tiny walled-in town with uninterrupted movement and a provincial quality. The hilltop location also offers panoramic views of the neighboring countryside and Río Minho, and the cannons and remains of the fortress provide the young at heart with hours of fun. The old town is entirely encircled by the fortress, and within its walls are a number of beautiful churches and a myriad of market streets. Just outside the walls is **El Puente Internacional,** built in 1886. The iron bridge stretches across the Río Minho from Valença to TUY (p. 549), uniting Spain and Portugal. Staying the night in Valença may not be necessary, but if you do, head to **Pensão Rio Minho ❷,** Largo da Estação, s/n, right next to the train station. The rooms, complete with TV and bathroom, are cozy and have an antique feel. Some have balconies, and there is a restaurant downstairs. (☎251 80 92 40. Sept-June singles €20, doubles €30, July-Aug. 25/35.) The **tourist office,** Ave. de Espanha 4930, is right below the *fortaleza*. (☎251 82 33 29. Open M-Sa May-Sept. 9:30am-12:30pm and 2:30-6pm, Oct.-Apr. 9:30am-12:30pm and 2-5:30pm.)

THE THREE BEIRAS

The Three Beiras region offers a versatile sampling of the best of Portugal: the pristine beaches of the coast, the rich greenery of the interior, and the ragged peaks of the Serra da Estrela. The Costa da Prata (Silver Coast) lines the shore, passing through Aveiro on the way to Porto. Its countryside is dotted with red-roofed farmhouses surrounded by expanses of corn, sunflowers, and wheat. A mecca for youth since the days in which it boasted the only university in Portugal, Coimbra hosts an opinionated, lively population; its nightlife, folklore and gorgeous architecture continue to attract young people. Only recently discovered by tourists, the region retains a wealth of Portuguese traditions.

COIMBRA ☎239

The crown jewel of the three Beiras, Coimbra is a rollicking city of 200,000, but it possesses the vibe of a metropolis many times its size. Backpackers and local college students roam graffiti-lined streets, providing a youthful exuberance rare in the Portuguese interior. For centuries, the Universidade de Coimbra was the only university in Portugal, attracting young men from the country's elite. Though universities now abound in Portugal, Coimbra's university district maintains its historical appeal. Visitors may be surprised to see the outer facade of the university in a state of disrepair; the city's preservation efforts are aimed at the buildings' interior, so be sure to see the indoor splendor.

TRANSPORTATION

Trains: (Info ☎808 20 82 08; www.cp.pt). **Estação Coimbra-A (Nova)** is 2 blocks from the lower town center, on the river. **Estação Coimbra-B (Velha)** is 3km northwest of town. Regional trains stop first in Coimbra-B, then some continue to Coimbra-A, departing in reverse order. Long-distance trains stop in Coimbra-B only; take a connecting train to Coimbra-A to reach the city (4min., right after trains arrive, €1.08 or free if transfer). To: **Braga** (2-3hr., 16 per day 5:45am-8:40pm, €10-20); **Figueira da Foz** (1hr., 20 per day 5:35am-12:10am, €2); **Lisboa's Sta. Apolonia** (2-3hr., 17 per day 5:30am-8:46pm, €12-30); **Porto** (1-2hr., 14 per day 5:45am-11:45pm, €6.90-20).

Buses: Joalto (formerly AVIC), R. João de Ruão, 18 (☎239 82 01 41; www.joalto.pt). Bus stops are in front of the Coimbra-A train station. To: **Condeixa** (25min., 6-15 per day 7:05am-11:30pm, €1.79) and **Conímbriga** (30min.; departs M-F 9:05, 9:35am, returns 1, 6pm; Sa-Su departs 9:35am, returns 6pm; €2.20). **RBL** (☎239 85 52 70; www.rede-expressos.pt), at the end of Av. Fernão de Magalhães and a 15min. walk past Coimbra-A. To: **Évora** (4-6hr., 9 per day 6:15am-2:15am, €15.80); **Faro** (8-9hr., 14 per day 6:15am-2:10am, €23); **Lisboa** (2hr., 18 per day 6:15am-2:15am, €13); **Luso** and **Buçaco** (45min., M-F 5 per day 7:35am-7:30pm, Sa 9am; €2.90); **Porto** (1hr., 14 per day 7am-3am, €11).

Public Transportation: SMTUC buses and street cars (☎239 81 02 47; www.smtuc.pt). 1-way on the bus €1.60, 3-trip ticket €2, 1-day pass €3, book of 11 €6. Sold at vending machines in Lg. da Portagem, Pr. da República, and in local shops like mini-markets and bookstores.

Taxis: Politaxis (☎239 49 90 90), outside Coimbra-A and the bus station.

Car Rental: Avis (☎239 83 47 86, reservations toll-free 800 20 10 02; www.avis.com), in Coimbra-A train station. 21+. From €80 per day. Manual transmission only. Open M-F 8:30am-12:30pm and 3-7pm. AmEx/MC/V.

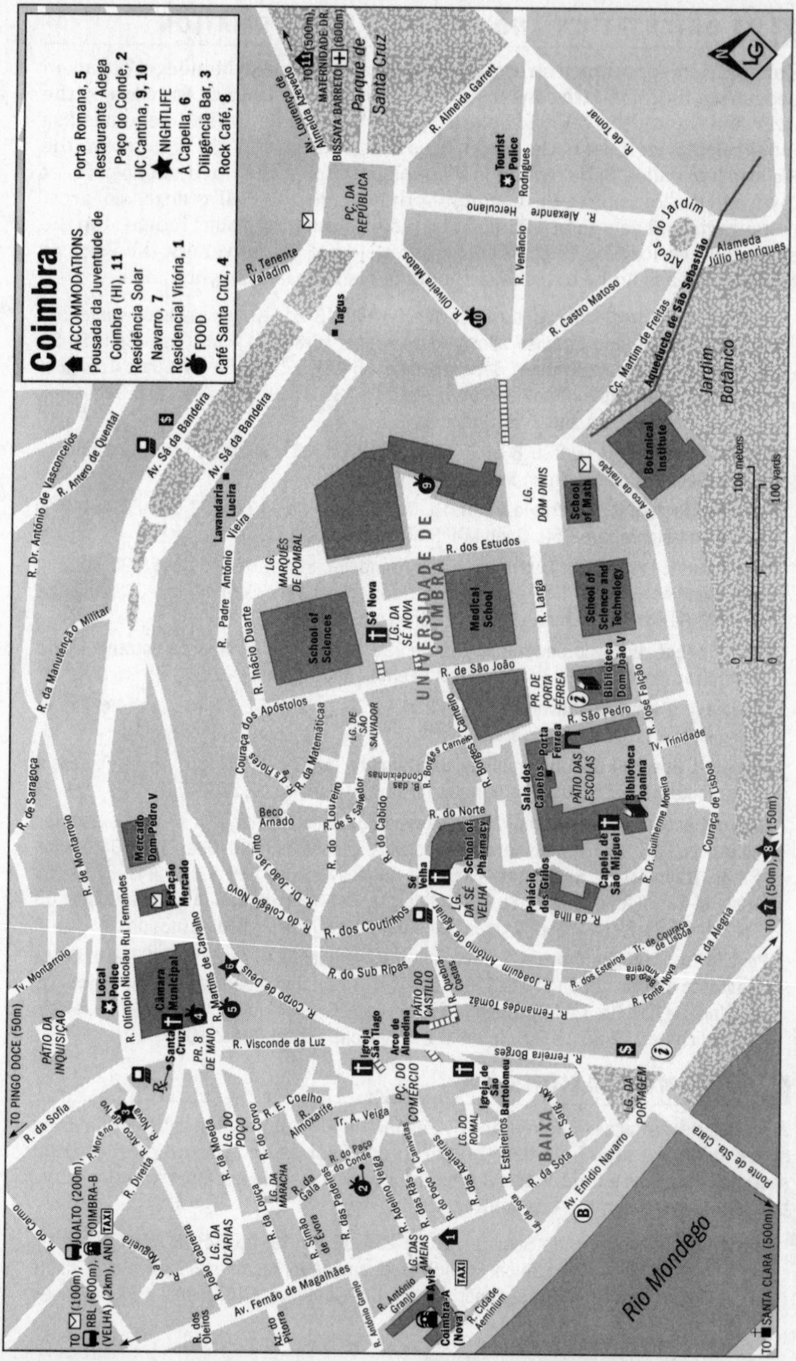

Coimbra

ACCOMMODATIONS
- Pousada da Juventude de Coimbra (HI), **11**
- Residência Solar Navarro, **7**
- Residencial Vitória, **1**

FOOD
- Café Santa Cruz, **4**
- Porta Romana, **5**
- Restaurante Adega Paço do Conde, **2**
- UC Cantina, **9, 10**

NIGHTLIFE
- A Capella, **6**
- Diligência Bar, **3**
- Rock Café, **8**

ORIENTATION AND PRACTICAL INFORMATION

Coimbra's steep, cobbled streets rise in tiers above the Río Mondego. The main pedestrian thoroughfare runs from **Praça 8 de Maio** to **Largo da Portagem** by the river and the tourist office. It starts as **Rua Visconde da Luz** and becomes **Rua Ferreira Borges** as it nears the water. This road forms a triangle region with the **Rio Mondego** called **Baixa,** which is the most central of the three major parts of town and the location of the Coimbra-A train station, as well as dozens of great restaurants and accommodations. The historic **university district** looms atop the steep hill overlooking Baixa. On the other side of the university, the **Praça da República** area is home to cafes, a shopping district, and the youth hostel.

Tourist Office: Regional, Lg. da Portagem (☎239 48 81 20; www.turismo-centro.pt). English, French, and Spanish spoken. Open June 16-Sept. 14 M-F 9am-8pm Sa-Su 9:30am-1pm and 2:30-6pm; Sept. 15-June 15 M-F 9-5pm, Sa-Su 10am-1pm and 2:30-5pm. **Municipal,** Praça da Porta Férrea (☎239 85 98 84). Open M-F 9am-6pm, Sa-Su 9am-12:30pm and 2-5:30pm.

Budget Travel: Tagus (☎239 83 62 05) inside the A.A.C. building on R. Padre António Vieira. Sells ISIC cards. Open M-F 9:30am-6pm.

Currency Exchange: Montepio Geral, Lg. da Portagem (☎239 85 17 00 or 82 80 31). €5 commission above €50. Open M-F 8:30am-3pm.

Laundromat: Lavandaria Lucira, Av. Sá da Bandeira, 86. Wash and dry €5.90 per 6kg (full machine), €2 for 1kg. Specify if you don't want your clothing ironed (*passada*). Open M-Sa 9am-1pm and 3-7pm, Su 9am-1pm.

Police: Local, Av. Elisio de Moura, 155 (☎239 79 76 40). **Serviço de Estrangeiros e Fronteiras** (tourist), Loja do Cidadâo, Av. Fernão de Magalhâes (☎239 85 35 00).

Pharmacy: Farmácia Universal, Pr. 8 de Maio, 32 (☎239 82 37 44), in the center of town. Open M-F 8am-7pm, Sa 8am-1pm.

Hospital: Hospital da Universidade de Coimbra (☎239 40 04 00), at Pr. Professor Mota Pinto and Av. Dr. Bissaya Barreto. Take bus #6, 7, 7t, 29, 35, 36 or 37.

Internet Access: Casa Aninhas, Pr. 8 de Maio, 38. This free, city-run service is popular, so expect a 15-30min. wait. Passport or driver's license required. Open M-F 10am-8pm, Sa-Su 10am-10pm. **Sp@cenet,** Av. Sá da Bandeira, 67 (☎239 83 98 44). €2 per hr. Open M-Sa 10am-midnight, Su 1pm-midnight. **Web@aventura,** Rua Quebra Costas 63 (☎239 10 81 89). €2 per hr. Open M-F 10am-10:30pm, Sa noon-10:30pm.

Post Office: Estação Central, Av. Fernão de Magalhães, 223 (☎239 85 07 70). **Poste Restante** and **fax.** Open M-F 8:30am-6:30pm, Sa-Su 9am-noon. **Municipal Office,** Lg. D. Dinis (☎239 85 17 60). Open M-F 9am-6pm, Sa 9am-noon. **Branch office,** Pr. da República (☎239 85 18 20). Open M-F 9am-6pm. **Postal Code:** 3000.

ACCOMMODATIONS

Accommodations are packed on Av. Fernão de Magalhães. Their bright flashing signs make the area between the Largo das Olarias and the Coimbra-A train station seem like a mini Vegas strip. The youth hostel is a 20min. walk or short bus ride away from the city center.

Residencial Vitória, R. da Sota, 11-19 (☎239 82 40 49; fax 84 28 97). Convenient location next to the train station. Friendly staff, and newer rooms with bath, phone, cable TV, breakfast, and A/C. In summer singles €30, doubles €45, triples €60. In winter

€25/40/50. Older rooms without amenities are acceptably comfortable, with shower, sink, and TV. Breakfast €2.50. Singles €20, doubles €30. AmEx/MC/V. ❷

Residência Solar Navarro, Av. Emídio Navarro, 60-A, 2nd fl. (☎239 82 79 99). Rock-bottom prices, large rooms, and high ceilings. Ensuite bathrooms. Singles €15; doubles, triples, and quints €12.50 per person. Cash only. ❶

Pousada da Juventude de Coimbra (HI), R. Henrique Seco, 14 (☎239 82 29 55). Off R. Lourenço Azevedo, to the left of Parque de Santa Cruz. At the end of the road, take the 2nd right, or take the #6,7 or 29 bus from in front of the train station. Get off 2 stops after Pr. da República, on Bysseia Barreto. Kitchen, TV room (with pool table and foosball), impeccable bathrooms. Breakfast included. 24hr. bag drop-off. Dorms €11; singles with bath €16; doubles €26, with bath €28. AmEx/MC/V. ❶

FOOD

The side streets below Pr. do Comércio, the areas around R. Direita off Pr. 8 de Maio, and the university side of Pr. da República are a good bet for bargain eats. Restaurants offer local favorites: steamy portions of *arroz de lampreia* (rice with eel) and *cabrito* (young goat). The cheapest meals are at the **UC Cantinas** (full meal for under €2), the university student cafeterias, on the right side of R. Oliveiro Matos and up the stairs near Lg. Dom Dinis. You'll need an ISIC card, and you may want to leave your backpack at home. For groceries, stock up at **Mercado Dom Pedro V** on R. Olímpio Nicolau Rui Fernandes (open M-Sa 8am-1pm). The supermarket **Pingo Doce,** is on R. João de Ruão, 14, a 3min. walk up R. da Sofia from Pr. 8 de Maio (☎239 85 29 30; open daily 8:30am-9pm).

Restaurante Adega Paço do Conde, R. do Paço do Conde (☎239 82 56 05). Adored by locals. Abundant grilled meat and fish dishes for only €5-6. The giant restaurant is partly indoors, partly outdoors, and covered by a tin roof, and the entrance is marked by a large archway. Entrees €4-13. Open M-Sa 11am-10pm. MC/V. ❶

Café Santa Cruz, Pr. 8 de Maio, 5 (☎239 83 36 17; www.cafesantacruz.com). Formerly part of a church, this is the city's most famous cafe. A vaulted ceiling and carved wooden chairs distinguish the dining space. Outdoor seating is available with a view of the plaza and the Igreja de Santa Cruz. Sandwiches €1.60-3. Summer, open M-Sa 7:30am-2am, winter M-Sa 7:30am-midnight. Cash only. ❶

Porta Romana, R. Martins de Carvalho, 8/10 (☎239 82 84 58), tucked away behind Café Santa Cruz. A wide variety of pasta entrees for €6-8 and pizzas for €4-7. Half portions of local cuisine from €4.50. Try the *Fettucine Fantasia,* with Roquefort cheese, cream sauce, and ham (€6.50). Open Tu-Su 10am-2am. Cash only. ❶

SIGHTS

OLD TOWN. Take in Coimbra's old town sights by making the steep 15min. climb from the river up to the university. Begin at Pr. 8 de Maio, often a scene for folk music and dance, and the **Igreja de Santa Cruz.** The 16th-century church boasts an enormous center dome and *azulejo*-lined walls, though the centerpiece is the tomb of Dom Afonso Henriques, Portugal's first king. *(☎239 82 29 41. Open M-F 7:30am 6:30pm, Sa 7:30am-12:30pm and 2pm-7:30pm, Su 8:30am-12:30pm and 4pm-7:30pm. Check the schedule at the main door for mass times. Sacristia with royal tombs €2.50, students and seniors €1.50.)* The ascent continues to the ancient **Arco de Almedina,** a remnant of the Moorish town wall, one block uphill from Lg. da Portagem. The gate leads past several university bookstores to the steep, twisted, and aptly named R. Quebra-Costas (Back-Breaker Street). Up a narrow stone stairway looms the 12th-century Romanesque **Sé Velha** (Old Cathedral). *(☎239 82 52 73. Open M-Th 10am-1pm and 2pm-6pm, F 10am-1pm, Sa 10am-5pm. Cathedral free. Cloister €1, students*

€0.80). Follow the signs to the 16th-century **Sé Nova** (New Cathedral), whose mixed classical- and Baroque-style exterior was finished for the resident Jesuit community. Bring sunglasses: the gilded main altar can be blinding at certain times of day. *(☎239 82 31 38. Open Tu-Sa 8:30am-noon and 2pm-6pm. Free.)*

UNIVERSIDADE DE COIMBRA. Though many buildings have since been constructed from reinforced concrete, the original law school retains its spot on the architectural dean's list. Enter through the **Porta Férrea** (Iron Gate), off R. São Pedro, to the **Pátio das Escolas,** which sports an excellent view of the city. The staircase to the right leads up to the **Sala Grande dos Actos** or **Sala dos Capelos** (Graduates' Hall), where portraits of Portugal's kings (6 of whom were born in Coimbra) hang below a 17th-century ceiling; this is where graduates receive their diplomas. The magnificent **Capela de São Miguel,** adorned with intricate *talha dourada* carvings (especially the organ), is a sight to behold. *Azulejos*, gold, silver, paintings, or carved wood line every surface; almost no floor, wall, or ceiling space is left uncovered. At the end of the row of buildings is the oldest library in Portugal, the **Biblioteca Joanina,** which overwhelms visitors with gold-trimmed extravagance. The portrait of Louis XV stares at viewers from every angle, making sure they don't snatch any of the library's 300,000 ancient books. A small army of bats keeps the books bug free. The library's oldest book, a marriage guide for young men, dates back to 1523. *(☎239 85 98 84. www.uc.pt. Open daily Mar. 13-Oct. 8:30am-7pm; Nov.-Mar. M-F 9am-5pm, Sa-Su 10am-4pm. Tickets to all of the university sights can be purchased outside the Porta Férrea, in the Biblioteca Dom João V. General ticket €6, seniors and students €4.20. The Sala dos Capelos and Biblioteca Joanina are each €3.50, seniors and students €2.45. There is a limit to how many people can be in the library at a time, so expect a 15-20min. wait.)*

NIGHTLIFE

After dinner, the outdoor cafes surrounding Praça da República buzz until 2am, after which crowds move on to the bars and clubs farther afield. The scene is best October through July, when the students are around Figueira da Foz, an hour away, which offers more options and makes a popular night trip. Many take the train, party all night, and return in the morning.

A Capella, R. Corpo de Deus on Lgo. Victoria (☎239 833 985). From Pr. 8 de Maio, take R. V. da Luz for about 100m and make a sharp U-turn to the left on R. Corpo de Deus. A Capella is tucked off the road to the left. Built in 1364, A Capella is now a small late-night cafe and the best place to hear *fado*. Very touristy, so don't expect to see many locals around. The professional *fadistas* play *fado* classics with historic scenes from Coimbra projected on the background wall. Mixed drinks €4-5. Performances at 9:30, 10:30, and 11:30pm. Cover €10, includes 1 drink. Open daily 9pm-3am.

Diligência Bar, R. Nova, 30 (☎239 82 76 67). Touristy during the summer, yet still intimate and pleasant. Original *fado* performed by students and regulars after 10pm. Entrees €9-11. Sangria €9.50 per jug. Min. consumption €5. Open daily 7pm-2am. V.

Rock Cafe, Parque Verde do Mondego (☎239 63 60 38, fax 239 84 21 38). On the riverside in the park, about 500m from the Ponte de Santa Clara towards the white bridge. You can go for a snack or salad (€2-6) during the day or rock during the night. The place often gets packed, specially during the weekends, when live bands play popular hits in English and Portuguese. Open M-Th noon-3am, F-Sa noon-4am. Live music Th-Sa starting at midnight. AmEx/MC/V.

FESTIVALS

Students run wild during the **Queima das Fitas** (Burning of the Ribbons), Coimbra's infamous week-long festival in the first or second week of May. The festivities begin when graduating seniors set fire to narrow ribbons, gifts from friends and family to commemorate their graduation; they then receive wide, ornamental replacement ribbons. The fun continues with nights of music and food in the streets of Coimbra. The **Festas da Rainha Santa,** in the first week of July, brings live choral music to the streets and the city's largest fireworks display to the sky. During even-numbered years, there are two processions of the statue of Rainha Santa (one at the beginning, one at the end), which reflect the festival's religious roots. Elderly ladies line the streets hours before the event to claim their spot on the sidewalk. During this time, folklore dance groups sometimes organize shows in front of Igreja de Santa Cruz, where participants are dressed in traditional costumes that remember the city's rural past. The firework-punctuated **Feira Popular** in the second week of July involves a giant fair full of games and carnival rides that keep the people across the river laughing and screaming all night. (€1, rides €2.)

DAYTRIPS FROM COIMBRA

CONÍMBRIGA

Joalto buses (marked Joalto or AVIC. ☎239 23 87 69) run from Coimbra (30min.; M-F 9:05 and 9:35am, Sa-Su 9:35am; €2.10; return M-F 1 and 6pm, Sa-Su 6pm). The buses from Coimbra leave from the first bus stop on the left when facing the train station. The buses going to Conímbriga are often marked as Condeixa, so be sure to confirm the destination with the bus driver. Buses run more frequently to Condeixa, 2km from Conímbriga (25min.; M-F every 30min. 6:30am-8:30pm, Sa noon, 1pm; €1.79). Come on a weekday morning and leave at 1pm, or trek 25-30min. to Condeixa. The bus stop is across from the church tower. Taxis (☎239 94 12 43, about €5) are more expensive but a secure bet.

The Ruínas de Conímbriga is Portugal's largest preserved Roman site, and it was already a prosperous village prior to the arrival of the Romans in the second half of the first century BC. Unfortunately, the enormous town wall wasn't enough to protect the city from barbarian invasion after the fall of the Empire, and by the end of the AD fifth century, Conímbriga was abandoned. What remains are intricate floor mosaics and crumbling walls in the shape of the rooms they once divided. (Open daily Oct-May 10am-6pm, June-Sept. 9am-8pm. Ticket office closes 30min. before the ruins. €3; seniors, students under 25, and all under 14 free. Su before 2pm free.) The ticket for the ruins includes the **Museu Monográfico de Conímbriga,** which displays ancient weapons, coins and pottery, the oldest dating back to the Bronze Age in the 10th century BC. (☎239 94 91 10; www.conimbriga.pt. Open Tu-Su Oct-May 10am-6pm, June-Sept. 9am- 8pm.)

BUÇACO FOREST AND LUSO

Buses run from Coimbra to Luso (45min.; M-F 7:35am, 12:30, 3:30, 5:30, 7:30pm, Sa 9am; €2.90) and continue to Buçaco. Buses to Coimbra depart a few blocks from the Luso tourist office, by the fountain in front of the bathrooms. (45min.; M-F 7:28, 8:53, am, 2:20, 6:28 pm, Sa 10:28; €2.90.) To get to the palace and convent, walk straight up the hill from the bus stop, past the souvenir stands. At the end, a green national park sign will direct you up the stone steps to a dirt trail, which eventually runs into the road. Stay on the road until you reach a pond on the right and a stairway with a stream down its center. Take the steps up and turn left at the top. You'll reach a small parking lot; the road on the left goes to the hotel. It's a 25min. uphill climb from the bus stop to the palace. (☎231 93 92 26; fax 231 93 90 06. Open M-F 9am-7pm, Sa-Su 10am-1pm and 3-5pm.)

Nature lovers have never had it so good. Buçaco is home to Portugal's most revered forest, a 105 hectare hiking wonderland, and national monument since 1943. Portuguese have escaped to this forest for centuries: Benedictine monks settled the Buçaco area in the 6th century, established a monastery, and remained in control until the 1834 disestablishment of all religious orders. The forest owes its fame to the Carmelites, who arrived here, barefoot and set on a life of seclusion, nearly 400 years ago. Selecting the forest for their *desertos* (isolated dwellings for penitence), the Carmelites planted over 700 exotic types of trees and plants brought from around the world by missionaries. In the center of the forest, adjoining the old Carmelite convent, is Dom Carlos's exuberant **Palácio de Buçaco.** Now a luxury hotel, the building is an attention-grabbing display of neo-Manueline architecture. The *azulejos* depict scenes from Camões' Os Lusíadas, the great Portuguese epic about the Age of Discovery (see **Literature,** p. 576). (☎231 93 92 26. Palace interior open to guests only. Convent open Tu-Sa 9am-12:30pm and 2-5:30pm, €0.60) In the forest itself, landmarks include the lovely **Fonte Fria** (Cold Fountain), the **Vale dos Fetos** (Fern Valley), and the **Porta de Rainha** (Queen's Gate). A 1hr. hike along the Via Sacra leads past 17th-century chapels and the **Obelisco á Batalha do Buçaco** (Battle of Buçaco Monument) to a sweeping panorama from the **Cruz Alta.** If you find yourself addicted to the natural beauty of Luso, **Pensão Astória ❷**, down the street from the tourist office, has sparkling, modest rooms. (R. Emidio Navarro. ☎231 93 91 82. High season singles €25; doubles €40. Low season €20/30.)

Stop at Luso's **tourist office,** R. Emidio Navarro, 136, downhill from the bus stop, to pick up detailed maps outlining the different hikes and routes, ranging from a 1hr. nature walks to a 3hr. historical hike. Free **internet** access available. (☎231 93 91 33. Open July 1-Sept. 15 M-F 9:30am-12:30pm and 2-6pm, Sa-Su 10am-1pm and 3pm-5pm; Sept. 16- June 30 daily from 9:30am-12:30pm and 2-6pm.) Relax at **Termas do Luso,** a spa situated over natural hot springs in Luso. The spa offers reasonably priced massages (€17 for 30min.) and a wide variety of other services. (R. Apartado, 1. ☎231 93 79 10. www.termasdoluso.com. Open M-Sa 8am-noon and 4-7pm.) Fill your bottle with free natural spring water near the spa entrance.

AVEIRO ☎234

Small, tranquil canals detailed with footbridges and gondola-like *moliceiros* (curved boats) wind through the historic heart of Aveiro (pop. 80,000), the "Venice of Portugal." The Ria de Aveiro, a network of canals, industrial ports and salt pans that covers 65 sq. km, surrounds the city, but Aveiro has access to the sea at only one point: Barra. Many come to Aveiro to delight in its classic architecture, delicious pastries, and the Museu de Aveiro, the convent where the canonized princess Santa Joana once lived. Visited primarily by European tourists, Aveiro is still a hidden treasure to the rest of the world.

TRANSPORTATION

Trains: Lg. Estação (☎234 38 16 32), end of Av. Dr. Lourenço Peixinho. To: **Braga** (2hr., 26 per day 4:42am-9:15pm, €6-17.50); **Coimbra** (1hr., 32 per day 6:12am-2:27am, €5-13.50); **Lisboa** (5hr., 19 per day 6:50am-2:27am, €13-25); **Ovar** (every 20min., 33 per day 5:45am-11:30pm, €1.80); **Porto** (45min., 47 per day 5:45am-11:30pm, €2.10).

Ferries: TransRia (☎234 33 10 95) ferries (no cars) depart for the beach at **São Jacinto** from the dock next to the bus stop at Barra (15 per day M-F 6:30am-1am, Sa-Su 7:25am-1am, last return at 1am; €1.05 one-way). Take the bus that says Costa Nova across the canal from the tourist office to the stop at the Barra rotary. (20min.; 13 per day M-F 7:10am-12:45am, Sa-Su 8:25am-12:45am; bus and ferry €2.60 1-way.)

Taxis: Near the train station on Av. Lourenço Peixinho and along the canal in Pr. Humberto Delgado. **Central Radio** taxis, ☎234 38 57 99.

ORIENTATION AND PRACTICAL INFORMATION

The heart of Aveiro is split by the **Canal Central** and its parallel street, **Avenida Dr. Lourenço Peixinho,** which runs straight from the train station to **Praça Humberto Delgado,** a big rotary fed by eight different streets. The **tourist office** is next to this intersection, off to the right from the train station. The fishermen's quarter, **Beira Mar,** is behind the tourist office, between the canal and the river; its central square, **Praça do Peixe,** is surrounded by restaurants. The residential district, where Aveiro's monuments lie, is on the other side of the Canal Central. From Pr. Humberto Delgado, **Rua Coimbra** runs past **Praça de República** and **Praça Marquês de Pombal** before intersecting the large **Rua Miguel de Bombarda,** which leads to the museum and the youth hostel.

Tourist Office: R. João Mendonça, 8 (☎234 42 07 60; fax 42 83 26). From the train station, go straight on Av. Dr. Lourenço Peixinho until you reach the bridge and Pr. Humberto Delgado (15min.); the tourist office is just past the intersection, on the right. English, French, and Spanish spoken. Staff provides information, maps, and bus, ferry, and train schedules. Open daily 9am-8pm.

Currency Exchange: Banks lining Av. Dr. Lourenço Peixinho are generally open M-F 8:30am-3pm. **ATMs** can be found on Av. Dr. Lourenço Peixinho, Pr. Humberto Delgado, and Pr. Marquês de Pombal.

Laundromat: Lavanderias Popular, Pr. 14 de Julho, 6 (☎234 42 39 53). €2-3 per piece. Open M-F 9am-12:30pm and 2:30-7pm, Sa 9am-1pm.

Police: Pr. Marquês de Pombal (☎234 34 05 26).

Pharmacy: Farmácia Central, R. dos Mercadores, 26/28 (☎234 42 38 70). Around the corner from the tourist office. Open M-F 9am-7pm, Sa 9am-1pm.

Hospital: Hospital Distrital de Aveiro, Av. Dr. Artur Ravara (☎234 37 83 00), near the park across the canal from the tourist office.

Internet Access: Aveiro Digital (☎234 40 02 07) in Pr. da República behind the statue of José Estévão. Free. Sign up and hang around until your name is called. 30min. limit. Open M-F 9am-7pm, Sa 10am-6pm. **Instituto Português da Juventude,** in the same building as the youth hostel. Free internet access. Open daily 9am-8pm.

Post Office: Main office, Pr. Marquês de Pombal (☎234 38 08 40), across the canal and up R. Coimbra. Open M-F 8:30am-6:30pm. Second **branch,** Av. Dr. Lourenço Peixinho, 169B (☎234 38 04 90), 2 blocks from the train station. Open M-F 8:30am-6:30pm. **Postal Code:** North of the canal 3800, south 3810.

ACCOMMODATIONS AND CAMPING

Inexpensive *pensões* line the streets of the old town, north of Pr. Humberto Delgado, and on the side of the canal with the tourist office; look for signs for "*quartos*" or "*dormidas.*" Prices fall in winter. The youth hostal is the best budget option, a 15-20min. walk from the tourist office on R. das Pombas.

Pousada da Juventude de Aveiro (HI), R. das Pombas, 96 (☎234 42 05 36). On the backside of the yellow building. Simpler than most *pousadas* and far from the center, with unbeatable prices. Big breakfast. Internet included. Reception 8am-noon and 6pm-midnight. Lockout noon-6pm. Dorms €9; doubles €18, with bath €22. AmEx/MC/V. ❶

Residencial Palmeira, R. de Palmeira, 7-11 (☎234 42 25 21). On the corner with R. Salmeiras. Newly renovated rooms, all with dark wood furniture, cable TV, sparkling hardwood floors, bath, and hair dryer. Free internet access. Breakfast included. Reserve ahead for summer weekends. June-Sept. singles €30, doubles €40, triples €50, quads €60; Oct.-May €20/30/40/55. MC/V. ❸

Pensão Estrela, R. José Estévão, 4 (☎234 42 38 18). Well-located *residencial* with a family atmosphere and a huge winding staircase. Rooms are modestly decorated but meticulously cleaned. Breakfast included. July-Aug. singles €30, doubles €35-40; Sept.-May €20/30. Cash only. Across the street, **Hospedaria dos Arcos,** R. José Estevão, 47 (☎234 38 31 30), owned by family members of Estrela, offer similar accommodations for about €5 less. Cash only. ❸

Camping Municipal de São Jacinto (☎234 33 12 20), in São Jacinto. Take the bus to Barra (20min., 21 per day 7:10am-12:45am, €1.60), and then ferry to São Jacinto (16 per day 6:15am-11:50pm; €1, round-trip €1.70). Provides basic amenities, including free hot showers and baths. Electricity €0.75. Reception 8am-7pm in summer and 8am-5pm in winter. Open Feb.-Nov. €1.84 per person, €1.02 per tent and per car. ❶

FOOD

Aveiro is famous for its *ovos moles* (sweetened egg yolk wrapped in paper-thin casings), which are traditionally packed into small decorative wooden barrels. For something a little more substantial, check out the seafood restaurants which circle the fish market off Pr. do Peixe (Fish Square) in the old town, a few blocks behind the tourist office. **Supermercado Pingo Doce,** R. Batalhão de Caçadores, 10, is across the canal from the tourist office, inside the mall (☎234 38 60 42. Open daily 9am-10pm.)

Restaurante Zico, R. José Estévão, 52 (☎234 42 96 49), off Pr. Humberto Delgado. A friendly, diner-like restaurant marked by a dramatic yellow "Z," Zico cooks up delicious plates of typical Portuguese cuisine. Entrees €8-11, abundant half portions €5.50-6.50. Open M-Sa 8am-midnight. Cash only. ❶

Pizzico Pizzaria, Lg. da Pr. do Peixe, 24 (☎234 42 45 09). An Italian menu in the middle of "Fish Square," a stylish interior, and artistic plates all make Pizzico stand out. Pizza €6-9, entrees €8-12. Open daily noon-11pm. MC/V. ❷

SIGHTS

The old town's main attraction is the **Museu de Aveiro,** Av. Sta. Joana Princesa. The museum, housed in the former Mosteiro de Jesus, honors the devout princess who retreated to the monastery in 1472 against her father's will. In the **Sala do Túmulo de Santa Joana,** *azulejo* panels depict the story of her life, and beneath the magnificent gilded Baroque ceiling lies one of the most famous works of art in Portugal—Santa Joana's Renaissance tomb, supported by the heads of four angels. Renovations expected to finish in December 2008. (☎234 42 32 97; www.ipmuseus.pt. Open Tu-Su 10am-1pm and 2-5:30pm. €3, students and seniors €1.50, under 14 free. Su before 2pm free.) Another popular attraction is the 16th-century **Igreja da Misericórdia** in Pr. República, across the canal and a block uphill from the tourist office. Striking blue *azulejos* cover much of the wall space. (☎234 42 67 32. Open M-F 9am-5:30pm.) Take advantage of the **BUGA free bike rentals** in front of the shopping mall, and follow the canal to Aveiro's **salt pans.** You'll eventually be biking with water on both sides, and occasionally salt accumulates forming a miniature white desert. The salt pans were a source of wealth for the city until the 16th century, when storms raised the sand bars and blocked off access to the sea for nearly 200 years.

BEACHES AND ENTERTAINMENT

The beach towns near Aveiro boast beautiful sand dunes. **Barra** and **Costa Nova** can be reached by bus from the central canal or train station stops (20min., M-F 21 per day 7:05am-12:40am, €1.60). Distant beaches, like the pine-scented natural reserve at the Dunas de São Jacinto (10km), are accessible by ferry (see **Ferries, p. 690**). Other popular beaches are located in **Ovar,** accessible by train (every 20-30 min, €1.80).

At night, head to Beira Mar, where the bars around Praça do Peixe overflow with people. From the *praça*, follow the small canal to the Canal de S. Roque, which runs parallel to the lagoon and is lined with great places to bar hop. For live Latin music, head to the always popular **Azúcar&Salsa,** Cais de São Roque, 82, down the canal, just after the small white bridge. Wednesdays are salsa nights. (☎234 42 21 11. Open Tu-Su until 2am.) For dancing, check out **Club 8,** Cais do Paraíso, 19. From the tourist office, cross Pr. Humberto Delgado and go right along the canal. Where the canal splits, take the bridge over the left arm of the canal and go left. (☎917 75 58 61. Open Th-Sa midnight-6am.)

GUARDA ☎271

A granite stronghold situated over 1km above sea level, Guarda (pop. 27,000) is Portugal's highest city. Whether it's the chilly temperatures generated by the altitude or the icy feel of the cathedral and its Gothic architecture, things are colder here. Guarda's residents have survived centuries of physical isolation and notoriously harsh winters. Two of the town's epithets, *fria* (cold) and *fuerte* (strong), allude to this legacy. But don't be fooled by the cool breeze; Guarda's inhabitants are some of the most warm and friendly in Portugal. Guarda offers visitors relaxation, countryside, and a few remnants of centuries past.

The **Sé** (cathedral) is a blend of architectural styles, built over 150 years. One of its details speaks to the city's Portuguese pride; on the rooftop is a posterior-shaped fountain facing Spain, known to locals as the Cu de Guarda. (☎271 21 12 31. Open Tu-Su 9am-noon and 2-5pm. Free.) The nearby **Museu da Guarda** has an archaeological and ethnographic collection as well as regional painting and sculpture. (☎271 21 34 60; www.ipmuseus.pt. Open Tu-Su approx. 10am-12:30pm and 2-5:30pm. General admission €2, seniors €1, students and teachers free, and. Free Su before 12:30pm.) It's also worth scrambling up the rocks to the castle ruins for a 360° view; from Pr. Luis de Camões take R. Miguel Alarcão and go right at Lg. João Soares.

Inexpensive *pensões* and *residenciais* are plentiful Pr. Luis de Camões, but fill up quickly on weekends. **Residencial Filipe ❶,** R. Vasco da Gama, 9, has well-decorated, medium-sized rooms, all equipped with TV, phone, and spotless private bathrooms. It's only a block from Pr. Luis de Camões, 200m ahead of the public park. (☎271 22 36 58/9. Breakfast included. Singles €17.50-20, doubles 25-€30, triples €40. AmEx/MC/V.) Just down the street is **Pensão Aliança ❷,** R. Vasco da Gama, 8-A, which has comparable rooms for a few euro less, with private bath and TV. (☎271 22 22 35. Breakfast included. Singles €15, with A/C €20; doubles €25/40; triples €30/50; quads €40/60. €2 less without breakfast. MC/V.) Traditional restaurants abound in the historical district; the oldest and best is **Restaurante A Floresta ❶,** R. Francisco de Passos, 40. Try Guarda's *morcelas torradas* (barbecued black pudding) in the stone-walled interior. (☎271 21 23 14. Entrees €5-10. Open daily noon-4pm and 7-11pm. MC/V.)

Buses depart Guarda from Centro Coordenador de Transportes, R. António Sérgio (☎271 22 15 15), a 10min. walk from town. **Rede Expressos** runs to: **Braga** (4-5hr.; M-F 7 per day 8:10am-6:40pm, Sa 5 per day 8:10am-6:20pm, Su 6 per day 10:45am-6:40pm; €14); **Coimbra** (3hr.; M-F 4 per day 6:15am-6:40pm, Sa 8:05am,

Su 4 per day 10:45am-6:45pm; €11.80); **Faro** (9-10hr.; 9 per day M-F 6:15am-6pm, Sa-Su 5-6 per day, 8:30am-6pm; €22.50); **Lisboa** (4hr.; M-F 8 per day 7am-6pm, Sa 2 per day 8:30am, 2:15pm; Su 8 per day 8:10am-7:30pm; €14.50); and **Castelo Branco** (1hr.; 7 per day M-Th 7am-9:15pm, F-Su 7am-10:45pm; €9:20). **Taxis** (☎271 22 18 63 or 271 23 91 63) to town cost about €3.

The tourist office and Guarda's cathedral lie on either side Praça Luis de Camões. To get to the plaza from the bus station, exit from the upper level and turn right onto R. do Nuno Alvares Pereira, walking uphill for several blocks. Continue straight past Jardim José de Lemos on your left. At the peak of the park, continue straight until you reach Residencial Filipe, and then go left onto R. do Comércio, just past the white church. An open square will be ahead on the left; the **tourist office** is around the corner, and has free **internet** access and city and regional maps. (☎271 20 55 30. Open daily 9am-12:30pm and 2-5:30pm.) **Internet** access is also available at **CyberCentro Guarda** located directly across the tourist office on the other side of the Pç. Luis de Camões. (☎271 23 22 50. €1.50 per hr. Open M-F 9am-10pm.) The bank **Millennium BCP** is next door to Residencial Filipe and has a 24hr. **ATM** outside. (☎271 20 51 60. Open M-F 10am-3:30pm.) Local services include **Hospital Distrital,** on Av. Rainha D. Amelia (☎271 20 02 00), and the **police,** on Lg. Frei Pedro (☎271 22 20 22). The **post office,** Lg. São João de Deus, 24, behind the Museu da Guarda, can send and receive faxes. (☎271 20 00 30. Open M-F 8:30am-6pm, Sa 9am-12:30pm.) **Postal Code:** 6300.

DAYTRIP FROM GUARDA: SORTELHA. Sortelha is a ghostly medieval village seemingly in the middle of nowhere, especially those to the carless traveler. The town's name literally means "ring," a name chosen for the fortified 13th-century castle walls that enclose the old town. Inside, the cobblestone streets wind like snakes, creating a labyrinth reminiscent of Lisboa's Alfama district; indeed, both were founded during the Arabic occupation. Fortunately, the area is so small that it is nearly impossible to get lost. One of the town's highlights is its **castle,** whose ruins are perched on the edge of a dangerously steep cliff. The castle walls run the perimeter of the village—the vertigo-immune are free to meander the edges. In the center is **Igreja da Nossa Senhora das Neves,** also known as the Igreja Matriz, with its beautiful Arabic mudéjar-style ceiling (open Su 10am-noon). Sortelha's best party is on August 15, the **Festa de Santo António;** the celebration fills the street with returning emigrants, and sometimes includes a bullfight.

By the castle gate is **Dom Sancho I ❸,** Lg. do Corro, which advertises "medieval food" and isn't far off the mark; the menu draws heavily on meat and other timeless staples. Vegetarian options are limited to salads. (☎271 38 82 67. Entrees €11-17. Open Tu-Sa noon to 3pm and 7-10pm. AmEx/MC/V) The **tourist office** is in a kiosk to the left after entering the castle gate. (☎800 262 788; Open M and W-Su 10am-12:30pm and 2:30pm-4:30pm.) V. Monteiro buses to nearby Sabugal leave from platform 9 of the Guarda bus station (☎271 75 34 05. 1hr.; M-F 5 per day 10:15am-6pm, Sa 12:15pm, return M-F 6:45am-1:30pm, Sa 8:30am; €2.30). From the bus station in Sabugal, take a taxi to Sortelha. **Taxis** (☎271 38 81 82) gather in town, a 3min. walk from the bus station. Exiting the station through the cafe, go to the intersection on the right, then take a left onto Av. dos Bombeiros Voluntarios. About 50m later, take a right at the fire station and walk into Lg. da Fonte, where taxis congregate in the center. A ride to the castle gate in Sortelha costs about €10. You can ask the driver to return to the castle to pick you up a few hours later for no extra charge.

PARQUE NATURAL DA SERRA DA ESTRELA

With craggy, barren mountains lining the horizon and emerald green rivers that flow through timeworn glacial valleys, **Parque Natural da Serra da Estrela** has attracted thousands of visitors since its establishment in 1976. Several hiking trails run north-south through the park, passing small stone villages along the way. The three main **trails** are **T1** (indicated with a solid red line), **T2,** and **T3** (both marked with solid yellow lines). These three trails pass through the mountain ranges, rivers, and villages, and each covers a distance of about 80-90km. Six shorter trails—T11, T12, T13, T14, T31, and T32—marked with dotted lines—branch off the main routes.

Manteigas provides an opportunity to do several **day hikes** on portions of the trails that pass through the town. These include walking up a gradual incline along the **Rio Zezere** towards **Albergaria,** 14km south of Manteigas, as well as a more challenging 12km hike to the stunning **Poço de Inferno** waterfall. The park's weather is erratic: winter snowfall often obscures the trail markers, summer heat can be scorching, and rain is frequent. Check about weather conditions and be sure to bring extra waterproof layers and sunscreen.

In recent years, the park has played host to several other adventure sports such, including **skiing, kayaking, mountain climbing, rapelling,** and **mountain biking.** Near Manteigas, **SkiParque,** Relva da Reboleira, leads excursions into the mountains or through the Rio Zezere, and fills its slopes between December and March. (☎275 98 00 90; www.skiparque.pt. Open daily 9am- 5pm. Guided hikes €20-40 per day; kayaking €6 per hr., €17.50 per day; horseback riding €50 per day; mountain biking €12.50 per hr. Ski slopes with equipment €22-26 per day. 50min. ski classes €30 plus €5 per extra person.) **UniversoTT,** R. Almirante Gago Coutinho, 10, operates directly out of Guarda and provides similar services, including rapelling, dirt biking, and canoeing. (☎271 23 71 83; www.universott.pt.) The most popular skiing spot is **Torre,** a €15-20 cab ride from Manteigas. (☎275 31 47 08. Slopes open Nov. to mid-Apr.) **Parapente** (hang gliding) is also popular, and Serra da Estrela hosted the Parapente World Cup in 2005.

The cheapest beds in Manteigas are at **Pensão Serradalto ❸,** R. 1 de Maio, upstairs from the **restaurant ❷,** about 50m from the gas station, with bright rooms overlooking the valley and impeccable baths. (☎275 98 11 51. Breakfast included. Singles €30, doubles €35, triples €50. €5 discount two or more days. Restaurant open daily noon-3pm and 7-11pm. Entrees €7-13. Cash only.) **Camping** in the park is prohibited, except at designated sites. Consult the information offices in Guarda or Manteigas about campsites or cabins in the park. You can also camp at **SkiParque ❶,** located off the main road 6km from Manteigas. (Taxis from Manteigas €5-6. €4.25 per person, €2-2.50 per tent, €2 per car.) The best restaurant in Manteigas is **A Cascata ❷,** R. 1 de Maio, behind the gas station and down a staircase; enjoy their regional specialties. (☎275 98 21 39. Entrees €7-12. Open M-Sa noon-3pm and 7-9:30pm. Cash only.)

Buses from platform 1 of the Guarda bus station to the gas station in Manteigas run infrequently and only on weekdays (1hr.; M-F 11:30am, 5pm, return to Guarda M-F 7am, 12:50pm; €3.40). The Parque Natural da Serra da Estrela **information office** in **Guarda,** R. D. Sancho, 1, has books and detailed topographic maps of the park, with clearly illustrated trails and points of interest (☎271 22 54 54). Alternatively, the first place to get information in **Manteigas** is the information center across the street from the gas station where the bus arrives and departs. Both offices sell the invaluable *Discovering the Region of the Serra da Estrela* (€4.20), which includes maps and detailed descriptions of all trails, including altitude changes, walking times, and landmarks along the way. (☎275 98 00 60. Both offices open M-F 9am-12:30pm and 2-5:30pm.)

TRÁS-OS-MONTES

The country's roughest and most isolated region, Trás-Os-Montes ("beyond the mountains") is a land of extremes, with rugged, bewitching, landscapes and radical seasonal weather. Distinctive cultural identities have sprung up in these isolated hamlets, amongst vast expanses of wilderness, lush vegetation, rocky cliffs, and arid expanses. Trás-Os-Montes has long been home to Portugal's political and religious exiles. During the Inquisition, a sizable community of Jews chose to take shelter in these mountains. They created the area's famous vegetarian sausages, abstaining from the region's meat products in order to keep kosher. Transportation today is sparse and distances between villages can be vast; expect to spend hours on rickety buses. The difficulty in traveling through the region is not without its benefits, however, as Trás-Os-Montes remains one of the last outposts of traditional Portugal.

BRAGANÇA ☎273

Wedged in a narrow valley between two steep slopes, Bragança (pop. 37,000) is a wilderness outpost and the perfect base for exploring the Parque Natural de Montesinho, which extends into Spain. Its isolation is what makes Bragança special; it provides the chance to experience some of Portugal's best scenery as well as the hospitable culture that has thrived in this remote location.

TRANSPORTATION

The nearest train station is in **Mirandela**, 1hr. from Bragança by bus. The bus station (☎273 300 450) is at the top of Av. João da Cruz, on Rua da Estação. **Rodonorte** (☎273 30 01 80; www.rodonorte.pt) runs to **Braga** via Mirandela and **Vila Real** (4-5hr.; M-W 5 per day 6am-3:30pm, Th-F 6-8 per day 6am-5pm, Sa 8am, Su 3 per day 2-5pm; €12.50, students €11.20). Rede Expressos (☎273 33 18 26; www.rede-expressos.pt) runs to: **Coimbra** (5hr.; M-Sa 6-7 per day 6am-7pm, Su 7 per day 6am-9:30pm; €12.50); **Lisboa** (8hr.; M-Sa 9-10 per day 6am-7pm, Su 14 per day 6am-9:30pm; €16.50); **Porto** (3hr.; M-Sa 9-10 per day 6am-7pm, Su 14 per day 6am-9:30pm; €10.40); **Vila Real** (2hr.; every hr. 6am-7pm, Su until 9:30pm; €8.50); **Madrid** via **Zamora, España** (5hr.; Tu and F 1:30pm, Su 5:45pm; €42) **Santos** (☎273 30 01 80; www.santosviagensturismo.pt) goes to **Lisboa** via **Vila Real** and **Coimbra** (8hr.; M-F 5 per day 6am-4pm, Sa 4 per day 8:30am-4pm, Su 8 per day 8:30am-9:30pm; €16, students €14.40). **Taxis** (☎273 32 20 07) are at Av. João da Cruz, near the post office and bus station.

ORIENTATION AND PRACTICAL INFORMATION

The bus station is located blocks from the center of town. With your back to the station (facing bus spaces), walk left along R. da Estação. Turn left below the rotary and walk over the bridge. When you come to a grassy, plaza-like street, **Av. João da Cruz,** turn right. At the post office, bear left onto downward-sloping R. Almirante dos Reis, which leads to several budget *pensões* and the **Praça da Sé** at the heart of the old town. To reach the **fortress,** on the hill west of Pr. da Sé, take R. dos Combatentes da Grande Guerra, bear right at the fork, and continue uphill to enter through the opening in the walls.

Tourist Office: Av. Cidade de Zamora (☎273 38 12 73). From the bus station, instead of a right at Av. João da Cruz, continue straight until you reach R. de Santo António. Continue straight downhill, and turn right at the rotary. The office is downhill on the corner to your right. Offers short-term luggage storage. Open M-F 9am-12:30pm, 2-5pm, Sa 10am-12:30pm.

Currency Exchange: Caixa Geral, R. Almirante dos Reis (☎273 31 08 00), opposite the post office on the corner. Also has a 24hr. **ATM.** Open M-F 8:30am-3pm.

Police: On R. Dr. Manuel Bento (☎273 30 34 00).

Medical Services: Centro Hospitales do Nordeste, Av. Abade de Baçal (☎273 31 08 00), before the stadium on the road to Vinhais.

Internet Access: available at the **Biblioteca Municipal,** Pr. Mercado, just off Pr. da Sé (☎273 30 08 51). Open M-F 9am-12:30pm and 2-7pm. Max. 1hr. Also at **CyberCentro** (☎273 33 19 32), 2nd fl. of the *mercado municipal.* €1 per hr., students €0.72 per hr. Wi-Fi available. Open M-F 10am-11pm, Sa 10am-7pm, Su 2pm-7pm.

Post Office: Corner of R. Almirante dos Reis and R. 5 de Outubro (☎273 32 21 49). **Western Union.** Open M-F 8:30am-5:30pm, Sa 9am-12:30pm. **Postal Code:** 5300.

ACCOMMODATIONS

Cheap *pensões* and *residenciais* line Pr. da Sé and R. Almirante dos Reis. For camping a few miles outside of town on the edge of the Parque Natural de Montesinho, contact the **Parque de Campismo Municipal do Sabor** (☎273 32 26 33).

Pensão Poças, R. Combatentes da Grande Guerra, 200 (☎273 33 14 28), just off Pr. da Sé. Central location. Large and charming rooms in an old building. Reception in restaurant below. Singles €15, with bath €20; doubles €25 (all with full or ½-bath); triples without €30. AmEx/MC/V. ❶

Pousada de Juventude—Bragança (HI), Forte de São João de Deus (☎273 30 46 00, fax 30 46 01), off Av. 22 de Maio. A 15min. walk from the center of town. Plain, bunk-bed dorms with balconies. Breakfast included. Laundry €2.50. Internet €5 per hr. July-Aug. dorms €11; doubles €26, with bath €32. Sept.-June €9/22/28. AmEx/MC/V. ❶

FOOD

The region is celebrated for its *presunto* (cured ham), *salsichão* (sausages), and the local delicacy, *alheiradas* (sausages made with bread and various meats). The stores around the *mercado municipal,* several blocks up from **Pr. da Sé** (open M-Sa 8am-7pm, Su 8am-1pm) stock these and fresh produce.

Solar Bragançano, Pr. da Sé, 34, 1st fl. (☎273 32 38 75; www.solar-braganca.com). Enjoy a first-class meal in an elegant dining room complete with chandeliers, linen tablecloths and classical music. Overlooks Pr. da Sé. Entrees from €8.50-12.50. Try one of their delicious, economical omelettes (€6). *Menú* €14. Open Jan.-Oct. daily noon-3pm and 6-11pm. Nov.-Feb. Tu-Su noon-3pm and 6-11pm. AmEx/MC/V. ❷

Restaurante Poças, R. Combatentes da Grande Guerra, 200 (☎273 33 14 28), off Pr. da Sé, is popular with the local crowd. Here, you can get good, traditional Portuguese food on the cheap, mere steps from the town center. Entrees €4-9. Salads €2-4. *Menú* €10. Open 9am-11pm; meals served noon-3pm and 8-11pm. AmEx/MC/V. ❷

SIGHTS

Bragança's major sites are concentrated in the citadel on the hill above the town. From the Pr. da Sé continue down R. Combatentes da Grande Guerra, bear right at the fork, and head upwards to the fortress' walls. The 12th-century **castelo** offers a quiet reminder of the city's regal past, along with gorgeous views of the countryside. Its **Museu Militar** has a wide range of military paraphernalia, dating from medieval treaties with Spain to Portuguese campaigns in Africa. (☎273 32 23 78. Open 9-11:45am and 2-4:45pm. €1.50, Su morning free.) The *pelourinho* (pillory) in the square behind the castle has a granite pig at its base, a vestige of pagan tradition: sinners and criminals were bound there in the Middle Ages. The **Domus Municipalis,** behind the church across the square from the castle, once served as the city's municipal meeting house. The **Museu Ibérico da Máscara e do Traje,** located right across the street from the *castelo*, features an extensive collection of traditional dress and masks from the Trás-Os-Montes region and neighboring provinces. The colorful suits and fierce masks are unlike anything you would think to find in this seemingly somber region of Portugal. (Open Tu-Su 10am-12:30pm and 2-6pm. €1). The gray stone exterior of the **Igreja de Santa Maria** betrays nothing of the melding of centuries and architectural styles inside, including *mudéjar* columns and colorful Baroque carved wood. (Open daily 9am-6pm. Free.)

NIGHTLIFE AND FESTIVALS

A popular hangout, especially after 1am on weekends, is **Klaustrus Cafe,** Pr. da Sé, 16, located underground off the Pr. da Sé. A local crowd chills out in this dim, relaxed bar. (☎273 33 34 59. Beer €1. Open daily 8pm-2am.) The most important festival is the mid-August **Festa de Nossa Senhora das Graças,** which includes concerts, art exhibits, and ceramics fairs. It culminates in fireworks the night of the 21st and religious processions the following day (the local patron saint's day). For a week in mid-May, the **Festa do Estudante** celebrates students' graduation from the university.

DAYTRIP FROM BRAGANÇA

PARQUE NATURAL DE MONTESINHO. The **Parque Natural de Montesinho** covers 290 sq. mi. between Bragança and the Spanish border. Old mountain paths lead through rolling woodlands of oak, chestnut, pine, and cherry past the Rio Sabor. *Pombais pombales* (pigeon lofts) dot the landscape, and the park is home to many rare and endangered species, including the Iberian wolf, royal eagle, and black stork. Outdoor activities include horseback riding, trout fishing, and hiking. Horseback riding can be arranged at **França** (☎273 91 91 41; call ahead). Plenty of mapped hiking routes are available in the park information office in Bragança. If you have only one day, the most worthwhile trip is to **Rio de Onor,** a village near the northeast corner, on the Spanish border. Here, in accordance with an essentially communal lifestyle, the Portuguese and Spanish have lived together for centuries, intermarrying and even speaking their own dialect, *rionorés*. A stone post with a "P" for "Portugal" on one side and an "E" for "España" on the other, marks the border. The village of Sanabria, inspiration for Unamuno's *San Manuel Bueno, Martir*, is a 12km walk from Rio de Onor. Villagers cross into Spain for groceries and back into Portugal for coffee at **Cervejaria Preto,** the only bar in town. You may be fortunate enough to arrive during the **Festa dos Rapazes,** a Christmastime rite of passage for village bachelors during which they take care of the village for a week. Afterwards, their introduction to mutual responsibility is celebrated with food and dancing.

There are also several small towns that can serve as starting points for hiking trails. See the park tourism office for more information. Getting to the park is difficult without a car, and only worthwhile if you have a specific activity in mind. **Taxis** to the park run €20 one-way depending on your destination; arrange ahead for pick-up in the park. There are also rural **buses** (€1-2) that run to park destinations, including Rio de Onor. Be careful to tell the driver you want to return to Bragança later, because the bus may not run if there are no other passengers going to your specific location. Bus schedules are available at the tourist office. (☎800 20 76 09; www.stub.com.pt). For the **park information office** in Bragança at R. Cónego Albano Falcão, 5, walk downhill from the tourist office on Av. Cidade de Zamora, take the first left onto a paved street and the first left again; it's at the end of the street on the right. Park trails are unmarked, but the office has maps and can help plan hikes. (☎273 30 04 00. Open M-F 9am-12:30pm and 2-5:30pm.) Add an extra hour to your time calculation for any hike, as the trails in the park aren't well-marked and can take longer to complete than expected. The office rents out traditional houses, known as **Casas Abrigos ❹.** (☎273 30 04 00. Doubles €40; quads €80. Houses are fully equipped with kitchen and bathroom.) **Montesinho Aventura** (☎273 91 90 07; www.montesinhoaventura.com) organizes outdoor activities in the park, including camping, rock climbing, rappelling, and canoeing.

VILA REAL ☎259

Wiped out by Gothic and Muslim invasions, the region of Serra Marao was empty until the 12th century, when King Dinis established Vila Real (pop. 25,000). The medieval city overlooks the deep gorges of the Corgo and Cabril Rivers in the foothills of the Serra, and is the gateway to **Parque Natural do Alvãois,** Portugal's smallest natural park. Its 8,000 hectares of pine-covered paradise, only 15km north of Vila Real, offers excellent short hiking trails. Vila Real's most visited site is the **Casa de Mateus,** an 18th-century manor house designed to reflect symmetry and repetition wherever possible. The beautiful surrounding gardens are free for anyone to wander, but tours inside must be guided. (☎259 32 31 21. Open daily June-Sept. 9am-7:30pm; Oct. and Mar.-May 9am-1pm and 2-6pm; Nov.-Feb. 10am-1pm and 2-5pm. €7.50. Ticket to gardens €4. Gardens and guided tour of manor house and chapel. Last tour 45 min before closing.) To get there take the #1 bus from in from R. Gonçalo Cristovâo, two blocks uphill from the tourist office on your left. Get off at the Abambres stop, from there take the road directly across the rotary and walk for 10 min, the palace will be on your right. (Tours 10min. every 30 min., M-F 7:48am-8:21am. Sa 8:18am-8:21pm)

Tr. de S. Domingos, next to the Cathedral on Av. Carvalho Araújo, is full of cheap *pensões*. **Residencial S. Domingos ❶,** Tr. de S. Domingos, 33, offers charming, old-fashioned rooms with private bath, cable TV, and phone. (☎259 32 20 39. Singles €15; doubles €25; triples €30. Cash only.) **Churrasquería Real ❶,** R. Teixeira de Sousa, 14, located on a quiet street off the main thoroughfare, serves grilled meat and fish dishes to local crowds. (☎259 32 20 78. Entrees €4-7. Open M-Sa 9am-11pm. Cash only.) There is a **supermarket** (open M-F 10am-2pm and Sa 4-7pm) in the basement at Av. 1 de Maio and R. Nova, around the corner from **Espaço Internet.** The cafes along Av. Carvalho Araújo and the square offer some nightlife options.

Trains (☎808 20 82 08) run from Av. 5 de Outubro to **Porto** (3-4hr., 4-5 per day 7am-7:15pm, €9.65). From the train station, it's a 5min. walk to the town center; head up Av. 5 de Outubro, cross the bridge onto R. Miguel Bombarda, take the third left onto R. Roque da Silveira (labeled as Largo V. de Almeida on pharmacy wall), and then bear left until you reach Av. 1 de Maio. **Buses** are a quicker option. **Tamega** runs buses to **Agarez,** a small town at the entrance of of Alvâo's natural park. (☎259 32 29 28. To **Vila Merin** via Agarez 30min.; M-F 7 per day 7am-7:15pm; return trips to Vila Real M-F 7 per day 7:25am-7:40pm, Sa 8am; €1.47.) To reach the Tamega station from the Vila Real station on R. Don Pedro Castro, take a left out of the station onto R. Don Pedro Castro. When you come to a wall of barriers on your left, continue on the sidewalk and turn left onto Av. Cidade de Orense. At the end of the barriers, turn left into the parking lot, which serves as the Tamega station. **Rede Expressos** buses, R. D. Pedro de Castro, are located in the main bus station in town. Buses run to:

Bragança (2hr., 7-12 per day 10:45am-11pm, €9.40), **Lisboa** (6hr.; M-Sa 10 per day 7am-9:15pm, Su 14 per day 7:15am-9:15pm; €18), and **Porto** (1hr.; M-Sa 14 per day 7:15am-9pm, Su 8 per day 7:45am-11:15pm; €6.40). **Taxis,** including **Rádiotáxi Expresso** (☎259 32 15 31), gather along Av. Carvalho Araújo.

Most activity centers around Av. Carvalho Araújo, which forms a T with Largo Conde Amarante and Avenida 1 de Maio. The **tourist office** is on Av. Carvalho Araújo, 34. (☎259 32 28 19; www.rtsmarao.pt. Short-term luggage storage. Open Oct.-May M-Sa 9:30am-12:30pm and 2-6pm; June-Sept. M-F 9:30am-7pm, Sa-Su 9:30am-12:30pm and 2-6pm.) To reach the tourist office, turn right out of the bus station and continue down R. D. Pedro de Castro onto Av. Carvalho Araújo, a street separated in the middle by a grassy barrier. Cross to the left side of the street, and the tourism office is on the left. Local services include: **Caixa General de Depósitos,** Pr. Luís de Camões, at the end of Av. Carvalho Araújo (open M-F 8:30am-3pm); **laundry** at **Lavandaria Miracorgo,** R. Camilo Castelo Branco, 33-33A, on a small street off Av. 1 de Maio (☎259 37 28 16; open M-F 8am-1pm and 2-7pm, Sa 8am-1pm); **police,** (☎259 33 02 40), at the end of Lg. Conde Amarante; **Farmácia Almeida,** Av. Carvalho Araújo, 41-43 (☎259 32 28 74; open daily 8:30am-7:30pm); **Hospital Distrital Vila Real,** Av. da Noruega (☎259 30 05 00; from Lg. Conde Amarante, follow the road as it becomes Av. da Noruega); and the **post office,** Av. Carvalho Araújo, across and up the street from the tourist office. (☎259 33 03 00; open M-F 8:30am-6pm, Sa 9am-12:30pm). **Postal Code:** 5000.

MOROCCO

Morocco, the hazy spit of land across the Strait of Gibraltar, is 13km and worlds away from Europe. The nation contains unparalleled raw beauty, with lush valleys, enormous desert dunes, ancient imperial cities, and North Africa's highest mountains. While you may reach Morocco today by high-speed ferry rather than brigantine ship, your path has been well worn by years of cultural exchange. Moorish rule in southern Spain is manifest across the old land of *al-Andalus* in a legacy of breathtaking art, architecture, and technology, while even the Spanish language, with thousands of words derived from Arabic, testifies to centuries of fluidity between Iberia and northern Africa. Arab, African, and European influences come together gracefully in modern Morocco. Locals hawk *thuya* wood from the beaches of Essaouira next to Fez's famed blue pottery, along with movies from America and sandals from China. Donkeys hurtle down alleys past women who accessorize headscarves with Gucci shades. Today, the "Western Kingdom" continues to balance its ancient heritage with a contemporary struggle for national sovereignty, stability, and prosperity.

Let's Go coverage of Morocco is meant to feature selected highlights of the country as a side trip from Spain or Portugal, accessible from the most common travel hubs of Tangier, Casablanca, and Marrakesh. As you journey south through Iberia, skim across the strait to discover the roots of *al-Andalus* in this flourishing modern nation. It might just be the highlight of your trip.

LIFE AND TIMES

HISTORY

ANCIENT TIMES. Archaeological evidence along Morocco's Atlantic coast suggests that regions of the country have been inhabited since at least 125,000 BC. The **Berber** people arrived between 4000 and 2000 BC, and traces of their early civilization, particularly their tool use, can be seen in the High Atlas Mountains. Though the **Phoenicians** developed colonies along the coast in the ninth century BC, they exerted little control or influence over the area. After the sack of Carthage, near modern Tunis in Tunisia, the **Romans** came to control North Africa's agricultural supply. When the Pax Romana deteriorated in the AD fourth century, the Romans abandoned Morocco. By 420 the country was ruled by the **Vandals,** followed by a period of brief **Byzantine** rule. Each of these civilizations faced a similar problem: it was impossible to exert any control over the land without a reliable overland route. As a result, much of the country remained unexplored for centuries.

IMPERIAL ISLAM (AD 669-1554). Morocco achieved stability in the late seventh and early eighth centuries when **Muslim** armies invaded North Africa. Less than 50 years after the death of the prophet **Muhammed** in 632, Uqba bin Nafi al-Fihri had spread the religion and the rule of the Umayyad Dynasty across the Maghreb to Morocco. The native Berbers could not hold off the Muslim troops, making peace with Islamic governor **Musa ibn Nusayr.** Many converted to Islam, setting the stage for the invasion of Spain in 711. Arab rule was short-

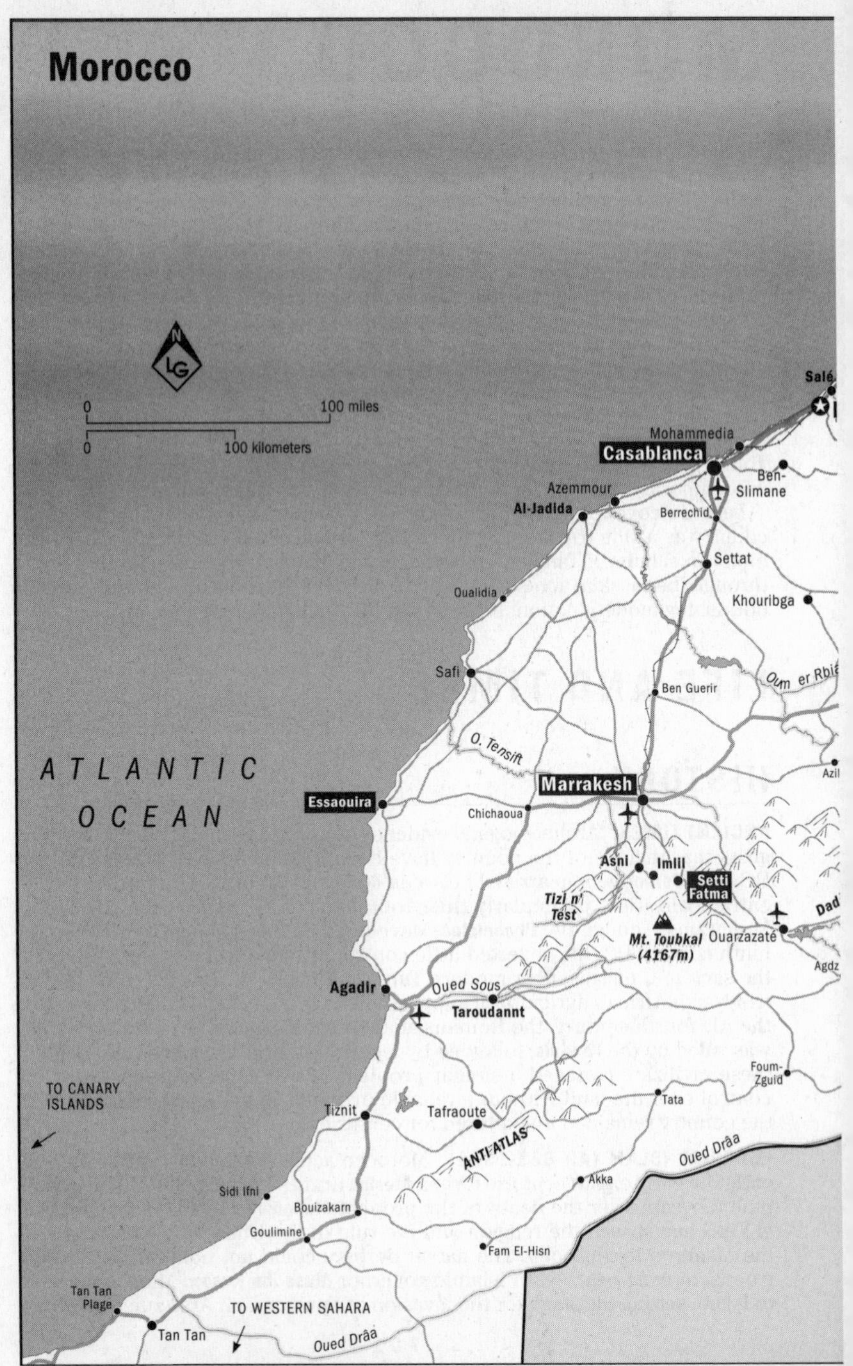
Morocco
0
100 miles
0
100 kilometers
Salé
Mohammedia
Casablanca
Ben-
Slimane
Azemmour
Al-Jadida
Berrechid
Settat
Khouribga
Oualidia
Safi
Oum er Rbia
Ben Guerir
O. Tensift
Azil
Marrakesh
ATLANTIC
OCEAN
Essaouira
Chichaoua
Asni
Imlil
Setti
Fatma
Tizi n'
Test
Mt. Toubkal
(4167m)
Ouarzazate
Dad
Agdz
Agadir
Oued Sous
Taroudannt
Foum-
Zguid
TO CANARY
ISLANDS
Tata
Tiznit
Tafraoute
ANTI-ATLAS
Oued Drâa
Akka
Sidi Ifni
Bouizakarn
Goulimine
Fam El-Hisn
Tan Tan
Plage
TO WESTERN SAHARA
Tan Tan
Oued Drâa

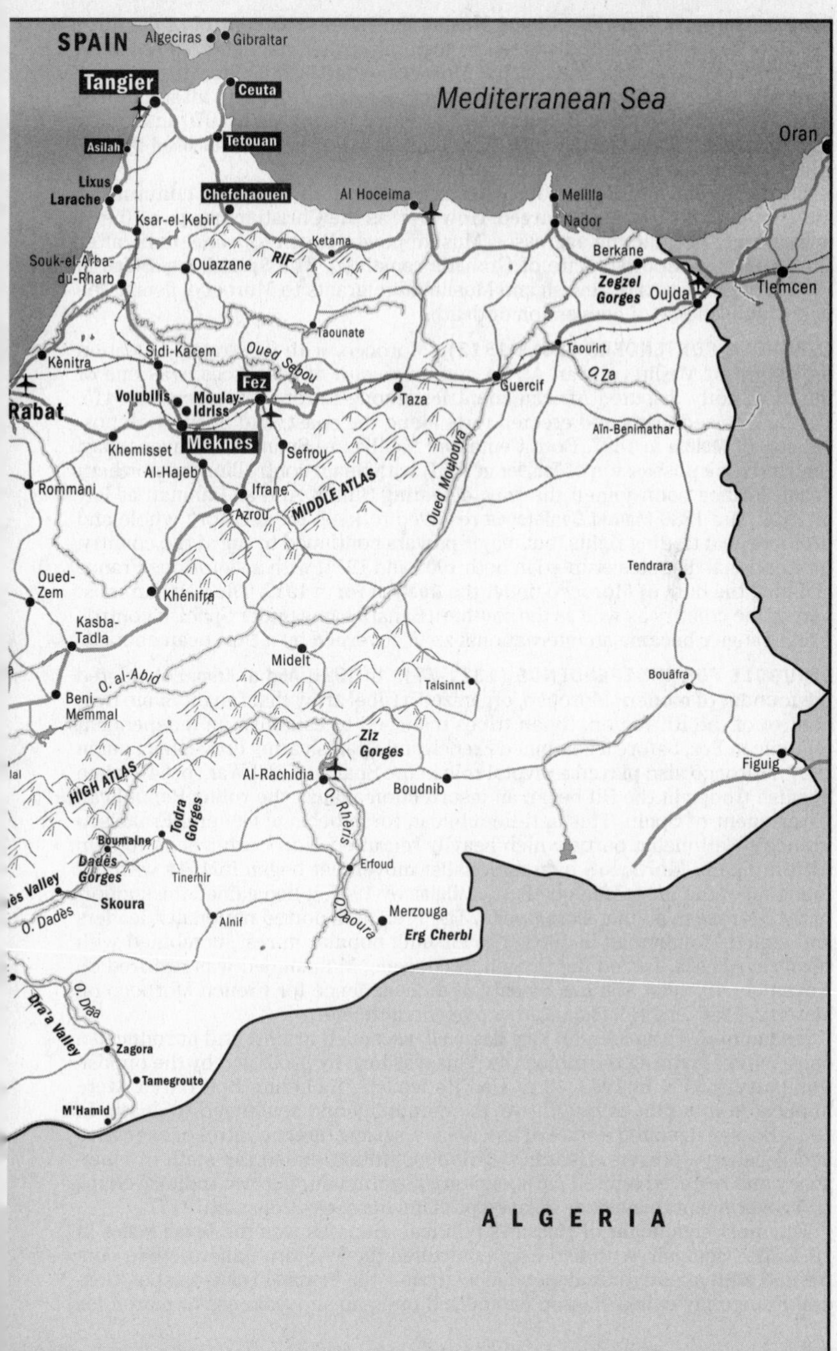
SPAIN
Algeciras
Gibraltar
Tangier
Ceuta
Mediterranean Sea
Oran
Asilah
Tetouan
Lixus
Larache
Chefchaouen
Al Hoceima
Melilla
Nador
Ksar-el-Kebir
Ketama
RIF
Berkane
Souk-el-Arba-du-Rharb
Ouazzane
Zegzel Gorges
Oujda
Tlemcen
Taounate
Kènitra
Sidi-Kacem
Oued Sebou
Taourirt
O. Za
Fez
Guercif
Taza
Volubilis
Moulay-Idriss
Rabat
Aïn-Benimathar
Meknes
Khemisset
Sefrou
Al-Hajeb
Oued Moulouya
Rommani
Ifrane
MIDDLE ATLAS
Azrou
Oued-Zem
Tendrara
Khénifra
Kasba-Tadla
Midelt
O. al-Abid
Talsinnt
Bouâfra
Beni-Memmal
Ziz Gorges
Figuig
HIGH ATLAS
Al-Rachidia
Boudnib
O. Rhèris
Todra Gorges
Boumaine
Dadès Gorges
Tinerhir
Erfoud
Skoura
O. Dadès
Alnif
O. Daoura
Merzouga
Erg Cherbi
O. Draa
Dra'a Valley
Zagora
Tamegroute
M'Hamid
ALGERIA

lived in Morocco. A series of local Muslim dynasties took control of the area, claiming descent from Muhammed to legitimize their rule. **Idris ibn Abd Allah,** after fleeing Arabia, founded the first Moroccan state in 789. Over the next few hundred years, Morocco was conquered by one minor dynasty after another, most notably the **Almoravid Dynasty,** which founded Marrakesh in 1070 and fought to repel the Christian advance in Iberian *al-Andalus*, and the **Almohad Dynasty,** which defeated the Almoravids in 1160.

During the reign of Berber dynasties in the 13th-16th centuries, cultural and intellectual links to **Iberia** resurged. However, as the Christian troops of Iberia increasingly became the aggressor, Muslim power began to wane, until, after 1248, only the Moorish state of Granada remained. The **Spanish Inquisition** in 1492 brought waves of Jewish and Muslim immigrants to Morocco, fleeing the unenviable choice of conversion or death.

EUROPEAN CONTENDERS (1415-1912). Morocco, with its strategic location on the tip of Mediterranean Africa and its wealth of resources, was one of the most hotly disputed African countries among European powers. In 1415, Portugal seized **Ceuta** and erected forts along the coast, and Spain took possession of **Melilla** in 1497. Both Ceuta and Melilla are Spanish exclaves today. England took possession of **Tangier** in 1661, with Spain controlling the northern coast. France soon joined the fray, defeating Sultan Abd-ar Rahman at Isly in 1844. The 1880 **Madrid Conference** resolved to keep the territory whole and protect equal trading rights, but major powers continued to tug at the country. International disputes erupted in both 1905 and 1911, with a victorious France claiming the bulk of Morocco under the **Treaty of Fez** in 1912. The northernmost part of the country as well as the southern Sahara came under Spanish control, while Tangier became an international zone governed by a European council.

STRUGGLE FOR INDEPENDENCE (1921-77). In 1921, **Abd al-Krim,** considered the founder of modern Morocco, organized a rebel army that fought Spain over control of the Rif region. Rifian tribes managed to establish an independent republic in Fez, before a combined French and Spanish army drove them out in 1927. Morocco also played a pivotal role in the Spanish Civil War (p. 64), when Spanish troops in the Rif began an insurrection against the ruling Republican government of Spain. This anti-Republican force became General Francisco Franco's Nationalist party, which heavily recruited Moroccan troops to help fight in Spain. Morocco's own nationalist movement began in 1944 with the founding of the Independence Party, **Istiqlal;** by 1947, it had gained the support of the Moroccan sultan, **Mohammed V.** The French deported nationalist leaders and exiled Mohammad in 1953. The ensuing popular unrest, combined with revolt in Algeria, forced the French to concede. Mohammed was restored on November 18, 1955, signing a treaty of independence for French Morocco on March 2, 1956, and Spanish Morocco one month later.

Mohammed V's successor, **King Hassan II,** ascended in 1961 and introduced a constitution favoring the monarchy. This was heavily protested by the opposition party, UNFP. In 1963, 10 of UNFP's leaders, including Ben Barka, were implicated in a plot to overthrow the monarchy and sentenced to death. In 1965, Hassan declared a state of emergency, seizing direct control of executive and legislative powers. Hassan's 1970 constitution ended the state of emergency and restored limited parliamentary government, but two military coups and governmental divisions delayed parliamentary elections until 1977.

The most significant of Hassan's political triumphs was the **Green March** in 1975. The Spanish, who had long controlled the Western Sahara, were confronted with a Saharan independence group—the **Polisario Front**—just as General Franco lay dying. Hassan capitalized on Spanish weakness to march his troops into the Sahara. He was victorious, partially due to the disorganization of the Polisario Front and the Spanish unwillingness to fight over the impoverished region. Unfortunately, a resolution to the Western Sahara dispute is still being sought. The Polisario Front gained support from Algeria, but war ravaged the Sahara until the UN declared a ceasefire in 1989.

MODERN MOROCCO (1977-2008). Today, Morocco is a constitutional monarchy. There is a parliament and Chamber of Representatives, but the king and his advisers make most important decisions. Under Hassan II, censorship squelched opposition from such groups as trade union activists and university radicals. Sluggish industrial growth, riots, drought, and the drain of war in the Western Sahara further sapped support for the government, but Morocco began to recover in the 90s. **Islamist** movements in North Africa caused concern, although Hassan's regime remained stable in comparison to those in neighboring countries. Morocco's relations with its neighbors were strained, particularly with Algeria, where illegal arms shuttling resulted in the closing of the Morocco-Algeria border in 1994. Southern Europe began to take a greater interest in Morocco, advocating tighter border controls in light of increased illegal **immigration** through Morocco.

The reign of current king **Mohammed VI** is considered to have brought progress and reform to Morocco. Not only did he release thousands of political prisoners, but in March 2002 Mohammed made waves with his semi-public marriage to a computer engineer. Traditionally, royal marriages were strictly kept secrets, and the public release of the name and photograph of the king's bride was widely seen as heralding an era of openness and modernity. Most notably, the king introduced a family code in 2004, the **Mudawana,** meant to give women more power and to equalize laws on divorce, custody, and consent. In the same year, Mohammed opened a commission investigating the human rights abuses of Hassan II, **Instance Equité et Réconciliation (IER).** Despite recent advances, a significant percentage of the Moroccan population lives below the poverty line, sometimes on less than a dollar a day. Morocco's social problems—unemployment, illiteracy, high infant mortality—remain deeply entrenched, but modernization and reform are the keywords today.

CURRENT EVENTS

The terrorist attacks of September 11, 2001, dealt a sharp blow to tourism in Morocco, as a public fear of flying and of visiting Muslim countries set in. Local authorities cracked down on suspected agents and affiliates of al-Qaeda, and in June 2002 the government arrested three Saudis on Moroccan soil, announcing that it had foiled an al-Qaeda plot to attack American and British ships in the Strait of Gibraltar. The spate of global terrorist activity since then, like the Madrid and London bombings, has not spared Morocco. Suicide bombings took place in Casablanca in 2003 and 2007, but, given the random and unpredictable nature of terrorism, travelers to Morocco face little elevated risk.

The dispute over control of the **Western Sahara** continues. In 2002, the European Union moved to send $13.3 million in aid to refugees from the Western Sahara, now displaced to southwestern Algeria. In 2007 and 2008, Morocco and the native Polisario Front undertook negotiations over the future of the region. Unfortunately, little progress has been made, with Saharan refugees facing an uncertain future and the disputed status of the territory likely to persist.

Border disputes have strained relations between Morocco and Spain, causing clashes over immigration, fishing rights, and oil exploration in disputed waters. The island of Perejil was occupied by Moroccan soldiers in late July

2002 before being retaken in a peaceful operation by an elite team of Spanish commandos. Morocco, which claims sovereignty over the island, justified sending troops there by establishing an observation post to tackle illegal immigration and drug smuggling across the Strait of Gibraltar, issues that continue to be salient for both countries.

PEOPLE AND CULTURE

LANGUAGE

Morocco is a paradise for polyglots. Although Classical Arabic is the official language of Morocco, it is rarely spoken and has become almost exclusively a written language. Most Moroccans speak French and the modern dialect of Arabic called **darija,** a compacted Arabic peppered with Spanish and French. In this book, city names appear first in English, then in Arabic. (Fez is written neither as Fès, the French spelling, nor Faas, the Arabic spelling.) A massive naming shift from French to Arabic is underway on street signs, so some of the streets mentioned in this book may go by a different title (here they are listed in both French and Arabic when necessary).

RELIGION

The religion of Islam was founded by the Arab prophet **Muhammed** in AD 622. Informed of his prophetic calling by the angel Gabriel, Muhammed is believed by Muslims to be the last of a long chain of visionaries that includes Abraham, Moses, Elijah, and Jesus. During his life, Muhammed's words and deeds were recorded in *hadith* (sayings) that make up the **Sunna,** or the "way of Muhammed." Following his death, the Muslim community split into two branches: the **Sunni** and the **Shi'a.** The Sunni wanted Muhammed's successor chosen by the Islamic community, while the Shi'ites insisted on a blood relative of the prophet. More than 99% of Moroccans are Sunni Muslim, though Morocco also has a small Jewish minority and an even smaller Christian one. Islam is the official state religion.

At the heart of the Islamic faith is the Arabic word islam, meaning submission. The believer accepts submission to the will of Allah (God) as embodied in the **Qur'an** (book of recitation). This Arabic text is considered by Muslims to be a miracle—perfect, immutable, and untranslatable. All practicing Muslims adhere to the **five pillars** of Islam: the formal profession of faith, prayer toward Mecca five times per day, alms-giving, fasting during the month of Ramadan, and, if possible, a pilgrimage to Mecca. While there is a difference between popular and orthodox Islam, Morocco is marked by a smaller theological gap between religious intellectuals and the general public than in other Arab countries. Another twist is the sect of **Sufism,** traditionally popular in Morocco. It takes a mystical approach to Islam that is based on the belief that Muslims will find the truth of God's love and knowledge through a personal experience with God. Sufis have seen a spiritual revival since the 1980s. Morocco has also had its share of Islamic **fundamentalist movements,** but the country faces substantially less religious unrest than other North African and Middle Eastern countries.

FOOD AND DRINK

EATING OUT

Moroccan chefs lavish aromatic and colorful spices on their dishes—ginger, cumin, saffron, honey, and sugar. Staples of Moroccan cuisine are couscous, tajine, and soups, with a blend of spices known as *ras al-hanut* lending the cuisine its distinctive flavor. **Tajine** is a stew of meat, vegetables, olives, and prunes named after the cone-shaped clay dish in which it is cooked. Vegetarian tajines are common as well. **Couscous** is a semolina-grain pasta about the size of sesame seeds, usually served with stewed meat or vegetables. Most Moroccan entrees include meat, but *couscous aux légumes* (couscous with vegetables) is a great vegetarian option. **Harira,** a chickpea soup, is very popular, and **baguettes, Moroccan breads,** and **honey-soaked pastries** are everywhere.

Common dishes include *poulet* (chicken), which can be prepared either *rôti* (roasted on a spit with olives) or *limon* (with lemon). Look for *kefta* (ground beef cooked in an array of herbs and spices), often served on a baguette. Other specialties include **mechoui,** whole lamb spitted over an open fire, and **pastilla,** a combination of pigeon or chicken, onions, almonds, eggs, butter, cinnamon, and sugar under a pastry shell. For a lighter treat, slurp sweet natural **yogurt** with mounds of peaches, nectarines, or strawberries, or try an oily Moroccan **salad** with finely chopped tomatoes, cucumbers, and onions. Snackers can munch on briny olives, roasted almonds, dried chickpeas, and cactus buds. **Lunchtime** runs from noon to 2pm, **dinner** from 7 to 9pm. If a service charge isn't automatically included, a 10% **tip** should suffice.

DRINKING

Despite the Islamic prohibition against **alcohol,** Moroccan, French, and Spanish wines can be found in supermarkets and restaurants. Moroccan bars are entirely male and often frequented largely by foreigners. More pleasant are the many **coffee houses** where you can relax with inexpensive Moroccan and French-pressed coffee and espresso. **Moroccan mint tea,** green tea steeped with mint leaves and saturated with sugar, defines the rhythm of the day in Morocco. Whether it is a steaming glass in the *kasbah* or a shared pot in an Atlas village, savor the ritual and the company. When you leave, you may discover you have become as addicted as most Moroccans.

CUSTOMS AND ETIQUETTE

TABOOS. Avoid clothing that exposes too much flesh. Modest clothing for both men and women is recommended, particularly in more rural areas. Even properly dressed non-Muslims are barred from entering many of Morocco's active mosques. Taboo topics to avoid in conversation with Moroccans include sex, Israel and Palestine, the royal family, and the Western Sahara.

PUBLIC BEHAVIOR. Tourists in larger areas are susceptible to the advances of Moroccans offering to guide them. If you refuse, be polite but insistent. Western women tend to attract attention from Moroccan men. In general, the best way to react is not at all. Toning down public visibility is always smart.

TABLE MANNERS. A traditional Moroccan meal begins with handwashing. Dinner may be served from a communal dish at a low, round table. Avoid directly using your left hand when eating, as this hand is traditionally reserved for personal hygiene. In more personal settings, such as in a Moroccan home, vocally praising the food is important.

THE ARTS

Art is a constant presence in Morocco. The traditional and contemporary art scene in Morocco has an undeniable vibrancy, whether through architecture, handicrafts, literature, dance, or song. Foreign fascination with Morocco is nothing new, as the country has entranced Western painters, writers, and travelers for centuries. Painters like Eugene Delacroix helped spread the idea of Orientalism with his exoticized, 19th century images of souks and sultans, but today's scene is one of hybrid literature, bursting colors, and thumping beats.

ART AND ARCHITECTURE

Moroccan **mosques** (sometimes called *djemma* or *masjid*) unite Islamic culture and devotion in elegant and functional places of worship. The *qibla* (wall) contains the *mihrab* (prayer niche) and faces Mecca. Attached to most mosques, Qur'anic *medersas* (schools, also *madrasas*) have classrooms, libraries, and a prayer hall around a central courtyard and fountain. **Islamic art** avoids portraying people, animals, and plants, and as a result it is rich in colorful geometric designs on tiles, woodwork, stone, and ceramics. **Calligraphy,** particularly elegant illuminations of Qur'anic verses, melds religious imagery with high art. Sultans reserved their most dazzling designs for imperial **palaces,** with long, symmetrical reception and dwelling rooms studded with decorative gates, hidden gardens, and tiny pools and fountains. **Berber architecture** in the Atlas Mountains and the southern desert, in contrast, is stark and enclosed. Kasbahs, monumental fortress-like structures, feature plain facades, thick walls, central courtyards, narrow passageways, and simple high towers. Walled Berber villages, known as *qsour* (or a *qsar*), house densely packed mud-brick houses.

R-E-S-P-E-C-T. Non-Muslims are usually prohibited from entering Moroccan mosques, although visitors may glimpse the splendor of interior courtyards from doorways. Non-Muslim guests should keep a respectful distance during prayers, which occur five times per day.

CRAFTS

Morocco is a paradise for **carpet** connoisseurs, with astounding regional patterns, colors, and materials, while the leather industry is equally renowned. The glazed tiles that make up a *zellij*, or **mosaic,** can be found on everything from mirrors to tables, but Moroccan **ceramics** are just as ubiquitous and just as striking. Vibrant swirls of blue, green, yellow, and turquoise mark dishes of all shapes and sizes, and Fez is particularly famous for its blue-and-white designs. Saharan and Berber **terra cotta** ware is also common. The south is known for **silver** jewelry, often inlaid with colorful stones or glass. Moroccan **woodwork,** too, is impressive; craftsmen transform blocks of cedar into delicate, intricately carved objets d'art. Moroccan *souqs* (markets) are filled with these local handicrafts. **Bargaining** is serious business, as much a cultural art form as an everyday activity. Engage with vigor: a reasonable final price should be about 50% of your seller's original quote. If you hit a standstill, walk out the door: the owner may just chase after you with a better offer.

MUSIC

In the north, a hybrid genre known as **Andaloussi** is played on instruments like the *bendir* (tambourine), *oud* (lute), and *darbuqa* (hand drum), setting classical poetry against complex musical structures. Developed in Granada in the ninth century, Arab-Andalucian music took hold in Morocco after the Muslim expulsion from Spain in 1492. **Berber** folk music is a communal, emotive celebration of life and art, often incorporating dance in village performances and rituals. **Gnaoua,** a style of hypnotic trance music with roots in sub-Saharan Africa, makes its mark with an annual festival in **Essaouira** (p. 748). Moroccan popular music is heavily influenced by **Rai,** a rebellious, polyglot pop born in urban Algeria. International superstars in the Maghreb canon include **Cheb Mami, Rachid Taha,** and **Cheb Khaled.**

LITERATURE

IN TRANSLATION. Moroccan intellectuals in the 1930s were instrumental precursors of the writers who are active today. Moroccan writers work in Arabic, French, and Spanish, and much of this work can be found in translation. Paul Bowles published the tales of storyteller **Mohammad Mrabet** in the 60s and 70s in books such as *The Lemon* and *M'hashis.* In *Dreams of Trespass: Tales of a Moroccan Girlhood,* **Fatima Mernissi** writes about the constraints facing women in a Fez harem in the 1950s. Contemporary, internationally acclaimed writers include **Mohamed Choukri, Driss Chraïbi, Mohamed Zafzaf,** and **Driss El Khouri.**

ON MOROCCO. Most foreign literature focuses on the country's intoxicating culture and landscape. *In Morocco,* by **Edith Wharton,** describes her travels through Rabat, Salé, Fez, and Meknes in the early 20th century. *The Voices of Marrakech,* by Bulgarian Nobel laureate **Elias Canetti,** eloquently records a European Jew's encounter with the Jewish community of Morocco in the 50s. In these same years, Morocco was a haven for expatriates and foreign writers like **Paul Bowles, Tennessee Williams, Jack Kerouac,** and **William S. Burroughs.** No reading list would be complete without *The Sheltering Sky, The Spider's House,* and *Days: Tangier Journal,* all by Bowles. For insight into the country's social history, pick up *The House of Si Abd Allah,* edited by noted scholar **Henry Munson,** which recounts an oral history of a Moroccan family.

SPORTS AND RECREATION

Moroccans are passionate about **soccer. Basketball** is a distant runner-up but has widespread appeal. The country also has a history of Olympic medalist track stars, and annual marathons in the Atlas Mountains and in Marrakesh make Morocco a prime destination for **runners. Skiing** is common in the Atlas Mountains (from late December to early March), and breathtaking **walking** and **trekking** can be undertaken across the country, particularly in the Rif and Atlas ranges. **Watersports** are popular on the Atlantic coast, and Morocco is also a popular destination for **cyclists** and **mountain bikers.**

NATIONAL HOLIDAYS

The following table lists national holidays. The dates of all Muslim holidays, which begin at sundown before the day listed, are based on the lunar calendar and are valid for 2009.

DATE	HOLIDAYS
January 1	New Year's Day
January 11	Independence Manifest
May 1	Labor Day
August 14	Reunification Day
August 20	Anniversary of the King's and People's Revolution
August 21	Young People's Day—celebrates the king's birthday
November 6	Anniversary of the Green March on Western Sahara
November 18	Independence Day
August 21-September 19	Ramadan
September 20	Eid al-Fitr
November 27	Eid al-Adha
December 18	Islamic New Year

ESSENTIALS

The information in this section is designed to help travelers get their bearings once they are in Morocco. For info about general travel preparations (including passports and permits, money, health, packing, international transportation, and more), consult the Essentials section at the beginning of this guide.

ENTRANCE REQUIREMENTS

Passport: Required for all citizens of United Kingdom, Canada, Australia, New Zealand, South Africa, Ireland, and the United States.

Visa: Required in addition to passport for citizens of South Africa.

International Driving Permit (p. 34). Required for all those planning to drive in Morocco, although foreign licenses with photo ID may be accepted.

EMBASSIES AND CONSULATES

In Morocco, most embassies and consulates are open Monday through Friday from around 8am to noon; some reopen after lunch until 6pm.

British Embassy: 28 Av. SAR Sidi Mohammed, Souissi, Rabat (☎+212 37 63 33 33). **Consulates:** Villa Les Sallurges, 36 Rue de la Loire, Polo, Casablanca (☎+212 022 85 74 00); Trafalgar House, 9 Rue Amerique du Sud, Tangier (☎+212 39 93 69 39).

Canadian Embassy: 13 bis, Jaafar As-Saddik, BP 709, Agdal, Rabat (☎+212 37 68 74 00; www.dfait-maeci.gc.ca/morocco).

Irish Honorary Consulate: COPRAGRI Bldg., Bd. Moulay Ismail km 6300, Route de Rabat, Aïn Sebaâ, Casablanca (☎+ 212 22 66 03 06).

Australian Embassy: Refer to the Canadian Embassy in Rabat (above). In case of emergency, contact any Commonwealth embassy.

New Zealand Embassy: Refer to the New Zealand Embassy in Spain (p. 11). In case of emergency, contact any Commonwealth embassy.

South African Embassy: 34 Rue de Saadiens, Rabat (☎+212 37 70 67 60).

US Embassy: 2 Av. de Mohammed El Fassi, Rabat (☎+212 037 76 22 65, after-hours 76 96 39). Consulate: 8 Bd. Moulay Youssef, Casablanca (☎+212 22 22 14 60).

TRANSPORTATION

BY PLANE

If you hope to see a lot of Morocco in a short time, flying may be your best option. **Royal Air Maroc** (www.royalairmaroc.com), Morocco's national airline, flies to and from most major cities in Europe, including Madrid and Lisboa. Domestically, a network of flights radiates from the Mohammed V Airport outside Casablanca. Flights connect Marrakesh, Rabat, Tangier, Fez, Agadir, and other Moroccan cities at least once per day. **Regional Airlines** (www.regionalmaroc.com) flies from Barcelona, Las Palmas, Lisboa, Madrid, and Málaga and offers many domestic routes, including Agadir, Casablanca, and Tangier. Some of the cheapest flights between Europe and Morocco, however, can be found on smaller budget carriers. For last-minute deals and internet specials, compare routes on airlines like **easyJet, Ryanair, Click Air,** and **Atlas Blue.**

BY FERRY

One of the most popular modes of travel between Spain and Morocco is by crossing the Strait of Gibraltar by ferry. Spanish government-run **Trasmediterránea** (☎902 16 01 80; www.balearia.net); leaves Algeciras's Estación Marítima for Ceuta and Tangier. Other companies include **EuroFerries, BuqueBus, Comanov, Comarit, FRS,** and **Limadet,** which operate upwards of sixteen weekly crossings per route. Crossing times vary from 30min. to 1½hr. depending on the ship. Passengers should expect to fill out a customs form and present their passport for an entry stamp before disembarking for Morocco.

BY TRAIN

Trains in Morocco are faster than buses, more comfortable, fairly reliable, and prompt. Second-class train tickets are slightly more expensive than corresponding CTM bus fares; first-class tickets cost around 20% more than those second-class. The main line runs from Tangier via Rabat and Casablanca to Marrakesh. A spur connects Fez, Meknes, and points east. Tickets bought on board cost at least 10% more and may cause trouble with the conductor.

BY BUS

Plan well ahead if you plan to use buses as your method of transport. They're not all that fast or comfortable, but they are extremely cheap and travel to nearly every corner of the country. **Compagnie de Transports du Maroc (CTM),** the state-owned line, has the fastest, most luxurious, most reliable, and generally most expensive buses. In many cities, CTM has a station separate from other lines; reservations are usually not necessary. *Let's Go* lists CTM stations in each city. Several dozen private companies operate as well. Other private companies, called *cars publiques* (a.k.a. *souq* buses), have more departures but are slower and much less comfortable. In bus stations, each company has its own info window; window-hop for information on destinations and schedules. The baggage check at CTM bus depots is usually safe. Your bags, however, may not be accepted for storage if you don't have padlocks on the zippers. Private bus companies also have baggage checkrooms.

BY TAXI

Two separate hordes of taxis prowl Moroccan streets: intra-urban *petit taxis* and inter-urban *grand taxis*, both dirt cheap by European standards. *Petit taxis* hold a maximum of three passengers and are all painted in one color depending on the municipality. Make sure the driver turns the meter on; they are required to do so by law. Otherwise, agree on the price before you go (around 50% of what the driver asks is fair). There is a 50% surcharge after 8pm in most localities. Don't be surprised if the driver stops for other passengers or picks you up with other passengers in the car, but, if you are picked up after the meter has been started, note the initial price. *Grand taxis* are the most expensive way to travel but go just about everywhere. Unlike their *petit* cousins, they don't usually cruise for passengers, congregating instead at a central area in town. They hold up to six passengers, but, if you're planning a long ride, you might buy two spaces to allow for extra room. A taxi won't go until it is filled, and ask other passengers what they are paying to avoid being ripped off.

BY CAR AND BY THUMB

There are two reasons to rent a car in Morocco: large group travel and destinations not reached by Morocco's public transportation system. Otherwise, rental is unnecessary. Roads can be very dangerous; reckless passing maneuvers, excessive speed, shoddy maintenance, and poorly equipped vehicles are all common. Multinational car rental chains **Hertz, Avis,** and **Europcar** all have branches in Morocco. Large local firms such as **Afric Car, Moroloc,** and **Locoto** offer cars for considerably less money but may also be less reliable. Both international and local firms are easy to find in all major cities. Before you leave the lot, make sure that you have a full spare, a complete toolkit, and a good map. Once on the road, you face a myriad of complications, the most serious being **security checks.** Virtually any trip will bring you to at least one checkpoint. Expect to be pulled over and asked to produce your passport and proof of rental. You also may be stopped for traffic violations, real or not. The fine is payable on the spot in dirhams. Whatever you do, do not travel with drugs in your car. **Hitchhiking** is very rare among travelers in Morocco, as transportation is already dirt cheap by European and North American standards. If Moroccans do pick up a foreigner, they will most likely expect payment. Hitching is more frequent in the south and in the mountains, where transportation is irregular. *Let's Go* does not recommend hitchhiking.

MONEY

In Morocco, banking hours are Monday through Friday 8:30 to 11:30am and 2:30 to 4:30pm, during Ramadan from 9:30am to 2pm. In the summer, certain banks close at 1pm and do not re-open in the afternoon. As in Europe, ATMs are the best way to change money. When changing large sums, keep in mind that it is very difficult to change currencies back upon departure. Taxes are generally included in prices, though in malls and *grandes surfaces* (larger superstores) you will find a 7% value added tax on food and a 20% tax on luxury goods.

SAFETY AND SECURITY

EMERGENCY ☎	Police: ☎19. Highway services: ☎177.

Morocco has received a bad rap, for the most part undeserved, among travelers. While the crime rate is higher than in Spain or Portugal, there is far more to Morocco than hustlers and drugs. Nevertheless, visitors should be careful. Large cities like Tangier and Fez are filled with fake guides offering tours of the city for a small price; they should be avoided. And as in all big cities, travelers should be wary of pickpocketers and aggressive panhandlers.

GLBT acceptance simply does not exist in the same way that it does in many Western countries. Travelers to Morocco should remember that homosexuality is technically a criminal offense in this country, and public displays of affection are not recommended. However, the cautious traveler will face little harassment or persecution. **Female travelers** will probably have extra difficulties traveling through Morocco without a male companion. At the very least, they should never travel alone. Visitors will feel safer and more comfortable (and will avoid offending local sensibilities) by not wearing short skirts, sleeveless tops, and shorts; moreover, females should always wear bras. Regardless, non-Moroccan women may be gawked at, commented upon, approached by hustlers, followed, or even groped. Moroccan woman may "hiss" at indecently clad female travelers. The best response to male harassers may be silence, but yelling *"shuma"* (meaning shame) may well embarrass them. If an uncomfortable situation persists, look out for a policeman.

Debates between the Moroccan government and the Algerian-based Polisario Front over possession of the **Western Sahara** resulted in a guerrilla war until the late 1980s. The UN called a cease-fire in 1991, but there are still unexploded landmines in the area. Travel to the Sahara is difficult and not recommended; clearance information can be obtained from Moroccan embassies.

HEALTH

All travelers in Morocco face a different set of health issues than in Spain and Portugal; food and waterborne diseases in particular are a common cause of illness. The CDC recommends that travelers drink only bottled or boiled water, avoiding tap water, fountain drinks, and ice cubes. It is also advisable to only eat only fruit and vegetables that are cooked and that you have peeled yourself. Stay away from food sold by street vendors and check to make sure that dairy products have been pasteurized. There is only a slight malaria risk in Morocco, but consult your doctor before leaving about the possibility of a vaccine.

While there is a public health system in Morocco, travelers should seek out private clinics, which offer the most dependent and affordable care. There are few English-speaking doctors, though French is widespread; learn a few basic words of medical vocabulary in French in case of an emergency. Private clinics are found in large cities and university towns with medical schools, such as Casablanca and Rabat. Travelers with significant medical problems that might need sudden and immediate attention are advised to stay in larger cities.

ACCOMMODATIONS

YOUTH HOSTELS

The Federation Royale des Auberges de Jeunesse (FRMAJ) is the Moroccan Hosteling International (HI) affiliate. Beds cost 45-60dh per night, and there is a surcharge for nonmembers everywhere but in Casablanca. Some hostels sell HI memberships on the spot. Call ahead for reservations. You'll probably need to bring your own sleepsack and towel, and there are usually curfew and lockout times. For hostel addresses, contact FRMAJ, Parc de la Ligue Arabe, BP 15998, Casa Principale, Casablanca 21000 (☎022 47 09 52). For more info on national youth hostel associations, see **Accommodations,** p. 40.

HOTELS

Although there is an official star system for rating hotels in Morocco, the rating reflects little more than price. Hotels that are not part of the system are not necessarily worse—standards vary greatly—but they are usually cheaper. Rooms can vary widely even within a particular hotel, so ask to see another room if you don't like the first. Cheap hotels in Morocco are extremely inexpensive—as little as 80dh per night. Listings are generally divided between medina and ville nouvelle establishments. Medina hotels are usually cheaper, but less comfortable and with fewer amenities. Hot showers, when available, may cost extra (usually less than 10dh). Many hotels offer laundry services.

CAMPING

Camping is popular and cheap (about 20dh per person), especially in the desert, mountains, and beaches. Like hotels, conditions vary widely. You can usually expect to find restrooms, but electricity is not as readily available. Use caution if camping unofficially, especially on the beaches, as theft is a problem.

KEEPING IN TOUCH

Useful communication information (including international access codes, calling card numbers, country codes, operator and directory assistance, and emergency numbers) is listed on the inside back cover of this book.

TELEPHONES. Morocco has invested hundreds of millions of dollars into modernizing its telephone system, markedly improving services. Phone offices (téléboutiques) are located in most cities. If you can't find one, head to the post office—they always have at least one phone for international calls. Remember that the initial zero (0) in city codes is dialed only when calling from another area within Morocco; from outside of Morocco the number is omitted. Local calls do not require dialing any portion of the city code. The most economical way to make international calls is with a calling card (see **By Telephone,** p. 37). To call home with a calling card, contact the operator for your service provider in Morocco by dialing the appropriate toll-free access number.

MAIL. Sending via airmail *(par avion)* can take a week to a month to reach the US or Canada. Less reliable surface mail *(par terre)* takes up to two months. Express mail *(recommandé* or *exprès postaux)*, is faster than regular airmail and more reliable. Post offices and tabacs sell stamps. For fast service (2 days to the US), your best bet is **DHL** (www.dhl.com), which has drop-off locations in major cities, or **FedEx** (www.fedex.com).

EMAIL. Cybercafes are common in major cities and more touristed towns. *Let's Go* lists internet access wherever possible.

EXPLORING MOROCCO

Northern Morocco is punctuated by ports and the occasional beach and bounded on the south by the high Rif mountains. Its valuable coastal cities, fought over by Moroccans, Berbers, Spaniards, and other European powers for centuries, have traditionally been the most common ports of entry to Morocco. This political back-and-forth, which continues today with Spanish exclaves Ceuta and Melilla, gives the north a strange flavor of a Morocco mingled with a touristed Europe. The aftertaste is not always the most pleasant, so for a better experience of an older, unadulterated Morocco, keep on pushing south.

TANGIER ☎039

For travelers venturing out of Europe for the first time, Tangier (pop. 600,000) can be overwhelming. The heat and the hustlers often leave uninspiring first impressions, but the energy and history, as well as the novelty for daytrippers, keep travelers coming. For centuries, the region bounced from one imperial power to the next, resulting in the 1923 with the declaration of Tangier as an "international zone" loosely governed by the US and eight European powers. Law enforcement dwindled, and the city began to attract rich heiresses, drug users, spies, and Beat Generation poets. When Morocco declared its independence in 1956, the new government tried to change Tangier's image, closing down most of the brothels and increasing police presence. Nowadays, the city has been reclaimed by Moroccans, and continues to thrive—its position as a gateway to Africa will keep the city moving, no matter who's in charge.

TRANSPORTATION

Flights: Royal Air Maroc, Pl. France (☎039 37 95 08). Domestic and international flights. **Iberia,** at the airport (☎039 39 34 33), flies daily to Madrid. A taxi to the airport, 16km from Tangier, costs 80-100dh for up to 6 people.

Trains: Trains leave from **Tanger Ville,** 4km south of the town center (not the old station on Av. d'Espagne). A *petit taxi* there costs around 10dh. To: **Asilah** (1hr., 4 per day, 8am-5:15pm, 15dh); **Casablanca** (7hr., 4 per day 8am-9pm, 118dh); **Fez** (5hr., 1 per day, 97dh) via **Meknes** (5hr., 81dh); and **Marrakesh** (11hr., 9:05pm, 275dh).

Buses: Non-CTM buses leave from Av. Yacoub al-Mansour at Pl. Jamia al-Arabia, 2km from the port entrance. Ask blue-coated personnel or check the boards for ticket information. The standard price for luggage is 5dh. A *petit taxi* from the port to the terminal costs around 8dh. From window #11 to: **Asilah** (11am, 4:30pm); from window #2 to **Casablanca** (6hr., every hr. 5am-1am) via **Rabat** (4-5hr.); **Marrakesh** (10hr., 6 per day, 6:45am-1am); from window #3 to: **Chefchaouen** (6 per day 5:45am-5:45pm); **Ceuta** (40min., 7 per day 6:15am-2:45pm); **Fez** (6hr., 5:30am, 6pm); **Tetouan** (21 per day, 5:30am-9:15 pm). The **CTM station** (☎039 93 11 72) near the port entrance offers pricier, less frequent service to the same destinations. To: **Casablanca** (6hr., 5 per day 5:30am-midnight, 140dh); **Chefchaouen** (3hr., 12:15, 8pm, 40dh); **Fez** (6hr., 5 per day 9:15am-9:15pm, 115dh) via **Meknes** (5hr., 100dh; **Marrakesh** (10hr.; 3 per day 11:15am, 2:45, 5:30pm; 220dh); and **Tetouan** (1hr.; 12:15, 8pm; 20dh).

Ferries: The cheapest and most convenient option is to buy a ticket at the very end of the ferry terminal, where company offices are located, though ticket agencies are

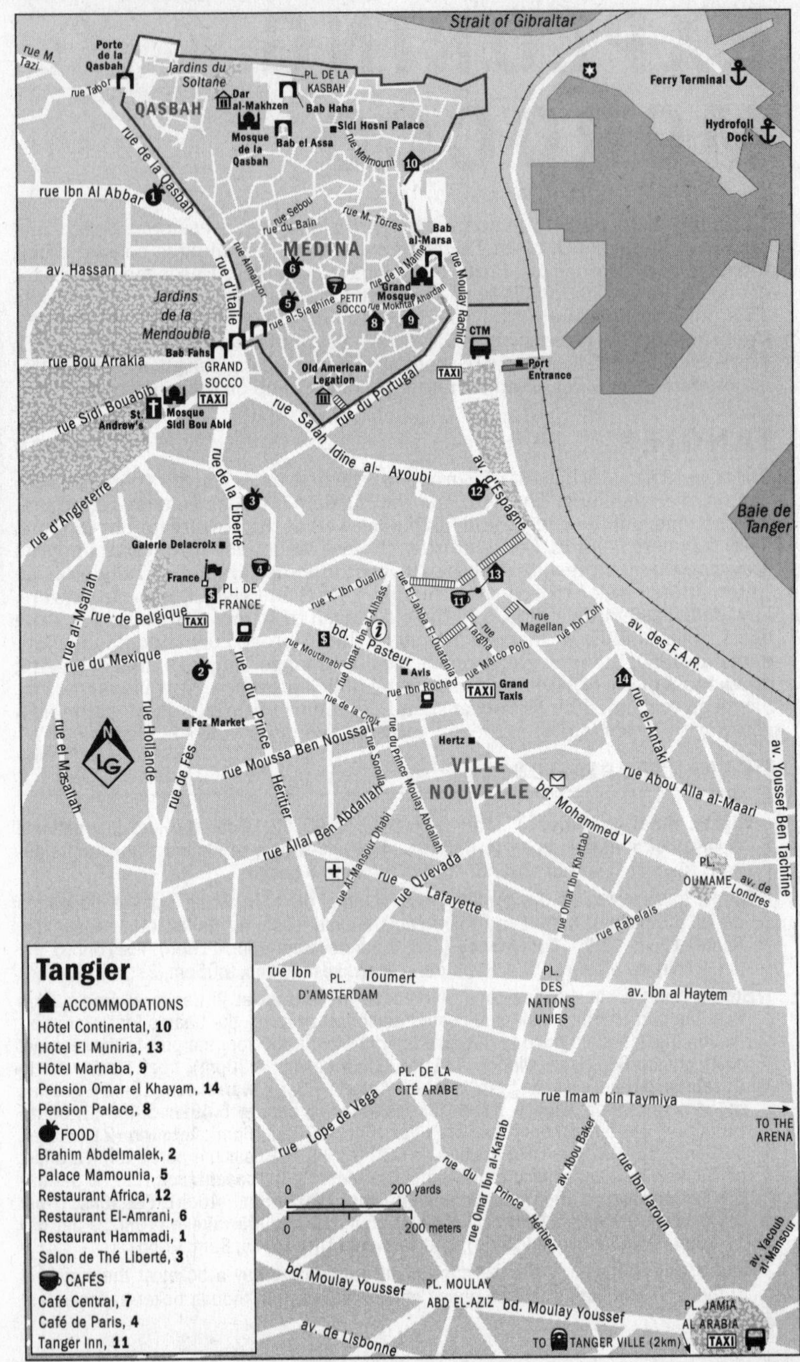

Strait of Gibraltar
Porte de la Qasbah
Jardins du Soltane
PL. DE LA KASBAH
QASBAH
Dar al-Makhzen
Bab Haha
Mosque de la Qasbah
Bab el Assa
Sidi Hosni Palace
Ferry Terminal
Hydrofoil Dock
MEDINA
Bab al-Marsa
Grand Mosque
PETIT SOCCO
Jardins de la Mendoubia
Bab Fahs
GRAND SOCCO
CTM
Port Entrance
Old American Legation
St. Andrew's
Mosque Sidi Bou Abid
Baie de Tanger
Galerie Delacroix
France
PL. DE FRANCE
Avis
Grand Taxis
Fez Market
Hertz
VILLE NOUVELLE
PL. OUMAME
PL. D'AMSTERDAM
PL. DES NATIONS UNIES
PL. DE LA CITÉ ARABE
TO THE ARENA
PL. MOULAY ABD EL-AZIZ
PL. JAMIA AL ARABIA
TO TANGER VILLE (2km)
200 yards
200 meters
Tangier
ACCOMMODATIONS
Hôtel Continental, 10
Hôtel El Muniria, 13
Hôtel Marhaba, 9
Pension Omar el Khayam, 14
Pension Palace, 8
FOOD
Brahim Abdelmalek, 2
Palace Mamounia, 5
Restaurant Africa, 12
Restaurant El-Amrani, 6
Restaurant Hammadi, 1
Salon de Thé Liberté, 3
CAFÉS
Café Central, 7
Café de Paris, 4
Tanger Inn, 11

located throughout the city. You'll need a boarding pass (available at any ticket desk) and a customs form (ask uniformed agents). Near the terminal, pushy men with ID cards will try to arrange your ticket and fill out your customs card for 10dh; just do it yourself. **FRS** (☎039 94 76 12) sends fast ferries to **Tarifa** (every 2hr. 8am-10pm; passenger 372 dh, car 920dh). **Euroferrys** (☎039 94 81 990) goes to **Algeciras** (7am and 4pm. Single ticket 526dh; car 1923dh).

Taxis: *Grand taxis* to nearby locations. Prices subject to bargaining; a fair price for 6 passengers is 20dh per person. Found everywhere, especially by the main bus stop, the Grand Socco, and the intersection of Blvd. Pasteur and Blvd. Mohammed V.

Car Rental: Avis, 54 Blvd. Pasteur (☎039 93 46 46). English spoken. Cars from 650dh per day with tax and insurance included. AmEx/MC/V. Min. age 25 for all cars. A special international license is not required. Open daily 8am-7pm.

ORIENTATION

Av. d'Espagne, a large boulevard that runs from the port along the waterfront to the train station 6km away, makes Tangier easy to navigate. Many of the *ville nouvelle* hotels are located about 1.5km down Av. d'Espagne away from the ferry terminal (a *petit taxi* should cost 5dh, but if you don't have a lot of baggage and you have your wits about you, just walk). Hustlers tend to swoop in here. Adjacent to the ferry terminal area on Ave. d'Espagne is the CTM station. **Rue du Portugal** heads uphill here and forms the border between the *ville nouvelle* and the medina. You can enter the medina and easily find some of its accommodations by turning right above the CTM station, continuing uphill on **Rue de la Plage.** You will reach the large, busy rotary known as the **Grand Socco,** which is the center of activity directly above the medina. From the Grand Socco, you can head down into the medina via **Rue al-Siaghin,** which leads to the **Petit Socco,** or walk down the bustling **Rue d'Italie** (if facing the medina, the street on the left through the large archway), which skirts the medina's western wall. The *ville nouvelle's* main commercial road is the **Blvd. Pasteur,** which connects the main square, **Pl. de France,** with **Blvd. Mohammed V.** Banks, the post office, and cafes can all be found on Blvd. Mohammed V.

PRACTICAL INFORMATION

Tourist Office: 29 Blvd. Pasteur (☎039 94 80 50). Some English, French, and Spanish spoken. Glossy brochures and basic map of the city, but nothing to get excited about. List of accommodations available. Open M-F 8:30am-noon and 2-7:20pm.

Currency Exchange: There is a branch of **BMCE** on most ferries and one in the port complex, although these only change cash. BMCE's main office in Tangier is located at 21 Blvd. Pasteur (☎039 93 11 25). No commission here, but other Moroccan banks charge fees for exchanging traveler's checks. Open M-F 9am-1pm and 3-7pm. Major banks line Blvd. Pasteur and Blvd. Mohammed V, several of which have **ATMs.** Travel agencies near the port are required to change money at official rates. There are **Western Union** locations at Pl. de France and the main post office.

Luggage Storage: At the train station (10dh per bag). Open 24hr. Also at the bus station (7dh per bag). Both open daily 6am-1am.

Police: ☎19. At the port and main train station. At the port, ask for the **Brigade Touristique,** which deal with issues and complaints from travelers.

Medical Services: Red Crescent, 6 Rue al-Mansour Dahbi (☎039 94 25 17), runs a 24hr. medical service. **Ambulance:** ☎039 31 27 27.

Internet Access: Several cafes in the *ville nouvelle,* including **Cyber Café Adam,** 2 Rue Ibn Roched, off Blvd. Pasteur and Blvd. Mohammed V. 10dh per hr. Open daily 8:30am-2am. **Espace Net** is on Ave. de Mexique, 1 block from Pl. de Paris.

Laundry: Pressing Jemelas, 20 Rue de las Once (☎063 22 21 98), off the Petit Socco and around the corner. 6-7dh per garment.

Post Office: 33 Blvd. Mohammed V (☎039 93 25 18), on the downhill continuation of Blvd. Pasteur. Poste Restante. Open M-Th 8:30am-6:30pm, Sa 8:30am-12:15pm. Parcels received around the corner from main entrance, on the back side of the building.

ACCOMMODATIONS

Whether you stay in the *ville nouvelle* or medina, you are bound to meet some hustlers "welcoming" you to Morocco. Your best bet is to ignore them and look like you know where you're going, even if you don't. In late summer, reservations are a good idea, as hotels fill up. Accommodations in the *ville nouvelle* generally offer more comfort and cleanliness, which is definitely worth the extra dirhams. Singles run from 50-80dh. In many places you'll have to pay for a hot shower, and you will definitely have to bring your own toilet paper.

MEDINA

The most convenient hostels are near Rue Mokhtar Ahardan, off the Petit Socco. From the Grand Socco, take the first right down Rue al-Siaghin to the Petit Socco, which is really a small intersection. Rue Mokhtar Ahardan begins at the end of the Petit Socco closest to the port. At night, the smaller streets off the medina can be unsafe.

Pension Palace, 2 Rue Mokhtar Ahardan (☎039 93 61 28). Downhill, on the alley exiting the Petit Socco to the right. The gorgeous courtyard, full of plants and tilework, starred in Bertolucci's adaptation of *The Sheltering Sky.* Clean, soft beds and one stark lightbulb. Communal toilets could use lids. Singles 50dh; doubles 100dh, with bath 150dh; triples 150/200dh; quads 200/260dh. ❶

Hotel Marhaba, 14 Rue de la Poste (☎039 93 88 02), to the left off of Mokhtar Ahardan. Set back off the madness of the medina, it's clean and not crumbling—a relief from some of the other budget options in the neighborhood. Big beds and sinks in all the rooms, and the showers are clean. Hot showers 7dh. Singles 80dh, doubles 100dh. ❷

Hôtel Continental, 36 Dar Baroud (☎039 93 10 24), overlooking the port. From the ferry terminal, bear right around the CTM station, and follow the many signs. A splurge for comfort and ambience. A grand hotel furnished with a mix of Moroccan ornament and Art Deco. Nice terrace overlooks less appealing port and warehouses. Wi-Fi available. Breakfast included. Showers hot only in the mornings. Reservations recommended. Singles 426dh, doubles 552dh, triples 668dh. MC/V. ❺

VILLE NOUVELLE

Hotels line Av. d'Espagne heading away from the port. The best values lie a few blocks uphill toward Blvd. Pasteur and Blvd. Mohammed V.

Hôtel El Muniria, Rue Magellan (☎039 93 53 37). From the port, walk south along the tree-lined pedestrian walkway. Take 1st right after Hôtel Biarritz on Av. d'Espagne walking away from the medina, and follow as it winds uphill. William Burroughs wrote *Naked Lunch* in room #9, and Jack Kerouac and Allen Ginsberg stayed in room #4. A great deal for Tangier, with spacious rooms, hot showers, and towels. Attached bar (**Tanger Inn,** see p. 720) is the hippest place in town. Singles 150dh, doubles 180dh. ❷

Pensión Omar El Khayam, 26 Ave. Antaki (☎063 71 84 60), up the hill from Av. d'Epagne past the port. In a distinctive yellow-brick imitation Moorish house, this *pensión* offers clean, neat, tiled rooms. Communal baths old, but clean and serviceable. Hot showers included—a plus. Singles 80dh, with bath 120dh; doubles 120/150dh. ❶

FOOD

MEDINA

The **Grand Socco** is home to fruit stalls, sandwich joints, and juice stands galore, so pick and choose before heading down to the **Petit Socco,** where there are cheap eateries on all sides. **La Rue d'Italie** is the place to go for a sit-down meal, with Moroccan and European fare side by side.

Restaurant Hammadi, 2 Rue de la Kasbah (☎039 93 45 14), the continuation of Rue d'Italie just outside the medina walls. Moroccan carpets, plush booths, and a group of local musicians set the ambience and attract tourists in droves. Specialties are *tajine* (40dh) and couscous (45dh). Beer and wine served. Entrees 40-60dh. 10% tax added to each meal. Open daily 11am-3pm and 7pm-midnight. MC/V. ❷

Restaurant El-Amrani, at the end of Rue Smihi. From the Grand Socco, walk down Rue d'Italie and head through the first gate (Bab Rahbat Zraa), and follow Smihi to the end. A hole-in-the-wall joint where old Moroccan men come to get heaping plates of beans and meat or fish (15-25dh) or the delicious **watermelon** (8dh). Unless you speak Arabic, ordering will involve a bit of charades, but it's worth it. ❶

Palace Mamounia, 4 Rue al-Siaghine (☎039 93 50 99), towards the Petit Socco. Elegant dining upstairs among wicker chairs, shady arbor, and huge Moroccan vases. Take note of the 15% service charge before you sit down. Massive Moroccan set menu 100dh. Open daily 8am-10pm. ❸

EXPLORING MOROCCO

VILLE NOUVELLE

The restaurants along **Av. d'Espagne** tout unspectacular and overpriced *menus touristiques* for 50dh and up. Beachfront restaurants run by high-end hotels are what you might expect—expensive and boring. You're better off scouting around **Pl. France** or grabbing a hot sandwich along **Blvd. Pasteur.**

Salon de Thé Liberté, 47 Rue de la Liberté. The cafe on the street is excellent for people-watching, but the secret garden, niftily hidden in the back, offers a better and quieter place to chow down on Moroccan favorites (meat dishes 35-45dh) and Western dishes alike. Spaghetti 15-35dh. Couscous 45dh. Open 8am-10:30pm. ❷

Brahim Abdelmalek, 14 Rue de Mexique (☎039 93 17 96), under an off-white awning. Cheap sandwiches in a hurry. King Hassan II allegedly lunched here; you can too, for less than 15dh. Open daily 10:30am-3am. ❶

Restaurant Africa, 83 Rue Salah Eddine al-Ayoubi (☎039 93 54 36), just off Av. d'Espagne near Pension Miami, opposite the old train station. A quiet, unassuming place with small tables sticks to international favorites (spaghetti, hamburgers) and Moroccan staples. Beer and wine served. Big 4-course *menu du jour* 50dh. Entrees 35-45dh. Open daily 9am-12:30am. ❷

SIGHTS

IN AND NEAR THE MEDINA

OLD AMERICAN LEGATION. The old legation is quirky and fascinating look at early American history. In 1821, this became the first foreign property acquired by the United States. The museum contains correspondence between George Washington and his "great and magnanimous friend" **Sultan Moulay ben Abdallah**—Morocco was the first nation to recognize America's independence. The legation displays a hilarious letter from the consul detailing his attempts to (unsuccessfully) refuse a gift of lions from the sultan. Visit the room dedicated to famous expat writer **Paul Bowles,** featuring photographs from Tangier's storied "interzone" days. The friendly curators will give excellent tours on request, but calling first is recommended. *(8 Rue d'America. Enter the medina via the large white steps on Rue du Portugal and look for the yellow archway emblazoned with the US seal. ☎039 93 53 17. Open M-F 10am-1pm and 3-5pm. Donation suggested.)*

ST. ANDREW'S CHURCH. In 1883 Moulay Hassan I granted this parcel of land to Great Britain to build an Anglican church. Out of respect for local architecture, it was built in a fusion of English and Moorish styles, with the roof above the altarpiece composed of intricately carved wood. A highlight is the Lord's Prayer inscribed in Arabic around the chancel arch. The cemetery outside is quiet and holds some English notables in North Africa. The church is kept locked but if you can find Mustapha, the happy, friendly caretaker, he will let you in and tell you a little about the church. *(At the end of Rue d'Angleterre. Open daily 9:30am-12:30pm and 2:30-4:30pm. Services Su at 8:30 and 11am. Donations recommended.)*

DAR AL-MAKHZEN. An opulent palace with handwoven tapestries, inlaid ceilings, and foliated archways, the Dar al-Makhzen was once home to the ruling pasha of Tangier and is now the **Museum of Moroccan Art.** The museum highlights the societies of Tangier from pre-Roman times to the Romans and Moors, with lead sarcophagi, funerary urns, pottery and musical instruments, and a gorgeous Roman mosaic depicting the voyage of Venus. It is all set around a lovely courtyard with a fountain and *zellij* tilework. The gardens in the middle are nicely shaded and a good place to hide from the heat. *(The easiest way to reach the museum and the Pl. de la Kasbah grounds is to enter the medina from Porte de la Kasbah gate and stick to the rampart wall until you reach the wide open space of Pl. de la Kasbah. The museum is to the right. ☎039 93 20 97. Open M and W-Su 9am-12:30pm and 3-5:30pm. 10dh.)*

MARKETS. The medina's commercial center is the **Grand Socco.** This busy square and traffic circle is cluttered with fruit vendors, parsley stands, and kebab and fish stalls. Off of Rue de Fez is the small, colorful **Fez Market,** where local merchants cater to Tangier's Europeans. *(Uphill on Rue de la Liberté, across Pl. France, and 2 blocks down Rue de Fez on the right.)* More pungent are the market stalls south of the Grand Socco, where saffron and a hundred other spices are on sale along with watermelons, dates, figs, olives, parsley, mint, melon, mango, and of course, tangerines—they originally came from Tangier, or, in French, Tanger. *(South of the Grand Socco along Rue Ayoubi and the streets off of it.)*

OTHER SIGHTS. Rue Riad Sultan runs alongside the Jardins du Soltane and continues to Pl. de la Kasbah, a sunny courtyard with a promontory offering spectacular views of Spain and the Atlantic Ocean. With your back to the water, walk toward the far right corner of the plaza. Just around the corner, to the right, the **Mosque de la Kasbah** rears its octagonal minaret. Outside the medina, 17th- and 18th-century bronze cannons hide in the **Jardins de la Mendoubia,** a welcome escape from the excitement of the Soccos. *(Opposite Rue de la Liberté, where Rue Bou Arrakia joins the Grand Socco, through the white gate marked #50.)* To laze about with a cold drink and stare across the glinting strait to Spain, head to the **Terrace des Parrasseux** (Idler's Terrace), which has benches with a clear view across to Europe. *(Off Pl. de France down Pasteur.)*

ENTERTAINMENT

The most popular evening activity in Tangier is sipping mint tea in front of a cafe on Pl. de France, in Blvd. Pasteur, or in Ville Nouvelle, which does have its share of small bars. The **Café de Paris,** 1 Pl. de France, hosted countless meetings between spies during WWII. Coming from the Grand Socco, look to the left. (☎039 93 84 44. Tea and coffee 5-6dh. Open daily 7am-11:30pm.) Inside the medina, **Café Central** was a favorite of William S. Burroughs, but today is mostly a hangout for middle-aged Moroccan men. (Off the Petit Socco; same hours and prices as Café de Paris). **Café Hafa,** an old Paul Bowles haunt, has a great view of Spain on a clear day. Sipping a mint tea (5dh) on one of the cafe's many terraces is a great way to clear your head of the city's bustle, and worth getting lost on the way there. (From the Kasbah, follow Rue Tabor for 10 minutes. When you can see the water through the buildings to the right, head toward it; it's down a street to the left. You may have to ask around to find it. Open daily 10am-8pm.) Cafes tend to attract a male crowd, but female tourists should not be afraid to grab a table and an orange juice, as it is perfectly acceptable. For a harder drink, there are few spots with ambience that attracts both genders in equal number. The hippest place in town is **Tanger Inn,** Rue Magellan, next to Hotel Muniria. Subdued house music attracts men and women, both local and foreign, for a nice cosmopolitan mix. A good place to sit back and nurse a drink (beer 20dh) at the end of the day. (Open daily 10pm-1am, until late Th-Sa.)

TETOUAN ☎039

For a small city, Tetouan (pronounced tet-ta-wan; pop. 350,000) has a lot of history and a lot of hustle. Controlled by the Spanish for much of the 20th century, the city's buildings and church attest to a long colonial presence, as do Spanish newspapers and the dominance of Spanish as a second language. The hustlers speak it, too, and it's hard to get far without an "Hola, amigo." Aside from its medina, packed with mosques and a *mellah*, the old Jewish quarter, there's not much to do—but plenty of buses to Chefchaouen.

Tetouan is bisected by **Av. Mohammed V,** which runs through the center, connecting the two main Pl.zas, **Pl. Moulay el-Mehdi** and **Pl. Hassan II,** and continues on into the winding streets of the old medina. To reach Pl. Moulay al-Mehdi, the heart of the *ville nouvelle*, from the CTM bus station, cross the street and turn left on Rue Moulay Abbas. Walk two blocks, turn right on Ave. al-Ourouba, and it's two blocks up. From the other bus station, it's best to take a taxi (8dh). Otherwise, walk up Rue de Torreta and bear left at the fork to get to the CTM station and then to the center. Pl. Moulay el-Mehdi is home to **Pension Iberia,** the **BMCE bank,** the **post office** (open M-F 8:30am-12:15pm and 2:30-6:30pm, Sa 8:30-11:30am) and **telephones.** Internet (5dh per hr.) can be found at **Remote Studios,** on Mohammed V in between the two plazas (open daily 10am-midnight.) The **tourist office** is a half block down Av. Mohammed V toward the medina, and has a map and info on guides. (☎039 96 19 15. Spanish and French spoken.) Open M-F 8:30am-noon and 2:30-6:30pm.) Reach **police** at ☎19.

Buses leave CTM's station to: **Casablanca** (7hr., 4 per day 5:45am-midnight, 140dh); **Chefchaouen** (1hr., 5 per day 5am-9:30pm, 20dh); **Fez** (5hr.; 11am, 1:45, 4:30pm; 93dh); **Marrakesh** (11hr.; 5:45am, noon, midnight; 235dh); and **Tangier** (1hr., 6am and 4:45pm, 20dh). **CTM** buses (☎039 93 24 15) provide a receipt for luggage (5dh). Non-CTM buses leave from a station south of the city. It's best to take a **petit taxi** (8dh), but to walk, head left of the CTM station and continue walking down Rue de Torreta across the highway; it's on the left. Departures to the locations above are relatively frequent as several companies run out of Tetouan. **Grand taxis** (15-20dh) to **Ceuta** also leave from near the CTM station. Taxis to **Chefchaouen** (25dh when full) run from a stand 10min. away: walk from Pl. Moulay al-Mehdi away from the bus station along Rue 10 de Mai and bear left onto Rue al-Jazair.

For accommodations, by far the best option is **Pension Iberia ❶**, Pl. Moulay al-Mehdi, on the third floor above BMCE. Clean, breezy rooms make up for a long walk upstairs. Fills up quickly. (☎039 96 36 79. Hot showers 10dh. Singles 50dh; doubles 80dh, triples 120dh.) **Hotel Príncipe ❶**, 20 Rue Youssef, has archaically furnished rooms with bath and toilet. Try to get a window overlooking the street. (☎039 96 27 95. Singles 70dh, with shower 90dh; doubles 100/120dh; triples 140/180dh). Cheerfully tacky whitewashed trees and plastic chairs decorate **Restaurant Restinga ❶**, 21 Ave. Mohammed V. The only place that serves alcohol in the area, it is dominated by Moroccan businessmen drinking Special Flag (14dh) and eating olives. Meat and fish dishes 40-50dh. (Open daily noon-3pm and 6:30-10pm.) The pocket-sized *pastillas* (lamb-filled pastries; 6dh) at **Café-Patisserie Smir ❶**, 17 Calle Mohammed V, make a perfect lunch-on-the-go, though there's also a balcony on which to linger (1-5dh). Popular with Moroccan families, it's also comfortable for women. (Open daily 6am-9pm.)

CEUTA (SEBTA) ☎039

Travelers hoping to avoid Tangier altogether may opt to ferry to the Spanish enclave Ceuta (pop. 75,000; called Sebta within Morocco) and from there cross the Moroccan border, only 5km away. There isn't much to keep you in Ceuta, and little to see besides some old walls and a monument to Franco. It is advisable to keep moving on immediately to Tetouan (35min.) or Chefchaouen (allow 4hr.), but if you're stuck in Ceuta, try the helpful **tourist booth** (☎956 50 62 75) in the ferry terminal, which has a map. Ceuta doesn't have much in the way of budget options, but if you're here overnight, try **Pensión la Bohemia ❸**, Paseo de la Revellín, 16. To get here, follow the water to Pl. de la Constitución and then head half a block down Po. de la Revellín. A dark hallway leads up to clean, small rooms. (Singles and doubles €35. Cash only.)

BORDER CROSSING. To reach the Moroccan border from Ceuta, grab a taxi from the town center (€6-7) or take bus #7 (€0.70); to reach the bus stand from the ferry (5min.), exit the terminal and take a left onto the main street. At the end of the street, near a roundabout with a fountain in the middle (and near the water), take a right up the hill, and then another right to the stand. Taxis and buses stop short of the border; you must cross on foot and have your passport stamped. Expect to be accosted by guides wanting to escort you to their cousin's rug emporium. Head straight to the parking lot, where *grand taxis* await (p. 711). Cash exchange is available at the border; do it here rather than in Ceuta. From the border, full *grand taxis* to Tetouan are 15-20dh per person. From there you can connect to the more mellow Chefchaouen by catching a bus or taxi. If you are heading to **Algeciras** from Ceuta, you can use one of several ferry companies (**Balearia** and **Acciona Trasmediterranea** among them) that offer fast service (35min., every hr. 7am-9pm, €40-45). Don't forget about the **time difference** between Spain and Morocco—Spain is 1hr. ahead, and 2hr. during daylight savings time.

CHEFCHAOUEN (CHAOUEN) ☎039

Tucked high in the Rif is the small, gleaming town of Chefchaouen (pop. 50,000). The town's laid-back ambience, excellent location for gorgeous hiking and mountain treks, and ready availability of *kif* (hashish) have lured backpackers for decades, but the breeze and blinding blue of its enchanting medina are more than worth a few days' rest.

TRANSPORTATION

The **bus station** (☎039 98 95 73) is a long hike downhill from town; **taxis** (10-15dh) pass along the road next to the station. Most buses are just passing through, and they fill up, so get tickets as early as possible. **CTM** and other buses go to: **Fez** (5hr.; 1, 3:15, 6pm; 65 dh); via **Ouzzane,** the best bet for connections (1hr.; 25dh); **Marrakesh** (8-9hr., 4 per day 1:30-8pm); **Casablanca** (8hr., 7pm) via **Rabat** (7hr.); **Tangier** (3:15pm, 40dh); and **Tetouan** (1hr., noon, 3:15pm, 25dh). To get to **Ceuta,** you must go through **Tetouan.** Private companies also have daily buses to **Fez** and **Meknes. Grand taxis** are the easiest way to get to **Tetouan** (30dh) and **Ceuta,** although they often take a while to fill. Taxis leave a block downhill from Pl. Mohammed V on **Av. al-Massira al-Khadra.**

PRACTICAL INFORMATION

From the bus stations, head up the steep hill and turn right after several blocks onto **Av. Mohammed V,** which leads to the tree-filled, circular **Pl. Mohammed V;** the center of town is a 20min. walk (or 10-15dh cab ride). Cross the plaza and continue east on Av. Hassan II, the main road of the *ville nouvelle.* Here you'll find **currency exchange** at the **BMCE** (open M-F 8:15am-2:15pm), the **post office** with telephones (open M-F 8am-4:30pm, Sa 8am-noon) and **internet** at **IRIC,** 10 av. Hassan II. (☎039 98 97 15. 10dh per hr. Open daily 9am-midnight.) Chefchaouen has no tourist office. Down Av. Hassan II is the **Bab al-Ain,** the main gate into the medina. From Bab al-Ain, the main street twists uphill to place **Uta al-Hammam,** the plaza at the heart of the medina. Just east of Uta al-Hammam is **Place el-Majzen,** the end of Av. Hassan II, which runs past Bab al-Ain and skirts the southern edge of the medina. **Hospital Mohammed V** (☎039 18 62 28) is a block west from Pl. Mohammed V on Av. al-Massira al-Khadra, down a flight of stairs from the plaza and on the left, and **police** can be reached at ☎19.

ACCOMMODATIONS

Chefchaouen has a slew of colorful budget hotels. Inside the medina, head uphill from **Bab al-Ain.** Lodgings are clustered along these streets and around **Pl. Uta al-Hammam.** Firmly a backpackers town, Chefchaouen is full of establishments that have social common rooms and rooftop terraces.

Hotel Andaluz, 1 Rue Sidi Salem (☎039 98 60 34). Directly behind Credit Agricola on Pl. Uta al-Hammam, in the medina. Small but comfortable rooms are set around a beautiful central courtyard filled with handcrafted Moroccan furniture. Friendly owners know a great deal about the town and good local hikes. Excellent roof terrace and free book exchange. Room includes hot showers. Singles 30dh; doubles 100dh; triples 150dh. Ask to sleep on the terrace for 30dh. ❶

Pension la Castellana, 4 Sidi Ahmad Bouhali (☎039 98 62 95). Walk to the end of Pl. Uta al-Hammam. Next to a *hamman,* this place caters to backpackers and encourages long stays. Communal kitchen and common room with stereo. Free hot showers. Singles 30dh; doubles 60dh; triples 90dh; quads 120dh. ❶

Pension Anaia (☎039 88 30 19). Along Hassan II, just below Place el-Majden. Common rooms on each floor feel like hip hookah dens, with funky couches and plush cushions everywhere. Rooms vary from spacious to cramped, but all are clean. Hot water in communal showers. Singles 60dh; doubles 120dh. ❶

Hotel Rif, Rue Hassan II (☎039 98 69 82). Just outside the medina walls. Follow Rue Hassan II to the right around the medina; Hotel Rif will be on your left. American

KIF IN THE RIF

With an army of backpackers passing through and something called the "Hippie River" in Chefchaouen, you might expect a little hash to be passed around in the Rif. How about as much as one-third of the world's supply?

The hills in the Rif are excellent for growing kif, the bright green shoot-like plant that can be refined into hashish. Kif has long been smoked by locals, as a milder form of hash mixed with tobacco, but it wasn't until the 60s that local farmers began to realize that the plant could be concentrated into hash and sold for enormous profit to recreational drug users all around the world.

Since then, kif has become the dominant force in the economy of the Rif, despite the fact that it's technically illegal. The ramifications have gotten more serious due to increased pressure from the US and the European Union, Morocco's primary trading partners. Nevertheless, authorities have largely turned a blind eye to the massive production and export of kif that goes on in the mountains. Perhaps, some suggest, it is a tacit acknowledgement of the crop's importance to what is otherwise a struggling and very limited local economy.

Still, when you're dealing with kif, you're playing with fire. Penalties for kif possession include up to 10 years in jail. While the locals might all be selling, kif is a risky game to play in the Rif.

kitsch meets Moroccan vistas at Hotel Rif. The terrace offers great views, especially of the mountains to the south. Rooms are standard but clean. Staff can help with hikes. Singles 160dh, with shower 200dh; doubles 190/240dh. Breakfast included. MC/V. ❶

FOOD

Inside the medina, outdoor seating is available in Pl. Uta al-Hammam at various restaurants, which have largely identical menus but good ambience.

Chez Aziz, just outside Bab al-Ain, the medina's gate. For a quick bite, stop by for a hearty egg and meat sandwich (10-15dh). Open daily noon-midnight. ❶

Al Kasaba, just off the plaza. Al Kasaba's secluded booths are candle-lit and decked out in Berber finery. The excellent three-course menu (60dh) provides a great way to while away the evening. The savory kebabs are a good bet for dinner. ❶

Restaurant Fuentes, in Pl. Uta al-Hammam, but set back from the hustle of the plaza. Get lost in the patterned intricacies of the ceiling as hip music plays, complementing the blue light at this quiet spot. Serves up traditional Moroccan fare and pasta dishes. Plates 35-50dh. Open daily 6-10:30pm. ❶

SIGHTS

Chefchaouen's steep **medina** is one of Morocco's best to explore, perhaps because it is less crowded and more relaxed than those of larger cities. Enter through Bab al-Ain and walk uphill toward **Pl. Uta al-Hammam,** the center of the medina. The side streets are worth a look, too, as some are drenched in exquisite bright blue paint, giving the town a fresh, Mediterranean feel unlike any other in Morocco. Also worth seeing is the 17th-century **kasbah** built by Moulay Ismail, Morocco's famous rogue. Inside is a **museum** with traditional Berber garments and pictures of Chefchaouen during the Rif War. The old jail cells, with rusty leg irons on the walls, are open, as is the tower. The view of the city is worth all the stairs. (Open M and W-Su 9am-1pm and 3-6:30pm. 10dh.)

HIKING

For information on maps, trails, or contacting guides, see Ahmed at **Hotel Andaluz** or the reception at **Hotel Rif.** Follow the **Ras al-Ma River** (still known as Hippie River from the days Chefchaouen attracted many) upstream into the hills for just a few kilometers for spectacular results. For a view of the city, hike to the **Hotel Asmaq** (follow signs for the *ville* *nouvelle*). Behind the hotel, there's a path that winds up the peak to the left, then runs down into the valley. Try reaching the "Spanish mosque," the ruins of a mosque built by the Spanish but abandoned in the Rif War. It's about 3km up the path on a hill overlooking the town. **Jebel el-Kalaa** (1616m), the peak that towers over Chefchaouen, is a reasonable one-day hike for anyone in decent shape. To get to the trailhead, head out **Bab el-Majarrol** at the end of the medina and walk up to **Hotel Atlas Chaouen.** Alternatively, you can walk up **Moulay Ali ben Rachid** (outside Bab al-Ain) and hike through the cemetary. Walk past the hotel along the road until you reach the entrance to **Talassemtane National Park.** The gravel path (marked with a sign reading "El-Kalaa and Izelan") is the start of the trail. The first hour is a series of switchbacks through pine groves. Once you clear them, it's scrub and flowers, along with lots of grazing goats. After 2-2½hr., the trail cuts sharply to the left (almost 180°) while the 4WD track continues past the mountain. You may pass *kif* plantations along the way (look for the short, densely growing bright green shoots, the only plants being watered), but farmers generally ignore you. The final 2-3hr. to the summit follow small switchbacks through large boulders and arid scrub. The path falls apart toward the top and some scrambling may be required, but the way is clear. The hike to the summit should take 5-6hr. at a moderate pace, and the descent is obviously much quicker. Berbers frequent and live along the lower trails, and a *"la bes"* or friendly wave will be warmly reciprocated. If you do continue straight and miss the turn (you are far from alone in this club), the hiking is still gorgeous, leading though several Berber villages and past the **Sfiha Telj,** huge rocky crags that stick out of the mountains. There are a few campsites but no large settlements for at least another day's hike, so plan accordingly.

THE MIDDLE ATLAS

The Middle Atlas is Morocco's heartland, an arid stretch where empires grew and political dynasties rose and fell. Home to Fez and Meknes, the region sees ancient medinas traversed by donkeys and modern cities growing side-by-side. Modernization has created dramatic contrasts, from the ancient Roman ruins of Volubulis outside Meknes to the satellite dishes on Fez's medina homes.

MEKNES ☎055

After uniting Morocco under his brutal rule, the rogue Sultan Moulay Ismail chose Meknes as his seat of power in 1672 and tried to turn this relative backwater into a capital to rival Versailles. Underrated and overshadowed by Fez, its colorful neighbor to the east, Meknes offers gorgeous imperial architecture, ostentatious sights, and a little more peace for visitors to take their time and enjoy the city free of hassle and hustle. A short ride away, equally hidden away from the tourist trail, are the stunning Roman ruins of Volubilis.

TRANSPORTATION

Trains: Meknes has 2 stations with nearly identical service. Use the **Meknes al-Amir Abdelkader Station,** Rue d'Alger (☎055 51 61 35), 2 blocks from Av. Mohammed V. (The **Meknes Main Station** is farther from the center of town.) To: **Casablanca** (3-4hr., 11 per day 2:50am-7:30pm, 86dh) via **Rabat** (2-3hr., 60dh); **Fez** (50min., 10 per day 9:30am-1:30am, 18dh); **Marrakesh** (8hr., 8 per day 3:15am-5:30pm, 160dh); **Tangier** via **Sidi Kacem** (4hr., 4 per day 7:50am-2:15am, 80dh).

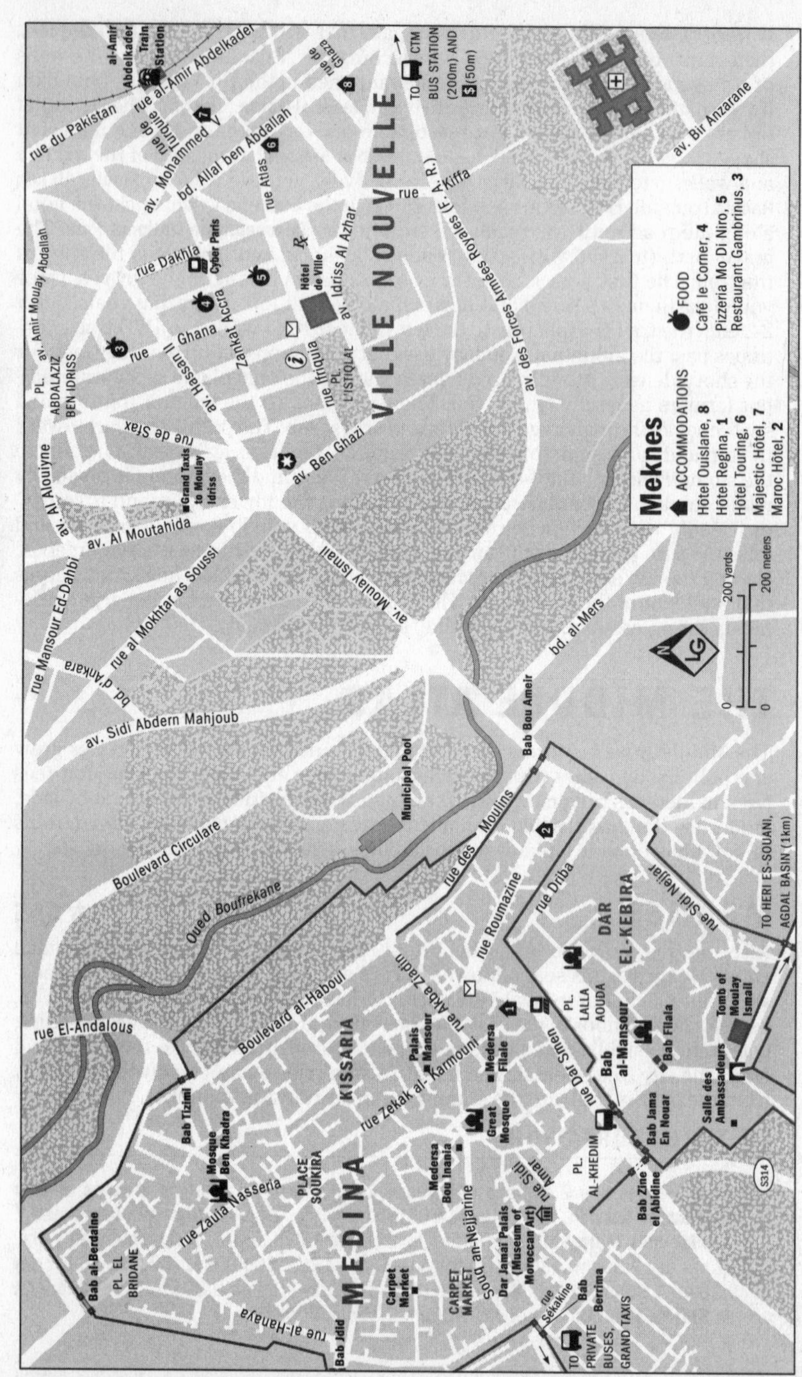

Meknes
ACCOMMODATIONS
Hôtel Ouislane, 8
Hôtel Regina, 1
Hôtel Touring, 6
Majestic Hôtel, 7
Maroc Hôtel, 2
FOOD
Café le Corner, 4
Pizzeria Mo Di Niro, 5
Restaurant Gambrinus, 3
200 yards
200 meters
VILLE NOUVELLE
MEDINA
KISSARIA
DAR EL-KEBIRA
Train Station
al-Amir Abdelkader
rue du Pakistan
rue al-Amir Abdelkader
rue de Ghaza
TO CTM BUS STATION (200m) AND $ (50m)
rue de Tunisie
av. Mohammed V
bd. Allal ben Abdallah
rue Atlas
rue Kiffa
av. des Forces Armées Royales (F.A.R.)
av. Bir Anzarane
av. Amir Moulay Abdallah
rue Dakhla
Cyber Paris
Hôtel de Ville
av. Idriss Al Azhar
PL. ABDALAZIZ BEN IDRISS
rue Ghana
Zankat Accra
rue Ifriquia
PL. L'ISTIQLAL
av. Hassan II
rue de Sfax
av. Al Alouiyne
Grand Taxis to Moulay Idriss
av. Ben Ghazi
av. Al Moutahida
rue Mansour Ed-Dahbi
rue al Mokhtar as Soussi
av. Moulay Ismail
bd. d'Ankara
bd. al-Mers
av. Sidi Abdern Mahjoub
Bab Bou Ameir
Municipal Pool
Boulevard Circulare
Oued Boufrekane
rue des Moulins
rue Roumazine
rue Driba
rue Sidi Nejjar
TO HERI ES-SOUANI, AGDAL BASIN (1km)
rue El-Andalous
Boulevard al-Haboul
rue Akba Ziadin
Palais Mansour
Medersa Filale
PL. LALLA AOUDA
Bab al-Mansour
Bab Filala
Tomb of Moulay Ismail
rue Dar Smen
rue Zekak al-Karmouni
Great Mosque
Bab Tizimi
Mosque Ben Khadra
PLACE SOUKIRA
rue Zaula Nasseria
Medersa Bou Inania
Bab Jama En Nouar
Salle des Ambassadeurs
rue Sidi Amar
PL. AL-KHEDIM
Bab Zine el Abidine
S314
Bab al-Berdaine
PL. EL BRIDANE
Carpet Market
CARPET MARKET
Souq an-Nejjarine
Dar Jamaï Palais (Museum of Moroccan Art)
rue Sekakine
Bab Berrima
rue al-Hanaya
Bab Jdid
TO PRIVATE BUSES, GRAND TAXIS

Buses: CTM, Av. des F.A.R. (☎055 51 47 59), a shiny, new station about 5 blocks from Av. Mohammed V (take a left when exiting the station; Av. Mohammed V will be to the right). To: **Casablanca** (4hr., 5 per day 3am-7pm, 80dh) via **Rabat** (3hr., 55dh); **Fez** (1hr., 4 per day, 4am-10:30pm, 25dh); **Marrakesh** (8hr., 7pm, 170dh); **Tangier** (5hr.; 12:15pm, 2am, 90-100 dh). **Private companies** depart from a station on Av. Mellah just outside Bab al-Khemis, on the far side of the medina from the *ville nouvelle.* A *petit taxi* is necessary. From window #5: **Casablanca** (11 per day, 5:30am-4pm) and **Rabat** (6, 11am, 12:15pm). From window #7: **Fez** (every hr. from 9am-6pm). From window #8: **Moulay Idriss** (every hr. 8am-6pm). From window #9: **Marrakesh** (4 per day 5:30am-6:30pm). From window #6: **Tangier** (7 per day, 4:45am-3pm) and **Tetouan** (4 per day, 5am-midnight) via Chefchaouen.

Taxis: *Grand taxis* cluster, among other places, on Av. des F.A.R., across from **Hotel Continental,** next to the private bus station, and outside the al-Amir Abdelkader train station. To: **Fez** (20dh), **Moulay Idriss** (10dh), **Rabat** (40dh).

ORIENTATION AND PRACTICAL INFORMATION

The river Oued Boufrekane divides the *ville nouvelle* from the medina and the adjacent imperial city. The train and CTM buses deposit passengers in the *ville nouvelle.* Tree-lined **Avenue Mohammed V,** the new city's main drag, intersects with **Avenue Hassan II** at a large roundabout surrounded by cafes and shops. From the intersection, follow Av. Hassan II, which turns into Av. Moulay Ismail, to approach the medina via Bab Bou-Amir. To reach **Bab al-Mansour** (the entrance to the imperial complex) and **Plaza al-Khedim** (the medina's main square), head uphill from Bab Bou-Amir, take a right on Rue Roumazine and then a left on Rue Dar Smen. It's a 20min. walk between the *ville nouvelle* and Bab Mansour. A *petit taxi* costs about 10dh. The private bus station drops you on the west side of the medina at Bab al-Khemis.

Tourist Office: 27 Pl. l'Istiqlal (☎055 52 44 26). Right next to the post office. Some English and Spanish spoken. Brochure with basic map of city. Guides are only necessary if you want more historical information about the sites, as Meknes is quite easy to navigate. Tours ½-day 150dh, full day 250dh. Open July-Sept. M-F 8am-6:30pm, Oct.-June M-F 8:30am-noon and 2:30-6:30pm.

Currency Exchange: BMCE, 98 Av. des F.A.R. (☎035 52 03 52), has **ATMs.** Exchange window open daily 9am-1pm and 4-7pm. Banks line Mohammed V and Hassan II.

Late-Night Pharmacy: Red Crescent Emergency Pharmacy (☎035 52 33 75), in Pl. l'Istiqlal, located in the south side of the Hotel de Ville, the town's administrative building. Open daily 8:30am-8:30pm.

Hospitals: Hôpital Moulay Ismail (☎035 52 28 05 or 52 28 06), down Rue Kiffa and up a flight of stairs.

Internet Access: Many choices in the *ville nouvelle,* including **Cyber Paris,** Rue de Accra. 6dh per hr. Open daily 9am-late. In the medina, try **Cyber Bab Mansour,** Rue Dar Smen just east of the gate. Fast connection. 10dh per hr. Open 10am-11pm.

Post Office: Pl. l'Istiqlal. Poste Restante at the side entrance. Open M-F 8am-4:15pm, Sa 8:30am-noon. Parcel service and exchange open M-F 8am-7pm. Branch office on Rue Dar Smen, near the medina.

ACCOMMODATIONS

MEDINA

Rue Roumazine and Rue Dar Smen house most of the medina's budget hotels, some of which are stunningly cheap. But you get what you pay for, and the primitive comforts might leave you longing for the *ville nouvelle.*

Hotel Regina, 19 Rue Dar Smen (☎035 53 02 80). The best option among the beaten-up budget hotels along the road. Beds are large and firm and rooms come with sinks. A sunny patio downstairs is nice to sit around and chat. Luggage storage 5dh per bag per day. Laundry 50dh per load. Hot showers 5dh. Singles 70dh, doubles 100dh, triples 150dh, quads 180dh. ❶

Maroc Hôtel, 7 Rue Roumazine (☎035 53 00 75). The *petit* garden outside is cute and peaceful but the interior is a little tacky—the carpet is like a fake putting green. For all that, a good value at its price, with hot showers and sinks in the rooms. Breakfast 20dh. Singles 90dh, doubles 180dh. Sleep on the terrace for 50dh. ❶

VILLE NOUVELLE

The *ville nouvelle* offers greater comfort and value and easier access to banks, CTM buses, and trains, but prices are higher than in the medina. Most of the cheapest hotels lie around Av. Mohammed V and Rue Allal ben Abdallah.

Majestic Hôtel, 19 Av. Mohammed V (☎035 52 20 35), near the train station. Bursting with personality—some rooms with leather furniture, others with elegant black wood. All are clean and spacious, some with huge, gleaming white baths—a major luxury. There's also an airy patio and a quiet little rooftop terrace. Breakfast included. Singles 140-200dh, doubles 215-300dh. Off-season 10% discount. ❶

Hotel Ouislane, 54 Rue Allal ben Abdallah (☎035 52 48 28). An upscale option with huge beds, shower, phone, and toilet. Immaculate rooms not particularly exciting but very comfortable, as they should be at this price. Singles 231dh, doubles 276dh, triples 359dh, quads 428dh. ❷

Hôtel Touring, 34 Rue Allal ben Abdallah (☎035 52 23 51), on the street parallel to Mohammed V away from the train station, near the intersection with rue Atlas. One of the cheapest places in the *ville nouvelle,* offers dim but spacious and uncluttered rooms. Singles 70dh, with shower 90dh; doubles 95/110dh. ❶

FOOD

MEDINA

The medina here has a disappointing lack of sit-down restaurants, trying to compensate with huge quantities of snack bars and rotisserie chicken. Food in the medina is a cheap, quick affair; if you want a dining experience, head to the *ville nouvelle.* That said, Pl. al-Khedim is full of vendors selling tasty smoked sausage sandwiches (20dh), fries, and corn on the cob, accompanied by the requisite orange juice stands. Rue Dar Smen is home to innumerable chicken places that give you a quarter of a chicken and fries for 25dh. Try to eat at places where you can see the food prepared, so you know that it is fresh.

VILLE NOUVELLE

The *ville nouvelle* is crammed with *patisseries,* pizza restaurants, and foreign imports. It can be difficult to find good Moroccan food, but the dining is more relaxed here than in the medina.

Restaurant Gambrinus, Rue Zankat Omar ibn Ass (☎035 52 02 58). Small tables make for quiet, intimate conversation over excellently cooked Moroccan favorites. Carefully origami-folded napkins and paintings add a bit of class. Come for the breakfast omelettes (20dh) or a slow, laid-back dinner. Couscous and *tajines* 60-70dh. 3-course menu 77dh. Open M-F 11am-3pm and 7-11pm, Sa 7-11pm. ❷

Pizzeria Mo Di Nero, 14 Rue Antserape (☎035 51 76 76). Hamburgers (16dh) and pizza (36-60dh) are the order of the day in this sleek, modern restaurant, with Moroccan soaps playing in the background. After eating, head to the swanky leather chairs in front for a coffee. Italian dishes 35-40dh. Open daily noon-3pm and 7-11pm. ❷

Café le Corner, 16 Rue Zankat Accra. Join the old men sipping tea on the terrace, a perfect corner spot to watch the crowds roll by. Women might feel more comfortable at the indoor seating. Specializes in tea and coffee but serves up traditional Moroccan *tajine* breakfasts (18dh) for a quick bite in the morning. Open daily 9am-11pm. ❶

SIGHTS

Almost all of Meknes' sights are located in and around the Bab Mansour, Morocco's most impressive gateway, built in 1732 by Moulay Ismail's son. Through the gate are the imperial monuments; behind it, across the plaza, is the medina.

IMPERIAL MEKNES

Weakened by war, weather, and the Great Earthquake of 1755, the ramparts of the Dar al-Kebira (Imperial City) testify to Meknes's former glory. Sultan Moulay Ismail, who, along with Hassan II, is perhaps Morocco's most revered visionary, personally supervised the building of over 25km of protective walls for his city within a city. Strolling about the site with a pick-ax and whip in hand, the sultan criticized and occasionally decapitated the enslaved Christian workers who displeased him. Scavenging materials from monuments all over Morocco, including Roman marble from the ruins at Volubilis, Moulay Ismail created a capital worthy of a conqueror of his stature. His grandson moved the capital to Marrakesh and the imperial city fell into neglect and dereliction, remembered and restored only well into the 20th century.

TOMB OF MOULAY ISMAIL. A series of simply tiled courtyards lead into a beautiful inner courtyard with a bubbling fountain where people perform ablutions before praying. The tomb itself is roped off in a richly carpeted room to the right, flanked by two functioning grandfather clocks, a consolation prize from Louis XIV after he refused Moulay Ismail's proposal to his daughter (no real tragedy for Moulay; he already had over 300 lovers). As usual, the carpets, stucco work, cedar ceilings, and the tomb itself are artisanal masterpieces, fit for a grand figure of Morocco's history. *(Through the 2 blue arches, and then immediately to the left. Open M-Th and Sa-Su 9am-noon and 3-6pm. Remember to take off your shoes inside, as people pray here. No pictures. Free, but donations requested in the room of the tomb.)*

SALLE DES AMBASSADEURS. Standing by itself in an open court is the green-tiled roof of the recently restored **Salle des Ambassadeurs,** where Ismail conducted affairs of state. Now it holds a plaque celebrating Meknes's status as an UNESCO World Heritage site. The building holds little else of note, so head down the stairs to the right to the so-called **"Christian Dungeon,"** a 6 sq. km underground storehouse and granary for the Sultan, his entourage, and their horses. More than one local might tell you that it once held some 50,000-100,000 Christian prisoners, but it was probably just a granary. There's not much down there, but it's fun to walk around the musty caverns. Since the "dungeon" remains a cool 15°C even in summer, it is the perfect place to avoid the midday sun. *(From*

Pl. al-Khedim, go through Bab al-Mansour or one of the nearby smaller gates, walk straight, and follow the wall on the right around the bend. Open daily 9am-noon and 3-6pm. 10dh.)

OTHER IMPERIAL CITY SIGHTS. A short trek from Moulay Ismail's tomb is the **Heri al-Souani** (storehouse), a granary with immense cisterns designed for prolonged sieges. It was also used to provide stabling and food for an incredible 12,000 horses. *(Open daily 9am-noon and 3-6pm. 10dh.)* Below lies the Agdal Basin, once Moulay Ismail's private country club and his reservoir in case of siege. His wives (more than 300) and their 800 kids were said to swim here to escape the stifling summer heat. Today, it is a nice place for an evening stroll. *(To get to the Heri al-Souani and Agdal Basin from Bab al-Mansour, walk down the road past his tomb for 15min., or take a petit taxi for 7dh. Free.)*

MEDINA

Meknes's medina is more pleasant, tranquil, and compact than those of the other imperial cities, thanks to the long years of neglect which kept its size manageable. Facing the Museum Dar Jamaï, take the alley to the left of the entrance. Push straight ahead to **Souq al-Nejjarine,** a major street. Heading left here brings you first to the textile souq, the carpenters' souq, and the carpet market. The rest of the medina is best explored like any other: wander until you get lost, then try to find your way out.

GREAT MOSQUE AND MADRASA MEDERSA BOU INANIA. While the Great Mosque is off-limits to non-Muslims, the semi-hidden 14th-century Medersa Bou Inania across from it is not. A college of theology and Muslim law, this *medersa* is another example of the glorious Merenid style, a wonderful melange of stucco, cedar, and *zellij* tilework handcrafted with stunning precision. Upstairs are a number of cells, each of which snugly hosted at least two students. The roof, which you may have to unlock yourself, offers a splendid view of the minaret of the Great Mosque and the rooftops of Meknes. *(Face Dar Jamaï in pl. al-Khedim, turn right onto rue Sidi Amar, and enter the medina. Follow the alley as it turns left, then fork right. Madrasa open daily 9am-noon and 3-6pm. 10dh.)*

MUSEUM DAR JAMAÏ. Once a palace belonging to a family of viziers to Moulay Hassan I, the building later became a hospital until 1920, when it was converted into this museum. The inner rooms are gorgeously decorated in stucco and cedar woodwork. On display is a decent collection of Berber carpets, old rifles, jewelry, and pottery, along with the obligatory displays of fantastic handwrought wooden doors. Check out the saddles and rifles used for *fantasia*, the traditional cavalry charge still performed at local festivals. *(At the far end of pl. al-Khedim. Open M and W-Su 9am-noon and 3-6pm. 10dh.)*

DAYTRIP FROM MEKNES

VOLUBILIS

There are no direct buses to Volubulis. A taxi is the most convenient and reliable method of transportation. While you can hire a grand taxi near the private bus station in Meknes, you need a 6-person party to get the cheapest fare, and taxis rarely fill up. Alone it will cost 150-180dh. The surest way is to take a grand taxi to Moulay Idriss (30min., 10dh per place). They leave from a lot on Av. des Nations Unies, 2 blocks north of the intersection of Av. Moulay Ismail and Av. Hassan II in the ville nouvelle. From Moulay Idriss, either walk if it's not too hot (4km. 40min., straight from junction with Moulay Idriss and then left at the sign for Oualili), or save your energy and take another taxi from Moulay Idriss (20dh total). To get back to Meknes, flag down a taxi back to Moulay Idriss (5dh). Just up the hill on the left are the grand taxis to Meknes. Don't try to return too late: rides become scarcer the later it gets. In general, leave yourself at least 1½hr. to enjoy the ruins.

Set among olive groves 33km from Meknes are the best-preserved Roman ruins in North Africa: **Volubilis.** Declared a World Heritage site in 1997, the stunning **mosaics** and crumbling columns are a must-see if you're passing through Meknes. Don't be surprised to see archaeologists and diggers, as 16 hectares remain totally unexcavated, but the ruins are often wonderfully empty.

The oldest continuous inhabitants of Volubilis were the Carthaginians. The city became a major center for the olive oil trade under Roman rule, reaching its zenith in the AD second and third centuries when it became the capital of the kingdom of Mauritania. The Romans, who viewed their North African possessions as a bread basket for their citizens, ordered the deforestation of the area to make room for grain crops; from that point on, local resources dwindled and the city began to decline. When Moulay Idriss took control of the city in the 18th century, he siphoned off much of the residential population to Fez and Meknes and ransacked the city for materials to build his palace. The same earthquake that ravaged Lisboa in 1755 destroyed what was left of Volubilis, and it remained forgotten and abandoned until the 20th century.

Head past the ticket office and over a small bridge, take a left and follow the path up the steps to the right, toward the ruins of a cluster of houses and olive presses. Follow the stone path to the two tall cypresses, under which sits the **House of Orpheus.** At left are the first collection of mosaics, one depicting the myth of Orpheus and Eurydice, the other showcasing a collection of sea creatures. Just uphill is a completely restored stone building, which houses a model of an **olive press.** This liquid gold wasn't just for cooking: the Romans used it to scrub themselves down after bathing. While the **baths** across the way are crumbling, they're a testament to the advanced plumbing systems the Romans employed. Continue uphill to the columned **capitol** and **basilica.** Once used as a court, the arcaded basilica is the most delightfully picturesque part of the ruins. Now's the time to remember those elementary school orations. Further along the path is the **House of the Acrobat,** with two great mosaics. In the middle of town looms the **Triumphal Arch,** built in AD 217. The gate marks the beginning of the town's main street, Decumanus Maximus. The houses along the street, including the **House of the Ephebus** and the **House of the Knight,** have impressive mosaics depicting scenes from Greco-Roman mythology. The best ones are in the **House of Venus,** off the road toward the lonely cypress tree. Walk to the right of the placard and up the three steps to see the *Abduction of Hylas by the Nymphs* and *Diana Bathing,* which retain much of their original color. Walk to the **Tangier Gate** at the top of the road for panoramic views of the ruins.

The ruins are open daily sunrise to sunset (admission 10dh; bring exact change). They are more peaceful and scenic in the early morning or late afternoon. Bring a hat, sunscreen, water, and sunglasses if you plan on visiting in the afternoon, and you may want to pack lunch, as there is only one small cafe. When US General George C. Patton visited the ruins, he declined an offer of a guided tour—he believed he had been stationed here as a Roman centurion in his previous life and thus knew his way around. Unless you have been similarly blessed, you might consider hiring a guide (available through the ticket office for roughly 150dh per small group).

FEZ ☎055, 035

The colorful, chaotic medina of Fez beats at its own crazy pace. Donkeys rush by with refrigerators on their backs, old men weave carpets and dance around dye pits with huge stacks of leather, children lead lost tourists out of alleyways, and everyone is selling something. Since UNESCO designated Fez a World Heritage Site in 1981, the city's walls have been largely restored, rebuilding a link

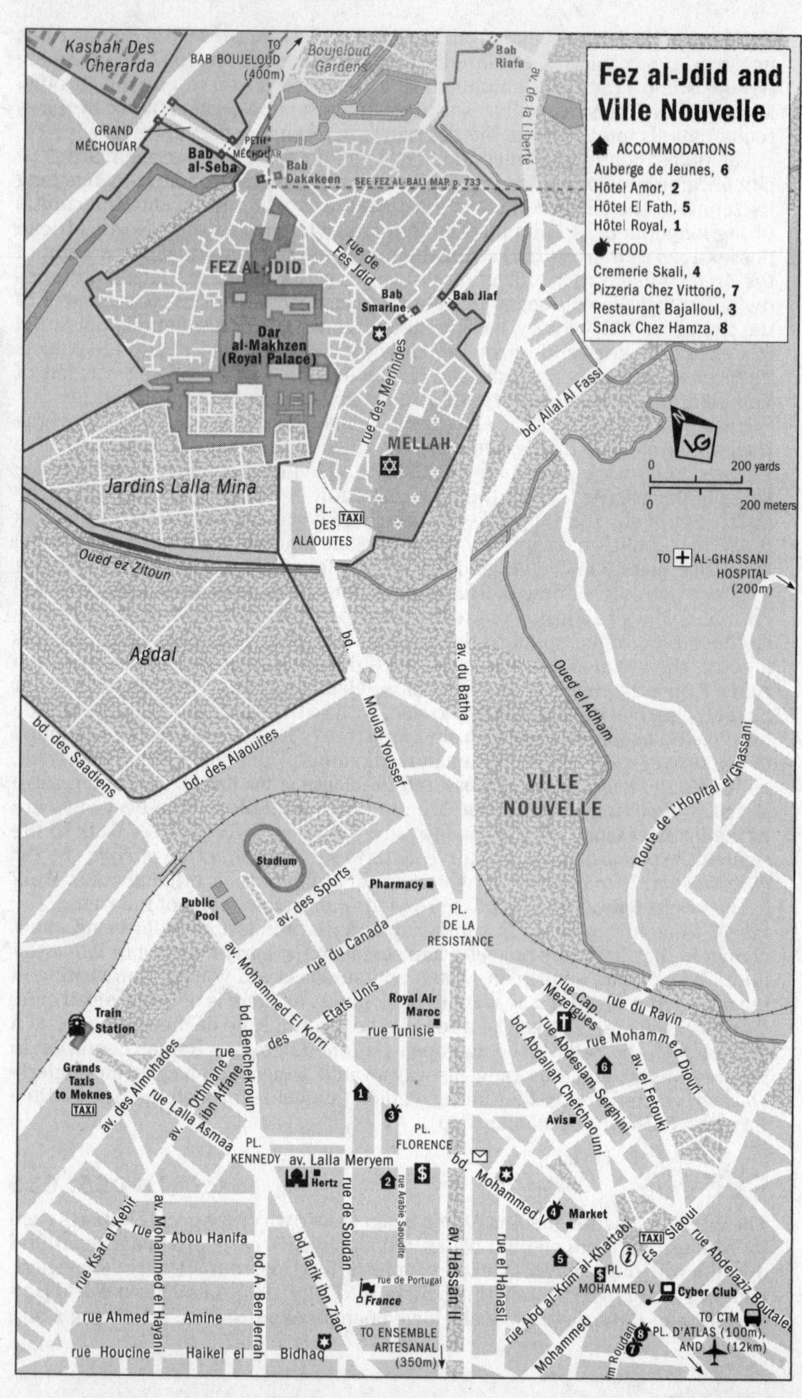

Fez al-Jdid and Ville Nouvelle
ACCOMMODATIONS
Auberge de Jeunes, 6
Hôtel Amor, 2
Hôtel El Fath, 5
Hôtel Royal, 1
FOOD
Cremerie Skali, 4
Pizzeria Chez Vittorio, 7
Restaurant Bajalloul, 3
Snack Chez Hamza, 8
Kasbah Des Cherarda
TO BAB BOUJELOUD (400m)
Boujeloud Gardens
Bab Riafa
av. de la Liberté
GRAND MÉCHOUAR
PETIT MÉCHOUAR
Bab al-Seba
Bab Dakakeen
SEE FEZ AL-BALI MAP, p. 733
FEZ AL-JDID
rue de Fes Jdid
Bab Smarine
Bab Jiaf
Dar al-Makhzen (Royal Palace)
rue des Merinides
MELLAH
bd. Allal Al Fassi
Jardins Lalla Mina
PL. DES ALAOUITES
0 200 yards
0 200 meters
Oued ez Zitoun
TO AL-GHASSANI HOSPITAL (200m)
Agdal
bd. Moulay Youssef
av. du Batha
Oued el Adham
VILLE NOUVELLE
Route de L'Hopital el Ghassani
bd. des Saadiens
bd. des Alaouites
Stadium
Pharmacy
Public Pool
av. des Sports
PL. DE LA RESISTANCE
rue du Canada
av. Mohammed El Korri
des Etats Unis
Royal Air Maroc
rue Tunisie
rue Cap. Mezergues
rue du Ravin
rue Mohammed Diouri
Train Station
bd. Benchekroun
rue Othmane ibn Affane
bd. Abdallah Chefchaouni
rue Abdeslam Serghini
av. el Fetouki
Grands Taxis to Meknes
av. des Almohades
rue Lalla Asmaa
Avis
PL. FLORENCE
PL. KENNEDY
av. Lalla Meryem
Hertz
bd. Mohammed V
rue Arabie Saoudite
Market
rue Ksar el Kebir
av. Mohammed el Hayani
rue Abou Hanifa
rue de Soudan
bd. Tarik ibn Ziad
av. Hassan II
rue el Hanasli
rue Abd al-Krim al-Khattabi
Es Slaoui
rue Abdelaziz Boutaleb
bd. A. Ben Jerrah
rue de Portugal
France
PL. MOHAMMED V
Cyber Club
TO CTM
rue Ahmed Amine
TO ENSEMBLE ARTESANAL (350m)
Mohammed
PL. D'ATLAS (100m), AND (12km)
rue Houcine Haikel el Bidhaq

EXPLORING MOROCCO

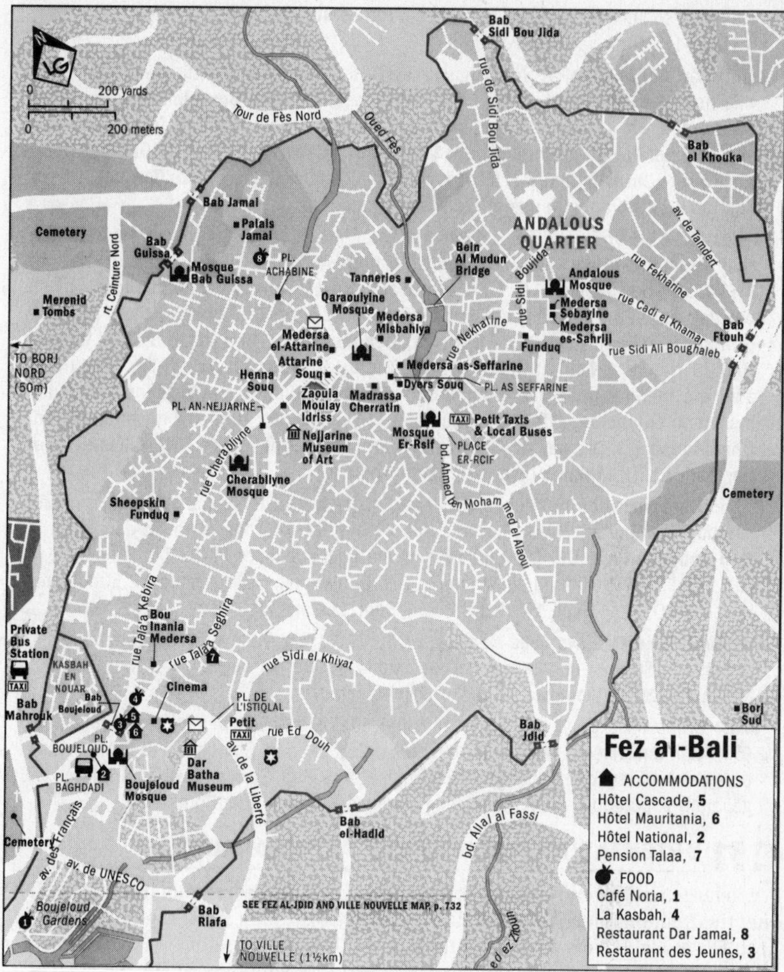

with its long and illustrious past. Founded in the 8th century by Moulay Idriss I, Fez rose to prominence with the construction of the Qaraouiyine, one of the world's first universities, in the 9th century. Fez emerged as the Maghreb's preeminent city, nurturing political dynasties and handing down legal rulings to the rest of the region. Fez reconciles its identity as the oldest town in Morocco with the demands of a modern city in the *ville nouvelle*, all while managing to remain at the artistic, intellectual, and spiritual helm of the nation.

TRANSPORTATION

Flights: Aérodrome de Fès-Saïs (☎035 62 48 00), 12km out of town on the road to Immouzzèr. Bus #16 leaves from Pl. Mohammed V (3dh). *Grand taxis* (120dh) also run there. **Royal Air Maroc,** 54 Av. Hassan II (☎035 62 55 16), flies daily to **Casa-**

blanca. Also services **Tangier, Marrakesh, Marseilles, London,** and **Paris.** Open daily 8:15am-12:30pm and 3:30-7:30pm.

Trains: Av. Almohades, at Rue Chenguit (☎055 93 03 33), a 5min. taxi ride to the ville nouvelle (5dh) or a 10min. ride to the medina's **Bab Boujeloud** (10dh). 2nd-class trains are a little pricier than buses but more than worth it. To: **Casablanca** (4hr., 15 per day, 2:10am-6:50pm); **Marrakesh** (7-8hr., 9 per day, 2:30am-6:50pm) via **Rabat** (3hr.); **Meknes** (1hr., 11 per day 2:10am-6:50pm). For **Tangier,** take a westbound train and change at Sidi Kacem junction.

Buses: CTM (☎055 73 29 92) stops near Pl. d'Atlas, at the far end of the *ville nouvelle.* From Pl. Florence, walk down Blvd. Mohammed V for 15min. and turn left onto Av. Youssef ben Tachfine. At Pl. d'Atlas, take the 1st right. To: **Casablanca** (5hr., 8 per day 6am-2am, 105dh) via **Rabat** (3hr., 75-80dh); **Chefchaouen** and **Tetouan** (4hr.; 8, 11:15am, 11:45pm; 75-90dh); **Meknes** (1hr., 9 and 11pm, 25dh); **Tangier** (6hr., 4 per day 11am-1:30am, 115dh). The **private bus station** in Fez is just outside the medina near **Bab Boujeloud,** and seems like it was designed to cause maximum confusion, with a huge number of windows for different destinations. To: **Casablanca** (25 per day 4:30am-1pm, 76dh) via **Rabat** (54dh); **Marrakesh** (5 per day 5am-9pm); **Meknes** (every 2hr. 6am-8pm).

EXPLORING MOROCCO

Public Transportation: Pl. Mohammed V and Pl. de la Résistance are the major hubs for city buses. Important routes include: bus **#9** and **11** from the Syndicat d'Initiative to **Bab Boujeloud** and **Dar Batha; #19** from the train station to **Pl. Rcif** in the middle of Fez al-Bali; **#47** from the train station to **Bab Boujeloud.** City buses cost 2.50dh; fares increase 20% July-Sept. 15 after 8:30pm, Sept. 16-June after 8pm.

Car Rental: Hertz, 1 Ave. Lalla Meryem (☎035 62 28 12). Open M-Sa 8:30am-noon and 2-6:30pm, Su 9am-noon. Cars start at around 500dh per day, 20% tax not included. Minimum age 25. Domestic drivers' license required.

Taxis: *Grand taxis* go to the airport (120dh), **Meknes** (20dh per person), and **Rabat** (60-70dh per person) along with other local destinations. Stands are at the train station, the bus station, Place de la Resistance, and Bab Guissa. **Petit taxi** drivers are generally good about using the meter. Fares increase 50% after 8pm.

ORIENTATION AND PRACTICAL INFORMATION

Fez is large and spread-out but still manageable. It is essentially three cities in one: the fashionable, French-built *ville nouvelle,* 1.5km from the medina; the Arab **Fez al-Jdid** ("New Fez"), containing the Jewish cemetery and the palace of Hassan II, next to the medina; and the enormous medina of **Fez al-Bali** ("Old Fez") housing nearly 500,000 residents. The *ville nouvelle* is most convenient for services, with the quietest accommodations, and is based on **Av. Hassan II** and **Blvd. Mohammed V,** which intersect at the more central **Pl. Florence,** the center of activity. Walking down Av. Moulay Youssef from the *ville nouvelle* brings you to **Pl. Alaouites** in Fez al-Jdid, directly in front of the king's palace, **Dar al-Makhzen.** After passing through Bab Smarine on the left, Rue Fez al-Jdid follows the length of the palace. At the end, a right through Bab Dakakeen leads to Fez al-Bali and its main gate Bab Boujeloud. The two main streets of Fez al-Bali heading down from the gate are **Tala'a Kebira** and **Tala'a Seghira,** although they are barely wide enough for its shops, a donkey, and your backpack.

Tourist Office: Syndicat d'Initiative, Pl. Mohammed V (☎055 62 34 60). You may need more guidance than their maps give, but luckily the staff is helpful and can answer most questions. Hire official guides for 150dh for half-day, 250dh for full day. Open M-F 8:30am-noon and 2:30-6:30pm, Sa 8:30am-noon.

Currency Exchange: BMCE, Pl. Mohammed V, opposite the Syndicat d'Initiative and to the right of main bank entrance. Handles MC/V and travelers check transactions. Has **ATMs.** Open M-F 8:15am-2:15pm. Pl. Florence has branches of most Moroccan banks.

Luggage Storage: At the train station. 10dh per bag, 6am-9pm. Also at the private bus station, 5 dh per bag. Open 6am-11pm.

Police: ☎19. Corner of Av. Mohammed V and Rue Allal Laoudiyi, next to the post office.

Late-night Pharmacy: Municipalité de Fès, Av. Moulay Youssef (☎035 62 34 93), off Pl. de la Résistance, 5min. uphill from royal palace. Open daily 9pm-6am.

Hospital: al-Ghassani (☎035 62 27 77), in the Dhar al-Mahrez district east of town. From Pl. Mohammed V, walk down Ave. Mohammed Slaoui as it becomes Ben Arbi Alaoui for 15 mins., and then turn left on Ave. al-Ghassani.

Internet Access: There are several internet cafes in the *ville nouvelle;* just look for a "Cyber" sign. **Cyber Club** is one block south of Pl. Mohammed V, on a corner on the left, above the teleboutique. 10dh per hour. Open daily 10am-8pm.

Post Office: At the corner of Av. Hassan II and Blvd. Mohammed V in the *ville nouvelle.* Branch offices at Pl. d'Atlas and in the medina at Pl. Batha. All branches open July-Sept. 15 M-F 8:30am-2:30pm, Sa 8-11:45am; Sept. 16-June M-F 8:30am-12:15pm and 2:30-6:30pm.

ACCOMMODATIONS

VILLE NOUVELLE

Accommodations in the *ville nouvelle* offer an escape from the madness of the medina and generally offer a little more value for your money. Pl. Florence and the southern end of Av. Mohammed V have good options for a cheap room.

Hotel Royal, 36 Rue de Soudan (☎035 62 46 56), off Pl. Florence. Perfect location in the center of the *ville nouvelle.* Good value—simple rooms are big and airy, all with showers and some with balconies over the street. Hot water in the morning only. Singles 100dh; doubles 140dh; triples 190dh; quads 230dh. ❶

Auberge de Jeunes (HI), 18 Rue de Abdeslam Serghini (☎035 62 40 85; www.fesyouth-hostel.com). High walls hide the shady, tree-filled courtyard. Rooms are small but well-maintained. Communal showers are sparkling, but cold. Single-sex dorms 55dh. Doubles 130dh. HI members pay 5dh less. ❶

Hôtel Amor, 31 Rue Arabie Saoudite (☎055 62 27 24), off pl. Florence. Quiet lobby leads to clean, well-furnished rooms with pretty beds. Private showers with hot water. Attached restaurant and bar is a convenient plus. Singles 170dh; doubles 192dh. ❷

Hotel El Fath, 107 Rue Mohammed El Hayani (☎035 94 46 50), on the corner of Blvd. Mohammed V. Higher floors are a hike and furniture is a little banged up, but years of scribbles add personality. Balconies offer nice views over the bustle of the *ville nouvelle.* Hot water all day long. Singles 100dh; doubles 150dh. ❶

FEZ AL-BALI

Just inside the Bab Boujeloud are a slew of budget hotels. They may be lacking in luxury (or hot water, even), and you'll be hassled as soon as you step out the door, but it is the place to stay if you want to be close to the action.

Hôtel Cascade, 26 Serrajine Boujeloud (☎055 63 84 42), just inside Bab Boujeloud and to the right. Hugely popular with backpackers and tourists, Cascade is a social place with friendly staff and simple, pretty rooms. Bathrooms are sparkling and showers are hot. The terrace, full of people playing cards and chatting around the snack bar, provides a bird's-eye view of Bab Boujeloud and the medina. Fills up quickly, so come early. Singles 80dh; double with shower 180dh; terrace 40 dh. ❶

Hôtel Mauritania, 20 Serrajine Boujeloud (☎055 63 35 18), to the right after the Bab Boujeloud. Whole place is a little battered, including the tiled rooms and shower, but it's right there in the medina. Beds are big with a strangely generous amount of bedding for the Fassi summer. Hot showers 10dh. Singles 80dh; doubles 150dh. ❶

Pension Talaa, 14 Talaa Seghira (☎035 63 33 59), right off the street. Rooms are absolutely minuscule but clean and newly-tiled, and management is friendly. Showers and modern toilet in wooden stalls, but clean and come with hot water. Watch yourself on the stairs to the top—they are unimaginably steep. Singles 75dh; doubles 150dh. ❶

Hotel National, Pl. Boujeloud, just before the gate on the left. Cracks in the floor and spare rooms are made up for by friendly owner and colorful tile and paintings on the way up. Shower could use a little more light. Singles 100dh; doubles 120dh. ❶

FOOD

VILLE NOUVELLE

Cheap sandwich shops and rotisserie places are the order of the day in the *ville nouvelle,* along with Italian spots, all of which offer a guilty getaway from Moroccan food. Pastry places and juice shops along Blvd. Mohammed V are top-notch, and perfect spots for a sweet breakfast. Or simply poke through stalls of fresh food at the central market on **Blvd. Mohammed V,** two blocks up from Pl. Mohammed V. (Open daily 8am-2pm.)

Pizzeria Chez Vittorio, 21 Rue Brahim Roudania (☎055 62 47 30), just down from Hotel Central. Does a convincing job of capturing the ambience of a small Italian joint—wine, conversation, red tablecloths, and a family feel. Beer (25-35dh), wine, and spirits served. 10% service charge. Pizza and spaghetti 60-75dh. Open daily noon-4pm and 7-11pm. MC/V. ❷

Restaurant Bajalloul, 22 Rue Arabie Saoudite, on the inside corner of Pl. Florence. Locals, families, and chatty women come for heaping meat plates (30-40dh), most served with salad. Open daily noon-midnight. ❷

Cremerie Skali, Blvd. Mohammed V, 3 blocks up from Pl. Mohammed V. A shaded breakfast spot on the corner that with pastries (5-10dh) and huge plates of fried eggs (15dh). The tropical juices (8-11dh) alone make a stop worthwhile. Open daily 7am-10pm. ❶

Snack Chez Hamza, 25 rue Brahim Roudani (☎055 93 02 14), across the street from Hotel Central. A no-frills sandwich shop. Good for a bite on the run. Sandwiches 15dh. *Tajines* and couscous 25-35dh. ❶

FEZ AL-BALI

Stalls line **Tala'a Kebira** and **Tala'a Seghira,** near the **Bab Boujeloud** and are scattered further down toward the sights. *Harira* (spicy lentil soup; 10dh) typically comes with potatoes and bread. Sandwiches will run you 15dh. Fresh-squeezed and cheap orange juice (3-4dh) is plentiful outside Bab Boujeloud. For some of the cheapest eateries in Morocco, go left from Tala'a Kebira at **Madrasa al-Atarrine,** and head into the medina toward **Pl. Achabine.** Other than the relatively cheap fare just inside the gate, sit-down dining in the medina consists of pricey "palace" restaurants done up in extreme Moroccan decor.

La Kasbah, Rue Serrajine just inside Bab Boujeloud. A sweet set of terraces overlooking the entrance to the medina offer shade, a breeze, and a beautiful view. Big helpings of standard Moroccan food. Plates 40dh, menu 70dh. Open daily 10am-11pm. ❷

Restaurant des Jeunes, 16 Rue Serrajine (☎055 63 49 75), next to Hotel Cascade. Quick and reliable Moroccan staples, right there by the Bab. Breakfasts (20dh) include omelette and crepe delights. Proximity to hotels guarantees more than a few tourists. Plates 40dh, menu 70dh. Open daily 9am-midnight. ❶

Restaurant Dar Jamai, 14 Foundouk Lihoudi (☎035 63 56 85), 100m from the Palais Jamai. Take a left past the hotel, then a right. Hang a left and follow the signs. Elegantly decked out with pillows and Berber rugs, a traditional restaurant without the excess of the other "palace" spots. Huge 4-course menu 100dh. Open daily noon-11pm. ❸

Café Noria, Boujeloud Gardens. Technically in Fez al-Jdid. At the end of Rue de Fez al-Jdid, head down the stairs; it's just inside the Boujeloud gardens. Known as the "Lover's Café," come here with or without your love to sip an orange juice or mint tea under the huge shady canopy of the trees. A getaway from the noise of the medina. Light menu available. Drinks 8-10dh. Salads 20dh. Open 8am-10pm. ❶

SIGHTS

FEZ AL-BALI

The medina here is a world of its own, a nest of 9000 unmarked streets packed with millennia-old *medersas*, *souqs*, and mosques, all withstanding the carnival of donkeys, artisans, and shopkeepers that own the narrow streets. While there are sights to be seen, wandering off down narrow alleys and taking a random turn can lead to colorful scenes just as worthwhile. The madness abates a little under the midday sun, so if you want to poke around when it is least crowded, come between noon and 3pm.

WITH A GUIDE. The easiest way to get to know the medina is with a guide. Official guides, speaking many languages, are available at the **Syndicat d'Initiative.** They'll save you time, discourage hustlers, and provide detailed explanations. (Don't assume that they'll help you bargain for goods, though.) You can hire a guide for half a day (3hr., 150dh) or a full day (5-6hr., 250dh). Though much cheaper, unofficial guides are illegal, often lack historical knowledge, and usually take travelers only to shops from which they will get a hefty commission. Whoever you hire, nail down an itinerary and price right off the bat.

WITHOUT A GUIDE. The bold and independent will find that with a little effort and research, the medina can be conquered (well, explored) without a guide. To keep hustlers and merchants at bay, ignore calls or hisses and simply say "*non, merci*" or "*la shokran*" to those who approach you directly. Remember: walking downhill will take you farther into the medina, while trekking uphill will lead you out to Bab Boujeloud. Without a guide, there are two classic approaches to exploring the medina. The first is to head to the main gateway **Bab Boujeloud** and wander down **Tala'a Kebira** from there. Virtually all of the sights in Fez's medina lie along the Tala'a Kebira (or the Grand Tala'a), old Fez's main street and an essential reference point for anyone attempting to navigate the medina. The Tala'a Kebira heads downhill from Bab Boujeloud to the **Qaraouiyine Mosque** area. The Bab Boujeloud is the main entrance to the medina; faux guides tend to gather here. Built in 1912 by the Frenchman Maréchal Lauyote, the *bab* is tiled in blue on one side (the color of Fez) and green on the other (the color of Islam). The square just inside the *bab* is where the Moroccan revolution against the French occupation began. Down to the right is the **Tala'a Seghira,** Fez's other main street, lined mostly by shops cater-

LES MUSIQUES DU MONDE

Every year in early June, people from all over the world pour into the ancient city of Fez to hear Sufi chants in Arabic, requiems in Latin, and popular songs in African patois and Hindi. This confusion of tongues has one common purpose—to share the world's sacred heritages through music.

The World Sacred Music Festival brings together performing artists from around the world in an effort to promote interfaith and intercultural dialogue. In the past, stars like Ravi Shankar of India have performed, but more traditionally smaller local groups are the headliners. Concerts are free to the public and take place in Dar Batha, outside Bab Boujeloud, and in the Bab Makina.

In addition, the Festival hosts Fez Encounters, a series of talks bringing together journalists, academics, and politicians to discuss global issues ranging from climate change to cultural identity in the face of globalization. The role of moral belief in the modern world is central here, but the art and music are what draw crowds and truly bring them together.

The World Sacred Music festival 2009 will take place May 29-June 6, 2009. While concerts and talks are free, finding accommodations during the festival can be difficult, so booking ahead is advisable. Visit www.fesfestival.com for more information on dates and events.

ing to locals. The second approach is to taxi inside the medina to the more centrally located **Place Rcif** nearby the Qaraouiyine Mosque. This choice puts you right near the center of the sights described below. The final option, for those with lots of time and even more patience, is simply to get lost in the magnificent atmosphere that is Fez's medina. You'll be vulnerable to hustlers, but you'll get to know the city on your own. When you're done, ask merchants or women how to get to Tala'a Kebira and follow it back uphill to Bab Boujeloud.

BOU INANIA MEDERSA. When Sultan Abu Inan was given the bill for the construction, he tore it up and threw it in the river that crossed the courtyard, claiming that no price could be put on beauty. And indeed, this *medersa* (a.k.a., madrasa, or religious school), built between 1350 and 1356, is Morocco's finest. Stunning stucco and cedar craftsmanship cover the walls of the recently renovated courtyard, and intricate *zellij* tilework complements the plasterwork. Once home to several hundred students who studied and prayed here, it is still used as a mosque, one of the few open to non-Muslims. The prayer room is off-limits, however. *(Open daily 9am-5:30pm. 10dh.)*

TANNERIES. Leather is dyed by hand here in huge earthen vats, with men treading the leather by foot. It is first washed in a greenish-blue liquid, then moved to a washing machine before being soaked in a mixture of pigeon excrement and cow urine to soften it up. The process takes up to a week, except for yellow garments, which are colored by hand with expensive saffron in two days. Red coloring comes from poppy flowers, blue from indigo, and brown from the henna plant. Feel free to take pictures of the men nimbly walking between the huge palette of dye pits below. With any luck, they will give you a sprig of mint to ward off the incredible stench of the dye pits—otherwise you'll have to stomach the smell, which intensifies on hot days. As you try to leave, they'll try to sell you something leather—jackets, pouffes (round footstools), or slippers. Unless you're armed for a bargaining battle, find the exit. *(Turn left at the end of Tala'a Kebira and follow the winding road until you reach a T-junction; turn right and follow the signs to Chouara tanneries, or wait to be accosted by a tannery "guardien", who will lead you up (20dh) to the terraces of a leather store to see Fez's iconic tanneries.)*

NEJJARINE MUSEUM OF ART. Dedicated to wood craftsmanship, the museum showcases an extensive collection of tools, massive wedding chairs, musical instruments, Qu'ranic tablets, and doors.

There is no shortage of finery on display—one entire room is dedicated to beautiful shelving. The tiled bathrooms are worth a visit, as they're the nicest around. The building itself is a beautifully restored warehouse originally built by Moulay Ismail. The rooftop terrace, affording a gorgeous view from the middle of the city, is perfect for a break and a bit of mint tea. *(The easiest way to get to the Place Nejjarine, with its tiled fountain, is to go all the way down Tala'a Seghira until it turns into Tala'a Kebira. Turn around, facing the direction you just came from, and go down the steps that are about 10m in front of you. At the bottom of the steps, follow the path to the small square; the museum is just off this small courtyard. Open daily 10am-5pm. 20dh, tea 10dh.)*

SPICE SOUQ AND OTHER MARKETS. Back on the Tala'a Kebira, the Attarine (Spice) Souq stretches several hundred meters to the end of the street. Now the domain of merchants hawking knock-off watches and personal hygiene items, it used to be a collection of shops, 150-170 in total, selling medicinal herbs and spices. Most were sold to physicians at the Maristan Sidi Frej, located in the Henna Souq (at the beginning of the Attarine Souq), where the depressed were treated with music, spices, and sex. The first psychiatric hospital in the Western world, opened in Valencia in 1410, was modeled on it. The Henna Souq, which is named for the dye that local women wear on their hands and feet for weddings, still sells a little of its namesake, but the *souq* is largely dominated by pottery shops today.

QAIRAOUINE MOSQUE. Exiting the *medersa*, turn left, and then left again; a few meters down is a little opening into the mosque, one of its 14 gates. The mosque also holds six fountains (3 for men and 3 for women), 300+ pillars, and can hold up to 20,000 worshippers (second only to the mosque of Hassan II in Casablanca). Founded in 857 by Fatima al-Fihri, a woman, the mosque is one of the oldest universities in the world. It trained students in logic, math, rhetoric, and the Qur'an while Europe stumbled through the Dark Ages. The Saadian pavilions are modeled on the Lion Court at the Alhambra in Granada, and the Almoravid *minbar* (pulpit) is made from ivory from Córdoba. What started as a small *medersa* grew in size and grandeur to encompass a huge plot of land in the medina. It is all off-limits to tourists, who must be satisfied by taking pictures through the archways.

THE DAR BATHA MUSEUM. The beautiful Dar Batha Museum, located by Hotel Batha, with its well-kept garden, makes an excellent diversion for those tired of endless, winding medina streets. The building itself, a 19th-century palace, may be turn out to be the highlight of the visit. The spacious Andalucian mansion hosted Sultan Hassan I and his son, Moulay Abd al-Aziz, during the last years of decadence before the French occupation. The museum, which hosts Moroccan music concerts in September, chronicles Fez's artistic history. The collection's centerpiece is the display of ceramics with the signature cobalt "Fez blue" adorning white enamel. *(Start at Bab Boujeloud, head straight down the Tala'a Seghira, take the right just before the next arch and follow the road to Pl. l'Istiqlal, home to the museum. Open W-Th and Sa-M 8:30am-noon and 2:30-6pm, F 8:30-11:30am and 3-6pm. 10dh.)*

FEZ AL-JDID

Fez al-Jdid, squarely between the medina and the *ville nouvelle*, was built in the 13th century by the Merenid sultan Youssef Yacoub to fortify himself against the world. The enormous **Dar al-Mahkzen,** his royal palace, is his gargantuan legacy to the city. The palace is not open to the public, and is in fact heavily guarded, but you can take a look at the gorgeous brass doors in front, at the end of the plaza. Just south of the plaza is the **mellah,** or Jewish quarter. In the 14th century the city's Jews were relocated here to offer them greater protection—and to more easily tax them. While there are few Jewish families remaining in the city, the architecture and neighborhood testify to their once significant presence. On the right as you head into Fez al-Jdid is an enormous **Jewish cemetery,** the final resting place for over 2,000 people. *(Open dawn-dusk; donations requested).* **Rue de Fez al-Jdid** is a sight in and of itself, a street absolutely choked with garment stalls. Locals flood in during the evening and it becomes an almost impassable mass of old women bargaining for clothing and young men calling out their wares like auctioneers. Bear left at the end of Rue de Fez al-Jdid into the **Petit Méchouar;** on the left is Bab Dakakeen, the back entrance to the Dar al-Makhzen. Bab al-Seba, an imperial gate, opens onto the **Grand Méchouar,** a roomy plaza lined with street lamps. From here it's an easy walk to Bab Boujeloud—turn through the opening to the right of Bab al-Seba, continue straight for 250m, veer to the right, and pass through a large arch at the end of the road. The entrance to the refreshing **Boujeloud Gardens,** a refuge from the midday sun, is on the right. *(Open Tu-Su. Free.)*

OUTSIDE THE MEDINA

There isn't much to see in Fez outside of the medina, but there are glorious views of the medina itself from the hills north of the city. The ramparts of the Borj Nord and the old Merenid tombs are on the same hill. Be careful after dark, as aggressive hustlers are known to frequent the area and there are plenty of dark and unsavory corners.

BORJ NORD AND THE MERENID TOMBS. To reach Borj Nord and the nearby tombs (they can be spotted from the ground), grab a *petit taxi* from the medina (5dh) or exit the medina through a small gate to the right on Pl. Baghdadi when walking from Bab Boujeloud toward Fez al-Jdid. Turn right on the main road, walk past the bus station 200m, then take a small path that winds its way up the hillside; the tombs are to the right and Borj Nord to the left. Thousands of white tombs, on the other side of Hotel des Merinides from Borj Nord, dot the hillside. Equally old and derelict are the **fortress ruins** above them, which you can wander around, marvel at, and climb on. Spectacularly old and neglected, they're amazingly accessible and worth a look. From the hills the panorama of the city, sprawled out in all its capricious sandstone antiquity, is especially impressive in the half-light of dawn or dusk; during calls to prayer, when over a hundred *muezzin* summon the faithful, the experience is almost mystical.

SHOPPING AND CRAFTS

As anyone hawking goods in the medina will tell you, Fez is the artisanal capital of Morocco. Notable goods include the blue pottery, made with cobalt; the selection of rugs and carpets; and the leather, made in the famous tanneries (see above). But really, everything is on offer: henna, herbal remedies for aging and impotence, daggers, brass tea services and sheepskins. Quality ranges from the handmade artisanry to shoddy, mass-produced stuff, but discerning the difference can be difficult for an untrained eye. In general, the stores along **Tala'a Kebira** offer cheaper but lower-quality items, while the *funduqs* and specialty stores will sell much better goods at significantly higher prices. If you do want to buy, bargain at a few stores first to get an idea of what something is worth. The first offer is always too much, often by twice, and only until the price is lowered for a third or fourth time are you usually getting a good deal. Do not let a middleman selling hats lead you to buy a *djellaba* or any other good—when he says he's negotiating the price, he's probably negotiating his commission. Lastly, a lot of the tannery and carpet showrooms are built in maze-like houses with many passageways, making it difficult to escape gracefully. But be firm; there's never an obligation to buy, no matter how many red carpets have been rolled out for you. Waiting until the end of the day, when shopkeepers are more inclined to make a sale rather than lose money, is a good time to try and buy.

THE ATLANTIC COAST

The towns along Morocco's Atlantic coast are more laid-back than their conservative cousins in the interior. Men and women alike sunbathe, swim, and surf. The west coast contains Morocco's industrial boom towns—Casablanca, the country's commercial center, and Rabat, its political capital—which, while very much part of the modern country, are best avoided by travelers with limited itineraries. If you're looking to relax by the sea, your best bets are smaller, more tranquil coastal cities, like Essaouira and Asilah.

ASILAH ☎039

The next stop south of Tangier, Asilah has a relaxed feel, white sand, and whitewashed medina walls, just miles away from the sweat and bustle of its northern neighbor. Carthage and Rome fought over the town in ancient times, while European powers failed many a time to wrest it from Moroccan pirates before it became a Spanish protectorate in 1911. There's no more fighting, and little going on here except at the beach. The town rouses from its slumber as droves of Spanish and French tourists come in late summer, reaching a peak during the huge international art festival that comes to town in August.

TRANSPORTATION. The **train station** (☎039 41 73 27) is a 25min. walk from town on the Tangier highway, past a strip of campgrounds. To get to town from the station, simply follow the road by the beach, keeping the sea to your right. A **taxi** to town costs about 15dh. Trains run to: **Marrakesh** (9hr., 5 per day 8:45am-10pm, 175dh) via **Rabat** (5hr., 78dh); **Casablanca** (6-7hr., 102dh); **Fez** (5-6hr., 1 per day, 82dh) via **Meknes** (4-5hr., 67dh); and **Tangier** (40min., 5 per day, 6:40am-10pm, 15dh). The onetime **bus station** is now abandoned, and all buses leave from a lot across from the Shell station east of the center. No schedules are posted, and often there are no officials around; while buses are cheaper, the train station is more reliable. To get to the bus station, follow Ave. Mauritania or Ave. Moulay Ismail from Pl. Mohammed V. **CTM Buses** run to: **Casablanca** via **Rabat** (4-5hr., 75-80dh); **Agadir** via **Marrakesh** (9hr., another 4hr. to Agadir; 200dh); **Meknes** (65dh) via **Fez** (3hr.-4hr., 70-75dh); and **Tangier** (1hr., 10dh). Private buses go to the same destinations and more with greater frequency. Buses leave for **Casablanca, Larache, and Tangier** at least once an hour 7am-7pm. **Taxis:** *Grand taxis* cluster in Pl. Mohammed V, by the bus station, and head to **Tangier** (15-20dh) and **Larache** (15-20dh).

ORIENTATION AND PRACTICAL INFORMATION. The main street into town is **Blvd. Mohammed V,** which ends at the town center, **Pl. Mohammed V** (a traffic circle). Here you'll find a **BMCE bank** and a **Banque Populaire,** both with **ATMs.** The main strip of restaurants, accommodations, and cafes are on **Rue Zallakah,** radiating from Pl. Mohammed V and the adjoining Av. Hassan II, which borders the medina. The town **market** sets up on Ave. Hassan II and extends into the medina. (Open daily 9am-6pm.) **Internet** can be found at **Cyber Monaco,** 124 on Av. Hassan II. (6dh per hr. Open daily 9am-late.) It's a 10min. walk down Hassan II from the town center, on the right. A **police** station is located at the corner of Ave. Mohammed V and Rue de la Liberté. (French spoken. In case of emergency, dial ☎19). To get to the **post office** from Pl. Mohammed V, take Blvd.

Mohammed V and turn right onto Pl. Nations Unies. The **post office** is 20m up on the left. (☎039 41 72 00. Open M-F 8am-noon and 2:30-6:30pm.)

ACCOMMODATIONS AND FOOD. Most hotels cluster around **Pl. Mohammed V** and off **Av. Hassan II.** In July and August, they brim with French and Spanish beachgoers; call at least a day in advance to reserve a room. For a bit of personality (at a price), try **Hotel Patio de la Luna ❸,** 12 Plaza Zelaka. Huge wicker chairs and massive beds furnish the rooms. The two roof terraces are excellent places to kick back and watch the sun set over the town. (☎039 41 60 74. Singles 350dh, doubles 550dh.) Back to normal budget fare, **Hôtel Sahara ❷,** 9 Rue Tarfaya, a block in from Av. Mohammed V and two blocks before Pl. Mohammed V, offers beautifully tiled but minuscule rooms around a sunny courtyard. Hot showers (5dh) are clean and cheap. (☎039 41 71 85. Singles 98dh, doubles 136dh, triples 186dh, quads 254dh.) **Hotel Mansour ❶,** 56 Av. Mohammed V, has old but clean rooms with slightly battered tile and showers. Firm beds and pleasant views over the garden across the street. (☎039 41 73 90. Singles 160dh, doubles 200dh.)

Asilah's restaurants do little to distinguish themselves. Hopeful waiters will call out to you in a Babel of tongues as you walk by the numerous restaurants that line the medina walls on Hassan II. Skip these: the food is cheap but middling, and every restaurant has an identical menu. For a classy sit-down experience, try **Casa Pepe ❷,** 8 Pl. Zallakah, a Spanish place that has been serving up seafood since 1914. The roses and candlelight inside are just as good a place to try the fish dishes (60-80dh) as the terrace outside. Beer, wine, and *aperitifs* are served. (☎039 41 73 95. Open daily noon-4pm and 8-11pm. MC/V.) For no-frills Moroccan food, try **Jawharat Achamal ❶,** at the corner of Liberté and Tarfaya, two blocks off Pl. Mohammed V. Hot *tajines* (30dh) are served up on the breezy sidewalk terrace. (Open daily noon-11pm, earlier in winter.) The cafes on Pl. Mohammed V fill with men sipping tea over heated card games. Join them at **Café Meknes ❶,** on the plaza, where you can sit and watch families stroll as your tea (6dh) cools. (☎039 41 73 29. Open daily 10am-10pm.)

SIGHTS AND BEACHES. Asilah's stunning medina is surrounded by heavily fortified 15th-century Portuguese walls. The walls inside alternate between pristine whitewash and vibrant murals painted each year during the festival (see below)—you're missing out if you don't take a walk through the old part of town. The Bab Kasaba, the gate off Rue Zallakah, leads past the Grand Mosque. Right across from the mosque is the modern and spacious **Centre Hassan II des Rencontres Internationales,** which houses art created during the great **International Festival,** held the first two weeks of August. (☎039 41 70 65. Normally closed, so call ahead before visiting.) Visiting studio artists are all given a white wall in the medina to cover with their creations, and over the course of several days the city's surfaces come alive in an act of collective pictorial expression. Musicians give concerts in the Centre, which also hosts symposia on international issues with visiting scholars and experts.

The town really comes to life on the beaches, though, which fill with families, children diving off of high rocks, and—everywhere—men playing massive beach soccer games. There are two popular beaches. The closest is toward the train station along the **Tangier-Asilah** highway (15min. from the medina), but the surf can be a little rough. The better of the two, in the opposite direction, is the enclosed **Paradise Beach,** an hour's walk from the medina along the road out of town. Horse-drawn wagons from the intersection of Av. Mohammed V run 150-200dh round-trip; or, try to persuade a taxi to make the bumpy trip.

For a more touristy activity, camels (big guys 40dh, small fries 20dh) will caravan you over the sands and through the surf for 15min.. The beach is dominated by men, but women and children are not uncommon. Many women wear their *djellabas* into the surf, but here and there a two-piece bathing suit can be spotted. Just be aware that as a westerner, you may attract a little more attention. Do not attempt to walk along the beach, or the sandy path that runs above it, to Paradise Beach. Massive layered-rock formations and the occasional sewage outlet are the only things that greet you, and the walk is long and dehydrating. Leave this area to the fishermen.

CASABLANCA ☎022

Though sprawling Casablanca (a.k.a. "Casa") has a famous name, there is little to see here other than the awe-inspiring Hassan II Mosque. Unfortunately, no one's looking at you, kid, except the hustlers who prowl the port and medina. A small city at the turn of the 20th century, the French built the wide boulevards and now-crumbling Art Deco buildings and made it into the booming commercial center it is today. A clash of desperately poor shantytowns and urban high-rises which dominate the skyline, Africa's largest port has little time for tourists and feels a little faded. Hidden on the western edge, though, is the Hassan II Mosque, the third-largest mosque in the world and a spectacular modern wonder.

TRANSPORTATION

The **Casa Port train station** is near the youth hostel and the city center; the **Casa Voyageurs** train station is a 50min. walk from Casa Port or a 25-30dh *petit taxi* ride. The private bus station is even farther away. To get from Casa Port to the convenient downtown **CTM bus station,** cross the street, and follow Blvd. Houphouet-Boigny to the head of Pl. Nations Unies. At the rotary, take a sharp left onto the wide **Av. des Forces Armées Royales** (known as Av. des F.A.R.), and turn on to the side street just before Hotel Farah; the station is right there. **Taxi** drivers at the station will often "forget" about the meter and ask for a ridiculous price upon dropping you off, so demand that they turn it on or settle for a price beforehand, despite their protests. Alternatively, walk a few blocks from the station for a taxi. Accommodations are almost all within walking distance, but be careful at night. Most of the major airlines and countless travel agencies are located on Av. des F.A.R. as you walk east from Pl. des Nations Unies.

Flights: Aéroport Mohammed V (☎022 53 90 40) handles all flights. Trains run between the airport terminal and the Casa Port train station (45min., 1 per hr., 6am-10pm, 30dh), stopping at Casa Voyageurs en route. You may have to change trains at Ain Sebaa, so check your ticket. Make sure to get on a train that runs to Casa Port. **Royal Air Maroc** (☎022 31 41 41), at the airport and 44 Av. des F.A.R. (☎022 31 11 12). Open M-F 8:30am-12:15pm and 2:30-7pm, Sa 8:30am-noon and 3-6pm.

Trains: There are 2 main train stations: **Casa Port** (☎022 27 18 37), undergoing massive construction, on the waterfront close to the heart of the city, and **Casa Voyageurs** (☎022 24 38 18), 4km outside the city center on Blvd. Ba Hammed. Casa Port has northbound service to **Rabat** (1hr., every 30min. 6:30am-9:30pm, 31dh). Casa Voyageurs has southbound service to **Fez** (5hr., 12 per day, 6:15am-10:30pm, 101dh) via **Meknes** (4hr., 86dh), **Marrakesh** (3hr., 9 per day, 4:50am-8:50pm, 84dh); **Tangier** (6hr., 4 per day 6:15am-12:15am, 124dh; transfer at **Sidi Kacem**).

Buses: Using CTM rather than a private company is worth the extra money and effort; the private bus station is a long taxi ride away from the city center. **CTM,** 23 Rue Léon L'Africain (☎022 45 80 00), off Blvd. Hassan Seghir. To: **Essaouira** (6hr.; 7, 7:30am,

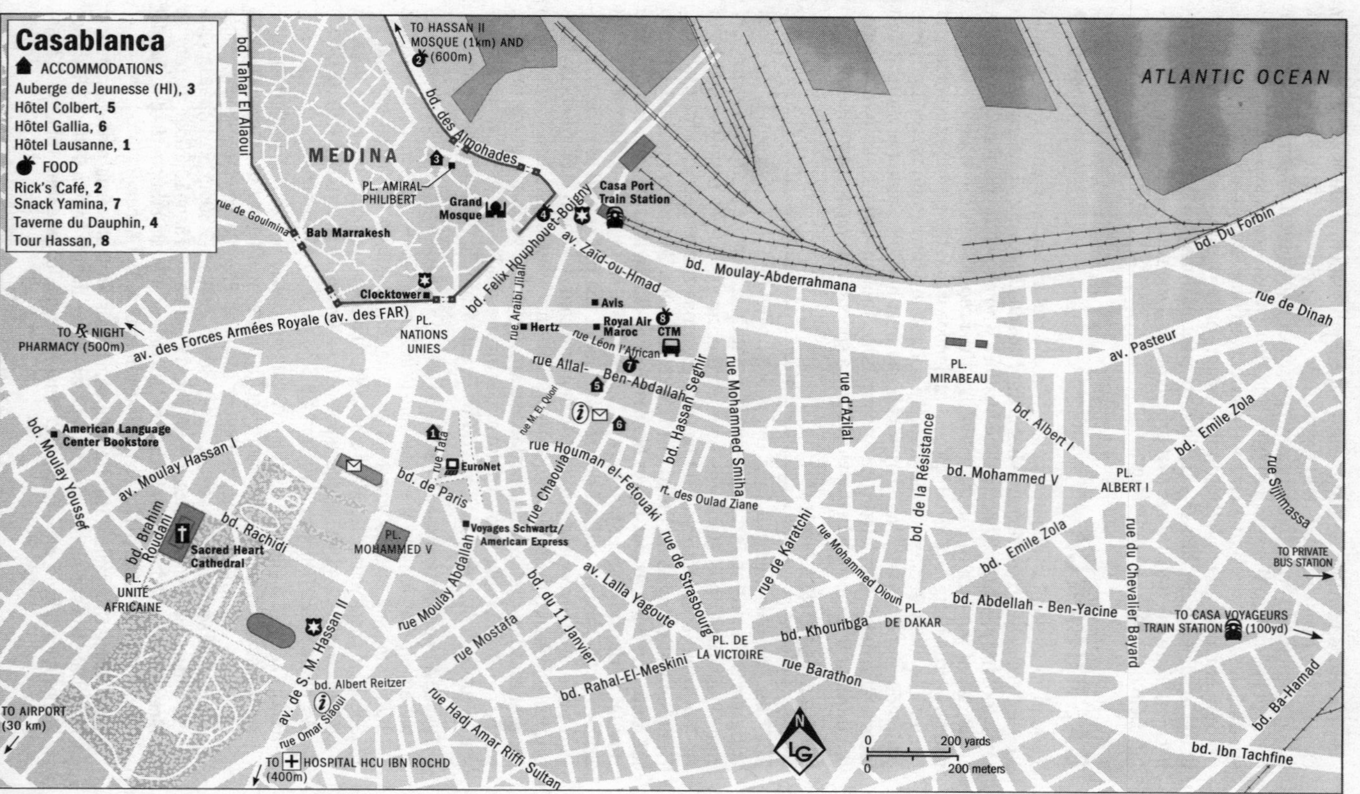
Casablanca
ACCOMMODATIONS
Auberge de Jeunesse (HI), 3
Hôtel Colbert, 5
Hôtel Gallia, 6
Hôtel Lausanne, 1
FOOD
Rick's Café, 2
Snack Yamina, 7
Taverne du Dauphin, 4
Tour Hassan, 8
ATLANTIC OCEAN
MEDINA
TO HASSAN II MOSQUE (1km) AND (600m)
bd. des Almohades
bd. Tahar El Alaoui
rue de Goulmina
Bab Marrakesh
PL. AMIRAL PHILIBERT
Grand Mosque
Clocktower
Casa Port Train Station
bd. Felix Houphouet-Boigny
av. Zaïd-ou-Hmad
bd. Moulay-Abderrahmana
bd. Du Forbin
rue de Dinah
av. Pasteur
PL. MIRABEAU
Avis
Royal Air Maroc
CTM
Hertz
rue Araibi Jilali
rue Léon l'African
rue Allal-Ben-Abdallah
PL. NATIONS UNIES
av. des Forces Armées Royale (av. des FAR)
TO NIGHT PHARMACY (500m)
rue M. El. Quori
rue Tata
EuroNet
bd. de Paris
rue Chaouia
rue Houman el-Fetouaki
bd. Hassan Seghir
rue Mohammed Smiha
rue d'Azilal
bd. de la Résistance
bd. Albert I
bd. Mohammed V
PL. ALBERT I
bd. Emile Zola
rue Sijilmassa
rt. des Oulad Ziane
American Language Center Bookstore
bd. Moulay Youssef
av. Moulay Hassan I
bd. Brahim Roudani
Sacred Heart Cathedral
bd. Rachidi
PL. MOHAMMED V
Voyages Schwartz/American Express
rue Moulay Abdallah
bd. du 11 Janvier
av. Lalla Yagoute
rue de Strasbourg
rue de Karatchi
rue Mohammed Diouri
PL. DE DAKAR
bd. Abdellah - Ben-Yacine
rue du Chevalier Bayard
TO PRIVATE BUS STATION
TO CASA VOYAGEURS TRAIN STATION (100yd)
PL. UNITÉ AFRICAINE
av. de S. M. Hassan II
rue Mostafa
PL. DE LA VICTOIRE
bd. Khouribga
rue Barathon
bd. Rahal-El-Meskini
bd. Albert Reitzer
rue Omar Slaoui
rue Hadj Amar Riffi Sultan
TO AIRPORT (30 km)
TO HOSPITAL HCU IBN ROCHD (400m)
bd. Ba-Hamad
bd. Ibn Tachfine
200 yards
200 meters

5pm; 135dh); **Fez** (6hr., 12 per day 7am-9pm, 100dh); **Marrakesh** (4hr., 9 per day, 8am-11pm, 85dh); **Meknes** (5hr., 11 per day 7am-7:30pm, 80dh); **Tetouan** (7hr. 6am, 4, 11:30pm; 125dh); **Tangier** (6hr., 6 per day 6am-11:45pm, 105dh).

Car Rental: Though travelers don't need a car in Casa, the city has dozens of rental companies. **Avis,** 19 Av. des F.A.R. (☎022 31 24 24). Open M-F 8am-7pm, Sa 8am-noon and 2-7pm, Su 8am-noon. AmEx/MC/V. **Hertz,** 25 Rue de Arabi Jilali (☎022 84 09 39), same hours. Min. age 25 for all cars at all dealerships.

METER MADNESS. In Casablanca, *petit taxi* drivers are particularly flagrant in taking "scenic routes" and failing to turn on the meter. Start with a sense of the route, and double-check the meter. The daytime rate should start at 1.40dh, the nighttime rate at 2.10dh. Taxi drivers are required by law to use their meter, and the surcharge by night is 50% of fare, not double.

ORIENTATION AND PRACTICAL INFORMATION

The city has two main squares, **Pl. Nations Unies,** below the landmark clock tower and a 5min. walk from Casa Port, and **Pl. Mohammed V.** Pl. Nations Unies spreads out in front of the Hyatt Regency. All the main arteries radiate from it; **Av. Hassan II** heads to Pl. Mohammed V six blocks south, **Blvd. Mohammed V** heads east toward Casa-Voyageurs, and just above it is **Rue Allal ben Abdallah,** around which lie many of the city's cheap lodgings and eateries. Along the top of Pl. Nations Unies runs **Av. Forces Armées Royales (F.A.R.),** which has all of the city's travel agencies and airlines. Turning right as you leave Casa Port will lead you along the medina walls and eventually bring you to **Hassan II Mosque.**

Tourist Office: Syndicat d'Initiative et de Tourisme, 98 Blvd. Mohammed V (☎/fax 022 22 15 24), at Rue Chaouia, about 4 blocks down from Pl. Nations Unies. English spoken. Open M-F 8:30am-6:30pm, Sa 8:30am-noon. **Office de Tourisme,** 55 rue Omar Slaoui (☎022 27 95 33 or 27 11 77). From Pl. Mohammed V, take Av. Hassan II, turn left on Rue Allal al-Fassi, and then right. Open M-F 8:30-4:30pm.

Currency Exchange: Many banks are closed on weekends and after 4pm; try the airport and larger hotels, which change money at Morocco's official rates. The **Hyatt Regency, Hôtel Suisse,** and **Hôtel Safir,** near Pl. des Nations Unies and the bus station, and the other big hotels near Pl. Nations Unies are all safe bets. **24hr. ATMs** are everywhere.

American Express: Voyages Schwartz, 112 Av. du Prince Moulay Abdallah (☎022 22 29 47). Offer standard services, but won't receive wired money. Open M-F 8:30am-noon and 2:30-6:30pm, Sa 8:30am-noon.

English Bookstore: American Language Center Bookstore, Blvd. Moulay Youssef (☎022 27 95 59), at Pl. Unité Africaine. Vast array of novels and reference books. Open M-F 9:30am-12:30pm and 3:30-6:30pm, Sa 9:30am-noon.

Emergency: ☎19. Police located by clock tower in the Pl. des Nations Unies. Tourist police handle travel-related issues. Located on Av. Hassan II and Blvd. Houphouet-Boigny.

Late-Night Pharmacy: Pharmacie des Generations, 53 Rue Jaber ibn Hayane (☎022 20 73 33). Walk down Hassan II and turn right on blvd. de Paris. It's a 15min. walk to Pl. Oued al-Makhazine, where the pharmacy is. Open 24hr. Other pharmacies with normal hours (8am-12:30pm and 2:30-8pm) are on almost any city block.

Medical Assistance: Centre Hospitalier Universitarire (CHU) Ibn Rochd (☎022 22 41 09), south of the city. Walk south on Hassan II past the parks and continue straight through the traffic circle. 4 blocks later, turn left and continue straight; the complex is one block up on the right. Served by buses #29 and 59.

Internet Access: EuroNet, 51 Rue Tata (☎022 26 57 21). 10dh per hr. Open daily 8am-11pm.

Post Office: Blvd. Paris, at Av. Hassan II. Poste Restante and telephones. Open M-F 8:30am-4:30pm, Sa 9am-noon. As always, packages are shipped and received from a separate office on the side of the building. Another **branch** located just to the left of the Syndicat d'Initiative. Same hours.

ACCOMMODATIONS

Casa's glory days are long gone by, and it shows in the crumbling façades and worn feel of all of its budget accommodations, which have seen grander times. The cheapest places are in the streets just southeast of Pl. des Nations Unies, particularly Rue Allal ben Abdallah and Rue Chaouia. Casa is very noisy, so try to get a room away from the street. Depending on where you are in Casa, a street name could be in French, Arabic with transliteration, or both; some listings below note particularly recent or confusing changes.

Hotel Gallia, 19 Rue ibn Batouta (☎022 48 16 94). Casa's best budget option is a hilarious mix-and-match of leather doors, pink walls, and Moroccan staples (look for the 6ft. hookah). Management is friendly, and rooms are big, bright affairs with faux flowers, large beds, and clean showers. Popular with backpackers. Breakfast (25dh) available, along with a computer for guest use. Singles 150dh, with shower 170dh; doubles 220/250dh; triples 295/330dh. ❶

Auberge de Jeunesse (HI), 6 pl. Ahmed Bidaoui (☎022 22 05 51). 10min. from Casa Port. Head right along Blvd. Almohades, which runs outside the medina wall, and go left up a small ramp-like street; blue signs point the way. A little removed in the medina, but an excellent value. Pleasant central lounge, clean dorms, and modern bathrooms with hot showers. Breakfast included (8-10am) and internet available. Reception open daily 8-10am and noon-11pm. Lock-out 10am-noon. Check-out 10am. Dorms 60dh doubles 130dh, triples 190dh. ❶

Hôtel Lausanne, 24 Rue Tata, formerly Rue Poincaré (☎022 26 86 90). A step up from similar small hotels, a sparkling and well-maintained place with excellent service. Catch up on Egyptian soap operas and Arab news in modern rooms with TV and hot showers. Singles 225dh, doubles 270dh, triples 350dh. ❷

Hôtel Colbert, 38 Rue Chaouia, formerly Rue Colbert (☎022 31 42 41). Comfy couches in reception and a leafy central courtyard lead up to spacious, spotless rooms. Communal showers are immaculate. Usually booked, so arrive early. Singles 115dh, with shower 150dh; doubles 150/185dh; each additional person 36dh. ❶

FOOD

Casa offers every cuisine under the sun, from McDonald's to Mexican, for those willing to look. But it can be strangely difficult to find Moroccan food in Morocco's largest city, with the center dominated by sandwich joints, *patisseries*, and pizzerias. The cheap eats capital is **Pl. de 16 de Novembre,** 2 blocks southeast of Pl. des Nations Unies. Glaring neon signs light the streets around it with snack places and cheap *tajine* restaurants. **Rue Chaouia** has a slew of rotisserie chicken places, always good bets. For fresh meats and produce, try haggling at the **central market,** 7 Rue Chaouia (open daily 8am-1pm).

Rick's Café, 248 Blvd. Sour Jdid (☎022 27 42 07). Follow the port road away from the center until the end of the medina walls; signs point to Rick's on the left. Fez-topped waiters serve pricey dishes to a largely tourist crowd in this nod to American cinema. The cheesecake alone (45dh) is worth a visit. Live jazz piano seals the deal. Roof terrace has nice views and expensive drinks. Wi-Fi hot spot. T-shirts and mugs for sale. Entrees 120-150dh. Open daily 1-3pm and 6pm-1am. AmEx/MC/V. ❹

Taverne au Dauphin, 115 Blvd. Felix Houphouet-Boigny (☎022 22 12 00), up the road from the port. A classy seafood place where fine wine mingles with the smell of briny oysters. Small fried dishes (40-60dh) are tasty but the Oualidia oysters (from 51dh) are the way to go. Serves wine and beer. Open M-Sa noon-3pm and 7-11pm. V. ❸

Tour Hassan, 136 Av. des F.A.R. (☎022 31 03 50). Glossy wood panelling, curves, and plants nod to the city's Art Deco past, compensating for the linoleum tables and soft rock. Sit inside, as the road is noisy. Good selection of alcohol, including the namesake Casablanca beer (35dh). Pizzas 40-50dh. Meat 70-90dh. Open 8am-12:30am. ❷

Snack Yamina, 35 Rue Chaouia. Not to be confused with the nearby Snack Amine. This king of roadside rotisseries serves up chicken plates (25dh) and fried fish specials (30-40dh) in a jiffy. Can't beat it for price or convenience. Open daily 9am-11pm. ❶

SIGHTS

HASSAN II MOSQUE. Taking the Qu'ranic verse literally that "the throne of God is built upon the water," former King Hassan II built his mosque, the third largest in the world, to hang dramatically over the Atlantic. It was designed by Frenchman Michel Pinseau, and construction began in 1986, with 10,000 workers and 2500 master craftsmen working in shifts nonstop (all day, every day) until 1993; it was opened the next year. The construction came to a total of US$800 million, much of it collected through public taxes. Guided tours let visitors into Pinseau's masterpiece, one of the few places in the country open to non-Muslims. Inside is the **prayer hall,** which accommodates 25,000 worshippers. Fabulously intricate stucco patterning covers the walls, and the hand-carved cedar roof, an engineering marvel, opens to the sky when the mosque is full and the weather is good. In winter, the floor is electrically heated. All of the materials to build the mosque came from Morocco, except the Italian glass for the 57 chandeliers and the Carrera marble that surrounds the *mihrab*, the prayer niche that points to Mecca. At one end of the prayer hall, silver electric gates weighing over 34 tons open only once a year—during the birthday celebration for the Prophet—for a grand entrance by his living descendant, the King himself. Downstairs are the ablution rooms for men and women, each containing 41 fountains, and the *hammams*, which one day (so they say) will be open for Muslims and non-Muslims alike. The plaza outside, blinding in midday, accommodates another 80,000 and offers the best views of the **minaret** (210m), the tallest in the world. Dominating the skyline during the day, the mosque glows brighter by night, shooting a 20 mi. long laser beam toward Mecca. *(Walk past the medina along the coastal road for about 15min., or take a petit taxi—should be no more than 10-15dh, though drivers will often ask for an unmetered 20dh. Tickets are sold to the left of the minaret, down the stairs. Guests must be modestly attired; women should cover their legs and shoulders. You'll have to take your shoes off before entering the prayer hall. Tours take 1hr. and are given M-Th and Sa 9, 10, 11am, noon, and 3pm, F 9, 10am, and 3pm. Tours in Arabic, English, French, and Spanish. 120dh, students 60dh.)*

NIGHTLIFE

Casa's Western feel might leave you hoping for a club scene, and the city doesn't disappoint. Avoid the center, full of slightly seedy, male-dominated bars. The real action is in **Aïn Diab,** a relatively wealthy neighborhood on the beach 4km west of the city center. The main drag, **Blvd. de la Corniche,** is lined with discos, upscale bars, and dance clubs. The young and sexy flock here on the weekends to flirt, drink, and show a little skin (or a lot). Most places get going after 1am and are open until the very early hours. Cover will probably run from 75-100dh, and up to 150dh at the *très chic* places. Dress codes require something more than shorts and sandals, so put on some nice shoes and a collar, or a skirt for women. While most places are fairly low-key, women will probably feel more comfortable in groups. Be wary of overly friendly Moroccan women, who might be out strolling for more than just a drink. Expect to pay 40-50dh each way for a cab from the center to Aïn Diab.

ESSAOUIRA ☎044

The siren song of Essaouira is inescapable. Its cool ocean breeze, sprawling beaches, local art and laid-back lifestyle are enough to make anyone want to go native. Notable as a dye-producing colony since Phoenician times, it was an important port throughout the ages, first for its secure ramparts, later and up to today for its sardines. The Gnaoua World Music Festival, held every year in June, and the city's numerous galleries all flaunt its artistic riches, but for most of the year its a quietly hip place. Jimi Hendrix and Cat Stevens liked the vibe in '69, and it hasn't changed much. Give yourself more than a day and you might find your visit slipping into weeks, months, and even years.

TRANSPORTATION

Buses: CTM runs from the station outside the medina, a 15min. walk from Pl. Moulay Hassan. Ticket window open 6:30am-10:30pm. To: **Agadir** (2hr., 2:30pm, 65dh), **Marrakesh** (3hr., 12:30 and 5pm, 55dh), and **Casablanca** (6hr.; 7:45, 11:10am, 4pm; 115dh). **Pullman du Sud** offers one overnight bus to **Casablanca** (7hr., midnight, 90dh). **Supratours** (☎024 47 53 17) buses leave from near **Bab Marrakesh;** to get to the ticket office and bus lot, walk past the post office from the beach and take the next left. In summer, it's best to buy a day or two in advance. Buses go to **Agadir** (2hr., 1:15pm, 65dh), **Marrakesh** (2hr., 5 per day 6am-6pm, 65dh), and **Safi** (3hr., 12:30pm, 40dh). Buy tickets at the office (open daily 5:30-6:30am, 9am-noon, and 3-6:45pm). Smaller companies offer frequent services to the cities above.

ORIENTATION AND PRACTICAL INFORMATION

The **bus station** is about 1km from the medina along Blvd. Industrie. Exit the rear of the station (where the buses park) and walk to the right, passing two *souqs* (or deserted wastelands, depending on the hour), to reach the medina gate, **Bab Doukkala** (10min.). The gate opens onto **Av. Mohammed Zerktouni,** one of two main arteries; the other is the parallel **Rue Mohammed ben Abdallah.** To reach the city center from Bab Doukkala, continue on Av. Mohammed Zerktouni as it becomes Av. l'Istiqlal (at an intersection surrounded by *souqs*). Walk until you see a clock tower and gate on the right. Go through the gate, pass through the square, and follow the road as it winds to Pl. Moulay Hassan, the heart of Essaouira. The ramparts line the streets of the plaza. To get to the beach, head left at the plaza and walk for 5min.

Tourist Office: Delegation Regionale de Tourisme, Rue de Caire (☎024 47 50 80). From the clocktower, walk 2 blocks toward the port and turn left on to Rue Caire. Some English spoken. Open M-F 9am-noon and 2:30-6:30pm.

Currency Exchange: Banks cluster around Pl. Moulay Hassan. **Bank Credit du Maroc,** Pl. Moulay Hassan (☎024 47 58 19), cashes traveler's checks and has an **ATM.** Open M-F 8:30am-3:45pm. **BMCE** (same hours as above) with an **ATM** is at the end of Pl. Moulay Hassan, near Ben Abdallah.

Luggage Storage: Available for 24hr. at the bus station (5dh per bag).

Police: ☎19. Station is on the same street as the tourist office.

Hospital: Hopital Sidi Mohammed ben Abdellah, Av. de l'Hopital (☎024 47 27 16), just past the post office away from the beach. Also **Croissant Rouge** (☎062 63 79 18), next to the tourist office. Open daily 9am-8pm.

Bookstore: Galerie Aida, 2 Rue de la Skala (☎024 47 62 90), off Pl. Moulay Hassan. Crafts, used books (in English and French), and art. Open daily 10am-8pm.

Internet Access: The area just above Pl. Moulay Hassan has a few *teleboutiques*. **Mogador Informatique** (☎024 47 50 65), on Av. l'Istiqlal to the right of the clocktower. 10dh per hour. Open daily 9am-midnight. **Internet Club,** right next to the tourist office, has Wi-Fi. 10dh per hour. Open daily 1am-11pm.

Post Office: Av. al-Moqamah at Lalla Aicha, the 1st left after Hôtel les Isles walking away from the medina by the shore. Poste Restante. Open 8:30am-noon and 2:30-6:30pm. **Branch** office on Rue Laalouj. **Postal Code:** 44000.

EXPLORING MOROCCO

ACCOMMODATIONS

Hotels in Essaouira are a little pricier than elsewhere in Morocco but generally better, most with pretty rooms, reliable hot water, and breezy roof terraces.

Hostel Essaouira, Derb Laghrissi. Walking away from the port on Av. de l'Istiqlal, turn right after the big mosque. Walk until you see signs for Dar Nafoura and turn left. Follow this to the big blue phone sign, turn right, and then take your first left. Grab a beer and make yourself at home with Bob Marley and a surfing crowd. Super friendly staff and guests chill out together in the kitchen/lounge downstairs, feasting and chatting on the couches and swings well into the night. Beautiful courtyard. Rooms clean and comfortable. Ask about working at the hostel or long-term stays. Beds 120dh. ❶

Hotel Cap Sim, 11 Ibu Rochd (☎024 78 58 34). Standing in pl. Moulay Hassam facing Credit du Maroc, make a left on rue Skala, the street along the ramparts right next to Banque Populaire. Make a right just before the archway and follow the street around to the hotel. Tall windows, a bright courtyard, and colorful rooms, along with a smiling staff, make it bright and cheerful. Attached bathrooms have clean tile and hot showers. Breakfast included. Singles and doubles 230dh, with shower 360dh. MC/V. ❸

Hôtel Tafraout, 7 rue Marrakesh (☎024 47 62 76). In pl. Moulay Hassan, walk past the restaurants and cafes and take a left onto the busy rue Sidi Mohammed ben Abdallah. Look for the sign a few blocks up. Lovely little brass sinks, traditional lamps, and Berber blankets on the beds lend great personality. Clean and well-maintained. Standard shower. Singles 180dh, with shower 280dh, doubles 280/400dh. Extra bed 100dh. ❸

Hôtel Smara, 26 rue Skala (☎024 47 56 55). Standing in Pl. Moulay Hassan, facing Credit du Maroc, make a left on rue Skala, right next to Banque Populaire (3min.). Arrive early—this is the most popular hotel among backpackers. Rooms are simple but adequate, with the perk of ocean waves crashing 100m away. Breakfast 10dh, served on an ocean terrace. Laundry 2dh per garment. Some English spoken. Singles 76dh; 1-bed doubles 104dh, 2-bed doubles 134dh; terrace suite with ocean views 196dh. ❷

FOOD

Some of the cheapest dining, as well as the best place to score some of Essaouira's daily catch, are the stalls at the port end of Pl. Moulay Hassan. Tasting menus (60dh) offer up 3 kinds of fish, squid, and shrimp. Sardines, the city's lifeblood, are cheapest (10h), while the rest of the catch (sea urchins, anyone?) will run you 30-40dh. Prices and selection are identical wherever you choose to eat, so just grab a table and dig in.

THE BEAT GOES ON

ssaouira sacrifices a little of its amous laid-back beach feel every une when musicians and music afiionados descend on the town for he four-day **Gnaoua World Music estival.** Gnaoua (pronounced guhow-a) is a North African fusion enre of spiritual music, formed s slaves from West Africa brought heir musical traditions to North frica and fused them with Moroccan and North African rhythms and nstrumentation. Traditionally, the musical groups, each of which was a spiritual brotherhood, would go hrough rituals to honor the seven saints of Islam or to invoke djinns nd spirits, as the performers would enter a trance-like state.

The spiritual aspect of the music remains, but has lost its overtly religious rituals. The fesival in Essaouira is famous for he creative interpretations of naoua, adding elements of jazz, eggae, and world music for 4 days of public performances. The most famous *maalems* (master musicians) perform at Bab Sbaa and Place Moulay Hassan. As if he town's relaxed attitude didn't already encourage brotherhood, he gnaoua brings together everyone present together for several days of musical and spiritual communion. The hippies felt the love here when they stopped by in the 70s, and it hasn't left yet.

The concert lasts 4 days and akes place in late June every ear. Visit the website, www.festial-gnaoua.net, for details.)

Taros Café, 2 Rue de Skala (☎024 47 64 07), right off of Pl. Moulay Hassan. Elegant fish and fowl are served among local art displays in this wonderful restaurant/café/gallery. The night isn't finished without a drink on the terrace, the hippest night spot in Essaouira (mixed drinks 50-70dh). Gaze over the railing to the ocean below, or just lounge and watch the live music and belly dancing. Plates 90-120dh. Desserts 50-60dh. Open daily 11am-4pm and 6pm-late. AmEx/MC/V for purchases over 300dh. ❸

Crêperie Mogador, Rue Laalouj, near the museum. A refreshing change from *tajines* and pizza; grab a *crêpe salée* (savory crepe; 45dh), huge affairs stuffed with meat, tomato, and egg. For dessert or a lighter snack, the sweet crepes (20-40dh) come in a glorious spectrum of sweetness, from honey or chocolate (30dh) to the enormous specialty peach melba (50dh). Open Sa-Th noon-3pm and 7-10pm. ❶

Restaurant Laayoune (☎024 47 46 43). From the top of Pl. Moulay Hassan (away from the port), take a right and continue past rue Sidi ben Mohammed Abdallah. Follow the road as it turns right; the restaurant is ahead on the left. Conversation and candlelight fill the air in this elegant but affordable local spot for Moroccan fare. All 4 set menus (58-78dh) are an excellent value. Fills up at night; be prepared to wait. Plates 50-70dh. Open daily noon-4pm and 7-11pm. ❷

SIGHTS

While it is possible to spend days lolling in cafes or napping away in the city's breezy air, Essaouira's ramparts, beaches, and galleries give the town its graceful beauty and should not be missed.

RAMPARTS AND PORT. The town's two *skalas* (forts) sit dramatically over the violent Atlantic, offering spectacular views of the ocean and the isles. The strange mixture of European and Moroccan military architecure, built by a Frenchman in the 18th century, is so picturesque that Orson Welles used it in his adaptation of Othello. **Skala de la Ville,** the more accessible of the two and free to the public, is down Rue de Skala from Pl. Moulay Hassan. The brass cannons, given to the city by European traders, are fun to climb and offer gorgeous views of the Atlantic crashing on the rocks below. The unoccupied nooks are popular with canoodling Moroccan couples, and it is easy to see why. The other, **Skala du Port,** offers incredible oblique shots of the old medina walls—don't forget your camera. On the other side are the colorful old fishing boats and the beach melting away into the horizon. *(Open M-Th and Sa-Su 9am-5:30pm, Fri 9am-12:30pm and 3-6pm. 10dh.)*

MEDINA SHOPS AND MUSEUMS. Under the ramparts are the cave-like woodshops that produce some of Morocco's finest crafts. The lovely, deep aroma of *thuya* wood wafts along the street, where all sorts of hand crafted finery are on display. the artisans inlay the *thuya* with cedar and ebony to produce the usual cups, chess sets, and drums, along with statues and masks, which make for incredible keepsakes. In addition to the wood, there's a great local painting scene in Essaouira, and galleries line the streets around the rampart. Quality is variable, but as most artists take their cues from the gorgeous landscapes, you can't go too wrong. For silver jewelry, head to the *souq* located just outside the medina walls on Av. Oqba ben Nafil. Look for the sign that says "*bijoux*" above the entrance on the right, about a block from rue de Caire on the right. **Museum Mohammed ben Abdallah,** near the Hôtel Majestic on Rue Derb Laalouj, is in the former residence of a pasha. It features antique woodwork and important manuscripts, including a 13th-century Qur'an. *(☎024 47 53 00. Currently closed for restorations, so call ahead. Open M and W-Su 9am-noon and 3-6:30pm. 10dh.)*

BEACHES. Essaouira's soft sand stretches for miles to the south, but the same lovely winds that keep the town cool make sunbathing difficult. That said, it's still one of Morocco's best, and offers up a slew of activities. Kitesurfing, beach soccer, and swimming are all excellent. The beach is crowded but unguarded, so be careful if you do take a dip. To reach the sand, head to the port and veer left; you can't miss it. You'll have to walk past the crowds near the port to get a decent spot in the sand. Windsurfing clubs cluster on the beach and rent boards. **UCPA Maroc,** right along the boardwalk, offers rentals and lessons. (☎061 34 33 04. Surfboards 50dh per hr., 200dh per day. Windsurfing 250dh per hr., 600dh per day. Surfing lessons 125dh per hr. Windsurfing lessons 220dh per hr. Kitesurfing lessons start at 1600dh for 6hr. of instruction.)

PURPLE ISLES. The dramatic, rocky islets visible from the ramparts, despite their modest appearance, have been a valuable commodity for several millennia. A Berber king from Mauritania, Juba II, set up dye factories here around 100 BC, producing the purple dye used to color Julius Caesar's cape, among other things, and giving the Isles their name. In 1506, the Portuguese, under King Manuel, built a fortress, and Moulay Hassan added a prison. Nowadays they are home to the rare Eleonora's falcons. Visiting them is possible but discouraged during breeding season (roughly Mar.-Oct.). You must first receive a free permit from the Port Office, which can take several days to process. Then you must arrange transportation with a fisherman or someone who owns a boat. Try to bargain for 400-500dh.

THE HIGH ATLAS

The High Atlas is among the most striking and varied landscapes in the world, embracing snow-capped mountains, unearthly pink rock fortresses, and gargantuan waterfalls alike. So diverse is this region that movies set in locales as disparate as Tibet and Arabia have been filmed here. At the feet of the High Atlas lies Marrakesh, a city overflowing with unique architecture, exotic bazaars, and magical energy. Falling southeast from the Atlas ranges and stretching through Ouarzazate to the sand-dune seas of the Sahara is Morocco's own desert. Mountainous and desolate, its deep reds and oranges are softened only by the rare, green veins of oases that creep through the valley floors. Set into

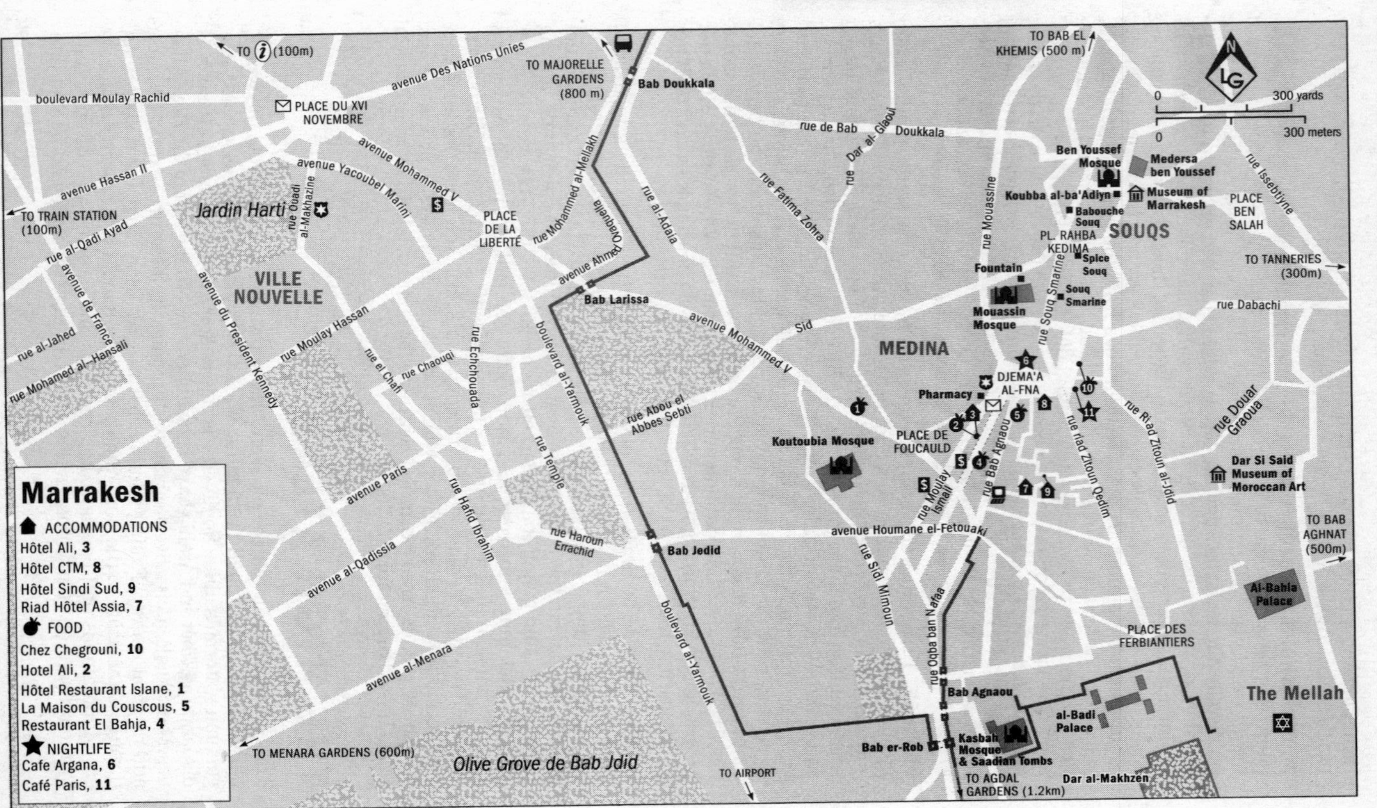

Marrakesh
ACCOMMODATIONS
Hôtel Ali, 3
Hôtel CTM, 8
Hôtel Sindi Sud, 9
Riad Hôtel Assia, 7
FOOD
Chez Chegrouni, 10
Hotel Ali, 2
Hôtel Restaurant Islane, 1
La Maison du Couscous, 5
Restaurant El Bahja, 4
NIGHTLIFE
Cafe Argana, 6
Café Paris, 11
0 300 yards
0 300 meters
N
LG
TO (100m)
TO MAJORELLE GARDENS (800 m)
Bab Doukkala
TO BAB EL KHEMIS (500 m)
boulevard Moulay Rachid
PLACE DU XVI NOVEMBRE
avenue Des Nations Unies
rue de Bab Doukkala
rue Dar al-Glaoui
Ben Youssef Mosque
Medersa ben Youssef
Koubba al-ba'Adiyn
Museum of Marrakesh
PLACE BEN SALAH
rue Issebtiyne
Babouche Souq
SOUQS
PL. RAHBA KEDIMA
Spice Souq
TO TANNERIES (300m)
avenue Hassan II
avenue Yacoubel Marini
avenue Mohammed V
TO TRAIN STATION (100m)
Jardin Harti
rue Oualdi al-Makhazine
PLACE DE LA LIBERTÉ
rue Mohammed al-Mellakh
rue Ahmed Oqaquella
rue al-Adaia
rue Fatima Zohra
rue Mouassine
Fountain
Souq Smarine
rue Souq Smarine
rue Dabachi
rue al-Qadi Ayad
avenue de France
VILLE NOUVELLE
avenue du President Kennedy
Bab Larissa
avenue Mohammed V
Sid
Mouassin Mosque
MEDINA
rue al-Jahed
rue Mohamed al-Hansali
rue Moulay Hassan
rue el Chafi
rue Chaouqi
rue Echchouada
boulevard al-Yarmouk
rue Abou el Abbes Sebti
DJEMA'A AL-FNA
Pharmacy
rue Riad Zitoun al-Jdid
rue Douar Graoua
Koutoubia Mosque
PLACE DE FOUCAULD
rue Bab Agnaou
rue riad Zitoun Qedim
Dar Si Said Museum of Moroccan Art
avenue Paris
rue Hafid Ibrahim
rue Temple
rue Moulay Ismail
rue Haroun Errachid
Bab Jedid
avenue Houmane el-Fetouaki
TO BAB AGHNAT (500m)
avenue al-Qadissia
rue Sidi Mimoun
Al-Bahia Palace
boulevard al-Yarmouk
rue Oqba ban Nafaa
PLACE DES FERBIANTIERS
avenue al-Menara
Bab Agnaou
al-Badi Palace
The Mellah
TO MENARA GARDENS (600m)
Olive Grove de Bab Jdid
TO AIRPORT
Bab er-Rob
Kasbah Mosque & Saadian Tombs
TO AGDAL GARDENS (1.2km)
Dar al-Makhzen

this landscape are fantastic Berber towns and *kasbahs*, where *pizid* (mud and straw) castles tower over the road. Excursions are possible by local transportation, but a rental car is best for exploring this region.

MARRAKESH ☎044

In a world gradually losing its magic and mystery, old Marrakesh has both in abundance. It all centers around Djema'a al-Fna, an incredible outdoor spectacle with snake charmers, charlatans, mystics, and healers, apparent holdouts from an earlier age. The Red City was founded in 1062 by the Almoravids and with its mosques and *medersas* quickly became an important center of culture and learning in North Africa. The Almohads destroyed much of the city upon succeeding them, hiring Andalucian artisans to rebuild it and giving the city its distinctive Moroccan-Spanish flavor. The city served as capital under various dynasties and remains the the tourism capital to this day, attracting droves of foreigners to its medina and *souqs*. The city's absurd heat leaves many begging for an escape, but the region doesn't disappoint. Hikes into the nearby Atlas mountains and camel treks into the desert are both a short drive away. Its location in the heart of Morocco, along with its old world allure, has made Marrakesh the hotspot it is today. And if you believe the clairvoyants in the square, the city will remain so for many years to come.

TRANSPORTATION

Flights: Aéroport de Marrakesh Menara (☎024 44 79 10 or 024 44 78 65), 5km south of town. Taxi from town 80-90dh, but they'll ask for 100dh. Bus #11 from the Koutoubia Mosque to the airport (about 7am-10pm, 3dh). Domestic and international flights on **Royal Air Maroc,** 197 Av. Mohammed V (☎024 42 55 00). Open M-F 8:30am-12:15pm and 2:30-7pm.

Trains: Av. Hassan II (☎024 44 65 69). Going away from the medina on Av. Mohammed V, turn left on Av. Hassan II (40min.). A taxi to or from pl. Djema'a al-Fna costs 10dh. To: **Rabat** (5hr., 9 per day 5am-9pm, 100-120dh) via **Casablanca** (4hr., 84dh); **Fez** (8hr., 8 per day 5am-7pm, 180dh) via **Meknes** (7hr., 160-170dh); **Tangier** via **Sidi Kacem** (6hr., 8 per day 5am-7pm, 200dh). 2nd class is often overbooked; pay attention when boarding so that you don't end up in an unnecessarily overcrowded car.

Buses: (☎024 43 39 33), a 25min. walk outside the medina walls by Bab Doukkala. To get there, walk out of the medina on Av. Mohammed V, pass through Bab Larissa, and then turn right, continuing along the walls to Bab Doukkala. The station is to the left. Arrive 30-60min. early, as seats fill quickly. Ignore the vagrants who want a tip for leading you to the right window; they will be fairly easy to find. **CTM** is window #10. To: **Casablanca** (4hr.; 4 per day 6:30am-6:30pm, 80dh); **Fez** (10hr.; 7am, 12, 11:45pm; 150dh); **Essaouira** (3hr.; 8am, 12:30pm; 65dh); **Ouarzazate** (4hr., 4 per day 7am-12:30am, 75dh); **Rabat** (5hr.; 2:30, 6:30am, 12:30pm; 65dh); **Tangier** (11hr., 2:30am) via **Tetouan** (9hr.). Private companies run frequently to destinations throughout Morocco, including **Essaouira** (window #7; 3hr., 13 per day, 4am-5pm, 35dh), **Rabat** (window #2; 5-6hr., 15 per day, 80-90dh), **Fez** (window #1; 10hr., 20 per day 4am-5pm, 125dh), and **Azilal** (window #18; 3hr., 8:30am, 12:30, 3:30pm, 60dh)

Grand Taxis: It's best to start from Bab al-Rob, where you can share a taxi to **Asni** (15dh) or **Setti Fatma** (20dh). There is another *grand taxi* stand on Av. Houmane el-Fetouaki; walk down Rue Bab Agnaou, turn left on Houmane el-Fetouaki, and walk for 2min. As always, you have to wait for the taxi to fill up. If you already have a group assembled, there's no need to head to Bab al-Rob; take one of the *grand taxis* at Djema'a al-Fna.

Car Rental: Hertz, 154 Blvd. Mohammed V (☎024 43 99 84). Open M-Sa 8am-noon and 2:30-6:30pm, Su 9am-noon. AmEx. **Avis,** 137 Blvd. Mohammed V (☎024 43 37 27). Same hours. AmEx/MC/V. Rentals at both agencies start at about 300dh per day for a Fiat Uno, plus 2.50dh per km. Min. age 25 for all cars, though many offices don't require proof of age. No special license required. Many hotels arrange rentals.

Moped/Scooter Rental: Rental stands dot the sidewalks around Pl. de 16 Novembre and back towards the medina. Rental fees are approx. 150dh per 6hr., or 300dh for the whole day. The only requirement is knowing generally how to drive one, so there's no insurance. Moped traffic in the city is always a little crazy, so drive at your own risk.

ORIENTATION AND PRACTICAL INFORMATION

Marrakesh and its medina are less crowded and maze-like than Morocco's other imperial cities, but just as crowded and noisy. Most of the excitement, as well as budget food and accommodation, centers around **Djema'a al-Fna** and the medina streets directly off of it. The *souqs* are on the streets leading north off of Djema'a al-Fna, and past them are several of the city's sights. The bus and train stations, administrative buildings, and luxury hotels are in **Guéliz,** the central neighborhood in the *ville nouvelle*, down **Av. Mohammed V;** from Djema'a al-Fna, walk to the towering **Koutoubia Minaret,** turn right, and walk for 20min. to reach **Pl. de 16 Novembre,** the central plaza. Also in Guéliz are most of the car rentals, newsstands, banks, and travel agencies. Bus #1 runs between the minaret and the heart of Guéliz (3dh). Or, take one of the many *petits taxis* (10dh) or horse-drawn carriages (15dh within the medina walls, 25dh to locations outside, sometimes more at night).

Tourist Office: Delegation Regionale de Tourisme, Av. Mohammed V (☎024 43 61 79), at Pl. Abdel Moumen ben Ali, a 30min. walk from Djema'a al-Fna. Take a *petit taxi* for about 15dh. Most helpful if you speak French; but all visitors can pick up glossy maps. (There is a better map on sale for 15dh at many tobacco shops and hotels.) Official guides, worthwhile in Marrakesh, can be booked here (½-day 150dh, full day 250dh). Visit a travel agency for Atlas or other excursions. Open daily 8:30am-noon and 2:30-6:30pm, summer 7:30am-3pm, Ramadan 9am-3pm.

Currency Exchange: Banks with 24hr. **ATMs** line Av. Mohammed V and Av. Hassan II in Guéliz. **Banque Populaire,** Av. Mohammed V, changes money. Open M-F 8:15am-3:45pm. In the medina, Rue Bab Agnaou, left of the post office, has plenty of banks and 24hr ATMs. Many hotels will change money 24hr. Try **Hôtel Ali** or **Hôtel Essaouira.**

Police: ☎19, off Djema'a al-Fna. In the *ville nouvelle,* the station is on Rue Ouadi al-Makhazine, off Pl. de 16 Novembre.

Late-Night Pharmacy: ☎024 44 54 26, off Djema'a al-Fna, on the way to Av. Mohammed V, on the right. Open Tu-Su 9pm-6am.

Medical Emergency: Doctor on call until 10pm at the late-night pharmacy. For more extensive service and 24hr. emergency service, try **Polyclinique du Sud,** 2 Rue Yougoslavie (☎024 44 79 99 or 024 42 57 51), in the *ville nouvelle.* From Pl. de 16 Novembre, walk 3 blocks down Av. Mohammed V away from the medina. Bear right onto Rue de Yougoslavie; it's 2 blocks down on the right. Private clinic with a range of specialists.

Internet Access: Many good internet cafes with A/C are on Bab Agnaou, the pedestrian mall off Djema'a al-Fna. **Hassan Internet,** just off Bab Agnaou, has a fast connection. 8dh per hr. Open 8am-midnight.

Post Office: Pl. 16 Novembre (☎024 43 09 77), off Av. Mohammed V. A madhouse. Unreliable Poste Restante. Open M-F 7:30am-3pm. Branch offices (☎024 44 09 77) in Djema'a al-Fna and near Bab er-Rob. Open M-F 7:30am-3pm. **DHL** and **FedEx** locations at Residence Al Mouhandiz, 113 Av. Abdel Karim El Kahattabi. **Postal Code:** 40000.

ACCOMMODATIONS

Marrakesh's inexpensive accommodations are in abundant supply near Djema'a al-Fna. Budget hotels clump along the *derbs* (side streets) just south of the place, as do *riads,* which are palatial, opulent restored medina homes with gorgeous terraces and home-cooked meals. Staying at a *riad* doesn't come cheap, but if you have a few extra dirhams, consider treating yourself to a night in one. On the far other end of the spectrum, many hotels allow you to sleep on the terrace for 30-40dh, a good option if you can't find a room, are desperately broke, or simply can't stand the ridiculous summer heat.

Hotel CTM, Djema'a al-Fna (☎024 44 23 25). Location, location, location: steps from the monkeys and mystics of the square, Hotel CTM offers elegant rooms in the front courtyard and less expensive, simpler rooms in the back. Communal shower is cold, but good for midday salvation from the heat. Terrace cafe and parking (30dh) to boot. Singles 120dh, with shower 160dh; doubles 190/230dh; triples 350dh. Newer rooms with A/C and shower 320/430/650dh. ❶

Hôtel Ali, Rue Moulay Ismail (☎044 44 49 79), past the post office off Djema'a al-Fna. A small mall of tourist services available here–currency exchange, Atlas excursions, two restaurants, massage services and shiatsu (150-200dh), and the good old-fashioned *hammam* (120dh) on the 2nd fl. Rooms are furnished with big, comfy beds, many with A/C. Showers are clean. The common areas are social, and the hotel is always bustling. English spoken. Call ahead or get here early. Singles 200dh, doubles 300dh, triples 400dh, quads 500dh. Terrace 40dh. ❶

Hôtel Sindi Sud, 109 Riad Zitoun al-Qedim (☎024 44 33 37), down Derb Sidi Bouloukat. From Djema'a al-Fna, face Hotel CTM and walk down the street to the left of it. Sindi Sud is down the first alley to the right. Psychedelic doors guard neat little rooms around a central courtyard. Reception arranges trips to Ouzoud and the desert; prices vary based on duration and group size. Breakfast 20dh. Singles 60dh, doubles 100dh, triples 150, with shower 300dh, quads 200/400dh. Terrace 30dh. ❶

Riad Hôtel Assia, 32 Rue de la Recette (☎024 39 12 85; www.hotel-assia-marrakech.com). Walk down Rue Bab Agnaou (left of the post office) and turn left when you see the signs. Modern convenience meets traditional Moroccan style in this lovely *riad.* Hand-worked *zellij* adorns the bathroom floor in simple but elegant air-conditioned rooms, all around a leafy central courtyard. The terrace has stunning views of the Koutoubia mosque. Shower, toilet, TV, and phone in rooms. Singles 250dh, doubles 380dh, triples 550dh, quads 650dh. ❷

FOOD

A small city of food stalls sprouts up in the early evening at Djema'a al-Fna, dishing up cheap fare from nightfall until well after midnight. Follow the crowds to the best *harira* (spicy bean and chickpea soup), served with dates and *chabakia* (a gooey honey-coated pastry), all for 3dh. The snails (5dh) are for the truly intrepid. Kebabs and sausages (25-30dh) are also on offer, but beware hidden garnish charges. You can't miss the orange juice (3dh), available all day and night, as the juicemen jockey for your business. On the other end of the price spectrum, Marrakesh also boasts many "palace restaurants" where music, outrageous portions, and liquor combine for a memorable, if expensive, evening (usually 300-600dh per person). The usual rotisserie places and snack bars, popular lunch stops, line Bab Agnaou.

Chez Chegrouni, 4 Pl. Djema'a al-Fna (☎024 47 46 15). Top *tajines* come at decent prices in this unobtrusive plaza-corner joint. The excellent chicken *tajine* with lemon and onion (50dh) is best taken on the terrace as you watch the action unfold. Salads 15dh. *Tajines* 50-60dh. Terrace prices slightly higher. Open daily 9am-late. ❶

Hôtel Restaurant Islane, Av. Mohammed V (☎024 44 00 81), on the roof of Hôtel Islane across from the Koutoubia Mosque. Wicker chairs and quality Italian food, with a stunning wide-angle view of the mosque. Pizzas (55-70dh) are spectacular. *Tajines* 80-90dh. F-Sa buffet 140dh. Open daily noon-3pm and 7-11pm. MC/V. ❷

Restaurant El Bahja, 41 Rue Bani Marine (☎024 44 03 43), to the right of the post office. Their motto is *"Le meilleur de la rue"* (the best of the street), and they serve up Moroccan staples at unbeatable prices. Sit down and grab a *tajine* or *grillade* (meat plate 25-30dh). 3-course menus 55-65dh. Open daily noon-11pm. ❶

Hôtel Ali (see **Accommodations,** p. 756). A tasty all-you-can-eat Moroccan buffet dinner situated 4 floors above the bustle of Djema'a al-Fna on the rooftop of Hôtel Ali, with a good variety of couscous, meat, salads, and fruit. A good place for women traveling alone. 70dh for hotel guests, 80dh for all others. Served daily 6:30-10pm. ❷

La Maison du Couscous, 53 Rue Bab Agnaou (☎024 38 68 92; www.couscousmarrakech.com), just off the plaza. Caters largely to tourists, but a very reliable option for couscous. Try the exotic *couscous du Sahara,* served with dried figs, dates, and camel meat. Dishes 70-100dh. Open daily 11am-11pm. AmEx/MC/V, min. 100dh. ❷

SIGHTS

DJEMA'A AL-FNA. Welcome to Djema'a al-Fna (Assembly of the Dead), arguably the most fantastic open-air spectacle in the world. Once the sight of public executions, it has been given over to a loose fraternity of storytellers, dancers, and entertainers. By day, old women will tattoo you with henna, while Barbary apes dance on chains next to men charming snakes. But the real entertainment comes at night, when food stalls come out and smoke fills the air, lending a mystical quality to the men muttering stories and women chanting over tarot cards. Sit down and listen to a story, watch a boxing match, or just stand amidst the commotion, marveling at the ebb and flow of the menagerie around you.

MEDINA AND SOUQS. Marrakesh's medina is less overwhelming than that of Fez, but almost as big and brash, stuffed with tanneries, *babouche* stalls, carpet bazaars, sheepskin vendors, and all manner of crafts. A survey of the medina (primetime for crowds is 5-8pm) begins at the *souqs.* From Djema'a al-Fna, enter the medina directly across from the **Café-Restaurant-Hôtel de France**. Walk past the first line of touristy places and take a quick left through the archway, which marks the beginning of **Rue Souq Smarine,** the main thoroughfare through the markets. This street is home to the **fabric souq,** with gorgeous silky woven blankets, and their owners, calling out to you to buy them. There's also the usual range of lamps, hookahs, and leather stores. A few minutes later you'll come to a large alley to the right heading into the **Rahba Kedima.** You might smell it first: the square is full of stalls selling herbs, spices, and soaps for all variety of cuisines and illnesses. Deeper in the square is **La Criée Berbère,** once home to a slave auction and now full of friendly men using impressive skills of persuasion to sell you carpets. Back on **Rue Souq Smarine** the road quickly forks. The right fork leads past more of the same shops, and eventually to the **Medersa ben Youssef.** The left fork is the *babouche souq*, a small universe of stalls selling traditional Moroccan slippers. When you reach a huge, sharp left turn, head down it to find the dyers' *souq,* full of huge bubbling vats. Pushing through them will lead you to the 16th-century **Mouassine Fountain,** a grimy but character-laden sight. Those with strong stomachs can visit the tanneries: continue through the *souqs* and take a right after the Medersa ben Youssef. Head straight for 10min.

through a run-down stretch of the medina, and the tanneries are on your right. If you get lost in the medina, ask a merchant for directions, or ask a child to lead you out of the maze for a few dirhams.

AL-BAHIA PALACE. The grandest palace in all of Marrakesh was built by the vizier Si Ahmed ibn Musa, better known as Bou Ahmed, who named it Al-Bahia ("the Brilliance"). Indeed, this seemingly never-ending network of courtyards, rooms, and sleeping quarters is a masterpiece. Every cedar-wood ceiling is spectacularly carved, making it easily one of the best displays of such craftsmanship in the country. Look for the five-piece ceiling in the side annex. From time to time it also holds contemporary art exhibits. *(From Djema'a al-Fna, walk down rue Riad Zitoun al-Qedim to its end at pl. Ferbiantiers, then turn left and follow the road as it curves to a red archway, which opens onto a long, tree-lined avenue leading to the palace door. Open M-Th and Sa-Su 8:30-11:45am and 2:30-5:45pm, F 8:30-11:30am and 3-5:45pm. 10dh.)*

MEDERSA BEN YOUSSEF. In 1565, Sultan Moulay Abdallah al-Ghalib raised the Medersa ben Youssef in the medina center; it was the largest Qur'anic school in the Maghreb until its closing in 1960. The *medersa* is a glorious example of the Merenid style, with *zellij* tile, stucco work, and carved cedar in layers on the courtyard walls. A huge arch opens on to the *mihrab* (prayer niche) and the prayer room. Upstairs are 132 cells, which they claim once accommodated all 900 of the students. *(Walk down the main souq street, Rue Souq Smarine, and bear right onto Rue Souq al-Kebir. Follow it to its end. Open Tu-Su, June-Aug. 9am-1pm and 2:30-6pm; Sept.-May 9am-6:30pm. 20dh, children 10dh. Combined admission for medersa, Museum of Marrakesh, and Koubba al-Ba'adiyn 60dh.)*

EXPLORING MOROCCO

DAR SI SAID. This 19th-century palace, built by the younger brother of Bou Ahmed, houses the Museum of Moroccan Arts, a superb collection of traditional handicrafts from around the country. The highlight of the collection is a 10th-century marble basin dating from the year 1000, brought to Marrakesh from Córdoba by Ali ben Youssef—it is the oldest preserved object in the city. Rugs, leatherwork, pottery, and weapons are all on display here as well. If you tire, head out to the courtyard's cool gazebo-covered fountain. *(Go toward al-Bahia, and continue on Rue Zitoun al-Jadid, taking the 2nd right heading toward Djema'a al-Fna and the 1st left down the alley where the museum resides. ☎024 38 95 64. Open M, W-Th, and Sa-Su 9-11:45am and 2:30-5:45pm, F 9-11:30am and 3-5:45pm. 10dh.)*

MUSEUM OF MARRAKESH. Collections of daggers, Fassi ceramic, and Berber clothing complement a contemporary art gallery showcasing work by Moroccan painters. The building itself, a 19th-century palace, is lavish and contains a traditional *hammam* to explore. *(Off the open plaza at the end of Rue Souq Smarine in the back of the medina, around the corner from the medersa and Koubba al-Ba'adiyn. ☎024 39 09 11. Open daily 9am-6pm. 40dh, students 20dh. Combined admission for 3 monuments 60dh.)*

KOUTOUBIA MOSQUE. Dominating the medina's skyline is the finest and best-preserved remnant of the Almohad dynasty, which ruled from 1130 to 1213. The 70m-tall minaret, built by the sultan Yacoub al-Mansour, is topped by four golden lanterns; legend has it that the sultan's wife melted her gold jewelry to gild the fourth. The mosque was the model for its sisters, one in Rabat and the other—the Giralda—in Sevilla (see p. 209). *(Entrance is forbidden to non-Muslims.)*

KOUBBA AL-BA'ADIYN MONUMENT. Next to the *medersa* is the bizarrely protruding cupola of the 12h-century Koubba al-Ba'adiyn, Marrakesh's oldest monument. Despite the destruction of all other Almoravid relics by the succeeding Almohads, their influence is undeniable here—this is the structure on which much of Morocco's architecture is modeled. It was excavated in the 20th century, and much remains hidden underground or by other structures. While the exterior of the cupola is unpainted, the curves and interior decoration are definitely distinct from later architecture and are worth a look. *(Walk down the main souq street, Rue Souq Smarine, bear right onto Rue Souq al-Kebir, and turn left at the madrasa. Open daily 9am-5:30pm. Bang on the door if it's closed. 10dh. 60dh for all 3 monuments.)*

SAADIAN TOMBS. Modeled after the interior of Granada's Alhambra, the Saadian Tombs served as the royal Saadian necropolis during the 16th and 17th centuries, and three halls of tombs have been preserved in much of their splendor. The first room is home to the children of Sultan Ahmed al-Mansour, followed by the **Hall of the Twelve Columns,** covered in marble, a gold-inlaid dome, and stucco work. The sultan, along with his descendants, are buried here. The last and smallest room is home to his mother and father. The unmarked tombs in the garden belong to women, while those of men are covered in Arabic calligraphy. The minaret of the Mosque of the Kasbah, al-Mansour's personal mosque, towers above the complex. *(From Djema'a al-Fna, walk down rue Bab Agnaou 5min. to Bab er-Rob, take a left through Bab Agnaou, and follow the signs into an alley just past the mosque. English tours (15-20dh) available from the guides near the entrance. Open daily 8:30-11:30am and 2:30-5:45pm. 10dh.)*

GARDENS. Since the 12th century, rulers have dealt with the sun by constructing massive gardens irrigated with water from the Atlas. The **Majorelle Gardens** were designed by French painter Jacques Majorelle in the 1920s, and are owned and maintained today by the Yves Saint-Laurent Foundation. Buried in the back is a lone column fragment, a memorial to the famous French designer, born in North Africa in 1936. On the same site is the small **Museum of Islamic Art.** *(From Djema'a al-Fna, walk toward Koutoubia Mosque and take a right on av. Mohammed V. After exiting the medina, take a right and follow the walls to the bus station. Bear left onto Blvd. Safi and turn right onto Av. Yacoub al-Mansour; the gardens are on the left. Better yet, take a petit taxi for 15dh (drivers will ask for 30). Open daily June-Aug. 8am-noon and 3-7pm, Sept.-May 8am-noon and 2-5pm. Gardens 30dh, museum 15dh.)* Winston Churchill and King Mohammed VI have both enjoyed the gardens of **La Mamounia,** perhaps the poshest hotel in the city, and you can too. The hotel allows the public to visit the gardens, but you'll have to dress appropriately and act the part. *(The hotel is 5min. from Djema'a al-Fna on Av. Houman el Fetouaki just before exiting through Bab Jedid. Open to the public until 2pm, although the doormen will often turn you away even earlier.)*

NIGHTLIFE

Most travelers hang around Djema'a al-Fna or in one of the terrace cafes that overlooks it for most of the night. **Café Argana** is a quiet spot with amazing views. Drinks 10dh. **Café Paris** is another pleasant option. Not much distinguishes the terrace bars: they all have great views. For a hard drink, try the bars at the **Tazi** (☎024 44 27 87) and **Foucauld** (☎024 44 54 99) hotels, where locals and tourists mix with the help of 25dh Spéciale Flag. (Both bars open at 9pm. To find the Tazi, head away from Djema'a al-Fna 200m down the street to the left of the Banque du Maroc. For Foucauld, turn right by the Tazi onto the road that becomes Av. Mohammed V and walk two blocks.) Young, pretty Marrakeshis like to party, and they support a thriving club scene. Most clubs pick up on the weekends after 1 or 2am. **Diamant Noir,** in **Hôtel Marrakech** on Av. Mohammed V, is a fairly popular, playing a good mix of current house and hip-hop jams. (Open 10pm-late. Cover 90-120dh.) **Pacha,** the famous Ibiza club, now rages through the night in Morocco, too. Features famous DJs and epically large dance floors. (☎024 38 84 05. Cover 150dh, weekends 300dh. Open 9pm-dawn.) Both are an expensive cab ride away from the medina in Guéliz.

DAYTRIPS FROM MARRAKESH

Marrakesh could not be better located for excursions to the coast, into the High Atlas, or into the oases of the southern deserts. The entire Atlas range offers lush valleys with waterfalls like the **Cascades d'Ouzoud,** gorgeous hiking through meadows and Berber villages, and the tallest mountain in the Atlas, **Jebel Toubkal** (4167m), whose trailhead is only an hour from Marrakesh. South are the **Dadès** and **Draa valleys,** full of secluded villages and age-old *ksours* (desert fortresses). Just past them are the first *ergs* (wind-swept desert expanses) into the **Sahara,** which you can enjoy on camelback. The tourist office can recommend a travel agency that will tailor trips according to your itinerary and group size. Many hotels, including **Hotel Ali,** also organize excursions, so ask around.

SETTI FATMA

To get to Setti Fatma, grand taxis (25dh) are the best bet. To find them, head out Bab er-Rob and turn right. Walk for 15 minutes down a dusty road until you see them on ther right. Minibuses (15dh) leave intermittently from 6am-noon from just outside Bab er-Rob, but aren't the most reliable. If you have a car, go 57km south on S513; ignore the first "P" (for parking) sign in Asgaour, even if men try to tell you you can't drive farther. You can in fact drive right to Setti Fatma, where you can find a limited number of free parking spaces.

The Ourika Valley, one hour southeast of Marrakesh, is an Eden away from the unrelenting heat of the city. The Atlas mountains seem to grow out of the sweltering haze, hiding the lush greenery of the valley, a favorite picknicking spot during the summer and home to Morocco's only ski resort, **Oukaïmden.** Setti Fatma, a small town at the end of the road, draws visitors with its waterfalls, small natural pools, and riverside eating. After lounging away on the lawn at one of the numerous restaurants, the easy hike to the first pool is a perfect way to cool off. To get there, cross one of the two primitive wooden bridges at the end of town. Head past the camels and find your way up to the path above the line of cafes. Head to the left, following the rough-cut stairs and stony path. Follow the path uphill past all the juice stands. After a while you may have to start clambering a little, but the climb is not overly taxing. In 20-30 minutes you'll reach the first *cascade* and the pool below it, filled with loud Moroccan boys and surrounded by picnickers. The steep climb to the right brings you above the *cascade* to a solitary spot with an exceptional view with the valley. While it may look easy, the climb is difficult and potentially dangerous, particularly the first part. It is best attempted, if at all, without shoes or camera. On the way back make sure to grab a cold drink from one of the **Berber refrigerators,** the waterworks spraying cold spring water onto the drinks below.

To find the other *cascades* or plan more secluded hikes and excursions around Setti Fatma, you'll need a guide. Ask for the highly-respected Ahmed Ait Kaid at the helpful **Bureau des Guides** on the main road or the main parking lot, both in the town center. All the waterfalls can be explored in just a few hours. Longer treks can be arranged to the Berber villages in the valleys and local mountains nearby. The closest are located down the river at the end of town (away from Marrakesh). They are almost completely secluded. Getting there requires local knowledge and is best done with a guide, who can also arrange a night's stay with a Berber family. If you're spending the night in the area, first try the clean and adequate **Café-Restaurant Asgaour ❶** near the bridge (☎024 48 52 94. Singles 80dh; doubles 100dh; triples 140dh). Most of the restaurants along the road have a few simple rooms upstairs—cheap, but don't expect many amenities. The only time you might have difficulty finding a roomis during the early August *moussem* (festival), when hundreds of Moroccans descend on the tiny town.

APPENDIX

CLIMATE

Climate on the Iberian Peninsula varies hugely by both region and season. While Asturians mull cider to keep warm as the cold rain falls, Sevilla's patios fill with sangria drinkers trying to stay cool under the sweltering afternoon sun. Like Spain, Portugal has both warm inland plains and a temperate coast. That coastal Mediterranean climate that blesses Spain and Portugal extends south to Morocco, which, although generally regarded as a desert, has a wealth of green mountains and fertile expanses. The following table contains average temperature ranges and rainfall for selected cities.

SPAIN	JANUARY			APRIL			JULY			OCTOBER		
	°C	°F	mm	°C	°F	mm	°C	°F	mm	°C	°F	mm
Barcelona	6-13	43-55	31	11-18	52-64	43	21-28	70-82	27	15-21	59-70	86
Madrid	2-9	36-48	39	7-18	45-64	48	17-31	63-88	11	10-19	50-66	53
Santander	7-12	45-54	119	10-15	50-59	83	16-22	61-72	54	12-18	54-64	133
Sevilla	6-15	43-59	66	11-24	52-75	57	20-36	68-97	1	14-26	57-79	70
PORTUGAL												
	°C	°F	mm	°C	°F	mm	°C	°F	mm	°C	°F	mm
Faro	9-15	48-59	70	13-20	55-68	31	20-28	68-82	1	16-22	61-72	51
Lisboa	8-14	46-57	111	12-20	52-68	54	15-25	59-77	3	14-22	57-72	62
Porto	5-13	41-55	159	9-18	48-64	86	15-25	59-77	20	11-21	52-70	105
MOROCCO												
	°C	°F	mm	°C	°F	mm	°C	°F	mm	°C	°F	mm
Marrakesh	4-18	39-64	25	11-26	52-79	31	19-38	66-100	3	14-28	57-82	23
Rabat	8-17	46-63	66	11-22	52-72	43	17-28	63-82	0	14-25	57-77	48

To convert from degrees Fahrenheit to degrees Celsius, subtract 32 and multiply by 5/9. To convert from Celsius to Fahrenheit, multiply by 9/5 and add 32.

°CELSIUS	-5	0	5	10	15	20	25	30	35	40
°FAHRENHEIT	23	32	41	50	59	68	77	86	95	104

MEASUREMENTS

Like the rest of the rational world, Spain, Portugal, and Morocco use the metric system. The basic unit of length is the meter (m), which is divided into 100 centimeters (cm) or 1000 millimeters (mm). One thousand meters make up one kilometer (km). Fluids are measured in liters (L), each divided into 1000 milliliters (mL). A liter of pure water weighs one kilogram (kg), which is divided into 1000 grams (g). One metric ton is 1000kg.

MEASUREMENT CONVERSIONS	
1 inch (in.) = 25.4mm	1 millimeter (mm) = 0.039 in.
1 foot (ft.) = 0.305m	1 meter (m) = 3.28 ft.
1 yard (yd.) = 0.914m	1 meter (m) = 1.094 yd.
1 mile (mi.) = 1.609km	1 kilometer (km) = 0.621 mi.
1 ounce (oz.) = 28.35g	1 gram (g) = 0.035 oz.
1 pound (lb.) = 0.454kg	1 kilogram (kg) = 2.205 lb.
1 fluid ounce (fl. oz.) = 29.57mL	1 milliliter (mL) = 0.034 fl. oz.
1 gallon (gal.) = 3.785L	1 liter (L) = 0.264 gal.

SPANISH PHRASEBOOK

Each vowel has only one pronunciation: *a* ("ah" in "father"); *e* ("eh" in "pet"); *i* ("ee" in "eat"); *o* ("oh" in "oat"); *u* ("oo" in "boot"); *y*, by itself, is pronounced the same as the Spanish i ("ee"). Most consonants are the same as in English. Important exceptions are: *j* ("h" in "hello"); *ll* ("y" in "yes"); *ñ* ("ny" in "canyon"); and *r* at the beginning of a word or *rr* anywhere in a word (trilled). *H* is always silent. *G* before *e* or *i* is pronounced like the "h" in "hen;" elsewhere it is pronounced like the "g" in "gate." *X* has a bewildering variety of pronunciations: depending on dialect and word position, it can sound like the English "h," "s," "sh," or "x." *B* and *v* have similar pronunciations. Spanish words receive stress on the syllable marked with an accent. In the absence of an accent mark, words that end in vowels, *n*, or *s* receive stress on the penultimate syllable. For words ending in all other consonants, stress falls on the last syllable. The Spanish language has masculine and feminine nouns, and gives a gender to all adjectives. Masculine words generally end with an *o*, feminine words generally end with an *a*. Pay close attention—slight changes in word ending can have drastic changes in meaning. For instance, when receiving directions, mind the distinction between *derecho* (straight; more commonly *recto*) and *derecha* (right). Sentences that end in ? or ! are also preceded by the same punctuation upside-down: *¿Cómo estás? ¡Muy bien, gracias!*

APPENDIX

ESSENTIAL PHRASES

ENGLISH	SPANISH	PRONUNCIATION
Hello.	Hola.	OH-la
How are you?	¿Cómo está?	KOH-mo es-TA
Good, thanks.	Muy bien, gracias.	MWEE bee-en, GRA-see-ahs
Goodbye.	Adiós.	ah-dee-OHS
Yes/No	Sí/No	SEE/NO
Please.	Por favor.	POHR fa-VOHR
Thank you.	Gracias.	GRA-see-ahs
You're welcome.	De nada.	DAY NAH-dah
Do you speak English?	¿Habla inglés?	AH-blah een-GLAYCE
I don't speak Spanish.	No hablo español.	NO AH-bloh ehs-pahn-YOHL
Excuse me.	Perdón.	pehr-DOHN
I don't know.	No sé.	NO SAY
Can you repeat that?	¿Puede repetirlo?	PWEH-day reh-peh-TEER-lo
Let's dance.	Bailamos.	by-lah-MOHS

ON ARRIVAL

ENGLISH	SPANISH	ENGLISH	SPANISH
I am from (the US/ Europe).	Soy de (los Estados Unidos/Europa).	What's the problem, sir/ madam?	¿Cuál es el problema, señor/señora?
Here is my passport.	Aquí está mi pasaporte.	I lost my passport.	Perdí mi pasaporte.
I will be here for less than six months.	Estaré aquí por menos de seis meses.	I have nothing to declare.	No tengo nada para declarar.
Where is customs?	¿Dónde está la aduana?	Where do I claim my luggage?	¿Dónde puedo reclamar mi equipaje?
I don't know where that came from.	No sé de donde vino eso.	Please do not detain me.	Por favor no me detenga.

DIRECTIONS

ENGLISH	SPANISH	ENGLISH	SPANISH
(to the) right/left	(a la) derecha/izquierda	across from	enfrente de/frente a
next to	al lado de/junto a	near/far	cerca/lejos
straight ahead	derecho	turn (command)	doble
on top of/above	encima de/arriba	beneath/below	bajo de/abajo
traffic light	semáforo	corner	esquina
street	calle/avenida	block	cuadra

SURVIVAL SPANISH

ENGLISH	SPANISH	ENGLISH	SPANISH
How can you get to...?	¿Cómo se puede llegar a...?	Is there anything cheaper?	¿Hay algo más barato/ económico?
Does this bus go to (Italy)?	¿Va este autobús a (Italia)?	I'm in a hurry!	¡Tengo prisa!
Where is (Azorín) street?	¿Dónde está la calle (Azorín)?	What bus line goes to..?	¿Qué línea de buses tiene servicio a...?
When does the bus leave?	¿Cuándo sale el bús?	From where does the bus leave?	¿De dónde sale el bús?
I'm getting off at...	Bajo en...	I have to go now.	Tengo que ir ahora.
Can I buy a ticket?	¿Podría comprar un boleto?	How far is...?	¿Qué tan lejos está...?
How long does the trip take?	¿Cuántas horas dura el viaje?	Please let me off at the zoo/hostel.	Por favor, déjeme en el zoológico/hostal
I am going to the airport.	Voy al aeropuerto.	The flight is delayed/ cancelled.	El vuelo está atrasado/ cancelado.
Where is the bathroom?	¿Dónde está el baño?	Is it safe to hitchhike?	¿Es seguro pedir aventón?
I lost my baggage.	Perdí mi equipaje.	I'm lost.	Estoy perdido(a).
How much does it cost per day/week?	¿Cuánto cuesta por día/ semana?	Does it have (heating/air-conditioning)?	¿Tiene (calefacción/aire acondicionado)?
Where can I buy a cell-phone?	¿Dónde puedo comprar un teléfono celular?	Where can I check e-mail?	¿Dónde se puede chequear el email?
Could you tell me what time it is?	¿Podría decirme qué hora es?	Are there student dis-counts available?	¿Hay descuentos para estudiantes?

ACCOMMODATIONS

ENGLISH	SPANISH	ENGLISH	SPANISH
Is there a cheap hotel around here?	¿Hay un hotel económico por aquí?	Are there rooms with windows?	¿Hay habitaciones con ventanas?
Do you have rooms available?	¿Tiene habitaciones libres?	I am going to stay for (four) days.	Me voy a quedar (cuatro) días.

APPENDIX

ENGLISH	SPANISH	ENGLISH	SPANISH
I would like to reserve a room.	Quisiera reservar una habitación.	Are there cheaper rooms?	¿Hay habitaciones más baratas?
Can I see a room?	¿Podría ver una habitación?	Do they come with private baths?	¿Vienen con baño privado?
Do you have any singles/doubles?	¿Tiene habitaciones sencillas/dobles?	Does it have (heating/A/C)?	¿Tiene (calefacción/aire acondicionado)?
I'll take it.	Lo tomo.	Who's there?	¿Quién es?
I need another key/towel/pillow.	Necesito otra llave/toalla/almohada.	The shower/sink/toilet is broken.	La ducha/pila/el servicio no funciona.

EMERGENCY

ENGLISH	SPANISH	ENGLISH	SPANISH
Help!	¡Socorro!/¡Ayúdeme!	Call the police!	¡Llame a la policía!
I am hurt.	Estoy herido(a).	Leave me alone!	¡Déjame en paz!
It's an emergency!	¡Es una emergencia!	They robbed me!	¡Me han robado!
Fire!	¡Fuego!/¡Incendio!	They went that way!	¡Fueron en esa dirección!
Call a clinic/ambulance/doctor/priest!	¡Llame a una clínica/una ambulancia/un médico/un padre!	I will only speak in the presence of a lawyer.	Sólo hablaré en presencia de un abogado(a).
I need to contact my embassy.	Necesito contactar mi embajada.	Don't touch me!	¡No me toque!

MEDICAL

ENGLISH	SPANISH	ENGLISH	SPANISH
I feel bad/better/fine/worse.	Me siento mal/mejor/bien/peor.	What is this medicine for?	¿Para qué es esta medicina?
I'm sick/ill.	Estoy enfermo(a).	Where is the nearest hospital/doctor?	¿Dónde está el hospital/doctor más cercano?
I'm allergic to...	Soy alérgico(a) a...	Here is my prescription.	Aquí está la receta médica.
I have a cold/a fever/diarrhea/nausea	Tengo gripe/una calentura/diarrea/náusea.	Call a doctor, please.	Llame a un médico, por favor

OUTDOORS/RECREATION

ENGLISH	SPANISH	ENGLISH	SPANISH
Is it safe to swim here?	¿Es seguro nadar aquí?	Do you have sunscreen?	¿Tiene crema solar?
What time is high/low tide?	¿A qué hora es marea alta/baja?	Is there a strong current?	¿Hay una corriente fuerte?
Where can I rent a surfboard/bike?	¿Dónde puedo alquilar un planeador de mar/bicicleta?.	Where is the trail?	¿Dónde está el rastro?
Do I need a guide?	¿Necesito una guía?	Can I camp here?	¿Puedo acampar aquí?

EATING OUT

ENGLISH	SPANISH	ENGLISH	SPANISH
Do you have anything vegetarian/without meat?	¿Hay algún plato vegetariano/sin carne?	Can I see the menu?	¿Podría ver la carta/el menú?
I would like to order (the eel).	Quisiera (el congrio).	Table for (one), please.	Mesa para (uno), por favor.
Check, please.	¡La cuenta, por favor!	Do you take credit cards?	¿Aceptan tarjetas de crédito?
Where is a good restaurant?	¿Dónde está un restaurante bueno?	Delicious!	¡Qué rico!

NUMBERS, DAYS, AND MONTHS

ENGLISH	SPANISH	ENGLISH	SPANISH	ENGLISH	SPANISH
0	cero	20	veinte	last night	anoche
1	uno	21	veintiuno	weekend	(el) fin de semana
2	dos	22	veintidos	morning	(la) mañana
3	tres	30	treinta	afternoon	(la) tarde
4	cuatro	40	cuarenta	night	(la) noche
5	cinco	50	cincuenta	month	(el) mes
6	seis	100	cien	year	(el) año
7	siete	1000	mil	early/late	temprano/tarde
8	ocho	1 million	un millón	January	enero
9	nueve	Monday	lunes	February	febrero
10	diez	Tuesday	martes	March	marzo
11	once	Wednesday	miércoles	April	abril
12	doce	Thursday	jueves	May	mayo
13	trece	Friday	viernes	June	junio
14	catorce	Saturday	sábado	July	julio
15	quince	Sunday	domingo	August	agosto
16	dieciseis	today	hoy	September	septiembre
17	diecisiete	tomorrow	mañana	October	octubre
18	dieciocho	day after tomorrow	pasado mañana	November	noviembre
19	diecinueve	yesterday	ayer	December	diciembre

APPENDIX

CATALAN/BASQUE/GALLEGO

ESSENTIAL PHRASES

ENGLISH	CATALAN	BASQUE	GALLEGO
Hello.	Hola.	Kaixo.	Ola.
Goodbye.	Adéu.	Agur.	Adeus.
Yes/No.	Sí/No.	Bai/Ez.	Si/Non.
Please.	Si us plau.	Mesedez.	Por favor.
Thank you.	Gràcies.	Eskerrik asko.	Graciñas.
You're welcome.	De res.	Ez horregatik.	De nada.
Do you speak English?	Parles anglès?	Ingelesez hitz egiten al duzu?	Falas inglés?
I don't understand.	No ho entenc.	Ez dut ulterzen.	Eu non entendo.
Excuse me.	Perdoni.	Barkatu.	Perdóeme.
I don't know.	No sé.	Ez dakit.	Eu non sei.
Can you repeat that?	Pot repetir?	Errepikatu ahal duzu hori?	Pode repetilo?
Where is...?	On és...?	Non dago...	Onde está...?
Who/What/When/Why	quem/que/quando/porque	nor/zer/noiz/zergatik	quen/que/cando/por qué
How do I get to (Madrid)?	Com puc arribar a (Madrid)?	Nola joaten da (Madril) era?	Como vou a (Madrid)?
Do you have any rooms available?	Teniu alguna habitació disponibile?	Badaukazu logelik?	Ten habitacións?
Help!	Ajuda!	Lagundu!	Axuda!
What is your name?/My name is...	Com et dius?/Em dic...	Nola duzu izena?/...dut izena.	Como te chamas?/Me chama...
Let's be friends.	Estiguem amics.	Izan dezagun lagunak.	Sexamos amigos.

NUMBERS

	CATALAN	BASQUE	GALLEGO		CATALAN	BASQUE	GALLEGO
1	u/una	bat	un/unha	20	vint	hogei	vinte
2	dos/dues	bi	dous/dúas	30	trenta	hogeita hamar	trinta
3	tres	hiru	tres	40	quaranta	berrogei	corenta
4	quatre	lau	catro	50	cinquanta	berrogei hamar	cincuenta
5	cinc	bost	cinco	60	seixanta	hirurogeita	sesenta
6	sis	sei	seis	70	setanta	hirurogeita hamar	setenta
7	set	zazpi	sete	80	vuitanta	larogei	oitenta
8	vuit	zortzi	oito	90	noranta	larogeita hamar	noventa
9	nou	bederatzi	nove	100	cent	ehun	cen
10	deu	hamar	dez	1000	mil	mila	mil

PORTUGUESE PHRASEBOOK

Portuguese words are often spelled like their Spanish equivalents, although the pronunciation is different. In addition to regular vowels, Portuguese, like French, has nasal vowels: those with a *tilde* (*ã*, *õ*, etc.) or before an *m* or *n* are pronounced with a nasal twang. At the end of a word, *o* is pronounced "oo" as in "room," and *e* is sometimes silent (usually after a *t* or *d*). The consonant *s* is pronounced "sh" or "zh" when it occurs before another consonant. The consonants *ch* and *x* are pronounced "sh," although the latter is sometimes pronounced as in English; *j* and *g* (before *e* or *i*) are pronounced "zh"; *ç* sounds like "es." The combinations *nh* and *lh* are pronounced "ny" as in "canyon" and "ly" as in "billion." The masculine singular definite article is "o" and the feminine singular definite article is "a."

APPENDIX

ESSENTIAL PHRASES

ENGLISH	PORTUGUESE	PRONUNCIATION
Yes/No.	Sim/Não.	see/now
Hello.	Olá.	oh-LAH
Good day/afternoon/night.	Bom dia/tarde/noite.	bom DEE-ah/TARD/NOYT
Goodbye.	Até logo.	ah-TEH low-go
Please.	Por favor.	pohr fa-VOHR
Thank you.	Obrigado/a.	oh-bree-GAH-doh/dah
Sorry/excuse me.	Desculpe.	dish-KOOLP-eh
Do you speak English?	Fala inglês?	FAH-lah een-GLAYSH?
I don't understand.	Não entendo	now ehn-TEHN-doh
Where is...?	Onde é...?	OHN-deh eh...?
How do you get to...?	Como chego à...?	COH-moo SHEH-go ah...?
How much does this cost?	Quanto custa?	KWAHN-too KOOST-ah?
Do you have a single/double room?	Tem um quarto individual/duplo?	tem oom KWAR-too EEN-dee-vee-doo-WAHL/DOO-ploh?
That is very cheap/expensive.	É muito caro/barato.	eh MUY-toh CAH-roh/bah-RAH-toh
Help!	Socorro!	soh-HOH-roh!
Who/what	quem/que	KEHM/KEH
When/why	quando/porque	KWAN-doh/pohr-KAY
I want/would like...	Eu quero/gostaria...	EH-oo KER-oh/gost-ar-EE-uh
What is your name? My name is...	Como se chama? O meu nome é...	COH-mo seh SHAH-mah? oh MEH-oo NO-meh eh...
I am (twenty) years old.	Eu tenho (vente) anos.	Eh-oo TEN-yo (VIN-teh) anyos.

NUMBERS, DAYS, AND MONTHS

ENGLISH	PORTUGUESE	ENGLISH	PORTUGUESE	ENGLISH	PORTUGUESE
0	zero	20	vinte	last night	ontem à noite
1	um/uma	21	vinte-um/uma	weekend	(o) fim-de-semana
2	dois/duas	22	vinte-dois/duas	morning	(a) manhã
3	três	30	trinta	afternoon	(a) tarde
4	quatro	40	quarenta	night	(a) noite
5	cinco	50	cinquenta	month	(o) mês
6	seis	100	cem	year	(o) ano
7	sete	1000	um mil	early/late	cedo/tarde
8	oito	1 million	um milhão	January	Janeiro
9	nove	Monday	segunda-feira	February	Fevereiro
10	dez	Tuesday	terça-feira	March	Março
11	onze	Wednesday	quarta-feira	April	Abril
12	doze	Thursday	quinta-feira	May	Maio
13	treze	Friday	sexta-feira	June	Junho
14	catorze	Saturday	sábado	July	Julho
15	quinze	Sunday	domingo	August	Agosto
16	dezasseis	today	hoje	September	Setembro
17	dezassete	tomorrow	amanhã	October	Outubro
18	dezoito	day after tomorrow	depois de amanhã	November	Novembro
19	dezanove	yesterday	ontem	December	Dezembro

APPENDIX

MOROCCO PHRASEBOOK

While Moroccan Arabic *(darija)* is historically related to standard Arabic, the dialect has evolved to such an extent that it could almost be considered a separate language. Berber, French, and even Spanish have had deep influences on the vocabulary and pronunciation of the language. Though Arabic is the official language and by far the most commonly spoken tongue, French remains widely understood, particularly in the governmental and tourist domain. Try out some Arabic—making the effort goes a long way towards being a respectful and engaged visitor—but speakers of English, Spanish, and other romance languages might have more luck sticking with French. Moroccan Arabic spellings are transliterated and should be pronounced phonetically.

ARABIC ESSENTIALS

ENGLISH	MOROCCAN ARABIC
Hello (polite).	es salaam alaykum
Hi/How are you?	la bas?
Fine, thanks.	la bas, barak
Yes/No	eeyeh/la
Please.	'afak (m)/'afik (f)
Thank you (very much).	shukran (bezzef)
You're welcome.	la shukran 'la wejb
Excuse me.	smeh leeyah
My name is...	esmee...
Goodbye	bessalama
God willing	ensha'llaah
I'm from...	ana men...

ENGLISH	MOROCCAN ARABIC
I don't speak Arabic.	makan'refsh l'arbeeyah
Do you speak English?	wash kat'ref negleezeeya?
Is this bus going to...?	wash had lkar ghaadee l...?
I'm looking for...	kanqellab 'la...
Get away from me!	ba'd mennee!
Help!	'teqnee!
I am sick.	ana mreed
I want (I would like)...	bgheet...
Where is the (train station)?	feen kayn (lagaar)?
What time does the...leave?	wufuqash kaykhrej...?
bus/train	otubees/tran
We like Morocco!	'azhebatna lmagreeb!

FRENCH ESSENTIALS

THE BASICS		
Hello (Good day)/Hi.	Bonjour/Salut	bohn-ZHOOR/sah-LU
Good evening.	Bon soir	bohn-SWAH
How are you?	Ça va?	sa-VA?
Goodbye	Au revoir	oh ruh-VWAH
Yes/No/Maybe	Oui/Non/Peut-être	wee/nohn/p'TET-ruh
Please	S'il vous plaît	see voo PLAY
Thank you	Merci	mehr-SEE
You're welcome	De rien/Je vous en prie	duh rhee-ehn/jh'VOOS on PREE
Pardon me	Excusez-moi/Pardon	ex-KU-zay-MWAH/pahr-DOHN
Help!	Au secours!	oh sek-OOR!
I'm lost	Je suis perdu(e)	jh'SWEE pehr-DU
I'm sorry	Je suis désolé(e)	jh'SWEE day-zoh-LAY
Do you speak English?	Parlez-vous anglais?	par-lay-voo ahn-GLAY?
I don't speak French.	Je ne parle pas français.	jh'ne parl pah frahn-SAY
I don't understand.	Je ne comprends pas.	jh'ne KOHM-prahn pas
Speak slowly.	Parlez moins vite.	par-lay mwehn veet
I would like...	Je voudrais...	jh'voo-DRAY
How much does this cost?	Combien ça coûte?	comb-YEN sa coot?
Leave me alone.	Laissez-moi tranquille	LESS-say-mwah trahn-KEEL
I need help.	J'ai besoin d'assistance.	jhay bezz-WEHN dah-SEE-stahnss
My name is ( ). What's your name?	Je m'appelle ( ). Comment vous appelez-vous?	JH'ma-PELL ( ). kuh-MAHN voo-za-pell-ay-VOO?
What is it?	Qu'est-ce que c'est?	kess-kuh-SAY?
Stop!	Arrêtez!	ahr-eh-TAY
It's just one step from the sublime to the ridiculous.	"Du sublime au ridicule il n'y a qu'un pas." (Napoléon)	doo soo-BLEEM oh ree-dee-CULE eel nee ah KHUN pah

APPENDIX

GLOSSARY

SPAIN: TRAVELING

abadía: abbey
abierto: open
ayuntamiento/ajuntament (C): city hall
albergue: youth hostel
alcazaba: Muslim citadel
alcázar: Muslim palace
arena: sand
autobús/autocar: bus
avenida/avinguda (C): avenue
bahía: bay
bakalao: Spanish techno
bandera azul: blue flag, EU award for clean beaches
baños: baths
barcelonés: of Barcelona
barrio viejo: old quarter
biblioteca: library
billete/boleto: ticket
buceo: scuba diving
cabo: cape
cajero automático: ATM
calle/carrer (C): street
cambio: currency exchange
capilla: chapel
castillo/castell (C): castle
catedral: cathedral
cerrado: closed
carretera: highway
casco antiguo/viejo: old city
chocolate: chocolate or hash
ciudad vieja/ciutat vella (C): old city
colegio: high school
consigna: luggage storage
Correos: post office
corrida: bullfight
cripta: crypt
cuarto: room
encierro: running of the bulls
entrada: entrance
ermita/ermida (C): hermitage
escuela: (elementary) school
estación: station
estanco: tobacco shop
estanque: pond
estany (C): lake
extremeño: of Extremadura
fachada: facade
feria: outdoor market, fair
ferrocarriles: trains
fiesta: holiday or festival
fuente/font (C): fountain
gallego: of Galicia
gitano: gypsy
glorieta: rotary
iglesia/església (C)/igrexa (G): church
IVA: value-added tax
jardín público: public garden
judería: Jewish quarter
librería: bookstore
lista de correos: poste restante
litera: sleeping car (in trains)
llegada: arrival
madrileño: Madrid resident
madrugada: early morning
manchego: from La Mancha
mercado/mercat (C): market
mezquita: mosque
mirador: lookout point
monestir (C): monastery
monte: mountain
mosteiro (G): monastery
mozárabe: Christian art style
mudéjar: Muslim architectural style
muelle/moll (C): wharf, pier
murallas: walls
museo/museu (C): museum
oficina: office
palacio/palau (C): palace
parador nacional: state-owned hotel
parte viejo: old town
páseo, Po./passeig, Pg. (C): promenade
pico: peak
playa/platja (C): beach
plaza/plaça, Pl. (C)/praza, Pr. (G): square, plaza
puente: bridge
quiosco: newsstand
rastro: flea market
real: royal
REAJ: Spanish youth hostel network
Reconquista: Christian reconquest of the Iberian peninsula from the Moors
refugio: shelter, refuge
reina/rey: queen/king
retablo: altarpiece
ría (G): estuary
río/riu (C): river
rua (G): street
sacristía: part of the church where sacred objects are kept
sala: room, hall

APPENDIX

salida: exit, departure
selva: forest
Semana Santa: Holy Week, leading up to Easter Sunday
sepulcro: tomb
seu (C): cathedral
sevillana: type of flamenco
SIDA: AIDS
sierra/serra (C): mountain range
Siglo de Oro: Golden Age
sillería: choir stalls
tienda: shop, tent
tesoro: treasury
torre: tower
universidad: university
v.o.: versión original, a foreign-language film subtitled in Spanish
valle: valley
zarzuela: Spanish light opera

SPAIN: FOOD AND DRINK

a la plancha/a brasa: grilled
aceite: oil
aceituna: olive
adabo: battered
agua: water
aguacate: avocado
aguardiente: firewater
ahumado/a: smoked
ajo: garlic
al horno: baked
albóndigas: meatballs
alloli: Catalan garlic sauce
almejas: clams
almendras: almonds
almuerzo: midday meal
anchoas: anchovies
angulla: eel
arroz: rice
arroz con leche: rice pudding
asado: roasted
atún: tuna
bacalao: salted cod
bistec: steak
bocadillo: sandwich
bodega: wine cellar
bollo: bread roll
boquerones: anchovies
brasa: chargrilled
cacahuete: peanut
café con leche: coffee w/milk
café solo: black coffee
calabacín: zucchini
calamares: calamari, squid
caldereta: stew
calimocho: red wine and cola
callos: tripe
camarones: shrimp
caña: beer in a small glass
canelones: cannelloni
cangrejo: crab
caracoles: snails
carne: meat
cava (C): sparkling white wine
cebolla: onion
cena: dinner
cerdo: pig, pork
cereza: cherry
cervecería: beer bar
cerveza: beer
champiñones: mushrooms
choco: cuttlefish
chorizo: spicy red sausage
chuleta: chop, cutlet
chupito: shot
churros: fried dough sticks
cocido: cooked, stew
conejo: rabbit
coñac: brandy
copas: drinks
cordero: lamb
cortado: coffee with little milk
croquetas: fried croquettes
crudo: raw
cuchara: spoon
cuchillo: knife
cuenta: the bill
desayuno: breakfast
dorada: sea bass
empanada: meat/fish pastry
ensaladilla rusa: vegetable salad with mayonnaise
entremeses: hors d'oeuvres
escabeche: pickled fish
espagueti: spaghetti
espárragos: asparagus
espinacas: spinach
fabada asturiana: bean soup with sausage and ham
flan: crème caramel
frambuesa: raspberry
fresa: strawberry
frito/a: fried
galleta: cookie
gambas: prawns
garbanzos: chickpeas
gazpacho: cold tomato soup with garlic and cucumber

APPENDIX

ginebra: gin
guisantes: peas
helado: ice cream
hielo: ice
horchata: sweet almond drink
horneado: baked
huevo: egg
jamón serrano: cured ham
jatetxea (B): restaurant
jerez: sherry
langosta: lobster
langostino: large prawn
leche: milk
lechuga: lettuce
lenguado: sole
lomo: pork loin
manzana: apple
manzanilla: dry, light sherry
mayonesa: mayonnaise
mejillones: mussels
melocotón: peach
menestra de verduras: vegetable mix/pottage
menú: full meal with bread, drink, and side dish
merienda: tea/snack
merluza: hake
migas: fried breadcrumb dish
mojito: white rum and club soda with mint and sugar
morcilla: blood sausage
muy hecho: well-done (steak)
naranja: orange
natillas: creamy milk dessert
navajas: razor clams
paella: rice and seafood dish
pan: bread
pasa: raisin
pastas: small sweet cakes
pastel: pastry
patatas bravas: potatoes w/spicy tomato sauce and mayo
patatas fritas: French fries
pato: duck
pavo: turkey
pechuga: chicken breast
pepino: cucumber
picante: spicy
pimienta (negra): (black) pepper
pimiento (rojo): (red) pepper
piña: pineapple
pintxo (B): Basque for tapa
plancha: grill
plátano: banana
plato del día: daily special plato combinado: entree and side dish
poco hecho: rare (steak)
pollo: chicken
pulpo: octopus
queso: cheese
rabo de toro: bull's tail
ración: small dish
rebozado: battered and fried
refrescos: soft drinks
relleno/a: stuffed
sal: salt
salchicha: pork sausage
sangría: red wine punch
seco: dried
servilleta: napkin
sesos: brains
setas: wild mushrooms
sidra: (alcoholic) cider
solomillo: sirloin
sopa: soup
taberna: tapas bar
tapa: bite-sized snack
tenedor: fork
ternera: beef, veal
terraza: patio seating
tinto: red (wine)
tocino: (Canadian) bacon
tomate: tomato
tortilla española: potato fritatta
tortilla francesa: omelette
tostada: toast
trucha: trout
trufas: truffles
tubo: tall glass of beer
txakoli (B): fizzy white wine
uva: grape
vaca, carne de: beef
vaso: glass
verduras: green vegetables
vino: wine
vino blanco: white wine
vino tinto: red wine
xampanyería (C): champagne bar
yema: candied egg yolk
zanahoria: carrot
zarzuela de marisco: shellfish stew
zumo: fruit juice

PORTUGAL: TRAVELING

alto/a: upper
autocarro: bus
bairro: neighborhood, district
baixo/a: lower

APPENDIX

berrões: stone pigs found in Trás-Os-Montes
bicicleta de montanha: mountain bike
bilhete: ticket
bilheteria: ticket office
câmara municipal: town hall
camioneta: long-distance bus
capela: chapel
casa de abrigo: shelter-house, usually in parks
castelo: castle
centro de saúde: state-run medical center
chegadas: arrivals
cidade: city
claustro: cloister
construção: construction
conta: bill
coro alto: choir stall
Correios: post office
cruzeiro: large stone cross; cruise
Dom, Dona: courtesy titles, usually for kings and queens
domingo: Sunday
entrada: entrance
esquerda: left (abbr. E, Esqa)
estação rodoviária: bus station
estrada: road
feriado: holiday
floresta: forest
fortaleza: fort
grutas: caves
horario: timetable
igreja: church
ilha: island
intercidade: inter-city train
lago: lake
largo: small square
ligação: connecting bus/train
livraria: bookstore
miradouro: lookout
mosteiro: monastery
mouraria: Moorish quarter
mudança: switch/change
palácio: palace
paragem: stop
partidas: departures
pelourinho: stone pillory
pensão (s.), pensões (pl.): pension(s)/guesthouse(s)
ponte: bridge
porta: gate/door
posto de informações turísticas: tourist office
pousada da juventude: youth hostel
pousada: guest house
praça: square
praça de touros: bullring
praia: beach
PSP: Polícia de Seguranca Pública, the local police force
quarta-feira: Wednesday
quarto de casal: room with double bed
quinta-feira: Thursday
quiosque: kiosk; newsstand
rés do chão (R/C): ground floor
residencial: guesthouse, more expensive than pensões
retábulo: altarpiece
ribeira: stream
ria: narrow lagoon
rio: river
romaria: pilgrimage-festival
rua: street
sábado: Saturday
saída: exit
sé: cathedral
segunda-feira: Monday
selos: stamps
sexta-feira: Friday
terça-feira: Tuesday
termas: spa
tesouraria: treasury
tourada: bullfight
velho/a: old
vila: town

PORTUGAL: FOOD AND DRINK

açorda: soup with bread and garlic
adega: wine cellar, bar
alface: lettuce
alho: garlic
almoço: lunch
ameijoas: clams
arroz: rice
arrufada de Coimbra: raised dough cake with cinnamon
assado: roasted
azeitonas: olives
bacalhau: cod
bacalhau à transmontana: cod braised with cured pork
balcão: balcony, or a counter in a bar or café
batata: potato
batido: milkshake
bem passado: well done (steak)
bica: espresso

APPENDIX

bitoque de porco: pork chops
bitoque de vaca: steak
bolachas: cookies
branco: white (wine)
cabrito: kid (goat)
café com leite: coffee with milk
café da manhã: breakfast
caldeirada: shellfish stew
caldo: broth/soup
camarões: shrimp
caneca: pint-size beer mug
caracóis: snails
carioca: coffee with hot water; like American coffee
carne: meat
carne de vaca: beef
cebola: onion
cerveja: beer
chocos: cuttlefish
chouriço: sausage
churrasco: BBQ
churrasqueira: BBQ house
cogumelos: mushrooms
conta: bill
couvert: charge added to bill for bread
cozido: boiled
cozido no forno: baked
doce: sweet
ementa: menu
ervilhas: green peas
esacalfado: poached
espadarte: swordfish
espetadas: skewered meat served with melted butter
esturjão: sturgeon
fatia: slice
feijão: bean
frango: chicken
frito: fried
galão: coffee with hot milk
gasosa: soda
gelado: ice cream
grão: chickpeas
grelhado: grilled
guisado: stewed
hambúrguer no prato: hamburger patty with fried egg
imperial: draft beer
jantar: dinner
lagosta: lobster
lampreia: lamprey
laranja: orange
legumes: vegetables
leitão: suckling pig
linguado: sole
linguiça: very thin sausage
lula: squid
maçã: apple
manteiga: butter
mariscos: shellfish
massapão: marzipan
mexilhões: mussels
ovo: egg
padaria: bakery
pão: bread
pastelaria: pastry shop
peru: turkey
pimentos: peppers
polvo: octopus
porco: pork
posta: slice of fish or meat
prato do dia: dish of the day
presunto: ham
queijo: cheese
recheado: stuffed
salmão: salmon
sande/sanduíche: sandwich
seco: dry
sobremesa: dessert
suco: juice
tasca: bistro/cafe
tigelada: egg custard
tinto: red wine
toucinho do ceu: cake made with pumpkin, egg-yolk, and bacon-drippings
uva passa: raisin
vinho de casa: house wine
vinho verde: sparkling wine
vitela: veal

MOROCCO

adhan (A): call to prayer
agneau (F): lamb
aguelmane (A): lake
alcazaba (A): citadel
alcázar (A): palace
al-kebir (A): leather
aourir (A): small mountain
attarine (A): perfume
aujourd'hui (F): today
azrour (A): rock
auberge de jeunesse (F): youth hostel
azib (A): shepherd's hut
bab (A): gate
beurre (F): butter
bière (F), birra (A): beer
billet (F): ticket
blanc (F): white

boeuf (F): beef
boulettes de viande (F): meatballs
brochette (F): shish-kebab
borj (A): tower
bus (F): bus
chambre (F): room
chameau (F): camel
chaud (F): hot
compris (F): included
consigne (F): left luggage
couscous (F): semolina grain
coûter (F): to cost
crevettes (F): shrimp
dar: palace
demain (F): tomorrow
djebel (A): mountain peak
djellaba (A): long Moroccan garment
djoutia (A): flea market
douche (F): shower
droite (F): right
erg (A): sand dune
fassi (A): resident of Fes
fermé (F): closed
froid (F): cold
gare (F): train station
gare routière (F): bus station
gauche (F): left
gite (F): gov't approved Berber houses used as shelters
haj (A): Mecca pilgrimage
hammam (A): public bath
kasbah (A): fort, citadel, medina
kif (A): marijuana
litham (A): veil
louer (F): to rent
madrasa (A): school
makhzen (A): government
medina (A): old Arabic city
mellah (A): Jewish quarter
mihrab (A): prayer niche
msalla (A): prayer area
mosquée (F): mosque
moussem (A): festival
muezzin (A): calls Muslims to prayer
musée (F): museum
nouveau/nouvelle (F): new
oued (A): river
ouvert (F): open
palais (F): palace
pastilla (A): pigeon pie
piscine (F): pool
poisson (F): fish
poste (F): post office
qsar, qsour (pl.) (A): fortified village with curved, white-washed houses
rue (F): street
salle de bain (F): bathroom
smarine (A): textiles
souq (A): market
tagine (A): Moroccan stew
timbre (F): stamp
tmer (A): dates
toilette (F): toilet
train (F): train
vieux/vielle (F): old
ville (F): city
voiture (F): car
zellij (A): decorative tiles

INDEX

A

Abd Allah, Idris ibn 704
A Coruña. See La Coruña.
Adolfo Suárez 65
Afonso III 567
A Guarda. See La Guardia.
AIDS 24
Aínsa (L'Ainsa) 449
Alacant. See Alicante.
A Lanzada. See La Lanzada.
Alas, Leopoldo 74
Alberti, Rafael 74
Albufeira 624
Alcalá de Henares 125
Alcazaba (Almería) 260
Alcazaba (Málaga) 254
Alcázar (Córdoba) 226
Alcázar (Sevilla) 209
Alcobaça 652
Alcúdia 333
Aleixandre, Vicente 74
Alentejo 630
Alfonso XII 64
Alfonso XIII 64
Algarve 616
Algarve and Alentejo 616
al-Gharb. See Algarve.
Alhambra, La 278
Alicante 306
al-Krim, Abd 704
Almería 259, 261
Almodóvar, Pedro 75
Almohad Dynasty 209, 212, 704
Almoravid Dynasty 704
al-Qaeda. See terrorism.
Altamira 72. See caves
Altea 314
Álvares Cabral, Pedro 567
Amadeo I 64
Andaloussi 709
Andalucía 220
Andorra 441
Andorra la Vella 441
Ansó 444
Antequera 270
Aragón 456
Aragonese Pyrenees 444
Aragón, La Rioja, and Navarra 456
Aranjuez 127
architecture
- Berber 708
- Churrigueresque 72
- Gothic 71
- Islamic 708
- Manueline 575
- Modernista 72
- mudéjar 71
- Plateresque 71
- Romanesque 71

Arcos de la Frontera 236
Armada 61
Armona 629
Asilah 741
Astorga 155
Asturias and Cantabria 506
ATMs 17
A Toxa. See La Toja
Aveiro 690
Ávila 137
azulejos 575, 599

B

Badajoz 196
banking. See money.
Baqueira-Beret 437
Barcelona 353
- accommodations 365
- daytrips 391
- entertainment 384
- festivals 391
- food 369
- nightlife 387
- shopping 386
- sights 375
- transportation, intercity 353
- transportation, local 361

Barcelos 677
bargaining. See money.
Barka, Ben 704
Basque
- language 67
- separatist movement 484, 496
- sports 76

Batalha 655
Bayona (Baiona) 551
BEJA 636
Belém 605
Benavente y Martínez, Jacinto 74
Benidorm 312
Berbers 701
Beyond Tourism 49
Bilbao (Bilbo) 492
Boabdil 280, 281
bodegas. See also wine.
- Jerez de la Frontera 233
- Logroño 468
- Sanlúcar de Barrameda 234

Boí 435
Bosch, Hieronymus 110, 115
Bowles, Paul 709
Braga 671, 675
Bragança 696
Bubión 287
bullfighting
- abolition of 51
- history of 76
- in Córdoba 227
- in Lisboa 601
- in Madrid 117
- in Murcia 318
- in Ronda 269
- in Santarém 641
- in Sevilla 216
- in Valencia 298

Bulnes 519
Buñuel, Luis 75, 111
Burgos 161
Burguete (Auritz-Burguete) 454
Burroughs, William S. 709

C

Cabo de Gata 262
Cabo Finisterre (Cabo Fisterra) 543
Cadaqués 418
Cádiz 238, 241
Caesar, Augustus 192, 456
Caesar, Julius 200, 579, 636, 751
Caetano, Marcelo 570
Calatrava, Santiago 72
Calderón de la Barca, Pedro 73
Calella de Palafrugell 409
Cambados 555

Camino de Santiago 468, 470, 536
Camões, Luís de 576
camping 42
Camprodon 427
Canetti, Elias 709
Cangas 552
Cangas de Onís 515
Cantabria 527
Cap de Formentor 332
Capela dos Ossos
Évora 634
Faro 628
Capileira 287
Carlist Wars 64
Carlos I 61. See Carlos V
Carlos II 64
Carlos V 61
Carmona, António 570
Carnation Revolution 570
Carnaval. See festivals
Carrión de los Condes 165
Cartagena 320
car travel
in Morocco 712
in Spain and Portugal 33
Casals, Pau (Pablo) 75
casas colgadas 179
Cascais 606
Castelló 301
Castelo Branco 662
Castilla La Mancha 172
Castilla La Mancha and Extremadura 172
Castilla y León 131
Castro, Rosalía del 74
Catalan Pyrenees 424
Cataluña (Catalunya) 394
cathedrals
Ávila 140
Braga 675
Burgos 164
Cádiz 241
Catedral de la Almudena 106
Catedral de San Isidro (Madrid) 102
Ciudad Rodrigo 149
Cuenca 183
Évora 634
Faro 628
Girona 413
Granada 283
Igreja de São Roque (Lisboa) 598
Igreja do Bom Jesus (Braga) 675
Lisboa 599
Oviedo 511
Sagrada Familia 380
Salamanca 146
Santander 532
Santiago de Compostela 541
Santuário de Fátima 658
Segovia 136
Sevilla 209
Toledo 177
TUY 550
cava 70, 369, 372
caves
Altamira 534
Covas d'en Xoroi (Menorca) 343
Cueva de la Pileta (Ronda) 270
Cueva del "Buxu" (Cangas de Onís) 517
Cuevas del Drach (Mallorca) 334
Cuevas de Nerja 284
Grutas de Mira de Aire (Batalha) 656
Grutas de Moeda (Fátima) 658
Guadix 285
Los Dólmenes (Antequera) 272
cellular phones 38
Celts 60, 304, 536, 566, 638
Cercedilla 129
Cernuda, Luis 74
Cervantes, Miguel de 73, 125, 126, 159
Ceuta 704
Ceuta (Sebta) 567, 722
Charlemagne 394, 441
Chefchaouen 722
Chopin, Frédéric 324
Choukri, Mohamed 709
Chraïbi, Driss 709
Churriguera family 72
cider (sidra) 70, 514
Cinco Villas 463
Ciudad Rodrigo 149
Ciutadella (Ciudadela) 339
Civil War. See Spanish Civil War.
climate 760
Coimbra 684
Columbus, Christopher 61, 105, 108, 131, 157, 189, 209, 210, 226, 234, 279, 289, 356, 376, 377, 551, 567
Comillas 535
Comunidad de Madrid 125
Conímbriga 689
consular services
Abroad 10
In Portugal 11
In Spain 11
Convento da Madre de Deus (Lisboa) 575, 599
Convento de Cristo (Tomar) 575, 661
Córdoba 220
Costa Blanca 304
Costa Brava 406
Costa de la Luz 229
Costa del Sol 250
Costa Dorada 394
Covadonga 522
credit cards 17
Cuenca 179
Culatra 630
currency exchange. See also money
current events
in Morocco 705
in Portugal 571
in Spain 66
customs 15

D

Dalí, Salvador
Casa-Museu Salvador Dalí 420
film collaborations 75, 111
painting 73, 111
personal life 419
Teatre-Museu Dalí 417
darija 706, 766
debit cards 17
Deià 331
Dénia 314
Dias, Bartolomeu 567
dietary concerns 47
Dinis I 567
disabled travelers 46
Dólmenes, Los. See caves.
Dom Afonso Henriques 567
Domènech i Montaner, Lluís 375, 378, 381
Don Juan 73
Douro and Minho 664
Douro Valley 573, 670
driving. See cars.

E

Echo. See Hecho.
ecotourism 44
Eivissa. See Ibiza.
Elche 321
El Cid 108, 149, 161, 164, 166

El Escorial. See San Lorenzo de El Escorial
El Greco 72, 110, 111, 140, 167, 177, 183, 187, 189, 417, 497
El Grove (O Grove) 556
El Khouri, Driss 709
El Torcal de Antequera. See Sierra de Torcal
Elvas 634
emergency medical services 24
entrance requirements 10
environmental conservation 51
Ericeira 608
Espot 434
Essaouira 709
Essentials 10
Estella 481
ETA. See terrorism.
Eurail passes 29
European Union 13, 15, 54, 571, 724
Euskadi. See Basque.
Évora 631
exchange rates. See money.
Extremadura 184

F

fado 577, 600
Falange 65, 125
Faro 626
Farol 630
Fátima 656
FC Barcelona 76
Felipe el Hermoso 61
Felipe González 66
Felipe II 61, 569
Felipe III 61
Felipe IV 61
Felipe V 64
female travelers 713
Feria de Abril. See festivals
Fernando and Isabel 61, 68, 104, 157, 189, 209, 226, 273, 282, 376, 462
Fernando I 567
Fernando VII 64
festivals
  Batalla del Vino (Haro) 471
  Bou a la Mar 316
  Carnaval 77, 117, 220, 243, 399
  Celtic Music Festival (Ortigueira) 563
  Concurs de Castells 402
  Feria de Abril 217
  Festa de Sant Jordi (Catalunya) 391
  Festa dos Rapazes (Bragança) 698
  Festival Internacional de Santander 533
  Fogueres de Sant Joan 311
  Ibiza and Formentera International Film Festival 348
  in Spain 77
  La Noche de San Juan 562
  Orgullo Gay (Madrid) 118
  Semana Santa 217
  World Sacred Music Festival (Fez) 738
Fez 731
Figueras (Figueres) 415
film 75
financial matters. See money.
flamenco
  history of 74
  in Jerez 234
  in Madrid 116
  in Sevilla 215
Fogueres de Sant Joan. See festivals.
Formentera 351
Franco, Francisco 65, 75, 111, 113, 114, 146, 147, 188, 484, 704
Fuente Dé 526
fútbol (futebol). See soccer.

G

Galicia 536
Galician (gallego). See languages
Garganta del Cares 519
Gaudí, Antoni 375, 376, 380, 381, 383, 535
gay and lesbian resources. See also GLBT travelers
  in Barcelona 364
  in Madrid 275
Gehry, Frank. See Museo Guggenheim
Generación de 1898 74
Generation of 1870 (Portugal) 576
Gibraltar 67, 247
Gijón 512
Girona (Gerona) 410
GLBT travelers 713
  in Morocco 713
  in Spain and Portugal 45
gnaoua 709, 750
Góngora, Luis de 73
Goya, Francisco de 72, 110
Granada 273, 704
Grandes, Almudena 74
Green March 704
Gris, Juan 111, 112
Guadalupe 189
Guadix 284
Guarda 693
Guernica 111
Guernica (Gernika) 498
Guillén, Jorge 74
Guimarães 676
Gulbenkian, Calouste 577, 598

H

hadith 706
Haro 471
Hassan II 704
health 22
  in Spain and Portugal 23
Hecho (Echo) 444
Hemingway, Ernest 74, 266, 454, 473, 477
Henry the Navigator 605
Hernández, Miguel 74
Herrera, Juan de 102, 103, 124, 128
hitchhiking 712
Hostelling International (HI) 40
Hotel Formentor 332
House of Bragança 569

I

Ibiza (Eivissa) 343
identification 14
  International Driving Permit (IDP) 34
  International Insurance Certificate 34
  International Student Exchange Card (ISE Card) 14
  International Student Identity Card (ISIC) 14
  International Teacher Identity Card (ITIC) 14
  International Youth Travel Card (IYTC) 14
  International Student Travel Confederation (ISTC) 14

INDEX

Ilhas Berlengas 649
immigration 51, 67, 705
Inquisition 61, 68, 704
Instance Equité et Réconciliation (IER) 705
International Brigades 65
International Festival (Asilah) 742
internet access 37
Iruña. See Pamplona.
Irving, Washington 281
Isabel de Castilla 61
Isabel II 64
Isabel la Católica. See Fernando and Isabel.
Islam 68
Islas Cíes (Illas Cíes) 549
Istiqlal 704
Itálica 218

J

Jaca 444
Jardim da Estrela (Lisboa) 598
Játiva. See Xàtiva
Jerez de la Frontera 230
Jiménez, Juan Ramón 74
João I 567
João V 569
João VI 569
José María Aznar 66
Juana la Loca 61
Juan Carlos I 65
Judaism 68
- in medieval Spain 227, 228, 265, 360, 376, 413, 463, 551
- in Morocco 704, 706
- in Portugal 628
- synagogues 178, 227, 376

K

Kerouac, Jack 709
Khaled, Cheb 709
Knights Templar 172, 567, 612, 659, 661
Koran. See Qur'an

L

La Coruña 557
Lagos 616
La Guardia 550
La Lanzada (A Lanzada) 557
L'Albufera 300
La Mezquita (Córdoba) 226
La Movida 65
languages 67. See also phrasebooks.
- Basque (euskera) 484
- Catalan 394, 405
- Galician (gallego) 536
- in Morocco 706
- Portuguese 571

La Rioja 467
La Sagrada Familia 380
Las Alpujarras 285
La Seu d'Urgell 439
Las Fallas. See festivals
Las Islas Baleares
- Formentera 351
- Ibiza (Eivissa) 343
- Mallorca (Majorca) 324
- Menorca 334
- transportation 322

La Toja (A Toxa) 556
Leiria 653
Lérida (Lleida) 421
Lisboa 579
- accommodations 587
- entertainment 600
- festivals 603
- food 592
- nightlife 601
- sights 595
- transportation, intercity 579
- transportation, local 585

Lisbon School 575
literature
- Generación de 1898 74
- Generación de 1927 74
- Siglo de Oro 73

Ilhas Armona 630
Logroño 468
Lope de Vega 73, 125
López García, Antonio 73
Lorca 319
Lorca, Federico García 74
Los Dólmenes (Antequera) 272
Louro 544
Lugo 562
Lusitania 566

M

Macau 571
Machado, Antonio 74, 135, 168
Madeira 567
Madinat al-Zahra 229
madrasas. See medersas.
Madrid
- accommodations 91
- daytrips 123
- entertainment 115
- food 95
- nightlife 119
- shopping 118
- sights 101
- transportation, intercity 78
- transportation, local 87

Madrid Conference 704
Mafra 607
Magellan, Ferdinand 569
Mahón (Maó) 334
mail services 39
Mairena, Antonio 74
Málaga 250
Mami, Cheb 709
Marbella 255
Marismas del Odiel 236
Marquês de Pombal 569
Martín Gaite, Carmen 74
measurements 760
medersas 708, 730, 737, 739, 756, 757
Medina del Campo 160
Meknes 725
Melilla 704
Mérida 192
Mernissi, Fatima 709
Mezquita (Córdoba) 226
minority travelers 47
Miró, Joan 73, 381
Modernisme 72, 375. See also architecture.
Mohammed V 704
Mohammed VI 705
Mojácar 263
Moneo, Rafael 72
money
- bargaining 708
- budget tips 18
- credit, debit, and ATM cards 17
- currency and exchange 15
- taxes 19
- tipping 19, 71, 707
- traveler's checks 16
- wiring money 18

Monsanto 663
Montjuïc 360
Montserrat 391
Moors 60, 68, 566

structures 260
mopeds. See transportation.
Morella 303
Morocco 701, 766
- accommodations 713
- communication 714
- consular services 710
- customs and etiquette 707
- food and drink 707
- history of 701
- language 706
- money 712
- national holidays 709
- religion 706
- the arts 708
- transportation 711

mosques 708
- Meknes 730
- Mezquita del Cristo de la Luz 178
- Qairaouine Mosque (Fez) 739

Mosteiro dos Jerónimos 575, 605. See also cathedrals.
Mosteiro Santa Maria da Vitória (Batalha) 656
Mosteiro Santa Maria de Vitória (Batalha) 575
motorcycles. See transportation
Mrabet, Mohammed 709
Mudawana 705
Muhammed, Prophet 701, 706
Mulhacén 1, 287
Munson, Henry 709
Murcia 316
Murillo, Bartolomé 72
Muros 544
Musa ibn Nusayr 701
Museo Guggenheim 497
Museo Nacional Centro de Arte Reina Sofía 111
Museo Thyssen-Bornemisza 111
Museu Calouste Gulbenkian 598
Museu Picasso (Barcelona) 378

N

Napoleon 64
Naranjo de Bulnes. See Bulnes
national holidays
- in Portugal 578
- in Spain 77

Nationalists 704
national parks 43
- Aigüestortes (Cataluña) 432
- Alvão (Trás-Os-Montes) 699
- Coto de Doñana (Andalucía) 234
- Parque Nacional de Ordesa 447
- Parque Natural da Serra da Estrela 695
- Parque Natural de Cabo de Gata-Níjar 262
- Parque Natural de Montesinho 698
- Parque Natural de Posets-Maladeta 452
- Parque Natural do Alvãois 699
- Peneda-Gerês (Douro and Minho) 678
- Picos de Europa 517
- Ria Formosa 630
- São Mamede (Alentejo) 635
- Serra da Estrela (The Three Beiras) 695
- Sierra Nevada 286

Navarra 473
Navarran Pyrenees 452
Nazaré 649
Nerja 284
North, The 664

O

O Castro de Baroña 544
O Grove. See El Grove.
Olhão 628
Oporto. See Porto.
Ortega y Gasset, José 74
Oviedo 507

P

packing 19
painting
- Cubism 73
- Siglo de Oro 72
- Surrealism 73

País Vasco (Euskadi) 484
Palacio Real (Madrid) 103
Palau de la Música Catalana 378
Palau Güell 380
Palencia 166
Palma 324
Pampaneira 286
Pamplona (Iruña) 473
Panteao Nacional (Lisboa) 599
Parc Güell 383
Parque das Nações 604
Parque del Buen Retiro 107
Parque del Monasterio de Piedra 463
Parque Doñana 217
passports 13
Peniche 645
Perejil 705
Pérez-Reverte, Arturo 74
Pessoa, Fernando 576
Phoenicians 220, 238, 255, 566, 701
phrasebooks
- Catalan/Basque/Gallego 764
- Portuguese 765
- Spanish 761

Picasso, Pablo 73, 111, 254, 378, 397, 561
Pizarro, Francisco 189, 191
police 20
Polisario Front 704, 705
Poncebos 523
Pontevedra 553
Popular Party (PP) 66
Port Lligat 418
Porto (Oporto) 664
porto (port) 573
Port Pollença 332
Portugal
- customs and etiquette 574
- food and drink 572
- history of 566
- language 571
- music 577
- religion 572
- sports 578
- the arts 575
- the media 577

Potes 524
Prado, Museo del 109
Primo de Rivera, José Antonio 125
Primo de Rivera, Miguel 64
Prince Henry the Navigator 567
Puigcerdá 429
Puig i Cadafalch, Josep 375, 381
Pyrenees, The 424

Q

Quinta de Marim 630
Qur'an 706

R

Rai 709
Real Madrid. See soccer.
Reconquista 61, 567
religion
- in Morocco 706
- in Portugal 572
- in Spain 68

INDEX

Reus 402
Reyes Católicos 61, 68, 172, 279, 462
Rías Altas 557, 564
Rías Bajas (Rías Baixas) 545
Ribadavia 551
Ribatejo and Estremadura 641
Rif Mountains 704
Ripoll 424
Rock of Gibraltar 249
Rodoreda, Mercè 74
roman ruins 71
- Badajoz 198
- Cartagena 320
- Conímbriga 689
- Itálica 218
- Lugo 562
- Segovia 135
- Tarragona 401
- Volubulis 730

Roncal 454
Roncesvalles 453
Ronda 266
Rossetti, Ana 74
Running of the Bulls. See under Festivals, San Fermín.
Ruta del Modernisme 375, 404

S

safety 20
safety and security 712
Sagres 622
Salamanca 141
Salardú 437
Salazar, Antonio 570
Salinas, Pedro 74
San Antonio de Portmany (Sant Antoni) 350
San Fermín. See festivals
San Lorenzo de El Escorial 123
Sanlúcar de Barrameda 234
San Sebastián (Donostia) 484
Santander 527
Sant Antoni. See San Antonio de Portmany
Santarém 641
Santa Teresa. See Teresa de Jesús.
Santiago de Compostela 536
Santillana del Mar 534
Saramago, José 576
sardana 75, 414, 421
saudade 566
Second Spanish Republic 64
Segovia 131
Segovia, Andrés 74
Semana Santa. See Festivals
separatist movement 65
Sert, Josep Lluís 72
Setúbal 613
Sevilla 200
- accommodations 206
- entertainment 215
- nightlife 214
- shopping 216
- sights 208
- transportation, intercity 200

sherry (jerez) 70, 233
Shi'a 706
Sierra de Guadarrama 129
Sierra de Torcal 272
Sierra Nevada
- see National Parks 286

Sines 638
Sintra 609
Sitges 394
skiing
- Andorra La Vella 443
- Baqueira-Beret 437
- Camprodon 428
- Oukaïmden 759
- Puigcerdà 429
- Sierra Nevada 286

Soares, Mario 570
soccer
- in Barcelona 385
- in Lisboa 601
- in Madrid 117
- in Morocco 709
- in Portugal 578
- in Sevilla 216
- in Spain 76

solo travelers 45
Soria 168
Sort 438
Sortelha 694
Spain
- current events 66
- customs and etiquette 70
- food and drink 68
- history 60
- language 67
- religion 68
- sports 76
- the arts 71

Spanish-American War 64
Spanish Civil War 65, 421, 704
- history of 147, 220

sports
- in Morocco 709
- in Portugal 578
- in Spain 76

Strait of Gibraltar 701, 705, 706
study abroad 53
Sufism 706
Sunni 706
synagogues. See Judaism

T

Taha, Rachid 709
Tangier 704, 715
Tàpies, Antoni 73, 381
Tarazona 464
Tarifa 244
Tarragona 399
telephone services 37
Teresa de Jesús 137
terrorism 21
- al-Qaeda 21, 66, 705
- ETA 21, 66

Teruel 465
Thirty Years' War 61
Three Tenors 75
time zones 39
tipping. See money.
- In Portugal 19
- In Spain 19

Toledo 172
Tomar 659
Torcal de Antequera 272
Torre de Belém 575, 606
Tossa de Mar 406
transportation
- airplanes 25, 30
- bicycles 36
- buses 31
- cars 33
- hitchhiking 37
- mopeds 36
- motorcycles 36
- trains 28, 32

Trás-Os-Montes 696
Treaty of Fez 704
Trevélez 288
Trujillo 189
TUY (Tui) 550

U

Umayyad Dynasty 701

INDEX

Unamuno, Miguel de 74, 147
UNFP 704
Urdón 526

V

Val d'Aran 436
Valdoviño 565
Valença do Minho 683
Valencia 289
Valencia and Murcia 289
Valladolid 157
Valldemossa 330
Valle de Benasque 450
Valle de los Caídos 125
Valle de Núria 428
Valle de Roncal 454
Vandals 701
Vasco da Gama 567
Vejer de la Frontera 243
Velázquez, Diego 72, 109
Viana do Castelo 680
Vielha 436
Vigo 545
Vila Real 699
visas 14
Visigoths 60, 566
Vitoria-Gasteiz 500
Viveiro 564
volunteering 49
- environmental work 51
- immigration 51
- social activism 50

W

War of Spanish Succession 64
War of the Two Brothers 569
Western Sahara 704, 705, 713
Western Union. See money.
Wharton, Edith 709
Williams, Tennessee 709
wine
- La Rioja 468
- Porto 671
- Potes 526

women travelers 45
working abroad 56
work permits 14

X

Xàtiva (Játiva) 300

Z

Zafzaf, Mohamed 709
Zamora 149
Zapatero, José Luis Rodríguez 66
Zaragoza 456
zarzuela 116

MAP INDEX

A Coruña 560
Alfama 591
Algarve and Alentejo 617
The Alhambra 280
Alicante 305
Andalucia 221
Andorra La Vella 443
Aragón, La Rioja, and Navarra 457
Asturias and Cantabria 507
Àvila 138
Bairro Alto 589
Baixa 588
Barcelona 354-355
Bilbao (Bilbo) 493
Braga 673
Burgos 162
Cáceres 185
Cadiz 239
Casablanca 744
Castilla La Mancha and Extremadura 173
Castilla y León 132
Cataluña (Catalunya) 395
Ciutat Vella 358
Coimbra 685
Comunidad de Madrid 127
Cordoba 222
Çuenca 180
Évora 632
Fez al-Bali 733
Fez al-Jdid and Ville Nouvelle 732
Galicia 537
Gibraltar 249
Girona (Gerona) 412
Granada 274
Ibiza City (Eivissa) 345
Las Islas Baleares 323
Jerez 231
Lagos 618
León 152
Lisboa 582
Lisboa and Vicinity 580
Lisboa Metro 585
La Macarena 213
Madrid 82
Madrid Overview 80
Malaga 252
Mahon (Mao) 336
Marbella 256
Marrakesh 752
Meknes 726
Mérida 194
Morocco 702
Northern Portugal 665
Oviedo 509
País Vasco (Euskadi) 485
Palma 325
Pamplona 472
Picos de Europa 518
Porto 666
Portugal 568
Ribatejo and Estremadura 642
Salamanca 143
San Sebastián (Donostia) 486
Santa Cruz 210
Santander 528
Santarém 644
Santiago de Compostela 538
Segovia 133
Sevilla 203
Sintra 610
Spain 63
Spain and Portugal Chapters XIV
Spain and Portugal Transportation XVI
The Pyrenees 425
Tangier 716
Toledo 174
Valencia 292
Valencia and Murcia 290
Vitoria-Gasteiz 502
Zaragoza 458

SUGGEST ITINERARIES

Al-Lovin Al-Andalus 9
Best of Spain and Portugal 6
The Cultured Life 8
Off the Beaten Camino 5

MAP LEGEND

Point of Interest
Accommodation
Camping
Food
Shopping
Museum
Sight
Nightlife
Airport
Arch/Gate
Bank
Beach
Bus Station/Stop
Castle
Church
Consulate/Embassy
Convent/Monastery
Ferry Landing
N-I Highway Sign
Hospital
Internet Café
Library/Bookstore
M M Metro Station
Mountain
Ski Area
Pharmacy
Police
Post Of ce
Synagogue
Theater
Tourist Of ce
Train Station
Park
Water
Beach
Pedestrian Zone
Stairs
N LG The Let's Go compass always points NORTH.